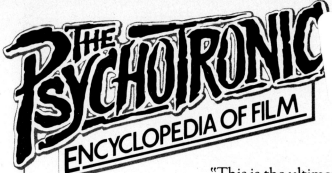

MW00860792

"This is the ultimate guide to *cine mauvaise*, lavishly illustrated, scrupulously researched, and entertainingly written... Author Michael Weldon has truly left no rock unturned...The book is full of small delights...both a scintillatingly weird look at the underside of Western culture and a thoroughly researched reference book."

The San Francisco Chronicle

"What Weldon's produced is nearly unputdownable...for cult film freaks, horror fans, and oddity buffs, *The Psychotronic Encyclopedia*, with its more than 3,000 listings, is a perfect buyer's (or renter's) guide to the decidedly offbeat."

The Washington Post

"An absolute must for those who lust after the slime and sleaze of B-movies. Loose, lecherous, and totally offbeat."

Cinefantastique

"By far the wittiest and most comprehensive attempt at creating a resource book on the murky field of the grade-Z/exploitation/cult film."

Film Quarterly

"The reviews are delightfully unabashed in their prejudices; they are informative, irreverent, and very, very funny."

Adam Film World

MICHAEL WELDON

with CHARLES BEESLEY,
Bob Martin and Akira Fitton

BALLANTINE BOOKS • NEW YORK

To

The Beachcliff
The Detroit (still there!)
The Embassy
The Granada
The Hilliard
The Hippodrome
The Homestead
The Madison
The Roxy
The Standard

and all the other great American movie theaters that are or soon will be parking lots, discos, and gutted firetraps.

Cover design by James R. Harris

Book Design by Michaelis/Carpelis Design Associates, Inc.

Cover stills, clockwise from upper left: From "HELLCATS OF THE NAVY" Copyright © 1957 Columbia Pictures Corporation. Courtesy of Columbia Pictures. From the MGM release "KISSIN' COUSINS" Copyright © 1964 Metro-Goldwyn-Mayer, Inc. and Four Leaf Productions, Inc. From "THE RATS ARE COMING! THE WEREWOLVES ARE HERE!" Copyright © William Mishkin Motion Pictures, Inc. From "THE BEACH GIRLS AND THE MONSTER." Background still: From "THE INCREDIBLE MELTING MAN" Copyright © 1977 Quartet Productions. Courtesy of Max J. Rosenberg, Producer. Back cover photo of the author by Jessica Raimi

Full photo credits may be found at the back of the book.

CONTENTS

ACKNOWLEDGMENTS

*M*uch of the early research for this book was done by Charles Beesley, who also wrote the entries marked –CB. Bob Martin of *Fangoria* magazine (–BM) also contributed many of the entries. Akira Fitton (–AF) wrote several of the reviews and designed the ad for *The Kirlian Witness* (a.k.a. *The Plants Are Watching*).

Special thanks are also due to Christopher Cerf, Michael Marsh, Sally Eckhoff, and Howard Smith and Lin Harris of *The Village Voice*. This book would not have been possible without their efforts.

Thanks to director Frank Henenlotter, for supplying screen credits and many of the rarest stills and pressbooks from his collection; to John Donaldson, for credits and stills; to Richard Bojarski and Barry Gillam, for digging up hard-to-find credits; and to Bill Landis and Rick Sullivan, for illustrations.

Other sources of the illustrations in the book were rock 'n' roll expert Alan Betrock, Pauline Klaw's *Movie Star News* (New York), *Cine 2000* (Paris), and various shops in Amsterdam.

Thanks to Joëlle Delbourgo, Liz Sacksteder, Fred Dodnick, Jimmy Harris, Stephen McNabb, and Nancy Burke at Ballantine, and to Don Chase, the copy-editor, for useful information.

The following people were also helpful during the preparation of this book: Lucas Balbo and the staff of *Heretic/Nostalgia* magazine (Paris); Nat Adriani of UPI; Gene Gromeck of Donald Velde, Inc.; Nancy Nuttall of New World; Sam Sherman of Independent-International; Lester Bangs; John and Geraldine Mead; Louise Gikow; and Katya Pendill.

Finally, I'd like to thank everybody who bought, wrote for, reviewed and supported *Psychotronic* magazine; and my family and everybody else in Cleveland who supported my movie mania.

—Michael Weldon
New York City
May 1983

FOREWORD

One morning in 1981, my wife, Geneviève, and I opened our mail to discover a hand-drawn rendition of an ancient Philco television set, on the screen of which was scrawled the following message:

MR & MRS CERF —
YOU NOW HAVE A SUBSCRIPTION TO PSYCHOTRONIC!
FROM MICHAEL MARSH

Following this information (just above the brightness knob on the Philco) was an undecipherable signature.

All very mysterious. And a call to our friend Mr. Marsh was anything but enlightening. "Just what is *Psychotronic?*" I asked. "You'll find out," he replied. "Let's just say I wanted to give you the opportunity to study, on a week-to-week basis, the development of a truly unique American mind."

About a week later, the postman delivered our first opportunity for study. It consisted of several Xeroxed sheets of paper, each filled with tiny, and impeccably neat, hand-printed script, broken only by the occasional odd illustration. And when I say "odd," I mean it quite literally. The cover sheet, for example, was graced by the photograph of a tiny soldier holding a huge hypodermic needle. Next to him, another soldier was bellowing into a megaphone which, incredibly, was pointing almost straight up into the sky. The object of their attention: a 60-foot tall totally bald man dressed only in a sarong, clutching a blonde in a low-cut evening dress.

Psychotronic, it seemed, was "New York's weekly guide to television movies—especially forgotten junk." And the cover illustration was a still of the memorable "world's largest fix" scene from *The Amazing Colossal Man*, the "unbeatable '50s hit" that was editor Michael Weldon's choice of what TV had to offer us this week. *The Amazing Colossal Man*, the painstakingly block-lettered text explained, was an attempt by producer Bert I. Gordon (the celebrated "Mr. B.I.G." himself!) to cash in on the success of

The fateful issue of Psychotronic magazine that first sparked Christopher Cerf's interest in Michael Weldon. The original Psychotronic logotype was designed by Sally Eckhoff.

Jack Arnold's *The Incredible Shrinking Man*. Bert's credits, we soon learned, included "producer, director, special effects (they're real shoddy), and co-writing the script" with Mark Hanna, whose involvement in the creation of *Attack of the 50 Ft. Woman* apparently made him the most experienced candidate for the job.

We watched *The Amazing Colossal Man*, of course. We also watched *The Angry Red Planet*, filmed in Cinemagic ("which means things change color a lot"), *Run of the Arrow* ("I could explain how Rod Steiger manages to shoot Ralph Meeker twice with the same bullet, but you wouldn't believe me"), and even *Los Monstruos del Terror* ("Sound dumb? Try to imagine what was going through Michael Rennie's mind while he was acting in this dubbed mess.") In short, we were hooked.

Our next insight into Michael Weldon's "truly unique American mind" came a few weeks later. I was in front of the television set, dutifully watching *Frankenstein Meets the Space Monster* ("You really owe it to yourself to watch this—it's *the worst*"). The evil Princess Marcuzan and her dwarf assistant Nadir had just arrived in Puerto Rico when my wife, who was downstairs reading *next* week's *Psychotronic*, called to me. "Gadzooks!" she exclaimed. "He's got *Gone With the Wind* in here!"

Jonathan Becker

Michael Weldon at home.

"He *does*!" I answered. "What's he got to say about it?"

"He says it's worth watching because the guy who designed the sets also worked on *The Man in the Iron Mask*."

"My God, what consistency!" I marvelled. "I've got to meet this Michael Weldon!"

And so it was that, the following Saturday, Michael Marsh and I found ourselves standing in front of a dilapidated brownstone on New York's East 9th Street, shouting up at a third-floor window ("The doorbell's out of order," Michael Weldon had told us on the phone, " but I'll be watching for you …"). Moments later, we were sitting in a tiny walk-up apartment, wedged between a shelf full of old movie books, several piles of magazines (including what seemed like thousands of copies of *Psychotronic*), and Weldon's remarkably cluttered worktable. "I'm really sorry about the doorbell," our host explained. "We're on a rent strike now, so I can't get it fixed."

"Will the strike end soon?" we asked.

"I hope not," he answered. "If I had to pay rent, I couldn't afford to put out my magazine."

With the preliminaries out of the way, Weldon proceeded to tackle our long list of questions about *Psychotronic*. "The name, as you've probably guessed, was originally meant to suggest a combination of weird horror films and electronic gadget-filled science fiction movies," he told us. "I thought I'd made it up, but it later turned out I'd stolen it from *The Psychotronic Man*, a Chicago-made film about a maniac barber who kills people with psychic energy. After a while, I began to use the term 'psychotronic' as an adjective, to describe all the different kinds of movies that interest me." And what, specifically, were those? "Well, monster and science-fiction films, of course. But exploitation films of any sort, really: biker movies, rock 'n' roll movies, musclemen movies, 3-D movies, '60s beach movies, Mexican movies with subtitles—you get the idea. . . ."

Particularly fascinating to Weldon are what he termed "grade-Z" movies: films produced so incompetently, or on such impoverished budgets, that they have no chance of being released through even the sleaziest of regular distribution channels. "Well, sometimes they open on 42nd street for a couple of days," Weldon said, " but they close right away, never to be seen in a theater again. The rest of them never make it to theaters at all. To earn back at least some of their money, the producers are forced to sell their product directly to TV. As a result, there's almost no information available about these films." Except, of course, for that which Weldon has culled from poring through thousands of outdated "fanzines" and promotion pieces—and, not surprisingly, from countless all-night marathons in front of the TV screen.

What triggered Michael Weldon's peculiar obsession? "It's kind of hard to say," he told us. "When I was growing up in Cleveland, my grandfather had a friend who owned a theater, and, as a result, I got in free every Wednesday night. They didn't show many 'psychotronic' films, though—they specialized more in your John Frankenheimer-type mainstream adventures. But, when I got older, I used to sneak out of school and go to the Hippodrome or the Embassy Theaters, where you could see several films a day—most of them really junky ones—without having to spend more than a dollar or so. I got really addicted to monster maga-

Jonathan Becker

zines, too—monsters, as you may recall, were very big in the '60s. My grades got worse and worse all the time, of course, and finally one day my dad gathered up all my monster magazines and tossed them in the garbage."

When *I* was a kid, *my* father once squeezed his way into my junk-filled bedroom and threw out my entire collection of New York Rangers hockey programs. So I had immediate sympathy. "And it was the scars of this horrible experience that made off-beat films the focus of your entire life!" I theorized.

"I don't think so," Weldon responded. "But I guess what happened made me more determined than ever to play hooky and go to the movies."

Whatever factors first contributed to Michael Weldon's taste in cinema, there is no question that he was profoundly influenced by a performer named "Ghoulardi," the host of a late-night horror-movie show on Cleveland's local CBS affiliate. "When a TV station wants to buy the rights to show a particular movie," Weldon explained, "they're almost always forced to invest in a couple of clinkers, too, as part of the package. Ghoulardi was the guy who had to show the clinkers." Ghoulardi, it seemed, had made the best of his unenviable fate by adopting a weird costume and an anarchist-beatnik persona; after a while, he even began cutting himself into the films his employers ordered him to show. Before he knew it he had become a cult hero, at least among a certain segment of Cleveland's youth. "One day," Weldon reminisced, "Ghoulardi made a special live appearance at the auditorium near my school—the very same auditorium where the Great Lakes Shakespeare Festival is usually held. He showed some terrible film clips, and then, using firecrackers, he blew up some skulls and model cars right on the stage. Kids were throwing their own firecrackers, too; it was really terrific!"

Perhaps the most important event in Weldon's career—even more important, if such is possible, than his discovery of Ghoulardi—was the fortuitous purchase, by his friend Gary Dumm, of fifty year's worth of bound volumes of the *Middletown* (Ohio) *News*. "Gary bought them only for the comic strips," Weldon told us, "and he didn't care at all about anything else in the paper. So, as long as they weren't on the backside of the comic pages, I was allowed to clip out any movie ads or articles I wanted. That's where a lot of the data in my files—and many of the illustrations I've used in *Psychotronic*—originally came from."

So much for history. What of the future? Weldon sighed deeply, and got up to fetch Michael Marsh and me some tea. "Well," he said dreamily, "first of all I'd like to make enough money so I could actually get my magazine printed, instead of having to Xerox it each week at the office where Sally, my girlfriend, works.

"Then, there's the book. I'd love to compile a reference book, so people could look up any 'psychotronic' films they were interested in on a title-by-title basis. A book like that would also make it possible for people to trace the careers of actors and directors—not just the ones who've fallen on hard times and can only get parts in Z pictures, but also film-makers and performers who got their start in exploitation films and then went on to do really important things. Did you know, for example, that Francis Ford Coppola once made a 3-D nudie movie called *The Playgirls and the Bellboy*?

"Then, finally, I'd like to do something about 42nd Street. There are a lot of developers and politicians these days who want to "clean up" 42nd Street; you know, tear down all the old $2.50-for-a-triple-bill movie theaters and replace them with hotels and boutiques and things like that." Weldon's eyes grew misty. "Wouldn't it be great," he said, "if we could start a 'Save 42nd Street Committee'—one whose goal was to keep things there *just* the way they are now?"

Almost three years have passed since the day I first met Michael Weldon. The rent-strike in his building ended many months ago, bringing with it a newly-repaired doorbell, but, sadly, at least a temporary end to the regular publication of *Psychotronic* magazine.

Weldon's other plans, however, are faring considerably better. Little progress has been made on New York City's ambitious plan to clean up 42nd Street. And, far more important, the incredible volume you now hold in your hands has been researched, written, and published. No longer need you worry about missing a terrific "scientist-kills-beautiful-women-in-order-to-graft-their-skin-onto-his-horribly-scarred-wife/girlfriend/daughter" movie simply because your local paper failed to appreciate its true value. Never again need you risk watching *Necromancy* without realizing that the fat actor with the beard and fake nose is actually Orson Welles. Maybe—just maybe —there's hope yet for commercial TV. . . .

—Christopher Cerf
New York City
1983

INTRODUCTION

*t*he *Psychotronic Encyclopedia of Film* celebrates over 3,000 movies often treated with indifference or contempt by other movie guides. Most of them are considered exploitation films. Some of them were made with such impossibly low budgets that they have never been released through regular channels of distribution. Many are now considered classics or cult films despite unfavorable critical response or initial box office failure. Critics searching for art condemn most of these features for the very reasons that millions continue to enjoy them: violence, sex, noise, and often mindless escapism.

Psychotronic films range from sincere social commentary to degrading trash. They concern teenagers, rock 'n' roll, juvenile delinquents, monsters, aliens, killers, spies, detectives, bikers, communists, drugs, natural catastrophes, atomic bombs, the prehistoric past, and the projected future. They star ex-models, ex-sports stars, would-be Marilyns, future Presidents (and First Ladies), dead rock stars, and has-beens of all types.

Although we have tried to be encyclopedic, we cannot claim to have included every potentially *Psychotronic* film ever released in America, nor have we seen all of the ones listed in the book. Some films are released only regionally; some are here and gone in a matter of days; some are so obscure that it's hard to track down any information about them at all. We've had to be somewhat arbitrary in deciding what to include. We've concentrated on the genres that we enjoy the most: horror, teen movies, and science fiction. We've also tried to document the careers of significant *Psychotronic* actors and actresses. Films in which they appear are noted throughout, even if the movies are otherwise unremarkable.

Certain horror greats receive special attention: Boris Karloff, Peter Lorre, Bela Lugosi, and Vincent Price. These actors have such a powerful and immediate presence that anything they appear in becomes special in a way that has nothing to do with the subject matter or quality of the film. So while we're more concerned with *Panic in the Year Zero* and *Hot Rods to Hell*, don't be surprised to find reviews for *Ninotchka* (with Lugosi) and *Keys of the Kingdom* (with Price) in this book. The mere participation of these stars makes these films *Psychotronic*.

The same applies to certain behind-the-scenes personalities. Whether good or bad, the films of many producers and directors are consistently *Psychotronic*, so we've included representative features from the entire range of their work. Many of these filmmakers are known for only a small part of their output, an unfair perception which we've tried to correct. If you like Roger Corman's *Little Shop of Horrors* or *The Pit and the Pendulum*, you should try his gangster, rock 'n' roll, and Western features. Albert Zugsmith directed the notorious *Sex Kittens Go to*

College, but he also produced *The Incredible Shrinking Man* and *Touch of Evil*.

The Psychotronic Encyclopedia of Film includes features made in the early '30s through 1982, but since we grew up in the '50s and '60s, our favorites mostly come from those two decades. Films made from the time of television's mass acceptance in the '50s to the creation of the current (inadequate) rating system in November 1968 are often the most interesting. During this period Hollywood was desperately trying to lure audiences away from their home screens and compete with the European imports while putting up with an outdated, puritanical censorship board. Theatergoers were rewarded with teenage rebellion, worldwide destruction, a potent but acceptable dose of sex and sadism, and gimmickry of all kinds, including 3-D and Cinerama. The so-called "adults-only" movies of the period are so tame that today they'd probably be rated R or PG, but they remain fascinating historical documents of a more innocent time.

Today there are more ways to watch *Psychotronic* films than ever before. We're in the midst of an astounding boom in the cable television and home video industries. Movies that most people didn't bother to see in the theater turn up within months on cable. Movies that would have remained unreleased or unseen except by collectors are now available to a vast market of viewers in the comfort of their homes. The promotional hype that once lured or tricked a person into spending a few bucks to see a movie is now being used to convince him to spend $60 to buy a videocassette of a film that in many cases would have put him to sleep or sent him to the exit doors in a theater. The lack of information available about the obscure films now being watched and even purchased by millions of bored consumers is staggering. This book attempts to remedy that problem for discriminating viewers of the more bizarre, shocking, and unclassifiable movies available.

We've made every effort to include as much interesting and relevant information as possible, while keeping the entries brief and to the point. We've also tried to illustrate the text where possible with original ad mats and unusual stills, most of which have not been used in any other film book and many of which have never before been seen in print anywhere. Many of these illustrations were acquired over the years from still shops and junk sales; many others were borrowed or rented from film collectors.

We hope that *The Psychotronic Encyclopedia of Film* will introduce you to new realms of cinematic enjoyment.

HOW TO USE THIS BOOK

All films reviewed in this book are listed alphabetically by title. If the film was originally released in a foreign country, the original foreign-language title is also indicated in the entry. If the film was released under several English-language titles, it is listed by the title it was originally released under or the one it is best known by, and the alternate titles are indicated in the entry. If you look it up under one of the alternate titles, you will be referred to the title it is discussed under.

Below the title, the year of the film's release is given. If the film was never released theatrically or released years after its completion, the year it was made is given. Following the date is the name of the American distributor, preceded where applicable by well-known foreign production companies such as Hammer and Toho. When a film was distributed by more than one company over the years, the original distributor is listed when possible. Made-for-television movies are indicated by "TV" instead of a distributor. When the film was not made by an American production company, the country of origin or the co-producing nations are also indicated.

Since color has been the norm for so long, we note when a film was made in black-and-white or in partial color. If the film was made in 3-D, that is also indicated, even if it was issued flat.

For each entry, we have made every effort to cite the producer, director, and screenwriter of the film. However, complete screen credits proved impossible to find for some of the more obscure features that were never reviewed by trade publications or have incomplete credits in the prints. Sometimes we have given a substitute credit—for example, "Associate Producer" instead of "Producer"—when the one we were looking for was unavailable.

After the review, we give the MPAA rating if it was R, X, or M (for "mature"—a rating used briefly instead of PG in 1968–1969). Films released before November 1968, made-for-television movies, and features released directly to television or videocassette companies are unrated.

Some of the reviews in the book were written by Charles Beesley, Bob Martin, and Akira Fitton. Their initials appear at the end of each entry they wrote.

We base our reviews on theatrical viewing whenever possible. Films made after the late '60s obviously suffer when cut for commercial television, and no film benefits from constant interruption for commercials.

We've tried to indicate throughout which movies have sound track albums in print. Most of those that remain in print for longer than a few months are on the Varèse Sarabande label.

Unlike many movie guides, this book does not give star ratings. If a film is especially good, bad, laughable, or boring we say so. Otherwise, we prefer to give you the facts and let you decide. People who enjoy the more unusual features tend to select them on the basis of the subject matter, stars, director, or company rather than somebody else's arbitrary and simplistic rating system.

THE STUDIOS

Knowing which company released a film can often tell you what to expect, but sometimes just knowing the name of the official distributor isn't enough. The relationships between many film companies featured prominently in this book have been obscured over the years by company name changes, the creation of subsidiaries, and corporate takeovers. This section outlines the history of some of the major distributors of *Psychotronic* films.

Probably the most important company in this book is American International Pictures (AIP). Founded in 1954 as American Releasing Corporation (ARC) by Samuel Z. Arkoff and the late James Nicholson, AIP (1956-1980) defined the postwar youth-oriented feature. Shortly after its 25th anniversary, the company was purchased by outsiders and renamed Filmways. Soon thereafter, Filmways was engulfed by Orion. The current regime may pretend to be disengaged from its exploitative past, but recent releases like *Amityville 3-D* indicate that its AIP origins linger.

During its heyday, AIP had several subsidiaries. Filmgroup made some of the more offbeat features (often produced or directed by AIP standby Roger Corman). By the late '60s more lurid features dealing with sex and drugs were released by Trans-American. During the '70s, Hallmark released the most shocking of the (mostly European) horror acquisitions. AIP-TV released dozens of Mexican, Japanese, and European films directly to American television. It also sometimes made extremely cheap features to be sold as part of TV package deals.

Many favorites that fans assume to be from AIP were actually made by Allied Artists, a company whose latter history and output were similar to AIP's. Monogram (1930-1953), the well-known king of Hollywood's poverty row studios, changed its name to Allied Artists in 1953 and continued making cheap youth-oriented features and releasing foreign horror films until the late '70s.

Producers Releasing Corporation (PRC), an even smaller studio founded in the '30s, became Eagle Lion in 1947. By 1951 that company had been swallowed up by United Artists. The (mostly awful) UA horror films of the '50s have their roots in PRC.

Other studios releasing more than their share of *Psychotronic* films are the old Republic (1935-1959) and RKO (1929-1959). During the '50s, Astor, DCA, Howco, and Lippert were quite active. Realart, a company that began as a vehicle for re-releasing old Universal horror films, also made its own features. James Nicholson, a co-founder of AIP, was a high-ranking executive at Realart.

Important independent companies active in the '60s include Box Office International, Fairway International, Fanfare, Geneni, Hemisphere, Barry Mahon, and Woolner Brothers. Larry Woolner later helped Roger Corman start New World, then left to form Dimension. Other defunct firms well represented here are Cinerama and Jerry Gross' Cinemation. Crown International, an exploitation company going back to the '50s, is still going strong. Small companies currently turning out *Psychotronic* films include Independent-International, Motion Picture Marketing (MPM), World Northal, United, 21st Century, Film Ventures, Group I, and Jensen Farley. Cannon and New World (recently sold by Roger Corman) are today's biggest independents.

Major studios that lost their identities years ago are Universal (the oldest studio in existence, founded in 1912), Paramount (1930-   ), 20th Century-Fox (founded as Fox in 1915, which merged with the new 20th Century corporation in 1935), and Columbia (1924-   ). MGM (1924-   ) and United Artists (1919-   ) are now merged as MGM/UA. Warner Brothers (1923-   ) purchased First National in 1928, which released films through Warner Brothers until 1938. During 1967-1968, Warner Brothers was known as Warner Brothers-Seven Arts or just Seven Arts.

Embassy was founded in the late '50s by Joseph E. Levine and later purchased to become Avco Embassy. It released foreign features directly to television as well as the familiar domestic releases. The company was recently purchased by

Norman Lear and is now known once again as Embassy.

Foreign studios of note include Japan's Toho and its rival, Daei. In England the international success of Hammer Studios set the stage for Amicus and Tigon, all of which specialized in horror features. Some of the most interesting British horror films of the '50s and '60s, however, were from the little-known Anglo Amalgamated.

ABBOTT AND COSTELLO GO TO MARS

1953 Universal (B&W)
PRODUCER: Howard Christie
DIRECTOR: Charles Lamont
SCREENWRITERS: John Grant,
    D.D. Beauchamp

Dumb comedy with the team (known as *deux nigauds*—two nitwits—in France) accidentally taking off in a rocket ship and landing in New Orleans during Mardi Gras. (They think it's Mars.) They take off again, this time with two unwanted convicts, and land on Venus, populated by beautiful women and ruled by Queen Alura (Mari Blanchard of *She-Devil* fame). The Venusians are played by contestants in the '53 Miss Universe pageant, including Anita Ekberg—Miss Sweden. The same year, the incredible *Cat Women of the Moon* explored similar territory. With Martha Hyer, Robert Paige, Horace MacMahon, and Jack Kruschen. Aren't you tired of movie books beginning with *Abbott and Costello*?

UPI 8/25/52: The "flying saucer" ideas are beginning to land in the costume jewelry business and some have come to rest on actress Mari Blanchard, star of Abbott and Costello Go To Mars. The "saucer" necklace and earrings couldn't have picked a better place between here and Mars. A prediction that more males will volunteer as spotters will be in order if saucers continue to travel along with heavenly bodies.

ABBOTT AND COSTELLO MEET DR. JEKYLL AND MR. HYDE

1953 Universal (B&W)
PRODUCER: Howard Christie
DIRECTOR: Charles Lamont
SCREENWRITERS: Leo Loeb, John Grant

Boris Karloff plays the Dr. but not the Mr. (famous stuntman Eddie Parker does). The stars are called Slim and Tubby, which should give you an idea of the level of comedy. When Costello becomes a monster he bites a group of bobbies, who all become identical monsters. With a fake Frankenstein monster, a giant mouse, Craig "Peter Gunn" Stevens, and Helen Westcott.

ABBOTT AND COSTELLO MEET FRANKENSTEIN

1948 Universal (B&W)
PRODUCER: Robert Arthur
DIRECTOR: Charles T. Barton
SCREENWRITERS: John Grant,
    Frederic I. Renaldo, Robert Lees

After achieving lasting fame as Count Dracula in 1931, Bela Lugosi had to wait 17 years to repeat the role. After Universal exhausted the possibilities of multimonster epics they decided to pit their three most popular creatures against a comedy team. The results aren't bad at all. Glenn Strange (later seen as the bartender on *Gunsmoke*) played the Karloff clone monster for the third time. Lon Chaney, Jr., played Larry Talbot the Wolfman for the fifth time. Lugosi was working for his old studio for the first time in years but soon returned to cheap quickies. Lenore Aubert wants Costello's brain for the monster. The Wolfman wants to be cured. Dracula turns into a cartoon bat. Vincent Price is heard briefly as the Invisible Man. Remade in Mexico as *Frankenstein, el Vampiro y Cia.*

ABBOTT AND COSTELLO MEET THE INVISIBLE MAN

1951 Universal (B&W)
PRODUCER: Howard Christie
DIRECTOR: Charles Lamont
SCREENWRITERS: John Grant,
Frederic I. Renaldo, Robert Lees

The boys are back again—as inept detectives involved with an invisible prizefighter played by Arthur Franz (*Monster on Campus*). With William Frawley (Fred Mertz on "I Love Lucy") and Sheldon Leonard.

ABBOTT AND COSTELLO MEET THE KILLER, BORIS KARLOFF

1949 Universal (B&W)
PRODUCER: Robert Arthur
DIRECTOR: Charles T. Barton
SCREENWRITERS: Hugh Wedlock, Jr.,
Howard Snyder, John Grant

The inferior follow-up to *Abbott and Costello Meet Frankenstein*, with the same director and female star (Lenore Aubert). Boris Karloff is wasted as the mad swami in a mystery-comedy about two dumb hotel employees who discover dead bodies. Boris hypnotizes Lou the bellboy and commands him to commit suicide. Lou refuses. With Roland Winters, Percy Helton, Alan Mowbray, and Billy Gray. The star-in-the-title idea cropped up again in *Bela Lugosi Meets a Brooklyn Gorilla* and *Sabu and the Magic Ring*.

ABBOTT AND COSTELLO MEET THE MUMMY

1955 Universal (B&W)
PRODUCER: Howard Christie
DIRECTOR: Charles Lamont
SCREENWRITER: John Grant

The last of the meet-the-monsters series, next-to-the-last movie for Abbott and Costello. In Egypt they discover the Mummy (Eddie Parker), now called Klaris. The mummy costume is awful. With Marie Windsor, Michael Ansara, Richard Deacon, and Mel Welles.

ABBY

1974 AIP
PRODUCERS: William Girdler, Mike Henry,
Gordon C. Layne
DIRECTOR: William Girdler
SCREENWRITER: G. Cornell Layne

"Blacula" William Marshall is now the black exorcist. As a bishop/archaeologist, he unknowingly brings back a demon from Africa that takes over Carol Speed, wife of minister Terry Carter. When possessed, she goes through the expected transformations while swearing and spewing. With Austin Stoker and Juanita Moore. From the director of *The Manitou*. Carol sings the theme song. Warner Brothers sued over similarities to *The Exorcist* and won. **(R)**

THE ABOMINABLE DR. PHIBES

1971 AIP (England)
PRODUCERS: Louis M. Heyward,
Ronald S. Dunas
DIRECTOR: Robert Fuest
SCREENWRITERS: James Whiton,
William Goldstein, George Bant

Clever art deco revenge film with Vincent Price as an ex-vaudevillian madman living in a secret underground mechanical world while killing off the team of surgeons that unsuccessfully operated on his late wife. Due to injury in an auto accident, Phibes has no face or voice, so he constructs an imitation face for himself and talks by plugging a cord from his neck into a Victrola. His ingenious methods of killing are inspired by the ten plagues visited upon the Pharoah in the Old Testament. Enemies die in horrible ways involving locusts, bats, and frogs. Joseph Cotten has a good role as the chief surgeon. With Virginia North as Vulnavia, Terry-Thomas, Hugh Griffith, and Caroline Munro seen mostly in photos as the late Mrs. Victoria Phibes. Great line: "Love means never having to say you're ugly!" It was billed as Price's 100th film. The sequel was *Dr. Phibes Rises Again*.

THE ABOMINABLE SNOWMAN OF THE HIMALAYAS

1957 Hammer/20th Century-Fox (England) (B&W)
PRODUCER: Aubrey Baring
DIRECTOR: Val Guest
SCREENWRITER: Nigel Kneale

An intelligent, restrained look at two men with opposing views who encounter a monster that turns out to be friendly (and frightened). Peter Cushing is the dedicated scientist. Forrest Tucker is a money-hungry showman. The giant yeti appears very briefly in an unforgettable scene. It was Cushing's first role after *The Curse of Frankenstein*. Based on a BBC television play. American ads warned viewers to "bring your own tranquilizers!"

THE ABSENT-MINDED PROFESSOR

1960 Buena Vista (B&W)
PRODUCER: Walt Disney
DIRECTOR: Robert Stevenson
SCREENWRITER: Bill Walsh

Fred MacMurray as Prof. Brainard develops "flubber," a super rubber that may have been the inspiration for the "Superballs by Whammo" that were bouncing all over the country. Flubber bounces the college basketball team to victory and helps Fred's Model T fly. Keenan Wynn is the villain (so is the Pentagon). With Tommy Kirk, Ed Wynn, and Nancy Olson. They all return in *Son of Flubber*.

ADVENTURES OF CAPTAIN FABIAN

1951 Republic (B&W)
PRODUCER/DIRECTOR: William Marshall
SCREENWRITER: Errol Flynn

Fading star Errol Flynn wrote the screenplay for this cheap period adventure set in New Orleans. As a sea captain, he rescues a Creole servant girl (Micheline Presle), who seeks revenge on the local corrupt rich people (Vincent Price and Victor Francen). With Agnes Moorehead as her "octoroon" companion, Howard Vernon, and Reggie Nalder.

THE ADVENTURES OF CAPTAIN MARVEL

1941 Republic (B&W)
PRODUCER: Hirram S. Brown
DIRECTORS: William Witney, John English
SCREENWRITERS: Ronald Davidson, Norman S. Hall, Arch B. Heath, Joseph Poland, Sol Shor
ALSO RELEASED AS: *The Return of Captain Marvel*

One of the best serials ever made. When young Billy Batson says "Shazam" he becomes the mighty Captain Marvel. Tom Tyler (*The Mummy's Hand*) doesn't say much as Marvel but he flies through the air and treats bad guys rougher than Superman ever did. The villain is the Scorpion. If he can steal five magical lenses he can rule the universe. Frank Coghlan, Jr., is Billy. The entire 12 chapters were re-released to be shown consecutively during the '60s. *Batman* was shown in its entirety too; in '66 a condensed feature version was released.

THE ADVENTURES OF SHERLOCK HOLMES

1939 20th Century-Fox (B&W)
PRODUCER: Darryl F. Zanuck
DIRECTOR: Alfred Werker
SCREENWRITERS: Edwin Blum, William Drake

The follow-up to *The Hound of the Baskervilles* is the best of the Basil Rathbone–Nigel Bruce Holmes films. Ida Lupino shows up with a sketch of a man with an albatross around his neck, a club-footed killer with bolas lurks in the fog, and Professor Moriarty (George Zucco) steals the crown jewels. Mary Gordon is Mrs. Hudson. Three years later the detective showed up in the 20th century at Universal for a series of 12 films.

THE ADVENTURES OF SHERLOCK HOLMES' SMARTER BROTHER
1976 20th Century-Fox
PRODUCER: Richard A. Roth
DIRECTOR/SCREENWRITER: Gene Wilder
Sort of a follow-up to *Young Frankenstein* with fewer laughs and no Mel Brooks. Director Wilder is Sigi Holmes, aided by Marty Feldman as a Scotland Yard detective in helping a blackmailed singer (Madeline Kahn). Leo McKern is a comical Moriarty. Douglas Wilmer and Thorley Walters are Holmes and Watson. With Dom DeLuise and Roy Kinnear.

ADVENTURES OF THE QUEEN
1975 TV
PRODUCER: Irwin Allen
DIRECTOR: David Lowell Rich
SCREENWRITER: John Gay
Robert Stack is the captain of a luxury cruiser that is about to be destroyed in order to kill millionaire passenger Ralph Bellamy. The worried passenger and crew list includes David Hedison, Bradford Dillman, Russell Johnson, and Sorrell Booke. By the director of *Have Rocket Will Travel*.

AFTER JENNY DIED: See TERROR FROM UNDER THE HOUSE

AFRICA SCREAMS
1949 United Artists (B&W)
PRODUCER: Edward Nassour
DIRECTOR: Charles Barton
SCREENWRITER: Earl Baldwin
Pretty bad Abbott and Costello quickie with non-actor stars like Frank ("Bring 'em back alive") Buck, lion tamer Clyde Beatty, and heavyweights Max and Buddy Baer. Also starring Hillary Brooke, stooge Shemp Howard, and future stooge Joe Besser. A bit with a giant gorilla was a nod to the same year's hit, *Mighty Joe Young*.

AFRICAN TREASURE
1952 Monogram (B&W)
PRODUCER: Walter Mirisch
DIRECTOR/SCREENWRITER: Ford Beebe
From the ads: "Jungle drums echo the dangers of ruthless fortune seekers!" Bomba (Johnny Sheffield) fights diamond smugglers. With Laurette Luez, Arthur Space, Lyle Talbot (*Glen or Glenda*), and Woody Strode.

AGAINST ALL ODDS: See KISS AND KILL.

AGENT FOR H.A.R.M.
1966 Universal
PRODUCER: Joseph F. Robertson
DIRECTOR: Gerd Oswald
SCREENWRITER: Blair Robertson
A low-budget American James Bond imitation by a director known for his *Outer Limits* episodes. Mark Richman stars as agent Adam Chance. H.A.R.M. chief Wendell Corey sends him to investigate a plot to import an alien spore that turns human flesh to fungus. Martin Koslek as Malko is the star villain. With Barbara Bouchet, Alizia Gur, Rafael Campos, and Donna Michelle, *Playboy's* Miss December 1963.

(Above) UPI 8/1/80: Kareem Abdul-Jabbar (left), playing the co-pilot, and Peter Graves, in the role of pilot, show young Rossie Harris how they check out the controls before the wild flight in Airplane! Kareem, best known for his starring role in professional basketball, says: "I like making movies. It's one of the things I might do when I quit playing basketball."

(Right) UPI 7/29/69: Veteran performers Helen Hayes and Van Heflin are reunited on the screen in Airport for the first time since they appeared together in My Son, John 17 years ago. But it isn't their reunion that prompts this embrace. Heflin plays a mad bomber on a plane and she's the little old lady stowaway who tries to stop him.

AIRPLANE

1980 Paramount
PRODUCER: John Davidson
DIRECTORS/SCREENWRITERS: Jim Abrahams, David and Jerry Zucker

A real surprise—a modern comedy with too many funny gags to catch in one viewing. A major hit, with a great cast of neglected B-movie and TV standbys, and some great anarchistic humor. For no reason at all, a watermelon splats on a desk. A framed photograph assumes the same pose as its subject standing in front of it. If that's not exactly funny, watch Robert Stack punch and judo-kick Hari Krishnas, Moonies, and other pests in an airport, or Lloyd Bridges float to the ceiling, his hair on end, after sniffing glue. The stars, Robert Hays and Julie Haggerty, are good, but the supporting cast is wonderful. Including Peter Graves (as a pilot who likes little boys), Leslie Nielsen, Barbara Billingsley (Beaver's mom), Kenneth Tobey, Kareem Abdul-Jabbar, Ethel Merman, and Maureen McGovern. A spoof of all the films in the ridiculous Airport series, the plot is based on Zero Hour, a 1957 film. There is a sequel, Airplane II, but the original creative team was not directly involved with it.

AIRPORT

1970 Universal
PRODUCER: Ross Hunter
DIRECTOR/SCREENWRITER: George Seaton

Burt Lancaster, the general manager of Lincoln International Airport, is having an affair with Jean Seberg. His wife (Dana Wynter) wants a divorce, Van Heflin is threatening a jet in flight with a bomb, Helen Hayes is a stowaway, and the weather's terrible. Burt's brother-in-law, the pilot (Dean Martin), finds out his lover, stewardess Jacqueline Bisset, is pregnant, and the bomb goes off in the plane's bathroom. This maverick disaster movie led to three sequels and countless imitations. The cast includes George Kennedy, Barry Nelson, Whit Bissell, Barbara Rush, Virginia Grey, Lloyd Nolan, and Barbara Hale. From the Arthur Hailey bestseller of the same title. In 70mm Todd-A O.

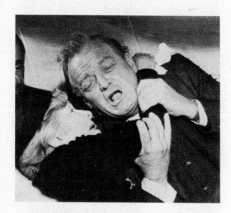

AIRPORT '75

1974 Universal
PRODUCER: William Frye
DIRECTOR: Jack Smight
SCREENWRITER: Don Ingalls

The first big laugh-filled follow-up to Airport stars Charlton Heston leaping from a helicopter to a disabled in-flight jet being flown by Karen Black. Along for the bumpy ride are George Kennedy (also in *Airport*), Helen Reddy as a singing nun, Dana Andrews, Roy Thinnes, Sid Caesar, Linda Blair (just after *The Exorcist*), Efrem Zimbalist, Jr., Gloria Swanson (in her first film in 16 years), Myrna Loy, Susan Clark, Ed Nelson, Larry Storch, Eric Estrada, Jerry Stiller, Norman Fell, Beverly Garland, and Guy Stockwell.

AIRPORT '77
1977 Universal
PRODUCER: William Frye
DIRECTOR: Jerry Jameson
SCREENWRITERS: Michael Scheff,
   David Spector
It's got everything: the Bermuda triangle, an undersea rescue, and an art heist. Jack Lemmon is the pilot and James Stewart is the art magnate. Also with your other favorites, including Lee Grant, Brenda Vaccaro, George Kennedy (in all *Airport* movies), Christopher Lee (as a hero), Joseph Cotten, Monte Markham, Darren McGavin, Olivia deHavilland, and Michael Pataki. By the director of *The Bat People*. The TV version includes over an hour of footage not shown in theaters!

ALABAMA'S GHOST
1972 Bremson International
PRODUCER/DIRECTOR/SCREENWRITER:
   Frederic Hobbs
"If you dug *Blacula*, you gonna love *Alabama's Ghost*." See a vampire rock group on motorcycles battle a ghost. As the ads said, "A super hip horror movie." With the Turk Murphy jazz band. Watch for it.

ALIAS JOHN PRESTON
1956 Associated Artists (England)
   (B&W)
PRODUCER: Sid Stone
DIRECTOR: David MacDonald
SCREENWRITER: Paul Tabori

Christopher Lee, in an early psychological horror film, stars as a man troubled by nightmares who becomes a Jekyll-Hyde type. Betta St. John is his wife. Alexander Knox is the psychiatrist.

ALIAS NICK BEAL
1949 Paramount (B&W)
PRODUCER: Endre Bohem
DIRECTOR: John Farrow
SCREENWRITER: Jonathan Latimer
Ray Milland is great as the devil in human form. He uses Audrey Totter to help corrupt honest politician Thomas Mitchell. With George Macready, Darryl Hickman, Fred Clark, King Donovan, and Nestor Paiva.

ALICE, SWEET ALICE
1976 Allied Artists
PRODUCER: Richard K. Rosenberg
DIRECTOR: Alfred Sole
SCREENWRITERS: Rosemary Ritvo,
   Alfred Sole
ALSO RELEASED AS: *Holy Terror, Communion*
Because of Brooke Shields' small role, this shocker has been re-released twice with new titles, each time disappointing folks who go to a film just because a famous underage model is in it. Well, forget about that because this movie is excellent despite the misleading hype. It's the best-made and most unsettling psycho-shocker in ages. A violently anti-Catholic feature, it takes place during the early '60s in Paterson, New Jersey (where it was filmed). The murders, although not overly gory, are hard to look at, and the audience is clearly thrown off track. You won't be sure who did it until the end, and you won't believe Mr. Alphonse! Brian DePalma's derivative hits pale by comparison. With Lillian Roth (*I'll Cry Tomorrow* was a film of her life story), Linda Miller, Mildred Clinton, and Niles McMaster. **(R)**

ALIEN

1979 20th Century-Fox (England)
PRODUCERS: Gordon Carroll, David Giler, Walter Hill
DIRECTOR: Ridley Scott
SCREENWRITER: Dan O'Bannon

Of course it's an expensive B-movie, but it's also fascinating, well made, and the scariest science-fiction film in ages. A welcome hit after all the dismal *Star Wars* clones, although the much-publicized effects are not as shocking as you've been led to believe. Too bad it was cut some before release. Sigourney Weaver as Ripley emerges as the survivor/star. Not only is it refreshing to have a female star in this kind of film, but there are no unnecessary, unrealistic subplots showing romantic or sexual situations. None! A real breakthrough. With Tom Skerritt, Veronica Cartwright (sister of Angela, who was *Lost in Space*), John Hurt (*The Elephant Man*), Ian Holm (as the science officer-robot), Yaphet Kotto, and Harry Dean Stanton. **(R)**

ALIEN CONTAMINATION

1981 Cannon (Italy)
PRODUCER: Charles Mancini
DIRECTOR: Lewis Coates (Luigi Cozzi)
SCREENWRITER: Luigi Cozzi

A bad Italian *Alien* copy by the director of *Starcrash*, a *Star Wars* copy. The story opens in New York City (like many recent Neapolitan shockers) but quickly shifts to a Colombian coffee factory, where space eggs that look like watermelons are being incubated for use in conquering Earth. The eggs squirt out a sticky liquid that causes people to explode. A slimy, badly constructed monster makes a token appearance. The dubbing is terrible. The music is by Goblin. With Ian McCulloch (of *Dr. Butcher, M.D.*). It was never released theatrically in America.

ALIEN DEAD: See IT FELL FROM THE SKY.

ALL THAT MONEY CAN BUY

1941 RKO (B&W)
PRODUCER/DIRECTOR: William Dieterle
SCREENWRITERS: Dan Totheroh, Stephen Vincent Benet
ORIGINALLY RELEASED AS: *The Devil and Daniel Webster*

Classic American fantasy set in 1840s New Hampshire. Walter Huston as Scratch (the Devil) buys the soul of farmer Jabez Stone (James Craig) for a pot of gold and seven years' good luck. As the Devil's emissary, Simone Simon acts as a nursemaid for Jabez's baby and steals him away from his wife. A man is danced to death at a party attended by demons and the farmer tricks the Devil into going to court over their deal. The courtroom is filled with a jury of damned American killers, pirates, and traitors. With Edward Arnold, H.B. Warner, Jeff Corey, and a fiddle-playing Devil. Music by Bernard Herrmann.

ALL THROUGH THE NIGHT

1942 Warner Brothers (B&W)
PRODUCER: Hal B. Wallis
DIRECTOR: Vincent Sherman
SCREENWRITERS: Leonard Spigelgass, Edwin Gilbert

From the ads: "Gangdom turns its gats on the Gestapo." Nazi saboteurs (Conrad Veidt, Peter Lorre, and Judith Anderson) plan to blow up a battleship in New York Harbor. A patriotic gangster named Gloves Donahue (Humphrey Bogart) stops them in a wartime comedy-thriller with Frank McHugh, Karen Verne, William Demarest, Phil Silvers, and Wallace Ford. Lorre, who had just been in *The Maltese Falcon* with Bogart, stands out as the sadistic spy Pepi.

ALLIGATOR

1980 Group I
PRODUCER: Brandon Chase
DIRECTOR: Lewis Teague
SCREENWRITER: John Sayles

Thanks to the screenplay by John Sayles, here is a giant-monster film that's as good or better than the best of the '50s films it resembles. The cast (especially tough-guy detective Robert Forster) is believable and the humor works. "Ramone," a 36-foot gator hiding in a Missouri sewer, even chomps on a sewer worker named Ed Norton. Robin Riker is a famous scientist romantically involved with the loner detective. Jack Carter is the mayor, Henry Silva a macho mercenary type, Dean Jagger (in his 70s) is the tycoon indirectly responsible for the alligator's growth. With Perry Lane and bits by Sidney Lassick, Mike Mazurki, Angel Tompkins, and Sue Lyon. Proof that low budget doesn't have to mean bad. (R)

THE ALLIGATOR PEOPLE

1959 20th Century-Fox (B&W)
PRODUCER: Jack Leewood
DIRECTOR: Roy del Ruth
SCREENWRITER: O.H. Hampton

Down in the Louisiana swamp, Beverly Garland finds her missing husband (*Rocky Jones—Space Ranger* series star Richard Crane) at the home of a doctor (Bruce Bennett). The poor man has horrible scaly skin and after another operation turns into an upright alligator (with pants on and no tail)! The unlikely alligator man (designed by the man who made the Fly) is one of the more outrageous screen monsters. Lon Chaney, Jr., as an unshaven drunk with a hook hand and sinister George Macready are on hand to make matters worse. With Frieda Inescort. Originally released with *Return of the Fly.*

ALPHAVILLE

1965 Pathe Contemporary Films
(France/Italy) (B&W)
PRODUCER: André Michelin
DIRECTOR/SCREENWRITER: Jean-Luc Godard
ORIGINALLY RELEASED AS: *Alphaville, Une Etrange Aventure de Lemmy Caution*

Godard took the well-known French film detective Lemmy Caution and put him in the present/future where you can drive to the planet Alphaville in a Ford Galaxie. Assigned to bring back or liquidate Professor Von Braun (Howard Vernon), Lemmy is tricked by his daughter (Anna Karina), an emotionless citizen ruled by Alpha-60, the ulti-

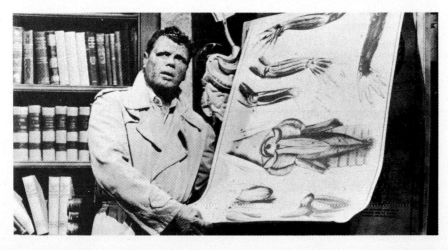

Richard Crane shows how he's supposed to look in The Alligator People.

mate control computer. The required dictionary/Bible is rewritten daily, changing the meanings of some words and banning others. A great confusing science-fiction/detective film full of references to Nosferatu, Hekyll and Jekyll, Flash Gordon, and other invented heroes. American-born Eddie Constantine starred in a series of French Lemmy Caution adventures. One, *Attack of the Robots*, was even directed by Jesse Franco. With Akim Tamiroff.

ALTERED STATES

1980 Warner Brothers
PRODUCER: Howard Gottfried
DIRECTOR: Ken Russell
SCREENWRITER: Sidney Aaron

Drugs and Darwinism are the excuse for a version of Jekyll and Hyde that seems tailored specifically for acid heads under the age of 16. Lots of pretty colors to watch, and some grotesque make-up effects by Dick Smith make it worthwhile—but that's about it. Part of *Altered States'* problems can be traced to the fact that director Arthur Penn, production designer Joe Alves, and effects supervisor John Dykstra were all replaced shortly before the start of principal photography. When Russell came in, radical changes were made that prompted screenwriter Paddy Chayefsky to use the pseudonym "Sidney Aaron" in the credits. William Hurt nevertheless is likable in his role as a young scientific researcher who pursues the process of de-evolution as if it were the Holy Grail and is rewarded by his own transformation into apeman and worse. Blair Brown is always lovable, and here she struggles gamely with the part of Hurt's wife, mad with jealousy over his dedication to truth-seeking. As one critic was brave enough to point out, *Monster on Campus* was a lot more sincere. With Drew Barrymore.**(R)** –BM

THE AMAZING CAPTAIN NEMO

1978 TV
PRODUCER: Irwin Allen
DIRECTOR: Alex March
SCREENWRITERS: Norman Katkov, Preston Wood, Robert Dennis, William Keys, Mann Rubin, Robert Bloch, Larry Alexander
ORIGINALLY RELEASED AS: *The Return of Captain Nemo*

This three-part miniseries loosely based on Jules Verne is Irwin Allen's attempt to duplicate the success of his *Voyage to the Bottom of the Sea.* It features a typical Allen cast. As the good Captain Nemo, José Ferrer takes the *Nautilus* to the lost city of Atlantis and battles a modern supersub owned by a mad professor (Burgess Meredith) who plans to destroy Washington, D.C. Also on hand are Mel Ferrer (for a *Star Wars*–inspired battle of the Ferrers), Horst Buchholz, Lynda Day George, Warren Stevens, Tom Hallick, robots, and all the old flashing lights and control panels from the *Seaview.* It was a theatrical release in Europe.

THE AMAZING COLOSSAL MAN

1957 AIP (B&W)
PRODUCER/DIRECTOR: Bert I. Gordon
SCREENWRITERS: Bert I. Gordon, Mark Hanna

As soon as *The Incredible Shrinking Man* proved to be a hit, director-producer-writer-effects man Bert Gordon rushed out his opposite popular hit. The opening is strong. Colonel Manning (Glenn Langan) walks right into the explosion of a plutonium bomb in the desert. The radiation burns his body, but it heals overnight and starts to grow rapidly. Soon the colossal colonel is losing his mind and feeling like "less than a man" since his wife (Cathy Downs) can only look up at him in disbelief. He gets tired of hanging around all the tiny props so he puts on his best giant diaper and heads for Las Vegas where he tears down oversize signs advertising casinos. He's finally shot down by the army at Hoover Dam. The special effects stink but who can resist Gordon's cheesy '50s movies? Look for the scene with the giant syringe. With Russ Bender, Judd Holdren, and William Hudson. The colonel was back the next year in *War of the Colossal Beast*. The theme music is available on the *Fantastic Film Music of Albert Glasser* album.

THE AMAZING DR. X: See THE SPIRITUALIST.

THE AMAZING TRANSPARENT MAN

1960 AIP (B&W)
PRODUCER: Lester D. Guthrie
DIRECTOR: Edward G. Ulmer
SCREENWRITER: Jack Lewis

This science-fiction/crime film was made simultaneously with Ulmer's *Beyond the Time Barrier*. Both were shot in Dallas on the site of the Texas State Fair, using exhibits of futuristic art and design as backdrops. Marguerite Chapman (*Flight to Mars*) is the moll of an invisible bank robber. With Douglas Kennedy and James Griffith.

THE AMBUSHERS

1967 Columbia
PRODUCER: Irving Allen
DIRECTOR: Henry Levin
SCREENWRITER: Herbert Baker

Dean Martin and Janice Rule go to Mexico to recover a flying saucer that never gets off the ground in the third of the Matt Helm films. Lots of stupid jokes and a shooting bra (copied from *The Tenth Victim*) keep Dino busy while dealing with villains Kurt Kasznar, Albert Salmi, and friendly Senta Berger.

With series regulars James Gregory and Beverly Adams. Tommy Boyce and Bobby Hart sing the theme song. Filmed in Mexico. Fashions by Oleg Cassini.

AN AMERICAN WEREWOLF IN LONDON

1981 Universal
PRODUCER: George Folsey, Jr.
DIRECTOR/SCREENWRITER: John Landis

Two traveling New York University students are attacked by a werewolf on the English moors. One dies; the other (former Dr. Pepper song-and-dance man David Naughton) survives, to receive the care of a beautiful nurse played by Jenny Agutter, and regular visits from his dead friend, who warns him that the werewolf's bite will take its toll at the next full moon. Sure enough, the lunar cycle brings about the strange transformation of man into wolf, accompanied by the strains of Creedence Clearwater and Elmer Bernstein's music, and engineered by special makeup effects man Rick Baker. (For his work here, Baker won the first Academy Award for Best Makeup when it was established as a regular Oscar category in 1981.) The wolflike creature soon comes to an abrupt end under the guns of the London police force. The guy who goes through the window during the *Blues Brothers*-styled car-wreck scene is writer-director John (*Animal House*) Landis. Landis tried to get Cat Stevens' "Moonshadow" and Bob Dylan's version of "Blue Moon" for the rock soundtrack, but both crooners found the script too irreverent to be graced by their work. **(R)** –BM

AMERICATHON

1979 United Artists
PRODUCER: Joe Roth
DIRECTOR: Neil Israel
SCREENWRITERS: Michael Mislove,
  Monica Johnson

Very few people flocked to the theaters to see this unfunny comedy set in 1998 and centered around a telethon to save America. The cast is strictly TV talent—John Ritter, Harvey Korman, Fred Willard, with Elvis Costello performing two songs, a Vietnamese punk rocker, and Chief Dan George. For some reason, John Carradine's part was cut out.

THE AMITYVILLE HORROR
1979 AIP
PRODUCERS: Ronald Saland, Elliot Geisinger
DIRECTOR: Stuart Rosenberg
SCREENWRITER: Sandor Stern
A young Long Island couple, played by Margot Kidder and James Brolin, face black muck in the basement and flies in the parlor of their new home. It must be haunted. Prelate Rod Steiger futters and sputters until the house kills him. With Murray Hamilton, Michael Sachs, Helen Shaver, Natasha Ryan, and Don Stroud. It was AIP's biggest hit. The company subsequently changed its name to Filmways. *Amityville: The Possession* is the 1982 sequel. **(R)**   –BM

AMITYVILLE II: THE POSSESSION
1982 Orion
PRODUCERS: Ira N. Smith,
    Stephen R. Greenwald
DIRECTOR: Damiano Damiani
SCREENWRITER: Tommy Lee Wallace
This sleazy Italian-American prequel to the popular *Amityville Horror* features unintentional laughs, a mass slaughter, incest, and another weak *Exorcist*-inspired script. This is what we get from Dino De Laurentiis for not turning out in droves for his *Flash Gordon* movie. As a priest who keeps trying to go fishing with hack actor Andrew Prine, James Olson gets the funniest lines. Burt Young mumbles his way through his role as the sadistic father, and Jack Magner stars as a possessed teen who sleeps with his younger sister after hearing the voice of the Devil on his Sony Walkman. Later he kills his whole family with a shotgun and develops ugly boils on his face. With Rutanya Alda as the mom. Orion absorbed Filmways, the short-lived successor to AIP. Damiani also directed *A Witch In Love*. *Amityville 3-D* is next. **(R)**

AMOK: See SCHIZO.

AMONG THE LIVING
1941 Paramount (B&W)
PRODUCER: Sol C. Siegal
DIRECTOR: Stuart Heisler
SCREENWRITERS: L. Cole, Garrett Fort
A low-budget psychological thriller, often cited as one of the great B-pictures. Albert Dekker stars in two roles, as a businessman in a poor Southern town and as his insane homicidal twin, hiding from the authorities. The good brother is married to Frances Farmer (in real life she did one more feature, then was committed to an asylum by her mother). The bad twin hangs out with young flirtatious Susan Hayward, pretending to help her catch the escaped killer for reward money. With Harry Carey and Maude Eburne.

AMONG THE THORNS: See THE YOUNG SINNER.

THE AMPHIBIAN MAN
1962 NTA (U.S.S.R.)
DIRECTORS: Gennadi Kazansky/
    Vladimir Chebotaryov
SCREENWRITERS: Alexander Xenofontov,
    Alexei Kapler, Akiba Golburt
An evil scientist tries to kill a young man with gills. A Soviet adventure released directly to television in America. With William Koren and Anastasia Virten. The estate of Edgar Rice Burroughs sued to prevent use of the name

Tarzan in the French release title (*Tarzan des Mers*).

AMUCK: See *MANIAC MANSION*.

ANATOMY OF A PSYCHO
1961 Unitel of California (B&W)
PRODUCER/DIRECTOR: Brooke L. Peters
SCREENWRITERS: Jane Mann, Larry Lee
Darrell Howe has a list of the people who sent his brother to the state gas chamber. With help from sadistic girlfriend Judy Howard, he plans to take care of them one by one. George and Gracie's son Ronnie Burns becomes the victim of a frame-up when his girl tries to talk sense into a twisted mind and makes things worse. From the director of *The Unearthly*. With Pamela Lincoln, Russ Bender, Don Devlin, Robert W. Stabler, and Pat McMahon.   –CB

ANATOMY OF A SYNDICATE: See *THE BIG OPERATOR*.

AND NOW THE SCREAMING STARTS
1973 Amicus/Cinema Releasing (England)
PRODUCERS: Milton Subotsky, Max J. Rosenberg
DIRECTOR: Roy Ward Baker
SCREENWRITER: Roger Marshall
As Dr. Pope, Peter Cushing tries to unravel the mystery surrounding the house of Fengriffen, where the very pregnant Stephanie Beacham and her husband (Ian Ogilvy) are being terrorized by a dismembered hand and an axe-wielding farmer. Herbert Lom plays an evil ancestor. Patrick Magee is the country doctor. With Guy Rolfe. (R)

AND SOON THE DARKNESS
1970 Levitt Pickman
PRODUCER/SCREENWRITER: Brian Clemens
DIRECTOR: Robert Fuest
Fuest made this British thriller about two vacationing British nurses cycling through rural France who are menaced by a sex murderer (Sandor Eles), just before he did *The Abominable Dr. Phibes*. Star Pamela Franklin has been starring in scary movies since she was a little girl (*The Innocents*, 1961).

AND THEN THERE WERE NONE
1945 20th Century-Fox (B&W)
PRODUCER/DIRECTOR: René Clair
SCREENWRITER: Dudley Nichols
Excellent adaptation of Agatha Christie's *Ten Little Indians*, a classic whodunit, set on a deserted island off the Devonshire coast. Directed in Hollywood by Frenchman Clair (*I Married a Witch*) with Barry Fitzgerald, Walter Huston, Louis Hayward, Roland Young, June Duprez, and C. Aubrey Smith. Two less effective remakes were made in '65 and '74.

ANDROMEDA STRAIN
1971 Universal
PRODUCER/DIRECTOR: Robert Wise
SCREENWRITER: Nelson Gidding
An excellent big-budget technological thriller, based on Michael Crichton's bestselling novel. Everyone in a small town is killed by a virus brought back by a space probe, except for a baby and an old derelict. A group of scientists in a vast underground laboratory complex study the survivors and attempt to avoid a worldwide epidemic. With great special effects by Douglas Trumbull and an exciting climax with James Olson vs. a computerized laser beam. A pretty terrifying look at the future (present?). With David Wayne, Arthur Hill, and Kate Reid.

The soundtrack of electronic music by Gil Melle was issued by Kapp Records on a six-sided disc which caused untold destruction to the nation's automatic turntables, whose cartridges were smashed by the record's corners. It was recalled and reissued safe and round.

ANDY WARHOL'S BAD

1977 New World
PRODUCER: Jeff Tornberg
DIRECTOR: Jed Johnson
SCREENWRITERS: Pat Hackett, George Abagnalo

Carroll Baker stars as a Queens electrolysist who manages a female dial-a-murder organization. Perry King and Stefania Cassini are L.T. and P.G. It looks like an unsuccessful attempt to make a John Waters movie. With Susan Tyrrell, Brigid Polk, Lawrence Tierney, and Soho art humor. Music by the late Michael Bloomfield. **(X)**

ANDY WARHOL'S DRACULA

1974 Bryanston (Italy)
PRODUCER: Andrew Braunsberg
DIRECTOR/SCREENWRITER: Paul Morrissey
ALSO RELEASED AS: *Blood for Dracula, Young Dracula*

Three of the stars of *Andy Warhol's Frankenstein* return in a co-feature made the same year. Udo Kier is the palest, weakest, sickest vampire ever seen on screen. His assistant (Arno Juerging) loads the coffin on his vintage 1930s car and they head for Italy looking for virgins' blood. They stay with impoverished nobleman Vittorio De Sica, his wife (Maxime McKendry), and their four beautiful daughters. The parents think Dracula is an eccentric but rich foreigner and want him to marry into the family. He finds out that three of the girls aren't "wirgins," retching each time he bites one. The fourth one (the real virgin) is "saved" by Communist handyman Joe Dallesandro before Dracula can drink her "pure" blood. Roman Polanski has a great bit as a villager, winning a game of "You can't do what I can do." In a scene nearly duplicated in *Monty Python and the Holy Grail*, Kier has his arms and legs hacked off but continues to move and hiss. A soundtrack album is available. **(R)**

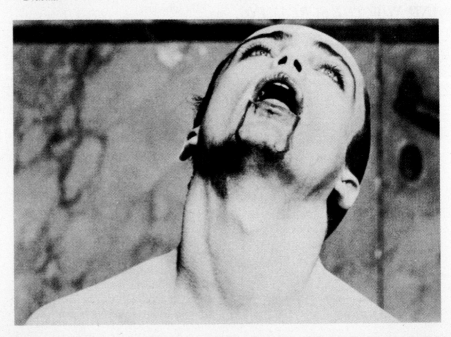

Udo Kier in Andy Warhol's Dracula.

ANDY WARHOL'S FRANKENSTEIN

1974 Bryanston (Italy) (3-D)
PRODUCER: Andrew Braunsberg
DIRECTOR: Paul Morrissey
SCREENWRITERS: Paul Morrissey,
   Antonio Margheriti
ALSO RELEASED AS: *Flesh for Frankenstein*

Andy probably didn't have to do anything more strenuous than sign a contract, but who cares. It's a comedy-gore-sex-horror movie that delivers—and it's in 3-D! Totally sick and disgustingly wonderful. Udo Kier (previously in *Mark of the Devil* and more obscure Euro-horrors) is the Baron, obsessed with his beautiful female creation (Dalila di Lazzaro), who needs a mate in order to create perfect beings. He uses giant shears to decapitate a handsome farmer (Srojan Zelenovic) and sews the head onto a new body. The Baron's sister/wife (Monique Van Vooren) seduces servant Joe Dallesandro and the monster. Otto (Arno Juerning) is the ultimate degenerate, Lorre-voiced assistant. The height of absurdity is reached at the end, with Joe Dallesandro dangling from the ceiling while the Baron (whose heart on the end of a spear seems about to drop on the audience) delivers an endless speech. All the while, the Addams Family-styled children watch and wait. A box-office winner in its original release, it was successful again during a 1982 re-release. The soundtrack album is in print. **(X)**

ANGEL, ANGEL, DOWN WE GO

1969 AIP
PRODUCER: Jerome F. Katzman
DIRECTOR/SCREENWRITER: Robert Thom
ALSO RELEASED AS: *Cult of the Damned*

A Hollywood decadence-and-murder story directed by the guy who wrote *Wild in the Streets*. Jordan Christopher and his rock group (including Roddy McDowall and singer Lou Rawls) move in on a wealthy family. Christopher seduces the shy daughter, Angel (Holly Near), and her mother (Jennifer Jones), a former stag-movie star. Jennifer is taken sky-diving with a faulty parachute and her husband, who had once been Christopher's lover, is found hanging from the swimming-pool diving board. Jordan Christopher sings all the songs, including "Mother Lover" and "Hey, Hey, Hey, and a Hi Ho." Lyrics by Barry Mann and Cynthia Weil. Reviewers noted similarities between the events in this feature and the Manson murders, but it was produced (by Sam Katzman's son) before Charlie made the front pages. **(R)**

AN ANGEL FOR SATAN

1966 (Italy)
PRODUCERS: Liliana Biancini,
   Giuliano Simonetti
DIRECTOR: Camillo Mastrocinque
SCREENWRITERS: Camillo Mastrocinique,
   Giuseppe Mangione
ORIGINALLY RELEASED AS: *Un Angelo per Satan*

A little-known and fairly perverse Barbara Steele movie that was released directly to television. Playing one of her many dual roles, she's a woman on vacation in a European village who seems to become possessed by the spirit of a 200-year-old statue. She also is the model for the statue in flashbacks. The evil woman seduces a number of people, unleashing jealousy and murders. With Antonio De Teffe and Ursula Davis.

ANGEL UNCHAINED

1970 AIP
PRODUCER/DIRECTOR: Lee Madden
SCREENWRITER: Jeffrey Alladin Fiskin

After rescuing his friend Shotgun (Bill McKinney) from an ambush, Angel (Don Stroud) leaves gang life behind for a leisurely cross-country tour. He makes it as far as Arizona, where he meets Tyne Daly in a gas station and joins a pacifist commune to be near her. The hippies' feud with local rednecks on dune buggies turns into major warfare when Angel takes down one attacker with a pitchfork. Shotgun and reinforcements are called in for the final confrontation. Co-starring Luke Askew, with Larry Bishop as Pilot, Bud Ekins as Speed, and Aldo Ray as the local sheriff. Madden also directed *Hell's Angels '69*. —CB

ANGELS DIE HARD!

1970 New World
PRODUCER: Charles Beach Dickerson
DIRECTOR/SCREENWRITER: Richard Compton

Angels vs. militant townspeople as cyclists honor the memory of a comrade run down after being released from the local jail. Despite the peace-making efforts of sheriff's daughter Connie Nelson and Deputy Frank Leo, the hour of confrontation arrives; much blood is spilled, and as Sheriff Carl Steppling bears down on head Angel Tom Baker, a bullet from Leo sends the squad car into an embankment where it explodes. Filmed in Kerrville, California. The cast includes William Smith, R.G. Armstrong, Alan DeWitt, and producer Beach Dickerson. Baker is the star of Andy Warhol's *I, a Man*. Custom bikes by Gary Littlejohn. **(R)** —CB

ANGELS FROM HELL

1968 AIP
PRODUCER: Kurt Neumann
DIRECTOR: Bruce Kessler
SCREENWRITER: Jerome Wish

Mike (Tom Stern), a biker, returns to California after serving in Vietnam. He uses his war-hero experience to organize a new, united super outlaw gang. When one member is shot by police because he killed a girl at a pot orgy, an all-out cop vs. biker war results. Mike "defiantly dies opposing the establishment for which he fought in 'Nam!" Music by the Peanut Butter Conspiracy and the Lollipop Shoppe. It was executive producer Joe Solomon's follow-up to *Hell's Angels on Wheels*. With Jack Starrett.

ANGELS' WILD WOMEN

1972 Independent International
PRODUCER/DIRECTOR: Al Adamson
SCREENWRITER: D. Dixon, Jr.

From the ads: "Too tough for any man! They'll beat 'em, treat 'em and eat 'em alive!" Four female bikers beat a rapist, go to a "free love colony," meet devil worshipers, and fight with chains and whips. Regina Carrol (the director's wife) stars as Margo. With Maggie Bemby (a Diana Ross look-alike with a 48-inch bust), Kent Taylor, Ross Hagen, and Vicki Volante. From the makers of *Blood of Dracula's Castle*. **(R)**

THE ANGRY BREED

1968 Commonwealth United
PRODUCER/DIRECTOR/SCREENWRITER:
David Commons

The adventures of an aspiring actor who is given a prize script after saving the life of a Hollywood screenwriter in Vietnam. On his return, Johnny Taylor has trouble finding a studio that will let him play the lead until he saves producer's daughter Lori Martin from a cycle-gang attack. The grateful father sends him to agent Jan Murray, but Murray wants the script for gang leader Deek Stacy (James MacArthur). Deek and his agent feed Johnny LSD and drag him away to the dungeon during the producer's Halloween party. Starring Murray MacLeod, with William Windom as Vance Patton, Jan Sterling as his alcoholic wife Gloria, and Melody Patterson as April Wilde. (M)   –CB

THE ANGRY RED PLANET

1959 AIP
PRODUCERS: Sidney Pink, Norman Maurer
DIRECTOR: Ib Melchior
SCREENWRITERS: Sid Pink, Ib Melchior

Mars as recalled by a woman astronaut under the influence of drugs. Since everything is supposed to be distorted and dreamlike, a process called Cinemagic was used. Giant creatures like three-eyed Martians, an intelligent amoeba, and a rat/spider/crab monster sometimes resemble cartoons, and the colors keep changing. An imaginative use of cheap special effects to highlight some silly science fiction. With Les Tremayne, Gerald Mohr, Jack Kruschen, and Nora Hayden. Similar drugged images were found in the Pink/Melchior team's next project, *Journey to the Seventh Planet*.

ANIMAL WORLD

1955 Warner Brothers
PRODUCER/DIRECTOR/SCREENWRITER:
Irwin Allen

Advertised as: "Two Billion Years in the Making!!" Despite scenes with dinosaurs designed by Willis O'Brien and animated by Ray Harryhausen, this Irwin Allen pseudo-documentary is probably as comical as his later, better-known disaster-film hits. *Animal World* was a follow-up to his *The Sea Around Us*. After animals, Irwin Allen summed up human life with *The Story of Mankind*. The dinosaur battle scenes were considered violent and a bit too gory at the time. Cuts were made before the film's release. Part of the battle segment later showed up in *Trog*.

THE ANNIVERSARY

1968 Hammer/20th Century-Fox (England)
PRODUCER/SCREENWRITER: Jimmy Sangster
DIRECTOR: Roy Ward Baker

A great black comedy starring Bette Davis in top form as Mrs. Taggart, the ultimate mom (with a black eyepatch). Every year she demands the presence of her three grown sons at the celebration of her wedding anniversary. But the father has been dead for years and Bette dominates and manipulates her sons so they won't stray. The one who managed to marry plans to move to Canada. Mom teaches him a lesson by telling him his children have been killed in an accident. She puts her glass eye under the pillow of another son's fiancée whom she claims has deformed ears and encourages her eldest son, who doesn't like women, to dress up in pretty underthings he steals from neighbors' clotheslines. (An early Pink Floyd song, "Arnold Layne," is about this panty fan). With Sheila Hancock, Jack Hedley, Christian Roberts, James Cossins, and Elaine Taylor. Theme by the New Vaudeville Band. Based on a London stage hit.

APACHE WOMAN
1955 ARC (AIP)
PRODUCER/DIRECTOR: Roger Corman
SCREENWRITER: Lou Russoff

From the ads: "Call her halfbreed and all hell breaks loose!" Government man Lloyd Bridges is sent to investigate an outbreak of lawlessness blamed on the local Apaches. While on assignment, he falls in love with a redskin beauty, then finds out the crime wave is the work of her renegade brother (Lance Fuller). Can Bridges save a peaceful reservation from the vengeance of angry pioneers without losing the woman he loves? The cast includes Chester Conklin and Paul Dubov, with AIP stock players Paul Birch, Dick Miller (as Tall Tree), Jonathan Haze, and Bruno Ve Sota. Joan Taylor (who ran the general store on *Rifleman*) is the Apache woman. Alex Gordon was executive producer.   –CB

APARTMENT ON THE THIRTEENTH FLOOR
1974 Atlas International (Spain)
PRODUCER: Joe Truchado
DIRECTOR: Eloy De La Iglesia

A slaughterhouse employee goes bonkers and begins killing people. When the bodies in his apartment begin to stink, he chops them up and pulverizes the remains. Vincent Parra stars in this charming import. (R)

A–P–E
1976 Worldwide (Korea) (3-D)
PRODUCERS: K.M. Yeung, Paul Leder
DIRECTOR: Paul Leder
SCREENWRITERS: Paul Leder, Ruben Leder

A terrible quickie *King Kong* imitation with a good first few minutes. A man in a gorilla suit destroys an ocean liner and kills a giant shark. Then it's the usual story in terrible 3-D. A Jack Harris presentation.

THE APE
1940 Monogram (B&W)
PRODUCER: Scott R. Dunlap
DIRECTOR: William Nigh
SCREENWRITERS: Curt Siodmak, Richard Carroll

Nine Boris Karloff films were released in 1940. He followed the dull Mr. Wong films at Monogram with this, probably the silliest movie of his entire career. Karloff plays another kindly doctor, trying to cure a polio victim (Maris Wrixon). He needs human spinal fluid for the miracle serum, so kills an escaped circus gorilla, skins it (off-screen), and disguised as the ape goes after more spines. What a brilliant idea!

Ten Tons of Animal Fury Leaps from the Screen

3D

- * defy a Giant Shark
- * destroy a teeming City
- * demolish an Ocean Liner
- * vanquish a Monster Reptile

JACK H. HARRIS presents

NOT TO BE CONFUSED WITH KING KONG

A*P*E

Starring ROD ARRANTS • JOANNA DE VARONA • ALEX NICOL • Directed by Paul Leder • Produced by K.M. Yeung and Paul Leder • LEE MING FILM CO.

Nobody would notice a gorilla killing people. And you thought only Bela Lugosi made movies this dumb.

THE APE MAN
1943 Monogram (B&W)
PRODUCERS: Sam Katzman, Jack Dietz
DIRECTOR: William Beaudine
SCREENWRITER: Barney Sarecky

An unbeatable combination: Beaudine and Lugosi! William "one-shot" Beaudine directed over 150 movies (from 1929 to 1966). Some of our favorites are *Voodoo Man* (1944), *Bela Lugosi Meets a Brooklyn Gorilla* (1952), and *Billy the Kid vs. Dracula* (1966). This incredible, typically ridiculous Monogram Studios horror features Bela as a scientist who injects himself with ape spinal fluid, becomes a werewolflike monster, and sends his pet gorilla out to murder humans for *their* spinal fluid so he can revert to normal. Reporters Wallace Ford and Louise Currie interfere. His sister (Minerva Urecal) approves; great stuff! A running gag features a man always peering through windows. At the end he says, "I'm the guy who wrote this picture!"

THE APE WOMAN
1963 Embassy (Italy/France)
PRODUCER: Carlo Ponti
DIRECTOR: Marco Ferreri
SCREENWRITERS: Marco Ferreri, Rafael Azcona
ORIGINALLY RELEASED AS: *La Donna Scimmia*

A depressing satire about a woman (Annie Girardot) covered with hair who is passed off as an African ape-woman stripteaser by fast-buck showman Ugo Tognazzi (*La Cage Aux Folles*). He discovers her at a poorhouse run by nuns where he is giving a "cultural" slide show of naked African women. When she threatens to leave him, he marries her. He finally agrees to have sex with her to keep her around, but she gets pregnant and dies giving birth. The promoter displays the corpses of his wife and baby. The show must go on. The American version has a special cowardly happy ending: her excess hair vanishes and the family lives happily and is supported by the reformed dad. It wasn't really that long ago that we were still being sheltered from the "excessive sex and violence" of decadent foreign films. Based on a true story.

THE AQUA SEX: See MERMAIDS OF TIBURON.

AN ARABIAN ADVENTURE
1979 Associated Film Distribution (England)
PRODUCER: John Dark
DIRECTOR: Kevin Connor
SCREENWRITER: Brian Hayles

Christopher Lee, as the wizard Alquazar, rules the city of Jaddur with an iron hand in this reshuffled version of *Thief of Baghdad* from producer John Dark (*At the Earth's Core, Warlords of Atlantis*). As usual, Dark's effects are more ambitious than they are effective (lots of little dolls on little flying carpets doing loop-the-loops in imitation of *Star Wars'* dogfights), but there's lots of action, a good comic performance by Mickey Rooney, and a brief cameo appearance by Peter Cushing.   –BM

ARE YOU DYING YOUNG MAN: See BEAST IN THE CELLAR.

THE ARENA
1973 New World
PRODUCER: Mark Damon
DIRECTOR: Steve Carver
SCREENWRITERS: Joyce and John Corrington,

From the ads: "See wild women fight to the death!" It's black slave Pam Grier (with a trident) vs. white slave Margaret Markov in this '70s drive-in version of *Spartacus*. The female slaves are really friends and turn on their decadent male captors for a bloody finish. A sometimes amusing departure from the women's prison movie cycle. Filmed in Italy. (R)

ARNOLD
1973 Cinerama
PRODUCER: Andrew J. Fenady
DIRECTOR: George Fenady
SCREENWRITERS: Jameson Brewer,
   John Fenton Murray
Horror/black comedy starring Stella Stevens as the new golddigging wife of a corpse. She marries Arnold at his funeral and continues to get his money as long as she stays by the coffin. Meanwhile various oddball relatives after Arnold's wealth are being killed in a variety of ways. With Roddy McDowall, Elsa Lanchester, Victor Buono, Farley Granger, and Patrick Knowles. From BCP (Bing Crosby Productions).

AROUND THE WORLD IN EIGHTY DAYS
1956 United Artists
PRODUCER: Michael Todd
DIRECTOR: Michael Anderson
SCREENWRITER: S.J. Perelman
Academy Award winning wide-screen all-star adventure comedy epic based on Jules Verne's novel of the same name, with the 1902 *Voyage to the Moon* as a prologue. David Niven stars as Phineas Fogg. With Cantinflas, Shirley MacLaine, Marlene Dietrich, Peter Lorre (as a Japanese steward), John Carradine (as a reporter), Ronald Colman, Frank Sinatra, Edward R. Murrow, Joe E. Brown, Noel Coward, Cedric Hardwicke, Buster Keaton, George Raft, Charles Boyer, Mike Mazurki, Edmond Lowe, Caesar Romero, Red Skelton, and many others. In 70mm Todd-AO. William Cameron Menzies was the associate producer.

AROUND THE WORLD, UNDER THE SEA
1966 MGM
PRODUCER/DIRECTOR: Andrew Marton
SCREENWRITERS: Arthur Weiss, Art Arthur
The hydronaut, an atomic submarine of fools, tries to stop a worldwide earthquake and encounters a giant moray eel. The stellar cast in this adventure brought to us by Ivan (*Flipper*) Tors includes Lloyd Bridges, Brian Kelly, David McCallum, Shirley Eaton, Marshall Thompson, Gary Merrill, Keenan Wynn, and Celeste Yarnall (*The Velvet Vampire*).

THE AROUSERS: See SWEET KILL.

ARSENIC AND OLD LACE
1941 Warner Brothers (B&W)
PRODUCER/DIRECTOR: Frank Capra
SCREENWRITERS: Julius J. Epstein,
   Philip G. Epstein
A wonderful, fast-paced ghoulish comedy starring a manic Cary Grant as Mortimer Brewster, a drama critic. He plans to marry Priscilla Lane but discovers that his kindly old aunts in Brooklyn have been poisoning lonely old men and having them buried in the basement by an uncle who thinks he's Teddy Roosevelt digging the Panama Canal. His brother, the long-lost Jonathan (Raymond Massey), shows up with the drunken Dr. Einstein (Peter Lorre). Jonathan is hiding from the law and, thanks to Lorre's inept plastic surgery, "looks like Boris Karloff." (Karloff played the role in the Broadway version, by Joseph Kesselring.) In the end Mortimer is relieved to discover he was adopted. With Josephine Hull, Jean Adair, and John Alexander, all from the play, and Edward Everett Horton, Jack Carson, and James Gleason. Music by

Max Steiner. For legal reasons, the release was held up over two years until the play ended its run.

ASPHYX

1972 Paragon (England)
PRODUCER: John Brittany
DIRECTOR: Peter Newbrook
SCREENWRITER: Brian Comport

Fascinating, unique science-fiction film set in the 1870s. A photographer/inventor (Robert Stevens) discovers he can photograph the spirit of death, which briefly enters the body when it dies. He photographs a man being publicly hung, and accidentally gets a picture of his own son drowning. The spirit, shown as a protoplasmic floating shape, is captured and used in experiments to achieve immortality. Convincing and well-acted. With Robert Powell (*Mahler*).

ASSAULT OF THE REBEL GIRLS: See CUBAN REBEL GIRLS

ASSAULT ON PARADISE: See MANIAC!

ASSAULT ON PRECINCT 13

1976 Turtle Releasing Corporation
PRODUCER: J.S. Kaplan
DIRECTOR/SCREENWRITER: John Carpenter

A great action-packed low-budget sleeper about the siege of an L.A. police station. On the last functioning night of the precinct, some unexpected prisoners are brought in and the phones are disconnected. All hell breaks loose when unrelenting urban guerrillas with silencers attack. The dark photography and Carpenter's repetitious four-note synthesizer score actually add to the appeal of this modern exploitation classic. With Austin Stoker, Darwin Johnson, and Laurie Zimmer. (**R**)

ASSIGNMENT: ISTANBUL: See THE CASTLE OF FU MANCHU.

ASSIGNMENT OUTER SPACE

1960 AIP (Italy)
PRODUCER: Hugo Grimaldi
DIRECTOR: Antonio Margheriti
(Anthony Daisies)
SCREENWRITER: Vassily Petrov
ALSO RELEASED AS: *Space Men*

The Alfa II, run by a malfunctioning computer, is about to crash into and destroy Earth. A group of international astronauts take off in another ship to stop it but spend most of the time arguing and fighting over a female crew member. Pretty dull stuff. With Rik von Nutter, Gabriella Farinon, Archie Savage, and Dave Montresor.

ASSIGNMENT TERROR

1970 Spain/Italy/W.Germany
PRODUCER: Jaime Prades
DIRECTORS: Tulio Demicheli, Hugo Fregonesé
SCREENWRITER: Jacinto Molina
ORIGINALLY RELEASED AS: *El Hombre Que Vino del Ummo*
ALSO RELEASED AS: *Dracula vs. Frankenstein*

A ridiculous horror/science-fiction movie starring the king of Spanish monsters, Paul Naschy. Starting with *Frankenstein's Bloody Terror*, Naschy played a vicious wolfman in a series of nine features. In this, the fourth, Michael Rennie plays an alien who revives the werewolf (Naschy, who wrote the script using his real name), the Frankenstein monster, Dracula, and the Mummy in order to conquer earth. Sound dumb? Try to imagine what went through Rennie's mind while he was acting in this dubbed mess. (Rennie died the next year.) With Karin Dor and Patty Shepard.

Tura Satana languidly scans newspaper for latest murderous exploits of The Astro Zombies.

THE ASTOUNDING SHE-MONSTER

1958 AIP (B&W)
PRODUCER/DIRECTOR: Ronnie Ashcroft
SCREENWRITER: Frank Hall

Wonderful ultra-cheap junk starring Robert Clarke as a geologist living in the woods with his trusty dog. A pair of crooks (Kenne Duncan and Jeanne Tatum) arrive with a kidnaped heiress (Marilyn Harvey) and take over the house. Soon a crash nearby turns out to be a spaceship containing a sexy blonde alien with a skintight metallic suit, high heels, lipstick, and incredible eyebrows (Shirley Kilpatrick). The plot is advanced by an offscreen narrator. Watch for it on your local Monster Chiller Horror Theater.

THE ASTRO-ZOMBIES

1968 Geneni Film Distributors
PRODUCER/DIRECTOR: Ted V. Mikels
SCREENWRITERS: Wayne Rogers,
   Ted V. Mikels

One of the all-time worst. John Carradine, as the mad Dr. DeMarco, works in a basement making zombies (actors with skeleton masks), with the help of a typically deformed assistant. The zombies like to mutilate people by ripping out their vital organs. Wendell

Also released as: Asylum.

Corey (who died just after filming) is a CIA chief on the case. Foreign agents (mostly Mexican) led by the incredible pasty-faced ex-stripper Satana, star of *Faster, Pussycat! Kill! Kill!*, are after DeMarco's creations. With Rafael Campos and Wally Moon. Wayne Rogers of *M. A. S. H.* co-wrote the script and was the executive producer.

ASYLUM

1972 Amicus/Cinerama (England)
PRODUCERS: Max J. Rosenberg,
   Milton Subotsky
DIRECTOR: Roy Ward Baker
SCREENWRITER: Robert Bloch
ALSO RELEASED AS: *House of Crazies*

"You have nothing to lose but your mind." Four horror stories (originally written and then adapted by Robert Bloch) are told by mental patients to explain why they "lost it." In "Frozen Fear," Richard Todd dismembers his wife (Sylvia Sims) and puts her wrapped-up parts in the freezer. Later, various arms, legs . . . attack. In "The Weird Tailor," Peter Cushing brings

some magic cloth to tailor Barry Morse to make a suit to bring his dead son back to life. "Lucy Comes to Stay" is a schizo-murder tale with Charlotte Rampling and Britt Ekland. "Mannikins of Horror" features tiny murdering robot dolls, with Herbert Lom, Patrick Magee, and Robert Powell. When reissued in theaters, this better-than-average anthology was advertised without even mentioning its many well-known stars. With Barbara Parkins.

ASYLUM EROTICA: See SLAUGHTER HOTEL.

ASYLUM OF SATAN
1972 Studio One
PRODUCER: J. Patrick Kelly III
DIRECTOR/SCREENWRITER: William Girdler
A very low-budget movie about a devil's disciple running a hospital and offering a female patient to his master. With "axed chopped bodies" and a robot snake. Filmed in Louisville, Kentucky. It was the first effort by the director of *The Manitou*. Charles Kissinger stars. **(R)**

AT THE EARTH'S CORE
1976 Amicus/AIP (England)
PRODUCER: John Dark
DIRECTOR: Kevin Connor
SCREENWRITER: Milton Subotsky
A childish version of Edgar Rice Burroughs' adventure, with Peter Cushing and his iron mole machine drilling into earth and arriving at Pellucidar. Pudgy Doug McClure is the hero. Caroline Munro is the princess Dia. With lots of odd man-in-suit monsters that look like Toho rejects.

ATLANTIS, THE LOST CONTINENT
1960 MGM
PRODUCER/DIRECTOR: George Pal
SCREENWRITER: Daniel Mainwaring

Silly adventure film set in the distant past on the scientifically advanced lost continent. A Greek sailor (Anthony Hall) rescues a princess (Joyce Taylor) whose father's kingdom has been taken over by the evil Zaren (John Dall, the star of *Gun Crazy*). The villain transforms slaves into animal men and uses atomic power to kill the opposition. The various bull-, dog-, and bear-headed slaves are the film's highlight. With Edward Platt, Barry Kroeger, Frank deKova, and William Smith.

An axe-chopped body from Asylum of Satan.

ATLAS
1960 Filmgroup
PRODUCER/DIRECTOR: Roger Corman
SCREENWRITER: Charles Griffith
A minimalist *Hercules* copy filmed in Greece by budget-minded Americans. Michael Forest as a thin Olympic champion fights the evil Praximedes (Frank Wolff). You might remember them in *Beast from Haunted Cave*. Barboura Morris (*Bucket of Blood*, *The Wasp Woman*) is the mistress Candia. Tiny armies including director Corman cross swords in front of ancient ruins. Frank and Barboura exchange wisecracks. Un-

like any other muscleman epic you've ever seen.

ATLAS AGAINST THE CYCLOPS

1961 Medallion (Italy)
PRODUCERS: Ermanno Donati,
   Luigi Carpentieri
DIRECTOR: Antonio Leonuiola
SCREENWRITERS: O. Biancoli, Gino Mangini
ORIGINALLY RELEASED AS: *Maciste nella Terra dei Ciclopi*

Gordon Mitchell as Maciste/Atlas fights an evil queen and saves a baby from a one-eyed giant.

ATOM AGE VAMPIRE

1961 Topaz Films (Italy) (B&W)
PRODUCER: Mario Fava
DIRECTOR/SCREENWRITER:
   Anton Giulio Masano

A professor (Alberto Lupo) who does research on Hiroshima bomb victims restores the horribly scarred face of a woman (Susan Loret) who had a car accident. He falls in love with her and has to kill women for their glands to keep her beautiful. For some unexplained reason, the doctor occasionally becomes a horrible reptile-faced creature. He also has to deal with his jealous female assistant and his patient's boyfriend, who arrives in a trench coat and sports car looking for his lost girl. A late night favorite.

THE ATOMIC BRAIN

1963 Emerson Films (B&W)
PRODUCERS: Jack Pollexfen,
   Dean Dillman, Jr.
DIRECTOR: Joseph V. Mascelli
SCREENWRITER: Vi Russell, Sue Dwiggens,
   Dean Dillman, Jr., Jack Pollexfen
ALSO RELEASED AS: *Monstrosity*

The cinematographer of *The Incredibly Strange Creatures* and other Ray Dennis Steckler films steps out and makes his own cheap horror film. A wealthy widow hires a mad doctor to transfer her brain into a beautiful young body. Three young European girls are imported as candidates but the doctor and his mutant assistant stray from their mission. Two girls become zombies and the third has a cat's brain placed in her head! You won't believe it! Meeeooooow!

THE ATOMIC CAFE

1982 Libra
PRODUCERS/DIRECTORS: Kevin Rafferty,
   Jayne Loader, Pierce Rafferty

A devastating documentary edited from 1950s U.S. Government films. Soldiers are subjected to atomic bomb tests, island paradises are wiped off the map, and schoolchildren are taught how to hide under desks to avoid nuclear fallout. Such respected figures as Chet Huntley and Hugh Beaumont (Beaver's dad) are onscreen pawns in the lunatic conspiracy to convince a trusting nation that an inevitable atomic showdown would be survivable and even worthwhile. Audiences react with nervous laughter and stunned disbelief. Then they go home and read about increased military spending, current underground bomb tests, weapons being launched into space, the planned evacuation of New York City, and a president who blames the entire antinuke movement on the Communists. Not recommended for viewers with weak hearts. An excellent sound-track album of '50s bomb-theme songs is available on Rounder. (No Rating)

THE ATOMIC KID

1954 Republic (B&W)
PRODUCER: Mickey Rooney
DIRECTOR: Leslie H. Martinson
SCREENWRITERS: Benedict Freeman,
   John Fenton Murray

While other films were demonstrating the unleashed horrors of atomic bombs with revived monsters and mutations, Mickey Rooney walks into an A-bomb blast and emerges a comical radioac-

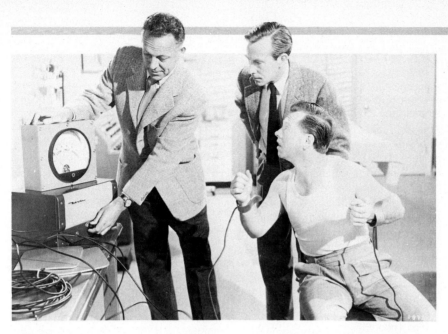

Whit Bissell watches as Mickey Rooney (The Atomic Kid) is tested for radioactivity.

tive "kid" who can win at Las Vegas slot machines just by standing alongside them. He goes to a testing-area house filled with mannequins and lives because of some peanut butter he ate. Blake Edwards wrote the story. With Whit Bissell.

THE ATOMIC MAN

1956 Allied Artists, (England) (B&W)
PRODUCER: Alec C. Snowden
DIRECTOR: Ken Hughes
SCREENWRITER: Charles Eric Maine
ORIGINALLY RELEASED AS: *Timeslip*

An atomic scientist, thought dead, is found alive and well by fellow scientists Gene Nelson and Faith Domergue. Due to an overdose of radiation, his mind works seven seconds ahead. He can't speak coherently but always knows the immediate future. Gangsters try to exploit his incredible powers for their own gains. Clever idea but a slow film. It originally played with *Invasion of the Body Snatchers.*

ATOMIC MONSTER: See *MAN MADE MONSTER.*

ATOMIC MONSTER — THE BEAST OF YUCCA FLATS: See *THE BEAST OF YUCCA FLATS.*

ATOMIC RULERS OF THE WORLD

1956-9 Manly TV (Japan) (B&W)
PRODUCER: Mitsugi Okura
DIRECTORS: Tervo Ishii, Akira Mitsuwa, Koreyoshi Akasaka
SCREENWRITER: Ichiro Miyegawa

Starman (also known as Supergiant) was the alien superhero of a series of nine short Japanese films. In 1964, four dubbed features edited from the originals were released on American television. The fast-paced seriallike action includes martial-arts fighting, back flips, and colorful costumes. In this feature, Starman battles American gangsters who threaten to destroy Japan with an atomic bomb. Funny excitement that shouldn't be missed. Ken Utsui is Starman.

ATOMIC SPACESHIP: See *FLASH GORDON.*

THE ATOMIC SUBMARINE

1959 Allied Artists (B&W)
PRODUCER: Alex Gordon
DIRECTOR: Spencer G. Bennet
SCREENWRITER: O.H. Hampton

A flying saucer that can travel underwater is destroying Earthships. An atomic sub discovers the saucer is alive, can self-repair any damage, and has a giant hairy eyeball inside. Arthur Franz, Dick Foran, Brett Halsey, Tom Conway, Paul Dubov, and Joi Lansing are submarine crew members. The best part comes when some of the men explore the saucer's interior. Bennet had directed mostly westerns since the silent era.

ATRAGON

1963 Toho/AIP
DIRECTOR: Inoshiro Honda
SCREENWRITER: Shinichi Sekizawa
ORIGINALLY RELEASED AS: *Kaitei Gunkan*

A superior Japanese science-fiction/fantasy film. The ancient undersea Mu kingdom has harnessed all the energy from the center of the Earth. The Mu queen decides to conquer the surface world by causing devastating earthquakes. The world's only hope is Captain Shinguji's incredible land/sea/air supership *Atragon*, built but not used by Japan during World War II. The captain doesn't get involved until his daughter and her boyfriend are kidnapped by the Mu kingdom. *Atragon* destroys the warring kingdom (and a giant serpent) in an orgy of great special effects. Tomoyuki Tanaka was the executive producer.

ATTACK FROM SPACE

1956–59 Manly TV (Japan) (B&W)
PRODUCER: Mitsugi Okura
DIRECTORS: Tervo Ishii, Akira Mitsuwa, Koreyoshi Akasaka
SCREENWRITER: Ichiro Miyegawa

Starman fights a Nazi-style alien in outer space. Unlike any other Japanese science fiction. See *Atomic Rulers of the World*.

ATTACK OF THE CRAB MONSTERS

1957 Allied Artists (B&W)
PRODUCER/DIRECTOR: Roger Corman
SCREENWRITER: Charles Griffith

One of Corman's delightful little science-fiction co-features. The giant atomic mutation crab looks pretty realistic except for its big eyes and the human feet you can sometimes spot underneath it. The crab decapitates scientists stranded on an isolated island, eats their heads, and assimilates their brains. The voices of previous victims coming through the crab attract new human food. With Richard Garland, Pamela Duncan, Russell Johnson, Mel Welles, Beech Dickerson, Leslie Bradley, Jonathan Haze, and Ed Nelson (in the crab). Originally co-billed with the equally essential *Not of This Earth*. It's only 64 minutes long.

ATTACK OF THE 50-FOOT WOMAN

1957 Allied Artists (B&W)
PRODUCER: Bernard Woolner
DIRECTOR: Nathan Hertz
SCREENWRITER: Mark Hanna

From the ads: "See a female colossus . . . her mountainous torso, skyscraper limbs, giant desires!" A legendary absurd classic starring statuesque Allison Hayes as a wealthy woman who is able to teach her cheating husband a lesson after a transparent bald alien turns her into a giant. Doctors chain her in the house and give her injections with an elephant syringe, but she breaks out and heads for the bar where her husband (William Hudson) is smooching and plotting with Yvette Vickers (*Playboy*'s Miss July 1959). She squeezes him to death before the cops close in and kill her. Harry! Nathan Hertz (Juran) also directed Ronald and Nancy Reagan in *Hellcats of the Navy* the same year.

ATTACK OF THE GIANT LEECHES

1959 AIP (B&W)
PRODUCER: Gene Corman
DIRECTOR: Bernard Kowalski
SCREENWRITER: Leo Gordon
ALSO RELEASED AS: *The Giant Leeches*

The intelligent, bloodthirsty leeches living in the swamp are actually men in suction-cup-covered suits that didn't quite fit over their air tanks. Besides the unconvincing monsters, this fun cheapie has a cast of no-good swamp dwellers. A bartender (Bruno Ve Sota) discovers his sexy tramp wife (Yvette Vickers) passionately kissing Michael Emmet; he forces them at gunpoint into the swamp—leech food. With Ken Clark, Gene Roth, Jan Shepard, and Tyler McVey. It's only 62 minutes long and originally played with *Bucket of Blood*. Roger Corman was executive producer.

ATTACK OF THE KILLER TOMATOES

1978 N.A.I. Entertainment
PRODUCERS: Steve Peace, John DeBello
DIRECTOR: John DeBello
SCREENWRITER: Costa Dillon

A science-fiction comedy with intentionally bad special effects and ludicrous dialogue. Scenes of various-sized tomatoes chasing people and bobbing in the water "attacking" a swimmer are funny, but it doesn't really make it as a midnight cult film. The only striking effect is a helicopter crashing (it was a real accident). A modern *Invasion of the Star Creatures*. With David Miller and Jack Riley.

ATTACK OF THE MAYAN MUMMY

1963 Medallion (Mexico/U.S.) (B&W)
PRODUCER/DIRECTOR: Jerry Warren
SCREENWRITERS: Gilberto Solares, Alfredo Salazar

Warren took scenes from the *Aztec Mummy* series and re-edited them with new scenes shot in America. The resulting mess about a woman regressing to a former life as a Mayan princess features Nina Knight, Richard Webb, and Bruno Ve Sota.

ATTACK OF THE MONSTERS

1969 Daiei/AIP-TV (Japan)
PRODUCER: Hidemasa Nagata
DIRECTOR: Noriaki Yuasa
SCREENWRITER: Fumi Takahashi
ORIGINALLY RELEASED AS: *Gamera tai Guiron*

An alien spaceship kidnaps two Earth boys. Gamera, the friendly giant flying turtle, races to a world on the other side of the sun to save them from the clutches of alien women who eat brains. He also battles Guiron, a ridiculous giant monster with a head shaped like a knife. The fifth Gamera movie.

ATTACK OF THE MUSHROOM PEOPLE

1963 Daiei/AIP-TV (Japan)
PRODUCER: Daiei
DIRECTORS: Inoshiro Honda, Giji Tsuburaya
SCREENWRITER: Takeshi Kimura
ALSO RELEASED AS: *Curse of the Mushroom People* and *Matango, the Fungus of Terror*

A real find for bored late-night TV viewers. It's a fungus frenzy as shipwrecked Japanese tourists are trapped on a fog-shrouded tropical island. One by one they turn into human toadstools. A survivor tells the story from a padded cell.

ATTACK OF THE PHANTOMS: See KISS MEETS THE PHANTOM OF THE PARK.

Stuffy John Agar refuses to join the fun in Attack of the Puppet People.

ATTACK OF THE PUPPET PEOPLE

1958 AIP (B&W)
PRODUCER/DIRECTOR: Bert I. Gordon
SCREENWRITER: George W. Yates

John Hoyt is a doll manufacturer and he's lonely. In order to have constant (and obedient) company he takes unsuspecting people into the back room of his shop and shrinks them. The little people are kept (sleeping) in glass tubes and taken out for champagne parties and rock 'n' roll dancing on the table. One little woman likes her existence—no worries or obligations, just sleep until the master wakes her for fun and games—but the recently shrunk John Agar is a rebel and leads five others on an escape plot. (Before being shrunk, John and his new girl go to a drive-in and make out during *The Amazing Colossal Man!* What irony!) The effects by Bert Gordon are good for one of his movies (if a little out of scale), but Hoyt is hilarious as the kind/mean puppet master, and you've got to see a briefcase full of John Agars in tubes! Hoyt stages a show in which little people are forced to act with marionettes; Agar violently attacks and destroys the Dr. Jekyll puppet! With June Kenney, Bert's little girl Susan (with a tiny cat), a "giant" dog, and a woman who bathes in a coffee can. Do-it-all Gordon also wrote the story.

ATTACK OF THE ROBOTS

1962 AIP-TV (France/Spain) (B&W)
DIRECTOR: Jesse Franco
SCREENWRITER: Jean-Claude Carrière
ORIGINALLY RELEASED AS: *Cartes sur Table*

Far from *Alphaville* in terms of quality, this is an earlier adventure starring Eddie Constantine as Interpol agent Lemmy Caution. He saves the world from a scientist whose killer robot-men are targeted to eliminate various heads of state. With Fernando Rey and Sophie Hardy.

AUDREY ROSE

1977 United Artists
PRODUCERS: Joe Wizan, Frank de Felitta
DIRECTOR: Robert Wise
SCREENWRITER: Frank de Felitta

John Beck and Marsha Mason live on New York's Central Park West with their 12-year-old daughter Ivy (Susan Swift). They're reasonably happy until Anthony Hopkins shows up and claims Ivy is a reincarnation of his daughter Audrey Rose, who was burned alive. A hypnotist is used to bring Hopkins' girl "back." Reincarnation has never been a very popular movie theme. This feature was a box-office flop for UA. Despite its bad reviews, it's probably a lot better than *The Reincarnation of Peter Proud* (1975). Robert Wise's long and diverse career can survive an occasional failure. From Frank de Felitta's novel of the same name. With Norman Lloyd, Robert Walden, and John Hillerman.

AUTOPSIA DE UN FANTASMA

1967 (Mexico)
PRODUCER/DIRECTOR: Ismael Rodriguez

It's really amazing that this Mexican horror-comedy film was never released here, because it features three American stars. John Carradine plays a traditional-looking Satan with horns. Basil Rathbone (in his last role) is a ghost looking for a perfect love. Cameron Mitchell is a mad scientist. A blond female robot falls for the 75-year-old Rathbone. The comedy ends with a nuclear holocaust! Those funny Mexicans!

AUTOPSY

1978 Brenner (Italy)
PRODUCER: Leonardo Pescarola
DIRECTOR: Armando Crispini

A mystery known for its graphic footage of an autopsy which was later cut out. Mimsy Farmer (*Hot Rods to Hell*) stars with Ray Lovelock and Barry Primus. Music by Ennio Morricone. **(R)**

AVALANCHE

1978 New World
PRODUCER: Roger Corman
DIRECTOR: Corey Allen
SCREENWRITER: Claude Pola

Advertised as: "6 million tons of icy terror!" This disaster got terrible reviews and didn't do so well at the box office. It couldn't be any worse than your average Irwin Allen movie. Rock Hudson stars as the rich developer of the resort in danger. Mia Farrow, his ex-wife, goes for naturalist photographer Robert Forster until Rock rescues her from a wrecked bridge. With Jeanette Nolan, Anthony Carbone (all right!), and X brands. A jet crash causes the avalanche. Director Corey Allen is a popular character actor.

Howard Vernon and his human robot in The Awful Dr. Orloff.

THE AVENGER

1960 UCC-TV (W. Germany) (B&W)
PRODUCER/SCREENWRITER: Kurt Ulrich
DIRECTOR: Karl Anton
ORIGINALLY RELEASED AS: *Der Raecher*
Based on the Edgar Wallace novel of the same name. An ugly hunchbacked ape man decapitates people and mails the heads to Scotland Yard. Heinz Drache stars with Ingrid Van Bergen. Dozens of the stories of Wallace (1875–1932) were filmed in Germany during the 60s. They all involve Scotland Yard investigating bizarre crimes. Klaus Kinski is in about fifteen of them. Christopher Lee and Gert Fröbe turned up in a few. Most were released directly to American television.

THE AVENGER

1962 Medallion, (France/Italy)
PRODUCERS: Albert Band, Giorgio Venturini
DIRECTOR: Giorgio Rivalta
SCREENWRITER: Ugo Liberatore
ORIGINALLY RELEASED AS: *La Leggende di Enea*
ALSO RELEASED AS: *The Last Glories of Troy*

Steve Reeves repeats his Aeneas role from *The Trojan Horse*. This time the muscular hero is involved with Etruscans, more Trojans, another princess, and a stampede of bulls. With Giacomo Rossi Stuart and Carla Marlier.

THE AWAKENING

1980 Warner Brothers
PRODUCERS: Robert Solo, Andrew Scheinman, Martin Shafer
DIRECTOR: Mike Newell
SCREENWRITERS: Allan Scott, Chris Bryant, Clive Exton
Charlton Heston stars as an archaeologist whose daughter (Jill Townsend) is possessed by the spirit of an evil Egyptian queen. It's based on *The Jewel of Seven Stars* by Bram Stoker, which was previously filmed under the title *Blood from the Mummy's Tomb*. A fairly dull big-budget production with Susannah York, Stephanie Zimbalist, and some pretty bloody scenes. The soundtrack is available. (R)

THE AWFUL DR. ORLOFF

1962 Sigma III Corporation (Spain/
France) (B&W)
PRODUCER: Serge Newman
DIRECTOR/SCREENWRITER: Jesse Franco
ORIGINALLY RELEASED AS: *Gritos en la Noche*

Here's the hit that got Jesse Franco's
incredible career off the ground. Maybe
you've heard how bad it is. It spawned
four sequels. Howard Vernon stars as
the demented Dr. Orloff, another European surgeon with a horribly disfigured
daughter. Of course he has to kidnap
beautiful women in order to perform
skin-graft operations. The real star,
though, is his brother Marius (Ricardo
Valle), a blind human robot with a
cartoonish face. Marius had been caught
with the Doc's wife, killed, and turned
into a handy slave. As a brave ballerina,
Diana Lorys puts a stop to the killings.
Originally co-billed with *The Horrible Dr.
Hichcock*. A tranquilizing experience.

THE AZTEC MUMMY

1957 Azteca (Mexico) (B&W)
PRODUCER: William Calderon Stell
DIRECTOR: Rafael Lopez Portillo
ORIGINALLY RELEASED AS: *La Momia*

Most Mexican films were pretty prim-
itive-looking in the '50s. Their '30s-style
horror films made with '30s techniques
are a strange and unique breed. The
same director made three in a row about
a long-haired walking corpse. Ramon
Gay is the hero in all three. The next
one, *Robot vs. the Aztec Mummy*, got
more north-of-the-border exposure. The
mummy's name is Popoca.

BABES IN BAGHDAD

1952 United Artists
PRODUCER: Edward J. Danziger
DIRECTOR: Edgar G. Ulmer
SCREENWRITER: Harry Lee Danziger

The main babes are Paulette Goddard and Gypsy Rose Lee. The eleven wives of the Kadi of Baghdad revolt because of neglect. With Richard Ney, John Boles, Sebastian Cabot, and Christopher Lee as a slave driver. Ulmer made *The Man From Planet X* for the same studio in '51. Filmed in Spain.

BABES IN TOYLAND

1934 MGM (B&W)
PRODUCER: Hal Roach
DIRECTORS: Gus Meins, Charles Rogers
SCREENWRITERS: Frank Butler, Nick Grinde
ALSO RELEASED AS: *March of the Wooden Soldiers*

A funny musical-comedy version of Victor Herbert's operetta with Laurel and Hardy as dimwitted heroes working for the toymaker. Instead of 600 one-foot soldiers they make 100 six-foot soldiers that later help fight the evil Barnaby (Henry Brandon) and his bogeymen. With Charlotte Henry, Angelo Rossitto, and Marie Wilson.

BABES IN TOYLAND

1961 Buena Vista
PRODUCER: Walt Disney
DIRECTOR: Jack Donohue
SCREENWRITERS: Joe Rinaldi, Ward Kimball, Lowell S. Hawley

A disaster from the Disney Studios, full of teen stars and forgettable songs. Annette Funicello has her sheep stolen by Ray Bolger, who has Tommy Sands kidnaped while Ed Wynn makes toys. With Tommy Kirk (*The Man With the Synthetic Brain*).

THE BABY

1974 Scotia International
PRODUCERS: Milton Polsky, Abe Polsky
DIRECTOR: Ted Post
SCREENWRITER: Abe Polsky

Ruth Roman plays a deranged mother who hates men. She takes it out on her full-grown teenaged son whom she's raised to remain an infant. As the baby, David Manzy wears diapers and crawls and gurgles in his crib. Anjanette Comer plays a social worker who shows up to spoil Mom's fun. With Marianna Hill and a twist ending. Roman is great but the film overall is an uneven mixture of horror clichés and reality (scenes of real retarded kids), and "baby's" crying is badly dubbed. From the director of *Whiffs*, a terrible nerve gas comedy.

BACHELOR OF HEARTS

1958 Continental (England)
PRODUCER: Vivian A. Cox
DIRECTOR: Wolf Rilla
SCREENWRITERS: Leslie Bricusse, Frederic Raphael

Hardy Kruger stars in this comedy as a German exchange student at Cambridge who becomes a victim of the pranks of the exclusive Dodo Club. Twenty-one-year-old Barbara Steele appears in her first role.

BACK DOOR TO HELL

1964 20th Century-Fox (U.S./Philippines) (B&W)
PRODUCER: Fred Roos
DIRECTOR: Monte Hellman
SCREENWRITERS: Richard A. Guttman, John Hackett

Hellman made two of these island cheapsters with Jack Nicholson after his useless *The Beast From Haunted Cave*. In this World War II story, Nicholson and John Hackett help Lieutenant Jimmie Rodgers sign up native guerrillas to fight the Japanese occupation. Annabelle Huggins, Conrad Maga, and Johnny Monteiro co-star. Filmed with the cooperation of the Philippine Department of National Defense. The follow-up is *Flight to Fury*. Nicholson also starred in *The Shooting* and *Ride the Whirlwind* for Hellman.   –CB

BACK FROM THE DEAD

1957 20th Century-Fox (B&W)
PRODUCER: Robert Stabler
DIRECTOR: Charles Marquis Warren
SCREENWRITER: Catherine Turney
Peggie Castle is possessed by the spirit of husband Arthur Franz's first wife! From the director of *The Unknown Terror*. With Marsha Hunt.

BACKGROUND TO DANGER

1943 Warner Brothers (B&W)
PRODUCER: Jerry Wald
DIRECTOR: Raoul Walsh
SCREENWRITER: W. R. Burnett
More *Casablanca*-style foreign intrigue set in Turkey, based on an Eric Ambler novel of the same name. George Raft and Brenda Marshall star with Peter Lorre as Zalenkoff, a Russian agent, and Sidney Greenstreet, who is working for the Nazis. With Turhan Bey and Kurt Katch. Ambler's *Journey Into Fear* had been a hit film the year before.

BAD CHARLESTON CHARLIE

1973 International Cinema
PRODUCER: Ross Hagen
DIRECTOR: Ivan Nagy
SCREENWRITERS: Ross Hagen, Ivan Nagy, Stan Kamber
Ross Hagen stars as a comic gangster. John Carradine is a drunk newspaper reporter. With Ultra Violet.

BAD GIRL: See TEENAGE BADGIRL.

BAD RONALD

1974 TV
PRODUCER: Philip Capice
DIRECTOR: Buzz Kulik
SCREENWRITER: Andrew Peter Martin
A psycho teen lives hidden in a house that a family with three daughters has just moved into. With Scott Jacoby, Pippa Scott, and Kim Hunter. By the director of *The Explosive Generation*.

THE BAD SEED

1956 Warner Brothers (B&W)
PRODUCER/DIRECTOR: Mervyn LeRoy
SCREENWRITER: John Lee Mahin
Eleven-year-old Patty McCormack received an Academy Award nomination for her portrayal of Rhoda, a pigtailed young murderess who seems to be inherently evil. After drowning a little boy at a picnic and burning the half-witted gardener to death, she's struck dead by lightning (an ending not in the play, which also starred Patty). A silly curtain call featuring Rhoda being spanked was also added because of the censor. With Nancy Kelly, Henry Jones, William Hopper, Eileen Heckart, Jesse White, and Evelyn Varden. Based on Maxwell Anderson's play of the same title.

BAFFLED!

1973 TV
PRODUCER/DIRECTOR: Philip Leacock
SCREENWRITER: Theodore Epstein
Leonard Nimoy as a race driver with ESP joins psychiatrist Susan Hampshire to try to prevent tragedies seen in his visions. With Vera Miles and Rachel Roberts. Filmed in England. Available on videocassette.

BAGHDAD

1949 Universal
PRODUCER: Robert Arthur
DIRECTOR: Charles Lamont
SCREENWRITER: Robert Hardy Andrews
As an Arabian princess, red-haired Maureen O'Hara sings and dances. Vincent Price, as Pasha Ali Nadim, is a comic-strip villain. Paul Christian is Hassan, the hero.

BAIT

1954 Columbia (B&W)
PRODUCER/DIRECTOR: Hugo Haas
SCREENWRITERS: Samuel W. Taylor,
Hugo Haas

The devil (Cedric Hardwicke) introduces and narrates this important moral lesson. Old prospector Hugo Haas marries young Cleo Moore and moves her into the cabin he shares with John Agar. Hugo hopes John will make a play for his wife so he can shoot him, but they fall in love discreetly and make their own plays. The fourth cheap drama starring Hugo and Cleo. John Agar returned with Cleo in Haas' *Hold Back Tomorrow*. With Bruno Ve Sota.

BALLAD IN BLUE: See *BLUES FOR LOVERS*.

A serious moment in Bait with Cleo Moore, Hugo Haas, and John Agar.

BAMBOO SAUCER

1967 World Entertainment
PRODUCER: Jerry Fairbanks
DIRECTOR/SCREENWRITER: Frank Telford
ALSO RELEASED AS: *Collision Course*

Dan Duryea and his team are searching for a downed saucer somewhere in Tibet; at the same time the Red Chinese discover the spaceship has a deadly side effect. Duryea finds the saucer and takes off in it. Little action before the end of this film; the results are only passable. With John Ericson, Lois Nettleton, and Bob Hastings.　　　　–AF

THE BANANA MONSTER: See *SCHLOCK*.

BANG BANG: See *THE BANG BANG KID*.

THE BANG BANG KID

1968 Ajay Films (Spain Italy)
PRODUCER: Sidney Pink
DIRECTOR: Luciano Lelly
SCREENWRITER: Jose L. Bayonas
ALSO RELEASED AS: *Bang Bang*

Happy Days' Tom Bosley stars as a malfunctioning comic gunslinger/robot. A hard-to-believe feature from the producer of *The Angry Red Planet*. With Guy Madison and Sandra Milo.

BARBARELLA

1968 Paramount (France/Italy)
PRODUCER: Dino De Laurentiis
DIRECTOR: Roger Vadim
SCREENWRITERS: Terry Southern,
Roger Vadim, Jean-Claude Forest,
Vittorio Bonicelli, Brian Degas,
Claude Brule, Tudor Gates,
Clement Biddlewood

A colorful, corny science-fiction adventure starring Jane Fonda as the heroine of the popular French comic strip. After an in-flight antigravity striptease, Barbarella lands on Lythion and sets out to find Duran Duran (Milo O'Shea). Anita Pallenberg makes a perfect black queen; she seduces the blind angel (John Phillip Law). Barbarella has sex with a revolutionary (David Hemmings) by taking pills and touching fingers. She also shorts out a pleasure machine, is trapped in the queen's chamber of nightmares, and is attacked by deadly birds, cannibalistic dolls, and hollow leather guards with whip arms. Lots of great clothes and ideas. With Marcel Marceau and Claude Dauphin. Sunday newspapers got a lot of criticism from parents for running full-color cartoon ads in their comic supplements.

BARBED WIRE DOLLS
1975 Burbank Int. Pictures Corp.
(W. Germany)
PRODUCER: E. C. Dietrich
DIRECTOR: Jesse Franco
ORIGINALLY RELEASED AS: *Frauen Gefängnis*
ALSO RELEASED AS: *Caged Women*
Bondage, beatings, rape, humiliation, and sadism in a gross prison film from the director of *99 Women* and *Wanda the Wicked Warden*. A popular 42nd Street item. With Lina Romay. **(R)**

BARN OF THE NAKED DEAD
1973 Twin World
PRODUCER/DIRECTOR: Gerald Cormier
SCREENWRITERS: Roman Valenti, Ralph Harolde
ALSO RELEASED AS: *Terror Circus*
Andrew Prine, formerly *Simon, King of the Witches*, continues his low-budget horror career as a maniac who tortures women. Meanwhile, his father, a monster transformed by radiation, roams the Nevada desert killing people. Incompetent cheap thrills with Jennifer Ashley.

BARON BLOOD
1972 AIP (Italy)
PRODUCER: Alfred Leone
DIRECTOR: Mario Bava
SCREENWRITER: Vincent Forte
ORIGINALLY RELEASED AS: *Gli Orrori del Castello di Noremberga*
When a hotel firm starts restoring an old Austrian castle, a centuries-old baron with a moldly face puts his torture chamber to good use. Joseph Cotten stars both as the contemporary baron in a wheelchair, and as the horrible ancient creature (he looks like Vincent Price in *The House of Wax*). Elke Sommer is on hand to scream a lot, and others enjoy the stretching rack and spike-lined coffins. With Rada Rassimov (also known as Sarah Bay). Filmed in Austria.

THE BARON OF ARIZONA
1950 Lippert (B&W)
PRODUCER: Carl K. Hittleman
DIRECTOR/SCREENWRITER: Sam Fuller
Fuller's second film is unlike any of his others, but it's a fascinating if slow-moving story of James Reams (Vincent Price), a 19th-century American who devises a complicated scheme involving forgeries and passing as a monk in Europe in order to "legally" claim the Arizona Territory as his own and establish his own country. He also raises Ellen Drew to be his future adoring wife. Supposedly based on a true story. With Beulah Bondi, Vladimir Sokoloff, Gene Roth, and Angelo Rossitto. Cinematography by James Wong Howe.

BARRACUDA
1978 Republic
PRODUCERS/SCREENWRITERS: Wayne Crawford, Harry Kerwin
DIRECTOR: Harry Kerwin
ALSO RELEASED AS: *The Lucifer Project*

Chemicals in the ocean make fish attack and people go crazy. Jason Evers (*The Brain That Wouldn't Die*) stars with Wayne David Crawford and Bert Freed. Filmed in Florida. Title theme by the Frankfurt Radio Symphony Orchestra. Other music by Klaus Schultze. It uses a one-shot revival of the old Republic logo.

BASKET CASE
1982 Analysis
PRODUCER: Edgar Ievins
DIRECTOR/SCREENWRITER: Frank Henenlotter
This imaginative independent feature is a twisted gem about the ultimate split personality. Kevin Vanhentenryck stars

THE TENANT IN ROOM 7 IS VERY SMALL, VERY TWISTED AND VERY MAD.

BASKET CASE

an IEVINS / HENENLOTTER production starring KEVIN VanHENTENRYCK TERRI SUSAN SMITH BEVERLY BONNER
Director of Photography BRUCE TORBET Music GUS RUSSO Executive Producers ARNIE BRUCK TOM KAYE
Production Executive RAY SUNDLIN Produced by EDGAR IEVINS Written and Directed by FRANK HENENLOTTER

as Duane, a seemingly innocent young man from Glen Falls, New York, who arrives at a seedy 42nd Street hotel clutching a mysterious wicker basket. Inside is Belial, his grotesque telepathic mutant twin. Duane tries to have a relationship with a nurse, but the vengeful, domineering brother makes him help slaughter the unethical doctors who had separated them. With animated sequences, gore, humor, and lots of surprises for horror fans. Also starring Robert Vogel, Beverly Bonner, and Terri Susan Smith.

THE BAT
1958 Allied Artists (B&W)
PRODUCER: C. J. Tevlin
DIRECTOR/SCREENWRITER: Crane Wilbur
An old-fashioned mystery play by Mary Roberts Rinehart that had already been filmed three times was made once more with Agnes Moorehead starring as a writer staying at a summer home. A hooded figure with a claw hand known as the Bat murders some of the cast, money is stolen, and a real bat shows up to terrorize a group of women. Vincent Price as Dr. Wells is the prime suspect. Grown-up "Little Rascal" Darla Hood is a victim of the mysterious killer. With Gavin Gordon and Lenita Lane. At the time of release, newspaper ads said: "Make a double date! People in pairs don't mind the scares!"

THE BAT PEOPLE
1974 AIP
PRODUCER/SCREENWRITER: Lou Shaw
DIRECTOR: Jerry Jameson
While exploring a cave in the desert, biologist John Beck is bitten by a bat and slowly mutates into a deadly bat/man. The makeup is pretty convincing in this low-budget thriller. With Marianne McAndrew and Michael Pataki as the sheriff.

THE BAT WHISPERS

1931 United Artists (B&W)
PRODUCER/DIRECTOR/SCREENWRITER:
Roland West

Director West remade his own *The Bat* (1926), about a masked killer in an old mansion. Chester Morris stars with Una Merkel and Gustav von Seyffertitz. A third version starred Vincent Price. They all were based on a popular play of the same title.

BATMAN

1966 20th Century-Fox
PRODUCER: William Dozier
DIRECTOR: Leslie H. Martinson
SCREENWRITER: Lorenzo Semple, Jr.

It's Batman—the Movie! It's longer and dumber than the TV show ever was! Four villains team up against the dynamic duo and steal a dehydrator that turns nine kidnaped diplomats to dust. With Cesar Romero as the Joker, Burgess Meredith as the Penguin, Frank Gorshin as the Riddler, and Lee Meriwether (Miss America 1955) playing Kitka the Catwoman for the first and last time. With all the show's regulars (Adam West, Burt Ward, Neil Hamilton, Alan Napier, Stafford Repp, and Madge Blake), a Bat-Copter, a Bat-Cycle, Reginald Denny, and Sterling Holloway. Holy economics, Batman, this lousy feature must have taken a week to film, edit, and release!

BATMEN OF AFRICA: See DARKEST AFRICA.

BATTLE BENEATH THE EARTH

1968 MGM (England)
PRODUCER: Charles Reynolds
DIRECTOR: Montgomery Tully
SCREENWRITER: L. Z. Hargreaves

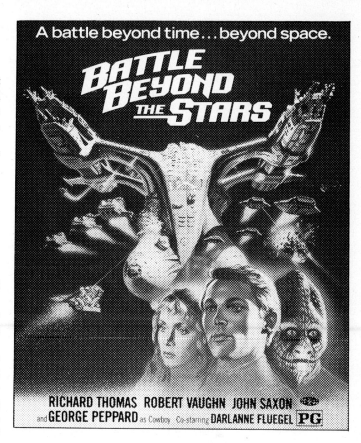

A battle beyond time...beyond space.

BATTLE BEYOND THE STARS

RICHARD THOMAS ROBERT VAUGHN JOHN SAXON and GEORGE PEPPARD as Cowboy Co-starring DARLANNE FLUEGEL **PG**

The Red Chinese use a laser-beam tank to drill a tunnel under the Pacific, so they can invade California with atom bombs! Kerwin Matthews leads a small American army to battle a small Chinese army in the tunnel. With Bessie Love, some classic dialogue, and an Anglo playing the Oriental leader.

BATTLE BEYOND THE STARS

1980 New World
PRODUCER: Ed Carlin
DIRECTOR: Jimmy T. Murakami
SCREENWRITER: John Sayles

The Seven Samurai done *Star Wars*-style with a script by John Sayles. Richard Thomas (*The Waltons*) recruits seven space fighters to save his peaceful planet from villain John Saxon. Robert Vaughn reprises his *Magnificent Seven* role. George Peppard is an actual space cowboy. Sybil Danning is a Valkyrie with the best space costume since *Barbarella*. Darlanne Flugel is the beautiful daughter of what's left of Sam Jaffe. The last two ships are manned by a lizard man and five white clones called Nestor. Some of the gags were cut out and the editing could have been better, but it's a lot more memorable and more fun than *The Empire Strikes Back*. With Jeff Corey. Roger Corman was executive producer. Music by James Horner. A soundtrack album is available.

BATTLE BEYOND THE SUN
1959/63 AIP/Filmgroup
PRODUCER: Thomas Colchart
DIRECTORS: Alexander Kozyr, Thomas Colchart
SCREENWRITERS: Nicholas Colbert, Edwin Palmer

Roger Corman bought a Russian film (*Nebo Zowet*) that featured Soviet cosmonauts triumphing over cowardly American astronauts. Young Francis Ford Coppola was called into action to re-edit, write new dialogue, and shoot a battle scene with monsters. The cold-war politics vanished as the scenario was projected into the future, when Earth is divided into two countries, North and South Hemis. The good-guy Russians became citizens of North Hemis. Unless you're a big fan of monster fights, it's pretty dull. It shows a tall, hastily constructed penis monster battling a round vagina monster! Only very young kids wouldn't notice. The reconstructed version does not play in the Soviet Union. Corman takes the executive producer credit.

BATTLE FOR THE PLANET OF THE APES
1973 20th Century-Fox
PRODUCER: Arthur P. Jacobs
DIRECTOR: J. Lee Thompson
SCREENWRITERS: Paul Dehn, John William Corrington, Joyce Hooper Corrington

Finally—the last chapter of the apes story. It's good apes vs. militant gorillas and it all leads up to the post-holocaust gorilla-ruled Earth of the first film. Roddy McDowall is back with Natalie Trundy from *Conquest*. . . . France Nuyen and Severn Darden are mutants. The ape casting gets funnier than ever. Have fun spotting hairy John Huston, Claude Akins, Paul Williams, and Lew Ayres. The human hero is Austin Stoker (*Assault on Precinct 13*). With Sam Jaffe as the lawgiver. The next stop for Roddy and the apes was a flop TV series which was re-edited into five phony features. Real fans went to drive-ins and watched all five ape films in a row.

BATTLE IN OUTER SPACE
1959 Toho/Columbia (Japan)
PRODUCER: Tomoyuki Tanaka
DIRECTOR: Inoshiro Honda
SCREENWRITER: Shinichi Sekizawa
ORIGINALLY RELEASED AS: *Uschi dai Senso*

Made as a sort of follow-up to *The Mysterians*, it's an all-out space-battle movie with flying saucers launched from the Moon by the pint-sized Natalians, fighting Earth spacecraft. With lasers, a space wheel, and Earth astronauts with transistor devices planted in their brains by the nasty aliens.

BATTLE OF BLOOD ISLAND
1960 Filmgroup (B&W)
PRODUCER: Roger Corman
DIRECTOR/SCREENWRITER: Joel Rapp

On a remote island in the South Pacific, two stranded American soldiers struggle to stay alive under impossible conditions in the late days of World War II. Filmed in the Caribbean. Ron Kennedy and Richard Devon are the leads. Rapp also directed *High School Big Shot*. —CB

THE BATTLE OF THE RIVER PLATE: See *PURSUIT OF THE GRAF SPEE*.

BATTLE OF THE WORLDS

1960 Topaz (Italy)
PRODUCTION SUPERVISOR: Thomas Sagone
DIRECTOR: Antonio Marghetti (Anthony Dawson)
SCREENWRITER: Vassily Petron
ORIGINALLY RELEASED AS: *Il Pianeta degli Uomini Spenti*

Seventy-two-year-old Claude Rains went to Italy to star as Professor Benjamin. A dead planet run by computers is trying to destroy Earth. The old professor and his crew travel to the planet and discover giant skeletons of a dead race. Thanks to a good performance by Rains and interesting sets, it's easier to take than most dull Italiano space flicks.

BATTLE TAXI

1955 United Artists (B&W)
PRODUCERS: Ivan Tors, Art Arthur
DIRECTOR: Herbert L. Strock
SCREENWRITER: Malvin Ward

Former jet pilot Arthur Franz learns the value of his new assignment with the Air Force helicopter rescue service during the Korean hostilities—searching for lost patrols, taking part in daring ocean rescues, and mixing it up with contentious enemy tanks. Stock footage courtesy of the 42nd Air Rescue Squadron. With Sterling Hayden, Marshall Thompson, and John Goddard. See *The Crawling Hand*. —CB

BATTLESTAR GALACTICA

1979 Universal
PRODUCERS: John Dykstra, Leslie Stevens
DIRECTOR: Richard A. Colla
SCREENWRITER: Glen Larson
ALSO RELEASED AS: *Mission Galactica: The Cyclon Attack*

The three-hour (with commercials) pilot for TV's *Star Wars* clone was cut to two hours and released in Canada as a feature. It was a hit, so a few more minutes were added and it got released in A-2can theaters, too. The recycled TV movie features "the super reality of Sensurround" (!) and a different ending from the original epic's. Starring Lorne Greene as the ship's commander, Maren Jensen as his daughter, Richard Hatch, Dirk Benedict, Cyclon warriors, and a robot bear that rivals the monkey in *Lost in Space*. The guest stars are Ray Milland, Lew Ayres, Wilfred Hyde White, Jane Seymour, and Robyn Douglas. The makers of *Star Wars* sued on grounds of plagiarism and lost.

BAYOU: See *POOR WHITE TRASH*.

BEACH BALL

1965 Paramount
PRODUCER: Bart Patton
DIRECTOR: Lennie Weinrib
SCREENWRITER: David Malcolm

Edd Byrnes tries to get an ethnic-music-studies grant to buy instruments for his sensations, the Wigglers. College-finance-committee members Chris Noel, Gail Gilmore, Mikki Jameson, and Brenda Benet uncover the scam and tear up the check, but the Wigglers play a custom-car show in drag and win first prize. The Supremes do "Come to the Beach Ball With Me," and The Four Seasons, Righteous Brothers, Walker Brothers, and Hondells play themselves. Robert Logan, Don Edmonds, and Aron Kincaid are the Wigglers. Swimsuits by Rose Marie Reed. Gary Kurtz of *Star Wars* fame was the assistant director. With Dick Miller.　　　　　　　　　–CB

BEACH BLANKET BINGO

　　1965 AIP

PRODUCERS: James H. Nicholson,
　　Samuel Z. Arkoff
DIRECTOR: William Asher
SCREENWRITERS: William Asher,
　　Leo Townsend

Frankie and Annette star in their fourth beach movie. A gang led by Eric Von Zipper (Harvey Lembeck) kidnaps a singing star managed by Paul Lynde, who hires sky-diving surfers for a publicity stunt. *Big Valley* regular Linda Evans is Sugar Kane. With the usual

Former matinee idol Jon Hall makes an impressive comeback in The Beach Girls and the Monster.

gang of idiots (Deborah Walley, John Ashley, Jody McCrea, Don Rickles, etc.), Marta Kristen as a mermaid, and Donna Michelle (*Playboy*'s Miss December 1963) as Animal. Music by the Hondells. Buster Keaton and Earl Wilson play themselves.

THE BEACH GIRLS AND THE MONSTER

　　1965 AIP-TV (B&W with color
　　sequence)
PRODUCER: Edward Janis
DIRECTOR: Jon Hall
SCREENWRITER: Joan Gardner
ALSO RELEASED AS: *Surf Terror, Monster
　　From the Surf*

Famous '40s movie hero Jon Hall returns to direct himself as Otto Lindsay, an oceanographer who likes to dress up like a sea monster and kill frivolous teens. The monster suit has a pointed head, bulging eyes, and seaweed hanging from it. The color sequence is stock footage of people surfing. A cheap laugh riot with lots of bongos, murders, and girls in bikinis. Music by Frank Sinatra, Jr.

BEACH PARTY

　　1963 AIP

PRODUCERS: James H. Nicholson, Lou Rusoff
DIRECTOR: William Asher
SCREENWRITER: Lou Rusoff

This is the one that started the Frankie and Annette beach series. William Asher directed five in a row, all inane, all very popular. Anthropology professor Robert Cummings and his secretary (Dorothy Malone) are studying the sex habits of teenagers. The surfing teens don't have much sex but they sing, battle the motorcycle rats and mice of Eric Von Zipper (Harvey Lembeck), and dance to Dick Dale and the Del-Tones. Dale, the king of the surf guitar, practically invented surf music and stands out here with his large earring; on one of his albums, the liner notes

explain that he was the only one in the film who didn't need bronze body makeup. Series regulars Jody McCrea and John Ashley mostly just stand around. Eva Six is the sexy waitress who dances with Frankie while Annette fumes. With Morey Amsterdam, *Playboy* foldouts Dolores Wells and Yvette Vickers (as a Yogi girl), and Brian Wilson of the Beach Boys as a surfer. Vincent Price has a surprise bit part. Karloff and Lorre did the same in later beach films. Look for Peter Falk as a biker.

BEAR ISLAND

1980 Columbia (England/Canada/U.S.)
PRODUCER: Peter Snell
DIRECTOR: Don Sharp
SCREENWRITERS: Don Sharp, David Butler, Murray Smith

"At a remote U.N. outpost in the frozen North Sea . . . something has gone terribly wrong," read the ad copy. Something has gone wrong when stars continue to make ignored or unreleased tax-shelter movies in Canada. This one, which few people have seen, has Donald Sutherland, Christopher Lee, Lloyd Bridges, Richard Widmark, Vanessa Redgrave, and Barbara Parkins. I'm sure they all tried real hard. Based on an Alistair Maclean mystery.

THE BEAST

1974 Argos (France)
PRODUCER: Anatole Dauman
DIRECTOR/SCREENWRITER: Walerian Borowczyk

A reworking of *Beauty and the Beast*, originally made as a segment of *Immoral Tales*. Hailed as an erotic classic, it features Sirpa Lane having sex with a hairy beast who dies of pleasure. Lisabeth Hummel dreams the whole story. **(X)**

BEAST FROM HAUNTED CAVE

1959 Filmgroup (B&W)
PRODUCER: Gene Corman
DIRECTOR: Monte Hellman
SCREENWRITER: Charles Griffith

"See: screaming young girls sucked into a labyrinth of horror by a blood-starved ghoul from hell!" If you believe that hype, you deserve to be disappointed by this story of gangsters in a ski lodge confronting an immobile "snow beast" in a cave. The creature (Chris Robinson) is covered in spiderwebs and encases a few cast members in cocoons. A painless 65 minutes. With Michael Forrest, Frank Wolff, Sheila Carol, and Wally Campo. Filmed in South Dakota. Originally co-billed with *The Wasp Woman*. Roger Corman was executive producer. The same cast appeared in *Ski Troop Attack* for Corman.

THE BEAST FROM 20,000 FATHOMS

1953 Warner Brothers (B&W)
PRODUCER: Jack Dietz
DIRECTOR: Eugene Lourie
SCREENWRITERS: Louis Morheim, Fred Frieberger

A milestone feature that spawned countless imitations. Derived partially from Ray Bradbury's short story "The Foghorn," the plot concerns a prehistoric dinosaur who is revived by an atomic blast in the Arctic. The (fictional) rheasauros, first seen vaguely

Annette and Frankie pose for a publicity photo to promote one of their early '60s beach party movies.

through a heavy snowstorm, was animated by Ray Harryhausen. It was his first film after assisting on *Mighty Joe Young*. The atomic beast swims to New York City, tramples people in Times Square and Wall Street, and ends up at Coney Island, where he takes bites out of the Cyclone roller coaster. Lee Van Cleef (in a small role) shoots it up with an atomic isotope, ending the destruction. The next year Japan released the similar *Godzilla*, and by the late '50s the monster unleashed by atomic energy was an overworked cliché. *Beast* stars Paul Christian and Paula Raymond as the romantic leads. Cecil Kellaway is the elderly paleontologist who sees the beast from a diving bell. With Kenneth Tobey (*The Thing*) and King Donovan (*Invasion of the Body Snatchers*). Director Lourie practically remade his monster hit twice with *The Giant Behemoth* and *Gorgo*. *Beast* was made for $200,000!

THE BEAST IN THE CELLAR
1971 Tigon/Cannon (England)
PRODUCER: Graham Harris
DIRECTOR/SCREENWRITER: James Kelly
ORIGINALLY RELEASED AS: *Are You Dying Young Man?*

Typical Filipino gore in Beast of Blood.

Two spinster sisters (Flora Robson and Beryl Reid) hide a terrible family secret in a talky modern Lovecraft-style horror film. (R)

THE BEAST MUST DIE
1974 Amicus/Cinerama (England)
PRODUCERS: Max J. Rosenberg, Milton Subotsky
DIRECTOR: Paul Annett
SCREENWRITER: Michael Winder
A werewolf mystery movie starring Calvin Lockhart as a millionaire hunter who invites a group of people to his isolated mountain lodge. One of them is a werewolf. During a 30-second "werewolf break," the audience is supposed to guess who it is. Prime suspects are Peter Cushing, Marlene Clark, and Charles Gray. Anton Diffring monitors the action on closed circuit television.

BEAST OF BLOOD
1970 Hemisphere (Philippines/U.S.)
PRODUCER/DIRECTOR/SCREENWRITER: Eddie Romero
ALSO RELEASED AS: *Beast of the Dead*
John Ashley returns to Blood Island in a horrible sequel to *The Mad Doctor of Blood Island*. Dr. Lorca (Eddie Garcia), now disfigured, has the body of the monster with green blood, but its head won't stay on. The headless creature terrorizes Celeste Yarnall. At original showings, "survival kits" containing airplane barf bags were thoughtfully handed out.

THE BEAST OF HOLLOW MOUNTAIN
1956 United Artists (U.S./Mexico)
PRODUCERS: Edward & William Nassour
DIRECTORS: Edward Nassour, Ismael Rodriguez
SCREENWRITERS: Robert Hill, Ismael Rodriguez, Carlos Orellana
ALSO RELEASED AS: *La Bestia de la Montāna*

King Kong creator Willis O'Brien always wanted to do a cowboys vs. dinosaurs movie. He sold his story idea to the Nassour brothers, but they did not hire him to do the stop-motion animation, so the combat scenes between the tyrannosaur and the cowboys are substandard. Guy Madison stars with Patricia Medina (*Phantom of the Rue Morgue*). The same idea was much better executed by Ray Harryhausen in *The Valley of Gwangi*.

BEAST OF MOROCCO: See THE HAND OF NIGHT.

BEAST OF PARADISE ISLAND: See PORT SINISTER.

BEAST OF THE DEAD: See BEAST OF BLOOD.

BEAST OF THE YELLOW NIGHT

1971 New World (U.S./Philippines)
PRODUCERS: Eddie Romero and John Ashley
DIRECTOR/SCREENWRITER: Eddie Romero
Co-producer John Ashley stars as a disciple of the Devil who kills people and absorbs their evil. He is transformed into an unconvincing, snarling, crusty-faced monster who wonders about the nature of God and the Devil when he is not murdering or having sex. Roger Corman was executive producer.

THE BEAST OF YUCCA FLATS

1961 Crown International (B&W)
PRODUCER: Anthony Cardoza
DIRECTOR/SCREENWRITER: Coleman Francis
ALSO RELEASED AS: *Atomic Monster—The Beast of Yucca Flats*
You might have been appalled (and delighted) watching *The Creeping Terror* because it had no dialogue, just

offscreen narration. Well, this hour-long amateur movie uses the same silent technique and it's even worse! The "star" is the huge and famous Tor Johnson who, as a Russian atomic scientist, is chased into the desert by Communist agents with guns. They actually miss his 300-pound-plus body from about 30 feet away. When Tor walks right into the blast of an atomic bomb, he is reduced to "nothing." He lives in a cave, carries a big stick, kills people, and eats hair. The narrator repeats absurd philosophical lines over and over ("Flag on the Moon—how did it get there?") and informs us of things after they've happened on the screen. The actors stare blankly waiting for direction. At the end, as Tor is dying, he is shown holding and being licked by a rabbit. A senseless nonmovie, worse than anything Tor did for Ed Wood, Jr. With Douglas Meller, Tony Cardoza, and Barbara Francis. Director Coleman Francis also edited the film.

THE BEAST THAT KILLED WOMEN

1965 Barry Mahon
PRODUCER/DIRECTOR/SCREENWRITER: Barry Mahon
A misogynist gorilla kills women at a nudist camp. Mahon made 10 other features for "adults only" the same year.

THE BEAST WITH FIVE FINGERS

1946 Warner Brothers (B&W)
PRODUCER: William Jacobs
DIRECTOR: Robert Florey
SCREENWRITER: Curt Siodmak
Peter Lorre gets a chance to act deranged in the last decent American horror film made for at least another decade. Lorre is in top form strangling himself and trying to nail an imaginary crawling hand to a table. A wonderful

special effect, the hand is at its best playing the piano and strangling Lorre. Luis Buñuel helped to film the powerful hand sequences. The story, set in Italy, features Robert Alda (Alan's dad), Andrea King, Victor Francen (as the dead pianist), J. Carrol Naish as a police captain, and John Abbott. From the director of the original *Murders in the Rue Morgue*.

THE BEAST WITH 1,000,000 EYES

1955 ARC (B&W)
PRODUCER/DIRECTOR: David Kramarsky
SCREENWRITER: Tom Filer

The alien/beast/puppet created by Paul Blaisdell has only two actual eyes but it has the added advantage of seeing through the eyes of the Earth animals it controls. That explanation out of the way, this is an effective little science-fiction movie in which the family of rancher Paul Birch is attacked by cows, birds, and even the formerly faithful pet dog. Living in the desert, the beast controls lower life forms and a retarded farm hand affectionately known as "Him." Lorna Thayer and Donald Cole complete Birch's terrified family. Silent comedy star Chester Conklin is old man Webber. Roger Corman was executive producer.

THE BEAST WITHIN

1982 United Artists
PRODUCERS: Harvey Bernhard, Gabriel Katzka
DIRECTOR: Phillipe Mora
SCREENWRITER: Tom Holland

Forget logic and you may enjoy this dark tale of a teenaged boy (Paul Clemens) who turns into a cannibalizing insect. The MacClearys neglected to tell their son that he was conceived when Mom was raped by a swamp monster. Now 17, he's starting to shed his skin ("Just like a cicada," says one character). This revolting transformation is squeezed for all it's worth, particularly when—for no reason other than cinema thrills—his head starts to blow up like a moldy, wet balloon. This silly premise for a horror movie is saved by a cast that plays it for real; director Mora helps by casually tossing off explanations of the weird occurrences, while concentrating on the dark aspects of the story and the atmosphere of a tiny, incestuous Southern town. The end product of the boy's transformation—a slimier, more believable version of dozens of rubber-suited creatures that stalked the 1950s B-movies—decapitates, skewers, and eats everyone in his path. Credit for the gory effects goes to Thomas Burman's makeup studio—the folks behind *Prophecy* and *Cat People*. Music by Les Baxter. With L.Q. Jones. **(R)**   –BM

THE BEASTMASTER

1982 MGM/UA
PRODUCERS: Paul Pepperman, Sylvio Tabet
DIRECTOR: Don Coscarelli
SCREENWRITERS: Don Coscarelli, Paul Pepperman

A sword-and-sorcery epic, directed by the 28-year-old creator of *Phantasm*, that sent most viewers over 12 to the exits. Rip Torn, a good actor in danger of becoming a permanent fixture on the nation's drive-in screens, plays Maax, an evil cult priest with a large false nose. Under Maax's influence, the blond hero (Marc Singer), whose surrogate mother is a cow, is able to communicate with and command animals. His best friends are two cute ferrets that hang from his belt and ex-*Charlie's Angel* star Tanya Roberts as a slave girl. John Amos (the dad on the *Good Times* series) has a Mohawk haircut and helps Maax control his barbarian warriors and zombie guards, who wear spiked leather bondage gear.

BEAT GENERATION
1959 MGM (B&W)
PRODUCER: Albert Zugsmith
DIRECTOR: Charles Haas
SCREENWRITERS: Richard Matheson,
   Lewis Meltzer
ALSO RELEASED AS: *This Rebel Age*

A lurid cop-after-a-rapist story with a
beatnik-coffee-house background.
Steve Cochran stars as the detective
who will stop at nothing to catch "the
aspirin kid" (Ray Danton), a wealthy
young rapist who considers himself
above the law and mentally superior.
To show the detective that he can get
away with anything, he picks Cochran's
new wife (Fay Spain) as his next victim.
The amazing oddball cast includes
Mamie Van Doren as an almost-victim;
Jackie Coogan as Cochran's partner
(seen in drag while staking out lovers'
lane); Jim Mitchum as Danton's eager
trainee; and Louis Armstrong and his
band, who perform on screen. And
then there are the beats—Vampira as
a poetess, Maxie Rosenbloom as a
wrestler, Charles Chaplin, Jr., and
Grabowski, the "Beat Beatnik." Also
with William Schallert, Guy Stockwell,
Regina Carrol, and Irish McCalla as
Coogan's wife.

BEAT THE DEVIL
1954 United Artists (B&W)
PRODUCER/DIRECTOR: John Huston
SCREENWRITERS: John Huston, Truman Capote

A satire recalling *The Maltese Falcon*,
starring Humphrey Bogart and Gina
Lollobrigida. Peter Lorre has blond hair
and calls himself O'Hara. Robert Morley takes the Sidney Greenstreet role.
A big flop when first released, it was
billed as a "serious" adventure movie.
Capote was still working on the script
while it was being filmed (in Italy).
Cinematography by Freddie Francis.

BEAT GIRL: See *WILD FOR KICKS*

THE BEATNIKS
1960 Barjul (B&W)
PRODUCER: Ron Miller
DIRECTOR: Paul Frees
SCREENWRITERS: Arthur Julian, Paul Frees

Talent scout hears leader of hipster terrorist gang singing along with jukebox
and offers him a shot at stardom. Our
hero tries to break from the gang and
gets entangled in murder committed by
resident maniac Peter Breck (Nick
Barkley on *The Big Valley*). "The intimate secrets of the beat generation!"

*Jackie Coogan and Steven
Cochran check out a cof-
fee house in* The Beat
Generation.

*UPI 1954: Movie bogey-
man Peter Lorre, just re-
turned from four years in
Europe, holds Katherine,
born September 21 in
Hamburg, Germany, for
her first photographs. Her
mother is the former Anna
Maria Brenning of Ham-
burg. Friend Humphrey
Bogart, with whom Lorre
starred in his most recent
motion picture,* Beat the
Devil, *cooperates in the
photo taking.*

45

the ads promised. Tony Travis stars, with Karen Kadler, Joyce Terry, and Charles Delaney.   —CB

BEATSVILLE: See THE REBEL SET.

BEAUTY AND THE BEAST
1946 Lopert (France) (B&W)
PRODUCER: Emile Darbon
DIRECTOR/SCREENWRITER: Jean Cocteau
ORIGINALLY RELEASED AS: *La Belle et La Bête*
A beautiful artistic fantasy classic that makes one wonder why other movies can't look like this. Josette Day and Jean Marais star.

BEAUTY AND THE BEAST
1963 United Artists
PRODUCER: Robert E. Kent
DIRECTOR: Edward L. Cahn
SCREENWRITERS: George Bruce,
    Orville H. Hampton
A forgotten quickie version of the famous fairy tale. It features the stars from *The House of Usher* (Mark Damon as the beast) and *Atlantis, the Lost Continent* (Joyce Taylor). If the beast resembles Lon Chaney as the Wolfman, it's because Jack Pierce, Universal's famous makeup artist, designed the face and hands. With Michael Pate and Merry Anders. It was the last feature by Edward Cahn, who died the same year.

BEAUTY AND THE BEAST
1976 TV
PRODUCER: Hank Moonjean
DIRECTOR: Fielder Cook
SCREENWRITER: Sherman Yellen
The Beast looks like a runaway from the *Island of Dr. Moreau* remake. As played by George C. Scott, he resembles a boar instead of the usual werewolf. John Chambers created the makeup, complete with tusks and snout. Trish Van Devere is Beauty. Bernard Lee is her father. Not very magical.

BEAUTY AND THE BODY
1963 Manson
PRODUCER/DIRECTOR: Paul Mart
SCREENWRITER: Richard Tyler
A romance travelogue that follows two vacationing teenagers who meet on the beach in Santa Monica and share three exciting days attending sports events in Southern California and Mexico. Swimming, sky diving, ice skating, karate, bullfights, and rodeos provide plenty of action. Physique star Kip Behar and Judy Miller part tenderly. She returns to her car-hop job, and an elaborate lie surfaces.   —CB

BEAUTY AND THE BRAIN: See SEX KITTENS GO TO COLLEGE.

BEAUTY AND THE ROBOT: See SEX KITTENS GO TO COLLEGE.

BECAUSE THEY'RE YOUNG
1960 Columbia (B&W)
PRODUCER: Jerry Bresler
DIRECTOR: Paul Wendkos
SCREENWRITER: James Gunn
"Because . . . they're driven by strange new desires they don't understand!" shrieked the ads. Because . . . *American Bandstand* host Dick Clark is driven to play the new teacher at Harrison High who understands the kids and their problems. Tuesday Weld is "scared by an experience" with Michael Callan. The teacher wants to experience the principal's secretary. Everyone ends up happy, including James Darren, who acts and sings, Roberta Shore, Warren Berlinger, Chris Robinson, and Doug McClure. Bobby Rydell sings the hit "Swinging School" over the credits, and Duane Eddy and the Rebels perform "Shazam" and the theme song, which was also a hit. I'd give the picture a 10. Rydell and Clark get a 5.

THE BED SITTING ROOM

1969 United Artists (England)
PRODUCER/DIRECTOR: Richard Lester
SCREENWRITER: Jean Antrobus

The comic side of postnuclear-holocaust life, British style. Civilization has disappeared and the few remaining inhabitants gradually mutate into inanimate objects and non-human life forms. Dad (Arthur Lowe) becomes a parrot, Mum (Mona Washbourne) turns into a chest of drawers. Daughter Rita Tushingham is seventeen months pregnant. Dudley Moore and Peter Cook represent the government. Marty Feldman is a Communist. With Spike Milligan (who wrote the play it was based on), Ralph Richardson, and Harry Secombe.

BEDAZZLED

1967 20th Century-Fox (England)
PRODUCER/DIRECTOR: Stanley Donen
SCREENWRITER: Peter Cook

Short-order cook Stanley Moon (Dudley Moore) sells his soul to George Spiggot (Peter Cook) and receives seven wishes. Trying to impress Eleanor Bron, Moon becomes a rock star (singing "Love Me"), a fly, and a nun. Raquel Welch is Lust. Cook sings the theme song. A great comedy.

THE BEDFORD INCIDENT

1965 Columbia (U.S./England) (B&W)
PRODUCER/DIRECTOR: James B. Harris
SCREENWRITER: James Poe

Harris, formerly producer of Stanley Kubrick features, made this film a year after *Dr. Strangelove.* Richard Widmark plays a navy captain who discovers a Russian sub off the coast of Greenland and decides to play cat and mouse with it. He arms a nuclear missile and warns the Russians that he'll use it if they don't give themselves up. This creates a tense situation aboard ship—and the threat of World War III. With Sidney Poitier as a newspaperman, Martin Balsam, James MacArthur, Wally Cox, and Donald Sutherland. —AF

BEDLAM

1946 RKO (B&W)
PRODUCER: Val Lewton
DIRECTOR: Mark Robson
SCREENWRITERS: Val Lewton, Mark Robson

In the last of Lewton's unique low budget RKO films, Boris Karloff stars as Master Sims, the sadistic ruler of a notorious London asylum. Set in 1761 and inspired by the engravings of William Hogarth, the story concerns Anna Lee, an actress sent to Bedlam after displeasing the fat Lord Mortimer (Billy House). At an inmate party, a man (Glenn Vernon) dies of asphyxiation after being painted gold to impersonate "Reason." Inmates have descriptive names like Dan the Dog (Robert Clarke) and Queen of the Artichokes (Ellen Corey). One inmate is judged insane because he invented motion pictures. There isn't much action, but some of the characters and situations are priceless. With Richard Fraser (as a Quaker), Elizabeth Russel (as Karloff's wife), and Skelton Knaggs. The year it was released, Boris got married for the fifth time.

BEDTIME FOR BONZO
1951 Universal (B&W)
PRODUCER: Michael Kraike
DIRECTOR: Frederick De Cordova
SCREENWRITERS: Val Burton, Lou Breslow
Don't miss President Reagan in his best-loved role. The story is based on the premise that "even a monkey brought up in the right surroundings can learn the meaning of decency and honesty." When Bonzo pulls off a jewel heist, his scientist-trainer (Ronald Reagan) gets blamed. Soon after this blockbuster was released, its screenwriter was labeled a Communist; he never wrote another movie! Director De Cordova is best known for directing the *Tonight Show.* He also did Elvis' *Frankie and Johnny,* an awful Bob Hope flop called *I'll Take Sweden,* and *Bonzo Goes to College.* Ron refused to star in the sequel because the plot wasn't believable! With Walter Slezak and Diana Lynn.

THE BEES
1978 New World (U.S./Mexico)
PRODUCER/DIRECTOR/SCREENWRITER:
Alfredo Zacharias
Except for an impressive shot of bees attacking the UN, this is a terrible/funny disaster film with misfire humor and ridiculous dialogue. Hero John Saxon and heroine Angel Tompkins find themselves covered with bees the

first night they go to bed together. Angel's Uncle Ziggy (John Carradine) putters around looking for a solution to the Brazilian bee attacks, and gets stung to death for his trouble. President Ford, shown in actual footage of the Rose Bowl Parade, lives. This and TV's *The Savage Bees* beat Irwin Allen's *The Swarm* onto the nation's screens.

BEFORE I HANG

1940 Columbia (B&W)
PRODUCER: Wallace McDonald
DIRECTOR: Nick Grinde
SCREENWRITER: Robert D. Andrews
Boris Karloff is a brilliant scientist driven to murder. Sentenced to death for a mercy killing, he continues his old-age–stopping experiments in prison, with the help of the prison doctor (Edward Van Sloan.) He's given a full pardon and becomes younger because of a blood injection. The blood was from a condemned criminal and causes him to murder indiscriminately. With Evelyn Keyes (*Gone With the Wind*) and Bruce Bennett.

BEGINNING OF THE END

1957 Republic (B&W)
PRODUCER/DIRECTOR: Bert I. Gordon
SCREENWRITERS: Fred Freiberger, Lester Gorn
"The screen's first full-length science-fiction thriller with real live creatures!" The ads assured you of this fact so you wouldn't be cheated by any phony stop-motion characters. Real grasshoppers shown on a rear projection screen are magically made to attack Chicago! It all started with the good old U.S. Government dumping radioactive material in the soil to improve crops. They grow to immense sizes, as do the creepy hoppers. Peter Graves stars with Peggie Castle, Thomas B. Henry, and Morris Ankrum. Graves saves the day by luring the bugs into the lake with a tape of the grasshopper's mating call. "You'll

Is Boris Karloff the strangler? Before I Hang.

be shocked out of your skin!" Bert was back with another real live creature the next year in *The Spider*. The theme song is available on *The Fantastic Film Music of Albert Glasser* album.

BEGINNING OR THE END

1947 MGM (B&W)
PRODUCER: Samuel Marx
DIRECTOR: Norman Taurog
SCREENWRITER: Robert Considine
Wow! The first real film about the A-bomb! It's quite serious and the production was overseen by the U.S. Government. The title comes from a statement by President Truman. Brian Donlevy (later Professor Quatermass) is the head of the Manhattan Project. Tom Drake (*Master of Lassie*) is the wimp scientist who thinks it should be used only for peace. But the majority rules and Hiroshima is destroyed. In *Science Fiction in the Cinema* John Baxter says, "Hilarious—Donlevy strides about pointing at unseen installations and saying, 'Put

the cyclotron over here!'" With Robert Walker, Hurd Hatfield, and Ludwig Stossel as Einstein.

BEHEMOTH THE SEA MONSTER: See THE GIANT BEHEMOTH.

BEHIND THE MASK

1932 Columbia (B&W)
DIRECTOR: John Francis Dillon
SCREENWRITERS: Jo Swerling, Dorothy Howell

Made in early 1931, this Secret Service film was released after *Frankenstein* and advertised as a horror movie. It features Boris Karloff working for Dr. X, a masked master criminal running a dope ring who turns out to be Edward Van Sloan. Jack Holt stars as an undercover agent almost operated on by the underworld doctor. With Constance Cummings.

BELA LUGOSI MEETS A BROOKLYN GORILLA

1952 Realart (B&W)
PRODUCER: Maurice Duke
DIRECTOR: William Beaudine
SCREENWRITER: Tim Ryan
ALSO RELEASED AS: *The Boys From Brooklyn*

Bela Lugosi is Dr. Zabor, a mad scientist on a tropical island who meets a team of Martin-and-Lewis imitators. Duke Mitchell takes the Dean Martin role. He's no big deal, but Sammy Petrillo, who looks and acts like a young Jerry Lewis, is amazing. It was Bela's last role before his famous Ed Wood, Jr., features. From the company that made *Bride of the Gorilla*. Jerry sued Sammy for copying him, and Mitchell and Petrillo disappeared from the screen.

BELL FROM HELL

1973 Avco Embassy-TV (Spain)
PRODUCER/DIRECTOR: Claudio Hill
SCREENWRITER: Santiago Moncada

A man is placed in an asylum. Greedy relatives want his money. He plucks out his eyes. A lot of the story centers around a bell tower. On the last day of shooting, the director jumped (fell?) to his death from that very tower. The film was released directly to American television. With Viveca Lindfors.

THE BELLBOY AND THE PLAYGIRLS: See THE PLAYGIRLS AND THE BELLBOY.

BEN

1972 Cinerama
PRODUCER: Mort Briskin
DIRECTOR: Phil Karlson
SCREENWRITER: Gilbert Ralston

The army of rats from *Willard* are still on the loose. A detective (Joseph Campanella) is investigating the murders in the first movie. Little Lee Hartcourt Montgomery makes friends with Ben the rat leader. Acting with Ben were Arthur O'Connell, Meredith Baxter, and Kenneth Tobey. "Ben's Song" was a hit single by Michael Jackson. The first 500 lucky patrons at first-run theaters in many cities got free photos of Ben! Like *Willard*, *Ben* was a Bing Crosby Production.

BENEATH THE PLANET OF THE APES

1970 20th Century-Fox
PRODUCER: Arthur Jacobs
DIRECTOR: Ted Post
SCREENWRITERS: Paul Dehn, Mort Abrahams

A good sequel to *Planet of the Apes*. It opens with Charlton Heston finding the Statue of Liberty and falling into a hole. Astronaut James Franciscus teams with mute Linda Harrison and friendly ape scientist Kim Hunter to find him. They all end up in the buried ruins of Grand Central Station, where masked telepathic mutants led by Victor Buono worship a live atom bomb that soon explodes, destroying what's left of the world. This did not, however, put a stop to the lucrative *Apes* series. Three increasingly silly sequels followed. This one also stars Maurice Evans (again), James Gregory as the brutal gorilla leader, Jeff Corey, Thomas Gomez, Gregory Sierra, and the voice of Roddy McDowall. Roddy wasn't in it because he was busy directing *Devil's Widow*.

THE BERMUDA DEPTHS
1978 TV
PRODUCERS: Rankin, Bass
DIRECTOR: Tom Kotani
SCREENWRITER: William Overgard
ALSO RELEASED AS: *It Came Up From the Bermuda Depths*
A prehistoric sea creature—a big turtle—and a woman who seems to have returned from death threaten Burl Ives in the Bermuda Triangle. A theatrical release in Europe. With Leigh McCloskey and Connie Selleca.

BERSERK
1968 Columbia (England)
PRODUCER: Herman Cohen
DIRECTOR: Jim O'Conolly
SCREENWRITERS: Aben Kandel, Herman Cohen
Herman Cohen returns to his *Horrors of the Black Museum* idea of gruesome, bizarre murders, but now he's got a real star—Joan Crawford! She's Monica Rivers, owner and ringmaster of a traveling circus who'll do anything to draw bigger audiences. When some performers die during shows, profits soar. As a young tightrope walker, Ty Hardin becomes Joan's lover and dies falling on bayonets. Michael Gough, as Joan's partner, has a spike driven through his head. Diana Dors is sawed in half! Robert Hardy is called in from Scotland Yard and, in a ludicrous ending, discovers who the killer is. With Judy Geeson, Milton Reid, a

midget, and intelligent poodles. Although not overly gory, it was the tackiest yet for Joan, who with her hair in a tight bun manages to outyell the other actors. Newspaper ads offered a "shock-limit test." Example: "Saw-teeth savagely slashing a girl apart rips my nerves." Check yes or no. Next stop for Joan: *Trog*.

THE BEST MAN WINS
1935 Columbia (B&W)
PRODUCER: Columbia
DIRECTOR: Erle C. Kenton
SCREENWRITERS: Ethel Hill, Bruce Manning
Bela Lugosi is a bearded villain who smuggles rare gems while pretending to catch fish. Hero Jack Holt and Edmund Lowe are deep-sea divers.

THE BEST OF SEX AND VIOLENCE
1981 Wizard
PRODUCER: Charles Band
DIRECTOR: Ken Dixon
A feature made from 40 trailers of the 1970s with onscreen commentary by John Carradine. Some of the films represented are *Zombie*, *Tourist Trap*, *Terminal Island*, *Tanya's Island*, *Truck Stop Women* and *Bury Me An Angel*. Watch for it on cable. Also with David and Keith Carradine.

BETRAYED WOMEN
1955 Allied Artists (B&W)
PRODUCER: William F. Broidy
DIRECTOR: Edward L. Cahn
SCREENWRITER: Steve Fisher
"Love-starved gun molls make a break for freedom!" the ads screamed. Detective Tom Drake is sent to investigate conditions in a ladies' death camp where Esther Dale inflicts cruelties upon Carole Mathews and Beverly Michaels as well as Drake's one-time fiancée, Peggy Knudsen. He arrives in time for a crashout and is forced to accompany

the three into swamp country as they search for Mathews' buried fifty grand. The cops know just where to look, but Carole would rather eat lead than surrender. "These babes were plenty tough!"   —CB

BETRAYER: See REBELLION IN CUBA.

BETWEEN TWO WORLDS
1944 Warner Brothers (B&W)
PRODUCER: Mark Hellinger
DIRECTOR: Edward A. Blatt
SCREENWRITER: Daniel Fuchs
Second version of *Outward Bound*, Sutton Vane's play about a ship of people who don't know they're dead and heading for Heaven(?). They spend the entire cruise bickering and judging each other's lives. Sound familiar? Great Warner Brothers cast includes John Garfield, Sidney Greenstreet, Paul Henreid, George Coulouris, and Eleanor Parker. Music by Erich Wolfgang Korngold.

BEWARE MY BRETHREN
1972 Cinerama (England)
PRODUCER/DIRECTOR: Robert Hartford-Davies
SCREENWRITER: Brian Comport
Patrick Magee is the minister of the Brethren, a religious sect whose finances come from the late mother of Tony Beckley. The young man kills women so they can be reborn and "communicates" with his mother. Magee ends up crucified. With Ann Todd. By the director of *Corruption*. **(R)**

BEWARE THE BLOB: See SON OF BLOB.

BEWITCHED
1945 MGM (B&W)
PRODUCER: Jerry Bresler
DIRECTOR/SCREENWRITER: Arch Oboler
The first feature by the creator of the *Lights Out* radio show. Psychiatrist Edmund Gwenn uses hypnosis to separate the split personality of Phyllis Thaxter. Oboler later made *Five*, *Bwana Devil*, and *The Twonkey*.

BEYOND ATLANTIS
1973 Dimension Pictures (Philippines)
PRODUCERS: Eddie Romero, John Ashley
DIRECTOR: Eddie Romero
SCREENWRITER: Charles Johnson
Possibly the worst of the John Ashley Filipino films. Ashley plays a baby-faced tough guy who is involved with bald gangster Sid Haig in a scheme to seize sacred pearls from the population of an uncharted island. They join forces with good guy Patrick Wayne and Lenore Stevens to plunder and loot. Nereus, the leader of the ancient islanders, is none other than George Nader (he starred in *Robot Monster*, for God's sake). He orders the beautiful "Syrene" (Leigh Christian) to mate with one of the strangers in order to continue their race. The results mix hilarity with boredom. Most of the natives have eyes like Ping-Pong balls and carry Syrene around in a giant clamshell. Ashley is incredible as usual. Dimension Pictures was run by Stephanie Rothman and her husband Charles Swartz.

BEYOND EVIL
1980 IFI-Scope III
PRODUCERS: David Baughn, Herb Freed
DIRECTOR: Herb Freed
SCREENWRITERS: Herb Freed, Paul Ross
Crummy *Exorcist*-type film, set on an island. With John Saxon, Lynda Day George, and Michael Dante. A laughable 100-year-old female spirit tries to possess George. Music by Pino Donaggio (*Carrie*). Director Freed next put Lynda's husband, Christopher George, in *Graduation Day*. **(R)**

BEYOND THE BERMUDA TRIANGLE

1975 TV
PRODUCER: Don Roth
DIRECTOR: William A. Graham
SCREENWRITER: Charles A. McDaniel
Retired businessman Fred MacMurray loses his fiancée (and his three sons?) in the famous triangle. With Donna Mills, Sam Groom, and Woody Woodbury. A Playboy production.

BEYOND THE DOOR

1975 Film Ventures (U.S./Italy)
DIRECTOR: Ovidio Assonitis (Oliver Hellman)
SCREENWRITER: Richard Barrett
(R. D'E Piazzoli)
Although partially filmed in California and with English stars, this is very much a shoddy Italian *Exorcist* clone. Juliet Mills (sister of Hayley and Nanny of the *Nanny and the Professor* TV show) stars as a pregnant woman who duplicates all of Linda Blair's green-puke convulsions and levitation tricks. The rest is filler. With trash actor Richard Johnson as her husband. It made enough money for the producers to fake a sequel. Presented by Edward L. Montoro. **(R)**

BEYOND THE DOOR 2

1979 Film Ventures (Italy)
PRODUCER: Juri Vasili
DIRECTOR: Mario Bava
SCREENWRITERS: Lamberto Bava,
Franco Barbieri
ALSO RELEASED AS: *Shock*
Advertised in America as a sequel to *Beyond the Door*, it's the last feature of horror specialist Mario Bava and, like its predecessor, it's about possession. Only one cast member, David Colin, Jr., remains from the original. He stars as a little boy possessed by a supernatural power. An amnesia victim, his mother (Daria Nicolodi) has horrible nightmares and a mysterious second husband (John Steiner), who isn't what he seems. This nonsequel is much more original than the first *Door* movie. **(R)**

BEYOND THE FOG: See HORRORS ON SNAPE ISLAND.

BEYOND THE GATE: See HUMAN EXPERIMENTS.

BEYOND THE LIVING: See NURSE SHERRI.

BEYOND THE POSEIDON ADVENTURE

1979 Warner Brothers
PRODUCER/DIRECTOR: Irwin Allen
SCREENWRITER: Nelson Gidding
Maker of science-fiction schlock and overcrowded disaster epics Irwin Allen brings us a sequel to his earlier sinking-ship hit. Michael Caine (also in Allen's *The Swarm*) stars as a thief trying to loot the boat, containing the bodies of an all-star cast, before it sinks. The sinking cast includes Sally Fields, Telly Savalas, Peter Boyle, Angela Cartwright, Shirley Jones, Karl Malden, Slim Pickens, Shirley Knight, and Jack Warden. Twenty-two minutes were added to the television version, to fill a three-hour time slot.

BEYOND THE TIME BARRIER

1960 AIP
PRODUCER: Robert Clarke
DIRECTOR: Edgar G. Ulmer
SCREENWRITER: Arthur C. Pierce
One of the last efforts of cult director Edgar G. Ulmer, it stars Robert Clarke as a pilot who breaks the time barrier and finds himself on a post-World War III Earth, where he's captured by mutants and rescued by a princess of the new underground civilization. Ulmer

Robert Clarke in Beyond the Time Barrier.

UPI 8/27/71: Many a girl can be taught the rudiments of acting, but how many are endowed with the natural gifts of a Raquel Welch or Marilyn Monroe? One of them is Edy Williams, a girl who could rejuvenate the inhabitants of Sun City simply by strolling through in a bikini filled out with her ample 39-23-37 form. Edy is now studying with famed drama coach Lee Strasberg. Her most recent motion picture is Beyond the Valley of the Dolls.

filmed it on the site of the 1959 Texas State Fairgrounds in Dallas, using an exhibit of futuristic art and design for sets. (He found time to make *The Amazing Transparent Man* there, too.) Both films, shot in a matter of weeks, are ultimate examples of minimalist filmmaking at its strangest. Star Robert Clarke was also in Ulmer's *Man From Planet X* (1950). With stock footage from *Island of Lost Souls.*

BEYOND THE VALLEY OF THE DOLLS
1970 20th Century-Fox
PRODUCER/DIRECTOR: Russ Meyer
SCREENWRITERS: Russ Meyer, Roger Ebert

The incredible story of the Carrie Nations, an all-girl rock group, in a funny look at Hollywood decadence. Dolly Read (*Playboy*'s Miss May '66 and wife of *Laugh In*'s Dick Martin), Cynthia Myers (Miss December '68), and Marcia McBroom make up the band. The most memorable character is John Lazar as Z-Man Bar-ell the Teen Tycoon, who at one point pretends he's Superwoman and decapitates Lance (Michael Blodgett). Blodgett now goes out with President Reagan's daughter Patti Davis. The screenplay is by Russ Meyer and Roger Ebert of *Sneak Previews*. Music by the

Strawberry Alarm Clock (who also appear on screen) and the Sandpipers. With Edy Williams, Erica Gavin, Haji, Pam Grier, and Charles Napier. Meyer did one more major-studio film (*The Seven Minutes*), and then went back to making his own distinctive macho fantasies. (X)

THE BIBLE...
IN THE BEGINNING
1966 20th Century-Fox (U.S./Italy)
PRODUCER: Dino De Laurentiis
DIRECTOR: John Huston
SCREENWRITER: Christopher Fry

Before Dino gave us his versions of *King Kong, Flash Gordon,* and *Orca,* we were blessed with his version of the first 22 chapters of Genesis. Director John Huston stars and narrates as Noah. Michael Parks (*Then Came Bronson*) is Adam. He and Ulla Bergryd begat us all. Richard Harris is Cain. Stephen Boyd is Nimrod (the Tower of Babel). George C. Scott is Abraham. Ava Gardner is his wife, Sarah. Peter O'Toole plays the three angels. Filmed in Italy and Egypt.

BIG BAD MAMA

1974 New World
PRODUCER: Roger Corman
DIRECTOR: Steve Carver
SCREENWRITERS: William Norton,
Francis Doel

In the tradition of *Bloody Mama*, Angie Dickinson stars as a 1930s Texas gangster/mother. Audiences were surprised at her pre-*Police Woman* nude love scene with William Shatner, who in non-*Star Trek* roles always seems like Captain Kirk caught in a time warp. I was more surprised at the nude scenes with Susan Sennett (as one of Angie's daughters), who had just been Ozzie and Harriet's innocent roomer on *Ozzie's Girls*. Anyway, it's a fun movie with the usual machine guns, banjo music, Tom Skerritt, Robbie Lee, Royal Dano, Joan Prather, and Dick Miller. Some of the music is by Woody Guthrie and Pete Seeger. The next year Cloris Leachman took her turn as *Crazy Mama*. (**R**)

MEN, MONEY and MOONSHINE
WHEN IT COMES TO VICE, MAMA KNOWS BEST!

HOT LEAD
HOT CARS
HOT DAMN!

ANGIE DICKINSON in
BIG BAD MAMA

BIG BEAT

1957 Universal
PRODUCER/DIRECTOR: Will Cowan
SCREENWRITER: David P. Harmon

A record-company exec who likes the old sounds lets his rockin' son (William Reynolds) start a subsidiary label. A musical demonstrating that Fats Domino (performing "I'm Walkin' "), the Diamonds (doing "Little Darling"), the Del-Vikings, and the Four Aces are as entertaining as the Mills Brothers, Harry James, Cal Tjader, and George Shearing. Bridging the generation gap, '50s style. To a kid in the '80s, it probably all sounds equally foreign. With Hans Conried, Gogi Grant, and Rose Marie. Originally billed with *The Thing That Couldn't Die*.

THE BIG BUS

1976 Paramount
PRODUCERS/SCREENWRITERS: Fred Freeman,
Lawrence J. Cohen
DIRECTOR: James Frawley

Before *Airplane*, we got this less-popular disaster-film parody about a giant nuclear-powered bus containing a swimming pool and a bowling alley. The cast includes Joseph Bologna, Stockard Channing, John Beck, José Ferrer, Larry Hagman, Sally Kellerman, Ruth Gordon, Lynn Redgrave, and Vic Tayback.

THE BIG CHASE

1953 Lippert (B&W)
PRODUCER: Robert Lippert, Jr.
DIRECTOR: Arthur Hilton
SCREENWRITER: Fred Freiberger

Glenn Langan of *The Amazing Colossal Man* is a rookie cop who passes up a promotion because his pregnant wife (Adele Jergens) wants him alive. But life on the juvenile squad has its risks. He gets into a railroad-yard shootout with payroll robber Lon Chaney, Jr., then helicopters to Mexico in pursuit of the rest of the gang. When he gets back he and his wife have a new baby girl. With Douglas Kennedy and Jim Davis. Hilton, more often an editor, also directed *Cat Women of the Moon*. —CB

THE BIG CIRCUS

1959 Allied Artists
PRODUCER/SCREENWRITER: Irwin Allen
DIRECTOR: Joseph M. Newman

This all-star cliché circus adventure climaxes when Gilbert Roland crosses Niagara Falls on a tightrope. Victor Mature stars with Rhonda Fleming, Kathryn Grant (*The Seventh Voyage of Sinbad*), Red Buttons, Vincent Price (the ringmaster), Peter Lorre (a sad-faced, drunken clown), Steve Allen, David Nelson (a deranged aerialist), the Human Cannonball, the Jungleland Elephants, Tex Carr and his Chimpanzees, and the Movieland Seals (as themselves).

THE BIG CUBE

1969 Warners, (U.S./Mexico)
PRODUCER: Lindsley Parsons
DIRECTOR: Tito Davison
SCREENWRITER: William Douglas Lansford

Retired Broadway star Adriana Roman (Lana Turner) lands in an asylum after stepdaughter Karin Mossberg spikes her nightly sedatives with LSD. Karin confesses to playwright Richard Egan when she realizes co-conspirator George Chakiris is only after her late father's fortune. The Finks perform "Lean On Me"; Regina Torne is the mysterious Queen Bee. With Dan O'Herlihy. Filmed in Mexico. In real life Lana Turner celebrated *The Big Cube*'s release by marrying her seventh husband. —CB

BIG ENOUGH AND OLD ENOUGH: See SAVAGES FROM HELL.

THE BIG OPERATOR

1959 MGM (B&W)
PRODUCER: Albert Zugsmith
DIRECTOR: Charles Haas
SCREENWRITER: Robert Smith
ALSO RELEASED AS: *Anatomy of a Syndicate*

Mickey Rooney plays Little Joe, a tough gangster being investigated by the FBI in another all-star oddity. With most of the cast of the previous Zugsmith/Haas opus, *The Beat Generation* (Mamie Van Doren, Ray Danton, Jackie Coogan, Vampira, and Steve Cochran). Also with Mel Torme, Jim Backus, Ziva Rodann, and little Jay North. Real serious stuff.

BIGFOOT

1969 Ellman Enterprises
PRODUCER: Anthony Cardoza
DIRECTOR: Robert F. Slatzer
SCREENWRITERS: Robert F. Slatzer,
James Gordon White

"Breeds with anything! Greatest monster since King Kong!" the ads claimed. Actually, it's the second worst Bigfoot movie (see *The Curse of Bigfoot*). A totally ridiculous story about a Northwestern missing link (a skinny man in a battered gorilla suit) who kidnaps women for breeding purposes. Highlights include a fight between Bigfoot and a real bear, and a motorcycle gang (led by famous nonstar star's sons Chris Mitchum and Lindsay Crosby) racing to the rescue of Joi Lansing. John Carradine and another Mitchum (John) want to capture the monster for a side show. With Ken Maynard, Doodles Weaver, Haji, and lots of girls in bikinis to tempt the poor lonely creature.

BIKINI BEACH

1964 AIP
PRODUCERS: James H. Nicholson,
Samuel Z. Arkoff
DIRECTOR: William Asher
SCREENWRITERS: William Asher,
Leo Townsend, Robert Dillon

Frankie and Annette on the beach —Part III. Avalon gets to air his personal hatred of the Beatles (and other British groups who were then ruling the airwaves) by playing the Potato Bug, a British recording star. Frankie also plays Frankie. He had enough trouble with one role, let alone two. His Bug portrayal, complete with long wig and "yeah-yeahs," is really embarrassing. Keenan Wynn is the manditory adult star who tries to prove that his chimp, Clyde, is more intelligent than American teenagers. Martha Hyer disagrees. Annette is torn between the two Frankies, and Eric Von Zipper (Harvey Lembeck) shows up to aid Wynn's antiteen campaign. The highlights are provided by Little Stevie Wonder, the Exciters, and the great surf band the Pyramids (they're all bald and one is black). With Don Rickles (as Big Drag), John Ashley, Jody McCrea, Meredith MacRae, Donna Loren, Boris Karloff (in a gag bit part), and Val Warren as a werewolf. Warren won a makeup contest in *Famous Monsters* magazine to land the small part.

BILLION DOLLAR BRAIN

1967 United Artists (England)
PRODUCER: Harry Saltzman
DIRECTOR: Ken Russell
SCREENWRITER: John McGrath
Michael Caine as Harry Palmer, the reluctant British agent, is back for the third time in the last and weirdest of the series. Karl Malden as Leo Newbegin works for Ed Begley as General Midwinter, a Texas oil billionaire planning to destroy Communist Russia by starting a revolution from a base in Latvia. The title computer is used to plan the uprising. Palmer gets involved with double agent Françoise Dorleac (who died in a car crash the year this was released) and some deadly eggs. Oscar Homolka reprises his Colonel

Stock role from *Funeral in Berlin*. Filmed in Latvia and Finland.

THE BILLION DOLLAR THREAT

1979 TV
PRODUCER: Jay Daniel
DIRECTOR: Barry Shear
SCREENWRITER: Jimmy Sangster
A comic James Bond-style pilot film with Patrick Macnee as Horatio Black, who threatens to destroy the world if he doesn't get one billion dollars real quick. Dale Robinette is the hero. With Ralph Bellamy, Keenan Wynn, and Harold Sakata, still redoing his *Goldfinger* role. Written by Jimmy Sangster of Hammer Films.

BILLY THE KID
VS. DRACULA

1966 Embassy Pictures
PRODUCER: Carroll Case
DIRECTOR: William Beaudine
SCREENWRITER: Carl K. Hittleman

John Carradine (in a top hat and a goatee) is Dracula for the first time since 1945. If you think 60-year-old John looks like a rather feeble vampire here, see him in *Nocturna* 14 years later. This time he poses as the uncle of pretty blond Betty (Melinda Plowman), owner of the Bar-B ranch. Her foreman is re-formed outlaw Billy the Kid (Chuck Courtney). Funny dialogue and low production values in this hopeless horror Western. With Roy Barcroft and Harry Carey, Jr. Filmed in "Shockorama"(?). This and co-feature *Jesse James vs. Frankenstein's Daughter* were the last two movies of superprolific William Beaudine, who directed over 175 films.

BIRD WITH THE CRYSTAL PLUMAGE

1970 U.M.C. Distributors
(Italy/W. Germany)
PRODUCER: Salvatore Argento
DIRECTOR/SCREENWRITER: Dario Argento
ALSO RELEASED AS: *L'Uccello dalle Piume di Cristallo, Phantom of Terror*

Except for Mario Bava's films, anything from Italy involving modern horror and crime has become synonymous with dull. This first effort by Dario Argento comes as a nice surprise because it's visually exciting and always interesting. Although based on an Edgar Wallace story, it's closer to Hitchcock than to the formula Wallace mysteries. An American writer in Rome (Tony Musante) witnesses a murder through a large window in a modern art gallery. The police refuse to let him leave until the murder (one of a series) is solved, and a caller threatens to kill his girlfriend (Suzy Kendall) if he doesn't leave. His investigation finally leads to the killer. Produced by Dario's father, Salvatore. With Eva Renzi. The soundtrack album with music by Ennio Morricone is still available.

THE BIRDS

1963 Universal
PRODUCER/DIRECTOR: Alfred Hitchcock
SCREENWRITER: Evan Hunter

Hitchcock followed the ground-breaking *Psycho* with another departure— a nature-turns-on-mankind story by Daphne Du Maurier. During a slowly developing relationship between lawyer Rod Taylor and an aggressive Tippi Hedren (a model in her first movie), birds begin to attack people randomly in an isolated California community. A teacher (Suzanne Pleshette) and schoolchildren are pecked at. Birds enter houses through chimneys. No explanation is ever given. The special effects (Albert J. Whitlock) are a combination of real birds, animation, and models. With young Veronica Cartwright, Jessica Tandy, and a bit with Hitchcock walking pet poodles. No music.

UPI 4/20/62: Director Alfred Hitchcock inspects some of the 1,300 finches appearing in one of the scare sequences for his new film, The Birds. The birds, shipped over from Japan, cost Hitchcock $1.50 per head. "Many people are afraid of birds," Hitchcock said. "Some women are more afraid of birds than they are of mice. There is no term for this phobia. Perhaps ornithobia would be correct usage."

BIRDS DO IT

1966 Columbia
PRODUCER: Stanley Colbert
DIRECTOR: Andrew Martin
SCREENWRITERS: Arnie Kogen, Art Arthur
Cape Kennedy janitor Soupy Sales (*Two Little Bears*) accidentally becomes "negatively ionized" so he can fly around with Judi the astro chimp. He also becomes magically irresistible to women (especially Beverly Adams). With Tab Hunter, Arthur O'Connell, and Edward Andrews.

BIRTHPLACE OF THE HOOTENANNY: See GREENWICH VILLAGE STORY

BLACK ANGEL

1946 Universal (B&W)
PRODUCERS: Roy William Neill, Tom McKnight
DIRECTOR: Roy William Neill
SCREENWRITER: Roy Chanslor
A good mystery based on a Cornell Woolrich novel. Dan Duryea's treacherous estranged wife is found murdered. June Vincent enlists his aid to help prove that her cheating husband, convicted of the crime, is innocent. Suspecting Marko (Peter Lorre), a very suspicious night club owner, they get a job at his club as a pianist/singer duo. Broderick Crawford is Captain Flood of the police department. With Wallace Ford. Lorre next starred in an Ambler adaptation, *The Chase*.

THE BLACK ANGELS

1970 Merrick International
PRODUCER: Leo Rivers
DIRECTOR/SCREENWRITER: Lawrence Merrick
"God forgives ... the Black Angels don't!" the ads read. An extremely violent biker film with a white gang (the Serpents) vs. a black one (the Choppers). The Choppers, a real California gang, played themselves. Johnny Reb (played by King John III) joins the Serpents. The gang soon learns the horrible truth—he's a Chopper member passing for white! An all-out war results. With Des Roberts, Linda Jackson, James Whitwirth (*The Hills Have Eyes*), and a lot of bad songs, "What's Going On" and "Military Disgust" among them. Director Merrick made *Guess What Happened to Count Dracula* the same year with many of the same actors. **(R)**

BLACK BELLY OF THE TARANTULA

1971 MGM (Italy)
PRODUCER: Marcello Danon
DIRECTOR: Paolo Cavara
SCREENWRITER: Lucille Saks
A confusing who's-the-killer movie probably inspired by the success of *Bird With the Crystal Plumage*. Victims are killed with a knife dipped in deadly spider venom. They're paralyzed, "so they must lie awake and watch themselves die!" Featuring three often-nude starlets of James Bond fame: Barbara Bouchet (*Casino Royale*), Claudine Auger (*Thunderball*), and Barbara Bach (*The Spy Who Loved Me*). With Giancarlo Giannini (*Seven Beauties*). The soundtrack by Ennio Morricone is available. **(R)**

THE BLACK BUCCANEER: See RAGE OF THE BUCCANEERS

THE BLACK CAMEL

1931 20th Century-Fox (B&W)
ASSOCIATE PRODUCER: William Sistrow
DIRECTOR: Hamilton MacFadden
SCREENWRITERS: Hugh Strange, Barry Conners
The second Warner Oland/Charlie Chan film. Made right after *Dracula*, it features a turbaned Bela Lugosi

as Tarneverro, a fortune-teller, and Dwight Faye in a bit part as a butler who actually did it. The only Chan film shot on location (Hawaii), it shows Charlie eating breakfast with his wife and ten children. The cast includes Sally Eilers, Robert Young, and Mary Gordon.

BLACK CASTLE
1952 Universal (B&W)
PRODUCER: William Alland
DIRECTOR: Nathan Juran
SCREENWRITER: Jerry Sackheim
Tame, dull Gothic horror with Boris Karloff as the captive physician of the murderous lord of a castle (Stephen McNally with a black eye patch). Richard Greene arrives to avenge a killing and faces a moat filled with alligators, a torture chamber, and a drug that makes people appear dead. With questionable characters played by Michael Pate and John Hoyt, and Lon Chaney, Jr., as a halfwit. Also with Mara Corday.

THE BLACK CAT
1934 Universal (B&W)
PRODUCER: Carl Laemmle, Jr.
DIRECTOR: Edgar Ulmer
SCREENWRITER: Peter Rurk
ALSO RELEASED AS: The Vanishing Body
Karloff and Lugosi together for the first time—and what a great movie! As devil cult leader/engineer Hjalmar Poelzig, Boris Karloff lives in an ultramodern European home, built on top of "the greatest graveyard in the world." He had stolen the wife of Dr. Vitus Werdegast (Bela Lugosi), and when she died he married her young daughter. When Lugosi arrives, he is shown his wife's dead body floating in a glass tank and told his daughter is also dead. After stopping a sacrificial ceremony, Lugosi skins Karloff alive and the whole unholy place blows up. Inspired more by Aleis-

ter Crowley than Poe, it combines classical music, art deco sets, and clever camerawork under the direction of the 30-year-old Ulmer. With David Manners, Jacqueline Wells (a.k.a. Julie Bishop), and none other than John Peter Richmond, later known as John Carradine, as the organist. Note Boris' black lipstick and haircut. A great Lugosi line: "Supernatural, perhaps— baloney, perhaps not."

THE BLACK CAT
1941 Universal (B&W)
PRODUCER: Burt Kelly
DIRECTOR: Albert S. Rogell
SCREENWRITERS: Robert Lees, Fred Rinaldo, Eric Taylor, Robert Neville
An unfunny old-dark-house murder-mystery comedy with a good cast. Bela Lugosi is a grizzly handyman who has many pet cats. Basil Rathbone and Gale Sondergaard play relatives living in a mansion. Hugh Herbert and Broderick Crawford provide the laughs. With Anne Gwynne and Gladys Cooper. When it was re-released, bit player Alan Ladd received top billing in newspaper ads.

THE BLACK CAT
1966 Hemisphere (B&W)
PRODUCER: Patrick Sims
DIRECTOR/SCREENWRITER: Harold Hoffman
Clever, original title for a gory exploitation film that is actually closer to the Poe story than the other earlier versions. A man thinks his father is reincarnated in a kitty, so he gouges its eye out and then kills it. He later kills his wife and walls her up in the basement—you know the rest. With a decapitation and an axe in a skull. The stars are Robert Frost and Robyn Baker. From the director of Underage and Love and the Animals (a documentary showing how animals mate).

BLACK CHRISTMAS: See SILENT NIGHT, EVIL NIGHT.

BLACK DRAGONS

1942 Monogram (B&W)
PRODUCERS: Sam Katzman, Jack Dietz
DIRECTOR: William Nigh
SCREENWRITER: Harvey M. Gates

Wartime madness, released shortly after Pearl Harbor. Bela Lugosi as a bearded Nazi plastic surgeon turns Japanese spies into Caucasians. Ads featured a signed testimonial by Bela stating, "Never have I worked in a story so startling or so blood-chillingly shocking. See it if you dare!" With Joan Barclay and George Pembroke.

BLACK FRANKENSTEIN: See BLACKENSTEIN.

BLACK FRIDAY

1940 Universal (B&W)
PRODUCER: Burt Kelly
DIRECTOR: Arthur Lubin
SCREENWRITERS: Curt Siodmak, Eric Taylor

A cheat Karloff/Lugosi film in which they have no scenes together and Stanley Ridges really stars. As a doctor, Karloff saves the life of his professor friend (Ridges) by giving him part of a dying gangster's brain. The man "becomes" the crook under hypnosis and kills underworld rival Lugosi and some of his men. Everybody's after the stolen money stashed by the dead gangster. For a publicity gimmick, Lugosi was actually hypnotised on the set for his death scene. With Ann Nagel and Anne Gwynne.

THE BLACK HOLE

1979 Buena Vista
PRODUCER: Ron Miller
DIRECTOR: Gary Nelson
SCREENWRITERS: Jeb Rosebrook, Gerry Day

Manley Hall hypnotizes Bela Lugosi for his role in Black Friday.

This film came out the same month as *Star Trek: The Motion Picture* and was mostly ignored even though it is far more enjoyable, with highly original and impressive special effects. A space probe, the *Palomino*, discovers another spaceship, the *Cygnus*, commanded by Hans Reinhardt (Maximilian Schell) and his killer robot, Max, on the edge of a black hole. The entire crew of the *Cygnus* is made up of mindless human slaves and robots (they look like a bunch of Darth Vaders). The big drawbacks to the film are two cutesy robots (voices by Roddy McDowall and Slim Pickens). But don't miss scenes of a meteor rolling down a main corridor, Anthony Perkins up against Max's rotary blades, and a large impressionistic bridge set. The story is loosely based on Jules Verne's *20,000 Leagues Under the Sea*. With Robert Forster, Ernest Borgnine, Joseph Bottoms, and Yvette Mimieux. John Barry wrote the score.   —AF

THE BLACK KLANSMAN

1966 U.S. Films (B&W)
PRODUCER/DIRECTOR: Ted V. Mikels
SCREENWRITERS: John T. Wilson,
Arthur Names
ALSO RELEASED AS: *I Crossed the Color Line*

Racial-tension exploitation by one of the world's worst directors. Richard Gilden stars as a light-skinned Negro entertainer who discovers that his daughter has been killed in a Ku Klux Klan church bombing. Passing for white, he joins the Klan and has an affair with the local leader's daughter. His white mistress and a black friend arrive to find him and are about to be hanged when.... At the happy ending the bad guys are exposed and racial harmony becomes a reality. Made with the sensitivity of Mikels' *The Astro-Zombies*. Presented by Joe Soloman.

BLACK MAGIC II: See REVENGE OF THE ZOMBIES.

BLACK NOON

1971 TV
PRODUCER/SCREENWRITER: Andrew J. Fenady
DIRECTOR: Bernard Kowalski

TV's first occult Western! A traveling preacher (Roy Thinnes) and his wife (Lynn Loring) arrive in a town where witchcraft rules. They should have known something was amiss when they spotted Yvette Mimieux (a mute), Henry Silva (a gunfighter), Gloria Grahame, and Ray Milland (as Deliverance). By the director of *Sssssss*.

BLACK PIT OF DR. M

1958 United Releasing (Mexico) (B&W)
PRODUCER: Alfred Ripstein, Jr.
DIRECTOR: Fernando Mendez
SCREENWRITER: Raymond Obon
ORIGINALLY RELEASED AS: *Misterios del Ultratumba*

A pretty wild horror film about an asylum doctor using a medium to contact his dead co-worker. A girl arrives to claim an inheritance, falls for a physician she saw in her dreams, and stays on as a nurse. An attendant who was recently scarred with acid dies, only to return to life with the spirit of the doctor who had been executed for a murder he didn't commit. The ugly revived corpse (who likes to play the violin) loves the nurse and wants to make her ugly, too. With Raphael Bertrand, Mary Cortez, and Gaston Santos.

THE BLACK RAVEN

1943 PRC (B&W)
DIRECTOR: Sam Newfield
SCREENWRITER: Fred Myton

The stars of *The Mad Monster* return in a story of murders at a roadside inn. Villain George Zucco owns it. Dumb handyman Glenn Strange does what he's told. With Robert Livingston and Charles Middleton.

THE BLACK ROOM

1935 Columbia (B&W)
PRODUCER: Robert North
DIRECTOR: Roy William Neill
SCREENWRITERS: Arthur Strawn,
Henry Meyers

Boris Karloff is great as 19th-century Czech twin brothers. A legend says that the kind younger brother will slay the older sadistic one in the black room. It happens as predicted in a round-about way after the bad twin kidnaps local women, throws enemies into a pit, and gives up his title of baron under mob pressure. With Marian Marsh, Katherine DeMille, and Edward Van Sloan.

BLACK SABBATH

1964 AIP (Italy)
PRODUCER: Salvatore Billitteri
DIRECTOR: Mario Bava
SCREENWRITERS: Marcello Fondato,
Alberto Bervilacqua, Mario Bava
ORIGINALLY RELEASED AS: *I Tre Volti della Paura*

Bava at his best. This excellent three-part horror story was labeled *Black Sabbath* by AIP to remind you of their previous Bava hit, *Black Sunday*. They also added a new Les Baxter sound track and Boris Karloff as a *Thriller*-type host. In "The Drop of Water" (from a story by Chekhov), a nurse (Jacqueline Pierreux) takes a diamond ring from the hand of a dead clairvoyant. But the terrifying corpse seeks revenge. In "The Telephone" (by F. G. Synder), a prostitute (Michelle Mercier) receives threatening phone calls from a dead man she had betrayed. In the best story, "The Wurdalak" (from a Tolstoy story), Boris Karloff is Gorca, a Balkan hunter who becomes a vampire and must prey on his loved ones. His first victim is his little grandson, who returns from the dead and cries to lure the family members. It has a great chilling ending. Also with Mark Damon (*House of Usher*).

THE BLACK SCORPION

1957 Warner Brothers (B&W)
PRODUCERS: Frank Melford, Jack Dietz
DIRECTOR: Edward Ludwig
SCREENWRITERS: David Duncan, Robert Blees
A low-budget feature shot in Mexico that includes excellent stop-motion animation effects (done in a rush) by Willis O'Brien and Peter Peterson. The terrifying huge scorpions make the monsters in most other films look pathetic.

Hoping to cash in on the previous year's *Tarantula*, its star Mara Corday is on hand with perennial hero Richard Denning as a geologist. A scorpion battles a helicopter and a train, and other animated wonders appear, like a spider and a worm with claws.

THE BLACK SLEEP

1956 United Artists
PRODUCER: Howard W. Koch
DIRECTOR: Reginald LeBorg
SCREENWRITER: John C. Higgens
ALSO RELEASED AS: *Dr. Cadman's Secret*
Never before (or since) have so many horror actors been brought together and told to act like mongoloids. Never have so many actors been so wasted. Only Basil Rathbone and Akim Tamiroff get to play semirational humans. Rathbone, as Dr. Cadman (in 19th-century England), tries to cure his cataleptic wife by experimenting on people provided by Otto the gypsy (Tamiroff). His lobotomy victims are kept in the basement except for Casmir the mute butler (74-year-old Bela Lugosi). Other brainless characters are John Carradine as Borg, a bearded nut always spouting verse; Lon Chaney, Jr., as Mongo, a witless idiot who strangles people; Tor Johnson as Curry, a big, blind retard kept in chains; a guy with a skull-like half-face; and a token bald woman with tufts of hair all over her body. In the end, the army of mutants escapes, chanting "Kill, kill, kill." They do. It was the last film Lugosi made. He died in August 1956.

BLACK SUNDAY

1960 AIP (Italy)
PRODUCER: Massimo Derita
DIRECTOR: Mario Bava
SCREENWRITERS: Ennio Deconcini,
  Mario Bava, Marcello Coscia,
  Mario Seranore
ORIGINALLY RELEASED AS: *La Maschera del Demonio*

Bela Lugosi (left) and John Carradine (right) dine with the cast of The Black Sleep.

English-born beauty Barbara Steele begins her horror career in this classic first feature by former cinematographer Bava. As Princess Asa, a witch, she has a metal mask with spikes pounded into her face and is burned at the stake. When she's revived a hundred years later by drops of blood, she summons her vampire servant (Arturo Dominici) from his grave and tries to take over Princess Katia (also Steele). Don't miss this atmospheric horror classic inspired by Gogol's "The Viy." Music (U.S. version) by Les Baxter. With John Richardson. After its American success, AIP brought Steele to America for *The Pit and the Pendulum*. *Black Sunday* premiered in Cleveland at the Allen Theatre. Patrons were given a special card with a protective chant.

Vic Morrow in Blackboard Jungle.

BLACK TORMENT
1964 Governor (England)
PRODUCER/DIRECTOR: Robert Hartford-Davis
SCREENWRITERS: Donald and Derek Ford
A British Lord (John Turner) remarries after his wife's suicide and returns to his gloomy old castle. Witness murder, a ghost on horseback, and an unbelievable trick ending. With Heather Sears.

BLACK ZOO
1963 Allied Artists
PRODUCER: Herman Cohen
DIRECTOR: Robert Gordon
SCREENWRITERS: Aben Kandel,
   Herman Cohen
L.A. zoo owner Michael Gough sends his various jungle cats (and a man in a gorilla suit left over from *Konga*) to maul his enemies. He loves the animals so much that he plays an organ recital for them while they lounge on the living-room furniture; he even wears a tiger-skin rug for ceremonies. Jeanne Cooper is his wife. Rod Lauren is a mute keeper Gough likes to beat. Virginia Grey, Jerome Cowan, and Elisha Cook, Jr., are all victims. With Marianna Hill. Edward Platt is a detective. Look for the rare photo/comic book of *Black Zoo* put out by *Horror Monsters* magazine.

BLACKBOARD JUNGLE
1955 MGM (B&W)
PRODUCER: Pandro S. Berman
DIRECTOR/SCREENWRITER: Richard Brooks
This top-notch look at an inner-city New York vocational school features rampant juvenile delinquency and "Rock Around the Clock" by Bill Haley and the Comets as its theme song. Although a pre-rock 'n' roll mania film, it did more than any other to spread the word. Glenn Ford stars as the teacher called Mr. Daddy-O by his students. Most of them don't seem interested in learning and act like prison-

ers striking out at their wardens, a shocking revelation to many older filmgoers. Vic Morrow, making his film debut as the main tough guy, beats up Ford, threatens his wife (Anne Francis), and smashes his math teacher's collection of jazz 78s. Other students are Sidney Poitier, Paul Mazursky, Raphael Campos, Jamie Farr (then known as Jameel Farah), and Allison Hayes. Margaret Hayes is a teacher. With John Hoyt, Louis Calhern, Richard Kiley, Horace MacMahon, and Richard Deacon. Based on a best-selling novel of the same title by Evan Hunter. *Rebel Without a Cause* was released the same year.

BLACKENSTEIN

1973 Exclusive International
PRODUCER/SCREENWRITER: Frank R. Saletri
DIRECTOR: William A. Levy
ALSO RELEASED AS: *Black Frankenstein*

After *Blacula* this was inevitable, but *nobody* could have guessed how bad it would be. It's a totally inept mixture of the worst horror and blaxploitation films—and Liz Renay (*Desperate Living*) is in it! A crazed scientist creates a beefy black monster with an afro. The creature likes to tear open the shirts of his female victims before killing them. If you think aging actors have it bad, how about an old special effects expert? Ken Strickfaden, the man who created the incredible electronic gadgets in the original Universal *Frankenstein* movies, made some token zaps in this equal-opportunity landmark. With John Hart, Ivory Stone, and Andrea King. (**R**)

BLACKOUT

1978 New World (Canada/France)
PRODUCERS: Nicole Boisuert, Eddy Matalon
DIRECTOR: Eddy Matalon
SCREENWRITER: John Saxton

A violent all-star look at New York's 1977 blackout. It disappeared from the-aters real fast. Cheap thrills with Robert Carradine, Jim Mitchum, Ray Milland, June Allyson, Belinda Montgomery, and Jean-Pierre Aumont. (**R**)

BLACULA

1972 AIP
PRODUCER: Joseph T. Naar
DIRECTOR: William Crain
SCREENWRITERS: Joan Torres, Raymond Koenig

Better than most of the black horror films, but besides the initial novelty, it's pretty ordinary. William Marshall is good as Manuwalde, a vampire in modern L.A. As a former African prince bitten by the original Dracula, he's appalled by contemporary customs and morals, putting the bite on drug dealers and homosexual antique dealers to help clean things up. Thalmus Rasulala finally defeats him. With Denise Nicholas (*Room 222*), Elisha Cook, Jr. (with a mechanical hook hand), Vonetta McGee, and Gordon Pinsent. It was billed as the first black horror film. It wasn't. *Scream, Blacula, Scream* was the sequel. Music by The Hues Corporation.

Thalmus Rasulala battles a gay vampire in an open grave while Denise Nicholas watches in Blacula.

BLADE

1973 Joseph Green Pictures
PRODUCER: George Mansse
DIRECTOR: Ernest Pintoff
SCREENWRITERS: Ernest Pintoff,
  Jeff Lieberman

"A psycho-karate killer brutalizes his victims and your emotions!" the ads promised. John Marley stars as a detective stalking a killer in New York City, where this confusing thriller was shot. With William Prince, Keene Curtis, and Marshall Efron. Co-written by Jeff Lieberman (*Squirm*). Pintoff also directed *Dynamite Chicken* and *Lunch Wagon Girls*. **(R)**

BLADE RUNNER

1982 Warner Brothers
PRODUCER: Michael Deeley
DIRECTOR: Ridley Scott
SCREENWRITERS: Hampton Fancher,
  David Peoples

The director of *Alien* returns with another superior big-budget ($27 million) science-fiction feature. A futuristic *film noir* adventure based on *Do Androids Dream of Electric Sheep?* by Phillip K. Dick, it's a much more difficult film than *Alien* or any of star Harrison Ford's other action hits. In 21st-century Los Angeles, Ford is forced to continue terminating out-of-control superhuman replicants, primarily beautiful Sean Young and Aryan killer Rutger Hauer. Some fans will recognize the unique Bradbury Building previously used in "The Sixth Finger" episode of *The Outer Limits*. Most of *Blade Runner* takes place on massive, incredibly detailed sets of towering megastructures built above the crumbling old buildings. The stunning visual effects are by Douglas Trumbull. Music by Vangelis. With Joe Turkel (the bartender in *The Shining*). A fascinating, sadistic movie marred by an unrealistic happy ending. The videocassette version contains five minutes of gore and violence cut from the theatrical print. **(R)**

THE BLANCHEVILLE MONSTER

1963 AIP-TV (Spain/Italy)
PRODUCER: Alberto Aguilera
DIRECTOR: Alberto deMartino
SCREENWRITERS: Bruno Corbucci,
  Giovanni Grimaldi, Natividad Zaro
ALSO RELEASED AS: *Horror*

Forgettable horror loosely based on Poe's "The House of Usher" and "The Premature Burial." An insane disfigured Englishman has buried his daughter alive. With Gerard Tichy and Joan Mills.

BLAST-OFF GIRLS

1967 Dominant/Boxoffice Spectaculars
PRODUCER/DIRECTOR/SCREENWRITER:
  Herschell Gordon Lewis

The Big Blast rock combo vs. crooked manager Boojie Baker (Dan Conway), who bribes promoters, hires girls to rip the boys' clothes off, and takes half of everything. He tries to blackmail the group into an even better deal following a phony drug raid, but his plan backfires and they tear up their contract. Featuring Ray Sager and Colonel Harlan Sanders. The band is actually the Faded Blue—Tom Tyrell, Ron Liace, Dennis Hickey, Chris Wolski, and Ralph Mullin. —CB

THE BLIND DEAD

1972 Hallmark (Spain)
EXECUTIVE PRODUCER: Salvadore Romero
DIRECTOR/SCREENWRITER: Armando De Ossorio
ORIGINALLY RELEASED AS: *La Noche del Terror
  Ciego*
ALSO RELEASED AS: *Tombs of the Blind Dead*

A 13th-century religious sect called the Templarios were executed and blinded (by crows) for killing women during blood rituals. They return from their graves as mummified bloodthirsty skel-

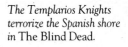

The Templarios Knights terrorize the Spanish shore in The Blind Dead.

etons on horseback and attack 20th-century Spaniards. This atmospheric horror film was so popular in Europe that three sequels resulted. *Return of the Blind Dead* was next. Starring Lone Fleming and Cesar Burner. **(R)**

BLIND MAN'S BLUFF: See *CAULDRON OF BLOOD*

THE BLOB

1958 Paramount
PRODUCER: Jack H. Harris
DIRECTOR: Irvin S. Yeaworthy
SCREENWRITERS: Theodore Simonson, Kate Phillips

Ingenious teen science-fiction classic with 28-year-old Steve McQueen in his first starring role. The ever-growing blob, bright red with the blood of the humans it absorbs, terrorizes a small American town by overtaking its most treasured institutions—a supermarket, a diner car, and a movie theater. The theater scene is especially great: the gelatinous mass makes its way to the projection booth, engulfs the projectionist, and oozes through the holes in the wall onto the patrons below (busy watching *Daughter of Horror*). A perfect effect to unsettle the theater audience watching *The Blob*! After consuming some of the people, it grows so big it's forced out the front lobby doors. McQueen and his girlfriend try to warn parents and police, but hey, they're just drunk kids, right? With Olin Howlin as the first victim (an old man) and Aneta Corseaut (best known as Helen Crump on *The Andy Griffith Show*) as McQueen's girl.

BLONDE PICKUP

1955 Globe Roadshows (B&W)
PRODUCER: George Weiss
DIRECTOR: Robert C. Dertano

Gym owner Timothy Farrell tampers with horses and sets up crooked lady-wrestling matches while dodging syndicate hit men and investigators from the Senate Crime Commission. He's skipping town with a suitcase full of money when his number comes up. Seamy mat action features Clare Mortensen, Rita

SHOCK AFTER **SHOCK** AFTER **SHOCK**
as Desire drives
a bargain with
MURDER!

BLOOD
AND **LACE**

STARRING
GLORIA GRAHAME
A CONTEMPORARY FILMAKERS/CARLIN COMPANY PRODUCTION released by AMERICAN INTERNATIONAL PICTURES

COLOR BY MOVIELAB **GP**

his lover (Eva Bartok) own a luxurious fashion salon and traffic drugs on the side. One by one, their beautiful models are killed by a masked man with a horrible metal claw glove. Featuring "30 of the world's most glamorous girls!" Bava's imaginative shockers were treated like cancer when shown in America's inner-city theaters. Today similar but inferior films are treated as major, even respectable releases.

BLOOD AND LACE
1971 AIP
PRODUCERS: Ed Carlin, Gil Lasky
DIRECTOR: Philip Gilbert
SCREENWRITER: Gil Lasky

One of the sickest PG-rated films ever made, starring Gloria Grahame. Set in an orphanage, the plot involves torture, starvation, murder (with hammers), blackmail, rape, incest, and frozen corpses. Vic Tayback (from the *Alice* show) makes a surprise appearance. Newspaper ads featured a big bloody hammer and promised "shock after shock after shock." With Melody Patterson and Milton Selzer.

BLOOD AND ROSES
1960 Paramount (France/Italy)
PRODUCER: Raymond Eger
DIRECTOR/SCREENWRITER: Roger Vadim
ORIGINALLY RELEASED AS: *Et Mourir de Plaisir*

An atmospheric, bloodless version of Sheridan le Fanu's *Carmilla*, which had previously been the basis for *Vampyr* (1932). Annette Vadim is Carmilla, a woman in modern-day Rome obsessed with her vampire ancestor Mircalla. Her aristocrat cousin (Mel Ferrer) puts on a masked ball celebrating his impending marriage to Elsa Martinelli. Carmilla/Mircalla kills a servant girl and bites her cousin's fiancée. The version dubbed for American audiences omitted all references to lesbianism, pretty much destroying the story.

Martinez, and Peaches Page. Globe, an art-house outfit, also released *Dance Hall Racket*. Farrell appears in *Jail Bait*. –CB

BLOOD!
1974 Bryanston
PRODUCER: Walter Kent
DIRECTOR/SCREENWRITER: Andy Milligan

Horrible horrors from Staten Island. In 1899 Dracula's daughter and the Wolfman's son marry and move to America and grow carnivorous plants. **(R)**

BLOOD AND BLACK LACE
1964 Woolner (Italy/France/W. Germany)
PRODUCERS: Massimo Patizi, Alfred Mirabel
PRODUCER (English version): Lou Moss
DIRECTOR: Mario Bava
SCREENWRITERS: Mario Bava, Marcello Fondato, Giuseppe Barilla
ORIGINALLY RELEASED AS: *Sei Donne per L'Assassino*

Even Cameron Mitchell is good in this beautifully photographed ahead-of-its-time gore-murder thriller. Mitchell and

BLOOD BATH

1966 AIP (B&W)
PRODUCER/SCREENWRITER: Jack Hill
DIRECTORS: Jack Hill, Stephanie Rothman
ALSO RELEASED AS: *Track of the Vampire*

A confusing but interesting horror film with an even more confusing history. William Campbell is Antonio Sordi, a crazed artist living in Venice, California. He believes he becomes his 15th-century ancestor, a vampire/artist who was burned at the stake. He stalks girls and kills them, or sometimes lures them to his bell-tower studio and drops them into a vat of boiling wax, then paints them. Sordi is in love with Lori Saunders, a ballerina whom he believes to be a reincarnation of his ancestor's mistress. He kills her friend Marissa Mathes (*Playboy*'s Miss June 1962), whose sister (Sandra Knight) shows up only to be killed herself. In the unlikely ending, his wax-covered victims come to life and kill him. Executive producer Roger Corman fired director Hill. Stephanie Rothman was given his footage plus old footage from a Yugoslavian vampire film and told to shoot new footage and have it all make sense. Sources conflict, but I'm sure this contains scenes from a 1965 feature called *Portrait in Terror* with Patrick Magee. In any case, Rothman shot the footage with Sandra Knight. Also with Corman regulars Jonathan Haze and Sid Haig. Sound by Gary Kurtz, who later produced the *Star Wars* movies.

BLOOD BATH

1976 Cannon
PRODUCER: Anthony Fingleton
DIRECTOR/SCREENWRITER: Joel Reed

This very local New York anthology of weird tales by the director of *Blood Sucking Freaks* shouldn't be confused with the '60s film of the same name. It consists of short *Twilight Zone*-like sequences and features Harve Presnell as a horror-movie director. You might want to endure it for the film debut of P.J. Soles of *Rock 'n' Roll High School* fame. Otherwise, take a nap.

BLOOD BEACH

1981 Jerry Gross Organization
PRODUCER: Steven Nalevansky
DIRECTOR/SCREENWRITER: Jeffrey Bloom

People are sucked into the sand by a ridiculous creature you only get to see for a few seconds. In one attempt at humor, a rapist is castrated by the unseen monster. A slow, uneventful '50s-style movie with John Saxon and Burt Young as contrasting cops, and Marianna Hill and David Huffman as troubled lovers. (R)

BLOOD BEAST FROM OUTER SPACE

1966 World Entertainment Corporation (England) (B&W)
PRODUCER: Ronald Liles
DIRECTOR: John Gilling
SCREENWRITER: Jim O'Connolly
ALSO RELEASED AS: *The Night Caller From Outer Space*

Detective John Saxon on the job in Blood Beach.

A disguised mutant alien (Robert Crewsdon) arrives from Jupiter's third moon in a glowing orb, rents a shop in Soho, and places ads in *Bikini Girl* magazine for models. The beautiful women are replenishing his world with healthy babies. A female scientist poses as a model to find out what's goin' on. Her co-scientists are Maurice Denham and American John Saxon. With Saxon as a hero it's no wonder that the undercover scientist/model gets killed. Don't miss the theme song.

THE BLOOD BEAST TERROR: See *THE VAMPIRE BEAST CRAVES BLOOD.*

BLOOD CEREMONY: See *FEMALE BUTCHER.*

BLOOD COUPLE: See *GANJA AND HESS.*

BLOOD CREATURE: See *TERROR IS A MAN.*

BLOOD DEMON

1967 Hemisphere (W. Germany)
PRODUCER: Wolfgang Kuhnlenz
DIRECTOR: Harold Reinl
SCREENWRITER: Manfred R. Köhler
ORIGINALLY RELEASED AS: *Die Schlangengrube und das Pendel*
ALSO RELEASED AS: *The Torture Chamber of Dr. Sadism*

This is supposed to be based on Poe's "The Pit and the Pendulum" but forget that and enjoy the outrageous story. Christopher Lee is Count Regula, who had been beheaded and dismembered for killing 12 virgins. Forty years later, his indestructible servant puts him back together and he's ready for virgin number 13. A baroness (Karin Dor), her attorney (ex-Tarzan Lex Barker), her maid, and a monk (who is really a thief) arrive at the castle. Karin is suspended

over a pit of spiders and snakes and Lex is strapped down under a razor-sharp pendulum. Lee really looks dead and there are some striking visual treats like an impressionistic forest full of corpses.

THE BLOOD DRINKERS

1966 Hemisphere (U.S./Philippines)
PRODUCER: Cirio H. Santiago
DIRECTOR: Gerardo de Leon
SCREENWRITER: Cesar Amigo
ALSO RELEASED AS: *The Vampire People*

It's nice to see that they can make a monster movie in the Philippines without John Ashley. Marco the Vampire (Ronald Remy) has a girl and a dwarf for assistants. He also has a bat that acts as a carrier pigeon. The girl he loves is dying, so he goes after her twin sister, planning a heart transplant. Amelia Fuentes, who plays the twins, returned as a vampire in *Creatures of Evil* a few years later. It's partially in real color and mostly in tinted black and white.

THE BLOOD FEAST

1963 Box Office Spectaculars
PRODUCER: David F. Friedman
DIRECTOR: Herschell Gordon Lewis
SCREENWRITER: A. Louise Downe

This is it! The infamous first gore film. If you can stand the sight of guts, it's hilarious. In Miami, Fuad Ramses, an Egyptian caterer, worships a goddess (a mannequin) and murders women for their body parts. A tongue, brains, and a leg are removed in disgusting and convincing full-color detail. As the limping caterer, Mal Arnold is a determined bug-eyed psycho. Connie Mason, *Playboy*'s blond June 1963 playmate, is given an "Egyptian feast" by her mother. Guess who the caterer is. A weird-looking cop (Thomas Wood) saves Connie just in time and Fuad ends up crushed in a garbage truck compacter. The acting is terrible. If the actors were as good as the effects it would be nearly

impossible to watch. The girl whose head is ripped open on the beach is Ashlyn Martin, another *Playboy* Playmate of the Month (April 1964). Lewis was the first, and for years the only, person making offensive films like this. He had previously made nudie films, but after this rural drive-in hit he did *2,000 Maniacs*, also with the untalented Miss Mason. Lewis is also credited with the music, the photography, and the special effects. In "Blood Color."

BLOOD FEAST

1976 Cannon (Italy)
DIRECTOR: Emil P. Miragala
SCREENWRITER: Frank Pitto
ALSO RELEASED AS: *Feast of Flesh*
The original feature bearing the title *Blood Feast* deserved it. This extremely boring police mystery starring Barbara Bouchet should be called *Living Room Furniture* because the chairs and lamps are more interesting than the actors.

BLOOD FIEND: See THEATER OF DEATH.

BLOOD FOR DRACULA: See ANDY WARHOL'S DRACULA.

BLOOD FROM THE MUMMY'S TOMB

1972 Hammer/AIP (England)
PRODUCER: Howard Brandy
DIRECTORS: Seth Holt, Michael Carreras
SCREENWRITER: Christopher Wicking
This mummy is female, unwrapped, and from a Bram Stoker story. The soul of Queen Tara is transferred to the daughter (Valerie Leon) of one of the archeologists who desecrated her tomb. Andrew Kier and George Coulouris lead the modern-day expedition that leads to death. The same story was remade as *The Awakening*.

BLOOD LEGACY: See LEGACY OF BLOOD.

Sandra Harrison is no typical vampire. She becomes a vampire when the evil headmistress of her girls' boarding school hypnotizes her. And her looks! She can hardly close her mouth for the long pointy teeth sticking out. Her long hair comes to a point on her forehead. She has jets of hair behind her ears, enormous winged eyebrows, and a white face. Really hot stuff! (She also wears the required '50s tight sweater.) With Louise Lewis, Gail Ganley, Thomas B. Henry, and Richard Devon. Ads warned: "In her eyes—desire! In her veins—the blood of a monster!"

BLOOD OF DRACULA'S CASTLE

1967 Paragon Pictures
PRODUCERS: Al Adamson, Rex Carlton
DIRECTORS: Jean Hewitt, Al Adamson
SCREENWRITER: Rex Carlton
ALSO RELEASED AS: *Dracula's Castle*

Not only is this a typically laughable Adamson Z-movie—star John Carradine doesn't even play Dracula. He's George the butler. Alex D'Arcy and

BLOOD MANIA

1971 Crown International
PRODUCERS: Peter Carpenter, Chris Marconi
DIRECTOR: Robert O'Neil
SCREENWRITERS: Toby Sacher, Tony Crechales

Lousy sleaze about an abortion doctor, drugs, blackmail, and a plot to gain an inheritance. The "shocking climax" during the last 15 minutes is supposed to "jolt you out of your seat." You've been warned. Starring co-producer Peter Carpenter and Maria De Aragon. (R)

BLOOD OF DRACULA

1957 AIP
PRODUCER: Herman Cohen
DIRECTOR: Herbert L. Strock
SCREENWRITER: Ralph Thorton

You can't tell from the bland title, but this is the female counterpart to *I Was a Teenage Frankenstein* and *I Was a Teenage Werewolf*. All were Cohen productions from the wonderful year of 1957. (At least it was a wonderful year for drive-in movies and rock 'n' roll.) Young

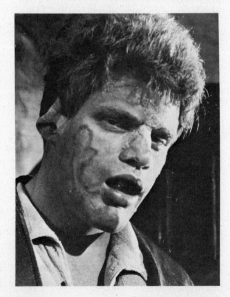

Note the terrific make-up job on the ear of this Blood of Dracula's Castle *star.*

Paula Raymond (star of *The Beast From 20,000 Fathoms*) are the Count and Countess Townsend (Dracula) living in present-day America. George and Mango (Ray Young), a halfwit hunchback, keep young women chained up in the basement, occasionally sacrificing them to the great god Luna(!). The girls' blood is drained with a syringe and served to the Draculas as cocktails. With Vicki Volante, Robert Dix (as a werewolf), John Cardos, and Kent Osborne. Cinematography by Laszlo Kovacs.

BLOOD OF FRANKENSTEIN: See DRACULA vs. FRANKENSTEIN

BLOOD OF FU MANCHU: See KISS AND KILL.

BLOOD OF GHASTLY HORROR
1965/71 Hemisphere
PRODUCER/DIRECTOR: Al Adamson
SCREENWRITERS: Dick Poston, Chris Martino
ALSO RELEASED AS: *Man With the Synthetic Brain*

An amazingly incoherent mess. The story, about jewel thieves using a Vietnam vet (with an electronic control device in his brain) as their zombie/hit man, was made by Adamson in 1965 as *Psycho-a-Go-Go*. New scenes were added in 1969 and it was released as *Fiend With the Electronic Brain*. Still more scenes were added in 1971 and the title changed again. The tacked-on star footage involves Kent Taylor, John Carradine (as the mad Dr. Vanard), and the stunning Regina Carrol as his daughter. (Regina is happily married to Al Adamson in real life.) The best scene involves ex-Disney star Tommy Kirk as a detective getting sick when he opens a gift box containing a sev-

ered head. With go-go-dancer victims and music by the Vendells! Cinematography by Vilmos Szigmund.

BLOOD OF THE MAN DEVIL: See HOUSE OF THE BLACK DEATH.

THE BLOOD OF NOSTRADAMUS
1960 AIP-TV (Mexico) (B&W)
PRODUCER: Victor Parra
DIRECTOR: Frederick Curiel
SCREENWRITERS: Charles Taboada, Alfred Ruanova

German Robles (*The Vampire*) played a bearded Mexican vampire descendant of the famous prophet (with a hunchback servant) in a ten-part serial. It was re-edited and dubbed into four features that were released directly to television in America. Try and tell one from another. A K. Gordon Murray presentation.

BLOOD OF THE UNDEAD: See SCHIZO.

BLOOD OF THE VAMPIRE
1958 Universal (England)
PRODUCERS: Robert S. Baker, Monty Berman
DIRECTOR: Henry Cass
SCREENWRITER: Jimmy Sangster

Dr. Callistrastus (Sir Donald Wolfit) is executed, returns to life, and runs an insane asylum. The revived doctor needs blood to stay alive, so he kills (and tortures) inmates. The most memorable aspect of the movie is the make-up. The doctor is a Lugosi-like fiend with pointed sideburns, upturned eyebrows, and a streak of white hair. His assistant Carl (Victor Maddern) is an unshaven cripple with bangs and a dead eye that bulges out an inch too low. Some torture-chamber scenes are fairly gruesome for the time. Barbara Shelley and Vincent Ball are a captive couple.

THE BLOOD ON SATAN'S CLAW

1970 Tigon/Cannon (England)
PRODUCERS: Peter L. Andrews,
Malcolm B. Heyworth
DIRECTOR: Piers Haggard
SCREENWRITERS: Robert Wynne-Simmons,
Piers Haggard
ALSO RELEASED AS: *Satan's Skin*

An effective, serious witchcraft thriller set in 17th-century England. Linda Hayden (*Taste the Blood of Dracula*) stars as Angel Blake, a seductive blonde serving the devil (seen as a hairy creature with claws). A coven of possessed children is formed. As a judge, Patrick Wymark tries to put a stop to the evil. With Barry Andrews. (**R**)

BLOOD ORGY: See GORE GORE GIRLS.

BLOOD ORGY OF THE SHE-DEVILS

1973 Gemini
PRODUCER/DIRECTOR/SCREENWRITER:
Ted V. Mikels

Mara the witch queen (Lila Zaborin) lives in California and practices the black arts. She even contacts an American Indian spirit during a seance and has a "wolf pack of voluptuous virgins." From the man responsible for *The Astro-Zombies*, so don't expect quality of any kind.

THE BLOOD ROSE

1969 Allied Artists (France)
PRODUCER: Edgar Oppenheimer
DIRECTOR: Claude Mulot
SCREENWRITERS: Claude Mulot,
Edgar Oppenheimer, Jean Carriaga
ORIGINALLY RELEASED AS: *La Rose Escorchée*

The doctor-kills-to-restore-the-face-of-a-beautiful-woman theme was really overworked in European films during the '60s. The best (and first) was *Horror*

A TERRIFYING, SCREAMING PLUNGE TO THE DEPTHS OF HELL!

TED V. MIKELS presents

BLOOD ORGY OF THE SHE-DEVILS

GENENI FILM DISTRIBUTING CO. INC.

Chamber of Dr. Faustus. This time, a wealthy painter (Frédéric Lansac) lives in a secluded château with his wife (Anny Duperey). Her face had been horribly burned so a plastic surgeon wanted by the police (Howard Vernon) is blackmailed into performing grafting operations. Of course, beautiful women are needed to "donate" their faces. This strange, atmospheric production is more warped than usual, thanks to two dwarf servants who wear animal skins, are sexually active, and generally get underfoot. With Elizabeth Teissier. Lesbian scenes were supposedly deleted for American release, where it was billed as "the first horror-sex film." (**R**)

THE BLOOD SEEKERS: See CAIN'S WAY.

THE BLOOD SPATTERED BRIDE

1974 Europix (Spain)
PRODUCER: Antonio Perez Olea
DIRECTOR/SCREENWRITER: Vincent Aranda
ORIGINALLY RELEASED AS: *La Novia Esangentada*

One of several versions of Sheridan le Fanu's *Carmilla* made after the success of *The Vampire Lovers*. This one deals more with the lesbian vampire aspects and includes bizarre scenes like a woman buried in the sand with a diving mask on and her breasts showing, and a female vampire couple sleeping in a coffin built for two. Maribel Martin stars with Alexandra Bastedo. **(R)**

BLOOD SUCKERS: See DR. TERROR'S GALLERY OF TERRORS.

BLOOD SUCKING FREAKS: See THE INCREDIBLE TORTURE SHOW.

BLOOD WATERS OF DR. Z

1972 Barton
PRODUCER/DIRECTOR: Don Barton
SCREENWRITERS: Lee Laren, Ron Kivett
ALSO RELEASED AS: *Zaat*

Florida is an unheralded center of grade Z filmmaking. This swamp movie features a mad doctor developing a race of super amphibian monsters. The creature has a scaly (and hairy) body and an immobile face that looks like (maybe) a good Halloween mask. The stars who probably returned to raising alligators after this one came out are Marshall Graver, Nancy Lien, and Paul Galloway.

BLOODEATERS

1980 Parker National
PRODUCER/DIRECTOR/SCREENWRITER: Chuck McCrann
ALSO RELEASED AS: *Forest of Fear*

A gory film inspired by *Night of the Living Dead*. Government agents are using a weed killer on marijuana crops. Young drug-dealing "farmers" are transformed into crazed cannibalistic zombies who attack people with machetes. Pretty strong stuff despite the mostly terrible acting. With John Amplas (*Martin*) as an FBI agent who looks like he should be in high school. Filmed in Pennsylvania. **(R)**

BLOODLUST

1959 Crown International
PRODUCER/DIRECTOR/SCREENWRITER: Ralph Brooke

Cheap exploitation version of *The Most Dangerous Game* in which the perverse Dr. Balleau (Wilton Graff) keeps his teenage victims' bodies in glass tanks. With June Kenney, Robert Reed (later the dad on *The Brady Bunch*), and Lilyan Chauvin.

THE BLOODSUCKERS

1971 Chevron (England)
PRODUCER: Graham Harris
DIRECTOR: Robert Hartford-Davies
SCREENWRITER: Julian More
ALSO RELEASED AS: *Incense for the Damned, Doctors Wear Scarlet*

Patrick Macnee (*The Avengers*) stars as a retired Greek major helping a young woman find her lost fiancé, who is under the influence of devil worshipers. The man (Patrick Mower) practices vampirism as an extension of his sexual perversion. Peter Cushing has a small role in this little-seen film. With Imogen Hassall. Based on Simon Raven's novel, *Doctors Wear Scarlet*. **(R)**

BLOODTHIRSTY BUTCHERS

1970 Constitution
PRODUCER: William Miskin
DIRECTOR/SCREENWRITER: Andy Milligan

Pathetic remake of *The Demon Barber of Fleet Street* with Sweeney Todd and his baker friend selling human meat pies. Filmed in England. Writer-director Milligan also photographed the film. (R)

THE BLOODY BROOD

1959 Sutton (Canada) (B&W)
PRODUCER/DIRECTOR: Julian Roffman
SCREENWRITERS: Elwood Ullman, Ben Kerner, Des Hardman

Peter Falk is Nico, the leader of a drug-dealing beatnik gang who feeds a messenger boy a hamburger full of ground glass—for kicks. When the local Mounties are unable to crack the case, the victim's brother (Jack Betts) cuts in. Ronald Hartmann, Barbara Lord, William Brydon, and Michael Zenon are Nico's sidekicks, and Robert Christie is Detective McLeod. —CB

BLOODY JUDGE: See NIGHT OF THE BLOOD MONSTER.

BLOODY MAMA

1969 AIP
PRODUCER/DIRECTOR: Roger Corman
SCREENWRITER: Robert Thom

Corman's psychological gangster movie stars Shelley Winters, machine gun in hand, as Ma Barker. Her dedicated gang (her sons) have every perversion, addiction, and problem imaginable. The sadistic Herman (Don Stroud) sleeps with Ma. When Fred (*Lou Grant* regular Robert Walden) is released from prison, he brings home his cellmate/lover (Bruce Dern), who also sleeps with Ma. Lloyd (Robert DeNiro) is a spaced-out drug addict who sniffs glue if nothing better is around. With Clint Kimbrough as the fourth brother, Pat Hingle, Diane Varsi, Scatman Crothers, and some alligators. Shelley had already played Ma "Parker" on *Batman* in 1966 in an episode called "The Biggest Mother of Them All." Filmed in the Ozarks. (R)

Shelley Winters and machine gun in Roger Corman's Bloody Mama.

THE BLOODY PIT OF HORROR

1965 Pacemaker (Italy)
PRODUCER: Francesco Merli
DIRECTOR: Massimo Pupillo (Max Hunter)
SCREENWRITERS: Roberto Natale,
Romano Migliorini
ALSO RELEASED AS: *The Crimson Executioner,
The Red Hangman*

A classic of silly sadism and bad acting.
While in Italy filming *Primitive Love*
with his wife Jayne Mansfield, muscleman Mickey Hargitay found time also
to star as the Crimson Executioner. His
castle is visited by a publisher and a
writer of horror novels. They bring
along a secretary, a photographer, and
five sexy models for the book jackets.
When they enter the forbidden torture
chamber for some cheesecake torture
shots, Mickey loses his cool, dons tights
and mask, and "becomes" the castle's
original owner. He spends a lot of time
stretching, burning, and cutting the
uninvited guests. These laughable,
unconvincing horrors are based on the
writings of the Marquis de Sade, who
is quoted as saying "my vengeance needs
blood" in the artful newspaper ads.

THE BLOODY VAMPIRE

1962 AIP-TV (Mexico) (B&W)
PRODUCER: Rafael Perez Grouas
DIRECTOR/SCREENWRITER: Michael Morata
ORIGINALLY RELEASED AS: *El Vampiro
Sangriento*

Count Cagliostro, a Mexican Van
Helsing type, disguises his own daughter as a servant to gain entrance into
the home of the vampire Count Frankenhausen (Carlos Agosti). The vampire survives. He was also in *Invasion
of the Vampires*. A K. Gordon Murray
Production.

BLOW OUT

1981 Filmways
PRODUCER: George Litto
DIRECTOR/SCREENWRITER: Brian DePalma

John Travolta works in Philadelphia as
a sound effects man for cheap horror
films. While taping wind effects for
Coed Frenzy, he inadvertently obtains
evidence of a political murder and a
cover-up conspiracy. What starts as
DePalma's best in years ends up with a
mindless comic car chase and a sick
twist ending that doesn't work. Mixed
intentions, still more Hitchcock references, and spinning camera shots help
sink Travolta's acting career. With
Nancy Allen as a naive prostitute in
her fourth role for her director-husband
and John Lithgow as a vicious ice-pick
murderer. Music by Pino Donaggio.
Trash movie fans will enjoy seeing all
the posters for hits like *Squirm* on the
wall in Travolta's office. (**R**)

THE BLUE BIRD

1940 20th Century-Fox
PRODUCER: Darryl F. Zanuck
DIRECTOR: Walter Lang
SCREENWRITER: Ernest Pascal

Shirley Temple lost the lead in *The Wizard of Oz* but got to star in this similar
fantasy, which pretty much ruined her
career. Over the hill at 12. It also stars
Gale Sondergaard, who had lost the
Wicked Witch role in that other film.
Shirley goes to the land of death to see
her grandparents. Along for the ill-fated
search for the bird of happiness are
Nigel Bruce, Sterling Holloway, Spring
Byington, and Scotty Beckett. Director Lang ended his career with *Snow
White and the Three Stooges*. Shirley
ended hers by marrying John Agar.
Later, she married Charles Black and
turned to politics.

THE BLUE BIRD

1976 20th Century-Fox (U.S.S.R./U.S.)
PRODUCER: Paul Maslansky
DIRECTOR: George Cukor
SCREENWRITERS: Hugh Whitemore, Alfred
Hayes

This second version of Maurice Maeterlinck's fantasy was the first American/Russian co-production and was a bigger commercial flop than the first version. Very few people paid to see Elizabeth Taylor, Jane Fonda, Ava Gardner, Cicely Tyson, Robert Morley, and Will Geer dressed up as witches and animals.

BLUE DENIM

1959 20th Century-Fox (B&W)
PRODUCER: Charles Brackett
DIRECTOR: Philip Dunne
SCREENWRITERS: Edith Sommer, Philip Dunne
ALSO RELEASED AS: *Blue Jeans*

Fifteen-year-old Carol Lynley: "Maybe I could just disappear somewhere or —just kill myself!" Sixteen-year-old Brandon De Wilde: "I'm responsible and I know a way out!" A look at a common teenage problem, featuring Macdonald Carey and Marsha Hunt as parents faced with being grandparents. With Warren Berlinger. The two young stars were actually 17 at the time. Carol had also starred in the Broadway play of the same title. Music by Bernard Herrmann.

BLUE HAWAII

1961 Paramount
PRODUCER: Hal B. Wallis
DIRECTOR: Norman Taurog
SCREENWRITER: Hal Kanter

From 1961 to 1968 Elvis Presley starred in 21 movies. This one started that series of mostly mindless musicals: Elvis stars as Chad Gates, who defies his wealthy pineapple-growing parents (Roland Winters and Angela Lansbury) by refusing to work for them. Instead, he takes a job with a tourist agency where his girlfriend (Joan Blackman) works. While escorting a group of girls around an island he gets in a fight and thrown in jail but emerges singing to marry and start an agency with his wife. Songs include "Ito Eats" and "Aloha

Oe." "Can't Help Falling in Love" was the hit.

BLUE JEANS: See BLUE DENIM.

BLUEBEARD

1944 PRC (B&W)
PRODUCER: Leon Fromkess
DIRECTOR: Edgar G. Ulmer
SCREENWRITER: Pierre Gendron

From the ads: "To love him meant death!" In one of his best roles John Carradine is Gaston Morel, an opera-singing puppet show operator in 19th-century Paris who kills women. He gives a marionette version of Faust singing several of the parts himself (with a dubbed voice). With Jean Parker, Nils Asther, and Ludwig Stossel. A popular B-film from the director of *The Man From Planet X.*

BLUEBEARD

1972 Cinerama (Italy/Hungary)
PRODUCER: Alexander Salkino
DIRECTOR: Edward Dmytryk
SCREENWRITER: Ennio Di Concini

UPI 4/27/72: Raquel Welch is a "nun" in her latest film effort, Bluebeard, filmed recently in Budapest. In the movie, she falls afoul of the amorous and wicked Bluebeard, played by Richard Burton.

Richard Burton marries seven women. He kills six of them in various ways for various reasons. Six of them have nude scenes, which is the excuse for this unlikely comedy. Karin Schubert is shot. Virna Lisi gets guillotined. Agostina Belli is "falconated." Marilu Tolo is drowned (after kicking Richard in the balls). Raquel Welch plays a nun who is suffocated. (Raquel doesn't do nude scenes.) Miraculously, Joey Heatherton survives. The dead wives are all kept lined up in a freezer. With Natalie Delon and Sybil Danning. Shot in four different European countries. Ads proclaimed: "Burton is Bluebeard." Burton is a Hack. Music by Ennio Morricone. **(R)**

BLUEBEARD'S TEN HONEYMOONS
1960 Allied Artists (England) (B&W)
PRODUCER: Roy Parkinson
DIRECTOR: Lee Wilder
SCREENWRITER: Myles Wilder
George Sanders is Landru the French wife-killer. It's by the director of *Killers From Space*, so you know what to expect. With Corinne Calvet, Patricia Roc, and Jean Kent.

BLUE SUNSHINE
1978 Cinema Shares
PRODUCER: George Manasse
DIRECTOR/SCREENWRITER: Jeff Leiberman
Leiberman's script concerns a group of ordinary middle-class citizens who turn into psychotic murderers as a result of bad LSD ingested some ten years earlier, when they were students at Stanford. First they lose their hair, then they lose their cool as they erupt into violence, which ends only with their deaths. Zalman King stars as Zipkin, a lone avenger determined to capture a living Blue Sunshiner and end the epidemic of psychedelic psychosis. From the director of *Squirm*. With Robert

Walden (*Lou Grant*), Mark Goddard (*Lost in Space*), and Alice Ghostley. **(R)** –BM

BLUES FOR LOVERS
1965 20th Century-Fox (England) (B&W)
PRODUCER: Herman Blaser
DIRECTOR: Paul Henreid
SCREENWRITER: Burton Wohl
ALSO RELEASED AS: *Ballad in Blue*
If you can get around the soap-opera plot with Ray Charles (as himself) helping to reunite young composer Tom Bell with Mary Peach and to cure her little boy's blindness, you'll be rewarded by Charles performing some of his classic hits. The songs include "Unchain My Heart," "Hallelujah, I Love Her So," "What'd I Say," "I Gotta Woman," and "Let the Good Times Roll."

THE BODY BENEATH
1971 Nova International
PRODUCER/DIRECTOR/SCREENWRITER: Andy Milligan
More terrible junk from Staten Island's Andy Milligan, who even photographed this movie. The Reverend Ford leads a family of 19th-century vampires. Originally filmed in 16mm "in the graveyards of England."

THE BODY SNATCHER
1945 RKO (B&W)
PRODUCER: Val Lewton
DIRECTOR: Robert Wise
SCREENWRITERS: Philip MacDonald, Val Lewton
A classic historical/horror movie based on Robert Louis Stevenson's short story. In 19th-century Edinburgh, Boris Karloff as Gray the cabdriver supplies bodies to Dr. Macfarlane (Henry Daniel) at the medical school. Second-billed Bela Lugosi has a small role as a dull-witted servant who tries unsuccessfully to blackmail Gray. Karloff and Daniel are excellent. The famous end shock

features Daniel imagining a corpse becoming Karloff and coming to life during a lightning storm. Karloff's voice is heard repeating, "You'll never get rid of me!" With Russell Wade, Edith Atwater, Robert Clarke, and Donna Lee as a little girl who sings Scottish folk songs.

BODY SNATCHER FROM HELL

1969 Pacemaker (Japan)
PRODUCER: Shochiko
DIRECTOR: Hajime Sato
SCREENWRITERS: Susumu Tataku, K. Kobayashi
ORIGINALLY RELEASED AS: *Kyuketsuki Gokemidoro*
ALSO RELEASED AS: *Goke, the Body Snatcher From Hell*

A pretty amazing airplane disaster/horror/science-fiction movie. When a plane crashes, the survivors are killed by a space vampire that takes over their bodies. Lots of surprising grisly makeup and shots of an oozing liquid entering a man through his smashed nose.

THE BODY STEALERS

1969 Tigon/Allied Artists (England)
PRODUCER: Tony Tenser
DIRECTOR: Gerry Levy
SCREENWRITER: Mike St. Clair
ALSO RELEASED AS: *Thin Air, Invasion of the Body Stealers*

Parachutists pass through a red mist and disappear in midair. It's the work of an alien (Maurice Evans) who puts the parachutists in suspended animation and substitutes duplicates. George Sanders (in a cameo role) discovers the dastardly plot. With Hillary Dwyer, Robert Flemyng, and Neil Connery. **(R)**

BOMBA AND THE ELEPHANT STAMPEDE

1951 Monogram (B&W)
PRODUCER: Walter Mirisch
DIRECTOR/SCREENWRITER: Ford Beebe

Bomba saves elephants from crooks (Myron Healey and John Kellog). With Donna Martell.

BOMBA AND THE HIDDEN CITY

1950 Monogram (B&W)
PRODUCER: Walter Mirisch
DIRECTOR: Ford Beebe
SCREENWRITER: Carroll Young

"Ruthless killers stalk human prey in Africa's citadel of mystery!" the ads promised. Bomba saves Sue England, a jungle orphan. With Paul Guilfoyle.

BOMBA AND THE JUNGLE GIRL

1952 Monogram (B&W)
PRODUCER: Walter Mirisch
DIRECTOR/SCREENWRITER: Ford Beebe

"Savage darts and white man's bullets split the Congo . . ." the ads proclaimed. Bomba finds the skeletons of his parents! With Karen Sharpe and Kimba the chimp.

BOMBA ON PANTHER ISLAND

1949 Monogram (B&W)
PRODUCER: Walter Mirisch
DIRECTOR/SCREENWRITER: Ford Beebe

Natives think a panther is really the devil. Bomba helps an agriculturist and fights the devil-cat. With Lita Baron and Allene Roberts.

BOMBA, THE JUNGLE BOY

1949 Monogram (B&W)
PRODUCER: Walter Mirisch
DIRECTOR: Ford Beebe
SCREENWRITER: Jack Dewitt

Two years after being kicked out of the *Tarzan* series, 18-year-old Johnny Sheffield started playing Bomba, based on Roy Rockwood's juvenile books written in the '20s. Footage from *Africa Speaks*, a 1930 documentary, was used in all 12 of the quickie features. Ex-child star Peggy Ann Garner plays the daughter of photographer Onslow Stevens. Bomba helps them. Ford Beebe (*The Invisible Man's Revenge*) directed all of them, wrote most of them, and produced the last four. Jungle Jim, over at Columbia, was a lot funnier.

THE BONNIE PARKER STORY

1958 AIP (B&W)
PRODUCER/SCREENWRITER: Stanley Shpetner
DIRECTOR: William Witney

Sharpie waitress teams up with brainless petty thief. Dorothy Provine, Pinky Pinkham on TV's *The Roaring Twenties*, nine years before Faye Dunaway. The cast includes Jack Hogan, Richard Bakalyan, Douglas Kennedy, Joseph Turkel, and Stanley Livingston (*My Three Sons*). When originally released (with *Machine Gun Kelly*) it was advertised as being "filmed in Superama," whatever that is.   —CB

THE BOOGENS

1982 Jensen Farley
PRODUCER: Charles E. Sellier, Jr.
DIRECTOR: James L. Conway
SCREENWRITERS: David O'Malley, Bob Hunt

The Sunn Classics documentary people branch out, making a horror film that's considerably less wholesome than their usual fare. A tentacled monster in a Utah mine shaft kills locals but is kept hidden from view in the '50s tradition until the last reel. More fun than *The UFO Incident*. With Rebecca Balding (*Silent Scream*). (**R**)

THE BOOGEY MAN

1980 Jerry Gross Organization
PRODUCER/DIRECTOR/SCREENWRITER:
Ulli Lomel

A bizarre, sometimes funny movie about a woman (Suzzana Love) who is haunted by the spirit of her mother's lover, killed years ago by her now-mute

A possessed piece of a broken mirror in The Boogey Man.

brother. A doctor (John Carradine) advises her to go back to her childhood home (the scene of the murder) to see there's nothing to be afraid of. A piece of broken mirror in which she saw the dead man glows and follows people around, inciting them to kill. People levitate, get pitchforks thrust through their stomachs (it takes place in the country), and die in various gory ways. Director Lomel (*Cocaine Cowboys*) used to work with Fassbinder. (**R**)

THE BOOGIE MAN WILL GET YOU

1942 Columbia (B&W)
PRODUCER: Colbert Clark
DIRECTOR: Lew Landers
SCREENWRITER: Edwin Blum

A silly comedy with Boris Karloff as a white-haired scientist who tries to turn people into supermen. Peter Lorre co-stars as an interested investor. "Slapsie" Maxie Rosenbloom is a victim of the malfunctioning transformation device. With Larry Parks. Karloff and Lorre were starring in *Arsenic and Old Lace* on Broadway at the time this was released. This feeble imitation beat the *Arsenic* film to the nation's screens.

BOP GIRL GOES CALYPSO

1957 United Artists (B&W)
PRODUCER/DIRECTOR: Howard Koch
SCREENWRITER: Ed James

Bobby Troup, as a university psychologist, tries to prove that calypso music is replacing rock 'n' roll. He visits clubs and falls in love with a calypso singer. With Nino Tempo, Lord Flea and his Calypsonians, the Cubanos, Judy Tyler, and Lucien Littlefield. A brief rush of calypso movies failed to duplicate the success of the similar rock counterparts. By the director of *Frankenstein 1970*.

THE BORN LOSERS

1967 AIP
PRODUCER/DIRECTOR/SCREENWRITER: Tom Laughlin

Billy Jack battles outlaw motorcyclists terrorizing small-town California girls. Coed Vicky Barrington (Elizabeth James) attracts the animals with wet-look bikini and boots. Jane Russell's daughter Jodell (Janice Miller) is attacked while doing a sultry striptease for a stuffed dog (really). Local cops help Billy by throwing him in jail and shooting him in the back. Bikers include Jeremy Slate as Danny, Bill Wellman, Jr., as Child, Robert Tessier as Cueball, Jeff Cooper as Gangrene, Paul Prokop as Speechless, and Edwin Cook as Crabs. With Jonathan Haze. Laughlin used pseudonyms (Donald Henderson and T.C. Frank) for his production credits.   –CB

BORN RECKLESS

1959 Warners (B&W)
PRODUCER: Aubrey Schenck
DIRECTOR: Howard W. Koch
SCREENWRITER: Richard Landau

Mamie Van Doren stars as a rodeo trick rider in love with a bronco-busting traveling companion who hasn't noticed. Jeff Richards gets mixed up with Carol Ohmart in a huge Imperial convertible; Mamie seeks advice from Jeff's grizzled sidekick, Arthur Hunnicut. Hear Mamie sing the title song for a steak dinner. Koch didn't direct again for 14 years.   –CB

BORN WILD: See YOUNG ANIMALS

BORN TO BE LOVED

1959 Universal (B&W)
PRODUCER/DIRECTOR/SCREENWRITER: Hugo Haas

Elderly music instructor Hugo Haas helps rich widow Vera Vague and poor Carol Morris (Miss Universe of 1957) find romance. Hugo gets a new baby grand piano and a wife. In earlier Haas films he gets murdered, cheated on, and used. They were more fun to watch. The 13th film directed by Hugo Haas (he starred in 10 of them). *Paradise Alley* was his next.

BOURBON ST. SHADOWS: See THE INVISIBLE AVENGER.

BOWERY AT MIDNIGHT

1942 Monogram (B&W)
PRODUCERS: Sam Katzman, Jack Dietz
DIRECTOR: Wallace Fox
SCREENWRITER: Gerald Schnitzer

A psychology professor (Bela Lugosi) runs a Bowery mission as a front for criminal activities. Although it's considered one of the better Monogram films, nobody seems to quite understand the plot. A doctor revives a group of dead bums in the basement and they kill Bela. The cast includes Wanda McKay, John Archer, and Tom Neal.

THE BOWERY BOYS MEET THE MONSTERS
1954 Allied Artists (B&W)
PRODUCER: Ben Schwalb
DIRECTOR: Edward Bernds
SCREENWRITERS: Elwood Ullman,
Edward Bernds

Cheap laughs and scares as Huntz Hall gets turned into a werewolf monster. There's the usual man in a gorilla suit, a clunky robot, even a vampire. With Lloyd Corrigan, Ellen Corby, and the usual crew (Leo Gorcey, his father as Louie, and his brother as Chuck). The Bowery Boys averaged four features a year. Most are just over an hour. On television you'll get about 25 minutes of commercial interruptions in a 90-minute slot.

BOWERY TO BAGHDAD
1955 Allied Artists (B&W)
PRODUCER: Ben Schwalb
DIRECTOR: Edward Bernds
SCREENWRITERS: Elwood Ullman,
Edward Bernds

The Bowery Boys find a magic lamp and a genie appears (Eric Blore in one of his last roles). With Leo, David, and Bernard Gorcey, Huntz Hall, and the rest of the gang. Leo Gorcey quit the series in 1956, at age 40, when his father Bernard Gorcey died. He had been playing basically the same role since 1937's *Dead End*. Huntz Hall continued in seven more movies without his former partner. Even with Gorcey, all but diehard fans of the series agree that sitting through most Bowery Boys features is moider.

BOXCAR BERTHA
1972 AIP
PRODUCER: Roger Corman
DIRECTOR: Martin Scorsese
SCREENWRITERS: Joyce H. and John W.
Corrington

Scorsese's second feature stars Barbara Hershey/Hertzstein/Seagull and her then real-life boyfriend David Carradine as Depression era train robbers. David's dad John is a railroad boss. With Barry Primus and Bernie Casey. Scorsese did *Mean Streets* the next year with more Carradine sons (David and Keith). **(R)**

A BOY AND HIS DOG
1975 LQ/JAF
PRODUCER: Alvy Moore
DIRECTOR/SCREENWRITER: L.Q. Jones

After making interesting little shockers like *The Witchmaker* and *The Brotherhood of Satan*, the Alvy Moore–L.Q. Jones team took on the risky job of filming a straightforward adaptation of Harlan Ellison's warped postnuclear novel, *A Boy and His Dog*. The result has become a campus and midnight-movie favorite. Don Johnson (*The Magic Garden of Stanley Sweetheart*) roams what's left of America with his telepathic, wisecracking dog, Blood. He escapes the brutal surface world, only to find himself in a ghoulish underground recreation of middle-class society run by Alvy Moore and Jason Robards. Escaping android farmers and a future of forced stud work, he takes Susan Benton to the surface where a dejected, starving Blood awaits him. The twist ending is effective. **(R)**

THE BOY AND THE PIRATES
1960 United Artists.
PRODUCER/DIRECTOR: Bert I. Gordon
SCREENWRITERS: Lillie Hayward,
Jerry Sackheim

A juvenile fantasy. A genie sends a young boy back in time, where he meets Blackbeard the Pirate. With Charles Herbert, Susan Gordon, Murvyn Vye, and Mickey Finn. Filmed in "Perceptovision," a nonexistent process. The theme music is available on *The Fantastic Film Music of Albert Glasser* album.

THE BOY WHO CRIED WEREWOLF

1973 Universal
PRODUCER: Aaron Rosenberg
DIRECTOR: Nathan Juran
SCREENWRITER: Bob Homel

Kerwin Matthews becomes a werewolf with surprisingly long facial hair. His 12-year-old son knows but nobody believes him. They go camping together. Contemporary nonsense is added by a group of Jesus freaks trying to exorcise the monster. With Elaine Devey and Scott Sealey.

THE BOY WITH GREEN HAIR

1948 RKO
PRODUCERS: Adrian Scott, Stephen Ames
DIRECTOR: Joseph Losey
SCREENWRITERS: Ben Barzman, Alfred Lewis Levitt

Losey's first feature is an antiwar film that was ordered cut by Howard Hughes when he purchased RKO. The original producer (Adrian Scott) quit when he was branded one of the Hollywood Ten. Twelve-year-old Dean Stockwell stars as a war orphan ostracized because of the color of his hair, which is later shaved off. Robert Ryan is a police psychiatrist. With Pat O'Brien, Barbara Hale, Dwayne Hickman, Rusty (later Russ) Tamblyn, and Ann Carter. In one scene orphan children in a poster come to life.

THE BOYS FROM BRAZIL

1978 20th Century-Fox
PRODUCERS: Martin Richards, Stanley O'Toole
DIRECTOR: Franklin J. Schaffer
SCREENWRITER: Heywood Gould

Not too long ago, Nazi-revival horror movies were shoddy, low-budget affairs, universally condemned for their questionable taste. Well, times have changed. This one was a major release with high production values and big-name stars. I'd rather watch *The Frozen Dead* or *I Saved Hitler's Brain* than this "respectable" exploitation feature with glossy gore. Gregory Peck as Dr. Mengele, the Angel of Death at the Auschwitz concentration camp, is living in South America, heading a project developing Hitler clones. He surgically experiments with local peasant children and plots with fellow Nazi James Mason. An aging Nazi hunter (Laurence Olivier) manages to topple the entire, complex worldwide conspiracy with the aid of some giant dogs in Pennsylvania. With Lilli Palmer, Uta Hagen, Michael Gough, and Linda Hayden. From a silly book by Ira Levin. Almost half an hour was cut out for television. **(R)**

THE BOYS FROM BROOKLYN: See *BELA LUGOSI MEETS A BROOKLYN GORILLA.*

BOYS OF THE CITY: See *GHOST CREEPS.*

THE BRAIN

1962 Governor (W. Germany/England) (B&W)
PRODUCER: Raymond Stross
DIRECTOR: Freddie Francis
SCREENWRITERS: Robert Stewart, Phil Mackie
ALSO RELEASED AS: *Vengeance, Ein Toter Sucht Seinen Mörder*

The third version of Curt Siodmak's *Donovan's Brain.* Peter Van Eyck stars as the doctor who keeps the brain of a ruthless tycoon alive after a plane crash. The living brain takes over the doctor's mind and uses him to discover who caused the "accident." Anne Heywood is the dead man's daughter. With Bernard Lee.

THE BRAIN EATERS
1958 AIP (B&W)
PRODUCER: Edwin Nelson
DIRECTOR: Bruno Ve Sota
SCREENWRITER: Gordon Urquhart

The special effects are laughable, but this is a good, imaginative low-budget science-fiction movie. Based on *The Puppet Masters* by Robert Heinlein, it concerns a strange drill-shaped craft from the center of the earth turning up in a small town. Hairy parasites take over the bodies of locals while scientist Ed Nelson (also the producer) battles thick-headed military personnel to stop the invasion. When he finally figures out how to enter the ship, he's confronted by a bearded old man you might not recognize. The voice, however, is unmistakable. It belongs to Leonard Nimoy! Only an hour long. With Jody Fair and Joanna Lee (*Plan 9 From Outer Space* alien).

THE BRAIN FROM PLANET AROUS
1958 Howco (B&W)
PRODUCER: Jacques Marquette
DIRECTOR: Nathan Hertz (Nathan Juran)
SCREENWRITER: Ray Buffum

The ultimate John Agar film! A hugely enjoyable invasion-attempt story with a large hamburger-like floating brain (called Gor) taking over nuclear physicist Agar. Using his shiny new black eyes, Agar destroys an airplane by staring at it, grinning and laughing at a job well done. A rival alien brain (called Vol) arrives and takes over Agar's dog. Gor-Agar and Vol-Rover battle until the exciting climax when girlfriend Joyce Meadows attacks the bad brain with an ax. With Robert Fuller and Thomas B. Henry. For more topical Nathan Hertz/Juran fare see *Hellcats of the Navy*.

BRAIN OF BLOOD
1971 Hemisphere
PRODUCERS: Al Adamson, Sam Sherman
DIRECTOR: Al Adamson
SCREENWRITERS: Joe Van Rodgers, Kane W. Lynn
ALSO RELEASED AS: *The Creature's Revenge*

Eddie Romero made a series of awful "Blood Island" films in the Philippines. The producers decided they weren't quite bad enough, so they hired Al Adamson to direct a similar mad-scientist film. Sure enough, it's worse than the others. Al manages to do everything wrong again. Kent Taylor (also in *Brides of Blood*) stars as the nut whose brain-transplant experiments produce Gor (John Bloom), a big ugly monster who gets to carry Regina Carrol around. Dwarf assistant Angelo Rossitto laughs a lot and pokes at chained women. Grant Williams is the hero. With Reed Hadley, Vicki Volante, and Zandor Vorkov. Partially filmed in the Philippines.

THE BRAIN SNATCHER: See *THE MAN WHO LIVED AGAIN.*

THE BRAIN THAT WOULDN'T DIE
1959 AIP (B&W)
PRODUCER: Rex Carlton
DIRECTOR/SCREENWRITER: Joseph Green

A great, absurd movie with Jason Evers (also known as Herb) as a brilliant surgeon whose fast driving causes an accident that decapitates his fiancée Jan (Virginia Leith). He wraps her head in his jacket and takes it to his upstate New York "mansion" (we see one barren room and an entranceway), attaches some coils and puts it/her in a film developing tray. The living head wants to die but talks too much, so he puts tape over her mouth and goes body-

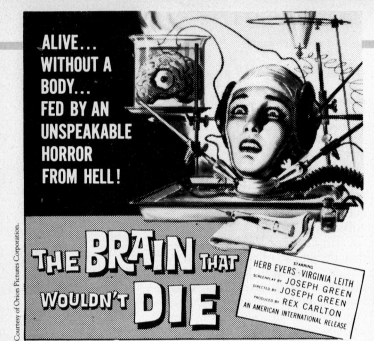

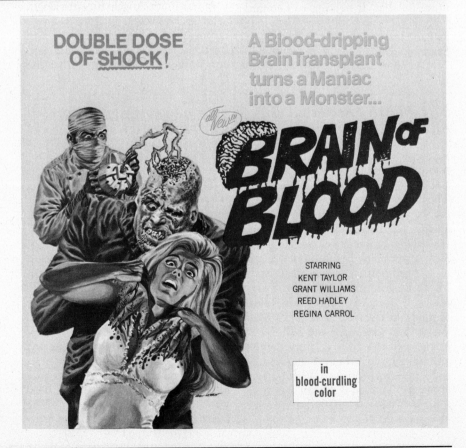

shopping. Driving around in his convertible eying asses isn't good enough, so the Doc visits a really stacked model who poses for photographers in a leopard-print bikini. Because her face is scarred and he promises to fix it, she agrees to go to the lab. When Jan finds out what's going on she uses her telepathic power to tell the giant pinhead mutant in the closet to break out. The creature tears the arm off the crippled assistant, kills the doctor by taking a big bloody bite out of his shoulder (and spitting it out), and sets the lab on fire. The blood-covered monster rescues the model as Jan laughs. Filmed in Tarrytown, New York, it took three years to reach an appalled public.

The horrible long-tongued terror of The Brainiac.

THE BRAINIAC
1961 AIP-TV (Mexico) (B&W)
PRODUCER: Abel Salazar
DIRECTOR: Chano Urveta
SCREENWRITER: Adolpho Portillo
ORIGINALLY RELEASED AS: *El Baron del Terror*
A 300-year-old Baron who was burned at the stake returns to life. The incredible creature sucks out victims' brains with a long tongue and has a big inflatable head. A surprisingly surreal horror movie with producer Abel Salazar and German Robles. If you can't find it on television, rent the videocassette.

THE BRASS BOTTLE
1964 Universal
PRODUCER: Albert Arthur
DIRECTOR: Harry Keller
SCREENWRITER: Oscar Brodney
Architect Tony Randall buys an antique bottle containing genie Burl Ives. Ives ruins Randall's life by being overhelpful and producing a female genie (Kamala Devi). Barbara Eden (soon to become a TV genie) is Tony's angry fiancée. A silly comedy, which had previously been filmed in 1914 and 1923.

BRAVE NEW WORLD
1980 TV
PRODUCER: Jacqueline Babbin
DIRECTOR: Burt Brinkerhoff
SCREENWRITER: Doran William Cannon
An adaptation of Aldous Huxley's satiric novel, this was originally a two-part special later cut to a three-hour version shown in one night. Kristopher Tabori (John Savage) is brought into the supercivilized world of artificial births (babies born in Glad plastic bags), outlawed love (everyone must "engage" in sex), and a "soma"-popping populace. Fine performances and clever scripting. With Julie Cobb, Keir Dullea, Bud Cort, Ron O'Neal, and Marcia Strassman. —AF

BREAKFAST AT MANCHESTER MORGUE: See DON'T OPEN THE WINDOW.

THE BRIBE
1949 MGM (B&W)
PRODUCER: Pandro S. Berman
DIRECTOR: Robert Z. Leonard
SCREENWRITER: Marguerite Roberts.

A federal agent (Robert Taylor) tells his story in flashback. Sent to a small South American island to break up a postwar weapons ring, he faces impossible odds against Charles Laughton and syndicate boss Vincent Price. Ava Gardner is the bait. Taylor is drugged, seduced, and thrown to the sharks. With John Hodiak, John Hoyt, and a song from Miss Gardner. Several scenes from *The Bribe* later turned up in Steve Martin's *Good Guys Don't Wear Plaid*.

THE BRIDE

1973 Unisphere (Canada)
PRODUCER: John Grissmer
DIRECTOR: Jean-Marie Pelissie
SCREENWRITERS: John Grissmer,
Jean-Marie Pelissie
ALSO RELEASED AS: *The House That Cried Murder*

A strange and vengeful wife (Robin Strasser, a soap opera actress) makes life hell for her husband (Arthur Roberts) and his lover. John Beal (*The Vampire*) is her father.

THE BRIDE AND THE BEAST

1958 Allied Artist (B&W)
PRODUCER/DIRECTOR: Adrian Weiss
SCREENWRITER: Ed Wood, Jr.
ALSO RELEASED AS: *Queen of the Gorillas*

Lance Fuller and wife Charlotte Austin are camping out in a tent in Africa. Charlotte seems to have a strange effect on the jungle animals and is especially attracted to gorillas. Scenes with the woman in her sheer nightgown or an ultra-tight sweater being embraced by a man in a gorilla suit provided the titillating publicity shots for this laughable film written by none other than Ed Wood, Jr.! The straying wife turns out to be the reincarnation of an ape. She reverts to a gorilla and ambles off into the jungle to mate with her furry friends. Poor Lance! With Johnny Roth and Jeanne Gerson. The music is by Les Baxter. Most of this short film is safari stock footage.

THE BRIDE OF FRANKENSTEIN

1935 Universal (B&W)
PRODUCER: Carl Laemmle, Jr.
DIRECTOR: James Whale
SCREENWRITERS: John Balderston,
William Hurlbut

The Frankenstein monster (Boris Karloff) returns, learns to talk, drink, and smoke, and forces his creator (Colin Clive) to piece together a mate in this fascinating, humorous horror classic. Frankenstein cries, is rejected by his mate, and gets carried Christlike on a cross. The film's most incredible performance is from Ernest Thesiger as the brittly eccentric Dr. Pretorious, creator of miniature beings; Elsa Lanchester is also pretty amazing as the hissing bride with electric hair (and as Mary Shelley in the prologue). Valerie Hobson is Mrs. Frankenstein. Dwight Frye is Karl, Pretorious' murderous servant. O.P. Heggie is the blind hermit. With Una O'Connor, John Carradine, and, in there somewhere, Walter Brennan. Franz Waxman wrote the effective musical score.

BRIDE OF THE ATOM: See BRIDE OF THE MONSTER.

BRIDE OF THE GORILLA

1951 Realart (B&W)
PRODUCER: Jack Broder
DIRECTOR/SCREENWRITER: Curt Siodmak

Plantation owner Raymond Burr is cursed by a witch doctor. He thinks he's a gorilla. His wife (Barbara Payton) is awfully upset, and Lon Chaney, Jr., as a local police officer, is confused by the killings. With Tom Conway, Paul Cavanaugh, and Woody Strode in his film debut. Watching Burr go through his apish changes is a rare treat. The venerable Herman Cohen was assistant producer on this epic.

BRIDE OF THE MONSTER
1956 Banner (B&W)
PRODUCER/DIRECTOR: Ed Wood, Jr.
SCREENWRITERS: Ed Wood, Jr., Alex Gordon
ALSO RELEASED AS: *Bride of the Atom*

Seventy-three year-old Bela Lugosi plays Dr. Vornoff in his last speaking role. Three of his last four releases were piloted by the notorious transvestite director Ed Wood, Jr. In his minimal lab deep in the swamps, Bela uses atomic energy to create superbeings. Most of his experiments die, but mindless giant Tor Johnson (once a normal man) survives and is called Lobo. As the barefoot bald giant, Tor wears a makeshift torn jacket and a big facial scar. Tony McCoy gets to play the hero because his dad financed the film. To give you an idea of the budget, poor Bela went home with $1,000! Loretta King is a nosy reporter whom Bela wants to mate with Lobo. Victims are transformed by being strapped to a table with a metal light-bulb shade on their heads and shot with atoms. When Bela is given the shock treatment himself he becomes superstrong and fights Lobo, only to fall into a pit containing a deadly octopus. The battling Bela is obviously a stunt man (Eddie Parker); the lifeless rubber octopus is a left-over prop from an old John Wayne film. When shot, the octopus releases an explosive mushroom cloud. The posters showed a young-looking Lugosi (with vampire teeth) carrying a beautiful woman and claimed it was "more horrifying than *Dracula* and *Frankenstein*." It was. The original co-feature was an obscurity called *Macumba*, similar to but not the same as *Macumba Love*.

BRIDES OF BLOOD
1968 Hemisphere (U.S./Philippines)
PRODUCER: Eddie Romero
DIRECTORS: Eddie Romero, Gerrardo de Leon
ALSO RELEASED AS: *Grave Desires, Island of Living Horror*

The first of a series of "Blood Island" films starring American teen actor John Ashley. Radiation causes animals and men to become monsters. The main

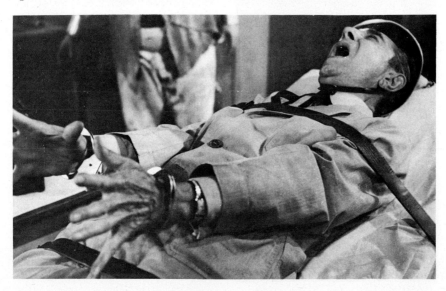

Bela Lugosi being turned into an atomic superman in Bride of the Monster.

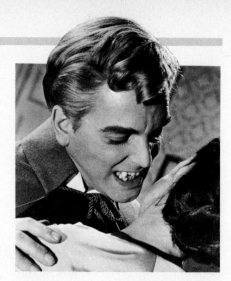

monster is an unbelievable cartoonish mess of dripping blobs that looks like the Michelin tire man's cousin. It eats naked girls. With Kent Taylor and Beverly Hills (any relation to Holly Woodlawn?). At original screenings, female patrons were given free plastic wedding rings. It was re-released in 1979 with an unbelievably misleading title and ad campaign. Three sexy women lean on a tombstone under the words: "They rise at night for more than a bite" and a warning about the "the unusual subject matter and explicit presentation." Terrible.

BRIDES OF DRACULA

1960 Hammer/Universal (England)
PRODUCER: Anthony Hinds
DIRECTOR: Terence Fisher
SCREENWRITERS: Jimmy Sangster, Peter Bryan, Edward Percy

Radiation mutant and one of the Brides of Blood.

Christopher Lee didn't want to repeat his *Horror of Dracula* role, but Peter Cushing returned as the sensible Dr. Van Helsing in this underrated sequel. Beginning with the actual exciting ending of the previous film, the story involves Baron Meinster, a handsome young blond man kept chained up by his old mother at their château. A young French schoolteacher (Yvonne Monlaur) spending the night releases the perverse man, who shows his pointy teeth, turns into a bat, and collects vampire brides. With Freda Jackson and Martita Hunt. It's hard to believe that David Peel, the star vampire, was 40 at the time.

THE BRIDES OF FU MANCHU

1966 Anglo Amalgamated/7 Arts Pictures (England)
PRODUCERS: Oliver Unger, Harry Alan Towers
DIRECTOR: Don Sharp
SCREENWRITERS: Harry Alan Towers, Don Sharp

Christopher Lee in his second outing as Fu Manchu. This time, stationed in North Africa, he has kidnaped twelve beautiful women, each the daughter of an international political figure. Publicity centered on the dozen "contest" winners, each from a different country, who are thrown into snake pits and appear in topless fight scenes (cut from the American version). Sir Nayland Smith (Douglas Wilmer), Dr. Petrie (Howard Marion-Crawford), and Heinz Drache as the fiancé of kidnaped Marie Versini arrive at the secret temple and use a death ray to blow it up. The dead (?) villain claims, "You will hear from me again!" You did. With Tsai Chin and Burt Kwouk.

BRIGHAM YOUNG — FRONTIERSMAN

1940 20th Century-Fox (B&W)
PRODUCER: Darryl Zanuck
DIRECTOR: Henry Hathaway
SCREENWRITER: Lamar Trotti

Vincent Price as the founder of the Mormon church! On the way to Salt Lake City in 1846 he's tried for treason and killed. Dean Jagger (as Brigham Young) takes over. The real stars are Tyrone Power and Linda Darnell. John Carradine is a scout. With Brian Donlevy, Mary Astor, Charles Middleton, and Chief Big Tree.

THE BRIGHTON STRANGLER

1945 RKO (B&W)
PRODUCER: Herman Schlom
DIRECTOR: Max Nosseck
SCREENWRITERS: Arnold Phillips, Max Nosseck

John Loder is an amnesiac English actor who assumes the identity of a murderous character he plays on stage. With June Duprez, Miles Mander, and Ian Wolf.

BRITISH INTELLIGENCE

1940 Warner Brothers (B&W)
ASSOCIATE PRODUCER: Bryan Foy
DIRECTOR: Terry Morse
SCREENWRITER: Lee Katz

Boris Karloff is a master spy working for the Germans during World War I. The scared Karloff poses as a butler for a British war officer. Double agent Margaret Lindsay manages to gain his trust and stop him from setting off a time bomb at a cabinet meeting. With Holmes Herbert and Maris Wrixon. A remake of *Three Faces West*, filmed in 1926, then in 1930 with Erich von Stroheim.

BROADMINDED

1931 First National (B&W)
DIRECTOR: Mervyn Leroy
SCREENWRITERS: Bert Kalmar, Harry Ruby

Joe E. Brown plays chaperon to his playboy cousin in a comedy featuring Bela Lugosi as a South American who actually gets a girlfriend (Thelma Todd) without having to kidnap or vampirize her. Bela was menacing only in publicity photos.

THE BROOD

1979 New World (Canada)
PRODUCER: Claude Heroux
DIRECTOR/SCREENWRITER: David Cronenberg

Oliver Reed is Dr. Hal Raglan, a mad psychotherapist whose catch phrase is "the shape of rage." It refers to his technique of encouraging patients to develop boils, welts, and other physical manifestations of their emotional turmoil. His greatest success is with Samantha Eggar, whose anger has given birth to a small army of nonhuman children who run off to kill another of her relatives every time Sam gets a little ticked off. Husband Art Hindle is understandably upset. (R)   —BM

BROTHERHOOD OF SATAN

1971 Columbia
PRODUCERS: L.Q. Jones, Alvy Moore
DIRECTOR: Bernard McEveety
SCREENWRITER: William Welch

Famous screen scum Strother Martin has his first starring role as the leader of a modern California devil cult. The elderly members arrange to transfer their souls to the bodies of kids, displayed on pedestals in a crypt. Some clever special effects show children's toys enlarged to life size by black magic. The producers, L.Q. Jones (who appeared with Martin in some Peckinpah films) and Alvy Moore (the *Green Acres* TV show) also act. Also with Charles Bateman and Ahna Capri.

THE BRUTE MAN
1946 PRC (B&W)
PRODUCER: Ben Pivar
DIRECTOR: Jean Yarbrough
SCREENWRITERS: George Brickern,
   M. Coates Webster

Rondo Hatton, in his last role, is a formerly handsome scientist who becomes an ugly killer when acid is thrown in his face. In real life, he was a formerly handsome actor with acromegaly, which distorted his features. The disease killed him after he made this feature for Universal. They washed their hands of the distasteful exploitation by selling

it to PRC. "His brain cried Kill! Kill! Kill!" ran the ads. With Tom Neal (*Detour*) and Jane Adams as a blind girl who isn't afraid of Rondo.

THE BUBBLE
1966 Midwestern Magic
PRODUCER/DIRECTOR/SCREENWRITER:
   Arch Oboler
ALSO RELEASED AS: *The Fantastic Invasion of Planet Earth*

In 1952 Arch Oboler made the first major 3-D feature (*Bwana Devil*). Fourteen years later he gave it another try, this time in "Spacevision." Special glasses were required. A little money and a better cast would have helped a lot. Only one projector was used. Ex-AIP starlet Deborah Walley, future *Mod Squad* star Michael Cole, and Johnny Desmond go to a strange community filled with old movie props and citizens repeating the same lines over and over. A huge transparent dome covers the whole town. The best 3-D effect is a floating beer mug. The worst includes a floating old rubber scare mask. It's like an expanded *Twilight Zone* episode that they couldn't find an end for. Recommended only to patient fans of bad 3-D movies.

BUCK ROGERS
1939 Universal (B&W)
ASSOCIATE PRODUCER: Barney Sarecky
DIRECTORS: Ford Beebe, Saul Goodkind
SCREENWRITERS: Norman S. Hall,
   Ray Trampe
ALSO RELEASED AS: *Destination Saturn*

If you haven't already seen the complete 12-chapter serial go for the condensed action-packed 90-minute version (released in 1965); it's much simpler than the Flash Gordon serials but almost as fun. Buster Crabbe stars as the hero who wakes up in the year 2500 and faces the space-age gangsters of Killer Kane. Constance Moore (as

Buck Rogers (*Buster Crabbe*) watches as Wilma Deering (*Constance Moore*) receives the latest in handguns.

Wilma Deering), C. Montague Shaw (as Dr. Huer), and Jackie Moore (as Buddy) fight along with Buck. Kane's men wear strap-on hoods decorated with lightning bolts and put mind-control helmets that look like paint cans on their enemies. On Saturn, Prince Tallen (Philson Ahn) and his men wear capes and bullet-shaped helmets. Buck wears his popular studded belt. The mutant Zuggs dress the best—loose pants with legs that don't match. Wilma looks like she's ready to go riding.

BUCK ROGERS IN THE 25TH CENTURY

1979 Universal
PRODUCER: Richard Caffey
DIRECTOR: Daniel Haller
SCREENWRITERS: Glen A. Larson, Leslie Stevens

Here's a TV pilot that people actually paid money to see. The same producers pulled the same stunt with their *Battlestar Galactica* movie. Both are *Star Wars*-influenced camp space operas. Gil Gerard as Buck battles Killer Kane (Henry Silva) and Draco (Joseph Wiseman). He trades sexual wisecracks with the evil but beautiful princess Ardala (Pamela Hensley), yet stays faithful to Wilma Deering (Erin Gray). Mel Blanc provided the voice for the cute robot. A soundtrack album is available. A TV series resulted. There was also a 1950 *Buck Rogers* TV show.

A BUCKET OF BLOOD

1959 AIP (B&W)
PRODUCER/DIRECTOR: Roger Corman
SCREENWRITER: Charles B. Griffith

A wonderful beatnik horror comedy shot in five days. Dick Miller, a familiar Corman stock-company player, is perfect as Walter Paisley, a coffeehouse busboy who wants to be as hip as the poetry-spouting beats he waits on. He

You'll be sick, sick, sick —from LAUGHING!

"Are you together?"

"All I said was, Bucket of Blood was coming on, lady. Please remove your hat."

"What a night! Fourteen people shrieked...nine people fainted and one of our ushers is missing!"

"Okay, let's get a bite to eat...but nothing with tomato sauce."

JAMES H. NICHOLSON and SAMUEL Z. ARKOFF present an AMERICAN-INTERNATIONAL PICTURE
A BUCKET OF BLOOD
STARRING DICK MILLER · BARBOURA MORRIS · ANTONY CARBONE · B GRIFFITH PRODUCED AND DIRECTED BY ROGER CORMAN WRITTEN BY CHARLES

accidentally kills his cat with a knife and covers it with plaster; the resultant "sculpture" is declared an artistic masterpiece. A lovely beatnik girl (Barboura Morris) falls in love with him, a woman gives him heroin, and everyone wants to see his next work of art. Contorted dead humans bring more recognition, respect, and money until the unfortunate status seeker is nabbed for his (mostly unintentional) crimes. An all-time classic. With Anthony Carbone, Ed Nelson, and Bert Convy. Corman followed it with the similar, better known *Little Shop of Horrors*. Both used the same comical jazz score by Fred Katz. Paul Horn on sax.

BUG

1975 Paramount
PRODUCER/SCREENWRITER: William Castle
DIRECTOR: Jeannot Swarc

An earthquake in a small Western town unleashes three-inch insects that cause fires. A scientist (Bradford Dillman) experiments on the bugs and mates them with cockroaches, resulting in giant meat-eating cockroaches. They also learn to fly and spell out words by forming the letters with their bodies. Patty McCormack (star of *The Bad Seed*) dies while a roach eats her eye. With Joanna Miles and Richard Gilland. It was the last production of "horror king" William Castle, who also wrote the screenplay based on the novel *The Hephaestus Plague*. Director Swarc went on to *Jaws II*.

BUNNY LAKE IS MISSING

1965 Columbia (England) (B&W)
PRODUCER/DIRECTOR: Otto Preminger
SCREENWRITERS: John and Penelope Mortimer

A psychological thriller with a "surprise" ending based on a novel of the same title by Evelyn Piper, whose *The Nanny* was filmed the same year. Carol Lynley goes to England and enrolls her little girl Bunny in a nursery school. When she goes to pick her up, the child is not there—and nobody has ever seen or heard of her. Laurence Olivier is the police inspector. As Lynley's brother, Keir Dullea has the Anthony Perkins role. With Noel Coward, Adrienne Corri, Anna Massey, Clive Revill, Finlay Currie (as the dollmaker), and on a television in a bar—the Zombies as themselves.

THE BURGLAR

1956 Columbia (B&W)
PRODUCER: Louis W. Kellman
DIRECTOR: Paul Wendkos
SCREENWRITER: David Goodis

Jayne Mansfield film noir! She helps her half-brother Dan Duryea steal a diamond necklace from a wealthy spiritualist. A crooked cop (Stewart Bradley) resorts to kidnaping and murder to obtain the jewels. It was a serious role for the actress, who next starred in *Will Success Spoil Rock Hunter?* on Broadway. *The Burglar* was filmed in Philadelphia and Atlantic City. It was the first film directed by Wendkos. With Martha Vickers and Mickey Shaughnessy. In 1972 it was remade in France as *The Burglars*.

BURN OUT: See JOURNEY INTO FEAR.

BURN WITCH BURN

1962 Anglo Amalgamated/AIP (England)
PRODUCER: Albert Fennell
DIRECTOR: Sidney Hayers
SCREENWRITERS: Charlie Beaumont, Richard Matheson, George Baxt
ORIGINALLY RELEASED AS: *Night of the Eagle*

A well-made scary tale of witchcraft based on Fritz Leiber's "Conjure Wife." A university professor (Peter Wyngarde) discovers that his wife (Janet Blair) is using voodoo and witchcraft to further his career. Being a rational man, he destroys all her spiders, skulls, and dolls —and his life falls apart. A student accuses him of rape, he almost dies in a car crash, and he finds his wife nearly dead in a graveyard. A stone eagle comes to life in an effective climax. For protection, American theater audiences were given a special pack of salt and words to an ancient incantation. *Weird Woman*, a 1944 Lon Chaney film, was based on the same story. The director of this version had previously done *Circus of Horrors*.

THE BURNING

1981 Filmways
PRODUCER: Harvey Weinstein
DIRECTOR: Tony Maylam
SCREENWRITERS: Peter Lawrence,
Bob Weinstein

A *Friday the 13th* copy about a disfigured man who had been burned by kids while he was a gardener at a summer camp. He returns to the camp to maul and decapitate with giant hedge shears. Lots of modern teens get killed to the music of Rick Wakeman. Filmed around Buffalo, New York. Tom Savini did the gore effects, which were mostly cut to avoid an X rating. The soundtrack is available. (R)

BURNT OFFERINGS

1976 United Artists
PRODUCER/DIRECTOR: Dan Curtis
SCREENWRITERS: William F. Nolan,
Dan Curtis

A family rents an old house for the summer. The house is possessed; deaths occur from a gas-filled room, a swimming pool, a falling chimney, "live" trees. Oliver Reed and Karen Black play the parents of 12-year old Lee Montgomery (the human star of *Ben*). Bette Davis is the aunt. Burgess Meredith and Eileen Heckart are the house owners. The ghost of a chauffeur driving a hearse haunts them. Dan Curtis is better off making TV films.

BURY ME AN ANGEL

1972 New World
PRODUCER: Paul Norbert
DIRECTOR/SCREENWRITER: Barbara Peters

"A howling hellcat humping a hot hog on a roaring rampage of revenge!" the ads promised. Dixie Peabody (*Angels Die Hard*), a six-foot blonde, gets on her bike with a sawed-off shotgun and, aided by two men, goes after the killer of her brother. With Dan Haggerty (*Grizzly Adams*) and Beach Dickerson. The first biker film directed by a woman. Peters later did *Humanoids From the Deep*. (R)

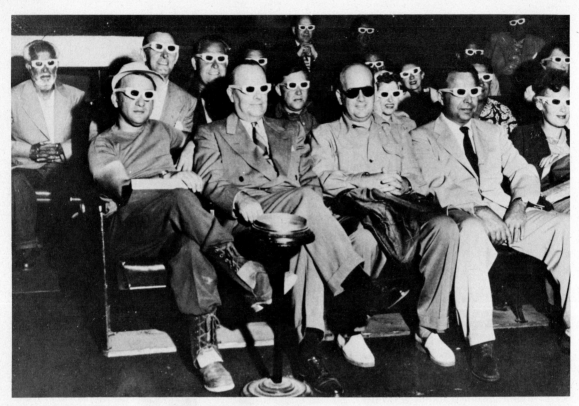

UPI 2/5/53: *A screening-room audience views* Bwana Devil *in Hollywood. Each spectator wears polarized spectacles, which are needed to produce the third-dimensional effect, for without them the viewer would see two images on the screen.*

THE BUSTER KEATON STORY

1957 Paramount (B&W)
PRODUCERS/SCREENWRITERS: Robert Smith,
   Sidney Sheldon
DIRECTOR: Sidney Sheldon
A mostly Hollywood-ized biography, concentrating on the great comedian's rise and fall. Donald O'Connor plays him. Keaton was hired as "technical advisor." Peter Lorre and C.B. DeMille play directors. With Ann Blyth as a fictional wife, Rhonda Fleming, and Jackie Coogan. Watching this probably made Keaton drink more heavily than he already had been.

THE BUSY BODY

1967 Paramount
PRODUCER/DIRECTOR: William Castle
SCREENWRITER: Ben Starr

A gangster comedy in which Sid Caesar is sent by gang leader Robert Ryan to find a corpse buried in a suit lined with money. With Anne Baxter, Kay Medford, Jan Murray, Richard Pryor, Dom Deluise, Godfrey Cambridge, Marty Ingels, Bill Dana, and George Jessel. Castle's next was a Sid Caesar ghost comedy, *The Spirit is Willing.*

BUTCHER, BAKER (NIGHTMARE MAKER)

1982 International Film Marketing
PRODUCERS: Stephen Breimer,
   Eugene Mazzola
DIRECTOR: William Asher
SCREENWRITERS: Stephen Breimer,
   Alan Jay Glueckman, Boon Collins
ALSO RELEASED AS: *Night Warning,
   Nightmare Maker*

AIP beach-movie director Asher is back with Kristy McNichol's brother (and ex-singing partner) Jimmy as a boy raised by his aunt (Susan Tyrrell). She turns the boy into a "surrogate husband" and becomes a psychopathic killer to keep him around the house. With Bo Svenson as a cop and "graphic violence." Asher also used to direct *I Love Lucy* episodes. (R)

BWANA DEVIL
1952 United Artists (3-D)
PRODUCER/DIRECTOR/SCREENWRITER:
Arch Oboler

A lousy film but it was the first 3-D feature released during the early 50's boom and it made piles of money. Railroad workers in Africa fight off lions and natives. Try to imagine this being the most publicized and talked-about movie playing in your town. "Newer than Television!" "A lion in your lap! A lover in your arms!" the ads screamed. With Robert Stack, Barbara Britton, and Nigel Bruce. In 1966 Oboler made *The Bubble*, another bad 3-D movie.

THE CABINET OF CALIGARI
1962 (B & W)
20th Century-Fox
PRODUCER/DIRECTOR: Roger Kay
SCREENWRITER: Robert Bloch

If this psychological horror film had a different title and weren't compared to the 1919 German film of the same title, it would have a much better reputation. It was Robert Bloch's second screenplay after *Psycho*. Glynis Johns experiences a series of terrifying hallucinations involving her psychiatrist, torture, and an unhelpful lover. As in the earlier film, we realize in the end that everything was in the mind of the patient, who is undergoing treatment in an asylum. With lots of distorted sets. Dan O'Herlihy is Dr. Caligari. With Estelle Winwood and Richard Davalos. A Lippert Production.

CAGED
1950 Warners (B&W)
PRODUCER: Jerry Wald
DIRECTOR: John Cromwell
SCREENWRITERS: Virginia Kellogg, Bernard C. Shoenfeld

Eleanor Parker didn't know her husband was robbing the gas station while she waited in the car. She lands in prison, where she is corrupted by Jan Sterling, Gertrude Michael, Jane Darwell, Ellen Corby, and the other tramps. Most threatening is a six-foot two-inch guard played by Hope Emerson, who throws Eleanor into solitary and shaves her head. Agnes Moorehead is the despairing warden who advises an aide to keep Parker's file active as she watches her walk out of the gates: "She'll be back." See *Women's Prison*, *Reform School Girl*, and *Caged Heat*. –CB

CAGED HEAT!
1974 New World
PRODUCER: Evelyn Purcell
DIRECTOR/SCREENWRITER: Jonathan Demme

Audiences expecting another forgettable women's-prison drive-in feature were a bit surprised to find politics and feminism mixed with the usual skin, shocks, and lowbrow humor in this cult film. Female inmates escape the sexual abuse and "corrective physical therapy" of Connorville Maximum Security Prison, rob a gang of bank robbers, take over the jail, and rescue their friends. Barbara Steele is McQueen, the repressed, crippled, sadistic warden who has a sexy cabaret-number dream. Inmates include Juanita Brown (*Foxy Brown*), Roberta Collins, Russ Meyer star Erica Gavin, and Rainbeaux Smith. Porn star Desirée Cousteau is in there somewhere, too. The music, a mixture of moody viola and country harmonica, is by John Cale. Evelyn Purcell, the producer, was the wife of Jonathan Demme, here making his first film. (R)

CAGED VIRGINS: See VIRGINS AND VAMPIRES.

CAGED WOMEN: See BARBED WIRE DOLLS.

TO THE UNSHOCKABLES:
IT SHOCKS, SHOCKS, SHOCKS, SHOCKS, S
SHOCKS, SHOCKS, SHOCKS, SHOCKS, S
SHOCKS, SHOCKS, SHOCKS, SHOCKS,
SHOCKS, SHOCKS, SHOCKS, SHOCKS,
SHOCKS, SHOCKS, SHOCKS, SHOCKS,
SHOCKS, SHOCKS, SHOCKS, SHOCKS,
SHOCKS, SHOCKS, SHOCKS, SHOCKS,
SHOCKS, SHOCKS, SHOCKS, SHOCK
SHOCKS, SHOCKS, SHOCKS, SHOCK

The Cabinet of CALIGARI
GLYNIS JOHNS · DAN O'HERLIHY
CINEMASCOPE

NO ONE PERMITTED OUT OR IN DURING THE LAST **13** NERVE-SHATTERING MINUTES!

CAIN'S CUTTHROATS: See CAIN'S WAY.

CAIN'S WAY

1970 Fanfare
PRODUCERS: Kent Osborne, Budd Dell
DIRECTOR: Kent Osborne
SCREENWRITER: Wilton Denmark
ALSO RELEASED AS: *Cain's Cutthroats, The Blood Seekers*

Inept violent sickness during the Civil War. Scott Brady tracks down the Confederate gang who had raped and killed his black wife. With a bounty hunter/preacher (John Carradine) at his side, he decapitates members of Robert Dix's gang and keeps their heads. The story is intercut with scenes showing a modern-day biker gang terrorizing a town. Important statements about history, racial problems, and violence from the people who gave us *Blood of Dracula's Castle.* **(R)**

CALIFORNIA HOLIDAY: See SPINOUT

CALL HIM MR. SHATTER

1974 Hammer/Avco Embassy (Hong Kong/England)
PRODUCERS: Michael Carreras, Vee King Shaw
DIRECTOR: Michael Carreras
SCREENWRITER: Don Houghton
ALSO RELEASED AS: *Shatter*

A spy/kung fu film made in Hong Kong. Hammer made *Legend of the 7 Golden Vampires*, a good kung fu/horror film, at the same time, also starring Peter Cushing. With Stewart Whitman, Anton Diffring, and a Bruce Lee clone. The original director, Seth Holt, died during production. Whitman is awful and Cushing's part is small. **(R)**

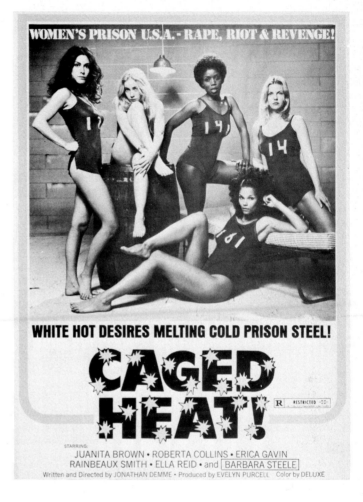

CALLING DR. DEATH

1943 Universal (B&W)
PRODUCER: Ben Pivar
DIRECTOR: Reginald LeBorg
SCREENWRITER: Edward Dein

A floating head introduces us to the first of five Lon Chaney, Jr., films inspired by the popular *Inner Sanctum* radio show. Chaney is a neurologist who uses hypnotism to solve his wife's murder. J. Carrol Naish is the police inspector. With Patricia Morrison, David Bruce (*The Mad Ghoul*), Fay Helm, and Holmes Herbert.

CALTIKI, THE IMMORTAL MONSTER

1959 Allied Artists (Italy) (B&W)
PRODUCER: Samuel Schneider
DIRECTOR: Riccardo Freda (Robert Hampton)
SCREENWRITER: Filippo Sanjust (Phillip Just)

An Italian movie set in Mexico, though filmed in Spain and pawned off as being American, even in Italy! Caltiki, a radioactive mass, is discovered in a subterranean pool near Mayan ruins in Mexico. A dead diver surfaces with only the bones of his arm left. Another man who touches the killer glob goes on a murder spree, strangling people with his new skeletal hand. Some good shocks. The cinematographer was Mario Bava (under the name John Foam). With John Merivale, Dioi Perego (Sullivan), and Giacomo Rossi-Stuart.

CAN ELLEN BE SAVED?

1974 TV
PRODUCER: Everett Chambers
DIRECTOR: Harvey Hart
SCREENWRITER: Emmett Roberts

John Saxon is hired by Leslie Nielsen and Louise Fletcher to deprogram their cult-disciple daughter, little Cathy Cannon. Religious fanatics, exorcism, and Michael Parks—all in a dull TV movie. By the Canadian director of *Dark Intruder*.

THE CANDIDATE

1964 Atlantic Pictures
PRODUCER: Maurice Duke
DIRECTOR: Robert Angus
SCREENWRITER: Joyce Ann Miller

No, it's not a Robert Redford hit. Two of America's most successful breast-fetish queens, Mamie Van Doren and June Wilkinson, star in a scandalous tale of political corruption in Washington, D.C., with none other than Ted ("Baxter") Knight. It's typical sleaze from a company known for its nudie films. Ted, a senatorial candidate, is involved with both beauties. At a party, he gets another girl pregnant. Mamie takes her to an abortionist who rapes her. Ted plans to marry June but dies of a heart attack when he sees her in a stag film. Has Mary Tyler Moore seen this one?

CANDY

1968 Cinerama Releasing
(U.S./France/Italy)
PRODUCER: Robert Haggiag
DIRECTOR: Christian Marquand
SCREENWRITER: Buck Henry

Terry Southern's novel is turned into a series of guest-star bits. Pouty Ewa Aulin is the sexual goal of an alcoholic Welsh poet (Richard Burton), the Mexican gardener (Ringo Starr), a general/pilot (Walter Matthau), a long-haired guru (Marlon Brando), a hunchback (Charles Aznavour), and finally her own father (John Astin). With James Coburn and John Huston as crazed doctors, Sugar Ray Robinson, Elsa Martinelli, Florinda Bolkan, and Anita Pallenberg. Some of the music was by the Byrds and Steppenwolf. Special effects expert Douglas Trumbull did the impressive opening and closing sequences. Filmed in Rome and New York. (R)

CANNIBAL ATTACK

1954 Columbia (B&W)
PRODUCER: Sam Katzman
DIRECTOR: Lee Sholem
SCREENWRITER: Carroll Young

For the last three "Jungle Jim" movies the cartoon-hero name was dropped and Johnny Weissmuller played . . . Johnny Weissmuller! Johnny battles a tribe of crooks that wear crocodile skins. Judy Walsh is the daughter of a princess in a tribe that *used* to be cannibals. With David Bruce.

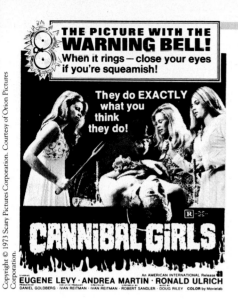

THE PICTURE WITH THE
WARNING BELL!
When it rings — close your eyes
if you're squeamish!

They do EXACTLY
what you
think
they do!

CANNiBAL GiRLS

An AMERICAN INTERNATIONAL Release

EUGENE LEVY · ANDREA MARTIN · RONALD ULRICH
DANIEL GOLDBERG · IVAN REITMAN · IVAN REITMAN · ROBERT SANDLER · DOUG RILEY   COLOR by Movielab

CANNIBAL GIRLS

1972 AIP (Canada)
PRODUCER: Daniel Goldberg
DIRECTOR: Ivan Reitman
SCREENWRITER: Robert Sandler
Second City TV fans: this horror spoof stars Eugene Levy and Andrea Martin. As in *Chamber of Horrors*, there's a warning bell that rings to induce the audience to close their eyes. Reitman, the director, later hit with *Meatballs* and *Stripes* after producing early David Cronenberg hits. **(R)**

CANNIBAL ORGY: See SPIDER BABY.

CANNIBALS IN THE STREETS

1982 Almi Cinema Five (Italy)
PRODUCERS: Maurizio Amati, Sandro Amati
DIRECTOR/SCREENWRITER:
Antonio Margheriti (Anthony Dawson)
ALSO RELEASED AS: *Invasion of the Flesh Hunters*
An extremely gory orgy of flesh-munching filmed in Atlanta, Georgia, with an Italian crew. John Saxon stars as an ex-Green Beret who was infected by a cannibal virus in Vietnam. He joins two other soldiers and a nurse on a rampage of maiming, killing, and eating until the police arrive to slaughter the hungry "heroes" in the sewer. Saxon's always interesting exploitation career goes back to 1955 when he made his debut in *Running Wild* with Mamie Van Doren. Director Margheriti has been churning out Italian junk movies for almost as long. Originally rated X for violence. **(R)**

CANNONBALL

1976 New World (U.S./Hong Kong)
PRODUCER: Samuel W. Gelfman
DIRECTORS/SCREENWRITERS: Paul Bartel, Donald C. Simpson
A follow-up to *Death Race 2000*. David Carradine as Cannonball Buckman participates in a present day illegal cross-country race. With Gerrit Graham, Robert Carradine, Judy Canova, Belinda Balaski, Bill McKinney, lots of mangled cars, and Martin Scorsese representing the Mafia. With bits by Roger Corman and Joe Dante. Run Run Shaw was the executive producer. In '78 Carradine was projected into the future again in *Deathsport*.

CAPE CANAVERAL MONSTERS

1960 CCM (B&W)
PRODUCER: Richard Greer
DIRECTOR/SCREENWRITER: Phil Tucker
Acts of sabotage are carried out against a fledgling U.S. space program by a married couple killed when their Buick hit a tree. Their energized bodies piece together an intergalactic communications center from faucets and broken speedometers. As long as they keep their arms from falling off, they do fine. Missiles go up, missiles come down. With lots of terrific NASA footage of same. Featuring Scott Peters, Linda Connell, Katherine Victor, Jason Johnson, and Frank Smith. As with *Robot Monster*,

worth spending an extra night in Wilkes-Barre for. —CB

CAPONE
1975 20th Century-Fox
PRODUCER: Roger Corman
DIRECTOR: Steve Carver
SCREENWRITER: Howard Browne
A quickie gangster bio, Corman style! Ben Gazzara is pretty ridiculous in his portrayal of Al Capone as a violent psychopath. Corman only produced this one but it includes scenes from his *St. Valentine's Day Massacre*. With Harry Guardino, John Cassavetes, Frank Campanella, Susan Blakely, and Sylvester Stallone as Frank "The Enforcer" Nitti. Blakely and Stallone had just been in *The Lords of Flatbush*. (R)

CAPRICORN ONE
1978 Warner Brothers
PRODUCER: Paul N. Lazarus III
DIRECTOR/SCREENWRITER: Peter Hyams
NASA fakes a manned flight to Mars. The capsule is destroyed and the astronauts who were supposed to be inside are marked for death to insure their silence. James Brolin, Sam Waterston, and O. J. Simpson are the astronauts fleeing from the government. Hal Holbrook is the mission commander who devises the deception, which is discovered by investigative reporter Elliott Gould and TV commentator Karen Black with the help of crop duster Telly Savalas. With David Doyle and Brenda Vaccaro. Director Hyams later did *Outland*.

CAPTAIN AMERICA
1979 TV
PRODUCER: Martin Goldstein
DIRECTOR: Rod Holcomb
SCREENWRITER: Don Ingalls
Dismal pilot film with Reb Brown as Captain America's son, saving Phoe-

nix from a neutron bomb. With Heather Menzies and Len Birman.

CAPTAIN AMERICA II
1979 TV
PRODUCER: Allan Balter
DIRECTOR: Ivan Nagy
SCREENWRITERS: Wilton Schiller, Patricia Payne
Reb Brown returns as the new Captain America in a second pilot film. Christopher Lee is a kidnaped scientist capable of accelerating the aging process. With Len Birman, Lana Wood, and Connie Selleca. It was a theatrical release in Europe.

CAPTAIN CLEGG: See NIGHT CREATURES

CAPTAIN KRONOS, VAMPIRE HUNTER
1973 Hammer/Paramount (England)
PRODUCERS: Albert Fennel, Brian Clemens
DIRECTOR/SCREENWRITER: Brian Clemens
Too bad this fun vampire adventure got lost on a double bill with the inferior *Frankenstein and the Monster From Hell*, because it's really good. Horst Janson is the swashbuckling hero, killing vampires with the aid of the odd, hunchbacked Professor Grost (John Carson) and Caroline Munro. The vampire lore is mostly new and the film works as an adventure and a comedy. When a friend (Ian Hendry) becomes a vampire they try to kill him by using a cross, bullets, a sword, and hanging. Nothing seems to work. They figure out how to knock him off just in time for a whole family of aristocratic bloodsuckers to be discovered. With Shane Bryant. Director Clemens wrote many of the best *Avengers* shows. The theme song is available on *The First Man on the Moon* L.P., which features music by Laurie Johnson.

CAPTAIN MEPHISTO AND THE TRANSFORMATION MACHINE: See *MANHUNT ON MYSTERY ISLAND.*

CAPTAIN MILKSHAKE
1970 Richmark (B&W)
PRODUCER/DIRECTOR: Richard Crawford
SCREENWRITERS: Richard Crawford,
　Barry Leichtling
Marine Geoff Gage is introduced to drugs and free love while home on leave. He breaks off with hippie girl Andrea Cagan and returns to Vietnam, where he dies in action. Music by the Steve Miller Band, Country Joe and the Fish, Quicksilver Messenger Service, and Kaleidoscope. With David Korn, Ronald Barca, and Belle Greer.
　　　　　　　　　　　　　　　　–CB

CAPTAIN NEMO AND THE UNDERWATER CITY
1969 MGM (England)
PRODUCER: Bertram Oster
DIRECTOR: James Hill
SCREENWRITERS: Pip and Jane Baker,
　R. Wright Campbell
Robert Ryan, as Captain Nemo, in his only fantasy film. A passable adaptation of Jules Verne, it features an underwater city threatened by a giant manta ray. With Luciana Paluzzi, Nanette Newman, and Chuck Connors as the senator.

CAPTAIN SINBAD
1963 MGM
PRODUCERS: Frank and Herman King
DIRECTOR: Byron Haskin
SCREENWRITERS: Samuel B. West, Harry Relis
Guy Williamson, TV's Zorro (and Professor Robinson in *Lost in Space*), stars as Sinbad in an overlooked fantasy with some great special effects. The villain/dictator (Pedro Prinendariz) keeps his heart in an ivory tower so he can't be killed. Abraham Sofaer is his court

magician. Sinbad encounters a giant fist with a spike-glove, an invisible monster, birdmen, a multiheaded monster, and a man-eating crocodile. Almost as good as *The Seventh Voyage of Sinbad.* Filmed in Germany.

CAPTIVE GIRL
1950 Columbia (B&W)
PRODUCER: Sam Katzman
DIRECTOR: William Berke
SCREENWRITER: Carroll Young
Jungle Jim (Johnny Weissmuller) rescues a blond girl (Anita Lhoest) who had grown up in the jungle. Buster Crabbe is the villain. Johnny and Buster, both former Tarzans, had also been in *Swamp Fire* (1946) together.

CAPTIVE WILD WOMAN
1943 Universal (B&W)
PRODUCER: Ben Pivar
DIRECTOR: Edward Dmytryk
SCREENWRITERS: Henry Sucher, Griffith Jay
The success of *Cat People* inspired Universal to make this ape-woman movie, a mindless but fun variation on the theme. John Carradine as Dr. Sigmund Walters turns a man in a gorilla suit into the beautiful Acquanetta. When sexually aroused, she becomes a hairy, snarling killer. Milburn Stone (Doc on

UPI 3/31/50: New York: Johnny Weissmuller (right), now appearing in Captive Girl, *is met by nine swimming beauties from his "watercade" show, on his arrival at La Guardia Field. The girls braved low temperatures to display their strapless bathing suits. The Weissmuller watercade opens in Cincinnati.*

Gunsmoke) is the animal-trainer hero. Evelyn Ankers is his girl. Circus footage from *The Big Cage* (1933) with Clyde Beatty helped fill out the 61-minute feature. With Lloyd Corrigan and Fay Helm. There were two sequels; *Jungle Woman* was next.

One of the Captive Women in the New York City of 3000 A.D.

CAPTIVE WOMEN
1952 RKO (B&W)
PRODUCERS/SCREENWRITERS: Aubrey Wisberg, Jack Pollexfen
DIRECTOR: Stuart Gilmore
ALSO RELEASED AS: *1,000 Years from Now*
New York in the 29th century is a post-atomic heap of rubble. The remaining people are either norms (led by Robert Clarke) or mutes (led by Ron Randall). The disfigured mutes are the peaceful good guys, the norms are barbaric. Clarke and co-stars William Schallert and Margaret Field had just been in *The Man from Planet X*. Pretty laughable stuff. Albert Zugsmith was associate producer.

CAPTURE THAT CAPSULE:
See *SPY SQUAD.*

THE CAR
1977 Universal
PRODUCERS: Elliot Silverstein, Marvin Birot
DIRECTOR: Elliot Silverstein
SCREENWRITERS: Dennis Shryack, Michael Butler, Lane Slate
Unintentional laughs highlight this thriller patterned after *Jaws.* A big black car without a driver chases Sheriff James Brolin and his family through the desert. After many deaths, the car blows up.

THE CARETAKERS
1963 United Artists (B&W)
PRODUCER/DIRECTOR: Hall Bartlett
SCREENWRITER: Henry F. Greenberg
Don't miss the powerful beginning of this good psycho-ward movie. Polly Bergen walks down the street (past associate producer Jerry Paris, doing a cameo) into a movie theater showing a state-of-the world newsreel, and has a nervous breakdown. She runs up to the stage, staring at the screen until the men in white coats arrive. In the mental hospital, it's Robert Stack as the liberal doctor vs. hard-liner Joan Crawford (in a support role). Joan teaches her nurses karate and considers Polly too dangerous to stay with others. The inmates include Janis Paige, Ellen Corby, and Barbara Barrie as a mute pyromaniac. Herbert Marshall runs the hospital where Van Williams and Susan Oliver work. Robert Vaughn is Bergen's weak husband.

CARNIVAL OF BLOOD
1971 Kirk Films
PRODUCER/DIRECTOR/SCREENWRITER: Leonard Kirman
I dare anybody to stay awake through *Carnival of Blood.* Some fools have been trying lately after putting down about $50 for the videocassette. Burt Young owns a copy. He's in it, though. It was his first film. Some women get killed and there's a guy named Gimpy. Most

of the time people sit on a couch and talk or try to break balloons. It was filmed at Coney Island, which is not a boring place. Originally co-billed with the equally unwatchable *Curse of the Headless Horseman*.

CARNIVAL OF SOULS

1962 Herts-Lion (B&W)
PRODUCER/DIRECTOR: Herk Harvey
SCREENWRITER: John Clifford

Organist Mary Henry (Candace Hilligoss) drowns when a girlfriend's car breaks through a rural Kansas bridge railing and sinks into a swollen river. Hours later, she reappears on the shore and makes her way to the town of Lawrence, where she starts her new job playing the organ at the church. Strange things begin to happen. She is drawn to an abandoned lakeside pavilion on the outskirts of town—where the dead walk. And dance. Farmers in ghoul makeup block every path of escape. Mary is back in the front seat of the old Chevy when it's dragged from the river. Frances Feist is the landlady, Sidney Berger the man next door. Director Harvey leads the dead eyes of Lawrence. Required viewing. —CB

CARNIVAL ROCK

1958 Howco (B&W)
PRODUCER/DIRECTOR: Roger Corman
SCREENWRITER: Leo Lieberman

"The pent-up fury of today's rock 'n' rollers—hungry for kicks!" was the ad copy on this one. Gambler Brian Hutton wins a nightclub and singer Susan Cabot; obsessed loser David Stewart stays on as a baggy-pants comic and torches the club on the eve of the wedding. With Dick Miller and Jonathan Haze. Musical guests include Bob Luman, David Houston, the Platters, and the Blockbusters. Originally a package deal with *Teenage Thunder*. Cabot

sings "Ou-shoo-bla-d." The Shadows (with guitarist James Burton) do the creep. —CB

CAROUSEL

1956 20th Century-Fox
PRODUCER: Wendy Ephron
DIRECTOR: Henry King
SCREENWRITERS: Phoebe and Henry Ephron

A musical version of *Liliom*, which Fritz Lang had directed in 1935. If Gordon Macrae and Shirley Jones singing "You'll Never Walk Alone" doesn't thrill you, watch for performances by Cameron Mitchell, Angelo Rossitto, and Tor Johnson!

CARRIE

1976 United Artists
PRODUCER: Paul Monash
DIRECTOR: Brian DePalma
SCREENWRITER: Lawrence D. Cohen

A horror film brilliantly conceived to appeal to the vast American teenage moviegoing population. The much-copied plot is about a naive girl (Sissy Spacek) who uses her psychic powers to punish her many tormentors, including her religious fanatic mother (Piper Laurie). The modern thrills include a menstruation-in-the-school-shower scene, a shock ending copied from *Deliverance*, and Nancy Allen (then the director's girlfriend, later his wife) giving John Travolta a blow job. Amy Irving, William Katt, Travolta, Allen, and P. J. Soles all went on to other teen-related projects. With Sidney Lassick. Based on Stephen King's first novel. Music by Pino Donaggio. **(R)**

CARRY ON SCREAMING

1966 Audio Film Center (England)
PRODUCER: Peter Rogers
DIRECTOR: Gerald Thomas
SCREENWRITER: Talbot Rothwell

The revived Dr. Watt (Kenneth Williams) and his vampirish sister (Fenella

Fielding) create twin Frankenstein monsters called Oddbod, who kidnap women. Bungling detectives investigate. A mummy and a Dr. Jekyll join in the fun. It was the 12th in the long-running series.

CASABLANCA
1943 Warner Brothers (B&W)
PRODUCER: Hal B. Wallis
DIRECTOR: Michael Curtiz
SCREENWRITERS: Julius J. and Philip G. Epstein
Ronald Reagan and Ann Sheridan almost played the Humphrey Bogart and Ingrid Bergman roles in this all-time favorite. Everybody's seen it and knows the plot and cast, which includes Peter Lorre in a great small role (Bogart calls him a "cut-rate parasite"), Sidney Greenstreet, and Conrad Veidt.

CASANOVA'S BIG NIGHT
1954 Paramount
PRODUCER: Paul Jones
DIRECTOR: Norman Z. McLeod
SCREENWRITER: Aubrey Wisberg
As a cowardly tailor's assistant, Bob Hope is mistaken for Casanova (Vincent Price in a small role). He encounters a Who's Who of screen villains and oddities, including Basil Rathbone, John Carradine, Lon Chaney, Jr., Raymond Burr, Skelton Knaggs, Primo Carnera, John Hoyt, Henry Brandon, Lucien Littlefield, and a group of midgets. With Joan Fontaine, Audrey Dalton, Frieda Inescort, and Robert Hutton.

CASBAH
1948 Universal (B&W)
PRODUCER: Nat C. Goldstein
DIRECTOR: John Berry
SCREENWRITER: L. Bushfekete
A musical remake of *Algiers* (1938) with the dubious charms of Tony Martin and Yvonne DeCarlo. Peter Lorre is Slimante, a singing police inspector. With

Hugo Haas, who soon decided he could direct as well as the guy who did this, as Omar.

CASE OF THE FULL MOON MURDERS
1971 Newport
PRODUCER/DIRECTOR: Sean Cunningham
SCREENWRITERS: Bud Talbot, Jerry Hayling
ALSO RELEASED AS: *Sex on the Groove Tube, Case of the Smiling Stiffs*
An episodic *Dragnet*-style parody of sexploitation films made in Florida by the director of *The Last House on the Left, Friday the 13th,* and *A Stranger Is Watching.* It features a vampire girl who likes oral sex and Harry Reems of *Deep Throat* fame. Originally released as a hard core feature with a self-imposed X rating. (R)

CASE OF THE SMILING STIFFS: See CASE OF THE FULL MOON MURDERS.

CASH ON DEMAND
1961 Hammer/Columbia (England)
PRODUCER: Michael Carreras
DIRECTOR: Quentin Lawrence
SCREENWRITERS: David T. Chantler, Lewis Greifer
Peter Cushing, in a rare '60s non-horror role, plays a strict bank manager. André Morell kidnaps his wife and son to force him to help commit a robbery.

CASINO ROYALE
1967 Columbia (England)
PRODUCERS: Charles K. Feldman, Jerry Bressler
DIRECTORS: John Huston, Ken Hughes, Val Guest, Robert Parrish, Joseph McGrath
SCREENWRITERS: Wolf Mankowitz, John Law, Michael Sayers, Billy Wilder, Ben Hecht, John Huston, Val Guest, Joseph Heller, Terry Southern

The only Ian Fleming Bond novel that producers Saltzman and Broccoli didn't own was his first. Charles Feldman decided to throw out the plot, use the title, and make this all-star comedy mishmash that looks like an adult *Monkees* show. David Niven stutters as the "real" Sir James Bond, coming out of retirement to save the world from SMERSH. Woody Allen, as his inept nephew Jimmy Bond, has some of the best scenes and provides the surprise ending. As a gambling expert, Peter Sellers has a big casino scene playing against Orson Welles, a SMERSH agent. The two actors disliked each other so much that they filmed on different days playing to doubles. Including a takeoff on German expressionistic films, a nod to the producer's earlier *What's New Pussycat* (with Peter O'Toole), a flying saucer, Frankenstein's monster (David Prowse), music by the Tijuana Brass, and Dusty Springfield singing "The Look of Love." With Ursula Andress, Joanna Pettet, Daliah Lavi, Barbara Bouchet, Deborah Kerr, William Holden, Charles Boyer, John Huston, George Raft, Jean-Paul Belmondo, and Jacqueline Bisset (as Miss Goodthighs). It's over two hours long.

CASTLE OF BLOOD

1964 Woolner (France/Italy) (B&W)
PRODUCERS: Frank Belty, Walter Sarch
DIRECTOR: Antonio Margheriti
(Anthony Dawson)
SCREENWRITERS: Jean Grimaud,
Gordon Wilson, Jr.
ORIGINALLY RELEASED AS: *Danza Macabra*
ALSO RELEASED AS: *Castle of Terror*
A writer (George Rivière) meets Edgar Allan Poe and Lord Blackwood at an inn. They bet him that he can't spend the night alone in a certain castle on All Soul's Eve. On that night, every person who ever died there re-enacts his deaths. He meets the beautiful Elizabeth Blackwood (Barbara Steele) and discovers she has no heartbeat. He sees several horrible murders replayed by the dead inhabitants. When he discovers that they plan to kill him for his blood he runs outside and is impaled on an iron fence. Poe and Blackwood arrive and collect their money from his pocket. One of Barbara Steele's best. A great ghost story with some tame (probably cut) lesbian scenes. Margheriti liked it so much he remade it as *Web of the Spider* with Tony Franciosa. American theater patrons who won a promotional contest got "one frozen dead corpse and one female scalp"!

CASTLE OF DOOM: See VAMPYR.

CASTLE OF EVIL

1966 World Entertainment Corporation
PRODUCER: Earle Lyon
DIRECTOR: Francis D. Lyon
SCREENWRITER: Charles A. Wallace
Kovec, a mad scientist who was disfigured by phosphorus salts, is dead. His heirs arrive at his Caribbean island castle and are killed by a robot created by the clever Kovec in his own image (rotted face, missing eye). This laughable horror features Scott Brady as the hero, Virginia Mayo as Kovec's ex-mistress, Hugh Marlowe, David Brian, and Lisa Gaye. A free funeral was promised "if you D.D. (Drop Dead) while watching."

THE CASTLE OF FU MANCHU

1968 International Cinema
(W. Germany/Spain/Italy/England)
PRODUCER/SCREENWRITER: Harry Alan Towers
DIRECTOR: Jesse Franco
ALSO RELEASED AS: *Assignment: Istanbul*
This final cheap Christopher Lee/Fu Manchu number was so bad it wasn't released for several years and then on

the bottom of a double bill. The main cast is the same as *Kiss and Kill* with the addition of European beauties Maria Perschy and Rosalba Neri.

CASTLE OF THE LIVING DEAD

1963 Woolner Bros. (Italy/France) (B&W)
PRODUCER: Paul Maslansky
DIRECTOR: Luciano Ricci (Herbert Wise)
SCREENWRITER: Warren Kiefer
ORIGINALLY RELEASED AS: *Il Castello de Morti Vivi*

A surprisingly good film about a small, picturesque group of performers who agree to travel by wagon to the castle of Count Drago (Christopher Lee with a goatee and blackened eyes). His realistic collection of stuffed animals is really the result of a drug that he also uses on humans to "preserve" their beauty. It's not a great role for Lee but the plays and magic shows put on by the performers are interesting. The dwarf emerges as the film's hero. Donald Sutherland plays two roles, a dimwitted soldier and, in old woman drag, a witch

who gives a charm to the dwarf. There are discrepancies in reports as to who actually directed, but the end scenes with the enormous statues were directed by Michael Reeves, a young Englishman who later made his own features.

CASTLE OF TERROR: See CASTLE OF BLOOD.

CASTLE OF TERROR: See HORROR CASTLE.

THE CAT AND THE CANARY

1939 Paramount (B&W)
PRODUCER: Arthur Hornblow, Jr.
DIRECTOR: Elliott Nugent
SCREENWRITERS: Walter De Leon, Lynn Starling

A comedy version of the old masked-killer play. Bob Hope and Paulette Goddard star with Gale Sondergaard, George Zucco, John Beal, and Douglass Montgomery. The escaped-inmate killer with the clutching hand stalked for the fourth time in 1978. Hope and Goddard returned in a better follow-up hit (*The Ghost Breakers*) in 1940.

THE CAT AND THE CANARY

1978 Quartet (British)
PRODUCER: Richard Gordon
DIRECTOR/SCREENWRITER: Radley Metzger

Based on a 1922 stage play, this was the fourth version of the reading-of-the-will mystery. It's a comic version set in 1934, by a director previously known for his enjoyably arty sex films (like *The Lickerish Quartet*). Carol Lynley is named the sole heir to a fortune left by Wilfrid Hyde-White. All the relatives are spending the night in an old mansion and an insane killer is loose in the neighborhood. With Honor Blackman, Michael Callan, Edward Fox, Wendy Hiller, Olivia Hussey, and Daniel Massey.

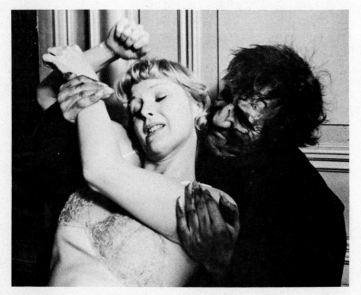

Carol Lynley struggles in the newest version of The Cat and the Canary.

THE CAT CREATURE

1973 TV
PRODUCER: Douglas S. Cramer
DIRECTOR: Curtis Harrington
SCREENWRITER: Robert Bloch

Okay attempt to recreate a Val Lewton '40s mood. Gale Sondergaard (who had only appeared in one film since 1949 because of the Communist scare blacklist) is Hester Black, a mysterious shopkeeper. John Carradine, Key Luke, Kent Smith (*Cat People*), and John Abbott (*The Vampire's Ghost*) are all on hand to remind you of the B-movie roots. Starring Meredith Baxter and David Hedison. With Stuart Whitman and Peter Lorre, Jr. (actually Eugene Weingand, an unrelated imposter once taken to court by Lorre for illegal use of his name).

THE CAT CREEPS

1930 Universal (B&W)
PRODUCER: Carl Laemmle, Jr.
DIRECTOR: Rupert Julian
SCREENWRITERS: Gladys Lehman, William Hurlbut

A talkie remake of *The Cat and the Canary* (1927). Helen Twelvetrees stars with Neil Hamilton, Jean Hersholt, and Montague Love. A Spanish-language version was shot simultaneously with a different cast. Universal did the same with *Dracula* the next year.

THE CAT CREEPS

1946 Universal (B&W)
PRODUCER: Howard Welsch
DIRECTOR: Earle C. Kenton
SCREENWRITERS: Edward Dein, Jerry Warner

Forgettable horror film with a murdered woman's spirit living in a cat. With Paul Kelly, Lois Collier, Noah Beery, Jr., Douglas Dumbrille, and Jonathan Hale. No relation to the 1930 film of the same name.

THE CAT GIRL

1957 AIP (England) (B&W)
PRODUCERS: Lou Rusoff, Herbert Smith
DIRECTOR: Alfred Shaughnessy
SCREENWRITER: Lou Rusoff

A film about a family curse which can turn a girl (Barbara Shelley) into a killer leopard. With Robert Ayres and Kay Callard. Originally co-billed with *The Amazing Colossal Man*.

THE CAT O'NINE TAILS

1971 National General Pictures (Italy/France/W. Germany)
PRODUCER: Salcatore Argento
DIRECTOR/SCREENWRITER: Dario Argento

The "Italian Hitchcock" returns with another clever, sometimes bloody mystery. Reporter James Franciscus teams with a blind professional crossword-puzzle solver (Karl Malden) to find a murderer. The XY factor in chromosomes causes the man to kill. Music by Ennio Morricone.

CAT PEOPLE

1942 RKO (B&W)
PRODUCER: Val Lewton
DIRECTOR: Jacques Tourneur
SCREENWRITER: Dewitt Bodeen

"Kiss me and I'll claw you to death!" read the ads. Irene (Simone Simon), a Serbian-born fashion artist living in New York, is haunted by the fear that she is descended from a race of cat-women who turn into panthers when sexually aroused. Her architect husband (Kent Smith) is having an affair with Jane Randolph and her psychiatrist (Tom Conway) wants to have one with her. The first of Lewton's great, subtly atmospheric B-movies. It deals more with the fear of sex than with a cliché monster. With Alan Napier and Elizabeth Russell as the mysterious woman who calls Irene "moya sestra." *The Curse of the Cat People* was a very different semi-sequel.

CAT PEOPLE
1982 Universal
PRODUCER: Charles Fries
DIRECTOR: Paul Schrader
SCREENWRITER: Alan Ormsby

Whenever Malcolm MacDowell has an orgasm, he turns into a panther. His sister, Nastassia Kinski, is under the same curse, but she doesn't know it 'cause she's a virgin. Since "cat people" can mate with each other without being transformed, MacDowell proposes an incestuous solution. Nasti is in love with zoo keeper John Heard, so she won't go for it—instead she goes off with Heard, who eventually finds a solution that's even more depraved. A radically revisionist remake of the Val Lewton moldy oldy set in New Orleans. Music by Giorgio Moroder and David Bowie. Screenplay by Alan Ormsby of *Children Shouldn't Play with Dead Things* fame. With Ruby Dee and Ed Begley, Jr. (R) –BM

CAT WOMEN OF THE MOON
1953 Astor (3-D)
PRODUCER: Al Zimbalist
DIRECTOR: Arthur Hilton
SCREENWRITER: Roy Hamilton
ALSO RELEASED AS: *Rocket to the Moon*

Sonny Tufts leads a mini-expedition to the Moon, inhabited by beautiful telepathic women in tights. Crew member Victor Jory causes trouble. A giant spider threatens. Sonny and Earth woman Marie Windsor love each other. The "cat women" let the Earth people go. A terrible but well-loved and trend-setting feature from the producer of the same year's ground-breaking *Robot Monster*. Both were in thrilling 3-D. *Cat Women* was remade in '58 as *Missile to the Moon*. Music by Elmer Bernstein (*The Magnificent Seven*).

CATALINA CAPER
1967 Crown International (B&W)
PRODUCERS: Bond Blackman, Jack Bartlett
DIRECTOR: Lee Sholem
SCREENWRITER: Clyde Ware

Vacationing divers Tommy Kirk and Brian Cutler are hired to retrieve a rare Chinese scroll dropped overboard during a scuffle between thieves. The two college friends help get the artifact back to the museum after girl-chasing and musical fun. Little Richard does "Scuba Party," and Mary Wells does "Never Steal Anything Wet." With Del Moore, Peter Duryea, Lyle Waggoner, Sue Casey, Carol Connors, the Cascades, Michael Blodgett, and the Adrian Teen Models. Filmed on location on Catalina Island and in Malibu. T.V. Mikels was the director of photography. Sholem directed *Louisiana Hussy*. –CB

CATASTROPHE 1999: THE PROPHECIES OF NOSTRADAMUS: See LAST DAYS OF PLANET EARTH.

CATCH US IF YOU CAN: See HAVING A WILD WEEKEND.

CATHY'S CURSE
1977 21st Century (Canada)
PRODUCERS: Eddy Matalon, N. Mathieu, Nicole Boisvert
DIRECTOR: Eddy Matalon
SCREENWRITERS: Myra Clement, Eddy Matalon, A. Sens-Cazenave
ORIGINALLY RELEASED AS: *Cauchemares*

Slow-moving *Exorcist* copy about a little girl with a possessed rag doll. Little Randi Allen gets to act like Linda Blair. Filmed in snowy Canada.

CATHY'S CURSE

SHE HAS THE POWER
...TO TERRORIZE.

Nicole Mathieu Boisvert and Eddy Matalon present "CATHY'S CURSE"
starring ALAN SCARFE BEVERLY MURRAY and RANDI ALLEN as CATHY

Directed by EDDY MATALON
Eastmancolor

THE CATMAN OF PARIS

1946 Republic (B&W)
PRODUCER: Marek M. Libkov
DIRECTOR: Lesley Selander
SCREENWRITER: Sherman L. Lowe

A man wearing a top hat and a cape becomes a cat. He basically looks like an unshaven guy with vampire teeth and Spock ears who went wild with an eyebrow pencil. With Lenore Albert, Carl Esmond, Douglas Dumbrille, and Gerald Mohr.

CATTLE QUEEN OF MONTANA

1954 RKO
PRODUCER: Benedict Borgeans
DIRECTOR: Allan Dwan
SCREENWRITERS: Robert Blees,
Howard Estabrook

Ronald Reagan plays a hired thug traitorously in love with his boss's enemy, cattle queen Barbara Stanwyck. In the end he turns out (surprise!) to be a good guy working for the government. It's said to be one of Reagan's best. The next year Dwan directed him in *Tennessee's Partner*. After that he only made one more theatrical release—*Hellcats of the Navy* with Nancy Davis. This one has Gene Evans, Lance Fuller, Jack Elam, Morris Ankrum, Myron Healy, and Paul Birch.

CAULDRON OF BLOOD

1967 Cannon (Spain)
PRODUCER/DIRECTOR/SCREENWRITER:
Santos Alcocer (Edward Mann)
ORIGINALLY RELEASED AS:
El Coleccionista de Cadavres
ALSO RELEASED AS: *Blind Man's Bluff*
Boris Karloff is a famous blind sculptor who unwittingly uses real bones as the foundations for his work. His wife (Viveca Lindfors) is the crazed killer who supplies the bones. Jean-Pierre Aumont is a writer fooling around with a potential model/victim. Boris spends most of the film in a wheelchair. For Viveca Lindfors fans only. Karloff was long gone by the time the movie was released here in '71. By the director of *Hallucination Generation*.

Tender Flesh
Burning Acid

THE CAULDRON OF DEATH

Color by MOVIELAB ©1979 FVI Inc.

THE CAULDRON OF DEATH

1979 Film Ventures (Italy)
DIRECTOR: Tulio Montoro
SCREENWRITER: Joe Maesso

Q.—What's worse than a boring Italian Mafia movie disguised as a horror film?

A.—A boring Italian Mafia movie with vacationing American stars. In this case, Arthur Kennedy and Chris Mitchum. Also with the ever-popular and very busy Barbara Bouchet. Presented by Edward L. Montoro. **(R)**

CAVALRY COMMAND

1963 Parade Pictures (U.S./Philippines)
PRODUCER: Cirio H. Santiago
DIRECTOR/SCREENWRITER: Eddie Romero

The Philippines—1902. John Agar struggles to convert a local fanatic who has organized a rebellion against American occupation. Richard Arlen, Myron Healey, William Phipps, Alicia Vergel, and Eddie Infante co-star. See *Brides of Blood.*   –CB

CAVE MAN: See ONE MILLION B.C.

CAVE OF THE LIVING DEAD

1964 Trans-Lux (Yugoslavia/
W. Germany) (B&W)
PRODUCER/DIRECTOR: Akos Von Rathony
SCREENWRITER: C. Von Rock
ORIGINALLY RELEASED AS: *Der Fluch der Gruenen Augen*

A professor and his secretary conducting experiments in a cave under an ancient castle. With the help of a witch (?) an Interpol inspector (Adrian Hoven) discovers seven missing girls in the cave. They're all living dead and the professor is really a vampire. With Karin Field and Erika Remberg. Richard Gordon was the executive producer.

CAVEMAN

1981 United Artists
PRODUCERS: Lawrence Turman, David Foster
DIRECTOR: Carl Gottlieb
SCREENWRITERS: Rudy De Luca, Carl Gottlieb

Since *Candy* in '68, Ringo Starr has been acting in movies most people never saw or quickly forgot. Then finally—a hit! He stars in this prehistoric comedy with his new wife Barbara Bach and the animated dinosaurs of David Allen. Well done Stone Age chuckles with Jack Gilford, Avery Schreiber, Dennis Quaid, and Shelly Long. Filmed in Mexico.

Siamese twins Daisy and Violet Hilton after their stage show in Chained for Life.

CELL 2455, DEATH ROW

1955 United Artists (B&W)
PRODUCER/DIRECTOR: Fred F. Sears
SCREENWRITER: Jack Dewitt

William Campbell, later the star of *Blood Bath* and *Dementia 13*, gets practice playing a killer as Caryl Chessman, a real life sex murderer on death row. Chessman was known as the "Lover's Lane Bandit." With Kathryn Grant, Vince Edwards, and Robert Campbell, William's brother. From the director of *Earth vs. the Flying Saucers*.

CHAINED FOR LIFE

1950 Classic Films (B&W)
PRODUCER: George Moscov
DIRECTOR: Harry L. Fraser
SCREENWRITER: Nat Tanchuck

Violet and Daisy Hilton, real Siamese twins who appeared in *Freaks*, sing and dance in this exploitation drama in which one of them is accused of murder. It's nothing compared to their real story. Born in England in 1908, they were sold by their barmaid mother to a woman who treated them little better than slaves and became rich by showing them off at freak shows in America. In the '30s they were taken to court by a woman who named them as correspondents in a divorce suit! The spectacular trial ended with the dismissal of their suit, and long-awaited freedom. By the time they made *Chained for Life*, they were owners of a hotel in Pittsburgh. By the '60s, the money was gone and they operated a fruit stand in Florida until they died in 1964. The nearly plotless film contains endless ordinary novelty acts for padding. With Allen Jenkins, once a popular member of the Warner Brothers stock company. Originally shown in adults-only theaters.

THE CHALLENGE: See IT TAKES A THIEF.

CHALLENGE TO SURVIVE: See LAND OF NO RETURN.

CHAMBER OF HORRORS

1941 Monogram (England) (B&W)
PRODUCER: John Argyle
DIRECTOR: Norman Lee
SCREENWRITERS: Norman Lee, Gilbert Gunn
ALSO RELEASED AS:
The Door with Seven Locks

"A woman's scream was music to his ears!" Leslie Banks, who had seen better days as the star of *The Man Who Knew Too Much* and *The Most Dangerous Game*, is a mad doctor who experiments in an underground lab and torture chamber (with an iron maiden). Lilli Palmer is an intended victim. It was remade in Germany in 1962. Based on an Edgar Wallace mystery.

CHAMBER OF HORRORS
1966 Warner Brothers
PRODUCER/DIRECTOR: Hy Averback
SCREENWRITER: Stephen Kandel
A great neglected shocker that was originally made as a TV pilot but was considered too lurid for home screens at the time. New scenes, including William Castle-style breaks, were added for a theatrical release. Whenever a gory scene is about to begin, the "Fear Flasher" and the "Horror Horn" spare us the blood. The TV series, based on *The House of Wax*, would have featured Cesare Danova and Wilfrid Hyde-White as turn-of-the-century crime-solving Baltimore wax-museum owners, along with a dwarf sidekick (Tun Tun). The real star here, though, is Patrick O'Neal, who is wonderful as Jason Cravatte, a demented killer who chopped off his own manacled hand to escape hanging. Cravatte has a special wooden hand stump, which can be fitted with a horrible selection of hooks, knives, and cleavers to hack up his enemies. With Laura Devon, Patrice Wymore, Suzy Parker, Yvonne Romain, Wayne Rogers, and guest stars Marie Windsor, Jeanette Nolan, and Tony Curtis.

CHAMPAGNE FOR CAESAR
1950 United Artists (B&W)
PRODUCER: George Moskov
DIRECTOR: Richard Whorf
SCREENWRITERS: Hans Jacoby, Fred Brady

Comedy about radio quiz shows, with Vincent Price in one of his best roles as a crazed soap tycoon who sponsors a show hosted by Art Linkletter(!). Ronald Colman plays an unemployed genius named Beauregard Bottomly, who becomes an overnight celebrity when he gets all the right answers to questions on the popular show. Price sends Celeste Holm to distract him and save his company's money. Recommended. With Lyle Talbot and the voice of Mel Blanc (Caesar is a talking bird).

CHANDU ON MAGIC ISLAND
1934 Principal (B&W)
PRODUCER: Sol Lesser
DIRECTOR: Ray Taylor
SCREENWRITER: Barry Barringer
See *The Return of Chandu*.

CHANDU THE MAGICIAN
1932 Fox (B&W)
DIRECTORS: Michael Varne,
William Cameron Menzies
SCREENWRITERS: Barry Connors, Phillip Klein
Impressive Egyptian sets and Bela Lugosi's evil turbaned villain Roxor highlight this filmed version of a radio adventure series. Edmund Lowe, looking like a silent-movie idol, stars as Chandu, who must stop Roxor from conquering the world with his death ray. With Irene Ware and Henry B. Walthall. James Wong Howe was the cinematographer. Audiences were confused when Bela showed up in a 1934 serial playing the hero Chandu.

CHANGE OF HABIT
1970 Universal
PRODUCER: Joe Connelly
DIRECTOR: William Graham
SCREENWRITERS: James Lee, S.S. Schweitzer, Eric Bercovici

Elvis Presley's 31st, last, and possibly worst film. As John Carpenter, a hip free-clinic ghetto doctor, he falls in love with a nurse (Mary Tyler Moore). What he doesn't know is that she's a nun. Elvis saves Sister Mary from a rape. She has to choose between God and Elvis. Elvis sings "Let Us Pray" and "Rubberneckin'." Edward Asner plays a cop (*The Mary Tyler Moore Show*, which debuted later that year, got its start here). Regis Toomey is a priest and Richard Carlson is a bishop. Don't miss the inspiring rock 'n' roll mass scene.

CHANGE OF MIND
1969 Cinerama
PRODUCERS/SCREENWRITERS: Seeleg Lester, Dick Wesson
DIRECTOR: Robert Stevens
The brain of a liberal white district attorney dying of cancer is implanted in the body of a recently deceased black man (Raymond St. Jacques). The man with a new body is rejected by his wife, mother and former associates. He becomes a community hero after breaking a controversial case involving the murder of Sheriff Leslie Nielsen's black mistress. Filmed in Toronto. With Susan Oliver, Cosette Lee, and Janet MacLachlan. **(R)**   —CB

THE CHANGELING
1981 Associated Film Distribution (Canada)
PRODUCERS: Joel B. Michaels, Garth H. Drabinsky
DIRECTOR: Peter Medak
SCREENWRITERS: William Gray, Diana Maddox
After he witnesses a road accident that kills his wife and daughter, a music teacher (George C. Scott) moves to a new town and rents an old decaying mansion. He communes with a ghost-child, and learns that a respected sena-

tor (Melvyn Douglas) was involved in the child's death.

The Changeling's basic story is pretty vapid, but Medak's style is definitely not, particularly in the seance sequence and the scenes immediately following. Medak's early films, *Negatives*, *A Day in the Death of Joe Egg*, and *The Ruling Class*, are bizarre classics, but box-office failures. Subsequently, he directed two comedies, *Ghosts in the Noonday Sun* with Peter Sellers and *The Odd Job* with Graham Chapman—both successful in Britain but unreleased here. He then chose to direct this ghost tale as a bid for large-scale commercial success. "I'd like to make a civilized sort of picture, that people would still go and see," he said at the time. "A friend of mine said that I should make *Hamlet* on roller skates." **(R)**   —BM

CHARIOTS OF THE GODS?
1969 Sunn Classics (W. Germany)
PRODUCER: Guentler Eulau
DIRECTOR: Harold Reinl
SCREENWRITER: Wilhelm Pogersdorff
ORIGINALLY RELEASED AS: *Erinnerungen an die Zukunft*
The original Sunn Classic release tries to convince us that all gods worshiped on earth were prehistoric aliens. Newer Sunn "classics" go about proving the existence of Christ and Noah's Ark. One thing you *can* be sure of—these boring, unconvincing documentaries make lots of easy bucks for Sunn Classics. From the director of over 50 W. German features. Based on the book of the same name by Erich Von Daniken.

CHARLIE CHAN AND THE CURSE OF THE DRAGON QUEEN
1981 American Communications
PRODUCER: Jerry Sherlock
DIRECTOR: Clive Donner
SCREENWRITERS: Stan Burns, David Axelrod

Roddy McDowall is the butler in Charlie Chan and the Curse of the Dragon Queen.

A dreadful comedy with Peter Ustinov as Chan and Richard Hatch as his inept grandson, who acts a lot like Jerry Lewis. Angie Dickinson looks awful as the dragon queen, often in black and white flashbacks. Roddy McDowall is a crippled butler. Brian Keith is an overboiling cop. With Lee Grant and Rachel Roberts. Chinese-American groups protested the film's ethnic stereotyping, but they needn't have bothered: hardly anyone saw this box-office dud.

CHARLIE CHAN AT THE OPERA

1937 20th Century-Fox (B&W)
PRODUCER: John Stone
DIRECTOR: H. Bruce Humberstone
SCREENWRITERS: Scott Darling,
Charles S. Belden

In one of the more elaborate Chan films, Boris Karloff is Gravelle, an ex-operatic baritone who escapes from a mental institution and is blamed for the murder of his wife and her lover. Chan (Warner Oland) figures the plot out with help from number-one son (Key Luke) and a police sergeant (William Demarest). Karloff sings (with a dubbed voice) and appears as Mephistopheles in *Faust*. With Charlotte Henry as his daughter.

CHARRO

1969 National General
PRODUCER/DIRECTOR/SCREENWRITER:
Charles Marquis Warren

Elvis plays a bearded reformed outlaw accused of stealing a cannon in 1870. It was a big move for Elvis to star in a serious nonmusical role. Not surprisingly, it flopped. Elvis only made two more movies, both terrible musical comedies. With Ina Balin and Victor French. By the director of *The Unknown Terror*. Music by Hugo Montenegro.

THE CHASE

1946 United Artists (B&W)
PRODUCER: Seymour Nebenzal
DIRECTOR: Arthur Ripley
SCREENWRITER: Philip Yordan

Dark version of a Cornell Woolrich novel (*Dream in a Dream*). Robert Cummings chauffeurs for Steve Cochran, a wealthy Miami "businessman" whose right-hand man is Gino (Peter Lorre). Cummings helps his employer's unhappy wife (Michèle Morgan) escape to Havana and is haunted by a nightmare involving his own death. With Don Wilson and Lloyd Corrigan. From the producer of *M*.

THE CHECKERED FLAG

1963 Mercury
PRODUCER: Herb Vendig
DIRECTOR/SCREENWRITER: William Grefe

Lust and murder on the hot-wheels circuit. Alcoholic track wife Evelyn King talks a promising rookie into helping dispose of her millionaire playboy husband. Joe Morrison manages to kill Charles G. Martin by triggering a pile-up, but loses both legs in the process. King is horribly burned in an explosion when she tries to pull Joe from the wreckage. Grefe's first. Financed by Herb Vendig, featuring Peggy Vendig as Joe's girl Ginger. Morrison and Martin appear in *Racing Fever* and *Safe at Home*. Live action filmed at Sebring.

–CB

THE CHILD

1977 Valiant International
PRODUCER: Robert Dadashian
DIRECTOR: Robert Voskanian
SCREENWRITER: Ralph Lucas
ALSO RELEASED AS: *Kill and Go Hide!*

A badly edited and shot story about a little girl (Rosalie Cole) who lives in the woods with her older brother and eccentric father. A young woman (Laurel Barnett) discovers that the difficult child can command dead bodies to rise from a nearby cemetery and kill. Things are pretty boring until the mummylike corpses attack and mutilate what's left of the small cast. Music by Michael Quatro. (R)

THE CHILDREN

1980 World Northal
PRODUCERS: Max Kalmanowicz,
   Carlton J. Albright
DIRECTOR: Max Kalmanowicz
SCREENWRITERS: Carlton J. Albright,
   Edward Terry

Some unintentional hilarity in this story about a nuclear-plant leak that turns a school bus of kids into atomic zombies with black fingernails. The cute, wide-eyed tykes walk up to adults, arms outstretched for a hug, and fry them on contact. A small-town sheriff encounters a series of uncaring, divorced, stoned, decadent parents (lots of social commentary here), although there is one wholesome couple whose kid is missing. The pregnant mom is played by Gale Garnett, who once hit top-40 charts with "We'll Sing in the Sunshine." She survives but gives birth to a mutant baby with black fingernails. The only way to kill the children is to cut their hands off! Scenes of hands littering the ground while kids with ob-viously phony stumps fall over make the viewer optimistic about the immediate future of bad cinema. (R)

CHILDREN OF THE DAMNED

1964 MGM (England) (B&W)
PRODUCER: Ben Arbeid
DIRECTOR: Anton M. Leader
SCREENWRITER: John Briley

A semi-sequel to the great *Village of the Damned*. They're both based on *The Midwich Cuckoos* by John Wynham, who also wrote *The Day of the Triffids*. Six of the alien kids from the original film are being studied by scientists and threatened by the military. Some people think this forgotten follow-up is as good as the original. The cast includes Ian Hendry and many competent British actors. "Beware the eyes that paralyze!"

CHILDREN SHOULDN'T PLAY WITH DEAD THINGS

1972 Geneni
PRODUCER/DIRECTOR: Benjamin Clark
   (Bob Clark)
SCREENWRITERS: Benjamin Clark,
   Alan Ormsby

An odd horror comedy starring Alan Ormsby (as a director) and his wife Anya. He and his actor friends go to an island and act out a satanic rite using a corpse they name Orville, which is the source of some strained comedy.

Ghouls enjoy dinner in Children Shouldn't Play with Dead Things.

The rite actually works, causing the dead to rise out of the earth in an excellent *Night of the Living Dead*–inspired sequence. When the dead begin to walk, the comedy (thankfully) disappears and the scares begin. Made in Florida. Bob Clark's next project was the incredible *Deathdream*.

CHOMPS

1979 American International
PRODUCER: Joseph Barbera
DIRECTOR: Don Chaffey
SCREENWRITERS: Dick Robbins, Duane Poole

Chomps is short for "Canine Home Protection System." A young electronics genius invents a robot dog in order to stop a crime wave, please his boss, and marry his boss's daughter (played by rock-star wife and former Spielberg girlfriend Valerie Bertinelli). He accomplishes all three by the time this bionic Benji tale is over. Jim Backus, Chuck McCann, Regis Toomey, and Red Buttons are around, but they can't save *Chomps* from its producer, Joseph Barbera of Hanna-Barbera (*The Flintstones*) fame.   —BM

THE CHOPPERS

1961 Fairway-International (B&W)
PRODUCER/SCREENWRITER: Arch Hall, Sr.
DIRECTOR: Leigh Jason

Arch Hall, Jr., and his car-stripping commandos outmaneuver authorities until an insurance investigator's secretary finds a chicken feather at the scene of a crime. Hall, as Cruiser, sings his own "Konga Joe" and "Monkey in My Hatband," and kills fence Moose McGill to keep him from squealing. The gang includes Robert Paget as Torch, Rex Holman as Flip, and Mickey Hoyle as Snooper. With Marianne Gaba (*Playboy's* Miss September 1959), Tom Brown, Chuck Barnes, and Bruno Ve Sota as McGill. Written and produced by Arch Hall, Sr. of *Eegah!* fame. –CB

THE CHOSEN

1977 AIP (England/Italy)
PRODUCER: Edmondo Amati
DIRECTOR: Alberto de Martino
SCREENWRITERS: Sergio Donati,
  Aldo Di Martino
ALSO RELEASED AS: *Holocaust 2,000*

A European mixture of *The Omen* and *The China Syndrome* (which hadn't been made yet). Kirk Douglas stars as a man who designed seven domed nuclear power plants. His son (Simon Ward) turns out to be the Antichrist; he plans to destroy the world with a chain of nuclear explosions. Poor Kirk even has a Biblical nightmare with a seven-headed serpent-monster destroying the world. If you haven't noticed, Kirk has become quite the exploitation/horror star lately. With Agostina Belli as Kirk's mistress. Also with Anthony Quayle. The soundtrack album by Ennio Morricone is available. (R)

CHOSEN SURVIVORS

1974 Columbia
PRODUCERS: Charles Fries, Leon Benson
DIRECTOR: Sutton Roley
SCREENWRITERS: H.B. Cross, Joe Reb Moffly

A group of 11 people take an elevator down 1,700 feet under the desert in order to survive a thermonuclear war. They don't realize that it's only a test. The safety chamber fills up with blood-sucking vampire bats and the people can't get out. Jackie Cooper stars in his first fake post-holocaust/vampire movie. With Bradford Dillman, Richard Jaeckel, Alex Cord, and Diana Muldaur. Filmed in Mexico.

CINDERELLA 2000

1977 Independent International
PRODUCER/DIRECTOR: Al Adamson
SCREENWRITER: Bud Donnelly

Al Adamson tops his previous efforts with this soft-core science-fiction sex musical version of *Cinderella*. With men in tights and bunny masks, a "fairy" godfather, and sets and makeup that will bring back memories of *Santa Claus Conquers the Martians*. Starring Catherine Erhardt, a former model and actress on *Search for Tomorrow*. Not to be confused with *Cinderella*, another X-rated film made the same year. (**X**)

CIRCLE OF IRON

1978 Avco Embassy (English)
PRODUCERS: Paul Maslansky, Sandy Howard
DIRECTOR: Richard Howard
SCREENWRITERS: Stirling Silliphant, Stanley Mann
ALSO RELEASED AS: *The Silent Flute*
Bruce Lee, James Coburn, and Stirling Silliphant originally wrote this martial-arts fantasy for Lee. But David Carradine ended up as the star of this philosophical adventure-fable. Most of the time, he is Chang-sha, guide to a knowledge-seeking fighter (Jeff Cooper); he also appears as a blind man, a monkey man, and Death. Christopher Lee is Zetan, keeper of the Book of Enlightment. With Eli Wallach, Roddy McDowall, and Erica Creer. It was a box-office failure. Filmed in Israel. (**R**)

CIRCUS OF FEAR: See PSYCHO-CIRCUS.

CIRCUS OF HORRORS

1960 Anglo Amalgamated/AIP (England)
PRODUCERS: Julian Wintle, Leslie Parkyn
DIRECTOR: Sidney Mayers
SCREENWRITER: George Baxt
Along with the superior *Peeping Tom* and the sillier *Horror of the Black Museum*, this is one of the big three among unforgettable sick British shockers dealing with voyeurism, physical deformities, and murders. All were made within a year of one another. Anton Diffring stars as Dr. Goethe, a plastic surgeon who is wanted by the police for aiding criminals and now runs a circus. He reconstructs the scarred features of otherwise beautiful women but forbids them to leave his little circus world. When they try, "accidents" occur. A knife-throwing act ends when the female target gets stuck in the neck. A lion tamer is mauled, an acrobat plunges to her death, etc. Goethe has a perverse fascination with the flawed women he treats, fondling their scars while praising their beauty. With Erika Remberg, Yvonne Molaur, Jane Hylaton, Yvonne Romain, and Donald Pleasence. Screenwriter George Baxt also wrote *Horror Hotel*. Don't miss the "temple of beauty."

CITY ACROSS THE RIVER

1949 Universal (B&W)
PRODUCER/DIRECTOR/SCREENWRITER: Maxwell Shane
A toned-down version of Irving Shulman's *The Amboy Dukes* that pre-dates the '50s juvenile-delinquency movies. Two members of a Brooklyn gang kill their shop teacher (they only wanted to rough him up). With zip guns, pool halls, and "Crazy," an incredible funny/scary psychotic geek teen in a zoot suit (Joshua Shelley). With young Tony Curtis, Richard Jaeckel, Jeff Corey, Stephen McNally, and Thelma Ritter.

CITY BENEATH THE SEA

1953 Universal
PRODUCER: Albert J. Cohen
DIRECTOR: Budd Boetticher
SCREENWRITERS: Jack Harvey, Ramon Romero
Robert Ryan and Anthony Quinn salvage a gold shipment from the sunken city of Port Royal. Bad guys and sharks get in the way. With Mala Powers (*The Colossus of New York*), Karel Stepanek, and Woody Strode. Filmed in the West Indies.

CITY BENEATH THE SEA

1971 TV
PRODUCER/DIRECTOR: Irwin Allen
SCREENWRITER: John Meredyth Lucas
ALSO RELEASED AS: *One Hour to Doomsday*

Typical Allen nonsense. In 2050 A.D. the vast underwater city of Pacifica is threatened by meteors and sea monsters. A TV pilot film shown theatrically in Europe, it features past Irwin Allen stars Richard Basehart (*Voyage to the Bottom of the Sea*) and James Darren (*The Time Tunnel*). Also starring Stuart Whitman, Robert Wagner, Joseph Cotten, Whit Bissell, Sugar Ray Robinson, and Rosemary Forsyth.

CITY ON FIRE

1979 Astral (Canada)
PRODUCER: Claude Heroux
DIRECTOR: Alvin Rakoff
SCREENWRITERS: Jack Hill, David P. Lewis, Céline La Frenière

A Midwestern American town burns to the ground in a cut-rate disaster movie filmed in Montreal. The hot cast includes Henry Fonda, Shelley Winters, Ava Gardner, Barry Newman, Susan Clark, Leslie Nielsen, and James Franciscus. Fonda's previous hits were *Rollercoaster*, *Tentacles*, *Swarm*, and *Meteor*.

CITY OF THE DEAD: See HORROR HOTEL.

CITY STORY

1954 Davis (B&W)
PRODUCER: Paul F. Heard
DIRECTOR: William Beaudine
SCREENWRITER: Margaret Fitts

From the man responsible for *Jesse James Meets Frankenstein's Daughter*, this is the story of a clergyman who seeks advice from a teenage jailbird when he is forced to do something about slack attendance. The result: "Wider community services bring young and old together in the house of God." Ann Doran of *Riot in Juvenile Prison* and *Hot Car Girl* June Kenney co-star with Warner Anderson and Herbert Lytton. Produced by Paul F. Heard of the Protestant Film Commission.   –CB

CITY UNDER THE SEA: See WAR-GODS OF THE DEEP.

THE CLAIRVOYANT

1935 Gaumont (England) (B&W)
PRODUCER: Charles Bennett
DIRECTOR: Maurice Elvey
SCREENWRITERS: Charles Bennett, Bryan Edgar Wallace
ALSO RELEASED AS: *Evil Mind*

"The Invisible Man makes the future visible . . . ," the ads promised. Claude Rains as a fake fortune-teller discovers his powers are real. He foresees his own death and is unable to prevent it. *The Night Has a Thousand Eyes* ('48) with Edward G. Robinson has a similar plot. With Fay Wray and Jane Baxter.

CLAMBAKE

1967 United Artists
PRODUCERS: Jules Levy, Arthur Gardner, Arnold Laven
DIRECTOR: Arthur Nadel
SCREENWRITER: Arthur Brown, Jr.

Elvis Presley, a Texas oil heir, goes to Florida, where he switches identities with a poor water-skiing instructor (Will Hutchins) and falls for his first student (Shelley Fabares). Bill Bixby, a playboy boat racer, is a rival for her charms. Elvis races a boat designed by Gary Merrill and sings "Who Needs Money." With Angelique Pettyjohn.

CLASH OF THE TITANS

1981 MGM/UA
PRODUCERS: Ray Harryhausen, Charles H. Schneer
DIRECTOR: Desmond Davis
SCREENWRITER: Beverley Cross

Harryhausen's biggest animation fantasy got an enormous publicity push and was a summer hit, which is nice. It cost more than twice as much as *Sinbad and the Eye of the Tiger*, but most of the budget must have gone to the big-name stars because it's a disappointment that's good more for laughs than for thrills. The Mount Olympus scenes (similar to those in *Jason and the Argonauts*) feature Laurence Olivier, Claire Bloom, Ursula Andress, and Maggie Smith, later seen as a giant talking head. Harry Hamlin stars as Perseus. (He and Ursula had a kid together.) With Burgess Meredith, Judi Bowker, and a robot owl. Jim Danforth helped with the effects, which often fail to convince.

CLASS OF '84
1982 United Film Distribution (Canada)
PRODUCER: Arthur Kent
DIRECTOR: Mark Lester
SCREENWRITERS: John Saxton, Tom Holland
In this sick updating of *The Blackboard Jungle*, the pregnant wife of a nice Chicago high school music teacher (Perry King) is raped by some of his doped-up punk students. King fights back, killing the guilty kids one at a time. Roddy McDowall is an alcoholic biology teacher whose favorite rabbits are skewered alive by students under the leadership of Timothy Van Patten. Timothy's brother, Vincent, starred in *Rock 'n' Roll High School*. Their proud dad is Mr. Bradford on *Eight Is Enough*. With Steven Arngrim, the star of *Fear No Evil*. By the director of Linda Blair's *Roller Boogie*. Music by Lalo Schifrin and Alice Cooper. (R)

THE CLAW MONSTERS:
See *PANTHER GIRL OF THE CONGO.*

THE CLIMAX
1944 Universal
PRODUCER/DIRECTOR: George Waggner
SCREENWRITERS: Curt Siodmak, Lynn Starling
Boris Karloff is Dr. Hohner, the physician of the royal opera who preserves the body of his dead wife and uses hypnosis on the singer he believes to be her reincarnation (Susanna Foster). Miss Foster, an opera singer, had been featured in the previous year's hit remake of *The Phantom of the Opera* (by the same director), which inspired this Technicolor thriller. With Turkish heartthrob Turhan Bey, the great Gale Sondergaard, ex-Little Rascal Scotty Beckett, Thomas Gomez, and June Vincent. It was a remake of a 1930 film.

A CLOCKWORK ORANGE
1971 Warner Brothers (England)
PRODUCER/DIRECTOR/SCREENWRITER:
Stanley Kubrick
This future-shock hit based on Anthony Burgess's novel doesn't look as innovative today as it did when it first came out. Like all Kubrick films, it has moments of brilliance, and Malcolm McDowell is great as Alex, the cured

Zeus (Laurence Olivier) plays with dolls on Mt. Olympus in Clash of the Titans.

Malcolm McDowell makes friends in a record store of the future in A Clockwork Orange.

"droog." Patrick Magee is Mr. Alexander. Adrienne Cori is his unfortunate wife. David Prowse is Julian, the muscular servant. With Anthony Sharp. Music by Walter (now Wendy) Carlos. Note the *2001* sound track in the record shop. The X rating demonstrated how unfair and unfocused our rating system is. Many newspapers refuse to carry ads for any and all X-rated films, grouping hard-core sex movies together with ambitious efforts like this. An R rating was later achieved by cutting out a few seconds of film, making it acceptable to self-censoring papers. **(X)**

THE CLONE MASTER
1978 TV
PRODUCER/SCREENWRITER: John D.F. Black
DIRECTOR: Don Medford
Art Hindle as a biochemist clones 13 exact replicas of himself in a desperate attempt to create a new television series. A dumb pilot, with Ralph Bellamy in his 17th made-for-TV movie.

CLONES
1973 Film Makers International
PRODUCER: Paul Hunt
DIRECTORS: Paul Hunt, Lamar Card
SCREENWRITER: Steve Fisher

Gregory Sierra, an early defector from the *Barney Miller* show, chases around clones of government scientists for about two hours (with commercial breaks). Also with Bruce Bennett, John Barrymore, Jr., and Angelo Rossitto.

THE CLONUS HORROR: See PARTS — THE CLONUS HORROR.

CLOSE ENCOUNTERS OF THE THIRD KIND
1977 Columbia
PRODUCERS: Julia Phillips, Michael Phillips
DIRECTOR/SCREENWRITER: Steven Spielberg
Jaws star Richard Dreyfuss discovers a UFO with friendly little musically inclined beings from outer space. In the tradition of remixed 12-inch disco singles, the confused consumer was offered three different versions of this box-office bonanza. In order to catch every frame, real fans watched the original, the Special Edition (available on videocassette), and the complete network television version (which includes all footage from both others). With Teri Garr, François Truffaut, and Roberts Blossom. Cinematography by Vilmos Zsigmond, Laszlo Kovacs, Douglas Trumbull, and others. Music by John Williams.

C'MON LET'S LIVE A LITTLE
1967 Paramount
PRODUCERS: June Starr, John Hertelandy
DIRECTOR: David Butler
SCREENWRITER: June Starr
Lots of ridiculous liberal movies about campus unrest were released in the '60s. Here's one that took a more conservative view. Singer Bobby Vee (no longer very popular by '67) plays Jesse Crawford, an Arkansas folk singer who gains entrance into a college after saving the dean's daughter (singer Jackie Deshannon) from a car accident. After being

used by campus radical John Ireland, Jr., to draw a crowd at a free-speech rally, Bobby punches him. The dean shows up and "completely wins over the student body." A fantasy? With Eddie Hodges and Patsy Kelly. By the director of many of Shirley Temple's best known features.

COBRA WOMAN

1944 Universal
PRODUCER: George Waggner
DIRECTOR: Robert Siodmak
SCREENWRITERS: Gene Lewis, Richard Brooks
Don't miss this extraordinary Hollywood Technicolor fantasy. Maria Montez stars as the queen of a mythical kitsch kingdom—and as her evil sister who has taken over the throne. With Jon Hall as Ramu, Lon Chaney, Jr., as the tongueless captain of the guards, Sabu, and Edgar Barrier as a bad guy who ends up in a pit of sharp spikes. The most outrageous of the Montez-Hall adventures. *Cobra Woman*'s director, Robert Siodmak, worked here during the war, turning out *films noirs* like

The Phantom Lady, The Killers, and *Crisscross.* He later returned to his native Germany, where he directed until his death in 1973.

CODE NAME: MINUS ONE: See GEMINI MAN.

CODE NAME: TRIXIE: See THE CRAZIES.

CODE OF SILENCE

1960 Sterling (B&W)
PRODUCER: Berj Hagopian
DIRECTOR: Mel Welles
SCREENWRITERS: Norman Toback, Allan Adrian
ALSO RELEASED AS: *Killer's Cage*
A quiet Mexican village erupts as syndicate hit men and Senate committee investigators fight over a former racketeer given to dropping names in his fiction. Terry Becker (Chief Sharkey on *Voyage to the Bottom of the Sea*) stars, with Elisa Loti and Welles' AIP friends Ed Nelson and Bruno Ve Sota. Filmed on location.   –CB

On the set of College Confidential, *producer Al Zugsmith (in T-shirt), Steve Allen, Mamie Van Doren, and Conway Twitty (standing).*

A COLD NIGHT'S DEATH

1973 TV
PRODUCER: Paul Junger Witt
DIRECTOR: Jerrold Freedman
SCREENWRITER: Christopher Knopf

Psychological science fiction about snowbound research scientists studying monkeys. With Robert Culp and Eli Wallach. The chimps surprise everyone in the end.

COLLEGE CONFIDENTIAL

1960 Universal (B&W)
PRODUCER/DIRECTOR: Albert Zugsmith
SCREENWRITER: Irving Shulman

The producer of *High School Confidential* steps out and directs the inevitable sound-alike follow-up. This time the small-time scandals involve sex instead of drugs. Steve Allen stars as a professor arrested for corrupting the minds of minors. Even his real-life wife Jayne Meadows can't stop him from ogling Mamie Van Doren! Conway Twitty sings. Walter Winchell, Earl Wilson, and Sheilah Graham play themselves. With Rocky Marciano, Elisha Cook, Jr., Ziva Rodann, and Mickey Shaughnessey (*Jailhouse Rock*). Zugsmith made *Sex Kittens Go to College* next.

A crazed but successful artist paints with his own blood in H. G. Lewis' Color Me Blood Red.

COLLISION COURSE: See BAMBOO SAUCER.

COLONEL MARCH INVESTIGATES

1954 Criterion (England) (B&W)
PRODUCER: Donald Ginsberg
SCREENWRITER: Led Davis

A feature made from episodes of *Colonel March of Scotland Yard*, a British television series. As Colonel March, Boris Karloff sports an eyepatch.

COLOR ME BLOOD RED

1965 Box Office Spectaculars
PRODUCER: David Friedman
DIRECTOR/SCREENWRITER:
Herschell Gordon Lewis

The third of Lewis' notorious gore films made in Florida stars Don Joseph, who bears a resemblance to Anthony Hopkins, as an artist who becomes a local celebrity after he starts painting with his own blood. When it finally dawns on him that he has only so much, he starts killing his models for their blood. Like *Blood Feast* and *2000 Maniacs* before it, it contains some graphic scenes, still shocking today. With the usual inept acting and a hydro-bike. "They say Gauguin was obnoxious too!" proclaims the mad painter. Lewis was also the film's cinematographer.

THE COLOSSUS OF NEW YORK

1958 Paramount (B&W)
PRODUCER: William Alland
DIRECTOR: Eugene Lourie
SCREENWRITER: Thelma Schnee

When renowned scientist Ross Martin dies, brother Otto Kruger transplants his brain in a robot (played by Ed Wolff). The eyeless, 12-foot-tall robot, wearing a cape and metal braces on his shoes to support his great weight, is one of the screen's finest science-fiction creations. The brain malfunctions and the formerly peaceful scientist becomes a lethal creature. Only his little son (Charles Herbert) can relate to the scary giant. His wife (Mala Powers) doesn't understand at all. With Robert Hutton and John Baragrey.

COLOSSUS: THE FORBIN PROJECT

1969 Universal
PRODUCER: Stanley Chase
DIRECTOR: Joseph Sargent
SCREENWRITER: James Bridges

A well-made and scary science-fiction film with a plot similar to *Demon Seed*'s. Dr Forbin (Eric Braeden of *Rat Patrol*) develops Colossus, the ultimate computer. The thinking machine demands that it be able to communicate with the equally powerful Soviet computer, Guardian. Together they launch missiles, destroying major cities as a part of a plan to take over the world. With Susan Clark and William Schallert. Music by Michael Colombier.

COMA

1978 United Artists
PRODUCER: Martin Erlichman
DIRECTOR/SCREENWRITER: Michael Crichton

Thriller about black-market organ transplants. The cast (including Geneviève Bujold, Richard Widmark, Rip Torn, Michael Douglas, Elizabeth Ashley, and Lois Chiles) is good and there are some chilling moments, but on the whole the film is forgettable.

THE COMEBACK

1978 Bedford (England)
PRODUCER/DIRECTOR: Pete Walker
SCREENWRITER: Murray Smith
ORIGINALLY RELEASED AS: *The Day the Screaming Stopped*

Popular (?) crooner Jack Jones in his first horror movie! He plays a middle-of-the-road hitmaker who loses his mind while recording a new album in a mansion. In one cheat scene designed to throw you off the track of the killer, his manager (David Doyle) is shown wearing a wig, a dress, and makeup. Otherwise it's a pretty good feature, with Richard Johnson, Sheila Keith (*The Confessional*), and Pamela Stephenson. Walker did *The House of Long Shadows* next. (R)

COMEDY OF TERRORS

1964 AIP
PRODUCERS: James H. Nicholson, Samuel Z. Arkoff
DIRECTOR: Jacques Tourneur
SCREENWRITER: Richard Matheson
ALSO RELEASED AS: *The Graveside Story*

Despite all appearances, this is not a Corman film. It's a lesser effort by the director of classics like *Cat People* and *I Walked With a Zombie*. Vincent Price stars as Waldo Trumbull, a lazy New England funeral parlor owner. He blackmails Felix (Peter Lorre, in his last featured role) to aid him in helping business by killing people, including the landlord (Basil Rathbone), a Shakespeare-spouting cataleptic who keeps "returning to life." Boris Karloff doesn't have much to do as Price's grizzly, senile father-in-law. Joyce Jameson is Price's opera-singing wife. Joe E. Brown shows up long enough to yell.

COMIN' AT YA!

1981 Filmways (Italy) (3-D)
PRODUCER: Tony Anthony
DIRECTOR: Ferdinanco Baldi
SCREENWRITERS: Lloyd Battista, Wolf Lowenthal, Gene Quintano

The first 3-D movie of the '80s was a big hit. It's a terrible spaghetti Western produced by its star, Tony Anthony. His woman (and dozens of other beauties) are kidnaped by two slobbering brothers, Gene Quintano (the executive producer) and Richard Palacius (*The Good, the Bad, and the Ugly*). The white slavers are so dumb that they leave the women on the desert to die. Almost everybody in the cast dies. The flaming arrows are very effective, but the endless shots of everything imaginable dribbling, falling, or shooting at the audience gets pretty tedious. Look out for the bats, rats, playing cards, and more bad 3-D movies to follow. *Revenge of the Shogun Women*, a re-release from Hong Kong, and *Parasite* also ran in '81. **(R)**

THE COMING

1980 International Films
PRODUCER/DIRECTOR/SCREENWRITER:
Bert I. Gordon

Teen terror idol Susan Swift, who screamed her way into your heart as *Audrey Rose*, returns as Loreen. Her teen routine is suddenly interrupted when her father from another life leaps the time barrier to enlist her aid in saving his daughter from being burned as a witch. Meanwhile, Loreen is being invaded by a strange evil force that gives her the ugliest case of acne ever captured on film, as well as a slimy, blood-thirsty parasite that creeps out of her every once in a while. Though at this writing there has not been a U.S. release, this could crop up on TV when you least expect it. With Guy Stockwell and Tisha Sterling. **(R)**   –BM

COMMUNION: See ALICE, SWEET ALICE.

COMPUTER KILLERS: See HORROR HOSPITAL.

CONAN, THE BARBARIAN

1982 Universal
PRODUCER: Edward Summer
DIRECTOR: John Milius
SCREENWRITERS: John Milius, Oliver Stone

This expensive entry in the early '80s sword-and-sorcery sweepstakes is a sprawling adaptation of Robert E. Howard's pulp stories starring non-actor muscleman Arnold Schwartzenegger (previously in *Hercules in New York*). It features a convincing giant snake, a tough female love interest (dancer Sandahl Bergman), and a few fun characters (surfing champ Gerry Lopez as a thief and Mako as a cowardly magician), but most of the epic scenes look like Dino De Laurentiis showing off again and wasting millions. As the evil Thulsa Doom, James Earl Jones turns into a snake. Max Von Sydow (fresh from Dino's *Flash Gordon*) is a Viking king. Conan's dad is action film star William Smith. Most of the blood and gore was cut prior to the release. It might have helped. Schwartzenegger, who looks perfect for the role, will be remembered mostly for punching out a camel. Four sequels are planned. **(R)**

THE CONCORDE — AIRPORT '79

1979 Universal
PRODUCER: Jennings Lang
DIRECTOR: David Lowell Rich
SCREENWRITER: Eric Roth

Airport No. 4 and funnier than ever. On the way to the 1980 Moscow Olympic Games, a plane with a bomb on board is shot at by missiles and flies upside down in *Star Wars*–influenced scenes. Some of the big stars with mouths above their noses are: George Kennedy (again) and Alain Delon as pilots, Mercedes McCambridge as a Russian coach, Susan Blakely, Robert Wagner, Eddie Albert, Bibi Andersson, Cicely Tyson, Martha Raye, Jimmy Walker, David Warner, John Davidson(!) and Charro(!!). With more bedroom scenes and suicides than any other disaster film. What happened to *Airport '81* and *Airport '83*?

THE CONFESSIONAL

1976 Atlas (England)
PRODUCER/DIRECTOR: Peter Walker
SCREENWRITER: David McGillivray
ALSO RELEASED AS: *House of Mortal Sin*

A violently anti-Catholic horror film. Anthony Sharpe as a demented old priest tape-records confessions so he can blackmail young women. Later, he kills the people who are on to him by strangling one with a rosary, giving one a poisoned host, and bashing another with an incense burner. Sheila Keith is his glass-eyed servant. It's the most unsettling of Walker's well-made features. With Stephanie Beacham and Mervyn Johns. Sharpe played a minister in *A Clockwork Orange*. Earlier Walker features included *School for Sex* and *Hot Girls for Men Only*. **(R)**

CONFESSIONS OF AN OPIUM EATER

1962 Allied Artists
PRODUCER/DIRECTOR: Albert Zugsmith
SCREENWRITER: Robert Hill, Seton I. Miller
ALSO RELEASED AS: *Souls for Sale, Secrets of a Soul, Evil of Chinatown*

Incredible, trashy drug adventure starring Vincent Price as Thomas de Quincy, an early 19th-century adventurer involved with helping runaway slave girls and victims of a tong war in San Francisco. Garbed in black from head to toe, Price narrates his adventures. The highlight: a long, unbelievable, violent, slow-motion drug trip/fight scene—worth the price of admission! In the late '60s this Albert Zugsmith epic was a favorite of drugged patrons at midnight shows. At the slave auction where beautiful Oriental girls are displayed in hanging bamboo cages, Vincent befriends a tiny wisecracking female Oriental dwarf. The tong leader turns out to be a woman in drag and the story ends in a sewer. At least real Orientals were given major roles for a change. With Philip Ahn, Linda Ho, Richard Loo, Victor Sen Yung, and Alicia Li (as Ping Toy). It was Zugsmith's last production shown legally to viewers under 18. His next was *Fanny Hill*, directed by Russ Meyer.

CONFIDENTIAL AGENT

1945 Warner Brothers (B&W)
PRODUCER/SCREENWRITER: Robert Buckner
DIRECTOR: Herman Schumlin

Charles Boyer is a Spanish loyalist in England involved with Lauren Bacall (in her second film). Peter Lorre is a double-crossing Spaniard. With George Coulouris, George Zucco, Victor Francen, and Wanda Hendrix. The cloak-and-dagger plot came from a Graham Greene novel of the same title. Cinematography by James Wong Howe.

CONGO CROSSING

1956 Universal
PRODUCER: Howard Christie
DIRECTOR: Joseph Pevney
SCREENWRITER: Richard Alan Simmons

George Nader and Virginia Mayo star in an African adventure about crooks, tsetse flies, and construction by the ex-actor director of *Female on the Beach*. Peter Lorre is the smiling Colonel Orlanda of Congotanga. Rex Ingram is a doctor and Michael Pate is a bad guy.

THE CONQUEROR

1956 RKO
PRODUCER/DIRECTOR: Dick Powell
SCREENWRITER: Oscar Millard

John Wayne in a spiked helmet as Genghis Khan and Susan Hayward as a Tartar princess provide lots of laughs, but the story behind this historical mess makes it even more interesting. The multi-million-dollar epic was the last personal project of that reclusive eccentric Howard Hughes. After its release (beginning with premieres in capital cities all over the world), Hughes sold RKO, then bought back *Jet Pilot* (an earlier Wayne film) and this epic for $12 million so only he could see them. *The Conqueror* was shot in Utah, near the site of atomic-bomb tests. Evidence is mounting that the director and several of the cast and many crew members, not to mention the local Indians who were hired to play Mongol warriors, have died slow painful deaths because of exposure. Multi-leveled madness, now unspooled for the masses again. With Agnes Moorehead, William Conrad, Thomas Gomez, Pedro Armendariz, John Hoyt, and Lee Van Cleef.

THE CONQUEROR WORM

1968 Tigon/AIP (England)
PRODUCER: Arnold Lewis Miller
DIRECTOR/SCREENWRITER: Michael Reeves
ALSO RELEASED AS: *The Witchfinder General*

AIP took this excellent tale of witch-hunting in 17th-century England, changed the title, and had Vincent Price recite Poe's "The Conqueror Worm" over the credits. It has nothing to do with Poe. Price, in one of his most restrained and humorless roles, is Matthew Hopkins, the Witchfinder General. The corrupt "public servant" tortures and blackmails female victims for money, power, and sex. When a young soldier (Ian Ogilvy) discovers that his fiancée (Hillary Dwyer) has been raped by Hopkins' brutal assistant (Robert Russell), he vows to track and kill the guilty pair. The violence ends when Price is hacked to death by an axe. With Patrick Wymark (as Cromwell), Rupert Davies, and Wilfrid Brambell (Paul's granddad in *A Hard Day's Night*). It was the third and last feature by 24-year-old Michael Reeves, who apparently killed himself in '69. Ian Ogilvy stars in all three of Reeves' unique films.

CONQUEST OF MYCENE

1963 Avco Embassy-TV (Italy/France)
PRODUCER: Bruno Turchetto
DIRECTOR: Giorgio Ferroni
SCREENWRITERS: Remigio Del Grosso, Giorgio Ferroni
ORIGINALLY RELEASED AS: *Ercole Contro Moloch*

Gordon Scott plays Glauco, the son of the late king of Mycene. He calls himself Hercules (to insure a better European box office) and fights the evil queen's son, Moloch. Scott eventually played the real thing in *Hercules and the Princess of Troy*, a 1967 TV pilot. With Rosalba Neri, Michel Lemoine, and Arturo Dominici.

CONQUEST OF SPACE

1955 Paramount
PRODUCER: George Pal
DIRECTOR: Byron Haskin
SCREENWRITER: James O'Hanlon

George Pal never forgave Paramount for cutting the budget and adding a love-story subplot to his planned follow-up to *Destination Moon*. Based on *The Mars Project* by Werner Von Braun, it still managed to depict wonders like an orbiting wheel-shaped space station. The story includes an only-in-the-'50s ending. The captain (Walter Brooke) decides that a trip to Mars is a blasphemy against God and tries to sabotage the landing. When the crew lands on Christmas day and is about to die of thirst, the friendly guy in the sky shows his approval by making it snow! With Eric Fleming (soon visiting *The Queen of Outer Space*), William Hopper, Mickey Shaughnessy, Phil Foster, Ross Martin, Benson Fong, and Joan Shawlee.

CONQUEST OF THE PLANET OF THE APES

1972 20th Century-Fox
PRODUCER: Arthur P. Jacobs
DIRECTOR: J. Lee Thompson
SCREENWRITER: Paul Dehn

The baby chimp from *Escape From...* grows up to be Roddy McDowall (formerly the dad). Roddy as Caesar becomes a slave/pet to Governor Don Murray and leads all the other apes in a revolt. Ricardo Montalban returns from the previous film. The ape makeup looks inferior the fourth time around. With Natalie Trundy, wife of Arthur P. Jacobs, who produced the entire series.

THE CONSPIRATORS

1944 Warner Brothers (B&W)
PRODUCER: Jack Chertok
DIRECTOR: Jean Negulesco
SCREENWRITERS: Vladimir Pozner,
Leo Rosten

Another of Warner's "remember *Casablanca*" films, with Paul Henried as a Dutch guerrilla leader in Lisbon. He meets mysterious Hedy Lamarr, suspicious Sidney Greenstreet, and mute Peter Lorre. With Victor Francen and Carol Thurston.

THE CONSTANT NYMPH

1943 Warner Brothers (B&W)
PRODUCER: Henry Blanke
DIRECTOR: Edmund Goulding
SCREENWRITER: Kathryn Scola

A British woman (Joan Fontaine) living in an alpine retreat falls in love with her piano teacher, an unsuccessful composer (Charles Boyer). Peter Lorre, in a rare non-menacing role, is a musician. With Alexis Smith, Brenda Marshall, and Charles Coburn. Based on a romantic novel by Margaret Fennedy which had already been filmed twice in England.

CONTINENTAL TWIST: See TWIST ALL NIGHT.

CONVICTS FOUR

1962 Allied Artists (B&W)
PRODUCER: A. Ronald Lubin
DIRECTOR/SCREENWRITER: Millard Kaufman

Ben Gazzara stars as John Resko, a troublesome convict in prison for life. When his artistic ability is discovered and encouraged, he becomes rehabilitated, famous, and paroled! The story is said to be true! Vincent Price plays the art critic who helps make him famous. Stuart Whitman is a guard. Ray Walston is Iggy, a comical psychotic, and Sammy Davis, Jr., is Wino, "the Halloween bandit." With Rod Steiger, Broderick Crawford, Dodie Stevens, Jack Albertson, and Reggie Nalder.

THE COOL AND THE CRAZY

1958 AIP (B&W)
PRODUCER: E. C. Rhoden, Jr.
DIRECTOR: William Witney
SCREENWRITER: Richard C. Sarafian

Dick Bakalyan looking for pot money in The Cool and the Crazy.

The second E.C. Rhoden production filmed in Kansas City, after Robert Altman's *The Delinquents*. Old-timer Witney has trouble keeping up with Scott Marlowe, Gigi Perreau, Richard Bakalyan, and Dick Jones in this high school dope exposé. Eddie the pusher gives the local kids a taste; service-station holdups and murder follow. Or: "Seven savage punks on a binge of violence!" as the ads promised. Nice, unfamiliar locations. Originally released with *Dragstrip Riot*. —CB

THE CORPSE GRINDERS
1971 Geneni
PRODUCER/DIRECTOR: Ted V. Mikels
SCREENWRITERS: Arch Hall,
  Joseph L. Cranston

An odd little horror comedy from the creator of *The Astro-Zombies*. A cat-food company with crippled derelict employees buys bodies from a grave-robbing couple to can and sell. Cats eating the tasty meat become savage, attacking their owners, which leads to an investigation by undercover veteri-narians. The machine of the title is a painted cardboard box. A body goes in one end and hamburger meat is pushed through holes in the other, falling into a bucket. The dialogue, acting, and sets are typically bad. Producer-director Mikels was also editor and music direc-tor on the film. It was often co-billed with TV's *The Worm Eaters*.

THE CORPSE VANISHES
1942 Monogram (B&W)
PRODUCER: Sam Katzman
DIRECTOR: Wallace Fox
SCREENWRITER: Harvey Gates

"Horror to make your hair stand on end!" the ads enticed. Bela Lugosi is Dr. Lorenz, a botanist who sends or-chids to young brides and then kidnaps them to provide glandular injections for his young-looking 80-year-old wife

(Luana Walters). Bela is aided by an old lady (Minerva Urecal), her idiot son (Frank Moran), and a dwarf (An-gelo Rossitto). Bela and his wife sleep in matching coffins. Like all of Bela's Monogram quickies, a must.

CORRIDOR OF MIRRORS
1948 Universal (England) (B&W)
PRODUCER: Rudolph Cartier
DIRECTOR: Terence Young
SCREENWRITERS: Rudolph Cartier,
  Edana Romney

Eric Portman thinks he and Edana Romney are reincarnated lovers from 400 years ago. Christopher Lee makes his film debut in a small part. Filmed in France.

CORRIDORS OF BLOOD
1958 MGM (England) (B&W)
PRODUCERS: John Croydon, Charles Vetter
DIRECTOR: Robert Day
SCREENWRITER: Jean Scott Rogers
ORIGINALLY RELEASED AS: *The Doctor from Seven Dials*

In 1840s London, Dr. Bolton (Boris Karloff) experiments with anesthesia. He becomes addicted to his experimental drugs and is humiliated when a patient rises from the operating table, attacking doctors. The well-meaning Bolton is blackmailed by two loathsome grave robbers, Black Ben (Francis de Wolff) and Resurrection Joe (Christopher Lee), who force him to sign false death certificates. Francis Mathews is the doctor's son. With Adrienne Corri, Betta St. John, and Nigel Green. Lee is good in his small role. Made at the same time as *The Haunted Strangler,* but not released theatrically here until 1963. Richard Gordon was executive producer.

CORRUPTION

1968 Columbia (England)
PRODUCER: Peter Newbrook
DIRECTOR: Robert Hartford-Davies
SCREENWRITERS: Donald Ford, Derek Ford
A laughably sleazy gem that had a great American ad campaign: "This Is Not a Woman's Picture! No women will be allowed in alone!" The ad shows a crowd of unescorted female would-be filmgoers being turned away by a cop. A brilliant surgeon (Peter Cushing) takes his beautiful model/fiancée (Sue Lloyd) to a party. He gets in a jealous fight with a photographer and a hot floodlight disfigures her face. Using a laser beam and new skin, he can restore her beauty—temporarily. Cushing decapitates topless prostitutes and stores their heads in the refrigerator. One day his house is besieged by a group of demented hippies, and the laser beam goes out of control, zapping and killing everybody around. At the end, Cushing wakes up from a dream and takes his beautiful model/fiancée (Sue Lloyd) to a party . . . . **(R)**

THE COSMIC MAN

1958 Allied Artists (B&W)
PRODUCER: Robert A. Terry
DIRECTOR: Herman Green
SCREENWRITER: Arthur C. Pierce
A mini-budget film influenced by *The Day the Earth Stood Still.* John Carradine plays a friendly, misunderstood alien who arrives in a giant golf ball. He has black skin and a white shadow! He passes as an earthling by wearing a trenchcoat, sunglasses, and a hat. Besides passing for white, he can become invisible. He also cures a crippled kid. Only scientists Bruce Bennett and Angela Greene believe in his peaceful mission. With Lynn Osborne and Jean Hagen.

COSMIC MONSTERS

1958 DCA (England) (B&W)
PRODUCER: George Maynard
DIRECTOR: Robert Gunn
SCREENWRITERS: Paul Ryder, Joe Ambor
A scientist (Forrest Tucker) accidentally makes a hole in the ionosphere. Giant killer insects from another dimension invade Earth. An alien (Martin Benson) arrives in a saucer and saves the world. With Gaby André. Based on a BBC-TV serial, *The Strange World of Planet X.* The same company (Eros) made a better film with Tucker the same year, *The Crawling Eye.*

THE COUCH

1962 Warner Brothers (B&W)
PRODUCER/DIRECTOR: Owen Crump
SCREENWRITER: Robert Bloch
Grant Williams plays an ice-pick killer undergoing treatment with psychiatrist Onslow Stevens. He picks the shrink as the victim of his next killing. From a story by Blake Edwards and the director. With Shirley Knight, Anne Helm, and Hope Summers.

COUNT DRACULA

1971 World Entertainment (Spain/
England/Italy/W. Germany)
PRODUCER: Harry Alan Towers
DIRECTOR: Jesse Franco
SCREENWRITERS: Jesse Franco,
August Finochi, Harry Alan Towers,
Carlo Fadda, Milo G. Cuccia,
Dietmar Behnke.

After five films, Christopher Lee was tired of playing Dracula the Hammer Company way. He wanted to do it by the book. The results are okay for a Franco film, but it's still a Franco film and that can't be too good. Lee plays Dracula as an older man with white hair and a mustache who gets younger after drinking blood. Herbert Lom is Professor Van Helsing. Klaus Kinski gives the standout performance as the mad Renfield eating insects in a padded cell. With Franco regulars Soledad Miranda, Maria Rohm, and Fred Williams. The music sounds like outtakes from *The Third Man*. Franco soon returned to more typical fare like *Vampyros Lesbos*.

COUNT DRACULA

1978 TV (England)
PRODUCER: Morris Barry
DIRECTOR: Philip Seville
SCREENWRITER: Gerald Savory

Louis Jourdan is the count in a surprisingly good three-hour videotape presentation originally shown in three parts. Frank Finlay is Van Helsing. With Susan Penhaligon and Judi Bowker. It's fairly faithful to the book and contains some good shocks.

COUNT DRACULA AND HIS VAMPIRE BRIDE: See THE SATANIC RITES OF DRACULA.

COUNT DRACULA'S GREAT LOVE: See DRACULA'S GREAT LOVE.

COUNT YORGA, VAMPIRE

1970 AIP
PRODUCER: Michael Macready
DIRECTOR/SCREENWRITER: Robert Kelljan

This successful low-budget "vampire in modern L.A." movie was originally planned as a sex film. Some of you older male perverts should recognize various of the vampire brides (including Marsha Jordon) as veterans of countless '60s soft-core sex movies. It was wisely turned into a sleazy but PG-rated hit. Star Robert Quarry, a former child actor, was elevated to a brief horror career. Roger Perry, Michael Murphy, and Michael Macready are the heroes. Macready, who also produced, got his more famous father George to narrate. Judith Lang is memorable as a recently bit victim who eats a kitty. With Donna Anders, and Edward Walsh as Brudah, the Count's idiot servant. *The Return Of Count Yorga* showed up the next year. Director Kelljan also acts in movies like *Hell's Angels on Wheels*.

COUNTDOWN

1967 Warner Brothers
PRODUCER: William Conrad
DIRECTOR: Robert Altman
SCREENWRITER: Loring Mandel

Astronaut James Caan is rushed into space when NASA learns the Russians are circling the Moon and are about to land. After personal problems on Earth are resolved, he lands on the Moon and discovers dead Russians. With Robert Duvall, Ted Knight, and Joanna Moore. It was Altman's first theatrical feature since *The James Dean Story* in '57.

COUNTESS DRACULA

1970 Hammer/Fox (England)
PRODUCER: Alexander Paal
DIRECTOR: Peter Sasdy
SCREENWRITER: Jeremy Paul

After playing Carmilla the vampire in *Vampire Lovers*, Ingrid Pitt shows up as a different kind of vampire. As Hungarian Countess Elizabeth Bathory, she remains youthful and beautiful by bathing in the blood of virgins whose nude corpses keep turning up in the nearby village. Nigel Green is a police captain who helps her find victims. Sandor Eles is her young lover. With Lesley-Anne Down and Maurice Denham.

COUNTRY MUSIC U.S.A.: See LAS VEGAS HILLBILLYS.

CRACK IN THE WORLD
1965 Paramount
PRODUCERS: Bernard Glasser,
Lester A. Sansom
DIRECTOR: Andrew Marton
SCREENWRITER: Jon Manchip
Searching for a new source of energy, scientist Dana Andrews sets off an atomic bomb at the center of the Earth that threatens to crack the world in two. Dana's sorry but he's old, has cancer, and suspects his wife (Janette Scott) is fooling around with another scientist (Kieron Moore), so he won't personally miss life too much. The world is barely saved. Part of it breaks off and forms a new moon. Filmed in Spain.

THE CRACK-UP
1936 20th Century-Fox (B&W)
PRODUCER: Samuel G. Engels
DIRECTOR: Mal St. Clair
SCREENWRITERS: Charles Kenyon, Sam Mintz
Brian Donlevy stars as Ace Martin, a pilot planning to steal the design of a revolutionary new war plane. The airport's feeble-minded, bugle-blowing mascot, Col. Gimpy (Peter Lorre), is actually Baron Taggart, a spy also after the plans, which are owned by Ralph Morgan. J. Carrol Naish and Helen Wood co-star.

CRASH!: See DEATH RIDE.

CRASH
1978 TV
PRODUCER: Edward J. Montague
DIRECTOR: Barry Shear
SCREENWRITERS: Donald S. Sanford,
Steve Brown
ALSO RELEASED AS: *The Crash of Flight 401*
A made-for-TV airline-disaster story with William Shatner, Adrienne Barbeau, Eddie Albert, George Maharis, Brooke Bundy, Brett Halsey, Ed Nelson, and band leader Artie Shaw—based on a real crash in the Florida Everglades. Two TV movies were made the same year about the same event. *The Ghost of Flight 401* substituted Ernest Borgnine for Captain Shatner. Take your pick or suffer through both!

CRASH LANDING
1958 Columbia (B&W)
PRODUCER: Sam Katzman
DIRECTOR: Fred Sears
SCREENWRITER: Fred Freiberger
A plane is about to crash in the ocean! Nancy Davis' husband is on it! With Gary Merrill as her husband, the pilot, Roger Smith, and Irene Hervey. By the director of *The Giant Claw* and *Teenage Crime Wave*. One of our First Lady's funniest features.

THE CRASH OF FLIGHT 401: See CRASH.

THE CRATER LAKE MONSTER
1977 Crown International
PRODUCER/DIRECTOR: William R. Stromberg
SCREENWRITERS: William R. Stromberg,
Richard Cardella
For animation fans only. A low-budget, badly acted independent feature starring a briefly seen animated dinosaur. A meteor reactivates the dormant creature; its final battle is with a snow-

plow. It was animated in "Fantamation" by David Allen, who has done good work on other low-budget films such as *Equinox* and *Flesh Gordon* and does great TV ads with Poppin Fresh, the Swiss Miss, and Mrs. Butterworth.

THE CRAWLING EYE
1958 DCA (England) (B&W)
PRODUCERS: Robert S. Baker, Monty Berman
DIRECTOR: Quentin Lawrence
SCREENWRITER: Jimmy Sangster
ALSO RELEASED AS: *The Trollenberg Terror*
A strange cloud is lurking around the Swiss village of Trollenberg, where mountain climbers have been found dead—with their heads ripped off! A lady with ESP (Janet Munro) contacts aliens in the clouds, who have long, deadly tentacles attached to their singular eyeball bodies. She joins with American Forrest Tucker to save humanity from the ghastly alien invasion. This popular and scary film was adapted from a British TV serial. *F-Troop* star Tucker also appeared in *The Cosmic Monsters* and *The Abominable Snowman*, made in England about the same time.

Forrest Tucker rescues a little girl from The Crawling Eye.

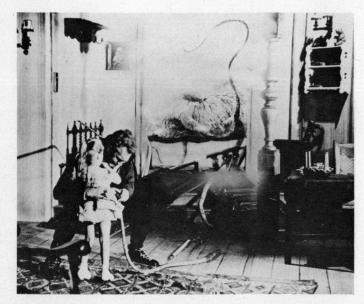

THE CRAWLING HAND
1963 AIP (B&W)
PRODUCER: James F. Robertson
DIRECTOR/SCREENWRITER: Herbert L. Strock
Young Peter Breck (*Shock Corridor*) is a confused teen taken over by the living hand of an astronaut who exploded in space. The hand kills people on its own, then gets the kid to help. The standout memory of this cheap little horror (by the director of *I Was a Teenage Frankenstein*) is the soundtrack. The ultimate rock song—"Papa Oom Mow Mow" by the Rivingtons—is heard twice! With Kent Taylor, Rod Lauren, Alan Hale, Jr., Richard Arlen (*Island of Lost Souls*), Tris Coffin, and Allison Hayes. Also introducing "the sex iceberg" Sirry Steffen. A cat eats the hand in the end. A landmark production.

CRAZE
1974 Warner Brothers (England)
PRODUCER: Herman Cohen
DIRECTOR: Freddie Francis
SCREENWRITERS: Aben Kandel, Herman Cohen
ALSO RELEASED AS: *The Infernal Idol*
Jack Palance stars as an antiques dealer who sacrifices women to his favorite idol, Chuku. Jack keeps Chuku in the cellar. With Diana Dors, Martin Potter, Trevor Howard, Hugh Griffith, Julie Ege, and Suzy Kendall. From the producer of *Berserk!*

CRAZED VAMPIRE: See VIRGINS AND VAMPIRES.

THE CRAZIES
1973 Cambist
PRODUCER: Alvin C. Croft
DIRECTOR/SCREENWRITER: George A. Romero
ALSO RELEASED AS: *Code Name: Trixie*
Box-office flop from Pittsburgh cult director George A. Romero. Panic, paranoia, and general madness prevail after a U.S. Army plane carrying a bac-

terial virus crashes near Evans City, Pennsylvania. The virus gets in the drinking water, transforming the locals into killers. When the army arrives in alienlike suits to save the few remaining sane citizens, they're met by highly hostile and confused folk. In one scene a kind-looking old lady calmly stabs a soldier with a long knitting needle. Like *Night of the Living Dead*, this low-budget local feature relies a lot on gore effects, so theatrical viewing is advised. With Lynn Lowrey. The theme song is "Heaven Help Us."

CRAZY HOUSE
1943 Universal (B&W)
ASSOCIATE PRODUCER: Erle C. Kenton
DIRECTOR: Edward Cline
SCREENWRITERS: Robert Lees,
　Frederic L. Rinaldo
Ole Olsen and Chic Johnson followed their hit *Hellzapoppin'* with another great anarchistic musical comedy. This time they're trying to get money to make a movie. When Universal refuses to back them, they make it independently. Martha O'Driscoll and Patrick Knowles star in a cast including Lon Chaney, Jr., Shemp Howard, Basil Rathbone and Nigel Bruce as Holmes and Watson, Billy Gilbert, Franklin Pangborn, Hans Conreid, the Count Basie Band, the Five Hertzogs, and New York Mayor Fiorello La Guardia.

CRAZY HOUSE: See NIGHT OF THE LAUGHING DEAD.

CRAZY KNIGHTS
1944 Monogram (B&W)
PRODUCER: Sam Katzman
DIRECTOR: William Beaudine
SCREENWRITER: Tim Ryan
ALSO RELEASED AS: *Ghost Crazy*
Shemp Howard, Billy Gilbert, and "Slapsie" Maxie Rosenbloom (the new Three Stooges?) star in this haunted-house comedy. With a gorilla, fake ghosts, and Minerva Urecal. One of 11 (!) Beaudine movies released in '44.

Cloris Leachman takes the law into her own hands as Crazy Mama.

CRAZY MAMA
1975 New World
PRODUCER: Julie Corman
DIRECTOR: Jonathan Demme
SCREENWRITER: Robert Thom
In between *The Mary Tyler Moore Show* and *Phyllis*, Cloris Leachman played a 1950s widow turning to a comic life of crime when she loses her Long Beach beauty parlor. She's joined by her partner (Ann Sothern), her pregnant daughter (Linda Purl), and her daughter's boyfriend (*Happy Days'* Donny Most). They head for Arkansas in a stolen Cadillac and a wood-panelled station wagon with an old lady, a greaser, and a defecting sheriff (Stuart Whitman). The sound track is made up of great '50s hits, including "Black Slacks" and "Transfusion." Director Demme (*Melvin and Howard*) had previously done *Caged Heat*. With Jim Backus, Dick Miller, Beach Dickerson, and director John Milius. Written by Demme's wife, Evelyn Purcell. **(R)**

CREATION OF THE HUMANOIDS

1962 Emerson Films
PRODUCERS: Wesley E. Barry, Edward J. Kay
DIRECTOR: Wesley E. Barry
SCREENWRITER: Jay Simms

An incredible little film about the sterile future after World War III. The small group of remaining humans use super-intelligent, obedient, purplish-green hairless robots to do all the work. Don Megowan (the monster in *The Creature Walks Among Us*) is Craigus, a security officer who distrusts the mechanical men. A scientist has been injecting blood into the emotionless androids, making them more human, and Craigus's girlfriend falls in love with one. The furious Craigus soon gets even more shocking news. Filmed on minimal sets as if it were a play, this short (75-minute) hit has been called "Andy Warhol's favorite movie." With Dudley Manlove (*Plan 9 From Outer Space*).

CREATURE FROM BLACK LAKE

1976 Howco International
PRODUCER: Jim McCollough
DIRECTOR: Joy Houck, Jr.
SCREENWRITER: Jim McCollough, Jr.

A surprisingly effective Bigfoot film with screen veterans Jack Elam and Dub Taylor helping the unknown cast move things along. Two eager college students drive a van to Louisiana to document the sighting of a mythical creature. The production was a happy family affair. The director's famous father owns Howco, the distributor. The producer's son, Jim McCullough, Jr., wrote the screenplay, and also acts and sings.

THE CREATURE FROM THE BLACK LAGOON

1954 Universal (3-D/B&W)
PRODUCER: William Alland
DIRECTOR: Jack Arnold
SCREENWRITER: Harry Essex, Arthur Ross

Richard Denning whomps the unfortunate Creature from the Black Lagoon.

The ads announced: "Centuries of Passion Pent Up in His Savage Heart!" A star is born! After the success of the 3-D film *It Came from Outer Space*, the same production team and star appeared in this 3-D hit featuring a newly created monster that enjoyed fame (and sequels) missing from the screen since the '40s. Members of an archaelogical expedition discover and then are mostly killed off by a prehistoric man/fish. Dedicated scientist Richard Carlson, rich greedy showoff Richard Denning, and the ancient graceful creature all want lovely Julie Adams in her white one-piece bathing suit. The creature, played underwater by swimming champ Ricou Browning, was a masterful creation by Bud Westmore and Jack Keven. Ben Chapman played the ancient monster on land. With Whit Bissell, who spends most of the movie wrapped up like a mummy, and Nestor Paiva. The new star was back a year later in *The Creature Walks Among Us*. A 1980s remake has been announced and cancelled several times.

CREATURE FROM THE HAUNTED SEA

1961 Film Group (B&W)
PRODUCER/DIRECTOR: Roger Corman
SCREENWRITER: Charles Griffith

A quickie horror comedy in the tradition of *Bucket of Blood* and *Little Shop of Horrors*. Corman decided at the last minute to use the same small cast and crew that had just done *The Battle of Blood Island* and *Last Woman on Earth* in Puerto Rico for a third feature there. When a Caribbean island has a revolution, American crook Sparks Moran (Anthony Carbone) plans to help loyalists (and the national treasury) escape on his boat, then kill the men and blame their deaths on a mythical sea monster. Trouble is, there really is a silly-looking monster that eats all of the cast except

for Robert Towne/Edward Wain and his girl Mango. Carbone uses his best Bogey voice. Robert Bean, acting for the first time, gives a stellar performance as a guy who communicates with animal noises. Cubans on the boat dance nonstop, never missing their murdered friends. It should've been a hit. With Betsy Jones-Moreland, Beach Dickerson, and Roger Corman. Music by Fred Katz.

CREATURE OF DESTRUCTION

1967 AIP-TV
PRODUCER/DIRECTOR: Larry Buchanan
SCREENWRITER: Enrique Touceda

Buchanan made four uncredited remakes of AIP '50s science-fiction movies. They all belong on anybody's top ten worst list. This isn't the worst of them, but it's still rotten to the core. If you ever saw *The She Creature* ('56) you know the plot. You also know the dialogue and the music. Instead of Chester Morris as the hypnotist who causes a beautiful girl to become her previous incarnation (a murdering prehistoric monster), we've got worn-out-looking Les Tremayne. Instead of the scary monster in the original, we get a man in a wet suit (look for the zipper) with a fishman mask with fangs and ping-pong ball eyes. The same monster turns up in Buchanan's *It's Alive*. With Aron Kincaid.

CREATURE OF THE WALKING DEAD

1960/65 A.D.P. Productions (Mexico) (B&W)
PRODUCER (U.S. Version): Jerry Warren
DIRECTOR: Fernando Cortés
SCREENWRITERS: Alfredo Varela, Jr., Fernando Cortés
ORIGINALLY RELEASED AS: *La Marca del Muerto*

A scientist revives the body of his dead grandfather. The walking corpse kills for blood to stay strong. In new footage edited into the American release, Katherine Victor conducts a seance and Bruno Ve Sota is a police inspector. The two-in-one movie, in the Jerry Warren tradition, makes little sense. With Rock Madison.

THE CREATURE WALKS AMONG US

1956 Universal (B&W)
PRODUCER: William Alland
DIRECTOR: John Sherwood
SCREENWRITER: Arthur Ross

The creature from the black lagoon returns for a final bash. After being harpooned and burned, he's operated on, leaving him a gill-less, bulky land creature with clothes. The new-model creature (Don Megowan) is after the human female charms of Leigh Snowden this time. Jeff Morrow and Rex Reason are the scientists. They had just starred in *This Island Earth*. Ricou Browning was again the creature in the opening underwater scenes.

THE CREATURE WASN'T NICE

1981 Almi Cinema 5
PRODUCER: Mark Haggard
DIRECTOR/SCREENWRITER: Bruce Kimmel
ALSO RELEASED AS: *Spaceship*

A low-budget spoof of *Alien* starring director Kimmel and Cindy Williams of *Laverne and Shirley*. Patrick Macnee is a mad scientist. Leslie Nielsen is the spaceship commander. Gerrit Graham is the co-pilot. With Kenneth Toby. An alien monster on board the ship sings "I Want to Eat Your Face." Kimmel also directed Williams in *The First Nudie Musical*.

CREATURE WITH THE ATOM BRAIN

1955 Columbia (B&W)
PRODUCER: Sam Katzman
DIRECTOR: Edward L. Cahn
SCREENWRITER: Curt Siodmak

The screen's first mass atomic zombie attack feature. A scientist creates superstrong robot men (with stitches where their skulls were cut open). The zombielike killers are used by gangsters to

Local police and the army battle super-human zombies in The Creature with the Atom Brain.

kill off rivals and meddlesome public officials. It was the first of many fun horrors from director Cahn. In 1981 Roky Erickson recorded a song based on this movie complete with dialogue and a radio report of a killing by a man impervious to bullets.

CREATURE WITH THE BLUE HAND

1967 New World (W. Germany)
PRODUCERS: Horst Wendlandt,
Preben Philipsen
DIRECTOR: Alfred Vohrer
SCREENWRITER: Alex Berg

One of the few German Edgar Wallace thrillers released here in theaters. Klaus Kinski stars (as twins) with Diana Korner and Harold Lepnvitz. The story concerns a cloaked killer stalking a castle and an asylum. It was Kinski's 15th appearance in the Wallace series.

THE CREATURES FROM BEYOND THE GRAVE: See FROM BEYOND THE GRAVE.

CREATURES OF EVIL

1970 Hemisphere (U.S./Philippines)
PRODUCER: Amalia Muhlach
DIRECTOR: Gerardo de Leon
SCREENWRITERS: Ben Feleo, Pierre L. Salas
ALSO RELEASED AS: *Curse of the Vampires*
A man keeps his vampire mom chained in the basement. In the end God cures her. Praise the Lord! A sequel to *The Blood Drinkers*. With a dwarf and a bald vampire.

CREATURES OF THE PREHISTORIC: See HORROR OF THE BLOOD MONSTERS.

THE CREATURE'S REVENGE: See BRAIN OF BLOOD.

UPI 1/7/71: Actress Julie Ege of Norway, who has embarked on a new career as a pop singer. Her first record, on the CBS label, written by John Lennon of Beatles fame, is called "Love." Julie became famous after films like Creatures the World Forgot.

CREATURES THE WORLD FORGOT

1971 Hammer/Columbia (England)
PRODUCER/SCREENWRITER: Michael Carreras
DIRECTOR: John Chaffey
After producing two prehistoric caveman hits with stop-motion dinosaurs, Hammer decided to skip the monsters and concentrate on the sexy cavewomen. Julie Ege, a former Miss Norway, was the selling point, slipping out of a wardrobe of revealing bikinis and furs. To insure bigger audiences of bored kids, they cut the R-rated movie to a PG, making it even more vacant and pointless. Filmed in Africa.

THE CREEPER

1948 20th Century-Fox (B&W)
PRODUCERS: Bernard Small, Ben Pivar
DIRECTOR: Jean Yarborough
SCREENWRITER: Maurice Tombragel
The only American horror film released during dull '48. Onslow Stevens becomes a killer with cat paws. With Eduard Cianelli, Julie Vincent, Ralph Morgan, and Philip Ahn.

Peter Cushing examines the finger of a prehistoric monster in The Creeping Flesh.

Copyright © 1972 World Services Limited. Courtesy of Columbia Pictures.

THE CREEPING FLESH
1972 Tigon/Columbia (England)
PRODUCER: Mike Redbourn
DIRECTOR: Freddie Francis
SCREENWRITERS: Peter Spenceley,
   Jonathan Rumbold

Partially effective gothic science-fiction horror, which seems to be the result of mixing two or more scripts together. Peter Cushing is a scientist who owns an incredible giant skeleton that grows flesh when touched by water. Christopher Lee, an unscrupulous half-brother, steals the skeleton and carries it out in the rain. The resulting creature provides some real shocks. Meanwhile, Cushing has injected his daughter (Lorna Heilbron) with a serum from the skeleton. She becomes a vicious killer and is faced with another homicidal maniac who has just escaped from an asylum—where her dad ends up.

THE CREEPING TERROR
1964 Crown International (B&W)
PRODUCER/DIRECTOR:
   Argyle (Art J.) Nelson, Jr.
SCREENWRITERS: Robert and Alan Silliphant
ALSO RELEASED AS: *Dangerous Charter*

A legendary silent monster movie. That is, there's almost no dialogue, only lame narration. The story of two hairy monsters resembling giant erect penises with suction mouths at the base is undoubtedly one of the top five worst movies of all time. One of the monsters goes to Lake Tahoe (where this was filmed) and eats a fisherman and his son, a chorus girl, patrons at a drive-in movie, and, best of all, some teens at a rock 'n' roll party. The victims have to fake being dragged inside the monster by pushing themselves into its hole/mouth. The feet of people playing the alien are visible. The director (?) later worked as an editor on big-budget films like *The Greatest Story Ever Told.* Co-writer Robert Silliphant also wrote *The Incredibly Strange Creatures . . .* Star Vic Savage is actually director Art J. Nelson.

THE CREEPING UNKNOWN
1956 Hammer/United Artists
   (England) (B&W)
PRODUCER: Anthony Hinds
DIRECTOR: Val Guest
SCREENWRITERS: Richard Landau, Val Guest
ALSO RELEASED AS: *The Quatermass Xperiment*

Hammer Films' first international hit was based on a television series featuring the superscientist Quatermass. American Brian Donlevy ably took over the role for this feature. The only surviving astronaut of a rocket crash (Richard Woodsworth) has a fungus on his hand that slowly consumes him. The resulting giant blob with tentacles is killed in Westminster Cathedral during a live TV broadcast. With Margia Dean and Lionel Jeffries. *Enemy from Space* was the sequel.

CREEPSHOW
1982 Warner Brothers
PRODUCER: Richard Rubenstein
DIRECTOR: George A. Romero
SCREENWRITER: Stephen King

This anthology of stories based on old *E.C.* comic books is sometimes closer to the feel of the originals than the British attempts (*Tales from the Crypt, Vault of Horror*, etc.), but it's a minor effort by Romero. "Something To Tide You Over" is about a jealous husband (Leslie Nielsen) who buries his wife (Gaylen Ross of *Dawn of the Dead*) and her lover (Ted Danson) neck-deep on a beach below tideline. In "Father's Day," a ghoulish surprise guest (John Amplas of *Martin*) visits Viveca Lindfors and Carrie Nye while they're celebrating the anniversary of the death of the family patriarch. College professor Hal Holbrook tries to get rid of his nagging wife (Adrienne Barbeau) after a friend (Fritz Weaver) discovers the living contents of "The Crate." Scriptwriter Stephen King plays a backwoods boy strangely affected by a meteor in "Weeds." A reclusive billionaire (E.G. Marshall) tries to stamp out the vermin of the world in the best episode, "They're Coming to Get You." The tales are humorous but ugly, moralistic, and suitably gory, and all feature "surprise" endings. Makeup by Tom Savini, seen here as a garbage man. A sound track is available. **(R)**

THE CREMATORS
1972 New World
PRODUCER/DIRECTOR/SCREENWRITER:
Harry Essex
An alien sphere absorbs human beings. A low-budget ($40,000) adaptation of *The Dune Rollers* from *Astounding Science Fiction* magazine. By the director of *Octaman*.

CRESCENDO
1969 Hammer/Warner Brothers
PRODUCER: Michael Carreras
DIRECTOR: Alan Gibson
SCREENWRITERS: Jimmy Sangster,
Alfred Shaughnessy

Stephanie Powers goes to France to do research on a deceased composer and runs into James Olson as his crippled dope-addicted son. Untold horrors turn out to be a mad twin locked in the attic. With Margaretta Scott. Similar to Hammer's early *Paranoiac*.

CRIME AND PUNISHMENT
1935 Columbia (B&W)
PRODUCER: B.P. Schulberg
DIRECTOR: Joseph von Sternberg
SCREENWRITERS: S.K. Lauren, Joseph Anthony
Following *Mad Love*, Peter Lorre got another great role, as Raskolnikov, Dostoyevsky's intellectual killer. Edward Arnold co-stars as the detective Porfiri. With Marian Marsh as Sanya, a prostitute. By the director of *The Blue Angel* and later Marlene Dietrich classics.

CRIME IN THE STREETS
1956 Allied Artists (B&W)
PRODUCER: Vincent M. Fennelly
DIRECTOR: Don Siegel
SCREENWRITER: Reginald Rose
Siegel followed *Invasion of the Body Snatchers* with low-budget street realism and juvenile delinquency. John Cassavetes plots to have his gang kill a witness to a crime. He practices the murder on a drunk. Sal Mineo (who had just been in *Rebel Without a Cause*) follows him faithfully. Mark Rydell, later the director of *The Rose* and *On Golden Pond*, is an unhinged gang member. James Whitmore is the understanding social worker.

THE CRIME OF DR. CRESPI
1935 Republic (B&W)
PRODUCER/DIRECTOR: John Auer
SCREENWRITERS: Lewis Graham,
Edwin Olmstead
A lowbudget bastardization of *The Premature Burial*, filmed in New York and starring Erich von Stroheim in his most outrageous role after *The Great Gabbo*.

As Dr. Andre Crespi, he injects a rival with a drug to make him appear dead and has the unfortunate man buried alive. Co-star Dwight Faye is a doctor friend who tries to stop Erich von's mad plan. With Edward Van Sloan.

CRIMES IN THE WAX MUSEUM: See NIGHTMARE IN WAX.

THE CRIMSON ALTAR: See THE CRIMSON CULT.

THE CRIMSON BLADE
1963 Hammer/Columbia (England)
PRODUCER: Anthony Nelson-Keys
DIRECTOR/SCREENWRITER: John Gilling
ALSO RELEASED AS: *The Scarlet Blade*
Cromwell vs. King Charles loyalists in 17th-century England. Lionel Jeffries stars as a ruthless bald bad guy. Oliver Reed is his aide. Jack Hedley and June Thorburn are loyalist lovers.

THE CRIMSON CULT
1968 Tigon/AIP (England)
PRODUCER: Louis M. Heyward
DIRECTOR: Vernon Sewell
SCREENWRITERS: Mervyn Haisman, Henry Lincoln
ALSO RELEASED AS: *Curse of the Crimson Altar, The Crimson Altar*
A pretty pathetic all-star version of H.P. Lovecraft's *The Ordeals in the Witch House*. Christopher Lee is J.D. Morley, owner of Greymarsh Lodge and a reincarnation of Lavina (Barbara Steele), a witch who was burned at the stake 300 years before. Boris Karloff as professor Marsh, an occult expert, helps Mark Eden and Virginia Wetherell escape from the witches. Eighty-one-year-old Karloff, acting in a wheelchair, caught a chest cold during production that led to his death in 1969. When released here in 1970, it was billed as Boris' last. It wasn't. He made four

quickies in Mexico afterward. Barbara Steele looks good with green skin and a goat's horn headdress, but mostly just sits watching nude and S&M scenes that were cut before the release. Michael Gough has his worst role ever as a butler. (M)

THE CRIMSON EXECUTIONER: See THE BLOODY PIT OF HORROR.

THE CRIMSON GHOST
1946 Republic (B&W)
PRODUCER: Ronald Davidson
DIRECTORS: William Witney, Fred C. Brannon
SCREENWRITERS: Alfred DeMono, Basil Dickey, Jesse Duffy, Sol Shor
ALSO RELEASED AS: *Cyclotrode X*
The Crimson Ghost, a great-looking serial villain, uses death rays and control collars to gain control of Cyclotrode X, a device that short circuits all electricity. The Ghost wears a black shroud and a scary skull mask. Charles Quigley and Linda Sterling star. Clayton Moore (*The Lone Ranger*) is the main thug. The condensed version came out in '66.

THE CRIMSON PIRATE
1952 Warner Brothers (England)
PRODUCER: Harold Hecht
DIRECTOR: Robert Siodmak
SCREENWRITER: Roland Kibbee
Burt Lancaster stars in a pirate spoof featuring a submarine and machine guns (in the 18th century). Torin Thatcher and Christopher Lee are villains. With Eva Bartok (*The Gamma People*). It's become a cult film.

CROCODILE
1979 Cobra Media (Hong Kong)
PRODUCERS: Dick Randall, Robert Chan
DIRECTOR: Sompote Sands
Ridiculous special effects and dialogue, lots of spurting blood, and a rear-projection croc make this one of the

worst in years. Filmed in Thailand and Korea. Presented by Herman Cohen. With Tany Tim. (R)

THE CROSS OF LORRAINE
1943 MGM (B&W)
PRODUCER: Edwin Knopf
DIRECTOR: Tay Garnett
SCREENWRITERS: Michael Kanin, Ring Lardner, Jr., Alexander Esway, Robert D. Andrews

Jean-Pierre Aumont and Gene Kelly are prisoners of war at odds with the Nazis. With Hume Cronyn, Wallace Ford, and Peter Lorre as the sadistic Nazi, Sergeant Berger, who shoots priest Cedric Hardwicke during church services. It was considered a bloody film in the '40s.

CROWHAVEN FARM
1970 TV
PRODUCER/DIRECTOR: Walter Grauman
SCREENWRITER: John McGreevey

Horror story about reincarnated witches who make life miserable for a couple (Hope Lange and Paul Burke) living on an old farm. Lloyd Bochner and John Carradine are warlocks. With an interesting flashback segment and William Smith.

CRUCIBLE OF HORROR
1971 Cannon (England)
PRODUCER: Gabrielle Beaumont
DIRECTOR: Viktor Ritelis
SCREENWRITER: Olaf Pooley
ALSO RELEASED AS: Velvet House

Michael Gough plays a sadistic man who torments his wife (Yvonne Mitchell) and daughter (Sharon Gurney). They kill him but he apparently returns from the dead. It was double-billed here with Cauldron of Blood.

CRUCIBLE OF TERROR
1971 Scotia/Barber (England)
PRODUCER: Tom Parkinson
DIRECTOR: Ted Hooker
SCREENWRITERS: Ted Hooker, Tom Parkinson

BBC-disc-jockey-turned-actor Mike Raven has his first starring role as a mad artist possessed by the spirit of a dead girl who covers bodies in bronze. With Mary Maude and Melissa Stribling.

CRUEL SWAMP: See SWAMP WOMEN.

CRUISE INTO TERROR
1979 TV
DIRECTOR: Bruce Kessler

Dirk Benedict (Battlestar Galactica) and Frank Converse (Movin' On) star in a tale of evil emanating from an ancient sarcophagus brought aboard a pleasure-cruise ship. Who brought the damned thing on in the first place? Was it Christopher George or Lynda Day George (in their third big TV-movie together)? How about Ray Milland, Marshall Thompson, John Forsythe, Hugh O'Brian, Stella Stevens, or Lee Meriwether?

THE CRY BABY KILLER
1958 Allied Artists (B&W)
PRODUCER: Roger Corman
DIRECTOR: Justus Addiss
SCREENWRITER: Leo Gordon

After shooting two hoods in a brass-knuckles attack, 21-year-old Jack Nicholson (in his first role) holes up in a drive-in theater storeroom with three hostages. Television crews arrive and the concession stand cleans up on hot dogs and pop until the police bring in tear gas. Harry Lauter, Leo Gordon, Carolyn Mitchell, Brett Halsey, Ed Nelson, and Mitzi McCall appear; Dick Kallman sings "Cry Baby Cry." Look for Roger Corman as a television cameraman on top of a van. A combo with Hot Car Girl. —CB

A CRY IN THE NIGHT

1956 Warners (B&W)
PRODUCER/SCREENWRITER: David Dortort
DIRECTOR: Frank Tuttle

"A frenzied search, a madman's whim, a girl's life in the balance!" the ads shouted. Infantile psycho Raymond Burr is discovered spying on a couple in Lovers' Loop. After knocking out the boyfriend, he drags policeman's daughter Natalie Wood away to his secret playhouse, where she is dismayed to find a dead puppy under the bed. Tuttle followed this with *Mesa of Lost Women.* The cast includes Brian Donlevy, Edmond O'Brien, and Richard Anderson. —CB

CRY OF THE BANSHEE

1970 AIP (England)
PRODUCER/DIRECTOR: Gordon Hessler
SCREENWRITERS: Jim Kelly,
  Christopher Wicking

An unsatisfying, confused 16th-century witch story. After torturing innocents as witches in *The Conqueror Worm,* Vincent Price is now faced with the real thing. Oona (Elisabeth Bergner), the leader of a Druid cult, sends a demon werewolf in the form of a handsome young man (Patrick Mower) to terrorize and kill Lord Whitman's (Price's) family. With Essy Persson (*I, A Woman*), Hillary Dwyer, Sally Geeson, and Hugh Griffith. The music by Les Baxter is available on a sound track album.

CRY OF THE BEWITCHED

1956 AIP-TV (Mexico)
PRODUCER: Ruben A. Calderon
DIRECTOR: Alfredo Crevena
SCREENWRITER: Julio Albo
ORIGINALLY RELEASED AS: *Yambao*
ALSO RELEASED AS: *Young and Evil*

The granddaughter of a witch uses voodoo to make the overseer of a sugar plantation fall in love with her. Nina Sevilla stars with Ramon Gay. In color.

CRY OF THE WEREWOLF

1944 Columbia (B&W)
PRODUCER: Wallace McDonald
DIRECTOR: Henry Levin
SCREENWRITERS: Griffin Jay, Charles O'Neal

As Queen Celeste of the gypsies, Nina Foch turns into a wolf and kills villagers. With Barton MacLane, Fritz Leiber, Milton Parsons, Blanche Yurka, and Stephen Crane.

CRYPT OF HORROR: See TERROR IN THE CRYPT.

CRYPT OF THE LIVING DEAD

1973 Coast Industries
PRODUCER/SCREENWRITER: Lou Shaw
DIRECTOR: Ray Danton

One of three obscure little horror films directed by actor Ray Danton. This one takes place on Vampire Island, where a 13th-century undead female wearing a tiara is revived by an American engineer. With Mark Damon, Andrew Prince, and Patty Sheppard. One ad shows a skull saying: "She's 700 Years Old And Still Going Strong!" Another shows a woman in a bikini with a wolf head.

CUBAN REBEL GIRLS

1960 Brenner (B&W)
PRODUCER/DIRECTOR: Barry Mahon
SCREENWRITER: Errol Flynn
ALSO RELEASED AS: *Assault of the Rebel Girls.*

Errol Flynn (playing himself) and 17-year-old girlfriend Beverly Aadland help

Castro guerrillas overthrow the Batista regime by smuggling arms to outposts in the Cuban countryside. Featuring "actual footage shot during the star's real-life adventures with Castro rebels!" The cast includes Marie Edmund, Jackie Jackler, and John Mackay. This was Flynn's last film. Producer-director Mahon, also Flynn's agent, became a sex movie tycoon; Aadland worked in nightclubs for a while and married a car dealer from Van Nuys.   –CB

CUCKOO PATROL

1965 Grand National (England) (B&W)
PRODUCER: Maurice J. Wilson
DIRECTOR: Duncan Wood
SCREENWRITER: Lew Schwarz

After musicals starring the Beatles, the Dave Clark Five, and Gerry and the Pacemakers, this film featured the worst of all the British invasion groups— Freddie and the Dreamers—doing the Freddie and dressing up like boy scouts. They also were in *Every Day's a Holiday*, *Seaside Swingers*, and *Out of Sight*.

CULT OF THE COBRA

1955 Universal (B&W)
PRODUCER: Howard Pine
DIRECTOR: Francis D. Lyon
SCREENWRITERS: Cecil Maiden,
    Richard Collins

Faith Domergue is a high priestess who can change into a cobra. Five American GIs who photographed her secret ritual in Asia are surprised to find her in America—out for revenge. All five were later forced to act in TV series: Richard Long (*77 Sunset Strip*), Marshall Thompson (*Daktari*), William Reynolds (*The FBI*), Jack Kelly (*Maverick*), and David Janssen (*The Fugitive*). With Kathleen Hughes. Originally double-billed with *Revenge of the Creature*.

CULT OF THE DAMNED: See *ANGEL, ANGEL, DOWN WE GO*.

CURFEW BREAKERS

1957 Screen Guild (B&W)
PRODUCER: Charles E. King
DIRECTOR: Alex Wells

"Pent-up punks on a penthouse binge!" the ads promised. An obscure youth-on-the-rampage shocker starring Regis Toomey and Paul Kelly as community leaders who investigate teenage drug traffic following the murder of a gas-station attendant by a crazed addict. Cathy Downs, Marilyn Madison, and Sheila Urban are too cool to be careful and "too young to be scared." A Presley stand-in performs "Baby Baby Blues" and "Jump for George." —CB

THE CURIOUS FEMALE

1969 Fanfare
PRODUCER/DIRECTOR: Paul Rapp
SCREENWRITER: Winston R. Paul
Science-fiction sex. In 2177 a master computer runs a sexually liberated world without love, romance, or families. Two people illegally view a 1969 film, *The Three Virgins*, about the only three students at a university who refuse to have premarital sex and why. The viewers are arrested for watching subversive material. Bunny Allister and David Westberg star in both films. With Angelique Pettyjohn. Joe Solomon was executive producer.

CURLEY AND HIS GANG IN THE HAUNTED MANSION: See WHO KILLED DOC ROBIN?

THE CURSE OF BIGFOOT

1975 Universal Entertainment
DIRECTOR: Don Fields
SCREENWRITER: J. T. Fields
Advertised as: "The story of five students who will never be the same!" The shysters at Universal Entertainment took an unreleased (or very obscure) students-on-field-trip monster thing from the early '60s and spliced new footage onto both ends in an attempt to make drive-in audiences think they were getting their money's worth. A creaky specialist lectures a high school class on the limits of knowledge. Flash back to his most horrifying experience, ten years before. William Simonsen and Robert Clymire star. The older section is fairly amusing if you can get that far. Not just another lame speculation movie. —CB

CURSE OF DRACULA: See THE RETURN OF DRACULA.

THE CURSE OF FRANKENSTEIN

1957 Hammer/Warner Brothers (England)
PRODUCER: Anthony Hinds
DIRECTOR: Terence Fisher
SCREENWRITER: Jimmy Sangster
While America was being overrun by atomic monsters and teenagers, the small British Hammer film company singlehandedly revived traditional gothic horror with their hit version of Mary Shelley's famous novel. It was made for $250,000 and grossed millions. It made Peter Cushing (as Dr. Frankenstein) an international star, but Christopher Lee, in his 36th film, hidden under makeup as the creature, didn't achieve star billing in an English-language production until 1964. Unlike the Universal films, it was in color, with blood, severed body parts, and a doctor who didn't just think about his work. Hazel Court as a housekeeper/mistress and Valeree Grant as a maid take Cushing's mind off his ugly creation. Robert Urquhart is the assistant. It was Terence Fisher's 25th feature. He spent the rest of his life directing horror films. Cushing starred in five sequels.

THE CURSE OF KING TUT

1980 TV (England)
PRODUCER: Peter Graham Scott
DIRECTOR: Philip Leacock
SCREENWRITER: Herb Meadows

The discovery of the tomb of Tutankhamen, TV-style, with Raymond Burr as a ridiculous villain. With Eva Marie Saint, Tom Baker, and Robin Ellis.

THE CURSE OF NOSTRADAMUS

1960 AIP-TV (Mexico) (B&W)
PRODUCER: Victor Parra
DIRECTOR: Frederick Curiel
SCREENWRITERS: Charles Toboada, Alfred Ruanova
ORIGINALLY RELEASED AS: *La Maldición de Nostradamus*
See *The Blood of Nostradamus.*

CURSE OF SIMBA: See CURSE OF THE VOODOO.

CURSE OF THE AZTEC MUMMY

1959 AIP-TV (Mexico) (B&W)
PRODUCER: William Calderon Stell
DIRECTOR: Raphael Portillo
SCREENWRITER: Alfredo Salazar
ORIGINALLY RELEASED AS: *La Maldicion de la Momia Azteca*

A lot of American kids were packed off to Saturday matinees to see K. Gordon Murray productions like this one in the '60s. At the time, his name was as well known as Walt Disney or William Castle, thanks to saturation television promotion. The youngsters didn't know they were seeing substandard Mexican films that K. got for a few pesos. In this follow-up to *The Robot vs. the Aztec Mummy*, the evil Dr. Krupp is back after the treasure in a pyramid guarded by Popoca, the tattered Mexican mummy. It was his third appearance. A few years later he returned in *Wrestling Women vs. the Aztec Mummy.*

CURSE OF THE BLACK WIDOW

1977 TV
PRODUCER: Steven North
DIRECTOR: Dan Curtis
SCREENWRITERS: Robert Blees, Earl Wallace
ALSO RELEASED AS: *Love Trap*

A Spider Lady "thriller" with pretty terrible makeup and the following cast: June Lockhart as the mother of Patty Duke and Donna Mills; Vic Morrow as a cop; Tony Franciosa, June Allyson (as Olga), Jeff Corey, Sid Caesar, and Roz Kelley. When even TV movies start changing titles in between showings things can get confusing. Would you be more likely to watch this under its alternate title?

CURSE OF THE BLOOD GHOULS: See SLAUGHTER OF THE VAMPIRES.

THE CURSE OF THE CAT PEOPLE

1944 RKO (B&W)
PRODUCER: Val Lewton
DIRECTORS: Robert Wise, Gunther V. Fritsch
SCREENWRITER: DeWitt Bodeen

Advertised as: "A tender tale of terror!" The stars of *Cat People* return! This "sequel" is a fantasy starring a beautiful little girl (Ann Carter) who sees the friendly ghost of her father's first wife (Simone Simon). It has nothing to do with cat people, but it's a sensitive classic on its own. Kent Smith and Jane Randolph are the dull parents.

CURSE OF THE CRIMSON ALTAR: See THE CRIMSON CULT.

THE CURSE OF THE CRYING WOMAN

1961 AIP-TV (Mexico) (B&W)
PRODUCER: Abel Salazar
DIRECTOR/SCREENWRITER: Rafael Baledon
ORIGINALLY RELEASED AS: *La Maldicion de la Llorona*

"The crying woman" is at the center of a Mexican legend that had already been filmed three times when this version came out. A descendant of the original crying woman inherits a house with ghosts and witches. With Abel Salazar and Rosita Arenas. Imagine paying to see it in a theater in 1969 (when K. Gordon Murray imported it). Now you can pay to see it on video-cassette.

CURSE OF THE DEMON

1956 Columbia (England) (B&W)
PRODUCER: Frank Bevis
DIRECTOR: Jacques Tourneur
SCREENWRITERS: Charles Bennett, Hal F. Chester
ORIGINALLY RELEASED AS: *Night of the Demon*

Classic devil-cult thriller from the director of *Cat People*. As in his Val Lewton features, Tourneur wanted to avoid showing a monster. The producers insisted on adding a demon based on old woodcuts, which is pretty scary but overused. Sensible American psychic investigator Dana Andrews is cursed by accepting a runic parchment from cult leader Niall MacGinnis. The photography and acting is mostly top-notch in a film that almost surpasses the earlier RKO-Lewton hits. With Peggy Cummins.

CURSE OF THE DEVIL

1973 Goldstone (Spain/Mexico)
PRODUCER: Luis Gomez
DIRECTOR: Charles Aured
SCREENWRITER: Jacinto Molina
ORIGINALLY RELEASED AS: *El Retorno de la Walpurgis*

Paul Naschy is *El Hombre Lobo* for the seventh time. Female gypsy devil-worshipers, descended from witches killed by an executioner (also Naschy) 400 years before, turn him into a snarling hairy beast. Most recent Spanish horror movies have had to be cut to get an American R rating. **(R)**

THE CURSE OF THE DOLL PEOPLE

1960 AIP-TV (Mexico) (B&W)
PRODUCER: William Calderon Stell
DIRECTOR: Benito Alazraki
SCREENWRITER: Alfredo Salazar
ORIGINALLY RELEASED AS: *Muñecas Infernales*

Midgets in dark suits and fright masks are delivered to the Mexico City homes of four who must pay for witnessing a forbidden Haitian voodoo ceremony. In the night, the mute death messengers crawl out of their boxes for revenge. The dubbed dialogue will give you a laugh but the little folks are quite another story. Not the average piece of junk. —CB

CURSE OF THE FACELESS MAN

1958 United Artists (B&W)
PRODUCER: Robert E. Kent
DIRECTOR: Edward L. Cahn
SCREENWRITER: Jerome Bixby

A crusty faceless mummylike creature (actually a slave buried in Pompeii when Vesuvius erupted) returns to life and escapes from a box in the back of a truck. He carries off Elaine Edwards. Richard Anderson is the hero.

CURSE OF THE FLY

1965 Lippert/20th Century-Fox (England) (B&W)
PRODUCERS: Robert Lippert, Jack Parsons
DIRECTOR: Don Sharp
SCREENWRITER: Harry Spalding

The only connection between this and the American "fly" films is a teleportation device, the Delambre family name, and a publicity still from *Return of the Fly*. On its own, it's a pretty good horror film. Brian Donlevy continues matter-transmission experiments, with disgusting results. People arrive in a glass case as completely mixed-up mutants, some just blobs of pulsating flesh. One of his sons (George Baker) marries a girl (Carole Gray) who is an escapee from a mental institution. She really doubts her sanity when she discovers her husband's first wife and a few lab assistants, all mutants, locked in the stables. When police arrive looking for the girl, Donlevy tries to escape in the machine and gets lost in the fourth dimension. Actually, he showed up in California, acting in *How to Stuff a Wild Bikini*. With Yvette Rees as the Chinese housekeeper and Burt Kwouk of the *Pink Panther* series.

CURSE OF THE LIVING CORPSE

1963 20th Century-Fox (B&W)
PRODUCER/DIRECTOR/SCREENWRITER:
Del Tenney

A gothic horror film made in Stamford, Connecticut. A millionaire vows to kill all his relatives if he is buried alive. He is, and various in-laws drown, are burned to death, disfigured, etc., as a hooded figure stalks around. The best death is the maid's. Her head is found on the dinner table. This laughable early gore movie stars Roy Scheider in his film debut! With Candace Hilligoss, star of *Carnival of Souls*. When co-billed with *The Horror of Party Beach* (by the same director), patrons were asked to sign a "Fright Release."

CURSE OF THE LIVING DEAD: See KILL BABY KILL.

CURSE OF THE MUMMY'S TOMB

1964 Hammer/Columbia (England)
PRODUCER/DIRECTOR: Michael Carreras
SCREENWRITER: Henry Younger

In the 1920s, American showman Fred Clark brings a mummy to England. The mummy of Ra-Antef (Dickey Owen) goes on a killing spree and kidnaps Jeanne Roland and carries her through the sewers until the final battle with the reincarnation of his brother (Terence Morgan), who killed him. One of Hammer's routine and unrelated mummy films.

CURSE OF THE MUSHROOM PEOPLE: See ATTACK OF THE MUSHROOM PEOPLE.

CURSE OF THE STONE HAND

1946/59/65 Associated Distributors Pictures (Mexico/Chile) (B&W)
PRODUCER/DIRECTOR (U.S. version):
Jerry Warren
DIRECTORS: Carl Schleipper, Carlos Hugo Christensen
SCREENWRITERS: Amos Powell, Marie Laurent

A two-part horror film with new American footage resulting in amusing chaos. John Carradine is an evil hypnotist. Katherine Victor is somebody's sister. With Lloyd Nelson. Narrator Bruno Ve Sota tries vainly to hold the plot together. The title story is a shortened 1959 Mexican film. "The Suicide Club" is a condensed 1946 film from Chile. Probably your only chance to see a Chilean horror movie.

CURSE OF THE SWAMP CREATURE

1966 AIP-TV
PRODUCER/DIRECTOR: Larry Buchanan
SCREENWRITER: Tony Huston

A mad doctor in the Florida Everglades creates bulky reptile monsters with ping-

The exciting climax of Larry Buchanan's Curse of the Swamp Creature.

Courtesy of Orion Pictures Corporation.

pong ball eyes. Most of them live about three minutes. John Agar arrives, sits in an easy chair, and smokes cigarettes. The black natives dance and burn a likeness of the evil doctor. A new swamp creature (who used to be the doctor's wife) leaves the lab and promptly falls into a pit of gators after being called a hag. An all-time favorite of American insomniacs. With Francine York (*Space Monster*).

CURSE OF THE UNDEAD
1959 Universal (B&W)
PRODUCER: Joseph Gershenson
DIRECTOR: Edward Dein
SCREENWRITERS: Edward and Mildred Dein
The first vampire Western! Rancher Kathleen Crowley hires a gunslinger who turns out to be a bloodsucker. Eric Fleming, as a minister, kills him with a bullet with a cross carved on it. Michael Pate, a minor villain in many films, stars as the vampire, Don Drago Robles, in all-black clothes, of course. With John Hoyt and Bruce Gordon.

CURSE OF THE VAMPIRE: See *THE PLAYGIRLS AND THE VAMPIRE.*

CURSE OF THE VAMPIRES: See *CREATURES OF EVIL.*

CURSE OF THE VOODOO
1965 Allied Artists (England/U.S.) (B&W)
PRODUCER: Kenneth Rice
DIRECTOR: Lindsay Shonteff
SCREENWRITER: Tony O'Grady
ALSO RELEASED AS: *Curse of Simba*
Game hunter Bryant Halliday is cursed by Chief M'Gobo when he kills a sacred lion. Back in England, he suffers physical and mental anguish, hallucinates, and is constantly feverish. He returns to South Africa and runs over M'Gobo with a jeep, ending the curse. With Dennis Price and Lisa Daniely. A Richard Gordon Production.

THE CURSE OF THE WEREWOLF
1961 Hammer/Universal (England)
PRODUCER: Anthony Hinds
DIRECTOR: Terence Fisher
SCREENWRITER: John Elder
As popular as the Wolfman is, this is the only really good serious Wolfman movie made since the 1941 Chaney version. Except for silver bullets, it has little in common with the accepted lycanthrope lore. It all starts with a pathetic beggar in 18th-century Spain, thrown into prison to rot by a cruel marquis. Years later, a mute servant girl (Yvonne Romain) is locked in with the now crazed, animal-like man. She is raped, escapes, and is found drowning by a professor. On Christmas Eve she dies giving birth to a little Leon, whose

adoptive parents have to put up bars to keep him in at night. As a young man, Leon (Oliver Reed) is sent to a monastery, but he escapes to be with his girlfriend and becomes a powerful snarling monster again. Reed is terrifying as the demonic werewolf and effective as the confused, tortured Leon. The makeup (by Roy Ashton) is great. The film was banned in Spain until 1976. Screenwriter Elder is actually the same person as producer Hinds. Based on *The Werewolf of Paris* by Guy Endore.

CURTAIN CALL AT CACTUS CREEK

1950 Universal (B&W)
PRODUCER: Robert Arthur
DIRECTOR: Charles Lamont
SCREENWRITER: Howard Dimsdale

In the Old West, a performing troupe does skits about the use of alcohol. Vincent Price is a hammy actor. Eve Arden as the mother of Gale Storm and stagehand Donald O'Connor complete the troupe. Walter Brennan is a bank robber.

Oliver Reed stars in Curse of the Werewolf.

HOT STEEL BETWEEN THEIR LEGS...
THE WILDEST BUNCH OF THE 70's!

ROARING THROUGH THE STREETS ON CHOPPED DOWN HOGS!

They steal women...
initiate them into the
pack...sell them
on the black
market of crime!

A MAURICE SMITH & RAY DORN production

THE CYCLE SAVAGES

Starring
BRUCE DERN · CHRIS ROBINSON
MELODY PATTERSON COLOR BY MOVIELAB

Written & Directed by **BILL BRAME** Produced by **MAURICE SMITH**
Associate Producers **ARTHUR GILBERT & FRANK RAGUSA**
Executive Producers **MIKE CURB & CASEY KASEM**
A TRANS AMERICAN FILMS RELEASE

R RESTRICTED Under 17 Requires Accompanying Parent or Adult Guardian

man wearing horns, claws, and a beak) story. John Bromfield (who had just been in *Revenge of the Creature*) stars with Beverly Garland and Tom Payne. Filmed in Brazil. Originally double-billed with *The Mole People*.

CYBORG 2087
1966 Features Film Corporation
PRODUCER: Earle Lyon
DIRECTOR: Franklin Andreon
SCREENWRITER: Arthur C. Pierce
As Garth the Cyborg, Michael Rennie travels back in time to 1965 to prevent Professor Marx (Eduard Franz) from developing radio telepathy that made possible a future dominated by a small ruling class—a world of torture without free thought. The slyly anti-Communist film was originally made for television on an extremely low budget. Garth also finds the time to fall in love with the professor's daughter (Karen Steele). With Wendell Corey (who was in *The Astro-Zombies* next) and Warren Stevens.

THE CYCLE SAVAGES
1969 AIP
PRODUCER: Maurice Smith
DIRECTOR/SCREENWRITER: Bill Brame
Bruce Dern doing what he does best, playing a sadistic mental case. As Keeg, he and his motorcycle gang run a white slavery operation in Las Vegas. High school girls are kidnaped, given LSD, and raped by the bikers before being sold. The hero (Chris Robinson) is an artist who joins up with a gang defector (Melody Patterson). Dern tortures him by putting his hands in a vise. Scott Brady and Steve Brodie are cops. *America's Top 10* host Casey Kasem (also an executive producer) plays Dern's brother. The other executive producer was Mike Curb, now Lieutenant Governor of California. Don't forget to look for the sound track. **(R)**

CURUCU, BEAST OF THE AMAZON
1956 Universal
PRODUCERS: Richard Kay, Harry Rybnick
DIRECTOR/SCREENWRITER: Curt Siodmak
A plantation in the Amazon is the setting of this phony monster (it's just a

CYCLOPS

1957 Allied Artists (B&W)

PRODUCER/DIRECTOR/SCREENWRITER:
Bert I. Gordon

Gloria Talbot hires pilot Lon Chaney, Jr., to take her to Mexico and find her lost husband. Thanks to radiation, her man (and some nearby snakes and animals) are giants. The 50-foot monster is Bert Gordon's dumbest/weirdest special effect. His mutated face is half covered with flabby flesh, half the mouth shows oversize teeth, and of course there is one oversized eye. If he resembles the guy in *War of the Colossal Beast* it's because it's the same actor (Dean Parkins). A trash classic! With James Craig and Tom Drake. It was originally part of an incredible double bill with *Daughter of Dr. Jekyll*—another Gloria Talbot triumph. The theme music is available on *The Fantastic Film Music of Albert Glasser* album.

CYCLOTRODE X: See THE CRIMSON GHOST.

THE D.I.

1957 Warner Brothers (B&W)
PRODUCER/DIRECTOR: Jack Webb
SCREENWRITER: James Lee Barrett

Dragnet creator and star Jack Webb is perfect as a maniacal Parris Island drill sargeant. A recruit (Don Dubbins), desperately trying to get thrown out of the Corps, almost costs Webb his reputation. The boy's mother (Virginia Gregg) visits and asks the sergeant to show no mercy (she had previously lost two sons and her husband in combat). With Lin McCarthy, little Melody Gale, 19 genuine U.S. Marines and Monica Lewis, who sings "(If'n You Don't) Somebody Else Will" in an officer's hangout.

DADDY'S GONE A-HUNTING

1969 National General
PRODUCER/DIRECTOR: Mark Robson
SCREENWRITERS: Larry Cohen,
Lorenzo Semple, Jr.

Mark Robson, once a Val Lewton director, followed his smash *Valley of the Dolls* with this psycho tale concerning the previously off-limits topic of abortion. In San Francisco a British woman (Carol White) discovers she's pregnant. She realizes that her photographer boyfriend (Scott Hylands) is violent and unstable. He wants to get married. She has an abortion. Later she marries a lawyer (Paul Burke), has a baby, and is generally happy. Guess who shows up? The crazed almost-dad demands that she kill her baby and then kidnaps it. Co-writer Larry Cohen later directed his own baby movies, *It's Alive* and its sequel. With Mala Powers. Music by Johnny (later John) Barry. (M)

THE DAFFODIL KILLER: See THE DEVIL'S DAFFODIL.

DAGORA THE SPACE MONSTER

1964 Toho (Japan)
DIRECTOR: Inoshiro Honda
SCREENWRITER: Shinichi Sekizawa
ORIGINALLY RELEASED AS: *Uchu Daikaiju Dogora*

Giant alien flying jellyfish attack in this odd Japanese film involving gangsters and diamonds (which the creatures like to eat). The animated monsters use their tentacles to rip up bridges and buildings.

DALEKS-INVASION EARTH 2150 B.C.

1966 Amicus/Continental (England)
PRODUCER: Max J. Rosenberg,
Milton Subotsky
DIRECTOR: Gordon Flemying
SCREENWRITER: Milton Subotsky

The second feature starring Peter Cushing as Dr. Who, based on the BBC television series. A police constable, thinking the doctor's time machine (the T.A.R.D.I.S.) is a phone booth, accidentally joins Who, his niece, and a grandmother in the future. The alien Daleks use mind control to make slaves out of humans and plan to blast out Earth's core and use it for a spaceship. The doctor, with the help of resistance fighters, wins again. With Andrew Keir, Roberta Tovey, Bernard Cribbins, and Jill Curzon.

DAMIEN OMEN II

1978 20th Century-Fox
PRODUCER: Harvey Bernard
DIRECTOR: Don Taylor
SCREENWRITERS: Stanley Mann, Mike Hodges

Damien the Antichrist is now 13 and played by Jonathan Scott Taylor. William Holden and Lee Grant, his new foster parents, die just as the previous ones did. A helpful raven pecks out the eyes of reporter Elizabeth Shepard and kills old aunt Marion (Sylvia Sidney). Lew Ayres drowns under ice. Damien goes to military school and lots of funerals. With Robert Foxworth and Alan Arbus. *The Final Conflict* became the next, and last, stop for the hit concept. Fox originally planned a longer series but this one didn't make enough money. **(R)**

DAMNATION ALLEY

1977 20th Century-Fox
PRODUCERS: Jerome M. Zeifman, Paul Maslansky
DIRECTOR: Jack Smight
SCREENWRITERS: Alan Sharp, Lukas Heller
Jan Michael Vincent and George Peppard drive around the postholocaust United States in a big tank, fight giant scorpions and cockroaches, pick up Dominique Sanda, and head for Albany. A flop version of Roger Zelazny's novel. With Paul Winfield and Murray Hamilton.

THE DAMNED: See THESE ARE THE DAMNED.

DANCE HALL RACKET

1956 Globe Roadshows (B&W)
PRODUCER: George Weiss
DIRECTOR: Phil Tucker
Lenny Bruce appears in this borderline art-house feature about an FBI operative planted in a dime-a-dance joint to get information on the murder of a merchant seaman. The club is a front for diamond smugglers, honky-tonk hostesses involved in the white slave trade, etc. Tucker made a series of bawdy *After Midnight* adults-only features and then tried to break Hollywood with his incredible *Robot Monster*. See also *Cape Canaveral Monsters*.   —CB

DANGER: DIABOLIK

1968 Paramount (France/Italy)
PRODUCER: Dino De Laurentiis
DIRECTOR: Mario Bava
SCREENWRITER: Dino Maivri
ALSO RELEASED AS: *Diabolik*
John Phillip Law, who had just been in *Barbarella*, stars as the international supercriminal Diabolik. He wears a skintight, head-to-toe black leather suit, from which he emerges to make love to his beautiful assistant (Marisa Mell) under a blanket of stolen bills. An inspector (Michel Piccoli) sets a trap, turning Diabolik into a gold-covered statue. A stylishly futuristic adventure based on the European *Diabolik* comic books. With Terry-Thomas.

DANGER ISLAND: See MR. MOTO ON DANGER ISLAND.

DANGER ROUTE

Amicus/United Artists (England)
PRODUCERS: Max J. Rosenberg, Milton Subotsky
DIRECTOR: Seth Holt
SCREENWRITER: Meade Roberts
Richard Johnson, a busy European B-picture actor, is a secret-service man

UPI 5/13/66: A Radcliffe College girl, known only as "Miss Box 2000," and her date, a metal robot named "The Dalek," which is the star of an English television series and the movie Daleks: Invasion Earth 2150 A.D., draw some amused glances from onlookers as they arrive at New York's Empire State Building for a visit. Miss Box 2000 recently drew national attention with her ad, in the Harvard Crimson, appealing for a temporary husband to free her from dormitory life. "The Dalek" applied for the job and may get it. "The Dalek" is, incidentally, the first monster to visit the Empire State Building with his girl since King Kong, carrying a reluctant Fay Wray, climbed to the skyscraper's pinnacle the hard way, up the outside of the building.

involved with the usual double agents, defecting scientists, and beautiful women, including Carol Lynley, Barbara Bouchet, and Diana Dors, who plays his helpful housekeeper. Sam Wanamaker is a CIA agent.

DANGEROUS CHARTER

1962 Crown International
PRODUCERS: Robert Gottschalk, John R. Moore
PRODUCER/DIRECTOR: Robert Gottschalk
SCREENWRITER: Paul Strait

The high seas adventures of three goofball fishermen who find a dead man and a half-million in heroin aboard the adrift yacht *Medusa.* "What kind of woman?! Snakes for hair!" exclaims one as they find a namesake bust in the master stateroom. A likely story develops as the Coast Guard tells Chris Warfield, Chick Chandler, and Wright King that the vessel is theirs if they will help set a trap for the dope dealers. Richard Foote bites and sings "The Sea Is My Woman" and "Lonely Guitar" repeatedly before his pals arrive for the dope. Sally Fraser, John Zaremba, Peter Forster, and John Pickard co-star. Location scenes filmed in 1958 off Santa Catalina Island.   —CB

DANGEROUS CHARTER: See THE CREEPING FLESH.

DANGEROUS FEMALE: See THE MALTESE FALCON.

DANGEROUS MISSION

1954 RKO (3-D)
PRODUCER: Irwin Allen
DIRECTOR: Louis King
SCREENWRITERS: Horace McCoy, W. R. Burnett, Charles Bennett

Forest fires and avalanches at Glacier National Park in a 3-D Irwin Allen movie! Piper Laurie, who has witnessed a gangland murder, flees to the park.

Victor Mature and Vincent Price soon show up there. One of them is there to kill her. The thickheaded woman can't figure out which. With William Bendix and Betta St. John.

DANGEROUS YOUTH

1958 Warner Brothers (England) (B&W)
PRODUCER: Anna Neagle
DIRECTOR: Herbert Wilcox
SCREENWRITER: Jack Trevor Story
ALSO RELEASED AS: *These Dangerous Years*

A tough Liverpool gang leader (Frankie Vaughan) becomes a popular singer, is drafted, marries his partner (Carole Lesley), and is happy ever after. The would-be Elvis sings top hits like "Cold Cold Shower." With Anna Neagle.

DANTE'S INFERNO

1935 Fox (B&W)
PRODUCER: Sol M. Wurtzel
DIRECTOR: Harry Lachman
SCREENWRITERS: Philip Klein, Robert M. Yost

A carnival disaster movie with an incredible look at Hell. Spencer Tracy as a successful showman brings on the deaths of patrons because of hasty construction. He has a wonderful 10-minute vision of writhing souls that was apparently taken from a silent Italian feature. With Claire Trevor, Henry B. Walthall, Ray "Crash" Corrigan, and Rita Hayworth (then Margarita Cansino) as a dancing girl.

DARBY O'GILL AND THE LITTLE PEOPLE

1959 Buena Vista
PRODUCER: Walt Disney
DIRECTOR: Robert Stevenson
SCREENWRITER: Lawrence Edward Watkin

As Darby, Albert Sharpe meets leprechauns who give him a fiddle. Sean Connery (who sings) and Janet Munro co-star with Estelle Winwood, Jack McGowran, and Kieron Moore. This Irish fantasy with howling banshees, a headless coach driver, and a ghost horse is one of Disney's best.

DAREDEVIL
1971 George Montgomery

From the ads: "I'm waiting for you to die! Die!" Another Southern stock-car epic, starring Dinah Shore's former husband George as a driver plagued by voodoo after being blamed for a track fatality. Lots of steamy action, as is usual with Montgomery's one-man shows. Co-starring Terry Moore of *Why Must I Die?*   —CB

THE DARK
1979 Film Ventures International
PRODUCERS: Dick Clark, Edward L. Montoro
DIRECTOR: John (Bud) Cardos
SCREENWRITER: Stanford Whitmore

A confusing science-fiction monster movie. A creature is stalking L.A., ripping the heads off victims. It also burns people to death with laser vision. The killings are always predicted by a mystic. Apparently the producers decided to make the supernatural monster an alien by adding new scenes. William Devane as an author, Cathy Lee Crosby as a TV newscaster, and Richard Jaeckel as a cop are all involved with the mysterious deaths. With Keenan Wynn, Vivian Blaine, and Casey Kasem. Tobe Hooper was originally set to direct this ill-fated movie. (R)

DARK EYES: See SATAN'S MISTRESS.

DARK EYES OF LONDON: See THE HUMAN MONSTER.

DARK INTRUDER
1965 Universal
PRODUCER: Jack Laird
DIRECTOR: Harvey Hart
SCREENWRITER: Barré Lydon

A superior supernatural story set at the turn of the century. As an occult investigator, Leslie Nielsen discovers a horrible-looking demon from Hell played by Werner Klemperer (*Hogan's Heroes*). The makeup is great. With Judi Meredith and Mark Richman. Originally made as a pilot for the projected *Black Cloak* TV series, but shown in theaters.

DARK PLACES
1972 Cinerama (England)
PRODUCER: James Hanna, Jr.
DIRECTOR: Don Sharp
SCREENWRITERS: Ed Brenan,
  Joseph Van Winkle

Joan Collins, Herbert Lom, and Christopher Lee as a greedy psychiatrist, are involved in a search for hidden money left to Robert Hardy, who is possessed by a murderous ancestor's spirit. With Jan Birkin and Jean Marsh.

THE DARK SECRET OF HARVEST HOME
1978 TV
PRODUCER: Jack Laird
DIRECTOR: Leo Penn
SCREENWRITERS: Jack Guss, Charles E. Israel

A New York City family moves to a New England farm community where the old-fashioned residents, led by Bette Davis as Widow Fortune, practice occult rituals to insure a good harvest. Originally a two-part, five-hour special, it was filmed at Holden Arboretum in Kirkwood, Ohio, and featured a number of Cleveland girls (including Jill Adams) dressed in sheets, moaning through the rituals. Based on Tom Tryon's novel, it has the look of the more recent *Deadly Blessing*. With David Ackroyd, Joanna Miles, Rosanna Arquette, Lina Raymond, Earl Keyes (Cleveland's "Mister Jingaling") as the sherriff, and the voice of Donald Pleasence.

DARK STAR

1972 Bryanston
PRODUCER: Jack H. Harris
DIRECTOR: John Carpenter
SCREENWRITERS: John Carpenter,
Dan O'Bannon

An impressive accomplishment that started as a USC project shot in 16mm and running around 45 minutes. Jack H. Harris put up additional funds, so the original footage was blown up to 35mm and 43 minutes were added. The whole thing cost about $60,000. It received a limited theatrical release in '75, and has since become a midnight and college favorite. Young spacemen fight boredom while on a protracted mission to destroy unstable suns. Except for a purposely laughable beachball alien, the special effects are excellent. Co-scriptwriter Dan O'Bannon also stars as Pinback. He later wrote *Alien*, a somewhat similar film but without *Dark Star*'s comedy. Carpenter went on to demonstrate his directorial skill in *Assault on Precinct 13* and *Halloween*. A soundtrack album is available.

DARK VENTURE

1956 First National Film Distributors
DIRECTOR/SCREENWRITER: John Calvert
Calvert (using the name John Trevlac) directs himself as an adventurer in Africa. John Carradine is a "deranged white mystic" guarding the elephants' graveyard. With Ann Cornell. Pretty obscure.

THE DARKER SIDE OF TERROR

1979 TV
PRODUCER: Al Ramus, John Herman Shaner
DIRECTOR: Gus Trikonis
SCREENWRITERS: Al Ramus,
John Herman Shaner

Robert Forster (*Alligator*) is a professor who has himself cloned. His troublemaking duplicate also wants his wife Adrienne Barbeau (*Swamp Thing*). Ray Milland (*The Thing With Two Heads*) regrets everything. From the director of *The Evil*.

DARKEST AFRICA

1936 Republic (B&W)
PRODUCER: Barney Sarecky
DIRECTORS: Breeves Easton, Joseph Kane
SCREENWRITERS: John Rathmell,
Barney Sarecky, Ted Parsons
ALSO RELEASED AS: *Batmen of Africa*,
King of the Jungleland

Famous animal trainer Clyde Beatty stars as himself in this fantastic serial, the first from Republic Studios. Clyde goes to a hidden jungle city with jungle boy Manuel King (a chubby kid hailed as "the world's youngest animal trainer") to rescue the boy's sister. The lost civilization is guarded by great flying batmen. Clyde and his pal also encounter dinosaurs (back-projection lizards). With a friendly gorilla. A 100-minute TV feature was released in 1966.

DATE BAIT

1960 Filmgroup (B&W)
PRODUCER/DIRECTOR: O'Dale Ireland
SCREENWRITERS: Robert Slaven,
Ethel Mae Page

Gary Clarke of *The Virginian* and Marlo Ryan star as teenagers determined to marry. Their plans are held up by two sets of parents as well as Marlo's former boyfriend and his doper-psycho brother. Some sources claim gangsters are working against them as well. Richard Gering co-stars. Co-billed with Ireland's *High School Caesar*.   –CB

A DATE WITH DEATH

1959 Pacific International
PRODUCER: William S. Edwards
DIRECTOR: Harold Daniels

Liz Renay was up for a contract with Warners when funny business with Mickey Cohen put her off limits. Her screen test was shelved and she landed in Arizona to make this picture, playing a jailed gang moll opposite Gerald Mohr of the *Foreign Intrigue* series. Mohr plays a vagrant who borrows the identity of a murdered police agent and stays on to break the local rackets and find his namesake's killer. The subliminal image process "Psychorama" carries over from Daniels' *Terror in the Haunted House*. With Harry Lauter, Robert Clarke, and Stephanie Farnay. Liz attended the premiere facing a grand jury indictment for perjury. She also appears in *The Thrill Killers* and *Desperate Living*.

—CB

DAUGHTER OF DR. JEKYLL

1957 Allied Artists (B&W)
PRODUCER/SCREENWRITER: Jack Pollexfen
DIRECTOR: Edward G. Ulmer

Gloria Talbot is the titular daughter. Her fiancé is John Agar and he's going crazy! The murders she's blamed for are actually committed by a werewolf doctor played by Arthur Shields, lookalike brother of Barry Fitzgerald. Gloria was in *The Cyclops* the same year.

DAUGHTER OF HORROR: See DEMENTIA.

DAUGHTER OF THE MIND

1969 TV
PRODUCER/DIRECTOR: Walter Grauman
SCREENWRITER: Luther Davis

Phony supernatural thriller with Ray Milland as a professor who thinks his dead daughter (Pamelyn Ferdin) is trying to communicate with him. It's all an elaborate plot devised by spies. Gene Tierney is the mom, Don Murray is a psychic investigator. With Edward Asner, George Macready, John Carradine, as a hypnotist, and Virginia Christine.

DAUGHTERS OF DARKNESS

1971 Gemini (Belgium/France/
W. Germany/Italy)
PRODUCERS: Alain Guilleaume, Paul Collet
DIRECTOR: Harry Kümel
SCREENWRITERS: Harry Kümel, Pierre Drouot
ORIGINALLY RELEASED AS: *Les Lèvres Rouges*

An excellent erotic vampire art film with Delphine Seyrig as the countess Elisabeth Bathory. She and her companion-lover Illona (Andrea Rau) stay at a huge luxurious European hotel by the sea. They seduce a sadistic young man and his beautiful bruised wife. The wife becomes the countess's new companion after her husband is killed and Illona dies from the water of a shower, which is deadly to a vampire. **(R)**

DAUGHTERS OF SATAN

1972 United Artists (Philippines)
PRODUCER: Aubrey Schenck
DIRECTOR: Hollingsworth Morse
SCREENWRITER: John C. Higgins

A man's wife becomes a witch. It was billed with *Superbeast* as "his and her horror!" Terrible, but Tom Selleck, now a top television heartthrob on *Magnum P.I.*, stars as an art collector in the Philippines. **(R)**

Vampire Countess Delphine Seyrig in Daughters of Darkness.

DAVID AND GOLIATH

1960 Allied Artists (Italy)
PRODUCER: Emimmo Salvi
DIRECTORS: Fernando Baldi, Richard Pottier
SCREENWRITERS: Umberto Scarpelli, Gino Mancini, Emimmo Salvi, Ambrogio Molteni
ORIGINALLY RELEASED AS: *David e Golia*

Orson Welles wasn't in a movie this bad again until *Necromancy* or *Butterfly*. If you don't want to sit through this cut-rate Biblical epic in which Welles plays King Saul, maybe you can find a copy of the comic-version (with color stills from the movie on the cover!). As David, Ivo Payer kills the badly made-up giant named Kronos who plays Goliath.

DAWN OF THE DEAD

1979 United Film Distributors
PRODUCERS: Richard Rubenstein, Dario Argento
DIRECTOR/SCREENWRITER: George Romero

An often devastating continuation of *Night of the Living Dead*. The story centers on two National Guardsmen called out to rekill the always growing number of flesh-eating ghouls and features the involvement of a television technician and her boyfriend. This time the exploding heads and ripped-open bodies are in bright color. The action starts in ghetto tenements and then switches brilliantly to a large brightly lit suburban mall complex where zombies ride escalators while Muzak plays. The important if overlong hit throws in vicious bikers that actually make you pity the zombies and some intentional humor, and borrows a bit from *The World, the Flesh, and the Devil*. As in *Night of the Living Dead*, the hero (Ken Foree) is black. Romero, who still ignores Hollywood and works out of Pittsburgh, fought the MPAA by releasing this unrated. It would have gotten a deadly X. Special makeup effects by Tom Savini. Italian director Dario Argento co-produced and made it a big hit in Europe. Goblin, heard in several Argento movies, provide part of the sound track. With Howard Smith of the *Village Voice*. For full impact see it in a multiplex theater at your nearest shopping mall. A slightly longer version sometimes plays at better theaters. (self imposed X)

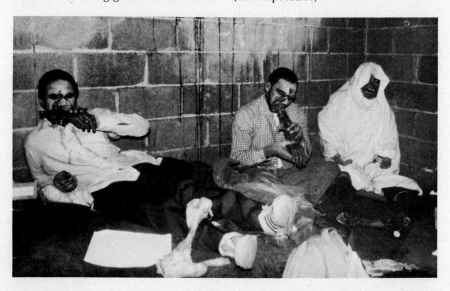

Hungry ghouls in Dawn of the Dead.

DAWN OF THE MUMMY
1981 Goldfarb (Italy)
PRODUCER/DIRECTOR: Frank Agrama
SCREENWRITERS: Daria Price, Ronald Dobrin

The first mummy gore movie! A fashion photographer and his models disturb the burial site of a mummy and his eight flesh-eating zombie followers. The highlight is an attack on a wedding party in which all the guests are disemboweled and devoured. Filmed in Egypt. Bad acting provided by Brenda King and Barry Sattels. (**X**)

THE DAY AFTER HALLOWEEN
1979 Group 1 (Australia)
PRODUCER: Anthony I. Ginnane
DIRECTOR: Rod Handy
SCREENWRITERS: Chris and Everett De Roche
ALSO RELEASED AS: *Snapshot*

Obscure European crime movies have been passed off as horror films in America for years. Here's an obscure Australian drama about a young fashion model that some people actually paid money to see, thinking it was a sequel to *Halloween*. With Chantal Contouri (*Thirst*). Music by Brian May (*Road Warrior*). (**R**)

THE DAY MARS INVADED EARTH
1963 20th Century-Fox (B&W)
PRODUCER/DIRECTOR: Maury Dexter
SCREENWRITER: Harry Spalding

Screen favorites Kent Taylor and Marie Windsor play husband and wife in this fun cheapie filmed at Greyston Mansion in Beverly Hills. Taylor, a Cape Canaveral scientist responsible for landing a communications device on Mars, returns home from a vacation and finds doubles of his family and himself! The Martian look-alikes reduce the originals to ashes. Some of his family is

found in the form of human-shaped ashes floating in the swimming pool. Poor Kent loses the battle against the devious aliens. With William Mimms and Betty Beall.

A DAY OF THE ANIMALS
1977 Film Ventures
PRODUCER: Edward L. Montoro
DIRECTOR: William Girdler
SCREENWRITERS: William Norton, Eleanor E. Norton
ALSO RELEASED AS: *Something Is Out There*

Animals of all kinds attack and kill people in the High Sierras. Why? Something about ecology and the sun. Who cares? With lots of humans too: Christopher and Lynda Day George, Richard Jaeckel, Leslie Nielsen, Michael Ansara, Paul Mantee, Andrew Stevens, and special guest Ruth Roman. It was director Girdler's follow-up to his dumb *Grizzly*.

DAY OF THE NIGHTMARE
1965 Herts-Lion (B&W)
PRODUCER: Leon Bleiberg
DIRECTOR: John Bushelman
SCREENWRITER: Leonard Goldstein

A seldom seen *Psycho* copy. A male commercial artist is suspected of murder, but no one can produce the dead woman's body. The artist reappears disguised as the missing woman and tries to kill his wife and father, then falls in front of a speeding yacht during a police chase. With John Ireland, Elena Verdugo, John Hart, and Liz Renay of *A Date with Death*. The director of photography is T.V. Mikels.　　　　—CB

DAY OF THE TRIFFIDS
1963 Allied Artists (England)
PRODUCER: George Pitcher
DIRECTOR: Steve Sekely
SCREENWRITER: Philip Yordan

Ex-musical star Howard Keel plays an American seaman who is one of the few people on Earth not blinded by a meteor shower. The meteors also bring plant spores that grow into giant mobile carnivorous plants which easily sting blind Earthlings to death. The sailor rescues a little girl and with a Frenchwoman (Nicole Maurey) they flee to Spain for a final confrontation with hordes of killer plants. Meanwhile Janette Scott and Kieron Moore (both of whom went on to face *A Crack in the World*) are being attacked in a lighthouse. Two simple ways of killing the aliens are discovered and Earth is saved again. From John Wyndham's novel of the same name. With Mervyn Johns. Screenwriter Yordan was also executive producer.

DAY OF THE WOMAN: See *I SPIT ON YOUR GRAVE.*

THE DAY THE EARTH CAUGHT FIRE
1961 Universal (England)
PRODUCER/DIRECTOR/SCREENWRITER:
　Val Guest
SCREENWRITER: Wolf Mankowitz

Excellent end-of-the-world drama centering on London *Daily News* writers who discover that recent unexplained disasters and the constantly rising temperature are the results of atomic testing. The U.S. and the U.S.S.R. had both set off test bombs at the same time, knocking the Earth out of orbit and hurling it toward the Sun. The film is mostly concerned with personal reactions to the disaster, and there's more talk than action, but the cast is always convincing. Leo McKern plays the science editor, Edward Judd is an alcoholic reporter, and Janet Munro is his girlfriend. As the world sweats and waits for a likely end, teenagers enjoy rock 'n' roll riots in the streets. When more bombs are exploded to try to reverse the damage, two headlines are prepared by the *News*: WORLD SAVED and WORLD DOOMED.

THE DAY THE EARTH FROZE
1959 AIP (Finland/U.S.S.R.) (B&W)
PRODUCER: Gregg Sebelious
DIRECTORS: Alekandr Ptushko,
　Julius Strandberg

A fantasy about a magic mill, a witch queen, a field of snakes, and a hero logger. When the witch steals the sun, everything freezes until the sound of sacred harps turns her to stone. In typical AIP fashion, dialogue scenes were reshot in '64 featuring American actors. Marvin Miller narrates.

THE DAY THE EARTH MOVED
1974 TV
PRODUCERS: Bobby Sherman, Ward Sylvester
DIRECTOR: Robert Michael Lewis
SCREENWRITERS: Jack Turley, Max Jack

Earthquake, television-style, with Jackie Cooper and Cleavon Little warning small-town residents to get out. The shook-up cast includes Beverly Garland (*It Conquered the World*), Stella Stevens, and William Windom.

THE DAY THE EARTH STOOD STILL

1951 20th Century-Fox (B&W)
PRODUCER: Julian Blaustein
DIRECTOR: Robert Wise
SCREENWRITER: Edmund H. North
Classic antiwar science fiction based on *Farewell to the Master* by Harry Bates. Michael Rennie as Klaatu, the Christ-like alien, arrives in Washington, D.C., with a warning: stop using nuclear weapons or the Earth will be destroyed. Sam Jaffe, as the Einstein character, and Patricia Neal seem to be the only ones convinced until he causes all power to stop for one hour. Patricia Neal later starred in a British semi-remake, *Immediate Disaster* ('54). Rennie was to be cast as an alien again in *Cyborg 2087* ('65), *Assignment Terror*, and even *Lost in Space*. Hugh Marlowe and Harry Lauter both found themselves back in Washington five years later in *Earth vs. the Flying Saucers*. The robot Gort was played by Lock Martin, a seven-foot-seven former doorman at Grauman's Chinese Theatre. Drew Pearson plays himself. Also with Billy Gray (*Father Knows Best*), Francis Bavier (*The Andy Griffith Show*), and Stuart Whitman. Special effects man Ray Kellogg later directed *The Killer Shrews*. The powerful music is by Bernard Herrmann. A remake was announced in 1982.

THE DAY THE FISH CAME OUT

1967 International Classics (England/Greece)
PRODUCER/DIRECTOR/SCREENWRITER:
Michael Cacoyannis

Bizarre nuclear disaster story from the director of *Zorba the Greek*. Wearing a pop-art bikini, Candice Bergen space-dances on an island in the Aegean while half-naked soldiers search for a downed plane's jettisoned warheads. Tom Courtenay, Ian Ogilvy, Colin Blakely, and Sam Wanamaker co-star. Atom-age swim-wear designed by the director.   –CB

THE DAY THE SCREAMING STOPPED: See COMEBACK.

THE DAY THE SKY EXPLODED

1958 Excelsior (France/Italy) (B&W)
PRODUCER: Guido Giambartolomei
DIRECTOR: Paolo Heusch
SCREENWRITERS: Marcello Coscia,
     Alessandro Continenza
An Earth rocket hits the Sun, sending asteroids hurling toward Earth. Heat waves, tidal waves, and assorted disasters result. Most scientists panic, give up, or go mad. The hero (Paul Hubschmid) saves Earth by organizing all countries to fire all their atomic weapons into space, thus destroying the asteroids. Not as exciting as it sounds. Cinematography by Mario Bava.

THE DAY THE WORLD ENDED

1956 AIP (B&W)
PRODUCER/DIRECTOR: Roger Corman
SCREENWRITER: Lou Rusoff
"A new high in naked shrieking terror!" proclaimed the ads. It was also the real beginning for the new American International Pictures (formerly A.R.C.). Roger Corman's first science-fiction film cost a whopping $65,000, was a big success, and is still a fondly remembered movie about T.D. Day. That's Total Destruction. After an atomic war, radiation turns survivors into horrible mutants. Hero Richard Denning, Lori Nelson (who had just been in *Revenge*

of the Creature), and the well-prepared Paul Birch are protected in a cabin surrounded by mountains, but their sanctuary is taken over by Michael "Touch" Connors and Paul Dubov. It's the wholesome good folk vs. the gun-wielding toughs and their wild moll (Adele Jergens). Outside, the telepathic, cannibalistic, three-eyed, four-horned, four-armed mutants are getting closer. The main mutant is played by Paul Blaisdell, who designed his outrageous suit. Jonathan Haze is one of the new, still part-human mutants. Alex Gordon was executive producer. An uncredited remake was *In the Year 2889*.

THE DAY TIME ENDED

1978 Compass International (Spain)
PRODUCERS: Wayne Schmidt, Steve Neill
DIRECTOR: John Cardos
SCREENWRITERS: Wayne Schmidt, J. Larry Carroll, David Schmoeller
ALSO RELEASED AS: *Vortex*

A pretty cheap, mixed-up science-fiction adventure about UFOs, a time warp, a desert home transplanted to an alien planet, and three animated creatures. With Chris Mitchum (the son of Robert and a star in Europe), Dorothy Malone, Jim Davis (*Dallas*), and little Natasha Ryan (*The Amityville Horror*). The one friendly alien is of the *Close Encounters* variety. The other two resemble an elephant mixed with a gorilla and a turtle without its shell respectively. A soundtrack album is available.

THE DAYDREAMER

1966 Embassy Pictures
PRODUCER/SCREENWRITER: Arthur Rankin Jr.
DIRECTOR: Saul Bass
Animagic feature (stop-motion puppets) based on Hans Christian Andersen stories, with Ray Bolger, Margaret Hamilton, and Jack Gilford in the live-action scenes. Boris Karloff provides the voice of the rat. Other voices are Hayley Mills, Ed Wynn, Patty Duke, Tallulah Bankhead, Terry-Thomas, Victor Borge, Robert Goulet, and Sessue Hayakawa. Most of them sing. Filmed in Japan, America, and various European countries.

DAYS OF THRILLS AND LAUGHTER

1961 20th Century-Fox (B&W)
PRODUCER/SCREENWRITER: Robert Youngson
Aside from the comedy, this compilation of rare silent footage includes Boris Karloff in a Ruth Roland serial, Warner Oland in a Pearl White serial, and Houdini in a scene from *Man From Beyond*.

DAYTONA BEACH WEEKEND

1965 Dominant
PRODUCER/DIRECTOR: Robert Welby
College students on vacation with legendary rock 'n' roll star Del Shannon, Houston & Dorsey, the Offbeats, and Sue Skeen. Shot on location in 16mm. Dominant also distributed *Blast-off Girls*.   –CB

D-DAY ON MARS: See THE PURPLE MONSTER STRIKES

DEAD AND BURIED

1981 Avco Embassy
PRODUCERS: Robert Shusett, Robert Fentress
DIRECTOR: Gary A. Sherman
SCREENWRITERS: Robert Shusett, Dan O'Bannon
A confusing, stupid, gory horror movie about reconstructed corpses living in a New England town. Everybody there seems to know what's going on except for Sheriff James Farentino. Jack Albertson, in his last role, plays an eccentric old mortician/zombie master who at one point is seen operating on himself. With Melody Anderson (*Flash Gordon*) providing beauty and laughs, Michael Pataki, and a syringe through

an eyeball. By the director of *Raw Meat* and the writers of *Alien*. **(R)**

THE DEAD ARE ALIVE
1972 NGP (Yugoslavia/Germany/Italy)
PRODUCER: Mondial Tefi
DIRECTOR: Armando Crispino
SCREENWRITERS: Lucio Battistrada, Armando Crispino

A series of gory killings seem to have been committed by Tuchulka, an Etruscan god. Samantha Eggar and Alex Cord are digging where they shouldn't. With Horst Frank. **(R)**

THE DEAD DON'T DIE
1975 TV
PRODUCER: Henry Coleman
DIRECTOR: Curtis Harrington
SCREENWRITER: Robert Bloch

A tribute to the poverty-row horrors of the '30s that tries hard to be as ridiculous as the originals. A group of West Indians in Chicago plots to rule the world with zombies. Involves hammy acting from George Hamilton as hero Don Drake. With Ray Milland, Ralph Meeker, John Blondell, Linda Cristal, Reggie Nalder, Milton Parsons, and Yvette Vickers. Robert Bloch (*Psycho*) wrote the teleplay.

DEAD EYES OF LONDON
1961 Magna (W. Germany) (B&W)
PRODUCER: Herbert Sennewald
DIRECTOR: Alfred Vohrer
SCREENWRITER: Trygve Larsen
ORIGINALLY RELEASED AS: *Die Toten Augen von London*

One of the best of many Edgar Wallace mysteries filmed in Germany. As a Scotland Yard inspector, Joachim Fuchsberger investigates the deaths of heavily insured old men. A gang of blind men led by a crooked reverend are behind the murders. With Klaus Kinski, Karin Baal, and Ady Berber as a monstrous bald and blind killer. The story was also filmed in 1939, as *The Human Monster* with Bela Lugosi.

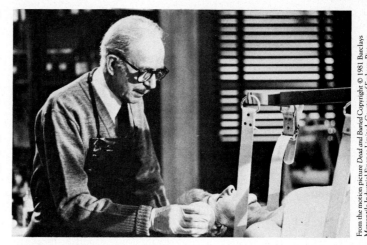

Dead and Buried stars Jack Albertson in his last role as a mortician.

DEAD KIDS: See STRANGE BEHAVIOR.

DEAD MAN'S EYES
1944 Universal (B&W)
PRODUCERS: Ben Pivar, Will Cowan
DIRECTOR: Reginald Le Borg
SCREENWRITER: Dwight Babcock

Acquanetta (as Tanya, sister of Satan!) is jealous because artist Lon Chaney, Jr., loves Jean Parker, so she throws acid in his face. Lon gets an eyeball transplant, is accused of a murder, and pretends he's still blind. Detective Thomas Gomez sorts things out. An "Inner Sanctum" mystery with Paul Kelly and Jonathan Hale.

DEAD MEN WALK
1943 PRC (B&W)
PRODUCER: Sigmund Neufeld
DIRECTOR: Sam Newfield
SCREENWRITER: Fred Myton

As a living-dead vampire, George Zucco menaces his twin brother Dr. Clayton (also Zucco). Zucco number one is aided by Zolarr, a hunchback (Dwight Frye). Frye died of a heart attack the next year. From the makers of *The Mad Monster*.

DEAD OF NIGHT
1945 Universal (England) (B&W)
PRODUCER: Michael Balcon
DIRECTORS: Alberto Cavalcanti,
 Basil Dearden, Robert Hamer,
 Charles Crichton
SCREENWRITERS: John Baines,
 Angus MacPhail, T.E.B. Clarke

No other horror compilation film has come close to the power of this classic, which has a strong linking story about an architect (Mervyn Johns) visiting the country home of his nightmares. When he tells the inhabitants that he knows them all from dreams they each relate a chilling story. All the characters and stories come together in a terrifying final sequence and the man's nightmare starts again. The best story features Michael Redgrave as a schizophrenic ventriloquist controlled by Hugo, his dummy. The ending obviously influenced *Psycho*. Other tales involve the ghost of a little boy at a Christmas party, a haunted mirror, a comical ghost on a golf course, and a waiting hearse.

DEAD OF NIGHT: See DEATHDREAM.

DEAD OF NIGHT
1977 TV
PRODUCER: Dan Curtis
DIRECTOR: Dan Curtis
SCREENWRITER: Richard Matheson

The second pilot for the projected *Dead of Night* series. *Trilogy of Terror* ('75) was the first. The first story, "No Such Thing as a Vampire," stars Horst Buchholz, Patrick Macnee, and Anjanette Comer. "Second Chance," about an antique car transporting its driver into the past, features Ed Begley, Christina Hart, and Ann Doran. The third tale is "Bobby."

THE DEAD ONE
1961 Favorite Films
PRODUCER/DIRECTOR/SCREENWRITER:
 Barry Mahon

The extremely prolific Barry Mahon made dozens of nudie films, some children's films, and this obscure voodoo-zombie horror movie. Monica Davis, afraid of losing a property inheritance, uses voodoo to resurrect her brother and sends the zombie after her cousin's new bride. With John McKay (*Cuban Rebel Girls*) and Linda Ormond. From the ads: "See the voodoo princess call on the dead ones to Kill! Kill! Kill!"

DEAD PEOPLE
1974 Bedford Enterprises
PRODUCER/DIRECTOR/SCREENWRITERS:
 Gloria Katz, Willard Huyck
ALSO RELEASED AS: *Messiah of Evil, Return of the Living Dead, Revenge of the Screaming Dead*

The writers of *American Graffiti* made their own *Night of the Living Dead* imitation. It's a confusing, badly edited story about zombies in a California coastal town. Marianna Hall stars as a woman searching for her father, a surrealist painter. With Joy Bang, Royal Dano, Elisha Cook, and Michael Greer. When the film was re-issued, ads carried a copy line used to promote *Dawn of the Dead*—"When there is no more room in hell the dead will walk the earth." George Romero sued. **(R)**

DEAD RINGER

1964 Warner Brothers (B&W)
PRODUCER: William H. Wright
DIRECTOR: Paul Henreid
SCREENWRITER: Albert Beich

"Double Davis Means Double Dynamite!" the ads shrieked. Fifty-six-year-old Bette Davis, heavily made up to look years younger, played twin sisters in this contrived mystery. After her sister's husband's funeral, the Bette that runs a bar learns that her rich twin had tricked her way into marriage with the man she also loved. Poor Bette kills identical rich Bette and assumes her identity and life-style. Her life is complicated by her late sis's lowlife boyfriend (Peter Lawford) and a cop (Karl Malden) who loved the "dead" cocktail lounge owner. Directed by her *Now Voyager* co-star, Paul Henreid. With Philip Carey, Jean Hagen, George Macready, and Estelle Winwood. A remake of a Mexican Dolores Del Rio film, it was Davis's first film after *Whatever Happened to Baby Jane?* It's usually cut by 10–12 minutes to fit a two-hour TV time slot, sacrificing the scene in which Davis sings "Shufflin' Off to Buffalo". This rendition has to be seen/heard to be believed.

DEADLIER THAN THE MALE

1966 Universal (England)
PRODUCER: Betty E. Box
DIRECTOR: Ralph Thomas
SCREENWRITER: Jimmy Sangster

Bulldog Drummond, the investigator hero of at least 20 films from the '20s to the '50s was revived again in the era of James Bond films, but he didn't resemble the original much. Richard Johnson stars. Nigel Green is the villain, living in a castle on a Mediterranean island. His all-female assassination ring includes Elke Sommer and Sylva Koscina. They lure the playboy detective to the island for a giant chess

The monster in Barry Mahon's The Dead One.

game of death. With Suzanna Leigh. *Some Girls Do* was a sequel.

THE DEADLY BEES

1967 Amicus/Paramount (England)
PRODUCERS: Max J. Rosenberg,
Milton Subotsky
DIRECTOR: Freddie Francis
SCREENWRITERS: Robert Bloch,
Anthony Marriott

Bee movie fans!—this one was the first. An exhausted pop singer (Suzanna Leigh) goes to a small British island to rest. Her rented cottage is on the farm of a beekeeper (Guy Doleman). A neighbor (Frank Finlay) also raises bees. Soon a dog, then a woman are found stung to death. And next the bees attack the girl.

DEADLY BLESSING

1981 United Artists
PRODUCERS: Micheline and Max Keller,
Pat Herskovic
DIRECTOR: Wes Craven
SCREENWRITERS: Glenn M. Benest,
Matthew Barr, Wes Craven

A beautifully photographed but confusing movie that pits three big city women against a strict Midwestern religious sect. Maren Jensen is joined by two gorgeous friends (Susan Buckner and Sharon Stone) after her ex-Hittite husband is killed. Ernest Borgnine is the strict religious leader. The few good parts involve a snake in a bathtub, a spider in someone's mouth (only a dream), goony-looking Michael Berryman from *The Hills Have Eyes*, and two characters going to see *Summer of Fear* (Craven's TV movie). The ending is a last-minute mixture of the supernatural and *Psycho* that satisfies no one. Music by James Horner (*Humanoids From the Deep*). **(R)**

THE DEADLY CIRCLE: See HONEYMOON OF HORROR.

THE DEADLY DREAM
1971 TV
PRODUCER: Stan Shpetner
DIRECTOR: Alf Kjellin
SCREENWRITER: Barry Oringer
Poor Lloyd Bridges thinks his dreams about people trying to kill him are real. They are. Janet Leigh is his wife. With Don Stroud, Richard Jaeckel, Leif Erickson, and Carl Betz. Directed by a Swedish actor.

THE DEADLY MANTIS
1957 Universal (B&W)
PRODUCER: William Alland
DIRECTOR: Nathan Juran
SCREENWRITER: Martin Berkeley
Released by an earthquake in the Arctic, a giant praying mantis hops to the East Coast, causing destruction in Washington, D.C., and New York City before being gassed to death in the Holland Tunnel. It dies on a pile of smashed-up paneled station wagons, hot rods, and trucks. Military man Craig Stevens, scientist William Hopper, and newswoman Alix Talton make up the requisite love triangle. A dumb film

with lots of stock footage. Producer Alland wrote the story.

DEADLY RAY FROM MARS: See FLASH GORDON'S TRIP TO MARS.

THE DEADLY TOWER
1975 TV
PRODUCER: Antonio Calderon
DIRECTOR: Jerry Jameson
SCREENWRITER: William Douglas Lansford
Ex-Disney star Kurt Russell plays a sniper who kills 13 people at random in this critically acclaimed TV movie based on a true 1966 event in Austin, Texas. With Ned Beatty, Pernell Roberts, John Forsythe, and Richard Yniguez. Earlier, similar films were *The Sniper* and *Targets*.

DEADMAN'S CURVE
1978 TV
PRODUCER: Pat Rooney
DIRECTOR: Richard Compton
SCREENWRITER: Darlene Young
A TV movie about Jan and Dean! Richard Hatch (*Battlestar Galactica*) plays Jan Berry, whose 1966 car crash left him comatose for several years. Bruce Davison (*Willard*) is Dean Torrance. Mike Love and Bruce Johnston of the Beach Boys play themselves, as do Dick Clark and Wolfman Jack (here calling himself "The Jackal.") See the real hit-making duo in *The T.A.M.I. Show*. Also be sure to get your Jan and Dean "Little Old Lady" skateboard, available at stores everywhere (information from the back of their *Command Performance* album). Director Compton usually works for New World.

DEADWOOD '76

1965 Fairway-International
PRODUCER: Nicholas Merriwether
DIRECTOR: James Landis
SCREENWRITERS: Arch Hall, Sr.,
William Watters

Fairway's next-to-last picture takes place in the old Dakota Territory. A young cowboy played by Arch Hall, Jr., rescues Tennessee Thompson (Jack Lester) from the Pawnees. Together they set out for Deadwood. Arch is mistaken for Billy the Kid and later captured by the redskins, but he runs into his father (Arch, Sr.) and falls in love with Little Bird (LaDonna Cottier) at the reservation. A showdown with Wild Bill Hickock (Robert Dix) follows his escape. Melissa Morgan plays Poker Kate and Rex Holman sings the title song. With John Cardos and Little Jack Little. Photography by William (Vilmos) Zsigmond. See *Airborne* and *The Nasty Rabbit*.   –CB

DEAFULA

1975 Signscope (B&W)
PRODUCER: Gary Holstrom
DIRECTOR/SCREENWRITER: Peter Wechsberg

The world's first feature film in sign language and it *had* to be about a vampire. You're not likely to have a chance to view this very low-budget effort, but it features a limited sound track for hearing audiences, a hunchback servant with tin-can hands, and a very theatrical-looking vampire. The director, who is deaf, started the first TV news program in sign language (in San Francisco).

DEAR DEAD DELILAH

1972 Avco Embassy TV
PRODUCER: Jack Clement
DIRECTOR/SCREENWRITER: John Farris

A cheap, pathetic axe-murder film set in the Deep South. Agnes Moorehead is the dying, wheelchair-bound owner of a mansion where lots of cash is buried. Various relatives and servants with atrocious Southern accents are decapitated while racing to get the loot. With Michael Ansara, Will Geer (*The Waltons*), and Dennis Patrick. Filmed in Nashville. Director Farris later wrote *The Fury*.

DEATH AT LOVEHOUSE

1976 TV
PRODUCER: Hal Sitowitz
DIRECTOR: E.W. Swackhamer
SCREENWRITER: Jim Barnett

A writer and his wife (Robert Wagner and Kate Jackson) stay at the mansion of a dead '30s movie star to research her life for a screenplay. Trouble is, her spirit rises from a glass tomb to destroy them. With film vets Sylvia Sidney, Joan Blondell, Dorothy Lamour, and John Carradine. Filmed at the Harold Lloyd estate.

DEATH BY INVITATION

1971 Paragon
DIRECTOR/SCREENWRITER: Ken Friedman

A witch decapitates the descendants of her killers with an axe. Real low-budget and enjoyed by few. **(R)**

DEATH CORPS: See SHOCK WAVES.

DEATH CRUISE

1974 TV
PRODUCERS: Aaron Spelling,
Leonard Goldberg
DIRECTOR: Ralph Senesky
SCREENWRITER: Jack B. Sowards

Three couples win ocean voyages. Will Richard Long, Polly Bergen, Edward Albert, Kate Jackson, Celeste Holm, and Tom Bosley sink? More TV disasters with Cesare Danova.

DEATH CURSE OF TARTU

1967 Thunderbird International
PRODUCERS: Joseph Fink, Juan Hidalgo-Gato
DIRECTOR/SCREENWRITER: William Grefe

Horrible Seminole witch doctor tracks four archaeology students who disturb his grave. Doug Hobart is Tartu, able to stalk victims as shark, snake, or alligator as well as zombie. Native prophecy comes true as dread creature is swallowed by quicksand during struggle with Fred Pinero. Fred and wife Babette Sherrill survive; the dead students are Mayra Christine, Sherman Hayes, Gary Holtz, and Maurice Stewart. Filmed on location in the Florida Everglades. Also from Grefe: *The Devil's Sisters* and *The Hooked Generation.*
—CB

DEATH DRIVE: See FER-DE-LANCE.

DEATH FLIGHT: See SST DEATH FLIGHT.

DEATH HOUSE: See SILENT NIGHT, BLOODY NIGHT.

DEATH IN SMALL DOSES

1957 Allied Artists (B&W)
PRODUCER: Rick Heermance
DIRECTOR: Joseph Newman
SCREENWRITER: John McGreevey

Chuck Connors (just before he went to small-screen fame as *The Rifleman*) is an amphetamine-popping '50s truck driver in this must-see feature. It would make a great triple bill with Chuck's *The Mad Bomber* and his *Tourist Trap.* Peter Graves stars as a U.S. Food and Drug Administration investigator. With Mala Powers and Merry Anders.

THE DEATH KISS

1933 Worldwide (B&W with tinted scenes)
PRODUCER: KBS
DIRECTOR: Edwin L. Marin
SCREENWRITERS: Barry Barringer, Gordan Kahn

Three of the stars of *Dracula* and a misleading ad campaign made '30s audiences expect a new horror movie. But this interesting independent feature is a murder mystery about Hollywood, with Bela Lugosi as a studio manager. David Manners is a scriptwriter. Edward Van Sloan is a director. Besides the mystery, it's a fascinating behind-the-scenes look at a real studio (the Tiffany Studios on Sunset Boulevard). With Adrienne Ames.

DEATH MOON

1978 TV
PRODUCER: Jay Benson
DIRECTOR: Bruce Kessler
SCREENWRITER: George Schenck

A werewolf-in-Hawaii movie. Vacationing Robert Foxworth falls for France Nuyen and is cursed. The best werewolf movie of April '78.

DEATH RACE 2000

1975 New World
PRODUCER: Roger Corman
DIRECTOR: Paul Bartel
SCREENWRITERS: Robert Thom, Charles B. Griffith

In the fascist America of the near future five drivers enter the transcontinental death race, gaining points for each person they hit and kill along the way. This cartoonish fantasy-comedy remains a popular favorite while its serious and expensive model, *Rollerball*, is forgotten. David Carradine stars as the partially bionic Frankenstein, a driver with a black leather suit and cape and a monster car with fangs. His navigator (Simone Griffith) is actually a revolutionary spy. His chief opponents are

Sylvester Stallone (as Machine Gun Joe Viterbo), Mary Woronov, and Roberta Collins. With deejay Don Steele as the fast-talking announcer and Louisa Moritz. From a story by Ib Melchior. Director Bartel had previously done *Private Parts*. He followed this with *Cannonball*, in which Carradine plays a similar role. (R)

DEATH RIDE
1977 Band Ltd.
PRODUCER: Brandon Chase
DIRECTOR: Charles Band
SCREENWRITER: Marc Marais
ALSO RELEASED AS: *Crash!*

Terrible psychic–car wreck movie featuring a crippled José Ferrer in one of his worst roles and Sue "Lolita" Lyon as his wife. She uses an idol to control a car that kills her enemies. With John Carradine, John Ericson, Leslie Parrish, and lots of crashes.

DEATH SHIP
1980 Avco Embassy (Canada)
PRODUCERS: Derek Gibson,
 Harold Greenberg
DIRECTOR: Alvin Rakoff
SCREENWRITER: John Robins

George Kennedy stars as the mad captain of a Nazi torture ship! Frozen sailors, rotting corpses, and stock footage are featured in this dull, cheap-looking horror film. With Richard Crenna, Sally Ann Howes, Kate Reid, and Nick Mancuso. (R)

DEATH SMILES ON A MURDERER
1973 Avco Embassy-TV (Italy)
DIRECTOR: Aristide Massaccesi
ORIGINALLY RELEASED AS: *La Morte a Sorriso All Assassino*

A doctor (Klaus Kinski) brings the dead back to life. See Ewa Aulin (*Candy*) turn into a rotting corpse! An incomprehensible feature.

DEATH TAKES A HOLIDAY
1934 Paramount (B&W)
PRODUCER: E. Lloyd Sheldon
DIRECTOR: Mitchell Leisen
SCREENWRITERS: Maxwell Anderson,
 Gladys Lehman

As Prince Sirki (Death), Fredric March arrives at a Riviera society party wearing a monocle and a bow tie. He falls in love with Evelyn Venable and lingers on earth. While he's here nobody dies. This popular fantasy is basically a filmed stage play, but March is great as usual. With Edward Van Sloan, Kent Taylor, and Sir Guy Standing.

DEATH TAKES A HOLIDAY
1971 TV
PRODUCER: George Eckstein
DIRECTOR: Richard Butler
SCREENWRITER: Rita Lakin

A bad remake of the '34 film. As Death, Monte Markham falls in love with Yvette Mimieux. Her wealthy family includes Melvyn Douglas, Myrna Loy, Kerwin Matthews, and Maureen Reagan. Typically TV-movie boring.

DEATH TRAP: See EATEN ALIVE.

DEATH VALLEY
1982 Universal
PRODUCER: Elliot Kastner
DIRECTOR: Dick Richards
SCREENWRITER: Richard Rothstein

Skinny David Carradine punches out Sylvester "Rocky" Stallone in Paul Bartel's Death Race 2000.

A boy goes from New York to Phoenix to visit his mother (Catherine Hicks). Upon his arrival he sees a murder but nobody believes him. A series of graphic knife slashings follows. Paul LeMat (*Melvin and Howard*) is Mom's boyfriend. Stephen McHattie is neurotic desert scum. (R)

DEATH WEEKEND: See THE HOUSE BY THE LAKE.

THE DEATH WHEELERS: See PSYCHOMANIA.

DEATHDREAM
1972 Europix (Canada)
PRODUCER/DIRECTOR: Bob Clark
SCREENWRITER: Alan Ormsby
ALSO RELEASED AS: *Dead of Night, Night Walk*

A great low-budget reworking of *The Monkey's Paw*. A woman wishes her son Andy (Richard Backus), who died in Vietnam, were back. He returns, a confused bloodthirsty walking corpse who kills his own dog and uses a syringe to obtain nourishment. He ends up in a graveyard after attending a drive-in movie with his girlfriend, his sister, and her date—who think he's just acting strange because of the war. Screenwriter Alan Ormsby also did the makeup. Additional makeup by Tom Savini. Fast becoming a late-night-TV cult classic. Don't miss.

DEATHLINE: See RAW MEAT.

THE DEATHMASTER
1972 AIP
PRODUCER: Fred Sadoff
DIRECTOR: Ray Danton
SCREENWRITER: R.L.Grove

A coffin containing a long-haired vampire is washed ashore on the Southern California coast. He becomes a Manson-esque guru to a sorry group of hippies.

A ridiculous, dated follow-up to the Count Yorga films; like them, it stars Robert Quarry as a vampire. Also starring Betty Anne Rees, John Fielder, and Bob Picket. With a *Billy Jack*—inspired kung fu fighter.

DEATHSPORT
1978 New World
PRODUCER: Roger Corman
DIRECTORS: Henry Suso, Allan Arkush
SCREENWRITERS: Henry Suso, Donald Stewart

David Carradine and Claudia Jennings star in this *Star Wars*—meets—*Death Race 2000* feature. As "range guides," the two escape after being forced to battle "statesmen" on futuristic motorcycles. Lots of fiery crashes on the desert and fights with cannibal mutants result. Jennings, *Playboy's* Miss November 1969 and Playmate of the year and a drive-in movie queen of the '70s, died in a car crash not long after this was released. With Richard Lynch and Jesse Vint. (R)

THE DECEIVERS: See INTIMACY.

DECOY FOR TERROR: See PLAYGIRL KILLER.

DEEP RED
1976 Mahler (Italy)
PRODUCER: Salvatore Argento
DIRECTOR: Dario Argento
SCREENWRITER: Giuseppe Bassan
ORIGINALLY RELEASED AS: *Profundo Rosso*
ALSO RELEASED AS: *The Hatchet Murders*

Another stylish and imaginative shocker by the director of *Suspiria*. David Hemmings stars as an Englishman in Rome who witnesses the murder of a psychiatrist. He flees from the mass killer and stumbles on clues, including some macabre childish drawings. Bloody fun with music by the Goblins. With Dario Nicolodi. (R)

A DEGREE OF MURDER

1967 Universal (W. Germany)
PRODUCER: Rob Houwer
DIRECTOR/SCREENWRITER: Volker Schlöndorff
ORIGINALLY RELEASED AS: *Mord und Totschlag*
The late Brian Jones of the Rolling Stones wrote the music for this modern murder story starring Stones girlfriend Anita Pallenberg, more recently involved in the real-life possible suicide of a young man at her American home. She plays a waitress who accidentally kills a former lover and finds a new one to help get rid of the body. From the director of *The Tin Drum*.

THE DELINQUENTS

1957 United Artists (B&W)
PRODUCER/DIRECTOR/SCREENWRITER:
Robert Altman
Altman's first feature, made in Kansas City in the summer of '55. The cast is local except for Peter Miller from *The Blackboard Jungle*, Richard Bakalyan, and Tommy Laughlin—who gets involved in a drive-in brawl after a showdown with his girlfriend's folks. Miller and Bakalyan introduce themselves to Laughlin after the free-for-all and seem to be nice enough guys. Then they turn around and kidnap his girl (Rosemary Howard), force liquor down his throat, and frame him for a gas-station holdup. Altman's wife and daughter appear along with Jet Pinkston and Lotus Corelli. Altman's next was *The James Dean Story*. —CB

DELUGE

1933 RKO (B&W)
PRODUCER: Samuel Bischoff
DIRECTOR: Felix E. Feist
SCREENWRITERS: John Goodrich, Warren B. Duff
The ads read: "Earth doomed!" Decades before most end-of-the-world movies, this spectacle showed New York flooded by a tidal wave. Sidney Blackmer stars as the last man on Earth. With Edward Van Sloan, Peggy Shannon, and Matt Moore. Footage of New York in ruins later turned up in Republic serials. Director Feist later did *Donovan's Brain*.

Originally released as: Deep Red.

DEMENTIA

1955 Van Wolf-API (B&W)
PRODUCER/DIRECTOR/SCREENWRITER:
John Parker
ALSO RELEASED AS: *Daughter of Horror*

A fascinating expressionistic hour-long horror film. Adrienne Barrett glides through dark alleys and into a vicious confrontation between a drunk and a passing policeman. She is led to the safety of Bruno Ve Sota's limousine. After a struggle with Adrienne in his apartment, Bruno lands on the street several floors down, his dead fingers clutching a necklace. The girl breaks through the gathering crowd, pulls the knife out of his stomach, and begins sawing off the hand when she is unable to loosen its grip. She flees into a jazz club. Suddenly, crazed laughter, pointing fingers, stares. She awakens in a cheap hotel room and moves to the dresser. Inside a drawer is the hand. Narration by Ed McMahon. Declared "inhuman, indecent, and the quintessence of gruesomeness" by the New York State Board of Censors. Scenes from the film and its '57 re-release poster turned up in The Blob. With Angelo Rossitto.   —CB

Luana Anders in Francis Ford Coppola's Dementia 13.

DEMENTIA 13

1963 AIP/Filmgroup (B&W)
PRODUCER: Roger Corman
DIRECTOR/SCREENWRITER: Francis Ford Coppola
ALSO RELEASED AS: *The Haunted and the Hunted*

From the opening scene of a woman dumping her heart-attack-victim husband into a lake, you know this is no ordinary quickie shocker. His body slowly sinks to the bottom of the lake alongside his transistor radio—still blaring bubbly rock'n'roll. While in Europe doing the sound for Roger Corman's *The Young Racers*, Coppola wrote the script for a film Corman wanted to make that would be like *Homicidal* (which was William Castle's attempt to make a film like *Psycho*). Because he had to go home and do *The Raven*, Corman gave Coppola $22,000 and three of *The Young Racers* stars and said, "You direct it." Good move, Roger. Luana Anders devises a bizarre scheme to gain control of her late husband's family's money. Patrick Magee is the mysterious family doctor, and William Campbell is Anders' brother-in-law. With a great trick ending, some truly shocking gory axe murders, and lots of inventive photography. Despite what you've heard, not Coppola's first film, but a minor horror classic from a master filmmaker. Watch for it. Filmed in Ireland. Original theater patrons had to take a "D-13 test" to get in. Scenes from this shocker turned up in Coppola's *You're a Big Boy Now*.

DEMON: See GOD TOLD ME TO.

THE DEMON BARBER OF FLEET STREET

1936 Select (England) (B&W)
DIRECTOR: George King

Tod Slaughter (1885–1956), billed as "the horror man of Europe" in this country, was a theatrical villain who starred in a series of campy features. In this, his best-known (in America), he plays Sweeney Todd, the barber who opens a trap door under the barber chair to dump victims into the basement where they're made into meat pies to be sold in the bake shop next door.

THE DEMON FROM DEVIL'S LAKE

1964 Phillips-Marker (B&W)
PRODUCER/DIRECTOR/SCREENWRITER:
Russ Marker

Operation Noah's Ark crash-lands in Lake Texoma on its way to space. Leaking radiation causes the birds, mammals, and reptiles to transmutate into one awful beast. Starring Dave Heath and made in Sherman, Texas.   –CB

THE DEMON LOVER

1976 21st Century
PRODUCERS/DIRECTORS/SCREENWRITERS:
Donald Jackson, Jerry Younkins

An independent release filmed in Jackson, Michigan, by horror fans and featuring Gunar Hansen (Leatherface in *The Texas Chainsaw Massacre*) and "Howard the Duck" artist Val Mayerick. Considering the lack of budget, this occult thriller got some surprisingly positive reviews, and a short (*Demon Lover Diary*) was made about the confusion behind the scenes and the dubious financial backers. The characters are all named after comic book and film personalities (Frazetta, Gould, Ormsby, Ackerman, Romero, Kirby, etc.). **(R)**

DEMON PLANET: See PLANET OF VAMPIRES.

DEMON RAGE: See SATAN'S MISTRESS.

DEMON SEED

1977 MGM/UA
PRODUCER: Herb Jaffe
DIRECTOR: Donald Cammell
SCREENWRITERS: Robert Jaffe, Roger Ohirson

Overlooked in the year of *Star Wars* and *Close Encounters*, this science-fiction thriller is worth re-evaluating. Scientist Fritz Weaver works on Proteus IV, an artificial brain (with Robert Vaughn's voice). He installs a terminal in his ultramodern house. The superintelligent computer takes over the house, seals all exits, and terrorizes the scientist's wife (Julie Christie). The results are like a mechanized version of *Rosemary's Baby*. The special effects, including an incredible flexible metal pyramid structure, are great. With Gerrit Graham (*Phantom of the Paradise*). Based on a novel by Dean R. Koontz. Director Donald Cammell was co-director of *Performance*. Electronic music by Ian Underwood and Lee Ritenour. (**R**)

DEMON WITCH CHILD
1974 Coliseum (Spain)
DIRECTOR: Armondo De Ossorio
Terrible *Exorcist* copy with a little girl turning ugly, doing awful things, then becoming an old witch. (**R**)

DEMONOID
1979 American Panorama
PRODUCER/DIRECTOR: Alfred Zacharias
SCREENWRITERS: David Lee Fein, Alfred Zacharias
ALSO RELEASED AS: *Macabra*
One of the worst horror films in years. Samantha Eggar and her husband go to Mexico and accidentally unleash a possessed severed hand found in a silver mine. Each person taken over by the five-fingered demon tries to get rid of his own left hand. One actor shuts his hand in a car door, one lets a train run over his, another uses a blowtorch. . . . A possessed cop to a plastic surgeon: "Either you cut my hand off or I'll kill you!" Stuart Whitman, as a priest who attempts an exorcism, has never been worse or funnier. His accent changes from Spanish to Irish to American. First-run theater patrons were given "Demonoid diplomas" to sign. This movie sat around for three years until somebody figured out what to do with it.

DEMONS OF THE MIND
1972 Hammer/Cinemation (England)
PRODUCER: Frank Godwin
DIRECTOR: Peter Sykes
SCREENWRITER: Christopher Wicking
An interesting and intelligent Hammer film set in 19th-century Bavaria. A baron keeps his children (Shane Briant and Gillian Hills) locked up because he thinks they're possessed. Doctor Patrick Magee discovers the down-to-earth facts concerning the family's incest and the baron's madness. With Paul Jones (star of *Privilege* and lead singer of the original Manfred Mann group), Yvonne Mitchell, Robert Hardy, and Virginia Wetherell (she and Magee were both in *Clockwork Orange*).

DEN OF DOOM: See *THE GLASS CAGE*.

DERANGED
1974 AIP (Canada)
PRODUCER: Tom Karr (Bob Clark)
DIRECTORS: Bob Clark, Alan Ormsby
SCREENWRITER: Alan Ormsby
Psycho and *The Texas Chainsaw Massacre* were both partially based on the real-life Wisconsin killer Ed Gein. But this movie comes closer to what actually happened. Robert Blossom is Ezra Cobb, "the butcher of Woodside," a neurotic middle-aged mama's boy who kills and stuffs people. As in the novel

Psycho, he studies occult books, and as in the movie *Psycho*, he preserves his mother's body when she dies. Tom Savini created the mummified corpses Ezra has sitting around the dinner table. The sickest part comes when he wears the skin of a woman he has just killed. A semi-humorous treatment of a real-life horror story. Ed Gein is in the state pen. **(R)**

DE SADE

1969 AIP
PRODUCERS: Samuel Z. Arkoff, James H. Nicholson
DIRECTOR: Cy Endfield
SCREENWRITERS: Richard Matheson, Peter Berg

A major financial flop for AIP, this "biographical" horror/sex film was partially directed by Roger Corman and Gordon Hessler. Screenwriter Richard Matheson claims his script was ruined. Nobody liked the results. The reviews called it "silly," "low-grade," "incomprehensible," and "embarrassing." John Huston, who plays the Marquis' cruel father, is used to embarrassing roles. Kier Dullea followed *2001: A Space Odyssey* with this. I guess this is probably supposed to be an odyssey into a depraved mind. If your taste in film is depraved enough you might love watching such ridiculously tame scenes as Keir putting jam on a girl's nipples, whipping a bare ass, and chasing topless beauties around his ornate bedroom. With Senta Berger, Lilli Palmer, and Anna Massey. Music by Billy Strange. Made in Berlin. **(R)**

DESTINATION INNER SPACE

1966 United Pictures
PRODUCER: Earle Lyon
DIRECTOR: Francis D. Lyon
SCREENWRITER: Arthur C. Pierce

The same team that brought you *Castle of Evil* is back with more mediocrity

starring tough guy Scott Brady. This time he's a navy commander in charge of an undersea lab being terrorized by an alien amphibian monster. Brady argues a lot with chief scientist Gary Merrill and tries to convince Sheree North (in a nice checkered diving outfit) that he's just the guy for her if they don't get slaughtered before the movie ends.

DESTINATION MOON

1950 Eagle-Lion
PRODUCER: George Pal
DIRECTOR: Irving Pichel
SCREENWRITERS: Rip van Ronkel, Robert A. Heinlein, James O'Hanlon

This historically important science-fiction hit usually surprises first-time viewers with its corny humor and dated look. It features a moon surface like the bottom of a dried-up lake, and was

UPI 1950: *The movie Destination Moon received some peculiar publicity when it was shown in West Berlin. Even "moon men" are subject to thirst. Here they are seen pausing at a side-walk cafe for a stein of beer. The ruins in the background are those of Berlin's Kurfuerstendamm.*

considered scientifically accurate at the time. John Archer stars with Warren Anderson, Tom Powers, and Dick Wesson. Also incorporating a Woody Woodpecker cartoon. George Pal considered Woody good luck and referred to him in several features. Directed by the co-star of *Dracula's Daughter*. The score by Leith Stevens has been reissued several times.

DESTINATION NIGHTMARE: See *THE VEIL*.

DESTINATION SATURN: See *BUCK ROGERS*.

DESTINY
1944 Universal (B&W)
PRODUCERS: Howard Benedict,
Roy William Neill
DIRECTORS: Reginald Le Borg, Julian Duvivier
SCREENWRITERS: Roy Chanslor, Ernest Pascal
A film within a film. A segment of the anthology *Flesh and Fantasy* was cut out before the film's release and expanded and re-edited by another director (Le Borg). The new and old sequences are easy to identify. Alan Curtis stars in the new beginning and in the superior main part. A fugitive, he hides out at a farm owned by Frank Craven, whose blind daughter (Gloria Jean) can commune with nature. When the crook attacks her (after shooting her father), a dog attacks him, a storm starts, trees grab at him, and he runs terrified into a river and drowns.

DESTROY ALL MONSTERS
1968 Toho/AIP (Japan)
PRODUCER: Tomoyuki Tanaka
DIRECTOR: Inoshiro Honda
SCREENWRITERS: Kaoru Mabunchi,
Ishiro Honda
ALSO RELEASED AS: *Kaiju Soshingeki*
The ultimate Japanese monster movie! In the future all of Earth's monsters are kept under control on Ogaswara Island. Aliens from Kilaak, stationed on the Moon, use remote-control devices and order the monsters to destroy! Godzilla attacks New York! Mothra invades Peking! Rodan destroys Moscow! There's also Manda (the snake from *Atragon*), Angurus (from *Godzilla vs. The Fire Monster*), Baragon (from *Frankenstein Conquers the World*), Spigas (the spider from *Son of Godzilla*). No more! Stop! Too many monsters! Aaaaaieeee! By the way, Earth regains control, the aliens send Ghidrah, who is defeated by the Earth monsters, and order is fully restored!

DESTROY ALL PLANETS
1968 Daiei/AIP-TV (Japan)
PRODUCER: Hidemasa Nagata
DIRECTOR: Noriaki Yuasa
SCREENWRITER: Fumi Takahashi
ALSO RELEASED AS: *Gamera Tai Virus*
Gamera the flying turtle is back for the fourth time. Aliens land in a spaceship made of four striped balls and turn into a giant flying squid. Gamera saves the world (and two little boys) by defeating the invaders. Not to be confused with *Destroy All Monsters*—now *that's* a movie to reckon with.

THE DESTRUCTORS
1967 United Pics
PRODUCER: Earle Lyon
DIRECTOR: Francis D. Lyon
SCREENWRITERS: Arthur C. Pierce,
Larry E. Jackson
Spy action about a super laser beam called the Cyclops. Richard Egan as hero Dan Street battles bad guys Michael Ansara, John Ericson, Joan Blackman, and Khigh Dhiegh, familiar faces all. Patricia Owens (*The Fly*) plays the hero's ex-wife. From the makers of *Castle of Evil*.

THE DEVIL AND DANIEL WEBSTER: See ALL THAT MONEY CAN BUY.

THE DEVIL AND MISS SARAH

1971 TV

PRODUCER: Stan Shpetner
DIRECTOR: Michael Caffey
SCREENWRITER: Calvin Clements

Boring occult Western with outlaw Gene Barry possessing Janice Rule's soul through hypnotism. James Drury is her husband. With Slim Pickens.

THE DEVIL BAT

1941 PRC (B&W)

PRODUCER: Jack Gallagher
DIRECTOR: Jean Yarbrough
SCREENWRITER: John Thomas Neville
ALSO RELEASED AS: Killer Bats

As Dr. Carruthers, Bela Lugosi gets revenge by giving out samples of his special shaving lotion. The aroma attracts his giant bat, usually kept in his secret lab. A wonderfully ridiculous chiller from the cheapest studio in the business. Bela says a cheery good-bye to his victims after making sure they sample his lotion. With hero Dave O'Brien and Suzanne Kaaren.

THE DEVIL BAT'S DAUGHTER

1946 PRC (B&W)

PRODUCER/DIRECTOR: Frank Wisbar
SCREENWRITER: Griffin Jay

A psychiatrist (Eddie Kane) tries to drive Rosemary Laplanche (Miss America of 1941) crazy. Rosemary is the daughter of the late Dr. Carruthers (played by Lugosi in The Devil Bat). The good doctor's name is cleared of the murders in that film and the "real" villain is exposed in this cheat sequel from the director of Strangler of the Swamp. John James is the hero.

THE DEVIL COMMANDS

1941 Columbia (B&W)

PRODUCER: Wallace McDonald
DIRECTOR: Edward Dmytryk
SCREENWRITERS: Robert D. Andrews, Milton Gunzberg

In Boris Karloff's weirdest unhinged-scientist film, he tries to communicate with the dead (specifically his late wife) by using electricity and stolen corpses. A whole table of seated, wired bodies in robotlike diving suits with neon lightning coming out of their helmets jerks spastically when Boris throws the switch. One manacled live human sits at the head of the table. After his medium-helper Anne Revere dies he decides to use his unwilling daughter (Amanda Duff). One standout scene has a maid locked in the room with the neatly arranged corpses. It was loosely based on "The Edge of Running Water," a popular story by William Sloane.

DEVIL DOG: THE HOUND OF HELL

1978 TV

PRODUCER: Lou Morheim
DIRECTOR: Curtis Harrington
SCREENWRITERS: Stephen and Elinor Karpf

A dog is possessed by the Devil! Its suburban-family owners (Richard Crenna, Yvette Mimieux, and kids) fall under its canine spell! With Victor Jory and Martine Beswick. TV's answer to Dracula's Dog?

THE DEVIL DOLL

1936 MGM (B&W)

PRODUCER: E.J. Mannix
DIRECTOR: Tod Browning
SCREENWRITERS: Garrett Fort, Guy Endore, Erich von Stroheim

A strange sentimental revenge story with Lionel Barrymore escaping from Devil's Island (where he was unjustly sentenced) and using the shrinking serum of his fellow prisoner Henry B. Walthall to make tiny people. He masquerades as a kindly old lady running a doll shop and sends 12-inch people to kill or rob his crooked ex-business partners. Maureen O'Sullivan is his impoverished daughter. Rafaela Ottiano is his crazed assistant. The special effects are better than in *Doctor Cyclops* or any other shrunken-people movie. Browning only did one more film (*Miracles for Sale*).

THE DEVIL DOLL

1963 Associated Film Distributors (England/U.S.)
PRODUCER/DIRECTOR: Lindsay Shonteff
SCREENWRITERS: George Barclay,
Lance Z. Hargreaves

Aside from a *Dead of Night* segment, this is the best ventriloquist's dummy film. Bryant Halliday is terrific as the Great Yorelli, whose act with the dummy Hugo is tense with insults and threats. A London newspaperman (William Sylvester) knows there's something unnatural about the act and determines to find out what it is. Hugo is scary enough just sitting there. But when he gets up and walks and talks on his own or threatens people with a knife, he's real nightmare material. There's an involved plot, plans for a female version of little Hugo, and a chilling ending. With Yvonne Romain. Richard Gordon was executive producer.

DEVIL GIRL FROM MARS

1954 Spartan (England) (B&W)
PRODUCERS: Edward J. and
Harry Lee Danziger
DIRECTOR: David MacDonald
SCREENWRITERS: John C. Mather,
James Eastwood

A Martian woman arrives on Earth to capture men for breeding purposes. Her tall robot companion is a unique creation that looks sort of like a thin white toaster with a police-car light on top. The alien herself is a real vision in boots, black tights, padded shoulders, cape, and a shiny black skullcap. The stuffy British males actually want to stay in England. With Hazel Court, Adrienne Corri, Hugh McDermott, and Peter Reynolds.

DEVIL GODDESS

1955 Columbia (B&W)
PRODUCER: Sam Katzman
DIRECTOR: Spencer Gordon Bennet
SCREENWRITER: George Plympton

African natives who look like Hawaiians worship a volcano. Johnny Weissmuller (as himself) guides an explorer and his daughter to their territory. It was the last of 16 Jungle Jim movies. For the last three the Jim name was dropped. Weissmuller, aged 51, retired from acting after this one, and producer Sam Katzman started aiming his movies at 16-year-olds instead of six-year-olds with *Rock Around the Clock* and other rock musicals.

THE DEVIL RIDES OUT: See THE DEVIL'S BRIDE.

THE DEVIL SHIP PIRATES

1964 Hammer/Columbia (England)
PRODUCER: Anthony Nelson-Keys
DIRECTOR: Don Sharp
SCREENWRITER: Jimmy Sangster

Even after 17 years of playing roles like Dracula, the Mummy, and Frankenstein's monster, it wasn't until this pirate film that Christopher Lee received top billing in an English-language film. He's the Spanish Captain Robles looting the coast of England. With Andrew Keir and Michael Ripper.

THE DEVIL WITHIN HER

1976 Hammer/AIP (England)
PRODUCER: Nato De Angeles
DIRECTOR: Peter Sasdy
SCREENWRITER: Stanley Price
ALSO RELEASED AS:
I Don't Want to Be Born

The Exorcist meets *It's Alive* as Joan Collins (cursed by a dwarf) gives birth to a killer baby. Donald Pleasence delivers the tiny terror. With Ralph Bates, Caroline Munro, and Eileen Atkins. **(R)**

DEVIL WOMAN

1976 Hallmark (Philippines)
PRODUCER: Jimmy Pasqual
DIRECTORS: Albert Yu, Felix Vila

An awful horror movie featuring a Gorgon. A woman with snakes for hair is harmless until superstitious villagers burn her home and kill her parents. She sends cobras (not the ones on her head) to kill the unfortunate locals.

THE DEVILS

1971 Warner Brothers (England)
PRODUCERS: Robert H. Solo, Ken Russell
DIRECTOR/SCREENWRITER: Ken Russell

Disturbing historical frenzy based on John Whiting's play of the same title and *The Devils of Loudon* by Aldous Huxley. Oliver Reed gives his best performance as the powerful father confessor of the walled 17th-century French town of Loudon who is destroyed by political manipulators. They hire an exorcist (Michael Gothard) to torture the mother superior (Vanessa Redgrave) until she makes slanderous accusations about the strong-willed religious leader she secretly lusts for. A stunning and fascinating film hurt at the box office by a misleading X rating. **(X)**

DEVIL'S ANGELS

1967 AIP
PRODUCER: Burt Topper
DIRECTOR: Daniel Haller
SCREENWRITER: Charles Griffith

From the ads: "Their god is violence . . . and like rabid dogs, Lust is the law they live by!" Cody (John Cassavetes) and his gang, the Skulls, have a run-in with a small-town sheriff following a fatality on the highway. The Skulls are deserted by their leader after a second gang's rescue attempt leaves the town in shreds. Beverly Adams, Leo Gordon, Wally Campo, Nai Bonet, Buck Kartalian, and Russ Bender co-star, with Mimsy Farmer as Marianne. It was a follow-up to the popular *Wild Angels*.   –CB

THE DEVIL'S BEDROOM

1964 Manson (B&W)
PRODUCERS: George Gunter, L.Q. Jones
DIRECTOR: L.Q. Jones
SCREENWRITERS: Claude Hall,
   Morgan Woodward

An early effort by the Alvy Moore–L.Q. Jones team (*The Witchmaker* and *A Boy and His Dog*). Moore, better known as Hank Kimball on the TV series *Green Acres*, was the associate producer and acts in the film. The story is about a couple driving a man insane to gain control of his Western property, located over an untapped oil well. With Valerie Allen and Dick Jones. Originally an adults-only release.

THE DEVIL'S BRIDE

1968 Hammer/Seven Arts (England)
PRODUCER: Anthony Nelson-Keys
DIRECTOR: Terence Fisher
SCREENWRITER: Richard Matheson
ALSO RELEASED AS: *The Devil Rides Out*

An excellent, imaginative horror story of good vs. evil, set in the '20s. Christopher Lee, representing the good for a change as the Duc De Richleau, discovers that his friend has joined a secret society of satanists. Charles Gray (narrator of *The Rocky Horror Picture Show*) plays Mocata, who has the knowledge and power to summon the

Devil. Lying in a protective circle with holy symbols, Lee and three others are subjected to every possible visual and psychological illusion of terror. Finally the Angel of Death arrives on horseback. Based on Dennis Wheatley's novel. With Nike Arrighi.

THE DEVIL'S COMMANDMENT
1956 RCIP (Italy) (B&W)
PRODUCERS: Ermanno Donati, Luigi Carpentieri
DIRECTOR: Riccardo Freda
SCREENWRITERS: Piero Regnoli, Rik Sjostrom
ORIGINALLY RELEASED AS: I Vampiri
ALSO RELEASED AS: Lust of the Vampires

This early Italian gothic horror film about a doctor using blood to restore the youth of a countess was released in America as an adults-only film. The U.S. distributor added an opening sequence in which an actress takes a bath and a mild rape scene. That's why this probably pretty interesting film, which was photographed by Mario Bava, is so hard to find now. With Gianna Maria Canale, Antoine Balpetre, and Paul Muller.

THE DEVIL'S DAFFODIL
1961 Goldstone Films (England/ W. Germany)
PRODUCERS: Steven Pallos, Donald Taylor
DIRECTOR: Akos Von Rathony
SCREENWRITERS: Basil Dawson, Donald Taylor
ALSO RELEASED AS: The Daffodil Killer, Das Geheimnis der Gelben Narzissen

An Edgar Wallace mystery which was shot with two different supporting casts, one English and the other German. Christopher Lee (who had to play a Chinese detective in German) stars in both. In the German version, Klaus Kinski is the main villain, an insane ex-con heroin addict who battles it out with Lee in a cemetery. With Joachim Fuchsberger. The less interesting English cast features William Lucas and Colin Jeavons (as the killer).

DEVIL'S DAUGHTER: See POCOMANIA.

THE DEVIL'S DAUGHTER
1972 TV
PRODUCERS: Thomas L. Miller, Edward K. Milkis
DIRECTOR: Jeannot Szwarc
SCREENWRITER: Colin Higgins

Shelley Winters as Satan! She tries to make the daughter of the title (Belinda J. Montgomery) marry a fellow demon. A Rosemary's Baby ripoff with Joseph Cotton, Jonathan Frid, Abe Vigoda, and Robert Foxworth. By the director of Bug and Jaws II.

DEVIL'S EXPRESS
1975 Mahler Films
PRODUCERS: Nick Patton, Steve Madoff
DIRECTOR: Barry Rosen
ALSO RELEASED AS: Gang Wars

A black New York City kung fu student somehow unleashes an ugly murdering demon in the subway system. A terrible, funny martial-arts monster movie with ideas taken from Raw Meat. In one scene you can see the camera crew! Starring Warhawk Tanzania and Sam DeFazio. (R)

THE DEVIL'S HAND
1959 Crown International (B&W)
PRODUCER: Alvis K. Bubis
DIRECTOR: William J. Hole, Jr.
SCREENWRITER: Jo Heims
ALSO RELEASED AS: The Naked Goddess, Live to Love

Robert Alda dreams about beautiful Linda Christian. He goes to a curio shop run by Neil Hamilton, a voodoo high priest, and is given the girl's address when he buys a doll of her. She convinces him to join the cult and his old girlfriend ends up in the hospital when her doll is used as a pincushion. Hamilton (Commissioner Gordon on *Batman*) has a nifty sacrifice machine, a wheel with sharp swords attached that descends from the ceiling onto the victim on a table. Pretty bad. From the director of *The Ghost of Dragstrip Hollow*.

THE DEVIL'S IN LOVE
1933 Fox (B&W)
PRODUCER: Fox Production
DIRECTOR: William Dieterle
Victory Jory stars as a doctor who joins the French Foreign Legion to avoid a murder charge. Bela Lugosi, in a small serious role, is a military prosecutor at a court-martial. With Loretta Young, David Manners, J. Carrol Naish, and Akim Tamiroff.

DEVIL'S ISLAND
1939 Warner Brothers (B&W)
ASSOCIATE PRODUCER: Bryan Foy
DIRECTOR: William Clemens
SCREENWRITERS: Kenneth Gamet, Don Ryan
A good exposé/adventure movie starring Boris Karloff as a curly-headed French surgeon accused of treason for treating an escaped convict. He's sent to the notorious island prison, where the sadistic commandant uses a miniature guillotine to clip his cigars. After leading a revolt, being put in solitary confinement, escaping, and being sentenced to death, Boris is helped by the commandant's wife for saving the life of her child. It was released a year late with some scenes cut and new footage added because of complaints from the French consulate. With James Stephenson and Nedda Harrigan.

THE DEVIL'S MASK
1946 Columbia (B&W)
PRODUCER: Wallace MacDonald
DIRECTOR: Henry Levin
SCREENWRITERS: Charles O'Neal,
  Dwight V. Babcock
An "I Love a Mystery" feature based on the CBS radio show. Private detectives Jim Bannon and Barton Yarborough investigate a murder involving shrunken heads, hypnotism, and a man who has returned from the grave. With Anita Louise and Mona Barrie.

THE DEVIL'S MESSENGER
1959/62 Herts-Lion International
  (U.S./Sweden) (B&W)
PRODUCER: Kenneth Herts
DIRECTOR: Herbert L. Strock, Curt Siodmak
SCREENWRITER: Leo Guild
Apparently Lon Chaney, Jr., went to Sweden and starred in a TV series called *No. 13 Demon St.*, written by Curt Siodmak. This is a re-edited version of three episodes. As the Devil, Chaney keeps a little revolving file of human sins. Karen Kadler is Satanya, his messenger. She helps three people on the road to Hell, then is reunited with the lover she had killed herself over. Chaney sends the damned couple back to Earth with an envelope. It contains the formula for the atomic bomb. Soon the human race is destroyed and everybody joins Lon Chaney in Hell! End. Same director as *I Was a Teenage Frankenstein*.

THE DEVIL'S NIGHTMARE
1971 Hemisphere (Belgium/Italy)
PRODUCER: Charles Lecocq
DIRECTOR: Jean Brismee
SCREENWRITERS: Patrice Rhomm,
  Charles Lecocq, André Hunebelle
ALSO RELEASED AS: *Vampire Playgirls*
Seven tourists (symbolizing the seven deadly sins) go to a remote European villa where they are seduced and killed

Erika Blanc helps enact
The Devil's Nightmare.

by a succubus (Erika Blanc). The deaths are various and gruesome. Daniel Emilfork, whom you might recognize from some Fellini movies, shows up as the Devil. With Jean Servais. It was released here in '74 in an attempt to cash in on the success of *The Exorcist*. (R)

THE DEVILS OF DARKNESS

1965 20th Century-Fox (England)
PRODUCER: Tom Blakely
DIRECTOR: Lance Comfort
SCREENWRITER: Lynn Fairhurst

Count Sinistre (Hubert Noel) is a vampire posing as an artist in modern-day Brittany. He leads a cult of Devil worshipers who met in a secret crypt under a graveyard. The cult enjoys sacrificing young female tourists and has an orgy with a snake dancer. William Sylvester is the hero. With Carole Gray.

THE DEVIL'S OWN

1966 Hammer/20th Century-Fox (England)
PRODUCER: Anthony Nelson-Keys
DIRECTOR: Carl Frankel
SCREENWRITER: Nigel Kneale
ALSO RELEASED AS: *The Witches*

Joan Fontaine owned the rights to an occult thriller and wanted to star in it, so she got Hammer Films to produce it. Reviews were less than enthusiastic. She retired from theatrical features for good. During the precredit sequence Joan is involved with voodoo in Africa. Returning to England, she finds a modern-day witches' coven led by Kay Walsh, who plans to sacrifice a virgin. Also with Martin Stevens (the lead kid in *Village of the Damned*).

THE DEVIL'S PARTNER

1958 Film Group (B&W)
PRODUCER: Hugh M. Hooker
DIRECTOR: Charles R. Rondeau
SCREENWRITERS: Stanley Clements, Laura J. Mathews

Ed Nelson has an interesting role: as an old man possessed by the Devil, he seems to die but returns as a younger version of himself. He sacrifices goats and uses magic to win Jean Allison from Richard Crane, who is savagely attacked by his own dog. When the sheriff investigates, the versatile evil one turns into a snake. With Edgar Buchanan and Byron Foulger.

THE DEVIL'S PEOPLE: See LAND OF THE MINOTAUR

THE DEVIL'S RAIN

1975 Bryanston
PRODUCERS: James V. Cullen, Michael S. Glick
DIRECTOR: Robert Fuest
SCREENWRITERS: Gabe Essoe, James Ashton, Gerald Hopman

Although it has a hard time living up to Hieronymus Bosch's "Garden of Earthly Delights," which is shown under the credits, this film might satisfy if you wait until the end. Ernest Borgnine as Corbis turns into a goat-headed demon and for about 15 minutes cast members are reduced to colorful oozing, melting puddles. The goat-demon is after an ancient book hidden by the Southwestern Preston family. A highlight is the screaming souls of doomed victims in a crystal ball that resembles one of those paperweights that snow when you turn them upside down. Not a highlight is the acting. With Ida Lupino and Keenan Wynn (they become eyeless soulless things), Eddie Albert, Tom Skerrit, William Shatner, Anton Levy (a "real witch"), and John Travolta (in a tiny role). When the film was rereleased, the hard-to-spot Travolta actually got top billing in the ads. Filmed in Mexico.

THE DEVIL'S SISTERS

1966 Thunderbird International (B&W)
PRODUCERS: Joseph Fink, Juan Hidalgo-Gato
DIRECTOR: William Grefe
SCREENWRITERS: John Nicholas,
William Grefe

Sharon Saxon answers a domestic-help-wanted classified in Tijuana and, with the help of sadistic Mildred Rodesky, is taken into a white slavery ring run by Velia Martinez and Anita Crystal (as the Alvarado sisters). Saxon is stripped and tied with barbed wire for her part in the murder of an Englishman but escapes after fellow captives rise in her defense. With Fred Pinero, Babette Sherrill, Toni Camel, Joan Jacobs, and Nora Alonzo. Filmed in Miami.   –CB

THE DEVIL'S SLEEP

1951 Screen Art (B&W)
DIRECTOR: Merle Connell

Leaders of a narcotics ring preying on teenagers try to stop the investigation of a crusading woman juvenile judge by tying her daughter into a blackmail scheme. Lita Grey Chaplin, John Mitchum, William Thomason, and Tracy Lynn star. Director Connell was the cinematographer on Phil Tucker's *Cape Canaveral Monsters*. He also directed *The Flesh Merchants*.   –CB

DEVIL'S TRIANGLE

1976 UFO Distribution
PRODUCER/DIRECTOR/SCREENWRITER:
Richard Winer

The best thing about this speculation film is its length. It's only 55 minutes. Vincent Price reads the silly narration. King Crimson provides the music. Viewers were offered $10,000 if they could solve the mystery of the triangle.

THE DEVIL'S WEDDING NIGHT

1973 Dimension (Italy)
PRODUCER: Ralph Zucker
DIRECTOR: Paul Solvay
SCREENWRITERS: Ralph Zucker,
Alan M. Harris

Italy's answer to *Countess Dracula*, starring Sara Bay of *Lady Frankenstein* fame as the countess who stays young by bathing in virgin's blood. American Mark Damon (*House of Usher*) shows up as both the good and bad brothers. The acting is all bad and there's lots of nudity. (**R**)

THE DEVIL'S WIDOW

1972 AIP (England)
PRODUCERS: Alan Ladd, Jr., Stanley Mann
DIRECTOR: Roddy McDowall
SCREENWRITER: William Spier
ALSO RELEASED AS: *Tam Lin*

Roddy McDowall directed a horror movie? Sure did, and it's an odd one. The story is based on an ancient Scottish folk song. Ava Gardner is an older woman who uses witchcraft to keep her young jet-set friends, including Madeline Smith, Stephanie Beacham, and Ian McShane. The film never got a general release and critics seem to agree that it's both awful and overarty. Filmed in Scotland. Music by Pentangle.

THE DIABOLICAL DR. Z

1966 U.S. Films (Spain/France) (B&W)
PRODUCERS: Serge Silberman, Michel Safra
DIRECTOR: Jesse Franco
SCREENWRITERS: Jesse Franco,
Jean-Claude Carrière
ORIGINALLY RELEASED AS: *Miss Muerte*

Howard Vernon is back as Dr. Orloff/ Dr. Von Zimmer. When he dies of a heart attack, his work is taken over by his devoted daughter (Mabel Karr). She discovers a cabaret dancer known as Miss Death (Estella Blain) who has abnormally long fingernails. The daughter figures they'd make good weapons, so she uses mind control to will the dancer to kill her dad's enemies. It was the third in a ridiculous series. Two were released only in Europe.

DIABOLIK: See DANGER: DIABOLIK.

DIABOLIQUE

1955 Seven Arts (France) (B&W)
PRODUCER/DIRECTOR: Henri-Georges Clouzot
SCREENWRITERS: Henri-Georges Clouzot,
Georges Geronimi, René Masson,
F. Grendel
ORIGINALLY RELEASED AS: *Les Diaboliques*

It's fitting that one of the first foreign features to make it big on the American art-theater circuit was a masterful psychological horror film. The twist-ending murder plot has been done countless times but never better. Simone Signoret helps Vera Clouzot (real-life wife of the director) drown her husband (Paul Meurisse), who "returns to life" in a terrifying scene. It all takes place at a school. The face of the would-be murderess/victim seeing her dead husband move was used in the effective newspaper ads. *Reflections of Murder* was a remake.

DIAL M FOR MURDER

1954 Warner Brothers (3-D)
PRODUCER/DIRECTOR: Alfred Hitchcock
SCREENWRITER: Frederick Knott

In a few years, stars Ray Milland and Robert Cummings would be working for AIP (in *Premature Burial* and *Beach Party* respectively), and Grace Kelly, in the first of her three Hitchcock roles here, would be the Princess of Monaco. All of them are excellent in this filmed version of Frederick Knott's suspense play. John Williams (the inspector) is now known for the TV commercials in which he pitches classical music LPs. Watch for director Alfred Hitchcock in a picture on Milland's wall. Kelly's hand reaching out for help as someone attempts to murder her is the best use of 3-D ever. The film was re-released in 1982.

DIAL M FOR MURDER

1981 TV
PRODUCER: Peter Katz
DIRECTOR: Boris Sagal
SCREENWRITER: John Gay

It's TV-movie remake time. (Before it was a play and a Hitchcock film it was a 1952 British television presentation.) Christopher Plummer is the husband who wants wife Angie Dickinson killed by Ron Moody. Inspector Anthony Quayle and Angie's lover Michael Parks solve the murder mystery. Angie had just starred in Brian DePalma's Hitchcock copy, *Dressed to Kill.*

DIAMONDS ARE FOREVER

1971 United Artists (England)
PRODUCERS: Albert R. Broccoli,
Harry Saltzman
DIRECTOR: Guy Hamilton
SCREENWRITERS: Richard Maibaum,
Tom Mankiewicz

After the failure of *On Her Majesty's Secret Service*, Sean Connery was lured back for one more Bond movie. He shouldn't have bothered. It's the worst. Everything leads to sausage king Jimmy Dean. 007 smashes cars, gambles, fights female gymnasts, loves Jill St. John, defeats Blofeld (Charles Gray—the third actor in the part), and strangles a woman with her bikini top. Lana Wood is thrown out a window. With *King Kong* star Bruce Cabot, who died in '72. Music by John Barry. Filmed largely in Las Vegas. Connery returned to the Bond role again in 1983 (*Never Say Die Again*).

DIARY OF A HIGH SCHOOL BRIDE
1959 AIP (B&W)
PRODUCER/DIRECTOR/SCREENWRITER:
 Burt Topper

Chris Robinson (of *Stanley*) stars as an unbalanced teenager trying to sabotage former girlfriend Anita Sands' marriage to law student Ronald Foster. She agrees to meet him for a talk on a deserted sound stage at his father's studio; he attacks. Foster, acting on a tip from another of Robinson's victims, races to the scene and there follows a hair-raising catwalk battle resulting in high-voltage electrocution. Title song written and performed by Tony Casanova. Originally billed with *Ghost of Dragstrip Hollow*. —CB

DIARY OF A MADMAN
1963 United Artists
PRODUCER/SCREENWRITER: Robert E. Kent
DIRECTOR: Reginald Le Borg

An effective low-key period horror piece based on "The Horla" by Guy de Maupassant. Vincent Price is Simon Cordier, a 19th-century French magistrate who inherits an invisible evil spirit when he kills a mad condemned prisoner in self-defense. The prisoner, whose eyes glow before he dies, provides an eerie scare. Cordier, now controlled by evil, tries to calm down by sculpting, but kills his model.

DICK TRACY
1945 RKO (B&W)
PRODUCER: Herman Schlom
DIRECTOR: William Berke
SCREENWRITER: Eric Taylor

After four popular Republic serials, Chester Gould's famous detective was featured in four full-length RKO films. In this, the first, Morgan Conway (as Tracy) captures a scarred Mike Mazurki (as Splitface). Anne Jeffreys plays Tess Trueheart. The newspaper ads, referring to the serials, promised "no waiting till tomorrow to see what's next!" Some consider these among the worst films ever made, but they were based on comic strips, aimed at kids attending matinees, and not intended to be taken too seriously. Director Martin Scorsese has announced a new Tracy feature.

DICK TRACY MEETS GRUESOME
1947 RKO (B&W)
PRODUCER: Herman Schlom
DIRECTOR: John Rawlins
SCREENWRITERS: Robertson White,
 Eric Taylor

In the best Dick Tracy feature, Boris Karloff plays Gruesome, who uses stolen paralyzing bombs to freeze everybody in banks while he robs them. Enemies are thrown in a furnace. Ralph Byrd is Dick Tracy. He was Tracy in four serials, two features, and on television. Anne Gwynne is Tess Trueheart. With Skelton Knaggs, Milton Parsons, Lex Barker, and Robert Clarke.

DICK TRACY'S DILEMMA
1947 RKO (B&W)
PRODUCER: Herman Schlom
DIRECTOR: John Rawlins
SCREENWRITER: Robert Stephen Brody

Boris Karloff (with gas bomb), Anne Gwynne, Ralph Byrd, and Skelton Knaggs in Dick Tracy Meets Gruesome.

After releasing two forgettable Tracy features, RKO got Ralph Byrd, the original serial Dick Tracy, to star in two more. These last two are even more cartoon-inspired than their predecessors. This one features Jack Lambert as a fur-stealing crook with a lethal hook hand. With Ian Keith and Lyle Latell.

DICK TRACY VS. CUEBALL

1946 RKO (B&W)
PRODUCER: Herman Schlom
DIRECTOR: Gordon Douglas
SCREENWRITER: Luci Ward

Morgan Conway as Dick Tracy and Anne Jeffreys as Tess Trueheart, for the second and last time. Typical ad campaign: "Dick the dauntless dares death to deliver diamonds!" The bald diamond-stealing crook is Dick Wessel. Includes characters with names like Filthy Flora and Percival Priceless. With series regulars Lyle Latell, Ian Keith, and Skelton Knaggs.

DIE, DIE MY DARLING

1965 Hammer/Columbia (English)
PRODUCER: Anthony Hinds
DIRECTOR: Silvio Narizzano
SCREENWRITER: Richard Matheson
ALSO RELEASED AS: *Fanatic*

Tallulah Bankhead in her last movie role (it was also her first in 12 years) as an old religious fanatic who keeps her dead son's fiancée (Stephanie Powers) prisoner. Tallulah plans to "cleanse" and then kill her so she can marry the dead son in Heaven! Stephanie is abused by every crazy member of the house, including Donald Sutherland as an imbecile handyman who reads his Bible upside down. A *Baby Jane* and *Psycho*-inspired drama.

DIE, MONSTER DIE

1965 AIP (U.S./England)
PRODUCER: Pat Green
DIRECTOR: Daniel Haller
SCREENWRITER: Jerry Sohl
ALSO RELEASED AS: *Monster of Terror*

Former AIP art director Daniel Haller directs for the first time with mixed results. Boris Karloff stars in a wheelchair as Nathum Witley, master of a strange house in Arkham, England, in this film based on an H.P. Lovecraft story. American Nick Adams arrives to marry Witley's daughter (Suzan Farmer) and discovers a huge, radioactive mutation-causing meteorite in the cellar. The plants and animals grow tremendously large, Mrs. Whitley (Freda Jackson) is disfigured, and Nathum becomes a glowing monster with a head like a raspberry. With Patrick Magee (as a doctor) and Terence De Marney. Haller tried filming Lovecraft again with *The Dunwich Horror*.

DIE SCREAMING MARIANNE

1970 (England)
DIRECTOR: Pete Walker

Susan George stars as a nightclub dancer pursued by killers out for her father's money. An early thriller by the director of *The Confessional*. With Christopher Sanford and Leo Genn.

DIMENSION 5
1967 Feature Film Corporation
PRODUCER: Earl Lyon
DIRECTOR: Franklin Adreon
SCREENWRITER: Arthur C. Pierce
Jeffrey Hunter, fresh from playing Captain Kirk in the *Star Trek* pilot, is secret agent Justin Power. He and France Nuyen wear time-travel belts and go a few weeks into the future to save Los Angeles from a Communist Chinese A-bomb. Harold Sakata is Big Buddah. With Donald Woods, Lindo Ho, and David Chon.

DINO
1957 Allied Artists (B&W)
PRODUCER: Bernice Block
DIRECTOR: Thomas Carr
SCREENWRITER: Reginald Rose
A confused 17-year-old juvenile delinquent (Sal Mineo) is paroled after serving time for a robbery in which a watchman was killed. Social worker Brian Keith tries to help. Susan Kohner is his girlfriend. Mineo had just played essentially the same role (as support) in *Rebel Without a Cause* and *Crime in the Streets*.

DINOSAURUS
1960 Universal
PRODUCER: Jack H. Harris
DIRECTOR: Irwin S. Yeaworth, Jr.
SCREENWRITERS: Jean Yeaworth,
Dan E. Weisburd
A children's film about a caveman, a brontosaurus, and a T. Rex revived by lightning on an island. A little boy befriends and rides the bronto, the T. Rex fights a steam shovel, and the caveman (Gregg Martel) has "comical" problems with modern appliances. The animation is pretty lousy. Dinosaur scenes later showed up on the *It's About Time* TV series.

DISC JOCKEY JAMBOREE:
See JAMBOREE

DISCIPLE OF DEATH
1972 Avco/Embassy (England)
PRODUCERS: Tom Parkinson,
Charles Fairman
DIRECTOR: Tom Parkinson
SCREENWRITERS: Tom Parkinson,
Churton Fairman
After being in several Hammer films and *Crucible of Terror*, ex-disc jockey Mike Raven starred in this low-budget Gothic shocker. He plays the Stranger, a living-dead ghoul who must sacrifice virgins to Satan. When the hero (Stephan Bradley) and a minister are unable to stop the killings, they go for help to an old Jewish cabalist with a magic mirror. With Virginia Wetherall (*A Clockwork Orange*).

THE DISEMBODIED
1957 Allied Artists (B&W)
PRODUCER: Ben Schwalb
DIRECTOR: Walter Grauman
SCREENWRITER: Jack Townley
Fun jungle nonsense with Allison Hayes as Tonda, who sneaks away from her doctor husband to dance wildly in a sarong and tooth necklace. The confusing voodoo feature also stars Paul Burke and John E. Wengraf. It originally played with *From Hell It Came*.

DISK-O-TEK HOLIDAY
1966 Allied Artists (England)
PRODUCER: Jacques De Lane
DIRECTORS: Douglas Hickox (U.K.)/
Vince Scarza (U.S.)
SCREENWRITER: David Edwards
ALSO RELEASED AS: *Just for You*

Released in Britain in 1964, this rock 'n' roll movie was reworked for American distribution with additional sequences featuring regional heroes like the Vagrants (with Leslie West) and the Rockin' Ramrods. With Peter and Gordon, the Chiffons, the Bachelors, Freddy Cannon, the Merseybeats, the Applejacks, the Orchids, Jackie and the Raindrops, Casey Paxton, and Millie Small. Arnie "Woo Woo" Ginsberg of Boston and Hy Lit of Philadelphia are the emcees. —CB

DOC SAVAGE — MAN OF BRONZE
1975 MGM
PRODUCER: George Pal
DIRECTOR: Michael Anderson
SCREENWRITERS: George Pal, Joe Morheim

Pal's last feature is a silly version of the '30s pulp magazine formula of a hero searching for killers in Africa. Blond ex-Tarzan Ron Ely stars. Look for Michael Berryman of *The Hills Have Eyes* fame in a small role. Director Anderson topped it the next year with *Logan's Run*.

DR. BLACK AND MR. HYDE
1975 Dimension
PRODUCER: Charles Walker
DIRECTOR: William Crain
SCREENWRITER: Larry LeBron
ALSO RELEASED AS: *The Watts Monster*

The director of *Blacula* returns with an even cheaper black horror film. Bernie Casey as "Dr. Pride" works at a Watts free clinic. When he becomes his monstrous other self he turns white! Looking like a black man who sneezed into a bag of flour, he kills women and leaves his nice girlfriend for a prostitute. Casey is an ex-Rams running back. With Rosalind Cash (*The Omega Man*), Ji-Tu Cumbuka, and disco music. It was originally going to be called *Dr. Black and Mr. White*. (R)

DOCTOR BLOOD'S COFFIN
1961 United Artists (England)
PRODUCER: George Fowler
DIRECTOR: Sidney J. Furie
SCREENWRITER: Jerry Juran

Dr. Peter Blood (Kieron Moore), a biochemist in Cornwall, decides to kill "worthless" people so he can use their hearts to revive "worthy" corpses. He experiments secretly in a mine, occasionally killing villagers. His father's nurse (Hazel Court), a widow, discovers his activities and threatens to call the authorities, so the perverse doctor revives the rotten, decomposed body of her dead husband (with the heart of a kidnaped hobo). Paul Stockman makes his debut as the unexpected hubby.

DR. BREEDLOVE OR HOW I LEARNED TO STOP WORRYING AND LOVE: See *KISS ME QUICK*.

DR. BUTCHER, M.D. (MEDICAL DEVIATE)
1979 Aquarius (Italy)
PRODUCER: Terry Levine
DIRECTOR/SCREENWRITER: Frank Martin (Francesco Martino)
ORIGINALLY RELEASED AS: *Queen of the Cannibals*

This extremely gory cannibal adventure became a big moneymaker when released in America with a new pretitle sequence (from an unreleased NYU film) tacked on. In 1982 an extensive traveling "Butchermobile" promotion in the New York City area helped spread the word that it was the best gut muncher in years. The disgusting effects are by the guy who did the honors for *Zombie*. As in that hit, the action begins in Manhattan but soon moves to a remote island. Very realistic flesh-eating Indonesian pygmies attack investigating Americans, while a

He is a depraved, homicidal killer.

...and He Makes House Calls!

DOCTOR BUTCHER M.D.

(Medical Deviate)

AQUARIUS RELEASING INC.

R

mad doctor performs lobotomies. Oriental natives provide comedy relief. Beautiful Alexandra Cole (a.k.a. Alexandria Delli Colli) is stripped and worshiped by the natives before the whole exhausting and incoherent feature ends. *Dr. Butcher II* (another re-edited Italian sickie) is promised. (R)

DR. CADMAN'S SECRET: See THE BLACK SLEEP.

DR. COOK'S GARDEN

1971 TV
PRODUCER: Bob Markell
DIRECTOR: Ted Post
SCREENWRITER: Art Wallace

In his only horror movie Bing Crosby plays Dr. Leonard Cook, who treats his small community just like his garden. He kills the weeds—the bad people. Based on an Ira Levin Broadway play. With Blythe Danner and Frank Converse.

DR. CYCLOPS

1940 Paramount
PRODUCER: Dale Van Every
DIRECTOR: Ernest B. Schoedsack
SCREENWRITER: Tom Kilpatrick

Dr. Thorkel, a bald, nearsighted scientist (Albert Dekker), lures five people and a burro to his jungle hideout and shrinks them. They're confronted by an impressive array of oversized props and an alligator. It's in Technicolor and is a lot of fun to watch. Janice Logan posed for countless great publicity shots, being crushed in a giant hand, stepped on by a giant boot, and examined by the cueball-headed doctor. From the director of *King Kong*.

DR. DEATH, SEEKER OF SOULS

1972 Cinerama Releasing
PRODUCER/DIRECTOR: Eddie Saeta
SCREENWRITER: Sal Ponti

Sure it's another stupid cheap horror movie, but the guest star is Moe Howard! It was the last role for the famous 77-year-old pie-thrower. John Considine stars as a youthful-looking but actually ancient soul transplanter. With his scarred assistant Thor he operates on female patients. With Barry Coe, Florence Marley (as Tanya), Cheryl Miller (from the *Daktari* series), Jo Morrow, Sivia Berg, and TV horror host Seymour. (R)

DOCTOR FAUSTUS

1968 Columbia (England/Italy)
PRODUCERS: Richard Burton, Richard McWhortor
DIRECTOR: Richard Burton
SCREENWRITER: Nevill Coghill

Burton shows his stuff directing himself as old Doctor Faustus, bargaining with Mephistopheles to sell his soul and become young to enjoy 24 hours of "voluptuousness" (and Elizabeth Taylor as Helen of Troy). An Oxford University production featuring members of their dramatic society. Richard was in *Candy* and *Boom!* the same year.

DR. FRANKENSTEIN ON CAMPUS

1970 Medfore (Canada)
PRODUCER: Bill Marshall
DIRECTOR: Gil Taylor
SCREENWRITERS: David Cobb, Bill Marshall, Gil Taylor
ALSO RELEASED AS: *Flick*

A young student who is a descendant of the famous doctor turns some of his classmates into zombies with drugs and a mind-control device. Starring Robin Ward. (R)

THE DOCTOR FROM SEVEN DIALS: See CORRIDORS OF BLOOD.

DR. GOLDFOOT AND THE BIKINI MACHINE

1965 AIP
PRODUCERS: James H. Nicholson, Samuel Z. Arkoff
DIRECTOR: Norman Taurog
SCREENWRITERS: Elwood Ullman, Robert Kaufman

An AIP joke starring Vincent Price as a mad doctor. He plans on taking over the world with his beautiful female robots, who seduce rich and powerful men. Susan Hart is sent after millionaire Dwayne Hickman. Secret agent Frankie Avalon tries to stop the plot but ends up in the torture chamber (with Hickman). The parody of *The Pit and the Pendulum* is the highlight of this nonsense, which also includes bits by Annette Funicello, Harvey Lembeck, Deborah Walley, and two *Playboy* Playmates. Title song sung by the Supremes. The made-in-Italy sequel makes this look like a classic.

DR. GOLDFOOT AND THE GIRL BOMBS

1966 AIP (Italy)
PRODUCERS: Louis M. Heyward, Fulvio Luciano
DIRECTOR: Mario Bava
SCREENWRITERS: Louis M. Heyward, Robert Kaufman, Castellano Pipolo
ORIGINALLY RELEASED AS: *Le Spie Vengona dal Semifreddo*

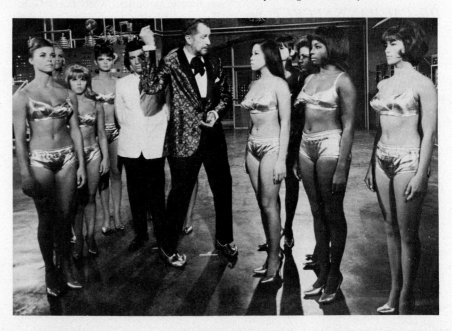

Vincent Price and his creations in Dr. Goldfoot and the Bikini Machine.

Incredibly bad, unfunny sequel to *Dr. Goldfoot and the Bikini Machine*. Vincent Price is back trying to start a war between Russia and America. His female robots have bombs in their navels that explode when they make love to NATO generals. Fabian, as an American spy, teams with two awful Italian comedians to stop Dr. Goldfoot. Laura Antonelli (now famous for taking off her clothes in "art" films) is the main girl bomb. Mario Bava's worst. It's even Fabian's worst. Includes footage from *Goldfoot No. 1*.

DR. HECKYL AND MR. HYPE
1980 Cannon
PRODUCERS: Menahem Golan, Yoram Globus
DIRECTOR/SCREENWRITER: Charles B. Griffith
Long-time Corman collaborator Charles Griffith made this comedy starring Oliver Reed as an incredibly ugly podiatrist who becomes a handsome murderer. Griffith, who wrote *Bucket of Blood* and *Little Shop of Horrors*, even uses Corman regulars Mel Welles and Dick Miller. Jackie Coogan is the desk sergeant at a dungeon/jail. With Sunny Johnson, Maia Danziber, and Corinne Calvert. (**R**)

DR. JEKYLL AND MR. HYDE
1932 Paramount (B&W)
PRODUCER/DIRECTOR: Rouben Mamoulian
SCREENWRITERS: Samuel Hoffenstein, Percy Heath
This classic adaptation of Robert Louis Stevenson's novel features Fredric March giving his Academy Award–winning performance. None of the countless other versions before or since has anything like the power of this quality production. Miriam Hopkins is Ivy the prostitute. Wally Westmore created the convincing makeup. A shocking adult treatment of a timeless theme. With Holmes Herbert and Rose Hobart. Cinematography by Karl Struss. Ten minutes were cut for a re-release and never restored.

DR. JEKYLL AND MR. HYDE
1941 MGM (B&W)
PRODUCER/DIRECTOR: Victor Fleming
SCREENWRITER: John Lee Mahin
Freudian version of the classic story. It was director Fleming's first movie after *Gone with the Wind*. Spencer Tracy stars without much makeup. With Lana Turner as his fiancée and Ingrid Bergman as Ivy the barmaid (obviously a prostitute in the superior '32 version). Worth watching just for Bergman's face and a brief sequence showing the two women as horses being whipped by Hyde. Two years later Tracy starred in Fleming's war-time fantasy, *A Guy Named Joe*.

UPI 8/7/41: The idea of this experiment is to test the female reaction to horror pictures. The movie was Dr. Jekyll and Mr. Hyde. Here is Josephine Seveck taking the test. She is hooked up to a recording apparatus presided over by Dr. W. Marston, eminent psychologist. While the gals get the horrors from the antics of Dr. J. (or maybe Mr. H.) on the screen, Dr. Marston checks his instruments and charts. He found that blondes are more emotional. As if we didn't know.

tertaining variation on an overused theme. Ralph Bates (who resembles Ray Davies of the Kinks) is the good doctor who becomes the evil and very beautiful Martine Beswick. Despite the obvious possibilities it had a PG rating. Ads carried this warning: "The sexual transformation of a man into a woman will actually take place before your very eyes!" The same line was later used more truthfully for *Let Me Die a Woman*, but that's another story. This one includes Burke and Hare, R.L. Stevenson's famous graverobbers, to supply bodies and a Jack the Ripper subplot.

DR. JEKYLL AND THE WOLFMAN

1971 International Cinema Films (Spain)
PRODUCER: Jose Frade
DIRECTOR: Leon Kaminsky
SCREENWRITER: Jacinto Molina
ALSO RELEASED AS:
    Dr. Jekyll y el Hombre Lobo
Paul Naschy as Valdemar the Wolfman—for the sixth time. Obviously running out of ideas, he goes to the grandson of Dr. Jekyll (Jack Taylor), who cures him of being a werewolf. An assistant then turns him into a new "Mr. Hyde" and he tortures women on a rack. (**R**)

DR. JEKYLL'S DUNGEON OF DEATH

1982 Rochelle
PRODUCER/DIRECTOR: James Wood
SCREENWRITER: James Mathers
A no-budget stinker made in Nevada about the grandson of Dr. Jekyll injecting captives in his house with an aggression serum. This results in long karate battles, torture, and various sadistic acts, all observed by the demented, voyeuristic doc. (**R**)

DR. JEKYLL AND SISTER HYDE

1971 Hammer/AIP (British)
PRODUCERS: Albert Fennell, Brian Clemens
DIRECTOR: Roy Ward Baker
SCREENWRITER: Brian Clemens
Brian Clemens, writer for the *Avengers* show, co-produced and wrote this en-

DR. MABUSE VS. SCOTLAND YARD

1963 UCC-TV (W. Germany) (B&W)
PRODUCER: Filmkunst
DIRECTOR: Paul May
SCREENWRITER: Ladislas Foder
ORIGINALLY RELEASED AS: *Scotland Yard Jagt Dr. Mabuse*

The spirit of Dr. Mabuse (Wolfgang Preiss) takes over the body of a professor and begins a new series of crimes. Peter Van Eyck (*The Wages of Fear*) stars with Klaus Kinski, Sabine Bethman, and Walter Rilla. It was the fifth and one of the best of a series of six Mabuse adventures made in the '60s.

DR. MANIAC: See THE MAN WHO LIVED AGAIN.

DR. NO

1963 United Artists (England)
PRODUCERS: Harry Saltzman, Albert R. Broccoli
DIRECTOR: Terence Young
SCREENWRITERS: Richard Maibaum, Johanna Harwood, Berkely Mather

Thirty-two-year-old Scot Sean Connery is Ian Fleming's 007 for the first time. James Bond is sent to Jamaica to investigate a murder and discovers a secret island base run by the diabolical Dr. No, who plans to destroy rockets launched from Cape Canaveral. He also discovers beautiful Ursula Andress as Honey, busy hunting shells on the beach. A winning combination of spies, sex, and science fiction, with a flame-throwing dragon (sort of) and a tarantula in bed. Joseph Wiseman is the Oriental Dr. No. Jack Lord is CIA agent Felix Leiter. Bernard Lee as M and Lois Maxwell as Miss Moneypenny continued their roles throughout the long series. With Anthony Dawson and Zena Marshall. Music by John Barry.

DOCTOR OF DOOM

1962 K. Gordon Murray (Mexico) (B&W)
PRODUCER: William Calderon Stell
DIRECTOR: Rene Cardona
SCREENWRITER: Alfred Salazar
ORIGINALLY RELEASED AS: *Las Luchadoras Contra el Médico Resino*

A classic of Mexican cinema. When a masked mad doctor steals the brain of a female scientist, her wrestling star sister vows to expose the culprit. Two beautiful, statuesque wrestling roommates, The Golden Rubi (Elizabeth Campbell) and Gloria Venus (Lorena Vasquez), eventually defeat the crazed surgeon, his super-strong ape man, Gomar, and his surgically created wrestling woman, Vendetta. They also have lots of fights in and out of the ring and rescue the bumbling male policemen. The first of a series of entertaining south-of-the-border wrestling women adventures. Don't miss it.

DR. ORLOFF'S MONSTER

1964 AIP-TV (Spain/Aus)
DIRECTOR: Jesse Franco
SCREENWRITERS: Jesse Franco, Nick Frank
ORIGINALLY RELEASED AS: *El Secreto del Dr. Orloff*

The Awful Dr. Orloff is back in his first sequel. Star Howard Vernon is missing, but the plot's the same as in the previous film. A mad scientist uses his human robot to kill for him. With Jose Rubio and Agnes Spaak. Pretty slow.

DR. PHIBES RISES AGAIN

1972 AIP (England)
PRODUCER: Louis M. Heyward
DIRECTOR: Robert Fuest
SCREENWRITERS: Robert Fuest, Robert Blees

Vincent Price returns as the ingenious doctor, now in Egypt searching for the

UPI 1972: *Last year's* Abominable Dr. Phibes *was such a well-received film that AIP is following it with another,* Dr. Phibes Rises Again. *Vincent Price depicts a scientist who is seeking a secret something which will bring his beloved deceased wife back to life. Of course he has to deliciously do away with a few bad guys and good guys along the way....*

Elixir of Life to revive his dead wife (Caroline Munro, in a glass coffin). Robert Quarry is after the same prize and, as in the original movie (*The Abominable Dr. Phibes*), people keep dying in horrible and sometimes hilarious ways. Especially good is a telephone receiver with a spike in it. Peter Cushing has a bit part as a ship's captain. With Hugh Griffith, Terry-Thomas, Fiona Lewis, Beryl Reid, and Valli Kemp as Vulnavia. Not as good as the first one but still fun.

DR. RENAULT'S SECRET
1942 20th Century Fox (B&W)
PRODUCER: Sol M. Wurtzel
DIRECTOR: Harry Lachman
SCREENWRITERS: William Bruckner, Robert F. Metzler

Mad scientist George Zucco turns a gorilla into an ape man (J. Carrol Naish). Monogram-style horror with a slightly higher budget. With Sheppard Strudwick, Lynne Roberts, and Mike Mazurki.

DR. SATAN'S ROBOT: See *THE MYSTERIOUS DR. SATAN.*

DR. SCORPION
1978 TV
PRODUCER: Alex Beaton
DIRECTOR: Richard Lang
SCREENWRITER: Stephen J. Cannell

As comic-book superhero Dr. Scorpion, Nick Mancuso saves the world from a mad doctor who steals atomic missiles. From the same TV season that brought us pilots for *Spiderman* and *The Incredible Hulk*, from the director of the pilots for *Fantasy Island* and *Vegas*. With Roscoe Lee Browne and Denny Miller.

DR. STRANGE
1978 TV
PRODUCER: Alex Beaton
DIRECTOR/SCREENWRITER: Philip DeGuere

After the success of *Superman*, the networks were anxious to turn comic-book heroes into series. This pilot is one interesting attempt. Peter Hooten is the psychiatrist hero. John Mills is his teacher, the ancient sorcerer Lindmar. Jessica Walter as Morgan Le Fay represents the forces of evil. From Stan Lee's Marvel comic. Hooten co-starred in Bo Derek's first film (*Fantasies*) and *Orca*.

DR. STRANGELOVE OR HOW I LEARNED TO STOP WORRYING AND LOVE THE BOMB
1963 Columbia (England) (B&W)
PRODUCER/DIRECTOR: Stanley Kubrick
SCREENWRITERS: Stanley Kubrick, Terry Southern, Peter George

Until *Atomic Cafe* was released, this was probably the most important film ever made. It looks less like a satire every year. As General Jack D. Ripper, Sterling Hayden sends B-52s to bomb Russia and stop Commies from putting fluoride in our water. The planes are recalled, but Texan Major "King" Kong (Slim Pickens) gets through, the Soviet doomsday device is triggered, and the world ends to the strains of "We'll Meet Again." Peter Sellers is in turn President Muffey, Captain Mandrake, and Dr. Strangelove, who eagerly awaits life underground where the ratio of women to men will be 5 to 1. George C. Scott is General "Buck" Turgidson, Keenan Wynn is Colonel "Bat" Guano. With Peter Bull, James Earl Jones, and Tracy Reed. Originally 102 minutes long. Music by Laurie Johnson.

DR. SYN
1937 Gaumont (England) (B&W)
DIRECTOR: Roy William Neill

In his last role, George Arliss is the smuggling Vicar of Dymchurch. The story was remade first as *Night Creatures* and then as *The Scarecrow of Romney Marsh*. Pink Floyd wrote a song about the character on their second album ("Corporal Clegg"). Director Neill later did most of the Rathbone /Holmes films.

DR. TARR'S TORTURE DUNGEON
1972 Group I (Mexico)
DIRECTOR: Juan Lopez Moctezuma

A reporter goes to an asylum run by inmates in a surreal version of Poe's "System of Dr. Tarr and Professor Feather." This film is stranger (and has more sex) than the usual south-of-the-border quickies. Director Moctezuma was the producer of Alexander Jodorowsky's *Fando y Lis*. **(R)**

DR. TERROR'S GALLERY OF HORRORS
1967 American General Pictures
PRODUCERS: David L. Hewitt, Ray Dorn
DIRECTOR: David L. Hewitt
SCREENWRITERS: David Prentiss, Gary Heacock, Russ Jones
ALSO RELEASED AS: *Blood Suckers, Return from the Past*

John Carradine and Lon Chaney, Jr., in a terrible five-part horror anthology made fast and cheap to cash in on the success of Hammer's *Dr. Terror's House of Horrors*. The sets look straight out of a play put on by a rural high school. The script is completely ludicrous. In other words—total entertainment! Don't miss it! Carradine is the narrator and a warlock in "The Witches Clock." Chaney is the narrator and a mad doctor bringing life to the corpse of a crazed murderer in "Spark of Life." Mitch Evans is "Count Alucard" (clever!) and gets to fight a werewolf. The other thrilling short stories are "Monster Raid" and "King Vampire." Rochelle Hudson, the other humiliated name star, was a leading lady back in the '30s and played Natalie Wood's mother in *Rebel Without a Cause*.

DR. TERROR'S HOUSE OF HORRORS
1943 National Road Show (B&W)

From the ads: "Now together for the first time on any screen! Zombies, vampires, ghouls, werewolves, voodoo rites, weird creatures, and the living dead!" The producers of this movie simply edited together scenes from five foreign or independent American features that they never paid rights for. See bits of *Le Golem* (French, '36), *Vampyr* (Danish, '31), *The Living Dead* (English, '33), and Bela Lugosi in *White Zombie* and *The Return of Chandu*.

DR. TERROR'S HOUSE OF HORRORS
1964 Amicus/Paramount (U.S./England)
PRODUCERS: Milton Subotsky, Max J. Rosenberg
DIRECTOR: Freddie Francis
SCREENWRITER: Milton Subotsky

The first and probably best of many Amicus horror anthology films. Dr. Sandor Schreck (Peter Cushing) uses tarot cards to tell the future of five doomed men. The first is killed by a female werewolf. The next is strangled by a vine. A jazz musician is killed by the Haitian god Dambala for playing music he heard at a secret ceremony. Donald Sutherland discovers his wife is a vampire, kills her, and hangs for it. As an art critic, Christopher Lee ruins artist Michael Gough's career, then runs him down with a car, severing his hand. The still living hand seeks revenge. With Bernard Lee.

DR. WHO AND THE DALEKS

1965 Amicus/Continental (English)
PRODUCERS: Milton Subotsky,
Max J. Rosenberg
DIRECTOR: Gordon Flemyng
SCREENWRITER: Milton Subotsky

The popular BBC-TV series *Dr. Who* was the longest-running science-fiction show in the world ('63-'75). Four different actors played the absent-minded doctor, but a fifth, Peter Cushing, was cast for the feature versions. In the future, the doctor, his two granddaughters, Barbara (Jennie Linden) and Susan (Roberta Tovey), and Ian (Roy Castle) boyfriend of Susan, fight the Daleks, creatures encased in short robotlike metal cones to avoid neutron-bomb radiation. The Thals, who are friendly humans, are hunted and destroyed by the Daleks. The sequel was *Daleks—Invasion Earth 2150 A.D.*, also with Jennie Linden and Roberta Tovey.

DOCTOR X

1932 First National
PRODUCER: First National
DIRECTOR: Michael Curtiz
SCREENWRITERS: Robert Tasker, Earl Baldwin

Lionel Atwill runs a scientific research lab on Long Island. Police suspect him of cannibalistic murders. Fay Wray screams. The killer is revealed to be Dr. Xavier (Preston Foster), a one-armed scientist who turns himself into a monster with synthetic flesh in a really scary scene. A great horror movie with dated comic relief, originally in "gorgeous Technicolor" (an early two-color process). The effective makeup was by Max Factor. The next year First National was absorbed by Warners, which made the better-known *Mystery of the Wax Museum* with the same stars, the same director, and the same color process. With Arthur Edmund Carew and Mae Busch. Michael Curtiz directed over 60 features in Europe, moved to America, and directed 62 more! Lots of them are very good.

DOCTORS WEAR SCARLET: See THE BLOODSUCKERS.

DOG EAT DOG

1963 Ajay Films (U.S./W. Germany/ Italy) (B&W)
PRODUCER: Carl Szokol
DIRECTORS: Ray Nazarro, Albert Zugsmith
SCREENWRITERS: Robert Hill, Michael Elkins

Jayne Mansfield and Cameron Mitchell together! In a nihilistic tale of greed, madness, and murder! Cameron is a gangster who steals a million dollars and flees to an Adriatic island with another crook and Darlene, a loose woman attracted by the loot (played by guess who?). There are double and triple crosses and a series of murders. One person is burned with gasoline, one is found strangled in a goldfish bowl (!), and eventually everybody on the island is dead except for an insane old woman who watches the money float out to sea. Obviously an important statement involving two of our most enduring stars.

THE DOLL SQUAD

1973 Geneni
PRODUCER/DIRECTOR: Ted V. Mikels
ALSO RELEASED AS: *Hustler Squad*

All-star action and hilarity about a team of female assassins hired by the CIA to stop foreign rocket saboteurs. With Anthony Eisley, Michael Ansara, Francine York (*Curse of the Swamp Creature*), Tura Satana (*The Astro-Zombies*), and Herb Robbins (*The Worm Eaters*). It's been reissued several times and is now popular on videocassette. Director Mikels (a goateed man who lives with ten women) claims the *Charlie's Angels* show was copied from this feature.

DOMINIQUE IS DEAD
1978 (England)
PRODUCERS: Milton Subotsky,
   Andrew Donally
DIRECTOR: Michael Anderson
SCREENWRITERS: Edward and
   Valerie Abraham

The first film presented by the ex-half of Amicus films, Milton Subotsky, is a thriller obviously inspired by *Diabolique*. Cliff Robertson (who had just done *Obsession*) tries to drive wife Jean Simmons insane so he can take her money, but she kills herself and haunts him. Jenny Agutter plays his half-sister. With Flora Robson, Judy Geeson, Simon Ward, and Ron Moody. By the director of *Logan's Run* and *Doc Savage—Man of Bronze*.

DONKEY SKIN
1971 Janus (France)
PRODUCER: Mag Bodard
DIRECTOR/SCREENWRITER: Jacques Demy
ORIGINALLY RELEASED AS: *Peau d'Ane*

A colorful musical fantasy starring Catherine Deneuve as a princess disguised as a pauper in a donkey skin to avoid having to marry her father (Jean Marais). Delphine Seyrig is her fairy godmother. With anachronisms like a helicopter. Parts are reminiscent of Cocteau's *Beauty and the Beast*. Like Demy's *Pied Piper*, it's a fairy tale for adults.

DONOVAN'S BRAIN
1953 United Artists (B&W)
PRODUCER: Tom Gries
DIRECTOR/SCREENWRITER: Felix Feist

From the ads: "A dead man's brain told him to kill kill kill kill kill . . . ." A good adaptation of Curt Siodmak's novel with the added attraction of our current First Lady, the former Miss Nancy Davis, as the heroine. Ron was busy making more down-to-earth Westerns at the time. Lew Ayres stars as the scientist whose mind is taken over by a pulsating living brain that he keeps in a fish tank. It belonged to a crooked tycoon. Nancy and fellow scientist Gene Evans worry about Lew's new personality and murderous tendencies. The story had previously been filmed in 1944 as *The Lady and the Monster*.

DON'T ANSWER THE PHONE
1980 Crown
PRODUCER/DIRECTOR: Robert Hammer
SCREENWRITERS: Robert Hammer,
   Michael Castle

If you like *really* trashy sick movies see this one. As an overweight Vietnam vet/porno photographer/rapist/strangler in L.A., Nicholas Worth gives an eccentric performance that outclasses

Tura Satana, Francine York, and two other members of T. V. Mikel's Doll Squad.

Chubby Checkers in Don't Knock the Twist.

DON'T BE AFRAID OF THE DARK
1973 TV
PRODUCER: Alan S. Epstein
DIRECTOR: John Newland
SCREENWRITER: Nigel McKeand

Kim Darby and Jim Hutton as Mr. & Mrs. inherit an old mansion, move in, and discover small goblin creatures with shriveled faces living underneath. Excellent makeup was used for this TV feature directed by the man who created the *One Step Beyond* series. With William Demarest and Barbara Anderson.

DON'T GO IN THE HOUSE
1980 Film Ventures
PRODUCER: Ellen Hammill
DIRECTOR: Joseph Ellison
SCREENWRITERS: Joseph Ellison,
Ellen Hammill, Joseph Masefield

A maniac who was burned by his mother as a child keeps charred corpses of women in his house. He scours discos for victims. At the end, the bodies come alive and attack him. A real sick one. For fans of *Maniac* only. **(R)**

DON'T KNOCK THE ROCK
1957 Columbia (B&W)
PRODUCER: Sam Katzman
DIRECTOR: Fred Sears
SCREENWRITER: Robert E. Kent

In the quick follow-up to *Rock Around the Clock*, Alan Dale plays a singing idol who puts on a rock 'n' roll show in his hometown to prove the new music isn't sinful. Alan Freed helps him. He also stages a 1920s dance and singing demonstration to show the mayor and the other old farts that their pop music was even lamer than rock. Besides Bill Haley and his Comets doing the title song, "Hot Dog Buddy Buddy," and others, the real reason to watch is Little Richard. The wildman of rock and his band blast through "Long Tall Sally" and "Tutti Frutti"—enough to scare any

all previous screen psychos. He calls a radio psychiatrist and rants on the air with a phony Mexican accent, constantly works out with weights (in slow motion), kills during mock-religious ceremonies—all of which he does to try and "measure up" to his father. The ads made it look like another baby-sitter-in-distress movie, but it's in a class all by itself. With James Westmoreland (*The Hills Have Eyes*). Worth later turned up in Craven's *Swamp Thing*. **(R)**

small-town old-timers. Also with the Treniers, Dave Appell and his Apple-jacks, some wild dancing, and a romantic subplot.

DON'T KNOCK THE TWIST
1962 Columbia (B&W)
PRODUCER: Sam Katzman
DIRECTOR: Oscar Rudolph
SCREENWRITER: James B. Gordan

Chubby Checker stars as himself in this inevitable quickie sequel to *Twist Around the Clock*. The plot concerns Lang Jeffries preparing a television twist special, an orphan summer camp, and the scandalous "Salome Twist." Musical highlights include Gene Chandler as and singing "The Duke of Earl," the Dovells doing "The Bristol Stomp," and Chubby and Dee Dee Sharp in "Slow Twistin." For some reason Vic Dana sings "Little Altar Boy." With Mari Blanchard.

DON'T LOOK IN THE BASEMENT
1973 Hallmark
PRODUCER/DIRECTOR: S. F. Brownrigg
SCREENWRITER: Tim Pope

Wes Craven and Sean Cunningham (the director and producer respectively of *Last House on the Left*) had nothing to do with this gore film. Hallmark Releasing Corporation just repeated their brilliant "it's only a movie" ad campaign from *Last House*. The only way to enjoy this trashy shocker is as a comedy. A female inmate takes over an experimental asylum when the director is axed. In what might be a nod to *Night of the Living Dead*, the last survivor is a black man named Sam, the guy who just wanted to eat popsicles. Don't miss the ridiculous end credits. It's only a movie—only a movie—only a movie —only a movie—only a movie—

DON'T LOOK NOW
1973 Paramount
PRODUCER: Peter Katz
DIRECTOR: Nicholas Roeg
SCREENWRITERS: Allan Scott, Chris Bryant

A psychic thriller based on a Daphne du Maurier novella set in Venice. After the daughter of Julie Christie and Donald Sutherland drowns, mysterious occurrences lead through the canals and alleys of Venice to a confusing ending. Roeg confused more audiences with *The Man Who Fell to Earth* and *Bad Timing*. *Don't Look Now* got considerable publicity when originally released because of a realistic love scene. Music by Pino Donaggio, who later scored De Palma hits. **(R)**

DON'T OPEN THE WINDOW
1974 Hallmark (Italy)
PRODUCER: Edmondo Amati
DIRECTOR: Jorge Grau
SCREENWRITERS: Jorge Grau,
  Sandro Continenza, Marcello Coscia
ORIGINALLY RELEASED AS: *Non Si Deve Profanane il Sonno dei Morti*
ALSO RELEASED AS: *Breakfast at Manchester Morgue*

The goriest and best *Night of the Living Dead* ripoff. Those of you who don't follow exploitation films might be surprised to see Arthur Kennedy as a mean cop surrounded by flesh-eating ghouls. A government device to kill insects also revives the dead. One body fresh from an autopsy is particularly gross. With Ray Lovelook and Christian Galbo. The misleading American title probably turned away potential patrons. A shocking film, which was drastically cut for its American release. **(R)**

DON'T TOUCH MY SISTER:
See *THE GLASS CAGE.*

DOOMED TO DIE
1940 Monogram (B&W)
PRODUCER: Paul Malvern
DIRECTOR: William Nigh
SCREENWRITERS: Michael Jacoby,
 Ralph Gilbert Bettinson

Boris Karloff, Grant Withers, and Marjorie Reynolds, as Mr. Wong, Captain Street, and reporter Bobby Logan respectively, solve the murder of a shipping magnate. It was the last of five Karloff/Wong movies, all directed by the same guy during '38–'40. When Karloff quit, they squeezed out one more without him (*Phantom of Chinatown*).

DOOMSDAY FLIGHT
1966 TV
PRODUCER: Frank Price
DIRECTOR: William A. Graham
SCREENWRITER: Rod Serling

Rod Serling wrote the teleplay for this early "World Premiere" TV-movie. Edmond O'Brien plays a maniac who plants a bomb on a jet that will activate below 5,000 feet. Special agent Jack Lord is the hero. Van Johnson is the captain. With John Saxon, Richard Carlson, Edward Asner, and Michael Sarrazin. Graham has directed an average of two TV movies a year ever since.

DOOMSDAY MACHINE
1967 First Leisure
PRODUCER: Harvey Rope
DIRECTOR: Lee Sholem
SCREENWRITER: Stuart James Byre

The planet Earth was totally destroyed in 1975! If you didn't know, it's because you missed this stunning thriller that wasn't released until it was five years old. A small group of people are in a spaceship en route to Venus when they notice some stock footage of tidal waves on their viewfinder. All of a sudden, Earth (resembling a papier-mâché ball on a string) burns to a crisp.

An atomic war and they missed it! In between scenes of a spaceship in flight (from *Warning from Space*, of 1956), the unlikely cast members argue, constantly walk through doors, and accept their "responsibility" to restart the human race. Grant Williams (*The Incredible Shrinking Man*) is a hot-tempered troublemaker trying to get into the pants of the females on board. Old Henry Wilcoxon is the self-sacrificing senior officer. Denny (*Tarzan*) Miller is handsome and sensible. With Mala Powers (*The Unknown Terror*), Ruta Lee, and Bobby Van (bad comedy relief). Also with Casey Kasem and Mike Farrell from M.A.S.H. in bit parts. From the director of *Superman and the Mole Men*.

DOOMWATCH
1972 Tigon (England)
PRODUCER: Tony Tenser
DIRECTOR: Peter Sasdy
SCREENWRITER: Clive Exton

In his second-to-last role George Sanders is a military officer investigating ecological horrors on an island. Fish eat chemicals dumped in the water. People eat the fish and become lumpy-faced mutants. Pretty dull. With Judy Geeson and Ian Bannen. It was based on a BBC series.

DOOR TO DOOR MANIAC: See FIVE MINUTES TO LIVE.

THE DOOR WITH SEVEN LOCKS: See CHAMBER OF HORRORS.

DOOR WITH THE SEVEN LOCKS
1962 UCC-TV (W. Germany) (B&W)
DIRECTOR: Alfred Vohrer
ORIGINALLY RELEASED AS: *Die Tür mit den Sieben Schlossern*

A remake of *Chamber of Horrors* ('40) with Klaus Kinski. It features a torture chamber, a treasure vault, and murder. An Edgar Wallace mystery with Heinz Drache, Ady Berber, and Sabine Sesselmann.

DORIAN GRAY

1970 AIP (Italy/W. Germany/ Liechtenstein/U.S.)
PRODUCER: Harry Alan Towers
DIRECTOR/SCREENWRITER: Massimo Dallamano
ALSO RELEASED AS: *Il Dio Chiamto Dorian, The Secret of Dorian Gray*

Helmut Berger, still hot from *The Damned*, stars in this tacky modern-day version of Oscar Wilde's novel. See Helmut stick it to an older rich woman in a horse stable and to Herbert Lom in a steambath! See mod Helmut in a striped fur coat. See lovely young Marie Liljedahl, naked as usual, as Dorian's innocent actress lover Sybil Vane. With Richard Todd, Margaret Lee, Maria Rohm, and Beryl Cunningham. Producer Towers was arrested in 1980 for running a sex-for-sale ring providing girls for politicians and UN diplomats. He was freed on probation and announced plans to produce a movie about his "other business." (**R**)

DOUBLE CONFESSION

1951 Stratford (England) (B&W)
PRODUCER/DIRECTOR: Harry Reynolds
SCREENWRITERS: William Templeton, Ralph Keene

A mystery set at a seaside resort with Peter Lorre and William Hartnell as gangsters. Derek Farr and Joan Hopkins star.

DOUBLE POSSESSION: See GANJA AND HESS.

DOUBLE TROUBLE: See SWINGIN' ALONG.

DOUBLE TROUBLE

1967 MGM
PRODUCERS: Judd Bernard, Irwin Winkler
DIRECTOR: Norman Taurog
SCREENWRITERS: Jo Heims, Marc Brandel

Elvis is Guy Lambert, a singer in London involved with Annette Day, jewels, detectives, and smuggling. Elvis, backed by the G-men, sings "Old MacDonald" and "Long-legged Girls with Short Dresses On." With Yvonne Romain, John Williams, and the Weire Brothers.

DRACULA

1931 Universal (B&W)
PRODUCER: Carl Laemmle, Jr.
DIRECTOR: Tod Browning
SCREENWRITER: Garrett Fort, Dudley Murphy

Having acted in films since 1917 (in Hungary, Germany, and America), 49-year-old Bela Lugosi (Bela Blasko) here plays his first starring role. He had been Dracula in the play since 1927. The phenomenal success of this, the first real talkie horror film, and *Frankenstein* later in the same year led to a cycle of similar hits. Edward Van Sloan, who had also been in the play, duplicated his Van Helsing role. The original version features Van Sloan warning the audience at the end, "There are such things as vampires!" Dwight Frye gained lasting fame as the lawyer Renfield, reduced to a crazed fly-eating slave to Dracula. A talky, bloodless filmed play that remains one of the best-loved films of all time. With Helen Chandler, David Manners, and some surprising armadillos. A Spanish-language version was filmed on the same sets with a different cast. Bela's immortal version, cautiously advertised as a strange love story, opened on Valentine's Day. Music by Tchaikovsky.

DRACULA: See HORROR OF DRACULA.

DRACULA
1974 TV
PRODUCER/DIRECTOR: Dan Curtis
SCREENWRITER: Richard Matheson

Curtis switches from Barnabas Collins to an ugly Dracula (Jack Palance) in love with Fiona Lewis. This talky TV movie was filmed in England and released as a theatrical feature in Europe. It followed Curtis' dull *Frankenstein* TV-movie. With Nigel Davenport as Van Helsing, Simon Ward, Virginia Wetherall, and romantic flashbacks. The original television showing was delayed by a Nixon speech announcing the resignation of Vice President Agnew.

DRACULA
1979 Universal
PRODUCER: Walter Mirisch
DIRECTOR: John Badham
SCREENWRITER: W. D. Richter

Frank Langella was popular as Dracula on Broadway (as was Lugosi), so why not hire him and the director of *Saturday Night Fever* and make the biggest-budgeted vampire movie of all time? Good question. Not the greatest movie, though. Lawrence Olivier is Van Helsing. With Donald Pleasence, Kate Nelligan, and some psychedelic special effects. Music by John Williams. (R)

DRACULA A.D. 1972
1972 Hammer/Warner Brothers (England)
PRODUCER: Josephine Douglas
DIRECTOR: Alan Gibson
ALSO RELEASED AS: *Dracula Today*

Van Helsing (Peter Cushing) destroys Dracula (Christopher Lee) during the 19th century. A century later, the vampire is conjured back to life in England during a black mass ritual. A descen-

A French actress tries to scare Christopher Lee in Dracula and Son.

dant of Van Helsing (Cushing again) carries on. Here, in Lee's sixth Dracula movie, Hammer Studios made a big mistake changing the setting to the 70s. The others are timeless. This one, full of mod young people, has already dated. A party sequence with the American band Stoneground is a real low point. Christopher Neame is another vampire called Johnny Alucard (clever). Dracula has lots of beautiful victims including Caroline Munro and Stephanie Beacham. Lee still looks as imposing as ever, but he claims he hated doing these final Dracula movies. At original openings, a short about The Count Dracula Society called *Horror Ritual* was shown. Barry Atwater starred.

DRACULA AND SON

1976 Quarter Films (France)
PRODUCER: Alain Poiré
DIRECTOR: Edouard Molinaro
SCREENWRITERS: Edouard Molinaro, Jean-Marie Poiré, Alain Godard
ORIGINALLY RELEASED AS: *Dracula, Père et Fils*

The first feature by the director of *La Cage aux Folles* is a vampire comedy and obviously the inspiration for *Love at First Bite*, which stole whole scenes from it. The reason they got away with it is that the American version of *Dracula and Son* had the worst dubbing and re-editing job in memory. The whole script was rewritten to include inane jokes. Bernard Menez as the son was given an imitation Don Adams voice and goes around saying "Sorry about that," and "Would you believe . . . ." One scene of Dracula (Christopher Lee with gray hair) opening a door is repeated endlessly, each time with a new dubbed-in unfunny gag supposedly spoken by actors whose mouths don't even move. The cretins that acquired the U.S. rights blew their

chances to make any money from a reportedly funny film.

DRACULA HAS RISEN FROM HIS GRAVE

1969 Hammer/Warner Brothers-7 Arts (England)
PRODUCER: Aida Young
DIRECTOR: Freddie Francis
SCREENWRITER: Anthony Hinds

The third Christopher Lee/Dracula film is also the most religious-oriented. A weak priest provides the blood to revive the vampire and becomes its servant. A girl, drained of her blood, is found hanging upside down inside a church bell. The hero tries to kill Dracula with a stake but he's an atheist who can't recite the required prayer. Dracula eventually dies, impaled on a crucifix. Except for *The Horror of Dracula*, this is the strongest and best-looking entry in the series. The publicity centered on starlet Veronica Carlson and silly ad lines like, "Boy, does he give a good hickey." One ad showed a pretty neck with two Band-Aids. With Rupert Davies, Ewan Hooper, Barry Andrews, and Barbara Ewins.

DRACULA IS DEAD AND WELL AND LIVING IN LONDON: See *THE SATANIC RITES OF DRACULA.*

DRACULA, PRINCE OF DARKNESS

1966 Hammer/20th Century-Fox
PRODUCER: Anthony Nelson-Keys
DIRECTOR: Terence Fisher
SCREENWRITER: John Sansom, Jimmy Sangster

Hammer waited eight long years before putting Christopher Lee in a follow-up to *Horror of Dracula*. The story follows two couples on vacation in the Carpath-

Zandor Vorkov bites Regina Carrol in Al Adamson's Dracula vs. Frankenstein.

ian Mountains and unfortunate enough to find themselves at Dracula's castle. Klove, the butler, kills one man, hangs him upsidedown over the vampire's ashes and slits his throat. Result: an instant vampire who gets to work right away and turns Barbara Shelley into a creature of the night. The remaining couple escapes to a monastery and soon it's vampires vs. monks (led by Andrew Kier as Father Sandor). Lee is awesome enough, but has no dialogue. The most memorable scene shows Barbara Shelley hissing and struggling as the brothers drive a stake through her heart. Filmed at about the same time as *Rasputin, The Mad Monk*, using the same sets and part of the same cast. With Francis Mathews, Susan Farmer, and Thorley Walters.

DRACULA (THE DIRTY OLD MAN)

1969 Art Films
PRODUCER/DIRECTOR/SCREENWRITER:
Williams Edwards
A sex comedy/horror film with Count Alucard (Vince Kelly) and his jackal-man assistant kidnaping naked virgins. Adults only!

DRACULA TODAY: See DRACULA A.D. 1972.

DRACULA VS. FRANKENSTEIN: See ASSIGNMENT TERROR.

DRACULA VS. FRANKENSTEIN.

1969/71 Independent-International
PRODUCER/DIRECTOR: Al Adamson
SCREENWRITERS: William Pugsley, Samuel M. Sherman
ALSO RELEASED AS: *Blood of Frankenstein, They're Coming to Get You*

Al Adamson's most famous celluloid atrocity is an embarrassing mixture of old actors and ideas with modern exploitation devices. Like many of Al's films, it was made in bits and pieces over a period of several years. Two stars, J. Carrol Naish and Lon Chaney, Jr., played their last parts in it. Naish, feeble and in his 70s, came out of retirement to play Dr. Frankenstein, who runs an amusement park horror show under an alias. He had to act in a wheelchair. Chaney, in his 60s, had a terrible role as Groton, an imbecile sent out to decapitate pretty young girls in miniskirts. Angelo Rossitto, a dwarf actor as old as the others, helps. Meanwhile, Dracula (played by a ridiculous-looking actor with a goatee and curly hair who calls himself Zandor Vorkov) arrives and forces the doc to revive "Frankenstein" (big John Bloom with a mutant mask and wig). The silly creature kills *Famous Monsters* editor Forrest J. Ackerman, a special guest star. As if that weren't enough, Adamson's busty blond wife Regina Carrol sings, dances, and takes L.S.D., and Anthony Eisley and Russ Tamblyn (as a biker) manage to show their acting talents. Some electrical props from *The Bride of Frankenstein* were dug up for atmosphere. It was released on a big double bill with *Frankenstein's Bloody Terror*. With Jim Davis (*Dallas*).

DRACULA'S CASTLE: See BLOOD OF DRACULA'S CASTLE.

DRACULA'S DAUGHTER
1936 Universal (B&W)
PRODUCER: E.M. Asher
DIRECTOR: Lambert Hillyer
SCREENWRITER: Garrett Fort

In the often-forgotten moody sequel to the 1931 *Dracula*, Edward Van Sloan's Van Helsing returns to face Gloria Holden, the screen's first female vampire star, as Countess Marya Zaleska. Sandor (Irving Pichel) is her strikingly pale servant with hair parted down the middle. The countess wants to be cured but she also wants young model Marguerite Churchill. Otto Kruger is the hero. By the director of *The Invisible Ray*. With Hedda Hopper and Nan Grey. Based on *Dracula's Guest* by Bram Stoker.

DRACULA'S DOG
1978 Crown International
PRODUCERS: Charles Band, Frank Ray Perilli
DIRECTOR: Albert Bano
SCREENWRITER: Frank Ray Perilli

Some people thought this title was just a joke. Zoltan, the title canine, is a vampire dog, accidentally resurrected in Transylvania. He pulls the stake out of vampire Reggie Nalder (also the vampire in *Salem's Lot*) and they go to America to serve the last of the Draculas, Michael Pataki (a vampire in *Grave of the Vampire*). Trouble is Pataki doesn't know his ancestry and José Ferrer (an actor who will appear in just about anything these days) as a Van Helsing type is after the bloodsucking pair. Zoltan chews a hole in the roof of Pataki's summer cabin and . . . As you can see this is no joke. **(R)**

DRACULA'S GREAT LOVE
1972 Cinema Shares (Spain)
PRODUCER: F. Laura Polop
DIRECTOR: Javier Aguirre
SCREENWRITERS: Jacinto Molina, Javier Aguirre
ORIGINALLY RELEASED AS: *Gran Amore del Conde Dracula*
ALSO RELEASED AS: *Count Dracula's Great Love, Vampire Playgirls*

Four unwary travelers seek refuge in a nursing home operated by the strange Dr. Wendell, played by Paul Naschy. Wendell, who is actually Dracula, puts the bite on three of his visitors and attempts to enlist the fourth, beautiful Karin, in a plan to bring his dead daughter back to life. Pretty tame for Spanish horror. **(R)** —BM

DRACULA'S LAST RITES: See LAST RITES.

DRAGNET
1954 Warner Brothers
PRODUCER: Stanley Meyer
DIRECTOR: Jack Webb
SCREENWRITER: Richard L. Breen

From the ads: "Siren-screaming out of the police files—the untold story of the Red Spot Gang!" Sgt. Friday (director Webb) and sidekick Smith (Ben Alexander) investigate the shooting of a former syndicate debt collector via four empty shotgun shells and the plaster impression of a left foot. An instrumental "Foggy Night in San Francisco" is heard. With Richard Boone, Ann Robinson, Gregg Weaver, Dub Taylor, and Virginia Gregg, who has a great scene as a sad one-legged widow. See -30-, also by Webb. —CB

DRAGNET
1966 TV
PRODUCER/DIRECTOR: Jack Webb
SCREENWRITER: Richard L. Breen

The pilot film for the revived *Dragnet* show (1967–'70), filmed in '66, wasn't shown until '69. In their typical no-nonsense fashion, Joe Friday (Webb) and his new partner Bill Gannon (Harry Morgan) track down the killer of two models. The new series, a high point of late '60s television, featured a stock company of actors playing different characters each week and often centered on misguided hippies and drugged-out kids. Joe set them all straight with a short sensible speech. With Gene Evans, Vic Perrin, and Bobby Troup.

DRAGONSLAYER

1981 Paramount/Buena Vista
PRODUCER: Hal Barwood
DIRECTOR: Matthew Robbins
SCREENWRITERS: Hal Barwood,
Matthew Robbins

The King of Urland has made an uneasy truce with the dragon that besieges his Kingdom by agreeing to sacrifice virgins to it on a regular basis. The people, however, are unhappy with the arrangement and call on Sir Ralph Richardson, a doddering wizard, to face the dragon in magical combat. When Richardson is knifed by an agent of the king, the task falls to young Galen, a not-quite-competent sorcerer's apprentice (Peter McNichol). Despite the dragons, the PG rating, and the fact that the Disney organization co-produced, don't dismiss this as kid-stuff till you've seen it — it's got true medieval grit, cynical humor, and incredible effects by the *Star Wars* people, and it's the only picture we can think of that kills off its two most endearing characters (one of 'em twice!). Vertithrax, the dragon, brought to life through a computer-controlled form of stop motion, is worth the price of admission by itself. —BM

DRAGONWYCK

1946 20th Century-Fox (B&W)
PRODUCER: Darryl F. Zanuck
DIRECTOR/SCREENWRITER:
Joseph L. Mankiewicz

Vincent Price is Nicholas Van Ryn, a wealthy eccentric who lives with his wife on an estate in the Hudson Valley in the 1840s. A distant cousin (Gene Tierney) who was raised by a puritanical father (Walter Huston) arrives to care for the Van Ryns' daughter. After the wife succumbs, Price and Tierney marry and have a child that dies. Price becomes even more sadistic and brooding, taking drugs and hiding in the attic. Tierney suffers until a young doctor (Glen Langdon) comes to the rescue. Gothic murder and madness from Anya Seton's novel. With Henry Morgan and Spring Byington.

DRAGSTRIP GIRL

1957 AIP (B&W)
PRODUCER: Alex Gordon
DIRECTOR: Edward L. Cahn
SCREENWRITER: Lou Russof

Frank Gorshin and Fay Spain in Dragstrip Girl.

The ads call her: "Car crazy, speed crazy, boy crazy!" John Ashley and poor but honest Steve Terrell fight for the hand of Fay Spain. Ashley tries to run his rival off course during the big race, then realizes there's a girl under that helmet. More ad copy: "Thrill-hungry teens on a reckless rampage!" Featuring action footage of Roman-riding, chicken runs, legal and illegal drags. With Frank Gorshin, Russ Bender, and quarter-mile champ Tommy Ivo — a regular on *My Little Margie*. Originally a twin bill with *Rock All Night*. More Cahn: *Invasion of the Saucer Men* and *Jet Attack*. —CB

DRAGSTRIP RIOT
1958 AIP (B&W)
PRODUCER: Dale Ireland
DIRECTOR: David Bradley
SCREENWRITER: George Hodgins
Gary Clarke and Yvonne Lime are pursued by motorcycle gang following altercation. Mystery wrench misses intended target, sending cyclist out of control over cliff. Clarke is blamed. On to beach riot, 'twixt four and two wheelers, where culprit is unmasked and retaliates with spear gun! Featuring Connie Stevens, *King Kong* screamer Fay Wray in her last role, and rare railroad-track drag footage. A dual release with *The Cool and the Crazy*. By the director of *They Saved Hitler's Brain*. —CB

THE DREAM MAKER
1963 Universal (England)
PRODUCER: Norman Williams
DIRECTOR: Don Sharp
SCREENWRITER: Leigh Vance
ALSO RELEASED AS: *It's All Happening*
A nice teen musical with nice-guy record-company talent scout Tommy Steele putting on a show for orphans. Tommy himself pitches in and sings

when Shane Fenton and the Fentones, John Barry, and the Clyde Valley Stompers show up late.

DRESSED TO KILL
1946 Universal (B&W)
PRODUCER/DIRECTOR: Roy William Neill
SCREENWRITER: Leonard Lee
The last of the 12 modern-day Holmes movies is about a music box and missing engraving plates. Basil Rathbone, Nigel Bruce, and Mary Gordon play their usual roles. With Patricia Morison. Holmes was off the screen for 13 years, next appearing in the Hammer version of *The Hound of the Baskervilles*.

DRESSED TO KILL
1980 Filmways
PRODUCER: George Litto
DIRECTOR/SCREENWRITER: Brian De Palma
See Michael Caine as a psychiatrist in drag kill with a razor. See Angie Dickinson naked again (although it was really a double in the shower). See the director's wife Nancy Allen play prostitute. The best *Psycho* movie of 1980. With Keith Gordon (from De Palma's *Home Movies*) and a look inside Bellevue. The sound track by Pino Donagio (*Carrie*) is available. When released, the Catholic Film and Broadcasting Review gave it a condemned rating, so if you're Catholic, watch at your own risk. The European version (also on videocassette in America) is longer and more explicit. A Samuel Z. Arkoff presentation. (**R**)

DRILLER KILLER
1979 Rochelle
PRODUCER: Rochelle Weisberg
DIRECTOR: Abel Ferrara
SCREENWRITER: Nicholas St. John

From the ads. "Several pints of blood will spill when teenage girls confront his drill!" New York art/exploitation film with an alienated young surrealist painter (director Ferrara) going berserk and attacking downtowners with his Black and Decker. A gory midnight movie, it was re-released (with *Drive-in Massacre*) when Ferrara hit with *Ms. 45*.

DRIVE-IN MASSACRE

1976 New American
PRODUCER/DIRECTOR: Stuart Segall
SCREENWRITERS: John Goff, Buck Flower
A very low-budget California horror movie about a madman killing off patrons of a drive-in. A bit better than you'd expect from the crummy ads. With funny characters and gore murders. A gimmick ending features a voice (supposedly the manager of the theater you're watching this in) warning you that the killer is loose and you might be the next victim! Made by people who usually do porn films. **(R)**

DRIVERS TO HELL: See WILD ONES ON WHEELS.

DUEL

1971 TV
PRODUCER: George Eckstein
DIRECTOR: Steven Spielberg
SCREENWRITER: Richard Matheson
This TV film was so popular that 15 minutes were added on so it could be released as a feature in Europe. As a travelling salesman Dennis Weaver is pursued by an oil tanker that seems to have a life of its own. It created an unwelcome new subgenre of possessed vehicle movies. Spielberg followed it with a TV horror movie (*Something Evil*), a TV pilot film (*Savage*), *The Sugarland Express*, and then the big time with *Jaws*.

DUEL OF THE TITANS

1961 Paramount (Italy)
PRODUCER: Alessandro Jacouoni
DIRECTOR: Sergio Corbucci
SCREENWRITERS: Sergio Corbucci, Luciano Martino, Sergio Leone, Giorgio Prosperi, Franco Rossetti, Ennio De Concini, Duccio Tessari
ORIGINALLY RELEASED AS: *Romolo e Remo*
More history reworked to star Steve Reeves as Romulus and Gordon Scott as Remus. The brothers raised by a wolf grow up and fight side by side until they both decide they want Julia, the daughter of the King of the Sabines (Virna Lisi). Romulus kills his brother and starts the Roman Empire.

DUNGEONS OF HARROW

1964 Herts-Lion
DIRECTOR: Pat Boyette
SCREENWRITER: Henry Garcia
ALSO RELEASED AS: *Dungeons of Horror*
In this wild feature made in San Antonio, Texas, a shipwreck survivor named Mr. Fallon awakens in the lost-island castle of Count Lorente De Sade, a spiteful old fool who can't even pronounce his own name right. Fallon's introduction to the count's captive family and morbid routines is enough to turn his hair gray. He meets the countess — leprous and insane, locked away in her wedding gown for the past twenty years; Miss Cassandra — "I used to be a nurse, now I'm not much of anything"; Mantis — a Nubian slave; little Anne — whose tongue was cut out by pirates and who bears the "scars and bruises of mistreatment." Cassandra and Fallon conspire to murder the horrible De Sade and escape to freedom, but the dingy cardboard hell proves difficult to leave behind. Featuring Russ Harvey, Helen Hogan, Bill McNulty, Maurice Harris, Ron Russell, Lee Morgan, and the director. Impossibly cheap, genuinely creepy, and about as close to standard

art and glamour as case notes from an asylum. Look for related features *The Weird Ones* and *No Man's Land*, which are just as unbelievable. —CB

DUNGEONS OF HORROR: See DUNGEONS OF HARROW.

THE DUNWICH HORROR

1969 AIP

PRODUCERS: James H. Nicholson, Samuel Z. Arkoff
DIRECTOR: Daniel Haller
SCREENWRITERS: Curtis Lee Hanson, Henry Rosenbaum, Ronald Silkosky

As a student at Miskatonic U., Sandra Dee is lured away and drugged by an extremely crazed Dean Stockwell, who has just stolen the Necronomicon from the library. Ed Begley (in his last role) is a professor who discovers that Stockwell has an invisible brother and a mother in an asylum. Stockwell is about to sacrifice Sandra at the devil's hopyard during a particularly druggy scene when the prof shows up with the proper curse. Based on H.P. Lovecraft's story. With Sam Jaffe as Stockwell's father, Lloyd Bochner, Talia Coppola (later Shire), Barboura Morris, and Beach Dickerson. Peter Fonda was originally set to play the Stockwell part. Roger Corman was executive producer. **(M)**

E.T.: THE EXTRA-TERRESTRIAL
1982 Universal
PRODUCERS: Steven Spielberg,
Kathleen Kennedy
DIRECTOR: Steven Spielberg
SCREENWRITERS: Steven Spielberg,
Melissa Mathison

Spielberg's uplifting science-fiction blockbuster has not only surpassed the domestic box-office take of his *Close Encounters*, *Raiders*, and *Jaws*, but also of *Star Wars*. Henry Thomas stars as Elliott. Little Drew Barrymore (a granddaughter of John) is his sister. Dee Wallace, of *The Hills Have Eyes*, *The Howling*, and *10*, is their divorced mom. They live a normal upper-middle-class suburban American existence until E.T. arrives and the Disney-inspired kid adventures begin. Despite the baggy-skinned alien's uncuddly appearance, mass-merchandised E.T. paraphernalia easily surpassed the Smurfs in popularity and went on to overpower even the *Star Wars* robots. John Williams, who also scored *Jaws* (I and II), *Star Wars* (and sequels), *Superman*, *Close Encounters*, and *Raiders*, provided the music. Hearing "Papa Oom Mow Mow" over a radio in an early scene provides a welcome relief from Williams' overly familiar score. With a film clip from *This Island Earth*. E.T. will not go away. Can you stand it?

THE EARTH DIES SCREAMING
1964 Lippert/20th Century-Fox (England)
PRODUCERS: Robert L. Lippert, Jack Parsons
DIRECTOR: Terence Fisher
SCREENWRITER: Henry Cross

Although it doesn't quite live up to its title, this is a good alien-invasion film. A test pilot returns to England and finds almost the entire population dead. Large robots with clear-domed heads roam the streets killing with their touch, then reviving the dead as eyeless zombies. The pilot discovers a few other survivors and they frantically search for a way to stop the invaders. With Willard Parker, Virginia Field, and Dennis Price.

EARTH II
1971 TV
PRODUCERS/SCREENWRITERS:
William Read Woodfield, Allan Balter
DIRECTOR: Tom Gries

A space station with 2,000 inhabitants becomes an independent country. An orbiting bomb and personal squabbles threaten the peace. Some of the 2,000 are Gary Lockwood, Anthony Franciosa, Lew Ayres, Mariette Hartley, and Gary Merrill.

EARTH VS. THE FLYING SAUCERS
1956 Columbia (B&W)
PRODUCER: Charles H. Schneer
DIRECTOR: Fred F. Sears
SCREENWRITERS: George Worthing Yates,
Raymond T. Marcus

The destruction of Washington, D.C., by Ray Harryhausen's incredible spinning flying saucers is the highlight of this alien-invasion film. Hero scientist Hugh Marlowe (back in the capitol after *The Day the Earth Stood Still*) develops an antisaucer weapon to defeat the aliens and gets to ride in a saucer (with new bride Joan Taylor). But before the battle is over the Capitol Building, the Lincoln Memorial, and other landmarks are realistically smashed. The featureless invaders wear "suits of solidified electricity" and resemble bullet-headed robots. Morris Ankrum is the general. With Thomas B. Henry, Donald Curtis, and Harry Lauter. Sam Katzman was executive producer.

EARTH VS. THE SPIDER: See THE SPIDER.

EARTHQUAKE

1974 Universal
PRODUCER/DIRECTOR: Mark Robson
SCREENWRITERS: George Fox, Mario Puzo

"In Sensurround!" which felt and sounded something like a very large vacuum cleaner being turned on. "The management assumes no responsibility for the physical or emotional reactions of the individual viewer." Some doctors claimed the process definitely damaged eardrums. It also ruined the movies playing next door in twin theaters all over the country. Charlton Heston is the hero, but models of Los Angeles are the real stars. With Ava Gardner, Lorne Greene, George Kennedy, Lloyd Nolan, Genevieve Bujold, Richard Roundtree, Barry Sullivan, Marjoe Gortner, Victoria Principal, and Gabriel Dell. Music by John Williams. It battled for audience attention with that other timeless classic, *The Towering Inferno*. '74 was a bad year.

THE EAST SIDE KIDS MEET BELA LUGOSI: See GHOSTS ON THE LOOSE.

EASY COME, EASY GO

1967 Paramount
PRODUCER: Hal Wallis
DIRECTOR: John Rich
SCREENWRITERS: Allen Weiss, Anthony Lawrence

Elvis Presley competes with the drug-crazed hippie modern world by singing "Yoga Is as Yoga Does" and playing a frogman doubling as a singer at a discotheque. Elsa Lanchester is a yoga teacher. Dodie Marshall owns a sunken ship that might contain a treasure. *Munsters* star Pat Priest is a wealthy playgirl. The instrumentals are called "Freakout" and "Go-Go-Jo."

UPI 4/27/74: Actor Charlton Heston and Ava Gardner grimace in panic as they duck under an automobile to avoid falling debris during a scene in the filming of Earthquake at Universal Studios.

EASY RIDER

1969 Columbia
PRODUCER: Bert Schneider
DIRECTOR: Dennis Hopper
SCREENWRITERS: Peter Fonda, Dennis Hopper, Terry Southern

Peter Fonda, Dennis Hopper, and Jack Nicholson, all involved in *The Trip*, got back together for this low-budget, much-praised counterculture hit. Dennis Hopper has been directing increasingly obscure and self-indulgent movies ever since. Here, playing Billy, he and Captain America (Fonda) sell coke to rich pusher Phil Spector, smoke a lot of grass, visit a commune, get arrested in a small town for riding their motorcycles in a parade, leave with an alcoholic civil rights lawyer (Nicholson), and smoke more grass. When the lawyer is beaten to death, they go to New Orleans during Mardi Gras where they have a bad acid trip with some prostitutes in a graveyard (Karen Black and Toni Basil of "Hey Micky" fame), then head for Florida. En route they're shot by rednecks. With Luana Anders, Robert Walker, Jr., and Michael Pataki. Background music by Steppenwolf, the Electric Prunes, Jimi Hendrix, Roger McGuinn, and others. Cinematography by Laszlo Kovacs. **(R)**

EATEN ALIVE

1976 New World
PRODUCER: Mardi Rustam
DIRECTOR: Tobe Hooper
SCREENWRITERS: Alvin Fast, Mardi Rustam
ALSO RELEASED AS: *Starlight Slaughter, Death Trap, Horror Hotel*

Veteran villain Neville Brand is a crazed Louisiana hotel owner who kills off most of the cast with his large scythe and an alligator. Star victims include Mel Ferrer, Carolyn Jones, and Stuart Whitman. With Marilyn Burns from Hooper's earlier cult hit, *The Texas Chainsaw Massacre*. Because of numerous title changes and bad distribution, *Eaten Alive* hasn't gained the reputation it deserves. (R)

ECCO

1963 AIP (Italy)
PRODUCER: Francesso Mazzei
DIRECTOR: Gianni Proia
SCREENWRITER: R. W. Cresse

George Sanders narrates a *Mondo Cane*–type documentary. Highlights include Nairobi tribesmen doing the twist, an L.A. roller derby, reindeer being castrated, duels in Berlin, a karate demonstration, and the last performance of the Grand Guignol theatrical troupe in Paris.

EDEN CRIED

1967 Continental (B&W)
PRODUCERS: Shael Young, Charles Ellis
DIRECTOR/SCREENWRITER: Fred Johnson
ALSO RELEASED AS: *In the Fall of '55 Eden Cried*

James Dean seems to be the inspiration for this 1955-set story of two Malibu neighbors who share good times until their parents force the relationship underground following a street-racing fatality. Starring Tom Pace, Carol Holland, and Victor Izay—who appears with Pace in *Girl in Gold Boots* and *The Astro-Zombies*.   —CB

EDGE OF FURY

1958 United Artists (B&W)
PRODUCER/SCREENWRITER: Robert Gurney, Jr.
DIRECTORS: Irving Lerner, Robert Gurney, Jr.
A sick beachcomber (Michael Higgins) slaughters a family at their summer home after talking them into renting him the adjacent guest cottage. When the police arrive, the killer is painting a family portrait. Jean Allison, Lois Holmes, Doris Fesette, and Malcolm Lee Beggs co-star.   –CB

EDGE OF HELL

1956 Universal (B&W)
PRODUCER/DIRECTOR/SCREENWRITER:
  Hugo Haas
A beggar (Hugo Hass) comes to America with his trickster dog Flip, and through a waitress friend's chauffeur fiancé they get a job entertaining at a wealthy child's birthday party. The youngster is much taken with Flip and Haas is offered $500 for the pooch by the boy's grandfather. He refuses and he and Flip use the day's wages to throw a party for their hobo friends. Some time later, weakened by asthma and unable to provide for Flip's well-being, Haas accepts $20 for his companion and is promptly beaten and robbed. Rescued by fellow vagrants, he clings to life until, on receiving word of dog's demise, he sets off for a rendezvous in Heaven, where he and friend will perform tricks for the Almighty. Francesa De Scaffa, Ken Carleton, and Syra Marti co-star. See *Pickup*.   –CB

EEGAH!

1962 Fairway-International Films
PRODUCER/DIRECTOR: Nicholas Merriwether
SCREENWRITER: Bob Wehling
The man responsible for this laugh riot is also known as William Watters (he plays Mr. Miller in *Eegah!* under that name) and Arch Hall, Sr. His son, 16-year-old Arch, Jr., stars here as Tom, the boyfriend of Mr. Miller's daughter Roxy. Richard Kiel ("Jaws" in recent James Bond films) excels as the title giant in an early featured role. Roxy discovers Eegah in a cave, befriends him, and gives him a clean shave. The idiot caveman falls in love with her. The sad love story ends in Palm Springs, where poor Eegah is shot by insensitive police while Arch, Jr., and the Archers play. Amazing. From the people who later released the classic *Incredibly Strange Creatures Who Stopped Living and Became Crazy Mixed-up Zombies*. That movie's director-star Ray Dennis Steckler is the man Eegah throws in the pool. With Carolyn Brandt.

EERIE MIDNIGHT HORROR SHOW: See TORMENTED.

EFFECTS

1980 The Image Works
PRODUCERS: John Harrison, Pasquae Buba
DIRECTOR/SCREENWRITER: Dusty Nelson
ALSO RELEASED AS: *The Manipulator*
Several film technicians best known for their work with George A. Romero contributed to this low-budget shocker about a manipulative film director who is working on a Grade-Z horror opus. The film project is entitled "Something's Wrong"—appropriately: cast and crew are unaware that they are also going to star in a "snuff" movie called "Duped," worked on by an undercover crew headed by the mad director. Unfortunately, the opportunities for black humor in the situation are mostly ignored; Nelson goes instead for the metaphysical implications of film-with-in-film-within-film. Tom Savini worked on the gore effects and has an acting role. Made in Pittsburgh. **(R)**   –BM

$8^{1}/_{2}$

1963 Embassy (Italy) (B&W)
PRODUCER: Angelo Rizzoli
DIRECTOR: Federico Fellini
SCREENWRITERS: Federico Fellini,
Tullio Pinelli, Ennio Flaiano,
Brunello Rono

Barbara Steele plays Gloria Morin.

EIGHTEEN AND ANXIOUS

1957 Republic (B&W)
PRODUCER: Edmund Chevie
DIRECTOR: Joe Parker
SCREENWRITERS: Dale and Katherine Runson
ALSO RELEASED AS: *No Greater Sin*

Mary Webster and her high school sweetheart (William Campbell) are forced to marry secretly in Mexico. He subsequently dies in a car crash, taking the only proof of the ceremony with him. With Martha Scott, Jim Backus, Jackie Coogan, Slick Slavin, and TV Batgirl Yvonne Craig. Songs by Phil Tuminello include "Teach Me How to Cry," "Bye Baby Bye," "Step Out of That Dream," and "Someday We'll Love Again." It was later re-released as part of an adults-only birth-of-a-baby show. —CB

ELECTRONIC MONSTER

1957 Anglo Amalgamated/Columbia (England) (B&W)
PRODUCER: Alec C. Snowden
DIRECTOR: Montgomery Tully
SCREENWRITERS: Charles Eric Maine,
J. MacLaren-Ross

Rod Cameron discovers that patients at a clinic are being given electronically induced hallucinations by unscrupulous doctors. An interesting, neglected feature based on the novel *Escapement* by Charles Eric Maine. The dream sequences involve dancing girls and torture. With Mary Murphy. By the director of *Battle Beneath the Earth*. Electronic music by Soundrama. Richard Gordon was executive producer.

THE ELEPHANT MAN

1980 Paramount (England) (B&W)
PRODUCER: Jonathan Sanger
DIRECTOR: David Lynch
SCREENWRITERS: Christopher DeVore,
Eric Bergren, David Lynch.

A surprise success from the director of *Eraserhead* that shares the bleak industrial-ruin look of that underground classic. Director of photography Freddie Francis was a director at Hammer and photographed *Sons and Lovers* and *The Innocents*. Freddie Jones, who plays the man who "owns" the elephant man, acted in many Hammer films. It's a beautifully made feature about John Merrick (John Hurt), the world's ugliest man, and sticks very close to the true story written by Dr. Frederick Treves (played by Anthony Hopkins). With Anne Bancroft, John Gielgud, and Wendy Hiller. Produced by Mel Brooks' company. It was nominated for eight Academy Awards.

ELVIS

1979 TV
PRODUCER/SCREENWRITER:
Anthony Lawrence
DIRECTOR: John Carpenter
ALSO RELEASED AS: *Elvis, the Movie*

Elvis is shown growing up, hitting the big time in records and movies, returning to live performances, and becoming a Las Vegas phenomenon. One character refers to him as a walking drugstore. Shelley Winters is Elvis' beloved Ma. Pat Hingle is Colonel Tom Parker. Season Hubley is Priscilla. Ronnie McDowell provides the singing voice for star Kurt Russell, backed by the original Jordanaires. With Melody Anderson, Ed Begley, Jr., and actors portraying Ed Sullivan, Natalie Wood, Bill Black, and Hank Snow. A theatrical release in Europe, it originally filled a three-hour TV time slot. Busy execu-

,tive producer Dick Clark also backed *The Birth of the Beatles* television movie the same year. Former Disney kid Kurt Russell went on to more Carpenter projects (*Escape from New York* and *The Thing*).

ELVIS, THE MOVIE: See ELVIS.

THE EMBALMER
1965 Europix (Italy) (B&W)
PRODUCERS: Christian Marvel, Walter Manley
DIRECTOR: Dino Tavella
SCREENWRITERS: Dino Tavella, G. Muretta
ORIGINALLY RELEASED AS: *Il Mostro di Venezia*

In Venice a madman who wears a monk's robe and a skull mask lives in the crypt of a secret underwater monastery. He occasionally dons frogman gear and swims through the canals looking for beautiful women to kill and embalm (to preserve their beauty, of course). A meddlesome architect turns up dead on stage as part of a magic act. With Maureen Brown and Gin Mart.

EMBRYO
1976 Cine Artists
PRODUCERS: Arnold H. Orgolini, Anita Doohan
DIRECTOR: Ralph Nelson
SCREENWRITERS: Anita Doohan, Jack W. Thomas

A real howl! Rock Hudson is hopeless as a brilliant scientist who grows the fetuses of a dog and a woman outside of their mothers' wombs. The woman (Nicaraguan Barbara Carrera) grows to maturity in four and a half weeks. Thanks to Rock's prenatal tapes, she is superintelligent and a perfect, totally devoted virgin lover for her "creator." Lots of embarrassing and repulsive scenes of fetuses bouncing on the floor

and the nubile superwoman deteriorating while injecting herself with some of Rock's special chemicals. Roddy McDowall and Dr. Joyce Brothers put in stupid appearances at a party scene. Rock is best at the end, crying and holding on to a withered old corpse he has just killed. With Diane Ladd as a repressed spinster type. (R)

EMPIRE OF THE ANTS
1977 AIP
PRODUCER/DIRECTOR/SCREENWRITER: Bert I. Gordon

Terrible science fiction about a group of suckers being shown a phony unfinished housing development on an island. Soon they're attacked by laughable giant ants created by radiation. Joan Collins is the head swindler. Robert Lansing is the bearded boat owner. Lots of boredom as the survivors bicker while trying to escape. The script is said to be based on an H.G. Wells book. With Albert Salmi, John David Carson, and Robert Pine. Somebody should tell Bert you can't bring back the '50s.

THE EMPIRE STRIKES BACK
1980 20th Century-Fox
PRODUCERS: George Lucas, Gary Kurtz
DIRECTOR: Irvin Kershner
SCREENWRITERS: Leigh Brackett, Lawrence Kasdan

The sequel to *Star Wars* is the number-three film rental champ of all time as of this writing. Guess what number two is. (*E.T.* is number one.) From the director of *Stakeout on Dope Street* and *Eyes of Laura Mars. Return of the Jedi* is the next step for this phenomenal series/industry. Music by John Williams. Williams, who has scored over 60 films, replaced Arthur Fiedler as conductor of the Boston Pops Orchestra the year *Empire* was released.

ENCOUNTER WITH THE UNKNOWN

1973 Centronics International
PRODUCER: Joe Glass
DIRECTOR: Harry Thomason

An anthology film partially narrated by a hard-up Rod Serling. It stars Rosie Holotik and Gene Ross of *Don't Look in the Basement*. The stories are about a cursed trio of teenagers, a mysterious hole in the earth on a farm, and a ghost on a bridge. A lot of money was saved by repeating certain segments over and over again as flashbacks, dreams, and subjects of serious discussion by one of the narrators. The dialogue was all dubbed in after the film was shot. From the makers of *So Sad About Gloria*.

THE END OF THE WORLD: See *PANIC IN THE YEAR ZERO*.

END OF THE WORLD

1977 Irwin Yablans Co.
PRODUCER: Charles Band
DIRECTOR: John Hayes
SCREENWRITER: Frank Ray Perelli

A priest (Christopher Lee) and some nuns in a convent are really aliens out to destroy the world! The disguised invaders resemble *Close Encounters* leftovers. The wonderful has-been cast includes Sue Lyon (the original *Lolita*), Lew Ayres, MacDonald Carey, Dean Jagger, and Kirk Scott.

ENEMY FROM SPACE

1957 Hammer/United Artists (England) (B&W)
PRODUCER: Anthony Hinds
DIRECTOR: Val Guest
SCREENWRITERS: Nigel Kneale, Val Guest
ALSO RELEASED AS: *Quatermass II*

Alien life forms take over a research plant and infiltrate the government. Dr. Quatermass (Brian Donlevy) is the only earthling smart enough to stop them.

From David Lynch's Eraserhead.

Good science fiction based on a British TV serial called *Quatermass II*. With Vera Day, Bryan Forbes, Sidney James, and Michael Ripper.

EQUINOX

1967/71 VIP
PRODUCERS: Dennis Muren, Jack Harris
DIRECTORS/SCREENWRITERS: Mark McGee, Jack Woods

A unique feature originally shot in 16mm to which producer Harris added new scenes. The cast of amateur unknowns and writer Fritz Leiber (as a missing scientist) face an incredible array of giant animated demons emerging from a dimensional barrier to hunt a necronomiconlike book. The special effects by Jim Danforth and David Allen include a flying devil and an apelike monster. Forrest J Ackerman supplies the voice on a tape. With Frank Bonner of the "W.K.R.P. in Cincinnati" show.

ERASERHEAD

1977 Libra (B&W)

PRODUCER/DIRECTOR/SCREENWRITER:
David Lynch

An amazing, almost indescribable nightmare, meticulously filmed over a period of five years with partial financing from the American Film Institute. Anyone who has lived in a once-thriving Northeastern city will be familiar with the decayed industrial surroundings. Others will identify with the completely alienated, sexually retarded characters. Many viewers (usually female) walk out of the theater in disgust. Many others watch it faithfully every week at midnight showings. You probably wouldn't feel comfortable alone in a room with one of the frequent viewers. Jack Nance stars. The gradual success of Lynch's debut feature led to *The Elephant Man*. A sound track album was finally released in 1982.

ERIK THE CONQUEROR

1961 AIP (Italy/France)

DIRECTOR: Mario Bava

SCREENWRITERS: Oreste Biancoli, Mario Bava, Piero Pierotti

ORIGINALLY RELEASED AS: *Gli Invasori*

ALSO RELEASED AS: *Fury of the Vikings*

Cameron Mitchell is Iron, a Viking chieftain. His brother Erik (Giorgio Giovannini) was raised by the British Queen. Iron's woman is Erik's wife's twin (Alice and Ellen Kessleri). The brothers fight. The first of three Viking movies Mitchell did in Europe in the '60s. The others were *Last of the Vikings* (1962) and *Knives of the Avenger* (1968).

THE EROTIC ADVENTURES OF SNOW WHITE: See GRIMMS FAIRY TALES FOR ADULTS.

ESCAPE

1971 TV

PRODUCER: Bruce Lansbury

DIRECTOR: John Llewellyn Moxey

SCREENWRITER: Paul Playdon

Christopher George as a magician/escape artist stops Avery Schreiber from taking over the world! With Gloria Grahame, Huntz Hall, William Schallert, William Windom, and human robots. Director Moxey has done over two dozen TV movies since 1970.

From the motion picture Escape from New York Copyright © 1981 Embassy Pictures. Courtesy of Embassy Pictures.

A future citizen in Escape from New York.

ESCAPE FROM NEW YORK

1981 Avco Embassy

PRODUCERS: Debra Hill, Larry Franco

DIRECTOR: John Carpenter

SCREENWRITERS: John Carpenter, Nick Castle

In 1997 Manhattan is a maximum security prison. Prisoner Snake Plissken (Kurt Russell) is hauled in by Warden Lee Van Cleef and offered a reprieve if he can rescue the President of the U.S., whose plane has crashed in the city. Although flawed, it's the best use of a New York City-in-ruins setting so far. Donald Pleasence is the ineffectual kidnaped President. Ernest Borgnine is a cabbie who knows his way around the prison/city. Isaac Hayes is "The Duke." Henry Dean Stanton as "Brain" and Adrienne Barbeau reluctantly help the grizzly hero. With obvious nods to Clint Eastwood Westerns and punk fashions. The girl in the ruins of a Chock Full O'Nuts is Season Hubley. *Escape from New York* games and sound tracks are available. With professional wrestler Ox Baker. (R)

in his last role) escape the end of the world in *Beneath* . . . by traveling back in time to L.A. in the 1970s. They're destroyed by greedy humans but Kim's chimp baby (played by a real chimp) survives in a circus and grows up to star in *Conquest* . . . With Bradford Dillman, Jason Evers, and Ricardo Montalban (as humans).

ESCAPE TO WITCH MOUNTAIN

1975 Buena Vista
PRODUCER: Jerome Courtland
DIRECTOR: John Hough
SCREENWRITER: Robert Malcolm Young
Two orphaned aliens with psychic pow-

Marie Liljedahl takes a bath in Eugénie . . . The Story of Her Journey Into Perversion.

ESCAPE FROM THE PLANET OF THE APES

1971 20th Century-Fox
PRODUCER: Arthur P. Jacobs
DIRECTOR: Don Taylor
SCREENWRITER: Paul Dehn
Apes Part III. Three apes (Roddy McDowall, Kim Hunter, and Sal Mineo

ers are exploited by an evil tycoon (Ray Milland) and a psychic investigator (Donald Pleasence). A nice guy (Eddie Albert) helps them escape. Eventually they're saved by a flying saucer from their homeland. The alien kids were back in *Return to Witch Mountain*, facing new villains.

EUGÉNIE... THE STORY OF HER JOURNEY INTO PERVERSION
1969 Distinction Films (Spain/
W. Germany/England)
PRODUCER/SCREENWRITER:
Harry Alan Towers
DIRECTOR: Jesse Franco
ALSO RELEASED AS: *Philosophy in the Boudoir*

Christopher Lee is Dolmance, the onscreen narrator of this inept sex sickie. He claims he never saw the rest of the film or knew what it was about. His role was supposed to be played by George Sanders, who "got sick." Maria Rohm is a wealthy jaded De Sade fan who lets a man seduce her on the condition that his beautiful young virginal daughter be sent to her private island for a weekend. Marie Liljedahl, star of some highly publicized European softcore epics like *Inga* and *Ann and Eve*, is the innocent Eugénie. But not for long. She's drugged, beaten, forced to participate in orgies (involving all the guests and the hired help), drinks blood, and kills Jack Taylor. In the clever ending she wakes up from a nightmare—and prepares to go to a private island for the weekend. An X-rated relic, which would probably get an R now. (**X**)

EVE
1968 Commonwealth United
(Spain/England/U.S.)
PRODUCER/SCREENWRITER:
Harry Alan Towers
DIRECTOR: Jeremy Summers
ALSO RELEASED AS: *The Face of Eve*

A really shoddy "female Tarzan" film with an interesting international cast. As an American pilot, Robert Walker, Jr. crashes in the jungles of Peru and is rescued by Eve (Celeste Yarnall) who is worshiped as a goddess by the natives. Soon there's a big search for her. Christopher Lee (in a wheelchair) is a famous explorer and Eve's grandfather.

Herbert Lom is a villain who has been passing off his mistress as the lost jungle woman. Fred Clark is an American sideshow operator. They all want Eve. Meanwhile the natives decide to torture her for helping the pilot.

THE EVE OF ST. MARK
1944 20th Century-Fox (B&W)
PRODUCER: William Perlberg
DIRECTOR: John M. Stah
SCREENWRITER: George Seaton

American soldiers train and go off to fight in the Philippines. Anne Baxter and William Eythe star. Vincent Price is a Shakespeare-quoting Southern-bred good guy. With Dickie Moore.

EVERYTHING YOU ALWAYS WANTED TO KNOW ABOUT SEX (BUT WERE AFRAID TO ASK)
1972 United Artists
PRODUCER: Charles H. Joffe
DIRECTOR/SCREENWRITER: Woody Allen

Seven segments based on questions in Dr. Reuben's bestselling sex manual. In one episode a mad sex-research doctor (John Carradine) who has created a 400-foot diaphragm is visited by Allen, who unleashes a giant breast. An Antonioni movie parody about frigidity stars Louise Lasser. In "What Happens During Ejaculation?" Tony Randall is a microscopic operator who sends out the nervous Woody Allen as sperm No. 2. A sometimes funny comedy that's best when Woody Allen is in it (four of the segments). With Gene Wilder, Lynn Redgrave, Burt Reynolds, and Lou Jacobi.

THE EVICTORS
1979 AIP
PRODUCER/DIRECTOR: Charles B. Pierce
SCREENWRITERS: Charles B. Pierce,
Garry Rusoff

More backwoods horrors from the creator of *The Legend of Bigfoot*. Vic Morrow stars as a real estate agent/killer. With Michael Parks, Jessica Harper, and Sue Ann Langdon. Very obscure.

THE EVIL

1978 New World
PRODUCER: Ed Carlin
DIRECTOR: Gus Trikonis
SCREENWRITER: Donald G. Thompson

An entertaining haunted-house thriller in the tradition of *The Haunting* but with more horrible deaths and a helpful ghost. Psychologist Richard Crenna, his doctor wife Joanna Pettet, and professor Andrew Prine go to a mansion with a group of students and patients. When Crenna unleashes a powerful force from the cellar, the horror never stops. The ending with Victor Buono (as the Devil) was cut from some prints. Opinions vary as to whether his presence ruined or made the film. Too bad some of the special effects are so shoddy.(R)

EVIL BRAIN FROM OUTER SPACE

1956–59 Manly TV (Japan) (B&W)
PRODUCER: Mitsugi Okora
DIRECTORS: Tervo Ishii, Akira Mitsuwa, Koreyoshi Akasaka
SCREENWRITER: Ichiro Miyagawa

See *Atomic Rulers of the World*. Starman battles deformed Marpetians ruled by the brain of Balazar, an evil scientist. Funnier than *Godzilla vs. the Smog Monster*.

THE EVIL EYE

1963 AIP (Italy) (B&W)
ASSOCIATE PRODUCER: Salvatore Billitteri
DIRECTOR: Mario Bava
SCREENWRITER: Ennio de Concini
ORIGINALLY RELEASED AS: *La Ragazza che Sapeva Troppo*

An American in Rome (Leticia Roman) can't convince anybody that she's witnessed a murder. Then her late aunt's house becomes occupied overnight by a couple who say they've always been there. A friendly doctor (John Saxon) becomes a suspect in a series of killings. A sometimes confusing mystery similar to the later Dario Argento films.

EVIL IN THE DEEP

1977 Selected
PRODUCERS: Virginia Stone, J.A.S. McCombie
DIRECTOR: Virginia Stone

"Rips your nerves to shreds!" the ads promised. Stephen Boyd (in his last role) is a brave scuba-diving shark hunter in this *Jaws*-inspired obscurity.

An ancient horror slept beneath the old haunted mansion... THE EVIL *nothing could stop its escape!*

Rosey Grier (*The Thing with Two Heads*) and Cheryl Stoppelmoor (soon to be Cheryl Ladd) co-star. Boyd died in '77.

EVIL MIND: See THE CLAIRVOYANT.

THE EVIL OF FRANKENSTEIN

1964 Hammer/Universal (England)
PRODUCER: Anthony Hinds
DIRECTOR: Freddie Francis
SCREENWRITER: John Elder

The third of Hammer's Peter Cushing/ Dr. Frankenstein films. It was the only one not directed by Terence Fisher and the only one in which the monster resembles the Universal/Karloff version. The doctor and his assistant Han (Sandor Eles) revive the monster, found frozen in an ice cave. The creature (Kiwi Kingston) has brain damage, so Zoltan, a mesmerist (Peter Woodthorpe), is called in to reactivate the brain with hypnotism. Zoltan takes total control and uses the lumbering monster to kill his enemies. With Katy Wild as a mute beggar. The American TV version has new scenes shot in the U.S. to replace scenes that were cut out.

EVILSPEAK

1982 The Moreno Co.
PRODUCERS: Sylvio Tabet, Eric Weston
DIRECTOR: Eric Weston
SCREENWRITERS: Joseph Garofalo, Eric Weston

Clint Howard, best known as a bear's best buddy on TV's *Gentle Ben*, plays a computer-obsessed nerd, abused and reviled by his classmates at an oh-so-oppressive military academy. As the butt of countless practical jokes, Howard has plenty of cause to whip up a bad case of anger before getting in touch (via computer hookup) with Satan and a hellish army of razor-tusked wild pigs. At first Howard, aided by the ancient black book he finds in the basement of the old chapel, tries to control his newfound powers. But when he finally decides that enough is too much, he lets the demonic porkers run riot over the campus and zaps drunken Sergeant R. G. Armstrong with a very nasty head twist. An energetic and promising terror film debut for Weston. (**R**)   –BM

EXCALIBUR

1981 Orion/Warner Brothers
PRODUCER/DIRECTOR: John Boorman
SCREENWRITERS: Rospo Pallenberg, John Boorman

Squeezing the whole of Thomas Mallory's *Le Morte d'Arthur* (with a few revisions) into one two-hour-forty-minute movie, Boorman takes the opportunity to discourse once again on cosmic duality (good-evil, pagan-Christian, Merlin-Morgana, Arthur-Mordred, etc.), with plenty of medieval pomp, hearty banqueting, and muddy, bloody battling. All well and good, but the dizzying pace of the film leaves little time for characterization (except for the characters that interest Boorman). It helps if you're already familiar with the events of the legend. With Nicol Williamson, Nigel Terry, Helen Mirren, and some wonderful iron masks. (**R**)
–BM

EXO-MAN

1977 TV
PRODUCER: Lionel E. Siegel
DIRECTOR: Richard Irving
SCREENWRITERS: Martin Caidin, Howard Rodman

When a professor (David Ackroyd) is paralyzed by gangsters, he creates an "exo-suit" and becomes a superhero in

WOMEN CAGED LIKE ANIMALS...
living only for the pleasure of their keepers!

HOUSE OF INSANE WOMEN

Originally released as: Exorcism's Daughter.

this TV pilot film featuring José Ferrer as Kermit Haas. With Harry Morgan and Kevin McCarthy. From the guy who made the *Six Million Dollar Man* pilot.

EXORCISM AT MIDNIGHT

1966/73 Independent International (England) (B&W tinted)
PRODUCER: Michael F. Johnson
DIRECTOR/SCREENWRITER: Stanley Goulder
ALSO RELEASED AS: *Naked Evil*

To cash in on the *Exorcist* craze, a surprisingly good old British voodoo movie was re-released in 1973 with some new American scenes. The story is about West Indians in England who believe in possession. An old black servant named Amazan is actually a witch doctor practicing in a hidden basement room. A detective (Richard Coleman) investigates a series of murders and a priest performs an exorcism. The embarrassing new scenes using actors with obvious American accents show doctors (including Lawrence Tierney) studying a possessed man. The entire film was tinted! The process was called "MultiColor." Remember, this was released in the '70s!

EXORCISM'S DAUGHTER

1974 National Forum Corporation (Spain)
DIRECTOR/SCREENWRITER: Rafael Morena Alba
ALSO RELEASED AS: *House of Insane Women*

A fairly interesting movie about a 19th-century asylum. Francisco Rabal (*Nazarin*) discovers that Amelia Gade is insane because as a child she saw her mother die during an attempted exorcism.

THE EXORCIST

1973 Warner Brothers
PRODUCER/SCREENWRITER:
William Peter Blatty
DIRECTOR: William Friedkin

Friedkin, known for such flops as *Good Times* (with Sonny and Cher) and *Cruising,* helped make this influential vomit fest the most popular horror film of all time. William Peter Blatty, who later turned unsuccessful director with *Twinkle Twinkle Killer Kane,* adapted his novel into an Oscar-winning screenplay. How much little Linda Blair really contributed to her part has been in question. Mercedes McCambridge supplied the possessed voice. Actress Eileen Smith doubled in the vomiting sequences and later had to sue for credit. Max Von Sydow and playwright Jason Miller are the priests. Ellen Burstyn is the actress mom. With Lee J. Cobb and Jack MacGowran (*Cul-de-Sac*). Dick Smith and Rick Baker were responsible for the trend-setting special makeup effects. The sound track, taken from Mike Oldfield's *Tubular Bells,* is still being copied in other features. (**R**)

EXORCIST II: THE HERETIC

1977 Warner Brothers
PRODUCERS: John Boorman, Richard Lederer
DIRECTOR: John Boorman
SCREENWRITER: William Goodhart

Everybody's new favorite bad Richard Burton movie, also starring 18-year-old Linda Blair being wired, studied, and probed by Louise Fletcher. Max Von Sydow is Father Merrin in flashbacks. Burton is Father Lamont, the heretic. Paul Henried is the cardinal and James Earl Jones is Kokumo. With Ned Beatty, music by Ennio Morricone, and a view through a fly's eye. A major financial and critical disaster, it was recalled and re-edited after audiences laughed at the very serious deviltry. Ads suggested buying the sound track and "The Making of . . ." book. (R)

THE EXOTIC ONES

1968 Ormond (B&W)

PRODUCER/DIRECTOR/SCREENWRITER:
Ron Ormond

Marijuana monster terrorizes strippers in New Orleans! The director and his wife June star. Ormond made at least nine other features from 1951 on, including *Mesa of Lost Women*, *King of the Bullwhip*, *Untamed Mistress*, and *Forty Acre Feud.*   –CB

THE EXPLOSIVE GENERATION

1961 United Artists (B&W)

PRODUCER: Stanley Colbert
DIRECTOR: Buzz Kulik
SCREENWRITER: Joseph Landon

Teacher William Shatner is suspended after having his high-schoolers write sexual autobiographies. The students protest his dismissal with a silence strike that culminates in a ghostly basketball game in the school gym. Featuring Patty McCormack, Lee Kinsolving, Billy Gray, and Beau Bridges; with Edward Platt, Jocelyn Brando, Steve Dunne, and Virginia Field as the PTA.   –CB

EXPRESSO BONGO

1959 Continental (B&W)

PRODUCER/DIRECTOR: Val Guest
SCREENWRITER: Wolf Mankowitz

Cliff Richards got his successful Elvis-of-England career started with this satirical musical based on the play of the same name. Laurence Harvey as a fast-talking small-time agent discovers him singing at the Tom Tom Club, backed by the Shadows. Bongo Herbert (Richards) rises to fame, sings religious ballads dedicated to his mother, suffers romantic confusion, and finally dumps his overbearing manager. A record company owner character refers to the whole business as "nausea."

THE EYE CREATURES

1965 AIP-TV

PRODUCER/DIRECTOR: Larry Buchanan
SCREENWRITERS: Robert Gurney, Jr.,
    Al Martin

If you've seen *Invasion of the Saucermen* and happen to catch this awful uncredited remake on TV while you're falling asleep, you'll probably doubt your sanity. The story is the same, but instead of scary little aliens, there are full-sized men in ill-fitting lumpy costumes with a lot of eyes, and John Ashley is the hero! Headlights make the creatures blow up real good. Add some voyeur army personnel and you've got the worst of the worst.

AN EYE FOR AN EYE: See THE PSYCHOPATH.

EYE OF THE CAT

1969 Universal

PRODUCERS: Bernard Schwartz,
    Philip Hazelton
DIRECTOR: David Lowell Rich
SCREENWRITER: Joseph Stefano

Cosmetologist Gayle Hunnicut plots with young heir Michael Sarazin to kill his wheelchair-ridden aunt (Eleanor Parker). Sarazin is deathly afraid of cats. The aunt owns dozens of them. The cats spoil the get-rich-quick plans. With Tullia the cat. (M)

EYE OF THE DEVIL
1966 MGM (England)
PRODUCERS: John Calley, Martin Ransohoft
DIRECTOR: J. Lee Thompson
SCREENWRITERS: Robin Estridge,
  Dennis Murphy
ALSO RELEASED AS: 13
British occult thriller set in France with David Niven as a wealthy vineyard owner who agrees to be sacrificed to improve the wine. His wife, Deborah Kerr, doesn't like the idea. Featuring David Hemmings as a warlock and Sharon Tate as a witch who turns a toad into a dove and hypnotizes people. Also with Donald Pleasence as a priest and Edward Mulhare. It was cut before the American release for reasons of "taste." Partially filmed in the Bordeaux country of France.

EYEBALL
1978 Brenner (Italy)
PRODUCER: Joseph Brenner
DIRECTOR: Umberto Lenzi
SCREENWRITER: Felix Tusell
ORIGINALLY RELEASED AS: *Gatto Rossi in un Labirinto do Vetro*
Another boring Italian murder mystery passed off as a horror film. John Richardson stars. The killer likes to cut out eyes. (R)

EYES OF A STRANGER
1980 Warner Brothers
PRODUCER: Ronald Zerra
DIRECTOR: Ken Wiederhorn
SCREENWRITERS: Mark Jackson, Eric L. Bloom

This boring film is just another standard rapist-killer movie, but there are a few nice touches. A TV anchorwoman who lives with her deaf, dumb, and blind sister (she became that way because she was raped as a child) discovers that a neighbor is the rapist-murderer but can't prove it. Even though well shot and edited, this dreamlike movie doesn't rise above its dull handling. At one point in the film a *Dawn of the Dead* poster can be seen in front of a movie theater. With Lauren Tewes and Jennifer Jason Leigh. By the director of *Shock Waves*. Gore effects by Tom Savini were mostly cut before the film's release.   –AF

THE EYES OF CHARLES SAND
1972 TV
PRODUCER: Hugh Benson
DIRECTOR: Reza Badiyi
SCREENWRITERS: Henry Farrell,
  Stanford Whitmore
Peter Haskell can see into the future in this TV-pilot film. He helps solve a murder. From a story by Henry Farrell. With Joan Bennett, Barbara Rush, Bradford Dillman, Sharon Farrell, Adam West, and Gary Clarke. Boring. The music was "borrowed" from *Wait Until Dark*. Henry Mancini sued.

EYES OF EVIL: See THE 1,000 EYES OF DR. MABUSE.

EYES OF HELL: See THE MASK.

EYES OF LAURA MARS
1978 Columbia
PRODUCER: Jon Peters
DIRECTOR: Irvin Kershner
SCREENWRITERS: John Carpenter,
  David Zelag Goodman

Former hairdresser Jon Peters originally planned to produce this psychic thriller as a vehicle for Barbra Streisand (she sings the theme song). Faye Dunaway ended up playing the title role of a fashionable New York photographer who can see through the eyes of a psycho who is murdering her friends. Tommy Lee Jones is a detective on the case. With Brad Dourif, Rene Auberjoinois, and Raul Julia. John Carpenter cowrote the screenplay from his story. Jack Harris (*The Blob*) was the executive producer. Helmut Newton did Faye's photographs. The director went on to *The Empire Strikes Back*. **(R)**

THE FABULOUS BARON MUNCHAUSEN

1961 Teleworld (Czechoslovakia)
DIRECTOR: Karel Zeman
SCREENWRITERS: Karel Zeman, Joseph Kainan
ORIGINALLY RELEASED AS: *Baron Prasil*

Live action is blended with backdrop scenery and props based on the engravings of Gustav Dore. The first modern man on the Moon finds the famous boasting baron already there enjoying tea with Jules Verne. The baron takes the astronaut on an incredible world tour using an airship held by birds. Terry Gilliam, who used similar techniques on *Monty Python,* promises to do a remake.

THE FABULOUS WORLD OF JULES VERNE

1958 Warner Brothers (Czechoslovakia)
PRODUCER: Ceskos Lovenskv Films
DIRECTOR: Karel Zeman
SCREENWRITERS: Karel Zeman, Frantisek Hrubin

The best-known of Zeman's poetic mixtures of live action and 19th-century engravings was released here with anglicized credits and promoted as being in "Mystimation." It's based on several Verne novels and features submarines, airships, and a giant squid. In the tradition of the silent films of George Méliès. Hugh Downs is in the tacked-on intro.

THE FACE BEHIND THE MASK

1941 Columbia (B&W)
PRODUCER: Wallace McDonald
DIRECTOR: Robert Florey
SCREENWRITERS: Allen Vincent, Paul Jarrico

Peter Lorre is perfect as Janos Szaby, an immigrant Hungarian watchmaker having a difficult time in America. He becomes horribly burned in a tenement fire and has made an expressionless mask of his face that he can't pay for. He grows increasingly bitter and easily takes over an underworld operation he joined to make money. When he helps out and falls in love with a blind girl (Evelyn Keyes) who considers him kind and honest, the gang thinks he's betrayed them and more tragedy results. A classic B-picture with George E. Stone and Don Beddoe. Florey directed Lorre again in *The Beast with Five Fingers.*

Gangsters watch their ex-boss Peter Lorre in The Face Behind the Mask.

THE FACE OF EVE: See EVE.

THE FACE OF FEAR: See PEEPING TOM.

FACE OF FIRE

1959 Allied Artists (U.S./Sweden) (B&W)
PRODUCERS: Albert Band, Louis Garfinkle
DIRECTOR: Albert Band
SCREENWRITER: Louis Garfinkle

Promoted as a horror movie, this filmed-in-Sweden feature is based on Stephen Crane's "The Monster." James Whitmore's face is badly burned while rescuing a boy from a fire. The ordeal also affects his mind and the townspeople become terrified of him. With Cameron Mitchell, Bettye Ackerman, and Royal Dano.

THE FACE OF FU MANCHU

1965 Anglo Amalgamated/Seven Arts (England)
PRODUCER/SCREENWRITER: Harry Alan Towers
DIRECTOR: Don Sharp

Christopher Lee is the archvillain Fu Manchu whose secret headquarters are right under the Thames (the water is handy for drowning his victims). With his beautiful but evil daughter Lin Tang (Tsai Chin) at his side, he plans to conquer the world with a new poison gas developed by a German professor he holds prisoner (Walter Rilla). The professor's daughter (Karin Dor) is also Fu's prisoner. Sir Nayland Smith (Nigel Green) stops the horrendous plot and Fu Manchu dies in an explosion. (Or did he? He was back the next year in *The Brides of Fu Manchu.*) With Howard Marion-Crawford as Dr. Petrie.

FACE OF MARBLE

1946 Monogram (B&W)
PRODUCER: Jeffrey Bernard
DIRECTOR: William Beaudine
SCREENWRITER: Michael Jacoby

UPI 9/13/65: *This portrait of evil represents the return of the sinister Fu Manchu. He is being portrayed in the new film* The Face of Fu Manchu *by British actor Christopher Lee.*

Professor Randolph (John Carradine) and his assistant (Robert Shayne) return some dead people to life. They also revive a Great Dane who is soon walking through walls. Meanwhile, the Haitian housekeeper uses voodoo love potions and Willie Best shivers and hides. With Claudia Drake and Maris Wrixon. A forerunner of *Dracula's Dog*. Bad as only a Monogram horror movie could be.

FACE OF THE SCREAMING WEREWOLF

1959/65 Associated Distributors Pictures (Mexico) (B&W)
PRODUCER (english version): Jerry Warren
DIRECTORS: Gilberto Martinez Solares, Jerry Warren
SCREENWRITERS: Gilberto Martinez Solares, Juan Garcia, Fernando de Fuentes
ALSO RELEASED AS: *House of Terror*

In 1959 Lon Chaney, Jr., went south of the border to star in a horror comedy called *La Casa del Terror* with Mexican funnyman Tin Tan. When Jerry Warren bought it for dubbing and a U.S. release, all the comedy was left out — or was it? A mad scientist finds a mummy and revives it, but under the bandages it's a werewolf! Lon, wearing makeup similar to the old Universal look, got to revive two of his '40s characters at once. A rarity.

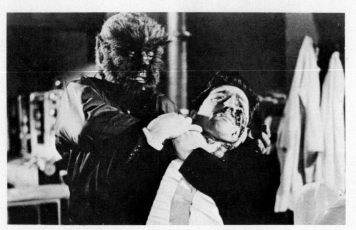

Lon Chaney plays the wolfman one more time in The Face of the Screaming Werewolf.

FADE TO BLACK

1980 Compass International
PRODUCERS: George Braunstein, Roy Hamady
DIRECTOR/SCREENWRITER: Vernon Zimmerman

Wimpy Eric Binford (played by wimpy Dennis Christopher) is a movie fan who kills people in the style of his heroes—Dracula, Richard Widmark, and Hopalong Cassidy among them. Unless you count the clips from old movies, poor Linda Kerridge—a talented actress doomed to be typed forever as a Marilyn Monroe look-alike—is the only asset in this attempt at a horror film by the director of the classic roller-derby epic *Unholy Rollers.* With a film clip from *Night of the Living Dead.* **(R)** —BM

FAHRENHEIT 451

1967 Universal (England)
PRODUCER: Lewis M. Allen
DIRECTOR/SCREENWRITER: François Truffaut

Truffaut tackles Ray Bradbury's world of totalitarianism. Montag (Oscar Werner) has a job burning books and a wife (Julie Christie) who watches a giant propaganda screen all day. He leaves both when his consciousness is raised by a teacher (Julie Christie with a different haircut). He hides out with the "book people" who keep busy reciting novels by memory (including *The Martian Chronicles*). Nicholas Roeg was the director of photography. Bernard Herrmann wrote the music. With a great dream sequence, wordless comic-book newspapers, and Anton Diffring.

FAIL-SAFE

1964 Columbia (B&W)
PRODUCER: Max E. Youngstein
DIRECTOR: Sidney Lumet
SCREENWRITER: Walter Bernstein

This nuclear-mistake movie was released a year after *Dr. Strangelove.* When Moscow is accidentally wiped off the map by American bombers, president Henry Fonda has New York City destroyed to avoid a war that would destroy all. The action ends with a freeze frame of children playing. With Dan O'Herlihy, Walter Matthau, Larry Hagman, and Dom DeLuise.

THE FAKERS: See HELL'S BLOODY DEVILS.

THE FALL GUY: See WHAT'S UP FRONT.

THE FALL OF THE HOUSE OF USHER ('60): See HOUSE OF USHER.

THE FALL OF THE HOUSE OF USHER

1980 Sunn Classics
PRODUCER: Charles E. Sellier, Jr.
DIRECTOR: James L. Conway
SCREENWRITER: Stephen Lord

A bearded Martin Landau and Ray Walston star in this new Poe adaptation from the people who brought us *In Search of the Gods* and an endless number of similar docudramas. They must have run out of psychic phenomena to explore because they're making more all-fiction duds like this. Filmed in Salt Lake City.

FALSE FACE

1976 United International
PRODUCERS: John Grissmer,
Joseph Weintraub
DIRECTOR/SCREENWRITER: John Grissmer
ORIGINALLY RELEASED AS: *Scalpel*

Robert Lansing is a murdering plastic surgeon in New Orleans who turns a go-go dancer into a duplicate of his runaway daughter (Judith Chapman). With a surprise ending. (**R**).

FAMILY PLOT

1976 Universal
PRODUCER/DIRECTOR: Alfred Hitchcock
SCREENWRITER: Ernest Lehman

Hitchcock's last film (his 53rd) about a kidnaping and two couples after money and diamonds is very lighthearted. It's entertaining but could almost be a Disney film. The crooked couple are William Devane and Karen Black. Spiritualist Barbara Harris and boyfriend Bruce Dern are the nice couple. Dern was put to much better use by Hitchcock on several episodes of *The Alfred Hitchcock Hour.* Alfred is seen for the last time as a familiar shadow on a glass door. Music by John Williams.

FANATIC: See DIE, DIE MY DARLING.

FANGS OF THE LIVING DEAD: See MALENKA THE VAMPIRE.

FANNY HILL: MEMORIES OF A WOMAN OF PLEASURE

1964 Famous Players (U.S./
W. Germany) (B&W)
PRODUCER: Albert Zugsmith
DIRECTOR: Russ Meyer
SCREENWRITER: Robert Hill

A one-shot collaboration between Meyer and Zugsmith. Neither has anything good to say about it. Leticia Roman is Fanny, the country girl who

UPI 1975: Famed motion picture director Alfred Hitchcock, who has just completed his 53rd motion picture, Universal's Family Plot, *celebrated his 76th birthday with a Spirit of '76 birthday cake in red, white, and blue in his office. The master of suspense was born on August 13, 1899, in Leytonstone, Essex, England. He directed his first film,* The Pleasure Garden, *on Italian and German locations in 1925. Hitchcock came to the United States in 1940 to direct* Rebecca *for David O. Selznick and remained in this country to become an American citizen.*

goes to London and has her life taken over by a madame played by Miriam Hopkins (star of the 1932 *Dr. Jekyll and Mr. Hyde,* here in her 60s). This rather tame version of the famous banned novel has a happy ending uniting Fanny with her sailor-lover Ulli Lommel. With Alex D'Arcy as the admiral and producer Zugsmith as a duke. The location scenes were filmed in Berlin.

THE FANTASTIC INVASION OF PLANET EARTH: See THE BUBBLE.

FANTASTIC VOYAGE

1966 20th Century-Fox
PRODUCER: Saul David
DIRECTOR: Richard Fleischer
SCREENWRITER: Harry Kleiner

In 1995 five people and a submarine are miniaturized and injected into the bloodstream of a dying defecting Czech scientist to perform brain surgery on him. Tiny Arthur Kennedy is the surgeon. Minuscule Raquel Welch is his

Dorothy Malone and John Ireland in Fast and Furious, *the first feature released by AIP.*

assistant in a tight diving suit. Minute Stephen Boyd is a secret agent. Little William Redfield is the submarine captain. Wee Donald Pleasence is an enemy agent killed by white corpuscles! They attack Raquel too and hero Boyd has to peel them off her quivering body. Lots of enlarged guts, a voyage through the ventricles, and a lung-induced tornado. With Edmond O'Brien and James Brolin.

FANTOMAS

1964 (France/Italy)
PRODUCER/DIRECTOR: André Hunebelle
SCREENWRITERS: Jean Halain, Pierre Foucaud
ORIGINALLY RELEASED AS: *Fantomas Contro Scotland Yard*

Jean Marais, the star of several Cocteau films, is the supercriminal Fantomas. Fandor, a newspaper reporter (also Marais), infuriates the criminal by printing stories saying there is no such person, that the police just made him up to have someone to blame for unsolved crimes. Fantomas, who has a metal face, is a master of disguises. He commits crimes as Fandor and as Jove, the police inspector (Louis de Funes).

With Marie-Hélène Arnaud. One of the three comical Fantomas adventures made in the early '60s with the same cast and director.

THE FAST AND THE FURIOUS

1954 ARC (AIP) (B&W)
PRODUCER: Roger Corman
DIRECTORS: John Ireland, Edwards Sampson
SCREENWRITERS: Jerome Odlum, Jean Howell

The second film from Roger Corman's Palo Alto productions and the first to be distributed by American Releasing Corporation, soon to be known as AIP. Blacklisted by the trucking industry after a mysterious fatality, teamster John Ireland is having coffee in a roadside café when he meets Dorothy Malone—on her way to compete in the annual Pebble Beach road race into Mexico. Ireland gets into a fistfight with a stranger, locks Malone in a shed, then takes her Jaguar and heads for the border. Running another driver off the course results in a flashback and a change of heart. With Bruce Carlisle, Marshall Bradford, Jean Howell, and Bruno Ve Sota. —CB

FASTER PUSSYCAT! KILL! KILL!

1965 Russ Meyer Associates (B&W)
PRODUCERS: Russ and Eve Meyer
DIRECTOR: Russ Meyer
SCREENWRITER: Jack Moran
ALSO RELEASED AS: *Leather Girls, Mankillers, Pussycat*

Partly because director John Waters has declared it's his favorite movie, this outrageous, ahead-of-its-time, adults-only feature has found a new, younger audience and a notoriety equaling Meyer's major-studio *Beyond the Valley of the Dolls.* Three psychotic go-go dancers race their Porsches in the California desert searching for cheap thrills. Tura Satana, an awesome part-Apache part-Japanese woman, wears a tight jumpsuit as Varla, the dyke leader of the pack. She leads Lori Williams and Haji in a funny, non-stop barrage of sex and violence while searching for an old man's hidden money. With martial-arts battles, a chicken run, a musclebound guy called Vegetable, Sue Bernard, *Playboy*'s Miss December 1966, as a kidnap victim, and the best dialogue you've heard in years. The Bostweeds provide the memorable theme song.

THE FASTEST GUITAR ALIVE

1967 MGM (B&W)
PRODUCER: Sam Katzman
DIRECTOR: Michael Moore
SCREENWRITER: Robert E. Kent

Roy Orbison stars as a Confederate spy who gives guitar lessons to the governor's daughter and then robs a Union mint before finding out the war is over. See Roy use his shotgun guitar to get himself and his companion Sammy Jackson and the dancing Chestnut Sisters out of a scrape with a band of renegades. Co-starring Joan Freeman and Maggie Pierce, with Lyle Bettger,

Ben Cooper, Poupee Gamın, Iron Eyes Cody, and Sam the Sham. Songs include "Pistolero," "Good Time Party," "Whirlwind," and "Rollin' On." –CB

THE FAT SPY

1966 Magna Pictures
PRODUCER: Everett Rosenthal
DIRECTOR: Joseph Brun
SCREENWRITER: Matthew Andrews

Would you believe a comedy (with music) about a search for the fountain of youth starring Jack E. Leonard (in two roles)? Brian Donlevy, a cosmetics tycoon, sends fat Jack E. to an island off Florida to find the fountain. Leonard's twin brother (in love with cosmetics manufacturer Phyllis Diller) shows up, too. As if that weren't bad enough, the island is loaded with singing teenagers and Jayne Mansfield as Donlevy's seductive daughter. Ponce de Leon turns up to put an end to the nonsense. With Jordan Christopher, Johnny Tillotson, and the Wild Ones, a group that actually played in New York City.

THE FATAL HOUR

1940 Monogram (B&W)
PRODUCER: William T. Lackey
DIRECTOR: William Nigh
SCREENWRITERS: Scott Darling, Joseph West

Another forgettable Mr. Wong detective film with Boris Karloff and Grant Withers solving a murder. With Marjorie Reynolds, Jason Robards, Sr., and Jack Kennedy.

THE FEAR CHAMBER

1968 Azteca (U.S./Mexico)
PRODUCER: Louis Enrique Vergara
DIRECTORS: Juan Ibañez, Jack Hill
SCREENWRITER: Jack Hill
ORIGINALLY RELEASED AS: *La Camara del Terror*

One of four Mexican features that Boris Karloff shot scenes for in Los Angeles.

These seldom-seen films were his last. As a kind scientist, he becomes ill after about 15 minutes of experimenting with a "living rock" and goes to bed. No more Boris. His assistants (including a dwarf) continue the experiments by feeding the blood of girls to the rock in an effort to rule the world. With Julissa, Santanon, and Carlos East. Boris' other south-of-the-border horrors were *House of Evil*, *The Incredible Invasion*, and *The Snake People*.

FEAR IN THE NIGHT

1947 Paramount (B&W)
PRODUCERS: William H. Pine,
    William C. Thomas
DIRECTOR/SCREENWRITER: Maxwell Shane
DeForest Kelly of *Star Trek* fame is a man who can't decide whether he killed somebody with a drill in a mirrored room or just dreamed it. His police-detective brother-in-law (Paul Kelly) helps sort out the facts. With Ann Doran. This Cornell Woolrich story was remade in 1956 as *Nightmare* by the same director.

FEAR IN THE NIGHT

1972 Hammer/International (England)
PRODUCER/DIRECTOR: Jimmy Sangster
SCREENWRITERS: Jimmy Sangster,
    Michael Syson
Peter Cushing stars as a one-armed headmaster of a private school. A young teacher (Ralph Bates) plots with Cushing's wife (Joan Collins), who is his mistress, to drive his own wife (Judy Geeson) insane and have her murder Cushing. Got that?

FEAR NO EVIL

1969 TV
PRODUCER/SCREENWRITER:
    Richard Alan Simmons
DIRECTOR: Paul Wendkos
The first and best made-for-TV occult movie. Louis Jourdan and Wilfrid Hyde-White star as occult investigators. Bradford Dillman becomes possessed by a full-length antique mirror. When he dies in a car crash, he returns through the mirror. His fiancée (Lynda Day George) seeks the help of the expert team. With Carroll O'Connor. It was a pilot film for a series to be called *Bedevilled*. *Ritual of Evil* was a second try.

FEAR NO EVIL

1981 Avco Embassy
PRODUCERS: Frank and Charles M. La Loggia
DIRECTOR/SCREENWRITER: Frank La Loggia
An interesting attempt to make a modern fantasy horror movie with strong religious overtones. Avco picked up the independent feature and added a lot of colorful optical effects. The confusing story features Andrew, a quiet high school student who is really the Antichrist. An old woman and a young girl are really angels sent to defeat him. Andrew destroys a local passion play and unleashes a horde of revived corpses. Most of the sound track is borrowed new wave and punk rock music, including Johnny Rotten snarling "I Am the Anti-Christ . . ." Pretty silly, but the guy who made it (in Rochester, New York) was only 23 at the time. One of Andrew's male high school tormentors is punished by being given instant breasts. A true oddity. Star Stefan Arngrim was the little boy on *The Land of the Giants* TV show. (R)

FEARLESS FRANK

1967 AIP
PRODUCER/DIRECTOR/SCREENWRITER:
    Philip Kaufman
ALSO RELEASED AS: *Frank's Greatest
    Adventure*
Frank, a country boy (Jon Voight), comes to the big city, falls in love with a girl named Plethora (Monique Van Vooren), is killed by gangsters and brought back to life as a superhero by a

doctor. The doctor's brother creates False Frank (also Voight), an inferior duplicate, to fight Frank. The original revived Frank becomes corrupt and overconfident while the imitation becomes the hero. A seldom shown satire filmed in Chicago by the director of the remake of *Invasion of the Body Snatchers*. With Joan Darling, Severn Darden (both in *The President's Analyst*), and David Steinberg as the Rat.

THE FEARLESS VAMPIRE KILLERS, OR PARDON ME BUT YOUR TEETH ARE IN MY NECK

1967 MGM (England)
PRODUCER: Gene Glitowski
DIRECTOR: Roman Polanski
SCREENWRITERS: Gerald Brach,
  Roman Polanski

Polanski's vampire spoof isn't his best effort, but like all his films it's at least partially brilliant. As Alfred, Polanski accompanies Professor Abronsius (Jack MacGowran), an enthusiastic old vampire hunter, to the castle of Count Von Krolock (Ferdy Mayne). MacGowran also starred in Polanski's *Cul-de-Sac* and was in *How I Won the War* and *The Exorcist*. Mayne repeated his excellent vampire role in an obscure 1971 German comedy, *Vampire Happening*. Although the idea of an organized colony of vampires attending a ball had been used in Hammer's *Kiss of the Vampire*, Polanski's film featured two firsts—a Jewish vampire (Alfie Bass) unaffected by the crucifix and a homosexual vampire (Ian Quarrier). Sharon Tate, who was featured in a *Playboy* pictorial promoting the film, is Rebecca, the beautiful red-haired peasant girl kidnaped (from one of her many baths) by the count. MGM cut 20 minutes out against Polanski's wishes and added a cartoon introduction. With awesome sets and striking color photography.

Shot on location 6,000 feet high in the Italian Alps.

THE FEARMAKERS

1958 United Artists (B&W)
PRODUCER: Martin Lancer
DIRECTOR: Jacques Tourneur
SCREENWRITERS: Elliot West, Chris Apple

Dana Andrews returns home from the Korean War and discovers his ad agency is unknowingly promoting communism. Their client, "The Sons of the Patriotic Pioneers" (an antiatomic warfare group), is a front for reds. With Dick Foran, Mel Torme, and Veda Ann Borg. Andrews had just been in Tourneur's *Curse of the Demon*.

FEAST OF FLESH: See BLOOD FEAST.

FEMALE: See THE VIOLENT YEARS.

THE FEMALE ANIMAL

1958 Universal
PRODUCER: Albert Zugsmith
DIRECTOR: Harry Keller

Hedy Lamarr plays a fading Hollywood sex symbol who decides to keep *Robot Monster* star George Nader around for company. She hires him as a caretaker but he falls for her adopted daughter Jane Powell. Lamarr retired after this nonhit. With Jan Sterling and Jerry Paris.

THE FEMALE BUNCH

1969 Burbank International
PRODUCER: Ralph Nussbaum
DIRECTOR: Al Adamson
SCREENWRITERS: Jale Lockwood,
  Brent Nimrod
ALSO RELEASED AS: *A Time to Run*

A gang of man-hating women living in the desert have problems with seduc-

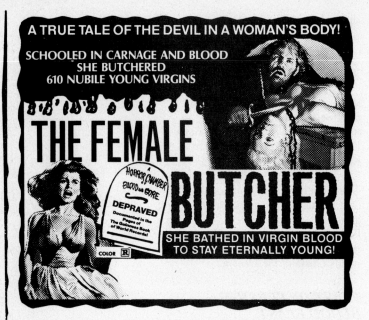

tive Russ Tamblyn. Lon Chaney, Jr., (in his last released film) is a hired-hand drug pusher. With Regina Carrol and Jennifer Bishop. Russ, Lon, and Regina were next seen in Adamson's *Dracula vs. Frankenstein*. For fitting atmosphere this sleazeball feature was shot on the Manson ranch. (**R**)

THE FEMALE BUTCHER

1972 Film Ventures (Italy/Spain)
PRODUCER: José Maria Sonzalez Sinde
DIRECTOR: Jorge Grau
SCREENWRITERS: Juan Tabar,
Sandro Contenenza
ORIGINALLY RELEASED AS: *Ceremonia Sangrienta*
ALSO RELEASED AS: *Legend of Blood Castle, Blood Ceremony*

"She butchered 610 nubile virgins!" the ads screamed. Lucia Bose, in another version of the Countess Elizabeth Bathory legend, stays eternally young by bathing in the blood of virgins. It was made after the producers studied the profits of *Countess Dracula*. With Ewa Aulin (*Candy*). (**R**)

THE FEMALE JUNGLE

1955 AIP (B&W)
PRODUCER: Burt Kaiser
DIRECTOR: Bruno Ve Sota
SCREENWRITERS: Burt Kaiser, Bruno Ve Sota
ALSO RELEASED AS: *The Hangover*

Jayne Mansfield in her first film role! She made $150 for playing a nymphomaniac. "It was finished in two weeks and led to nothing," she claimed later. The story starred Lawrence Tierney (the real-life brother of Scott Brady) as a police sergeant found drunk at the scene of an actress's murder. With John Carradine as a gossip writer, Kathleen Crowley, and director Ve Sota. Jayne then moved to even smaller roles at Warner Brothers before starring in *Will Success Spoil Rock Hunter?* on Broadway and returning to Hollywood and a starring contract at 20th Century-Fox.

FER-DE-LANCE

1974 TV
PRODUCER: Dominic Frontière
DIRECTOR: Russ Mayberry
SCREENWRITER: Leslie Stevens
ALSO RELEASED AS: *Death Drive*

Television's dumbest disaster film. It's about snakes on a submarine. With David Janssen, Hope Lange, Jason Evers, and Ivan Dixon. The British had to pay to see it. Leslie Stevens (*The Outer Limits*) was executive producer.

FERRY CROSS THE MERSEY

1964 United Artists (England) (B&W)
PRODUCER: Michael Holden
DIRECTOR: Jeremy Summers
SCREENWRITER: David Franden

Gerry and the Pacemakers, a popular Liverpool group of the early '60s, star in their own *Hard Day's Night*. After being welcomed by screaming fans, Gerry Marsden reminisces about the old prefame days going to art school during the day and playing the Cavern at night. After equipment complications they win a big-beat contest and achieve (short-lived) international fame. They perform the title hit, "It's Gonna Be All Right," and others. Cilla Black, the Fourmost, and others you never heard of also play. Executive producer Brian Epstein managed the Beatles and the Pacemakers. Note the way Gerry holds his guitar.

FIEND OF DOPE ISLAND

1961 Essanjay (B&W)
PRODUCER: J. Harold Odell
DIRECTOR: Nate Watt
SCREENWRITERS: Bruce Bennett,
Mark Carabel

Caribbean island baron Bruce Bennett lives by dealing in stolen firearms and local marijuana, paying his native laborers slave wages. The fiend imports a white female for fun, but she and his assistant (Robert Bray) unite to end the tyranny. With Tania Velia as Glory La Verne.   –CB

FIEND WITHOUT A FACE

1958 Anglo Amalgamated/MGM
(England) (B&W)
PRODUCER: John Croydon
DIRECTOR: Arthur Crabtree
SCREENWRITER: Herbert J. Leder

A rocket base in Canada is being sabotaged by an invisible force created by some scientists experimenting with the materialization of thought. This film starring Marshall Thompson might seem pretty ordinary for a while, but stick with it. The thought creatures eventually materialize as flying brains with spinal cords attached. The scenes of these partially animated creatures choking their screaming victims with their cords while sucking their brains out are the most nightmarish and shocking you'll ever see. Real breathtaking stuff! The

Living brains attack in this British release still from Fiend Without A Face.

special effects were created by a team of Austrians. The film was directed by the guy who did *Horror of the Black Museum.* Two hits in a row for Mr. Crabtree. Richard Gordon was executive producer.

THE FIENDISH GHOULS: See MANIA.

THE FIFTH FLOOR

1980 Film Ventures
PRODUCER/DIRECTOR: Howard Avedis
SCREENWRITERS: Meyer Dolinsky,
Howard Avedis

A cocktail waitress at a disco lounge is slipped a powerful drug and ends up in a mental asylum on the dreaded fifth floor. As a leering, demented attendant, Bo Hopkins makes sure she doesn't regain her sanity. Mel Ferrer is the guest-star doctor. Casablanca Records provided the disco music. With Dianne Hull, Patti D'Arbanville, Sharon Farrell, and Julie Adams. Pretty Bad. (**R**)

52 MILES TO TERROR: See HOT RODS TO HELL.

FIGHTING DEVIL DOGS
1938 Republic (B&W)
PRODUCER: Robert Beche
DIRECTORS: William Witney, John English
SCREENWRITERS: Barry Shipman, Franklyn Adreon, Ronald Davidson, Sol Shor
ALSO RELEASED AS: *The Tornado of Doom*

The Lightning, an impressive villain with lightning bolts all over his costume, destroys with his artificial thunderbolt. U.S. Marine hero Lee Powell saves the world and Eleanor Stewart. With Herman Brix (Bruce Bennett) and Montague Love. A condensed feature version was released to TV in '66.

THE FINAL CONFLICT
1981 20th Century-Fox (England)
PRODUCER: Harvey Bernhard
DIRECTOR: Graham Baker
SCREENWRITER: Andrew Birkin

The Omen, Part Three. Damien (Sam Neill) is now grown up, running a large corporation and about to become U.S. Ambassador to England. Some monks led by Rossano Brazzi try to stop him from killing Don Gordon's baby, a possible future obstacle. The monks die in a number of contrived ways. The baby is killed by a steam iron. The public didn't seem too interested in the last installment of this stupid series and it didn't even have celebrity deaths to help it along. With Charles Durning. **(R)**

THE FINAL COUNTDOWN
1980 United Artists
PRODUCER: Peter Vincent Douglas
DIRECTOR: Don Taylor
SCREENWRITERS: David Ambrose, Gerry Davis, Thomas Hunter, Peter Powell

Kirk Douglas, firmly established as a horror/science fiction star after *The Fury*, *The Chosen*, and *Saturn 3*, stars as the skipper of a nuclear aircraft carrier (the Nimitz) in this silly *Twilight Zone*-style feature. Kirk and his ship are suddenly time-warped to Pearl Harbor before the attack! With Katharine Ross, Martin Sheen, James Farentino, Charles Durning, and Ron O'Neal.

FINAL EXAM
1981 Avco Embassy
PRODUCERS: John L. Chambliss, Myron Meisel
DIRECTOR/SCREENWRITER: Jimmy Huston

Another *Halloween* copy, this one set at a college. A homicidal maniac fatally knifes all the main characters except the heroine. The victims get a lot of screen time but the murders are too tame to please the hardened fans of this type of film in the '80s. **(R)**

THE FINAL PROGRAMME: See *THE LAST DAYS OF MAN ON EARTH*

THE FINAL WAR
1960 Toei/Same Lake Enterprises (Japan) (B&W)
PRODUCER: Toei
DIRECTOR: Shigeaki Hidaka
SCREENWRITERS: T. Yasumi, Takeshi Kimura
ORIGINALLY RELEASED AS: *Dai Sanji Sekai Taisen*
ALSO RELEASED AS: *World War Three Breaks Out*

End-of-the-world paranoia from a Japanese point of view. The U.S. accidentally detonates a nuclear bomb over Korea. South Korea blames North Korea. Japan mobilizes. An American jet is shot down over the Soviet Union. Tokyo is totally leveled by Soviet H-bombs. The film's hero finds his nurse girlfriend dead and dies from radiation. Every country in the world is destroyed except for Argentina. A great kiddie-matinee feature.

FINGERS AT THE WINDOW
1942 MGM (B&W)
PRODUCER: Irving Star
DIRECTOR: Charles Lederer
SCREENWRITERS: Rose Caylor,
  Lawrence P. Bachmann

"The Mystery of the Robot Murders!" the ads promised. Basil Rathbone is a magician who impersonates the head of an asylum and hypnotizes inmates so they'll commit axe murders. With Lew Ayres and Laraine Day (known at the time as stars of the *Dr. Kildare* series).

FIRE!
1977 TV
PRODUCER: Irwin Allen
DIRECTOR: Earl Bellamy
SCREENWRITERS: Norman Katkov,
  Arthur Weiss

A hot one from disaster master Irwin Allen, executive producer of this story about a mountain community threatened by a blaze started by an escaped con. Ernest Borgnine stars. Others risking burned makeup include Patty Duke Astin, Neville Brand, Erik Estrada, Lloyd Nolan, Vera Miles, Donna Mills, Gene Evans, Ty Hardin, and Alex Cord. A short (90-minute) version was paired with a cut-down *Flood!* as television's first double-disaster bill!

FIRE IN THE SKY
1978 TV
PRODUCER: Hugh Benson
DIRECTOR: Jerry Jameson
SCREENWRITERS: Dennis Nemec,
  Michael Blankfort

Astronomer Richard Crenna warns the people of Phoenix that a fiery comet will destroy them. It does. With Elizabeth Ashley and 5,700 extras! An Emmy winner for special destructo effects! It aired before *Meteor* was released. *Meteor* was funnier.

FIRE MAIDENS FROM OUTER SPACE
1956 Topaz Films (England) (B&W)
PRODUCER: George Fowler
DIRECTOR/SCREENWRITER: Cy Roth

Sort of a British version of *Cat Women of the Moon* and just as ridiculous. America's instant has-been Anthony Dexter (star of *Valentino*) is the astronaut leader who finds a lost all-female civilization on a moon of Jupiter. These descendants of the citizens of Atlantis wear bathing suits with little skirts and lie around in flames for extra energy. A lumpy-faced monster in tights attacks the five Earth men. The alien beauties dance to Borodin's *Polovetsin Dances*.

FIREBALL 500
1966 AIP
PRODUCERS: James H. Nicholson,
  Samuel Z. Arkoff
DIRECTOR: William Asher
SCREENWRITERS: William Asher,
  Leo Townsend

Frankie Avalon plays into the hands of whiskey runners by agreeing to drive in a cross-country race. Annette Funicello and Fabian assist. With Chill Wills, Harvey Lembeck, Julie Parrish, and Vin Scully. Music by the Don Randi Trio Plus One and the Carole Lombard Singers. Track action filmed at the Ascot and Saugus Raceways near Los Angeles, local color shot in Charlotte, North Carolina. Featuring four *Playboy* Playmates. —CB

FIREBALL JUNGLE
1968 Americana
PRODUCER: G. B. Roberts
DIRECTOR: Jose Priete
SCREENWRITER: Harry Whittington
ALSO RELEASED AS: *Jungle Terror*

Stock-car racing infiltrated! Cateye Meares (Alan Mixon) helps mobster Nero Sagittarius (John Russell) take

Modern horrors in Lon Chaney's last film, Fireball Jungle.

over a string of Southern tracks, slaughtering as many troublemakers as necessary. Drivers are sent careening, and junkyard owner Lon Chaney, Jr., becomes a human torch. Cateye is eventually undone by the brother of one of his earlier victims. With Randy Kirby, Chuck Daniel, Nancy Donohue, Babs Beatty, and Herman the Wonder Dog. Thrill driving by Joie Chitwood. Made in Tampa. Director Priete is also known as Joseph Prieto. —CB

FIRST MAN INTO SPACE

1959 Anglo Amalgamated/MGM (England) (B&W)
PRODUCERS: John Croydon, Charles F. Vetter, Jr.
DIRECTOR: Robert Day
SCREENWRITERS: John C. Cooper, Lance Z. Hargreaves

Another scary hit from the people who made *Fiend Without a Face* (Amalgamated). Somebody there knew how to deliver uneasy shocks. An astronaut returns to Earth bloated and totally covered with space dust except for one eye. The crazed man needs blood to survive. He soon graduates from cattle to people.

The commander (Marshall Thompson) gets him in a glass booth and tries to communicate. No such luck. With Marla Landi. Richard Gordon was executive producer.

FIRST MEN IN THE MOON

1964 Columbia (England/U.S.)
PRODUCER: Charles H. Schneer
DIRECTOR: Nathan Juran
SCREENWRITERS: Nigel Kneale, Jan Read

Fun Victorian science fiction based on H.G. Wells' novel. When UN astronauts land on the moon they find a British flag from 1899 there. Flashbacks show eccentric professor Cavor (Lionel Jeffries) using his antigravity paint on a spherical metal ship that takes him to the Moon with playwright Edward Judd and Judd's fiancée, Martha Hyer. They're captured by Selenites (insect men). Most of them are men in suits, but a special feature is stop-motion animation by Ray Harryhausen of the Grand Lunar and a giant Moon calf (caterpillar). Peter Finch has a tiny role as a messenger in England. Newspaper ads featured a signed endorsement from Col. John "Shorty" Powers. A sound track album by Laurie Johnson is available.

FIRST SPACESHIP ON VENUS

1960 Crown International (E. Germany/Poland)
PRODUCERS: Newton P. Jacobs, Paul Schreibman, Edmund Goldman
DIRECTOR: Kurt Maetzig
SCREENWRITERS: J. Barckhausen, J. Fethke, W. Kohlasse, K. Mätzig, G. Reisch, G. Rücker, A. Stenbock-Fermor
ORIGINALLY RELEASED AS: *Der Schweigende Stern*

A critically acclaimed serious space film with good special effects, which was released here by Hugo Grimaldi minus 30 minutes of footage. Based on a book by Stanislaw Lem, it tracks a multi-racial/national flight to Venus in 1985. The picturesque but dead world they find has been destroyed by nuclear warfare. Try and imagine a 1960 American movie with a black astronaut.

FIVE

1951 Columbia
PRODUCER/DIRECTOR/SCREENWRITER:
Arch Oboler

The original postholocaust hit. Five survivors come together in a Frank Lloyd Wright cliff house and talk about the nuclear holocaust. They are a pregnant woman, a black doorman, a bank cashier who is dying, a frustrated idealist, and a mountain climber who is a murderer. With William Phipps, Susan Douglas, James Anderson, Charles Lampkin, and Earl Lee. —AF

FIVE BLOODY GRAVES

1969 Independent International Pictures
PRODUCER/DIRECTOR: Al Adamson
SCREENWRITER: Robert Dix
ALSO RELEASED AS: *The Gun Riders,*
Lonely Man

From the ads: "Passionate playgirls meet sick gunmen in a savage and sensuous slaughter!" Actor-screenwriter Robert Dix (who also was associate producer) stars as "The Messenger of Death" in this cheap allegorical Western. Death himself (Gene Raymond) narrates the action: Yacqui Indians attack, bathing prostitutes are watched by a lecherous old preacher (John Carradine), a squaw is raped and tortured, a man is left to die on an ant hill. Heavy thought from entertaining hack Al Adamson. With Scott Brady, John Cardos, Jim Davis (*Dallas*), Paula Raymond, and Vicki Volante. Cinematography by Vilmos Zsigmund. **(R)**

FIVE GOLDEN DRAGONS

1968 Warner Brothers (England)
PRODUCER/SCREENWRITER: Harry Alan Towers
DIRECTOR: Jerry Summers

Robert Cummings stars in his last theatrical feature as an American in Hong Kong in this international crime adventure. With George Raft, Brian Donlevy, Dan Duryea, Christopher Lee, Maria Rohm, and Margaret Lee. From the director of *The Vengeance of Fu Manchu.*

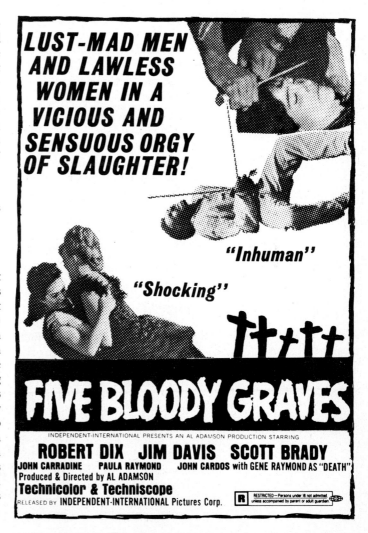

241

FIVE GUNS WEST

1955 ARC (AIP) (B&W)
PRODUCER/DIRECTOR: Roger Corman
SCREENWRITER: R. Wright Campbell

Corman's first time out as director. A cavalry-escorted stagecoach carries a defecting intelligence network head toward Union headquarters. Jailbird commandos help a Confederate captain stop it. With John Lund, Dorothy Malone, Bob Campbell, Jonathan Haze, Paul Birch, Larry Thor, and Michael "Touch" Connors. —CB

FIVE MILLION YEARS TO EARTH

1967 Hammer/Warner Brothers (England)
PRODUCER: Anthony Nelson-Keys
DIRECTOR: Roy Ward Baker
SCREENWRITER: Nigel Kneale
ALSO RELEASED AS: *Quatermass and the Pit*

The Quatermass series created by Nigel Kneale was originally serialized on British TV. Hammer made two excellent features about the superscientist in the '50s (*The Creeping Unknown* in '56 and *Enemy from Space* in '57—U.S. titles). Andrew Kier stars in this, the best of the series and one of the better science-fiction movies ever made. A Martian spaceship containing long-dead insectlike creatures is discovered under the London subway. The ship is protected by a mental energy which when unleashed begins destroying the city. The scientists discover that the aliens had instigated human evolution by their experiments on ancient apes (they were trying to make them into better slaves). When the Martians died the humans were left on their own. Some of these ideas were explored the next year in *2001: A Space Odyssey*. With Barbara Shelley and James Donald. In 1980, *The Quatermass Conclusion* starring John Mills was produced

as a British TV movie, but it hasn't shown up here yet.

FIVE MINUTES TO LIVE

1961 Sutton (B&W)
PRODUCER: James Ellsworth
DIRECTOR: Bill Karn
SCREENWRITER: Cay Forester
ALSO RELEASED AS: *Door-to-Door Maniac*

Johnny Cash poses as a salesman to trap housewife Cay Forester while his partner extracts $70,000 ransom from her banker husband. Featuring Donald Woods, Pamela Mason, Ronny Howard (who was Opie on *The Andy Griffith Show* at the time), Vic Tayback, and Merle Travis. Cash sings "I've Come to Kill" and "Five Minutes to Live." Rereleased by AIP in 1966 as *Door-to-Door Maniac* with an added rape scene. —CB

FIVE STAR FINAL

1931 Warner Brothers (B&W)
PRODUCER: Hal B. Wallis
DIRECTOR: Mervyn Leroy
SCREENWRITER: Byron Morgan

A film version of a play written by the managing editor of the *New York Evening Graphic*, the *Post* of its day. Managing editor Edward G. Robinson hires Boris Karloff to pose as a priest and photograph and spy on a family previously involved in a sensational murder. New sensational stories result in a double suicide and death threats aimed at the publisher. With H.B. Warner, Marian Marsh, Frances Starr, and Ona Munson. *Two Against the World* was a remake.

FIVE THE HARD WAY

1969 Crown International
PRODUCER: Ross Hagen
DIRECTOR: Gus Trikonis
SCREENWRITER: Tony Houston
ALSO RELEASED AS: *The Sidehackers*

A competition cyclist (Ross Hagen) seeks revenge for the sex slaying of his fiancée (Diane McBain). The man responsible is Michael Pataki (*Grave of the Vampire*). He and his boys prepare for a confrontation with Hagen and friends Crapout (Hoke Howell), Nero (Edward Parrish), and Jake (Robert Tessier). When the title was later changed to *The Sidehackers*, most people drew a blank. Director Trikonis was a Shark in *West Side Story*.   —CB

THE 5000 FINGERS OF DR. T

1953 Columbia
PRODUCER: Stanley Kramer
DIRECTOR: Roy Rowland
SCREENWRITERS: Dr. Seuss, Alan Scott

This children's nightmare co-written by Dr. Seuss is one of the best surrealistic fantasies ever made. Tommy Rettig (later star of TV's *Lassie*) dreams he is sent to a music school run by Dr. Terwilliker (Hans Conreid), a mad piano instructor who hopes to have his 500 pupils play with their 5000 fingers on his piano, the world's largest. Tommy, with the help of Peter Lind Hayes, fights two men on rollerskates connected by their beards and builds a bomb (possibly atomic), which absorbs sounds right out of the air. With Mary Healy.   —AF

FIVE WEEKS IN A BALLOON

1962 20th Century-Fox
PRODUCER/DIRECTOR: Irwin Allen
SCREENWRITERS: Charles Bennett, Irwin Allen, Albert Gail

Jules Verne was hot box office in the early '60s, so Irwin Allen made this fairly entertaining Verne adventure about a balloon voyage in Africa. Cedric Hardwicke (the balloon's inventor), Fabian (his young assistant who also sings the title song), Red Buttons (a playboy reporter), Barbara Luna (a runaway slave), and Richard Haydn float into uncharted West Africa. They rescue Barbara Eden (*I Dream of Jeannie*) from a drunken sultan (Billy Gilbert) and take on Ahmed, a cowardly Arab slave trader (Peter Lorre). With Herbert Marshall, Henry Daniel, Mike Mazurki, and Chester the Chimp. Allen soon jumped over to TV, where he produced *Voyage to the Bottom of the Sea*, based on his previous hit film.

UPI 12/12/52: The set is ready as shooting is resumed for the giant piano courtyard sequence in the fantasy, The 5,000 Fingers of Dr. T. *Menacing guards, small boys, and a 100-yard-long piano make up the scene. Camera and sound crews are at lower right.*

THE FLAME BARRIER

1958 United Artists (B&W)
PRODUCERS: Arthur Gardner, Jules V. Levy
DIRECTOR: Paul Landers
SCREENWRITERS: Pat Fielder,
George W. Yates

Arthur Franz and Kathleen Crowley go to the jungle to find a fallen satellite. It's covered by a hot mass of living protoplasm that can melt humans. Originally billed with *The Return of Dracula*.

FLAMING STAR

1960 20th Century-Fox
PRODUCER: David Weisbart
DIRECTOR: Don Siegel
SCREENWRITERS: Clair Huffaker,
Nunnally Johnson

Elvis Presley's best films had good directors. After *King Creole* (Michael Curtiz) and this serious, violent Western, he usually got busy but pedestrian Norman Taurog. In this one, Elvis is Pacer Burton, a half-breed tragically caught between the world of his father (John McIntyre) and his Indian mother (Dolores Del Rio). Steve Forrest is his brother. With Barbara Eden, L.Q. Jones, and Richard Jaeckel. Elvis sings the title song over the credits and one other song at a birthday party. Elvis' fans were not very pleased. His part was originally intended for Brando. Barbara Steele was later cast as the female lead but quit over wardrobe differences.

THE FLAMING TEEN-AGE

1956 Truman (B&W)
DIRECTORS: Ervin S. Yeaworth,
Charles Edwards

Noel Reyburn, Ethel Barrett, Jerry Frank, and Shirley Holmes star in this semidocumentary look at booze and dope. A concerned father takes his son out for a night on the town to show him the evils of alcohol. Part Two is the allegedly true story of a dope addict-turned-evangelist. Originally co-billed with *Lost Women*.   —CB

FLASH GORDON

1936 Universal (B&W)
PRODUCER: Henry MacRae
DIRECTOR: Frederick Stephani
SCREENWRITERS: Frederick Stephani,
George Plympton, Basil Dickey,
Ella O'Neill
ALSO RELEASED AS: *Rocket Ship, Spaceship to
the Unknown, Space Soldiers, Atomic
Rocketship*

The best-loved, most imaginative serial of all time deserves to be viewed in its entirety (13 chapters), but various feature versions (with various titles) exist. In this one, Buster Crabbe (in his best role) leaves Earth with Dale Arden (Joen Rogers) and Dr. Zarkov (Frank Shannon) and heads for Mongo to stop attacks on Earth. Charles Middleton is the wonderful bald Ming the Merciless, whose beautiful daughter Princess Aura wants Flash for herself. Richard Alexander is the helpful Prince Barin. With hawk men, shark men, dinosaurs, a horned gorilla, electric torture, a lobster monster, lion men, monkey men, soldiers in armor, great costumes and sets, and lots of spaceships on wires. The great god Tao was borrowed from *The Mummy*. The exciting music and some sets were from *The Bride of Frankenstein*. A timeless classic.

FLASH GORDON

1980 Universal (England)
PRODUCER: Dino DeLaurentiis
DIRECTOR: Mike Hodges
SCREENWRITER: Lorenzo Semple, Jr.

Despite a repetitive rock score by Queen and a terrible campy attitude, this Flash Gordon from executive producer Dino DeLaurentiis is often visually impressive, and Max Von Sydow does a good Charles Middleton impersonation. Basically it's about as good as *Battlestar Galactica*. Sam Jones is a pretty bad hero. Dino discovered the star of his new epic on *The Dating Game*! His lines had to be dubbed over

Dr. Zarkof, Princess Aura,
Flash Gordon *carrying
Dale Arden, and Ming the
Merciless.*

by another actor! Buster Crabbe probably got more money than he made during his entire acting career for endorsing the new version and making TV appearances to plug it. With Melody Anderson of *Battlestar Galactica* as Dale, Chaim Topol as Dr. Zarkov, Brian Blessed as Vultan, chief of the Hawkmen, and some Nazi-style villains, including Mariangela Melato of Lina Wertmuller film fame. This *Flash* cost 22 million earth dollars.

FLASH GORDON CONQUERS THE UNIVERSE

1940 Universal (B&W)
PRODUCER: Henry MacRae
DIRECTORS: Ford Beebe, Ray Taylor
SCREENWRITERS: George H. Plympton, Basil Dickey, Barry Shipman
ALSO RELEASED AS: *Purple Death from Outer Space, Space Soldiers Conquer the Universe, Perils from the Planet Mongo*

Buster Crabbe is Flash Gordon for the third and final time. Carol Hughes is the new Dale Arden. Roland Drew is the new Prince Barin. Charles Middleton is, as always, Ming. Anne Gwynne is the evil Sonia. Frank Shannon is again Dr. Zarkov. Flash and his comrades travel to Frigia, encounter rock men, and dress like characters from Robin Hood. Originally a 12-chapter serial, it was condensed for a TV feature.

FLASH GORDON'S TRIP TO MARS

1938 Universal (B&W)
PRODUCER: Barney Sarecky
DIRECTORS: Ford Beebe, Robert F. Hill
SCREENWRITERS: Ray Trompe, Norman S. Hall, Wyndham Gittens, Herbert Dolmas
ALSO RELEASED AS: *Mars Attacks the World, Deadly Ray from Mars*

Buster Crabbe is back fighting Ming the Merciless and stopping a war between the tree men and the clay men. All the stars from *Flash Gordon* are back and except for the comedy relief of new character Happy Hapgood (Donald Kerr), it's almost as great as the original. Montague Shaw is the popular clay king. Originally a 15-chapter serial, it was later condensed into a feature. Beatrice Roberts is Queen Azura.

FLESH AND BLOOD SHOW
1973 Entertainment Ventures (England) (Part 3-D)
PRODUCER/DIRECTOR: Pete Walker
SCREENWRITER: Alfred Shaughnessy
ORIGINALLY RELEASED AS: *Asylum of the Insane*
"An appalling amalgam of carnage and carnality," as the ads put it, from the director of *The Comeback* and *The Confessional*. Following the phenomenal success of *The Stewardesses* there was a mostly ignored early '70s glut of bad 3-D and partially 3-D sex films. This was the only 3-D horror film released at that time. It features a bit of sex and a group of actors and actresses at an audition being attacked by a hooded killer. Ray Brooks and Jenny Hanley star. It's been given a new lease on life via the miracle of videocassettes. **(R)**

FLESH AND FANTASY
1943 Universal (B&W)
PRODUCERS: Julien Duvivier, Charles Boyer
DIRECTOR: Julien Duvivier
SCREENWRITERS: Ernest Pascal, Samuel Hoffenstein, Ellis St. Joseph
One of the earliest and best compilation fantasy films. In the first story a girl who is considered ugly goes to a strange toy shop and purchases a mask that changes her life. The second, based on Oscar Wilde's "The Crime of Lord Saville," stars Edward G. Robinson as a man whose life is determined by a palm reader. In the third story a psychic trapeze artist is haunted by a woman. A fourth story was removed and expanded into the feature *Destiny*. With Charles Boyer (the co-producer), Barbara Stanwyck, Robert Cummings, Thomas Mitchell, and Robert Benchley (in the connecting sequences).

FLESH AND FLAME: See THE NIGHT OF THE QUARTER MOON.

THE FLESH AND THE FIENDS: See MANIA

FLESH AND THE SPUR
1956 AIP (B&W)
PRODUCER: Alex Gordon
DIRECTOR: Edward L. Cahn
From the ads: "Death stalked the ant hill!" A vengeance patrol led by dirt farmer John Agar tracks escaped killer Michael "Touch" Connors. Agar rescues Indian girl Marla English from the ant hill where her tribesmen left her to die. With Raymond Hatton, Maria Monay, Joyce Meadows, and Kenne Duncan of *The Sinister Urge*. Title song by Chipmunks creator Ross Bagdasarian. A double bill with *Naked Paradise*.
–CB

THE FLESH EATERS
1964 Cinema Distributors of America (B&W)
PRODUCERS: Jack and Terry Curtis, Arnold Drake
DIRECTOR: Jack Curtis
SCREENWRITER: Arnold Drake
A prime example of an outrageous early '60s independent shocker. A plane containing an alcoholic film star (Rita Morly) and her secretary crashes on a small island (actually Long Island) inhabited only by a crazed scientist (Martin Koslek) experimenting with tiny carnivorous sea creatures able to strip the flesh of humans in seconds! Koslek was a bottom-of-the-barrel villain at Universal during the '40s and played Joseph Paul Goebbels at least three times. The film's other standout performer is Ray Tudor as the jive-talking, shipwrecked beatnik Omar.

CREEPING, CRAWLING, FLESH-EATING MAGGOTS

LIVING BODIES USED FOR THE MOST VILE EXPERIMENT EVER DEVISED!

VIKING INTERNATIONAL PICTURES PRESENTS

MORBID HORROR IN VIVID COLOR

FLESH FEAST

starring VERONICA LAKE

WITH
PHIL PHILBIN
HEATHER HUGHES
MARTHA MISCHON
YANKA MANN
DIAN WILHITE
CHRIS MARTELL

The flesh eaters were created by scratching the film with pins, but the makeup job on the victims is pretty good. Don't miss the unexpected and ambitious ending. Filmed (as early as 1961) by sex-film vets. The director also made hits like *The Pink Pussy* and *We Are All Naked.* Famous sex director Radley Metzger was the editor. Theater patrons were offered packs of "instant blood" for protection.

FLESH FEAST

1970 Cine World Corporation
PRODUCERS: Veronica Lake, Brad F. Ginter
DIRECTOR: Brad F. Ginter
SCREENWRITERS: Brad F. Ginter,
   Thomas Casey
Except for *Footsteps in the Snow,* an ob-

scure feature made in Montreal, this very cheap horror film was Veronica Lake's first film in 22 years. While other middle-aged female stars were busy with axe murders and psychological problems in England and Hollywood, Veronica went to Miami Beach where she co-produced, and starred as an ex-mental-patient scientist experimenting with restoring youth. First the old skin tissue is removed with flesh-eating maggots! They used real ones, raised in garbage cans (rice was added for crowd shots). The big surprise is that her secret new patient turns out to be Hitler! Since her mother had died in a concentration camp, the scientist destroys the exiled dictator with a swarm of maggots. This film is still available for theatrical showings. Veronica Lake, who was born in Brooklyn, died in 1973. (R)

FLESH FOR FRANKENSTEIN: See *ANDY WARHOL'S FRANKENSTEIN*.

FLESH GORDON

1972 Grafitti Productions
PRODUCERS: Bill Osco, Howard Ziehm
DIRECTOR/SCREENWRITER: Mike Light
The acting's bad and the humor is pretty sophomoric, but the faithfully recreated spoof of the Flesh Gordon legend with

standout animation sequences and sex made this a natural hit. The plot borrows from all the old serials. Flesh's spaceship, on a wire like the one in the '30s serials, is shaped like a penis. So are the guns. Zarkoff is Jerkoff, Ming is Wang, the Forest Men from *Flash Gordon Conquers the Universe* are gay, there's a lesbian land, a great metal beetle man with a sword, a giant monster with hooves that talks, and a penisaurus with a blinking eye at the end—all animated by Dave Allen, Jim Danforth (his name is spelled backward in the credits), and other talented artists. With porn queen Candy Samples as a space dyke with a hook hand, hilarious robots with cock drills, and John Hoyt! The original hardcore sex scenes have been cut a lot since '72. (X)

FLICK: See DR. FRANKENSTEIN ON CAMPUS.

THE FLIGHT THAT DISAPPEARED

1961 United Artists (B&W)
PRODUCER: Robert E. Kent
DIRECTOR: Reginald LeBorg
SCREENWRITERS: Ralph and Judith Hart, Owen Harris
U.S. scientists who have developed a new superbomb are taken to another dimension and put on trial for plotting to destroy Earth. The jury is made up of unborn future generations. The scientists are found guilty, but released when the judge decides only prayer can save the human race. Craig Hill stars with Paula Raymond and Dayton Lummis.

FLIGHT TO FURY

1966 Feature Film (U.S./Philippines) (B&W)
PRODUCER: Fred Roos
DIRECTOR: Monte Hellman
SCREENWRITER: Jack Nicholson

Passenger plane crash-lands in the jungle en route to Manila, depraved passengers fight over stolen diamonds. Jack Nicholson wins, but throws the gems into a river when he realizes he's going to die. Dewey Martin, Vic Diaz, John Hackett, and Jacqueline Hellman co-star, with Fay Spain as Destiny Cooper. Follow-up to *Back Door to Hell*.   –CB

FLIGHT TO HOLOCAUST

1977 TV
PRODUCER: A.C. Lyles
DIRECTOR: Bernard Kowalski
SCREENWRITERS: Robert Heverly,
   Anthony Lawrence

A private plane crashes into the side of a skyscraper! Sons of famous actors (Patrick Wayne, Christopher Mitchum, and Desi Arnaz, Jr.) star as professional troubleshooters in this cut-rate *Towering Inferno*. By the director of *Attack of the Giant Leeches*. With Sid Caesar, Rory Calhoun, Greg Morris, Lloyd Nolan, and Paul Williams.

FLIGHT TO MARS

1951 Monogram
PRODUCER: Walter Mirisch
DIRECTOR: Lesley Selander
SCREENWRITER: Arthur Strawn

The first space-flight movie in color, a surprise from the last days of the Monogram Studios. Cameron Mitchell starts his long career of low-budget weirdness by joining Arthur Franz as the leaders of the first Martian landing. They discover a vast, advanced underground civilization led by Morris Ankrum as the council leader. His beautiful daughter (in a silver minidress with pointy shoulders) saves the handsome Earthmen from imprisonment and death. The impressive city was mostly well-done paintings. Filming took 11 days. The space suits were left over from *Destination Moon*. In amazingly unreal Cinecolor.

FLOOD!

1976 TV
PRODUCER: Irwin Allen
DIRECTOR: Earl Bellamy
SCREENWRITER: Don Ingalls

Executive producer Irwin Allen's first made-for-TV disaster movie! As a cynical helicopter pilot, Robert Culp comes to the rescue when a dam bursts. The soggy cast includes favorites like Cameron Mitchell, Leif Garrett, Whit Bissell, Richard Basehart, Barbara Hershey, Martin Milner, Carol Lynley, and Roddy McDowall. *Fire!*, Irwin's clever companion piece, aired the next year.

THE FLY

1958 20th Century-Fox
PRODUCER/DIRECTOR: Kurt Neumann
SCREENWRITER: James Clavell

A brilliant, sick, absurd hit based on a *Playboy* short story. Patricia Owens, a seemingly mad woman who keeps looking for flies, crushes her French Canadian scientist husband André Delambre (Al Hedison) in a hydraulic press—twice. In a confrontation with brother-in-law Vincent Price, she confesses the killing and explains why she did it. Matter-transmitter experiments had resulted in Andre trading his head and an arm with a fly. The tiny "white fly" with a human head must be found! When little Philip Delambre finds his fly dad screaming "Help me! Help me!" in a squeaky little voice while a spider moves in to eat him, Herbert Marshall as the police inspector picks up a rock and smashes him/it. Unforgettable. Screenwriter James Clavell is the author of *Shogun*.

20th Century-Fox presents the last word in excitement— the last word in thrills!

THE FLY with the head of a man..and the man with the head of THE FLY!

It's the terror-topper first introduced to the public in "Playboy" Magazine!

For your own good we won't let you see it alone... unless you sign a waiver in our lobby absolving the management for the unpredictable effects of "The Fly" on your nervous system!

"Once it was human... even as you and I!"

$100 if you prove it can't happen!

Terror-COLOR by DE LUXE
CINEMASCOPE

starring
AL HEDISON · PATRICIA OWENS
VINCENT PRICE · HERBERT MARSHALL
Produced and Directed by
KURT NEUMANN
Screenplay by
JAMES CLAVELL

James Craven repeats his role as Dr. Bryant. Scenes from *King of the Rocketmen* ('49) were used. (The incoherent feature version consists of random 13-minute chapters strung together in '58.)

THE FLYING SAUCER

1950 Film Classics (B&W)
PRODUCER/DIRECTOR: Mikel Conrad
SCREENWRITERS: Mikel Conrad, Howard Irving Young

Practically a one-man show with producer-director Mikel Conrad starring in his own story as an agent sent to Alaska. There he finds the saucer of the title and Communist scientists. It was the first movie about UFOs and supposedly had to be viewed officially by the FBI before its release. Imagine a roomful of our country's finest watching a special preview. The saucer isn't even from outer space. With Denver Pyle.

THE FLYING SAUCER

1964 Avco Embassy-TV (Italy)
PRODUCER: Dino DeLaurentiis
DIRECTOR: Tinto Brass
SCREENWRITER: Rudolpho Sonego
ORIGINALLY RELEASED AS: *Il Disco Volante*

An unfunny comedy from the director of *Caligula*. A Martian lands and kidnaps Italians. Alberto Sordi plays four different roles. With Monica Vitti.

FLYING DISC MAN FROM MARS

1951 Republic (B&W)
PRODUCER: Franklin Adreon
DIRECTOR: Fred C. Brannon
SCREENWRITER: Ronald Davidson

From the ads: "A Republic serial in 12 atomic chapters!" Mota the Martian (Gregory Gay), originally seen in *The Purple Monster Strikes*, returns to Earth in his one-man bat-wing spaceship, hides in a volcano, and starts conquering again! His new weapon is the thermal disintegrator. Aviator Walter Reed and secretary Lois Collier save Earth.

THE FLYING SERPENT

1946 PRC (B&W)
PRODUCER: Sigmund Neufeld
DIRECTOR: Sherman Scott (Sam Newfeld)
SCREENWRITER: John T. Neville

George Zucco is an insane archaeologist who uses Quetzalcoatl, the ancient Aztec bird/god, to murder his enemies. He simply puts a feather on somebody and the bird/god kills to get it back. The monster bird was an interesting idea, but you know that at a studio like PRC the wires will show and uncontrolled acting will do in any attempt at seriousness. If it looks overly familiar, maybe you've seen *The Devil Bat* from the same studio. With Mantan Moreland.

THE FOG

1980 Avco Embassy
PRODUCER: Debra Hill
DIRECTOR: John Carpenter
SCREENWRITERS: John Carpenter, Debra Hill
The Elizabeth Dane, a ghost ship with rotted pirate corpses, invades a coastal town. Though a hit in its own right, Carpenter's horror follow-up to *Halloween* failed to duplicate the earlier film's sensational scares or astronomical box office. With Adrienne Barbeau as a deejay, Hal Holbrook as a priest, Jamie Lee Curtis, her real-life mother Janet Leigh, Nancy Loomis, and John Houseman, who tells the story around a campfire. **(R)**

FOG ISLAND

1945 PRC (B&W)
PRODUCER: Leon Fromkess
DIRECTOR: Terry Morse
SCREENWRITER: Pierre Gendron
Lionel Atwill and George Zucco star in a tale of hidden treasure on an island. With Jerome Cowan and Veda Ann Borg. Zucco made five poverty-row cheapies for PRC. Director Morse later did the American scenes for *Godzilla*.

THE FOLKS AT RED WOLF INN

1972 Scope III
PRODUCER: Michael Macready
DIRECTOR: Bud Townsend
ALSO RELEASED AS: *Terror at Red Wolf Inn*; *Terror House*
In '72, the year of the cannibal, we were offered *Raw Meat*, *Cannibal Girls*, and this—all of them basically comedies about eating people. Dumb jokes about spare ribs and lady fingers go back to *The Undertaker and His Pals*. A young cannibal (John Nelson) who lives with his loving grandparents falls for Linda Gillin, who is on the week's menu. Producer Michael Macready, who presented the *Count Yorga* films, also acts in this one. By the director of *Nightmare in Wax*. It was advertised as "a grotty bedtime story."

FOLLOW THAT DREAM

1962 United Artists
PRODUCER: David Weisbart
DIRECTOR: Gordon Douglas
SCREENWRITER: Charles Lederer
Elvis Presley as Toby Kwimper, a homeless army vet, settles down on a Florida beach with his father (Arthur O'Connell) and four orphans. One of them (Ann Helm) loves Elvis. The homesteaders start a profitable fishing business and tangle with gangsters and the government. One of Elvis' dullest. With Joanna Moore, Simon Oakland, and Roland Winters.

FOOD OF THE GODS

1976 AIP
PRODUCER/DIRECTOR/SCREENWRITER:
Bert I. Gordon
Animals of all kinds become giants after eating a special growth food raised by a farmer on an island. It was the second time Bert Gordon used ideas from H.G. Wells' novel of the same title (see *Village of the Giants*). Some of the special effects are great compared with Bert's other efforts (Rick Baker built some of the creatures), but the dialogue and script are laughable as usual. As the hero, Marjoe Gortner confronts giant chickens and wasps. As a businessman out to exploit the phenomena, Ralph Meeker is chewed up by giant rats. Ida Lupino is attacked in her home by some disgusting insects. With Pamela Franklin.

Nancy Sinatra and Bob Denver meditate in For Those Who Think Young.

THE FOOL KILLER

1963 Allied Artists/AIP (B&W)
PRODUCER: David Friedkin
DIRECTOR: Servando Gonzalez
SCREENWRITERS: Morton Fine, David Friedkin
ALSO RELEASED AS: *Violent Journey*

In post–Civil War America, a 12-year-old orphan (Edward Albert, Jr.) leaves his foster home and meets an oldster (Henry Hull) who tells him the legend of a tall man with an axe who kills the fools of the world. The boy later befriends an odd, introverted, antireligious veteran played by Anthony Perkins. He takes Perkins to a revival meeting. Afterward the preacher is found hacked to death. A great, unique Americana/psycho movie which was released first in '65 and then in a badly cut version in '69.

FOR PETE'S SAKE

1966 World-Wide (B&W)
PRODUCER: Frank R. Jacobson
DIRECTOR/SCREENWRITER: James F. Collier

Robert Sampson, Pippa Scott, and son Johnny Jensen attend a Billy Graham revival; later God and Jesus help Sampson shut down a teenage cycle gang. With Sam Groom, Bob Beach, and Harry Lauter. Graham also appears in *The Restless Ones* and *Wiretapper*. Not to be confused with the dismal 1974 Barbra Streisand comedy of the same name.   –CB

FOR SINGLES ONLY

1968 Columbia
PRODUCER: Sam Katzman
DIRECTOR: Arthur Dreifuss
SCREENWRITERS: Hal Collins, Arthur Dreifuss

Musical comedy, Katzman style. Lana Wood attempts suicide and is gang-raped. John Saxon seduces Mary Ann Mobley to win a bet. Milton Berle, the social director of the singles-only building where they all live, throws a party at the end. The Nitty Gritty Dirt Band, the Sunshine Company, the Lewis and Clark Expedition, the Walter Wanderley Trio, and the Cal Tjader Band provide the swingin' music for the under-30s.

FOR THOSE WHO THINK YOUNG

1964 United Artists
PRODUCER: Hugh Benson
DIRECTOR: Leslie H. Martinson
SCREENWRITER: James O'Hanlon

Surfing college students hang out at a club watching comedian Woody Woodbury and drinking Cokes. James Darren, as rich playboy "Ding" Pruitt III, falls for Pamela Tiffin. His grandfather tries to have the club closed but is exposed as an ex-bootlegger. The comic cast includes Tina Louise and Bob Denver, both lost on *Gilligan's Island* later that year, Nancy Sinatra, Paul Lynde, Roger Smith, George Raft, Robert Armstrong, Anna Lee, Jack LaRue, and Alan Jenkins.

FOR YOUR EYES ONLY

1981 United Artists (England)
PRODUCER: Albert R. Broccoli
DIRECTOR: John Glen
SCREENWRITER: Richard Maibaum

After *Moonraker* James Bond (Roger Moore) returns to earth in a simpler, low-key entry with a lot of skiing, mountain climbing, and scuba diving. Carole Bouquet (*That Obscure Object of Desire*) is a sympathetic heroine. With Chaim Topol as Columbo, Lynn-Holly Jackson, Michael Gothard, Jill Bennett, sharks, and a Margaret Thatcher imitator. Sheena Easton sings the hit theme song. One cast member, Tula Cossey, made news when a London paper discovered she used to be named Barry. William Grefe (*The Death Curse of Tartu*) was the second unit director. The next Bond adventure is *Octopussy*.

FORBIDDEN LOVE: See FREAKS.

FORBIDDEN PLANET

1956 MGM
PRODUCER: Nicholas Nayfack
DIRECTOR: Fred McLeod Wilcox
SCREENWRITER: Cyril Hume

Special effects are the stars of this science-fiction version of Shakespeare's *The Tempest*. A flying saucer from Earth is sent to rescue a space mission on Altair IV. The starship commander (Leslie Nielsen) discovers only two survivors, Morbius (Walter Pidgeon) and his beautiful daughter Alta (Anne Francis); the rest have been killed by some unknown terror still roaming the planet. Morbius lives in a house constructed above the last remains of the ancient Krell civilization. The film, shot entirely on sound stages at MGM, features electronic music by Louis and Bebe Baron. Still one of the finest science-fiction films ever. The highlights are the tour of the Krell city, the Id monster, Robby the Robot, the landing of United Planets Cruiser C-57D, and the laser battle with the monster. With Warren Stevens and Earl Holliman. A sound track album is available.

—AF

FORBIDDEN WORLD

1982 New World
PRODUCER: Roger Corman
DIRECTOR: Alan Holzman
SCREENWRITER: Jim Wynorski
ALSO RELEASED AS: *Mutant*

A cut-rate follow-up to New World's *Galaxy of Terror* featuring sets from that film, space-battle scenes lifted from *Battle Beyond the Stars*, and an *Alien*-inspired flesh-eating and vomiting tentacled monster. The creature is the result of an extraterrestrial rape, which was cut to avoid an X rating. The new sets are the cheapest in years, constructed mainly of cardboard and egg cartons. A living scientist's cancerous liver is cut out by star Jesse Vint and fed to the alien killer in a key scene. A pretty sick quickie for the legions of undiscriminating science-fiction/gore fans. **(R)**

THE FORCE BEYOND

1978 Film Ventures
DIRECTOR: William Sachs

If you loved *Galaxina* and *The Incredible Melting Man*, here's an earlier attempt at low-budget thrills by their director. Find out why "100,000 people disappear off the face of the Earth each year." See a "mysterious creature in Oregon"!

FOREST OF FEAR: See THE BLOODEATERS.

THE 4D MAN

1959 Universal
PRODUCER: Jack Harris
DIRECTOR: Irwin S. Yeaworth, Jr.
SCREENWRITERS: Theodore Simonson,
Cy Chermak
ALSO RELEASED AS: *Master of Terror*
A science-fiction hit from the team that made *The Blob*. Scientist Robert Lansing discovers a way to pass through solid matter. With no support from colleagues or his cheating wife, he turns to a brief life of easy crime. When he passes through other humans, they die of old age while he becomes younger. The special effects are great and it's really strange to see Patty Duke at age 12. With Lee Meriwether and James Congdon.

FOUR FLIES ON GREY VELVET

1972 Paramount
PRODUCER: Salvatore Argento
DIRECTOR/SCREENWRITER: Dario Argento
ORIGINALLY RELEASED AS: *Quatro Mosche di Velluto Gris*
A psychological murder mystery with the added attraction of a laser-beam device able to photograph the last image on the retina of a dead person's eye. Michael Brandon stars as a rich rock star married to Mimsy Farmer. Includes

some surprising camerawork and some gruesome killings. Music by Ennio Morricone. **(R)**

FOUR FOR TEXAS

1963 Warner Brothers
PRODUCER/DIRECTOR: Robert Aldrich
SCREENWRITERS: Theodore Simonson,
Cy Chermak
Frank Sinatra and Dean Martin in a stupid Western comedy. Director Aldrich hates it. The Three Stooges are in it. They destroy a nude painting of Anita Ekberg. With Ursula Andress, Victor Buono, Charles Bronson, Jack Elam, and Arthur Godfrey.

THE FOUR MUSKETEERS

1974 20th Century-Fox (England)
EXECUTIVE PRODUCER: Alexander Salkind
DIRECTOR: Richard Lester
SCREENWRITER: George McDonald Fraser
The Three Musketeers—Part Two. More swashbuckling fun with basically the same cast. Christopher Lee as the nasty Rochefort (with an eye patch and flowing hair) and Faye Dunaway as Milady (with long curls) have larger roles this time. The closest Richard Lester has come to duplicating the spirit of his Beatles movies.

FOUR SIDED TRIANGLE

1953 Hammer/Aster (England) (B&W)
PRODUCER: Alexander Paal
DIRECTOR: Terence Fisher
SCREENWRITERS: Paul Tabori, Terence Fisher
Bride of the Gorilla star Barbara Payton is loved by two scientists, but she only loves one of them. So, being civilized Englishmen, they do the only sensible thing—make a duplicate of her. Dials twirl, neon tubes glow, and finally a twin blonde emerges from the glass-enclosed table. Being identical, both Barbaras love the same man! With James Hayter and Stephen Murray.

THE FOUR SKULLS OF JONATHAN DRAKE

1959 United Artists (B&W)
PRODUCER: Robert E. Kent
DIRECTOR: Edward L. Cahn
SCREENWRITER: Orville H. Hampton

A classic ghoulish cheapie with expert screen villain Henry Daniell as the title head shrinker. Members of a certain family all die of decapitation at the age of 60. The heads, brought to Drake by his tall, long-haired servant (whose mouth is sewn shut with visible sutures), are carefully treated and shrunken. In the end we discover that Drake is a 200-year-old man whose head is sewn on to the body of a witch doctor! With Eduard Franz, Valerie French, and Grant Richards.

FRANCIS IN THE HAUNTED HOUSE

1956 Universal (B&W)
PRODUCER: Robert Arthur
DIRECTOR: Charles Lamont
SCREENWRITERS: Herbert Margolis,
William Raynde

After six Francis the Talking Mule comedies, Donald O'Connor said, "Enough!" So did director Arthur Lubin. Universal decided to squeeze out one more, so they got a director of Ma and Pa Kettle and Abbott and Costello films (it was Lamont's last feature) and Mickey Rooney to fill in. Imagine Mickey on a talking mule hiding from phony ghosts and a cast that includes David Janssen. The worst. With Virginia Welles.

FRANCIS JOINS THE WACS

1954 Universal (B&W)
PRODUCER: Ted Richmond
DIRECTOR: Arthur Lubin
SCREENWRITER: Devery Freeman

Francis the Talking Mule and army lieutenant Donald O'Connor help some WACs with a camouflage mis-sion. The cast includes a who's who of '50s B-movie beauties (Julie Adams, Mamie Van Doren, Mara Corday, and Allison Hayes). Also with Zasu Pitts, Chill Wills, and Lynn Bari. Mamie sings "She'll Be Comin' 'Round the Mountain." It was the fifth of six Francis movies directed by Lubin, who later transferred the concept to TV with *Mr. Ed.*

FRANKENSTEIN

1931 Universal (B&W)
PRODUCER: Carl Laemmle, Jr.
DIRECTOR: James Whale
SCREENWRITERS: Garrett Fort, Robert Florey,
Francis Edward Faragoh

After 12 years of acting obscurity, 44-year-old Boris Karloff became a household name by playing the monster made from dead bodies. It's still powerful today, despite the lack of music and some prerelease censoring by the studio. When Dr. Frankenstein (Colin Clive) has his great "It's alive!" scene, he originally continued, "Now

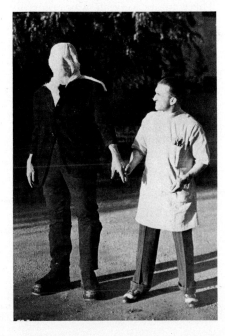

Makeup expert Jack Pierce with Boris Karloff before the public was allowed to see the face of Franken-stein.

I know what it's like to be God!" The monster was also shown throwing the little girl into the water. Two endings were filmed. In one, the doctor dies when thrown from the windmill; in the other, he lives. With Edward Van Sloane, Mae Clarke, and Dwight Faye as the hunchback Fritz, snatcher of the famous bad brain. Some original prints were tinted green, "the color of fear." Karloff worked for director Whale a year later in *The Old Dark House*. *The Bride of Frankenstein* had to wait until '35.

FRANKENSTEIN
1973 TV
PRODUCER: Dan Curtis
DIRECTOR: Glenn Jordan
SCREENWRITERS: Sam Hall, Richard Landau
Bo Svenson plays the sympathetic stitched-up creature. Robert Foxworth (*Questar*) is the doctor. With Susan Strasberg and Robert Gentry. A cheap little production that was quickly forgotten when *Frankenstein: The True Story* was aired later the same year. Three hours long, it was originally shown on two nights.

FRANKENSTEIN AND THE MONSTER FROM HELL
1973 Hammer/Paramount (England)
PRODUCER: Roy Skeggs
DIRECTOR: Terence Fisher
SCREENWRITER: John Elder
Peter Cushing plays the infamous baron in the sixth and final entry in the Hammer Frankenstein series. It's also the worst. As played by David Prowse (later Darth Vader in *Star Wars*), the monster is a hairy apelike creature made from parts of inmates of an asylum where Frankenstein works. A laughable model of the asylum ruins any attempt at reality, and scenes of skulls being cut open are ludicrous. Shane Briant is the doctor's assistant. Madeline Smith is Angel. With Bernard Lee. **(R)**

FRANKENSTEIN CONQUERS THE WORLD
1964 AIP (Japan/U.S.)
PRODUCER: Tomoyuki Tanaka
DIRECTOR: Inoshiro Honda
SCREENWRITER: Kaoru Mabuchi
ORIGINALLY RELEASED AS: *Fuharankenshutain tai Baragon*
In this ridiculous monster-battle film a young Japanese boy eats the heart of the Frankenstein monster that had been sent from Germany during the war and mutated in Hiroshima. The boy grows into a friendly bucktoothed giant dressed like a caveman and saves the day by destroying a troublesome dinosaur called Baragon. Add confused American actor Nick Adams as Dr. James Brown and you get a new low in horror. Scenes of a giant octopus were removed for the American release.

FRANKENSTEIN CREATED WOMAN
1967 Hammer/20th Century-Fox (England)
PRODUCER: Anthony Nelson-Keys
DIRECTOR: Terence Fisher
SCREENWRITER: Anthony Hinds
Even if you're not a fan of the Hammer Dr. Frankenstein series, you might like this offbeat entry. Peter Cushing (playing the doctor for the fourth time) and his assistant (Thorley Walters) are experimenting with the transfer of souls. A crippled girl with a large birthmark on her face drowns herself after her lover is guillotined for a murder for which he was framed. The clever doctors put the boy's soul/brain in the girl's body, fix her face and limp, and dye her hair blond. The result is *Playboy*'s Miss August 1966, Susan Denberg, a beautiful woman with the mind of her bitter boyfriend! Out for revenge, she/he lures her/his enemies to remote places, promising sex and delivering a few chops with a cleaver. More psychologi-

cally oriented horror is displayed when the girl imagines talking with her/his decapitated head. A few years later Hammer tried another dual-sex "monster" with *Dr. Jekyll and Sister Hyde.*

FRANKENSTEIN MEETS THE SPACE MONSTER
1965 Allied Artists (B&W)
PRODUCER: Robert McCarty
DIRECTOR: Robert Gaffney
SCREENWRITER: George Garret
ALSO RELEASED AS: *Mars Invades Puerto Rico*
Don't miss. It's the worst. The evil but beautiful Princess Marcuzan and her bald effeminate dwarf assistant Nadir arrive in Puerto Rico to kidnap women to use in repopulating their dying planet. Meanwhie Frank, an American astronaut who is actually an android, crash-lands near the aliens. He becomes Frankenstein, a crazed killer with only half a face. While wildly go-going girls are kidnaped from a poolside party, scientists track down Frank, and a rock combo plays hits like "That's the Way It's Got to Be." The rewired Frank battles the horrible alien mutant Mull and rescues the kidnaped Earth girls. Lots of rock music, stock footage, and laughs. Filmed in Puerto Rico. The actors are mostly New Yorkers. With James Karen (star of *Poltergeist* and Pathmart television commercials), David Kerman, and Nancy Marshall.

FRANKENSTEIN MEETS THE WOLFMAN
1943 Universal (B&W)
PRODUCER: George Waggner
DIRECTOR: Roy William Neill
SCREENWRITER: Curt Siodmak
The fifth Frankenstein feature in the Universal series is really a sequel to *The Wolfman.* It's great to see Lon Chaney, Jr. back as Larry Talbot and Maria Ouspenskaya as Maleva the gypsy, but casting Bela Lugosi as the Frankenstein

monster was a big mistake. As Dr. Frank Mannering, Patric Knowles revives the monster and tries to cure the wolfman, but they escape, fight, and are drowned by villagers who explode a dam. Ilona Massey is Baroness Elsa Frankenstein. With Lionel Atwill as the mayor, Dwight Frye as a villager, and Dennis Hoey, who basically plays his Inspector Lestrode role from the Holmes films (also directed by Neill). A favorite segment shows a distraught Chaney stopping a big gypsy production number with lyrics about wanting to live.

FRANKENSTEIN MUST BE DESTROYED
1969 Hammer/Warner Brothers (England)
PRODUCER: Anthony Nelson-Keys
DIRECTOR: Terence Fisher
SCREENWRITER: Bert Batt
In the fifth of the Hammer Dr. Frankenstein series, the doctor (Peter Cushing) more than ever is shown to be the real monster. He blackmails a younger physician (Simon Ward) into helping him and takes over the life (and body) of his fiancée (Veronica Carlson). The "monster" is a pathetic bald guy (Freddie Jones—recently in *The Elephant Man*) with stitches around his head. A scene with a buried body bursting through the soil because of a broken water pipe is memorable, but some of the (tame) gore effects get a little silly, especially when the doctors use a drill and saw to remove a brain.

FRANKENSTEIN 1970
1958 Allied Artists (B&W)
PRODUCER: Aubrey Shenck
DIRECTOR: Howard W. Koch
SCREENWRITERS: Richard Landau, George W. Yates
In the future year of 1970, Boris Karloff's baron lets a TV crew film a show about Frankenstein at his castle. Meanwhile

the scarred Germanic nobleman plays spooky tunes at his pipe organ and tries to duplicate his famous ancestor's experiments down in the lab. Using atomic energy and his servant's brain, he builds a wrapped-up creature that looks like a mummy with a garbage can on its head. In a surprising finale the monster is revealed to have the face of . . . Boris Karloff! A strange mixture of gothic and atomic-age horrors with one of Boris' hammiest performances. With Tom Duggan, Jana Lund, and Mike Lane as the TV-show monster. Howard W. Koch, who also directed *Bop Girl*, *Untamed Youth*, and *The Girl in Black Stockings*, later produced *The Odd Couple* and Frank Sinatra films.

FRANKENSTEIN: THE TRUE STORY

1974 TV (England)
PRODUCER: Hunt Stromberg, Jr.
DIRECTOR: Jack Smight
SCREENWRITERS: Christopher Isherwood, Don Bachardy

Maybe not the "true" story, but an excellent epic version of the legend that was shown theatrically in Europe. Dr. Frankenstein (Leonard "Romeo" Whiting) creates the creature (Michael Sarrazin) with the help of Clerval (David McCallum). Unfortunately, they don't know how to keep the monster's flesh from rotting. James Mason, as the eccentric Dr. Polidorv, demands the creation of a mate. They use the head of the creature's true love, farm girl Jane Seymour, to create Prima. The degenerating creature breaks into a party where Prima is being introduced and rips her head off. With Agnes Moorehead in her second-to-last role, Sir Ralph Richardson as a blind hermit, Sir John Gielgud, Tom Baker, Nicola Paget, Michael Wilding, and Margaret Leighton. Originally four hours long.

FRANKENSTEIN'S BLOODY TERROR

1968 Independent International (Spain)
PRODUCER: Maxper
DIRECTOR: Enrique L. Equiluz
SCREENWRITER: Jacinto Molina
ORIGINALLY RELEASED AS: *La Marca del Hombre Lobo*

Waldemar Daninsky (Paul Naschy) is a werewolf who goes to an occult-specialist couple for a cure. They turn out to be vampires. In Spain this was a big hit (in 3-D) and led to eight more films with horror star Naschy as El Hombre Lobo. In America it was released (usually in 2-D) with a totally misleading title, a silly prologue, and about 45 minutes of footage missing. Basically an atmospheric old-fashioned monster movie with '60s blood, it has an undeservedly bad reputation. In super-70mm "Chil-o-rama." Naschy uses his real name, Jacinto Molina, to write his scripts.

FRANKENSTEIN'S CASTLE OF FREAKS: See *HOUSE OF FREAKS*.

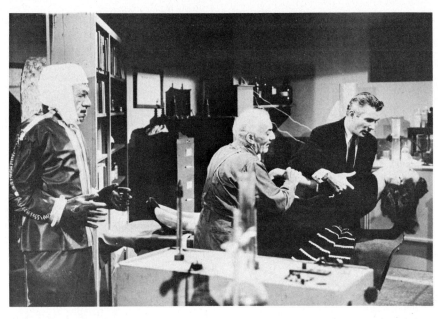

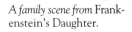
A family scene from Frankenstein's Daughter.

FRANKENSTEIN'S DAUGHTER

1958 Astor (B&W)
PRODUCER: Marc Frederic
DIRECTOR: Dick Cunha
SCREENWRITER: M.E. Barrie

Incredibly shoddy teenage-monster movie from the director of *Missile to the Moon*. Oliver Frankenstein (Donald Murphy), another descendent of the original doctor, makes a creature with half its face melted away and uses drugs to turn a girl (Sandra Knight) into a buck-toothed monster. Both creatures are played by men. Talented John Ashley and Sally Todd are teen lovers. With the great Harold Lloyd, Jr., and Robert Dix.

FRANKIE AND JOHNNY

1966 United Artists
PRODUCER: Edward Small
DIRECTOR: Fred De Cordova
SCREENWRITER: Alex Gottlieb

In this retelling of the famous song, gambler-singer Johnny (Elvis Presley) loves Frankie (Donna Douglas, taking a break from *The Beverly Hillbillies*). Anthony Eisley hires them to sing on his showboat. Harry Morgan is their piano player. Elvis thinks red-haired Nancy Kovack brings him luck. Jealous Frankie shoots Johnny, who lives anyway. Elvis sings "Petunia, the Gardener's Daughter" and "What Every Woman Lives For." De Cordova directed both Bonzo films.

FRANK'S GREATEST ADVENTURE: See FEARLESS FRANK.

FRANTIC

1958 Times Films (France) (B&W)
PRODUCER: Jean Thuillier
DIRECTOR: Louis Malle
SCREENWRITERS: Louis Malle, Roger Nimier
ORIGINALLY RELEASED AS: *Ascenseur pour l'Échafaud*

In 1961 Americans were offered this first effort by French New Wave director Malle with a new title designed to compete with the then recent *Psycho*, *Mania*, and *Homicidal*. It does share some elements with those shockers. Jeanne Moreau and lover Maurice Ronet plan the perfect crime, the murder of her husband. After the deed, Ronet's car, gun, and camera are stolen by a pair of wild teenagers while he is trapped in a stalled elevator. The teenagers use his gun in a double homicide for which he's blamed. More plot twists slowly unfold to the music of Miles Davis. Although filmed before the Malle-Moreau team's *The Lovers, Frantic* wasn't shown here until after. Times Films also released *Mondo Cane* and *Wild for Kicks*.

FREAKS

1932 MGM (B&W)
PRODUCER/DIRECTOR: Tod Browning
SCREENWRITERS: Willis Goldbeck,
Leon Gordon, Edgar Allan Woolf,
Al Boasberg
ALSO RELEASED AS: *Forbidden Love; Nature's Mistakes; The Monster Show*

This incredible feature, banned for decades, is a powerful morality tale with a thunderstorm scene that is still strong enough to induce nightmares. Tod Browning, who had directed many of Lon Chaney's best films, put his future on the line by making this unconventional, unflinching oddity—and lost. Tiny Harry Earles (in both versions of Browning's *The Unholy Three*) is Hans, the star. When a cruel trapeze artist (Olga Baclanova) marries him, publicly humiliates him, and tries with her strong-man lover (Henry Victor) to kill him for an inheritance, the circus freaks band together to avenge their friend. Wallace Ford is a sympathetic clown who charms Leila Hyams. The actual circus freaks include the Hilton Sisters (Siamese twins later in the exploitative *Chained for Life*), Johnny Eck, "the living half-boy," Prince Randian, "the living torso," pinheads, Josephine/Joseph, and a living skeleton. Except for the vengeance scene they're portrayed as gentle beings sometimes tormented by cruel outsiders. Daisy Earles (the real-life sister of Harry) is Hans' dejected girlfriend. With Angelo Rossitto. "But for an accident of birth, you might be as they are."

Prince Randian and Johnny Eck in Tod Browning's Freaks.

FREE GRASS

1969 Hollywood Star Pictures
PRODUCER: John Lawrence
DIRECTOR: Bill Brame
SCREENWRITERS: John Lawrence,
James Gordon White, Gerald Wilson
ALSO RELEASED AS: *Scream Free*

How did you miss this dynamite combination of *West Side Story* stars and *Easy Rider*–inspired plot? Richard Beymer falls in love with Lana Wood (sister Natalie wasn't available). They need cash, so he agrees to help Russ Tamblyn and his gang smuggle grass from Mexico to L.A. on motorcycles. When Beymer objects to narcotics agents being killed, his long-haired pal from the Jets puts LSD in his drink, tries to burn him alive, and has the Natalie substitute kidnaped. Too bad it wasn't a musical. Also with Bing's son Lindsay Crosby, Joel's son Jody McCrea, and obnoxious deejay Casey Kasem. Director Brame also did *The Cycle Savages*. **(R)**

FREE, WHITE AND 21
1963 AIP (B&W)
PRODUCER/DIRECTOR: Larry Buchanan
SCREENWRITERS: Larry Buchanan, Hal Dwain, Cliff Pope

Texas rape trial involving a black hotel owner and a Swedish freedom rider. Frederick O'Neal is Ernie Jones, Annalena Lund is Greta Mae Hansen, you are the jury. With George Edgley, George Russell, and John Hicks. More Buchanan: *Creature of Destruction* and *The Trial of Lee Harvey Oswald*. **–CB**

FRENZY
1972 Universal (England)
PRODUCER/DIRECTOR: Alfred Hitchcock
SCREENWRITER: Anthony Shaffer

At age 72, Hitchcock returned to England to do his first picture there in 22 years. It's a mix of elements from a lot of his earlier hits. Barry Foster is a very active psycho rapist-murderer. His friend Jon Finch (*The Vampire Lovers*) is accused of the heinous crimes. One of the pathetic victims is Anna Massey, star of *Peeping Tom*. The "necktie stranglings" are more graphic than anything Hitchcock had done and the dark humor is a bit darker than usual. It was Hitchcock's only R-rated film. **(R)**

FRIDAY THE 13TH
1980 Georgetown Films/Paramount
PRODUCER/DIRECTOR/SCREENWRITER: Sean Cunningham

Camp Crystal Lake has been closed for several years, ever since the occurrence of a brutal, unsolved murder. Seven counselors gather to reopen the camp for business; only one survives. A good film for those on the lookout for a no-frills catalogue of killings. Sean Cunningham, who also produced and co-wrote *Last House on the Left*, says he did it because he needed a hit. Tom Savini, also known for his work on several George A. Romero films, solidified his reputation as a master of gore effects with this one. The big surprise for many was seeing wholesome early-television celebrity Betsy Palmer playing a major role and losing her head. Also with Bing Crosby's son Harry, who is shot in the eye with an arrow. As the ads explained, "They are Doomed". **(R)** **–BM**

FRIDAY THE 13TH PART II
1981 Paramount
PRODUCERS: Steve Miner, Dennis Murphy
DIRECTOR: Steve Miner
SCREENWRITER: Ron Kurz

Five years after the *Friday the 13th* killings, the body count starts again at Camp Crystal. This sequel was cut to avoid an X rating, so it's not as shocking or disgusting as the original. You do, however, get to see lots of shots of Betsy Palmer's mongoloid son Jason's feet. **(R)**

FRIDAY THE 13TH, PART III
1982 Paramount (3-D)
PRODUCER: Frank Mancuso, Jr.
DIRECTOR: Steve Miner
SCREENWRITERS: Martin Kitrosser, Carol Watson

It's the same old story again. Jason is back, this time in a hockey mask, chopping up dope-smoking teens at Camp Crystal. Dana Kimmel is the only survivor of slaughter No. 2. The "surprise" ending is copied from No. 1. The gore effects aren't as good as in the previous entries but the 3-D effects are excellent. The best is achieved when an eyeball is squeezed out of a head and seemingly thrust into the audience. With a flashback performance by Betsy Palmer in 2-D, some bikers, and the first issue of *Fangoria*. Paramount tends to act a little embarrassed by the success of these moneymakers. They released *An Officer and a Gentleman* during the same month. **(R)**

FRIDAY THE 13TH . . . THE ORPHAN
1980 World Northal
DIRECTOR/SCREENWRITER: John Ballard
ALSO RELEASED AS: *Killer Orphan*
Clever title, huh? A 10-year-old boy retaliates against the adult world in a bloody fashion. At some showings, the old gimmick of offering an insurance policy against death by shock was used. Mark Owens stars with Joanna Miles and Peggy Feury. The theme song is by Janis Ian (*Society's Child*). **(R)**

FRIGHT: See SPELL OF THE HYPNOTIST.

FRIGHT
1972 Allied Artists (England)
PRODUCERS: Harry Fine, Michael Style
DIRECTOR: Peter Collinson
SCREENWRITER: Tudor Gates
ALSO RELEASED AS: *Night Legs*
More psycho killings from director Collinson (*The Penthouse*). Susan George is hired as a babysitter by mother Honor Blackman. Father Ian Bannen, who has just escaped from the asylum, seems sane enough to the babysitter, but he's already killed her boyfriend (Dennis Waterman) and is after her. When the police finally arrive, he threatens to take the life of his own son unless they let him escape.

FRIGHTMARE
1974 Miracle (England)
PRODUCER/DIRECTOR: Peter Walker
SCREENWRITER: David McGillwray

A gory film about an elderly British farm couple (Sheila Keith and Rupert Davies) who are cannibals. Like other Walker projects, it's well acted, effectively gruesome, and didn't receive a decent release in America. Sheila Keith, a stage actress who appeared in several of Walker's movies, is pretty memorable. **(R)**

FROGS
1972 AIP
PRODUCERS: Peter Thomas, George Edwards
DIRECTOR: George McCowan
SCREENWRITERS: Robert Hutchison, Robert Blees
A rich family led by cantankerous, wheelchair-ridden Ray Milland suffers from bad ecological karma. Snakes, lizards, insects, all led by intelligent frogs, attack the clichéd upper-class types on their private island. "Millions of slimy bodies squirming everywhere—millions of gaping mouths!" is the way the ads put it. The film often played with its Japanese cousin *Godzilla vs. the Smog Monster*. Filmed in Eden State Park, Florida. With Sam Elliott, Joan Van Ark, and Adam Roarke (*Psych-Out*).

FROM BEYOND THE GRAVE
1974 Amicus/Warner Brothers (England)
PRODUCERS: Max J. Rosenburg, Milton Subotsky
DIRECTOR: Kevin Conner
SCREENWRITERS: Robin Clarke, Raymond Christodqulow
ALSO RELEASED AS: *The Creatures from Beyond the Grave*
An especially good anthology horror film based on four stories by R. Chetwynd-Hayes. Peter Cushing holds it all together as an antiques dealer who sells surprisingly potent objects to various characters. With David Warner, Donald Pleasence, his look-alike daughter Angela, Diana Dors, Ian Ogilvy, Lesley-

Originally released as:
From Beyond the Grave.

THE CREATURES
THEY CAME FROM BEYOND THE GRAVE!
They weren't born!!
They were kicked out of HELL!!!

Anne Down, Margaret Leighton, Ian Bannen, Nyree Dawn Porter, and Ian Carmichael.

FROM EAR TO EAR

1971 Cinemation (France)
PRODUCER: Jerry Gross
DIRECTOR: Louise Soulanes
ORIGINALLY RELEASED AS: *Les Cousines*
A pair of bisexual female cousins torture a girl with sex, drugs, and a mummified baby. A French exploitation shocker re-edited and greatly altered for American release. With Jean Gavin.

FROM HELL IT CAME

1957 Allied Artists (B&W)
PRODUCER: Jack Milner
DIRECTOR: Dan Miller
SCREENWRITER: Richard Bernstein
When South Sea island Prince Kimo is killed by the tribal chief and the witch doctor for fraternizing with visiting scientists, he returns as Tabanga, a walking tree! Tabanga, who looks like the star of a six-year-old's bad dream, is a classic example of the anything-goes monsters of the '50s. The scientists, led by Tod Andrews and Tina Carver, dig up the tree-man growing out of

Kimo's grave, put him on an operating table, and stimulate his heart. Then the awkward Tabanga (ever see a tree try to walk?) drops some enemies in quicksand and eventually joins them there. With native dances, girl fights, and a half-assed explanation involving an atom bomb of how all this came to be. Paul Blaisdell created the incredible creature from Hell.

FROM RUSSIA WITH LOVE

1964 United Artists (England)
PRODUCERS: Harry Saltzman, Albert Broccoli
DIRECTOR: Terence Young
SCREENWRITER: Richard Maibaum
Sean Connery is back in the second and best of the James Bond films. 007 goes to Istanbul and falls into the arms of Tatiana (Daniela Bianchi), a Russian agent who is unknowingly leading him into a Spectre death trap. Bond battles the incredible Rosa Klebb (Lotte Lenya), a Russian who works for Spectre and carries a poisonous switchblade in her shoe, and a big blond psycho hit man (Robert Shaw) on the Orient Express. Martine Beswick and Aliza Gur

UPI 3/7/64: To travel lightly, but effectively, every youngster will want BARK, the James Bond Assault and Raider Kit that is being introduced by Multiple Toymakers at the Toy Fair. Among other things, BARK has in its molded plastic attaché case a missile launcher with three missiles, a rocket-firing pistol, and a cap-firing pocket gun. The rocket firing pistol also can be operated while the case is closed. BARK is only one of five new James Bond products that Multiple is adding to its highly successful 007 line of toys to coincide with the release of the new Bond film, From Russia with Love.

have a great girl-fight scene. With Pedro Armendariz as Kerim Bey, and series regulars Bernard Lee and Lois Maxwell. Filmed in Istanbul and London. Theme song by Matt Monro. Music by John Barry.

FROM THE EARTH TO THE MOON

1958 RKO
PRODUCER: Benedict Bogeaus
DIRECTOR: Byron Haskin
SCREENWRITERS: Robert Blees, James Leicester
A pretty dull Jules Verne adventure about a 19th-century spaceship fired from a cannon. The passengers are Joseph Cotten, George Sanders, Debra Paget, and Don Dubbins. They all belong to the Gun Club. With Henry Daniell, Patric Knowles, Morris Ankrum, and Carl Esmond as Jules Verne.

FROZEN ALIVE

1964 Magna Pictures
(W. Germany/England) (B&W)
PRODUCERS: Ron Rietti, Arthur Brauner
DIRECTOR: Bernard Knowles
SCREENWRITER: Evelyn Frazer
ORIGINALLY RELEASED AS: *Der Fall X701*
A scientist is accused of killing his unfaithful wife while he is frozen in suspended animation. Mark Stevens stars with Marianne Koch and Yoachim Hansen.

THE FROZEN DEAD

1967 Warner Brothers (England)
PRODUCER/DIRECTOR/SCREENWRITER:
Herbert J. Leder
An incredible film starring Dana Andrews as a postwar Nazi scientist in England trying to revive Hitler's top officials, now hanging (in uniform) in a walk-in freezer. Dana can get the Third Reichers to walk, but their brains don't work. His colleague kills a girl and keeps her pathetic-looking shaved head alive

on a table. As in *The Brain That Wouldn't Die*, the heroine develops mental telepathy and warns her American friends about what's going down. In a totally weird ending the two Nazi scientists are strangled by dismembered arms hanging on a wall, activated by the telepathic head! An unheralded wonder of silliness. With Ann Polk, Philip Gilbert, and Kathleen Breck as the bodiless girl.

THE FROZEN GHOST
1945 Universal (B&W)
PRODUCER: William Cowan
DIRECTOR: Harold Young
SCREENWRITERS: Bernard Schubert, Luci Ward
Lon Chaney, Jr., is a mentalist accused of causing the death of an audience member he hypnotized. It's no *Hypnotic Eye*, just another "Inner Sanctum" mystery. With Martin Kosleck as a weird wax-museum owner, Evelyn Ankers, Elena Verdugo, Douglas Dumbrille, and Milburn Stone.

FULL CIRCLE: See THE HAUNTING OF JULIA.

FULL MOON: See MOON CHILD.

FULL MOON HIGH
1982 Filmways
PRODUCER/DIRECTOR/SCREENWRITER: Larry Cohen
Adam Arkin goes to Transylvania with his father (Ed McMahon). He becomes a teenage werewolf who likes to bite girls on the ass. This seldom-seen comedy was released right after *An American Werewolf in London*. Also with Adam's real-life father Alan as a psychiatrist, Demond Wilson (*Sanford and Son*), Elizabeth Hartman, Louie Nye, and Kenneth Mars. Director Cohen

next started work on *I, the Jury*, got fired, and finally found some success with *Q*.

THE FUN HOUSE: See LAST HOUSE ON DEAD END STREET.

FUN IN ACAPULCO
1963 Paramount
PRODUCER: Hal Wallis
DIRECTOR: Richard Thorpe
SCREENWRITER: Alan Weiss
Ex-trapeze artist Elvis Presley becomes a lifeguard and singer at a resort hotel where Ursula Andress is the social director. Ursula and lady bullfighter Elsa Cardenas both want Elvis. Diving champ Alejandro Rey wants Ursula. A cute Mexican boy is Elvis' manager. Elvis sings songs like "No Room to Rhumba in a Sportscar" and conquers his fear of heights.

FUNERAL IN BERLIN
1966 Paramount (England)
PRODUCER: Charles Kasher
DIRECTOR: Guy Hamilton
SCREENWRITER: Evan Jones
Michael Caine is back as Harry Palmer, a spy involved with double-crossing ex-Nazi Communists and an Israeli agent. Oscar Homolka has one of his best roles as the colonel whose funeral is faked in order to get him through the Berlin wall. With Eva Renzi and Paul Hubschmid. Hamilton had directed *Goldfinger* and went on to other Bond films.

THE FUNHOUSE
1981 Universal
PRODUCERS: Derek Powers, Steven Bernhardt
DIRECTOR: Tobe Hooper
SCREENWRITER: Larry Block
A cleft-headed albino (played by professional mime Wayne Doba) whose favorite apparel is a Frankenstein monster

mask stalks the dark corners of a carnival funhouse, picking off young stoned students locked in for the night in routine slaughter-film style.

Funhouse was plagued by cost and schedule problems during the entire shoot—which started with the transportation of an entire carnival from Akron, Ohio, to the Ivan Tors studio (home of *Flipper*) in Florida. The monster, designed and built by Rick Baker and Craig Reardon, is costumed badly, and the picture doesn't seem finished. Not the film hoped for from the director of *The Texas Chainsaw Massacre*. With Sylvia Miles, Kevin Conway, and a clip from *The Bride of Frankenstein*. Hooper next did *Poltergeist* for Steven Spielberg. **(R)** —BM

THE FURY

1978 20th Century-Fox
PRODUCER: Frank Yablans
DIRECTOR: Brian De Palma
SCREENWRITER: John Farris

Can the witchdoctor save Jungle Jim (Johnny Weissmuller) in Fury of the Congo?

Author/scriptwriter John Farris wrote this after seeing *Carrie*. John Cassavetes kidnaps Andrew Stevens (the real life son of Stella) for his psychic powers. Stevens' dad Kirk Douglas tries to rescue him. Amy Irving (*Carrie*) uses her powers to blow Cassavetes apart. Bits of his bloody body fly all over a nicely furnished room; his head ends up on the floor, his legs on a couch. Another highlight is Carrie Snodgress' head splattering into a pulpy mass after smashing through a car windshield. This rather confused movie made money because of these scenes. Another crowd pleaser is a timely scene with Arabs on a revolving carnival ride that goes so fast they're thrown up in the air and crash through a wall to their deaths. De Palma really knows how to work his audience. With Fiona Lewis, Rutanya Alda, and Charles Durning. Music by John Williams. **(R)**

FURY AT SMUGGLERS BAY

1961 Embassy Pictures (England) (B&W)
PRODUCER/DIRECTOR/SCREENWRITER:
John Gilling

As Squire Trevenyan, Peter Cushing is after Black John (Bernard Lee), leader of a gang that lures ships onto the rocks to be wrecked and then loots them. The 19th-century adventure set in Cornwall stars John Fraser, Michele Mercier, and George Coulouris. By the director of *Mania*.

FURY OF THE CONGO

1951 Columbia (B&W)
PRODUCER: Sam Katzman
DIRECTOR: William Berke
SCREENWRITER: Carroll Young

The ads promised: "Barbaric beauties in fierce jungle war!" Jungle Jim (Johnny Weissmuller) saves a white native tribe from the clutches of a narcotics gang in hot pursuit of the Okongo, a giant spider that provides a powerful drug. With Lyle Talbot and Sherry Moreland.

FURY OF THE SUCCUBUS:
See *SATAN'S MISTRESS.*

FURY OF THE VIKINGS: See
ERIC THE CONQUEROR.

THE FURY OF THE
WOLFMAN

1970 Avco Embassy-TV (Spain)
PRODUCER: Plata Films
DIRECTOR: Jose Maria Zabalza
SCREENWRITER: Jacinto Molina

Paul Naschy plays the wolfman for the fourth time. A mad female scientist who turns into a werewolf and a trip to Tibet are involved. Includes scenes from *Frankenstein's Bloody Terror*. *Dr. Jekyll and the Wolfman* was next in the series.

FURY UNLEASHED: See
HOT ROD GANG.

FUTURE COP

1976 TV
PRODUCER/SCREENWRITER: Anthony Wilson
DIRECTOR: Jud Taylor

Old cop Ernest Borgnine gets a new partner—android Michael Shannon. With John Amos. It led to a short-lived television series. Taylor directs as many as three TV quickies a year.

FUTUREWORLD

1976 AIP
PRODUCERS: Paul Lazarus III, James T. Aubrey, Jr.
DIRECTOR: Richard T. Heffron
SCREENWRITERS: Mayo Simon, George Schenk

In this sequel to *Westworld*, Peter Fonda and Blythe Danner play reporters investigating a simulated space flight in Delos, an adult vacation park. They discover a world-domination plot and a clone of Fonda. With Arthur Hill, Allan Luden, and a brief appearance by Yul Brynner to remind you of the first movie.

G.I. BLUES

1960 Paramount
PRODUCER: Hal Wallis
DIRECTOR: Norman Taurog
SCREENWRITERS: Edmund Belan,
    Henry Garson

In 1960, Elvis returned from the army minus his sideburns, did a TV show with Frank Sinatra, and made this movie about a singing serviceman. Parts of it were filmed in Germany while he was still stationed there. As Tulsa McCauley, he forms a combo with two buddies and plays a big army show. A series of misunderstandings involving a bet to see who can seduce cabaret singer Juliet Prowse give way to marriage plans and a happy ending. Elvis sings "Wooden Heart," partially in German, and other tunes. The one-time threat to the youth of America plays with puppets and baby-sits. Still, media bluenoses complained at the time because teen idol Elvis was obviously hanging out at a whorehouse. Just imagine—an American soldier in such a place.

The late Dorothy Stratten as Galaxina.

GALAXINA

1980 Crown
PRODUCER: Marilyn J. Tenser
DIRECTOR/SCREENWRITER: William Sachs

A comedy science-fiction adventure with good special effects for a low-budget project, but the humor really doesn't work. Dorothy Stratten (Hoogstratten), the beautiful 20-year-old *Playboy* Playmate of the Year, stars as the robot Galaxina. Featuring parodies of *Alien* and *Star Wars*, Avery Schreiber, Angelo Rossitto as a small alien, and a film clip from *First Spaceship on Venus*. By the director of *The Incredible Melting Man*. Stratten was murdered by her sicko estranged husband the day the film premiered in Kansas City. **(R)**

GALAXY OF TERROR

1981 New World
PRODUCERS: Roger Corman, Marc Siegler
DIRECTOR: B. D. Clark
SCREENWRITERS: Marc Siegler, B.D. Clark
ALSO RELEASED AS: *Mindwarp: An Infinity of Terror, Planet of Horrors*

A science-fiction/horror movie patterned after *Alien*, with touches of *The Empire Strikes Back*. The story is confusing, sometimes ridiculous, but there are plenty of real shocks and a strange enough cast to make it worthwhile. Erin Moran (Joanie on *Happy Days*) gets disemboweled and explodes! Sid Haig cuts off his own arm after a small glass weapon burrows under his skin. A space woman is raped by a giant worm. These scenes are disgusting firsts and should please even veteran gross-out fans. With Edward Albert, Grace Zabriske, Ray Walston (*My Favorite Martian*), Zalman King, and Bernard Behrens. It played under various titles in different parts of the country. Take your pick. **(R)**

GAME OF DEATH
1946 RKO (B&W)
PRODUCER: Herman Schlom
DIRECTOR: Robert Wise
SCREENWRITER: Norman Houston
A remake of *The Most Dangerous Game*, with John Loder in the Count Zaroff role. Audrey Long uses tapes of Fay Wray's screams from the original and Noble Johnson repeats his role of 14 years earlier. With Edgar Barrier, Jason Robards, Sr., Russell Wade, Robert Clarke, and Gene Roth.

THE GAME OF DEATH
1978 Columbia (Hong Kong)
PRODUCER: Raymond Chow
DIRECTORS: Robert Clouse, Bruce Lee
SCREENWRITER: Jan Spears
After starring in four features, Bruce Lee died a cult hero, leaving behind about ten minutes of fight scenes he had directed and starred in with Kareem Abdul Jabbar. In the tradition of *Plan 9 from Outer Space* "starring" Bela Lugosi after his death, an entire feature was made around the valuable footage. Most of the time an unconvincing double masquerades as Lee, wearing dark glasses. Sometimes he's seen only from behind, or close-ups of Lee's face or eyes are cut in. Gig Young, Dean Jagger, and Hugh O'Brien all pretend to be in a Bruce Lee film. Future action star Chuck Norris appears in an outtake from *Return of the Dragon*. Ghoulish (and bad) cash-in projects featuring dead stars are inevitable. *The Trail of the Pink Panther* is a more recent example. **(R)**

GAMERA THE INVINCIBLE
1965 World Entertainment/Daiei
PRODUCER: Yonejiro Saito
DIRECTORS: Masaichi Nagata,
Sandy Howard (U.S. version)
SCREENWRITERS: Fumi Takahashi,
Richard Kraft
ORIGINALLY RELEASED AS: *Daikaiju Gamera*
ALSO RELEASED AS: *Gammera the Invincible*
Gamera, an unlikely movie star, was created in Japan to rival Godzilla. As in the first Godzilla film, new American footage was added here and the story severely altered. An atomic bomb unleashes a giant fire-breathing prehistoric turtle that flies by pulling into its shell and spinning. Albert Dekker (as the U.S. Secretary of Defense) and Brian Donlevy (as a general) confer with Japanese scientists to decide how to avert worldwide destruction. Earth is saved by using the ingenious "Plan 2" (Gamera is trapped in a rocket and sent to Mars). The superturtle caught on (in Japan, anyway). So far there have been eight Gamera adventures. Like Godzilla, the crushing monster became a friendly hero in later films.

GAMERA VS. MONSTER X
1970 Daiei/AIP-TV (Japan)
DIRECTOR: Noriaki Yuasa
SCREENWRITER: Fumi Takahashi
ORIGINALLY RELEASED AS: *Gamera tai Daimaju Jaiga*
The sixth and most outrageous Gamera-the-flying-turtle adventure. At Expo '70, Jiger, a female monster, lays an egg in Gamera's body. The offspring

sucks the hero monster's blood. The usual two little Japanese boys arrive and save Gamera so he can defeat the invaders and save the world again. It was the last big turtle movie to reach American shores.

GAMES

1967 Universal
PRODUCER: George Edwards
DIRECTOR: Curtis Harrington
SCREENWRITER: Gene Kearney

A bored art-collecting Manhattan couple (James Caan and Katharine Ross) invite an interesting aging cosmetics saleswoman to enliven their dull lives by directing sex and death "games." Simone Signoret stars in a *Diabolique*-style thriller featuring a corpse encased in plaster and displayed in the living room as art, and a triple-cross ending. One of Harrington's most effective films, it features Kent Smith, Florence Marly (star of his *Queen of Blood*), Don Stroud, Estelle Winwood, a bit by Luana Anders (*Night Tide*), and a scene of Lugosi in *Dracula*.

THE GAMMA PEOPLE

1956 Columbia (England) (B&W)
PRODUCER: John Gossage
DIRECTOR: John Gilling
SCREENWRITERS: John Gossage, John Gilling

An American (Paul Douglas) and an Englishman (Leslie Phillips from the *Carry On* series) travel to a mythical Eastern European country run by a dictator (Walter Rilla). The pair discover a secret project in which children are bombarded with gamma rays. Some become geniuses, others morons. A very unusual science-fiction film combining some humor with political horror. With Eva Bartok. It originally played in America with *1984*.

GAMMA 693: See *NIGHT OF THE ZOMBIES*.

GANG WARS: See *THE DEVIL'S EXPRESS*.

GANJA AND HESS

1973 Kelly-Jordan Enterprises
PRODUCER: Chiz Schultz
DIRECTOR/SCREENWRITER: Bill Gunn
ALSO RELEASED AS: *Double Possession, Blood Couple*

Duane Jones, star of *Night of the Living Dead*, is a modern vampire with visions of his native Africa. It's an interesting black-oriented horror film, both arty and exploitative, which was rereleased after being confusingly cut. Director Gunn plays a really odd victim of the rich decadent vampire. Marlene Clark (also in Russ Meyer films) becomes Jones' bride. One version substitutes soul music for the original haunting African music. Filmed at Croton-on-Hudson, New York, and the Brooklyn Museum. (R)

GAPPA THE TRIPIBIAN MONSTER: See *MONSTER FROM A PREHISTORIC PLANET*.

GARDEN OF THE DEAD

1972 Clover
PRODUCER: Daniel Cady
DIRECTOR: John Hayes
SCREENWRITER: John Jones

A low-budget *Night of the Living Dead*–inspired feature with prison inmates

Originally released as: Ganja and Hess.

who sniff formaldehyde to get high. They go crazy and are killed by guards. Returning from the dead, they attack with hoes and sharp rakes.

THE GARDENER: See SEEDS OF EVIL.

GARGOYLES
1972 TV
PRODUCERS: Robert W. Christiansen, Rick Rosenberg
DIRECTOR: B.W.L. Norton
SCREENWRITERS: Stephen and Elinor Karpf
An anthropologist (Cornel Wilde) and his daughter (Jennifer Salt) find a skeleton in Mexico. A group of ancient monsters show up to get their bones back. The unusual gargoyles (each one is different) won an Emmy. Bernie Casey, star of *Dr. Black and Mr. Hyde*, plays the gargoyle leader. With Grayson Hall (*Dark Shadows*).

GARU, THE MAD MONK: See GURU, THE MAD MONK.

GAS, OR HOW IT BECAME NECESSARY TO DESTROY THE WORLD IN ORDER TO SAVE IT: See GAS-S-S-S!

GAS-S-S-S!
1970 AIP
PRODUCER/DIRECTOR: Roger Corman
SCREENWRITER: George Armitage
ALSO RELEASED AS: *Gas, or How It Became Necessary to Destroy the World in Order to Save It*
Everybody over 25 dies after a nerve-gas leak. Corman says AIP ruined this youth-takeover musical comedy by cutting too much, including the character of God. Could be . . . but apart from the fun of spotting up-and-coming stars

in the cast, it's an excruciating hippie movie. With Robert Corff, Elaine Giftos, Bud Cort (*Harold and Maude*), Talia Coppola (later Shire), Ben Vereen, Cindy Williams, Marshall McLuhan, and Country Joe and the Fish. At the end, dead heroes (John Kennedy, Martin Luther King, Che, and Poe) emerge from a crack in the ground. Bring back the crab monsters! It was the second-to-last film Corman directed and his last for AIP.

GEMINI MAN
1976 TV
PRODUCER: Robert F. O'Neill
DIRECTOR: Alan Levi
SCREENWRITER: Leslie Stevens
ALSO RELEASED AS: *Code Name: Minus One*
A reworking of *The Invisible Man* TV show from the producers of *The Six Million Dollar Man*. Ben Murphy can become invisible for short amounts of time. The resulting series lasted a short amount of time.

GENESIS II
1973 TV
PRODUCER/SCREENWRITER: Gene Roddenberry
DIRECTOR: John Llewellyn Moxey
A pilot film, from the creator of *Star Trek*, for a series that never made it. Dylan Hunt (Alex Cord) wakes up in the year 2133 after being in suspended animation for 60 years. He finds a post–World War III universe with the usual mutants and scientists trying to rebuild things. He also makes friends with Mariette Hartley, who has two belly buttons. With Ted "Lurch" Cassidy. It's pretty standard stuff and a lot of confusion was later caused by two more pilots based on the same characters: *Planet Earth* and *Strange New World*.

THE GENII OF DARKNESS

1960 Azteca/AIP-TV (Mexico) (B&W)
PRODUCER: Victor Parra
DIRECTOR: Frederick Curiel
SCREENWRITERS: Charles Taboada,
   Alfred Ruandova
ORIGINALLY RELEASED AS: *Nostradamus, el
   Genio de las Tinieblas*
See *The Blood of Nostradamus.*

GENIUS AT WORK

1946 RKO (B&W)
PRODUCER: Herman Schlom
DIRECTOR: Leslie Goodwins
SCREENWRITERS: Robert E. Kent, Monte Brice
The last film starring Brown and Carney, RKO's imitation Abbott and Costello team, was also Lionel Atwill's last feature. He plays "The Cobra," a criminologist/killer who at one point disguises himself as an old woman. Bela Lugosi is wasted again as Atwill's servant. With Anne Jeffries. The team of Wally Brown and Alan Carney broke up after this, their eighth unfunny comedy. It was a remake of a 1937 Jack Oakie film, *Super Sleuth.*

THE GEORGE RAFT STORY

1961 Allied Artists (B&W)
PRODUCER: Ben Schwalb
DIRECTOR: Joseph M. Newman
SCREENWRITER: Crane Wilbur

Ray Danton as George Raft dunks Jayne Mansfield in The George Raft Story.

Not many actors have their life stories filmed while they're alive. I don't know what George thought of this little bio, but it's got plenty of gangsters and dames. Future horror-film director Ray Danton is Raft, shown growing up in Hell's Kitchen, dancing at casinos, hanging out with gangsters, making *Scarface,* fleeing Cuba after the revolution, and acting in *Some Like It Hot.* Barbara Nichols is his friend Texas, and Jayne Mansfield, Julie London, and Barrie Chase are fictional girlfriends. Neville Brand is Al Capone (as he was on *The Untouchables*). Brad Dexter is Bugsy Siegel. With Frank Gorshin, Herschel Bernardi, and Robert Strauss.

GET YOURSELF A COLLEGE GIRL

1964 MGM
PRODUCER: Sam Katzman
DIRECTOR: Sidney Miller
SCREENWRITER: Robert E. Kent
ALSO RELEASED AS: *The Swingin' Set*
Mary Ann Mobley, Miss America of 1959, stars as a student at a conservative college who secretly writes hit rock songs. On vacation at a Sun Valley resort, she and other students put on a show to help re-elect a senator. The lineup: the Dave Clark Five and the Animals, fresh from England, the Standells in their prehit days, Freddie Bell and the Bellboys (left over from Katzman's 50's musicals) and for the quieter moments—the Jimmy Smith Trio and Stan Getz and Astrud Gilberto. Also with Nancy Sinatra and Chad Everett.

THE GHASTLY ONES

1969 JER
PRODUCER/DIRECTOR: Andy Milligan
SCREENWRITERS: Andy Milligan,
   Hal Sherwood
A 16mm wonder about three couples going to an old mansion on an island

off the coast of Maine inhabited by two old ladies and a hunchback (who eats live rabbits). People are sawed in half, decapitated, stuck with pitchforks. The gore effects are so laughably bad that you can see a rubber leg bounce. Writer-director Milligan, who also photographed this film, remade it as *Legacy of Blood* in '78. If you're an Andy Milligan fan there's no hope for you. Filmed on Staten Island.

GHIDRAH, THE THREE HEADED MONSTERS

1965 Toho/Continental (Japan)
PRODUCER: Tomoyuki Tanaka
DIRECTOR: Inoshiro Honda
SCREENWRITER: Shinichi Sekizawa
ORIGINALLY RELEASED AS: *Sandai Kaiju Chikyu Saidai No Kessen*

The first of the "new" Godzilla films. The former terror of Japan, now a good guy, teams up with two other Toho monsters, Rodan and Mothra, to battle the new three-headed alien horror, Ghidrah. The huge fire-breathing winged dragon, who comes from a meteor, is an inspired creation. Add a subplot about a beautiful missing princess claiming she's a Martian and you've got one of the best Japanese monster bashes. With Mothra's little pals, the twin Alilenas.

THE GHOST

1963 Magna Pictures (Italy)
PRODUCERS: Luigi Carpentieri,
  Ermanno Donati
DIRECTOR: Riccardo Freda (Robert Hampton)
SCREENWRITERS: Oreste Biancoli,
  Riccardo Freda

Not just any ghost but the ghost of Dr. Hichcock (of *The Horrible . . .*), now a cripple with an unfaithful wife (Barbara Steele). She and her lover (Peter Baldwin) plot against the husband. The lover and the housekeeper plot against

Staten Island mayhem in The Ghastly Ones.

her. With seances, murder, insanity . . . but see it for Barbara Steele.

THE GHOST AND MR. CHICKEN

1966 Universal
PRODUCER: Edward J. Montagne
DIRECTOR: Alan Rafkin
SCREENWRITERS: James Fritzell,
  Everett Greenbaum

After leaving *Mayberry*, Don Knotts made a lot of movies you never saw. This one, although light, is actually pretty good. As Luther, a timid small-town newspaper typesetter, he becomes a hero after spending the night in a haunted house (complete with a blood-stained organ that plays itself) and tracking down a murderer. With Joan Staley (*Playboy*'s Miss November 1958), Liam Redmond, Dick Sargent, Skip Homeier, Cliff Norton, Ellen Corby, and Hope Summers.

THE GHOST AND MRS. MUIR

1947 20th Century-Fox (B&W)
PRODUCER: Fred Kohlmar
DIRECTOR: Joseph L. Mankiewicz
SCREENWRITER: Philip Dunne

An excellent romantic ghost story. Gene Tierney, a widow living in a beautiful New England home, is haunted by the charming ghost of a sea captain (Rex Harrison). With George Sanders and little Natalie Wood. Music by Bernard Herrmann. It was remade in '55 as *Stranger in the Night* and also became a 1968–70 TV series.

GHOST BREAKERS
1940 Paramount (B&W)
PRODUCER: Arthur Hornblow, Jr.
DIRECTOR: George Marshall
SCREENWRITER: Walter De Leon

Following the success of *The Cat and the Canary*, Bob Hope and Paulette Goddard were reunited in this superior horror comedy. Hiding out from gangsters, Hope and Willie Best go to Cuba, where Goddard has inherited a haunted castle. Noble Johnson is a great zombie and there's a real ghost. With Richard Carlson, Anthony Quinn, Pedro De Cordoba, and Paul Lukas. One of Bob Hope's best. In '53 it was remade as *Scared Stiff* with Martin and Lewis.

GHOST CATCHERS
1944 Universal (B&W)
PRODUCER/SCREENWRITER:
Edmund L. Hartmann
DIRECTOR: Edward F. Cline

An insane Olsen and Johnson comedy about a haunted house located next door to their nightclub. Real ghosts mix with gangsters trying to scare people away. Lon Chaney, Jr., is a bear, Andy Devine is a horse, Cliff Norton is a tap-dancing ghost, and Leo Carillo is a mummy. It's filled with unexpected gags, impressive special effects, an exorcism with swing music, and Ole Olsen and Chic Johnson facing the camera and talking to the audience. Gloria Jean

and Martha O'Driscoll also star. Look for Tor Johson and Mel Torme as a drummer.

GHOST CHASERS
1951 Monogram (B&W)
PRODUCER: Jan Grippo
DIRECTOR: William Beaudine
SCREENWRITER: Bert Lawrence

Leo Gorcey, Huntz Hall, and the other Bowery Boys chase ghosts and a mad doctor (Philip Van Zandt).

GHOST CRAZY: See CRAZY NIGHTS.

THE GHOST CREEPS
1940 Monogram (B&W)
PRODUCER: Sam Katzman
DIRECTOR: Joseph Lewis
SCREENWRITER: William Lively
ALSO RELEASED AS: *Boys of the City*

The East Side Kids (after they were the Dead End Kids, before they were the Bowery Boys) encounter ghosts that turn out to be fakes. The ghost footage was added at the last minute in an effort to parody the then current hit *Rebecca*. Leo Gorcey and Bobby Jordan star. Director Lewis later did classics like *Gun Crazy* and *The Big Combo*. Sam Katzman was associate producer.

THE GHOST GOES WEST
1936 United Artists (England) (B&W)
PRODUCER: Alexander Korda
DIRECTOR: René Clair
SCREENWRITERS: Robert E. Sherwood, Geoffrey Kerr

An excellent romantic comedy. A Scottish castle containing a ghost has been moved to America. As the castle's new inhabitant, Jean Parker falls in love with the ghost, who takes the human form of Robert Donat. With Eugene

Pallette and Elsa Lanchester. Original prints were tinted sepia.

GHOST IN THE INVISIBLE BIKINI
1966 AIP
PRODUCERS: James H. Nicholson, Samuel Z. Arkoff
DIRECTOR: Don Weis
SCREENWRITERS: Louis M. Heywood, Elwood Ullman

A beautiful ghost (Susan Hart) tells the dead Boris Karloff that in order to get to Heaven he must perform a good deed. Unfortunately the deed involves helping to keep Tommy Kirk from being swindled out of his inheritance by crooked lawyer Basil Rathbone. It's pretty much standard AIP mindlessness, with Deborah Walley, Nancy Sinatra (she sings), Aron Kincaid, more old-timers (Francis X. Bushman, Patsy Kelly, and Jesse White), Harvey Lembeck as Eric Von Zipper, some unconvincing monsters, good music by the Bobby Fuller Four, lots of girls, and a gorilla.

THE GHOST OF DRAGSTRIP HOLLOW
1959 AIP (B&W)
PRODUCER/SCREENWRITER: Lou Rusoff
DIRECTOR: William Hole, Jr.

A group of drag racers and their girls hold a Halloween rock 'n' roll costume bash in an abandoned mansion. "The She Creature" shows up wearing tennis shoes. Only her tits are gone, so now it's a he creature. The rockin' teens find out that the creature is really Paul Blaisdell, who cries when they find him out. Blaisdell created most of the best AIP '50s monsters, including the one for *The She Creature*, which showed up in three films. Russ Bender stars in this plotless-jive filler with Jody Fair, Martin Braddock, and Jack Geng. Music by the Renegades.

THE GHOST OF FLIGHT 401
1978 TV
PRODUCER: Emmet G. Lavery, Jr.
DIRECTOR: Steven Hilliard Stern
SCREENWRITER: Robert Malcolm Young

Ernest Borgnine as the ill-fated captain of a crashed jet reappears in ghost form on other flights. The same "real" incident provided the plot for *Crash*, another '78 TV-movie, but it didn't have Ernie the friendly ghost. With Gary Lockwood and Tina Chen.

THE GHOST OF FRANKENSTEIN
1942 Universal (B&W)
PRODUCER: George Waggner
DIRECTOR: Erle C. Kenton
SCREENWRITER: W. Scott Darling

In the follow-up to *The Son of Frankenstein*, the monster (Lon Chaney, Jr.) is revived by lightning and taken by Igor (Bela Lugosi) to another Frankenstein son (Sir Cedric Hardwicke). Frankenstein's assistant (Lionel Atwill) puts Igor's brain in the monster—who then kidnaps a little girl, takes her back, and goes to court in chains to stand trial. With Evelyn Ankers, Ralph Bellamy, and Dwight Frye as a villager. Characters who died in the previous film magically show up.

GHOST SHIP
1943 RKO (B&W)
PRODUCER: Val Lewton
DIRECTOR: Mark Robson
SCREENWRITER: Donald Henderson Clarke

The least known of Lewton's classic atmospheric films features Russell Wade as an officer on a sailing ship who discovers that his much-admired captain (Richard Dix) is a psychopathic killer. With Edith Barrett, Skelton Knaggs, Lawrence Tierney, and Sir Lancelot (*I Walked with a Zombie*).

GHOST STORY

1981 Universal
PRODUCERS: Burt Weissbourd,
Douglas Green
DIRECTOR: John Irvin
SCREENWRITER: Lawrence D. Cohen

Fred Astaire, Melvyn Douglas, John Houseman, and Douglas Fairbanks, Jr., star as old men upset when the ghost of a woman they accidentally drowned 50 years ago comes back to kill them one by one. Apparently, the problem of adapting Peter Straub's 600-page novel for the screen was solved by throwing the entire thing out the window; the novel was an admirable marriage of gothic style and modern horror, while this film has neither the atmosphere of *The Haunting*, nor the chill of *Carrie* (adapted from Stephen King's novel by screenwriter Cohen). It's more a soap opera than a horror film. With Alice Krige (*Chariots of Fire*) as the ghost, Craig Wasson, and Patricia Neal. **(R)**   –BM

GHOSTS ON THE LOOSE

1943 Monogram (B&W)
PRODUCER: Sam Katzman
DIRECTOR: William Beaudine
SCREENWRITER: Kenneth Higgins
ALSO RELEASED AS: *The East Side Kids Meet Bela Lugosi*

Bela Lugosi as Emil, a Nazi spy, pretends his hideout in New York is haunted. The East Side Kids show up and Huntz Hall and Leo Gorcey find themselves bound and gagged by Bela, Minerva Urecal, and Frank Moran. With a prestar Ava Gardner, Billy Benedict, Bobby Jordan, and Sunshine Sammy Morrison (the original black kid in *Our Gang* shorts from 1922 to 1924).

THE GHOUL

1933 Gaumont (England) (B&W)
DIRECTOR: T. Hayes Hunter
SCREENWRITERS: Roland Pertwee,
John Hastings Turner

Following *The Mummy*, Boris Karloff returned to his native England (which he had left in 1909) to star as an Egyptologist professor. He dies with a jewel called the Eternal Light in his hand and vows to return from the grave if it's stolen. Soon the house is teaming with heirs and criminals, the jewel is missing, and Karloff rises. Ernest Thesiger is the clubfooted servant. Cedric Hardwicke is a crooked lawyer. Ralph Richardson is a phony parson. It was remade as a comedy (*What a Carve Up*).

THE GHOUL

1975 Tyburn (England)
PRODUCER: Kevin Francis
DIRECTOR: Freddie Francis
SCREENWRITER: John Elder

In the '20s, a murdering cannibal is on the loose. Peter Cushing stars as Dr. Lawrence. With Veronica Carlson, Gwen Watford, and John Hurt as the gardener. Don Henderson is the ghoul. Never released theatrically in America but available on videocassette.

THE GIANT BEHEMOTH

1959 Allied Artists (England) (B&W)
PRODUCER: Ted Lloyd
DIRECTORS: Douglas Hickok,
Eugene Lourie
SCREENWRITER: Eugene Lourie
ALSO RELEASED AS: *Behemoth the Sea Monster*

Eugene Lourie recycles elements from his *Beast from 20,000 Fathoms*, sets them in England—and ends up with the scariest giant-monster-on-the-loose movie ever made. The giant brontosaurus, loose in London, was animated by King Kong's creator, Willis O'Brien, among others. This monster has a radioactive advantage over the original. As it smashes cars and knocks over the House of Parliament, it also burns the skin off screaming people. Even though the animation was rushed, the results are fine. With Gene Evans and Andre Morell as scientists, Leigh Madison, and Jack MacGowran.

THE GIANT CLAW
1957 Columbia (B&W)
PRODUCER: Sam Katzman
DIRECTOR: Fred F. Sears
SCREENWRITERS: Samuel Newman,
   Paul Gangelin

It's a giant marionette bird from outer space surrounded by an invisible force field and it's attacking New York! It likes to destroy airplanes and lays an egg in Quebec. Jeff Morrow and Mara Corday (*Playboy*'s Miss October 1958) as the star-crossed scientists team up with Morris Ankrum to defeat the floppy-winged horror (on visible wires). They all had recent experience in such matters, having fought Kronos, the Black Lagoon Creature, a tarantula, black scorpions, and flying saucers during the previous year. With Robert Shayne, film clips from *Earth vs. the Flying Saucers*, and the destruction of the U.N.

GIANT FROM THE UNKNOWN
1958 Astor (B&W)
PRODUCER: Arthur P. Jacobs
DIRECTOR: Richard E. Cunha
SCREENWRITERS: Frank Hart Taussig,
   Ralph Brooke

Buddy Baer, a professional fighter, plays a murdering Spanish conquistador revived by lightning in the 20th century. Inept shocks from the director of *Missile to the Moon* and the producer of the *Planet of the Apes* series. With Edward Kemmer, Sally Fraser, and Morris Ankrum.

THE GIANT GILA MONSTER
1959 McLendon Radio Pictures (B&W)
PRODUCER: Ken Curtis
DIRECTOR: Ray Kellog
SCREENWRITERS: Jay Sims, Ray Kellogg

Don Sullivan and his teenage friends battle a rear-projected gila monster in New Mexico. Rock music, hot rods, and laughs from the director of *The Killer Shrews* and *The Green Berets*. Produced by Ken Curtis (Festus on *Gunsmoke*). With Shug Fisher.

THE GIANT LEECHES: See ATTACK OF THE GIANT LEECHES.

GIANT OF MARATHON
1959 MGM (Italy)
PRODUCER: Bruno Vailati
DIRECTOR: Jacques Tourneur
SCREENWRITERS: Ennio De Concini,
   Augusta Frassimetti

After the popularity of two Hercules features and *Goliath and the Barbarians*, Steve Reeves returned as Philippides, defending Athens against Persian invaders. Mylene Demonget co-stars in this slow-moving spectacle. Director Tourneur soon returned to America to work for AIP. Cinematographer Mario Bava stayed in Italy and worked on Reeves' next adventure, *The White Warrior*.

GIANT OF METROPOLIS
1961 Seven Arts Associated (Italy)
PRODUCER: Emimmo Salvi
DIRECTOR: Umberto Scarpelli
SCREENWRITERS: Sabatino Ciuffino,
   Oreste Palella, Ambrogio Molteni,
   Gino Stafford, Emimmo Salvi
ORIGINALLY RELEASED AS: *Il Gigante di Metropolis*

Made during the Italian Hercules craze, this imaginative fantasy features a typical strongman (Gordon Mitchell as Obro) but looks more like a Flash Gordon film. A hidden, scientifically advanced supercity in 10,000 B.C. is the setting for experiments, torture, and palace intrigue. The costumes and sets are a great mixture of ancient and futuristic. With Roldana Luip and Bella Cortez.

GIANT SPIDER INVASION

1975 Group I
PRODUCER: William W. Gillette
DIRECTOR: Bill Rebane
SCREENWRITERS: Bill Rebane,
  Richard L. Huff

There hasn't been a movie with special effects so bad since *The Giant Claw*. Different-sized spiders jump out of a "black hole" and terrorize a small town. The big ones are stripped-down Volkswagens with legs and eyes added. Lots of laughs with Steve Brodie (*The Beast from 20,000 Fathoms*), Barbara Hale (*Perry Mason*), Alan Hale (*Gilligan's Island*), and Leslie Parrish.

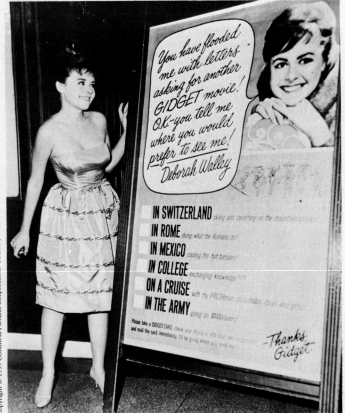

Deborah Walley starred in Gidget Goes Hawaiian, but the locations suggested on the Gidget-Cards in this promotion were left to her successors.

GIDGET

1959 Columbia
PRODUCER: Lewis J. Rachmil
DIRECTOR: Paul Wendkos
SCREENWRITER: Gabrielle Upton

Seventeen-year-old Sandra Dee loves surfer James Darren but is sidetracked by beach bum Cliff Robertson. With Arthur O'Connell, Joby Baker, Yvonne Craig, and Doug McClure. The success of this wholesome teenage sand-and-sex comedy led to a whole new genre of beach films in the '60s. If you liked this one, you'll probably also want to see *Gidget Goes Hawaiian* (Deborah Walley), *Gidget Goes to Rome* (Cindy Carol), *Gidget Grows Up* (Karen Valentine) or *Gidget Gets Married* (Monie Ellis).

THE GIFT OF GAB

1934 Universal (B&W)
PRODUCER: Carl Laemmle, Jr.
DIRECTOR: Karl Freund
SCREENWRITERS: Ryan James, Lou Breslow

After making *The Black Cat* together, Karloff and Lugosi both did bits in this musical comedy about a radio show. Boris, in a top hat, is the Phantom. Bela is an Apache dancer. Edmond Lowe and Gloria Stuart star. With a comedy trio called The Three Stooges (not the popular Howard, Fine, Howard team but a competing band of upstarts). Also with Chester Morris, Andy Devine, Alexander Wolcott, Sterling Holloway, Alice White, and Wini Shaw.

GIGANTIS, THE FIRE MONSTER

1955 Toho/Warner Brothers (Japan) (B&W)
PRODUCER: Tomoyuki Tanaka
DIRECTOR: Motoyoshi Odo
SCREENWRITERS: Takeo Murata,
  Sigeaki Hidaka
ORIGINALLY RELEASED AS: *Gujira No Gyakushyu*

The first Godzilla sequel, released here when it was four years old, used a new title for the star monster because Warner Brothers didn't own the rights to the name of Japan's most famous film export. Godzilla battles Angorus, a giant creature with a spiky back. They level pagodas and crush civilians. It was seven years before the atomic dinosaur returned in *King Kong vs. Godzilla.*

THE GIRL CAN'T HELP IT

1956 20th Century-Fox
PRODUCER/DIRECTOR/SCREENWRITER:
  Frank Tashlin

"She mesmerizes every mother's son—if she smiles then beefsteak becomes well done . . ." Little Richard sings the great theme song while Jayne Mansfield bumps down the street clutching her milk bottles. Gangster Edmond O'Brien forces press agent Tom Ewell to make Jayne a singing star. This classic '50s sex comedy depicts the influence of organized crime on the rock 'n' roll craze. It also shows some of the best rock acts performing in stereo, Cinemascope, and DeLuxe color. Fats Domino sings "Blue Monday." Gene Vincent and the Bluecaps do "Be Bop A Lula" in a studio, Eddie Cochran does "Twenty Flight Rock" on TV, and Little Richard does "She's Got It" in a nightclub. For the older members of the audience Julie London sings "Cry Me A River," O'Brien does comical songs in prison, and Jayne squeals.

GIRL HAPPY

1965 MGM
PRODUCER: Joe Pasternak
DIRECTOR: Boris Sagal
SCREENWRITERS: Harvey Bullock, R.S. Allen
Elvis is Rusty Wells. His combo (including Gary Crosby and Jimmy Hawkins) are hired by a Chicago gangster (Harold

J. Stone) to play in his Fort Lauderdale nightclub. Elvis also has to keep an eye on boss' daughter Shelley Fabares (who loves him) while trying to make it with Mary Ann Mobley. Watch for the mountains in the "Florida" background. With Jackie Coogan and Nina Talbot. Hear 11 songs including "She's the Meanest Girl in Town," "Fort Lauderdale Chamber of Commerce," and "Do the Clam."

UPI 1956: Jayne Mansfield as movie audiences will see her in The Girl Can't Help It. *20th Century-Fox has made her a cottony platinum blonde and raised her hairline a half-inch as the glamour build-up gets underway in earnest.*

GIRL HUNTERS

1963 Colorama (England) (B&W)
PRODUCER: Robert Fellows
DIRECTOR: Roy Rowland
SCREENWRITERS: Mickey Spillane, Roy Rowland, Robert Fellows

Mickey Spillane stars as his own creation, detective Mike Hammer. He also co-wrote the screenplay, based on his '62 bestseller. None of the Hammer films was a commercial hit when released, but they're great to catch on TV. This was the comeback story with Hammer emerging from a seven-year alcoholic stupor after the disappearance of his secretary, Velda. A plot involving communist assassins is discovered. Spillane/Hammer catches one killer and nails his hand to the floor! With Shirley Eaton as a suspicious widow, Lloyd Nolan as a federal agent, newspaper columnist Hy Gardner as himself, and Scott Peters as police captain Pat Chambers.

THE GIRL IN BLACK STOCKINGS

1957 United Artists (B&W)
EXECUTIVE DIRECTOR: Aubrey Schenck
DIRECTOR: Howard W. Koch
SCREENWRITER: Richard Landon

A murder mystery set at a resort in Utah, starring Lex Barker and Anne Bancroft. Mamie Van Doren (who also did *Untamed Youth* and *Born Reckless* for director Koch) is third-billed. With Marie Windsor, Ron Randall, and Stuart Whitman.

GIRL IN GOLD BOOTS

1968 Geneni (B&W)
PRODUCER/DIRECTOR: Ted V. Mikels
SCREENWRITERS: Leighton L. Peatman, Art Names, John T. Wilson

A whirlpool of crime and sin nearly swallows a draft dodger and his girl in Hollywood. Critter Jones and Michele take jobs as janitor and go-go girl in a sleazy dive, but they end up hitchhiking back to the induction center after tangling with robbery, drugs, and murder. Jody Daniels and Leslie McCrae star, with Bara Byrnes, Tom Pace, Mark Herron, and Victor Izay. Songs include "Cowboy Santa," "Minnie Shimmy," "Wheels of Love," and "You Gotta Come Down." —CB

THE GIRL IN LOVERS LANE

1960 Filmgroup (B&W)
PRODUCER: Robert Roark
DIRECTOR: Charles R. Rondeau
SCREENWRITER: Jo Heims

Runaway Lowell Brown is befriended on the road by Brett Halsey. Brett courts

too young to know...too reckless to care..
THE GIRL IN LOVERS' LANE

A ROBERT ROARK PRODUCTION/A FILMGROUP PRESENTATION

Joyce Meadows during a stopover in a small town and is nearly lynched when she turns up dead. Local vigilantes are defused when Brown talks a confession out of half-wit Jack Elam. "Too young to know, too reckless to forget!" is the way the ads described the dead girl. Emile Meyer plays her father. A package deal with *The Wild Ride*.   —CB

GIRL IN ROOM 13

1961 Astor Pictures (U.S./Brazil)
PRODUCER: Marc Frederic
DIRECTOR: Richard E. Cunha
SCREENWRITERS: H.E. Barre,
  Richard E. Cunha

The director of *Missile to the Moon* and *The She Demons* filmed this in Brazil with 62-year-old Brian Donlevy as Steve Marshall, private eye. He tracks counterfeiters and killers and faces a cast of unknowns.

THE GIRL IN THE KREMLIN

1957 Universal (B&W)
PRODUCER: Albert Zugsmith
DIRECTOR: Russell Birdwell
SCREENWRITERS: Harry Rushkin,
  DeWitt Bodeen

Stalin didn't die! He had his face remodeled and took lots of rubles to Greece where he hid out with his nurse (Zsa Zsa Gabor). Zsa Zsa plays twin sisters! Stalin (Maurice Manson) likes bald women! With Lex Barker, William Schallert, and Jeffrey Stone. Zsa Zsa had to wait for *Queen of Outer Space* to get another role this good. Originally billed with *The Deadly Mantis*.

GIRL IN THE LEATHER SUIT: See HELL'S BELLES.

THE GIRL ON THE BRIDGE

1951 20th Century-Fox (B&W)
PRODUCER/DIRECTOR/SCREENWRITER:
  Hugo Haas

Hugo Haas and Beverly Michaels seem worried in The Girl on the Bridge.

Producer-director-writer Hugo Haas also stars as a lonely middle-aged watchmaker whose obsessive involvement with an unwed mother (pouty Beverly Michaels) leads to suicide. Blackmail, death, and desperation abound in a trashy follow-up to *Pickup*. With Robert Dane and Johnny Close. Most of poor Hugo's features receive one-star (or lower) ratings in movie-review books.

THE GIRLS FROM THUNDER STRIP

1966 American General
PRODUCER/DIRECTOR: David L. Hewitt
SCREENWRITER: Pat Boyette

Motorcycle gang and moonshine war, from a script by Pat Boyette (*Dungeons of Harrow*). Maray Ayres, Jody McCrea, Mick Mehas, Lindsay Crosby, and deejay Casey Kasem star. American General distributed other Hewitt productions, including *Hell's Chosen Few* and *Wizard of Mars*.   —CB

GIRLS! GIRLS! GIRLS!

1962 Paramount
PRODUCER: Hal B. Wallis
DIRECTOR: Norman Taurog
SCREENWRITERS: Allan Weiss, Edward Anhalt

Elvis movie No. 11! Poor but honest Elvis works on a tuna boat in Hawaii and moonlights as a nightclub singer just so he can buy back his late father's sailboat. Singer Stella Stevens and Laurel Goodwin both want Elvis. Laurel is rich but pretends to be poor. She buys the boat for Elvis. His pride is hurt but, after saving her from the lecherous owner of the tuna boat, he marries her, makes her sell the boat, and builds his own! With at least one classic song —"Return to Sender"—and the usual dogs like "Song of the Shrimp."

GIRLS, GUNS AND GANGSTERS

1958 United Artists (B&W)
PRODUCER/SCREENWRITER: Robert E. Kent
DIRECTOR: Edward Cahn

Gerald Mohr, Lee Van Cleef, Paul Fix, and Grant Richards are gangsters with guns. Mamie Van Doren is a girl. The same year, Cahn also directed *Jet Attack*, *The Curse of the Faceless Man*, *Suicide Battalion*, *Hong Kong Confidential*, and *It! The Terror from Beyond Space*. Mamie wasn't in any of them.

GIRLS IN PRISON

1956 AIP (B&W)
PRODUCER: Alex Gordon
DIRECTOR: Edward L. Cahn
SCREENWRITER: Lou Rusoff

The ads promised: "1000 trapped women ripped from steel cages by a shattering earthquake!" Joan Taylor faces violent death at the hands of crazed inmates on the trail of holdup money they believe she has hidden. Featuring Richard Denning as the prison chaplain who opens his own investigation, with Adele Jergens, Helen Gilbert, Jane Darwell, Diana Darrin, and Mae Marsh. A "double-sock rock and thrill show" with *Hot Rod Girl*. —CB

THE GIRLS ON THE BEACH

1965 Paramount
PRODUCER: Harvey Jacobson
DIRECTOR: William Witney
SCREENWRITER: David Malcolm

Vacationing sorority girls are led to believe that the Beatles are flying in to headline their house benefit. They aren't, so Noreen Corcoran, Linda Marshall, and Anna Capri attempt a simulation. Lesley Gore does "Leave Me Alone," "It's Gotta Be You," and "I Don't Want to Be a Loser"; the Crickets perform "Lonely Sea" and "La Bamba"; the Beach Boys sing "Little Honda" and the title song. The cast includes Martin West, Peter Brooks, Arnold Lessing, Steve Rogers, Aron Kincaid, Lana Wood, Ron Kennedy, and Bruno Ve Sota. —CB

GIRLS ON THE LOOSE

1958 Universal (B&W)
PRODUCERS: Harry Rybnich, Richard Kay
DIRECTOR: Paul Henreid
SCREENWRITERS: Alan Friedman, Dorothy Raison, Allen Rivkin

From the ads: "Crime-crazy gang girls looting, lying, living only for thrills!" Mara Corday masterminds a $200,000 payroll robbery, her kid sister falls in love with the investigating officer, and the hellcats kill each other over the loot. Featuring Lita Milan, Mark Richman, Abby Dalton, and Barbara Bostock—who sings a couple of songs. Co-released with Henreid's *Live Fast, Die Young*. —CB

GIRLS TOWN

1959 MGM (B&W)
PRODUCER: Albert Zugsmith
DIRECTOR: Charles Haas
SCREENWRITER: Robert Smith
ALSO RELEASED AS: *The Innocent and the Damned*

Bad girl Mamie Van Doren is sent up for a crime she didn't commit. In the correctional institution she looks for the real culprit. Was it Mel Torme? Paul Anka? Ray Anthony? The Platters? What are they all doing in a female lockup? How about Gloria Talbot, Cathy Crosby, Gigi Perreau, Maggie Hayes, or Sheilah Graham? Also with the hysterical Charles Chaplin, Jr., and big Jim Mitchum.

GIRLY

1970 Cinerama Releasing (England)
PRODUCER: Ronald J. Kahn
DIRECTOR: Freddie Francis
SCREENWRITER: Brian Comport
ALSO RELEASED AS: *Mumsy, Nanny, Sonny and Girly*

A family of active psychopaths living in an old Victorian house murder a woman, convince her drunken boyfriend he was responsible, threaten to blackmail him, and force him to move in. The "new friend" (Michael Bryant) seduces Mumsy, Girly, and Nanny, causing family discord. With axe murders and a boiled head. Vanessa Howard is Girly; Howard Trever is her murderous brother. With Ursula Howells and Pat Heywood. (**R**)

THE GLASS CAGE

1964 Futurama (B&W)
PRODUCERS: John Hoyt, Paul Lewis
DIRECTOR: Antonio Santean
SCREENWRITERS: John Hoyt, Antonio Santean
ALSO RELEASED AS: *Den of Doom, Don't Touch My Sister*

An interesting experimental mystery co-written, co-produced, and starring busy character actor John Hoyt (*Attack of the Puppet People*). As a police detective, he sends Robert Kelljan to investigate the murder of a prowler. The accused is lonely Arline Sax, who also plays her own domineering sister. Elisha Cook, Jr. is their father. A shorter version of the film deletes a scene with a beatnik

Mara Corday stays cool in Girls on the Loose.

rapist (King Moody). A real find on late-night TV.

THE GLASS WEB

1953 Universal (3-D)
PRODUCER: Albert J. Cohen
DIRECTOR: Jack Arnold
SCREENWRITERS: Leonard Lee, Robert Blees

A murder mystery with an interesting behind-the-scenes look at early television production. Edward G. Robinson, a meticulous scriptwriter for a live crime show based on current true stories, gives himself away by using facts only the real killer could know. With John Forsythe, Richard Denning, and Kathleen Hughes. It was one of Arnold's four 3-D projects.

GLEN AND RANDA

1971 UMC Pictures
PRODUCER: Sidney Glazier
DIRECTOR: Jim McBride
SCREENWRITERS: Lorenzo Mans, Rudolph Wurlitzer, Jim McBride

A young post-nuclear-holocaust couple search vainly for the city of Metropolis, which they have discovered in an old comic book. A 16mm feature blown up to 35mm showing a horrible future where everybody looks like an early '70s hippie. A bit of nudity and sex got it an early X. (**X**)

Originally released as:
Glen or Glenda.

WHAT WAS "HIS" SEX...?

"I CHANGED MY SEX!"

A DARING EXPOSE OF A MODERN PROBLEM... ★ ADULTS ONLY!

GLEN OR GLENDA
1953 Screen Classics (B&W)
PRODUCER: George Weiss
DIRECTOR/SCREENWRITER: Edward D. Wood, Jr.
ALSO RELEASED AS: *I Led Two Lives,*
I Changed My Sex, He or She, The
Transvestite

Wood's first feature is a very personal look at transvestism and transsexuals, extremely taboo topics 30 years ago. Police Inspector Warren (Lyle Talbot) discusses the suicide of a transvestite with Dr. Alton (Timothy Farrell). The doctor relates two true stories. Ex-marine Alan (Tommy Haynes) undergoes a sex-change operation and becomes Ann. Glen (played by the director under the name Daniel Davis) is afraid to tell his wife (played by Dolores Fuller, the director's wife) that he enjoys dressing up in angora sweaters and going out at night as Glenda. Bela Lugosi—as a godlike figure called the Spirit, who sits in an easy chair in a room full of skulls, shrunken heads, and voodoo idols—interrupts the story with such profound comments as: "Pull the string! Dance to that which one is created for!" He also mentions "big green dragons that sit on your doorstep and eat little boys." Another (offscreen) narrator ponders life: "The world is a strange place to live in. All those cars. All going someplace. All carrying humans. . . ." This all takes place in 67 minutes and is padded with a staggering amount of stock footage of a World War II battle, lightning, and a highway. The producer, George Weiss, also made exploitation films like *Test Tube Babies.* Wood's next feature was *Jail Bait. Glen or Glenda* was actually rereleased by Paramount in 1981. The world still wasn't ready.

THE GLORY STOMPERS
1967 AIP
PRODUCER: John Lawrence
DIRECTOR: Anthony M. Lanza
SCREENWRITERS: James Gordon White,
John Lawrence

Dennis Hopper's Black Souls capture Stompers leader Jody McCrea and his girl Chris Noel. Jody is beaten and left for dead as the Souls drag Noel off to be sold on the white-slavery market in Mexico. Jock Mahoney discovers the injured McCrea and joins his former friend on a manhunt. With Saundra Gayle, Astrid Warner, Robert Tessier, Lindsay Crosby, and Casey Kasem as Mouth. Music by Sidewalk Productions.
—CB

GLUMP: See *PLEASE DON'T EAT MY MOTHER.*

GO-GO BIG BEAT!

1964 El Dorado Pictures (England)
PRODUCER: Kenneth Hume
DIRECTORS/SCREENWRITERS: Kenneth Hume, Frank Gilpin

Three color shorts strung together, giving an early look at the Beatles era in England. Millie Small sings "My Boy Lollipop," Lulu and the Luvvers do "Shout," the Animals do "Baby Let Me Take You Home," and the Hollies do "Here I Go Again." Other groups include the Merseybeats, Brian Poole and the Tremolos, the Tornados, and the great Swinging Blue Jeans. The last third is a modern ballet called "Mods and Rockers" with a café scene and a gangfight, set to early Beatle songs performed by a cover band. It was advertised so as to make you think the Fab Four themselves were in it.

GO GO MANIA

1965 AIP (England)
PRODUCER: Harry Field
DIRECTOR/SCREENWRITER: Frederic Goode
ALSO RELEASED AS: *Pop Gear*

Goofy London deejay Jimmy Saville introduces 16 top recording acts. The first 15 perform on stylized studio sets. The group everybody paid to see, the Beatles, are shown in a 1963 newsreel taken at a Manchester concert. You can *almost* hear "She Loves You" and "Twist and Shout" over the screams. It's still a great collection of performances by the likes of the Animals, the Spencer Davis Group, the Nashville Teens, the Honeycombs, Billy J. Kramer and the Dakotas, Herman's Hermits, Peter and Gordon, and others who never made

it on these shores. "It's the new international beat that's rockin' the world!"

GO, JOHNNY GO!

1959 Hal Roach Distribution Corp. (B&W)
PRODUCER: Alan Freed
DIRECTOR/SCREENWRITER: Paul Landres

The fictional rise of a poor orphan boy named Johnny Melody (Jimmy Clanton) to rock 'n' roll stardom. Alan Freed, playing himself as usual, and Chuck Berry, doing likewise, help him reach the top. Besides performances by Clanton, Berry, Eddie Cochran, the Cadillacs, the Flamingos, Harvey of the Moonglows, and a few others, this feature has two unique sequences. It's the only film with Richie Valens, who was dead by the time it was released. He seems like the nice, shy 18-year-old that he was reported to be. Then there's an absolutely heart-stopping performance by Jackie Wilson, obviously one of the coolest men in the business.

Originally released as: God Told Me To.

285

GOD TOLD ME TO
1976 New World
PRODUCER/DIRECTOR/SCREENWRITER:
Larry Cohen
ALSO RELEASED AS: *Demon*

A remarkable, seldom-seen feature made in New York by the director of *It's Alive*. The title was changed to *Demon* after TV stations refused to run the original trailer. A religious cop (Tony Lo Bianco) investigates a series of senseless sniper murders. The killers, when asked why they did it, answer with the film's title. "God" turns out to be a pale, long-haired half-breed alien (Richard Lynch) whose mother (Sylvia Sidney), now in a rest home, was impregnated by beings from a flying saucer (shown in a flashback). With more surprises and an appearance by Andy Kaufman as a cop who goes berserk in a parade. Sandy Dennis and Deborah Raffin also star. **(R)**

THE GODSEND
1980 Cannon (England)
PRODUCER/DIRECTOR: Gabrielle Beaumont
SCREENWRITER: Olaf Pooley

A slow *Omen* copy with a couple adopting a little blond girl who somehow kills all four of their natural children. Angela Pleasence is the natural mother of the hellish kid. **(R)**

GODZILLA, KING OF THE MONSTERS
1954 Toho/Embassy (Japan) (B&W)
PRODUCER: Tomoyuki Tanaka
DIRECTORS: Inoshiro Honda,
Terry Morse (U.S. version)
SCREENWRITERS: Takeo Murata,
Inoshiro Honda
ORIGINALLY RELEASED AS: *Gojira*

Right after *The Beast from 20,000 Fathoms* stomped New York, Japan countered with Gojira—"Makes King Kong look like a midget!" screamed the ads. The ancient dinosaur with radioactive breath totally destroys Tokyo. Unlike most of the Godzilla sequels, which are aimed at kids, this is a very somber, serious science-fiction film about the (fictitious) result of nuclear radiation. The American release features a lot of Raymond Burr as reporter Steve Martin. Most of the new scenes are made to fit in pretty well by using doubles for the original actors. But at the end, on the boat, Burr seems to stare continually at nothing. It's too bad so much of the original story about the Kamikaze scientist hero with the eye patch seems to be missing. He (Akira Takarada) uses his oxygen destroyer to kill the atomic terror. Dr. Yamano is played by Takashi Shimura of *The Seven Samurai*. Giji Tsuburaya developed the monster suit. Akira Ifukube wrote the haunting musical score.

GODZILLA ON MONSTER ISLAND
1971 Toho/Cinema Shares (Japan)
DIRECTOR: Jun Fukuda
SCREENWRITER: Shinichi Sekizawa
ORIGINALLY RELEASED AS: *Gojira Tai Gaigan*

Alien cockroaches use Ghidrah the three-headed dragon and Gaigan (a metal bird with a buzz saw in its stomach) to invade Earth. Godzilla teams up with Angorus (his foe from *Gigantis the Fire Monster*) to save it. In probably the worst Godzilla movie, the monsters actually talk to each other. It takes place at a children's amusement park.

GODZILLA VS. MEGALON

1973 Toho/Cinema Shares (Japan)
PRODUCER: Tomoyuki Tanaka
DIRECTOR/SCREENWRITER: Jun Fukuda
ORIGINALLY RELEASED AS: *Gojira Tai Megaro*
Another laughable Godzilla film. Stationed under an ocean, the Seatopians (left over from *Atragon*) plan to conquer Earth with Gaigan (the metal bird monster with a buzz saw in its stomach) and Megalon (a new metal insect monster with drill arms). Godzilla teams up with Jet Jaguar, a brightly colored Ultraman-like cyborg that can change its size to fight the bad monsters. The human star is a little boy. When the monsters battle it's on a barren desert; no more costly model cities to topple. When it came out here the Dino DeLaurentiis *King Kong* was playing, so ads showed Godzilla and Megalon on top of the World Trade Center Towers. It's almost as funny as the new Kong film. The dubbing includes some ridiculous mild swearing like "those damn Seatopians" and "shit, Jet Jaguar, what'll we do?"

GODZILLA VS. THE BIONIC MONSTER

1974 Toho/Cinema Shares (Japan)
PRODUCER: Tomoyuki Tanaka
DIRECTOR: Jun Fukuda
SCREENWRITERS: Jun Fukuda,
Hiroyasa Yamura
ORIGINALLY RELEASED AS: *Gojira Tai Meka-Gojira*
ALSO RELEASED AS: *Godzilla vs. the Cosmic Monster*

SPACE MONSTERS WAR WITH...

GODZILLA FOR THE EARTH!

In COLOR and WIDESCREEN

GODZILLA ON MONSTER ISLAND

For Godzilla's 20th anniversary (and 14th film) Toho studios created Mecha-Godzilla, a worthy metal adversary. Of course, by this time Godzilla movies looked like long Ultraman TV shows. This one's got ape aliens, cyborgs, Angurus, and a ludicrous new dog monster with floppy ears. The creators of television's Bionic Man sued over the Bionic Monster title. Bionic was changed to Cosmic.

GODZILLA VS. THE COSMIC MONSTER: See *GODZILLA VS. THE BIONIC MONSTER.*

GODZILLA VS. THE SEA MONSTER

1966 Toho/Continental (Japan)
PRODUCER: Tomoyuki Tanaka
DIRECTOR: Jun Fukuda
SCREENWRITER: Shinichi Sekizawa
ORIGINALLY RELEASED AS: *Nankai No Dai Ketto*
Godzilla teams with Mothra to battle Ebirah, an evil giant shrimp. The tiny twin Alilenas put in an appearance, too.

Godzilla (center), his young son, and a horned neighbor in Godzilla's Revenge.

GODZILLA VS. THE SMOG MONSTER

1971 Toho/AIP (Japan)
PRODUCER: Tomoyuki Tanaka
DIRECTOR: Yoshimitsu Banno
SCREENWRITERS: Kaoru Mabuchi,
Yoshimitsu Banno
ORIGINALLY RELEASED AS: *Gojira Tai Hedora*

Godzilla battles a stinking giant live pile of bilge and garbage called Hedora ("pollution" in Japanese). As in all the '70s Godzilla films, there's a cute little boy star, lots of comedy, cartoon sequences, and the usual silly special effects. This film has the added attraction of songs like "Save the Earth" and lots of teens rockin' out on Mount Fuji. It was sometimes co-featured with *Frogs* for a not-too-popular ecology-horror-comedy double bill. It was the 11th Godzilla movie.

GODZILLA VS. THE THING

1964 Toho/AIP (Japan)
PRODUCER: Tomoyuki Tanaka
DIRECTOR: Inoshiro Honda
SCREENWRITER: Shinichi Sekizawa
ORIGINALLY RELEASED AS: *Gojira Tai Mosura*

Pitting Godzilla against Mothra was a good idea. The fight scenes don't resemble Saturday night wrestling matches as the ones in *King Kong vs. Godzilla* do, and it's always fun to see Mothra's tiny twin guardians, the Alilenas. Godzilla kills Mothra, but her giant egg (in the hands of carnival promoters) hatches and two giant caterpillars emerge. They spin a cocoon around the menacing dinosaur and drop him in the ocean. An enjoyable sequel.

GODZILLA'S REVENGE

1969 Toho/UPA (Japan)
PRODUCER: Tomoyuki Tanaka
DIRECTOR: Inoshiro Honda
SCREENWRITER: Shinichi Sekizawa
ORIGINALLY RELEASED AS: *Ord Kaiju
Daishingeki*

A Godzilla film for six-year-olds (most of them are aimed at 10-year-olds). A little boy having trouble with bullies and some crooks dreams that he goes to Monster Island, where most of the *Destroy All Monsters* cast of creatures are in residence. Godzilla teaches the kid to be brave and win his battles. Godzilla's son Minya talks and blows smoke rings. The theme song is "March of the Monsters." Lots of money was saved by using battle scenes from *Son of Godzilla* and *Godzilla vs. the Sea Monster*.

GOG
1954 United Artists (3-D)
PRODUCER: Ivan Tors
DIRECTOR: Herbert L. Strock
SCREENWRITER: Tom Taggart
Communist spies take over a computer that controls two non-humanoid robots. The robots kill scientists and destroy most of Herbert Marshall's lab. The many-armed robot tank Gog and its "brother" Magog are the out-of-control stars. With Richard Egan working for the Office of Scientific Investigation, a fictional group also featured in *The Magnetic Monster*, Constance Dowling, William Schallert, and Philip Van Zandt. Producer Tors, who provided the original story, soon started a similar television series, *Science Fiction Theater*.

GOKE, THE BODY SNATCHER FROM HELL: See BODY SNATCHER FROM HELL.

GOLD OF THE AMAZON WOMEN
1979 TV
PRODUCER: Alfred Leone
DIRECTOR: Mark L. Lester
SCREENWRITER: Sue Donen
Anita Ekberg is Queen Na-Eela in a big comeback effort. Na, Lee-Leeo, and other Amazon women from South America "follow" fortune hunters Bo Svenson and Donald Pleasence back to Manhattan. With Jasmine and Sarita. You won't believe it. From the director of *The Class of '84*.

GOLD RAIDERS
1951 United Artists (B&W)
PRODUCER: Bernard Glasser
DIRECTOR: Edward Bernds
SCREENWRITERS: Elwood Ullmann, William Lively
A Three Stooges movie you never heard about. Larry, Shemp, and Moe are the heroes in this forgotten Western starring George O'Brien. With Sheila Ryan, Lyle Talbor, Fuzzy Knight, and Monte Blue.

THE GOLDEN ARROW
1962 MGM (Italy)
PRODUCER: Goffredo Lombardo
DIRECTOR: Antonio Margheriti
SCREENWRITERS: Bruno Vailati, Augusto Frassinetti, Filippo Sanjust, Giorgio Prosperi, Giorgio Alorio
ORIGINALLY RELEASED AS: *La Freccia d'Oro*
Hassan the thief (Tab Hunter) becomes Sultan of Damascus after he shows he is the only one who can shoot a magic arrow. With a flying carpet, several genies, and Rossana Podesta.

THE GOLDEN IDOL
1954 Allied Artists (B&W)
PRODUCER/DIRECTOR/SCREENWRITER: Ford Beebe
An Arab chief steals an idol from the Watusis. Bomba (Johnny Sheffield) gets it back. With Anne Kimbell and Paul Guilfoyle.

THE GOLDEN MISTRESS
1954 United Artists (B&W)
PRODUCERS: Richard Kay, Harry Rybnick
DIRECTOR: Joel Judge
SCREENWRITERS: Lew Hewitt, Joel Judge
John Agar stars in a tale of voodoo and a golden idol. With Rosemarie Bowe and Kiki. Filmed in Haiti.

THE GOLDEN NYMPHS: See HONEYMOON OF HORROR.

THE GOLDEN VOYAGE OF SINBAD

1973 Columbia
PRODUCER: Charles H. Schneer
DIRECTOR: Gordon Hessler
SCREENWRITER: Brian Clemens

Fifteen years after the classic *Seventh Voyage of Sinbad*, stop-motion master Ray Harryhausen brought the ancient fantasy world of Sinbad back to the screen. It's lots of fun, even though this voyage can't touch the first one. Some critics blamed the script by Brian Clemens. Maybe they should have singled out the direction of Gordon Hessler and the bland acting of star John Phillip Law instead. The animation is great, but unfortunately, unlike the original monsters, none of the creatures is enormous. A one-eyed centaur battles a winged griffin, the wooden siren figurehead of the ship and six armed female statues are brought to life by the Black Prince Koura (Tom Baker, "Dr. Who"), and a tiny winged homunculus spies on Sinbad. Caroline Munro is the slave girl with an eye tattooed on her palm. Douglas Wilmer is the Grand Vizier, who wears a golden mask to hide his scarred face. It was such a box-office hit that the first Sinbad film was re-released to theaters and a third (*Sinbad and the Eye of the Tiger*) was put into production. The live action scenes for all three were filmed in Spain. Music by Miklos Rosa.

GOLDFINGER

1964 United Artists (England)
PRODUCERS: Albert R. Broccoli, Harry Saltzman
DIRECTOR: Guy Hamilton
SCREENWRITERS: Richard Maibaum, Paul Dehn

The third James Bond hit features Gert Fröbe as the supervillain who drives a solid-gold Rolls Royce and plans to rob Fort Knox, then destroy it with an atom bomb. 007 (Sean Connery) arrives in his gimmick-laden Astin Martin DB5 and investigates. He lingers in Miami with Goldfinger's secretary (Shirley Eaton) and later finds her suffocated in a coat of gold paint. Goldfinger's karate expert pilot Pussy Galore (former *Avengers* star Honor Blackman) fights then joins Bond. He saves the gold supply after surviving a possible laser beam castration and electrocuting Oddjob (Harold Sakata with a razor-brimmed derby). Goldfinger ends up sucked through a hole in a jet plane. Music by John Barry. Shirley Bassey sings the great hit-single theme song. It was the biggest Bond movie at the time. The first two were rereleased and *The Man from U.N.C.L.E.* carried the whole idea (minus the sex) to new extremes on television.

GOLIATH AND THE BARBARIANS

1960 AIP (Italy)
PRODUCER: Emimmo Salvi
DIRECTOR: Carlo Campogalliani
SCREENWRITERS: Emimmo Salvi, Gino Mangini
ORIGINALLY RELEASED AS: *Il Terror dei Barberi*

UPI 1/20/81: It's a very special car so there's a very special parking place for it. Carol Lee stands next to the Aston Martin DB-5 that she and her husband, Jerry, own. The car is parked in the silver, black, and gray game room in their suburban Philadelphia home. Built in 1963, the "fabulous machine" was used by "superspy James Bond" in the movie Goldfinger. It's still in perfect working order.

290

After two Hercules hits, Steve Reeves plays a different hero pretty much the same way. With the hero of *King Kong*, Bruce Cabot, and Chelo Alonso. A sound track album by Les Baxter is available.

GOLIATH AND THE DRAGON

1960 AIP (Italy/France)
PRODUCERS: Archille Piazzi, Gianni Fuchs
DIRECTOR: Vittorio Cottafavi
SCREENWRITERS: Mario Piccolo,
Archibald Zounds, Jr.
ORIGINALLY RELEASED AS: *La Vendetta de Ercole*

The first two Hercules films to follow the Steve Reeves hits were clearly made with American audiences in mind. One starred Jayne Mansfield (*The Loves of Hercules*). In this one, Broderick Crawford, fresh from the *Highway Patrol* TV show, stars as the evil toga-wearing king. Both feature mythical (and quite phony) dragons. Watch Brod lower female victims into his pit of horror! Hercules (Reg Park), who is called Goliath in American prints, battles a three-headed dog, the one-headed dragon, a giant bat, and the wind goddess. Great stuff. Les Baxter did the music that AIP added.

GOLIATH AND THE SINS OF BABYLON

1963 AIP (Italy)
PRODUCER: Elio Scardamaglia
DIRECTOR: Michele Lupo
SCREENWRITERS: Roberto Gianviti,
Francesco Scardamaglia,
Lionello De Felice
ORIGINALLY RELEASED AS: *Maciste, L'Eroe Piu Grande del Mondo*

Mark Forest plays Maciste again. In the dubbed version he's called Goliath. He wins a chariot race and rescues 21 virgins, keeping one for himself.

Gordon Scott shows off in Goliath and the Vampires.

GOLIATH AND THE VAMPIRES

1961 AIP (Italy)
PRODUCER: Paolo Moffa
DIRECTOR: Giacomo Gentilomo
SCREENWRITERS: Sergio Corbucci,
Duccio Tessari
ORIGINALLY RELEASED AS: *Maciste Contro il Vampiro*
ALSO RELEASED AS: *The Vampires*

Former Tarzan Gordon Scott plays Italian hero Maciste. His name was changed to the more familiar Goliath in America. He saves slave women from a vampire who turns men into human robots. Gianna Maria Canale is an "amazon beauty." A Dino DeLaurentiis presentation. One of the more exciting *Hercules*-type pictures. Scott repeated the role in *Samson and the 7 Miracles*.

GOLIATH AWAITS

1981 TV
PRODUCERS: Hugh Benson, Richard Bluel
DIRECTOR: Kevin Conner
SCREENWRITERS: Richard Bluel, Pat Fielder

Action...Excitement...Spectacle beyond your wildest dreams!

GOLIATHON

A SHAW BROTHERS PRESENTATION • Starring LEE HASSEN and introducing EVELYNE KRAFT • Produced by RUNME SHAW
Directed by HOMER GAUGH • Special Effects by ANDREW RYAN • Released by WORLD NORTHAL CORPORATION
PG

Christopher Lee plays the captain/ dictator of 300 people who have managed to survive under the water ever since their ship sank 40 years ago. The cramped utopian society is invaded by divers and the power source malfunctions. Originally an overlong four-hour two-part special. With John Carradine as a ham actor, Eddie Albert, Frank Gorshin, Jean Marsh, Alex Cord, Robert Forster, Mark Harmon, and John McIntire. Filmed on the Queen Mary.

GOLIATHON
1977 World Northal (Hong Kong)
PRODUCER: Runme Shaw
DIRECTOR: Homer Gaugh
SCREENWRITER: Li Chen
ALSO RELEASED AS: *The Mighty Peking Man*

Hilarious *King Kong* copy with the addition of a beautiful blond jungle woman as the giant ape's friend. The jungle woman, who is always on the verge of losing her top, falls in love with an Oriental adventurer. His expedition takes the creature back to Hong Kong to exhibit it in an arena. All the Kong clichés are used. The effects are pathetic and the dialogue is priceless. Almost as funny as *Infra Man*. Evelyn Kraft, of the German *Lady Dracula*, stars.

GOMAR — THE HUMAN GORILLA: See NIGHT OF THE BLOODY APES.

GOOD TIMES
1967 Columbia
PRODUCER: Lindsley Parsons
DIRECTOR: William Friedkin
SCREENWRITER: Tony Barrett

Cher, not Chic. Sonny and Cher play themselves in a spoof of old movies directed by Friedkin before he turned to pea soup and hankies in left jeans pockets. Sonny dreams he and Cher star in a Western, a gangster movie, and a Tarzan film. As film tycoon Mordicus, George Sanders is the villain in each segment. Sonny distrusts him and decides to concentrate on their singing career. Too bad he didn't stick to his decision in real life. The once happily married couple sing a number of tunes, including their smash "I Got You, Babe." The worst was yet to come ("Chastity"). With China Lee (*Playboy*'s Miss August 1964) and Edy Williams (*Beyond the Valley of the Dolls*).

GOODBYE GEMINI

1970 Cinerama Releasing Corporation
(England)
PRODUCER: Peter Snell
DIRECTOR: Alan Gibson
SCREENWRITER: Edmund Ward

A nice little psychological study of incestuous twins. Martin Potter (who starred in *Satyricon* the same year) gets jealous of a man who pays too much attention to his live-in twin sister (Judy Geeson), so he gets him drunk, takes him to a homosexual orgy, and snaps pictures. The next step is to get his sister to help kill the intruder. Then he kills her and himself. With Sir Michael Redgrave. **(R)**

GORATH

1963 Toho/Columbia (Japan)
PRODUCER: Toho Co.
DIRECTOR: Inoshiro Honda
SCREENWRITER: Takeshi Kimuri
ORIGINALLY RELEASED AS: *Yosei Gorasu*

Inoshiro Honda found time between directing *Godzilla* features to do this little-known tale. In 1980 (the future) a massive runaway planet is about to collide with Earth. Quick-thinking Japanese scientists move Earth with large rockets, but resulting earthquakes unleash a tusked terror from the polar regions. Unfortunately the walrus scene was cut for the American release.

THE GORE GORE GIRLS

1972 Lewis Pictures
PRODUCER/DIRECTOR: Herschell Gordon Lewis
SCREENWRITER: Alan J. Dachman
ALSO RELEASED AS: *Blood Orgy*

Lewis' last horror film is a sick but humorous mixture of sex and gore, and is more offensive than any of his earlier hits (like *Blood Feast* and *2000 Maniacs*). Strippers who work for nightclub owner Henny Youngman (!) are slaughtered in various gross ways. An egotistical, fey detective and a female reporter investigate. A women's lib group attacks the strippers on stage. A Vietnam vet sits at the bar drawing faces on melons, then splatting them all over with his fist. Henny tells jokes. It was one of the first movies given an X for violence. **(X)**

GORGO

1961 MGM (England)
PRODUCER: Wilfred Eades
DIRECTOR: Eugene Lourie
SCREENWRITERS: John Loring, Daniel Hyatt

After directing the animated *Beast from 20,000 Fathoms*, which inspired *Godzilla*, Eugene Lourie directed this giant dinosaur film, Japanese style (man in a monster suit). Gorgo, a 65-foot-tall prehistoric dinosaur, is captured off the shore of Ireland and taken to London as a circus exhibit. Soon his 250-foot-tall mom arrives and destroys "Westminster Abbey, the tower of Big Ben, and the rosy red cheeks of the little children." Scenes with a diving bell and a roller coaster are direct throwbacks to *Beast*. With Bill Travers and William Sylvester.

THE GORGON

1964 Hammer/Columbia (England)
PRODUCER: Anthony Nelson-Keys
DIRECTOR: Terence Fisher
SCREENWRITER: John Gilling

After remaking everything in sight, the Hammer Studios decided to exploit mythology. In 19th-century Europe a doctor (Peter Cushing) protects a girl (Barbara Shelley) who becomes a mythical snake-haired creature at night. Men who gaze at her turn to stone! A professor (Christopher Lee) arrives to find out why so many stiffs are turning up and cuts the hissing, writhing serpent's head off.

THE GORILLA

1939 20th Century-Fox (B&W)
PRODUCERS: Darryl F. Zanuck,
Harry Joe Brown
DIRECTOR: Allan Dwan
SCREENWRITERS: Rian James, Sid Silvers

An old mystery-comedy play that had already been filmed twice (in '27 and '30) was revived yet again as a vehicle for the Ritz Brothers. The constantly mugging brothers play detectives investigating the monkey-suit murders. Bela Lugosi was thrown in as another sinister butler, but Lionel Atwill stars. With Anita Louise, Edward Norris, and comedienne Patsy Kelly.

GORILLA: See NABONGA.

GORILLA AT LARGE

1954 20th Century-Fox (3-D)
PRODUCER: Robert L. Jacks
DIRECTOR: Harmon Jones
SCREENWRITERS: Leonard Praskins,
Barney Slater

Unbelievable all-star stupidity about a "real" gorilla killing people at a circus. Of course you can't tell the real gorilla from the actor in a suit, since they're both actors in a suit. In case you didn't know the ending already—Anne Bancroft is the murderess in a gorilla suit! Her act consists of swinging over a cage of "real" gorillas. Cameron Mitchell (who is top-billed) also wears a gorilla suit. Raymond Burr had already been a gorilla in *Bride of the Gorilla*, so he doesn't. Also on hand for the 3-D hilarity are Lee J. Cobb as a detective, Lee Marvin, Billy Curtis, and Warren Stevens. With Goliath, "the hate beast that loves to kill." Director Jones went on to *Beast of Budapest* and *Don't Worry We'll Think of a Title*.

GRADUATION DAY

1982 Bedford
PRODUCER/DIRECTOR: Herb Freed
SCREENWRITERS: Anne Marisse, Herb Freed

Coach Christopher George roots for soon to be slaughtered teens in Graduation Day.

Yet another cliché *Halloween*-inspired body-count movie. Members of a high school track team are being killed. By the coach (Christopher George)? The principal (Michael Pataki)? Probably not. Interesting to note that the gore effects were done by a young woman (Jill Rockow). (R)

GRAVE DESIRES: See THE VAMPYRE'S NIGHT ORGY.

GRAVE OF THE VAMPIRE
1972 Entertainment Pyramid
PRODUCER: Daniel Cady
DIRECTOR: John Hayes
SCREENWRITERS: John Patrick Hayes, David Chase
ALSO RELEASED AS: *Seed of Terror*
In the opening of one of the more shocking movies you might catch on TV, Michael Pataki is a vampire who rapes a woman in an open grave. The pale, pathetic mother has a baby who drinks her blood (from a bottle) until she dies. The kid grows up into a very odd reluctant vampire (William Smith) and sets out to kill his father. He finds him teaching a college course on occultism. He also falls in love with a neighbor and tries to restrain his vampire urges when she wants to join the undead. William Smith had just appeared in the last season of *Hawaii Five-0*. Michael Pataki starred in *Dracula's Dog* a few years later. (R)

GRAVEYARD OF HORROR
1971 International Films (Spain)
DIRECTOR/SCREENWRITER: Miguel Madrid
ORIGINALLY RELEASED AS: *Necrophagus*
A man cares for his hairy ghoul brother by tending his grave and feeding him fresh corpses. A strange feature best viewed at 5:30 A.M. on television.

THE GRAVESIDE STORY: See COMEDY OF TERRORS.

GRAVEYARD TRAMPS: See INVASION OF THE BEE GIRLS.

GREAT ALLIGATOR
1980 (Italy)
PRODUCER: Lawrence Martin
DIRECTOR/SCREENWRITER: Sergio Martino
ORIGINALLY RELEASED AS: *Il Fiume del Grande Caimano*
A direct-to-American-network-TV quickie with the same main cast and crew as *Screamers*. Mel Ferrer thoughtlessly keeps his lucrative African resort open even while tourists and locals are being devoured by a giant alligator. (Mel also encountered gators in Tobe Hooper's *Death Trap*.) Barbara Bach co-stars and Richard Johnson has a ridiculous bit as a bearded hermit. Not as good as the same year's *Alligator* but better than *Crocodile*.

GREAT GABBO
1929 Sono-Art Worldwide (B&W and color)
PRODUCER/DIRECTOR: James Cruze
SCREENWRITER: F. Hugh Herbert
Incredibly awkward backstage drama/ musical! Erich von Stroheim (complete with monocle) gives an eccentric performance as an egocentric ventriloquist who abuses his devoted female helper (Betty Compton) and talks with his singing dummy Otto. The action halts periodically for awful song-and-dance numbers like "Caught in a Web of Love," in which chorus girls dangle from a giant web controlled by a man in a ridiculous spider costume. Scenes with Stroheim and Otto singing in a restaurant are priceless. You'll never forget this creaky old talkie based on "The Rival Dummy" by Ben Hecht.

THE GREAT HOUDINIS
1976 TV
DIRECTOR/SCREENWRITER: Melville Shavelson
Paul Michael Glaser stars in a pretty good bio of the famous escape artist/magician. Sally Struthers is his wife, Ruth Gordon his mother. With Peter Cushing as Arthur Conan Doyle, Vivian Vance (in a rare dramatic role), Adrienne Barbeau, Wilfrid Hyde-White, Clive Revill, Nina Foch, Jack Carter, and Bill Bixby.

THE GREAT RUPERT
1950 Eagle-Lion (B&W)
PRODUCER: George Pal
DIRECTOR: Irving Pichel
SCREENWRITER: Laslo Vadnay
George Pal's first feature production stars Jimmy Durante and Terry Moore (who had just been in *Mighty Joe Young*) in a light comic adventure about a squirrel who dances (in stop-motion animation) and finds hidden money in an old house. With Tom Drake.

GREAT WHITE
1982 Film Ventures (Italy)
PRODUCERS: Maurizio Amati, Ugo Tucci
DIRECTOR: Enzo G. Castellari
SCREENWRITER: Mark Princi
Seven years after *Jaws* those shark-attack movies keep on coming. This one stars James Franciscus (*Cat O' Nine Tales*) and Vic Morrow (*Humanoids of the Deep*). It's so close to its inspiration that Universal was able to obtain a preliminary injunction in court to stop any further showings. People who managed to catch it say it's pretty funny.

GREEN HELL
1940 Universal (B&W)
PRODUCER: Harry Edington
DIRECTOR: James Whale
SCREENWRITER: Frances Marion
An archaeological expedition to the Brazilian jungle finds lost Inca temples, head-hunting cannibals, and poison darts. Douglas Fairbanks, Jr., and Joan Bennett star. With George Sanders, Vincent Price (as Bennett's weak husband), Alan Hale, Noble Johnson (as an Indian chief), and Iron Eyes Cody (as a snake dancer). The Inca temple set became an Egyptian temple in *The Mummy's Hand*. Karl Freund was the cameraman. It was the second-to-last effort from the director of many classic Universal horror films. Most viewers, including star Price, found it hysterically funny.

THE GREEN HORNET
1974 Acquarius
PRODUCER: William Dozier
DIRECTORS: Norman Foster, Jerry Thomas
Three episodes of the short-lived 1966 TV series were thrown together to cash in on the popularity of Bruce Lee (who died in '73). Ads read "Bruce Lee as Kato—in *The Green Hornet*." He does get in a few fights, but the unrelated stories about rich game hunters killing gangsters, phony aliens with a bomb, and a tong war are pretty tedious. Some idiot made a few continuity switches in the editing, making things even more senseless. A drawing of a hornet is shown wherever commercials used to be. With Van Williams.

THE GREEN SLIME
1968 Toei/MGM (U.S./Japan)
PRODUCERS: Ivan Reiner, Walter Manley
DIRECTOR: Kinji Fukasaku
SCREENWRITERS: Charles Sinclair, William Finger, Tom Rowe
ALSO RELEASED AS: *Gamma Sango Uchu Daisakusen*
Green newspaper ads for this space disaster announced: "The Green Slime are coming!" then "The Green Slime are here." The Green Slime were the most laughably unconvincing monsters of any Japanese production in years.

The one-eyed creatures with stiff tentacles multiplied when shot! What should astronauts Richard Jaeckel and Robert Horton do? Fight over Luciana Paluzzi in her fetching minidress at an outerspace party, of course. Uncredited midgets played the slime monsters. The theme song was sold on a 45.

GREENWICH VILLAGE STORY

1963 Shawn International (B&W)
PRODUCER/DIRECTOR/SCREENWRITER:
Jack O'Connell
ALSO RELEASED AS: *Birthplace of the Hootenanny, They Love as They Please*

Robert Hogan and Melinda Plank belong to the beat generation. Robert promises to marry the ballet-dancing Melinda if his first novel is a success. The book is panned and Melinda dies from an abortion while Robert is in the country sulking. With Tani Seitz, James Frawley, John Brent, and John C. Avildsen, later the director of *Joe* and *Rocky*, as Alvie. O'Connell also directed *Revolution*.   –CB

GRIM REAPER

1981 Film Ventures (Italy)
PRODUCER: Oscar Santaniello
DIRECTOR: Joe D'Amato
SCREENWRITER: Lewis Montefiore
ORIGINALLY RELEASED AS: *Anthropophagous*

Tisa Farrow of *Zombie* fame is stuck on a Greek island this time. Most of the population has been devoured by a crusty-faced ghoul named Klaus. Director D'Amato should stick to sex films. Tisa is, of course, Mia's sister and a daughter of Maureen O'Sullivan and director John Farrow. **(R)**

GRIMM'S FAIRY TALES FOR ADULTS

1970 Cinemation (W. Germany)
DIRECTORS: Rolf Thiele; Helen Gray (U.S. version)
SCREENWRITER: Rolf Thiele
ORIGINALLY RELEASED AS: *Grimms Märchen Für Lusterne Pärchen*
ALSO RELEASED AS: *The Erotic Adventures of Snow White*

Jerry Gross imported and re-edited this sex fantasy in which Marie Liljadahl sleeps topless in a plastic coffin until she is revived by an amorous snake with a little crown. It has a lot of pretty sick scenes, including Cinderella's ugly stepsisters cutting their toes off in order to fit into her slipper (which is, incidentally, what happens in the original Grimm version of the tale). The first of many "adult" versions of famous children's stories. **(X)**

GRIZZLY

1976 Film Ventures
PRODUCERS/SCREENWRITERS: David Sheldon, Harvey Flaxman
DIRECTOR: William Girdler
ALSO RELEASED AS: *Killer Grizzly*

Girdler is best known for *Abby* (1974), his black version of *The Exorcist*. This is his bear version of *Jaws*. Starring with what the ads called "18 feet of gut-crunching, man-eating terror".

Marie Liljedahl as Snow White in Grimms Fairy Tales for Adults.

18 feet of gut-crunching man-eating terror!

GRIZZLY

CHRISTOPHER GEORGE • **ANDREW PRINE** • **RICHARD JAECKEL**

NOT SINCE JAWS!

PG

WARNING!
MAY BE TOO INTENSE FOR YOUNGER CHILDREN

are Christopher George and Richard Jaeckel, both of whom starred in Girdler's '77 feature *Day of the Animals*. Also with Andrew Prine.

GRUESOME TWOSOME

1968 Mayflower
PRODUCER/DIRECTOR: Herschell Gordon Lewis
SCREENWRITER: Louise Downe
An obscure gore film from the director of *Blood Feast*. A young imbecile (Rodney Bedell) scalps young women for his mother, a wigmaker. The victims are boarders in the twosome's home.

GUESS WHAT HAPPENED TO COUNT DRACULA

1970 Merrick International
PRODUCER: Leo Rivers
DIRECTOR/SCREENWRITER: Laurence Merrick
This terrible little quickie was slapped together and beat the better known *Count Yorga* to the nation's screens. Des Roberts stars as Count Adrian, a modern vampire at a discotheque called Dracula's Castle. Some scenes were filmed at the famous "Magic Castle" in Hollywood. There are rumored to be two other versions, an R-rated one with more orgy scenes and a homosexual one. Characters have names like Imp, Vamp, Hunch, and Rut. Writer-director-executive producer Merrick also made *Black Angels*.

A GUIDE FOR THE MARRIED MAN

1967 20th Century-Fox
PRODUCER: Frank McCarthy
DIRECTOR: Gene Kelly
SCREENWRITER: Frank Tarloff
Walter Matthau convinces friend Robert Morse that he should fool around with other women in order to preserve his marriage (to Inger Stevens). Matthau illustrates his point with a lot of humorous stories acted out by a lot of famous people (often in tiny roles). Among them are Jayne Mansfield in her first Hollywood film since 1961 (she only made one more—*Single Room Furnished*), Jackie Joseph (*Little Shop of Horrors*), Jack Benny, Lucille Ball, Jeffrey Hunter, Marty Ingels, Sam Jaffe, Wally Cox and Louis Nye. The Turtles sing the theme song. Music by Johnny (John) Williams.

THE GUN RIDERS: See FIVE BLOODY GRAVES.

GUNS, SIN, AND BATHTUB GIN: See THE LADY IN RED.

GUNSLINGER

1956 AIP (B&W)
PRODUCER/DIRECTOR: Roger Corman
SCREENWRITER: Charles Griffith
A *Johnny Guitar* remake involving a scramble for land in the path of a projected railroad and two strong frontier

women set on shooting each other out of the picture. Beverly Garland is the new marshal, having taken over after her husband was shot over breakfast; Allison Hayes is the land-scam mastermind who imports John Ireland to eliminate anyone who gets in the way. Big decision for Ireland when he is caught in a three-way showdown: "Hired to kill the woman he loves!" is the way the ads put it. With Martin Kingsley, Jonathan Haze, Bruno Ve Sota, and Chris Alcaide. —CB

GURU, THE MAD MONK

1971 Nova International

PRODUCER/DIRECTOR/SCREENWRITER:
Andy Milligan

ALSO RELEASED AS: *Garu, the Mad Monk*

Father Guru, his vampire mistress, and hunchback servant Igor torture prisoners on the island of Mortavia. Filmed on the island of Manhattan in St. Peter's Church. Sixty-two minutes that only seem like hours.

GUYANA, CULT OF THE DAMNED

1980 Universal (Mexico/Panama/Spain)

PRODUCER/DIRECTOR/SCREENWRITER:
René Cardona, Jr.

The ultimate laughable exploitation film by the director of *Survive*, a cannibal/disaster hit. The incredible cast flown down to profit from the mass suicide includes Stuart Whitman as Reverend Jim Johnson (the names were changed to protect the innocent?), Bradford Dillman as Dr. Gary Straw the Kool-Aid mixer, Joseph Cotten, John Ireland, Gene Barry, Yvonne De Carlo, and Jennifer Ashley. Extremely sleazy, even after cutting to get an R rating, and much more enjoyable than the TV feature that followed. It later made a perfect double bill with *Amin—The Rise and Fall*. **(R)**

GUYANA TRAGEDY: THE STORY OF JIM JONES

1980 TV

PRODUCERS: Ernest Tidyman, Sam Manners
DIRECTOR: William A. Graham
SCREENWRITER: Ernest Tidyman

Originally a four-hour, two-part epic, this version of the '78 Kool-Aid drinking festival won Emmies. The ads asked: "Why would 913 people put their lives in his hands? Why?" What I want to know is: Why would millions of people spend two nights glued to their TV sets to watch mass suicides? Powers Booth plays Jim Jones. Lots of drugs and implied sex. With Ned Beatty, Veronica Cartwright, James Earl Jones, Diane Ladd, Randy Quaid, Rosalind Cash (*The Omega Man*), Brenda Vaccaro (*Death Weekend*), and Meg Foster (*Tender Flesh*). Jones is portrayed as a drug-crazed idol who has frequent sex with female followers (like a rock star). Scriptwriter Ernest Tidyman also wrote *Shaft*.

Rev. Jim Johnson (Stuart Whitman) instructs his followers to leave San Francisco with him in Guyana, Cult of the Damned.

THE H MAN

1958 Toho/Columbia (Japan)
PRODUCER: Tomoyuki Tanaka
DIRECTOR: Inoshiro Honda
SCREENWRITER: Takeshi Kimura
ORIGINALLY RELEASED AS:
Uomini H; Bijyo to Ekitainingen

Men are turned into oozing green radioactive slime by an atomic bomb. The colorful killer goop dissolves and eats other people. The original title translates as "Beautiful Women and the Hydrogen Man." Sort of a more serious version of *The Blob*, which was released the same year.

HALF HUMAN

1955 Toho/DCA (Japan) (B&W)
PRODUCER: Tomoyuki Tanaka
DIRECTOR: Inoshiro Honda,
Kenneth G. Crane (U.S. Version)
SCREENWRITER: Takeo Murata
ORIGINALLY RELEASED AS: Jujin Yukiotako

In this abominable-snowman film a giant apelike creature (with a really creepy-looking baby) is discovered in the mountains of northern Japan. The film was Americanized with new scenes featuring John Carradine and Morris Ankrum. Director Honda, who had just done *Godzilla*, made *Rodan* next.

HALLOWEEN

1978 Compass International
PRODUCERS/SCREENWRITERS: John Carpenter,
Debra Hill
DIRECTOR: John Carpenter

America's film reviewers fell over themselves praising this influential low-budget ($300,000) horror film. It made countless millions and we're still suffering from all the inferior imitations ground out by every producer trying to make a quick buck. It's good, but Carpenter's *Assault on Precinct 13* was even better. Donald Pleasence is the grim psychiatrist after the indestructible mad killer. Jamie Lee Curtis is Laurie, the terrified, virginal, small town survivor. P.J. Soles and Nancy Loomis aren't so lucky. With clips from *The Thing* and *Forbidden Planet*. The director prepared new scenes for the '81 TV showing. The inevitable sequel also came out in '81. A *Halloween* video game is available. **(R)**

HALLOWEEN II

1981 Universal
PRODUCERS/SCREENWRITERS: Debra Hill,
John Carpenter
DIRECTOR: Rick Rosenthal

"All-New! MORE Of The Night He Came Home," read the posters, which should give you an idea of where this thing was coming from. Michael, the killer from *Halloween*, gets up and kills again and again and again, until Jamie Lee Curtis finds out that he's her brother and sets him on fire. It's miles ahead of the other *Halloween* imitations—but it's still an imitation.

Controversy raged about this film when director Rosenthal was quoted as saying that executive producer John Carpenter came in at the end of the filming and screwed it all up by shooting gore inserts. Members of Carpenter's loyal crew, however, indicate that Carpenter was only trying to straighten out Rosenthal's screw-ups. Carpenter, always the gentleman, kept out of the controversy, and after a few weeks nobody cared. With Donald Pleasence and a scene from *Night of the Living Dead*. A sound track album is available. **(R)**   –BM

HALLOWEEN III: SEASON OF THE WITCH

1982 Universal
PRODUCERS: Debra Hill, John Carpenter
DIRECTOR/SCREENWRITER: Tommy Lee Wallace

Not another slasher sequel, but a fun if farfetched new Halloween story with a cheat title. Irish actor Dan O'Herlihy plays a Druid descendant with a diaboli-

Upper Left: A production shot from Halloween.

Upper right: Jamie Lee Curtis in Halloween II.

Below: Tom Atkins and Stacey Nelkins visit her late father's costume shop in Halloween III.

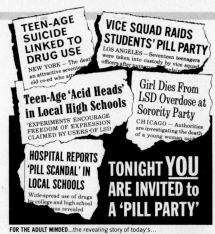

TEEN-AGE SUICIDE LINKED TO DRUG USE

NEW YORK — The death an attractive seventeen old co-ed who att...

VICE SQUAD RAIDS STUDENTS' PILL PARTY

LOS ANGELES — Seventeen teenagers were taken into custody by vice squad officers after numerous complain...

Teen-Age 'Acid Heads' in Local High Schools

'EXPERIMENTS' ENCOURAGE FREEDOM OF EXPRESSION CLAIMED BY USERS OF LSD

Girl Dies From LSD Overdose at Sorority Party

CHICAGO — Authorities are investigating the death of a young woman said...

HOSPITAL REPORTS 'PILL SCANDAL' IN LOCAL SCHOOLS

Wide-spread use of drugs by college and high school was revealed

TONIGHT **YOU** ARE INVITED to A 'PILL PARTY'

FOR THE ADULT MINDED...the revealing story of today's...

HALLUCINATION GENERATION STARRING GEORGE MONTGOMERY · DANNY STONE

cal plan. He has robots manufacture masks containing microchips from Stonehenge. The trick-or-treaters who buy them blow up in a mass of snakes, bugs, and slime while watching a television commercial for the masks on Halloween. The three glow-in-the-dark masks used in the film are actually for sale. They were made at the famous Don Post studio, which economically serves as the madman's mask factory in the movie. Stacey Nelkin and the hero doctor (Tom Atkins from *Escape from New York* and *The Fog*) race to save the nation's children from an explosive end. Annual Halloween features with unrelated plots are planned. (**R**)

HALLUCINATION GENERATION

1966 Trans-American (B&W with color sequences)
PRODUCER: Nigel Cox
DIRECTOR: Edward A. Mann
SCREENWRITER: Edward A. Mann
George Montgomery is the psychedelic advisor to a circle of young expatriates living on the Isle of Ibiza. Visitor Danny Stone, who avoids taking part in the

fun until his mother cuts off his allowance, seeks help in a monastery after an LSD-induced crime spree results in the murder of a Barcelona antiques dealer. The real world is black-and-white, the LSD trips are in color. Featuring Renate Kasche, Tom Baker, Marianne Kanter, and Steve Rowland. Filmed in Spain.   —CB

THE HALLUCINATORS: See THE NAKED ZOO.

THE HAND

1961 AIP (England) (B&W)
PRODUCER: Bill Luckwell
DIRECTOR: Henry Cass
SCREENWRITERS: Ray Cooney, Tony Hilton
Actually it's about a couple of hands. In Burma during World War II, captured British soldiers who refuse to talk have their right hands severed. Their captain (Derek Bond) is less patriotic. Years later, in contemporary London, a series of amputation murders are investigated by detectives. Who do you think did it? It's pretty chilling.

THE HAND

1981 Orion/Warner Brothers
PRODUCER: Edward R. Pressman
DIRECTOR/SCREENWRITER: Oliver Stone
After newspaper cartoonist Michael Caine loses his right hand and his career in a car wreck, wife Andrea Marcovicci pegs him as a loser, and he loses her, too. But he's not alone—his hand comes back to keep him company, and to help him kill off some of the people who've been bugging him. Another angry and depressing picture from Stone, who wrote and directed *Seizure* and won an Oscar for his *Midnight Express* screenplay. With Viveca Lindfors. (**R**)   —BM

HAND OF DEATH

1961 20th Century-Fox (B&W)
PRODUCER/SCREENWRITER: Eugene Ling
DIRECTOR: Gene Nelson

Working at his desert lab, scientist John Agar develops a gas he believes will avert nuclear war. Instead it turns him into a horrible bloated monster whose touch means instant death! The cracked face makeup in this low-budget film is a unique creation. With ex-Stooge Joe Besser and future Munster Butch Patrick. Paula Raymond (*Beast from 20,000 Fathoms*) is Agar's suffering wife.

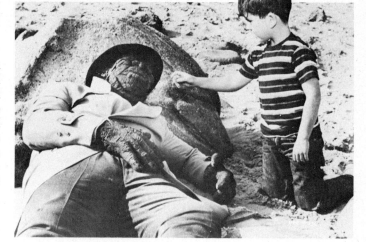

A bloated John Agar in Hand of Death.

THE HAND OF NIGHT

1966 Schoenfeld Films (England) (B&W)
PRODUCER: Harry Field
DIRECTOR: Frederic Goode
SCREENWRITER: Bruce Stewart
ALSO RELEASED AS: *Beast of Morocco*

William Sylvester visits an archaeologist in northern Africa, where he falls for a woman who turns out to be a vampire. With Aliza Gur, Terence De Marney, and Diane Clare. Filmed in Morocco.

HANDS OF A STRANGER

1962 Allied Artists (B&W)
PRODUCERS: Newton Arnold,
Michael DuPont
DIRECTOR/SCREENWRITER: Newton Arnold

An interesting American version of *The Hands of Orlac*. James Stapleton is a famous pianist whose mutilated hands are replaced surgically. Unable to play the piano anymore, he goes crazy and seeks revenge on the doctors who performed the operation and the cabdriver (now blind) who caused the accident. With Irish McCalla (*Sheena, Queen of the Jungle*), Sally Kellerman (in a small role), Paul Lukather, and Joan Harvey.

THE HANDS OF ORLAC

1961 Continental (France/England) (B&W)
PRODUCERS: Steven Pallos, Donald Taylor
DIRECTOR: Edmond T. Gréville
SCREENWRITERS: John Baines,
Edmond T. Gréville

Mel Ferrer is Orlac, a concert pianist whose hands are destroyed in a plane crash. A surgeon (Donald Wolfit) grafts the hands of a condemned strangler onto the confused Orlac, who now thinks he's a killer. In Marseilles, a magician named Nero (Christopher Lee) and his reluctant assistant (Dany Carrel) decide to blackmail him. With an odd haircut and eye makeup, Lee is the film's highlight: he nearly scares Ferrer to death and kills his assistant on stage by sticking swords through her in an upright "trick" coffin. With Donald Pleasence. Two versions were filmed simultaneously—one in French, one in English—a practice more common in the early '30s.

HANDS OF THE RIPPER

1971 Hammer/Universal (England)
PRODUCER: Aida Young
DIRECTOR: Peter Sasdy
SCREENWRITER: L.W. Davidson

A critically acclaimed thriller similar to *The Daughter of Dr. Jekyll*. Welsh actress Angharad Rees stars as the daughter of Jack the Ripper. She may or may not be following in dad's murderous footsteps. Eric Porter is a kind doctor who tries to help. **(R)**

HANGAR 18
1980 Taft International
PRODUCER: Charles E. Sellier, Jr.
DIRECTOR: James L. Conway
SCREENWRITER: Steven Thornley
Darren McGavin leads a group of scientists studying a flying saucer the government has hidden in a warehouse. Some post–*Close Encounters* aliens finally emerge to wake up the audience for a while. With Robert Vaughn, Joseph Campanella, Tom Hallick, William Schallert, and Gary Collins. From the Sunn Classics folks.

HANGOVER: See THE FEMALE JUNGLE.

HANGOVER SQUARE
1945 20th Century-Fox (B&W)
PRODUCER: Robert Bassler
DIRECTOR: John Brahm
SCREENWRITER: Barré Lydon
John Brahm directs a follow-up to his successful *The Lodger* with the same male leads playing similar roles. Laird Cregar stars as a schizophrenic concert pianist. George Sanders is a detective. By the time it was released 28-year-old Cregar was dead, a victim of excessive dieting. With Linda Darnell, Alan Napier, and Glenn Langan. With music by Bernard Herrmann and a memorable fiery finale.

HANNIE CAULDER
1971 Paramount (England)
PRODUCER: Patrick Curtis
DIRECTOR: Burt Kennedy
SCREENWRITERS: Burt Kennedy, David Haft
Robert Culp is a killer hired by Raquel Welch to track down the men who had raped her and killed her husband. Ernest Borgnine, Strother Martin, and Jack Elam play the Western slime who did it. In his first Western, Christopher Lee builds Raquel a special gun. Also with Diana Dors and Stephen Boyd. Watch it for the cast. Producer Curtis was Raquel's real-life husband. Filmed in Spain.

THE HAPPINESSS CAGE: See THE MIND SNATCHER.

HAPPINESS IS A WARM CLUE
1971 TV
PRODUCER: Jack Laird
DIRECTOR: Daryl Duke
SCREENWRITER: Gene Kearney
ALSO RELEASED AS: *The Return of Charlie Chan*
A pilot film with Ross Martin as Charlie Chan. It wasn't shown on American television until 1979. Protests about another white actor playing the Oriental detective might have had something to do with it. With Leslie Nielsen, Richard Haydn, and Louise Sorel.

HAPPY BIRTHDAY TO ME
1981 Columbia (Canada)
PRODUCERS: John Dunning, André Link
DIRECTOR: J. Lee Thompson
SCREENWRITERS: John Saxton, Peter Jobin, Timothy Bond
The most shocking thing about this film was the poster—a young man screaming with a shish-kabob skewer shoved down his throat. The star is Melissa Sue Anderson (*Little House on the Prairie*), a college student in New England whose preppy friends, all members of the "Top Ten Club," keep dying in various unusual ways. Melissa, who had brain surgery after an accident, thinks she might be the killer. Glenn Ford is

her psychiatrist. Except for the graphic surgery scene it's not as gory as some similar movies but has more plot twists and other surprises. (R)

HAPPY BIRTHDAY, WANDA JUNE

1971 Columbia
PRODUCER: Robert Goldman
DIRECTOR: Mark Robson
SCREENWRITER: Kurt Vonnegut, Jr.

Rod Steiger returns home after seven years and finds his wife (Susannah York) matured and engaged. Lots of black humor and some fantasy (one scene is set in Heaven) in a very stagy version of Kurt Vonnegut, Jr.'s play. With Don Murray, William Hickey, and Pamelyn Ferdin.

HAPPY MOTHER'S DAY, LOVE GEORGE

1973 Cinema 5
PRODUCER/DIRECTOR: Darren McGavin
SCREENWRITER: Robert Clouse
ALSO RELEASED AS: *Run, Stranger, Run*

In Nova Scotia Ron Howard (*Happy Days*) is the illegitimate son of café owner Cloris Leachman. His father, George, who was murdered, was married to his mother's sister (Patricia Neal). His mother's new boyfriend (Bobby Darin in his last role) beats him. A religious fanatic couple care for him and a series of gory murders take place. Simon Oakland and Thayer David round out the cast of this horror film directed by actor Darren McGavin after his *Kolchak, The Night Stalker* series was cancelled.

A HARD DAY'S NIGHT

1964 United Artists (England) (B&W)
PRODUCER: Walter Shenson
DIRECTOR: Richard Lester
SCREENWRITER: Alun Owen

Wilfred Brambell (Paul's grandad) starred in *Steptoe and Son*, a popular British TV show copied here as *Sanford and Son*. Norman Rossington (Norm, the manager) is also in *Saturday Night and Sunday Morning* and *A Night to Remember*. John Junkin (Norm's assistant) plays in Lester's *How I Won the War* with John Lennon. Victor Spinetti (the TV director) returned in *Help!* and is in *Start the Revolution Without Me*. With Patti Boyd and the Beatles.

HAREM HOLIDAY: See HARUM SCARUM.

HARLEQUIN

1980 Hemdale (Australia)
PRODUCER: Tony Ginnane
DIRECTOR: Simon Powell
SCREENWRITER: Everett DeRoche

Another imaginative Australian movie from the company that made *Thirst*. Robert Powell (*The Asphyx*) stars as Harlequin, a mysterious but benevolent modern Rasputin who cures the leukemia-stricken child of a wealthy senator (David Hemmings). The politician's wife (Carmen Duncan) is totally taken by the healer, who can also levitate and disappear, but a political manipulator (Broderick Crawford) tries to destroy him. Music by Brian May (*The Road Warrior*).

HAROLD ROBBINS' THE PIRATE

1978 TV
PRODUCER: Howard W. Koch
DIRECTOR: Ken Annakin
SCREENWRITER: Jules J. Epstein

Baydr Al Fay (Franco Nero) is a Jewish-born Arab oil sheik with a daughter in the PLO. Epic (four hours) TV trash with Christopher Lee as Samir, Olivia Hussey, James Franciscus, Stuart Whitman, Jeff Corey, Michael Pataki, Eli Wallach, Ferdy Mayne, Marjorie Lord, and a cast of dozens.

HARUM SCARUM

1965 MGM
PRODUCER: Sam Katzman
DIRECTOR: Gene Nelson
SCREENWRITER: Gerard Drayson Adams
ALSO RELEASED AS: *Harem Holiday*

Motion picture and singing star Johnny Tyronne (Elvis Presley) is kidnaped while on a tour of the Middle East. In between Arabian adventures he falls for Princess Shalimar (Mary Ann Mobley) and sings "Go East, Young Man," "Harem Holiday," and seven other hits. With Michael Ansara, Fran Jeffries, Jay Novello, and little Billy Barty. Nelson also directed Elvis in another Katzman cheapie, *Kissin' Cousins*, and John Agar in *Hand of Death*.

HATCHET FOR A HONEYMOON

1969 G.G.P. Pictures (Spain/Italy)
PRODUCER: Manuel Cano Sanciriaco
DIRECTOR: Mario Bava
SCREENWRITERS: Santiago Moncada, Mario Bava
ORIGINALLY RELEASED AS:
Il Roso Segno della Pollias

Debra Paget, Vincent Price, and Lon Chaney during the filming of The Haunted Palace.

Copyright © 1963 Alta Vista Productions. Courtesy of Orion Pictures Corporation.

A psycho designer (Stephen Forsyth) with a secret room of mannequins in wedding dresses can't get a divorce, so he begins hacking up young brides on their wedding night. He also likes to dress up as a bride himself and eventually kills his wife, who decides to return from the grave! A demented shocker, including a character watching Bava's *Black Sabbath* on television.

THE HATCHET MURDERS: See *DEEP RED.*

THE HAUNTED AND THE HUNTED: See *DEMENTIA 13.*

THE HAUNTED HOUSE OF HORROR: See *HORROR HOUSE.*

THE HAUNTED PALACE

1963 AIP
PRODUCER/DIRECTOR: Roger Corman
SCREENWRITER: Charles Beaumont

A good entry in the Corman/Price/Poe series. It was frauduently presented as a Poe adaptation, but actually it's based on "The Case of Charles Dexter Ward" by H.P. Lovecraft. Joseph Curwen (Vincent Price) is burned as a warlock by the villagers of Arkham in 1765. A century later his great-great grandson, Charles Dexter Ward (also played by Price), arrives with his wife (Debra Paget) to reopen the Curwen mansion. Arkham is filled with mutants (results of the Curwen curse). The spirit of Ward's ancestor takes over and Ward/Curwen, aided by warlocks (Lon Chaney, Jr., and Milton Parsons), resurrects his former witch partner and prepares to sacrifice his wife on the altar hidden in a massive basement. In the end, evil triumphs. With Elisha Cook, Jr., Leo Gordon, Barbara Morris, and Bruno Ve Sota.

THE HAUNTED STRANGLER

1958 Anglo Amalgamated/MGM (England)
PRODUCER: John Croydon
DIRECTOR: Robert Day
SCREENWRITERS: Jan Read, John Croydon

In this good old-fashioned horror movie Boris Karloff stars as a 19th-century criminologist investigating a 20-year-old murder case. Karloff periodically becomes a snarling killer repeating the original crimes, but he doesn't remember the transformations. To play the madman, he simply shuts one eye and bites his lower lip and stalks around as if it were the '30s again. Anthony Dawson is the Scotland Yard man who tracks him down. With Elizabeth Allan. Richard Gordon was executive producer.

THE HAUNTING

1963 MGM (U.S./England) (B&W)
PRODUCER/DIRECTOR: Robert Wise
SCREENWRITER: Nelson Gidding

You don't see any phantoms, but pulsating walls, loud pounding noises, a little girl's cries, and Julie Harris' hysteria should make you want to leave a night light on after seeing what is undoubtedly the scariest ghost movie ever made. An anthropologist (Richard Johnson), a lonely woman who had a traumatizing supernatural experience as a child (Harris), a cool lesbian with ESP (Claire Bloom), and a wisecracking heir (Russ Tamblyn) spend the night in a haunted New England mansion. The relentless horrors they're subjected to make this the best of Robert Wise's many popular hits—in glorious black-and-white. Based on *The Haunting of Hill House* by Shirley Jackson. Filmed in England.

THE HAUNTING OF JULIA

1977 Discovery (England/Canada)
PRODUCERS: Peter Fetterman, Alfred Pariser
DIRECTOR: Richard Loncraine
SCREENWRITER: Dave Humphries
ALSO RELEASED AS: *Full Circle*

Mia Farrow (with a *Rosemary's Baby* haircut) stars in a critically acclaimed supernatural story which was released here in '82. It's based on a novel by Peter Straub (*Ghost Story*). As Julia, Mia feels responsible for the death of her little girl, leaves her husband, and moves to a strange house. With Keir Dullea and Jill Bennett. (**R**)

HAUNTS

1976 Intercontinental
PRODUCERS: Herb Freed, Burt Weisbourd
DIRECTOR: Herb Freed
SCREENWRITER: Anne Marisse
ALSO RELEASED AS: *The Veil*

In this confusing low-budget mess, May Britt (from *The Blue Angel* remake) is a repressed but busy farm girl who seems to be going crazy. She thinks her mysterious uncle (Cameron Mitchell) is lurking around when he's really miles away. She also (maybe) kills somebody —and sleeps with her goat. Cameron Mitchell's hair changes color *three* times during the movie and Aldo Ray as the overweight alcoholic sheriff gets to mumble a lot and throw up. When an out-of-town killer is caught the murders continue. Even the poor goat dies.

Jack Palance in Hawk the Slayer.

HAUNTS OF THE VERY RICH
1972 TV
PRODUCER: Lillian Gallo
DIRECTOR: Paul Wendkos
SCREENWRITER: William Wood
A television mixture of *Outward Bound* and *No Exit* clichés with seven people stranded on a paradise island who discover they're dead. Lloyd Bridges, Cloris Leachman, Edward Asner, Anne Francis, Tony Bill, and Donna Mills are all in Hell!

HAUSER'S MEMORY
1970 TV
PRODUCER: Jack Laird
DIRECTOR: Boris Sagal
SCREENWRITER: Adrian Spies
Scientist David McCallum injects himself with a brain serum containing the memory of a dead German physicist. The "new man" spurns his wife (Susan Strasberg) and seeks revenge against former SS members who had punished him for rejecting Hitler. Lilli Palmer plays the dead man's wife. With Robert Webber and Leslie Nielsen. Based on a novel by Curt Siodmak—who wrote the similar *Donovan's Brain*. Filmed in Europe.

HAVE ROCKET, WILL TRAVEL
1959 Columbia (B&W)
PRODUCER: Harry Romm
DIRECTOR: David Lowell Rich
SCREENWRITER: Raphael Hayes
After making films for 28 years, the Three Stooges thought they were finished when their contract expired in '58. Television came to the rescue by showing 190(!) old shorts and making the Stooges more popular than ever. Moe and Larry were rehired by Columbia, recruited a new Stooge (Joe De Rita), and made this outer-space quickie complete with a trip to Venus, a talking unicorn, and duplicate Stooges. It made millions. Soon there were Three Stooges comic books, stamps, bubble-gum cards. . . . They starred in five more films.

HAVING A WILD WEEKEND
1965 Warner Brothers (England) (B&W)
PRODUCER: David Deutsch
DIRECTOR: John Boorman
SCREENWRITER: Peter Nichols
ALSO RELEASED AS: *Catch Us If You Can*
The Dave Clark Five, who were nearly as famous as the Beatles at the time, in *their* musical comedy by first-time director Boorman (*Deliverance*, *Zardoz*). They play disillusioned stuntmen doing TV commercials stressing "eat meat." Sick of the grind, they take a company car and an actress (Barbara Ferris) and head for her private island to get away from it all. Instead, they encounter beatniks, a Frankenstein monster, war games, and a stray missile. At a costume ball they dress as famous actors (and actresses) and dodge publicity-seeking

photographers. In a surprise ending Dave Clark (as Steve) abandons his friends and the girl, who go along with the publicity. The popular "Tottenham Sound" is on the sound track, but the group is never shown performing.

HAWK THE SLAYER

1980 ITC (England)
PRODUCER: Harry Robertson
DIRECTOR/SCREENWRITER: Terry Marcel

A sword-and-scorcery feature released too early to cash in on the craze, which didn't get off the ground for another two years. Jack Palance is everything that's evil as Voltan, disfigured half-brother of the noble Hawk (John Terry). They both want "The Power" (a magic flying sword). With lots of slow-motion swordfights, Shane Briant, Patrick Magee, Ferdy Mayne, Harry Andrews, and Roy Kinneger.

HE KNOWS YOU'RE ALONE

1980 Lansbury-Beruh/United Artists
PRODUCERS: George Manasse, Robert Di Milia, Nan Pearlman
DIRECTOR: Armand Mastroianni
SCREENWRITER: Scott Parker

A bride-to-be loses her bridesmaid and several of her guests to a knife-wielding maniac, which eventually leads to her own confrontation with the killer. No real surprises here, unless you count the fact that the director is Marcello's American cousin. Filmed on Staten Island. —BM

HE LIVED TO KILL: See A NIGHT OF TERROR.

HE OR SHE: See GLEN OR GLENDA.

THE HEAD

1959 Trans-Lux (West Germany) (B&W)
PRODUCER: Wolfgang Hartwig
DIRECTOR/SCREENWRITER: Victor Trivas
ORIGINALLY RELEASED AS: *Die Nackte und der Satan*

Amazing but true—the same year that *The Brain That Wouldn't Die* was produced, some Germans were making this similar decapitation epic. Michel Simon (a famous French actor who had seen better days) has invented serum Z. He uses it to keep a dog's head alive. His new co-worker, Dr. Ood (Horst Frank), cuts off Simon's chubby head and keeps it alive with the serum. Not wanting to be upstaged by the American counterpart, the director also has Ood put the pretty head of a crippled nurse onto the perfect body of a stripper. The nurse/stripper falls in love with the stripper's boyfriend, who recognizes the nurse but not the body! Incredible, to say the least, and the special effects are pathetic.

HEAD

1968 Columbia
PRODUCERS/SCREENWRITERS: Bob Rafelson, Jack Nicholson
DIRECTOR: Bob Rafelson

The Monkees Show ended in '68. Micky, Davy, Mike, and Peter really had nothing to lose by debunking their image in this major-company pseudo-underground plotless musical. Jack Nicholson, who hadn't even been in *Easy Rider* yet, co-wrote and produced with newcomer Rafelson. It's spotty, but there are some inspired moments, some great photography, really odd guest stars, and some of the Monkees' best songs. It's all very anti-establishment and drug-tinged. The irreverent group sprinkle dandruff on Victor Mature's head in one of the best scenes. Watch for Annette Funicello as Min-

COLUMBIA PICTURES presents the

monkees

and Victor Mature! and Sonny Liston!
and Annette Funicello! and Carol Doda!

"head"

"A movie for a
turned-on
audience!"
–Renata Adler, New York Times

G

**Suggested for
GENERAL
audiences.**

Copyright © 1968 Raybert Productions, Inc. Courtesy of Columbia Pictures.

Three teenagers meet ancient British ghosts in a haunted castle. You'll groan or sleep through this comedy featuring the title ghost chasing around after his floating head. With Richard Lyon, Lilliane Scotiane, and Clive Revill.

THE HEARSE
1980 Crown International
PRODUCERS: Mark Tenser, Charles Russel
DIRECTOR: George Bowers
SCREENWRITER: Bill Bleich

Trish Van Devere inherits an old mansion and is hounded by a 1953 Packard hearse. Not bad enough to be actually funny (like, for instance, *The Car*), but not good (like *Duel*), either. Joseph Cotten plays a drunken lawyer.   –BM

HEARTBEEPS
1982 Universal
PRODUCER: Michael Phillips
DIRECTOR: Allan Arkush
SCREENWRITER: John Hill

A sentimental comedy set in 1995 that was a major Christmas release flop. Andy Kaufman and Bernadette Peters play servant robots who fall in love, run away, and have a (real) robot baby. Melanie Mayron and Christopher Guest are the Gorts, a helpful couple who own the junkyard where the mechanical fugitives hide out. Randy Quaid and Kenneth McMillan are robot-factory employees. Jack Carter is the voice of Catskill 55602, an entertainment model. With Dick Miller. A setback for the director of *Rock 'n' Roll High School*, who returned to teens with *Get Crazy*. Music by John Williams.

THE HELICOPTER SPIES
1968 MGM
PRODUCER: Anthony Spinner
DIRECTOR: Boris Sagal
SCREENWRITER: Dean Hargrove

Two episodes of *The Man from U.N.C.L.E.* show edited into a feature.

nie, Frank Zappa (with a bull), Sonny Liston, Carol Doda (as Sally Silicone), T.C. Jones (as Mr. & Mrs. Ace), Abraham Sofaer, Teri Garr, and Tor Johnson. Old film clips feature Reagan, Lugosi (in *The Black Cat*), Ann Miller, and Charles Laughton. It did nothing to help the Monkees' quickly sinking career. Watch it and look for the sound track album (with the mirror cover).

THE HEADLESS GHOST
1959 AIP (England) (B&W)
PRODUCER: Herman Cohen
DIRECTOR: Peter G. Scott
SCREENWRITER: Kenneth Langtry

Napoleon and Ilya (Robert Vaughn and David McCallum) go to Greece to find the thermal prism, a new secret weapon owned by a sect of mystics. With Carol Lynley, Bradford Dillman, Lola Albright, Julie London, John Carradine, Sid Haig, and, of course, Leo G. Carroll.

HELL NIGHT
1981 Compass International
PRODUCERS: Irwin Yablans,
  Bruce Cohn Curtis
DIRECTOR: Tom DeSimone
SCREENWRITER: Randolph Feldman

Linda Blair is one of four new college students who have to spend the night in an old mansion that years before was the scene of a mass family murder/suicide. One retarded son supposedly survived and is back to kill. A ridiculous teenage slasher movie with Vincent Van Patten. Director DeSimone earlier did gay porn films. He later made the popular *Concrete Jungle*. (R)

HELL ON FRISCO BAY
1955 Warner Brothers
ASSOCIATE PRODUCER: George C. Bertholon
DIRECTOR: Frank Tuttle
SCREENWRITERS: Sydney Boehm,
  Martin Rackin

Ex-cop Alan Ladd is framed by waterfront hood Edward G. Robinson. With Joanne Dru, William Demarest, Fay Wray, Nester Paiva, and Jayne Mansfield as "a blonde." In Warnercolor and Cinemascope.

HELL ON WHEELS
1967 Crown International
PRODUCER: Robert Patrick
DIRECTOR: Will Zens
SCREENWRITER: Wesley Cox

John Ashley stars as a track mechanic who tries to get out of the shadow of stock-car-ace brother Marty Robbins by opening his own speed shop. Outfitting tankers for the local bootlegging ring becomes a lucrative sideline for John, but he and Marty are taken hostage when he tries to phase himself out. Their other brother, revenue agent Robert Dornan, arrives too late to stop a high-speed chase over winding mountain roads which ends in death. The Stoneman Family and Connie Smith play themselves, and Marty sings "Fly Butterfly" and "No Tears, Milady." With Gigi Perreau.   –CB

HELL SHIP MUTINY
1957 Republic (B&W)
ASSOCIATE PRODUCER: George Bilson
DIRECTORS: Lee Sholem, Elmo Williams
SCREENWRITER: De Vallon Scott

Jon Hall (also the executive producer) is a sea captain who helps a South Seas princess (Roberta Haynes) rid Tema Tangi island of thieves. With Peter Lorre as Lamouet, a crooked French judge, John Carradine, Peter Coe, and Mike Mazurki. The pits from Republic.

Linda Blair in Hell Night.

Ron and Nancy Reagan in
Hellcats of the Navy.

commander and shares his canteen in exchange for mine-field information, but the commander tries to double-cross him. "The guts and gore of desert war!" were promised by the ads. With Brandon Carroll, Fred Gavlin, and Greg Stuart. *Tank Battalion* was the original co-feature. —CB

HELLBORN:
See *THE SINISTER URGE*.

THE HELLCATS

1968 Crown International
PRODUCER: Anthony Cardoza
DIRECTOR: Robert F. Slatzer
SCREENWRITERS: Tony Houston,
    Robert F. Slatzer

A female motorcycle gang is infiltrated by the girlfriend of a murdered detective (Dee Duffy). She accompanies Sharyn Kinzie and Lydia Goya on a drug run into Mexico and is taken hostage by director Slatzer (as the mysterious Mr. Adrian) on her return. Thrilling dockside confrontation between Hellcats and authorities follows. Featuring Sonny West as Snake and Shannon Summers as Rita, with guests Pepper, Candy Cane, Moonfire, Mongoose, Scorpio, Scab, and Zombie. Davy Jones' Dolphins do "Hellcats," "Mass Confusion," and "I Can't Take a Chance"; Somebody's Children give us "Marionettes" and "I'm Up." Producer Cardoza also did *The Beast of Yucca Flats*. —CB

HELL SQUAD

1958 AIP (B&W)
PRODUCER/DIRECTOR/SCREENWRITER:
    Burt Topper

Five American soldiers, lost in the Tunisian desert during World War II, are unable to ask for directions because radio communications are being monitored by the enemy. The patrol is trapped by gunfire and strafed by hostile aircraft; eventually only Wally Campo is left. He meets up with a stranded German

HELLCATS OF THE NAVY

1957 Columbia
PRODUCER: Charles H. Schneer
DIRECTOR: Nathan Juran
SCREENWRITERS: David Lang,
    Raymond Marcus

Every American citizen should see this momentous screen teaming of our President and First Lady. As a submarine commander, Ronald Reagan has broken up with Nancy Davis (safe on shore). She had a fling with one of his men who keeps an 8 × 10 glossy of her under his pillow. When her admirer is out in a diving suit, the sub is attacked and Ron orders the hatch shut before he can get back in. He dies and Ron (now rid of his rival) is blamed by Arthur Franz (*Monster on Campus*) and some others for the unfortunate death. The awkward love scenes between Ron and Nancy are chilling. With Harry Lauter, Selmer Jackson, and an intro by Admiral Nimitz. It was Reagan's last theatrical feature. Director Juran, also known as Nathan Hertz, is better known for his *Attack of the 50 Ft. Woman* and *Brain from Planet Arous*.

THE HELLFIRE CLUB

1961 Embassy Pictures (England)
PRODUCERS/DIRECTORS: Robert S. Baker,
   Monty Berman
SCREENWRITERS: Leon Griffiths,
   Jimmy Sangster

In 18th-century London the wife of the leader of the Hellfire Club takes her son and flees to escape her husband's decadence. The boy (Keith Michell) returns years later and with the help of an attorney (Peter Cushing) fights the club's new leader, his cousin, for rights to the estate. With Kai Fisher, Adrienne Corri, and Skip Martin. American prints are in black-and-white. There's a club with the same name in New York City that makes this place look like *Mister Rogers Neighborhood*.

HELLO DOWN THERE

1968 Paramount
PRODUCER: George Sherman
DIRECTOR: Jack Arnold
SCREENWRITERS: Frank Telford,
   John McGreevey

An Ivan Tors, made-in-Florida production. It's a wholesome comedy about dad Tony Randall and mom Janet Leigh and their teen son and daughter and their rock band—all living and playing together in an undersea house. Besides great rock songs like "Glub" and "Hey Little Goldfish," it's got cute dolphins and seals, Merv Griffin (as himself), and an extensive cast, including Jim Backus, Roddy McDowall, Ken Berry, Richard Dreyfuss, Harvey Lembeck, Bruce Gordon, and Arnold Stang.

HELL'S ANGELS ON WHEELS

1967 U.S. Films
PRODUCER: Joe Soloman
DIRECTOR: Richard Rush
SCREENWRITER: R. Wright Campbell

Gas station attendant Poet (Jack Nicholson) joins the Angels and is jumped by four sailors in an amusement park. Head Angel Adam Roarke takes care of the attackers for his pal, but the relationship sours when Poet moves in on his girl (Sabrina Scharf) during the big orgy sequence. Roarke crashes through plate glass and dies in flames. The cast includes Jana Taylor, Mimi Machu, Jack Starrett, Bruno Ve Sota, Gary Littlejohn, and Sonny Barger, real-life Angels leader who brought along followers from Oakland and Daly City as well as the Nomads of Sacramento. The Poor perform "Study in Motion No. 1." Laszlo Kovacs was the cinematographer. Director Rush went on to do *Psych-Out* and *Too Soon to Love*, also with Nicholson. U.S. Films also released *The Beach Girls and the Monster*. —CB

HELL'S ANGELS '69

1969 AIP
PRODUCER: Tom Stern
DIRECTOR: Lee Madden
SCREENWRITER: Don Tait

Two East Coast rich kids (Tom Stern and Jeremy Slate) who have come to rob Caesar's Palace for kicks hoodwink Sonny Barger and his gang into supplying the perfect diversion. The job goes off as planned but Stern, Slate, and Angels defector Conny Van Dyke face death as angry Angels track them into the Nevada desert seeking revenge. Filmed on location. Featuring Steve Sandor, Terry the Tramp, G.D. Spradlin, and the Hell's Angels Oakland chapter. Producer-star Stern wrote the original story with Slate. Madden also directed *Angel Unchained*. –CB

HELL'S BELLES
1969 AIP
PRODUCER/DIRECTOR: Maury Dexter
SCREENWRITERS: James Gordon White, Robert McMullen
ALSO RELEASED AS: *Girl in the Leather Suit*
A motorcycle won in a desert enduro is stolen by Adam Roarke and his gang, and Jocelyn Lane is left in trade. When rancher Jeremy Slate regains consciousness he and his new friend Jocelyn head off across the Arizona desert for acts of revenge involving rope, chain, and snakepit. Gippo, Red Beard, Rabbit, Meatball, and Crazy John flee in terror; Slate sells the reclaimed bike to make a down payment on cactus-country love nest. With Angelique Pettyjohn, Michael Walker, and Astrid Warner. –CB

HELL'S BLOODY DEVILS
1967 Independent International Pictures
PRODUCER/DIRECTOR: Al Adamson
SCREENWRITER: Jerry Evans
ALSO RELEASED AS: *Operation M, The Fakers*
When released in 1970 the ads said "all new!" It was, of course, old and so were the usual Al Adamson stars, including Broderick (*Highway Patrol*) Crawford, Scott Brady, Kent Taylor, and John Carradine. Try and follow this story of Count Von Delberg, a Nazi war criminal who joins forces with the Mafia and outlaw bikers to circulate counterfeit money in Utah. The plan is undermined by undercover FBI and Israeli agents. With Keith Andes, Robert Dix, Vicki Volante, and Bambi Allen. Featuring "The Wild Rebellion Girls," California's Hessians biker gang, Colonel Harlon Sanders, film clips of Hitler, and trained dolphins. The violent biker segments are missing from the TV version. Cinematography by Laszlo Kovacs. Also with Anne Randall, *Playboy*'s Miss May 1967.

HELL'S CHOSEN FEW
1968 Thunderbird International
PRODUCER/DIRECTOR: David L. Hewitt
SCREENWRITERS: John K. McCarthy, David Prentiss
A returning Vietnam veteran (Joey Daniels) joins the motorcycle gang of his jailed brother (Gary Kent) to find out who really killed the sheriff's daughter's boyfriend. With help from the sheriff's daughter and the brother's girlfriend (Kelly Ross), the sheriff is proven guilty and killed. The "innocent" biker is released and proceeds to make a fool of his brother. With Titus Moody. Hewitt created *The Girls from Thunder Strip*, *Dr. Terror's Gallery of Horrors*, and others. –CB

HELL'S PLAYGROUND
1967 Commercial
PRODUCER: John Baron
DIRECTOR: Jesse Clark
SCREENWRITER: M. O'Neil
ALSO RELEASED AS: *Riot at Lauderdale*
Beach riot! Spring break in Fort Lauderdale with Jane Ashley, Skip Everett, the Surftones, and the Pebbles. More Florida fun: *Daytona Beach Weekend*, *Weekend Rebellion*, *Musical Mutiny*, and *Mondo Daytona*. –CB

HELLZAPOPPIN
1941 Universal (B&W)
PRODUCER: Jules Levey
DIRECTOR: N.C. Potter
SCREENWRITERS: Nat Perrin, Warren Wilson

Olsen and Johnson's anarchic stage play turned into an almost equally unstructured movie. It opens in Hell. Occasionally the stars "leave" the film, argue with its projectionist (Shemp Howard), and have him replay scenes. Sometimes the film jumps out of frame. With *Mad* magazine–type gags about potted plants and a character yelling "Mr. Jones!" for no apparent reason. Unfortunately an added romantic subplot slows things down. With Mischa Auer, Martha Raye, Hugh Herbert, a Frankenstein monster, and Elisha Cook, Jr., as the scriptwriter. Olsen and Johnson returned in the even better *Crazy House*.

HELP!

1965 United Artists (England)
PRODUCER: Walter Shenson
DIRECTOR: Richard Lester
SCREENWRITERS: Marc Behm, Charles Wood
Leo McKern (high priest Clang) is also in *X The Unknown*, *The Mouse That Roared*, and *The Day the Earth Caught Fire*. Eleanor Bron (priestess Ahme) is in *Alfie* and *Two for the Road*. Victor Spinetti (Prof. Foot) was the TV director in *A Hard Day's Night*. Roy Kinnear (Foot's assistant Algernon) is in *Taste the Blood of Dracula*, *The Three Musketeers*, and *How I Won the War*. With the Beatles singing seven great songs. Partially filmed in Austria and the Bahamas.

HERCULES

1957 Warner Brothers (Italy)
PRODUCER: Federico Teti
DIRECTOR: Pietro Francisci
SCREENWRITERS: Ennio de Concini, Gaio Frattini, Pietro Francisci
ORIGINALLY RELEASED AS: *La Fatiche de Ercole*
From the ads: "See the heroic Hercules rip down the Age of Orgy's lavish palace of lustful pleasure!" "See the seductive Amazons lure men to voluptuous revels and violent deaths!" The one that started the onslaught of Italian muscleman movies. Producer Joseph E. Levine made a bundle bringing it and *Hercules Unchained* to America. Star Steve Reeves was a former Mr. Universe from Montana. The story is basically "Jason and the Golden Fleece." Think about the "cost in millions" when you see the awful men-in-monster-suit dinosaurs. With Sylvia Koscina, Gianna Maria Canale, and Arturo Dominici (*Black Sunday*). Mario Bava was the cinematographer. A 1980's version is promised with Lou Ferrigno (*The Incredible Hulk*).

HERCULES AGAINST ROME

1964 AIP-TV (Italy/France)
DIRECTOR: Piero Pierotti
SCREENWRITERS: Arpad De Riso, Nino Scolaro
ORIGINALLY RELEASED AS: *Ercole Contro Roma*
Alan Steel, whose real name is Sergio Ciani, takes his turn as the musclebound Italian boulder-thrower. One of eight Hercules titles released directly to television by AIP.

HERCULES AGAINST THE MOONMEN

1964 Governor (Italy/France)
PRODUCER: Luigi Mondello
DIRECTOR: Giacomo Gentilomo
SCREENWRITERS: Arpad De Riso, Nino Scolaro, Giacomo Gentilomo, Angelo Sangarmano
ORIGINALLY RELEASED AS: *Maciste e la Regina di Samar*
Alan Steel as Hercules (actually Maciste) fights the Moonmen living in the Mountain of Death. With sacrifices, monsters, a metal-headed giant, and the best rock men of all time.

315

Fay Spain as the evil queen in Hercules and the Captive Women.

typical Woolner Brothers ads called this one *Hercules and the Huanted Women!* (No, that's not a typo.)

HERCULES AND THE HAUNTED WOMEN: See *HERCULES AND THE CAPTIVE WOMEN.*

HERCULES VS. THE HYDRA: See *THE LOVES OF HERCULES.*

HERCULES AGAINST THE SONS OF THE SUN

1964 Screen Gems (Italy/Spain)
PRODUCER/DIRECTOR/SCREENWRITER:
Osvaldo Civirani
ORIGINALLY RELEASED AS: *Ercole Contro i Figli del Sole*

A favorite title. Hercules (Mark Forest) fights Incas.

HERCULES AND THE CAPTIVE WOMEN

1961 Woolner Brothers (Italy/France)
PRODUCER: Achille Piazzi
DIRECTOR: Vittorio Cottafavi
SCREENWRITERS: Alessandro Continenza, Vittorio Cottafavi, Duccio Tessari
ORIGINALLY RELEASED AS: *Ercole alla Conquista della Atlantide*
ALSO RELEASED AS: *Hercules and the Haunted Women*

Hercules (Reg Park) goes to Atlantis— which is ruled by Fay Spain! She plays the sadistic Queen Antinea and has the power to control men. Herc rescues his son, fights an army of identical men and a weird upright dragon, then sinks Fay and her lost island. The same people made *Hercules in the Haunted World,* which is even better. When they were released here as a double feature the

HERCULES AND THE TYRANTS OF BABYLON

1964 AIP-TV (Italy)
DIRECTOR: Domenico Paolella
SCREENWRITERS: L. Martino, Domenico Paolella
ORIGINALLY RELEASED AS: *Ercole contro i Tiranni di Babilonia*

Rock Stevens takes over as the brainless body builder. With Helga Line.

HERCULES IN NEW YORK

1970 United Films
PRODUCER/SCREENWRITER: Aubrey Wisberg
DIRECTOR: Arthur A. Seidelman
ALSO RELEASED AS: *Hercules: The Movie*

Years after the Hercules movie mania had ended, some guys in New York decided we needed another one. Arnold Stang stars as the meek friend of Hercules (played here by Arnold Schwartzenneger, using an alias). The ancient hero is sent to modern Manhattan by his dad Zeus. He captures a bear that escapes from the Central Park Zoo, rides a chariot up Broadway, and makes a living as a professional wrestler. What else? Thirteen years later, it was shown under a new title to cash in on Arnold's *Conan* film.

HERCULES IN THE HAUNTED WORLD

1961 Woolner Brothers (Italy)
EXECUTIVE PRODUCER: Achille Piazzi
DIRECTOR: Mario Bava
SCREENWRITERS: Allesandro Continenza, Mario Bava, Duccio Tessari, Franco Prosperi

This is the only Hercules movie that really makes it as a fantasy. Depending on your mood (or age) it can be scary and exciting or pretty funny. Hercules (Reg Park) goes to Hell! Yes—he and a pal go to Hades to obtain a precious plant to cure an ailing princess. They encounter many wonders, including Christopher Lee as the evil Lichas, servant of Pluto, some great rock men, seas of lava, and a tempting naked maiden in chains. Hercules throws boulders and overcomes all obstacles. Lee does not play a vampire (as implied in some of the ads). *Hercules and the Captive Women*, also with Park, is worth catching as well.

HERCULES IN THE VALE OF WOE

1962 Avco Embassy-TV (Italy)
PRODUCER: Ignazio Luceri
SCREENWRITERS: Vittorio Metz, Marcello Marchesi
ALSO RELEASED AS: *Maciste Against Hercules in the Vale of Woe*

After seeing Hercules epics with Jayne Mansfield and Broderick Crawford, the world was ready for the first intentionally comic Hercules film. Two dumb Italian con men travel back in time where they encounter Hercules (Kirk Morris) and Maciste.

HERCULES, PRISONER OF EVIL

1964 AIP-TV (Italy)
PRODUCER: Adelpho Ambrosiano
DIRECTOR: Antonio Margheriti (Anthony Dawson)

Reg Park plays Hercules for the third time. The increasingly boring series is given a boost by a witch who turns men into werewolves. Park's Hercules films are the most imaginative.

HERCULES, SAMSON AND ULYSSES

1964 MGM (Italy)
PRODUCER: Joseph Fryd
DIRECTOR/SCREENWRITER: Pietro Francisci
ORIGINALLY RELEASED AS: *Ercole, Sfida e Sansone*

Hercules is mistaken for Samson after he and Ulysses battle a sea monster. You have to be a real muscle fan to tell Kirk Morris, Richard Lloyd, and Enzo Cervisco, as the three heroes, apart.

HERCULES: THE MOVIE: See HERCULES IN NEW YORK.

HERCULES UNCHAINED

1959 Warner Brothers (Italy)
PRODUCER: Bruno Vailati
DIRECTOR: Pietro Francisci
SCREENWRITERS: Pietro Francisci, Ennio De Concini
ORIGINALLY RELEASED AS: *Ercole e la Regina di Lidia*

Steve Reeves and Sylvia Koscina return in the hit sequel to *Hercules*. The

UPI 2/11/74: *The family of actor John Carradine (center) holds a reunion this week to celebrate the 68th birthday of the saturnine actor, who has played in 100 movies. Marking the second time in family history that the clan has gathered are, left to right: Robert, 19, Christopher, 26, Keith, 24, John, Bruce (in striped shirt), David, Barbara Seagull, and David's and Barbara's child, Free. John and Keith starred most recently in Hex.*

son of Jupiter loses his memory thanks to the evil Queen Lidia (Silvia Lopel), fights tigers and a giant (wrestler Primo Carnera), and pulls down the massive pillars he's chained to, demolishing a heathen temple. Lidia kills, then stuffs, her lovers. Over 20 Hercules films with different actors followed. Reeves went on to play other legendary heroes.

HERCULES VS. THE GIANT WARRIORS

1964 John Alexander Films (Italy/France)
PRODUCER: Alberto Chimins
DIRECTOR: Alberto De Martino
SCREENWRITERS: Roberto Gianviti, Alessandro Ferreau
ORIGINALLY RELEASED AS: *Il Trionfo di Ercole*
Zeus takes away Hercules' strength but thoughtfully restores it later. Don Vadis stars and battles a sorceress in Hades plus 10 giant bronze warriors.

HEX

1973 20th Century-Fox
PRODUCER: Clark Paylow
DIRECTOR: Leo Garen
SCREENWRITERS: Leo Garen, Steve Katz
In 1919 a biker gang goes to an isolated ranch where two sisters live. One is a witch who kills the intruders in various bizarre ways. Starring Keith Carradine and Robert Walker, Jr., as a mute. Norman Mailer liked it. 20th Century-Fox didn't. They decided not to release it. Filmed in South Dakota. With Gary Busey and John Carradine.

HEY, LET'S TWIST!

1961 Paramount (B&W)
PRODUCER: Harry Romm
DIRECTOR: Greg Garrison
SCREENWRITER: Hal Hackady
A fictionalized look at the rise of the Peppermint Lounge in New York. When their papa has a stroke, Joey Dee (as himself) and Teddy Randazzo (as his brother) take over the family restaurant, rename it, and introduce the twist there. Society columnist Zohra Lampert visits and soon it's a reservations-only club with the original teens crowded out by the twisting upper crust. This makes money but causes personal conflicts for poor Joey, who turns it back to a teen spot. Likely story. With Jo-Ann Campbell, Alan Arbus, the Starliters, and the Peppermint Loungers as themselves.

HIDDEN FACE: See JAILBAIT.

THE HIDDEN HAND

1942 Warner Brothers (B&W)
PRODUCER: William Jacobs
DIRECTOR: Ben Stoloff
SCREENWRITERS: Anthony Coldewey, Raymond Schrock
An old-fashioned mystery with creepy, pop-eyed Milton Parsons as an asylum escapee. Young Craig Stevens is the hero. The story has something to do with suspended animation. It features Julie Bishop, Elizabeth Fraser, Willie Best, Creighton Hale, and Monte Blue.

Robert Clarke as The Hideous Sun Demon.

THE HIDEOUS SUN DEMON

1959 Pacific International (B&W)
PRODUCER/DIRECTOR: Robert Clarke
SCREENWRITERS: E.S. Seeley, Jr., Doane Hoag

Robert Clarke, the guy who met *The Man from Planet X*, stars in his most famous low-budget science-fiction film. He plays a scientist exposed to radiation who becomes a monster when the sun shines on him. The scaly lizardman makeup is the highpoint of this great laughable hit. Some of the music later turned up in *Night of the Living Dead*. Clarke next went *Beyond the Time Barrier*.

HIGH PLAINS DRIFTER

1973 Universal
PRODUCER: Robert Daley
DIRECTOR: Clint Eastwood
SCREENWRITER: Ernest Tidyman

In a bizarre variation on his Western loner/avenger role, Clint Eastwood is featured as an angel of death. With some help from midget Billy Curtis (as Mordecai), he kills everyone in sight, paints the town red, burns it, and rides off. With Verna Bloom, Marianna Hill, and Jack Ging. **(R)**

HIGH SCHOOL BIG SHOT

1959 Filmgroup (B&W)
PRODUCER: Stan Bichman
DIRECTOR/SCREENWRITER: Joel Rapp

Tom Pittman is unpopular at school because of his high IQ. His naiveté makes him easy prey for a gold-digging classmate who wants him to write her term papers. He engineers a shipping-office heist for her, but she and her real boyfriend double-cross him. Death for many. With Virginia Aldridge, Howard Viet, Stanley Adams, and Malcolm Atterbury. Original co-feature: *T-Bird Gang*. Rapp also directed *Battle of Blood Island*. Roger Corman was executive producer.   —CB

HIGH SCHOOL CAESAR

1960 Filmgroup (B&W)
PRODUCER/DIRECTOR: O'Dale Ireland
SCREENWRITERS: Ethel Mae Page,
   Robert Slaven

John Ashley is unpopular at school because of his wealth. He organizes an in-school protection racket, but his brutal tactics result in public outrage and a fall from power. With Lowell Brown, Steve Stevens, Judy Nugent, and Gary Vinson of *McHale's Navy*. A dougle feature with the same director's *Date Bait*.
                —CB

HIGH SCHOOL CONFIDENTIAL

1958 MGM (B&W)
PRODUCER: Albert Zugsmith
DIRECTOR: Jack Arnold
SCREENWRITERS: Louis Meltzer, Robert Blees
ALSO RELEASED AS: *The Young Hellions*

From the opening with Jerry Lee Lewis singing the title song while pounding the keys of a piano on the back of a flat-bed truck to the absurd happy ending, this teen-dope-ring movie is a classic of its kind. As the new kid in school, Russ Tamblyn asks teacher Jan Sterling for a date, proves he's even cooler than jive-talking John Drew

Barrymore, and soon learns the local drug setup. Mr. A, the head pusher (Jackie Coogan!), spends spare hours cheerfully playing piano at a teen club. Tamblyn lives with his "aunt" (Mamie Van Doren), who is always trying to seduce him, and goes out with Mel Welles. Nice guy Michael Landon drag races with Tamblyn, who keeps joints hidden under his glove compartment and pretends to shoot up to impress his new boss Coogan. With Charles Chaplin, Jr., Lyle Talbot, William Wellman, Jr., Diana Darrin, and Ray Anthony. A serious look at the horrors of drug addiction.

HIGH SCHOOL HELLCATS
1958 AIP (B&W)
PRODUCERS: James H. Nicholson,
   Samuel Z. Arkoff
DIRECTOR: Edward Bernds
SCREENWRITERS: Mark and Jan Lowel
Yvonne Lime is new in town. She's not interested in smarting off to teachers or wild drinking parties. After a run-in with Jana Lund's outlaw sorority on her first day at a school, she seeks advice from the college boy who works at the malt shop: "What must a good girl say to belong?" The delinquent fun ends with death in an abandoned movie theater. With Brett Halsey and Suzanne Sydney. A dual release with *Hot Rod Gang*.   –CB

HIGH YELLOW
1965 Thunder (B&W)
EXECUTIVE PRODUCER: Clyde Knudsen
DIRECTOR: Larry Buchanan
The sordid confessions of a 17-year-old Negro maid who passes for white in a loveless nest of misfits and malcontents. Cynthia Hull's tyrannical employer is movie tycoon Bob Brown, who shares his palace with hypochondriac wife Anne MacAdams, hellcat daughter Kay Taylor, son Warren Hammack (kicked out of West Point for sexual deviancy), plus a blackmailing handyman and larcenous chauffeur. Filmed at the Frisco estate outside Dallas. See *Creature of Destruction*.   –CB

HIGHWAY DRAGNET
1954 Allied Artists (B&W)
PRODUCER: Willim F. Broidy
DIRECTOR: Nathan Juran
SCREENWRITERS: Herb Meadow,
   Jerome Odlum
Richard Conte as an ex-marine hitches a ride from a lady photographer and her model, then finds himself the object of a police manhunt on a murder charge. Can he prove his innocence? Young Roger Corman received his first screen credit as co-writer and associate producer. He became a real producer with *The Monster from the Ocean Floor*. The cast of this quickie includes Joan Bennett, Wanda Hendrix, and Reed Hadley. Some sources claim it was shot in 3-D. The title was inspired by *Dragnet*, then a hit on TV.

HILLBILLYS IN A HAUNTED HOUSE
1967 Woolner Brothers
PRODUCER: Bernard Woolner
DIRECTOR: Jean Yarbrough
SCREENWRITER: Duke Yelton
Two Country music stars (played by Country music star Ferlin Husky and nonstar Joi Lansing) spend the night in a haunted mansion used as a front for spies. Lon Chaney, Jr., is the bodyguard of Madame Wong (Linda Ho). Basil Rathbone as Gregor, John Carradine as the mad Dr. Kimmil, and George Barrows as a gorilla complete the spy ring. They're after an atomic formula. Musical-comedy nonsense which manages to waste three (count 'em) once-popular horror stars. Also with Sonny James, Merle Haggard, and Molly Bee. It was a fitting last film for

axle breaks in the desert they're faced with another family. The father, a mutant left to die on an atomic test site, is called Jupiter (James Whitworth—also in the sick *Don't Answer the Phone*). His wife is a fat ex-prostitute that "nobody in town ever missed." The "kids" are Pluto, Mars, Mercury, and Ruby—they're all cannibals who communicate with stolen C.B. radios! The Clevelanders are dying off quickly and the hill people have the baby, soon to be dinner. The seemingly hopeless situation is helped by one of the dogs and a few sacrifices by the frantic stranded family. It's an exciting, savage movie with touches of humor. Pluto is Michael Berryman, who played the bald terminal case in *One Flew Over the Cuckoo's Nest*. (R)

James Whitworth as Jupiter, the patriarch of the mutant family in The Hills Have Eyes.

director Yarbrough, who started out back at PRC doing *The Devil Bat* with Lugosi ('41). *Hillbillys* was a sequel to *Las Vegas Hillbillys*, also with Ferlin.

THE HILLS HAVE EYES

1977 Vanguard
PRODUCER: Peter Locke
DIRECTOR/SCREENWRITER: Wes Craven
Craven, known for his groundbreaking bad-taste revenge drama *Last House on the Left*, toned down a bit for this one, but it's still outrageous. The plot is similar to *Texas Chainsaw Massacre*, but *Hills* is more convincing and more subversive. A typical God-fearing middle-class American family with an ex-cop dad leaves the wilds of Cleveland and heads for California in a trailer and station wagon. Besides Mom and Dad Carter there are two pretty daughters (Susan Lanier and Dee Wallace of *E.T.*), a handsome son (Robert Houston), a son-in-law (Martin Speer), the new grandchild, and two family dogs (Beauty and the Beast). When the car's

THE HINDU

1953 United Artists
PRODUCER/DIRECTOR/SCREENWRITER:
Frank Ferrin
ALSO RELEASED AS: *Sabaka*
Boris Karloff plays a turbaned general in India faced with a murderous religious cult. With Victor Jory, Reginald Denny, and Lisa Howard. The real star is Nino Marcel as Gunga Ram, a young elephant trainer. Filmed in India.

HIPPIE HOLLYWOOD: THE ACID-BLASTING FREAKS: See MONDO HOLLYWOOD.

THE HIPPIE REVOLT

1967 Headliner
PRODUCER: Art Lieberman
DIRECTOR: Edgar Beatty
The Summer of Love, from Haight-Ashbury to Sunset Strip–filmed as it happened! Take a trip to the weird world of LSD! Witness the effects of POT on the male/female sex drive! Blow your mind to the sounds of the Love Generation! Plus body painting,

crash pads, love-ins, and freak-outs! Authentic hippie locale! —CB

HIS KIND OF WOMAN
1951 RKO (B&W)
PRODUCERS: Howard Hughes, Robert Sparks
DIRECTOR: John Farrow
SCREENWRITER: Frank Fenton

As a gambler just out of jail, Robert Mitchum is lured to Mexico where he is set up to be killed so deported syndicate boss Raymond Burr can assume his identity. Outrageous *film noir* with a vamping Jane Russell posing as an heiress, hammy Vincent Price as a matinee idol, and dialogue you won't believe. Russell wears a black bathing suit. Mitchum, who passes the time ironing money, is stripped, beaten, and offered a slow-death drug injection. With Tim Holt, Jim Backus, and Jane singing "Kiss and Run" and two other seductive tunes.

HIS WIFE'S HABIT: See WOMEN AND BLOODY TERROR.

HIT AND RUN
1957 United Artists (B&W)
PRODUCER/DIRECTOR/SCREENWRITER:
Hugo Haas

"Back from the grave for revenge!" Garage owner Hugo Haas is purposely killed by a hit-and-run driver. The murder was planned by a mechanic employee (Vince Edwards in his first starring role) to clear the way for romance with Hugo's young showgirl wife (Cleo Moore in her seventh Haas film). An unexpected twin-brother heir (Hugo again), just released from prison, shows up to straighten things out. Ella Mae Morse sings "What Good'll It Do Me."

HITLER'S HANGMAN: See HITLER'S MADMAN.

HITLER'S MADMAN
1943 MGM
PRODUCER: Seymour Nebenzal
DIRECTOR: Douglas Sirk
SCREENWRITER: Peretz Hirshbein
ALSO RELEASED AS: *Hitler's Hangman*

After fleeing Germany Douglas Sirk directed this, his first American film, for the tiny PRC company. It's based on the destruction of Lidice, Czechoslovakia, in retaliation for the assassination of Hitler's executioner Heydrich. Held up because of its similarity to Fritz Lang's *Hangmen Also Die*, Sirk's film was sold to MGM and released later. John Carradine stars as the war criminal. Alan Curtis is the hero. With Patricia Morison, Ralph Morgan, Edgar Kennedy, Peter Van Eyck, and Ava Gardner. It's one of the few PRC films anyone has anything good to say about.

HITLER'S SON
1978 (W. Germany)
ASSOC. PRODUCER: Burkhard Driest
DIRECTOR: Rod Amateau
SCREENWRITERS: Lukas Heller,
Burkhard Driest

Bud Cort, star of *Harold and Maude*, is Adolf's son Willy in this comedy, which didn't get released here. Peter Cushing's in it. The *Variety* ad says: "Ve haff vays of making you laff." Tasteful. Presented by Gerd Goering.

HOLD BACK TOMORROW
1955 Universal (B&W)
PRODUCER/DIRECTOR/SCREENWRITER:
Hugo Haas

John Agar sits in his death-row cell awaiting a late date with a noose. Somebody asks his last wish; he says get me a girl. Enter suicidal hooker Cleo Moore. Agar and friend, both hopelessly cynical, decide to be married by the prison chaplain. As John is being led away he mentions a dream in which the rope breaks, the prison bells ring, and he is pardoned because of the miracle. Moore waits in the prison chapel and as she prays, the bells begin to ring. With Frank De Kova and Harry Guardino.

–CB

HOLD ON!
1965 MGM
PRODUCER: Sam Katzman
DIRECTOR: Arthur Lubin
SCREENWRITER: James B. Gordon

Herman's Hermits were more popular here than in their native England. Even years after the departure of lead singer Peter Noone, the group continued to play small U.S. gigs. This wholesome American answer to the Beatles' *Help!* is based on the unlikely premise that NASA will name a spaceship after the group if they are deemed worthy. After a lot of screaming at a charity lawn party and a Rose Bowl show, they are. They do the hits "A Must to Avoid," "Leaning on a Lamppost," and others. With Shelley Fabares (in between Elvis films) and Sue Ann Langdon. The Hermits returned in *Mrs. Brown, You've Got a Lovely Daughter.*

HOLD THAT GHOST
1941 Universal (B&W)
ASSOCIATE PRODUCERS: Burt Kelly, Glenn Tryon
DIRECTOR: Arthur Lubin
SCREENWRITERS: Robert Lees, Fred Rinaldo, John Grant

The third of Abbott and Costello's hit wartime comedies featuring the Andrews Sisters. The newspaper ads advise you to "forget the news—shake the blues. . . . " It's a funny haunted house movie with Joan Davis as a professional radio screamer, Mischa Auer, Universal horror star Evelyn Ankers, young Richard Carlson, and Shemp Howard. Ankers and Carlson were married in real life. With Ted Lewis and his entertainers. Directed by Arthur Lubin,

John Agar shares his last meal with Cleo Moore in Hugo Haas' Hold Back Tomorrow.

who did the comedy team's best (their first five) and later was responsible for the *Mr. Ed* show.

HOLD THAT HYPNOTIST
1957 Allied Artists (B&W)
PRODUCER: Ben Schwalb
DIRECTOR: Austen Jewell
SCREENWRITER: Dan Pepper

The Bowery Boys jump on the *Bridey Murphy* bandwagon. Huntz Hall regresses to the 17th century, where he obtains a map from Blackbeard the Pirate (Mel Welles). With Stanley Clements.

HOLD THAT LINE
1952 Monogram (B&W)
PRODUCER: Jerry Thomas
DIRECTOR: William Beaudine
SCREENWRITERS: Tim Ryan, Charles R. Marion

The Bowery Boys go to college and use a super-strength formula to win the big game. With John Bromfield, Veda Ann Borg, Leo Gorcey, Huntz Hall, and the usual crew.

HOLIDAY IN SPAIN: See THE SCENT OF MYSTERY.

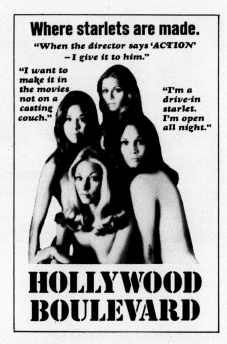

Where starlets are made.

"When the director says 'ACTION' — I give it to him."

"I want to make it in the movies not on a casting couch."

"I'm a drive-in starlet. I'm open all night."

HOLLYWOOD BOULEVARD

HOLLYWOOD BOULEVARD
1976 New World
PRODUCER: Jon Davidson
DIRECTORS: Joe Dante, Allan Arkush
SCREENWRITER: Patrick Hobby
The directors set out to parody drive-in features and make the lowest-budgeted, fastest New World picture in history. They succeeded. It's a crazed, fast-paced, paste-up job about filming *Machete Maidens of Maratau* for Miracle Pictures—with a masked killer on the set. Scenes from *The Terror* and *Battle Beyond the Sun* are used along with appearances by Robby the Robot, Dick Miller as Walter Paisley, Forrest J. Ackerman, director Paul Bartel as director Von Leppe, Commander Cody and his Lost Planet Airmen, and a final confrontation on top of the Hollywood sign. Mary Woronov and Candice Rialson star. This ultimate in-joke feature led to Arkush directing *Rock 'n' Roll High School* and Dante directing *Piranha* and *The Howling*. They had pre-

viously been editors on New World trailers. (R)

HOLLYWOOD CANTEEN
1944 Warner Brothers (B&W)
PRODUCER: Alex Gottlieb
DIRECTOR/SCREENWRITER: Delmer Daves
On sick leave from active duty, young Robert Hutton tries to pick up Joan Leslie at the canteen. Bette Davis explains how the establishment operates and endless stars sing, dance, or just appear. Some of them are: Peter Lorre, Sidney Greenstreet, Faye Emerson, and Zachary Scott (all had just been in *The Mask of Dimitrios*), Jack Benny, Roy Rogers and Trigger, Jimmy Dorsey and his band, the Andrews Sisters, Joan Crawford, Ida Lupino, Barbara Stanwyck, Jane Wyman, and Kitty Carlisle. It was Warners' biggest hit of the year.

HOLLYWOOD MEATCLEAVER MASSACRE: See *THE MEATCLEAVER MASSACRE*.

HOLOCAUST 2,000: See *THE CHOSEN*.

HOLY TERROR: See *ALICE, SWEET ALICE*.

HOMEBODIES
1974 Avco Embassy
PRODUCER: Marshal Blackar
DIRECTOR: Peter Brocco
SCREENWRITER: Larry Yust
A group of demented senior citizens threatened with eviction via urban renewal take desperate steps. Construction workers fry in an elevator cage, a knifed relocation hostess is dumped off a bridge into a freight car, and a capi-

talist contractor is buried alive in cement. Starring Frances Fuller, Ian Wolfe, Ruth McDevitt, and Kenneth Tobey. An excellent low budget oddity filmed in Cincinnati, where there's desperation to spare.   —CB

HOMESICK FOR ST. PAUL

1963 (W. Germany)
ORIGINALLY RELEASED AS: *Heimweh Nach St. Paul*

Jayne Mansfield sings in German, accompanied by accordions and glockenspiels. Her co-star is Freddy Quinn, an Elvis imitator. The film received a very limited American release in New York City.

HOMICIDAL

1961 Columbia (B&W)
PRODUCER/DIRECTOR: William Castle
SCREENWRITER: Robb White

Castle's classic! The first and most obvious *Psycho* imitation takes the transvestite theme a step further. The star (Jean Arless) plays Emily *and* her husband Warren. Arless' real sex is never revealed. Audiences weren't allowed in to see *Psycho* after the first five minutes of each showing. Audiences watching *Homicidal* were given a "fright break" five minutes before the end. They could "follow the yellow streak to the cowards' corner" and get their money back. Few people did. The film opens with Emily the icy blonde paying a confused bellboy (Richard Rust) to marry her. During the private nighttime ceremony she stabs the justice of the peace. The story gets more bizarre with the decapitation of an old mute woman, a trip to Denmark, and an unbelievable scheme to protect an inheritance. An incredible experience. Jean Arless, where are you? With Glenn Corbett, Patricia Breslin, and Hope Summers.

THE HONEYMOON KILLERS

1970 Cinerama (B&W)
PRODUCER: Warren Steibel
DIRECTOR/SCREENWRITER: Leonard Kastle
ALSO RELEASED AS: *The Lonely Hearts Killers*

Based on the true story of Ray Hernandez and Martha Beck, who met through

lonely-hearts correspondence and were executed in 1951 for the murders of Myrtle Young, Janet Fay, Delphine Downing and her 2-year-old daughter Rainelle. Between projects the immigrant gigolo and the overweight nurse from Mobile relax in a modest home on a quiet street in Valley Stream, Long Island. Starring Tony LoBianco and Shirley Stoler. Originally set for release by AIP in 1969 as *The Lonely Hearts Killers*. Definitely not made by the usual bozos. Required viewing. **(R)**   –CB

The Honeymoon Killers *caress.*

HONEYMOON OF HORROR

1964 Manson
PRODUCER: Herb Meyer
DIRECTOR: Irwin Meyer
SCREENWRITER: Alexander Panas
ALSO RELEASED AS: *The Deadly Circle, The Golden Nymphs, Orgy of the Golden Nudes*

Threatening phone calls and queer accidents plague sculptor Emile Duvre's new bride Lilli. It seems that each of Emile's friends has a reason to want her dead. The linkup with a series of statuettes seems to have been lifted from *Screaming Mimi*. Robert Parsons and Abbey Heller star as Emile and Lilli. Filmed in Miami and Coconut Grove, Florida. An adults only feature. Manson released *The Devil's Bedroom* and *Sinderella and the Golden Bra* the same year.   –CB

HONEYMOON WITH A STRANGER

1969 TV
PRODUCER: Robert Jacks
DIRECTOR: John Peyser
SCREENWRITERS: David P. Harmon, Henry Slesar

A pretty good mystery starring Janet Leigh. She wakes up from her wedding night alongside a stranger (Cesare Danova) who claims to be her husband. Nobody believes her. Rossano Brazzi is the police captain. Barbara Steele and Eric Braeden are in on the plot. Filmed in Spain, though the story takes place in Italy.

HONG KONG

1951 Paramount
PRODUCERS: William H. Pine, William C. Thomas
DIRECTOR: Lewis Foster
SCREENWRITER: Winston Miller

Ronald Reagan, dressed like Indiana Jones, is a crooked ex-GI in China after

World War II trying to steal a valuable antique from an orphan (Danny Chang). Rhonda Fleming helps him go straight. With Nigel Bruce and Marvin Miller as Tao Liang. The popular Ron-and-Rhonda team had just been in *The Last Outpost*. They returned in *Tropic Zone*.

THE HOOKED GENERATION

1968 Allied Artists
PRODUCER/DIRECTOR: William Grefe
SCREENWRITER: Quinn Morrison

Pushers Daisy (Jeremy Slate), Acid (John David Chandler) and Dum Dum (Willie Pastrano) are spotted murdering their Cuban suppliers and burning their boat. Intervening Coast Guardsmen are eliminated in turn; informers Steve Alaimo and Cece Stone are dragged away to a Seminole camp hideout. The nightmare ends as Daisy gets a hypo in the neck following the deaths of Acid and Dum Dum by bullet and snake. Camp scenes were filmed in the Everglades. With Socrates Ballis, Michael De Beausset, and William Kerwin of *Decoy for Terror*. Music by the Bangles. Alaimo was a regular on *Where the Action Is.* —CB

HOOTENANNY HOOT

1963 MGM (B&W)
PRODUCER: Sam Katzman
DIRECTOR: Gene Nelson
SCREENWRITER: James B. Gordon

Peter Breck (*Shock Corridor*, *The Crawling Hand*) plays a New York TV director who makes a star of Pamela Austin after hearing her lead a college hootenanny. He turns the show into a TV series (there really was a 1963–64 TV series) and gets back with his wife Ruta Lee (*Doomsday Machine*). Music is provided by Johnny Cash, Sheb Wooley, the Brothers Four, Judy Henske, and George Hamilton IV. With Chris Crosby and Joby Baker (the *Gidget* series).

THE HORRIBLE DR. HICHCOCK

1962 Sigma III (Italy)
PRODUCERS: Luigi Carpentieri, Ermano Donati
DIRECTOR: Riccardo Freda (Robert Hampton)
SCREENWRITER: Julyan Perry
ORIGINALLY RELEASED AS: *L'Orribile Segreto del Dottore Hichcock*

Dr. Hichcock (Robert Flemyng), a necrophiliac living in 1885, likes to drug his wife for sexual "funeral games." When he goes too far she dies. Twelve years later the sick doc marries the lovely Cynthia (Barbara Steele), but wife No. 1 returns from the grave, in terrible shape. He tries to restore the rotting first wife by hanging his second one upside down and draining her blood. An outrageous Euro-gothic horror film with some choice ad lines: "His secret was a coffin named desire!" And: "The candle of his lust burnt brightest in the shadow of the grave!" The American version is missing 12 minutes of sexual deviation. Barbara Steele returned in a sequel, *The Ghost*. The director was a former art critic.

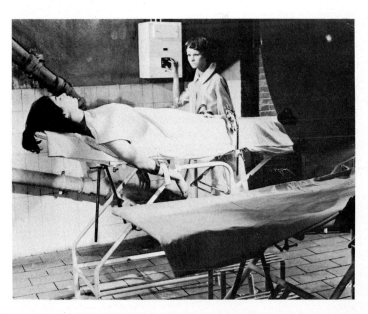

Edith Scob visits her father's lab in The Horror Chamber of Dr. Faustus.

THE HORRIBLE SEXY VAMPIRE

1970 Paragon (Spain)
PRODUCER: Edmondo Amanti
DIRECTOR: Jose Luis Madrid
ORIGINALLY RELEASED AS: *El Vampiro de la Utopista*

Waldemar Wohlfahrt plays the reincarnation of a vampire baron. The best horror movie title of 1970.

HORROR: See THE BLANCHEVILLE MONSTER.

THE HORROR AT 37,000 FEET

1973 TV
PRODUCER: Anthony Wilson
DIRECTOR: David Lowell Rich
SCREENWRITERS: Ron Austin, Jim Buchanan

A druid stone in the baggage compartment puts a jetliner and its passengers in danger and causes many strange happenings. On board are Chuck Connors, William Shatner, Roy Thinnes, Buddy Ebsen, France Nuyen, Russell Johnson, Tammy Grimes, Paul Winfield, Will Hutchins, and Lynn Loring.

HORROR CASTLE

1964 Zodiac Films (Italy)
PRODUCER: Marco Vicario
DIRECTOR: Antonio Margheriti (Anthony Dawson)
SCREENWRITERS: Antonio Margheriti, G. Green, Edmond T. Greville
ORIGINALLY RELEASED AS: *La Vergine de Norimberga*
ALSO RELEASED AS: *Terror Castle, Castle of Terror*

A haunted castle on the Rhine is the setting for this typical Euro-horror movie with Christopher Lee as the terribly scarred chauffeur/caretaker. Georges Rivière arrives at the family castle with his American wife (Rossana Podesta) and the mysterious mutilation murders begin. Some believe a 300-year-old executioner is using the still-intact and well-supplied torture chamber. The truth about the deaths turns out to be related to more recent torturers—Nazis.

HORROR CHAMBER OF DR. FAUSTUS

1959 Lopert (France/Italy) (B&W)
PRODUCER: Jules Borkon
DIRECTOR: Georges Franju
SCREENWRITERS: Georges Franju, Jean Redon, Claude Sautet, Pierre Boileau, Thomas Narcejac
ORIGINALLY RELEASED AS: *Yeux sans Visage*

A classic, poetic horror film with a much-copied plot about a plastic surgeon trying to revive his daughter's beauty. Pierre Brasseur sends his assistant (Alida Valli) to kidnap young female victims in Paris. As the scarred daughter, Edith Scob wears an immobile face mask with holes for her large sad eyes. One extremely shocking scene shows the doctor cutting around the face and eyes of a woman and slowly peeling off the skin. Even now, over 20 years later, modern gore makeup effects haven't duplicated that unsettling close-up. It ends with the masked daughter releasing cages of experimental dogs and doves. Music by Maurice Jarre.

HORROR CREATURES OF THE PREHISTORIC PLANET: See HORROR OF THE BLOOD MONSTERS.

HORROR EXPRESS

1972 Scotia International (Spain/England)
PRODUCER: Bernard Gordon
DIRECTOR: Eugenio Martia
SCREENWRITER: Arnaud D'Usseau
ORIGINALLY RELEASED AS: *Pancio en el Transiberiano*

Before groaning—not another Christopher Lee—Peter Cushing movie!—try

only wants to get laid. Then he develops a serum that turns him into a brutal monster! He dissolves the cruel janitor in a drum of chemicals! He removes his bitchy English teacher's hand with a paper cutter! As the part-time killer Potts, Pat Cardi is good, but the rest of the cast is pretty awful. The cops are all played by football pros. Don't let that stop you from watching this obscure teen epic. **(R)**

HORROR HOSPITAL

1973 Hallmark (England)
PRODUCER: Richard Gordon
DIRECTOR: Anthony Balch
SCREENWRITERS: Anthony Balch,
    Alan Watson
ALSO RELEASED AS: *Computer Killers*

Michael Gough, the British king of horror-film ranting and overacting, stars as Dr. Storm in a misfire comedy of decapitations and brain experiments. Robert Askwith is a Peter Noone lookalike pop singer who visits the hospital. It was re-released here with an ad campaign comparing it to *Coma*. With Dennis Price as a humorous homosexual and a scene-stealing dwarf (Skip Martin). **(R)**

HORROR HOTEL

1960 Trans-Lux (England) (B&W)
PRODUCERS: Milton Subotsky,
    Donald Taylor
DIRECTOR: John Moxey
SCREENWRITER: George Baxt
ALSO RELEASED AS: *The City of the Dead*

"Just ring for doom service!" the ads advise. A good witchcraft movie with an interesting plot similarity to *Psycho*, released the same year. A girl goes alone to an inn and is killed. Her boyfriend and brother arrive to look for her. Christopher Lee, a history professor, is part of a modern coven in Whitewood, Massachusetts. Patricia Jessel, proprietress of the inn, is really a centuries-

watching this fun science-fiction/horror story set on the Trans-Siberian express in 1906. Explorer Lee is returning from China with the body of an apelike "missing link" inhabited by an alien force. The alien can assimilate all the knowledge from people by staring at them. The process "boils" their brains, causes death, and makes their eyes bleed and turn white. The life force later takes over various passengers who appear normal but kill. Lee teams with rival Cushing to defeat the creature and saw the tops off victim's heads for brain inspections. In a *Night of the Living Dead*–style scene, all the dead passengers return as zombies and march through the train toward the terrified survivors. With Telly Savalas as an uncouth Cossack policeman. Made because the producer owned the model train used in *Nicholas and Alexander* (1971).

HORROR HIGH

1974 Crown International
PRODUCER: Tom Moore
DIRECTOR: Larry Stouffer
SCREENWRITER: Jake Fowler
ALSO RELEASED AS: *Twisted Brain*

Incredibly cheap production originally shot in 16mm. Werner Potts, an intelligent but wimpy chemistry student, is ridiculed by jocks, girls, even the janitor. His teachers are mean and his dad

The exciting climax of Horror Hotel.

old witch. The two men arrive in time for the sacrifice of a history student (Betta St. John) and in an exciting climax one of them manages, while dying, to kill the witches with the shadow of a cemetery cross. Recommended. Screenwriter Baxt also wrote *Circus of Horrors*.

HORROR HOTEL MASSACRE: See *EATEN ALIVE*.

HORROR HOUSE

1969 Tigon/AIP (England)
PRODUCER: Tony Tenser
DIRECTOR: Michael Armstrong
SCREENWRITERS: Michael Armstrong, Peter Marcus
ALSO RELEASED AS: *The Haunted House of Horror*

Just what we needed—30-year-old "kid" Frankie Avalon in a British haunted-house-party movie. One of the teens is killing the others with a Kukri knife. Who could it be? It's not Frankie; he dies a bloody death. With Jill Haworth, Mark Wynter, and Dennis Price. By the director of *Mark of the Devil*. It was sometimes part of a "Ghoul-a-rama" show with *The Conqueror Worm* and two other British horrors.

HORROR ISLAND

1941 Universal (B&W)
ASSOCIATE PRODUCER: Ben Pivar
DIRECTOR: George Waggner
SCREENWRITERS: Maurice Trombragel, Victor McLeod

"The Phantom" stalks a haunted castle where people are searching for a treasure. With Dick Foran, Peggy Moran, Leo Carrillo (*The Cisco Kid*), and Fuzzy Knight.

HORROR OF DRACULA

1958 Hammer/Universal (England)
PRODUCER: Anthony Hinds
DIRECTOR: Terence Fisher
SCREENWRITER: Jimmy Sangster
ALSO RELEASED AS: *Dracula*

The best vampire film ever made. Time hasn't diminished the impact of this ground-breaking hit. Christopher Lee is great as the tall caped count that the Victorian ladies swoon over. Based on Bram Stoker's novel, this version has just the right doses of blood, sex, and horror. Hammer made seven sequels, all but one starring Lee. Peter Cushing returned as Dr. Van Helsing in only three. Michael Gough's role as Arthur Holmwood led to a career in horror films. Holmwood's wife Mina (Melissa Stribbling) and sister Lucy (Carol Marsh) are both vampire victims. As Jonathan Harker, John Van Eyssen seems to be the main character until his untimely death. With Valerie Gaunt as the vampire who ages when staked by Harker. *The Brides of Dracula* was the immediate sequel.

THE HORROR OF FRANKENSTEIN

1970 Hammer/Continental (England)
PRODUCER/DIRECTOR: Jimmy Sangster
SCREENWRITERS: Jimmy Sangster, Jeremy Burnham

Before *Andy Warhol's Frankenstein* and Mel Brooks' *Young Frankenstein* (both

1974), England's Hammer Studios did the first real Frankenstein comedy, which is basically a remake of their own *Curse of Frankenstein*. Too bad it isn't funny. The doctor (Ralph Bates) brings a dead turtle back to life and assembles his monster by numbers. Scenes from *The Bride of Frankenstein* are parodied (as in Brooks' overrated version) and there's some sex and gore (as in the Warhol/Morrissey version). The silly-looking muscular creature is Dave Prowse, the body builder in *A Clockwork Orange* who went on to play Darth Vader in the *Star Wars* movies. Also with Hammer Studio beauties Veronica Carlson and Kate O'Mara, Dennis Price as a grave-robber, and future star Jon Finch as a student. (R)

THE HORROR OF IT ALL

1964 Lippert/20th Century-Fox (England)
ASSOCIATE PRODUCER: Margia Dean
DIRECTOR: Terence Fisher
SCREENWRITER: Ray Russel

Mr. Wholesome, Pat Boone (who sings the title song), is an American visiting the Marley mansion in England to ask permission to marry one of the family's daughters. It's a horror/comedy similar to *The Old Dark House*, which had just been remade. The murderous eccentric family includes Dennis Price, Andre Melly as a possible vampire (she was definitely one in *The Brides of Dracula*), a werewolfish madman, and a brother with an electric hearse.

HORROR OF PARTY BEACH

1964 20th Century-Fox (B&W)
PRODUCER/DIRECTOR: Del Tenney
SCREENWRITER: Richard L. Hilliard

Forget anemic teen horror films like *Ghost in the Invisible Bikini*. This low-budget gem from Stamford, Connecticut, features kids on the beach dancing to "The Zombie Stomp" and a girl who drinks hard liquor and strips for bikers. Meanwhile radioactive waste turns human skulls on the bottom of the ocean into horrible monsters! They kill the wayward girl on the beach, then all the girls at a slumber party. If you don't understand what's happening, newspaper headlines (MONSTERS STRIKE!, MONSTERS STRIKE AGAIN!, and MASS MURDER AT SLUMBER PARTY!) are shown to keep you informed. With great music by the Del-Aires, lame jokes, phony blood, a sportscar driven through New York City, and a maid named Eulabelle

David Prowse as the monster in Horror of Frankenstein.

The Del-Aires do the zombie stomp in Horror of Party Beach.

Filipino vampires in Horror of the Blood Monsters.

gating a vampire tribe that plans to conquer Earth! Narrator Theodore Gottlieb tries to help make sense of things. Vilmos Zsigmond was the cinematographer. Ten points for the title.

HORROR OF THE ZOMBIES

1974 Independent International (Spain)
PRODUCER: J.L. Bermuder De Castro
DIRECTOR/SCREENWRITER: Armando De Ossorio
ORIGINALLY RELEASED AS: *El Buque Maldito*

An exercise in tedium favored by late-night television starers, this sequel to *The Blind Dead* takes place almost entirely on a sailing boat. Bikini-clad fashion models are chased in endless circles by eyeless ghouls wearing hoods. Maria Perschy and Jack Taylor star. The Spanish zombies were back again in *Night of the Seagulls*.

HORROR ON SNAPE ISLAND

1971 Fanfare (England)
PRODUCER: Richard Gordon
DIRECTOR/SCREENWRITER: Jim O'Connolly
ALSO RELEASED AS: *Beyond the Fog,*
Tower of Evil

Bryant Halliday stars in a tale of murder, cannabalism, and an ancient Phoenician axe. With George Coulouris, Dennis Price, and Jill Haworth. It was rereleased in '81 with a new title to mislead people into thinking it might be a sequel to *The Fog*. Halliday also starred in *Devil Doll*, *Curse of the Voodoo*, and *The Projected Man* for producer Gordon. (**R**)

HORROR PLANET:
See INSEMINOID.

HORROR RISES FROM THE TOMB

1972 Avco Embassy (Spain)
PRODUCER: Profilms
DIRECTOR: Carlos Aured
SCREENWRITER: Jacinto Molina
ORIGINALLY RELEASED AS: *El Espanto Surge*
La Tomba

who saves the day by knocking over a beaker of sodium on a living monster hand, which promptly disintegrates. Billed as "the first horror monster musical!" it's a cool classic that was also turned into a photo comic book. EXTRA! EXTRA! FIVE MORE KILLED BY MONSTERS!

HORROR OF THE BLOOD MONSTERS

1970 Independent International Pictures
PRODUCER/DIRECTOR: Al Adamson
SCREENWRITER: Sue McNair
ALSO RELEASED AS: *Creatures of the Prehistoric Planet, Horror Creatures of the Prehistoric Planet, Space Mission of the Lost Planet, Vampire Men of the Lost Planet*

This paste-up science-fiction atrocity includes footage from a black-and-white Filipino movie with "snake men," "bat demons," and "claw creatures." To explain the tinted scenes the alien planet on which they take place is said to be poisoned with "chromatic radiation" that alters the colors of the spectrum! The phony color was even advertised as "Spectrum X!" The new scenes filmed in America feature Adamson regulars John Carradine, Robert Dix, and Vicki Volante as astronaut/scientists investi-

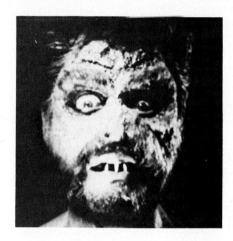

Paul Naschy, a 15th-century knight beheaded for witchcraft, returns to life in modern times and takes control of his identical descendant (Paul Naschy).

THE HORRORS OF SPIDER ISLAND

1959 Pacemaker
(W. Germany/Yugoslavia) (B&W)
PRODUCER: Gaston Hakim
DIRECTOR: Fritz Bottger (Jamie Nolan)
ORIGINALLY RELEASED AS: *Ein Toter im Netz*
ALSO RELEASED AS: *It's Hot in Paradise*

Egyptian actor Alex D'Arcy, the star of *Blood of Dracula's Castle*, plays a Hollywood talent scout who, along with seven pretty showgirls, survives a plane crash on a remote island. They discover a dead scientist caught in a giant spiderweb and (surprise!) giant spiders. Alex is bitten and becomes a giant, ugly, hairy-faced monster. The gruesome but tacky special effects resemble a Bert I. Gordon film, but it's all in German. An outrageous oddity.

HORRORS OF THE BLACK MUSEUM

1959 Anglo-Amalgamated/AIP
(England/U.S.)
PRODUCER: Herman Cohen
DIRECTOR: Arthur Crabtree
SCREENWRITERS: Aben Kandel,
Herman Cohen

The public loves to read the grisly details of sensational murders, so crime reporter Michael Gough provides the imaginative killings and then benefits from the detailed accounts he writes. This unforgettable sick film begins with a woman testing a new pair of binoculars, especially equipped with spikes that go right into her eyes. Gough displays the murder weapons in his museum and signs autographed copies of his bestseller *The Poetry of Murder* for his adoring fans. Using hypnotism, he turns his faithful young assistant into a lumpy-faced zombie who kills women and eventually rebels in an amusement-park climax. Gough, in his best role, puts bodies into an acid vat and kills with ice tongs and a guillotine/bed. With Graham Gurnow, June Cunningham, and Shirley Ann Field (who finds a body in a trunk in *Peeping Tom*). Originally advertised as being filmed in "Hypno-vision," which referred to a 13-minute lecture-prologue on hypnotism.

The giant German monster in The Horrors of Spider Island.

Ex-centerfold Barbi Benton emotes in The Hospital Massacre.

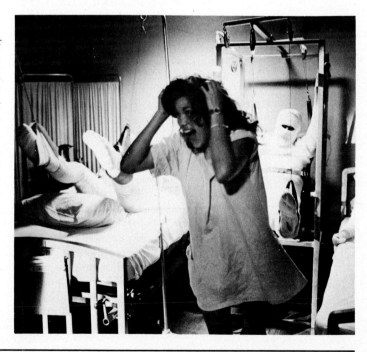

HOSPITAL MASSACRE

1982 Cannon
PRODUCERS: Menahem Golem,
Yoram Globus
DIRECTOR: Boaz Davidson
SCREENWRITER: Marc Behm
ALSO RELEASED AS: *Ward 13*

Playboy playmates in the past haven't done too well in movies. Remember *Galaxina, Blood Feast,* and *Twins of Evil?* Barbi Benton, Hugh Hefner's own one-time girlfriend, left her big Country music career for the inevitable exploitation movie career. See Barbi menaced by evil orderlies! See Barbi get a hypo in the neck! See Barbi take her clothes off! Box-office gold! **(R)**

THE HOSTAGE

1966 Crown International
PRODUCER/DIRECTOR:
Russell S. Doughton, Jr.
SCREENWRITER: Robert Laning

A six-year-old boy is locked in a moving van driven by two murderers. A low-budget adventure with Harry Dean Stanton as the weak-willed Eddie and Don O'Kelly as his violent, dominating partner Bull. John Carradine plays Otis Lovelace, a derelict. Filmed on location near Des Moines, Iowa. Ted V. Mikels was the cinematographer. Gary Kurtz was the editor and assistant director.

THE HOT ANGEL

1958 Paramount (B&W)
PRODUCER/SCREENWRITER: Stanley Kallis
DIRECTOR: Joe Parker

The ads promised: "Hot rod hot-shots and their tailgate babes!" A Korean war vet looks after his dead buddy's sister and kid brother while doing aerial survey work for a uranium prospector. The boy gets mixed up with a delinquent gang led by the son of a ruthless claim jumper, and the sister falls in love. Featuring Edward Kemmer, Mason Alan Dinehart, Jackie Loughery, and the Grand Canyon from above.   –CB

HOT CAR GIRL

1958 Allied Artists (B&W)
PRODUCER: Gene Corman
DIRECTOR: Bernard Kowalski
SCREENWRITER: Leo Gordon

"Defiant young trouble-mongers on the loose!" the ads shrilled. Richard Bakalyan and his pals make lunch money selling stolen auto parts to a crooked junk dealer. They have parties. Their downfall comes when a gang girl kills a cop in a chicken run. Bakalyan and June Kenney flee, leaving a trail of stolen cars and bodies; he sends his sidekick to safety before getting himself killed in a torrent of lead at the mouth of a cave. Originally distributed with *Cry Baby Killer.* Featuring John Brinkley, Robert Knapp, Jana Lund, Sheila McKay, Ed Nelson, Jack Lambert, and Bruno Ve Sota. Music by Cal Tjader. Roger Corman was executive producer.
      –CB

HOT CARS

1956 United Artists
PRODUCER: Howard Koch
DIRECTOR: Ranald MacDougall
SCREENWRITERS: Don Martin, Rich Landau

Used car salesman fired for refusing to foist reconditioned wreck on customer is forced to return to work as infant son's medical bills accumulate. John Bromfield soon comes under suspicion for the murder of a detective investigating his employer's scam, but he clears himself after a harrowing roller-coaster struggle with the real killer. Cast includes Joi Lansing, Mark Dana, Carol Shannon, and Dabbs Greer. Music by Les Baxter.   –CB

HOT MONEY GIRL: See LONG DISTANCE.

HOT ROD

1950 Monogram (B&W)
PRODUCER: Jerry Thomas
DIRECTOR: Lewis D. Collins
SCREENWRITER: Daniel Ullman

A judge's suspicions are confirmed when a hot rod belonging to his son (James Lydon, star of the Henry Aldrich films) is involved in a hit-and-run fatality. Lydon claims the car was stolen by the killer, whom he eventually gets to confess. Then James vindicates himself by using his flathead roadster to aid in the capture of a dangerous fugitive. With Gil Stratton, Jr., Myron Healey, and Gloria Winters of the *Sky King* TV series.   –CB

HOT ROD GANG

1958 AIP (B&W)
PRODUCER: Buddy Rogers
DIRECTOR: Lew Landers
SCREENWRITER: Lou Rusoff
ALSO RELEASED AS: *Fury Unleashed*

See "Crazy kids living to a wild rock and roll beat!" as advertised. While waiting for two aunts and their attorney to come through with his inheritance, John Ashley of *The Eye Creatures* uses his singing talents to finance hotcar projects. He is befriended by Gene Vincent, who does "Dance in the Street," "Dance to the Bop," "Baby Blue," and "Lovely Loretta" with the Bluecaps and unbilled Eddie Cochran. The cast includes Jody Fair, Steve Drexel, Dub Taylor, and Doodles Weaver. Originally shown with *High School Hellcats*.   –CB

HOT ROD GIRL

1956 AIP (B&W)
PRODUCER: Norman Herman
DIRECTOR: Leslie H. Martinson
SCREENWRITER: John McGreevey

The ads promised: "Teenage terrorists on a speed-crazy rampage!" Policeman Chuck Connors sets up a supervised hot-rod racing program with help from a young enthusiast, but John Smith withdraws his support following the death of his younger brother in a crackup. Back to street dragging and chicken runs for the local delinquents. Soon Smith is arrested in the hit-and-run death of a grade-schooler, and Connors chases down the truth. With Lori Nelson, Mark Andrews, Frank Gorshin, Roxanne Arlen, and Dabbs Greer. Originally a co-feature with *Girls in Prison*.   –CB

HOT ROD HULLABALOO

1966 Allied Artists
PRODUCERS: Martin T. Low,
  William T. Naud
DIRECTOR: William T. Naud
SCREENWRITER: Stanley Schneider

Terror stalks a nonsanctioned demolition derby. The hero, who needs to win money to pay his college tuition, doesn't know that his chief competitor intends to shoot anyone who gets in the way. A friend gets word to the student hero's girl before being run down in an amusement park. The girl sticks a pencil in the barrel of the gun. Featuring John Arnold, Arlen Dean Snyder, and Kendra Kerr, with Gene Bua, Val Bisoglio, and Marsha Mason. Location scenes shot in and around Washington, D.C. From the director of *Thunder in Dixie*.   –CB

HOT ROD RUMBLE

1957 Allied Artists (B&W)
PRODUCER: Norman Herman
DIRECTOR: Leslie H. Martinson
SCREENWRITER: Meyer Doblinsky

"Loudmouth" (Brett Halsey) is accused of murder when a street job carrying Leigh Snowden and another of her suitors is forced off the road, killing Loudmouth's rival. The truth leaks out amid live drag action from Pomona. A dual release with *Calypso Joe*. Richard Hartunian, Wright King, and Joey Forman appear. Director Martinson ended up at Warners TV doing *77 Sunset Strip*, *Cheyenne*, and *Bronco*.   —CB

HOT RODS TO HELL

1967 MGM
PRODUCER: Sam Katzman
DIRECTOR: John Brahm
SCREENWRITER: Robert E. Kent
ALSO RELEASED AS: *52 Miles to Terror*

"They're souped up for thrills and there's no limit to what they'll do!" the ads screamed. Dana Andrews, his wife (Jeanne Crain), their teenage daughter and little boy drive through the California desert heading for a new life running a restaurant-motel. Their dreams go bad when Mimsy Farmer and her two delinquent boyfriends chase the car, throw beer cans in the window, try to seduce the daughter, and finally drive Dana to take action. In the end, the trouble-makers promise to "behave like sensible adults." Music by Mickey Rooney, Jr., and his combo! Originally filmed as a television movie, it was deemed too sensational for that medium. So it played theaters and ended up on TV soon after. Mimsy did *Devil's Angels*, *Riot on Sunset Strip*, and *The Wild Racers*, then relocated to Europe.

HOTEL BERLIN

1945 Warner Brothers (B&W)
PRODUCER: Louis F. Edelman
DIRECTOR: Peter Godfrey
SCREENWRITER: Jo Pagano

Germans during the last days of the war, based on a novel by Vicki Baum (*Grand Hotel*). Helmut Dantine stars as an underground leader. Peter Lorre is Koenig, an alcoholic scientist. Faye Emerson is an actress. With Raymond Massey as a defecting Nazi general, George Coulouris as a Gestapo head planning the next war, Alan Hale, Henry Daniell, and Andrea King. Ads promised more of "the *Casablanca* kind of sensation."

HOUDINI

1953 Paramount
PRODUCER: George Pal
DIRECTOR: George Marshall
SCREENWRITER: Phillip Yordan

A highly fictionalized bio of the great magician and escape artist that relied on the real-life star couple of Tony Curtis and Janet Leigh to draw audiences. Houdini deserves better. With Torin Thatcher (the villain in *The Seventh Voyage of Sinbad*), Sig Ruman, and Ian Wolfe. Busy director Marshall made *Scared Stiff* and two other features the same year.

HOUND DOG MAN

1959 20th Century-Fox
PRODUCER: Jerry Wald
DIRECTOR: Don Siegel
SCREENWRITERS: Fred Gipson, Winston Miller

Call them punks...
Call them animals...
But you better get out of their way!

They're souped-up for thrills and there's no limit to what they'll do!

METRO-GOLDWYN-MAYER PRESENTS
HOT RODS TO HELL
DANA ANDREWS · JEANNE CRAIN
MIMSY FARMER · LAURIE MOCK · PAUL BERTOYA · GENE KIRKWOOD and MICKEY ROONEY, JR. AND HIS COMBO
ROBERT E. KENT · JOHN BRAHM · SAM KATZMAN A FOUR LEAF PRODUCTION IN METROCOLOR

UPI 8/26/59: Literally following in the footsteps of Elvis Presley (left), 16-year-old rock 'n' roll singer Fabian (right) is playing an almost identical role in his first movie. Appearing in Hound Dog Man, Fabian is even wearing some of the same clothes Elvis wore in his first movie. Among the other similarities: both made their debut at 20th Century-Fox; both played younger brothers; both wore the same blue jeans; both were named Clint in the films; and both wore the same shoes. Elvis is shown during the filming of Love Me Tender in 1956.

Sixteen-year-old Fabian Forte Bonaparte makes his acting debut in a period film with teen appeal. The story, set in 1912, features Carol Lynley, Dodie Stevens, Claude Akins, Edgar Buchanan, Arthur O'Connell, Jane Darwell, L.Q. Jones, Royal Dano, and Stuart Whitman. The theme song was a top-10 hit. Siegel directed Elvis in *Flaming Star* the next year. Fabian's only big hits came when Elvis was in the army. Curtis Harrington was associate producer.

THE HOUND OF THE BASKERVILLES

1939 20th Century-Fox (B&W)
ASSOCIATE PRODUCER: Gene Markey
DIRECTOR: Sidney Lanfield
SCREENWRITER: Ernest Pascal

Basil Rathbone and Nigel Bruce team as Holmes and Watson for the first time. For years it was unavailable for viewing, possibly because of a brief mention of Sherlock's cocaine habit. Richard Green is Sir Henry. Cast members under suspicion include Lionel Atwill as an occult doctor and John Carradine as a sinister overseer. Wendy Barrie loves Sir Henry. Mary Gordon is Mrs. Hudson. The Victorian era sleuth returned later that year in *The Adventures of Sherlock Holmes*. "Watson, the needle!"

THE HOUND OF THE BASKERVILLES

1959 Hammer/United Artists (England)
PRODUCER: Anthony Hinds
DIRECTOR: Terence Fisher
SCREENWRITER: Peter Bryan

The first Holmes film since the Universal series ended in '46 stars Peter Cushing as the famed detective. It shows more of the decadence and horror of Baskerville Hall than any other version and was the first Holmes in color. Christopher Lee is Sir Henry. Andre Morell is Dr. Watson. Lee next took the Holmes role in *Valley of Fear*.

THE HOUND OF THE BASKERVILLES
1972 TV
PRODUCER: Stanley Kallis
DIRECTOR: Barry Crane
SCREENWRITER: Robert E. Thompson
A weak pilot film for a series that would have alternated Holmes stories with the exploits of Nick Carter (Robert Conrad) and Hildegarde Withers (Eve Arden). Stewart Granger is Sherlock Holmes. Bernard Fox is Watson. With William Shatner, John Williams, and Anthony Zerbe.

THE HOUND OF THE BASKERVILLES
1978 Atlantic (England)
PRODUCER: John Goldstone
DIRECTOR: Paul Morrissey
SCREENWRITERS: Peter Cook, Dudley Moore, Paul Morrissey
This spoof, written by its stars, Peter Cook and Dudley Moore, wasn't released here until after Moore's new fame in *10*. It features an *Exorcist* takeoff, Terry-Thomas, Joan Greenwood, Kenneth Williams (from *Carry On* films), and Spike Milligan. From the director of *Trash*.

THE HOURS OF LOVE
1963 Cinema V (Italy) (B&W)
PRODUCERS: Isidoro Broggi, Renato Libassi
DIRECTOR: Luciano Salce
SCREENWRITERS: Luciano Salce, Franco Castellano
A comedy starring Ugo Tognazzi and Emmanuelle Riva as a couple whose romance ends when they marry. Barbara Steele is third-billed.

THE HOUSE BY THE LAKE
1976 AIP (Canada)
PRODUCER: Ivan Reitman
DIRECTOR/SCREENWRITER: William Freut
ALSO RELEASED AS: *Death Weekend*
While on vacation, Brenda Vaccaro and her boyfriend are attacked by a quartet of sadistic goons led by Don Stroud. It's sometimes billed with the similar but much stronger *Last House on the Left*. Freut later directed the dull *Funeral Home*. (R)

THE HOUSE IN MARSH ROAD: See THE INVISIBLE CREATURE.

HOUSE OF CRAZIES: See ASYLUM.

HOUSE OF DARK SHADOWS
1970 MGM
PRODUCER/DIRECTOR: Dan Curtis
SCREENWRITERS: Sam Hall, Gordon Russell
Dark Shadows series regulars Jonathan Frid and Joan Bennett appear as Barnabas and Elizabeth Collins. Grayson Hall, Kathryn Leigh Scott, and Roger Davis all repeat their TV roles. Nancy Barret stands out as a Hammer-style vampire who gets staked. The reason the 150-year-old Barnabas so closely resembles Dustin Hoffman in *Little Big Man* is that Dick Smith used basically the same latex appliance makeup in both films. Also with Thayer David. *Night of Dark Shadows* was the sequel. Some of the 1,000 original half-hour TV episodes are now in syndication. Thirteen years later, Curtis moved from cheap monsters to a multimillion-dollar mini-series called *Winds of War*.

HOUSE OF DRACULA
1945 Universal (B&W)
PRODUCER: Paul Malvern
DIRECTOR: Erle C. Kenton
SCREENWRITER: Edward T. Lowe

The superior follow-up to *The House of Frankenstein* stars the unbilled Onslow Stevens as Dr. Edelmann, a scientist who becomes a wide-eyed killer when Dracula's blood is mixed with his. He also revives the Frankenstein monster (Glenn Strange) and tries to "cure" the Wolfman (Lon Chaney, Jr.), and Dracula (John Carradine). Jane Adams is a pretty hunchbacked nurse, the perfect girl for Chaney. Lionel Atwill is another police inspector (he always seems to turn up with a new name and the same uniform in these films). Martha O'Driscoll is the other nurse. With Ludwig Stossel and Skelton Knaggs. Lots of stock footage and music can be recognized from earlier Universal horror hits. This was the end of the trail for the famous Universal monsters—until they met Abbott and Costello three years later.

HOUSE OF EVIL
1968 Columbia (U.S./Mexico)
PRODUCER: Luis Enrique Veraga
DIRECTORS: Juan Ibañez, Jack Hill
SCREENWRITER: Jack Hill
One of the four seldom-seen Mexican cheapies for which Boris Karloff shot scenes in Los Angeles shortly before he died. This one is a horror film involving a torture dungeon. American director Hill is an old hand at piecing together movies like this, having worked on *The Terror*, *Blood Bath*, and others for AIP.

THE HOUSE OF EXORCISM
1975 Peppercorn Wormser (Italy)
PRODUCER: Alfred Leone
DIRECTOR: Mickey Lion (Mario Bava)
SCREENWRITERS: Alberto Tintini, Alfred Leone
ORIGINALLY RELEASED AS: *La Casa dell' Exorcismo*
ALSO RELEASED AS: *Lisa and the Devil*
A confusing horror movie starring Elke Sommer, who discovers a mannequin of herself. There's a warped family with a sadistic husband and nympho wife, a necro son, and, as the butler, Telly Savalas (with a lollipop!). New "exorcist" scenes with Robert Alda as a priest and Elke spewing bile and frogs were added for the American release, but reportedly both versions can be seen on television. With Alida Valli and Sylva Koscina. It's Savalas' best Italian film. (R)

HOUSE OF FEAR
1939 Universal (B&W)
ASSOC. PRODUCER: Edmund Grainger
DIRECTOR: Joe May
SCREENWRITER: Peter Milne
A pretty tame remake of *The Last Warning* (1928), about a phony murderous ghost in a haunted theater. The creaky whodunit features William Gargan, Irene Hervey, El Brendel, Robert Coote, and Walter Woolf King.

THE HOUSE OF FEAR
1944 Universal (B&W)
PRODUCER/DIRECTOR: Roy William Neill
SCREENWRITER: Roy Chanslor
Sherlock Holmes (Basil Rathbone) and Watson (Nigel Bruce) go to a mansion in Scotland where members of "The Good Comrades" club are being murdered. Based on "The Five Orange Pips," a short story by Arthur Conan Doyle. With Dennis Hoey, Gavin Muir, and Paul Cavanaugh.

HOUSE OF FRANKENSTEIN
1945 Universal (B&W)
PRODUCER: Paul Malvern
DIRECTOR: Erle C. Kenton
SCREENWRITER: Edward T. Lowe
As a mad doctor, Boris Karloff escapes from prison with Daniel the hunchback (J. Carrol Naish) and seeks revenge plus Dr. Frankenstein's journal in this episodic all-star monster extravaganza. John Carradine is good playing Dracula

for the first time, but he's destroyed before Lon Chaney, Jr., as the Wolfman, shows up in search of a cure for lycanthropy. Debuting as the monster, Glenn Strange doesn't have much to do. As professor Lampini, George Zucco has his identity and traveling horror show stolen by Karloff. Elena Verdugo is a pretty gypsy who loves the unhappy werewolf. Lionel Atwill is a police inspector, Ann Gwynne a victim of the vampire. With Sig Ruman, Peter Coe, and Frank Reicher. The monsters were all back (minus Karloff) in *House of Dracula* later the same year.

HOUSE OF FREAKS

1973 Cinerama (Italy)
PRODUCER: Robert Randall
DIRECTOR: Robert Oliver
SCREENWRITER: Mario Francini
ORIGINALLY RELEASED AS: *El Castello dell' Orrore*
ALSO RELEASED AS: *Frankenstein's Castle of Freaks*

South Pacific star Rossano Brazzi plays Count Frankenstein in a cheap Euro sex horror film. Michael Dunn, the only dwarf actor to get good parts in major productions, sinks to the cliché evil dwarf role. With Edmund Purdom, Christiane Royce (star of *The Wolfwoman*), a giant, Ook the Neanderthal man, and lots of naked girls. It was the last release from Cinerama.

HOUSE OF FRIGHT

1960 Hammer/AIP (England)
PRODUCER: Michael Carreras
DIRECTOR: Terence Fisher
SCREENWRITER: Wolf Mankowitz
ALSO RELEASED AS:
    The Two Faces of Dr. Jekyll

An okay version of *Dr. Jekyll and Mr. Hyde* starring Paul Massie. This time an old and weak Jekyll becomes a young and handsome Hyde. As Hyde, he finds his wife (Dawn Addams) with his lecherous friend (Christopher Lee). In the dressing room of a snake dancer, Hyde lets a python crush his ex-friend to death. He then rapes his wife who kills herself. Later he convinces the police that Jekyll committed the murders, and that a burnt corpse is all that remains of the culprit.

HOUSE OF HORRORS

1946 Universal (B&W)
PRODUCER: Ben Pivar
DIRECTOR: Jean Yarbrough
SCREENWRITER: George Bricker

The incredible Rondo Hatton is the Creeper in his first starring role. Crazed sculptor Martin Kosleck rescues Rondo from drowning, makes a nice bust of him, and uses his unique bone-crushing powers to kill various enemies. Hatton's famous killer roles only lasted for two years, but he'll never be forgotten. You can now buy Rondo Hatton masks to wear when you're tired of your Tor Johnson mask. With Robert Lowery, Virginia Grey, Kent Taylor, Alan Napier, and Bill Goodwin.

HOUSE OF INSANE WOMEN: See *EXORCISM'S DAUGHTER.*

HOUSE OF MORTAL SIN: See *THE CONFESSIONAL.*

HOUSE OF 1,000 DOLLS

1967 AIP (W. Germany/Spain)
PRODUCER/SCREENWRITER: Harry Alan Towers
DIRECTOR: Jeremy Summers
ORIGINALLY RELEASED AS: *Das Haus der Tausend Freuden*

A ridiculous drama starring Vincent Price and Martha Hyer as stage magicians who drug young women in Tangiers for a white-slave ring. Hero George Nader (*Robot Monster*) finally figures out what's going on and kills bad-guy Price. With Maria Rohm, star of many trashy Harry Alan Towers films. When first released, it was double-billed with *Mary Jane*.

HOUSE OF PSYCHOTIC WOMEN

1973 Independent International (Spain)
PRODUCER: Modesto Perez Redondo
DIRECTOR: Carlos Aured
SCREENWRITER: Jacinto Molina
ORIGINALLY RELEASED AS: *Los Ojos Azules de la Muñeca Rota*

A bloody movie about three strange sisters and a sex murderer in the snow. With horror star Paul Naschy, Diana Lorys, and Eva Leon. **(R)**

THE HOUSE OF ROTHSCHILD

1934 United Artists (B&W with color sequences)
PRODUCER: Darryl F. Zanuck
DIRECTOR: Alfred Werker
SCREENWRITER: Nunnelly Johnson

During the Napoleonic wars Nathan Rothschild (George Arliss) tries to lend money to Napoleon's enemies. As the anti-semitic Prussian Ambassador Baron Ledrantz, Boris Karloff blocks his bid and later has Jews killed in the ghetto. Loretta Young is Rothschild's daughter. Robert Young is her suitor. Arliss, who also plays Rothschild's father, is publicly honored in the closing sequence filmed in three-strip Technicolor.

THE HOUSE OF SEVEN CORPSES

1974 International Amusement
PRODUCER/DIRECTOR/SCREENWRITER: Paul Harrison

Until Cameron Mitchell catches up, John Carradine will hold the record for cheap horror movies. This time he's the creepy caretaker of a haunted house where John Ireland is a director shooting an occult movie. The star of the film within a film is Faith Domergue (from *This Island Earth*), who conjures up a ghoul. The actors and crew members argue a lot and die one by one. The house was formerly the Governor's Mansion in Utah. Watching actors portraying actors is always a treat. Director Harrison wrote the Saturday morning *H.R. Puf'n'stuf* television series.

HOUSE OF SEVEN GABLES

1940 Universal (B&W)
ASSOC. PRODUCER: Burt Kelly
DIRECTOR: Joe May
SCREENWRITER: Lester Cole

George Sanders is the evil Jaffrey Pyncheon in Nathaniel Hawthorne's tale set in 19th-century Massachusetts. His brother Clifford (Vincent Price) is sent to prison so Jaffrey can get at the family fortune buried in the ancestral home. With Margaret Lindsay, Alan Napier, Cecil Kellaway, and Nan Grey. Price sings. Universal made an "exact" duplication of the actual house in Salem, but threw out much of the plot of the novel. The same year, German refugee Joe May also did *The Invisible Man's Revenge* with Price, Kellaway, and Grey.

HOUSE OF TERROR: See FACE OF THE SCREAMING WEREWOLF.

HOUSE OF THE BLACK DEATH

1965 Medallion/Taurus
PRODUCERS: William White, Richard Shotwell
DIRECTORS: Harold Daniels, Reginald Le Borge
SCREENWRITER: Richard Mahoney
ALSO RELEASED AS: *Blood of the Man Devil*, *Night of the Beast*

Lon Chancy, Jr., and John Carradine are the Desade brothers in this obscure horror film about witches. They don't have any scenes together. Andre, the good warlock (Carradine), spends the whole time in bed. Belial (Chaney with devil horns) is more active. Possibly each had his own director. With the incredible Katherine Victor, a werewolf, and '40s stars Tom Drake and Andrea King. Watch for it.

HOUSE OF THE DAMNED
1963 20th Century-Fox (B&W)
PRODUCER/DIRECTOR: Maury Dexter
SCREENWRITER: Harry Spalding

A couple visits an old mansion once owned by a recluse circus-sideshow owner. The house seems to be haunted and their friend's wife is found—decapitated! But don't be scared, it's only been faked by the shy inhabitants, all freaks hiding out after their boss died. Starring Merry Anders, Ron Foster, Erica Peters, and Richard Crane. With legless people and giant Richard Kiel. Director Dexter is also known for *The Day Mars Invaded Earth*, released the same year.

HOUSE OF USHER
1960 AIP
PRODUCER/DIRECTOR: Roger Corman
SCREENWRITER: Richard Matheson
ALSO RELEASED AS: *The Fall of the House of Usher*

The great success of this modest Poe adaptation freed Roger Corman from making black-and-white double-features. It was filmed in 15 days and cost about $200,000, both new highs for Corman. Vincent Price is effective as the white-haired supersensitive recluse Roderick Usher, who buries his sister (Myrna Fahey) alive. Mark Damon is her fiancé. It's a masterpiece of moody low-budget horror. Screenwriter Richard Matheson, cinematographer Floyd Crosby, art director Daniel Haller, and composer Les Baxter all did great jobs and continued to work on the Poe series.

HOUSE OF WAX
1953 Warner Brothers (3-D)
PRODUCER: Bryan Foy
DIRECTOR: André de Toth
SCREENWRITER: Crane Wilbur

This famous remake of *The Mystery of the Wax Museum* (1933) was one of the best 3-D movies and the one that launched Vincent Price's horror career. In turn-of-the-century Baltimore, Price is a horribly scarred sculptor left to die in his museum during an insurance fire. He survives and, for revenge, murders people, steals the bodies from the morgue, covers them with wax, and displays the incredibly life-like figures in his new Chamber of Horrors/Wax Museum. Carolyn Jones (Morticia on *The Addams Family*) ends up as Marie Antoinette. Charles Buchinsky/Bronson plays the mute Igor. The original junkie character is an alcoholic in this safer '50s version. With Phyllis Kirk, Frank Lovejoy, and the ever-popular paddle balls. Price starred in *The Mad Magician*, *Dangerous Mission*, and *Son* of *Sinbad*, also in 3-D. *House of Wax* was rereleased in 1982. The director was blind in one eye.

HOUSE OF WHIPCORD
1974 AIP (England)
PRODUCER/DIRECTOR: Peter Walker
SCREENWRITER: David McGillivray

An elderly couple runs a secret prison in the country and punishes "immoral" young women with whips, rats, and hanging. Their son (called Mark E. Desade) brings them a rather slow-witted young French model (Anne Michelle from *The Virgin Witch*). Sheila Keith (*Frightmare*) is the sadistic warden.

HOUSE ON BARE MOUNTAIN
1962 Olympic
PRODUCERS: Bob Cresse, David Andrew, Wesdon Bishop
DIRECTOR: Lee Frost
SCREENWRITER: Denver Scott

"20 terrified teen lovelies tastefully unattired!" were promised by the ads for this silly nudie film. Bob Cresse, a co-producer, stars as a voyeuristic bootlegger in drag running a girls' school. His/her assistant is a werewolf. At a Costume ball, Dracula and the Frankenstein monster show up and twist with "Miss Hollywood." By the makers of *One Million AC/DC*. Adults only, of course.

HOUSE ON HAUNTED HILL
1958 Allied Artists (B&W)
PRODUCER/DIRECTOR: William Castle
SCREENWRITER: Robb White

William Castle, doing what he did best: scaring the shit out of the kids in the audience! The much-publicized Emergo process—"more startling than 3-D!"—was really nothing more than a luminous skeleton that floated over the

Adults-only monster in House on Bare Mountain.

viewers' heads on a pulley. Firsthand reports reveal why many theaters didn't bother: the excited patrons, knowing what was going to happen, were well armed with candy boxes to throw at the battered and defenseless bones. The film itself stars Vincent Price, who gleefully tries to scare his overnight guests to death with a decapitated head, a witch, the skeleton, and an acid vat. His scheming wife (Carol Ohmart in a white nightgown) has other ideas. Elisha Cook, Jr., is the timid owner of the "haunted" house. *77 Sunset Strip* star Richard Long, Alan Marshall, and Carolyn Craig are some of the guests who receive guns in little coffins from their thoughtful host. Screenwriter Robb White worked on most of Castle's best movies.

THE HOUSE ON SKULL MOUNTAIN
1974 20th Century-Fox
PRODUCER: Ray Storey
DIRECTOR: Ron Honthaner
SCREENWRITER: Mildred Pares

Gary Clarke (teenage werewolf), Gary Conway (teenage Frankenstein), and Robert Harris (mad makeup man) in How to Make a Monster.

A black voodoo-horror movie from Atlanta. Businessmen there hired the ex-associate producer of the *Gunsmoke* series to direct. Jean Durand is a butler/witch doctor. Victor French is the token white victim. Janee Michelle is his wife. With Mike Evans of *All in the Family*. Georgia Senator Leroy Johnson plays the lawyer who reads the will. (R)

HOUSE THAT CRIED MURDER: See THE BRIDE.

THE HOUSE THAT DRIPPED BLOOD

1971 Amicus/Cinerama (England)
PRODUCERS: Max J. Rosenberg,
Milton Subotsky
DIRECTOR: Peter Duffell
SCREENWRITER: Robert Bloch
Four horror stories by Robert Bloch. The first features Delhom Elliott as a mystery writer facing his own fictional murderer. Next Peter Cushing is lured to a wax museum by a living statue. In the best segment Christopher Lee's incredibly cute and innocent little daugh-

ter (Chloe Franks) practices voodoo by sticking pins in a little daddy doll. Also with Nyree Dawn Porter. The last segment is a bit of silly comedy with Jon Pertwee as an actor who becomes a real vampire when he puts on a cape. Ingrid Pitt is a vampire/actress.

THE HOUSE THAT SCREAMED

1969 AIP (Spain)
PRODUCER: Arturo Gonzales
DIRECTOR: Narciso Ibanez Serrador
SCREENWRITER: Luis Verna Penafiel
ORIGINALLY RELEASED AS: *La Residencia.*
Lilli Palmer, a respected Austrian-born star, is Madame Fourneau, a widow who runs a correctional school for girls in 19th-century France. John Moulder Brown (*Deep End*) is her sexually repressed son. I wouldn't want to give away the end of this sick made-in-Spain movie, but . . . the son kills schoolgirls, cuts off parts of their bodies, and constructs a composite "mom" in the attic. Rated PG, but with scenes of girls being whipped, tied up, and locked in closets. It was cut before the American release.

THE HOUSE THAT VANISHED

1974 AIP (England)
PRODUCER: Diana Daubeney
DIRECTOR: Joseph Larraz
SCREENWRITER: Derek Ford
ALSO RELEASED AS: *Scream and Die*

A young model witnesses a murder at an old house, then later can't find the house. Her boyfriend turns out to be the killer. Another retitled movie from abroad advertised with the overused "It's only a movie!" line. It sometimes played with *Last House on the Left*. Andrea Allan and Karl Lanchbury star. From the director of *Vampyres*. (R)

THE HOUSE THAT WOULDN'T DIE

1970 TV
PRODUCER: Aaron Spelling
DIRECTOR: John Llewellyn Moxey
SCREENWRITER: Henry Farrell

Barbara Stanwyck inherits an Amish house with ghosts! With Richard Egan and Michael Anderson, Jr. Screenwriter Henry Farrell wrote the novel on which *Whatever Happened to Baby Jane?* was based.

THE HOUSE WHERE EVIL DWELLS

1982 MGM/UA
PRODUCER: Martin B. Cohen
DIRECTOR: Kevin Conner
SCREENWRITER: Robert A. Suhosky

The director of *Motel Hell* returns with a samurai ghost story filmed in Japan. Most viewers couldn't decide whether this one was supposed to be funny or not. An American couple (Susan George and Edward Albert) move to a haunted Japanese country house and are taken over by spirits of murder and hara-kiri victims. Their diplomat friend (Doug McClure) is decapitated and big crabs show up for an attack. (R)

HOW AWFUL ABOUT ALLAN

1970 TV
PRODUCER: George Edwards
DIRECTOR: Curtis Harrington
SCREENWRITER: Henry Farrell

This TV-movie suffers from too many familiar elements, including the *Baby Jane*–type title. Anthony (*Psycho*) Perkins plays a guilt-ridden, semiblind mental patient who is released from the hospital to stay with his psychotic sister Julie (*The Haunting*) Harris, who proceeds to torment him. Also with Joan Hackett (not known for playing stable types) and token "old-timer" Kent Smith. Teleplay by Henry (*Baby Jane*) Farrell.

HOW TO MAKE A DOLL

1968 Unusual Films
PRODUCER/DIRECTOR: Herschell Gordon Lewis
SCREENWRITERS: Bert Ray, Herschell Gordon Lewis

A science-fiction nudie comedy with a computer that creates beautiful women. After endless orgies with beautiful robots, a professor (Robert Wood) wants a real woman. His glasses break and he falls in love with an ugly one. She turns into a rabbit after he tells the computer he wants her to be his dream bunny. By the director of *Two Thousand Maniacs*.

HOW TO MAKE A MONSTER

1958 AIP (B&W with color sequence)
PRODUCER: Herman Cohen
DIRECTOR: Herbert L. Strock
SCREENWRITERS: Kenneth Langtry, Herman Cohen

Here's a movie especially for '50s monster movie fans! It's the behind-the-scenes story of a makeup artist who panics when the studio stops making horror movies—obviously a dumb idea. During his last production he puts special drugged makeup on the actors playing the teenage Frankenstein (Gary Conway, repeating his earlier role) and the teenage werewolf (Gary Clarke, not Michael Landon). The makeup makes them think they're really monsters! They kill the stupid studio execs who threatened their "master's" future! Our hero, the makeup man (Robert H. Harris), joins the murdering fun disguised as a caveman! This movie is littered with old props from other American International movies like *The She Creature* and *Invasion of the Saucermen*. Spot your favorites! Spot John Ashley! With Robert Shayne and Morris Ankrum. It originally played with *Teenage Caveman*.

HOW TO MAKE IT: See *TARGET: HARRY.*

HOW TO STEAL THE WORLD

1968 MGM
PRODUCER: Anthony Spinner
DIRECTOR: Sutton Roley
SCREENWRITER: Norman Hudis
The last of *The Man from U.N.C.L.E.* features, edited from TV episodes. Robert Vaughn and David McCallum are sent out by Leo G. Carroll to prevent Barry Sullivan from taking over the world with obedience gas. With Eleanor Parker, Leslie Nielsen, Tony Bill, Dan O'Herlihy, and Hugh Marlowe. The four-year series was over by the time this came out.

HOW TO STUFF A WILD BIKINI

1965 AIP
PRODUCERS: James H. Nicholson,
Samuel Z. Arkoff
DIRECTOR: William Asher
SCREENWRITERS: William Asher,
Leo Townsend
The last and most ridiculous of Asher's beach movies. Frankie Avalon, on naval-reserve duty in Tahiti, doesn't trust Annette Funicello to stay faithful, so he hires Bwana, a witch doctor, to help. Seventy-year-old Buster Keaton conjures up a floating bikini, "stuffs" it with Beverly Adams, and sends her to distract Dwayne (*Dobie Gillis*) Hickman from Miss Funicello. Series regulars Harvey Lembeck (as Eric Von Zipper), Jody McCrea (as Bonehead), and John Ashley are on hand, as well as Brian Donlevy and Mickey Rooney. The music is by the great frat-rock group the Kingsmen (who play "themselves"), and Brian Wilson can be spotted as one of the "beach boys." With four *Playboy* Playmates, including Marianne Gaba (Miss September 1959) as Animal.

HOW TO SUCCEED WITH SEX

1970 Medford Film Corporation
PRODUCER: Jerome F. Katzman
DIRECTOR/SCREENWRITER: Bert I. Gordon
Imagine a sex comedy by the guy responsible for *The Amazing Colossal Man* and *Attack of the Puppet People*. Too bad it doesn't include giant people terrorizing a major city with unusual sex acts or tiny people doing it by a giant telephone that keeps ringing. It's just softcore frolics with a guy who's frantic because his fiancée says—not till we're married. Following instructions in a book leads him through comical situations, including visiting a prostitute who turns out to be...guess who? With Bambi Allen and Victoria Bond. Producer Jerome Katzman's dad Sam was the executive producer. (X)

THE HOWLING

1981 Avco Embassy
PRODUCERS: Michael Finnell, Jack Conrad
DIRECTOR: Joe Dante
SCREENWRITERS: John Sayles,
Terence H. Winkless
A horror movie for horror movie fans by the director of *Piranha*. It's scary,

it's funny, and it has incredible transformation scenes, including one of humans turning into werewolves while making love under a moonlit sky. The plot concerns a California consciousness-raising group led by Patrick Macnee that's actually a coven of werewolves. A recently traumatized TV newswoman (Dee Wallace of *E.T.*) goes there with her husband. With clips from *The Wolfman*, lots of wolf gags, and countless film references. Characters are named after directors who made past wolfman movies, Forrest J. Ackerman visits an occult book shop run by Dick Miller, Roger Corman makes a phone call, etc. With Elizabeth Brooks as a leather-clad wolf woman, a very brief animated scene, John Carradine, Kevin McCarthy, Kenneth Tobey, Slim Pickens, and a script co-written by John Sayles, who appears in a morgue scene. Much better than the more successful *American Werewolf in London*. A sound track album by Pino Donaggio is available. Watch for a sequel. **(R)**

HUDSON'S BAY

1940 20th Century-Fox (B&W)
PRODUCER: Darryl F. Zanuck
DIRECTOR: Irving Pichel
SCREENWRITER: Lamar Trotti

Paul Muni as the French-Canadian Pierre Esprit Radisson, John Sutton as an Englishman, and Laird Cregar as a Canadian trap furs and take them back to the silly snobbish King Charles II (Vincent Price). Sutton gets the girl (Gene Tierney). With Nigel Bruce, Chief Thundercloud, and Chief Big Cloud. A very light and distorted look at history.

THE HUMAN DUPLICATORS

1965 Woolner Brothers/Allied Artists
PRODUCERS: Hugo Grimaldi,
Arthur C. Pierce
DIRECTOR: Hugo Grimaldi
SCREENWRITER: Arthur C. Pierce

Richard Kiel as Kolos, a giant alien, is sent to Earth to create android duplicates of humans to infiltrate the government. The whole cheap production takes

Effective advertising art for The Howling.

place in the mansion of a professor (George Macready) who is himself soon duplicated. Besides the thrill of having two of hero George Nader, this must-see nonsense includes sexy Barbara Nicols, Hugh "Ward Cleaver" Beaumont, silent movie star Richard Arlen, and a love interest (in a blind woman) for Kolos.

HUMAN EXPERIMENTS

1979 Crown International
PRODUCERS: Summer Brown,
  Gregory Goodell
DIRECTOR: J. Gregory Goodell
SCREENWRITER: Richard Rothstein
ALSO RELEASED AS: *Beyond the Gate*

A psychiatrist who believes that extreme mental shock can be used to curb criminal impulses sets up shop at a women's prison, exposing the residents to bugs, spiders, and the like. His subjects become well-behaved catatonics until he meets a charming country-and-western singer, who becomes the object of his attentions. The star-studded cast includes Jackie Coogan, Aldo Ray, and Ellen Travolta (yes, his sister). Theme song by Jerry Jeff Walker. **(R)**
—BM

George Nader and his android double in George Macready's basement in The Human Duplicators.

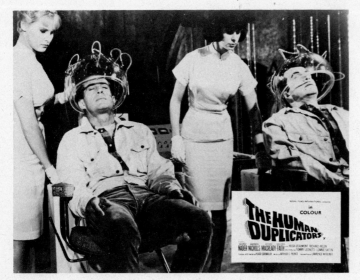

THE HUMAN MONSTER

1939 Monogram (England) (B&W)
PRODUCER: John Argyle
DIRECTOR: Walter Summers
SCREENWRITERS: Patrick Kirwin,
  Walter Summers, John Argyle
ALSO RELEASED AS: *Dark Eyes of London*

One of Bela Lugosi's best. He plays Dr. Orloff, an insurance swindler who disguises himself as a kindly old doctor running a home for the blind. The horror is stronger than in American movies made at the time. Bela and his ugly blind-brute assistant tie up, torture, and kill victims in scenes considered pretty tasteless at the time. Not at all like other Monogram films (they merely released it). Based on an Edgar Wallace story. Remade in Germany in '61.

THE HUMAN VAPOR

1960 Toho/Allied Artists (Japan)
EXEC. PRODUCER: Tomoyuki Tanaka
DIRECTOR: Inoshiro Honda
SCREENWRITER: Takeshi Kimura
ORIGINALLY RELEASED AS: *Gasu Ningen
  Daiichigo*

A Tokyo man robs banks for the love of Fujichiyo, a famous dancer. The crimes are simple because, thanks to a scientist, the robber can turn himself into a mist. Leaving his clothes in a rumpled pile, he goes under doors, through keyholes. . . .

THE HUMANOID

1979 Columbia (Italy)
PRODUCER: Georgio Venturini
DIRECTOR: George B. Lewis
SCREENWRITERS: Adriano Bolzoni, Aldo Lado

Richard Kiel and Corinne Clery, who had just been in *Moonraker*, star as space-age heroes battling bad guys Arthur Kennedy and Ivan Rassimov. Another *Star Wars* copy complete with a friendly robot dog. Kiel is the invincible giant humanoid. Also with Barbara Bach (*The Spy Who Loved Me*). Music by Ennio Morricone.

HUMANOIDS OF THE DEEP

1980 New World
PRODUCERS: Martin B. Cohen, Hunt Lowry
DIRECTOR: Barbara Peters
SCREENWRITER: Frederick James

The first major monster movie where we see the creatures actually doing what was always implied in all those old scenes showing women being carried offscreen. Many were offended by the rape aspect of this fast-paced thriller featuring lots of *Creature from the Black Lagoon*—inspired monsters. Eventually they tear apart a carnival before being killed by stars Doug McClure and Ann Turkel. Doug McClure is an Indian-tormenting bad guy. Directed by a woman, who claims Roger Corman had the controversial scenes added after she was finished with the project. Like it or not, it was a hit and is not dull. A sound track album is available. **(R)**

HUMONGUS

1982 Embassy (Canada)
PRODUCER: Anthony Kramreither
DIRECTOR: Paul Lynch
SCREENWRITER: William Gray

The writer and director of *Prom Night*, a post-*Halloween* Jamie Lee Curtis hit, return with more teens in peril. A yacht with a girl, her boyfriend, and her brother on board is shipwrecked on an island. A briefly viewed seven-foot-tall mutant, who has been eating dogs since his rape-victim mother died, stalks the potential meals. Janet Julian and David Wallace star. **(R)**

THE HUNCHBACK OF NOTRE DAME

1939 RKO (B&W)
PRODUCER: Pandro S. Berman
DIRECTOR: William Dieterle
SCREENWRITER: Sonya Levien

Classic version of the Victor Hugo novel, starring the wonderful Charles Laughton as the lovesick, deformed bellringer. Quasimodo watches the daily poverty and crime of the city from the heights of the gargoyle-laden cathedral, while the powerful, corrupt clergy manipulate, rob, and torture the powerless masses. He disrupts all of Paris when he rescues Maureen O'Hara from a public hanging and protects her by pouring molten lead on the mob below. Laughton's acting makes the character more pathetic than in the other versions. Very few shots of his grotesque makeup were ever released. Also with those two great cinema villains Sir Cedric Hardwicke and George Zucco, Edmond O'Brien, Thomas Mitchell, and a tiny bit by the real-life deformed Rondo Hatton (in the King of the Fools segment). A great film.

THE HUNCHBACK OF NOTRE DAME

1957 Allied Artists (France/Italy)
PRODUCERS: Robert and Raymond Hakim
DIRECTOR: Jean Delannoy
SCREENWRITERS: Jean Aurenche,
Jacques Prévert
ORIGINALLY RELEASED AS: *Notre Dame de Paris*

Some people think Anthony Quinn is a great actor and was a natural to follow Lon Chaney and Charles Laughton in the role of the deformed bellringer. They should've known better. Quinn was best playing heavies in bit parts. This remake is remembered mostly for some torture scenes involving Gina Lollobrigida. With Alain Cuny. For *really* bad Quinn, watch for *The Happening*.

THE HUNCHBACK OF NOTRE DAME

1978 TV (England)
PRODUCER: Cedric Messina
DIRECTOR: Alan Cooke
SCREENWRITER: Robert Muller

A BBC videotape presentation starring Warren Clarke as Quasimodo, Kenneth Haigh as the archdeacon, and Michele Newell as Esmerelda.

THE HUNCHBACK OF NOTRE DAME
1982 TV (England)
PRODUCER: Norman Rosemont
DIRECTOR: Michael Tuchner
SCREENWRITER: John Gay
Anthony Hopkins is an odd looking hunchback in love with Lesley-Anne Down as Esmerelda. Derek Jacobi is Dom Claude Frollo. With John Gielgud and Robert Powell. A Hallmark Hall of Fame presentation.

HUNCHBACK OF THE MORGUE
1972 Cinemation (Spain)
PRODUCER: F. Lara Polop
DIRECTOR: Javier Aquirre
SCREENWRITERS: Jacinto Molina, Albert Insua, Javier Aguirre
ORIGINALLY RELEASED AS: *El Jorbado de la Morgue*
Paul Naschy as a demented, sexually active hunchback supplies bodies to a scientist who feeds them to a living head attached to a glass tank full of guts. The star also keeps busy killing rats who try to eat his dead girlfriend. (R)

HUNGRY PETS: See PLEASE DON'T EAT MY MOTHER.

HUNGRY WIVES
1972
PRODUCER: Nancy M. Romero
DIRECTOR/SCREENWRITER: George A. Romero
ORIGINALLY RELEASED AS: *Jack's Wife*
ALSO RELEASED AS: *Season of the Witch*
A suburban housewife (Jan White) practices witchcraft, kills her husband, and joins a coven. This dated and slow feature should be viewed by Romero completists only. It was rereleased as *Season of the Witch* in 1982 to confused theater patrons who thought it was newer than *Dawn of the Dead* (as implied by the poster) or *Halloween: Season of the Witch*, also playing at the time. Here's the justification for the new title: When the main character visits an occult shop, Donovan's *Season of the Witch* is heard on the sound track. Romero was also the editor and cinematographer. Most versions of *Hungry Wives* are missing up to 40 minutes of its original 130-minute running time. His next feature, *The Crazies*, although another commercial disaster, was a return to the expected *Night of the Living Dead*–type thrills.

HURRICANE
1974 TV
PRODUCER: Edward J. Montagne
DIRECTOR: Jerry Jameson
SCREENWRITER: Jack Turley
Larry Hagman and Martin Milner are hurricane experts who react violently to rear-projected newsreel footage in this made-for-TV disaster (not to be confused with Dino DeLaurentiis' '79 remake of the '37 film of the same name). Also blown around are Jessica Walter, Barry Sullivan, Will Geer, and Frank Sutton (*Gomer Pyle*).

HUSH...HUSH, SWEET CHARLOTTE
1964 20th Century-Fox
PRODUCER/DIRECTOR: Robert Aldrich
SCREEWRITERS: Henry Farrell, Lukas Heller
The successful follow-up to *What Ever Happened to Baby Jane?* with the same producer/director, writers (adapting a Farrell story) and two of its stars (Bette Davis and Victor Buono). Joan Crawford was ill and was replaced by Olivia DeHavilland. Poor Bette, an aging Southern belle, is being driven crazy by greedy relatives. In flashbacks her

lover (Bruce Dern) is decapitated and her father (Buono) hushes up the scandal. More good casting includes Joseph Cotten as the family doc, Agnes Moorehead as the unkempt housekeeper, Cecil Kellaway as a retired insurance investigator, Mary Astor, William Campbell, George Kennedy, and Ellen Corby.

HUSTLER SQUAD: See DOLL SQUAD.

HYPNOSIS

1963 United Film Enterprises (W. Germany/Spain/Italy) (B&W)
PRODUCER: Alfons Carcasina
DIRECTOR: Eugenio Martin
SCREENWRITERS: Giuseppe Mangione, Eugenio Martin, G. Moreno Burgos, Francis Niewal, Gehrard Schmidt
ORIGINALLY RELEASED AS: *Nur Tote Zuegen Schweigen*

Jean Sorel is Erik Stein, a ventriloquist/hypnotist/murderer. He kills the original star of his stage act, but the man's fiancée (Eleonora Rossi-Drago) scares him into confessing by convincing him that Grog the dummy is alive. With Heinz Drache and Hildegard Knef.

THE HYPNOTIC EYE

1959 Allied Artists (B&W)
PRODUCER: Charles B. Bloch
DIRECTOR: George Blair
SCREENWRITERS:
Gitta and William Read Woolfield

A sleaze classic. Jacques Bergerac stars as the great Desmond, a hypnotist whose beautiful female volunteer subjects tend to go home and disfigure their faces. In a truly sick film that shows up on TV intact thanks to its pre-ratings "restraint," one woman washes her face in acid, one dries her hair over a lit burner, and another takes a scalding shower. The film features "Hypnomagic": Desmond hypnotizes his entire audience (including all of us unsuspecting movie fans) and makes them stamp their feet and lift balloons. This sequence is an amazing bit of nonsense that should be preserved in a time capsule. If that isn't enough, there's Allison Hayes (formerly a 50-foot woman) as Desmond's wife/assistant Justine, and the "king of the beatniks" reciting poetry accompanied by Ed "Big Daddy" Nord on bongos! Also with Fred Demara, the great impersonator (Tony Curtis played him in a movie), impersonating an actor impersonating a doctor. With Merry Anders and Carol Thurston. I will watch the hypnotic eye—I will watch the hypnotic eye— I will watch the hypnotic eye. . . .

HYSTERIA

1965 Hammer/MGM (England) (B&W)
PRODUCER/SCREENWRITER: Jimmy Sangster
DIRECTOR: Freddie Francis

An effective psychological drama with Robert Webber as an American accident victim with amnesia in London. In the hospital, Anthony Newlands is the doctor who tells him to expect hallucinations. Moving into an apartment donated by an anonymous benefactor, he imagines some horrifying things—or does he? With Jennifer Jayne, Maurice Denham, Sue Lloyd, and Kiwi Kingston.

Hypnotist Jacques Bergerac convinces a subject that he's freezing in The Hypnotic Eye.

I BURY THE LIVING

1958 United Artists (B&W)
PRODUCERS: Albert Band, Louis Garfinkle
DIRECTOR: Albert Band
SCREENWRITER: Louis Garfinkle

A cemetery caretaker (Richard Boone) discovers an interesting fact about the map of the grounds. The occupied plots are marked with black pins; owned but empty ones have white pins. By switching the pins around, he can cause the death of future tenants and revive current ones. A favorite of Stephen King. With Theodore Bikel, Peggy Maurer, and Russ Bender. By the director of *Face of Fire*.

I CHANGED MY SEX: See GLEN OR GLENDA.

I CROSSED THE COLOR LINE: See THE BLACK KLANSMAN.

I DIED A THOUSAND TIMES

1955 Warner Brothers
PRODUCER: Willis Goldbeck
DIRECTOR: Stuart Heisler
SCREENWRITER: W.R. Burnett

Viewers tired of *High Sierra* should watch for this cheesy remake starring Jack Palance as Mad Dog Earl. Shelley Winters is his moll. With Lee Marvin, Lon Chaney, Jr., Earl Holliman, Dennis Hopper, Lori Nelson, Mae Clark, Bill Kennedy, and Gonzalez-Gonzalez.

I DISMEMBER MAMA

1972 Europix
PRODUCER: Leon Roth
DIRECTOR: Paul Leder
SCREENWRITER: William Norton
ALSO RELEASED AS: *Poor Albert and Little Annie*

Zoey Hall plays Albert, a psycho in Hollywood who kills "impure women." He falls in love with nine-year-old Annie (Geri Reischl). With Greg Mullavey, the husband on *Mary Hartman, Mary Hartman*, as a detective. This retitled sickie played with *Blood Spattered Bride*. By the director of *Please Don't Eat My Mother*. **(R)**

I DON'T WANT TO BE BORN: See THE DEVIL WITHIN HER.

I DRINK YOUR BLOOD

1971 Cinemation
PRODUCER: Jerry Gross
DIRECTOR/SCREENWRITER: David Durston

An intense gore comedy (?) film. Hippie devil-cultists give LSD to an old man. His son retaliates by injecting rabid-dog blood into their meat pies. The cannibalistic longhairs kill each other and infect a group of construction workers. An extremely unpleasant film with Ronda Fultz, Jadine Wong, and Lynn Lowrey (*The Crazies*). It had to be cut to earn an R rating. Director Durston also made an entertaining venereal disease feature called *Stigma*. **(R)**

I EAT YOUR SKIN

1964 Cinemation (B&W)
PRODUCER/DIRECTOR/SCREENWRITER: Del Tenney

Producer Jerry Gross needed a co-feature for his *I Drink Your Blood*, so he bought a seven-year-old unreleased black-and-white film (*Voodoo Blood Bath*) made by the man responsible for *Horror of Party Beach* and gave it a new title. A mad doctor uses radioactive snake venom to produce killer humanoid zombies with fried-egg eyes and crusty faces. Starring William Joyce and Heather Hewitt. No skin is eaten. The ad campaign for the double feature insured large audiences—"2 great blood-horrors to rip out your guts!" Now available as part of a special bad videocassette series.

I HATE YOUR GUTS: See *THE INTRUDER*.

I LED TWO LIVES: See *GLEN OR GLENDA*.

I LOVE A MYSTERY
1944 Columbia (B&W)
PRODUCER: Wallace MacDonald
DIRECTOR: Henry Levin
SCREENWRITER: Charles O'Neal
An Oriental mystic uses black magic to drive people to suicide. Clairvoyant George Macready is afraid he'll be decapitated. Jim Bannon and Barton Yarborough star as the detective team popularized on the radio. They returned in two sequels. With Nina Foch and Carole Mathews.

I MARRIED A MONSTER FROM OUTER SPACE
1958 Paramount (B&W)
PRODUCER/DIRECTOR: Gene Fowler
SCREENWRITER: Louis Vittes
An overlooked, well-made science-fiction hit that should appeal especially to women. On her wedding night Gloria Talbot discovers that handsome new husband Tom Tryon is really an alien monster! And nobody will believe her!

Aliens working from their flying saucer kidnap Earthmen and make themselves into identical duplicates in an effort to repopulate their race. The memorable monsters have faces like mutated rhubarb with round white mouths and three-clawed hands. They'd fit right in on *The Outer Limits* show. One inspired scene shows the duplicated husbands lined up and floating in the air while hooked up to glowing white orbs in the saucer. With Ken Lynch, Maxie Rosenbloom, and a heroic German shepherd.

I MARRIED TOO YOUNG: See *MARRIED TOO YOUNG*.

I, MOBSTER
1958 20th Century-Fox (B&W)
PRODUCERS: Roger Corman, Gene Corman
DIRECTOR: Roger Corman
SCREENWRITER: Steve Fisher
The rise and fall of gangland leader Joe Sante (Steve Cochran), told in flashback. With once-innocent girlfriend Lita Milan, he goes from numbers to drugs to head of the syndicate. Burlesque queen Lili St. Cyr sings. With Yvette Vickers, Grant Withers, Celia Lovsky, and Robert Strauss. It was Corman's only modern-day gangster movie and was made after the popular *Machine Gun Kelly*.

I, MONSTER
1971 Amicus/Cannon (England)
PRODUCERS: Max J. Rosenberg, Milton Subotsky
DIRECTOR: Stephen Weeks
SCREENWRITER: Milton Subotsky
"Dr. Jekyll and Mr. Hyde" becomes Dr. Marlowe and Mr. Blake. Christopher Lee stars. As time goes on, his evil half gets uglier and uglier. Peter Cushing and Mike Raven are fellow doctors. With little Chloe Franks. It was originally planned as a 3-D feature, which would have been quite unusual in '71.

I NEVER PROMISED YOU A ROSE GARDEN

1977 New World
PRODUCERS: Edgar J. Sherick,
   Daniel H. Blatt, Terence F. Dean,
   Michael Hausman
DIRECTOR: Anthony Page
SCREENWRITERS: Gavin Lambert,
   Lewis John Carlino

Kathleen Quinlan suffers the horrors of schizophrenia. Bibi Andersson is her psychiatrist. With Silvia Sidney, Signe Hasso, Diane Varsi, Susan Tyrrell, and Barbara Steele. Based on Joanne Greenberg's bestseller. One of New World's best domestic releases.

I SAW WHAT YOU DID

1965 Universal (B&W)
PRODUCER/DIRECTOR: William Castle
SCREENWRITER: William McGivern

Ads warned that this feature was about uxoricide (look it up). It's a light thriller with two teenage girls passing their baby-sitting time making random crank calls. They speak the movie's title to John Ireland, who coincidentally had just killed his wife in the shower. Joan Crawford is wasted as the worried psycho's lover-neighbor who tries to blackmail him into living with her. With Leif Erickson and lots of fog. Some theaters had seat belts installed to keep scared patrons in place. It was Crawford's second Castle shocker. Next stop—Herman Cohen shockers!

I SPIT ON YOUR GRAVE

1977 Jerry Gross Organization
PRODUCERS: Joseph Zbeda, Meir Zarchi
DIRECTOR/SCREENWRITER: Meir Zarchi
ORIGINALLY RELEASED AS: *Day of the Woman*

Thanks to the PBS Sneak Previews show, which labeled it inhumane and sexist, this revenge exploitation feature has gained a new audience of videocassette buyers. Camille Keaton (Buster's grandniece) stars as a novelist spending the summer alone at an isolated lakeside house. Four locals (one retarded) beat and rape her. She eventually hangs, axes, or castrates the whole group. A humorless and disturbing movie shot in Connecticut. (R)

I, THE JURY

1953 United Artists (3-D, B&W)
PRODUCER: Victor Saville
DIRECTOR/SCREENWRITER: Harry Essex

The scriptwriter of *Creature from the Black Lagoon* and *It Came from Outer Space* writes and directs the first Mike Hammer movie (based on Mickey Spillane's bestselling 1946 novel). Biff Elliot gives the 3-D punches as he tracks the murderer of a friend who saved his life during the war. He falls in love with a lady psychiatrist who asks "How could you?" at the end. With Peggie Castle, Preston Foster, and Elisha Cook, Jr.

I, THE JURY

1982 20th Century-Fox
PRODUCER: Robert Solo
DIRECTOR: Richard Heffron
SCREENWRITER: Larry Cohen

Armand Assante was the screen's first Mike Hammer after Mickey Spillane himself took the role in *The Girl Hunters* ('63). This disappointing new version of the original Hammer novel features a psychotic slasher (Judson Scott) who hates redheads, and a sex clinic run by Barbara Carrera. Filmed in Manhattan and Glen Cove, Long Island. Screenwriter Larry Cohen was originally set to direct but was fired by the producer. With Laurene Landon as Velda, Alan King as a syndicate boss, and a group of porn stars in a mostly deleted orgy scene. (R)

I WALKED WITH A ZOMBIE

1943 RKO (B&W)
PRODUCER: Val Lewton
DIRECTOR: Jacques Tourneur
SCREENWRITERS: Curt Siodmak, Ardel Wray
According to the ads: "She's alive . . . yet dead! She's dead . . . yet alive!" Nurse Frances Dee goes to San Sebastian in the West Indies to care for the sick wife of plantation owner Tom Conway. Hoping for a cure, she takes the silent blond woman (Christine Gordon) to a secret voodoo ceremony and uncovers horrible family secrets. This classic, poetic film features James Ellison as Conway's half-brother, Edith Barrett as their mother, calypso singer Sir Lancelot, and Darby Jones as Carre-Four, the incredible zombie guard.

I WANT HER DEAD: See W.

I WAS A TEENAGE FRANKENSTEIN

1957 AIP (B&W with color sequence)
PRODUCER: Herman Cohen
DIRECTOR: Herbert L. Strock
SCREENWRITER: Kenneth Langtry
It's hard to believe this American teen hit was released the same year as the British gothic *Curse of Frankenstein*. They both used horrible mangled-face makeup for the monster but what a difference in the approach! As a cut-rate descendant of Dr. Frankenstein living in L.A., Whit Bissell creates a weight-lifting ugly-faced monster in the basement. He keeps the monster a secret from his fiancée (Phyllis Coates) and throws his assistant to the alligators when he gets in the way. Whit then sends the monster out for a new head. A handsome teenager (Gary Conway, later on *Burke's Law*) making out in his car is the surprised donor. A terrible but inevitable and amusing exploitation quickie follow-up to *I Was a Teenage Werewolf*. Originally billed with *Blood of Dracula*.

I WAS A TEENAGE WEREWOLF

1957 AIP (B&W)
PRODUCER: Herman Cohen
DIRECTOR: Gene Fowler, Jr.
SCREENWRITER: Ralph Thorton
Young Michael Landon (real name—Eugene Orowitz) will never be forgotten as the troubled high school student turned into a snarling drooling hairy monster by Whit Bissell. No full moons or crucifixes are involved. Hypnotism causes the retrogressive transformation whenever Landon is startled. Like when the school bell rings while he's watching a girl hanging from the parallel bars in the gym. A trend-setting hit with rock 'n' roll, dancing, fistfights, and teen traumas. With Yvonne Lime, Guy Williams (as a cop), and Vladimir Sokoloff. Bissell was back the same year creating a teenage Frankenstein. *Werewolf* originally played with *Invasion of the Saucer Men*.

I WAS AN ADVENTURESS

1940 20th Century-Fox (B&W)
PRODUCER: Darryl F. Zanuck
DIRECTOR: Gregory Ratoff
SCREENWRITER: Karl Tunberg

Erich von Stroheim, Peter Lorre (as Polo), and Vera Zorina are jewel thieves. She marries Richard Greene and tries to go straight, but Peter and Erich just won't go away. With Sig Ruman and a Swan Lake ballet sequence.

THE ICE HOUSE
1969 Hollywood Cinemart
PRODUCER: Dorrell McGowan
DIRECTOR: Stuart E. McGowan
ALSO RELEASED AS: *Cold Blood,*
   The Passion Pit
A psycho-killer movie starring twins (Robert and David Story) and good old Scott Brady as a police lieutenant. After being hit on the head with a bottle of booze by stripper Venus de Marco (Sabrina), brother No. 1 goes crazy, kills her, and freezes her body in his ice house. He puts some more beauties on ice, then kills nosy brother No. 2, a sheriff, and assumes his identity. In this no-budget cheapie, madness triumphs.

Sabrina was known for having her 40-plus bust insured.

I'LL GIVE A MILLION

1938 20th Century-Fox (B&W)
PRODUCER: Darryl F. Zanuck
DIRECTOR: Walter Lang
SCREENWRITER: Boris Ingster

Warner Baxter is an eccentric millionaire posing as a hobo on the Riviera. He searches for a kind person to give a million francs to. Peter Lorre as "Louie the Dope" and John Carradine are fellow hobos. A remake of an Italian film. With Marjorie Weaver and Jean Hersholt.

I'LL GIVE MY LIFE

1959 Howco (B&W)
PRODUCER: Sam Hersh
DIRECTOR: William F. Claxton
SCREENWRITER: Herbert Moulton

Construction magnate Ray Collins' son returns with his engineering degree and his decision to become a missionary. Father-son relations cool until years later, when the young man dies of jungle fever in New Guinea. Then Collins mounts a nationwide fund-raising tour in memory of his dead son. John Bryant, Donald Woods, and Angie Dickinson co-star. —CB

ILLEGAL

1955 Warner Brothers (B&W)
PRODUCER: Frank P. Rosenburg
DIRECTOR: Lewis Allen
SCREENWRITERS: W.R. Burnett,
    James R. Webb

Edward G. Robinson is a D.A. risking his career by defending Nina Foch on a homicide charge. Jayne Mansfield was 12th-billed as Angel O'Hara. She stayed around Warners for an appearance in *Hell on Frisco Bay*, Robinson's next film. With Hugh Marlowe, DeForest Kelly, Edward Platt, Albert Dekker, Ellen Corby, Henry Kulky, and Jonathan Hale. It was a remake of *The Mouthpiece* (1932).

THE ILLUSTRATED MAN
1969 Warner Brothers
PRODUCERS: Howard B. Kreitsek, Ted Mann
DIRECTOR: Jack Smight
SCREENWRITER: Howard B. Kreitsek
Most reviewers blasted this adaptation of three famous Ray Bradbury stories. Rod Steiger and Claire Bloom star in all three stories. In the connecting segments, set in 1933, Steiger is the tattooed man and Claire Bloom is the mysterious tattoo artist from the future. "The Long Rain" episode is great. It even features Jason Evers from *The Brain That Wouldn't Die!* "The Veldt" and "The Last Night of the World" are the other stories.

IMAGE: See MONDO HOLLYWOOD.

Paloma Picasso as Countess Bathory in Immoral Tales.

IMMEDIATE DISASTER: See STRANGER FROM VENUS.

IMMORAL TALES
1974 New Line (France)
PRODUCER: Anatole Dauman
DIRECTOR/SCREENWRITER: Walerian Borowczyk
ORIGINALLY RELEASED AS: *Contes Immoraux*
Four erotic stories comprise this European hit which was cut by 15 minutes for its American "art theater" release. The best segment, which got all the attention, stars Paloma Picasso as Erzebet Bathory, the legendary countess who bathed in the blood of virgins to retain her youth and beauty. Other segments include a young girl masturbating with a cucumber, a group of priests having sex with a woman on a table, and the story of Lucretia Borgia. A fifth segment, "The Beast," was expanded into a feature. (**X**)

THE IMMORTAL
1969 TV
PRODUCER: Louis Morheim
DIRECTOR: Joseph Sargent
SCREENWRITER: Robert Specht
Christopher George stars as a race-car driver with a rare blood factor that halts aging. A billionaire (Barry Sullivan) and his men chase him all over trying to drain his blood. A series of the same name resulted, lasting one season. George soon became a king of bad exploitation features. With Carol Lynley as his dying girlfriend, Ralph Bellamy, and Jessica Walter.

IMPULSE
1974 Conqueror Films
DIRECTOR: William Grefe
The ads proclaimed: "When the demons of evil take over all powers of reason only *impulse* remains!" When the director of *The Sting of Death* has William

Shatner play a possessed killer, only audience disbelief remains. Ruth "The Baby" Roman and Harold "Odd Job" Sakata also star. It was Grefe's follow-up to *Stanley*. He soon went on to become the second unit director on James Bond films.

IN LIKE FLINT
1967 20th Century-Fox
PRODUCER: Saul David
DIRECTOR: Gordon Douglas
SCREENWRITER: Hal Fimberg

James Coburn returns as secret agent Derek Flint. A secret society of women plan to take over the world. They kidnap the President and freeze three of Flint's girlfriends. He discovers their Fabulous Face Cold cream front in Europe and ends up in outer space. Disguised as a woman, Pentagon official Lee J. Cobb tries to help. With Jean Hale, Yvonne Craig, and Andrew Duggan. Music includes "Your Zowie Face." One of the few Bond spoofs worth watching.

IN SAIGON, SOME MAY LIVE
1966 Miracle (England)
DIRECTOR: Vernon Sewell
ALSO RELEASED AS: *Some May Live*

Joseph Cotten goes to Saigon to find out who tried to kill a U.S. senator, there on a secret visit. Peter Cushing is a journalist working for the Communists. As Cushing's wife, Martha Hyer helps Cotten and his assistant. It was actually filmed in Nam while the war was on.

IN SEARCH OF DRACULA
1971 Independent International (Sweden/U.S.)
PRODUCER/DIRECTOR: Calvin Floyd
SCREENWRITER: Yvonne Floyd

You might want to pretend this is a serious documentary filmed partially in Transylvania, with Christopher Lee playing Vlad the impaler, the "real" Dracula. And, it is—in part. A serious and fairly dull Swedish TV special was too short for theatrical release, so random scenes from various Hammer Dracula films and the then unreleased *Count Dracula* were edited in. The result is a bit of a mess, all narrated by Christopher Lee.

IN SEARCH OF HISTORIC JESUS
1980 Sunn Classics
PRODUCERS: Charles E. Sellier, Jr., James L. Conway
DIRECTOR: Gary Conway
SCREENWRITERS: Martin Wald, Jack Jacobs

Brad Crandell narrates a search for the Shroud of Turin. It followed similar searches for UFOs, Bigfoot, Noah's Ark, and other popular phenomena. By the director of *Beyond and Back*. John Rubinstein, star of *Zachariah* (the first rock Western) and *The Car*, plays Jesus and walks on water. With Nehemia Persoff, John Anderson, and Royal Dano.

IN THE DEVIL'S GARDEN
1971 Hemisphere (England)
PRODUCER: Peter Rogers
DIRECTOR: Sidney Hayers
SCREENWRITER: John Krause
ORIGINALLY RELEASED AS: *Tower of Terror*

A psycho rapist attacks schoolgirls in a feature often shown as a horror movie on Saturday morning TV. Suzy Kendall stars, with Frank Findlay, Lesley Anne Down, and Freddie Jones.

IN THE FALL OF '55 EDEN CRIED: See EDEN CRIED.

IN THE GRIP OF THE SPIDER: See WEB OF THE SPIDER.

IN THE YEAR 2889
1966 AIP-TV

PRODUCER/DIRECTOR: Larry Buchanan
SCREENWRITER: Harold Hoffman
ALSO RELEASED AS: *Year 2889*

Paul Petersen, teen star of *The Donna Reed Show* and singer of hits like "She Can't Find Her Keys" and "My Dad," stars in an actionless uncredited remake of Corman's *The Day the World Ended*. The people hiding out from postnuclear mutants have a nicer house in this version, but wait'll you see the monsters. Wow!

IN THIS OUR LIFE
1942 Warner Brothers (B&W)

ASSOCIATE PRODUCER: David Lewis
DIRECTOR: John Huston
SCREENWRITER: Howard Koch

Bette Davis ruins the life of her sister (Olivia de Havilland) by stealing her husband (Dennis Morgan). Both sisters have male first names (Roy and Stanley). John Huston's second film as a director is a fevered melodrama touching on themes of racial discrimination and incest. Watch for an amazing roadhouse sequence featuring the cast of *The Maltese Falcon* (Bogart, Astor, Greenstreet, Lorre, Cook, Bond, Maclane, and Walter Huston)! Lee Patrick (also in *Falcon*) has a real role.

A portrait of The Incredible Melting Man.

INCENSE FOR THE DAMNED: See THE BLOODSUCKERS.

THE INCREDIBLE HULK
1977 TV

PRODUCER/DIRECTOR/SCREENWRITER:
Kenneth Johnson

Johnson, who used to work on *The Six Million Dollar Man* and later created *The Bionic Woman*, showed more super slow-motion strength with this serious version of the Marvel comic-book character. Dr. David Bruce Banner (they added David because the network did not want a hero called Bruce), played by Bill Bixby, experiments with gamma rays and finds that under duress they change him into a green giant played by muscleman Lou Ferrigno. A modern *Dr. Jekyll and Mr. Hyde*. This was released as a feature in foreign countries.

–AF

THE INCREDIBLE INVASION
1968 Columbia (Mexico/U.S.)

PRODUCER: Louis Enrique Vergara
DIRECTORS: Juan Ibanez, Jack Hill
SCREENWRITERS: Karl Schanzer,
Louis Enrique Vergara
ORIGINALLY RELEASED AS: *Invasion Sinitestra*

Boris Karloff stars as a scientist with a death ray. Invisible aliens arrive and take over humans. The last of four quickies Karloff shot scenes for in L.A. before he died. With Maura Monti and Enrique Guzman. The ill, 81-year-old horror star is always shown sitting down or leaning against a support of some kind.

THE INCREDIBLE MELTING MAN

1977 AIP
PRODUCER: Samuel W. Gelfman
DIRECTOR/SCREENWRITER: William Sachs

Remember *The First Man Into Space?* Here's a modern variation on its theme. Upon his return from orbiting Saturn, astronaut Alex Rebar is a bloodthirsty creature. The skeleton covered with bloody oozing goop was created by Rick Baker and is a highpoint of this '50s retread. With grade-Z movie vet Myron Healy as a general, Rainbeaux Smith as a model, and Jonathan Demme in a bit part. (R)

THE INCREDIBLE MR. LIMPET

1964 Warner Brothers
PRODUCER: John C. Rose
DIRECTOR: Arthur Lubin
SCREENWRITERS: Jameson Brewer, John C. Rose

In the early 1940s Henry Limpet (Don Knotts), a mild-mannered Brooklyn bookkeeper who loves fish, goes to Coney Island, falls off a dock, and is turned into a dolphin. When World War II breaks out the cartoon Knotts dolphin (with wire-rim glasses) becomes a hero by helping track German U-boats. A good, partially animated fantasy. With Carole Cook and Jack Weston.

THE INCREDIBLE PETRIFIED WORLD

1959 Governor (B&W)
PRODUCER/DIRECTOR: Jerry Warren
SCREENWRITER: John W. Sterner

John Carradine (with a wig and beard) develops a diving bell and sends Robert Clarke and his crew down, down, down to a frozen cave. Most reviews claim it's the acting that's petrified. Who cares? Watch it anyway. With Phyllis Coates (Lois Lane in TV's *Superman*).

THE INCREDIBLE SHRINKING MAN

1957 Universal (B&W)
PRODUCER: Albert Zugsmith
DIRECTOR: Jack Arnold
SCREENWRITER: Richard Matheson

A classic, directed by the master of '50s science fiction, Jack Arnold, from the novel by Richard Matheson. Scott Carey (Grant Williams) begins slowly shrinking after passing through a radioactive cloud. Nobody can explain it—it just happens. On the way down, he sees his happy marriage fall apart and is terrorized by his pet cat and finally by a spider while he's locked in the basement. He escapes through a hole in the window screen and accepts his fate, looking forward to new worlds as he becomes infinitesimally small. With Randy Stuart as the wife, April Kent as an unconvincing "midget," William Schallert, and Billy Curtis.

Grant Williams as Scott Carey in Jack Arnold's The Incredible Shrinking Man.

THE INCREDIBLE
SHRINKING WOMAN

1981 Universal
PRODUCER: Hank Moonjean
DIRECTOR/SCREENWRITER: Jane Wagner

A pleasant satirical comedy in which air pollution, food additives, and other hazards of everyday life combine to turn Lily Tomlin into a tiny person, much to the dismay of ad-man husband Charles Grodin. A group of mad scientists kidnaps little Lily, with plans of shrinking the world into subjugation. With the help of Sidney the gorilla (effects man Rick Baker in his own ape suit), she sets out to expose the plot. Originally, John Landis of *Animal House* was to write and direct *Shrinking Woman*, but Universal found his plans to be too expensive by several million, and production was cancelled. Wagner, a close friend and associate of Tomlin's, suggested scaling down the film, and the project was revived. Cost overruns (mostly involving the film's adequate-to-excellent effects) brought things pretty much up to the level Landis had suggested in the first place, later justified by the film's moderate success.
—BM

THE INCREDIBLE TORTURE
SHOW

1978 Rochelle
PRODUCER/DIRECTOR/SCREENWRITER:
Joel M. Reed
ALSO RELEASED AS: *Blood Sucking Freaks*

A low-budget Manhattan-shot comedy/gore/sex movie set in a Soho Grand Guignol theater that's sicker than anything by H.G. Lewis. As Sardu, Seamus O'Brien kidnaps a Lincoln Center ballerina who later kicks a *New York Times* critic to death. A dwarf tends a cage of naked cannibal women. People are tortured and decapitated, and a woman has her brains sucked out through a straw. Filmed in "Ghoulovision." The

acting is much better than most of the effects. Originally rated X. With Niles McMaster (*Alice, Sweet Alice*). In 1982, it turned up as a midnight feature and was closed because of Women Against Pornography protests. **(R)**

INCREDIBLE TWO-HEADED
TRANSPLANT

1971 AIP
PRODUCER: John Lawrence
DIRECTOR: Anthony Lanza
SCREENWRITERS: James Gordon White,
John Lawrence

Even if you've see *The Thing with Two Heads*, you won't be prepared for this incredibly awful bad-taste epic. Bruce Dern, who was in *Bloody Mama* the same year, is crazier than ever as the doctor who grafts the head of a leering homicidal maniac onto the body of a large retarded handyman. The original head, played by John Bloom (the monster in *Dracula vs. Frankenstein*), cries and talks like a baby while the new insane head leads them on a rampage of killing. Dern even offers his wife (Pat Priest—Marilyn on *The Munsters*) to the horrible schizoid creature. Berry Kroger is suitably ludicrous as Dern's Germanic assistant. TV horror-movie host Seymour is the gardener. *America's-Top 10* host Casey Kasem is Dern's friend. Director Lanza was once an editor for Ray Dennis Steckler Films. The theme song is "It's Incredible"!

THE INCREDIBLY STRANGE
CREATURES WHO STOPPED
LIVING AND BECAME CRAZY
MIXED-UP ZOMBIES

1964 Fairway-International
PRODUCER/DIRECTOR: Ray Dennis Steckler
SCREENWRITERS:
Gene Pollock, Robert Silliphant
ALSO RELEASED AS: *Teenage Psycho Meets Bloody Mary*

"The first monster musical!" claimed the ads. At a Long Beach amusement park Madame Estrella the gypsy fortune-teller hypnotizes patrons, throws acid in their faces, and collects the now ugly monsters in cages in the basement. Ortega the hunchback and Carmelita the stripper help. Hero Cash Flagg (the director) visits the gypsy and is turned into a zombie in a hooded sweat shirt! The monsters break loose during an incredible dance number and kill everyone in sight until the police arrive. Hear "The Mixed-Up Zombie Stomp"! See the "1001 weirdest scenes ever!" "Not for sissies!" When the film was reissued, actors wearing the same horror masks used in the movie "crashed out of the screen to invade the audience and abduct girls from their seats"! At least that's how the ads described it. Filmed in Bloody Vision. Look for this unbelievably well-photographed oddity with Carolyn Brandt (the director's wife), Atlas King, and a hypnotic umbrella! Vilmós Zsigmond was the cinematographer.

INCUBUS
1965 Daystan (B&W)
PRODUCER: Anthony M. Taylor
DIRECTOR/SCREENWRITER: Leslie Stevens
In his last pre-Captain Kirk feature, William Shatner plays a man encountering demons both good and evil. The dialogue is spoken in Esperanto, an international language developed in 1887 which of course didn't get very far. There's a how-to-speak-Esperanto LP on ESP. You might need it to understand this movie. Both movie and album are quite rare. Directed by the creator of *The Outer Limits*.

INCUBUS
1982 Film Ventures (Canada)
PRODUCERS: Marc Boyman, Johnny Eckert
DIRECTOR: John Hough
SCREENWRITER: George Franklin
A sometimes funny, often disgusting demon-rape movie based on Ray Russell's novel of the same name. A doctor (John Cassavettes) investigates violent sex murders in a Wisconsin town. There's a female love interest, a movie-

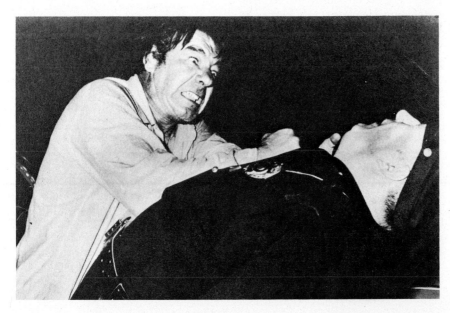

Lon Chaney is The Indestructible Man.

theater bathroom mauling, the required shower scene, and a briefly viewed, ugly, androgynous monster. John Ireland (*Satan's Cheerleaders*) lends his acting talents as the sheriff. With the rock group F.M. From the director of *The Legend of Hell House* and several recent Disney films. (R)

THE INDESTRUCTIBLE MAN
1956 Allied Artists (B&W)
PRODUCER/DIRECTOR: Jack Pollexfen
SCREENWRITERS: Sue Bradford, Vy Russel
The ads promised: "300,000 volts of horror!" Lon Chaney, Jr., made a lot of bad junky movies, but this one is *great* junk. The opening scene of a doctor (Robert Shayne) trying to stick a hypodermic needle into the arm of a butcher (Chaney) only to have it bend is so good that it's shown twice. As an electrocuted convict brought back to life, Chaney is silent and intense as he visits his old stripper girlfriend (Marian Carr) and kills the ex-cohorts (with names like Squeamy Ellis) who betrayed him. He ends up hiding in the sewer system and having his face burned by flamethrowers. Half the movie seems to be interminably held extreme close-ups of Chaney's baggy quivering eyes. This classic trashy film is narrated *Dragnet*-style by Ross Elliott as a detective. Originally billed with *World Without End*.

THE INFERNAL IDOL: See CRAZE.

INFERNO
1953 20th Century-Fox (3-D)
PRODUCER: William Bloom
DIRECTOR: Roy Baker
SCREENWRITER: Francis Cockrell
A wealthy businessman (Robert Ryan) is left to die on the desert by his wife (Rhonda Fleming) and her boyfriend (William Lundigan). Ryan survives by drinking cactus juice and catching an occasional rabbit. It's a serious, well-made 3-D feature, but near the end when Ryan throws an oil lamp, causing the inferno, you can clearly see the string. The effect might remind you of the 3-D shorts with the Three Stooges. With Henry Hull.

INFERNO
1980 20th Century-Fox (Italy)
PRODUCER: Claudio Argento
DIRECTOR/SCREENWRITER: Dario Argento
The follow-up to the popular *Suspiria*, with bloody special effects by Mario Bava (who died in '80). Leigh Mc-Closkey, Alida Valli, and Daria Nicolodi star. With music by Keith Emerson. (R)

INFRA-MAN
1975 Joseph Brenner Associates (Hong Kong)
PRODUCER: Runme Shaw
DIRECTOR: Hua-Shan
If you've ever watched the Japanese *Ultra-Man* TV show you'll have some idea of how outrageous and fun this Chinese production is. Super Infra-Man, a bionic superhero, battles endless incredible monsters sent by Princess Dragon Mom from Inner Earth. The lovely but evil blond Mom wears a dark shiny outfit with a skull belt and horns. Her talkative, hyperactive creatures include Octopus Man, Beetle Man, and several robots. The hero played by Li Hsiu-Hsien (*Fists of Fury*) not only flies but is a kung-fu expert. Almost non-stop laughs and excitement with some great special effects, lots of skulls, and a character reading a Dennis Wheatley occult novel.

THE INITIATION OF SARAH

1978 TV
PRODUCER: Jay Benson
DIRECTOR: Robert Day
SCREENWRITERS: Don Ingalls, Carol Saraceno, Kenette Gfeller

Kay Lenz is a quiet college student, rejected by snotty social climbers, in this *Carrie* imitation. She joins the sorority nobody wants to be in. Shelley Winters is the oddball house mother, who encourages her to use her psychic powers for revenge. With Tony Bill, Kathryn (Grant) Crosby, Morgan Fairchild, Tisa Farrow (*Zombie*), and the daughters or neices of Van Heflin, Martin Balsam, Robert Stack, Robert Ryan, and others. You won't know which is which, but it's an interesting concept.

INN OF FRIGHTENED PEOPLE: See TERROR FROM UNDER THE HOUSE.

THE INNOCENT AND THE DAMNED: See GIRL'S TOWN.

THE INNOCENTS

1961 20th Century-Fox (England/U.S.) (B&W)
PRODUCER/DIRECTOR: Jack Clayton
SCREENWRITERS: Truman Capote, William Archibald

Classic chiller based on Henry James' *The Turn of the Screw*. Miss Giddens (Deborah Kerr) is hired by Michael Redgrave to be governess for his nephew and niece. Young Martin Stevens (*Village of the Damned*) has been expelled from school for corrupting other students. He and his sister (Pamela Franklin) are under the control of Quint and Miss Jessel, former servants, now dead. The *excellent* photography is by Freddie Francis. With Megs Jenkins and Peter Wyngarde.

INSEMINOID

1981 Almi Cinema 5 Films (England)
PRODUCERS: Richard Gordon, David Speechley
DIRECTOR: Norman J. Warren
SCREENWRITERS: Nick and Gloria Maley
ALSO RELEASED AS: *Horror Planet*

A gory *Alien* copy with the selling point of rape by a monster and the birth of a killer alien baby. *To Sir with Love* star Judy Geeson is the expectant mother who kills for blood. With Jennifer Ashley, Stephanie Beacham, and Robin Clark. A Sir Run Run Shaw presentation. It was badly cut to avoid an X rating in America. (**R**)

INTERNATIONAL HOUSE

1933 Paramount (B&W)
DIRECTOR: Edward Sutherland
SCREENWRITERS: Francis Martin, Walter De Leon

A great antique comedy starring W. C. Fields as the inventor of a giant screen that shows radio programs visually! Bidders for the amazing device arrive at a hotel in China where they watch Cab Calloway sing "Reefer Man." Rudy Vallee and Baby Rose Marie also perform. Bela Lugosi shows up as a Russian general. It was a good role for Bela, who did *Island of Lost Souls* for Paramount the same year. With Burns and Allen, Franklin Pangborn as the desk clerk, Stuart Erwin, Peggy Hopkins Joyce, young Sterling Holloway dancing, and Fields driving his "Spirit of South Brooklyn" roadster up the stairs.

INTIMACY

1966 Goldstone (B&W)
EXECUTIVE PRODUCER: Felix J. Bilgrey
DIRECTOR: Victor Stoloff
SCREENWRITER: Harvey Flaxman
ALSO RELEASED AS: *The Deceivers*

Tragedy results from government-contract blackmail scheme. Businessman Barry Sullivan tries to ruin an honest

The leader of the Invaders *from Mars.*

mails a young girl into accusing a black student of rape. Robert Emhardt, a familiar overweight screen villain, is a wealthy supporter of the outside agitator. Shatner plays a real creep whose downfall is caused by the unwise seduction of the wife of a salesman (Leo Gordon). Citizens of Charleston, Missouri, play themselves; they probably did not realize that William Shatner is the story's villain. With screenwriter Charles Beaumont as a doctor. Critically acclaimed, it was too controversial at the time to receive much distribution. Corman returned to Poe films. It later played under more exploitable titles, sometimes with *Poor White Trash*.

INTRUDER WITHIN

1981 TV
PRODUCER: Neil T. Maffeo
DIRECTOR: Peter Carter
SCREENWRITER: Ed Waters
ALSO RELEASED AS: *Panic Offshore*

A blatant *Alien* copy set on an offshore oil rig. A snakelike creature hatches from an egg and attacks a crew member. The man then rapes a female co-worker (remember, this is a TV movie). She gives birth to a huge monster that kills off the rest of the crew. With Chad Everett, Joseph Bottoms, and the multitalented Jennifer Warren.

official by setting up a hidden movie camera in his hotel room and getting him a date with Washington hooker Jackie De Shannon. Sullivan dies of heart seizure after his own wife Joan Blackman's torrid screen debut. Jack Ging is the intended victim, Nancy Malone is his alcoholic wife Virginia. Stoloff produced *Of Love and Desire*.

—CB

THE INTRUDER

1961 Pathe-America (B&W)
PRODUCER/DIRECTOR: Roger Corman
SCREENWRITER: Charles Beaumont
ALSO RELEASED AS: *I Hate Your Guts, Shame*

A well-made, serious look at integration in the South, starring William Shatner as a visiting racist troublemaker who encourages the white citizens to harass the new black students at the local high school and to fight court orders permitting their enrollment. When speeches aren't enough he black-

INVADERS FROM MARS

1953 20th Century-Fox
PRODUCER: Edward L. Alperson
DIRECTOR: William Cameron Menzies
SCREENWRITER: Richard Blake

David (Jimmy Hunt) wakes up after a nightmare and sees a flying saucer land in the marsh below his window. His dad (Leif Erickson) investigates, disappears, and then returns, but with a new, cold personality. Soon David's mom (Hillary Brooke) and others also act strange. Nobody believes the boy's incredible story until he meets a Health Department physician (Helena Carter) and an astronomer (Arthur Franz). Giant green Martians who obey a tentacled head in a transparent globe kidnap the doctor and David, and are about to make them slaves when the army arrives, rescues the prisoners, and blows up the ship. David wakes up—it was only a dream—then looks out the window and sees a flying saucer land in the marsh. . . .

This movie has achieved a cult reputation because of its imaginatively distorted sets and nightmarish quality. The director, once an illustrator of children's books, was the set designer for *Gone with the Wind*. Originally planned as a 3-D project, *Invader* is shown in both color and black-and-white versions, sometimes with the only-a-dream ending missing. With Morris Ankrum, Milburn Stone, and the famous mutants with visible suit seams.

INVADERS FROM SPACE

1956–59 TV (Japan) (B&W)
PRODUCER: Mitsugi Okora
DIRECTORS: Teruo Ishii, Akira Mitsuwa, Koreyoshi Akasaka
SCREENWRITER: Ichiro Miyagawa
See *Atomic Rulers of the World*. Starman fights another army of bizarre alien invaders. Better than Ultra-Man.

INVASION

1965 Anglo Amalgamated/AIP-TV (England) (B&W)
PRODUCER: Jack Greenwood
DIRECTOR: Alan Bridges
SCREENWRITER: Roger Marshall
This interesting, small-scale science-fiction film deals with aliens who put an invisible force field around a secluded country hospital. The unwanted visitors are pretty Oriental women in spacesuits. Edward Judo, hero of many

British films, is a scientist. With Yoko Tani, Tsai Chin, Cali Raia, and Eric Young.

INVASION OF THE ANIMAL PEOPLE

1958/62 ADP (Sweden) (B&W)
PRODUCERS: Bertil Jernberg, Jerry Warren (U.S. version)
DIRECTOR: Virgel Vogel, Jerry Warren (U.S. version)
SCREENWRITER: Arthur C. Pierce
ORIGINALLY RELEASED AS: *Rymdinvasion i Lappland*
In this unusual feature filmed in Lapland, a woman is captured by a giant alien. In tacked-on American footage, she's rescued when her geologist uncle (John Carradine) and his assistant (Robert Burton) start an avalanche, scaring the creature away. With Barbara Wilson, Stan Gester, and Bengt Blomgren.

INVASION OF THE ASTRO-MONSTERS: See MONSTER ZERO.

INVASION OF THE BEE GIRLS

1973 Centaur
PRODUCER: Sequoia Pictures
DIRECTOR: Denis Sanders
SCREENWRITER: Nicholas Meyer
ALSO RELEASED AS: *Graveyard Tramps*
"They'll love the very lives out of your body!" Male research scientists are dying of sexual exhaustion. A government man (William Smith, usually seen in biker films) discovers that a group of women have turned themselves into sterile but sexually driven "bees" who leave the men smiling—and dead. Anita Ford (*The Big Bird Cage*) and Victoria Vetri (*When Dinosaurs Ruled the Earth*) are the queen bees who cover naked women recruits in sticky white goop and turn on the radiation. Beautiful killers in dark sunglasses emerge.

Screenplay by Nicholas Meyer, director of *Time After Time*. With René Bond. (R)

INVASION OF THE BLOOD FARMERS

1972 NMO Distributing
PRODUCER/DIRECTOR: Ed Adlum
SCREENWRITERS: Ed Adlum, Ed Kelleher

Inept cheapie with modern "druids" drawing the blood from victims with plastic tubes to keep their queen happy in her glass coffin. The lead villain is a queen of a different kind. The "shocking" ending is tinted red. A total grade-Z feature filmed in upstate New York that's gaining a bit of a bad-movie fan following. Ed Kelleher does reviews for *Creem* magazine and also wrote *Shriek of the Mutilated*. By the director of *Blonde on a Bum Trip*.

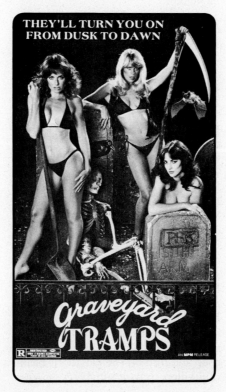

THEY'LL TURN YOU ON FROM DUSK TO DAWN

Graveyard TRAMPS

Originally released as: Invasion of the Bee Girls.

INVASION OF THE BODY SNATCHERS

1956 Allied Artists (B&W)
PRODUCER: Walter Wanger
DIRECTOR: Don Siegel
SCREENWRITERS: Daniel Mainwaring, Sam Peckinpah

When residents of Santa Mira tell psychiatrist Miles Bennell (Kevin McCarthy) that their relatives aren't really their relatives, he says they're just responding to "what's going on in the world today." He soon discovers a plot to turn everyone into emotionless equals. This chilling classic—based on Jack Finney's novel—had a safe happy ending added on when it was released right in the middle of Eisenhower's eight-year run. Dana Wynter is Becky, Miles' girlfriend and last human companion. King Donovan and Carolyn Jones are the couple who find an unfinished pod man on the pool table. Whit Bissell and Richard Deacon are in the phony ending. Sam Peckinpah, who cowrote the script, is a meter reader who joins the crowd that chases Miles to the highway at the original end of the film. "You're next!"

INVASION OF THE BODY SNATCHERS

1978 United Artists
PRODUCER: Robert Solo
DIRECTOR: Philip Kaufman
SCREENWRITER: W.D. Richter

A sequel/remake of Jack Finney's parable about people becoming unemotional zombies that starts where the other left off. The "pod people" are now in the big city. Kevin McCarthy (star of the great 1956 version) is still running and yelling, warning passing motorists about the invasion. Donald Sutherland and Brooke Adams flee from the pods in San Francisco. Also with Leonard Nimoy as a psychiatrist, Veronica Cart-

wright (*Alien*), a bit by the original's director Don Siegel as a cab driver, and Jeff Goldblum.

INVASION OF THE BODY STEALERS: See *THE BODY STEALERS*.

INVASION OF THE FLESH HUNTERS: See *CANNIBALS IN THE STREETS*.

INVASION OF THE NEPTUNE MEN

1961 Toei/TV (Japan) (B&W)
PRODUCER: Hiroshi Okawa
DIRECTOR: Koji Ota
SCREENWRITER: Shin Morita
ORIGINALLY RELEASED AS: *Uchu Kaisoku*

Sonny "Shinichi" Chiba stars as Iron-sharp, a superhero alien who saves Earth from the Neptune men. He travels in a custom space coupe.

INVASION OF THE SAUCER MEN

1957 AIP (B&W)
PRODUCERS: James H. Nicholson, Robert Gurney, Jr.
DIRECTOR: Edward L. Cahn
SCREENWRITERS: Robert Gurney, Jr., Al Martin

Great teen science-fiction comedy set in Hicksville, where the kids just want to make out in their cars. Aliens land in a flying saucer. They have hypo hands that inject alcohol into the innocent teens. Nobody believes the drunk kids, but two con men played by Frank Gorshin (*The Riddler*) and Lyn Osborne (Cadet Happy of *Space Patrol*) plan to keep a dead alien in their refrigerator. The giant-headed aliens with bulging exposed brains were created by Paul Blaisdell and played by midgets. A dismembered alien hand with an eye on its back slashes tires and terrifies a romantic couple in a hot rod. With Gloria Castillo, Steve Terrell, Russ Bender, and Ed Nelson. *The Eye Creatures* was the awful '65 remake.

Kevin McCarthy's pod develops in Invasion of the Body Snatchers.

INVASION OF THE STAR CREATURES

1962 AIP (B&W)
PRODUCER: Berj Hagopian
DIRECTOR: Bruno Ve Sota
SCREENWRITER: Jonathan Haze

A stupid science-fiction comedy written by Jonathan Haze, star of *Little Shop of Horrors*. Two idiot soldiers (Bob Ball and Frankie Ram) run into two vegetable monsters (men in tights with big stuffed heads). After being chased endlessly through a small cave, they manage to seduce the sexy female invaders, Professor Puna and Dr. Tanga, by giving them their first kisses. Gloria Victor and Dolores Reed are stacked better than *The Cat Women of the Moon* and *The Queen of Outer Space*. With director Ve Sota in a walk-on role.

BEAUTIFUL...DEADLY...IN THEIR VEINS THE BLOOD OF MONSTERS!

INVASION OF THE STAR CREATURES

STARRING
BOB BALL · FRANKIE RAY · WRITTEN BY JONATHAN HAZE · DIRECTED BY BRUNO VE SOTA · PRODUCED BY BERJ HAGOPIAN
AN AMERICAN INTERNATIONAL RELEASE

THE INVASION OF THE VAMPIRES

1961 K. Gordon Murray Productions (Mexico) (B&W)
PRODUCER: Raphael Grovas
DIRECTOR/SCREENWRITER: Miguel Morayta
ORIGINALLY RELEASED AS: *La Invasion de los Vampiros*

Count Frankenhausen (Carlos Agosti), a vampire in the 16th century, is stalked by Dr. Ulises. With some great visuals, including a misty cave filled with coffins of victims and huge vampire bats.

INVASION OF THE ZOMBIES

1961 Azteca (Mexico) (B&W)
PRODUCER: Fernando Osés
DIRECTOR/SCREENWRITER: Benito Alzraki

Santo, the silver-masked wrestling hero, defeats a mad scientist trying to conquer the world with an army of zombies. Wrestling movies have been popular in Mexico since the '50s. Santo, the most popular star, has been in over 40! Only a few have been dubbed into English (see *Samson . . .*) but others often show up on Spanish-language TV stations. You don't need to understand the language; just watch the outrageous action. Some of the more recent ones have featured armies of wrestling werewolves, space creatures, and naked vampire women. Santo is a real wrestler who can be followed on the screen, in the ring, and in comic books.

INVASION U.S.A.

1953 Columbia (B&W)
PRODUCERS: Albert Zugsmith, Robert Smith
DIRECTOR: Alfred E. Green
SCREENWRITER: Robert Smith

Cold-war hysteria with a cast including both of the actresses who played Lois Lane on TV (Phyllis Coates and Noel Neill), Dan O'Herlihy, Gerald Mohr, Peggie Castle, and Edward G. Robinson, Jr. Patrons drinking at a bar are hypnotized by O'Herlihy into believing America has been attacked by nuclear weapons. Afterward, they promise to be prepared. Ads claimed you would "see the mutant horror of the H-bomb!" "Operation H Bomb," a Pathé newsreel about Yucca Flats, was released the same month.

INVISIBLE AGENT

1942 Universal (B&W)
PRODUCER: Frank Lloyd
DIRECTOR: Edward L. Marin
SCREENWRITER: Curt Siodmak

The Invisible Man joins the war effort. As a son of the original, Jon Hall goes to Germany and makes fools out of Nazi leaders. Peter Lorre as Ikito, a Japanese agent who commits hara-kiri, and Cedric Hardwicke provide the real problems. With Ilona Massey and Key Luke.

THE INVISIBLE AVENGER

1958 Republic (B&W)
PRODUCERS: Eric Sayers, Emanuel Demby
DIRECTORS: John Sledge, James Wong Howe
SCREENWRITERS: George Bellak, Betty Jeffries
ALSO RELEASED AS: *Bourbon St. Shadows*

The Shadow (who can make himself invisible) becomes involved with an exiled Latin American dictator while investigating the murder of a New Orleans jazz-band leader. Rereleased with additional footage as *Bourbon St. Shadows* in 1962, crediting Ben Parker as producer-director. Richard Derr of *When Worlds Collide* stars, with Mark Daniels and Helen Westcott. Howe was an Oscar-winning cinematographer. Filmed in New Orleans.   –CB

THE INVISIBLE BOY

1957 MGM (B&W)
PRODUCER: Nicholas Nayfack
DIRECTOR: Herman Hoffman
SCREENWRITER: Cyril Hume

A preoccupied scientist dad gives his lucky son Robby the robot to play with.

The friendly robot makes the kid invisible for a while, gives him a ride in a superkite, and goes bad when an evil computer takes over. An underrated science-fiction fantasy with Richard Eyer (the genie in *The Seventh Voyage of Sinbad*), Philip Abbott, Diane Brewster, Harold J. Stone, and Robert H. Harris.

THE INVISIBLE CREATURE

1960 AIP-TV (England) (B&W)
PRODUCER/SCREENWRITER: Maurice J. Wilson
DIRECTOR: Montgomery Tully
ALSO RELEASED AS: *The House in Marsh Road*

A ghost saves a woman from her murderous husband. With Tony Wright and Patricia Dainton.

THE INVISIBLE DR. MABUSE

1962 Thunder Pictures (W. Germany) (B&W)
PRODUCER: Arthur Brauner
DIRECTOR: Harold Reinl
SCREENWRITERS: Ladislas Fodor
ORIGINALLY RELEASED AS: *Die Unsichtbaren Krallen des Dr. Mabuse*
ALSO RELEASED AS: *The Invisible Horror*

UPI 7/5/52: Stark realism in special film effects makes a mushrooming atomic blast in Manhattan seem like the real thing. This scene climaxes Invasion, U.S.A., *for which entire sections of downtown New York were built in miniature.*

Bela Lugosi is a kind doctor who thinks his beloved wife (Betty Compson) is dead. She just has amnesia and likes to roam around staring in windows. Whenever Bela sees her, he goes temporarily insane and strangles houseguests, servants, etc. With Peggy Ann Young, John McGuire, and Clarence Muse as a surprisingly dignified black butler. Lots of close-ups of Bela's eyes.

THE INVISIBLE HORROR: See: *THE INVISIBLE DR. MABUSE.*

INVISIBLE INVADERS
1959 United Artists (B&W)
PRODUCER: Robert E. Kent
DIRECTOR: Edward L. Cahn
SCREENWRITER: Samuel Newman
Invisible aliens arrive from the Moon in an invisible spaceship. They take over the bodies of dead men (including John Carradine as a nuclear physicist), who become white-faced zombies with blackened eyes marching arms outstretched to conquer the world! Who can save us? How about scientist John Agar and some high-frequency sounds? An early *Night of the Living Dead*–type story, but without the gore. With Robert Hutton and Jean Byron.

UPI 8/2/57: If the Brooklyn Dodgers ever make that move to Los Angeles, the Dodgers' famed catcher Roy Campanella had better look to his laurels. He may have competition in "Robby," Hollywood's mechanical man, who is serving as battery mate for young Richard Eyer, ardent Little Leaguer. The pair are also co-players in MGM's forthcoming science-fiction movie, The Invisible Boy.

A professor disfigured in a car crash invents "Operation X" to make himself invisible so he won't scare his girlfriend! Dr. Mabuse (Wolfgang Preiss) kidnaps the girl (Karin Dor) in order to get the secret. Later the invisible villain and his invisible thugs are stopped by a New York detective (Lex Barker) as they try to take over the world. Mabuse is returned to an asylum. Reinl directed *The Return of Dr. Mabuse* next.

THE INVISIBLE GHOST
1941 Monogram (B&W)
PRODUCER: Sam Katzman
DIRECTOR: Joseph H. Lewis
SCREENWRITERS: Helen and Al Martin

THE INVISIBLE KILLER
1940 PRC (B&W)
ASSOCIATE PRODUCER: Sigmund Neufeld
DIRECTOR: Sherman Scott (Sam Newfield)
SCREENWRITER: Joseph O'Donnell
A detective and a lady reporter solve a murder mystery involving sonic death by telephone. With Grace Bradley and Roland Drew. By the director of *Terror of Tiny Town.*

THE INVISIBLE MAN
1933 Universal (B&W)
PRODUCER: Carl Laemmle, Jr.
DIRECTOR: James Whale
SCREENWRITER: R.C. Sherriff

Claude Rains (or at least his familiar voice) makes his film debut as the invisible power-mad British scientist Jack Griffin. Good dialogue and special effects highlight the H.G. Wells story featuring Gloria Stuart, Una O'Connor, and—if you look hard—John Carradine and Dwight Frye. A major technical flaw: when the naked Invisible Man runs through the snow, he leaves shoe prints.

THE INVISIBLE MAN
1975 TV
PRODUCER/SCREENWRITER: Steven Bochco
DIRECTOR: Robert Michael Lewis

David McCallum, a modern scientist with an invisibility formula, tries to keep the military from discovering his secret. The pilot film for a very short-lived series. With Jackie Cooper and Melinda Fee.

THE INVISIBLE MAN RETURNS
1940 Universal (B&W)
ASSOCIATE PRODUCER: Kenneth Goldsmith
DIRECTOR: Joe May
SCREENWRITERS: Lester Cole, Curt Siodmak

Vincent Price, as the brother of the original Invisible Man, is wrongly accused of murder and condemned to death. A scientist (John Dutton) makes him invisible, too, so he can escape and trap the real killer. Nan Grey provides the love interest. Cedric Hardwicke is the villain, Cecil Kellaway a helpful detective. With Alan Napier. Featuring a photograph of Claude Rains.

THE INVISIBLE MAN'S REVENGE
1944 Universal (B&W)
PRODUCER/DIRECTOR: Ford Beebe
SCREENWRITER: Bertram Millhauser

Jon Hall (*The Invisible Agent*) is an invisible criminal aided by scientist John Carradine. With Gale Sondergaard, Evelyn Ankers, Leon Errol, and Alan Curtis. Also with an invisible dog. It

Is this a scene from Night of the Living Dads? *No, it's the revived corpses in* Invisible Invaders.

373

was the last of Universal's serious Invisible series.

THE INVISIBLE MENACE
1937 Warner Brothers (B&W)
ASSOCIATE PRODUCER: Bryan Foy
DIRECTOR: John Farrow
SCREENWRITER: Crane Wilbur
ALSO RELEASED AS: *Without Warning*
Murders at an isolated army post seem to have been committed by embezzler Boris Karloff. With Marie Wilson, Eddie Craven, and Regis Toomey. It was remade in '43 as *Murder on the Waterfront*.

THE INVISIBLE RAY
1936 Universal (B&W)
PRODUCER: Edmund Grainger
DIRECTOR: Lambert Hillyer
SCREENWRITER: John Colton
Good early science-fiction horror with Boris Karloff as Janos Rukh, a scientist who goes to Africa and discovers "radium X" in a meteor. As Dr. Benet, Bela Lugosi helps finance experiments with the healing alien substance. But Janos has touched it: he glows in the dark and begins to go insane when he discovers he can kill with his touch. To demonstrate his powers to the public, he melts a life-size statue representing one of the seven deadly sins each time he kills. His own mother (Violet Cooper) destroys the antidote, causing him to disintegrate. With Frances Drake, Beulah Bondi, and Snowflake. By the director of *Dracula's Daughter*.

INVISIBLE TERROR
1963 R&B (West Germany)
DIRECTOR: Raphael Nussbaum
SCREENWRITERS: Raphael Nussbaum, Wladimir Semitjof
ORIGINALLY RELEASED AS: *Der Unsichtbare*
A crook steals a scientist's invisibility drug. Similar to Edward G. Ulmer's *Amazing Transparent Man*. With Hanaes Hauser and Ellen Schwiers.

THE INVISIBLE WOMAN
1941 Universal (B&W)
ASSOCIATE PRODUCER: Burt Kelly
DIRECTOR: Edward Sutherland
SCREENWRITERS: Robert Lees, Fred Rinaldo, Gertrude Purcell
John Barrymore is wasted in one of his last roles, an old comic scientist with an invisibility machine. Virginia Bruce plays a fashion model who becomes the woman of the title and battles spies. John Howard is her love interest. With Charlie Ruggles, Oscar Homolka, Margaret Hamilton, Shemp Howard, and Maria Montez. Barrymore died the next year.

THE IPCRESS FILE
1965 Universal (England)
PRODUCER: Harry Saltzman
DIRECTOR: Sidney J. Furie
SCREENWRITERS: Bill Canaway, James Doran
Best of the three Michael Caine–Harry Palmer films. Unlike 007 and most spies that followed, this agent is a cockney who has to be blackmailed by the government before rendering services. He undergoes "brain drain" torture for his troubles. With Nigel Green (*The Ruling Class*) and Sue Lloyd (*Corruption*). Based on the novel of the same title by Len Deighton. Music by John Barry.

IS THIS TRIP REALLY NECESSARY?
1970 Hollywood Star Pictures
PRODUCER/DIRECTOR: Ben Bendit
SCREENWRITER: Lee Kalcheim
Has anybody seen this? John Carradine plays an insane director working on an epic sex film who gives actresses LSD, then kills them with an iron maiden in his private torture chamber. Marvin Miller (star of TV's *The Millionaire*) stars

with Peter Duryea, Carol Kane, and Barbara Mallory. (M)

ISN'T IT SHOCKING

1973 TV
PRODUCERS: Ron Bernstein,
Howard Rosenman
DIRECTOR: John Badham
SCREENWRITER: Lane Slate

Oddball pseudo-horror movie set (and filmed) in Mount Angel, Oregon. Edmond O'Brien is killing off 1928 high school grads with an electronic murder machine that leaves no traces. The sheriff (Alan Alda) and his wife (Louise Lasser) try to find out why the old folks are dying. With Ruth Gordon, Will Geer, and Lloyd Nolan.

THE ISLAND

1980 Universal
PRODUCERS: Richard D. Zanuck,
David Brown
DIRECTOR: Michael Ritchie
SCREENWRITER: Peter Benchley

A scary Bermuda Triangle movie that's worth watching. Seventeenth-century pirates are responsible for all the missing ships. They capture Michael Caine and turn his young son against him. David Warner leads the ritualistic out-of-time cutthroats. With Angela Punch McGregor. Based on Peter (*Jaws*) Benchley's novel of the same name. The music by Ennio Morricone is available on a sound track album. For some reason, *The Island* cost $22 million to film. (R)

THE ISLAND OF DR. MOREAU

1977 AIP
PRODUCERS: John Temple-Smith,
Skip Steloff
DIRECTOR: Don Taylor
SCREENWRITER: John Herman Shaner

A big mistake. A useless, boring remake of *Island of Lost Souls*, with Burt

Lancaster as Moreau. In this version, hero Michael York turns into a beast. Barbara Carrera is Maria. Nigel Davenport is Montgomery. Richard Basehart is a poor substitute for Bela Lugosi. Some good makeup is wasted. Filmed in the Virgin Islands.

ISLAND OF DOOMED MEN

1940 Columbia (B&W)
PRODUCER: Wallace MacDonald
DIRECTOR: Charles Barton

Peter Lorre is great as the sadistic, well-dressed ruler of an island where men become his slaves and the only woman (Rochelle Hudson) is kept as an uncooperative mistress. She cringes in disgust when Lorre touches her and hopes that prisoner Robert Wilcox will take her away. Charles "Ming" Middleton is one of the overseers. Lorre listens to Chopin before flogging more doomed men.

ISLAND OF LIVING HORROR: See BRIDES OF BLOOD.

ISLAND OF LOST MEN

1939 Paramount (B&W)
DIRECTOR: Kurt Neumann
SCREENWRITERS: William R. Lipman,
Horace McCoy

UPI 7/8/77: Actor Richard Basehart is a changed man — or changed wolf — in the film The Island of Dr. Moreau. At left is Basehart as he ordinarily looks. At right, he's made up for his part as "Sayer of the Law" in the film. He plays a wolf that has been given human characteristics and a half-human appearance as the result of one of Dr. Moreau's experiments.

Anna May Wong searches for a general held captive by J. Carrol Naish on a jungle island. With Anthony Quinn, Broderick Crawford, and Eric Blore. It was a remake of the 1933 *White Woman*, with Charles Laughton.

ISLAND OF LOST SOULS

1933 Paramount (B&W)
DIRECTOR: Erle C. Kenton
SCREENWRITERS: Waldemar Young,
Philip Wylie

It was banned in England for years. H.G. Wells, who wrote the novel it was based on, condemned it as being vulgar. It's also probably the best horror film ever made. No other film has as many different and scary faces as this one. The atmosphere (mostly created on sets) is remarkable. With his little goatee, a clean white suit, and an ever present whip, Charles Laughton is perfect as Dr. Moreau. He surgically turns animals into a grotesque array of beastmen and tries to get his ultimate creation, Lota the panther woman, to mate with shipwreck victim Richard Arlen. Nineteen-year-old Kathleen Burke played Lota; she was a Chicago contestant in a nationwide search for a girl with the right "animal" look. Bela Lugosi is also great as the Sayer of the Law. His tormented voice leading a chant of "What is the law—are we not men!" is unforgettable. With Leila Hyams (also in *Freaks*), Arthur Hohl, Stanley Fields, Komai Tetsu, and in there somewhere—Randolph Scott and Alan Ladd. Seventy-two fascinating minutes ending in the House of Pain. Cinematography by Karl Struss.

ISLAND OF LOST WOMEN

1959 Warner Brothers (B&W)
PRODUCER: Albert J. Cohen
DIRECTOR: Frank W. Tuttle
SCREENWRITER: Ray Buffum

An atomic scientist with deadly ray guns and three beautiful daughters has unwanted visitors on his island. Result —"They turned a forbidden paradise into a raging hell!" Or so the ads would have us believe. Alan Ladd was the executive producer. With Jeff Richards, Venetia Stevenson, Alan Napier, and Gavin Muir.

ISLAND OF TERROR

1966 Planet/Universal (England)
PRODUCER: Tom Blakeley
DIRECTOR: Terence Fisher
SCREENWRITERS: Allen Ramsen,
Edward Andrew Mann
ALSO RELEASED AS: *The Creepers*

Effectively scary story about slithery round tentacled creatures that live on bone marrow. When boneless corpses are discovered on an Irish island, two scientists (Peter Cushing and Edward Judd) are brought over to help. The disgusting creatures responsible for the carnage seem indestructible—and they divide and multiply! Soon nobody on the island will have any bones left! Richard Gordon was executive producer.

ISLAND OF THE BURNING DAMNED: See ISLAND OF THE BURNING DOOMED.

ISLAND OF THE BURNING DOOMED

1967 Maron/Planet
PRODUCER: Tom Blakeley
DIRECTOR: Terence Fisher
SCREENWRITERS: Ronald Liles,
Pip and Jane Baker
ALSO RELEASED AS: *Island of the Burning Damned, Night of the Big Heat*

The Planet Company of England somehow signed Hammer stars Christopher Lee and Peter Cushing along with Hammer director Fisher for this interesting little movie. Protoplasmic aliens take over a small island during the winter and cause an unbearable heat wave. It gets so hot that humans begin to incinerate. Most of the action takes place at an inn where the helpless inhabitants get on each other's nerves, to say the least. Based on John Lymington's novel, *Night of the Big Heat*. With Patrick Allen and Sarah Lawson.

ISLAND OF THE DAMNED
1976 AIP (Spain)
PRODUCER: Manuel Perez
DIRECTOR: Narciso Ibanez Serrador
SCREENWRITER: Luis Perafiel
ORIGINALLY RELEASED AS: *Quién Puede Matar a un Nino?*

A man and his pregnant wife arrive on an island for a vacation. The children there have killed all the adults and the visiting couple is next. A critically acclaimed movie by the director of *The House That Screamed*. **(R)**

ISLAND OF THE DOOMED
1966 Allied Artists (Spain/W. Germany)
PRODUCER: George Ferrer
DIRECTOR: Mel Welles
SCREENWRITER: Stephen Schmidt
ORIGINALLY RELEASED AS: *La Isla de la Muerte*
ALSO RELEASED AS: *Man Eater of Hydra*

As the mad botanist Baron Von Weser, Cameron Mitchell creates a vampire-tree that sucks blood with its tentacle-like branches. If that isn't enough to make you watch, the director played Gravis Muchnik in *Little Shop of Horrors*! With Elisa Montes and George Martin. Mitchell, who has a handy mute servant, ends up strangled by his own creation. Cameron Mitchell—the unheralded king of bad horror for three decades!

ISLE OF THE DEAD
1945 RKO (B&W)
PRODUCER: Val Lewton
DIRECTOR: Mark Robson
SCREENWRITERS: Ardel Wray, Josef Mischel

Ads promised "201 blood-curdling scenes you'll never tear out of your mind!" Well, there are some atmospheric frights in this grim tale of the plague during the Balkan Wars. As a Greek general, Boris Karloff walks around the bodies. The "Vrykolaka" is a woman who was buried alive, walking around ghostlike with a trident. With Ellen Drew, Jason Robards, Sr., Alan Napier, Katherine Emery, and Skelton Knaggs. It's the least interesting of the consecutive three movies Karloff did for Lewton.

ISLE OF THE FISHMEN: See SCREAMERS.

ISLE OF THE SNAKE PEOPLE: See THE SNAKE PEOPLE.

IT!
1967 Warner Brothers (England)
PRODUCER/DIRECTOR/SCREENWRITER:
Herbert J. Leder

A ridiculous updating of the legend of the golem, from the man behind *The Frozen Dead*. Roddy McDowall is a deranged assistant museum curator who keeps his mother's corpse at home for company (it looks just like Mrs. Bates in *Psycho*). He discovers how to control the ancient Hebrew statue, which resembles a skinny version of the tree monster in *From Hell It Came*. The golem kills Roddy's enemies and disappears under the sea after its temporary master is destroyed by an atom bomb. With Jill Haworth and Paul Maxwell. McDowall always plays crazy people

It Came from Outer Space and Kathleen Hughes has just seen it in this staged shot.

with a lot of conviction (see *Shock Treatment* and *Angel, Angel Down We Go*).

IT CAME FROM BENEATH THE SEA

1955 Columbia (B&W)
PRODUCER: Charles H. Schneer
DIRECTOR: Robert Gordon
SCREENWRITER: George Worthing Yates

A giant radioactive octopus (animated by Ray Harryhausen) is spotted by submarine captain Kenneth Tobey. The slimy suction-cup horror surfaces in San Francisco, where it destroys the Market Street Tower and the Golden Gate Bridge before being torpedoed to smithereens. While all this is going on, Tobey finds time to battle biologist Donald Curtis for the charms of lovely scientist Faith Domergue. Thanks to the ridiculous budget and time limitations, the

"octopus" has only five tentacles. The first of many enjoyable Schneer/Harryhausen collaborations. It originally played with *Creature with the Atom Brain*.

IT CAME FROM HOLLYWOOD

1982 Paramount
PRODUCERS: Susan Strausberg, Jeff Stein
DIRECTORS: Malcolm Leo, Andrew Solt
SCREENWRITER: Dana Olsen

Paramount purchased a "That's Hollywood" of B-movies made by film collectors and editors, re-edited it, and added new comic segments and insulting narration. It has lots of great and/or funny scenes from dozens of often unidentified old science-fiction, horror, and teen movies, but the condescending attitude sinks the project. Gilda Radner, Dan Aykroyd, John Candy, and Cheech and Chong are the marquee-value additions. Categories include gorillas, aliens, monsters, and brains.

IT CAME FROM OUTER SPACE

1953 Universal (B&W, 3-D)
PRODUCER: William Alland
DIRECTOR: Jack Arnold
SCREENWRITER: Harry Essex

Nobody believes astronomer Richard Carlson when he sees a huge space orb crash in the desert. The alien Xenomorphs make doubles of some townspeople to help repair their ship. Telephone line workers Joe Sawyer and Russell Johnson (the professor on *Gilligan's Island*) are the first to be duplicated. A superior science-fiction film based on "The Meteor" by Ray Bradbury. It was the first of several Alland-Arnold hits. With Barbara Rush as Carlson's fiancée, Charles Drake, and Morey Amsterdam.

IT CAME UP FROM THE BERMUDA DEPTHS: See THE BERMUDA DEPTHS.

IT CONQUERED THE WORLD

1956 AIP (B&W)
PRODUCER/DIRECTOR: Roger Corman
SCREENWRITERS: Lou Rusoff, Charles Griffith

Corman's second science-fiction movie features one of the screen's most unlikely monsters. The Venusian (played by its creator, Paul Blaisdell) looks like a pointed hat with arms, horns, and lots of teeth. Scientist Lee Van Cleef talks to Venus on his ham radio and serves the creature until his wife (Beverly Garland) is killed by it. Then Van Cleef battles the creature with a blowtorch. It falls on its side and dies. So does Lee. Peter Graves is the hero. He kills his own wife after she's attacked by one of the alien's bat helpers and turned into a slave. With Sally Fraser, Russ Bender, Dick Miller, Jonathan Haze, and Charles B. Griffith. Most people know Beverly Garland from TV's *My Three Sons*. See *Zontar, The Thing from Venus.*

IT FELL FROM THE SKY

1979 Firebird International
PRODUCER/DIRECTOR: Fred Olen Ray
SCREENWRITERS: Fred Olen Ray,
Allan Nicholas
ALSO RELEASED AS: *Alien Dead*

A feature starring Buster Crabbe (in his 70s) as Sheriff Kowalski. The characters' names were chosen because of connections with Roger Corman movies. The plot is about people on a houseboat turning into ghouls. From the director of *The Brain Leeches*. Filmed in Florida.

IT HAPPENED AT LAKEWOOD MANOR

1977 TV
PRODUCER: Peter Nelson
DIRECTOR: Robert Scheerer
SCREENWRITERS: Guerdon Trueblood,
Peter Nelson
ALSO RELEASED AS: *Panic at Lakewood Manor*

Buster Crabbe, still saving the world in It Fell from the Sky.

This was originally going to be called *Ants*. They crawl all over Suzanne Somers at a summer resort. With Robert Foxworth, Myrna Loy, and Lynda Day George. The same production company made *Tarantulas, the Deadly Cargo*, which premiered the same month. It was a feature release in Europe.

IT HAPPENED AT THE WORLD'S FAIR
1963 MGM
PRODUCER: Ted Richmond
DIRECTOR: Norman Taurog
SCREENWRITERS: Si Rose, Seamon Jacobs
Elvis Presley plays a grounded bush pilot who ends up taking a little Chinese girl to the World's Fair in Seattle, where he falls in love with a nurse (Joan O'Brien) and holds off confused child-welfare-board officers. Gary Lockwood is his partner. With Yvonne (*Batwoman*) Craig. Elvis sings "Cotton Candy Land" and "Happy Ending."

IT HAPPENED HERE
1966 Lopert (England) (B&W)
PRODUCERS/DIRECTORS/SCREENWRITERS:
Kevin Brownlow, Andrew Mollo
Germany wins World War II and England is occupied by Nazi soldiers. A British nurse (Pauline Murray) works for the fascist government but discovers that instead of being cured, her Russian and Polish patients are dying from injections. She's arrested and deported for objecting and eventually joins the resistance movement. A low-budget drama that took 10 years to complete. Filmed partially in 16mm.

IT HAPPENED IN ATHENS
1962 20th Century-Fox (Italy)
PRODUCER: James S. Elliot
DIRECTOR: Andrew Marton
SCREENWRITER: Laslo Vadnay

It's 1896 and Jayne Mansfield is Eleni Costa, Greece's most glamorous actress. The Olympic games are being revived in Athens and Eleni announces that she'll marry the winner of the 26-mile marathon, confident that it will be her lover, a lieutenant. A young shepherd named Spiridon (played by Trax Colton) is in love with Christina, Eleni's maid. He enters the contest and wins, causing some embarrassment for the actress. Filmed in Greece with a mostly Greek cast, it also features Bob Mathias as the American coach.

IT LIVES AGAIN
1978 Warner Brothers
PRODUCER/DIRECTOR/SCREENWRITER:
Larry Cohen
ALSO RELEASED AS: *It's Alive II*
It's Alive was such a hit that more killer mutant babies were ordered. The original's dad (John Ryan) and scientist (Andrew Duggan) return to help wipe out the new terror tots. Frederic Forrest (*Apocalypse Now*) and Kathleen Lloyd star as an expectant couple. Eddie Constantine (Lemmy Caution) plays a doctor. Bernard Herrmann had died in '75 but received credit for this, his "last" score, which was reworked by Laurie Johnson using leftovers from the '74 film. Like most of Herrmann's works, the sound track is still in print. Better than the original, it was still a financial flop. (**R**)

IT TAKES A THIEF
1960 Valiant Films (England)
PRODUCER: John Temple Smith
DIRECTOR/SCREENWRITER: John Gilling
ALSO RELEASED AS: *The Challenge*
Jayne Mansfield plays Billy Lacross, the leader of a gang of British crooks! An-

thony Quayle, a widower infatuated with Jayne, is talked into helping in a robbery. He's caught and gets sent up for five years. In the meantime Carl Mohner has taken over the gang and has Quayle's son kidnaped in order to find out where the hidden loot is. Jayne's straight now, so she helps retrieve the kid. Director Gilling is better known for his horror films.

IT! THE TERROR FROM BEYOND SPACE
1958 United Artists (B&W)
PRODUCER: Robert E. King
DIRECTOR: Edward L. Cahn
SCREENWRITER: Jerome Bixby
A stowaway blood-drinking Martian monster kills off astronauts. In a suit by Paul Blaisdell, Ray "Crash" Corrigan hides in the air shafts and can rip through metal with his claws. Marshall Thompson is the hero. A pretty scary space horror with Shawn Smith and Ann Doran.

IT'S A BIKINI WORLD
1967 Trans American Films
PRODUCER: Charles S. Swartz
DIRECTOR: Stephanie Rothman
SCREENWRITERS: Charles S. Swartz, Stephanie Rothman
A bragging beach jock can't win the girl he wants, so he poses as his own brother, a shy intellectual. She falls for the phony while beating the original in a series of races (surfing, skate boarding, car racing). A novel feminist theme for a beach-party movie —too bad Tommy Kirk and Deborah Walley were picked to star in it. The real reason to see it is the bands: the Gentrys, the Toys, and the Animals are all great, but the highlight is the Castaways (in their only film appearance) doing their wonderfully bizarre

"Liar, Liar." With Sid Haig as Big Daddy and Lori Williams (*Faster Pussycat! Kill! Kill!*).

IT'S A MAD, MAD, MAD, MAD WORLD
1963 United Artists
PRODUCER/DIRECTOR: Stanley Kramer
SCREENWRITERS: William Rose, Tania Rose
The only movie with animated figures of the Three Stooges (as firemen). It also has music by the Shirelles and too many stars. Everybody knows that some of them are Sid Caesar, Mickey Rooney, Edie Adams, Spencer Tracy, Milton Berle, and Ethel Merman. Not everybody knows that Paul Birch, Leo Gorcey, Sterling Holloway, Zasu Pitts, Stan Freberg, Jerry Lewis, Buster Keaton, Joe E. Brown, and Don Knotts are also in it.

IT'S A SMALL WORLD
1950 Eagle Lion (B&W)
PRODUCER: Peter Scully
DIRECTOR: William Castle
SCREENWRITER: Otto Schreiber
Even before his crummy 3-D movies and his great gimmick horror hits, William Castle was making unique exploitation films. This seldom-shown feature is a serious story of a midget and "his attempt to find a place in the world labeling him a misfit." Paul Dale, a Des Moines deejay, stars. With Will Geer (*The Waltons*) as his father, Steve Brodie, and Lorraine Miller.

IT'S ALIVE!
1968 AIP-TV
PRODUCER/DIRECTOR/SCREENWRITER:
Larry Buchanan
One of Buchanan's legendary awful quickie television movies. Tommy Kirk (*Mars Needs Women*) stars in this tale

SOMETHING'S GOT TO GIVE.........!

When the emotions and longings of a man are pent-up in the body of a child!

MOTION PICTURES, INC. presents

IT'S A SMALL WORLD

PAUL DALE · LORRAINE MILLER · WILL GEER · STEVE BRODIE

Produced by Peter Scully · Directed by William Castle

An Eagle Lion Films Release

of a man with a pet monster in a cave. It's alive; it needs people to eat; it has sharp teeth and a zipper up its back. It's also the same monster used in *Creature of Destruction!* With Shirley Bond and Billy Thurman. Based on a story by Richard Matheson about a dinosaur called a masasaurus.

IT'S ALIVE

1974 Warner Brothers
PRODUCER/DIRECTOR/SCREENWRITER:
   Larry Cohen
The screen's first monster baby seemed a bit shocking even after *The Exorcist*. It was Larry Cohen's biggest hit and benefits from Bernard Herrmann's score and Rick Baker's horrible fanged mutant infant. The baby doesn't waste any time slaughtering the doctor and nurses in the delivery room. Later it attacks a milk truck. With a PG rating and a seldom-shown creature, it's surprisingly "tasteful." With John Ryan as the

father, Sharon Farrell, Guy Stockwell, Andrew Duggan, and Michael Ansara. *It Lives Again* was a sequel.

IT'S ALIVE II: See IT LIVES AGAIN.

IT'S ALL HAPPENING: See THE DREAM MAKER.

IT'S HOT IN PARADISE: See THE HORRORS OF SPIDER ISLAND.

IT'S NOT THE SIZE THAT COUNTS

1975 Joseph Brenner (England)
PRODUCER: Betty E. Box
DIRECTOR: Ralph Thomas
SCREENWRITER: Sid Colin
ALSO RELEASED AS: *Percy's Progress*
A disguised sequel to *Percy*, a penis-transplant comedy. Denholm Elliott and Elke Sommer return from the original. They're joined by Vincent Price, Judy Geeson, Milo O'Shea, Julie Ege, and George Coulouris. A chemical in the water makes men impotent. Like the first one, this film was ignored in the States. **(R)**

I'VE LIVED BEFORE

1956 Universal (B&W)
PRODUCER: Howard Christie
DIRECTOR: Richard H. Bartlett
SCREENWRITERS: Norman Jolley,
   William Talman
Jock Mahoney stars as an airline pilot who, in the middle of a Chicago–New York flight, decides he's been hit and goes into a dive. Co-pilot Jerry Paris knocks him out and brings the plane in alone. When Mahoney wakes up in the hospital he explains to passenger Ann Harding that he is her long-lost fiancé, Lieutenant Peter Stevens, shot down over France in 1918. By relating

intimate details of their time together and revealing the inscription on a treasured locket, he convinces her that this is the case. John McIntire and Leigh Snowden co-star. *The Search for Bridey Murphy* made 1956 a big year for reincarnation; see *Spell of the Hypnotist* and *Hold That Hypnotist*.   –CB

IT'S TRAD DAD: See *RING-A-DING RHYTHM*

J.D.'S REVENGE

1976 AIP
PRODUCER/DIRECTOR: Arthur Marks
SCREENWRITER: Jaison Starkes

An all-black reincarnation-horror movie starring Glynn Turman as a law student possessed by the spirit of a '30s gangster. Lou Gossett is the preacher hero. With Joan Pringle. Prince (who has since made the big time) sings "I Will Never Let You Go." (R)

JACK AND THE BEANSTALK

1952 Warner Brothers
(color with B&W sequence)
PRODUCER: Alex Gottlieb
DIRECTOR: Jean Yarbrough
SCREENWRITER: Nat Curtis

Lou Costello dreams that he and Bud Abbott are characters in the famous fairy tale. A substandard musical-fantasy comedy with professional fighter Buddy Baer as the giant. With Dorothy Ford and William Farnum.

JACK THE GIANT KILLER

1962 United Artists
PRODUCER: Edward Small
DIRECTOR: Nathan Juran
SCREENWRITERS: Orville H. Hampton, Nathan Juran

Edward Small, a producer who had turned down the successful *Seventh Voyage of Sinbad*, later decided to make an almost exact duplicate. He hired that film's director (Nathan Juran), star (Kerwin Matthews), and villain (Torin Thatcher). For the animation he got Jim Danforth (who had worked on "Gumby" shorts). The animation is inferior to *Sinbad*'s, but the plot is virtually the same. The wicked sorcerer Pendragon (Thatcher) captures a princess (Judi Meredith). Hero Jack (Matthews) is faced with Cormoran, a creature similar to Harryhausen's cyclops but with two eyes; Galligantua, a similar creature with two heads; a flying dragon, a sea monster, witches, and ghouls. Two crew members are turned into a dog and a chimp, and a leprechaun (Don Beddoe) exits on a rainbow. Producer Small later offered *The Christine Jorgensen Story*.

JACK THE RIPPER: See THE VEIL.

JACK THE RIPPER

1959 Paramount (England)
(B&W with color sequence)
PRODUCERS/DIRECTORS: Robert Baker, Monty Berman
SCREENWRITER: Jimmy Sangster

Lots of people in America saw this because of the saturation ad campaign by promoter Joseph E. Levine (who also ballyhooed *Hercules* into a major success). With Lee Paterson, Eddie Byrne, and Ewen Solon. The film goes into color when Jack is crushed to death by an elevator. The Baker/Berman team also made *Mania*, *Blood of the Vampire*, and *The Hellfire Club*.

JACK THE RIPPER

1976 Cineshowcase
(W. Germany/Switzerland)
PRODUCER: Peter Baumgartner
DIRECTOR/SCREENWRITER: Jesse Franco
ORIGINALLY RELEASED AS: *Der Dirnenmörder von London*

Another shoddy Franco film. It was released here only after Klaus Kinski's newfound fame in Werner Herzog films. The Kinski Ripper is shown cutting out eyes and other body parts. Charlie's daughter Josephine Chaplin co-stars. With Herbert Fux and Lina Romay. (R)

THE JACKALS

1967 20th Century-Fox (South Africa)
PRODUCER/DIRECTOR: Robert D. Webb
SCREENWRITERS: Lamar Trotti, Austin Medord

A loose remake of *Yellow Sky* ('48) with Vincent Price as an old prospector losing his gold stakes to five fugitive bank robbers. It was sold directly to television in America. With Diana Ivarson and Robert Gunner.

JACK'S WIFE: See HUNGRY WIVES.

JACKTOWN
1962 Pictorial International (B&W)
PRODUCER/DIRECTOR/SCREENWRITER:
William Martin

A delinquent petty thief who gets two to five years after being caught in the back seat of a car with a fifteen-year-old girl is given garden work by the warden who believes his story. But warden Douglas Rutherford thinks again when inmate Richard Meade and his daughter (Patty McCormack) fall in love. Shot on location at Southern Michigan Prison in Jackson. Newsreel footage of the 1952 Jacktown riots furnishes an opportunity for the youngster to prove his good intentions. With Mike Tancredi, Johanna Douglas, and Gordon Grant.   —CB

JAGUAR
1956 Republic (B&W)
ASSOCIATE PRODUCERS:
Mickey Rooney, Maurice Duke
DIRECTOR: George Blair
SCREENWRITERS: John Fenton Murray, Benedict Freedman

Sabu stars with Chiquita in a murder mystery with Jonathan Hale, Barton McLane, and Michael "Touch" Connors. The Indian hero was next seen in *Sabu and the Magic Ring*, also directed by Blair.

JAGUAR LIVES
1979 AIP
PRODUCER: Derek Gibson
DIRECTOR: Ernest Pintoff
SCREENWRITER: Yabo Yablonsky

International intrigue starring Joe Lewis as an athletic spy. With John Huston as a crippled shipping magnate, Donald Pleasence as a South American dictator, Barbara Bach, Christopher Lee, Joseph Wiseman, Capucine, and Woody Strode.

JAIL BAIT
1955 Howco (B&W)
PRODUCER/DIRECTOR: Edward D. Wood, Jr.
SCREENWRITERS: Edward D. Wood, Jr., Alex Gordon
ALSO RELEASED AS: *Hidden Face*

Tim Farrell tries to get out from under a fatal theater holdup by forcing his partner's plastic-surgeon father to replace his face. But surgeon Herbert Rawlinson finds out that his son, sought for killing the night watchman, has already been eliminated to keep him from a confession. He gives Farrell the one face that will insure his undoing. Filmed in and around the Monterey Theatre in Monterey Park, California. With Steve Reeves, Lyle Talbot, Dolores Fuller, Theodora Thurman, and Clancy Malone. The minstrel show production number is from a 1951 Ron Ormond feature called *Yes Sir Mr. Bones*. Talbot, Farrell, and Fuller also starred in Wood's previous feature, *Glen or Glenda*. The

Elvis and Jennifer Holden in Jailhouse Rock.

amazing musical score was lifted from *Mesa of Lost Women* —CB

THE JAILBREAKERS
1960 AIP (B&W)
PRODUCER/DIRECTOR/SCREENWRITER: Alex Grasshoff

Robert Hutton and wife Mary Castle are held hostage in a ghost town by three escaped convicts searching for $400,000 in stolen currency. When another thug arrives, the convicts turn on each other and lose the money. With Michael O'Connell, Gabe Delutri, and Anton Van Stralen. Hutton directed and starred in *The Slime People*. —CB

JAILHOUSE ROCK
1957 MGM (B&W)
PRODUCER: Pandro S. Berman
DIRECTOR: Richard Thorpe
SCREENWRITER: Guy Trosper

Following his hit *Loving You*, Elvis basically plays himself again in this fictional account of the rise of a rock star. As Vince Everett, he accidentally kills a man in a bar (he was only defending a lady in distress), goes to the state prison, and gets a conniving ex-Country singer (Mickey Shaughnessy) as a cellmate. Note the Hank Williams picture on the cell wall. When Vince is released, his agent (Judy Tyler) helps him cut an independent single ("I Wanna Be Free"). Disc jockey Dean Jones plugs the record; Vince becomes a sensation, goes Hollywood, falls for an actress, hires his ex-cellmate as a flunky, forgets his friends, and almost loses his voice. The famous "Jailhouse Rock" dance scene is part of a TV special. Elvis also sings "Treat Me Nice" and "Baby, I Don't Care." With Scotty and Bill. For this film Colonel Parker managed to get Elvis $250,000 up front and 50 percent of all profits.

JALOPY
1953 Allied Artists (B&W)
PRODUCER: Ben Schwalb
DIRECTOR: William Beaudine
SCREENWRITERS: Tim Ryan, Jack Crutcher, Bert Lawrence

The Bowery Boys experiment with a combination love potion and super car fuel. Huntz Hall stars with Leo, David, and Bernard Gorcey. Robert Lowery is the villain. From the director of *Billy the Kid vs. Dracula*.

JAMBOREE

1957 Warner Brothers (B&W)
PRODUCERS: Max J. Rosenberg, Milton Subotsky
DIRECTOR: Roy Lockwood
SCREENWRITER: Leonard Kantor
ALSO RELEASED AS: *Disc Jockey Jamboree*

"17 great recording stars! 21 hit tunes!" There's a plot about divorced talent agents getting back together and their kids becoming recording stars. There's also endless music from a wide spectrum of entertainers. Besides the Count Basie Band with Joe Williams, there's Fats Domino, Jerry Lee Lewis in his first film, the incredible Slim Whitman, Buddy Knox, rockabilly greats Jimmy Bowen and Charlie Gracie, young Frankie Avalon, popular disc jockeys, and the dubbed-in voice of Connie Francis. Newspapers reported that theater ushers in Buffalo were stabbed while Jerry Lee did "Great Balls of Fire."

THE JAMES DEAN STORY

1957 Warner Brothers (B&W)
PRODUCERS/DIRECTORS: George W. George, Robert Altman

"Was he a rebel? Was he a giant?" This collection of stills, home movies, and interviews was released two years after Dean died (at 24). Uncle Marcus and Aunt Ortense reminisce about his life in Fairmont, Indiana. There's also news footage of his car crash and a screen test for *East of Eden*. Tommy Sands sings "Let Me Be Loved."

JASON AND THE ARGONAUTS

1963 Columbia (England)
PRODUCER: Charles H. Schneer
DIRECTOR: Don Chaffey
SCREENWRITERS: Jan Read, Beverly Cross

Another Ray Harryhausen animated masterpiece. Only his *Seventh Voyage of Sinbad* has as many great scenes. Watched over by the gods on Mt. Olympus and aided by Hera (Honor Blackman), Jason (Todd Armstrong) sails the *Argo* to the other side of the world to obtain the Golden Fleece. He encounters purple-winged harpies, Triton the merman, a seven-headed hydra whose teeth turn into amazing skeleton warriors, and the bronze giant Talos. A classic fantasy. With Nancy Kovack as Medea, Nigel Green as Hercules, Douglas Wilmer, and Michael Gwynn. The music is by Bernard Herrmann. Filmed in Italy. It was a box-office failure because most people thought it would be another routine muscleman feature.

JAWS

1975 Universal
PRODUCERS: Richard D. Zanuck, David Brown
DIRECTOR: Steven Spielberg
SCREENWRITERS: Peter Benchley, Carl Gottlieb

After four TV movies and *The Sugarland Express*, 28-year-old Spielberg became an industry giant and scared a lot of impressionable bathers out of the ocean with his effective shark-paranoia feature. Roy Scheider, Richard Dreyfuss, and Robert Shaw go after the convincing aquatic man-eater in a boat named *Orca*. With Lorraine Gary and Murray Hamilton. Based on Peter Benchley's best-selling novel. Academy Award-winning music by John Williams.

JAWS II

1978 Universal
PRODUCERS: Richard D. Zanuck,
  David Brown
DIRECTOR: Jeannot Szwarc
SCREENWRITERS: Carl Gottlieb,
  Howard Sackler

Roy Scheider is back. Lorraine Gary is back. Murray Hamilton is back. The shark is back. John Williams did the music again. Lots of teenagers are in it. By the director of *Bug* and 32 *Night Gallery* segments. *Variety* called it "the most expensive film that AIP never made." The next sequel has been announced as *Jaws 3-D*.

JAWS OF DEATH: See MAKO: JAWS OF DEATH.

THE JAYNE MANSFIELD STORY

1980 TV
PRODUCERS: Linda Otto, Joan Barnett
DIRECTOR: Dick Lowery
SCREENWRITERS: Charles Dennis,
  Nancy Gayle

WKRP in Cincinnati star Loni Anderson as Jayne Mansfield! Arnold Schwarzenegger as Mickey Hargitay, Jayne's true love! But it can't top *The Wild Wild World of Jayne Mansfield* for insight and good taste. This semifictional, romanticized account of the world's most famous decapitated dumb blonde leads up to the fatal car crash. Based on *Jayne Mansfield and the American Fifties* by Martha Saxon. Waiting to see who the networks pounce on next for quickie bios almost makes television in the '80s worthwhile.

JENNIFER

1978 AIP
PRODUCER: Steve Krantz
DIRECTOR: Brice Mack
SCREENWRITER: Kay Cousins

Terrible *Carrie* imitation with ideas from *Willard* (or maybe *Stanley*) thrown in. Jeff Corey is the religious-fanatic father of a schoolgirl (Lisa Pelikan) who conjures up giant snakes to kill her tormentors. Nina Foch is a teacher-victim. With John Gavin and Bert Convy.

JESSE JAMES MEETS FRANKENSTEIN'S DAUGHTER

1965 Embassy
PRODUCER: Carroll Case
DIRECTOR: William Beaudine
SCREENWRITER: Carl Hittleman

The last of over 150 cheapies directed by William Beaudine during his five-decade B and Z career. Despite the title, it's the famous doctor's *granddaughter* (Narda Onyx!) who puts her dad's creation's brain in the head of Jesse James' muscle-bound pal (Cal Bolder) and names him Igor. Bad acting and dialogue make this a joy to watch. With Nestor Paiva, John Lupton, Estelita, and Jim Davis. Its companion, *Billy the Kid vs. Dracula*, was also directed by Beaudine.

JET ATTACK

1958 AIP (B&W)
PRODUCER: Alex Gordon
DIRECTOR: Edward L. Cahn
SCREENWRITER: Orville Hampton
ALSO RELEASED AS: *Jet Squad*

From the ads: "Jet action blasts the screen!" Joe Hamilton, a scientist from U.S. Air Force radar, is captured when his experimental plane is shot down behind enemy lines in Korea. John Agar, James Dobson, and Gregory Walcott must rescue him before he is brainwashed. Russian nurse Audrey Totter helps. Agar and Hamilton escape in a Russian MIG while Dobson runs interference by crashing into an attacker. Originally shown with *Suicide Battalion*.   —CB

JET SQUAD: See *JET ATTACK.*

JIVARO

1954 Paramount (B&W)
PRODUCERS: William H. Pine,
William C. Thomas
DIRECTOR: Edward Ludwig
SCREENWRITER: Winston Miller
Gold hunters meet head hunters in South America. Fernando Lamas stars with Lon Chaney, Jr., Rhonda Fleming, Rita Moreno, and Brian Keith.

JOHNNY COOL

1963 United Artists (B&W)
PRODUCER/DIRECTOR: William Asher
SCREENWRITER: Joseph Landon
Outlaw Sicilian folk hero Henry Silva, in the States on a Mafia revenge mission, is picked up by divorcee Elizabeth (*Bewitched*) Montgomery after he shuts down a cocktail-lounge hood. "All men look like men, so few really are," she remarks admiringly. Together they embark on a 48-hour orgy of destruction from Idlewild Airport to Mulholland Drive. The direction may be half-baked but what a cast: Jim Backus, Joey Bishop, Brad Dexter, John McGiver, Mort Sahl, Telly Savalas, Sammy Davis, Jr., Joseph Calleia, Douglass Dumbrille, and Elisha Cook, Jr. Sammy sings "The Ballad of Johnny Cool." Montgomery was Mrs. Asher when this was made.   —CB

JONATHAN

1970 New Yorker (W. Germany)
PRODUCER: Iouna Films
DIRECTOR/SCREENWRITER:
Hans W. Geissendörfer
ORIGINALLY RELEASED AS: *Jonathan, Vampire Sterben Nicht*
A critically acclaimed period film with a decadent vampire (Jurgen Jung) feeding off the local peasants to the strains of classical music. It equates vampirism with fascism and features the bloody retaliation of the peasants. After initial showings, scenes of sex and violence were added to make the film more marketable.

JOURNEY BENEATH THE DESERT

1961 Avco Embassy-TV (France/Italy)
EXECUTIVE PRODUCER: Nat Wachberger
DIRECTOR: Edgar G. Ulmer
SCREENWRITERS: Ugo Liberatore,
Remigio Del Grosso, Andre Tabet,
Amedeo Nazzari
ORIGINALLY RELEASED AS: *L'Atlantide* (France), *Antinea, L'Amante della Citta Sepolta* (Italy)
A very low-budget version of the Atlantis legend featuring Haya Harareet as Antinea the evil queen. With Jean-Louis Tritignant and Georges Rivière. It was the second-to-last film for Ulmer, who replaced another director after filming had started. The story had been filmed several times before, once as *Siren of Atlantis* ('48). This modern version ends with an atomic bomb destroying the lost city.

JOURNEY INTO BEYOND

1977 Burbank International (color and B&W)
PRODUCER: Rudolph Kalmowicz
DIRECTOR: Rolf Olsen
SCREENWRITER: Paul Ross
Most recent documentaries on psychic phenomena are only good for dozing through. This one might keep you awake, if only to guess which segments are faked. A witch doctor performs bloodless eye surgery, statues cry, people float in midair, and an explicit "psychic" operation on an abdomen is shown. John Carradine is on hand to explain all the wonders. **(R)**

JOURNEY INTO DARKNESS
1968 Hammer (England)
PRODUCER: Joan Harrison
DIRECTORS: Peter Sasdy, James Hill
SCREENWRITERS: Oscar Millard, John Gould

Two episodes of *Journey to the Unknown*, the British anthology series produced by Hammer. "The New People" stars Robert Reed. "Paper Dolls" stars Michael Tolan and Jill Collins. With an introduction by Patrick McGoohan.

JOURNEY INTO FEAR
1974 Stirling Gold (Canada)
PRODUCER/SCREENWRITER: Trevor Wallace
DIRECTOR: Daniel Mann
ALSO RELEASED AS: *Burn Out*

Remake of Eric Ambler's suspense novel, first done in 1942 by Orson Welles. Sam Waterston stars as a research biologist involved in international intrigue with numerous guest stars, including Zero Mostel, Yvette Mimieux, Joseph Wiseman, Shelley Winters, Donald Pleasence, and Vincent Price. From the director of *Willard* and *Butterfield 8*.

JOURNEY INTO MIDNIGHT
1968 Hammer (England)
PRODUCER: Joan Harrison
DIRECTORS: Roy Ward Baker, Alan Gibson
SCREENWRITERS: Robert Bloch, Jeremy Paul

Two episodes of the *Journey to the Unknown* show, a British anthology series produced by Hammer Films that ran 17 weeks. "The Indian Spirit Guide" was written by Robert Bloch and stars Julie Harris and Tom Adams. "Poor Butterfly" stars Chad Everett. A rare chance to see part of this forgotten series.

JOURNEY TO FREEDOM
1957 Republic (B&W)
DIRECTOR: Robert C. Dertano

Soviet agents track a "Voice of Freedom" activist from Communist Bulgaria to L.A. via Istanbul, Paris, and New York. Jacques Scott falls in love with nurse Genevive Aumont while recovering from a construction-site mishap. Their love is threatened when the Reds spring a hit-and-run frame-up. George Graham, Morgan Lane, and Tor Johnson co-star; Dertano also directed *Gun Girls* and *Blonde Pick-up*. —CB

JOURNEY TO THE BEGINNING OF TIME
1954/67 New Trends
(U.S./Czechoslovakia)
PRODUCER: William Cayton
DIRECTOR: Karel Zeman
SCREENWRITERS: Karel Zeman, J. A. Novotny

New scenes shot in New York's American Museum of Natural History were added to this fantasy from the creator of *The Fabulous World of Jules Verne*. Young boys on a raft drift backward on the River of Time, encountering woolly mammoths and dinosaurs. In 1967, the matinee price was 50 cents.

JOURNEY TO THE CENTER OF THE EARTH
1959 20th Century-Fox
PRODUCER: Charles Brackett
DIRECTOR: Henry Levin
SCREENWRITERS: Walter Reisch,
    Charles Brackett

James Mason leads Arlene Dahl, Pat Boone, and a big Swede with a duck into a volcano in this effective Jules Verne adventure. Thayer David is a ruthless rival explorer. They find giant mushrooms and jewels, big lizards, an underground sea, and a lost city. With Diane Baker and Alan Napier. Great music by Bernard Herrmann.

JOURNEY TO THE CENTER OF THE EARTH: See WHERE TIME BEGAN.

JOURNEY TO THE CENTER OF TIME

1967 American General Pictures
PRODUCERS: Ray Dorn, David L. Hewitt
DIRECTOR: David L. Hewitt
SCREENWRITER: David Prentiss

Almost a remake of *The Time Travelers*, which David L. Hewitt co-wrote. Dr. Von Steiner (Abraham Sofaer—played by Preston Foster in '64) and his assistants (Anthony Eisley and Gigi Perreau) demonstrate their time capsule to the future owner of their research center (Scott Brady). A malfunction causes them to appear in 6968 A.D., when Earth is under attack by aliens, then brings them back to prehistoric times for a dinosaur attack. All these wonders are achieved by the use of stock footage. Despite the cheapness, the absurdity of endlessly ping-ponging back and forth in time makes this fun to watch. Shots and bits of dialogue are repeated and eventually the need for continuity and logic disappears. The editor must have had a great time. With Lyle Waggoner.

JOURNEY TO THE FAR SIDE OF THE SUN

1969 Universal (England)
PRODUCERS: Gerry and Sylvia Anderson
DIRECTOR: Robert Parrish
SCREENWRITERS: Gerry and Sylvia Anderson, Donald James

Gerry and Sylvia Anderson, the British team that brought us TV puppet shows like *Supercar* and *Thunderbirds* and the live-action shows *Space 1999* and *UFO*, produced and wrote this neglected feature starring Roy Thinnes, fresh from the *Invaders* series. An astronaut is sent to a planet hidden behind the sun with an orbit parallel to Earth's. The spaceship crash-lands and he finds himself back on Earth, except everything is backwards! Twenty minutes were cut for the American release. With

Herbert Lom, Patrick Wymark, and Ian Hendry.

JOURNEY TO THE LOST CITY

1958 AIP (W. Germany)
PRODUCER/DIRECTOR: Fritz Lang
SCREENWRITER: Werner Joerge Luedecke

Fritz Lang returned to Germany after 24 years in Hollywood and France to remake *Der Tiger von Eschnapur* and *Das Indische Grabmal*, two 1919 adventures directed by Joe May. American audiences got this badly condensed version of both. Debra Paget plays a dancer in India rescued by Paul Christian. Their serial-style adventures include lepers, snakes, elephants, and man-eating tigers.

JOURNEY TO THE SEVENTH PLANET

1962 AIP (U.S./Sweden)
PRODUCER/DIRECTOR: Sidney Pink
SCREENWRITERS: Ib Melchior, Sidney Pink

Mind-bending science fiction filmed in Sweden in Cinemagic(!). It's 2001. Five

Fritz Lang's Journey to the Lost City

astronauts on Uranus have their brains picked by a giant eye creature. Their fears, desires, and memories appear as realistic hallucinations. One of the weird monsters is a cyclops-dinosaur-rat animated by Jim Danforth. One of the dream women found lounging in a bikini is Greta Thyssen, seen in many of the final Three Stooges shorts. One of the astronauts is John Agar! What a movie!

JOY RIDE

1958 Allied Artists (B&W)
PRODUCER: Ben Schwalb
DIRECTOR: Edward Bernds
SCREENWRITER: Arthur Horman
An adaptation of an Ellery Queen story about a middle-aged sportscar enthusiast plagued by hot rodders set on a test drive. Regis Toomey of *Curfew Breakers* stars, with Rad Fulton, Ann Doran, and Nicholas King. More from Bernds: *Reform School Girl* and *Queen of Outer Space*.   –CB

JUDEX

1963 Continental (France/Italy) (B&W)
PRODUCER: Robert De Nesle
DIRECTOR: Georges Franju
SCREENWRITERS: Jacques Champreux, Francis Lacassin
A beautiful masked-superhero film by the director of *The Horror Chamber of Dr. Faustus*. It's based on a 1917 serial directed by Louis Fevillade, who also made the first Fantomas film. Judex, a master of disguises (played by American magician Channing Pollock), seeks revenge on an evil banker who drove his father to suicide. People are kidnaped, villainess Francine Berge disguises herself as a nun, and a circus aerialist (Sylva Koscina) helps Judex in his quest for retribution. With Edith Scob as the banker's daughter who loves Judex. Recommended.

JUGGERNAUT

1936 Grand National (England) (B&W)
PRODUCER: Julius Hagen
DIRECTOR: Henry Edwards
SCREENWRITERS: Cyril Campion, H. Fowler Mear, H. Fraenkel
As Dr. Sartorius, Boris Karloff needs funds to continue his experiments, so he agrees to poison an elderly millionaire in exchange for money from the man's wife (Mona Goya). While planning to murder another heir, a nurse discovers the plot and Boris injects himself with the poisonous needle.

JUKE BOX RACKET

1960 Brenner (B&W)
PRODUCERS: Jim Geallis, George Barris
DIRECTOR: Barry Mahon
Five teenagers help a friendly storekeeper fight mobsters bent on taking over local juke-box routes. With Arlene Corwin, Lou Anne Lee, Beverly Nazarow, Seymour Cassel, Peter Clune, and Steve Karmen who wrote the songs with Peter Szabo. Mahon directed six movies in 1960, *Cuban Rebel Girls*, *Rocket Attack U.S.A.*, and *Morals Squad* among them.   –CB

JUKE BOX RHYTHM

1959 Columbia (B&W)
PRODUCER: Sam Katzman
DIRECTOR: Arthur Dreifuss
SCREENWRITERS: Mary P. McCall, Jr., Earl Baldwin
A rock musical starring Jack Jones? He's a singer/student whose father (Brian Donlevy) uses foreign princess Jo Morrow in a publicity scheme to help his Broadway show "Juke Box Jamboree." Princess and student fall in love. It's worth watching for Johnny Otis doing "Willie and the Hand Jive". With Hans Conreid, the Earl Grant Trio, the Treniers, and George Jessel as himself.

JULIUS CAESAR
1970 AIP (England)
PRODUCER: Peter Snell
DIRECTOR: Stuart Burge
SCREENWRITER: Robert Furnival

You know the story. Charlton Heston is Marc Anthony, Jason Robards, Jr., is Brutus, and John Gielgud is Julius. The supporting cast is more interesting: Robert Vaughn, Diana Rigg, Christopher Lee, Michael Gough, Richard Johnson, Richard Chamberlain, and Jill Bennett.

THE JUNGLE
1952 Lippert (B&W)
PRODUCER/DIRECTOR: William Berke
SCREENWRITER: Carroll Young

In '51, the Lippert outfit made *Lost Continent* starring Cesar Romero, prehistoric monsters, and Acquanetta. This follow-up stars Romero, prehistoric monsters (elephants with hair glued on), and Sulchana! It was filmed on location in India and features Rod Cameron and Marie Windsor as a princess. By the director of *Zamba the Gorilla*. Filmed in sepia (a black-and-white print tinted in shades of brown).

JUNGLE CAPTIVE
1944 Universal (B&W)
ASSOCIATE PRODUCER: Morgan B. Cox
DIRECTOR: Harold Young
SCREENWRITERS: M. Coates, Webster and D.U. Babcock
ALSO RELEASED AS: *Wild Jungle Captive*

The second sequel to *Captive Wild Woman*, this one with a new cast. Paula the ape woman (Vicky Lane) is revived by scientist Otto Kruger. The female werewolf-style makeup is better this time and the assistant is Rondo Hatton! He plays Moloch the brute, making this a two-monster hit. With Jerome Cowan and a romantic subplot.

JUNGLE GENTS
1954 Allied Artists (B&W)
PRODUCER: Ben Schwalb
DIRECTOR: Edward Bernds
SCREENWRITERS: Elwood Ullman, Edward Bernds

When Huntz Hall goes to the jungle, he can smell diamonds. With Woody Strode, Clint Walker (as Tarzan), and Laurette Luez (*Prehistoric Women*). Leo Gorcey and the other Bowery Boys are there, too. Director Bernds later graduated to Three Stooges features.

JUNGLE GODDESS
1948 Lippert (B&W)
PRODUCER: William Stephens
DIRECTOR: Lewis D. Collins
SCREENWRITER: Joseph Pagano

A lost heiress (with a leopardskin outfit) rules a savage empire "against unbelievable odds!" Ex-Dick Tracy Ralph Byrd and future Superman George Reeves star in this laugh-filled adventure with Wanda McKay and Armida.

JUNGLE HELL
1956 Medallion TV (B&W)
PRODUCER/DIRECTOR/SCREENWRITER: Norman A. Cerf

Sabu stars in this low-budget obscurity along with a flying saucer, a death ray, and radioactive rocks! With David Bruce (*The Mad Ghoul*) and George E. Stone.

JUNGLE JIM
1948 Columbia (B&W)
PRODUCER: Sam Katzman
DIRECTOR: William Berke
SCREENWRITER: Carroll Young

For Johnny Weissmuller, going from playing Tarzan at RKO to Jungle Jim at Columbia was a short swing on the vine. Johnny made 16 low-budget adventures based on the comic strip in six years. This, the first, features Virginia Grey as a scientist in distress seeking a drug to combat polio. Future Superman George Reeves is the villain. Ads promise "devil doctors," "mad elephants," and a "monstrous sea serpent." Audiences got stock footage and a backlot jungle. Jim has a pet crow (Caw-Caw) and a little dog (Skipper). He later traded them in at the nearest pet shop for a more familiar chimp. Weissmuller, a great Tarzan, gets to talk too much in these ridiculous jungle adventures.

From Jungle Jim in the Forbidden Land.

JUNGLE JIM IN THE FORBIDDEN LAND

1952 Columbia (B&W)
PRODUCER: Sam Katzman
DIRECTOR: Lew Landers
SCREENWRITER: Samuel Newman

Johnny Weissmuller fights greedy ivory hunters and million-year-old "man monsters." Surprise—the tall, hairy "missing link" creatures (male and female) are actually effective; they look much better than anybody would expect in a low-budget series entry like this. With Angela Greene, Jean Willes, and Zamba ("the talented chimp").

JUNGLE MAN

1941 PRC (B&W)
PRODUCER: T.H. Richmond
DIRECTOR: Harry Fraser
SCREENWRITER: Rita Douglas

"1000 savage thrills" were promised in this cheapie starring Buster Crabbe as a doctor searching for a cure for jungle fever and fighting stuffed lions and rubber snakes. With Sheila Darcy.

JUNGLE MAN-EATERS

1954 Columbia (B&W)
PRODUCER: Sam Katzman
DIRECTOR: Lee Sholem
SCREENWRITER: Samuel Newman

Jungle Jim (Johnny Weissmuller) fights a diamond-smuggling ring and a cannibal tribe. With Karin Booth. This is one of the only Jungle Jim films with black Africans. Most of them feature natives who look like South Sea islanders.

JUNGLE MANHUNT

1951 Columbia (B&W)
PRODUCER: Sam Katzman
DIRECTOR: Lew Landers
SCREENWRITER: Samuel Newman

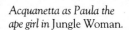
Acquanetta as Paula the ape girl in Jungle Woman.

Jungle Jim (Johnny Weissmuller) rescues a football player (real gridiron hero Bob Waterfield) who was lost in the jungle. Bad guys force natives to make synthetic diamonds. Two incredible men-in-suit dinosaurs show up. The creatures are man-sized and one fights Jim in a scene that must have inspired Japanese filmmakers. Laughable fun with Sheila Ryan, Lyle Talbot, and Tamba the chimp (not to be confused with Zamba the chimp).

JUNGLE MOON MEN
1955 Columbia (B&W)
PRODUCER: Sam Katzman
DIRECTOR: Charles S. Gould
SCREENWRITERS: Dwight V. Babcock,
Jo Pagano
A blond priestess (Helen Stanton) with the secret of eternal life rules over a tribe of white pygmies in skirts who worship the moon. Johnny Weissmuller as Johnny Weissmuller saves Jean Byron, an anthropologist, from the little bad guys. With Billy Curtis and Angelo Rossitto. A continuation of the Jungle Jim series.

JUNGLE TERROR: See FIREBALL JUNGLE.

JUNGLE WOMAN
1944 Universal (B&W)
PRODUCER: Will Cowan
DIRECTOR: Reginald Le Borg
SCREENWRITERS: Henry Sucher,
Edward Dein, Bernard Schubert
This quickie sequel to *Captive Wild Woman* finds J. Carrol Naish taking over

from John Carradine, reviving the dead gorilla, and turning her into Acquanetta again. The silent sexy ape woman again turns into a monster and is killed, only to return in *Jungle Captive*. With Milburn Stone, Evelyn Ankers, and many scenes from the first film. Also with Douglas Dumbrille and a retarded assistant.

JUST FOR FUN
1963 Amicus/Columbia (England) (B&W)
PRODUCER/SCREENWRITER: Milton Subotsky
DIRECTOR: Gordon Flemyng
In the near future, teenagers Mark Wynter and Cherry Roland organize their own political party and win a local election by using musical performers in the campaign. One of the last pre-Beatlemania musicals, full of Brylcreem, Italian suits, and beehive hairdos. Highlights include Bobby Vee singing "The Night Has a Thousand Eyes," the Springfields with Dusty Springfield, Freddie Cannon, the Crickets, and the Tremelos. With British rockers unheard of here, like Joe Brown and half of the Shadows.

JUST FOR THE HELL OF IT
1968 Unusual Films
PRODUCER/DIRECTOR/SCREENWRITER: Herschell Gordon Lewis
"Violence and vandalism—you've never seen anything like it!" the ads screamed. Three teenage boys and a girl (named Bitsy) go on a rampage of destruction. They disrupt a party, destroy a restaurant, fight baseball players, beat up girls, and force people to take drugs. "Destruction Inc.!" is the theme song. More unique madness from the director of *Blood Feast*. With Ray Sager, star of *The Wizard of Gore*.

JUST FOR YOU: See DISK-O-TEK HOLIDAY.

JUST IMAGINE
1930 20th Century-Fox (B&W)
ASSOCIATE PRODUCERS: Ray Henderson, B.G. Desylva, Lew Brown
DIRECTOR: David Butler
SCREENWRITERS: David Butler, Ray Henderson, B.G. Desylva, Lew Brown
Incredible science-fiction musical comedy set in the wonderful, then futuristic New York of 1980! El Brendel, an actor with a phony Swedish accent, wakes up Buck Rogers–style in the future where 19-year-old Maureen O'Sullivan is fought over by men who need government approval to marry her. Brendel and one of the suitors, John Garrick, blast off to Mars, where everyone is a twin. The sets of future Manhattan were so impressive that scenes were later used in *Flash Gordon* serials. The Prohibition humor and songs are unbelievably silly and the Martian costumes could start new fashion trends if this got widely shown. Lightning bolts, spikes, and metallic-print bikinis mixed with ridiculous wigs and eye makeup are part of the wackiest outfits in screen history. With Mischa Auer and Frank Albertson. Never has a movie been at once so ahead of its time and so dated.

JUSTINE
1969 AIP (Italy/Spain)
DIRECTOR: Jesse Franco
SCREENWRITER: Arpad De Riso, Erich Krohnke
ORIGINALLY RELEASED AS: *Marquis De Sade: Justine*
A story of black magic, sex, and sadism. Jack Palance sacrifices naked women on an altar. With Mercedes McCam-

bridge (99 *Women*), Sylvia Koscina, Maria Rohm, and Akim Tamiroff. Best of all is Klaus Kinski as the Marquis De Sade. Not to be confused with the George Cukor film of the same title also released in 1969.

JUVENILE JUNGLE

1958 Republic (B&W)
PRODUCER: Sidney Picker
DIRECTOR: William Witney
SCREENWRITER: Arthur T. Horman

Jazzed-out teenage gangsters on the beach. Corey Allen executes the perfect kidnaping and falls in love with the hostage. He gets three slugs in the belly when his partners realize the $40,000 ransom demand is off. With Rebecca Welles, Anne Whitfield, and Richard Bakalyan. Witney deserted Republic for AIP after this companion feature for *Young and Wild*. —CB

KARATE KILLERS
1967 MGM
PRODUCER: Boris Ingster
DIRECTOR: Barry Shear
SCREENWRITER: Norman Hudis

A *Man from U.N.C.L.E.* feature, edited from TV episodes. THRUSH is after a professor's formula for turning seawater into gold. This one really has the stars: Joan Crawford, Curt Jurgens, Herbert Lom, Telly Savalas, Diane McBain, Jill Ireland, and Kim Darby. Regulars Robert Vaughn, David McCallum, and Leo G. Carroll are back, too.

KEEP IT COOL: See LET'S ROCK.

THE KEEPER
1976 Lionsgate (Canada)
PRODUCER: Donald Wilson
DIRECTOR/SCREENWRITER: Tom Drake

Christopher Lee stars as a cripple who monitors the inmates in an asylum and tries to kill all the heirs to their fortunes. A horror spoof filmed in British Columbia with seven-foot-tall twins and a detective hero named Dick Driver.

THE KEYS OF THE KINGDOM
1944 20th Century-Fox (B&W)
PRODUCER: Joseph L. Mankiewicz
DIRECTOR: John M. Stahl
SCREENWRITERS: Joseph L. Mankiewicz, Nunnally Johnson

The story of a devout Catholic missionary priest (Gregory Peck) serving in China. His life is told in flashback from childhood, when he's played by Roddy McDowall. Vincent Price shows up as a snobbish worldly reverend who makes the peasants carry him around. With Thomas Mitchell, Edmund Gwenn, Cedric Hardwicke, Benson Fong, Philip Ahn, Richard Loo, Rosa Stradner, Peggy Ann Garner, and Anne Revere.

KID GALAHAD
1962 United Artists
PRODUCER: David Weisbart
DIRECTOR: Phil Karlson
SCREENWRITER: William Fay

A good remake of the 1937 Warner Brothers film (which was retitled *The Battling Bellhop*). Elvis Presley, a sparring partner at a Catskill training camp, is turned into a pro and set up by Gig Young, who tries to repay debts to gangsters. Lola Albright is Young's girlfriend. His sister (Joan Blackman) falls for Elvis. With Charles Bronson as an honest trainer who has his hands broken by crooks, Ned Glass, Richard Devon, and Michael Dante. Elvis sings "Home Is Where the Heart Is" and five other songs.

THE KIDNAPPING OF THE PRESIDENT
1980 Crown (Canada)
PRODUCERS: George Mendeluk, John Ryan
DIRECTOR: George Mendeluk
SCREENWRITER: Richard Murphy

When terrorists in Toronto grab President Hal Holbrook and demand $100 million in diamonds for ransom, Vice President Van Johnson has problems holding things together. Star William Shatner (working in his Canadian homeland) fixes everything. With Ava Gardner. An election year nonhit, quickly sold to television (R)

KILL AND GO HIDE!: See THE CHILD.

KILL BABY KILL
1966 Europix (Italy)
PRODUCERS: Nando Pisani, Luciano Catenacci
DIRECTOR: Mario Bava
SCREENWRITERS: Romano Migliorini, Roberto Natale, Mario Bava
ORIGINALLY RELEASED AS: *Operatione Paura*
ALSO RELEASED AS: *Curse of the Living Dead*

A small Transylvanian town is plagued by strange deaths. The revenge-seeking ghost of a seven-year-old girl shows up to drive people to suicide. Others are killed by a witch who thrusts gold coins through their hearts. Giacomo Rossi-Stuart plays a doctor and Erik Blanc is his assistant in this sometimes slow but rewarding thriller. One scene shows a man opening a door and walking through a room over and over again. The ghost child is reminiscent of the little boy in Bava's better-known *Black Sabbath*. Rereleased as part of the "Orgy of the Living Dead" triple bill.

KILLDOZER

1974 TV
PRODUCER: Herbert F. Solow
DIRECTOR: Jerry London
SCREENWRITERS: Theodore Sturgeon, Ed MacKillop
A bulldozer controlled by an alien force goes after confused construction workers Clint Walker, Carl Betz, and Neville Brand. Based on a story by Theodore Sturgeon.

KILLER APE

1953 Columbia (B&W)
PRODUCER: Sam Katzman
DIRECTOR: Spencer Gordon Bennet
SCREENWRITERS: Carroll Young, Arthur Hoerl
Wazuli tribesmen are selling animals to white hunters, who are producing mind-control drugs. Johnny Weissmuller as Jungle Jim stops them and battles a giant caveman (Max Palmer, a real giant) with fur booties. Carol Thurston is a native girl in distress. With Ray Corrigan and Nestor Paiva.

KILLER BATS: See DEVIL BAT.

A TRIPLE AVALANCHE
Revenge of the Living Dead
2nd Hit Mario Bava's
Curse of the Living Dead
3rd Hit
Fangs of the Living Dead
PG

WARNING: We, the producers, are providing a free insurance policy insuring the sanity of every patron attending this explosion of terror, you will receive free psychiatric care or be placed in an asylum for the rest of your life!
We urge you to take advantage of this protection!

KILLER BEES

1974 TV
PRODUCERS: Howard Rosenman, Ron Bernstein
DIRECTOR: Curtis Harrington
SCREENWRITERS: John William and Joyce Corrington
Seventy-seven year old Gloria Swanson came out of acting retirement to play Madame Von Bohlen, matriarch of a California winegrowing family. She rules her family (including Edward Albert, Roger Davis, and Craig Stevens) with an iron hand and sends out swarms of local bees to attack those who oppose her. Kate Jackson also stars in this routine "Movie of the Week."

KILLER FISH

1979 Associated Films (Italy/Brazil)
PRODUCER: Alex Ponti
DIRECTOR: Anthony Dawson (Antonio Marcheriti)
SCREENWRITER: Michael Rogers
After too many shark movies, we get piranha movies. This one stars Lee Ma-

The "2nd hit" of this "triple avalanche of grisly horror" was originally released as Kill Baby Kill.

Ingrid Goude spots The Killer Shrews.

jors and Karen Black diving for a sunken treasure, protected by the "killer fish." It's terrible. So are performances by James Franciscus, Margaux Hemingway, and Marisa Berenson. By the director of *Cannibals in the Street.*

KILLER FORCE
1977 AIP (U.S./S. Africa)
PRODUCERS: Nat and Patrick Wachsberger
DIRECTOR: Val Guest
SCREENWRITERS: Michael Winner, Val Guest
Professional killers at a South African diamond mine, with an all-star cast. Telly Savalas stars with Christopher and Maud Adams (both had just been in *Man with the Golden Gun*), Peter Fonda, Hugh O'Brian, and O.J. Simpson. **(R)**

KILLER GRIZZLY: See GRIZZLY.

THE KILLER INSIDE ME
1976 Warner Brothers
PRODUCER: Michael W. Leighton
DIRECTOR: Burt Kennedy
SCREENWRITERS: Edward Mann, Robert Chamblee
An unusual feature starring Stacy Keach as a psychotic deputy sheriff. With John Carradine, Susan Tyrrell, Tisha Sterling, Don Stroud, Keenan Wynn, Royal Dano, and Julie Adams. **(R)**

KILLER LEOPARD
1954 Allied Artists (B&W)
PRODUCER/DIRECTOR/SCREENWRITER: Ford Beebe
Bomba (Johnny Sheffield) leads a famous movie actress (*Not of This Earth* star Beverly Garland) through the jungle to find her lost husband. With Ross Conway and Bill Walker.

KILLER ORPHAN: See FRIDAY THE 13th . . . THE ORPHAN.

THE KILLER SHREWS
1959 McLendon Radio Pictures (B&W)
PRODUCER: Ken Curtis
DIRECTOR: Ray Kellogg
SCREENWRITER: Jay Sims
Ken Curtis (Festus on *Gunsmoke*) produces and stars in a homemade horror (in both senses of the word) from Texas. He creates and is later gobbled up by a couple of dogs with phoney fangs. James Best is the hero who loves Ingrid Goude (Miss Universe of '57). Watch the cast members escape while hiding in barrels! The best thing about this little disaster was the poster showing a giant shrew tail (nothing like the furry tails actually used) knocking over a high-heeled shoe. The same people made *The Giant Gila Monster* to complete a dynamite double

bill. With Baruch Lumet (Sidney's dad). Director Kellogg did second unit work for John Ford and Howard Hawks.

THE KILLERS

1964 Universal
PRODUCER/DIRECTOR: Don Siegel
SCREENWRITER: Gene L. Coon

After a seven-year absence from feature films, Ronald Reagan agreed to play his first real screen villain in a TV-movie version of Hemingway's *The Killers* (previously filmed in 1946). NBC decided it was too violent, so it was released in theaters. Lee Marvin and Clu Gulager play professional hit men trying to find out why their recent victim (John Cassavetes) accepted his death without resistance. Strong-arm "interviews" provide flashbacks showing the dead ex-race-car driver being manipulated and morally crushed by white-collar gangster Reagan and his double-crossing mistress Angie Dickinson as he helped in a robbery. Reagan slaps Angie around, kills people, and provides some unintentional laughs while discussing how to get ahead in the world with partner Norman Fell (of *Three's Company*). Nancy Wilson sings the title song.

KILLERS CAGE: See CODE OF SILENCE.

KILLERS FROM SPACE

1954 RKO (B&W)
PRODUCER/DIRECTOR: W. Lee Wilder
SCREENWRITER: Bill Raynor

While his brother Billy was working on *The Seven Year Itch*, Lee Wilder was busy churning out another substandard science-fiction film. This one features hilarious aliens with hooded sweat suits, mittens, striped belts, and eyes made out of Ping-Pong ball halves. They bring nuclear scientist Peter Graves back to life in a cave complete with used electronic equipment. To demonstrate their powers, they show Peter stock footage of lizards, lava, and giant insects. He figures out their futuristic VU meters and causes the secret headquarters to blow up. Earth is saved again! With Barbara Bestar and James Seay.

KILLERS THREE

1969 AIP
PRODUCER: Dick Clark
DIRECTOR: Bruce Kessler
SCREENWRITER: Michael Fisher

After World War II, two backwoods North Carolinians (Robert Walker, Jr., and Dick Clark) rob a bootlegger's safe, kill several people in the process, and head for California with Walker's wife (Diane Varsi). Merle Haggard appears as a sheriff and sings the title song and "Mama Tried." With John Cardos, Beach Dickerson, and Bunny Owens. *American Bandstand* host Clark, who plays a demolition expert with wire-

Peter Graves can't believe the makeup on the Killers *from Space.*

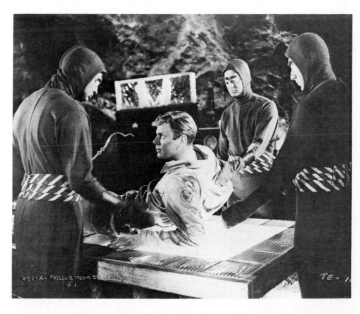

401

frame glasses, produced this post-*Bonnie and Clyde* fiasco. He also produced *Psych-out* and *The Savage Seven*. By the director of *Simon, King of the Witches*. (M)

THE KILLING KIND

1973 Media Cinema
PRODUCER: George Edwards
DIRECTOR: Curtis Harrington
SCREENWRITER: Lenny Crechalon

Young John Savage returns home from serving a prison term for a rape he didn't commit. He seeks revenge on his lawyer (Ruth Roman) and the girl who framed him, but his real problem is his overbearing mother (Ann Sothern), who keeps bringing him chocolate milk. Cindy Williams is a persistent boarder in the house. Luana Anders plays a drunken neighbor. A seldom-seen sickie.

KING CREOLE

1958 Paramount (B&W)
PRODUCER: Hal Wallis
DIRECTOR: Michael Curtiz
SCREENWRITERS: Herbert Baker,
Michael Vincent Gazzo

Don't miss the great Elvis in his fourth and best movie, based on the Harold Robbins novel *A Stone for Danny Fisher*. Danny, a busboy at a Bourbon Street nightclub, becomes a local singing star and gets mixed up with gangsters. He also gets involved with nice girl Dolores Hart and older woman Carolyn Jones, who is the mistress of hood Walter Matthau. As a young thug, Vic Morrow robs the drugstore where Elvis' downtrodden dad (Dean Jagger) works. Elvis is blamed. Some of the songs are: "Hard Headed Woman," "Trouble," "Dixieland Rock," and "As Long As I Have You." Buy the album! Elvis was granted a two-month deferment to make this film before being drafted. No new Elvis records or movies were released until 1960 and by then things just weren't the same.

KING DINOSAUR

1955 Lippert (B&W)
PRODUCERS: Bert I. Gordon, Al Zimbalist
DIRECTOR: Bert I. Gordon
SCREENWRITER: Tom Gries

Bert Gordon and co-producer Al Zimbalist (*Robot Monsters*) created the popular minicast-vs.-rear-projection-monsters trend with this low-budget hit. Four people fly to the planet Nova where a blown-up Gila monster and a giant armadillo chase them. Marvin Miller of *The Millionaire* narrates. The crew includes two women, so expect lots of interrupted love scenes. An exploding A-bomb ends the action.

KING KONG

1933 RKO (B&W)
PRODUCERS/DIRECTORS: Merian C. Cooper,
Ernest B. Schoedsack
SCREENWRITERS: James Creelman, Ruth Rose

A timeless classic made by a team of documentary filmmakers who patterned hero Carl Denham after themselves. Sets and stars (Fay Wray and Robert Armstrong) were from the previous year's *The Most Dangerous Game*. Willis O'Brien (*The Lost World*) animated the amazingly lifelike ape. Scenes showing Kong stepping on and biting natives and removing Wray's clothes were cut in the original version but were put back when the film was re-released in the '60s. With Bruce Cabot, Frank Reicher (the ship's captain), Noble Johnson (the native chief of Skull Island), dinosaurs, elevated trains, and the Empire State Building. Music by Max Steiner. From an original story by Edgar Wallace and co-producer/director Cooper.

Fay Wray and Bruce Cabot at the top of the Empire State Building at the conclusion of King Kong '33.

UPI 6/23/76: Jessica Lange, playing the part originally made famous by Fay Wray, stands in front of a model of King Kong during the shooting for the final scene in the Dino De Laurentiis production of King Kong. Thousands turned out to watch shooting of the final scene—and to serve as unpaid extras—at the World Trade Center plaza in New York late June 21st. According to publicists for the film, some 45,000 turned out late June 22nd for more location shooting.

KING KONG

1976 Paramount
PRODUCER: Dino De Laurentiis
DIRECTOR: John Guillermin
SCREENWRITER: Lorenzo Semple, Jr.

If defrauding the public were really a crime, Dino De Laurentiis would've gotten the chair for this atrocious $24 million deception—a Christmas present to gullible patrons in 2,200 theaters from sea to shining sea. *Variety* called it "brilliant." It got an Academy Award for special effects. Can Dino buy *anything*? Who could forget star Jessica Lange (a fashion model with no acting experience) reading lines like, "Put me down, you male chauvinist ape!" Were you one of the "45,000" New Yorkers who showed up at the World Trade Center to see a giant dead gorilla? Akira Fitton was! The fallout from this bomb lingers. Go to the Empire State Building where they still sell glasses showing Kong on the World Trade Center! The casting director *deserved* an award for getting John Agar to play the D.A. of New York City. (In real life, Agar later opened an amusement park called Agar's Land of Kong.) With Jeff Bridges and Charles Grodin. Music by John Barry.

KING KONG ESCAPES

1968 Toho (Japan)
PRODUCER: Tomoyuki Tanaka
DIRECTOR: Inoshiro Honda
SCREENWRITER: Kaoru Mabuchi
ORIGINALLY RELEASED AS: *Kingu Kongo No Gyakushu*

When the Toho Studios decided to revive their gorilla-suit Kong, they pitted him against Mekakong, a robot resembling a giant metal Magilla Gorilla. They also added a silly evil Dr. Who (no relation to the British *Who*), out to conquer the world, and Gorosaurus, a Godzilla substitute. To insure overseas success, J. Arthur Rank, Jr., directed new scenes with Rhodes Reason and Linda Miller. Star Mie Hama was also in *King Kong vs. Godzilla* and *You Only Live Twice*. Maximum laughs and excitement.

KING KONG VS. GODZILLA

1962 Toho/Universal (Japan)
PRODUCER: John Beck
DIRECTORS: Inoshiro Honda,
Thomas Montgomery, U.S. version
SCREENWRITERS: Shinichi Sekizawa,
Paul Mason, Bruce Howard
ORIGINALLY RELEASED AS: *Kingu Kongu Tai Gojira*

After a seven-year rest Godzilla returned, in color for the first time. In the film's best scene King Kong escapes, kills a giant octopus, and proceeds to step on terrified South Sea natives. Kong is drugged with narcotic berries and flown to Japan by balloon. Things get sillier as Godzilla emerges from an Arctic iceberg, destroys a nuclear sub, and heads for Japan. The two giants throw boulders at each other and act like professional wrestlers. They fall off Mount Fuji into the sea. Kong surfaces and swims away. In the original version Godzilla seems to win. With Mie Hama as a Fay Wray substitute, new American scenes with Michael Keith as a UN reporter, and lots of comic relief. The man-in-a-suit Kong outraged fans of the original, but after the '76 remake it didn't seem so bad.

KING OF THE JUNGLE

1933 Paramount (B&W)
DIRECTORS: Bruce Humberstone, Max Marcin
SCREENWRITERS: Philip Wylie,
Fred Niblo, Jr.

Buster Crabbe plays a Tarzan-like lion man raised in the jungle and taken to America as a circus attraction. With Francis Dee, Irving Pichel, and Douglass Dumbrille. Crabbe was *Tarzan the Fearless* later the same year.

KING OF THE JUNGLE LAND: See *DARKEST AFRICA*.

KING OF THE ROCKETMEN
1949 Republic (B&W)
ASSOCIATE PRODUCER: Franklin Adreon
DIRECTOR: Fred Brannon
SCREENWRITERS: Royal Cole, William Lively, Sol Shor
ALSO RELEASED AS: *Lost Planet Airmen*

Tristram Coffin plays the popular flying rocketman. Using his jet-propelled flying suit he stops Dr. Vulcan from destroying all of New York City with his decimator. When the mayor refuses to pay a billion dollars in ransom, parts of the city are destroyed by an earthquake and a tidal wave. The scenes of destruction were taken from *Deluge* ('33). Mae Clarke (*Frankenstein*, *Public Enemy*) is Glenda, photographer for *Miracle* magazine. Republic later reused the rocketman suit and the well-done flying scenes for Commando Cody serials. A feature condensation of this popular serial was released in '51.

KING OF THE ZOMBIES
1941 Monogram (B&W)
PRODUCER: Lindsley Parsons
DIRECTOR: Jean Yarbrough
SCREENWRITER: Edmund Kelso

Henry Victor (the strongman in *Freaks*) wears a cape and turns black men into zombies for "foreign" agents. Dick Purcell is the hero. Joan Woodbury screams. The real star of this outstanding example of inept wartime horror is comedian Mantan Moreland. Not to be missed.

KINGDOM OF THE SPIDERS
1977 Dimension
PRODUCERS: Igo Kanter, Jeffrey M. Sneller
DIRECTOR: Bud Cardos
SCREENWRITERS: Richard Robinson, Alan Caillou

When pesticides destroy their food, creepy tarantulas attack the town of Verde, Arizona. Five thousand live tarantulas were used. With William Shatner, Tiffany Bolling, Woody Strode, Nancy Lafferty (Mrs. Shatner), and Natasha Ryan (*Days of Our Lives*). Better than you'd think. Director Cardos used to act in Al Adamson movies. Music by Dorsey Burnette of The Johnny Burnette Trio.

Originally released as: The Kirlian Witness.

THE KIRLIAN WITNESS

1978 Sampson & Cranor, Inc.
PRODUCER/DIRECTOR: Jonathan Sarno
SCREENWRITERS: Jonathan Sarno,
Lamar Sanders
ALSO RELEASED AS: *The Plants Are Watching*

Antonioni's *Blow-Up* must have been a major influence on this first feature effort by Sarno, who used to do production work for Gerard (*Deep Throat*) Damiano. The cinematographer and music composer also came from a hardcore-movie background. The result is an intriguing, moody thriller about a woman with telepathic sensitivity to plants who tries to track down her sister's murderer. Shot entirely in New York. Kirlian photography is used to disclose who the killer is. With Nancy Snyder, Joel Colodner, Nancy Boykin, and Ted Leplat.   –AF

KISS AND KILL

1968 Commonwealth United (Spain/
W. Germany/U.S./England)
PRODUCER: Harry Alan Towers
DIRECTOR: Jess Franco
SCREENWRITERS: Harry Alan Towers,
Manfred Köhler, Jess Franco
ALSO RELEASED AS: *The Blood of Fu
Manchu, Against All Odds*

Christopher Lee is back as Dr. Fu Manchu for the fourth time. Now he's in Brazil and sends 10 native women, injected with snake poison, to give "the kiss of death" to his enemies. Richard Green takes over the role of Smith. Shirley Eaton is "the black widow." With Tsai Chin, Howard Marion-Crawford, and Maria Rohm. Not too bad for a Jesse Franco film.

KISS ME DEADLY

1955 United Artists (B&W)
PRODUCER/DIRECTOR: Robert Aldrich
SCREENWRITER: I.A. Bezzerides

Classic atomic-age *film noir* based on Mickey Spillane's novel of the same title. When Ralph Meeker as the best screen Mike Hammer gives a ride to an escapee from an asylum (Cloris Leachman), his car is run off the road and she's tortured and killed. Hammer wakes up in an L.A. hospital, drives a sportscar rigged with bombs, and is given sodium pentothal at the beach house of Dr. Soberin (Albert Dekker). The search for "The Great Whatsit" ends in a mushroom cloud. With Gaby Rodgers, Maxine Cooper (as Velda), Leigh Snowden, Jack Elam, and Strother Martin. Filmed on Los Angeles area locations. Music by Frank DeVol, Nat King Cole, and Caruso. Essential viewing.

KISS ME QUICK

1964 G&S Productions
PRODUCER/DIRECTOR/SCREENWRITER:
Russ Meyer
ALSO RELEASED AS: *Dr. Breedlove or How I
Learned to Stop Worrying and Love*

An "adults-only" nudie comedy/science-fiction/horror movie that would get an R rating if released today. Sterilox, an effeminate alien from an all-male planet, visits Dr. Breedlove, a mad scientist with a neck brace who manufactures women. The alien ignores the naked women and leaves with a vending machine. It's all shot on one mad lab set with a Frankenstein monster, Dracula, and a mummy. Even more fun that *Dr. Goldfoot and the Bikini Machine.* Cinematography by Laszlo Kovacs.

KISS MEETS THE PHANTOM OF THE PARK

1978 Avco Embassy
PRODUCER: Terry Morse, Jr.
DIRECTOR: Gordon Hessler
SCREENWRITERS: Jan-Michael Sherman,
Don Buday
ALSO RELEASED AS: *Attack of the Phantoms*

When the popular rock-spectacle group KISS released four solo albums at once, made a terrible movie, and lost their drummer all in the same year, everybody thought the end was near for the young New York millionaires. Working at an amusement park, evil scientist Anthony Zerbe creates KISS clones. Teenagers are lost in a fun house and the real KISS gives a concert! Produced by Hanna-Barbera of *Hey Queeksdraw!* fame and directed by the consistently bad Hessler. Shown here as a TV movie; lucky foreigners got to pay for it.

KISS OF EVIL: See KISS OF THE VAMPIRE.

KISS OF THE TARANTULA
1977 Omni
PRODUCER: Daniel Munger
DIRECTOR: Chris Munger
SCREENWRITER: Warren Hamilton
A cheap shocker in the tradition of *Carrie* and *Willard* about a tormented teenage girl (Suzanne Lini) whose family runs and lives in a mortuary. When other kids ridicule her, she unleashes her horde of obedient tarantulas. The best scene shows couples making out in a locked car, not noticing the eight-legged horrors crawling on them. (R)

KISS OF THE VAMPIRE
1963 Hammer/Universal (England)
PRODUCER: Anthony Hinds
DIRECTOR: Don Sharpe
SCREENWRITER: John Elder
ALSO RELEASED AS: *Kiss of Evil*
A superior vampire thriller set in the Bavaria of 1910. Dr. Ravena (Noel Willman) heads a vampire cult in a château. A vacationing young couple accepts a dinner invitation, then stays for a masquerade ball. The wife (Marianne Harcourt) becomes a vampire and the husband (Edward De Souza) enlists the aid of Professor Zimmer (Clifford Evans), a Van Helsing type. The American TV version is missing some of the best scenes and substitutes new, tamer ones. Even with the changes it's one of the best and obviously influenced *The Fearless Vampire Killers*. Producer Hinds and screenwriter Elder are one and the same person.

KISS THE GIRLS AND MAKE THEM DIE
1966 Columbia (Italy/U.S.)
PRODUCER: Dino De Laurentiis
DIRECTORS: Henry Levin, Dino Maiuri
SCREENWRITERS: Jack Pulman, Dino Maiuri
ORIGINALLY RELEASED AS: *Se Tuttle le Donne Del Mondor*
Mad industrialist Raf Vallone plans to conquer the world by bombarding Earth with a sterilization ray by satellite, and then using women from his hibernation harem to repopulate the planet. American CIA agent Mike Connors and English agent Dorothy Provine arrive in Brazil and find his secret undersea lab. The worst Bond imitation known to man. With Terry-Thomas, Margaret Lee, Beverly Adams, Marilu Tolo, Nazi scientists, and Communist Chinese. Filmed in Rio De Janeiro. Connors did *Mannix* next.

KISS THEM FOR ME
1957 20th Century-Fox
PRODUCER: Jerry Wald
DIRECTOR: Stanley Donen
SCREENWRITER: Julius Epstein
The historic meeting of Cary Grant and Jayne Mansfield in a flop comedy about naval officers on shore leave in San Francisco. Jayne plays a dumb blonde. With Suzy Parker, Ray Walston, Larry Blyden, and Leif Erickson.

Elvis and Elvis in Sam Katzman's Kissin' Cousins.

KISSIN' COUSINS

1964 MGM
PRODUCER: Sam Katzman
DIRECTOR: Gene Nelson
SCREENWRITERS: Gerald Drayson Adams, Gene Nelson

In his cheapest quickie musical, Elvis plays both Josh, an Air Force officer, and Jodie, his twin hillbilly cousin. Josh is trying to convince Tennessee moonshiner Arthur O'Connell to let the military install ICBMs in his mountain. Both Elvises sing ("One Boy, Two Little Girls," "Catchin' On Fast" and other nonhits), dance, find romance, and encounter the Kittyhawks, "13 man-starved women" from a nearby village. Glenda Farrell is the duo's Ma. Jack Albertson is a captain. Pamela Austin and Yvonne Craig are barefoot Daisy Mae types. Elvis really had a twin brother who died at birth.

KNIGHTRIDERS

1981 United Film Distribution
PRODUCER: Richard P. Rubenstein
DIRECTOR/SCREENWRITER: George A. Romero

A traveling commune of motorcyclists and craftsmen make their living by setting up a renaissance fair highlighted by motorcycle jousts in each of the towns they visit. King Billy, the leader of the troupe, finds that his own version of Camelot is threatened by showbiz promoters, internal strife, and financial crises. *Knightriders* was Romero's fourth departure from the splatter mold imposed by the success of his zombie films and *Martin*; and, for the fourth time, some critics raved while audiences stayed away in droves. Romero's people have expressed the opinion that *Knightriders* failed because audiences identified it as a dated motorcycle exploitation film; a more cynical view might be that the film, which celebrates idealism and independence, was just too naive for modern moviegoers. The cast includes Christine Forrest (Mrs. Romero), John Amplas, Steven King, and Tom Savini. **(R)** —BM

KNIVES OF THE AVENGER

1967 World Entertainment (Italy)
PRODUCER: P. Tagliaferri
DIRECTOR: John Hold (Mario Bava)
SCREENWRITER: Alberto Liberati
ORIGINALLY RELEASED AS: *Raffica di Coltelli*

Vikings battle each other, decapitate enemies, pillage, and rape. Cameron Mitchell stars as the vengeful Rurik in his second Viking drama directed by horror expert Bava. With Fausto Tozzi and Giaccomo Rossi-Stuart (Jack Stewart).

KONGA

1961 Anglo Amalgamated/AIP (England)
PRODUCER: Herman Cohen
DIRECTOR: John Lemont
SCREENWRITERS: Aben Kandel, Herman Cohen

Hilarious monkey business starring Michael Gough as Dr. Decker, a botany professor with a growth serum and a chimp. Soon the (real) chimp becomes a man in a gorilla suit, which the doctor hypnotizes and orders to kill! Meanwhile his live-in assistant/lover (Margo Johns) gets jealous of a pretty young thing in a tight sweater and gives Konga an overdose. Konga grows to Kong size, crashes through the ceiling, and heads for Big Ben with a Michael Gough doll. Also with pop singer Jess Conrad and some giant man- (and woman-) eating plants.

Michael Gough stars in Konga.

KRONOS

1957 20th Century-Fox
PRODUCER/DIRECTOR: Kurt Neumann
SCREENWRITER: Irving Block

Kronos, a giant, featureless, square alien robot with cylindrical legs, was a welcome change in a year of teen monsters and giant animals. Kronos is deposited in Mexico by a flying saucer and tramples everything in its path as it continues to grow and advance towards L.A. All of Earth's energy is absorbed by the conquering cube. Scientist John Emery is taken over by alien forces while his colleagues (Jeff Morrow and Barbara Lawrence) race to save Earth. *Kronos* was a great showcase for special effects experts Jack Rabin, Irving Block, and Louis Dewitt, who were also the associate producers. With Morris Ankrum and Robert Shayne.

KUNG FU

1972 TV
PRODUCER/DIRECTOR: Jerry Thorpe
SCREENWRITERS: Ed Spielman, Howard Friedlander

The pilot film for the popular series (1972–75). David Carradine is Kwai Chang Caine, the philosophical young Chinese-American martial-arts expert out West during the 1870s. He helps the ill-treated Oriental laborers working on the transcontinental railroad while hiding from enemies from China. Keith Carradine plays Caine as a younger man. The masters are played by Key Luke, Richard Loo, and Philip Ahn. With Victor Sen Yung and Benson Fong. Luke, Yung, and Fong all played sons of Charlie Chan. Barry Sullivan is the oppressive railroad boss. The series made Carradine a hero/star and led to the American release of Hong Kong kung-fu films. Bruce Lee was originally to star, but network officials decided we weren't ready for an Oriental TV star.

KWAIDAN

1963 Walter Reade-Sterling (Japan)
PRODUCER: Shigeru Wakatsuki
DIRECTOR: Masuki Kobayashi
SCREENWRITER: Yoko Mizuki

Fascinating trio of Japanese ghost stories, adapted from books by Lafcadio Hearn, an American who settled in Japan in 1890. A man in one episode is painted with symbols to repel ghosts. He forgot to paint his ear, so they rip it off! A fourth segment about a snow witch is usually missing from American prints.

L.A. 2017
1971 TV
PRODUCER: Dean Hargrove
DIRECTOR: Steven Spielberg
SCREENWRITER Philip Wylie
Newspaper publisher Gene Barry dreams he's in the Los Angeles of the future. Things are even worse than they are now. Nearly everybody lives underground because the pollution is so bad. A feature-length episode of *The Name of the Game* series. With Barry Sullivan, Edmond O'Brien, and Sharon Farrell.

ONLY THE MONSTER SHE MADE COULD SATISFY HER STRANGE DESIRES!

A MAD SURGEON'S MIND IN A WOMAN'S BODY

Lady FRANKENSTEIN

METROCOLOR

LABYRINTH: See REFLECTION OF FEAR.

THE LADY AND THE MONSTER
1944 Republic (B&W)
ASSOCIATE PRODUCER/DIRECTOR: George Sherman
SCREENWRITERS: Dane Lussier, Frederick Kohner
ALSO RELEASED AS: *Tiger Man*
This first version of *Donovan's Brain* stars Erich von Stroheim as the doctor who keeps the brain of a dead gangster alive. The brain takes over lab assistant Richard Arlen and makes him kill the gangster's enemies. Erich's other assistant is Czechoslovakian-born Vera Hruba Ralston, a former skating champion who married Herbert Yates, the president of Republic. She could barely speak English but he put her in over two dozen films. Nancy Davis played her role in the '53 version. With Sidney Blackmer and Billy Benedict.

LADY DRACULA: See LEMORA, THE LADY DRACULA.

LADY FRANKENSTEIN
1972 New World (Italy)
PRODUCER: Harry Cushing
DIRECTOR: Mel Welles
SCREENWRITER: Edward di Lorenzo
ORIGINALLY RELEASED AS: *La Figlia di Frankenstein*
Joseph Cotten as Dr. Frankenstein! His scientist daughter (Sarah Bay a.k.a. Rosalba Neri) creates a handsome new creature for her sexual pleasure!— "Only the monster she made could satisfy her strange desires!" A second monster looks like the closet mutant in *The Brain That Wouldn't Die*! Cotten

dies early in the picture, but scenes of the ugly monster in striped pants carrying naked women around and the good-looking one screwing his creator on the operating table make this an entertaining curiosity predating *Andy Warhol's Frankenstein*. Directed by the flower store owner in *Little Shop of Horrors!* With Mickey Hargitay! A similar Italian movie, *Frankenstein 1980*, was released the same year. **(R)**

LADY IN A CAGE

1964 Paramount (B&W)
PRODUCER/SCREENWRITER: Luther Davis
DIRECTOR: Walter Grauman
When wealthy widow Olivia de Havilland becomes trapped in a cagelike elevator, her mansion is invaded by a wino thief (Jeff Corey), a prostitute (Ann Sothern), and three young sickos wearing stockings over their faces. The trio, led by James Caan in an early role, have an orgy, murder the wino, and torment the caged woman with a note from her son threatening suicide. Olivia survived to return in *Hush Hush, Sweet Charlotte* within the year. Considered controversial and overly violent at the time, *Lady* was banned in England. By the director of *Disembodied*.

THE LADY IN RED

1979 New World
PRODUCER: Julie Corman
DIRECTOR: Lewis Teague
SCREENWRITER: John Sayles
ALSO RELEASED AS: *Guns, Sin and Bathtub Gin*
A retelling of the Dillinger legend focusing on his girlfriend Polly Franklin (Pamela Sue Martin). Robert Conrad is Dillinger. With Louise Fletcher and Dick Miller. Director Teague and writer Sayles later did *Alligator*. **(R)**

LADY IN THE IRON MASK

1952 20th Century-Fox
PRODUCERS: Walter Wanger, Eugene Frenke
DIRECTOR: Ralph Murphy
SCREENWRITERS: Jack Pollexfen, Aubrey Weisberg
A three-musketeers story with big Tor Johnson as the mad executioner. He wears a black costume with metal studs and keeps heroine Patricia Medina chained up in the dungeon. Louis Hayward stars. With Alan Hale.

LADY IN THE LAKE

1947 MGM (B&W)
PRODUCER: George Haight
DIRECTOR: Robert Montgomery
SCREENWRITER: Steve Fisher
Montgomery directs himself as Raymond Chandler's Philip Marlowe in a film shot almost entirely from the detective's subjective point of view. The ads made it sound like something akin to 3-D: "*YOU* accept an invitation to a blonde's apartment! *YOU* get socked in the jaw by a murder suspect!..." *YOU* star along with Montgomery as he submits a story to Audrey Totter for *Lurid Detective* magazine and tries to find her boss' missing wife. With Lloyd Nolan, Jayne Meadows, and Morris Ankrum.

LADYBUG LADYBUG

1963 United Artists (B&W)
PRODUCER/DIRECTOR: Frank Perry
SCREENWRITER: Eleanor Perry
A chilling low-budget film based on a true incident during the 1962 Cuban missile crisis. When an air-raid warning box at a small rural elementary school goes off, the teachers and students think there's been a nuclear attack. A group of children hide out in a family fallout shelter. They're afraid to let in a little girl (because of fallout), so she hides

in a discarded refrigerator and suffocates. It was Perry's first film after *David and Lisa*. Not many people have seen it.

LANCER SPY

1937 20th Century-Fox (B&W)
ASSOCIATE PRODUCER: Samuel G. Engel
DIRECTOR: Gregory Ratoff
SCREENWRITER: Philip Dunne

George Sanders in his first starring role disguises himself as a Nazi officer to get secret information. Peter Lorre as Major Siegfried Gruning is the real thing. Sanders and Lorre were together next in *Mr. Moto's Last Warning*. With Dolores Del Rio, Lionel Atwill, Sig Ruman, and Joseph Schildkraut.

LAND OF NO RETURN

1977 International Picture Show
PRODUCER/DIRECTOR/SCREENWRITER:
  Kent Bateman
ALSO RELEASED AS: *Challenge to Survive, Snowman*

A slow survival picture. A bearded Mel Torme plays a television animal trainer who crash-lands his private plane in Utah. Torme wears loud sports clothes and talks to his trusty eagle. William Shatner is a worried television producer.

LAND OF THE MINOTAUR

1976 Crown International (Greece)
PRODUCER: Frixos Constantine
DIRECTOR: Costa Carayiannis
SCREENWRITER: Arthur Rowe
ALSO RELEASED AS: *The Devil's People*

Peter Cushing sacrifices women and leads a modern Greek cult that worships the minotaur. As the village priest, Donald Pleasence tries to stop him. With a bit of sex, some gore, and music by Brian Eno! **(R)**

LAND OF THE PHARAOHS

1955 Warner Brothers
PRODUCER/DIRECTOR: Howard Hawks
SCREENWRITERS: William Faulkner,
  Harry Kurnitz, Harold Jack Bloom

Underrated CinemaScope epic about Cheops (Jack Hawkins) and the building of his incredible self-sealing eternal tomb. Criticized for not having enough action, it's still a fascinating account of how and why the pyramids were built. With Joan Collins ("Her treachery stained every stone of the pyramid!" according to the ads) and Charlie Chaplin's son Sidney. Music by Dimitri Tiomkin. Filmed in Egypt.

THE LAND THAT TIME FORGOT

1975 Amicus/AIP (England)
PRODUCER: John Dark
DIRECTOR: Kevin Conner
SCREENWRITERS: James Cawthorn,
  Michael Moorcock

The first and worst of a series of British Amicus Studios juvenile adventures based on Edgar Rice Burroughs novels. A World War I German sub with prisoners on board ends up in the lost land of Caprona with cavemen and the phoniest dinosaurs you've ever seen. They are really men in rubber suits and giant prop heads on poles. The pterodactyl doesn't use wings to fly; it uses easy-to-see wires! And the star is Doug McClure! The pits. *The People That Time Forgot* was the sequel.

THE LAND UNKNOWN

1957 Universal (B&W)
PRODUCER: William Alland
DIRECTOR: Virgel Vogel
SCREENWRITER: Laslo Gorog

Jock Mahoney and three others crashland a helicopter in a hidden prehistoric valley below the Antarctic. Shawn Smith is almost devoured by a carnivorous plant, and a tyrannosaur and a "flippersaurus" attack. The dinosaurs are better than usual for the man-in-a-suit variety, and the misty sets and matte-painting backgrounds make a pretty effective lost world. With Douglas Kennedy and William Reynolds.

LAS VEGAS BY NIGHT: See SPREE.

LAS VEGAS HILLBILLYS

1966 Woolner Brothers
PRODUCER/SCREENWRITER: Larry E. Jackson
DIRECTOR: Arthur C. Pierce
ALSO RELEASED AS: *Country Music U.S.A.*
Jayne Mansfield and Mamie Van Doren together! Ferlin Husky stars as Woody, a country bumpkin who inherits a casino in Las Vegas. When it turns out to be a dump, the singing barmaid (Mamie) helps fix it up and put on a music jamboree with Sonny James, Del Reeves, Bill Anderson, and Connie Smith. Both Mamie and Jayne (who plays a famous star) sing and dance. With Richard Kiel and "The Duke of Paducah." Ferlin returned in a sequel, *Hillbillys in a Haunted House.* It's really unfair that Northerners were denied the opportunity to see these cheap star oddities at the time of the original release.

LAS VEGAS STORY

1952 RKO (B&W)
PRODUCER: Robert Sparks
DIRECTOR: Robert Stevenson
SCREENWRITERS: Earl Felton, Harry Essex
Gambler Vincent Price takes sexy wife Jane Russell to Las Vegas, where she encounters her ex-lover Victor Mature, now a sheriff's deputy. Jane sings "My Resistance is Low," is kidnaped by a murderer, and ends up with Victor after all. With Brad Dexter, Hoagy Carmichael, and Milton Kibbe.

LASERBLAST

1978 Selected Pictures
PRODUCER: Charles Band
DIRECTOR: Michael Rae
SCREENWRITERS: Franne Schact, Frank Ray Perilli

The best part of this teen-revenge film are the turtle-headed aliens animated by David Allen. They leave a laser gun on the desert that is picked up by young Kim Milford (*The Rocky Horror Picture Show*). The taunted and troubled teen turns green and ugly and proceeds to blast everybody who made fun of him, from kids at a party to dopers in a van. He also blows apart a *Star Wars* poster. Roddy McDowall and Keenan Wynn put in typical brief cameos. Aimed at '70s junior high school students. With Cheryl Smith.

LASSIE'S GREAT ADVENTURE

1963 20th Century-Fox
PRODUCER: Robert Golden
DIRECTOR: William Beaudine
SCREENWRITERS: Monroe Manning,
   Charles O'Neal
Originally a four-part story (*The Journey*) on TV, this features the prime *Lassie* cast with good old June Lockhart as Mrs. Ruth Martin and lovable little Jon Provost as Timmy. Not only is it directed by William Beaudine, whose next feature was *Billy the Kid vs. Dracula*, but it stars giant Richard Kiel as Chinook Pete, a deaf-mute Indian! When Timmy and Lassie are carried off in a hot-air balloon and land in a tree somewhere in Canada, Chinook Pete decides Timmy is a perfect replacement for his dead son. Lassie has different ideas. With Walter Stocker, the hero of *They Saved Hitler's Brain.*

THE LAST CHASE

1981 Crown International
PRODUCERS: Martyn Burke, Fran Rosati
DIRECTOR: Martyn Burke
SCREENWRITERS: C.R. O'Christopher,
   Roy Moore, Martyn Burke
In the future, America is out of gas. There are no more cars. Rebel ex-race

driver Lee Majors reassembles his red Porsche and heads to California with a young electronics genius (Chris Makepeace). The oppressive government sends a Phantom jet to stop him. It's no *Death Race 2000*. With Burgess Meredith.

THE LAST CHILD
1971 TV
PRODUCER: Aaron Spelling
DIRECTOR: John Moxey
SCREENWRITER: Peter S. Fischer
Edward Asner is a population inspector in 1994. He's after Janet Margolin and husband Michael (*Mod Squad*) Cole, who broke the law by having a second child. Ven Heflin (in his last role) is a retired senator who helps the couple escape. With Harry Guardino and Kent Smith.

THE LAST DAYS OF MAN ON EARTH
1974 New World (England)
PRODUCERS: John Goldstone, Sandy Heberson
DIRECTOR/SCREENWRITER: Robert Fuest
ALSO RELEASED AS: *The Final Programme*
A science-fiction film with good intentions that doesn't really make it. Jon Finch stars as Jerry Cornelius, hero of futuristic popular novels by Michael Moorcock. After a number of cartoonish adventures, including one in which he kills his drug-crazed brother, the genetically superior Finch is sexually joined with Jenny Runacre to create a new messiah. The result is an ape man. The cast includes Sterling Hayden, Patrick Magee, George Coulouris, Harry Andrews, and Julie Ege. Music by Beaver and Krause. From the director of the Dr. Phibes movies. A failed attempt at a cult film. (R)

LAST DAYS OF PLANET EARTH
1974 Toho (Japan)
DIRECTOR: Shiro Moritani
SCREENWRITER: Shinobu Hashimoto
ORIGINALLY RELEASED AS: *Catastrophe 1999: The Prophecies of Nostradamus*
The makers of *Tidal Wave* assembled the same major cast to experience even worse disasters in this follow-up feature released directly to television in America. The end of the world looks pretty exciting this time. After atomic bombs drop, mutants, vampire bats, and other harder to define terrors attack, stoned teens on motorcycles commit mass suicide, and the sky turns into an endless mirror so everybody can get a better look. Kenju Kobayashi, Tetsuro Tanaba, and Hiroshi Fujioka star.

THE LAST DAYS OF POMPEII
1935 RKO (B&W)
PRODUCER: Merian C. Cooper
DIRECTOR: Ernest B. Schoedsack
SCREENWRITER: Ruth Rose
Exciting spectacle from the *King Kong* team, using much of the *Kong* score. Preston Foster stars as a blacksmith-turned-gladiator. *Last Days* features colosseum battles and mass destruction as the volcano erupts. With villain Basil Rathbone, Dorothy Wilson, Alan Hale, and Louis Calhern.

THE LAST DAYS OF POMPEII
1960 United Artists (Italy/Spain)
PRODUCER: Paolo Moffa
DIRECTOR: Mario Bonnard
SCREENWRITERS: Ennio de Concini, Sergio Leone, Duccio Tessari, Sergio Corbucci
ORIGINALLY RELEASED AS: *Ultimi Giorni di Pompeii*
Steve Reeves is the muscleman hero of this gladiator remake. With Christine Kaufmann and Fernando Rey. Reeves starred in fifteen Italian action films beginning with *Hercules*.

THE LAST DINOSAUR

1977 TV (U.S./Japan)
PRODUCERS: Arthur Rankin, Jr., Jules Bass
DIRECTORS: Alex Grasshoff, Tom Kotani
SCREENWRITER: William Overgard

A Rankin/Bass Production made in Japan. Richard Boone plays Masten Thrust, the richest man in the world. He takes a small crew in his Thrust Polar Borer (it's labeled on the side) to a lost world to capture a man-in-a-suit T. Rex. Looks like the Amicus Edgar Rice Burroughs films and is just as childish. With Joan Van Ark. A made-for-TV movie here, it was released theatrically in less fortunate countries.

THE LAST GENERATION

1971 R&S Films
PRODUCER: Luther Davis
DIRECTOR: William Graham
SCREENWRITER: Earl Hammer, Jr.

It's the 21st century and the world is overpopulated with Stuart Whitman, Vera Miles, Lew Ayres, Mercedes McCambridge, Pearl Bailey, Lee Grant, Michael Rennie, Connie Stevens, Phil Harris, and Cesar Romero.

LAST GLORIES OF TROY:
See THE AVENGER.

LAST HOUSE ON DEAD END STREET

1977 Cinematic
PRODUCER: Norman F. Kaiser
DIRECTOR: Victor Janos
SCREENWRITER: Brian Lawrence
ALSO RELEASED AS: *The Fun House*

This extremely gory feature about snuff films was released with "Cult Classic" stamped on the ads. It features a hunchback and footage of an animal slaughterhouse. Have you ever heard anyone even admit that they saw it? (**R**)

LAST HOUSE ON THE LEFT

1972 AIP/Hallmark
PRODUCER: Sean S. Cunningham
DIRECTOR/SCREENWRITER: Wes Craven

A controversial, popular rape/revenge movie. Is it a remake of Bergman's *Virgin Spring* illustrating the sickness of life in modern-day America? Is it a coarse, repulsive exploitation film for sickos? It's both. The producer, who previously did porno movies, later did *Friday the 13th*, another controversial and trend-setting hit. The director (an ex-high school teacher) also made a better though similar film (*The Hills Have Eyes*), as well as a few weaker features (including a TV-movie). *Last House* has

Courtesy of Orion Pictures Corporation.

The Last Man on Earth
(Vincent Price) shops for
garlic.

THE LAST MAN ON EARTH

1964 AIP (Italy) (B&W)
PRODUCER: Robert L. Lippert
DIRECTOR: Ubaldo Ragona
Sidney Salkow (U.S. Version)
SCREENWRITERS: Logan Swanson,
William P. Leicester
ORIGINALLY RELEASED AS: *L'Ultimo Uomo
della Terror*

An end-of-the-world vampire/zombie
thriller with an undeserved bad rep. It's
based on Richard Matheson's *I Am Legend*. He hated this adaptation, but when
have writers ever liked the way their
work ends up on the screen? It was
later remade as the weak *Omega Man*,
but this version and the book were obviously the inspiration for *Night of the
Living Dead*. Morgan (Vincent Price),
the only human left, passes the time
burning dead bodies and driving stakes
through the hearts of wandering pasty-
faced ghouls. His maddening routine
includes gathering garlic, sharpening
piles of stakes, and playing old records
to blot out the noise of the creatures
trying to break into his suburban house
at night. He later discovers a group of
people who avoid becoming vampires
by taking chemical injections. Because
he staked many of their cohorts, they
want him killed. No blood and guts,
but a terrifying look at the last of a dead
race. With Giacomo Rossi-Stuart.

LAST OF THE SECRET AGENTS?

1966 Paramount
PRODUCER/DIRECTOR: Norman Abbott
SCREENWRITER: Mel Tolkin

Marty Allen and Steve Rossi as Marty
and Steve, American tourists in France,
are given a multipurpose umbrella
weapon and pitted against an international band of art thieves. The Statue
of Liberty is among the stolen treasures.
Co-star Nancy Sinatra sings the title
song. With John Williams, Edy Wil-

been cut, recut, and had scenes replaced
and removed so many times that stories about various legendary shocking
scenes are hard to disprove. The effective ad campaign ("To avoid fainting
keep repeating: It's only a movie . . .
only a movie . . .") has been copied
many times. No matter what you think
about it, *Last House* is effective and
disturbing and still shows up periodically in theaters. David Hess, Jeremy
Rain, and Fred Lincoln star. **(R)**

LAST HOUSE ON THE LEFT PART II: See *TWITCH OF THE DEATH NERVE.*

liams, Lou Jacobi, Sig Ruman, Harvey Korman, and Ed Sullivan as himself. Would make a dynamite double bill with *The Magic World of Topo Gigo*.

THE LAST OUTPOST

1951 Paramount
PRODUCERS: William H. Pine,
 William C. Thomas
DIRECTOR: Lewis R. Foster
SCREENWRITERS: Geoffrey Holmes,
 George Worthing Yates, Winston Miller

Ronald Reagan and Bruce Bennett are brothers who were on opposite sides in the Civil War but join to fight a common enemy—injuns. Reagan rode his own horse (Tarbaby). With Rhonda

Fleming (also in *Hong Kong* and *Tropic Zone* with Reagan) and the late Hugh Beaumont.

LAST RITES

1980 Cannon
PRODUCER: Kelly Van Horn
DIRECTOR/SCREENWRITER: Domonic Paris
ALSO RELEASED AS: *Dracula's Last Rites*

A low-budget film made in upstate New York that tries to invent new vampire lore. The results are deadening. The town mortician (called Lucard) is a bald vampire. He works with the sheriff and a doctor, who bring him accident victims. After sucking their blood, he drives stakes through their hearts to avoid competition and covers the wounds for burial. An old lady somehow survives the ordeal and walks around scaring people, including her daughter and son-in-law (called the Fondas). Microphones, a camera-equipment box, and the tops of sets are clearly visible throughout the film. I sat through it twice. **(R)**

THE LAST TIME I SAW ARCHIE

1961 United Artists
PRODUCER/DIRECTOR: Jack Webb
SCREENWRITER: William Bowers

A civilian pilot pulled into action in the late days of World War II talks about a memorable acquaintance. Robert Mitchum is Archie, a shameless con man who bluffs his way through the service and into a head slot at a Hollywood movie studio while Jack Webb watches from the sidelines. Co-stars include Martha Hyer, France Nuyen, Joe Flynn, James Lydon, Del Moore, Louis Nye, Don Knotts, Robert Strauss, Harvey Lembeck, and Bob's son Jim. Location scenes filmed at California's Fort MacArthur.   –CB

Originally released as: Last Rites.

THE LAST TYCOON

1976 Paramount
PRODUCER: Sam Spiegel
DIRECTOR: Elia Kazan
SCREENWRITER: Harold Pinter

Robert DeNiro stars as a famous Hollywood producer in a fair adaptation of F. Scott Fitzgerald's unfinished novel. A long movie with a lot of people who don't usually get good roles anymore, like Ray Milland, Tony Curtis, Dana Andrews, John Carradine, Donald Pleasence, and Robert Mitchum. With Jeanne Moreau, Jack Nicholson, and Jeff Corey. DeNiro and Nicholson play Ping-Pong.

THE LAST WAR

1961 Toho/Medallion-TV (Japan)
PRODUCERS: Sanezumi Fusimoto,
Tomoyuki Tanaka
DIRECTOR: Shue Matsubayashi
SCREENWRITERS: Toshio Yazumi,
Takeshi Kimura
ORIGINALLY RELEASED AS: *Senkai dai Senso*

Nuclear missiles are fired by mistake. War breaks out, leading to the end of the world. Not to be confused with *The Final War*, a 1960 Japanese movie.

THE LAST WOMAN ON EARTH

1960 Filmgroup
PRODUCER/DIRECTOR: Roger Corman
SCREENWRITER: Edward Wain
(Robert Towne)

Corman produced three movies in five weeks in Puerto Rico. He directed this one and *Creature from the Haunted Sea* with the same cast. Robert Towne (who later wrote *Chinatown*) didn't have the script done in time, so he was brought along to finish it on location and play the second lead at the same time, even though he had never acted before. He plays crook Anthony Carbone's lawyer. As the only survivers of a nuclear war in Puerto Rico, they fight over the lucky woman of the title (Betsy Jones-Moreland). Towne used the name Edward Wain in the credits as both writer and actor.

THE LATE GREAT PLANET EARTH

1979 Pacific International
PRODUCERS: Robert Amram, Rober Riddell
DIRECTOR/SCREENWRITER: Robert Amram

"The ultimate disaster movie!" is what the ads promised. It was also the ultimate Sunn Classics–type documentary with none other than Orson Welles explaining how the world will end in our lifetime. No wonder he doesn't take good parts anymore—what difference does it make if nobody will be around to see him? It's based on Hal Lindsey's bestseller. Hal's in the movie too, along with biblical re-enactments, UFOs, Bermuda triangles, and scientific testimonies.

LATITUDE ZERO

1969 Toho/National General
(U.S./Japan)
PRODUCER: Tomoyuki Tanaka
DIRECTOR: Inoshiro Honda
SCREENWRITERS: Ted Sherdeman,
Shinichi Sekizawa
ORIGINALLY RELEASED AS: *Ido Zero Daisakusen*

Crazy Japanese fantasy-adventure with American stars. Cesar Romero as Malic the murderer and Patricia Medina as Lucretia try to destroy an underwater citadel and, with it, submarine captain Joseph Cotten. Malic sends a flying lion, giant rats, and batmen to kill the scientists. The other good guys are Richard Jaeckel (also in *The Green Slime*), Linda Haynes, and Akira Takarada.

LAURA

1944 20th Century-Fox (B&W)
PRODUCER/DIRECTOR: Otto Preminger
SCREENWRITERS: Jay Dratier,
Samuel Hoffenstein, Betty Reinhardt

Classic murder mystery with Dana Andrews as the New York detective haunted by the memory of a beautiful murder victim (Gene Tierney). Tierney later turns up alive. Clifton Webb, as radio personality Waldo Lydecker, is her mentor who can't stand the possibility of her marrying Shelby Carpenter (Vincent Price). Judith Anderson, who is in love with Price, doesn't like the idea, either. All are suspects in the murder of the model who was mistaken for Laura. Great dialogue and performances. From the novel by Vera Caspary. Direction was started by Mamoulian, taken over by Preminger. Theme song by Johnny Mercer.

LAW AND ORDER
1953 Universal (B&W)
PRODUCER: John W. Rogers
DIRECTOR: Nathan Juran
SCREENWRITERS: John and Owen Bagni, D.D. Beauchamp

Ronald Reagan as a retired U.S. Marshal brings kid brother Russell Johnson ("The Professor" on *Gilligan's Island*) to justice. Based on the Wyatt Earp legend. With Dorothy Malone. Juran had just directed Karloff in the boring *Black Castle*. His next, *Highway Dragnet*, was written by Roger Corman.

LEATHER GIRLS: See FASTER PUSSYCAT! KILL! KILL!

LEAVE HER TO HEAVEN
1945 20th Century-Fox
PRODUCER: William A. Bacher
DIRECTOR: John M. Stahl
SCREENWRITER: Jo Swerling

Technicolor *film noir* told in flashback. Gene Tierney will do anything to avoid sharing her writer husband (Cornel Wilde), who resembles her late father. She lets his crippled brother (Darryl Hickman) drown, throws herself down the stairs to induce miscarriage, and when Wilde threatens to leave, poisons herself and sets up her half-sister (Jeanne Crain) and husband to take the blame. Vincent Price is the prosecuting attorney, a former lover of the tragic, evilly possessive woman. With Ray Collins, Milton Parsons, and Chill Wills. Based on Ben Ames William's novel.

THE LEECH WOMAN
1960 Universal (B&W)
PRODUCER: Joseph Gershenson
DIRECTOR: Edward Dein
SCREENWRITER: David Duncan

A scientist's aging, neglected wife (Coleen Gray) discovers that she can stay young by killing men for their hormones. Sometimes called "an unsung feminist film." With the unsung Gloria Talbot and feminist Grant Williams. The leech woman regrets her jungle secrets at the end and turns to dust. Coleen Gray had previously starred in *Red River* and *The Killing*.

THE LEGACY
1979 Universal (England)
PRODUCER: David Foster
DIRECTOR: Richard Marquand
SCREENWRITERS: Jimmy Sangster, Patric Tilley, Paul Wheeler
ALSO RELEASED AS: *The Legacy of Maggie Walsh*

Californians Katharine Ross and Sam Elliott go to England and become involved with a group of satanists who begin dying in a variety of graphic ways. It's all being done by an ancient, ugly, bedridden man (John Standing). In one clever death scheme, the surface of a swimming pool turns solid while a woman drowns below. Pretty bad. Roger Daltrey of The Who is in it. Marquand directed *The Return of the Jedi*. **(R)**

LEGACY OF BLOOD

1973 Universal Entertainment
PRODUCER/DIRECTOR: Carl Monson
SCREENWRITER: Eric Norden
ALSO RELEASED AS: *Blood Legacy*

The children of a millionaire must spend a week in his house in order to gain their inheritance. John Carradine is the father. The cast members (including Faith Domergue and Jeff Morrow from *This Island Earth*) die. With Merry Anders and Buck Kartarian. See: *The Ghastly Ones* and *Legacy of Blood* (below).

LEGACY OF HORROR

1978 Ken Lane Films
PRODUCER/DIRECTOR/SCREENWRITER:
Andy Milligan

A Staten Island–shot period film about a group of people who gather to find out about an inheritance. One of them is a killer who wants to do in all the others. The trouble is that you have to sit through one of the worst written, acted, and directed films to reach the gory climax, where people get sawed, knifed, axed, and punctured. Milligan also served as editor and cinematographer on this film, which is a remake of his *The Ghastly Ones*. **(R)** —AF

THE LEGACY OF MAGGIE WALSH: See THE LEGACY.

LEGACY OF SATAN

1973 Damiano Films
PRODUCER/DIRECTOR/SCREENWRITER:
Gerard Damiano

A dull item from the pretentious creator of *The Devil in Miss Jones*. The sex has been mostly edited out and what's left is the usual satanic-cult stuff.

LEGEND OF BLOOD CASTLE: See FEMALE BUTCHER.

THE LEGEND OF BLOOD MOUNTAIN

1965 Craddock
PRODUCER: Don Hadley
DIRECTOR: Massey Cramer
SCREENWRITERS: Massey Cramer,
Don Hadley, Bob Corley

George Ellis of *The Old Guitar* is Bestoink Dooley, a small-town reporter who meets pretty girls and a monster while scouting for a story. Zenas Sears, Glenda Brunson of *Speed Lovers*, Erin Fleming, and Sheila Stringer co-star. Filmed on location at Stone Mountain and Lake Spivey, Georgia. —CB

THE LEGEND OF BOGGY CREEK

1973 Howco International
PRODUCER/DIRECTOR: Charles B. Pierce
SCREENWRITER: Earl E. Smith

A docudrama about a Bigfoot type in Fouke, Arkansas. Not bad for this sort of thing—until you see the creature. *Return to Boggy Creek* came out in '77.

LEGEND OF HELL HOUSE

1973 20th Century-Fox (England/U.S.)
PRODUCERS: Albert Fennell,
Norman T. Herman
DIRECTOR: John Hough
SCREENWRITER: Richard Matheson

Richard Matheson adapted his own novel for this good psychic phenomena thriller, which is very similar to *The Haunting* ('63). New Zealander Clive Revill plays the only psychic investigator who remains both alive and sane after spending time in Hell House. Years later, a dying millionaire convinces him to go back with a new team, including his wife (Gayle Hunnicut), a mental medium (Pamela Franklin), and a physical medium (Roddy McDowall). Locked in the windowless house, they're terrorized by ghosts and ectoplasmic materializations. British child star Franklin

(*The Innocents*, '61; *The Nanny*, '65; *Our Mother's House*, '67) participates in a horror-movie first—sex with an invisible ghost. The weird ending features an unbilled silent role by Michael Gough. It was the only film made by ex-AIP founder James Nicholson for his own Academy Pictures. Nicholson died in '73.

THE LEGEND OF HILLBILLY JOHN

1973 Jack Harris
PRODUCER: Barney Rosenzweig
DIRECTOR: John Newland
SCREENWRITER: Melvin Levy
ORIGINALLY RELEASED AS: *Who Fears the Devil?*

A wandering ballad singer in the Appalachians encounters a giant demon bird and black magic. Directed by the host of the *One Step Beyond* show. With Susan Strasberg, Denver Pyle, Hedge Capers, and Severn Darden. Special effects by Gene Warren (*The Time Machine*).

THE LEGEND OF LIZZIE BORDEN

1975 TV
PRODUCER: George LeMaire
DIRECTOR: Paul Wendkos
SCREENWRITER: William Bast

Elizabeth Montgomery stars as a 19th-century psycho who hacks up her parents with an ax after carefully removing her clothes to avoid bloodstains. Fairly shocking for a TV movie, it won several Emmies. With Don Porter, Fritz Weaver, Ed Flanders, and John Beal.

THE LEGEND OF SPIDER FOREST

1976 New Line (England)
DIRECTOR: Peter Sykes
ORIGINALLY RELEASED AS: *Venom*

A young painter on vacation in Bavaria encounters the "Spider Goddess" and scientists who kill with spider venom.

LEGEND OF THE SEVEN GOLDEN VAMPIRES

1973 Hammer/Shaw Brothers–
Dynamite Entertainment
(England/Hong Kong)
PRODUCERS: Don Houghton, Vee King Shaw
DIRECTOR: Roy Ward Baker
SCREENWRITER: Don Houghton
ALSO RELEASED AS: *The Seven Brothers Meet Dracula*

It's too bad the world's first kung-fu vampire film had to wait six years for a U.S. release. It's an exciting period action-fantasy starring Peter Cushing as Professor Van Helsing. He's joined by David Chiang, Julie Ege, and a family team of martial-arts experts who help him to defeat an endless supply of skeleton-faced peasant ghouls. The heroes chop the creatures kung fu–style and pull the hearts from their rotted bodies. The ghouls are slaves of a group of masked vampires aided by Dracula himself (John Forbes Robertson). Better than any of the last Hammer Dracula movies and an exciting martial-arts adventure. (R)

LEGEND OF THE WEREWOLF

1975 (England)
PRODUCER: Kevin Francis
DIRECTOR: Freddie Francis
SCREENWRITER: John Elder

A period film set in Paris with Peter Cushing as a police pathologist after a werewolf (David Rintoul). This wolf-man looks a lot like Oliver Reed did. With Ron Moody, Hugh Griffith, Roy Castle, and Pamela Green. Not released theatrically in America.

THE LEGEND OF
THE WOLF WOMAN

1977 Dimension (Spain)
PRODUCER: Diego Alchimede
DIRECTORSCREENWRITER: Rino Di Silvestro
ORIGINALLY RELEASED AS: *La Lupa Mannura*

A pretty sleazy sex-horror movie that begins with a naked woman growing hair all over her body, foaming at the mouth, and killing a villager. Two hundred years later another woman, supposedly possessed by her spirit, runs around murdering people and detectives try to solve the crimes. It was released here in '81 to compete with *The Howling*. (R)

LEGEND OF WITCH
HOLLOW: See THE
WITCHMAKER.

THE LEGENDARY CASE OF
LEMORA: See LEMORA,
THE LADY DRACULA.

THE LEMON GROVE KIDS
MEET THE MONSTERS

1966 Steckler
PRODUCER/DIRECTOR: Ray Dennis Steckler
SCREENWRITERS: Ron Haydock, Jim Harmon

A wacky Southern California imitation of the Bowery Boys from the makers of *The Incredibly Strange Creatures*. This homemade feature combines two 16mm shorts starring friends and neighbors of the director, who appears himself under the name Cash Flagg. Steckler/Flagg looks a *lot* like Huntz Hall. He and the gang have a race and run into a beatnik spy, a mummy, a gorilla, a vampire lady, and spacemen. When the film was first shown in theaters, people in monster costumes ran into the audience, probably delighting the kids attending. With Carolyn Brandt (Steckler's wife).

LEMORA, THE LADY
DRACULA

1974 Media Cinema
PRODUCER: Robert Fern
DIRECTOR: Richard Blackburn
SCREENWRITERS: Richard Blackburn, Robert Fern
ALSO RELEASED AS: *The Legendary Case of Lemora, Lady Dracula*

During the 1920s in Georgia a female vampire (Leslie Gilb) tricks a 13-year-old church singer (Cheryl Smith) into visiting her home in the woods. This interesting low-budget oddity features ghoul-like beast people and a sensual vampire whose followers are little children. The Catholic Film Board gave it a condemned rating. Director Blackburn also plays a preacher. Cheryl (Rainbeaux) Smith is also in *Caged Heat* and *Phantasm Comes Again*, an Australian porno feature.

THE LEOPARD MAN

1943 RKO (B&W)
PRODUCER: Val Lewton
DIRECTOR: Jacques Tourneur
SCREENWRITER: Ardel Wray

The ads promised: "The blood-racing story of a maniac who kills like a cat!" An unconventional, haunting film about a killer leopard loose in New Mexico. It includes the famous scene of a mother "punishing" her little girl by not unlocking the front door to let her in at night. All the audience sees during her ordeal is blood trickling under the door. With black-hooded monks and one of the best trapped-in-a-cemetery sequences ever. Dennis O'Keefe, Jean Brooks, and Margo star. Based on a Cornell Woolrich story.

LESBIAN TWINS: See THE VIRGIN WITCH.

LET ME DIE A WOMAN

1979 Hygiene Films

If you have a strong stomach and a taste for the bizarre, look for this tacky sexchange feature, a modern equivalent of *Glen or Glenda*. A humorless and sleazy documentary, it's hosted by a "real" doctor who shows interviews with real transsexuals before and after their operations (also shown), and stock footage from newsreels and grainy porno films. A *Let Me Die a Woman* paperback book was sold at the box office. For once, the hype ("See a man become a woman before your eyes") was true. **(Unrated)**

LET'S KILL UNCLE

1966 Universal
PRODUCER/DIRECTOR: William Castle
SCREENWRITER: Mark Rodgers

A 12-year-old orphan (Pat Cardi, later the star of *Horror High*) who has just inherited a fortune is trapped on an island with his uncle (Nigel Green), a former British intelligence commander who intends to kill him. A young girl (Mary Badham from *To Kill a Mockingbird*) is the boy's only ally against the sarcastic uncle, who uses hypnotism, a pool of sharks, fire, and poison mushrooms as weapons. It's different. With Nestor Paiva.

LET'S ROCK!

1958 Columbia (B&W)
PRODUCER/DIRECTOR: Harry Foster
SCREENWRITER: Hal Hackady
ALSO RELEASED AS: *Keep It Cool*

Phyllis Newman helps ballad singer Julius La Rosa sell records in a rock 'n' roll world. I doubt if this movie helped him much in real life. Watch it for the Royal Teens (doing "Short Shorts"!), Danny and the Juniors ("At the Hop"), Paul Anka, Roy Hamilton, Della Reese, and '50s deejay Wink Martindale, still grinning today on TV quiz shows.

Julius La Rosa in Let's Rock.

Zohra Lampert stars in Let's Scare Jessica to Death.

LET'S SCARE JESSICA TO DEATH

1971 Paramount
PRODUCERS: Charles B. Moss, Jr.,
William Badalto
DIRECTOR: John Hancock
SCREENWRITERS: Norman Jonas, Ralph Rose
Called an unsuccessful mixture of *Carnival of Souls* and *Night of the Living Dead*, this debut by director John Hancock (*Bang the Drum Slowly*) is an enjoyable shocker. Zohra Lampert, recently released from a mental hospital, purchases a farm in Connecticut with her classical musician husband. Her tenuous grip on reality crumbles with the arrival of a strange guest (Gretchen Corbett) who turns out to be a female vampire. Lampert stands out in a cast of stage and soap-opera actors.

LICENSED TO KILL: See THE SECOND BEST SECRET AGENT IN THE WHOLE WIDE WORLD.

LIFE BEGINS AT 17

1959 Columbia (B&W)
PRODUCER: Sam Katzman
DIRECTOR: Arthur Dreifuss
SCREENWRITER: Richard Baer
Edd Byrnes, then famous as "Kookie" on *77 Sunset Strip*, stars with Mark Damon and Ann Doran (Jimmy's mother in *Rebel Without a Cause*) in what was advertised as "a family drama of adolescent love." Watch for it. With Luana Anders and Dorothy Johnson.

LIGHTNING BOLT

1966 Woolner Brothers (Italy/Spain)
PRODUCER: Alfonso Balcazar
DIRECTOR: Antonio Margheriti
SCREENWRITERS: Alfonso Balcazar,
José Antonio de la Loma
ALSO RELEASED AS: *Operazione Goldman*
A spy thriller concerning sabotage at Cape Kennedy, an underwater city, and frozen women. Star Anthony Eisley is an unheralded hero of many cheap horrors.

LILA: See MANTIS IN LACE.

THE LION HUNTERS

1951 Monogram (B&W)
PRODUCER: Walter Mirisch
DIRECTOR/SCREENWRITER: Ford Beebe
Bomba (Johnny Sheffield) saves sacred cats from corrupt hunters played by Morris Ankrum and Douglas Kennedy. He also saves Ann Todd.

LISA AND THE DEVIL: See THE HOUSE OF EXORCISM.

THE LITTLE GIRL WHO LIVES DOWN THE LANE

1977 AIP (Canada)
PRODUCER: Zev Braun
DIRECTOR: Nicolas Gessner
SCREENWRITER: Laird Koenig
Fifteen-year-old Jodie Foster is the 13-year-old girl of the title. She lives alone

in an isolated house and kills people who threaten her. With Martin Sheen.

LITTLE RED RIDING HOOD AND THE MONSTERS

1960 K. Gordon Murray (Mexico)
PRODUCER/DIRECTOR: Roberto Rodriguez
SCREENWRITERS: Fernando Morales Ortiz, Aldolfo Torres Portillo
ALSO RELEASED AS: *Caperucita y Pulgarcito*
Little Red Riding Hood (Maria Garcia) and Tom Thumb fight a vampire and a witch in a haunted forest! One of three Hood movies made the same year in Mexico and shipped up here like clockwork in the mid-'60s to warp the minds of little kids whose parents wanted to go Christmas shopping or whatever. In color!

THE LITTLE SHOP OF HORRORS

1960 Filmgroup (B&W)
PRODUCER/DIRECTOR: Roger Corman
SCREENWRITER: Charles Griffith
Corman's cult-classic comedy was a follow-up to *Bucket of Blood*, and used the same music (by Fred Katz) and the same scriptwriter. Jonathan Haze, a familiar face in many Corman films, stars as Seymour Krelboing, a florist's delivery boy who gains respect, minor fame, and Audrey, an equally dimwitted girlfriend (Jackie Joseph), by nurturing Audrey, Jr., a rare plant that needs human blood. The 70-minute film, which was shot in two and a half days, is crowded with great gags and characters. Mel Welles is Gravis Mushnik, skid row flower-shop owner. (LOTS PLANTS —CHEAP, says the sign on the door.) *Bucket of Blood* star Dick Miller is Fouch, a customer who eats flowers. Jack Nicholson has a great bit as a masochistic dentist's patient named Wilbur Force. It all begins with a *Dragnet* parody: "My name is Sgt. Joe Fink. I work on a 24-hour shift down at homi-

cide. . . . " A wonder with the ultimate hypochondriac mother, a junkyard chase, and the world's most famous talking plant. Every time it's on television, school kids go around yelling, "Feed me! I'm hungry!" the next day. Not to be missed. In 1982, it became an Off-Broadway musical in New York. Scriptwriter Griffith had to sue for credit.

LIVE A LITTLE, LOVE A LITTLE

1968 MGM
PRODUCER: Douglas Lawrence
DIRECTOR: Norman Taurog
SCREENWRITER: Michael A. Hoey
As Greg, Elvis is a photographer leading a double life working both for a *Playboy*-type magazine (run by Don Porter) and for conservative publisher Rudy Vallee. In an attempt to be more "hep," Elvis sleeps with model Michelle Carey and says "dammit" a few times in this hopelessly out-of-it movie. With Dick Sargent, Sterling Holloway, and Celeste Yarnall. One of the four songs is "Edge of Reality."

LIVE AGAIN, DIE AGAIN

1974 TV
PRODUCER: Robert F. O'Neill
DIRECTOR: Richard A. Colla
SCREENWRITER: Joseph Stefano
Donna Mills is thawed out after 30 years in this futuristic soap opera. She has a tough time dealing with her old husband (Walter Pidgeon) and her grown-up kids (Vera Miles and Mike Farrell).

LIVE AND LET DIE

1973 United Artists (England)
PRODUCERS: Albert R. Broccoli, Harry Saltzman
DIRECTOR: Guy Hamilton
SCREENWRITER: Tom Mankiewicz
Roger Moore, TV's "Saint," takes over the 007 role. Following on the heels of comical David Niven, forgettable

George Lazenby, and out-of-shape Sean Connery, Moore looks pretty good. This time, the villains are all black. The action takes place in New Orleans, Harlem, and Jamaica. Yaphet Kotto, as Kananga, is flooding the U.S. with heroin. 007 stops him (I wonder who's supplying it now). Kotto is filled up like a balloon and explodes. The writers must have stolen that idea from a Three Stooges short where Curly is covered with tar and inflated. Attaining a new height of silliness, Jane Seymour as Solitaire can tell the future as long as she remains a virgin. Bond, of course, ruins her plans to tell fortunes for a living. The character of J.W. Pepper, a comic redneck sheriff, would fit right in on *The Dukes of Hazzard*, but in a spy movie? Geoffrey Holder is Baron Samedi, a voodoo god. David Hedison (*Voyage to the Bottom of the Sea*) takes the CIA-man role. With Madeline Smith. Paul McCartney wrote and performed the hit theme song, the best thing about this whole movie. Former Beatles producer George Martin scored the music.

LIVE FAST, DIE YOUNG

1958 Universal (B&W)
PRODUCERS: Harry Rybnick, Richard Kay
DIRECTOR: Paul Henreid
SCREENWRITERS: Allen Rivkin, Ib Melchior
Norma Eberhardt runs off to a sleazy San Francisco dive and almost gets mixed up in an armed robbery before older sister Mary Murphy catches up. The ads claimed it was the "sin-steeped story of today's beat generation!" With Mike Connors, Troy Donahue, and Dorothy Provine. Co-released with *Girls on the Loose*, also from director Henreid. —CB

LIVE IT UP: See SING AND SWING.

LIVE TO LOVE: See THE DEVIL'S HAND.

THE LIVER EATERS: See SPIDER BABY.

THE LIVING COFFIN

1958 K. Gordon Murray (Mexico)
PRODUCER: César Santos Galindo
DIRECTOR: Fernando Mendez
SCREENWRITER: Ramon Obón
ALSO RELEASED AS: El Grito de la Muerte

A girl has an alarm installed in her coffin in this "Premature Burial"-type story. Presented by the importer of *Little Red Riding Hood and the Monsters*.

THE LIVING GHOST

1942 Monogram (B&W)
PRODUCER: A.W. Hackel
DIRECTOR: William Beaudine
SCREENWRITER: Joseph Hoffman

A man becomes a "scientific killer" (a zombie). James Dunn clowns around and Joan Woodbury gets scared. With Minerva Urecal.

THE LIVING HEAD

1959 K. Gordon Murray
(Mexico) (B&W)
PRODUCER: Abel Salazar
DIRECTOR: Chanto Urueta
SCREENWRITERS: Frederick Curiel,
A. Lopez Portillo
ORIGINALLY RELEASED AS: La Cabeza Viviente

The heads of Catl, an Aztec chief, and his grand priest are found in a tomb. They come to life, placing a woman under a spell, and human sacrifices begin. With German Robles and Abel Salazar, both horror stars south of the border. It wasn't released in English until '69.

LIVING LEGEND

1980 E.O. Corporation
PRODUCER: Earl Owensby
DIRECTOR: Worth Keeter
SCREENWRITER: Tom McIntyre

Earl Owensby (who previously starred in eight of his own movies) plays a thinly disguised Elvis Presley-type character in a story about a Country rock star in a glitter jump suit. He has a manipulative manager, takes pills, and sings with the dubbed-in voice of Roy Orbison. His girlfriend is Ginger Alden, former fiancée of the real Elvis. If you live in the Northeast the only way you'll see Earl's low-budget North Carolina movies is on cable.

LIZZIE

1957 MGM (B&W)
PRODUCER: Jerry Bresler
DIRECTOR: Hugo Haas
SCREENWRITER: Mel Dinelli

Elizabeth (Eleanor Parker), a shy sickly museum employee, has a split personality. As Beth, she's a happy, well-adjusted woman. As Lizzie, she's a hell-raising party girl who writes threatening letters. Her alcoholic aunt (Joan Blondell) and a kind neighbor (director Haas) take her to a psychiatrist (Richard Boone), who discovers a sordid traumatic incident in her past. Songs by Burt Bacharach and Hal David, sung by Johnny Mathis. It's the only Haas movie that received any serious notice. Based on *The Bird's Nest* by Shirley Jackson. *The Three Faces of Eve* was released the same year.

LOCK UP YOUR DAUGHTERS

1956 New Realm (B&W)
PRODUCER: Sam Katzman

Bela Lugosi made nearly a dozen classically inept features for the Monogram studios. Fast-thinking Sam Katzman hired the quickly fading star to narrate this compilation film containing scenes from six of them (including *The Ape Man* and *The Voodoo Man*). In the "new" footage, Bela refers to this forgotten cash-in attempt as his obituary. He died the year it was released, not knowing his next and last film would be *Plan 9 from Outer Space*, which opens with a brief home-movie clip of him shot a few days before he died.

LOCUSTS
1974 TV
PRODUCER: Herbert Wright
DIRECTOR: Richard T. Heffron
SCREENWRITER: Robert Malcolm Young

Grasshoppers land on Ben Johnson, Ron Howard, and Belinda Balanski and destroy the harvest in their Midwestern farming community in this TV terror film.

THE LODGER
1932 Olympic (England) (B&W)
PRODUCER: Julius Hagan
DIRECTOR: Maurice Elvey
SCREENWRITERS: Paul Rotha, Miles Mander
ALSO RELEASED AS: *The Phantom Fiend*

Musician Ivor Novello, a lodger in an old couple's house, is suspected of a series of killings in this remake of Hitchcock's 1926 silent classic. Jack Hawkins is a reporter. The film was re-released with a more exploitable title (see above). Nonetheless, few in the U.S. have seen it.

THE LODGER
1944 20 Century-Fox (B&W)
PRODUCER: Robert Bassler
DIRECTOR: John Brahm
SCREENWRITER: Barré Lydon

Excellent remake of Alfred Hitchcock's 1926 film based on Marie Belloc-Lowndes' novel. In 19th-century England, Laird Cregar rents a room at the home of an old couple. Unlike earlier versions of the story, here he really is Jack the Ripper. With Merle Oberon, George Sanders, Sir Cedric Hardwicke, Sara Allgood, and Skelton Knaggs. The film was so popular (and big Laird Cregar was so good) that he and Sanders returned in a similar hit, *Hangover Square*.

LOGAN'S RUN
1976 MGM
PRODUCER: Saul David
DIRECTOR: Michael Anderson
SCREENWRITER: David Zeelag Goodman

Right up there with the same year's *Kong* remake. A much-publicized big-budget bust. Michael York did this in between his other terrible fantasy flops—*Lost Horizon* and *The Island of Dr. Moreau*. The futuristic togalike costumes are ugly, the sequence with Peter Ustinov living in the ruins of Washington, D.C., brings groans from the audience, and the robot (Roscoe Lee Brown) wouldn't make it in an old serial. Jenny Agutter also stars and gets to fight the film's best-loved star—Farrah Fawcett-Majors. The magnificent city of the future is actually a Dallas shopping mall. Hard to believe *Logan's Run* actually spawned a TV show.

LOLA'S MISTAKE: See THIS REBEL BREED.

THE LOLLIPOP COVER
1965 Continental (B&W with color sequences)
PRODUCER/DIRECTOR: Everett Chambers
SCREENWRITERS: Everett Chambers, Don Gordon

An abandoned nine-year-old girl (Carol Seflinger) is befriended by a boxer on his way to Los Angeles. He hopes to reclaim his life savings from his dead sister's drug-addict boyfriend. Color sequences result from young Seflinger's peering through candy wrappers, contrasting her rosy outlook with that of her world-weary friend. With Don Gordon, George Sawaya, John Marley, Midge Ware, and Lee Philips. Sally Kellerman sings "If You Love Me" and "When I See a Rainbow." —CB

THE LONELY HEARTS KILLERS: See *THE HONEYMOON KILLERS*.

LONELY MAN: See *FIVE BLOODY GRAVES*.

THE LONELY SEX
1959 Brenner (B&W)
PRODUCER/DIRECTOR/SCREENWRITER:
Richard Hilliard
A psychiatrist's daughter is taken to a forest hideout by a killer maniac. He finds her father's card in her purse and goes into town to confess, but is killed after being followed home by the psychiatrist and his brother—a notorious Peeping Tom. Director Hilliard later worked with Del Tenney in Connecticut, directing *Psychomania* and writing the screenplay for *The Horror of Party Beach*.   –CB

LONG DISTANCE
1959 Alan Enterprises (W. Germany/ England) (B&W)
DIRECTOR: Alvin Rakoff
ALSO RELEASED AS: *Hot Money Girl*, *The Treasure of San Teresa*
During the war, Eddie Constantine, an American O.S.S. man, hides some priceless jewels in a Czech monastery for a German resistance fighter. After the war, he returns to retrieve them, only to find that the monastery is now a Communist police station. With Dawn Addams, Christopher Lee, and Tsai Chin.

THE LONG NIGHT
1947 RKO (B&W)
PRODUCERS: Robert and Raymond Hakim, Anatole Litvak
DIRECTOR: Anatole Litvak
SCREENWRITER: John Wexley
Vincent Price is a second-rate blond(!) magician in a bleak Midwestern mill town. Ex-GI Henry Fonda kills him be-cause he had seduced his innocent girlfriend (Barbara Bel Geddes). The police don't understand. A remake of the French classic *Le Jour Se Lève* (1939). With Ann Dvorak and Elisha Cook, Jr.

A LONG RIDE FROM HELL
1968 Cinerama (Italy)
DIRECTOR: Alex Burks
SCREENWRITERS: Roberto Natale, Steve Reeves
ORIGINALLY RELEASED AS: *Vivo per la Tua Morte*
Former Hercules Steve Reeves co-wrote this Western in which he stars as a man who is unjustly jailed. He escapes and single-handedly kills all the real horse rustlers and killers. With Rosalba Neri and Silvana Venturelli. It was the last movie for the American hero of Italian-made adventures popular at Saturday matinees during the early '60s. He retired to a ranch to raise horses. **(R)**

THE LONG WAIT
1954 United Artists (B&W)
PRODUCER: Lesser Samuels
DIRECTOR: Victor Saville
SCREENWRITERS: Alan Green, Lesser Samuels
A Mickey Spillane adaptation about a hitchhiker who loses his memory and his face in a fiery highway smashup. Anthony Quinn, who is trying to clear himself of a robbery/murder charge, traces a photo of himself to a strange town where, after plastic surgery, he must figure out which of four women is his ex-wife. With Charles Coburn, Gene Evans, and Peggie Castle.   –CB

THE LONGEST DAY
1962 20th Century-Fox
PRODUCER: Darryl F. Zanuck
DIRECTORS: Ken Annakin, Bernhard Wicki, Gerd Oswald, Darryl F. Zanuck
SCREENWRITER: Cornelius Ryan

The cast of this famous D-day epic includes (to mention just a few) Curt Jurgens, Peter Van Eyck, and Gert Frobe as Germans; Jean Servais and Jean-Louis Barrault as Frenchmen; Sean Connery, Christopher Lee, Richard Todd, Leo Genn, and Richard Burton as Englishmen; and Ray Danton, Tommy Sands, Mark Damon, Tom Tryon, Sal Mineo, Paul Anka, Mel Ferrer, Richard Beymer, Fabian, and Stuart Whitman as Americans.

LOOK IN ANY WINDOW

1961 Allied Artists (B&W)
PRODUCERS: William Alland,
    Lawrence E. Mascott
DIRECTOR: William Alland
SCREENWRITER: Lawrence E. Mascott
Ruth Roman is watering her lawn when neighbor Jack Cassidy pulls up in his BMW 507 and offers a high time in Las Vegas. They embrace wildly. While they're away, Cassidy's daughter Gigi Perreau falls through a glass-top patio table while fleeing a Peeping Tom. And Ruth and alcoholic husband Alex Nicol examine their suburban lifestyle following son Paul Anka's capture by plainclothesmen. With Carole Mathews, Robert Sampson, and George Dolenz. Anka sings the title song. The swimsuits are by Rose Marie Reed.   –CB

LOOK WHAT'S HAPPENED TO ROSEMARY'S BABY

1976 TV
PRODUCER/SCREENWRITER: Anthony Wilson
DIRECTOR: Sam O'Steen
ALSO RELEASED AS: Rosemary's Baby II
Don't go out of your way to see this shoddy "sequel" with Ruth Gordon returning to repeat her original role. Ray Milland is her husband. Patty Duke takes over the Mia Farrow role and George Maharis is her husband. Stephen McHattie is the grown-up son

of Satan. The cast is rounded out by Broderick Crawford, Tina Louise, and Donna Mills. How about a TV sequel to Repulsion, too?

LOOKER

1981 Warner Brothers
PRODUCER: Howard Jeffrey
DIRECTOR/SCREENWRITER: Michael Crichton
More slick science fiction from the writer-director of Westworld and Coma. This yarn about subliminal advertising on TV is his silliest. Beautiful models are murdered and duplicated by a computer. Why? You got me. As the American plastic-surgeon hero, Albert Finney teams up with a model (Susan Dey of The Partridge Family) to find the killers. James Coburn heads the conglomerate behind the murders. Leigh Taylor-Young runs the research institute. With some Playboy playmates, stun guns, invisible bad guys, and Darryl Hickman.

LORD LOVE A DUCK

1966 United Artists (B&W)
PRODUCER/DIRECTOR: George Axelrod
SCREENWRITERS: Larry H. Johnson,
    George Axelrod
A sometimes-black comedy making fun of California '60s life-styles, exploitation movies, and rock music, by the writer of the plays Seven Year Itch and Will Success Spoil Rock Hunter? Roddy McDowall tells the story in flashback, from the psycho ward to which he's been committed after bulldozing a high school graduation ceremony. He had devoted his life to fulfilling every wish of Tuesday Weld. She gets her cashmere sweaters, joins a sorority, passes her courses, marries a handsome senior, and lands a starring role in Bikini Widow. With Lola Albright, Ruth Gordon, Harvey Korman, and Martin West.

Tuesday next played another perfect American girl in *Pretty Poison*.

LORD OF THE JUNGLE
1955 Allied Artists (B&W)
PRODUCER/DIRECTOR/SCREENWRITER:
Ford Beebe

Johnny Sheffield plays Bomba the Jungle Boy for the last time. He saves some more elephants. With Wayne Morris and Nancy Hale. Sheffield, then 24, retired from acting and invested his jungle money in California real estate.

LORD SHANGO
1975 Bryanston
PRODUCERS: Steve Bond, Ronald Hobbs
DIRECTOR: Raymond Marsh
SCREENWRITER: Paul Carter Harrison

A nonexploitative black horror film that suffered the same fate as *Ganja and Hess*—oblivion. In eastern Tennessee, Marlene Clark (also in *Ganja*) and her daughter (Avis McCarthur), who were raised as Christians, are faced with African superstitions and a tribal priest who returns to life. Lawrence Cook is top-billed as Shango. **(R)**

THE LOSERS
1970 Fanfare
PRODUCER: Joe Solomon
DIRECTOR: Jack Starrett
SCREENWRITER: Alan Cailou

Many consider this the ultimate biker film. Five Hells Angels with armored choppers are recruited by the CIA for special projects in Cambodia—everything from busting up native villages to rescuing a Presidential advisor from the Red Chinese. Dirty Denny (Houston Savage) wants to return to his favorite whorehouse, but he and friends Link (William Smith), Duke (Adam Roarke), Speed (Eugene Cornelius), and Limpy (Paul Koslo) die at the hands of the Cong. Captain Jackson is played by Bernie Hamilton of *Starsky and Hutch*. With Jack Starrett. **(R)** −CB

THE LOST CONTINENT
1951 Lippert (B&W)
PRODUCER: Sigmund Neufeld
DIRECTOR: Sam Newfield
SCREENWRITER: Richard H. Landau

An atomic rocket is lost on a plateau where animated dinosaurs roam. Cesar Romero organizes a who's who of '50s science-fiction film stars to join him in the search. John Hoyt, Hugh Beaumont, and Whit Bissell are all there, along with Hillary Brooke. They meet the still exotic and beautiful Acquanetta, who leads some of them to safety. The plateau sequences were tinted green. The spaceship scenes are from *RocketShip X-M*. By the director of *The Terror of Tiny Town*.

THE LOST CONTINENT
1968 Hammer/20th Century-Fox (England)
PRODUCER/DIRECTOR: Michael Carreras
SCREENWRITER: Michael Nash

An oddball adventure-fantasy based on *Uncharted Seas* by Dennis Wheatley. A lost race of conquistadors lives in a land of giant prehistoric crabs and jellyfish. A shipful of frantic Britishers is enticed there by living seaweed. With Eric Porter, Hildegard Knef, Suzanna Leigh, and Dana Gillespie.

THE LOST HORIZON
1937 Columbia (B&W)
PRODUCER/DIRECTOR: Frank Capra
SCREENWRITER: Robert Riskin

Classic version of James Hilton's novel with Ronald Colman leaving the war-torn real world for a 1930s Hollywood version of Shangri-la. Sam Jaffe is the High Lama. Margo is the woman who ages when she tries to leave. With Edward Everett Horton, Thomas Mitchell, Noble Johnson, and Jane Wyman.

LOST HORIZON

1973 Columbia
PRODUCER: Ross Hunter
DIRECTOR: Charles Jarrott
SCREENWRITER: Larry Kramer

A flop musical remake from the producer of *Airport*. Peter Finch and brother Michael York go to Shangri-la. Charles Boyer is the High Lama. John Gielgud is Chang. Olivia Hussey ages rapidly. Sally Kellerman is a reporter. George Kennedy (*Airport*) is the pilot. Bobby Van plays himself, a bad comedian. Liv Ullman dances and sings with kids. It's long, although a fertility dance sequence was removed after audiences laughed too much. With Kent Smith.

LOST, LONELY AND VICIOUS

1959 Howco (B&W)
PRODUCER: Charles M. Casinelli
DIRECTOR: Frank Myers
SCREENWRITER: Norman Graham

Ken Clayton stars as a young actor who uses the time between jobs for romantic hijinks. His dates include Sandra Giles, Lilyan Chauvin of *Bloodlust*, and Barbara Wilson of *Invasion of the Animal People*. Producer Casinelli also backed *Louisiana Hussy*.   —CB

THE LOST MISSILE

1958 United Artists (U.S./Canada)
PRODUCER: Lee Gordon
DIRECTOR: Lester William Berke
SCREENWRITERS: John McPartland, Jerome Bixby

The title ship, launched by unidentified Eastern Europeans, circles the globe at 5000 m.p.h., burning a 10-mile-wide groove across Earth's surface with New York and Ottawa in its path. Robert Loggia puts together an antimissile missile but juvenile delinquents steal the warhead. With Ellen Parker, Larry Kerr, Philip Pine, Marilee Earle, and Joe Hyams.   —CB

THE LOST PATROL

1934 RKO (B&W)
PRODUCERS: John Ford, Merian C. Cooper
DIRECTOR: John Ford
SCREENWRITER: Dudley Nichols

After Arabs kill most of a British patrol stranded in the Mesopotamian desert during World War I, only three men are left: the sergeant (Victor MacLaglen), Wallace Ford, and Boris Karloff. Karloff, a religious fanatic, is the first to crack. With Reginald Denny and Alan Hale.

LOST PLANET AIRMEN: See KING OF THE ROCKETMEN.

THE LOST TRIBE

1949 Columbia (B&W)
PRODUCER: Sam Katzman
DIRECTOR: William Berke
SCREENWRITERS: Arthur Hoerl, Don Martin

The ads promised: "Africa's most savage diamond hunt!" As Jungle Jim, Johnny Weissmuller battles crooks after the treasure of Dzamm. A man in a gorilla suit helps. With Myrna Dell, Elena Verdugo, and battles with a lion, a tiger, and a shark! The "lost" African natives are white.

THE LOST VOLCANO

1950 Monogram (B&W)
PRODUCER: Walter Mirisch
DIRECTOR: Ford Beebe
SCREENWRITER: Jack Dewitt

Bomba (Johnny Sheffield) saves a little boy who's been kidnaped. With Donald Woods, Marjorie Lord, and Elena Verdugo.

LOST WOMEN: See MESA OF LOST WOMEN.

THE LOST WORLD

1960 20th Century-Fox
PRODUCER/DIRECTOR: Irwin Allen
SCREENWRITERS: Irwin Allen, Charles Bennett

Arthur Conan Doyle's tale of a lost plateau discovered by stubborn old Professor Challenger. The 1925 version used stop-motion animation and includes scenes of a brontosaurus wrecking London. This one uses pet-store lizards with phony fins and never leaves the prehistoric world. In one of his last roles, Claude Rains is the professor whose expedition includes Michael Rennie, Jill St. John, David Hedison, Fernando Lamas, and Richard Haydn. Allen was obviously inspired by the previous year's similar hit, *Journey to the Center of the Earth*. Scenes of Hedison and a giant spider later turned up in Allen's *Voyage to the Bottom of the Sea* TV series.

THE LOST WORLD OF SINBAD

1964 Toho/AIP (Japan)
PRODUCER: Yuko Tanaka
DIRECTOR: Senkichi Tangiguchi
SCREENWRITER: Takeshi Kimura
ORIGINALLY RELEASED AS: *Daitozoku*
ALSO RELEASED AS: *Samurai Pirate*

As Luzon, a wealthy 16th-century Japanese citizen wrongly condemned to death for piracy, Toshiro Mifune escapes and seeks revenge. He saves the rulers of an island from real pirates and from a witch who changes into a flying insect and can turn people into stone. In the dubbed American version Mifune becomes the more familiar "Sinbad." With Mie Hama. From the makers of *Godzilla*.

LOUISA

1950 Universal (B&W)
PRODUCER: Robert Arthur
DIRECTOR: Alexander Hall
SCREENWRITER: Stanley Roberts

Remember the TV show *December Bride* (1954–59)? It was based on this movie featuring Ronald Reagan. He was billed after stars Spring Byington, Charles Coburn, and Edmund Gwenn. A romantic comedy, also with Piper (*Carrie*) Laurie (in her film debut as Ron's daughter) and Ruth Hussey. By the director of *Here Comes Mr. Jordan*.

LOUISIANA HUSSY

1960 Howco (B&W)
PRODUCER: Charles M. Casinelli
DIRECTOR: Lee Sholem
SCREENWRITER: Charles Lang

Dangerous Cajun beauty ruins every life she touches, breaking up families and eventually causing the suicide of a young bride. Starring Nan Peterson, with Robert Richards, Peter Coe of *Okefenokee*, Harry Lauter, and Betty Lynn (Barney Fife's girl Thelma Lou on *The Andy Griffith Show*). Howco also made *Girl with an Itch* and *My World Dies Screaming*. —CB

LOVE AT FIRST BITE

1979 AIP
PRODUCER: Joel Freeman
DIRECTOR: Stan Dragoti
SCREENWRITER: Robert Kaufman

A comic vampire movie for *Love Boat* fans. George Hamilton is the out-of-place Dracula in modern Manhattan. Arte Johnson does his Dwight Frye imitations. Susan Saint James is the fashion model who wakes up with "a dynamite hickey." Richard Benjamin is her psychiatrist lover and Dick Shawn is a cop. A scene at a Harlem funeral home with Sherman Hemsley seems really out of joint. Do you want to see Dracula disco dancing? The music includes "I Love the Nightlife" by Evelyn Champagne King. *Love at Second Bite* is the announced sequel. Scriptwriter Kaufman did other films for AIP, including *Dr. Goldfoot*. Director Dragoti (married to Cheryl Tiegs at the time) was busted for cocaine possession in Europe on the way to Cannes to promote *Love at First Bite*. He's also known for directing the "I Love New York" television spots.

LOVE BUTCHER

1975 Mirror
PRODUCERS: Gary Williams, Mickey Belski
DIRECTORS: Mikel Angel, Don Jones
SCREENWRITERS: Don Jones, James Evergreen
An extremely ridiculous psycho movie about Caleb, a balding, crippled gardener constantly mistreated by his female suburban Los Angeles employers. Whenever he's insulted or dismissed, he returns as his handsome, virile alter-ego "brother" Lester, who seduces and then kills the offenders. Eric Stern is great in both roles. Despite the title, the film is very tame by today's standards. The dialogue is often priceless and at one point Caleb shows up disguised as a Puerto Rican door-to-door record salesman! **(R)**

THE LOVE-INS

1967 Columbia
PRODUCER: Sam Katzman
DIRECTOR: Arthur Dreifuss
SCREENWRITERS: Hal Collins, Arthur Dreifuss
Amusing hippie/drug movie with Richard Todd as a Timothy Leary–type ex-professor who becomes a self-centered idol, wearing robes and advocating LSD. After he gets Susan Oliver pregnant, then rejects her, James MacArthur (as her ex-boyfriend and an underground newspaper publisher) assassinates the new messiah at a rally in a stadium! Oliver has a hilarious trip, imagining she's the star of *Alice in Wonderland*. And at one point Todd goes on the Joe Pyne show (Pyne plays himself). With Mark Goddard, the Chocolate Watchband, and the New Age. It was banned in England.

LOVE ME DEADLY

1972 Cinema National
PRODUCER: Buck Edwards
DIRECTOR/SCREENWRITER: Jacques Lacerte
A psychological horror film about a woman (Mary Wilcox) who loves corpses and a homosexual mortuary-attendant killer. Ther hero is Lyle Waggoner of the *Wonder Woman* series and *The Carol Burnett Show*.

LOVE ME TENDER

1956 20th Century-Fox (B&W)
PRODUCER: David Weisbart
DIRECTOR: Robert D. Webb
SCREENWRITER: Robert Buckner

Elvis Presley (then 21) was third-billed in his first feature, a Civil War story about four brothers. Richard Egan, William Campbell, and James Drury, all Confederate soldiers, rob a Federal payroll at the end of the war. Elvis, the youngest, stays home, sings four songs, and steals Debra Paget from missing big brother Egan. The original title was "The Reno Brothers," but it was wisely changed. With Neville Brand and Bruce Bennett. It was the first feature to recoup its entire cost in the first three days of release. Producer David Weisbart also brought us *Rebel Without a Cause*.

LOVE-SLAVES OF THE AMAZON
1957 Universal
PRODUCER/DIRECTOR/SCREENWRITER: Curt Siodmak

A tribe of female warriors captures some confused modern men. From the director of *Bride of the Gorilla*. With Eduardo Cianelli, Don Taylor, and Gianna Segale.

LOVE TRAP: See THE CURSE OF THE BLACK WIDOW.

THE LOVE WAR
1970 TV
PRODUCER: Aaron Spelling
DIRECTOR: George McGowan
SCREENWRITERS: Guerdon Trueblood, David Kidd

The first TV-movie with aliens. Big deal. Creatures from warring planets take human form on Earth. Lloyd Bridges is Kyle, an Argonian soldier who falls in love with Angie Dickinson, who is actually a Zinan spy!

LOVERS IN LIMBO: See THE NAME OF THE GAME IS KILL!

THE LOVES OF EDGAR ALLAN POE
1942 20th Century-Fox (B&W)
PRODUCER: Bryan Foy
DIRECTOR: Harry Lachman
SCREENWRITERS: Samuel Hoffenstein, Tom Reed

"He lived dramatically and loved intensely!" according to the ads. John Shepperd, who later changed his name to Shepperd Strudwick and acted in favorites like *The Monitors* and *Psychomania*, is Poe. Linda Darnell, Virginia Gilmore, and Jane Darwell influence his work.

THE LOVES OF HERCULES

1960 (Italy/France)
DIRECTOR: Carlo Ludonico Bragaglia
SCREENWRITER: Continenza, Doria
ALSO RELEASED AS: *Hercules vs. Hydra*

Jayne Mansfield in two roles, and her strongman husband Mickey Hargitay as Hercules! Mickey saves Jayne as a queen (with a black wig) by throwing axes at her bindings while she's tied spread-eagled to two trees. They fall in love.

An evil amazon queen has herself turned into Jayne (with a red wig) to fool lovesick Mickey. The dubbing, done in England, adds to the hilarity. So does a giant three-headed dragon floundering in a cave while Mickey decapitates it. The amazing scene was also used in *The Wild Wild World of Jayne Mansfield*. With a cyclops and incredible talking trees. Funnier than *The Three Stooges Meet Hercules*.

THE LOVING TOUCH: See PSYCHO LOVER.

LOVING YOU

1957 Paramount
PRODUCER: Hal Wallis
DIRECTOR: Hal Kanter
SCREENWRITERS: Herbert Baker, Hal Kanter

Elvis at his best, top-billed for the first time. As Deke Rivers, a truck driver, he's persuaded by press agent Lizabeth Scott to join the band of her ex-husband Wendell Corey as a singer. Elvis' wild rock singing and Scott's publicity stunts soon overshadow the Country-swing band. After some great concerts, fights, and misunderstandings, Elvis gets a TV contract and band singer Dolores Hart for a girlfriend. Elvis sings the hit theme song, "Let Me Be Your Teddy Bear," "Mean Woman Blues," "Let's Have a Party," and others. In VistaVision.

THE LUCIFER PROJECT: See BARRACUDA.

LURED

1947 Universal (B&W)
PRODUCER: Hunt Stromberg
DIRECTOR: Douglas Sirk
SCREENWRITER: Leo Rosten

As an American dance-hall hostess in London, Lucille Ball is used as bait by Scotland Yard to catch a murdering kidnaper of women. Suspects include fiancé George Sanders, fiancé's partner Sir

UPI 4/11/57: Elvis Presley, right, is engaged in some new and fancy gyrations here as he gets into a barroom fight with actor Ken Becker during a shooting of Hal Wallis' production Loving You.

Cedric Hardwicke, George Zucco, and crazed dress designer Boris Karloff. Erich von Stroheim played the Karloff role in the original 1929 French version, *Pièges*.

LUST FOR A VAMPIRE

1971 Hammer/Continental (England)
PRODUCERS: Harry Fine, Michael Style
DIRECTOR: Jimmy Sangster
SCREENWRITER: Tudor Gates
ALSO RELEASED AS: *To Love a Vampire*

In the sequel to *The Vampire Lovers*, blond Yvette Stensgaard is Mircalla, the lesbian vampire busy in an all-girl boarding school. Ralph Bates is a professor who offers to help. Mike Raven is Count Karnstein. Somebody sings a song called "Strange Love" as Mircalla seduces and vampirizes Michael Johnson in one of the sillier scenes. With Suzanna Leigh and Pippa Steel. It had to be cut to get an R rating. **(R)**

LUST OF THE VAMPIRES: See *THE DEVIL'S COMMANDMENT.*

LYCANTHROPUS: See *WEREWOLF IN A GIRL'S DORMITORY.*

M

1931 Paramount (Germany) (B&W)
PRODUCER: Seymour Nebenzal
DIRECTOR: Fritz Lang
SCREENWRITERS: Fritz Lang, Thea von Harbov

Peter Lorre (who was born Laszlo Löwenstein in Hungary) was acting in plays in Berlin when Lang cast him as the vampire of Düsseldorf, a child killer based on a real person, in this timeless film. Lorre's incomparable performance and Lang's innovative use of sound (it was his first talkie) made M an international classic. Lorre whistles "The Hall of the Mountain King" before committing the horrible crimes he later can't remember. It takes criminals (and the city's beggars) to catch him and take him to an old building for a "trial." A few years later Lorre (and Lang) fled Nazi Germany; both ended up in America. Lorre was the favorite actor of Goebbels.

M

1951 Columbia (B&W)
PRODUCER: Seymour Nebenzal
DIRECTOR: Joseph Losey
SCREENWRITERS: Norman Reilly Raine,
Leo Katcher

An almost exact remake of the Lang film produced by the same man. David Wayne stars as a flute-playing Los Angeles child murderer who collects children's shoes. Howard Da Silva is the inspector. With Steve Brodie and Raymond Burr. A grim film by Losey, who moved to England the next year after he was accused of being a Communist. M was banned in Ohio.

MA BARKER'S KILLER BROOD

1960 Filmservice (B&W)
PRODUCER: William J. Faris
DIRECTOR: Bill Karn
SCREENWRITER: F. Paul Hall

From dust-bowl days in Oklahoma to an opulent Florida hideout under siege, Lurene Tuttle leads her sons astray while maintaining a consultation sideline for the likes of Dillinger, Karpis, Baby Face Nelson, and Machine Gun Kelly. The cast includes Tris Coffin, Paul Dubov, Myrna Dell, Nelson Leigh, Vic Lundin, and Don Grady of My *Three Sons*. —CB

MACABRA: See DEMONOID.

MACABRE

1958 Allied Artists (B&W)
PRODUCER/DIRECTOR: William Castle
SCREENWRITER: Robb White

After 15 years of directing forgotten B-films William Castle made his first

NO. 1 FEMALE GANGSTER OF ALL TIME!

she taught and trained her four sons to be criminals!

TRUE! AUTHENTIC!

"MA BARKER's KILLER BROOD"

STARRING **LURENE TUTTLE** (as MA BARKER)

Charles Bronson stars in Roger Corman's Machine Gun Kelly.

horror movie and never looked back. He also started his series of gimmicks— "We insure you for $1,000 against death by fright!" It's a pretty dark plot about an attempt to scare a disgraced small-town doctor (William Prince) to death by convincing him that his little girl has been buried alive. Sort of like *Peyton Place* set in a graveyard. The script was based on *The Marble Forest*, a novel written by 13 people using a pseudonym. With Jim Backus, Ellen Corby, and Christine White.

MACBETH
1971 Columbia (U.S./England)
PRODUCER: Andrew Braunsberg
DIRECTOR: Roman Polanski
SCREENWRITERS: Roman Polanski, Kenneth Tynan

Playboy magazine financed this great version of Shakespeare's darkest work.

It was Polanski's first project after Sharon Tate was killed. Jon Finch plays the title role and Francesca Annis is Lady Macbeth. With music by the Third Ear Band and the screen's first convincing decapitation scene. **(R)**

MACHINE GUN KELLY
1958 AIP (B&W)
PRODUCER/DIRECTOR: Roger Corman

From the ads: "Without his gun he was naked yellow!" In one of Corman's most respected movies, Charles Bronson has his first starring role as the famous bank robber, seldom without his Thompson machine gun. The story opens with great jazzy music and a murder shown in shadows and ends with Kelly giving himself up to police after a botched kidnaping. As his moll, Susan Cabot is the driving force behind his exploits. He has an exaggerated fear of death and death symbols. The sight of a coffin makes him freeze during a bank job, causing Morey Amsterdam to lose his arm. Barboura Morris is a nurse kidnaped along with a little girl. Frank De Kova is a gas station owner who threatens Kelly with his caged wildcat. With Jack Lambert and Wally Campo. Corman followed this with *I, Mobster*.

MACISTE AGAINST HERCULES IN THE VALE OF WOE: See *HERCULES IN THE VALE OF WOE.*

MACUMBA LOVE
1960 United Artists
PRODUCER/DIRECTOR: Douglas Fowley
SCREENWRITER: Norman Graham
"Blood lust of the voodoo queen!" A steamy cheap voodoo movie made by actor-turned-director Douglas Fowley in Brazil. Serial actor Walter Reed shares billing with Ziva Rodann and June Wilkinson, a popular rival of Mamie Van Doren known for her *Playboy* shots. "In flaming Eastman color." Music by Simonetti.

MAD AT THE WORLD
1955 Filmakers (B&W)
DIRECTOR/SCREENWRITER: Harry Essex
The ads promised: "Trigger-happy teeners living for kicks!" And: "A true story of teenage wolfpacks on the prowl!" A sadistic joyride attack by young hoodlums leaves Keefe Brasselle's infant son fighting for life after being hit by a flying whiskey bottle. When Frank Lovejoy and assistant Paul Bryar are unable to come through with solid leads, the enraged parent investigates on his own. As he fishes for information, he is recognized and is on the verge of being eliminated by Paul Dubov, Stanley Clements, James Delgado, and Joseph Turkel at a deserted lumber mill when the police catch up. Lovejoy captures the baddies, but the baby dies. Prologue by Senator Estes Kefauver. —CB

THE MAD BOMBER
1973 Cinemation
PRODUCER/DIRECTOR/SCREENWRITER: Bert I. Gordon
Chuck Connors is the mad bomber. Neville Brand is a mad rapist. Vince (*Ben Casey*) Edwards is an angry L.A. cop who has to catch the rapist in order to find the bomber. Connors walks around with bombs in shopping bags, wears wire-frame glasses, and has a big chip on his shoulder. He gives a perfor-

UPI 6/15/60: Giving Chicago its biggest kick since Mrs. O'Leary's cow, British beauty June Wilkinson launches her heavenly body into orbit next to the Buckingham Fountain in the Windy City. The 19-year-old brown-eyed blond, whose lucky numbers are 44-20-36, stars in the United Artists release, Macumba Love.

mance that must have led to his role in *Tourist Trap*. Brand stays home and watches porno footage of his wife for inspiration. Better than most Gordon films but with the usual laughs.

THE MAD BUTCHER

1972 Ellman (Italy)
PRODUCER: Harry Hope
DIRECTOR: John Zuru
SCREENWRITER: Charles Ross
ALSO RELEASED AS: *Meat is Meat, Strangler of Vienna*

"Sausage lovers, don't see this movie!" the ads warned. Victor Buono stars in a Sweeney Todd–type role in this seldom-seen horror film. With Brad Harris, Karen Field, and John Ireland. (**R**)

THE MAD DOCTOR

1940 Paramount (B&W)
PRODUCER: George Arthur
DIRECTOR: Tim Whelan
SCREENWRITER: Howard J. Green

Not a horror movie but an amusing modern-day Bluebeard story set in New York City. Basil Rathbone is the killer psychiatrist who, with his admiring sidekick Martin Koslek, is always one step ahead of the law. One character refers to psychiatrists as soul meddlers and mind-reading quacks. Basil fits the description perfectly. With Ralph Morgan, Ellen Drew, John Howard, and Vera Vague.

THE MAD DOCTOR OF BLOOD ISLAND

1969 Hemisphere (Philippines/U.S.)
PRODUCER: Eddie Romero
DIRECTORS: Geraldo De Leon, Eddie Romero
SCREENWRITER: Reuben Conway
ALSO RELEASED AS: *Tomb of Living Dead*

"In blood dripping color." Hero John Ashley goes to Blood Island and discovers that a friend's father has been turned into a horrible monster with green blood. (The chlorophyll creature created by Dr. Lorca (Ronald Remy) later returned in *Beast of Blood*.) When this awful film played in theaters with *Brides of Blood*, customers were given some "green blood" (water) during a special prologue and told to drink it as an aphrodisiac. Co-star Angelique Pettyjohn must have taken some. She later changed her name to Heaven St. John and starred in porno features like *Body Talk* and *Titillation*.

THE MAD DOCTOR OF MARKET STREET

1942 Universal (B&W)
PRODUCER: Paul Malvern
DIRECTOR: Joseph H. Lewis
SCREENWRITER: Al Martin

Ferociously violent - unexpectedly kind. Ruthless bandit or rebel hero? An outlaw's outlaw with a score to settle.

MAD DOG MORGAN

beaten, branded, brutalized, but never broken.

the **true story** of the legendary Mad Dog Morgan... a jolting chapter in history.

Peter Lorre and Francis Drake in Mad Love.

Lionel Atwill, as a discredited doctor who can revive the dead, goes to a tropical island and impresses the natives. Noble Johnson is the chief. A pretty ridiculous one-hour feature with comedy relief from Nat Pendleton. Also starring Una Merkel, Claire Dodd, and Ann Nagel.

MAD DOG MORGAN

1976 British Empire (Australia)
PRODUCER: Jeremy Thomas
DIRECTOR/SCREENWRITER: Phillippe Mora
Dennis Hopper stars as a famous 19th-century Australian outlaw aided by a young aborigine (David Gulpilil of *The Last Wave* and *Walkabout*). The story is similar to *Ned Kelly* with Mick Jagger. With supervillain Michael Pate. Director Mora later did *The Beast Within*.

THE MAD EXECUTIONERS

1963 Paramount (W. Germany) (B&W)
PRODUCER: Arthur Brauner
DIRECTOR: Edward Willeg
SCREENWRITER: Robert A. Stemmle
ORIGINALLY RELEASED AS: *Der Henker von London*

An Edgar Wallace mystery about a group of vigilante killers, a sex maniac who decapitates women, and a mad surgeon. Scotland Yard investigates. Maria Perschy stars with Hansjorg Felmy.

THE MAD GENIUS

1931 Warner Brothers (B&W)
DIRECTOR: Michael Curtiz
SCREENWRITERS: J. Grubb Alexander, Harvey Thew
A follow-up to *Svengali* ('31) with its star, John Barrymore, in a similar dominating role as a clubfooted dance teacher who raises a young boy to be the famous ballet star he could never be. He succeeds in keeping the boy dancer (Donald Cook) away from the dancing girl (Marian Marsh) he loves. A drug-addict ballet master kills Barrymore with an axe and his body is discovered draped over a giant stage-prop demon. Boris Karloff plays the boy's cruel father in a brief scene.

THE MAD GHOUL

1943 Universal (B&W)
ASSOCIATE PRODUCER: Ben Pivar
DIRECTOR: James P. Hogan
SCREENWRITERS: Brenda Weisberg, Paul Gangelin
Fun nonsense with a professor (George Zucco) turning nice guy David Bruce into a white-faced living-dead ghoul who robs fresh graves and kills for new hearts. The ghoul follows around his singing star fiancée (Evelyn Ankers), but she's now interested in Turhan Bey, her pianist. Police detective Robert Armstrong catches the ghoul by hiding in a casket. With Milburn Stone.

MAD LOVE

1935 MGM (B&W)
PRODUCER: John W. Considine, Jr.
DIRECTOR: Karl Freund
SCREENWRITERS: P. J. Wolfson, John L. Balderston

One of the all-time classic horror films. In his first American movie, Peter Lorre stars as Dr. Gogol, a brilliant surgeon who attends "Le Théâtre des Horreurs" and becomes obsessed by its star actress (Frances Drake). She loves her husband, the famous pianist Orlac (Colin Clive), and finds the bald doctor (who also likes to watch convicts go to the guillotine) repulsive. Gogol buys a wax figure of her and stares at it in a mirror while playing his pipe organ, pretending she's there. The horror starts when Orlac is hurt in an accident and Gogol grafts on to the pianist the hands of a recently executed knife thrower. He convinces Orlac that he's being driven to kill by the new hands and, in an amazing scene, the crazed doctor shows up as the dead, decapitated knife thrower, complete with elaborate neck brace and shiny metal hands. It was the last film directed by the famous cinematographer Freund, who later photographed the *I Love Lucy* show. *Mad Love* is essentially a remake of *The Hands of Orlac* (1925), which was filmed in Germany with Conrad Veidt. With Ted Healy (originally a partner of the Three Stooges) as a reporter, Keye Luke as Gogol's surgeon assistant, and Billy Gilbert.

Vincent Price as The Mad Magician.

THE MAD MAGICIAN

1954 Columbia (B&W with color sequence; 3-D)
PRODUCER: Brian Foy
DIRECTOR: John Brahm
SCREENWRITER: Crane Wilbur

A *House of Wax* imitation with Vincent Price as a 19th-century illusionist who cracks when his ideas and his wife (Eva Gabor) are stolen. He kills the villains by decapitating one with a buzz-saw trick and putting another in his famous crematorium. Vincent is a master of disguises, too. For a while he looks like a devil with little curled hair pieces for horns. With Patrick O'Neal, Jay Novello, Corey Allen, and Mary Murphy. The producer and screenwriter were also responsible for the much better *House of Wax*. *The Mad Magician* was a big L.A. television hit when shown in 3-D by horror hostess Elvira in 1982.

MAD MAX

1979 Filmways (Australia)
PRODUCER: Byron Kennedy
DIRECTORS: George Miller,
Mel Gibson
SCREENWRITERS: George Miller,
James McCausland

Called a cross between *A Clockwork Orange* and *Walking Tall*, this Aussie exploitation hit was dubbed so slow Americans could understand the dialogue. In the near future, a cop (21-year-old Mel Gibson of *Gallipoli*) quits the force and goes on a vengeance spree after his family is murdered by a motorcycle gang. Lots of car chases. At the time of its release, it was the biggest

New York-born Australian star Mel Gibson in Mad Max.

commercial success in Australian film history. *Mad Max II* was retitled *Road Warrior* and was an even bigger hit in '82. The sound track by Brian May is still available (R)

MAD MAX II: See THE ROAD WARRIOR.

THE MAD MONSTER

1942 PRC (B&W)
PRODUCER: Sigmund Neufeld
DIRECTOR: Sam Newfield
SCREENWRITER: Fred Myton
A pretty funny no-budget film inspired by Universal's *The Wolfman*. Crazy George Zucco turns big dumb farmhand Glenn Strange into a big hairy monster in overalls who kidnaps a little girl. Injections of wolf blood do the trick. With Anne Nagel and Mae Busch. Zucco controls his new instrument of revenge with a whip, à la Dr. Moreau.

MAD MONSTER PARTY

1969 Avco Embassy
PRODUCER: Arthur Rankin, Jr
DIRECTOR: Jules Bass
SCREENWRITERS: Ken Korobkin, Harvey Kurtzman

Boris Karloff provides the voice for Baron Boris Von Frankenstein in a stop-motion puppet comedy filmed in "animagic." Forrest J. Ackerman contributed to the screenplay, which includes a hunchback (with a Charles Laughton imitation voice), the invisible man (with a Claude Rains voice), a creature with a Peter Lorre voice, and just about every other famous monster of filmland. Phyllis Diller provides the voice for her puppet, Boris' ugly wife. Also with the voice of Gale Garnett.

THE MAD ROOM

1969 Columbia
PRODUCER: Norman Maurer
DIRECTOR: Bernard Girard
SCREENWRITERS: Bernard Girard, A. Z. Martin
A remake of *Ladies in Retirement* (1941). Stella Stevens is the companion of a wealthy widow (Shelley Winters). When her teenage brother and sister are released from an asylum they come to live in Shelley's mansion. They had been suspected of killing their parents. When Shelley finds out their past and tells them to leave she's found hacked to death. A dog walking around with one of her severed hands in its mouth leads to the horrible truth! Nazz with Todd Rundgren is heard on the sound track. Filmed in British Columbia. (M)

MADAME SIN

1972 TV (U.S./England)
PRODUCERS: Julian Wintle, Lou Morkeim
DIRECTOR: David Greene
SCREENWRITERS: David Greene, Barry Oringer
In her first TV-movie Bette Davis plays a female Fu Manchu type living in a Scottish castle. She kidnaps an ex-CIA man (executive producer Robert Wagner) in an effort to steal a Polaris sub. Bette has sonic guns, mind-controlling

drugs, and an elaborate lab. It was a pilot film shown theatrically in Europe and now available on videocassette. With Delholm Elliott, Catherine Schell, and Roy Kinnear. From the director of *The Shuttered Room*.

MADHOUSE
1974 Amicus/AIP (England)
PRODUCERS: Max J. Rosenberg,
  Milton Subotsky
DIRECTOR: Jim Clark
SCREENWRITER: Greg Morrison
Vincent Price stars as horror actor Paul Toombes, famous for playing "Dr. Death." After suffering a nervous breakdown he goes to England to do a TV series, and cast and crew members start dying the way characters did in Toombes' old movies. Peter Cushing plays his scriptwriter. Robert Quarry is the producer. This meeting of three horror stars is pretty lame. The highlights are provided by clips of Price in earlier AIP films. With Adrienne Corri and Linda Hayden.

MADMAN
1982 Jensen Farley
PRODUCERS: Gary Sales,
  Joe Giannone
DIRECTOR/SCREENWRITER: Joe Gianonne
An abandoned summer camp is reopened as a training center for counselors. Over a campfire, the group leader recounts the incident that brought the closing of the camp: a heavyset woodsman named Madman Marz keeps himself well-hidden, but should anyone call his name he comes out swinging the nearest available sharp object. Of course, one wise guy must defy the legend—he calls out for the madman, who stirs out of the trees to deliver bloody death to all the residents of the camp. Routine stuff with so-so effects; but unique in that *all* the sympathetic characters get wiped out. Only the wise

guy who started all the trouble remains intact at the conclusion of the film —and of course the madman, ready to emerge once again in case of a sequel. Filmed on Long Island. With *Dawn of the Dead* star Gaylen Ross. **(R)**   –BM

MADMEN OF MANDORAS: See THEY SAVED HITLER'S BRAIN.

THE MAFU CAGE: See MY SISTER MY LOVE.

MAGIC
1978 20th Century-Fox
PRODUCERS: Joseph E. Levine,
  Richard P. Levine
DIRECTOR: Richard Attenborough
SCREENWRITER: William Goldman
An uneasy update of the old ventriloquist-taken-over-by-his-evil-dummy theme. Anthony Hopkins is a big success with his ugly foulmouthed dummy Fats. He goes to the Catskills to see his former love Ann Margret and kills her husband (Ed Lauter) and his agent (Burgess Meredith). It was a substantial hit and was nominated for Academy Awards. Big deal. **(R)**

THE MAGIC CARPET
1951 Columbia
PRODUCER: Sam Katzman
DIRECTOR: Lew Landers
SCREENWRITER: David Mathews
Lucille Ball and John Agar fly around on the title carpet and defeat evil Arab Raymond Burr. It was the end of this kind of nonsense for the 41-year-old Lucille Ball, who became a real star later in the year with *I Love Lucy*. Burr and Agar still had a few gorilla suits in their futures. With Patricia Medina and George Tobias.

THE MAGIC CHRISTIAN

1969 Commonwealth United (England)
PRODUCER: Denis O'Dell
DIRECTOR: Joseph McGrath
SCREENWRITERS: Joseph McGrath,
  Terry Southern, Peter Sellers

Peter Sellers and Ringo Starr star as Sir Guy Grand and his adopted son in this wild hit-and-miss satire based on Terry Southern's book. Sir Guy goes about proving how money corrupts all. Some of the guest-star bits are priceless. Highlights include: Raquel Welch as a galley slave driver with a whip; Laurence Harvey doing a striptease while performing Hamlet; Christopher Lee as a vampire running in slow motion; Yul Brynner in drag singing "Mad About the Boy" to a nervous Roman Polanski. With Richard Attenborough and Wilfrid Hyde-White. Graham Chapman and John Cleese from Monty Python appear and contributed to the screenplay. The excellent rock sound track is by Badfinger (who recorded for the Beatles' Apple label) and Thunderclap New-

man. The TV version usually omits the entire ending. (M)

THE MAGIC SERPENT

1966 Toei/AIP-TV (Japan)
DIRECTOR: Tetsuy Yamauchi
SCREENWRITER: Masaru Igami

A prince turns into a giant frog and battles a wizard who turns into a dragon in this nutty fantasy from Japan.

MAGIC SPECTACLES

1961 Fairway International
PRODUCER/SCREENWRITER: Arch Hall, Sr.
DIRECTOR: Bob Wehling
ALSO RELEASED AS: Tickled Pink

Hollywood advertising man uses title specs to see through women's clothes. Tommy Holden stars, with June Parr. Kay Cramer, Cindy Tyler, Danice Daniels, Jean Cartwright, and Carla Olson are the "go-go go-go" girls. –CB

THE MAGIC SWORD

1962 United Artists
PRODUCER/DIRECTOR: Bert I. Gordon
SCREENWRITER: Bernard Schoenfeld

This Bert I. Gordon sword-and-sorcery epic provides a great time for kids. If you're a bit older you can enjoy other aspects of the film, such as the oddball cast including Maila "Vampira" Nurmi as a hag, Richard Kiel as a giant pinhead, and Angelo Rossitto as a dwarf (surprise). Basil Rathbone is the evil magician Lodac who kidnaps a princess (Anne Helm) and devises seven challenges for her would-be rescuer Saint George (Gary Lockwood). With tiny people, Siamese twins, an unconvincing two-headed dragon, and a giant ogre among the director's special effects, and Estelle Winwood as the witch Sybil. It was the most action-packed fantasy since The Seventh Voyage of Sinbad and Bert's best.

THE MAGIC VOYAGE OF SINBAD

1952 Filmgroup, (U.S.S.R.)
PRODUCER: Art Diamond
DIRECTORS: Alexander Ptushko,
James Landis
SCREENWRITERS: Karl Isar,
Francis Ford Coppola
ORIGINALLY RELEASED AS: *Sadko*

No Sinbad here. This colorful Russian fantasy epic was released here in '61 with a new title and anglicized cast names—what kind of parents would send their kids to a commie film? It's really pretty impressive. The bearded hero from ancient Novgorod searches the world for the bird of happiness. The only real low point is a silly-looking octopus. Based on Rimski-Korsakov's opera. With Sergei Stolyarov and Anna Larionova.

THE MAGNETIC MONSTER

1953 United Artists (B&W)
PRODUCER: Ivan Tors
DIRECTOR: Curt Siodmak
SCREENWRITERS: Ivan Tors,
Curt Siodmak

The ads blared: "Cosmic Frankenstein terrorizes Earth!" An isotope grows while absorbing energy and giving off radiation. Similar to an idea used in an *Outer Limits* episode. The sequence with the giant cyclotron is from a 1934 German film, *Gold*. With Richard Carlson working for the Office of Scientific Investigation, King Donovan, Kathlene Freeman, and Strother Martin.

MAJIN, MONSTER OF TERROR

1966 Daiei/AIP-TV (Japan)
PRODUCER: Masaichi Nagata
DIRECTOR: Kimiyoshi Yasuda
SCREENWRITER: Teteuo Yoshida
ORIGINALLY RELEASED AS: *Daimasin*
ALSO RELEASED AS: *Majin, The Hideous Idol*

Transporting atomic materials in The Magnetic Monster.

A superior Japanese fantasy about a giant stone statue god that comes to life and helps a prince and princess regain their throne. Majin, the vengeful warrior, causes an earthquake and kills a cruel warlord. He turns into a statue again, but was back for more action in *The Return of Majin*.

MAJIN STRIKES AGAIN

1966 Daiei/AIP-TV (Japan)
PRODUCER: Masaichi Nagata
DIRECTORS: Issei Mori, Yoshiyuki
SCREENWRITER: Teteuo Yoshida

Majin, the stone idol, comes to life for the third and final time to right some wrongs.

MAJIN, THE HIDEOUS IDOL: See *MAJIN, MONSTER OF TERROR*.

MAKO: THE JAWS OF DEATH

1976 Selected
PRODUCER/DIRECTOR: William Grefe
ALSO RELEASED AS: *The Jaws of Death*

Shark exploitation gets Richard Jaeckel mad. When he tries to make a living by renting his finny friends out to a research facility and a roadhouse, the lessees betray him. See a beautiful woman locked in a ballet of death in a behind-the-bar aquarium showcase. As with *Stanley*, a pretty cheap shot. The co-stars are Jennifer Bishop, Harold "Odd Job" Sakata, Luke Nalperin (*Flipper*), John Davis Chandler (*The Hooked Generation*) and Buffy Dee. Producer/director Grefe went on to second unit direction of James Bond Films.   –CB

MALATESTA'S CARNIVAL

1973 Windmill Films
PRODUCERS: Richard Grosser,
    Walker Stuart
DIRECTOR/SCREENWRITER: Christopher Speeth

Pretty obscure gore horror comedy featuring Herve Villechaize (*Fantasy Island*). In one scene monsters and ghouls eat people while watching old horror movies on TV. The sound track was designed to produce terror psychologically! Somebody at *The Monster Times* liked it a lot.

MALENKA, THE VAMPIRE

1968 Europix (Spain/Italy)
PRODUCERS: Aubrey Ambert,
    Rossana Yani
DIRECTOR/SCREENWRITER: Armando De Ossorio
ORIGINALLY RELEASED AS: *La Nipote del Vampiro*
ALSO RELEASED AS: *Fangs of the Living Dead*

Anita Ekberg is terrorized by the niece of a woman who was burned as a witch at the castle of Count Wolduck. It was released here as part of the *Orgy of the Living Dead* show. With Rossana Yanni and Diana Lorys.

THE MALTESE BIPPY

1969 MGM
PRODUCERS: Everett Freeman, Robert Enders
DIRECTOR: Norman Panama
SCREENWRITERS: Everett Freeman, Ray Singer

Rowan and Martin's Laugh In was the talk of America's TV-watching population when this derivative mystery-comedy was released. It's a G-rated film about a New York nudie-movie producer (Dan Rowan) and his star (Dick Martin). They go to an old house on Long Island. Martin turns into a werewolf. Julie Newmar turns into an Afghan. Lots of people are murdered. Several different endings are offered. With Carol Lynley and Fritz Weaver. It was not a hit. "What's a bippy?"

THE MALTESE FALCON

1931 Warner Brothers (B&W)
DIRECTOR: Roy Del Ruth
SCREENWRITERS: Maude Fulton,
    Lucien Hubbard, Brown Holmes
ALSO RELEASED AS: *Dangerous Female*

It's amazing to see how closely the popular 1941 version follows this first attempt to film Dashiell Hammett's novel. Of course the cast makes a big difference. Ricardo Cortez is Sam Spade. Bebe Daniels is Brigid. Dudley Digges, Otto Matiesen, and Dwight Frye have the roles immortalized by Greenstreet, Lorre, and Cook. It's interesting to see Frye (who was Renfield in *Dracula* the same year) as Wilmer.

THE MALTESE FALCON

1941 Warner Brothers (B&W)
PRODUCER: Henry Blanke
DIRECTOR/SCREENWRITER: John Huston

It started as just another Warners remake: Dashiell Hammett's novel had been filmed in 1931 and again in 1936 (as *Satan Met a Lady*). Nobody expected Huston's first movie as a director to become an instant (and perennial) hit. George Raft turned down the leading role of Sam Spade. It was taken by Bogart, of course, and Mary Astor plays Brigid. It launched the screen career of 61-year-old Sidney Greenstreet (as Gutman) who continued to be paired with Peter Lorre in *Three Strangers*, *The Mask of Dimitrios*, and so on. As the frizzy-haired Joel Cairo, Lorre hands out perfumed calling cards and gets roughed up by Bogart. As Wilmer, Elisha Cook, Jr., completes the odd gang. With Gladys George, Ward Bond, Barton Maclane, Jerome Cowan (as Miles Archer), Walter Huston (he delivers the falcon), and Lee Patrick.

MAMA DRACULA

1980 Limelight Int. (France/Belgium)
PRODUCER/DIRECTOR: Boris Szulzinger
SCREENWRITERS: Boris Szulzinger,
Pierre Sterckx, Marc-Henri Wajnberg

Louise Fletcher (*One Flew Over the Cuckoo's Nest*) stars in a comedy version of the Countess Elizabeth Bathory legend. That means funny scenes of an aging woman killing young virgins and bathing in their blood. By the director of *Shame of the Jungle*, an X-rated cartoon. With Maria Schneider (*Last Tango in Paris*) and the Wajnberg Brothers (twins).

THE MAN AND THE MONSTER

1958 Distributor K. Gordon Murray
(Mexico) (B&W)
PRODUCER: Abel Salazar
DIRECTOR: Rafael Baledon
SCREENWRITER: Alfredo Salazar
ORIGINALLY RELEASED AS: *El Hombre y el Monstruo*

A concert pianist sells his soul to the Devil. Every time a certain classical piece ("Hooked on Classics"?) is played he turns into an ugly snarling hairy monster with long pointy fangs and kills people! With Abel Salazar.

MAN BEAST

1955 Favorite (B&W)
PRODUCER/DIRECTOR: Jerry Warren
SCREENWRITER: Arthur Cassidy
From the ads: "See: women stalked and captured for breeding by Yeti monsters!" And: "Bestial monster madness," with explorers in the Himalayas encounter-ing a hairy white beast. Starring the great Rock Madison. With Virginia Maynor. From the director of *Invasion of the Animal People.* You might have seen *Man Beast* billed with *Godzilla.* Some scenes were apparently shot in Mexico.

A MAN CALLED DAGGER

1967 MGM
PRODUCER: Lewis M. Horowitz
DIRECTOR: Richard Rush
SCREENWRITERS: James Peatman,
Robert S. Weekley

Absurd spy spoof with Jan Murray as Rudolph Koffman, a former concentration-camp commandant now using a meat-packing plant as a front to conquer the world. Paul Mantee (who can't act, either) is secret agent Dick Dagger, with a laser-beam wristwatch and girlfriend/fellow agent Terry Moore. Sue Ann Langdon plays Ingrid, Murray's mistress and partner in torture. The stellar cast is rounded out by Bruno Ve Sota and Richard Kiel. Music by Steve Allen. Cinematography by Laszlo Kovacs.

MAN CRAZY

1953 20th Century-Fox (B&W)
PRODUCERS/SCREENWRITERS:
Sidney Harmon, Philip Yordan
DIRECTOR: Irving Lerner
"It dares to tell the truth!" the ads claimed. Three teenaged girls who spend most of their time at a small-town drugstore find $28,000. Christine White, Irene Anders, and Coleen Miller (products of uncaring parents and broken homes) set out for the big time in Hollywood and burn their fingers instead. With Neville Brand.   —CB

MAN EATER OF HYDRA: See ISLAND OF THE DOOMED.

MAN FROM ATLANTIS

1977 TV
PRODUCER: Robert M. Justman
DIRECTOR: Lee H. Katzin
SCREENWRITER: Mayo Simon

The first pilot for the short-lived series starring Patrick Duffy (Bobby on *Dallas*) as the Aquaman-like swimming hero with gills. Belinda Montgomery helps him fight bad guys led by Victor Buono. A flop here, it was a big hit as one of the first American TV shows allowed in China. Directed by the man who made *The Phynx*. Several features were put together from re-edited episodes.

THE MAN FROM PLANET X

1951 United Artists (B&W)
PRODUCERS/SCREENWRITERS:
Aubrey Wisberg, Jack Pollexfen
DIRECTOR: Edgar G. Ulmer

This little science-fiction favorite, along with *The Thing* and *The Day the Earth Stood Still*, was one of the first serious movies to feature visiting aliens. Here the extraterrestrial is a short being with a haunting, immobile white face with slit eyes and a speaker-translator on his chest. When his spaceship lands on the misty moors of Scotland, a scientist captures him and tries to force him to tell all. The friendly being reacts by turning on a mind-control ray. Robert Clarke stars with Margaret Field and William Schallert. It was shot in six days. Director Ulmer was a busy man who directed low-budget films of every description in German, English, Yiddish, Ukrainian, and Italian. In the silent era he worked with Lang and Murnau. This is one of his best.

THE MAN IN HALF-MOON STREET

1943 Paramount (B&W)
PRODUCER: Walter MacEwen
DIRECTOR: Ralph M. Murphy
SCREENWRITER: Charles Kenyon

Nils Asther as a 120-year-old scientist looks 35 because of gland transplants. This love story/horror movie based on a play by Barré Lydon was remade as *The Man Who Could Cheat Death*. With Helen Walker, Brandon Hurst, and Reinhold Schuentzel.

THE MAN IN OUTER SPACE

1961 AIP-TV (Czechoslovakia) (B&W)
PRODUCER: Rudolph Wolf
DIRECTOR: Oldrich Lipsky
SCREENWRITERS: Oldrich Lipsky,
Zdenek Blaka
ORIGINALLY RELEASED AS: *Muzz Pryniho Stoleti*

A totally foreign science-fiction comedy about a 20th-century upholsterer (Milos Kopecky) who accidentally blasts himself into space. After being examined by aliens he returns to 25th-century Earth (with an invisible man). The dubbing has made this satire of technology and capitalism a bit hard to follow. By the director of *Lemonade Joe*.

MAN IN THE ATTIC

1953 20th Century-Fox (B&W)
PRODUCER: Robert L. Jacks
DIRECTOR: Hugo Fregonese
SCREENWRITERS: Robert Presnell, Jr.,
Barré Lydon

Jack Palance is Jack the Ripper (a role he was born to play) in a remake of *The Lodger*. Constance Smith is his can-can-dancer girlfriend. With Frances Bavier (Aunt Bee on *The Andy Griffith Show!*) and Rhys Williams.

MAN IN THE DARK

1953 Columbia (B&W, 3-D)
PRODUCER: Wallace MacDonald
DIRECTOR: Lew Landers
SCREENWRITERS: George Bricker,
Jack Leonard

The first major-studio 3-D film, a remake of *The Man Who Lived Twice*, was shot in 11 days and beat *The House of Wax* to the nation's screens. Edmond O'Brien is the criminal whose face is altered along with his memory. Lots of objects are hurled at the audience and there's a wild roller-coaster ride. With Audrey Totter, Ted De Corsia, and Horace McMahon. Original prints are tinted sepia.

MAN IN THE IRON MASK

1939 United Artists (B&W)
PRODUCER/DIRECTOR: James Whale
SCREENWRITER: George Bruce

Famous horror director Whale puts his mark of quality on this version of the Dumas classic. Louis Hayward stars as twin brothers. One is imprisoned in the iron mask and returns for revenge. With Warren William, Alan Hale, Joan Bennett, Dwight Frye, sword fights, torture chambers, and Peter Cushing making his film debut.

MAN IN THE MOON

1961 Trans-Lux (England) (B&W)
PRODUCER: Michael Relph
DIRECTOR: Basil Dearden
SCREENWRITERS: Michael Relph,
Bryan Forbes

Kenneth More, a professional guinea pig, is chosen as the first British astronaut. He's sent to the Moon but lands in Australia instead. A comedy with Shirley Ann Field and Charles Gray.

MAN MADE MONSTER

1941 Universal (B&W)
ASSOCIATE PRODUCER: Jack Bernhard
DIRECTOR: George Waggner
SCREENWRITER: Joseph West
ALSO RELEASED AS: *The Atomic Monster*

Lon Chaney, Jr., stars as Dynamo Dan the Electric Man, a circus performer who falls into the hands of mad doctor Lionel Atwill. The friendly man who can absorb electricity is transformed into a white-faced zombielike killer in a bulky rubber suit. Lon is sent to the electric chair but he survives, kills the warden, and escapes in time to rescue

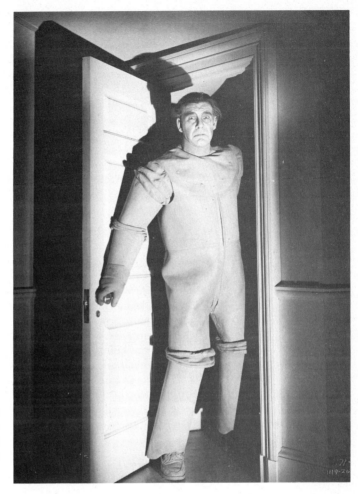

Anne Nagel from the crazed Atwill. A classic of its kind.

The Man Made Monster (Lon Chaney) in his rubber suit.

THE MAN OF A THOUSAND FACES

1957 Universal (B&W)
PRODUCER: Robert Arthur
DIRECTOR: Joseph Pevney
SCREENWRITERS: Ivan Goff,
R. Wright Campbell, Ben Roberts

This story of master makeup artist and actor Lon Chaney is, like all Hollywood biopics, full of fiction. James Cagney (who doesn't look anything like Chaney) gets to appear as the Hunchback and the Phantom in an entertaining portrayal of the perfectionistic actor. Raised by deaf-mute parents, he makes a career out of playing grotesque, deformed people and has marriage problems. With Dorothy Malone, Jane Greer, Jim Backus, Celia Lousky, Roger Smith as Lon Chaney, Jr., and Robert Evans, later more famous as a producer and studio head, as producer/studio head Irving G. Thalberg. A sound track album has been recently released.

MAN ON A SWING
1974 Paramount
PRODUCER: Howard B. Jaffe
DIRECTOR: Frank Perry
SCREENWRITER: David Zelag Goodman
Joel Grey is a clairvoyant who offers to help police track down a rapist/killer. Police inspector Cliff Robertson thinks that Grey is the killer. A little-known film directed by Frank Perry (*Play It As It Lays*, *Rancho Deluxe*) whose films are usually uniquely puzzling. This one got great reviews in some fairly obscure publications.

THE MAN THEY COULD NOT HANG
1939 Columbia (B&W)
PRODUCER: Wallace MacDonald
DIRECTOR: Nick Grinde
SCREENWRITER: Karl Brown
Kindly scientist Boris Karloff is executed by the state for his artificial-heart-transplant experiments. After being brought back to life by assistant Byron Foulger, Boris traps the judge and jury that condemned him in his specially rigged mansion and kills them one by one. One of many similar Karloff films. With Lorna Gray (as his daughter), Robert Wilcox, Roger Pryor, and Ann Doran.

THE MAN WHO CHANGED HIS MIND: See THE MAN WHO LIVED AGAIN.

THE MAN WHO COULD CHEAT DEATH
1959 Hammer/Paramount (England)
PRODUCER: Michael Carreras
DIRECTOR: Terence Fisher
SCREENWRITER: Jimmy Sangster
A good remake of *The Man in Half Moon Street* starring Anton Diffring as the eternally young man who needs gland transplants every few years. Christopher Lee is a doctor friend. With Hazel Court.

THE MAN WHO COULD WORK MIRACLES
1937 United Artists (England) (B&W)
PRODUCER: Alexander Korda
DIRECTOR: Lothar Mendes
SCREENWRITER: H.G. Wells
H.G. Wells himself wrote the script for this great fantasy comedy starring Roland Young as a meek clerk given unlimited powers by the gods. It starts out small-scale and whimsical and ends with incredible scenes showing what happens when Young stops Earth from rotating. It has great special effects, a strong antiwar theme, and an impressive British cast including Ralph Richardson, Ernest Thesiger, George Zucco, Torin Thatcher, Joan Gardner, and George Sanders playing a god in his first screen role. Richard Pryor is set to star in a remake.

THE MAN WHO FELL TO EARTH
1976 Cinema 5
PRODUCER: Deeley Spikings
DIRECTOR: Nicholas Roeg
SCREENWRITER: Paul Mayersberg
David Bowie stars as a cat-eyed bald alien in human disguise trying to return home to his desert planet and fam-

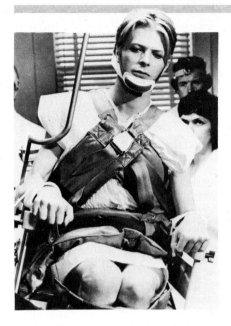

After an operation conservative British businessman Roger Moore is horrified to discover an extroverted exact duplicate of himself meddling in his affairs. With Hildegard Neil, Olga Georges-Picot, and Freddie Jones. It was Moore's last pre-Bond film. Based on an episode of the Alfred Hitchcock television show.

ily. With the help of a patent lawyer (Buck Henry) and a professor (Rip Torn) he makes untold millions marketing electronic inventions. His girlfriend (Candy Clark) and the lawyer are bribed by the government, his return flight is stopped, and, after extensive painful tests, he becomes an alcoholic recluse trapped on Earth. David Bowie makes a great alien and this fascinating science-fiction film (which spans 25 years) will be revived in the future long after most of his derivative rock albums land in the cut-out bins. John Phillips was the musical director. Some of Bowie's songs for the film (they weren't used) turned up on *Low*, which has a shot from the film on the cover (so does *Station to Station*). With Claudia Jennings. (R)

THE MAN WHO HAUNTED HIMSELF

1971 Levitt/Pickman (England)
PRODUCER: Michael Relph
DIRECTOR: Basil Dearden
SCREENWRITERS: Michael Relph,
Basil Dearden

THE MAN WHO KNEW TOO MUCH

1934 Gaumont (England) (B&W)
PRODUCER: Michael Balcon
DIRECTOR: Alfred Hitchcock
SCREENWRITER: A.R. Rawlinson

Leslie Banks and Edna Best play a couple vacationing in Switzerland who learn of an anarchist assassination plot from a dying Frenchman. The anarchists kidnap their little girl to insure their silence. Peter Lorre, in his first English-language film, stands out as the chief kidnaper. He has a big scar above one eye and a streak of blond hair. A well-timed scream during a concert at the Albert Hall stops the assassination. The villains lose in a shootout with police. It was the only Hitchcock movie that the director chose to remake (in 1956, with James Stewart and Doris Day).

THE MAN WHO
LIVED AGAIN

1936 Gaumont (England) (B&W)
DIRECTOR: Robert Stevenson
SCREENWRITERS: L. Du Garde Peach,
Sidney Gilliat, John L. Balderston
ALSO RELEASED AS: *The Man Who Changed
His Mind; The Brain Snatcher; Dr. Maniac*
Scientist Boris Karloff is in love with
assistant Anna Lee, but she loves John
Loder. Boris' solution is to use his elec-
tronic brain-transfer apparatus on Lod-
er. He'll get himself a younger body and
the girl. Boris' plans go wrong some-
where. This seldom-shown film is said
to be one of Karloff's best.

THE MAN WHO
LIVED TWICE

1936 Columbia (B&W)
PRODUCER: Ben Pivar
DIRECTOR: Harry Lachman
SCREENWRITERS: Tom Van Dycke,
Fred Niblo, Jr., Arthur Strawn
A horribly scarred gangster (Ralph
Bellamy) emerges from an operation
with a handsome face and amnesia. The
"new" man becomes a famous doctor
but his forgotten past catches up with
him. With Marian Marsh, Thurston
Halland, and Ward Bond. Edmond
O'Brien starred in *Man in the Dark*,
a remake.

THE MAN WHO RECLAIMED
HIS HEAD

1935 Universal (B&W)
PRODUCER: Carl Laemmle, Jr.
DIRECTOR: Edward Ludwig
SCREENWRITERS: Jean Bart, Samuel Ornits
Claude Rains stars as a pacifist whose
wife (Joan Bennett) and peace plans
are stolen by warmonger/munitions
manufacturer Lionel Atwill. Rains
forgets his love of peace and decapi-
tates Atwill. With Wallace Ford and
Baby Jane. It was remade as *Strange
Confession.*

THE MAN WHO SAW
TOMORROW

1981 Warner Brothers
PRODUCERS: Robert Guenette, Lee Kramer,
Paul Drane
DIRECTOR: Robert Guenette
SCREENWRITERS: Robert Guenette, Alan
Hopgood
In 1979 Orson Welles narrated *The Late
Great Planet Earth.* He's back again
prophesying doom and destruction, this
time as envisioned by the 16th-century
French physician Nostradamus. Film
clips are mixed with dramatizations and
interviews in the Sunn Classic style
(cheap). Wars, assassinations, and dis-
coveries were correctly predicted, according to Orson. The future holds a
massive earthquake in May 1988 and a
nuclear attack on Manhattan (by Mos-
lems) in 1999. Seven years of destruction will follow. Plan accordingly.

THE MAN WHO
TURNED TO STONE

1957 Columbia (B&W)
PRODUCER: Sam Katzman
DIRECTOR: Leslie Kardos
SCREENWRITER: Raymond T. Marcus
Victor Jory leads a group of 200-year-
old scientists who have managed to stay
alive by putting women in a tub of
chemicals and sapping their energy
through wires attached to headbands.
Without the stolen female energy they
turn to stone. With Ann Doran, Charlotte Austin, and Paul Cavanaugh.

THE MAN WHO WANTED
TO LIVE FOREVER

1970 TV (Canada)
PRODUCER: Terence Dene
DIRECTOR: John Trent
SCREENWRITER: M. Denker
ALSO RELEASED AS: *The Only Way Out Is
Dead*

A heart surgeon (Stuart Whitman) discovers that billionaire Burl Ives is using his private medical-research center to steal body parts from young men in order to prolong his life. With Sandy Dennis. It was a theatrical release in Europe.

THE MAN WITH NINE LIVES

1940 Columbia (B&W)
DIRECTOR: Nick Grinde
SCREENWRITER: Karl Brown

Another good-scientist-gone-bad role for Boris Karloff. As bearded Dr. Kravaal, he attempts to cure cancer victims by freezing them in his Canadian ice cave by piling large ice chips on their bodies. After being thawed out himself, he is stopped by the local mounties from icing Roger Pryor and Jo Ann Sayers. With Byron Foulger.

THE MAN WITH THE GOLDEN GUN

1974 United Artists (England)
PRODUCERS: Albert R. Broccoli, Harry Saltzman
DIRECTOR: Guy Hamilton
SCREENWRITERS: Richard Maibaum, Tom Mankiewicz

Christopher Lee hits a career peak (in terms of budget only) as Scaramanga, the million-dollar-a-hit assassin with an extra nipple. Little Herve Villechaize practices for his role as Tattoo on *Fantasy Island* by playing Nick Nack. Britt Ekland is Mary Goodnight. Maud Adams is Scaramanga's mistress. In his second outing as James Bond, Roger Moore goes to an island where there's a solar-energy laser beam and dodges some tacky but colorful psychedelic effects. Clifton James repeats his dumb sheriff role. Lulu sings the non-hit theme song. Music by John Barry.

UPI 12/13/74: Swedish-born actress Britt Ekland is the latest in a long line of lovely leading ladies for James Bond. Britt helps Bond, played by Roger Moore, track down the bad guy in the latest Bond film, The Man With the Golden Gun.

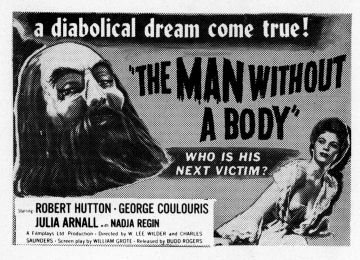

a diabolical dream come true!

"THE MAN WITHOUT A BODY"

WHO IS HIS NEXT VICTIM?

Starring ROBERT HUTTON · GEORGE COULOURIS
JULIA ARNALL with NADJA REGIN
A Filmplays Ltd Production · Directed by W. LEE WILDER and CHARLES
SAUNDERS · Screen play by WILLIAM GROTE · Released by BUDD ROGERS

THE MAN WITH THE POWER
1977 TV
PRODUCER/SCREENWRITER: Allan Baxter
DIRECTOR: Nicholas Sgarro
A schoolteacher who can move objects and bend iron through eye concentration is picked to guard a visiting Bengal princess. A pilot film with Vic Morrow, Roger Perry, and Persis Khambatta.

MAN WITH THE SYNTHETIC BRAIN: See BLOOD OF GHASTLY HORROR.

THE MAN WITH THE YELLOW EYES: See PLANETS AGAINST US.

THE MAN WITH TWO HEADS
1972 William Mishkin
PRODUCER: William Mishkin
DIRECTOR/SCREENWRITER: Andy Milligan
Not *The Thing with Two Heads* made the same year, but a terrible version of the Dr. Jekyll and Mr. Hyde story made by Staten Island's Milligan in England. Milligan was his own cinematographer. (R)

THE MAN WITHOUT A BODY
1957 Budd Rogers (England) (B&W)
PRODUCER: Guido Coen
DIRECTORS: W. Lee Wilder, Charles Saunders
SCREENWRITER: William Grote
Scientists revive the talking bearded head of Nostradamus. Hooked up to tubes on a table, it still makes accurate predictions. Robert Hutton decides the head needs a new body. Pretty terrible. With George Coulouris and Julia Arnall.

MANDRAKE
1979 TV
PRODUCER/SCREENWRITER: Rick Husky
DIRECTOR: Harry Falk
A pilot film about the comic-strip magician Mandrake (Anthony Herrera) stopping a series of roller-coaster murders. Ji-Tu Cumbuka is Lothar. With Harry Blackstone, Jr. Mandrake was also a serial in 1939.

MANFISH
1956 Universal
PRODUCER/DIRECTOR: W. Lee Wilder
SCREENWRITER: Joel Murcott
A modern adventure film about an undersea treasure, vaguely based on Poe's "The Gold Bug" and his "The Telltale Heart." With John Bromfield, Lon Chaney, Jr., Victor Jory, the always amusing Barbara Nichols in her first role, and calypso music. Filmed in Jamaica.

MANHUNT ON MYSTERY ISLAND
1945 Republic (B&W)
ASSOCIATE PRODUCER: Ronald Davidson
DIRECTORS: Spencer Bennet, Wallace Grissel, Yakima Canutt
SCREENWRITERS: Albert Demond, Basil Dickey, Jesse Duffy, Alan James, Grant Nelson, Joseph Poland
ALSO RELEASED AS: *Captain Mephisto and the Transformation Machine*

Using the "transformation chair," a man turns himself into the nefarious 18th-century pirate Captain Mephisto (Roy Barcroft). Mephisto attempts to gain control of the powerful radioatomic power transmitter, but hero criminologist Richard Bailey and inventor's daughter Linda Sterling stop him after about a dozen close calls. A condensed feature version of this serial was released in '66.

MANIA

1960 Pacemaker Films (England)
PRODUCERS: Robert S. Baker,
    Monty Berman
DIRECTOR: John Gilling
SCREENWRITERS: John Gilling, Leon Griffiths
ALSO RELEASED AS: *The Flesh and the Fiends*;
    The Fiendish Ghouls; *Psycho-Killers*

Although screened here as if it were an inferior exploitation film and obviously inspired by the success of Hammer's early horrors, this is an excellent atmospheric movie. As Dr. Knox, Peter Cushing scandalizes the medical profession by buying bodies for experiments. George Rose and Donald Pleasence are thoroughly convincing and disgusting as the Irish grave robbers Burke and Hare. They'll kill anybody, of any age, to get some money. The poverty and filth of 19th-century Edinburgh provide an unforgettable background for this unflinching film. The romantic couple (John Cairney and Billie Whitelaw) are, surprisingly enough, killed off. Scenes of explicit violence, including eyes being burned out, are shown. The original prints contained some nudity, unusual at the time, especially in England. Cushing inspects the corpses brought in by daintily holding his nose with a hankie and throwing some gold coins at the killers. Watch for it.

MANIAC

1934 Hollywood Producers and
    Distributors (B&W)
PRODUCER/DIRECTOR: Dwain Esper
SCREENWRITER: Hildegarde Stadie

Don't pass up an opportunity to see this incredible old adults-only oddity based in part on Poe's "The Black Cat." Bill Woods stars as a crazed vaudevillian who ends up killing and impersonating Dr. Meirschultz (Horace Carpenter), a mad scientist who could revive the dead. Highlights include the eating of a cat's eye, body snatching, two women locked in a cellar fighting with syringes, a rapist who thinks he's a gorilla, and a bit of nudity in defiance of the Hays Code. Including film clips from *Witchcraft Through the Ages* (Sweden, 1920) and *Siegfried* (Germany, 1923) to illustrate madness. You won't believe it. Esper and his scriptwriter wife Hildegarde also made *Marijuana, Weed with Roots in Hell* and *How to Undress in Front of Your Husband*.

MANIAC

1963 Hammer/Columbia (England)
    (B&W)
PRODUCER/SCREENWRITER: Jimmy Sangster
DIRECTOR: Michael Carreras

An American artist in France (*Seventh Voyage of Sinbad* star Kerwin Matthews) falls in love with a young woman but is seduced by her stepmother (Nadia Gray) and talked into helping her father escape from an insane asylum. It's obviously a bad move and he nearly becomes the victim of a nut with a blowtorch. An interesting *Psycho*-inspired thriller with a typical twist ending.

MANIAC!

1978 New World
PRODUCER: James V. Hart
DIRECTOR: Richard Compton
SCREENWRITER: John C. Broderick
ALSO RELEASED AS: *Ransom; Assault on Paradise*

An ex-Vietnam vet dressed as an Indian threatens to kill important people in a resort town unless he receives $5 million. Corrupt millionaire Stuart Whitman hires hit man Oliver Reed to put a stop to the murders. John Ireland is the sheriff, who also works for Whitman. With Deborah Raffin as a reporter and Jim Mitchum. Roger McGuinn of the Byrds sings the title song. An unrelated precredit scene with a masked-killer clown was tacked on and used in the horror ad campaign. Filmed in Phoenix, Arizona. By the director of *Angels Die Hard*.

MANIAC
1980 Analysis
PRODUCERS: Andrew Garroni, William Lustig
DIRECTOR: William Lustig
SCREENWRITERS: Z.A. Rozenberg, Joe Spinell
This low-budget New York City slasher movie starring the special makeup effects of Tom Savini (who appears as a victim) managed to offend even many gore fans. It's a project of busy character actor Joe Spinell (both *Godfather* films, *Taxi Driver*, *Cruising*, the *Rocky* films) who wrote the story, was the executive producer, and stars as Frank Zito, a repulsive schizophrenic killer. When he isn't trying to romance beautiful Caroline Munro (as a photographer), he kills women, scalps them, and puts the bloody hair on the mannequins in his filthy apartment. From the director of *The Violation of Claudia* and the distributors of *Caligula*. The sound track album is still available. (self-imposed **X**)

MANIAC MANSION
1978 Group I (Italy)
PRODUCER/DIRECTOR: Jurgen Goslar
ALSO RELEASED AS: *Amuck*
Maybe you remember Farley Granger in *Strangers on a Train* and thought he was pretty good. Watch this and think again. Farley kidnaps females and forces them to put on endless sex shows. Barbara Bouchet shows up looking for her sister. Farley gets crazier by the moment. (**R**)

THE MANIACS ARE LOOSE: See *THE THRILL KILLERS*.

MANIPULATOR: See *EFFECTS*.

THE MANITOU
1978 Avco Embassy
PRODUCER/DIRECTOR: William Girdler
SCREENWRITERS: William Girdler, Jon Cedar
Poor Susan Strasberg has an evil Indian midget growing out of her back! The 400-year-old medicine man is "reborn," terrorizes the all star cast, and ends up confronting hero Tony Curtis in a refrigerator. Curtis, in the silliest role of his career, is a phony spiritualist and former lover of Strasberg. Michael Ansara is Singing Rock. Stella Stevens is a gypsy. Based on a novel of the same title by Graham Masterson. With Ann Sothern, Burgess Meredith, Jeanette Nolan, Paul Mantee, and Jon Cedar, who co-wrote the screenplay. Only the

International queen of science fiction and horror Caroline Munro stars as a fashion photographer fated to meet the Maniac.

special effects make it worthwhile. Girdler, the 30-year-old producer-director, died in a helicopter accident before this was released. It was his ninth feature.

MANKILLERS: See FASTER PUSSYCAT! KILL! KILL!

MANOS, THE HANDS OF FATE
1966 Emerson
PRODUCER/DIRECTOR/SCREENWRITER:
Hal P. Warren

What kind of movie would a fertilizer salesman from El Paso, Texas, make? This kind: Warren is vacationing with his wife, little girl, and poodle Peppy when he takes a wrong turn to nowhere and stops at a phantasmagoric house to ask directions. Servant Torga answers and the nightmare begins. Peppy is torn to bits trying to escape, and his owners end up in a cheesy backyard temple witnessing the weird rites of revived master Manos and his harem queens. The presence of guests causes nothing but trouble; the bickering between Torga and Manos escalates until Manos makes a point by vaporizing Torga's hand in sacrificial fires. Meet Torga's replacement in the surprise conclusion. Made in El Paso. With Tom Neyman, John Reynolds, and Diane Mahree. –CB

MANSION OF THE DOOMED
1976 Group I
PRODUCER: Charles Band
DIRECTOR: Michael Pataki
SCREENWRITER: Frank Ray Perilli

Dr. Chaney (Richard Basehart) feels responsible for the accident that caused daughter Tisha Sterling to go blind. The doctor kidnaps people, surgically removes their eyes, and throws them in his dungeon. None of the operations work. The eyeless victims kill his assistant (Gloria Grahame). As the kind but crazed killer, Basehart is pretty funny. From the director of *Dracula's Dog*. With Vic Tayback and Arthur Space. Producer Band was 21 at the time.

THE MANSTER
1959 Lopert (U.S./Japan) (B&W)
PRODUCER: George P. Breakston
DIRECTORS: Kenneth B. Crane,
    George P. Breakston
SCREENWRITER: Walter J. Sheldon
ALSO RELEASED AS: *The Split*

The world's first double-headed-monster movie! An American reporter (Larry Stanford) is given an injection by the mad Dr. Suzuki (who keeps his mutant wife in a cage). An eye grows on the reporter's shoulder! It soon becomes an ugly head that resembles a carved coconut! The extra-headed monster kills people! Then it splits into two beings—man and ape man. Man throws ape man into a volcano! End.

MANTIS IN LACE
1968 Boxoffice International
PRODUCER/SCREENWRITER: Sanford White
DIRECTOR: William Rotsler
ALSO RELEASED AS: *Lila*

A psycho-killer-drug-nudie movie starring Susan Stewart as Lila, a topless go-go dancer who takes too much LSD. She lures a series of men to a candlelit warehouse for sex but kills them with garden tools while hallucinating. One man seems to turn into a giant insect; another's head becomes a bunch of bananas. Shot in New York City by cinematographer Laszlo Kovacs, who did *Easy Rider* the following year. Makeup by Mike Weldon (no relation). Harry Novak's Boxoffice Internatinal later made horror films like *Axe and the Child*. Director Rotsler writes for *Adam Film World* magazine. (**R**)

MARCH OF THE WOODEN SOLDIERS: See *BABES IN TOYLAND.*

MARK OF THE DEVIL

1970 Hallmark (W. Germany/England)
PRODUCER: Adrian Hoven
DIRECTOR: Michael Armstrong
SCREENWRITER: Sergio Cassner
ORIGINALLY RELEASED AS: *Brenn: Hexe, Brenn*

"Likely to upset your stomach!" the ads claimed. This is the one with the famous "stomach distress" bags given to viewers. Thanks to a brilliant American ad campaign stressing the gore ("rated V for violence"), this witch-hunt tale set in 18th-century Austria was a big moneymaker. Herbert Lom stars as the sadistic (and impotent) witch-trial judge. Tongues are ripped out; women (often topless) are burned, stretched, cut. . . . But if you're a fan of this kind of stuff, you're unlikely to find it "the most horrifying film ever made." With Udo Kier (from the Warhol horrors), ugly Reggie Nalder (*Salem's Lot*), Olivera Vuco, and Gaby Fuchs. **(R)**

Courtesy of Orion Pictures Corporation.

MARK OF THE DEVIL II

1972 AIP (W. Germany/England)
DIRECTOR: Adrian Hoven
SCREENWRITERS: Adrian Hoven, Fred Denger
ORIGINALLY RELEASED AS: *Hexen-Geschandet und Tode Gequalt*

What, no vomit bags? This sequel claims to include "10 scenes that you will *positively* not be able to stomach." The ads also say it was "banned in 19 countries." I'd like to see a list. Anton Diffring (*Circus of Horrors*) stars this time. Reggie Nalder returns from the original and its producer took over as director. With a beautiful countess (Erica Blanc) and some nuns being tortured and burned. **(R)**

MARK OF THE GORILLA

1950 Columbia (B&W)
PRODUCER: Sam Katzman
DIRECTOR: William Berke
SCREENWRITER: Carroll Young

Bad guys (including Onslow Stevens) disguise themselves as gorillas in order to steal buried Nazi loot. Only hero Jungle Jim (Johnny Weissmuller) can tell the crooks in ape suits from the "real" apes (in ape suits). He rescues a captive princess. With Trudy Marshall.

MARK OF THE VAMPIRE

1935 MGM (B&W)
PRODUCER: E.J. Mannix
DIRECTOR: Tod Browning
SCREENWRITERS: Guy Endore, Bernard Schubert

A sound remake of Browning's *London After Midnight*, which starred Lon Chaney. The vampires turn out to be actors hired to frighten people, but Bela Lugosi in a small part as Count Mora and Carroll Borland as his daughter Luna look great. With her long black hair and pale skin, the 21-year-old Borland set the precedent for Morticia and Vampira. Lionel Barrymore stars as a Ven Helsing type. Lionel Atwill is Inspector Neumann. With Elizabeth

Allen, Jean Hersholt, and Donald Meek. Cinematography by James Wong Howe. Only one hour long.

MARK OF THE VAMPIRE: See THE VAMPIRE.

MARNIE
1964 Universal
PRODUCER/DIRECTOR: Alfred Hitchcock
SCREENWRITER: Jay Presson Allen

Audiences had a hard time with this sexual/psychological horror film with a William Castle–style gimmick (the screen flashes red at stressful moments) and Sean Connery, who was known only as Bond to most viewers. Tippi Hedren is Marnie, a compulsive thief living under an assumed name who loves her horse and has an hysterical fear of thunderstorms, sex, and the color red. When her rich publisher employer (Connery) catches her robbing the safe he blackmails her into marrying him, forces her to have sex, and attempts to discover the cause of her problems. A visit to her crippled mother and a helpful flashback clear everything up. With Diane Baker, Bruce Dern, and Alan Napier. Music by Bernard Herrmann. Hitchcock is seen in a hotel lobby.

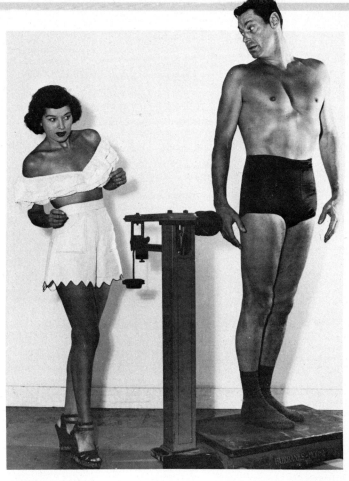

MAROONED
1969 Columbia
PRODUCER: M. J. Frankovich
DIRECTOR: John Sturges
SCREENWRITER: Mayo Simon

Three American astronauts (Gene Hackman, Richard Crenna, and James Franciscus) on an endurance mission are stranded in orbit and running out of oxygen. At Cape Kennedy, supervisor Gregory Peck tries to help while wives Lee Grant, Nancy Kovack, and Mariette Hartley fret. In an unlikely ending Russian cosmonauts arrive with oxygen. The story is basically an in-space remake of Sturges' *Jeopardy* ('53). *Marooned* won an Oscar for special

Above:
UPI 9/17/50: Johnny Weissmuller demonstrates the plunging waistline by tipping the scales at 199. According to his present contract Weissmuller had to report for his current picture, Mark of the Go-rilla, *weighing not more than 200 pounds or forfeit a thousand dollars for each pound over the mark. The interested young lady is co-star Trudy Marshall.*

Bela Lugosi and Carol Borland in Tod Browning's Mark of the Vampire.

461

effects. Also with Scott Brady in his first respectable production in years.

MARRIED TOO YOUNG
1962 Headliner (B&W)
DIRECTOR: George Moskov
SCREENWRITER: Nathaniel Tanchuck
ALSO RELEASED AS: *I Married Too Young*

Harold Lloyd, Jr., trades his dream of becoming a doctor for mechanic's overalls to support high school bride Jana Lund. Trouble comes when he tries to set up housekeeping away from meddlesome oldsters and gets involved in Anthony Dexter's hot-car ring. With Marianna Hill (still an exploitation film regular, in her debut role as a bad girl), Trudy Marshall, George Cisar, and Nita Loveless.   –CB

MARS ATTACKS THE WORLD: See FLASH GORDON'S TRIP TO MARS.

MARS INVADES PUERTO RICO: See FRANKENSTEIN MEETS THE SPACE MONSTER.

MARS NEEDS WOMEN
1966 AIP-TV
PRODUCER/DIRECTOR/SCREENWRITER: Larry Buchanan

Tommy Kirk (right) in Larry Buchanan's Mars Needs Women.

Courtesy of Orion Pictures Corporation.

Remember Tommy Kirk as an alien in *Pajama Party?* You'll love him in this made-for-television travesty from the director of *Zontar, the Thing from Venus* and *Goodbye Norma Jean.* Yvonne "Batgirl" Craig is a go-go dancing lady scientist in demand on Mars. With lots of stock footage and dubbed-in sound. Incredible.

MARTA
1971 Avco Embassy-TV (Spain/Italy)
DIRECTOR: José Antonio Conde
SCREENWRITERS: José Antonio Conde, J.J.A. Millan, Lopez Aranda

Stephen Boyd stars as a crazed killer with a torture chamber and a dead wife kept in a suit of armor. With Marisa Mell.

THE MARTIAN CHRONICLES
1980 TV
PRODUCERS: Andrew Donally, Milton Subotsky
DIRECTOR: Michael Anderson
SCREENWRITER: Richard Matheson

This not-too-successful, six-hour, three-part miniseries based on Ray Bradbury's book suffers from bad special effects, slow pacing, and uninspired direction. The ten stories were strung together by means of a main character, Colonel John Wilder (Rock Hudson), who links up the different segments. With Bernie Casey, Roddy McDowall, Darren McGavin, Maria Schell, Bernadette Peters, Michael Anderson, Jr., Fritz Weaver, Barry Morse, Joyce Van Patten, Gayle Hunnicutt, and Jon Finch (as Jesus Christ). One alien looks just like David Bowie in *The Man Who Fell to Earth.* It was a theatrical release in Europe.   –AF

MARTIN
1977 Libra
PRODUCER: Richard Rubinstein
DIRECTOR/SCREENWRITER: George A. Romero

Romero's *Living Dead* films are great but this is his best so far. It's too disturbing, bleak, and personal to have been a financial hit, even at midnight showings. John Amplas stars as Martin, a shy and severely confused 18-year-old "vampire" living with relatives in a dying Pennsylvania steel town. His elderly cousin (Lincoln Maazel, father of Lorin) believes he's a "Nosferatu" and tries to destroy him with crosses and garlic. The old man's defenses merely irritate Martin, a strictly modern sexual psycho who uses razor blades and syringes to drain the blood from his female victims. Romero appears as an ineffectual priest and makeup artist Tom Savini plays the fiancé of Martin's cousin (Christine Forrest). One inspired touch has Martin becoming a regular on an all-night phone-in radio show: he calls to talk about his problem. In years to come this will be considered a classic. The sound track is available on Varèse Saraband. (R)

MARYJANE

1968 AIP

PRODUCER/DIRECTOR: Maury Dextar
SCREENWRITERS: Richard Gautier,
  Peter L. Marshall

Has-been pop star Fabian plays a high school art teacher who is framed and busted while trying to convince the principal that maybe grass isn't so bad. Diane McBain (of the *Surfside Six* series) is a fellow teacher who turns out to be a pusher and a junkie who sleeps with her students. Written by the incredible turned-on team of Peter Marshall (*Hollywood Squares*) and Dick Gautier (Hymie the C.O.N.T.R.O.L. robot on *Get Smart*). With Patty McCormack, the by-then grown-up little girl from *The Bad Seed*, Kevin Coughlin, Russ Bender, Teri Garr, and a bit by Gautier. Exploitation tips from the original pressbook suggesting special screenings from the clergy: "Members of the clergy have a keen interest in their communities and are eager to assist with local problems. Marijuana is a growing problem in most communities, and after your clergyman has attended a screening of *Maryjane*, there is no doubt that he will

John Amplas stars in George Romero's Martin.

be forthcoming with favorable comment from the pulpit."

MARY, MARY, BLOODY MARY
1975 Translor (Mexico)
PRODUCER: Proa Films
DIRECTOR: Juan Lopez Moctezuma
SCREENWRITER: Malcolm Marmostein

Christina Ferrare stars as a lesbian vampire who stabs her lovers in the neck and drinks their blood. Ex-model Ferrare is now known as the wife of accused coke dealer, millionaire John Delorean. Guest star John Carradine (as her father) wasn't around long enough to finish the feature, so an unconvincing double was substituted. From the director of *Dr. Tarr's Torture Dungeon.*

THE MASK
1961 Warner Brothers (Canada)
(B&W; 3-D)
PRODUCER/DIRECTOR: Julian Roffman
SCREENWRITERS: Frank Taubes, Sandy Habner
ALSO RELEASED AS: *Eyes of Hell; The Spooky Movie Show*

One of the great gimmick films. An introduction explains the hallucinogenic powers of "The Mask." The viewers were instructed to put their masks on when the psychiatrist in the movie (Paul Stevens) does. The result is "Depth Dimension," 3-D sequences showing the horrors of the subconscious. A beautiful woman is carried to a sacrificial altar by hooded figures. A ragged ghoul rows a coffin through a sea of mist. This psychological horror film was originally a box-office flop but still gets reissued every few years. "Put the mask on—now!"

THE MASK OF DIJON
1946 PRC (B&W)
PRODUCERS: Max Alexander, Alfred Stern
DIRECTOR: Lew Landers
SCREENWRITERS: Arthur St. Clair,
    Griffin Jay

The outrageous Erich von Stroheim stars as a magician who hypnotizes enemies to make them kill and commit suicide. With Jeanne Bates and Edward Van Sloan.

THE MASK OF DIMITRIOS
1944 Warner Brothers (B&W)
PRODUCER: Henry Blanke
DIRECTOR: Jean Negulesco
SCREENWRITER: Frank Gruber

Peter Lorre, a meek, bow-tie-wearing mystery writer, is in Istanbul trying to reconstruct the life of a notorious villain (Zachary Scott in his film debut) who has been murdered. He's helped in an odd fashion by Sidney Greenstreet and a number of flashbacks revealing the deviousness of Dimitrios. Based on *A Coffin for Dimitrios* by Eric Ambler, whose *Background to Danger* had just been filmed with Lorre and Greenstreet. With Faye Emerson and Victor Francen. It promised and nearly delivered "the Maltese Falcon kind of thrill."

THE MASK OF FU MANCHU
1932 MGM (B&W)
PRODUCER: Irving Thalberg
DIRECTOR: Charles Brabin
SCREENWRITERS: Irene Kuhn,
    Edgar Allan Woolf, John Willard

A wonderfully outrageous adventure about the Oriental Fu (Boris Karloff) torturing and killing to obtain the mask and sword of Genghis Khan. With them (plus his electronic-ray machine) he can exterminate the white race and rule the world. Myrna Loy is Fu's daughter Fah Lo See. Lewis Stone is Nayland Smith of Scotland Yard. As a British museum scientist, Jean Hersholt is placed between two spiked walls, slowly closing in. Others face the alligator pit, decapitation, or the horrors of the incessant bell. With Charles Starrett and Karen Morley. The classic Fu Manchu movie.

THE MASQUE OF THE RED DEATH

1964 Anglo Amalgamated/AIP (England)
PRODUCER/DIRECTOR: Roger Corman
SCREENWRITER: Charles Beaumont

In what is probably Corman's best all-around serious feature, Vincent Price (as Prospero, a Satan-worshiping prince in plague-ridden 12th-century Italy) is the ultimate evil character. Everyone exists merely as a toy to be manipulated by the sadistic prince. Only the lowliest peasants have any morals. Although colorful and entertaining, it creates more of a feeling of doom and depression than any other Corman film. Making a pact with the Devil, Hazel Court brands her breast to impress Prospero; but he's only interested in the innocent Jane Asher, whose fiancé (David Weston) and father (Nigel Green) are imprisoned for future humiliation and entertainment. In a subplot lifted from Poe's "Hop Toad," a jester/dwarf (Skip Martin) gets revenge on a nobleman (Patrick Magee) by burning him alive in a gorilla suit during the masque. Nicholas Roeg (director of *The Man Who Fell to Earth*) was the director of photography. One impressive sequence follows the prince through a series of large chambers, each a different rich color. The dance of death sequence is less impressive—unless you take into account that the whole project was done in five weeks! Corman usually needed three or less but explained that "the English crews work slower than American crews."

MASTER MINDS

1949 Monogram (B&W)
PRODUCER: Jan Grippo
DIRECTOR: Jean Yarbrough
SCREENWRITERS: Charles R. Marion, Bert Lawrence

"Horror-iffic hilarity" abounds as a mad doctor (Alan Napier) searches for a new brain for his bearded ape man Atlas (Glenn Strange). The Bowery Boys show up at the lab and Huntz Hall is singled out and strapped to the operating table. With Skelton Knaggs, Jane Adams, Minerva Urecal, and the usual "boys" (Leo Gorcey, Billy Benedict, Gabriel Dell). Makeup by Jack Pierce, who created the classic Universal monsters during more prosperous times.

MASTER OF HORROR

1960 U.S. Films (Argentina)
PRODUCER: Nicolas Carreras
DIRECTOR: Enrique Carreras
SCREENWRITER: Louis Penafiel
ORIGINALLY RELEASED AS: *Obras Maestras del Terror*

A trilogy of Poe stories, including two Corman filmed as *Tales of Terror* a year later. The third segment, "The Telltale Heart," was deleted from this dubbed feature presented by Jack Harris. It was released with *Master of Terror*.

MASTER OF TERROR: See THE 4-D MAN.

UPI 5/22/64: Vincent Price just couldn't resist buying pastries and a loaf of French bread in one of the bakeries along London's Petticoat Lane. Sharing in the shopping fun is the actor's current co-star Jane Asher. They both took an afternoon off during the filming of The Masque of the Red Death *on location in England.*

MASTER OF THE WORLD
1961 AIP
DIRECTOR: William Witney
SCREENWRITER: Richard Matheson

In between Poe films, Vincent Price starred as Robur the Conqueror, a 19th-century inventor who plans to end war by destroying all man's weapons from his flying airship, the Albatross. Based on the stories of Jules Verne, it's like *20,000 Leagues Under the Sea* in the air. As a munitions maker, Henry Hull is held prisoner on the ship along with his daughter and her fiancé. The hero is Strock (Charles Bronson in a striped T-shirt). Bronson had also appeared with Price in *The House of Wax*. This low-budget production is spiced up with footage from various battle epics. With Mary Webster, David Frankham, and Wally Campo. A Roger Corman production. A sound track album is currently available.

MATANGO, THE FUNGUS OF TERROR: See *ATTACK OF THE MUSHROOM PEOPLE.*

MATCHLESS
1967 United Artists (Italy)
PRODUCERS: Ermanno Donati,
   Luigi Carpentieri
DIRECTOR: Alberto Lattuada
SCREENWRITERS: Dean Craif, Jack Pulman,
   Luigi Malerga, A. Lattvada

A New York journalist (Patrick O'Neal) is captured by the Chinese and tortured as a spy. A cellmate gives him an invisibility ring, but when he uses it to escape, he's caught and tortured by Americans. He later spies on international gangster Donald Pleasence for the U.S. With Ira Von Furstenburg and Henry Silva. Secret-agent weirdness presented by Dino De Laurentiis.

MATT HELM
1975 TV
PRODUCER/DIRECTOR: Buzz Kulik
SCREENWRITER: Sam H. Rolfe

Anthony Franciosa, in the old Dean Martin secret agent role, protects a movie star. A series resulted and lasted a few months. With Ann Turkel, Gene Evans, and Patrick Macnee.

A MATTER OF LIFE AND DEATH: See *STAIRWAY TO HEAVEN.*

THE MAZE
1953 Allied Artists (B&W, 3-D)
PRODUCER: Richard Heermance
DIRECTOR: William Cameron Menzies
SCREENWRITER: Dan Ullman

A slow-moving film that's fascinating to look at, thanks to the weird sets designed by the director and the most unusual ending you'll ever witness. Veronica Hurst marries Richard Carlson, who leaves for a Scottish castle he's inherited and tells her to stay away. She of course shows up with her aunt (Katherine Emery), determined to discover why her husband has turned cold and gray-haired. With Michael Pate and Hillary Brooke. Filmed in England.

MEAT CLEAVER MASSACRE
1977 Group I
EXECUTIVE PRODUCER: Steven L. Singer
DIRECTOR: Evan Lee
ALSO RELEASED AS: *The Hollywood Meat
   Cleaver Massacre*

A cheap gore film about a comatose professor of the occult conjuring up forces to wreak vengeance on the four thugs who killed his family. The massacre is too dark to see most of the time but an attack by cacti is a highlight. Christopher Lee shows he has the career sense of Lugosi or even John

Carradine by appearing as the onscreen narrator ("the host"). **(R)**

MEAT IS MEAT: See THE MAD BUTCHER.

THE MEDUSA TOUCH
1978 Warner Brothers (England)
PRODUCERS: Lew Grade, Arnon Milchan
DIRECTOR: Jack Gold
SCREENWRITERS: John Briley, Jack Gold
Once *Exorcist II: The Heretic* came out, nobody wanted to go see Richard Burton in this ESP disaster film from England. After having his skull cracked, Burton lies in bed attached to a support system and causes psychogenic havoc. A London cathedral collapses and a jet crashes into the city. Lee Remick (fresh from *The Omen*) is his psychiatrist. French detective Lino Ventura discovers the power behind the disasters. Imagine a combination of *Meat Cleaver Massacre* and an Irwin Allen movie. A Sir Lew Grade production.

MEET ME IN LAS VEGAS
1956 MGM
PRODUCER: Joe Pasternak
DIRECTOR: Roy Rowland
SCREENWRITER: Isobel Lennart
Cyd Charisse as a ballet star is good luck to gambler Dan Dailey. It's an overstuffed musical with Jim Backus and Agnes Moorehead. The Sands Club backdrop provides the justification for guest bits by Frank Sinatra, Sammy Davis, Jr., Lena Horne, Eddie Fisher, Debbie Reynolds, and Peter Lorre, who plays blackjack. His line: "Hit me, you creep."

MEGAFORCE
1982 20th Century-Fox
PRODUCER: Albert S. Ruddy
DIRECTOR: Hal Needham
SCREENWRITERS: Albert S. Ruddy, Hal Needham, James Whittaker, André Morgan

A major $27 million science-fiction flop from the director of Burt Reynolds' biggest action hits. It's a futuristic motorcycle-and-car-crash movie starring Barry Bostwick as Ace Hunter. Persis Khambatta, the bald alien woman in *Star Trek: The Motion Picture*, co-stars, with hair this time. Also with Edward Mulhare, Henry Silva, and Michael Beck (*Warlords of the 21st Century*). A Megaforce videogame was not a big seller. See *The Road Warrior* instead.

THE MEPHISTO WALTZ
1971 20th Century-Fox
PRODUCER: Quinn Martin
DIRECTOR: Paul Wendkos
SCREENWRITER: Ben Maddow
A TV producer, a TV director, and (mostly) TV stars make an occult thriller about souls being transferred all over the place. Elderly pianist Curt Jurgens takes over Alan Alda's body. As Alda's wife, Jacqueline Bisset has her mind transferred to Jurgen's lover. Barbara Parkins sits around in tights and lights candles, and a dog walks around in a human mask. With Bradford Dillman, little Pamelyn Ferdin, William Windom, and Khiegh Dhiegh. **(R)**

THE MERMAIDS OF TIBURON
1962 Art Films International
PRODUCER/DIRECTOR/SCREENWRITER: John Lamb
ALSO RELEASED AS: *The Aqua Sex*
Foolish undersea adventure concerning "unclassified" fish women thought to reign over a fortune in rare fire pearls. Marine biologist George Rowe, taken into confidence by the Mermaid Queen, supplies a running commentary through the bubbles. A typical remark: "It occurred to me to wonder just how feminine these creatures might be." That question is answered in an adults-

The Mermaids of Tiburon.

only revision called *The Aqua Sex* released in 1965. Diane Webber (a.k.a. Marguerite Empey of early *Playboy* magazine fame) is revealed in the added scenes. Both versions feature Timothy Carey, who kills charter-boat skipper Jose Gonzalez-Gonzalez and one of the amphibians in his lust for treasure. With Vicki Kantenwine, Nani Morissey, Judy Edwards, and Jean Carroll. Filmed mainly in La Paz, Mexico, and around Catalina Island by underwater photography specialist Lamb.   –CB

MESA OF LOST WOMEN
1952 Howco (B&W)
PRODUCERS: G. William Perkins, Melvin Gale
DIRECTORS: Herbert Tevos, Ron Ormond
ALSO RELEASED AS: *Lost Women*

A must-see item for fans of Uncle Fester and early-'50s girlie science fiction. Mad scientist Jackie Coogan creates a giant tarantula and superwomen with long fingernails. A lobotomized scientist doing a strange Elmer Fudd impersonation leads hero Allan Nixon (*Prehistoric Women*) from a Mexican bar to the mysterious mesa. Great grade-Z nonsense with Tandra Quinn (as Tarantella), Mary Hill, Katena Vea (later known as Katherine Victor of *Teenage Zombies*) and Mona McKinnon (*Plan 9 from Outer Space*). The incredible guitar-and-piano score was reused in Ed Wood, Jr.'s *Jailbait*.

MESSAGE FROM SPACE
1978 Toei/United Artists (U.S./Japan)
PRODUCERS: Banjiro Uemlura, Yoshinori Watanabe, Tan Takaiwa
DIRECTOR: Kinji Fukasaku
SCREENWRITER: Hiroo Matsuda

Vic Morrow and Sonny Chiba star in a Japanese *Star Wars*-inspired fantasy with a cute robot, a spaceship with sails, a miniskirted heroine (Peggy Lee Brennan), and a lot of ancient-looking warriors. The ad campaign featured the line "Help us!"

MESSIAH OF EVIL: See DEAD PEOPLE

METEOR
1979 AIP
PRODUCERS: Arnold Orgolini, Theodore Parvin
DIRECTOR: Ronald Neame
SCREENWRITERS: Stanley Mann, Edmund H. North

An $18 million all-star disaster-movie flop from the director of *The Poseidon Adventure*. Americans and Russians refuse to cooperate in time to stop a meteor from destroying New York (the World Trade Center buildings explode and subways collapse). Tidal waves destroy Hong Kong, avalanches kill skiers. Meanwhile, you can thrill to the personal tragedies of Sean Connery as an American scientist and Natalie Wood as a Russian astrophysicist, both of whom get covered by lots of icky mud. Also on the U.S. side are Karl Malden, Martin Landau (he's hilarious), Joseph Campanella, and Henry Fonda as a President even older than Reagan. Brian Keith only speaks Russian and Trevor Howard is a token Brit. With footage from *Avalanche*.

METEOR MONSTER: See TEENAGE MONSTER.

MICKEY SPILLANE'S MARGIN FOR MURDER

1981 TV
PRODUCER: Alex Lucas
DIRECTOR: Daniel Haller
SCREENWRITER: Calvin Clements, Jr.
A new version of *I, the Jury* was supposed to be released in '81. Endless behind-the-scenes problems held it up. This TV-movie, probably made to beat the theatrical feature, is surprisingly good. Updated to modern-day New York, the story takes a cynical look at crooked politicians and sleazy discos. Kevin Dobson (Lt. Crocker on *Kojak*) makes a good Mike Hammer, avenging a friend's death ("We had lots of beeahs and yeahs togetha") and discovering a far-reaching plot. Cindy Pickett (star of Vadim's *Night Games*) is Velda. With John Considine and Donna Dixon.

MIDNIGHT OFFERINGS

1981 TV
DIRECTOR: Rod Holcomb
SCREENWRITER: Juanita Bartlett
Rival high school girls battle it out in this *Carrie*-inspired supernatural drama. With Melissa Sue Anderson and Mary McDonough.

THE MIGHTY GORGA

1969 American General Pictures
PRODUCERS: Robert O'Neil, David Hewitt
DIRECTOR: David L. Hewitt
SCREENWRITERS: Joan Hewitt, David Prentiss
Anthony Eisley leads the search to find a 50-ton gorilla in this no-budget adventure. With Kent Taylor (as Bwana Jack), Scott Brady, dinosaurs, and a witch doctor. From the makers of *Dr. Terror's Gallery of Horrors* and *Spider Baby.*

MIGHTY JOE YOUNG

1949 RKO (B&W with tinted sequence)
PRODUCER: Merian C. Cooper
DIRECTOR: Ernest B. Schoedsack
SCREENWRITER: Ruth Rose

From the folks who gave us *King Kong*, a wonderful fantasy/love story about a girl and a gorilla. When Terry Moore and her pet "Mr. Joseph Young" are brought to Hollywood to star in an impressive but cheesy nightclub act, Joe gets harassed by drunks, escapes, and totally destroys the place. The act includes Terry playing "Beautiful Dreamer" on a grand piano while held above her chained, unhappy pet's head and 10 real wrestlers losing a tug o'war battle with the giant ape. *Kong* star Robert Armstrong returns as an exploitative showman. The film originally had a tinted sequence during the orphanage fire. Animation by Willis O'Brien and newcomer Ray Harryhausen. With Ben Johnson, Frank McHugh, Regis Toomey, and Nester Paiva. The wrestlers include Primo Carnera the Swedish Angel and Bomber Kulkavitch, who later submerged weekly on *Voyage to the Bottom of the Sea*.

THE MIGHTY PEKING MAN:
See *GOLIATHON*.

MILL OF THE STONE WOMEN

1960 Parade Pictures (France/Italy)
PRODUCER: Gianpaola Bigazzi
DIRECTOR: Giorgio Ferroni
SCREENWRITERS: Remigio Del Grosso, Ugo Liberatore, Giorgio Stegani, Giorgio Ferroni
ORIGINALLY RELEASED AS: *Il Mulino delle Donne di Pietra*

An interesting Euro-horror movie filmed in Holland. In 1912 an art student is researching a carousel of statues of beautiful women. He meets a scientist (Wolfgang Preiss) who owns the windmill that powers the exhibit and discovers that the man's daughter is being kept alive with the blood of murdered girls. The statues are really petrified corpses. Based on a story from *Flemish Tales*, not *Bucket of Blood*.

THE MILLION EYES OF SU-MURU

1967 AIP (England)
PRODUCER/SCREENWRITER: Harry Alan Towers
DIRECTOR: Lindsay Shonteff

From the producer of the Fu Manchu series, another low-budget Sax Rohmer adaptation. The beautiful and sadistic Su-muru (Shirley Eaton) plans to conquer the world with her army of women. The free world has to rely on the talents of Frankie Avalon and George Nader to stop her. As President Boong of Sinonesia, Klaus Kinski is turned to stone. With Wilfrid Hyde-White. Filmed in Hong Kong. If you can stand this one, look for the sequel, *Rio 70*.

THE MIND BENDERS

1963 Anglo Amalgamated/AIP (England) (B&W)
PRODUCER: Michael Relph
DIRECTOR: Basil Dearden
SCREENWRITER: James Kennaway

A believable, pre-psychedelic variation on the *Altered States* theme. Scientist Dirk Bogarde undergoes sensory-deprivation tests in a dark tank of water to prove the innocence of a professor who was labeled a traitor and committed suicide after the same treatment. Bogarde's "friends" brainwash him into hating his wife (Mary Ure) and he becomes violent and irresponsible.

THE MIND OF MR. SOAMES

1970 Amicus/Columbia (England)
PRODUCERS: Max J. Rosenberg, Milton Subotsky
DIRECTOR: Alan Cooke
SCREENWRITERS: Joan Hale, Edward Simpson

Terence Stamp stars as a man just brought out of a 30-year coma by an American neurosurgeon (bearded Robert Vaughn). Another doctor (Nigel Davenport) puts him through an accelerated educational program that is monitored by cameras for a television special. Things get a bit ridiculous when Stamp escapes in a white jump suit and confronts people as a full-grown baby. Eventually he is found hiding in a barn flooded with bright lights so the television director can get a clear shot of him killing Vaughn with a pitchfork.

THE MIND SNATCHERS
1972 Cinerama
PRODUCER: George Goodman
DIRECTOR: Bernard Girard
SCREENWRITER: Ron Whyte
ALSO RELEASED AS: *The Happiness Cage*
Army scientists experiment on volunteer servicemen by attaching electrodes to their pleasure centers and giving them shock treatments. Christopher Walken stars with Ronny Cox (as a victim) and Ralph Meeker (as a major). Filmed in Denmark

MINDWARP: AN INFINITY OF TERROR: See GALAXY OF TERROR.

THE MINI-SKIRT MOB
1968 AIP
PRODUCER/DIRECTOR: Maury Dexter
SCREENWRITER: James Gordon White
Biker Diane McBain wants to cause trouble for an ex-boyfriend (Ross Hagen) and his new bride (Sherry Jackson). The mischief escalates until sister Patty McCormack is killed by a Molotov cocktail and McBain finds herself hanging by one hand over a deadly chasm. Should Sherry Jackson let go before Hagen returns with the police? With Jeremy Slate and Harry Dean Stanton. Patty sits in with the American Revolu-

tion on the title track. Filmed in California and Arizona. The "bikers" ride Hondas. —CB

THE MINOTAUR
1960 United Artists (Italy)
PRODUCERS: Dino Mordini, Georgia Agliani, Rudolphe Solmsen
DIRECTOR: Silvio Amadio
SCREENWRITERS: Alessandro Continenza, Gian Paolo Callegari
ORIGINALLY RELEASED AS: *Teseo Contro il Minotauro*
Rosanna Schiaffino plays an evil princess and her twin sister. As Prince Theseus, Bob Mathias throws the bad sister to the dogs and saves the good one from the minotaur in a labyrinth.

Bob Mathias fights The Minotaur.

THE MIRACLE MAN
1932 Paramount (B&W)
DIRECTOR: Norman Z. McLeod
SCREENWRITERS: Waldemar Young, Samuel Hoffenstein
"They come to loot—and stay to love!"
A remake of a 1919 Lon Chaney film with Chester Morris and Sylvia Sidney

The giant spider in Missile to the Moon.

leading a band of crooks who use a faith healer as part of their racket. When they witness a real miracle they reform, helping to build a church. Boris Karloff plays Nikko, a crooked tavern owner. With Irving Pichel.

MIRACLES FOR SALE
1939 MGM (B&W)
DIRECTOR: Tod Browning
SCREENWRITERS: James Edward Grant, Marion Parsonnet, Harry Ruskin
Browning's last feature is an underrated mystery starring Robert Young as a magician/detective investigating fake seances and murder. With Henry Hull (as an escape artist), Gloria Holden, William Demarest, and Florence Rice. It followed *Mark of the Vampire*, which also has a bad reputation because it reveals the supernatural to be cheap tricks.

MIRANDA
1948 Eagle-Lion (England) (B&W)
PRODUCER: Betty E. Box
DIRECTOR: Ken Annakin
SCREENWRITER: Peter Blackmore

Miranda the mermaid (Glynis Johns) rescues a drowning man and is taken to London. *Mad About Men* was a sequel. *Mr. Peabody and the Mermaid*, an American film, came out the same year. With Googie Withers, Griffith Jones, and Margaret Rutherford.

THE MISADVENTURES OF MERLIN JONES
1963 Buena Vista
PRODUCER: Walt Disney
DIRECTOR: Robert Stevenson
SCREENWRITERS: Tom and Helen August
Tommy Kirk takes over the patented Walt Disney eccentric-inventor role from Fred MacMurray. His electronic helmet, attached to a record player, enables him to read minds. He and girlfriend Annette Funicello expose a crooked judge with the help of a hypnotized chimp (Stanley). They were all back in *The Monkey's Uncle*.

MISSILE MONSTERS: See FLYING DISC MAN FROM MARS.

MISSILE TO THE MOON

1959 Astor (B&W)
PRODUCER: Marc Frederic
DIRECTOR: Richard Cunha
SCREENWRITERS: H.E. Barre, Vincent Fotre

To provide a co-feature for his *Frankenstein's Daughter*, director Cunha remade the notorious *Cat Women of the Moon*. It's the old Earthmen-meet-a-lost-race-of-sexy-alien-women routine, but even more ridiculous and shoddy this time. With teenagers, hilarious "rock men," and a hairy spider puppet. With Richard Travis, Gary Clarke (*How to Make a Monster*), Laurie Mitchell (*The Queen of Outer Space*), and Cathy Downs.

MISSION GALACTICA: THE CYCLON ATTACK: See *BATTLESTAR GALACTICA.*

MISSION MARS

1968 Allied Artists
PRODUCER: Everett Rosenthal
DIRECTOR: Nicholas Webster
SCREENWRITER: Mike St. Clair

Darren McGavin and Nick Adams, the first U.S. astronauts on the Moon, find a dead Russian (who returns to life), a man-eating sphere, and a "polarite" weapon. Filmed in Miami. Released the same year as *2001*.

MISSION STARDUST

1968 Times Films (Spain/Italy/ W. Germany)
DIRECTOR: Primo Zeglio
SCREENWRITERS: Karl H. Volgeman, Federico D'Urrutia
ORIGINALLY RELEASED AS: *4 . . . 3 . . . 2 . . . 1 . . . Morte*

German pulp magazine space hero Perry Rhodan (Lang Jeffries) and a group of American astronauts rescue blonde alien Essy Persson (*I, a Woman*) and take her to Africa. She needs to find a blood specialist to save her dying race. Earth spies interfere but everything turns out okay. It was going to be the first of a series that never materialized. Pretty shoddy.

MISTER FREEDOM

1969 Grove Press (France)
PRODUCERS: Guy Belfond, Michel Zemer, Christian Thivat
DIRECTOR/SCREENWRITER: William Klein

A political fantasy-satire with John Abbey as the title character, a superpatriotic sheriff in football costume who takes his orders from Dr. Freedom (Donald Pleasence). Delphine Seyrig helps him save France from Communism, but she turns out to be a double agent. After fighting Red China Man and Christ Man, Abbey decides France isn't worth saving and blows it up with an atom bomb. Only in the '60s would anybody even think of releasing this here. With Philippe Noiret, Serge Gainsbourg, Yves Montand, and Simone Signoret. The director-screenwriter was a fashion photographer.

MR. DISTRICT ATTORNEY

1941 Republic (B&W)
ASSOCIATE PRODUCER: Leonard Fields
DIRECTOR: William Morgan
SCREENWRITER: Karl Brown

Dennis O'Keefe stars as the assistant D.A. in a lighthearted mystery based on a popular radio series. With Peter Lorre in a small but effective role as a corrupt city official, Florence Rice, and Stanley Ridges.

MR. HEX

1946 Monogram (B&W)
PRODUCER: Jan Grippo
DIRECTOR: William Beaudine
SCREENWRITER: Cyril Endfield

Raymond the hypnotist (Ian Keith) turns Sach (Huntz Hall) into a great boxer. Bowery Boys nonsense with Leo

Gorcey, Bobby Jordan, and Gabriel Dell. One of five Bowery Boys movies released in '46.

MR. MOTO IN DANGER ISLAND

1939 20th Century-Fox (B&W)
PRODUCER: John Stone
DIRECTOR: Herbert I. Leeds
SCREENWRITER: Peter Milne
ALSO RELEASED AS: *Danger Island*

Japanese detective Mr. Moto (Peter Lorre) traps a killer and diamond smuggler in Puerto Rico. With Jean Hersholt, Warren Hymer (comic relief), Amanda Duff, Robert Lowery, and Ward Bond. Lorre starred in eight quickly made mysteries based on John P. Marquand's *Saturday Evening Post* stories, but this was actually a remake of a non-Moto feature, *Murder in Trinidad* (1934), also filmed as *Caribbean Mystery* (1945).

MR. MOTO TAKES A CHANCE

1938 20th Century-Fox (B&W)
PRODUCER: Sol M. Wurtzel
DIRECTOR: Norman Foster
SCREENWRITERS: Lou Breslow, John Patrick

Posing as an archaeologist, Japanese detective Mr. Moto (Peter Lorre) goes to the ruins of Ankor Wat and discovers a fanatical native with an arsenal who plans to rid Asia of all whites. At one point Lorre/Moto disguises himself as an old Tibetan guru. With Rochelle Hudson, Robert Kent, and Chick Chandler.

MR. MOTO TAKES A VACATION

1939 20th Century-Fox (B&W)
PRODUCER: Sol M. Wurtzel
DIRECTOR: Norman Foster
SCREENWRITERS: Philip MacDonald, Norman Foster

In the last of his eight Mr. Moto films, Peter Lorre guards a priceless crown destined for San Francisco. The villain is a master of disguises. Could it be Lionel Atwill? With Virginia Fields and Joseph Schildkraut.

MR. MOTO'S GAMBLE

1938 20th Century-Fox (B&W)
PRODUCER: Sol M. Wurtzel
DIRECTOR: James Tingling
SCREENWRITERS: Charles Belden, Jerry Cady

Warner Oland was scheduled to star in *Charlie Chan at the Fights*. When he died, the studio didn't want to waste time or a script, so a few changes were made and it became a Mr. Moto film. Number one son Keye Luke co-stars with Peter Lorre. It's about murder by poison in the boxing ring. With Harold Huber, Lynn Bari, Ward Bond, Maxie Rosenbloom, and Lon Chaney, Jr.

MR. MOTO'S LAST WARNING

1939 20th Century-Fox (B&W)
PRODUCER: Sol M. Wurtzel
DIRECTOR: Norman Foster
SCREENWRITERS: Philip MacDonald, Norman Foster

Ricardo Cortez and George Sanders plan to blow up the French fleet at the Suez Canal. Mr. Moto (Peter Lorre) foils their plan while posing first as a meek antiques dealer and later as a clown. As a spy, John Carradine gets lowered into the ocean in an airless diving bell by the bad guys. With Virginia Field, and Robert Coote as comic relief.

MR. PEABODY AND THE MERMAID

1948 Universal (B&W)
PRODUCER/SCREENWRITER: Nunnally Johnson
DIRECTOR: Irving Pichel

There haven't been many real mermaid movies. This one was an imitation of *Miranda* ('48). William Powell, while vacationing in the Caribbean, finds Ann Blyth and decides to take her and her fish tail home to his pool in Boston. With Fred Clark and Andrea King.

MISTER ROCK AND ROLL

1957 Paramount (B&W)
PRODUCER: Ralph Siepe
DIRECTOR: Charles Dubin
SCREENWRITER: James Blumgarten

Lois O'Brien writes a positive article about "rock star" Teddy Randazzo but her magazine editor rewrites it and slanders rock 'n' roll! Alan Freed to the rescue! He explains the history of rock and arranges for his teen listeners to contribute to the nasty editor's favorite charity. History is altered slightly when Rocky Graziano is included in a scene in which Cleveland's Record Rendezvous owner Leo Mintz hips Freed to the new phenomenon—white kids buying "race" records. The music in this movie is by a great cross section of rock, Country, rhythm and blues, and jazz artists: Frankie Lymon and the Teenagers, Little Richard, Chuck Berry, Laverne Baker, the Moonglows, Ferlin Husky, Clyde McPhatter, Brook Benton, and Lionel Hampton.

MR. SARDONICUS

1961 Columbia
PRODUCER/DIRECTOR: William Castle
SCREENWRITER: Ray Russell

A macabre tale of a rich 19th-century man whose face is permanently fixed in a wide hideous grin. The baron (Guy Rolfe) resembles Conrad Veidt in *The Man Who Laughs*. He tricks his wife's doctor (Ronald Lewis) into operating on his face, with surprising results. Castle's gimmick is the "Punishment Poll." Patrons received a flourescent thumb card. As in the arena, it was thumbs up or thumbs down. There are supposedly two different endings—*you* decide what happens. Naturally everybody screamed, "Kill him!" Sardonicus died every time. A memorable plus is Oscar Homolka, the great Austrian villain, as the sinister one-eyed servant who spends his leisure hours tying up girls and applying live leeches to their faces. Based on a short story by Ray Russell, originally in *Playboy*. The same year Castle made his all-time sleaze hit—*Homicidal*.

MR. SUPERINVISIBLE

1964 K-tel (Italy/Spain/W. Germany)
DIRECTOR: Antonio Margheriti
   (Anthony Dawson)
SCREENWRITERS: M. Eller, Luis Marquina
ORIGINALLY RELEASED AS: *El Invencible Hombre Invisible*

K-tel, a company well known to TV viewers, tried real hard to convince gullible American parents that this dubbed movie was a Disney product. Besides changing the director's name, they offered chances for a free trip to Disneyland. The only thing American about this kid comedy is star Dean Jones. Walt wouldn't have liked it at all.

MR. WONG, DETECTIVE

1938 Monogram (B&W)
PRODUCER: Scott R. Dunlap
DIRECTOR: William Nigh
SCREENWRITER: Houston Branch

Mister Rock and Roll
(*Alan Freed*).

Boris Karloff starred in five quickies as the very British-looking and -sounding Chinese detective Mr. Wong. They were Monogram's pitiful attempts to duplicate the success of the Mr. Moto and Charlie Chan films being made at 20th Century-Fox. Wong discovers who has been killing people with poison gas bombs. With series regular Grant Withers and Evelyn Brent. The script was remade in '48 as a Chan film, *Docks of New Orleans.*

MR. WONG IN CHINATOWN

1939 Monogram (B&W)
PRODUCER: Scott R. Dunlap
DIRECTOR: William Nigh
SCREENWRITER: Scott Darling

A Chinese princess and her maid are murdered. Mr. Wong (Boris Karloff) discovers the culprit with the help of Grant Withers and his reporter girlfriend (Marjorie Reynolds). Top acting honors go to Angelo Rossitto as a mute Oriental dwarf. With Lotus Long. It was remade in '47 as *The Chinese Ring,* a Charlie Chan movie.

MRS. BROWN YOU'VE GOT A LOVELY DAUGHTER

1968 MGM (England)
PRODUCER: Allen V. Klein
DIRECTOR: Saul Swimmer
SCREENWRITER: Thaddeus Vane

Peter Noone and Herman's Hermits star in a musical comedy somehow inspired by their 1965 hit song. The damn movie's about dog racing! Mrs. Brown is a greyhound who gives birth to a daughter after winning a race. There's another Mrs. Brown (Mona Washbourne) and Herman/Peter falls for her lovely daughter, a model, but she leaves for an assignment in Italy. What excitement! The group sings "Kind of a Hush," "Holiday Inn" and "Daisy Chain." Producer Klein managed the Beatles for awhile.

MS. 45

1981 Rochelle
PRODUCER: Navaron Films
DIRECTOR: Abel Ferrara
SCREENWRITER: Nicholas St. John

A well-made low-budget New York revenge movie from the director of *Driller Killer.* It's sort of a female version of *Death Wish.* A mute garment-district worker (17-year-old Zoë Tamerlis) goes on a killing spree after she's raped twice in the same day. Tamerlis, wearing lots of makeup and black leather, looks great as she kills off all the male scum of the city. There's enough blood for exploitation fans, great jazz music, and some clever surprises. Recommended. (R)

MISTRESS OF THE APES

1981 CineWorld
PRODUCER: John F. Rickert
DIRECTOR/SCREENWRITER: Larry Buchanan

"Liberated at last!" said the ads. A woman in Central Africa searching for her lost husband decides to stay and live with the local "near men" after their only female is killed. The missing links look like football players with shag haircuts, loincloths, and a little ugly face makeup. The ape men respect her more than the neurotic scummy men on the safari and those back home in New York, so she's happy. Important social statements from the director of *Zontar, the Thing from Venus.* Starring Jenny Neumann and Barbara Leigh. Director of photography: Nicholas Josef Von Sternberg. (R)

MISTRESS OF THE WORLD

1959 CCC (Italy/France/W. Germany)
DIRECTOR: William Dieterle
SCREENWRITERS: Jo Esinger, M.G. Petersson
ORIGINALLY RELEASED AS: *Il Mistero dei Trei Continenti*

A shortened version of a two-part three-hour-plus international feature about a scientist who can control gravity. With

Martha Hyer, Sabu, Carlos Thompson, Lino Ventura, and Wolfgang Preiss. It was one of the last productions by the director of *The Hunchback of Notre Dame* ('39) and *All That Money Can Buy.*

MOBS INC.
1956 Premier (B&W)
PRODUCER: Hal Roach, Jr.
DIRECTOR: William Asher
SCREENWRITERS: Will Gould, Lee Loeb

Listen in as Reed Hadley lectures the young men of the Los Angeles Police Academy on the wiles of confidence men. These three unrelated bunco cases may have been lifted from the *Racket Squad* series on which they're based. (1) A taxi dancer and racketeer pose as a writer-photographer team to gain access to a wealthy man's home. (2) A glamour queen takes in $40,000 through a stock swindle. (3) Townspeople help a young arthritis victim fix up a $1,750 farm, then buy it back for $50,000 after the man claims to have discovered miracle spring waters. Douglass Dumbrille, Don Hagerty, Will Geer, and Marjorie Reynolds of *The Life of Riley* are the stars. Asher, best known for beach movies, also directed *Johnny Cool.*   —CB

MODESTY BLAISE
1966 20th Century-Fox (England)
PRODUCER: Joseph Janni
DIRECTOR: Joseph Losey
SCREENWRITER: Evan Jones

In her first English-speaking role, Monica Vitti plays the comic-strip secret agent. It's the closest thing to a comedy Losey has ever done. Movies like this improve with age. Dirk Bogarde as the totally white villain Gabriel and Rosella Falk as his sadistic assistant Mrs. Fothergill are really strange. Terence Stamp is Modesty's partner in mod clothes and spy fighting. With Harry

Andrews, Clive Revill, Tina Aumont (the daughter of Maria Montez), and Michael Craig. Filmed all over Europe.

THE MOLE PEOPLE
1956 Universal (B&W)
PRODUCER: William Alland
DIRECTOR: Virgil Vogel
SCREENWRITER: Laszlo Gorog

Dr. Frank Baxter, a guy whom kids were supposed to take seriously on "educational" TV specials, introduces

She was abused and violated.

It will never happen again!

MS•45

John Agar fights an albino Sumerian in The Mole People.

this favorite underground-civilization fantasy. One of the screen's finest hero teams (John Agar and Hugh Beaumont) climbs down a hole in Asia and discovers a race of superstitious albinos. Naturally John finds a pretty one (Cynthia Patrick) to fall in love with. Even farther down are the famous mole people, actually slaves of the albino Sumerians, who revolt and save the good guys from the surface. Great fun, it was later turned into a photocomic book. Don't forget your flashlight! With Alan Napier and Nestor Paiva.

MONDO BALORDO

1964 Crown International (Italy)
PRODUCER: Ivanhoe Productions
DIRECTOR: Roberto Bianchi Montero
Boris Karloff is the host/narrator for the English-dubbed version of this documentary of bizarre customs. See an Oriental opium den, a transvestite bar, child coke addicts in Ecuador, a man who says he's Rudolph Valentino reincarnated, a Las Vegas beauty pageant, and much, much more.

MONDO DAYTONA

1968 Craddock
PRODUCERS: Bill Packham, Gordon Craddock
DIRECTOR: Frank Willard
Students raise hell during spring break. Billy Joe Royal supplies narration and sings "These Are Not My People," "Hush," and "Down in the Boondocks"; Mike Sharp does "Spooky" and "Breakthrough"; the Tams do "What Kind of Fool" and "Laugh It Off"; the Swinging Medallions do "She Drives Me Out of My Mind" and their big frat house drinking hit "Double Shot (of My Baby's Love)". *Weekend Rebellion* was a new version of the same film. Sort of *Mondo Daytona: Special Edition.*   –CB

MONDO HOLLYWOOD

1967 Emerson
PRODUCER/DIRECTOR/SCREENWRITER: Robert Carl Cohen
ALSO RELEASED AS: *Image, Hippie Hollywood: The Acid-Blasting Freaks*
The way-out world of Hollywood scenemakers Lewis Beach Marvin III, Dale Davis, Jim Arender, Vito, Jay Sebring, Rudi Gernreich, Dee Dee Cartier, Hope Chest, Gypsy Boots, and many more. Featuring body painting, LSD, skydiving, hairstyling, and topless fashion. With music by Bobby Jameson, Davie Allan and the Arrows, and the Mugwumps.   –CB

MONDO MOD

1967 Timely
PRODUCER/DIRECTOR: Peter Perry
SCREENWRITER: Sherman Greene
Humble Harve explains motorcycles, go-karts, surfing, LSD, pot, coffee shops, and discotheques; Sam the Soul and the Inspirations, the Gretschmen, and the Group furnish sounds of protest and love. Photography by William (originally, and later, Vilmos) Zsigmond

and Laszlo Kovacs. Director Perry edited *Blood of Dracula's Castle.* —CB

MONDO TEENO: See TEENAGE REBELLION.

THE MONITORS

1969 Bell and Howell Productions
PRODUCER: Bernard Samlins
DIRECTOR: Jack Shea
SCREENWRITER: Myron S. Gold

A rambling filmed-in-Chicago cult item about aliens with derbies taking over and enforcing peace by outlawing emotions. They use TV ads with clever jingles and semifamous personalities to brainwash the population. Guy Stockwell stars and gets involved with Susan Oliver and Sherry Jackson. Shepperd Strudwick is the head alien. Avery Schreiber is a klutzy sidekick, Larry Storch and Keenan Wynn lead the right-wing underground. Some of the TV stars are Xavier Cougat, Stubby Kaye, Jackie Vernon, and Senator Everett Dirksen! Also with Alan Arkin and Ed Begley. Cinematography by Vilmos Zsigmond.

MONKEY'S UNCLE

1964 Buena Vista
PRODUCER: Walt Disney
DIRECTOR: Robert Stevenson
SCREENWRITERS: Tom and Helen August

In a sequel to *The Misadventures of Merlin Jones,* Tommy Kirk, Annette, and Stanley the chimp return with more inventions and misadventures. Merlin invents a man-powered flying machine, uses a strength-increasing drug, and saves the football team by helping idiot players pass exams with his brain machine. Annette and the Beach Boys sing the theme song. It was Annette's last for Uncle Walt. She was strictly AIP material for the rest of the decade.

THE MONOLITH MONSTERS

1957 Universal (B&W)
PRODUCER: Howard Christie
DIRECTOR: John Sherwood
SCREENWRITERS: Norman Jolley, Robert M. Fresco

A standout '50s science-fiction film based on a story by Jack Arnold. Like many of the movies Arnold directed, it takes place in a desert town. Meteor crystals growing out of the ground absorb moisture from humans, resulting in really stiff stiffs. When it rains the crystals grow until they tower over the town. They get too big and break, crushing buildings and people. New crystals grow from the pieces. Can Grant Williams and fiancée Lola Albright save the town? With Les Tremayne and William Schallert.

MONSTER

1979 Academy International
PRODUCER: Ken Herts
DIRECTOR: Herbert L. Strock, Ken Herts
SCREENWRITERS: Walter Robert Schmidt, Garland Scott, Herbert Strock, Ken Herts

An Italian *Jaws*-inspired obscurity filmed in South America and California. Original trade ads (in '75) list Andre Faro as the director. The cast includes John Carradine, Cesar Romero, Jim Mitchum, Keenan Wynn, Diane McBain, and Anthony Eisley. The monster is sort of a big dinosaur. Considering the cast and director (Strock did *The Crawling Hand* and *How to Make a Monster*), it's destined to become a favorite of bad movie fans.

MONSTER A GO-GO

1965 B.I.&L. (B&W)
PRODUCER: Herschell Gordon Lewis
DIRECTORS: Bill Rebane, Herschell Gordon Lewis

Herschell Gordon Lewis wanted a cofeature for his *Moonshine Mountain,* so he bought an unfinished science-fiction film called *Terror at Halfday,* added narration and some new scenes, and released it under the Sheldon Seymour pseudonym. Usually considered one of *the* worst, it featured Henry Height, "the tallest man in the world," as an astronaut who returns to Earth as a mutated giant. Ads said: "You've never seen a picture like this"—thank goodness! Unless you lived in the South in the '60s you probably still haven't seen it. Music by the Other Three.

THE MONSTER AND THE GIRL

1940 Paramount (B&W)
PRODUCER: Jack Moss
DIRECTOR: Stuart Heisler
SCREENWRITER: Stuart Anthony

When a man is wrongly executed, a doctor (George Zucco) saves his brain and puts it into a gorilla. The avenging ape goes after the scum who had sold his sister into prostitution (a daring theme at the time). Ellen Drew is the girl. With Paul Lukas, Rod Cameron, Onslow Stevens, Gerald Mohr, and hero Robert Paige. Philip Terry provides the brain. Not your typical '40s horror film. Also with Cliff Edwards, the voice of Jiminy Cricket.

THE MONSTER CLUB

1980 ITC (England)
PRODUCER: Milton Subotsky
DIRECTOR: Roy Ward Baker
SCREENWRITERS: Edward and Valerie Abraham

Vincent Price, who hadn't made a film in five years, unwisely returned in this retread. Price, as a vampire, is the link to three offbeat but weak horror stories. He takes John Carradine (as horror writer Chetwynd-Hayes) to a silly disco for monsters where the tales are related. The cast also includes Stuart Whitman, Donald Pleasence, Britt Ekland, Patrick Magee, Richard Johnson as a vampire, and Simon Ward. With onscreen appearances by the Pretty Things and UB 40.

THE MONSTER DEMOLISHER

1960 AIP-TV (Mexico) (B&W)
PRODUCER: Victor Paras
DIRECTOR: Frederick Curiel
SCREENWRITERS: Frederick Curiel, Charles Taboada
ORIGINALLY RELEASED AS: *Nostradamus y el Destructor de Monstruos*

See *The Blood of Nostradamus*.

MONSTER FROM A PREHISTORIC PLANET

1967 AIP-TV (Japan)
PRODUCER: Mideo Koi
DIRECTOR: Haruyasu Noguchi
SCREENWRITERS: Iwao Yamazak, Ryuko Nakan Ishi
ORIGINALLY RELEASED AS: *Daikyaju Gappa*
ALSO RELEASED AS: *Gappa the Tripibian Monster*

A one-shot giant-monster movie with a plot similar to *Gorgo*. A giant young reptile bird is taken to Tokyo. Its even larger angry parents arrive and level Tokyo before taking the baby back home to their happy island.

MONSTER FROM GREEN HELL

1957 DCA (B&W)
PRODUCER: Al Zimbalist
DIRECTOR: Kenneth Crane
SCREENWRITERS: Louis Vittes, Endre Bohem

Radiation in Africa produces giant buzzing wasps. The main one looks more like a beetle, but that figures since this movie was produced by the man responsible for *Robot Monster*. Eduardo Ciannelli and Vladimir Sokoloff are in it, but Jim Davis and Barbara Turner star. Includes footage from *Stanley and Livingstone* ('39). Also with some stop-motion animation wasps.

THE MONSTER FROM THE OCEAN FLOOR

1954 Lippert (B&W)
PRODUCER: Roger Corman
DIRECTOR: Wyott Ordung
SCREENWRITER: William Danch

Corman's first production effort is terrible, but it made back the $12,000 it cost pretty fast so he was happy. The director, who also acts in this laughable six-day wonder, had an impressive background (he wrote *Robot Monster*). A giant one-eyed octopus is kept off camera until the last few minutes when a one-man minisub rams it in the eye. Anne Kimball is the female-scientist star. With Stuart Wade and Dick Pinner.

MONSTER FROM THE SURF: See THE BEACH GIRLS AND THE MONSTER.

MONSTER ISLAND

1981 Fort Films (Spain/U.S.)
PRODUCER/DIRECTOR: J. Piquer Simon
SCREENWRITERS: Jorge Grau,
Juan Piquer Simon, R. Gantman

"The costliest film ever to be made in Spain" is a Jules Verne adventure with Terence Stamp as the evil Taskinar. With dinosaurs and horror stars Peter Cushing and Paul Naschy.

THE MONSTER MAKER

1944 PRC (B&W)
PRODUCER: Sigmund Neufeld
DIRECTOR: Sam Newfield
SCREENWRITERS: Pierre Gendron,
Martin Mooney

When phony doctor J. Carrol Naish is spurned by Wanda McKay he turns on her father, Ralph Morgan. With the help of strongman Glenn Strange he injects the pianist dad with acromegaly germs, turning him into an ugly-faced "monster."

THE MONSTER OF PIEDRAS BLANCAS

1959 Film Service Distributors (B&W)
PRODUCER: Jack Kevan
DIRECTOR: Irvin Berwick
SCREENWRITER: Haile Chace

A lighthouse keeper puts out food for a legendary monster he claims lives in a nearby cave. Nobody believes him until the creature shows up and rips the heads off a few people. With little horns, big claws, and a hellish snarling face, the monster resembles a scarier version of the Black Lagoon creature. It was created and played by the film's producer, Jack Kevan. Les Tremayne is a doctor. Jeanne Carmen and Don Sullivan hang out on "Lover's Beach" as potential headless teens.

MONSTER OF TERROR: See DIE, MONSTER DIE.

MONSTER OF THE ISLAND

1953 Romana Films (Italy) (B&W)
PRODUCER: Fortunato Misiano
DIRECTOR: Roberto B. Montero
SCREENWRITERS: Roberto B. Montero, ·
Alberto Vechietti
ORIGINALLY RELEASED AS: *Il Monstro dell Isola*

No monster. Just Boris Karloff as a good guy involved with dope smugglers who kidnap a bambino. It only played Italian-language theaters in America but later showed up dubbed on television.

MONSTER ON THE CAMPUS

1958 Universal (B&W)
PRODUCER: Joseph Gershenson
DIRECTOR: Jack Arnold
SCREENWRITER: David Duncan

Arthur Franz is a college professor who studies a prehistoric fish. A dragonfly stings the fish and grows a foot long. His dog is turned into a killer wolf. When the brainy teacher somehow gets

The Monster of Piedras
Blancas.

some fish into his pipe and smokes it
he becomes an ugly Neanderthal man
with an axe and a plaid work shirt! Troy
Donahue is a student. Eddie Parker
plays the monster. With Whit Bissell
and Joanna Moore. It was Arnold's last
monster film. He didn't like it.

THE MONSTER SHOW:
See FREAKS.

THE MONSTER THAT
CHALLENGED THE WORLD
1957 United Artists (B&W)
PRODUCERS: Arthur Gardner, Jules V. Levy
DIRECTOR: Arnold Laven
SCREENWRITER: Pat Fielder

This monster is a giant caterpillar.
Giant eggs are laid in California's Salton
Sea. One hatches and heads for scien-
tist Hans Conreid's lab. Tim Holt and

Audrey Dalton star with Milton Parsons and Jody McCrea.

THE MONSTER WALKS
1932 Mayfair (B&W)
PRODUCER: Cliff Broughton
DIRECTOR: Frank Stayer
SCREENWRITER: Robert Ellis

An old-dark-house mystery with murders blamed on an ape (actually a chimp) though Mischa Auer is the actual killer. Real old-fashioned stuff made after the success of *Dracula* and *Frankenstein*. With Rex Lease and Vera Reynolds. One of the rarer features now being sold on videocassette.

MONSTER ZERO
1966 Toho/Maron Films (Japan)
PRODUCER: Tomoyuki Tanaka
DIRECTOR: Inoshiro Honda
SCREENWRITER: Shinichi Sekizawa
ORIGINALLY RELEASED AS: *Kaiju Daisenso*
ALSO RELEASED AS: *Invasion of Astro-Monsters*

Godzilla in outer space! Nick Adams follows up his *Frankenstein Conquers the World* role as astronaut Glenn. He and Godzilla-film regular Akira Takarada make a deal with the citizens of Planet X. Godzilla and Rodan are taken in space bubbles carried by flying saucers to defeat the alien Ghidrah. But it's all a dirty trick! The spacemen with wraparound shades now have three monsters to attack Earth with. Nick falls in love with a toy saleswoman who's really a spy and there's a big outer-space battle. Earth wins! That didn't make Nick Adams happy, though. By the time this movie was released in America (1970) he had been dead for two years, a suicide.

THE MONSTERS ARE LOOSE: See THE THRILL KILLERS.

MONSTERS FROM THE MOON: See ROBOT MONSTER.

MONSTROSITY: See THE ATOMIC BRAIN.

MONTEREY POP
1969 Leacock Pennebaker
PRODUCERS: D.A. Pennebaker, Richard Leacock
DIRECTOR: D.A. Pennebaker

This mostly great documentary of the '67 Monterey International Pop Festival is a who's who of dead rock stars. The longest piece is by Ravi Shankar, excellent but just a passing fad in the Western world. The Mamas and the Papas do more songs than anybody, which figures since their manager, Lou Adler, and John Phillips produced the festival. Cass Elliot died from drugs, claims Phillips, who with his daughter Mackenzie recently reformed the group after going public with their drug addiction and rehabilitation. Hugh Masakela and Simon and Garfunkel perform. The San Francisco scene is represented by the Jefferson Airplane and Country Joe and the Fish. The Animals, not at their peak, do "Paint It Black." Two members of Canned Heat, Bob Hite and Al Wilson, are dead. The real highlights are provided by the Who (with the late Keith Moon), Big Brother and the Holding Company (featuring the late Janis Joplin), the late Jimi Hendrix, and the late Otis Redding. Watch for the late Brian Jones.

MOON OF THE WOLF
1972 TV
PRODUCERS: Everett Chambers, Peter Thomas
DIRECTOR: Daniel Petrie
SCREENWRITER: Alvin Sapinsley

Sheriff David Janssen hunts for a loup-garou in the bayou. Bradford Dillman is the hairy one. With Barbara Rush and Royal Dano.

MOON WOLF
1959 Allied Artists (Finland/
W. Germany) (B&W)
DIRECTOR: Martin Nosseck
ORIGINALLY RELEASED AS: *Und Immer Ruft das Herz*

A veterinarian allows his dog Wolf to be used in a space project. Wolf is launched in a rocket and lands near the Arctic Circle, close by the home of one of the vet's old flames. The vet and a woodsman fight over the woman, Wolf is rescued, and real wolves attack.

MOON ZERO TWO
1969 Hammer/Warner Brothers
(England)
PRODUCER/SCREENWRITER: Michael Carreras
DIRECTOR: Roy Ward Baker

The first outer-space Western. In 2121 astronaut James Olsen goes to a Moon hotel, shoots it out with bad guys, looks for sapphires, and helps Catherine Schell find her brother. With Adrienne Corri and the Gojos. It was made right after *2001*.

MOONCHILD
1971 Filmmakers Limited
PRODUCER: Dick Alexander
DIRECTOR/SCREENWRITER: Alan Gadney
ALSO RELEASED AS: *Full Moon*

An experimental feature filmed in Riverside, California. In the 1920s a young man goes to an inn whose residents have been repeating the same experiences since the 1700s. John Carradine plays the only mortal there. Victor Buono is the maître d'. Made for a USC Master of Arts degree.

MOONRAKER
1979 United Artists (England)
PRODUCER: Albert R. Broccoli
DIRECTOR: Lewis Gilbert
SCREENWRITER: Christopher Wood

"James Bond Meets *Star Wars*" or "The Return of *Jaws*." The 11th in the James Bond series was even bigger and costlier than its predecessor, *The Spy Who Loved Me*. Michael Lonsdale is Drax, the dullest villain of them all. He's planning to destroy the present population of Earth and then repopulate the planet with a superrace that he'll breed in space. Big Richard Kiel becomes the hero after falling in love in space. Lois Chiles is Mary Goodhead. With Corinne Clery and Bernard Lee as M for the last time. Roger Moore is 007. It made more money than any other Bond film, although Shirley Bassey did not enjoy a Goldfinger-style hit with her theme song. Music by John Barry. William Grefe was the second unit director.

MORE DEAD THAN ALIVE
1969 United Artists
PRODUCER: Hal Klein
DIRECTOR: Robert Sparr
SCREENWRITER: George Schenck

Despite Vincent Price and the title, this is a Western starring Clint Walker (TV's *Cheyenne*) as an out-of-place gunfighter in the 1890s. He's beaten by Mike (*Tarzan*) Henry's gang, nursed to health by Anne Francis, and joins a traveling sideshow owned by Price. After an apparently happy ending a man named Karma (!) shows up and kills the hero. (M)

MORE WILD WEST
1980 TV
PRODUCER: Robert L. Jakes
DIRECTOR: Burt Kennedy
SCREENWRITERS: William Bowers,
Tony Kayden

The networks are really scraping the bottom of the barrel for TV-movie subjects. This is the second time CBS has regurgitated this old TV series. Besides the regulars (Robert Conrad and Ross Martin) we've got Jonathan Winters trying to take over the world with invisibility, Harry Morgan, and Victor Buono. Not bad but get the guest stars— Jack La Lanne and Dr. Joyce Brothers, the TV shrink! She's also in *Embryo*, a bouncing-fetus epic.

MORGAN!

1966 Cinema V (England)
PRODUCER: Leon Clore
DIRECTOR: Karel Reisz
SCREENWRITER: David Mercer

David Warner in his best-remembered role as an eccentric London artist with a gorilla fixation. His mother wants him to be a Marxist and his wife (Vanessa Redgrave) wants a divorce. When not watching the ape at the zoo he watches *King Kong* or *Tarzan, the Ape Man*. He does everything possible to distract his ex-wife, from putting a skeleton in her bed to crashing her wedding to a second husband in a gorilla suit on a motorcycle. He ends up in a mental hospital creating a hammer-and-sickle-shaped garden.

MORGAN THE PIRATE

1960 MGM (France/Italy)
DIRECTOR: Primo Zeglio
SCREENWRITERS: Filippo Sanjust, Andre De Toth, Primo Zeglio
ORIGINALLY RELEASED AS: *Morgan il Pirata*

Steve Reeves as Morgan, an English pirate who attacks only Spanish ships. He takes over Panama, where he had been a slave, and wins the love of Valerie LaGrange. Presented by Joseph E. Levine.

MORO WITCH DOCTOR

1964 20th Century-Fox (U.S./ Philippines) (B&W)
PRODUCER/DIRECTOR/SCREENWRITER: Eddie Romero

A tale of drug smuggling, opium plantations, religious fanatics, and death in Manila from the folks who brought you *The Mad Doctor of Blood Island*. Jock Mahoney stars as CIA agent Jefferson Stark. With Margia Dean and Reed Hadley.

MOSS ROSE

1947 20th Century-Fox (B&W)
PRODUCER: Gene Markey
DIRECTOR: Gregory Ratoff
SCREENWRITERS: Jules Furthman, Tom Reed

Vincent Price as a turn-of-the-century Scotland Yard detective? Peggy Cummins is a Cockney girl who betters her social position by blackmailing killer nobleman Victor Mature. Ethel Barrymore is the rich killer's mother. Hero Price figures out who the "Bible murderer" is. With George Zucco and Patricia Medina.

THE MOST DANGEROUS GAME

1932 RKO (B&W)
PRODUCERS: Merian C. Cooper, Ernest B. Schoedsack
DIRECTORS: Ernest B. Schoedsack, Irving Pichel
SCREENWRITER: James A. Creelman

The creators of *King Kong* made this classic tale the year before their giant ape burst upon the scene. Leslie Banks plays the famous Count Zaroff who hunts humans with a bow and arrow on his misty island. Joel McCrea, Fay Wray, and Robert Armstrong are his latest shipwreck victims. One of Zaroff's men is Noble Johnson, the native chief of Kong Island, here playing a white man! Wray and Armstrong of course also went on to *Kong*, as did composer Max Steiner. Scenes with decapitated human heads are missing from some prints. RKO remade it as *A Game of Death* in '46.

THE MOST DANGEROUS MAN ALIVE

1961 Columbia (B&W)
PRODUCER: Benedict Bogeans
DIRECTOR: Allan Dwan
SCREENWRITERS: James Leicester, Philip Rock

Framed convict Ron Randell escapes, walks into a cobalt-bomb blast, and becomes impervious to bullets. He goes on a vengeance spree until getting burned to a crisp by a flamethrower. With Debra Paget, Morris Ankrum, and Anthony Caruso.

MOTEL HELL

1980 United Artists
PRODUCERS/SCREENWRITERS:
   Steven C. and Robert Jaffe
DIRECTOR: Kevin Connor

An unsuccessful major-studio attempt at cannibal comedy. A cheerful Rory Calhoun stars as Farmer Vincent, whose exclusive sausages are sold from his out-of-the-way motel. Victims are planted in the ground up to their necks and force-fed. The plump people, whose vocal cords have been slit, are dug up and slaughtered. Nina Axelrod as a young woman who wants to marry the crazed old Calhoun, *Playboy* centerfold Rosanne Katon, and a group of ridiculous "punk rockers" don't help much. With Nancy Parson (*Porky's*), Wolfman Jack, and a clip from *The Monster That Challenged the World.* From the director of all those British/Amicus/Edgar Rice Burroughs adventures. **(R)**

MOTHER GOOSE A GO-GO

1966 Jack H. Harris Enterprises
PRODUCER/DIRECTOR/SCREENWRITER:
   Jack H. Harris
ALSO RELEASED AS: *The Unkissed Bride*

This one's hard to believe, but . . . newlyweds (Tommy Kirk and Anne Helm) are staying at a hotel owned by the bride's uncle (Jacques Bergerac of *The Hypnotic Eye*). After having lovemaking problems, the husband visits a shrink and discovers that he has a "Mother Goose Complex" (?). The solution is to treat him with an LSD spray while he sleeps, causing his fairytale fantasies to enter into reality. You figure it out. From the man who brought you *The Blob.* Featuring TV talk-show bully Joe Pyne and Henny Youngman as themselves!

MOTHER'S DAY

1981 United Film Distribution
PRODUCER/DIRECTOR: Charles Kaufman
SCREENWRITERS: Charles Kaufman,
   Warren D. Leight

Ike (Holden McGuire) and Addley (Billy Ray McQuade) are brothers, two bad-natured slobs whose mushlike brains are far too sensitive to signals from the media. The house they live in is a riot of consumer products—they're collectors of *Sesame Street* and *Star Trek* paraphernalia, they eat Trix cereal by the bucket, and they have endless arguments as to whether punk is better than disco. And every once in a while, they rape and kill ("Just like I seen on TV," says Ike), while mother (Rose Ross) directs the show. Into the woods near their happy home

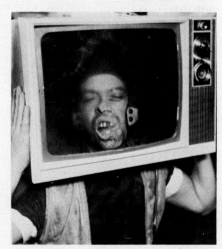

TV death in Mother's Day.

486

Emi and Yumi Ito as the Alilenas in Mothra.

comes a trio of young women, former roommates on their annual reunion. The demented brothers capture the girls and begin their torture show. Of all the violent films released in the past few years, none has received reviews so unfairly reviling as *Mother's Day*. None of the critics mentioned or even seemed to recognize the satirical point of this admittedly twisted comedy—that it is the "launderized" violence performed by the bland villains of television that makes a violent society livable, more than any gore show. (Self imposed X)

–BM

caterpillar emerges, goes to Tokyo, crushes buildings, spins a cocoon, becomes Mothra (a giant moth), causes tidal waves and windstorms with its wings, picks up the tiny twins at the airport and heads home. Mothra and the Alilenas returned as co-stars in four Godzilla movies. When not acting, the girls (Emi and Yumi Ito) have a singing career as the Peanuts. One of their albums, "The Peanuts Hit Parade" was released on London International in America. They do selections by Gene Pitney, Paul Anka, and Tchaikovsky.

MOTHRA

1962 Toho/Columbia (Japan)
PRODUCER: Tomoyuki Tanaka
DIRECTOR: Inoshiro Honda
SCREENWRITER: Shinichi Sekizawa
ORIGINALLY RELEASED AS: *Mosura*

One of the best Japanese monster movies. The Alilenas (twin six-inch princesses who sing and talk in unison) are kidnaped from Infant island by an evil showman and taken to Japan to sing in his nightclub. Back on the island a giant sacred egg hatches. A giant

MOTOR PSYCHO

1965 Eve Productions (B&W)
PRODUCER/DIRECTOR: Russ Meyer
SCREENWRITERS: William E. Sprauge, Russ Meyer

Alex Rocco (later in *The Godfather* and *Herbie Goes Bananas*, among others) joins the beautiful Haji in a vengeful battle against three murderous but clean-cut bikers on Hondas. This comic sex and violence feature set in the desert was originally co-billed with Meyer's more memorable *Faster Pussycat! Kill!*

Kill!, also featuring Haji. Meyer was a bit ahead of his time—the outlaw biker fad didn't start until a year later with *The Wild Angels*.

MOTORCYCLE GANG
1957 AIP (B&W)
PRODUCER: Alex Gordon
DIRECTOR: Edward L. Cahn
SCREENWRITER: Lou Rusoff

The evils of illegal street racing. Steve Terrell is goaded by girlfriend Anne Neyland into a runoff with a highway outlaw. John Ashley pays in the end. The cast includes Carl "Alfalfa" Switzer, Eddie Kafafian, and Jean Moorehead of *The Violent Years*. "Wild and wicked—living with no tomorrow!" is the way the ads described them all. AIP's 16th double feature, with *Sorority Girl*. –CB

MOULIN ROUGE
1952 United Artists
ASSOCIATE PRODUCER: Jack Clayton
DIRECTOR: John Huston
SCREENWRITERS: Anthony Veiller, John Huston

José Ferrer stars on his knees as Toulouse-Lautrec in this Oscar-winning biography. Zsa Zsa Gabor co-stars, and Christopher Lee (as Seurat) and Peter Cushing are both in there somewhere. Cinematography by Freddie Francis.

THE MOUSE THAT ROARED
1959 Columbia (England)
PRODUCER: Walter Shenson
DIRECTOR: Jack Arnold
SCREENWRITERS: Roger MacDougall, Stanley Mann

The Grand Duchy of Fenwick declares war on America, planning to lose and get financial aid. Peter Sellers and 20 men wearing armor and equipped with bows and arrows go to New York and capture the football-shaped Q bomb created by Jean Seberg's father. They win the war. Sellers also plays the Grand Duchess and a count. With William

Hartnell and Leo McKern. *The Mouse on the Moon* was a less effective sequel.

THE MOVIE MURDERER
1970 TV
PRODUCER: Jack Laird
DIRECTOR: Boris Sagal
SCREENWRITER: Stanford Whitmore

Good TV-movie about an arsonist (Warren Oates) who runs around torching buildings containing negatives of him in the act. Arthur Kennedy is a fire-insurance investigator. With lots of film clips and an amusing look at an underground movie. With Jeff Corey, Elisha Cook, Jr., and Robert Webber. From the director of *The Omega Man*.

MOVIE STAR, AMERICAN STYLE, OR LSD, I HATE YOU!
1967 Famous Players (B&W with tinted sequence)
PRODUCER: Robert Caramico
DIRECTOR: Albert Zugsmith
SCREENWRITERS: Albert Zugsmith, Graham Lee Mahn, Lulu Talmadge

Zugsmith's Hollywood acid-therapy "comedy," complete with a tinted trip sequence "in hilarious LSD color." A suicidal film star named Honey Bunny (Paula Lane) is sent by her producer (Robert Strauss) to a rest home run by the unhinged Dr. Horatio (Del Moore), who gives his patients LSD as a cure. The wacky patients include T.C. Jones as an effeminate dress designer, a midget, a fat lady, and lots of actors, directors, and producers, including *Schlock-meister* Albert Zugsmith himself. T.C. Jones, who plays both men and women in other films, also sings the title song.

MOVING VIOLATION
1976 20th Century-Fox
PRODUCER: Julie Corman
DIRECTOR: Charles S. Dubin
SCREENWRITERS: David R. Osterhout, William Norton

A car-chase movie with a sheriff chasing Stephen McHattie and Kay Lenz as a couple who witnessed a murder in a corrupt town. With Eddie Albert, Will Geer, and Dick Miller. Roger Corman is the executive producer.

THE MUMMY
1932 Universal (B&W)
PRODUCER: Stanley Bergerman
DIRECTOR: Karl Freund
SCREENWRITER: John L. Balderston
Cinematographer Karl Freund, who had worked on *Metropolis* and *The Last Laugh* in Germany, made his directoral debut with this moody horror classic. Boris Karloff stars as Im-ho-tep, the 3,700-year-old priest buried alive for stealing a sacred scroll. He emerges from his mummy wrap and, disguised as Ardeth Bey, a "modern" Egyptian, he offers eternal life to the reincarnation of the woman he loves (Zita Johann). Some of the best scenes are flashbacks shown in his pool of remembrance. Edward Van Sloan and David Manners play their usual roles. Noble Johnson is the Mummy's slave. Bramwell Fletcher has an unforgettable scene as the man whose mind snaps when he sees the wrapped body move. The statue of Isis plays an important role. Boris was billed as "Karloff the uncanny." Carl Laemmle, Jr. was executive producer.

THE MUMMY
1959 Hammer/Universal (England)
PRODUCER: Michael Carreras
DIRECTOR: Terence Fisher
SCREENWRITER: Jimmy Sangster
After playing the Frankenstein monster and Dracula, Christopher Lee turned to Kharis the Mummy. *Curse of Frankenstein, The Horror of Dracula*, and this hit restarted the horror-movie industry. All three were directed by Terence Fisher and co-starred Peter Cushing. Kharis is revived in the 19th century by an Egyptian fanatic as an instrument of revenge. The Mummy just wants archaeologist Cushing's wife: he thinks she's a reincarnation of the princess he died for. The wife/princess is Yvonne Furneaux, later in Polanski's *Repulsion*. Lee made a powerful, fast-moving Mummy. The opening sequence where he's condemned to be buried alive was a real shocker in 1959. One slave holds his tongue with pliers while another whacks it off with a knife. George Pastell is Mehemet the priest.

THE MUMMY'S CURSE
1944 Universal (B&W)
ASSOCIATE PRODUCER: Oliver Drake
DIRECTOR: Leslie Goodwins
SCREENWRITER: Bernardo Schubert
The reincarnations of Princess Ananka and Kharis the Mummy are dug out of the swamp they sunk into at the end of *The Mummy's Ghost*. Lon Chaney plays the Mummy for the last time. Ananka is played by Virginia Christine, famous as Mrs. Olsen on recent TV coffee commercials. Peter Coe and Martin Kosleck are the tana-leaf-brewing priests. With Kay Harding, Kurt Katch, Holmes Herbert, and lots of footage from earlier Mummy films. The worst of the series.

THE MUMMY'S GHOST
1944 Universal (B&W)
ASSOCIATE PRODUCER: Ben Pivar
DIRECTOR: Reginald Le Borg
SCREENWRITERS: Griffith Jay, Henry Sucher, Brena Weisberg
Since his disciple Turhan Bey failed in his mission in *The Mummy's Tomb*, the old priest (George Zucco) sends a new one, Youssef Bey (John Carradine), to New England to help Kharis (Lon Chaney) find the Princess Ananka. A college student with two white shocks of hair (Ramsey Ames) is the modern reincarnation of the Egyptian princess

who ends up in the swamp with Kharis. Robert Lowery is the hero. With Barton MacLane and Frank Reicher.

THE MUMMY'S HAND
1940 Universal (B&W)
PRODUCER: Ben Pivar
DIRECTOR: Christy Cabanne
SCREENWRITERS: Griffith Jay, Maxwell Shane
The first of the Kharis the Mummy films stars Tom Tyler in the bandages. Dick Foran and Wallace Ford are survivors of the expedition cursed by opening the sacred tomb. George Zucco is the high priest cooking tana leaves. Peggy Moran is the woman the Mummy wants. With Eduardo Ciannelli and Cecil Kellaway. The impressive temple set was left over from *Green Hell*. Tyler went on to play Captain Marvel and the Mummy role went to Lon Chaney. With over ten minutes of footage from *The Mummy* ('31) used as a flashback.

THE MUMMY'S REVENGE
1973 Avco Embassy-TV (Spain)
PRODUCER: Luis Mendez
DIRECTOR: Carlos Aured
SCREENWRITER: Jacinto Molina
ORIGINALLY RELEASED AS: *La Venganza de la Momie*
Paul Naschy plays the worst-looking Mummy since the one Abbott and Costello met. He also appears unwrapped.

THE MUMMY'S SHROUD
1967 Hammer/20th Century-Fox (England)
PRODUCER: Anthony Nelson-Keys
DIRECTOR/SCREENWRITER: John Gilling
The mummy of an Egyptian slave (Edie Powell) is revived when an early-20th-century expedition breaks into a tomb. This mummy (named Prem) was designed to resemble a real one instead of a Hollywood model, but the movie is still pretty forgettable. With Maggie Kimberley and Andre Morell. Peter Cushing narrates.

THE MUMMY'S TOMB
1942 Universal (B&W)
ASSOCIATE PRODUCER: Ben Pivar
DIRECTOR: Harold Young
SCREENWRITERS: Griffith Jay, Henry Sucher
The sequel to *The Mummy's Hand* finds high priest George Zucco, now an old man, sending his follower (Turhan Bey) to America with Kharis (Lon Chaney). Hiding out at a cemetery, they seek revenge on Dick Foran and Wallace Ford (also old men) who had defiled the tomb of Princess Ananka in the earlier film. Elyse Knox gets carried off this time. It opens with flashbacks to the 1940 film and includes shots of mad villagers from the original *Frankenstein*. In many of the scenes the Mummy was played by famous stuntman Eddie Parker.

MUMSY, NANNY, SONNY AND GIRLY: See GIRLY.

MUNSTER, GO HOME
1966 Universal
PRODUCERS: Joe Connelly, Bob Mosker
DIRECTOR: Earl Bellamy
SCREENWRITERS: George Tibbles, Joe Connelly, Bob Mosker
Half-hour TV situation comedies usually don't inspire very good feature-length films. This one was made for TV, but released theatrically at the last minute. At least it's better than the 1981 Munsters reunion TV-movie. The Munsters inherit a British estate that is being used as headquarters by counterfeiters. Hermione Gingold, her son (Terry-Thomas), and their sinister butler Cruikshan (John Carradine) vainly try to scare away the weird Americans. Herman wins a race in his custom-made Dragula coffin/car. With the TV cast (Fred Gwynne, Yvonne De Carlo, Al Lewis, Butch Patrick) except for Debbie Watson, one of four different Mari-

lyns. With Richard Dawson, Cliff Norton, and Robert Pine (From the *CHiPs* TV series) as Marilyn's boyfriend.

THE MUNSTER'S REVENGE

1981 TV
PRODUCER: Don Nelson
DIRECTOR: Don Weiss
SCREENWRITERS: Arthur Alsberg, Don Nelson
The Munsters was always inferior to the usually great *Addams Family*. Both shows started in '64 and ran exactly two seasons. I'd rather see a *Car 54 Where Are You?* TV-movie than this one. Universal produced the series, so Fred Gwynne as Herman can legally look like the Karloff monster. He still looks the same as he did in the series. So does Al Lewis as Grandpa. Yvonne De Carlo, on the other hand, will never recover in looks or credibility from movies like *Silent Scream*, *The Seven Minutes* and *Guyana: Cult of the Damned*. Eddie and Marilyn are played by newcomers. Sid Caesar is Dr. Diablo. The story is about robots disguised as wax figures. One wears a Tor Johnson mask.

MURDER BY DECREE

1979 Avco-Embassy (England/Canada)
PRODUCERS: Rene Dupont, Bob Clark
DIRECTOR: Bob Clark
SCREENWRITER: John Hopkins
It's a crime that this Sherlock Holmes vs. Jack the Ripper film didn't do better. It's the best all-around Holmes movie ever made. Christopher Plummer as Holmes and James Mason as Watson discover a cover-up plot implicating the entire government. David Hemmings, Anthony Quayle, and John Gielgud represent various arms of the law. Frank Finlay is Lestrade. Donald Sutherland plays a helpful psychic. Geneviève Bujold is especially good as an institutionalized victim. From the director of *Deathdream*. Don't miss.

Al Lewis, Fred Gwynne, and Yvonne De Carlo return for The Munsters' Revenge.

MURDER BY MAIL: See *SCHIZOID.*

MURDER BY TELEVISION

1935 Imperial Distributors
ASSOCIATE PRODUCER: Edward M. Spitz
DIRECTOR: Clifford Sanforth
SCREENWRITER: Joseph O'Donnell
A rare and boring independently produced mystery featuring Bela Lugosi as twin brothers. It turns out neither one is the killer of a professor who has invented a television set (a "science-fiction" idea in '35). This static talkie with a cast of unknowns wasn't shown much even in the '30s.

MURDER BY THE CLOCK

1931 Paramount (B&W)
DIRECTOR: Edward Sloman
SCREENWRITER: Henry Myers

A forgotten early horror movie centering on a crypt specially equipped with a horn that sounds if the woman buried inside is actually alive. A murder mystery involves a dead man brought back to life and a mysterious half-wit (Irving Pichel). With William Boyd, Lilyan Tashman, and Regis Toomey.

THE MURDER CLINIC

1966 Europix (France/Italy)
PRODUCER/DIRECTOR: Elio Scardamaglia (Michael Hamilton)
SCREENWRITERS: Ernesto Gastaldi, Luciano Martino
ALSO RELEASED AS: *La Lama del Corpo*, *The Murder Society*, *Revenge of the Living Dead*

Another European-plastic-surgeon-trying-to-restore-a-disfigured-woman's-face film. It also features a hooded killer at an asylum. Millions of Americans have seen it as part of the *Orgy of the Living Dead* triple bill. With William Berger and Françoise Prévost.

MURDER MANSION

1970 Avco Embassy-TV (Spain)
DIRECTOR: Francisco Lara Polop
ORIGINALLY RELEASED AS:
  La Mansion de la Niebla

A young couple spends the night in the home of the title. With "ghosts and vampires." Analia Gade, Ida Galli, Andres Resino.

MURDER ON FLIGHT 502

1975 TV
PRODUCER: David Chasman
DIRECTOR: George McCowan
SCREENWRITER: David P. Harmon

Airport '75, TV style. Robert Stack is the pilot of a jet being terrorized by a maniac. With Polly Bergen, Theodore Bikel, Sonny Bono(!), Fernando Lamas, George Maharis, Farah Fawcett-Majors(!), Hugh O'Brian, Walter Pidgeon, Danny Bonaduce(!), and Stack's real-life wife and daughters!

UPI 2/13/67: The "Great White Way" of yesteryear today is a place frequented mostly by the undesirable. This small portion of 42nd Street near Eighth Avenue is a jam of neon-lighted restaurants, amusement centers of questionable attractions, and small movie theaters that are open nearly all night. Currently efforts are being made to make the area more desirable.

THE MURDER SOCIETY: See THE MURDER CLINIC.

MURDERER'S ROW

1966 Columbia
PRODUCER: Irving Allen
DIRECTOR: Henry Levin
SCREENWRITER: Herbert Baker

The second Matt Helm adventure finds wise-cracking photographer/spy Dean Martin posing as a hit man working for hammy villain Karl Malden, who plans to destroy Washington, D.C. with a helio beam. Ann-Margret, as Karl's daughter, is usually found dancing wildly in one pop-art outfit or another. Tom Reese plays Ironhead, a killer who ends up hanging from a giant magnet. Dino's lucky son gets to play a few hot numbers as part of "Dino, Desi and Billy." It didn't help their record sales much. With Camilla Sparv, Beverly Adams, and an inflatable boat. Filmed on the Riviera. Dino sings, too!

MURDERS IN THE RUE MORGUE

1932 Universal (B&W)
PRODUCER: Carl Laemmle, Jr.
DIRECTOR: Robert Florey
SCREENWRITERS: Tom Reed, Dale Van Every

In his first horror film after *Dracula*, Bela Lugosi plays Dr. Mirakle. In turn-of-the-century Paris he exhibits "Erik, le gorille au cerveau humain" and secretly injects women with ape blood. Dead victims are dumped in the river. It doesn't have much to do with Poe, but the distorted sets are great and the plot is pretty lurid in a pre-Code fashion. *What's My Line?* regular Arlene Francis makes her film debut as a prostitute tied to a cross. Erik (Charles Gemora) kills people and stuffs their corpses up chimneys. Sidney Fox and Leon Waycroff (later known as Leon Ames) star as a romantic couple. Noble Johnson plays Bela's assistant. This quickie was sort of a favor to the rejected director of *Frankenstein* (Florey) and the actor who had turned down the monster role (Lugosi). The ape suit's better than most, but the illusion is ruined by close-ups of a real orangutan.

MURDERS IN THE RUE MORGUE

1971 AIP
PRODUCER: Louis M. Heyward
DIRECTOR: Gordon Hessler
SCREENWRITERS: Christophe Wicking, Henry Slesar

Jason Robards runs a horror theater in 19th-century France. Herbert Lom with a disfigured face, looking the way he did in *The Phantom of the Opera*, sets out to destroy Robards and his show. A totally confused movie with flashbacks and dream sequences galore. With Michael Dunn, Lilli Palmer, Christine Kaufmann, Maria Perschy, and a gorilla suit that looks like it was left over from *Trog*. Filmed in Spain.

MURDERS IN THE ZOO

1933 Paramount (B&W)
DIRECTOR: Edward Sutherland
SCREENWRITERS: Philip Wylie, Seton I. Miller

Kathleen Burke, the panther woman in *Island of Lost Souls*, returns as the wife of an insanely jealous and sadistic zookeeper (Lionel Atwill). Both films were condemned for excessively bad taste. People are thrown to alligators, snakes, and lions, and one man is left to die after Lionel sews his mouth shut. Randolph Scott is the hero. Charlie Ruggles provides comic relief. With Gail Patrick and John Lodge.

MUSCLE BEACH PARTY

1964 AIP
PRODUCERS: James H. Nicholson, Robert Dillon
DIRECTOR: William Asher
SCREENWRITER: Robert Dillon

Frankie and Annette on the beach—Part II. A wealthy contessa (Luciana Paluzzi of *The Green Slime*) wants muscleman Flex Martin (Rock Stevens a.k.a. Peter Lupus of the *Mission Impossible* series) for her own—until she meets Frankie. Annette gets jealous. Don Rickles trains the muscle builders. Buddy Hackett manages the contessa. With Morey Amsterdam, Jody McCrea, Donna Loren, and Dan Haggerty. If you can last through the unfunny beach antics you'll see Little Stevie Wonder, Dick Dale and his Del-tones, and a last look at Peter Lorre in a bit part as Mr. Strangdour. Lorre, who surely would have continued in AIP films, died that year.

MUSICAL MUTINY

1970 CineWorld
PRODUCER: Barry Mahon

A long-dead Caribbean buccaneer named Don Williams the Great visits Pirate's World amusement park where he tricks a guard into throwing open the gates to an Iron Butterfly concert. The group's manager pulls them off after one song and local bands fill in until a rich hippie promises to settle accounts if the Butterfly will finish their set. Doug, Ron, Erik, and Lee return to butcher "Soul Experience," "In the Time of Our Lives," and "In-A-Gadda-Da-Vida." The emergency guest bands include Fantasy, the New Society Band, and Grit.   –CB

MUTANT: See FORBIDDEN WORLD.

MUTATIONS

1972 Columbia (England)
PRODUCER: Robert Weinbach
DIRECTOR: Jack Cardiff
SCREENWRITER: Garson Raye

Donald Pleasence plays a doctor who crosses humans with plants. His best creation is a venus fly trap man. He sends his failures to a freak show operated by dwarf Michael Dunn in his last role (he died in '73). As in the famous *Freaks*, real sideshow people are featured: a human pincushion, a lizard lady, a frog boy, a monkey woman, and a pretzel boy. With Tom Baker as Dunn's sadistic deformed assistant, Julie Ege, Jill Haworth, and Brad Harris. The most memorable character is a man called Popeye. Director Cardiff was a former cinematographer (*The Red Shoes*, *Black Narcissus*).

MUTINY IN OUTER SPACE

1965 Allied Artists (B&W)
PRODUCERS: Hugo Grimaldi, Arthur C. Pierce
DIRECTOR: Hugo Grimaldi
SCREENWRITER: Arthur C. Pierce

Low-budget space-station problems originally shown with *The Human Duplicators*. A lunar fungus attacks astronauts, turning them hairy, ugly, and dead. William Leslie, Dolores Faith, and others worry a lot. With Glenn Langan and Harold Lloyd, Jr.

MY BLOOD RUNS COLD

1965 Warner Brothers (B&W)
PRODUCER/DIRECTOR: William Conrad
SCREENWRITER: John Mantley

Troy Donahue risks his good-guy image as an insane killer who convinces Joey Heatherton(!) that they are reincarnations of past lovers. Her father (Barry Sullivan) and ex-boyfriend (Nicolas Coster) find Troy hard to take. Directed by TV's *Cannon*. With Jeanette Nolan and John Holland (*They Saved Hitler's*

Brain). Troy later played a Charles Manson character in *Sweet Saviour*.

MY BLOODY VALENTINE

1981 Paramount (Canada)
PRODUCERS: John Dunning, André Link,
Stephen Miller
DIRECTOR: George Mihalka
SCREENWRITER: John Beard

A *Halloween* copy about a crazed miner who turns up for a Valentine's Day party, cuts people's hearts out with a pickax, and delivers them to local cops in candy boxes. Many gory scenes were cut before release to avoid an X rating. The stupid young people giving the party decide to move it to the mine where most of them work. With a surprise ending and lots of Molson's beer. **(R)**

MY BROTHER HAS BAD DREAMS

1977 American Pictures
PRODUCER/DIRECTOR: Robert Emery

A man is driven to homicide out of jealousy over his sister's lover. Nick Kleinholtz stars in a watchable no-budget quickie from the makers of *Scream Evelyn Scream*. A late-night TV favorite with a mannequin on a motorcycle.

MY FAVORITE BLONDE

1942 Paramount (B&W)
DIRECTOR: Sidney Lanfield
SCREENWRITERS: Don Hartman, Frank Butler

Bob Hope spy comedy featuring veteran villains George Zucco and Gale Sondergaard. With Madeleine Carroll. The trained penguin that shares Hope's vaudeville act was a good idea, but the bird gets thoughtlessly thrown around so much that the Society for Prevention of Cruelty to Penguins should have been notified. Director Lanfield later produced *The Addams Family*.

MY FAVORITE BRUNETTE

1947 Paramount (B&W)
PRODUCER: Daniel Dare
DIRECTOR: Elliott Nugent
SCREENWRITERS: Edmund Beloin, Jack Rose

In one of his best comedies, Bob Hope plays a baby photographer mistaken for a private detective. He tries to protect Dorothy Lamour from the likes of Lon Chaney, Jr. (as Willie), Peter Lorre (as Kismet), Elisha Cook, Jr., and John Hoyt. In a parody of his famous role in *Of Mice and Men* Chaney plays a dumb brute who cracks nuts with his hands. Also watch for Bing Crosby and Alan Ladd!

MY GUN IS QUICK

1957 United Artists (B&W)
PRODUCER: George White, Phil Victor
DIRECTOR: George White
SCREENWRITERS: Richard Collins,
Richard Powell

The third of UA's Mike Hammer films. As the famous private eye, Robert Bray is involved with a girl with an unusual ring who is murdered. With Whitney Blake, Pat Donahue, and Richard Garland. Spillane played his own creation six years later in *The Girl Hunters*.

MY SISTER MY LOVE

1979 American General
PRODUCER: Diana Young
DIRECTOR: Karen Arthur
SCREENWRITER: Don Christian
ORIGINALLY RELEASED AS: *The Mafu Cage*

A psychological drama based on a French play, rescued from oblivion by videocassette sales. Carol Kane is crazy and tortures and kills people. She's very close to sister Lee Grant, who joins her in eliminating intruders. The two stars made more commercial thrillers after this: *Damien: Omen II* (Grant) and *When a Stranger Calls* (Kane). With Will Geer, James Olson, and a gorilla. **(R)**

MY SON, THE HERO

1962 United Artists (Italy/France)
PRODUCER: Franco Cristaldi
DIRECTOR: Duccio Tessari
SCREENWRITERS: Ennio De Cocini,
Duccio Tessari
ORIGINALLY RELEASED AS: *Les Titans*

Several years before Woody Allen turned a Japanese spy movie into *What's Up, Tiger Lily?*, this mythological adventure was turned into a comedy via English dubbing. The hero fights in the arena, wears an invisibility helmet, does battle with the gorgon; statues come to life while saying supposedly funny lines with Jewish accents. T. Rowe wrote the new dialogue.

MY SON, THE VAMPIRE

1952 Blue Chip Productions (England)
(B&W)
PRODUCER/DIRECTOR: John Gilling
SCREENWRITER: Val Valentin
ALSO RELEASED AS: *Old Mother Riley Meets
the Vampire, Vampire Over London*

This infamous Bela Lugosi film isn't really that terrible when you consider its background. Arthur Lucan, a British music hall comedian, had been playing an Irish washerwoman named Old Mother Riley in a series of comedies going back to 1937 (this was the last). Lugosi's presence had previously helped the fading Abbott and Costello, so why not have him help out an aging drag act? Trouble was nobody in America wanted to know. By the time it came out here in '63 it had a new title and a theme song by Alan Sherman, who was riding high with his hit album "My Son the Folksinger." Bela plays Baron Van Housen, a criminal who thinks he's a vampire. His disassembled robot gets misplaced and Mother Riley gets in the way of his sinister plans. A weird movie for sure, but no worse than your average Monogram feature. The real crime was Bela's salary—$5,000.

MY SOUL RUNS NAKED: See *RAT FINK*.

MY WORLD DIES SCREAMING: See *TERROR IN THE HAUNTED HOUSE*.

MYRA BRECKENRIDGE

1970 20th-Century-Fox
PRODUCER: Robert Fryer
DIRECTOR: Michael Sarne
SCREENWRITERS: Michael Sarne, David Gilep

In a desperate effort to make back some of the money lost on this famous disaster it was rereleased as a midnight movie top-billing Farrah Fawcett "in her first erotic movie scandal." Any film that opens with John Carradine as a doctor surgically removing Rex Reed's cock has got the right idea even if it did go wrong. Seventy-seven-year-old Mae West in her first role in 26 years got the original top billing but not much to do. She's a "talent agent" after the young man whom Raquel Welch (formerly Reed) had strapped to a table and raped. John Huston follows up his great roles in *Candy* and *De Sade* by playing Myron/Myra's rich old ex-cowboy-star uncle. Lots of old Hollywood film clips are used as well as old actors like Andy Devine and Grady Sutton. With Jim Backus, Calvin Lockhart, William Hopper, Tom Selleck, and Genevieve Waite, whose husband John Phillips wrote the song Rex sings. The lovely Farrah, by the way, ends up in bed with Raquel. (X)

THE MYSTERIANS

1957 Toho/MGM (Japan)
PRODUCER: Tomoyuki Tanaka
DIRECTOR: Inoshiro Honda
SCREENWRITER: Jojiro Okami
ORIGINALLY RELEASED AS: *Chikyu Boeign*

"See! See! See! A daring attempt by love-starved men of another planet to steal our women!" That's the plot. The invaders from Mystroid wear capes, round helmets, and dark glasses. They bring a giant metallic tanklike robot bird and a whole fleet of flying saucers to aid them in their mission. Lots of massive destruction and good special effects make this an all-time favorite. *The Mysterians* was one of the last releases from RKO. When Howard Hughes closed down, it was sold to MGM.

MYSTERIOUS DOCTOR

1943 Warner Brothers (B&W)
PRODUCER: William Jacobs
DIRECTOR: Ben Stoloff
SCREENWRITER: Richard Weil
A headless ghost (actually a Nazi) stalks a mining village, sabotages the British war effort, and decapitates people. A reportedly hilarious horror with John Loder, Eleanor Parker, Matt Willis, and Creighton Hale.

THE MYSTERIOUS DR. SATAN

1940 Republic (B&W)
ASSOCIATE PRODUCER: Hiram S. Brown, Jr.
DIRECTORS: William Witney, John English
SCREENWRITERS: Franklyn Adreon, Ronald Davidson, Norman S. Hall, Joseph Poland, Sol Shor
ALSO RELEASED AS: *Dr. Satan's Robot*
Dr. Satan (Eduardo Ciannelli) terrorizes the world with his cute awkward robot. Robert Wilcox as the Copperhead, a hero wearing a sack over his head, intervenes. A feature version of this fun 15-chapter serial was released in 1966. With Ella Neal and C. Montague Shaw.

THE MYSTERIOUS MR. MOTO

1938 20th Century-Fox (B&W)
PRODUCER: Sol Wurtzel
DIRECTOR: Norman Foster
SCREENWRITERS: Philip McDonald, Norman Foster
Japanese detective Mr. Moto (Peter Lorre) poses as a Devil's Island prisoner and escapes with Leon Ames, a member of the League of Assassins. In London Moto becomes the killer's houseboy and breaks up the gang. With Mary Maguire, Henry Wilcoxon, and Harold Huber.

MYSTERIOUS ISLAND

1961 Columbia (U.S./England)
PRODUCER: Charles H. Schneer
DIRECTOR: Cy Endfield
SCREENWRITERS: John Prebble, Daniel Ullman, Crane Wilbur
During the Civil War some Union prisoners, a rebel sergeant, and a reporter escape in an observation balloon that drifts to a tropical island. Along with two female shipwreck survivors, they discover a giant crab (they boil and eat it), a giant baby bird, and giant bees. When pirates attack they're rescued by none other than Captain Nemo (Herbert Lom). The story is a sequel to Verne's *20,000 Leagues Under the Sea* and the wonderful special effects are by Ray Harryhausen. With Gary Merrill, Michael Craig, Joan Greenwood, Michael Callan, and an octopus. Music by Bernard Herrmann.

THE MYSTERIOUS ISLAND OF CAPTAIN NEMO

1973 Cinema Releasing (France/Spain)
PRODUCER: Alina Productions
DIRECTORS: Henri Colpi, Juan Antonio Bardem
SCREENWRITERS: Jean Antonio Barders, Jacques Champreaux
ORIGINALLY RELEASED AS: *L'Ile Mysterieuse*

A cut-rate version of the Jules Verne story with good sets and Omar Sharif as Captain Nemo.

THE MYSTERIOUS MR. WONG

1935 Monogram (B&W)
PRODUCER: George Yohalem
DIRECTOR: William Nigh
SCREENWRITER: Nina Howatt

Bela Lugosi with his usual accent plays an Oriental Fu Manchu–type villain in New York's Chinatown. He uses hatchetmen and a torture chamber to take possession of "the 12 coins of Confucius," which will make him ruler of China. Wallace Ford is the wisecracking reporter hero. With Arlene Judge and Lotus Long. It has nothing to do with the later Mr. Wong films Monogram made with Karloff.

THE MYSTERIOUS MONSTERS

1976 Sunn Classics
PRODUCER: Charles E. Sellier, Jr.
DIRECTOR/SCREENWRITER: Robert Guenette

Peter Graves narrates! With Bigfoot! The Loch Ness monster! The Abominable Snowman! Peter provides proof! Can you take it?

MYSTERIOUS SATELLITE: See WARNING FROM SPACE.

THE MYSTERY OF EDWIN DROOD

1935 Universal (B&W)
DIRECTOR: Stuart Walker
SCREENWRITERS: John L. Balderstein, Gladys Unger

Claude Rains plays a choirmaster opium addict in an adaptation of Charles Dickens' last (unfinished) novel about murder and a love triangle. With David Manners, Heather Angel, Douglas Montgomery, Valerie Hobson, and the crypt set from *Dracula* ('31).

THE MYSTERY OF MARIE ROGET

1942 Universal (B&W)
ASSOCIATE PRODUCER: Paul Malvern
DIRECTOR: Phil Rosen
SCREENWRITER: Michael Jacoby
ALSO RELEASED AS: *Phantom of Paris*

Poe's story is based on a real 1842 murder case. The film features Patrick Knowles as detective Pierre Dupin, aided by Lloyd Carrigan. Maria Montez is Marie. A stolen brain and the presence of Maria Ouspenskaya and Charles Middleton add horror touches. "Who is the phantom mangler of Paris?"

THE MYSTERY OF THE MARIE CELESTE

1935 Hammer (England) (B&W)
PRODUCER: M. Fraser Passmore
DIRECTOR: Denison Clift
SCREENWRITER: Charles Larkworthy
ALSO RELEASED AS: *Phantom Ship*

Bela Lugosi plays Anton Lorenzen, an unshaven crazed seaman, in the second film produced by England's Hammer Studios. The story is based on a true incident concerning a 19th-century American windjammer discovered adrift with no crew. No trace was ever found of them. With Shirley Grey.

THE MYSTERY OF MR. WONG

1939 Monogram (B&W)
PRODUCER: Scott R. Dunlap
DIRECTOR: William Nigh
SCREENWRITER: Scott Darling

Mr. Wong (Boris Karloff) exposes the murderer who has stolen "the eye of the daughter of the moon," a priceless sapphire. The second in the series. With Lotus Long, Ivan Lebedeff, Grant Withers, and Dorothy Tree.

THE MYSTERY OF THE 13TH GUEST

1943 Monogram (B&W)
PRODUCER: Monogram
DIRECTOR: William Beaudine
SCREENWRITERS: Charles Marion, Tim Ryan

Who is the fiendish killer? A remake of the 1932 Ginger Rogers movie with Helen Parrish and Dick Purcell as a detective.

MYSTERY OF THE WAX MUSEUM

1933 Warner Brothers
PRODUCTION SUPERVISOR: Henry Blanke
DIRECTOR: Michael Curtiz
SCREENWRITERS: Don Mullany, Carl Erickson

In his most famous role, Lionel Atwill is Henry Jarrod, the mad sculptor who covers bodies with wax to repopulate the museum that his partner set fire to. Fay Wray, his future Marie Antoinette, cracks off Atwill's false face to reveal the incredibly mangled features underneath. The real female star is Glenda Farrell, an underrated blond comedienne, as a wisecracking reporter who saves the day. Arthur Edmund Carewe plays a junkie suspected of murder who is tortured by the New York Police. A horror classic filmed in early Technicolor (two colors) with great sets and some real scares. The biggest flaw is the use of live people as the wax dummies: you can see them breathing and trying to stay still. *The House of Wax* was a close remake minus the reporter and the junkie.

NABONGA

1944 PRC (B&W)
PRODUCER: Sigmund Neufeld
DIRECTOR: Sam Newfield
SCREENWRITER: Fred Myton
ALSO RELEASED AS: *Gorilla*

Eighteen-year-old Julie London makes her screen debut as a jungle goddess. Her best friend is a big, bone-crushing ape until handsome Buster Crabbe shows up. Soon Julie (with flowers in her hair) convinces Nabonga that Buster's okay. And then they all defeat the villains played by Barton MacLane and Fifi D'Orsay. Newfield directed the similar *White Pongo* the next year.

NAKED ANGELS

1969 Crown International
PRODUCER: David R. Dawdy
DIRECTOR/SCREENWRITER: Bruce Clark

On his release from a Los Angeles hospital, Michael Greene leads his crazed Angels into Nevada to take care of the rival gang that put him away. They experience the standard desert hardships as they search for the Las Vegas Hotdoggers' old mine hideout. Jennifer Gan, Richard Rust, Art Jenoff, Tedd King, and Felicia Guy co-star; the Straight Records sound track features Jeff Simmons. Roger Corman was executive producer. **(R)** –CB

THE NAKED APE

1973 Universal
PRODUCER: Zev Bufman
DIRECTOR/SCREENWRITER: Donald Driver

Millions of years of evolution are explored with live action and animation in this oddity produced by the film-production arm of *Playboy* magazine. Ex-*Rifleman* co-star Johnny Crawford stars with Victoria Principal and Marvin Miller. A seldom-screened comic documentary-fantasy executive-produced by Hugh Hefner, the man who gave us airbrushed pubic hair.

UPI 3/13/72: Actor Johnny Crawford stands between pre-historic figures at the Field Museum of Natural History where a scene for the film The Naked Ape will be made. The figures were especially made for the film at a cost of about $10,000 each. Crawford, who starred as Chuck Connors' son in the "Rifleman" TV series, is making his motion-picture debut in the film.

NAKED EVIL: See *EXORCISM AT MIDNIGHT*.

THE NAKED GODDESS: See *THE DEVIL'S HAND*.

THE NAKED GUN

1956 Associated Film (B&W)
PRODUCER: Ron Ormond
DIRECTOR: Edward Dew
SCREENWRITERS: Ron Ormond, Jack Lewis

The story of an insurance man searching for the heiress to a stolen and thereby cursed Aztec fortune. It turns out to be Mara Corday of *The Giant Claw*. Jody McCrea co-stars, with veterans Barton MacLane, Tom Brown, Veda Ann Borg, and Morris Ankrum. –CB

THE NAKED JUNGLE

1954 Paramount
PRODUCER: George Pal
DIRECTOR: Byron Haskin
SCREENWRITERS: Philip Yordan, Ronald MacDougall

The Pal/Haskin team (*War of the Worlds*) turns to the real-life horror of South American soldier ants. Most of the story concerns Charlton Heston's rejection of mail order bride Eleanor Parker, but the scenes of his plantation being overrun by millions of ants make this one of the best insect-attack movies ever. A larger variety showed up only months later in *Them!*

THE NAKED KISS
1964 Allied Artists (B&W)
PRODUCER/DIRECTOR/SCREENWRITER:
Sam Fuller

After his powerful *Shock Corridor*, Fuller made this revealing look at American morals; then, except for *Shark Kill* (1970), which he disowns, he didn't direct again until *The Big Red One* in 1980. The feature that nearly ended his career opens with a bald prostitute (Constance Towers) killing her cruel pimp. She flees to the town of Grantville disguised as an Angel Foam champagne saleswoman, but soon switches to a respectable job as a nurse in the children's ward of a hospital. She discovers dark secrets about a respected, wealthy local man (Michael Dante) and stands up to the local madam (Virginia Grey) who is busy recruiting young girls. Anthony Eisley is the helpful but corrupt police chief. With Patsy Kelly and Edy Williams.

NAKED PARADISE
1957 AIP
PRODUCER/DIRECTOR: Roger Corman
SCREENWRITER: Charles B. Griffith
ALSO RELEASED AS: *Thunder Over Hawaii*

Beverly Garland falls in with mobsters planning to trick cruise-boat captain Richard Denning into a plantation payroll robbery. Leslie Bradley, Jonathan Haze, and Dick Miller are outwitted; Richard and Beverly live out their days exploring the South Seas. Filmed on location in the Islands. Wardrobe by Shaheen of Honolulu. *Flesh and the Spur* was the co-feature. —CB

NAKED TERROR
1961 Joseph Brenner Associates

Vincent Price narrates a documentary on African Zulus. See: murder by witchcraft, the dance of the deadly pythons, virgins being initiated into the tribe, and arms thrust into scalding water as a way of detecting liars.

NAKED YOUTH: See WILD YOUTH.

THE NAKED ZOO
1970 R&S Films
PRODUCER/DIRECTOR: William Grefe
SCREENWRITER: Roy Preston
ALSO RELEASED AS: *The Hallucinators*

Love and crime in Miami's Cocoanut Grove artist's colony. Swinging young writer Stephen Oliver has a falling-out with benefactress Rita Hayworth in the wake of a wild LSD party. Rita foolishly tries blackmail after Oliver's reconciliation attempt leaves her crippled millionaire husband dead. Fay Spain, Ford Rainey, and Willie Pastrano are the co-stars; the music is by Steve Alaimo and Canned Heat. This was Grefe's eighth feature. —CB

THE NAME OF THE GAME IS KILL!
1968 Fanfare Films
PRODUCER: Robert Poore
DIRECTOR: Gunnar Hellstrom
SCREENWRITER: Gary Crutcher
ALSO RELEASED AS: *Lovers in Limbo*

A weird one with Jack Lord, made just before the long-running *Hawaii Five-0* kept him permanently employed. Playing a transient Hungarian refugee in Arizona named Symcha Lipa, he becomes involved with the Terry family. Tisha Sterling is childlike and loves

Susan Strasberg in The Name of the Game is Kill.

spiders. Sister Collin Wilcox is "masculine-looking." Susan Strasberg is the normal one. The three strange siblings try to seduce, then kill Symcha. It turns out that their nervous mom (T. C. Jones) is actually their crazy dad, pretending he's his own murdered wife. Shades of *Homicidal!* T. C. Jones made a brief career out of playing sexually ambiguous roles and the same year played another Mr. and Mrs. in *Head* with the Monkees. Filmed in Jerome, Arizona. The Electric Prunes do "Shadows." Joe Solomon was executive producer. Vilmos Zsigmond was the cinematographer.

NANCY STEELE IS MISSING

1937 20th Century-Fox (B&W)
PRODUCER: Nunnally Johnson
DIRECTOR: George Marshall
SCREENWRITERS: Hal Long, Gene Fowler
A World War I pacifist (Victor McLaglen) kidnaps the baby daughter of a munitions manufacturer (June Lang). He leaves the child with unsuspecting friends and ends up in jail with a devious professor (Peter Lorre) as a cellmate.

By the time the girl is 17, she thinks McLaglen is her father and Lorre tries to collect a reward by passing off an imposter as the kidnaped girl. With John Carradine as a Cockney convict, Walter Connolly, and Jane Darwell.

THE NANNY

1965 Hammer/20th Century-Fox (England) (B&W)
PRODUCER/SCREENWRITER: Jimmy Sangster
DIRECTOR: Seth Holt
Bette Davis stars as a dowdy and proper nanny to little William Dix, just released from a home for disturbed children where he'd been put for drowning his sister. It was really Bette's fault, but only a neighboring friend (Pamela Franklin) believes the young boy. The whole family depends on the live-in servant and she's trying to kill them! With Wendy Craig and Jill Bennett.

NASHVILLE REBEL

1966 AIP
PRODUCER: Fred A. Niles
DIRECTOR: Jay Sheridan
SCREENWRITERS: Ira Kerns, Jay Sheridan
Waylon Jennings becomes a popular attraction around his small-town Tennessee home following an amateur hootenanny. A crooked agent tries to sabotage his marriage and career by sending him away to a posh Chicago nightclub. After being laughed off stage, he hits the bottle. His girl comes to the rescue by talking Tex Ritter into setting up a comeback appearance at the Grand Ol' Opry. Waylon does "Nashville Rebel," "Nashville Bum," "Silver Ribbons," and "Long Way from Home"; Tex sings "Hillbilly Heaven." Also with Henny Youngman, Sonny James, the Wilburn Brothers, Faron Young, Porter Wagoner, and Loretta Lynn (who sings "You Ain't Woman Enough"). —CB

502

THE NASTY RABBIT

1965 Fairway-International
PRODUCER: Nicholas Merriwether
DIRECTOR: James Landis
SCREENWRITERS: Arch Hall, Sr.,
    Jim Crutchfield
ALSO RELEASED AS: *Spies-a-Go-Go*

International agents invade a dude ranch to keep tabs on a Soviet saboteur sent to release a contaminated bunny on the Continental Divide. Mischa Terr stars, with both Arch Halls (Sr. and Jr.), Melissa Morgan, Little Jack Little, and assistant cameraman Laszlo Kovacs as the Idiot. Songs ("The Jackrabbit Shuffle," "The Robot Walk," "The Spy Waltz," and "Jackie") performed by Arch, Jr. and the Archers, and Pat and Lolly Vegas of Redbone. Filmed in Wyoming by Vilmos Zsigmond and Laszlo Kovacs. See *Eegah!* —CB

NATURE'S MISTAKES: See FREAKS.

NAUGHTY DALLAS

1964 Paul Mart Productions
PRODUCER/DIRECTOR/SCREENWRITER:
    Larry Buchanan

Some people will do absolutely anything. The man responsible for *The Eye Creatures* deals himself in by filming a standard strips-and-burlesque quickie in Jack Ruby's Carousel Club. Featuring resident exotics Kim Athas, Peggy Steele, Breck Wall, and Jada. Two months later, in April 1964, came *The Trial of Lee Harvey Oswald*, also by Buchanan. —CB

NAVAJO RUN

1964 AIP (B&W)
PRODUCER/DIRECTOR: Johnny Seven
SCREENWRITER: Jo Herms

A sick trap opens for half-breed Matthew Whitehawk when he seeks help at a frontier ranch after being bitten

Bette Davis is The Nanny.

by a rattler. Luke Grog, wife Sarah, and mute brother Jesse nurse him back to his feet so that Luke can drop him in the middle of the forest without food or water and hunt him down as he has 16 Indians before him. Producer-director Seven is Whitehawk; Warren Kemmerling, Virginia Vincent, and Ron Soble are the Grogs. —CB

NAVY VS. THE NIGHT MONSTERS

1966 Realart
PRODUCER: George Edwards
DIRECTOR/SCREENWRITER: Michael Hoey

A top must-see feature. The casting director deseves an award. Blond bombshell Mamie Van Doren (real name: Joan Olander) stars with suave Anthony Eisley (*Dracula vs. Frankenstein*), Pamela Mason, and Bill Gray (Bud on *Father Knows Best*). The multi-talented (and dead) Bobby Van also added humor to *Doomsday Machine* and the wonderful syndicated *Make Me Laugh* show. And you will probably recognize Russ Bender from countless '50s cheapies. They're all in the Navy, stationed at the South Pole, but it's hot! Acid-bleeding, walking plants are after the cast! The cast is after Mamie! In real life, Mamie now runs an antiques shop in California.

THE NEANDERTHAL MAN
1953 United Artists (B&W)
PRODUCERS/SCREENWRITERS:
Aubrey Wisberg, Jack Pollexfen
DIRECTOR: E. A. Dupont
A scientist (Robert Shayne) uses a serum to turn his pet kitty into a sabre-toothed cat and himself into an ugly beast man wearing one of the most expressionless masks ever created. Director Dupont was once a big name in Germany, where he did films like *Variety* ('26). With Richard Crane (television's *Rocky Jones, Space Ranger*) and Doris Merric.

NECROMANCY
1972 Cinerama
PRODUCER/DIRECTOR/SCREENWRITER:
Bert I. Gordon
Bert I. Gordon floundered through the '70s with junk like this modern-day witchcraft tale. He got Orson Welles to star (with a beard and fake nose) as Cato, the leader of a small town that manufactures occult toys. Orson uses Pamela Franklin (*The Legend of Hell House*) to help bring back his dead son. Although released with a PG rating, it originally contained nude coven scenes. Also with Lee Purcell, Harvey Jason, and *Playboy* Playmate Sue Bernard.

NED KELLY
1970 United Artists (England)
PRODUCER: Neil Hartley
DIRECTOR: Tony Richardson
SCREENWRITERS: Tony Richardson, Ian Jones
Mick Jagger is an Australian folk hero/outlaw who hanged after being practically forced into a life of crime by Brit-ish policemen. He and his brothers wear bulletproof suits of armor with masks. Waylon Jennings provides the soundtrack music. Jagger sings "The Wild Colonial Boy." Filmed in Australia. It was pretty much ignored when released here.

NEITHER THE SEA, NOR THE SAND
1974 Tigon/International Amusement (England)
PRODUCERS: Jack Smith, Pete Fetterman
DIRECTOR: Fred Burnley
SCREENWRITERS: Gordon Honeycomb, Rosemary Davies
Susan Hampshire leaves her husband for a young man (Michael Petrovich). He vows never to leave her, dies, and then returns from the grave. She's happy until he begins to rot. With Frank Finlay.

THE NEPTUNE DISASTER
1973 20th Century-Fox (Canada)
PRODUCER: Sanford Howard
DIRECTOR: Daniel Petrie
SCREENWRITER: Jack Dewitt
ALSO RELEASED AS: *The Neptune Factor*
Laughable all-star underwater mess with an obvious model sub and normal-sized eels and fish used to represent horrible giant sea monsters. With Yvette Mimieux, Ben Gazzara, Ernest Borgnine (*The Poseidon Adventure*), and Walter Pidgeon. From the director of *A Raisin in the Sun*.

THE NEPTUNE FACTOR: See THE NEPTUNE DISASTER.

THE NEST OF THE CUCKOO BIRDS
1965 Williams (B&W)
PRODUCER/DIRECTOR/SCREENWRITER:
Bert Williams

A revenue agent (Bert Williams) chasing moonshiners through the Everglades stumbles onto a strange inn run by a showgirl-turned-taxidermist who displays human trophies in the Chapel of the Dead. With Chuck Frankle, Ann Long, Jacky Scalso, and Larry Wright. Williams' wife Peggy wrote the title song performed by the Four Bits. –CB

THE NESTING

1981 Mature Pictures
PRODUCER/DIRECTOR: Armand Weston
SCREENWRITERS: Armand Weston, Daria Price
Agoraphobic mystery writer Robin Groves leaves New York to live in an old house haunted by the ghost of a madam (Gloria Grahame in her last role). The ex-brothel is the scene of slow-motion gore killings. With John Carradine in a small role. Weston previously directed hard-core sex movies. He should go back to them. **(R)**

THE NET: See PROJECT M–7.

NEUTRON AGAINST THE DEATH ROBOTS

1961 Commonwealth United-TV
(Mexico) (B&W)
PRODUCER: Luis Garcia de Leon
DIRECTOR/SCREENWRITER: Frederico Curiel
ORIGINALLY RELEASED AS:
  Los Automatas de la Muerte
Neutron (Wolf Ruvinskis), the Mexican wrestling hero with lightning bolts on his black mask, battles a monstrous blood-consuming brain, human robots, and the neutron bomb! At least seven Neutron adventures were produced. Many were sold directly to American TV in dubbed versions. Watch for *Neutron Battles the Karate Assassins*, *Neutron vs. the Maniac*, *Neutron vs. the Amazing Dr. Caronte*, etc.

Gloria Grahame in The Nesting.

THE NEW ADVENTURES OF TARZAN

1935 Burroughs-Tarzan Pictures (B&W)
PRODUCERS: George W. Stout,
  Ben S. Cohen, Ashton Dearholt,
  Edgar Rice Burroughs
DIRECTOR: Edward Kull
SCREENWRITER: Charles F. Royal
This historic oddity was produced by Edgar Rice Burroughs' own company. Originally a 12-chapter serial, it was the first Tarzan film shot on location (in Guatemala). A crude but fascinating production, it's been called the purest treatment of the ape man on the screen (as in the books, he speaks perfect English). Filmed in four months under impossible conditions in the jungle, the sound was so bad that it had to be redubbed back home. Crew members got sick from insect and snake bites. Many of the 650 native extras refused to act around Jiggs the chimp. Burroughs fell in love and ran off with the wife of his producer partner. She became his second wife. Herman Brix, an Olympic decathlon champ, was

paid $75 a week (!) to suffer in the jungle heat and do his own stunts as Tarzan. Brix later changed his name to Bruce Bennett and landed roles in stuff like *The Alligator People* and *The Cosmic Man.* Ula Holt co-stars. The plot concerns the Green Goddess, ruler of a lost city guarded by monster men. Actual Mayan ruins are used for the city. Theaters could run it as a serial or as a 75-minute feature. *Tarzan and the Green Goddess,* a different, re-edited feature, came out in 1938.

THE NEW HOUSE ON THE LEFT

1977 Hallmark (Italy)
PRODUCER/DIRECTOR: Aldo Ladd
ALSO RELEASED AS:
Second House from the Left

Murdering rapist attacks women on a train in a retitled co-feature with *Last House on the Left.* Kay Beal and Patty Edwards star. (R)

THE NEW ORIGINAL WONDER WOMAN

1975 TV
PRODUCER: Douglas S. Cramer
DIRECTOR: Leonard Horn
SCREENWRITER: Stanley Ralph Ross

Mental patients in New Year's Evil.

Wonder Woman pilot film, take two. Linda Carter is Diana Prince, actually Wonder Woman from Paradise Island. Lyle Waggoner is her co-star as Major Steve. The World War II–era adventure led to the popular series and Linda Carter trying to be taken seriously as an actress and singer. She had better luck on diet-soft-drink commercials. But she did make a striking-looking and sincere superheroine. The fitting guest stars in this live comic book were Red Buttons, Kenneth Mars, Fannie Flagg, Henry Gibson, Cloris Leachman, Stella Stevens, and Eric Braeden.

NEW YEAR'S EVIL

1981 Cannon
PRODUCERS: Menahem Golan,
Yoram Globos
DIRECTOR: Emmett Alston
SCREENWRITER: Leonard Neubauer
Roz Kelly (*Happy Days*) stars as an L.A. punk fan hosting a New Year's Eve concert attended by a maniac who kills one person every hour. Lots of bad heavy-metal "punk" music is heard in this ridiculous slasher movie. With John Alderman.

THE NEXT VOICE YOU HEAR

1950 MGM (B&W)
PRODUCER: Dore Schary
DIRECTOR: William A. Wellman.
SCREENWRITER: Charles Schnee
First Lady Nancy Davis is married to James Whitmore. They live in a small town, have a son (Gary Gray), and like to stay home nights and listen to God on the radio! Everybody's listening all over the world! In all languages! One God for all! High ratings for God! Despite the historic broadcasts, Nancy was soon facing death in *Donovan's Brain* and James got pinched by *Them.* With Jeff Corey and Lillian Bronson.

James Whitmore is upset by the voice of God in The Next Voice You Hear. *Nancy Davis is concerned.*

NIGHT CALLER FROM OUTER SPACE: See *BLOOD BEAST FROM OUTER SPACE.*

NIGHT CHILD
1975 Film Ventures (England/Italy)
PRODUCER: William C. Reich
DIRECTOR: Max Dallamano
SCREENWRITERS: Massimo Dallamano,
    Franco Marrottax

Another *Exorcist* copy. Richard Johnson's daughter is possessed. She kills all his girlfriends. Starring Nicole Elmi, the little girl in *Andy Warhol's Frankenstein*, *Baron Blood*, and *Deep Red*.

NIGHT CREATURE
1979 Dimension
PRODUCER: Ross Hagen
DIRECTOR: Lee Madden
SCREENWRITER: Hubert Smith
ALSO RELEASED AS: *Out of the Darkness*

A jungle adventure advertised as a horror film. Donald Pleasence, one of the screen's most overworked actors, is badly miscast as a macho hunter with a private Southeast Asian island on which a deadly panther is roaming free. Producer Hagen plays the hero. Nancy Kwan co-stars. Both were also in Hagen's *Wonder Women*.

NIGHT CREATURES
1962 Hammer/Universal (England)
PRODUCER: John Temple-Smith
DIRECTOR: Peter Graham Scott
SCREENWRITERS: John Elder,
    Barbara S. Harper
ALSO RELEASED AS: *Captain Clegg*

Peter Cushing poses as Dr. Blyss, an 18th-century vicar, but he's really the notorious Captain Clegg, who has given up piracy to operate a smuggling ring. His elaborate operation includes the marsh phantoms (men and horses dressed as skeletons) and a lookout scarecrow (Oliver Reed). Clegg turns out to be a good guy, helping the poor while breaking unreasonable laws—but his brutal past catches up with him in the form of a huge mulatto (Milton Reid) whose tongue was removed by the former pirate. With Yvonne Romaine. This story was also filmed in '37 as *Dr. Syn* with George Arliss, and by Disney in '63 as *The Scarecrow of Romney Marsh* with Patrick McGoohan. This version is considered the best.

THE NIGHT DIGGER
1971 MGM (England)
PRODUCERS: Alan D. Courtney, Norman S. Powell
DIRECTOR: Alistair Reid
SCREENWRITER: Roald Dahl
ORIGINALLY RELEASED AS: *The Road Builder*
A frustrated spinster (Patricia Neal) living in a Victorian mansion with her possessive blind foster mother (Pamela Brown) shields their young handyman from the police. He (Nicolas Clay) is a rapist/murderer who buries his victims in the path of a road being paved. Screenwriter Roald Dahl (author of *Charlie and the Chocolate Factory* and other sophisticated novels for children and adults) is Patricia Neal's husband. Music by Bernard Herrmann.

THE NIGHT EVELYN CAME OUT OF THE GRAVE
1971 Phase One (Italy)
DIRECTOR: Emilio P. Miraglia
SCREENWRITERS: Fabio Pittoru, Massimo Felisatti, Emilio P. Miraglia
ORIGINALLY RELEASED AS: *La Notte che Evelyn Usca dalla Tomba*
Anthony Steffen (his real name is Antonio DeTeffe) plays a disturbed playboy who likes to bring women home to his estate for fun in his little torture chamber. His first guest is Erika Blanc, whom he discovers in a nightclub doing a great strip act involving a velvet-lined coffin. Antonio thinks his dead wife Evelyn has returned to hinder his games. The TV censors will hinder your viewing of this R-rated Italian shocker. with Giocomo Rossi-Stuart.(R)

NIGHT GALLERY
1969 TV
PRODUCER: John Badham
DIRECTORS: Boris Sagal, Steven Spielberg, Barry Shear
SCREENWRITER: Rod Serling
The three-part pilot film that launched Rod Serling's *Night Gallery* series. (1) Roddy McDowall schemes to murder uncle George Macready. With Ossie Davis. Directed by Sagal. (2) Joan Crawford is a blind woman who steals the sight of Tom Bosley during a New York blackout. With Barry Sullivan. It was Spielberg's first professional film and the second-to-last feature for Crawford. (3) Richard Kiley is a Nazi war criminal obsessed with a painting in a museum. With Sam Jaffe. Directed by Shear. All have surprise endings and are introduced by Serling in his gallery.

THE NIGHT GOD SCREAMED
1973 Cinemation
PRODUCERS: Ed Carlin, Gil Lasky
DIRECTOR: Lee Madden
SCREENWRITER: Gil Lasky
Forties star Jeanne Crain returns to play a woman hunted by a murderous Manson-like hooded figure. You see, her testimony in court sent some Jesus freaks to death row. With Alex Nicol.

NIGHT HAIR CHILD: See WHAT THE PEEPER SAW.

NIGHT HAS A THOUSAND EYES

1948 Paramount (B&W)
PRODUCER: Endre Bohem
DIRECTOR: John Farrow
SCREENWRITERS: Barré Lyndon,
  Jonathan Latimer

A neglected psychological thriller in the *film noir* tradition. Edward G. Robinson is John Triton, a man cursed with the ability to foretell the future. But he's powerless to alter the doom-filled future he foresees: "I had become a reverse zombie; the world was dead and I was living." John Lund and Gail Russell (*The Uninvited*) hear Triton's incredible story over coffee in a café, then realize their own involvement. With Virginia Bruce, William Demarest, Jerome Cowan, John Alexander, and Richard Webb. From a story by Cornell Woolrich. Directed by Farrow just after he did *The Big Clock*.

NIGHT IS THE PHANTOM: See WHAT!

NIGHT KEY

1937 Universal (B&W)
ASSOCIATE PRODUCER: Robert Presnell
DIRECTOR: Lloyd Corrigan
SCREENWRITERS: Tristram Tupper,
  John C. Moffitt

Karloff plays a good guy—a nearsighted old scientist who invents the ultimate burglar alarm. Gangsters led by Ward Bond kidnap him, but Boris outwits them with his electric rays. With Jean Rogers, Warren Hull, Hobart Cavanaugh, and Frank Reicher.

NIGHT LEGS: See FRIGHT.

THE NIGHT MONSTER

1942 Universal (B&W)
PRODUCER/DIRECTOR: Ford Beebe
SCREENWRITER: Clarence Upson Young

Jeanne Crain in The Night God Screamed.

He only got fifth billing, but Ralph Morgan is the legless star of this supernatural murder mystery. Doctors who performed the double amputation are being killed. Who's responsible? The butler (Bela Lugosi)? Lionel Atwill? The Indian mystic (Nils Asther)? How about Don Porter, Frank Reicher, Leif Erikson, Irene Hervey, or perhaps a walking skeleton holding a miniature coffin?

NIGHT MUST FALL

1937 MGM (B&W)
PRODUCER: Hunt Stromberg
DIRECTOR: Richard Thorpe
SCREENWRITER: John Van Druten

Once you've seen Robert Montgomery here as a charming Cockney psycho carrying around a head in a hat box, he starts to seem demented in all his films. He successfully convinces 72-year-old Dame May Whitty (in a wheelchair) that he's the best son she never had. Rosalind Russell isn't fooled as easily.

Featuring several of the stars of the play by Emlyn Williams.

NIGHT MUST FALL
1964 MGM (England) (B&W)
PRODUCERS: Albert Finney,
Karel Reisz
DIRECTOR: Karel Reisz
SCREENWRITER: Clive Exton
The director of *Morgan!* does a disturbing remake of the '37 movie, this time with Albert Finney as a completely insane Welsh axe murderer. He moves in with a wealthy widow (Mona Washbourne) to redecorate the house. He plays "games" with her while sleeping with her daughter (Susan Hampshire) and maid (Sheila Hancock). He also performs rituals with the head in the box until the daughter finds out what's going on.

NIGHT OF A THOUSAND CATS
1972 Ellman Enterprises (Mexico)
PRODUCER: Avant
DIRECTOR: Rene Cardona
SCREENWRITER: Mario Marzac
ORIGINALLY RELEASED AS: *La Noche de los Mil Gatos*

A gross but funny south-of-the-border cannibal-cat movie from the director of *Survive!* (a cannibal-plane-crash movie). A crazed millionaire feeds people to his large collection of starving cats. He also decapitates women and preserves their heads. American actress Anjanette Comer (*Lepke, The Baby*) co-stars with Zulma Faiad and Hugo Stiglitz.

NIGHT OF BLOODY HORROR
1969 Howco International
PRODUCER/DIRECTOR: Joy N. Houck, Jr.
SCREENWRITERS: Joy N. Houck, Jr.,
Robert A. Weaver

Inept gore murder movie filmed in "Violent Vision" in New Orleans. The producers offered $1,000 cash to your family if you died while watching various meat-cleaver mutilations and an eye-gouging. Gerald McRaney stars as an often-jailed ex-mental-patient suspect. A *Psycho* ripoff in which the mother actually did it. With Evelyn Hendricks. Filmed in 16mm. Music by the Bored.

NIGHT OF DARK SHADOWS
1971 MGM
PRODUCER/DIRECTOR: Dan Curtis
SCREENWRITER: Sam Hall
Budgeted even lower than the first *Dark Shadows* feature (*House of Dark Shadows*), and Jonathan Frid and Joan Bennett are badly missed. Grayson Hall, Nancy Barrett, Thayer David, and John Karlen remain from *House of Dark Shadows*, joined by TV series regulars David Selby and Laura Parker, who is hanged as a witch. The new attraction is Kate Jackson. Even if you're a devoted fan of this Collinwood nonsense it's a real grade-Z dud.

NIGHT OF EVIL
1962 Astor Pictures (B&W)
PRODUCERS: Richard Gailbreath, Lou Perry
DIRECTOR: Richard Gailbreath
SCREENWRITER: Louis Perino
A high school girl (Lisa Gaye) on the road to ruin. After being wrongly sent to a girl's home she wins the Miss Colorado contest but has to withdraw from the Miss America contest when her recent marriage to an unreformed ex-con is made public. She becomes a stripper, tries to kill herself, holds up a drugstore . . . Featuring *Dementia 13* star William Campbell and a large cast of unknowns. Filmed in Fort Wayne, Indiana.

A NIGHT OF TERROR
1933 Columbia (B&W)
DIRECTOR: Benjamin Stoloff
SCREENWRITERS: Beatrice Van,
    William Jacobs, Lester Nielson
ALSO RELEASED AS: *He Lived to Kill*

At the end of this silly old murder mystery the dead killer rises and warns the audience not to reveal his identity, so I won't. However, the killer isn't Bela Lugosi, who appears as a swami complete with turban and earring, or his wife who keeps going into trances, or reporter Wallace Ford, or the black chauffeur or Sally Blane or George Meeker as a scientist who claims he can revive the dead. Watch it for Bela's eyes. "I am the maniac!"

NIGHT OF THE BEAST: See HOUSE OF THE BLACK DEATH.

NIGHT OF THE BIG HEAT: See ISLAND OF THE BURNING DOOMED.

NIGHT OF THE BLOOD BEAST
1958 AIP (B&W)
PRODUCER: Gene Corman
DIRECTOR: Bernard Kowalski
SCREENWRITER: Martin Varno

Roger Corman decided to help out his brother Gene by serving as the executive producer for three movies that Gene produced. The others were *Attack of the Giant Leeches* and *Beast from the Haunted Cave*. All were directed by Kowalski. In this one, astronaut Michael Emmet returns to Earth dead. His corpse is revived by an ugly crusty alien that likes to decapitate people. The monster has implanted its cells in the astronaut's bloodstream, making him an expectant mother! With Ed Nelson,

"NIGHT OF THE BLOOD BEAST": STARRING
Michael Emmet • Angela Greene • John Baer
AN AMERICAN-INTERNATIONAL PICTURE

Angela Greene, and Jean Hagen, who showed up next in *The Cosmic Man*.

NIGHT OF THE BLOOD MONSTER
1970 AIP (Spain/Germany/Italy)
PRODUCERS: Harry Alan Towers,
    Anthony Scott Veitch
DIRECTOR/SCREENWRITER: Jesse Franco
ORIGINALLY RELEASED AS: *El Proceso de las Brujas*
ALSO RELEASED AS: *Bloody Judge*

A cheap imitation of *The Conqueror Worm* with Christopher Lee (in a powdered wig) as the Lord Chief Justice of England in the 1600s. He condemns women as witches to further his political and sexual needs. Howard Vernon, as a hooded executioner, had most of his scenes (involving torture and nudity) cut in order to get an American PG rating. With Maria Schell, Leo Genn, Margaret Lee, and Maria Rohm.

Censored still from the Mexican Night of the Bloody Apes.

NIGHT OF THE BLOODY APES

1968 Jerand (Mexico)
PRODUCER: G. Calderon Stell
DIRECTOR: René Cardona
SCREENWRITERS: René Cardona,
  René Cardona, Jr.
ORIGINALLY RELEASED AS: *La Horriplante
  Bestia Humana*
ALSO RELEASED AS: *Gomar—The Human
  Gorilla, Horror y Sexo*

Totally tasteless and amateurish south-of-the-border horrors. A scientist puts the heart of a gorilla into his dead son who becomes a murdering and raping strongman resembling an ugly prize-fighter. A very gory film with real scenes of open-heart surgery and technical innovations like obvious rubber knives and makeup that falls off. It's basically a remake of *Doctor of Doom* (by the same director) with only one wrestling heroine this time. Her name is Lucy and her boyfriend is a Mexican cop.

NIGHT OF THE COBRA WOMAN

1973 New World (Philippines/U.S.)
PRODUCER: Kerry Magnus
DIRECTOR: Andrew Meyer
SCREENWRITERS: Kerry Magnus,
  Andrew Meyer

From the ads: "She sucks the life from the bodies of men!" Marlene Clark (*Putney Swope*) stars as a woman who can turn herself into a cobra. She needs constant lovemaking (and snake venom) to stay eternally young, so she steals the boyfriend of a young biology student (Joy Bang). With Roger Garrett and Slash Marks. Advertised as being in "Slitherama". (R)

NIGHT OF THE DARK FULL MOON: See SILENT NIGHT, BLOODY NIGHT.

NIGHT OF THE DEMON: See CURSE OF THE DEMON.

NIGHT OF THE DEMON: See THE TOUCH OF SATAN.

NIGHT OF THE EAGLE: See BURN WITCH BURN.

NIGHT OF THE GHOULS

1959 Crown International TV (B&W)
PRODUCER/DIRECTOR/SCREENWRITER:
  Edward Wood, Jr.
ALSO RELEASED AS: *Revenge of the Dead*

Plan 9 from Outer Space fans will love this follow-up tale about the walking dead. It opens in a cemetery. Criswell, the "real" medium, rises from his coffin to tell us of "monsters to be pitied . . . monsters to be despised." Kenne Duncan (a stunt man in serials) stars as Dr. Acula, a phony medium aided by Valda Hansen, a bogus ghost, and big Tor Johnson, wearing rags and horrible scar makeup as Lobo. The doctor swindles people by pretending to contact dead relatives, but then accidentally succeeds in reviving a bunch of corpses that bury him alive! Vampire (Maila Nurmi) is on hand as the real black ghost. The infamous Wood directed one more film (*Sinister Urge*, '61).

NIGHT OF THE HOWLING BEAST

1976 Independent International (Spain)
PRODUCER: Profilms
DIRECTOR: Miguel Iglesias Bonns
SCREENWRITER: Jacinto Molina
ORIGINALLY RELEASED AS: *La Maldicion de la Bestia*
ALSO RELEASED AS: *The Werewolf and the Yeti*

Paul Naschy is back as Waldemar the werewolf for the eighth time. In Tibet this time, he faces the famous Yeti, one of the most overworked creatures of the '70s. With Grace Mills.

NIGHT OF THE HUNTER

1955 United Artists (B&W)
PRODUCER: Paul Gregory
DIRECTOR: Charles Laughton
SCREENWRITER: James Agee

Robert Mitchum is a religious psychopath (with the words love and hate tattooed on his knuckles) who marries a former cellmate's widow. When Shelley Winters is unable to tell him where the holdup money is hidden, she winds up in a submerged Model T with a slit throat. Her two little ones, carriers of the secret, drift downriver with Mitchum in pursuit on horseback. With Lillian Gish, Evelyn Varden, Billy Chapin, Corey Allen, and Peter Graves. A classic.   –CB

NIGHT OF THE LAUGHING DEAD

1973 MGM (England)
PRODUCERS/SCREENWRITERS: Clive Exton, Terry Nation
DIRECTOR: Peter Sykes
ORIGINALLY RELEASED AS: *House in Nightmare Park*
ALSO RELEASED AS: *Crazy House*

Ray Milland stars in a mystery/comedy in the tradition of *The Old Dark House*. Comedian Frankie Howerd (*Sgt. Pepper's Lonely Hearts Club Band*) is the

SHE SUCKS THE LIFE FROM THE BODIES OF MEN.

NIGHT OF THE COBRA WOMAN

Starring
JOY BANG · MARLENE CLARK · ROGER GARRETT
Produced by KERRY MAGNESS and HARVEY MARKS
Directed by ANDREW MEYER   Metrocolor R

bumbling hero. With Kenneth Griffith, Hugh Burden, and lots of snakes.

NIGHT OF THE LEPUS

1972 MGM
PRODUCER: A. C. Lyles
DIRECTOR: William F. Claxton
SCREENWRITERS: Don Holliday, Gene R. Kearney

Giant carnivorous bunnies attack the population of Arizona! Sometimes real rabbits are shown hopping around miniature sets. Sometimes actors get to wear bunny suits. Who would agree to appear in such an absurd film? Stuart Whitman, Janet Leigh, Rory Calhoun, DeForest Kelly, and Paul Fix—that's who. By the way, the rascal rabbits roar. Producer Lyles is better known for his Westerns.

NIGHT OF THE LIVING DEAD

1968 Walter Reade (B&W)
PRODUCERS: Russell Streinger, Karl Hardman
DIRECTOR: George A. Romero
SCREENWRITER: John A. Russo

Great, terrifying flesh-eating-ghoul shocker with gore, priceless dialogue, and a refreshing lack of scientific explanations, romance, or happy endings. While Barbara and Johnny are visiting their father's grave, Johnny does a Karloff imitation, and a living corpse attacks and kills him. Barbara runs to a farmhouse where the terror never lets up. Romero's cult classic redefines the meaning of horror. He still makes his movies in Pittsburgh, where this one was shot. Duane Jones stars as Ben, Karl Hardman and Marilyn Eastman are Mr. and Mrs. Cooper. Romero plays an interviewer in Washington, D.C. The music was mostly "borrowed" from '50s science fiction movies. A sound track was issued 14 years after the film was released.

NIGHT OF THE QUARTER MOON

1959 MGM
PRODUCER: Albert Zugsmith
DIRECTOR: Hugo Haas
SCREENWRITERS: Frank Davis, Franklin Coen
ALSO RELEASED AS: *Flesh and Flame*

"I don't care about the color of her skin . . . she's mine!" A rich veteran of the Korean War (John Drew Barrymore) is taken on a Mexican fishing trip by his brother (Dean Jones). He falls for and marries a "quadroon" Hispanic woman (Julie London!) and people back home in San Francisco get upset. Zugsmith sleaze meets Haas trash with Agnes Moorehead, Nat King Cole, Jackie Coogan, Anna Kashfi, and Cathy Crosby.

NIGHT OF THE SEAGULLS

1975 Big Apple (Spain)
PRODUCER: José Angel Santos
DIRECTOR/SCREENWRITER: Amando De Ossorio
ALSO RELEASED AS: *La Noche de las Gaviotas*

The third sequel to *The Blind Dead*. The living-dead Templarios return on horseback to maim, mutilate, and kill modern Spaniards. The ads promised: "Seven Nights, Seven Victims, Seven Human Hearts!"

NIGHT OF THE SORCERERS

1970 Avco Embassy (Spain)
DIRECTOR: Armando de Ossorio

In the African jungle gorgeous vampire women in leopard skins sacrifice strangers. One foreigner is turned into a monster. With Jack Taylor.

Scene from George Romero's incredible Night of the Living Dead.

NIGHT OF THE WITCHES

1970 Medford
PRODUCERS: Keith Erik Burt, Vincent Forte
DIRECTOR/SCREENWRITER: Keith Erik Burt

Keith Larsen, star of *Women of Prehistoric Planet*, used a pseudonym to star in and make this sex/horror film with Charles Manson touches. Keith is a phony-preacher rapist who tries to blackmail a coven of California witches living in a mansion. **(R)**

NIGHT OF THE ZOMBIES

1981 N.M.D.
PRODUCER: Lorin E. Price
DIRECTOR/SCREENWRITER: Joel M. Reed
ALSO RELEASED AS: *Gamma 693*

The fantastic plot of this shoestring-budget New York City production involves living-dead World War II soldiers

still fighting (and eating) each other near Munich. It's all a senseless Nazi plot. Jamie Gillis, a porno star who can act better than most, plays a CIA agent. The director plays the guy behind the zombie scheme. **(R)**

NIGHT SCHOOL

1981 Paramount
PRODUCERS: Larry Babb, Ruth Avergan
DIRECTOR: Ken Hughes
SCREENWRITER: Ruth Avergan
ALSO RELEASED AS: *Terror Eyes*

Women are decapitated by a maniac in this slick-looking but forgettable horror film made in Boston. Heads turn up in a pool, a pot of stew, etc., and cops search for the villain. There's a surprise ending starring Rachel Ward. Rachel was also in *Final Terror*, released after she starred in *The Thorn Birds* on TV. *Night School* is by the director of *Chitty Chitty Bang Bang*. **(R)**

NIGHT SLAVES

1970 TV
PRODUCER: Everett Chambers
DIRECTOR: Ted Post
SCREENWRITERS: Everett Chambers,
  Robert Specht

Aliens use hypnotized residents of a small town to repair their spaceship. James Franciscus, an unaffected man with a metal plate in his head, falls in love with an alien (Tisha Sterling). With Lee Grant, Scott Marlowe, Leslie Nielsen, and Andrew Prine. A Bing Crosby production with a plot awfully similar to *They Came from Beyond Space*.

THE NIGHT STALKER

1971 TV
PRODUCER: Dan Curtis
DIRECTOR: John Moxley
SCREENWRITER: Richard Matheson

This well-made pilot film features Darren McGavin as a wise-guy reporter with a straw hat trying to prove the existence of and then destroy a vicious modern-day vampire (Barry Atwater) stalking Las Vegas. Unlike most dull Curtis projects, this one used a good director, John Moxley (*Horror Hotel*), and a tight script based on a Jeff Rice story. With Carol Lynley, Ralph Meeker, Claude Akins, Kent Smith, Elisha Cook, Jr., and series regular Simon Oakland as Kolchak's boss. *The Night Strangler* was the second pilot.

NIGHT STAR, GODDESS OF ELECTRA: See WAR OF THE ZOMBIES.

THE NIGHT STRANGLER
1973 TV
PRODUCER/DIRECTOR: Dan Curtis
SCREENWRITER: Richard Matheson
ALSO RELEASED AS: *The Time Killer*

Darren McGavin returns as reporter Carl Kolchak in the second pilot film for *The Night Stalker* series. Simon Oakland is once again his skeptical editor. In Seattle, Kolchak battles a centuries-old killer alchemist (Richard Anderson) who strangles women and lives in a weird house under the city. Another superior TV thriller scripted by Richard Matheson. With familiar horror faces Scott Brady, Margaret Hamilton, and John Carradine as a newspaper owner. Also with Jo Ann Pflug, Wally Cox, and Nina Wayne.

THE NIGHT THAT PANICKED AMERICA
1975 TV
PRODUCER/DIRECTOR: Joseph Sargent
SCREENWRITERS: Nicholas Meyer,
  Anthony Wilson

A good documentary-style look at the Halloween night in 1938 when Orson Welles and his Mercury Theatre dramatized *The War of the Worlds* on the radio and New Jersey residents were convinced it was real. Paul Shenar is Welles. With Vic Morrow, Cliff DeYoung, Tom Bosley, Will Geer, Meredith Baxter, Eileen Brennan, and Casey Kasem.

THE NIGHT THE BRIDGE FELL DOWN
1980 TV
PRODUCER: Irwin Allen
DIRECTOR: George Fenady
SCREENWRITERS: Arthur Weiss,
  Ray Goldstone, Michael Robert David

Desi Arnaz, Jr., probably your favorite TV-movie star, is a crazed bank robber holding people captive on a bridge. With Leslie Nielsen, James MacArthur, and Eve Plumb. Its U.S. debut was pre-empted by the 1980 World Series. After playing in England and Australia, it finally aired here in 1983. Not worth the wait.

THE NIGHT THE WORLD EXPLODED
1957 Columbia (B&W)
PRODUCER: Sam Katzman
DIRECTOR: Fred F. Sears
SCREENWRITERS: Luci Ward, Jack Natteford

"Nature goes mad!" the ads shouted. Bing Crosby's widow (Kathryn Grant) stars! (They were married the year this dull movie was released.) Pressure built up at the Earth's core threatens to end it all. Scientists save us. With William Leslie and Tristram Coffin.

THE NIGHT THEY KILLED RASPUTIN
1962 Brigadier (Italy/France)
PRODUCER: Vincent Forte
DIRECTOR: Pierre Chenal
SCREENWRITERS: Ugo Liberatore,
  Pierre Chenal, André Tabet
ALSO RELEASED AS: *The Nights of Rasputin*

John Drew Barrymore is Prince Yousoupoff, the man who killed Rasputin, a role his father had played in '32. Edmund Purdom (star of *The Egyptian*) is the long-haired Russian monk. Gianna Maria Canale is the czarina. A color film, it was released here in black and white.

NIGHT TIDE
1961 AIP (B&W)
PRODUCER: Aram Kantarian
DIRECTOR/SCREENWRITER: Curtis Harrington

An excellent low-budget fantasy(?) with Dennis Hopper as a sailor on leave in a small California seaside resort. He becomes obsessed with an orphan girl (Linda Lawson) who plays a mermaid at a sideshow. She believes herself to be a descendant of the "sea people" who must kill during the full moon. Avant-garde director Curtis Harrington did this odd *Cat People*–inspired movie after making a series of experimental shorts. He's now known as a TV horror-film director and seems to have lost most of what made *Night Tide* so memorable. Co-star Luana Anders later starred in Coppola's *Dementia 13*. With Gavin Muir and Bruno Ve Sota.

NIGHT TRAIN TO MUNDO FINE
1966 Hollywood Star Pictures (B&W)
PRODUCER: Anthony Cardoza
DIRECTOR/SCREENWRITER: Coleman Francis

John Carradine in a cheap adventure made by and starring the team responsible for *The Beast of Yucca Flats*! Director Francis stars as an escaped convict attempting to invade Cuba. Producer Anthony Cardoza helps. Carradine is a train engineer and sings the title song!

NIGHT UNTO NIGHT
1947 Warner Brothers (B&W)
PRODUCER: Owen Crump
DIRECTOR: Don Siegel
SCREENWRITER: Kathryn Scola

Siegel's second film stars 36-year-old Ronald Reagan (who was about to di-vorce Jane Wyman) as a doomed epileptic scientist in love with a mentally ill widow played by Viveca Lindfors (*Cauldron of Blood*) in her American film debut. The Swedish Lindfors sees ghosts. The film's release was held up for two years. With Broderick Crawford, Craig Stevens, and Rosemary DeCamp. Siegel also did Reagan's last film, *The Killers*, in '64.

THE NIGHT VISITOR
1970 Hemisphere (Sweden)
PRODUCER: Mel Ferrer
DIRECTOR: Laslo Benedek
SCREENWRITER: Gul Elmes

Hungarian director Benedek (*The Wild One*) went to Sweden to film this excellent revenge tale starring Max Von Sydow. As Salem, a farmer accused of a murder he didn't commit, Sydow is sent to an asylum where he uses an ingenious method to escape and kill the people who sent him there. Each time, the police find him back in his cell from which it seems he couldn't possibly have escaped. The well-known cast—Liv Ullmann, Trevor Howard, and Von Sydow—were left out of the cheap Hemisphere ads. Music by Henry Mancini.

NIGHT WALK: See DEATHDREAM.

THE NIGHT WALKER
1964 Universal (B&W)
PRODUCER/DIRECTOR: William Castle
SCREENWRITER: Robert Bloch

After his great, gimmicky '50s monster movies, director William Castle turned to *Psycho*-imitations. This one is pretty ridiculous. *Psycho* author Robert Bloch wrote the screenplay and Barbara Stanwyck (in her last theatrical feature) stars with real-life ex-husband Robert Taylor. Barbara has these nightmares, you see, and she starts thinking they're real.

The special effects during the dream sequences are great—for a few laughs. Hayden Rourke is her ugly blind husband. Lloyd Bochner is the man of her dreams. With Rochelle Hudson. This almost did for Barbara what *Trog* did for Joan Crawford.

NIGHT WARNING: See BUTCHER, BAKER (NIGHTMARE MAKER).

NIGHT WATCH
1973 Avco Embassy (England)
PRODUCERS: Martin Poll,
George W. George, Barnard S. Strauss
DIRECTOR: Brian G. Hutton
In this modern British *Gaslight*-type thriller Elizabeth Taylor is driven to the brink by husband Laurence Harvey and his mistress (Billie Whitelaw). This was Harvey's second-to-last film. In the last one, *Welcome to Arrow Beach*, he played a cannibal. Based on the play of the same title by Lucille Fletcher. With Linda Hayden (*Taste the Blood of Dracula*). By the director of another of Liz's flops, *X, Y and Zee*.

NIGHT WORLD
1932 Universal (B&W)
PRODUCER: Carl Laemmle, Jr.
DIRECTOR: Hobart Henley
SCREENWRITER: Richard Schayer
A nightclub, bootleg liquor, murder, and music in a drama with dances arranged by Busby Berkeley. Lew Ayres, a young drunk, is befriended by dance director Mae Clarke. Boris Karloff owns the club. Clarke and Karloff had just been in *Frankenstein*. With Hedda Hopper, Louise Beavers, and George Raft.

THE NIGHTCOMERS
1971 Avco Embassy (England)
PRODUCER/DIRECTOR: Michael Winner
SCREENWRITER: Michael Hastings
An attempt to show what happened to the children prior to the events narrated in Henry James' "The Turn of the Screw" (filmed as *The Innocents*). The selling point in this unsuccessful "prequel" was Marlon Brando just before *The Godfather* and *Last Tango in Paris* made him a big star (again). He plays Quint, the sadistic gardener who likes to abuse Miss Jessel, the governess (Stephanie Beacham). Little Flora and Miles easily come under Quint's influence. Despite his name, director Winner has turned out mostly forgettable misses like *I'll Never Forget Whatsisname*, *Won Ton Ton, the Dog That Saved Hollywood*, and *the Sentinel*. (R)

NIGHTMARE
1956 United Artists (B&W)
PRODUCERS: William Thomas, Howard Pine
DIRECTOR/SCREENWRITER: Maxwell Shane
Kevin McCarthy is a New Orleans jazz musician who dreams that he kills a man in a mirrored room in a strange mansion. His brother-in-law, police detective Edward G. Robinson, discovers there really was a murder there. Hypnotism and a record played at the wrong speed figure in the plot of this adaptation of a Cornell Woolrich short story. It was also filmed by the same director in 1947 as *Fear in the Night*. With Virginia Christine, Connie Russell, and Barry Atwater.

NIGHTMARE
1963 Hammer/Universal (England) (B&W)
PRODUCER/SCREENWRITER: Jimmy Sangster
DIRECTOR: Freddie Francis
A girl (Jennie Linden) has nightmares of a white-shrouded apparition leading her to a room containing a dead woman with a knife in her chest. It's a drive-the-heiress-crazy plot that backfires in

one of the more interesting post-*Pyscho* films. With David Knight and Moira Richmond.

NIGHTMARE: See NIGHTMARE IN BADHAM COUNTY.

NIGHTMARE
1981 21st Century
PRODUCER: John L. Watkins
DIRECTOR/SCREENWRITER: Romano Scavolini

A gore movie about a man who chopped up his father and a female dominatrix when he was young. The antipsychotic drugs he takes fail to work. He has recurring nightmares and leaves New York to kill his ex-wife in Florida. A lousy film any way you look at it. For real gore fans only. Since nobody ever heard of the cast, special makeup effects expert Tom Savini received top billing in the original ads. He informed the producers that he didn't even work on the film and would sue. His name was quickly covered with tape on all the posters. From a kung-fu movie distributor and a sex-movie director.

(self-imposed **X**)

NIGHTMARE ALLEY
1947 20th Century-Fox (B&W)
PRODUCER: George Jessel
DIRECTOR: Edmund Goulding
SCREENWRITER: Jules Furthman

Carnival operator Tyrone Power heads for the big time in Chicago by transforming himself into the Great Stanton, a spiritualist. He forces his wife (Coleen Gray) to pose as a millionaire's dead mistress and uses a sideshow fortune-teller (Joan Blondell), a psychologist (Helen Walker), and blackmail to become successful. The incredible ending finds Stanton, exposed and broken, back at the seedy carnival as a chicken-biting geek. A real carnival was authentically reconstructed in Hollywood. Lindsay Gresham, the man who wrote the novel it was based on, later killed himself. With Mike Mazurki, and Ian Keith. Unlike any other Hollywood product at the time, and look who produced it.

NIGHTMARE CASTLE
1965 Allied Artists (Italy) (B&W)
PRODUCER: Carlo Caiano
DIRECTOR: Mario Caiano (Alan Grunewald)
SCREENWRITERS: Fabio de Agostino, Mario Caiano
ORIGINALLY RELEASED AS: *Amanti d'Oltretomba*

Barbara Steele plays two roles in one of her best horror films. When scientist Paul Muller discovers his wife (Barbara) with the gardener, he chains them up in the crypt (after disfiguring the man with a hot poker), cuts their hearts out, and hides them in an urn. He also uses their blood to rejuvenate his mistress (Helga Line) and marries his wife's blond cousin (Barbara again) for her money. The dead couple return as ghosts and give the sadistic scientist what-for.

NIGHTMARE HONEYMOON
1973 MGM
PRODUCER: Hugh Benson
DIRECTOR: Elliott Silverstein
SCREENWRITER: S. Lee Pogostin

"Thank heavens it's only a movie!" the ads enticed. A sadistic low-budget thriller about newlyweds pursued and terrorized by a pair of killer rapists. Dack Rambo and Rebecca Dianna Smith are the unfortunate couple. One of the psychos is John Beck from the '60s group the Leaves ("Hey Joe"). With Pat Hingle and Jeanette Nolan. Filmed in Louisiana. Nicolas Roeg, the original director, was replaced after five days of shooting. Silverstein also directed *Cat Ballou*. Music by Elmer Bernstein.

NIGHTMARE IN BADHAM COUNTY

1976 TV
PRODUCER: William Lloyd Baums
DIRECTOR: John Llewellyn Moxey
SCREENWRITER: Jo Heims
ALSO RELEASED AS: *Nightmare*

This is a more serious variation on the plot of *Untamed Youth* (1957). Vacationing coeds Deborah Raffin and Lynne Moody are sent to a prison farm by a sadistic small town sheriff (Chuck Connors) and a weak judge (Ralph Bellamy). Suicide, murder, beatings, rape, and racism are everyday facts of their prison life. With Tina Louise as a very unglamorous guard, Della Reese, Lana Wood, and Robert Reed (*The Brady Bunch*), as a warden. It was offered as a theatrical release outside the U.S. and reportedly was a big hit in The People's Republic of China. The big screen version also shows on cable television.

NIGHTMARE IN BLOOD

1978 PFE
PRODUCERS/SCREENWRITERS: John Stanley, Kenn Davis
DIRECTOR: John Stanley

A low-budget horror comedy about an actor who plays vampires and turns out to be the real thing. A horror-film convention provides the background. Kerwin Matthews makes a cameo appearance. The director was a San Francisco TV-horror-movie host. (R)

NIGHTMARE IN WAX

1966 Crown International
PRODUCER: Martin B. Cohen
DIRECTOR: Bud Townsend
SCREENWRITER: Rex Carlton
ALSO RELEASED AS: *Crimes in the Wax Museum*

Don't miss Cameron Mitchell in his ultimate grade-z starring role as Vince Rinaud, the crazed, scarred owner of a Hollywood wax museum. He used to be a normal-looking makeup man for Paragon Pictures, but ever since studio owner Barry Kroeger disfigured him in a jealous rage over famous actress Anne Helm, he's thought only of revenge. He injects a secret formula into various Paragon stars. Result—instant statues. Cameron is in top form ranting and raving to sculptured heads, which are obviously the heads of real people stuck through holes in a table. Watch them breathe. Watch others trying to stand still and imitate wax figures. Scott Brady and John Cardos are thick-headed detectives investigating the obviously demented Mitchell. Victoria Carroll is a go-go dancer used to lure new victims to the museum. Keep watching till the totally senseless ending. With the T-bones. Filmed at the Movieland Wax Museum in L.A. Director Townsend later did the X-rated *Alice in Wonderland*.

Mad sculptor Cameron Mitchell talks to an actress with her head through a hole in the table in Nightmare in Wax.

NIGHTS IN A HAREM:
See *SON OF SINBAD.*

THE NIGHTS OF RASPUTIN:
See *THE NIGHT THEY KILLED RASPUTIN*.

THE NIGHTS OF
THE WEREWOLF
1968 (Spain/France)
PRODUCER: Plata Films
DIRECTOR: René Govar
SCREENWRITERS: Jacinto Molina, René Govar, C. Belard
ORIGINALLY RELEASED AS: *Las Noches del Hombre Lobo*

Paul Naschy as Waldemar Daninsky, Spain's famous werewolf, returns in a sequel to *Frankenstein's Bloody Terror*. Naschy wrote the script using his real name, Jacinto Molina. He fights a mad scientist. Not yet released in America.

NIGHTWING
1979 Columbia
PRODUCER: Martin Rensohoff
DIRECTOR: Arthur Hiller
SCREENWRITERS: Steve Shagan, Bud Shrake, Martin Cruz Smith

Bats are scary, right? Not this time. A New Mexican community of Maskai Indians is in uproar as cattle and people turn up dead, horribly mutilated by a horde of fake-looking rabid bats. Tribal deputy Nick Mancuso is joined in the battle against them by David Warner, a surly English biologist who's been tracking down the migratory beasts ever since they ate his father. With Strother Martin and George Clutesi, an Indian who played a similar role in *Prophecy*, another lousy '79 horror movie. —BM

1984
1956 Columbia (England) (B&W)
PRODUCER: N. Peter Rathvon
DIRECTOR: Michael Anderson
SCREENWRITERS: William P. Templeton, Ralph Bettison

"War is peace. Freedom is slavery." Edmund O'Brien defies Big Brother in this effective version of George Orwell's classic. The original film ends with O'Brien and his lover (Jan Sterling) being shot. For the U.S. release the ending was changed. They reform and become loyal to Big Brother! With Michael Redgrave, Mervyn Jones, Donald Pleasence (also in *THX 1138*), Michael Ripper, and Patrick Allen. By now the title is a bit dated but the message is increasingly relevant.

99 AND $^{44}/_{100}$% DEAD
1974 20th Century-Fox
PRODUCER: Joe Wizan
DIRECTOR: John Frankenheimer
SCREENWRITER: Robert Dillon

Frankenheimer (*The Manchurian Candidate*, *Seconds*) attempted to make a futuristic, comic-book-style gangster satire. The few who've seen it seem to agree he failed. Richard Harris is a hit man caught between warring gangsters Bradford Dillman and Edmond O'Brien. As Claw, Chuck Connors has detachable weapons that fit his metal-stump hand (an idea stolen from *Chamber of Horrors* of '66). A river is filled with cement shoe corpses and the sewers contain giant albino gators. There's lots of bizarre violence in the pop/camp style (perhaps a few years too late). With Harris' then-wife Ann Turkel (*Humanoids of the Deep*).

99 WOMEN
1969 Commonwealth United (Spain/Italy/W. Germany)
PRODUCER: Harry Alan Towers
DIRECTOR: Jesse Franco
SCREENWRITERS: Harry Alan Towers, Carlo Fadda, Milo G. Cuccia, Jesse Franco
ORIGINALLY RELEASED AS: *99 Mujeres*

Besides ridiculous horror movies, Jesse Franco sometimes makes women's prison films—a great excuse for sex scenes. Jesse also has good luck getting known performers to act in his sensational junk.

This one stars Mercedes McCambridge as Thelma, a sadistic supervisor of a women's prison on a Caribbean island. She's demoted to being an assistant to Maria Schell after too many prisoners die. Mercedes gets her job back by accusing the new warden of having a lesbian relationship with Maria Rohm, a prisoner. Meanwhile, on the same island, there's a men's prison run by Herbert Lom, who likes to borrow female inmates for nights of pleasure. Lots of floggings, torture . . . In 1983 Producer Towers announced a 3-D remake. **(X)**

NINOTCHKA
1939 MGM (B&W)
PRODUCER/DIRECTOR: Ernst Lubitsch
SCREENWRITERS: Charles Brackett,
Billy Wilder, Walter Reisch

This classic Garbo film features Bela Lugosi as Commissar Razn. Two years later, Greta was back in *Two Faced Woman*, her last movie. Two years later, Bela was back in *The Devil Bat*, *Spooks Run Wild*, *The Invisible Ghost*, etc.

NO BLADE OF GRASS
1970 MGM (England)
PRODUCER/DIRECTOR: Cornel Wilde
SCREENWRITERS: Sean Forestal,
Jefferson Pascal

Actor Cornel Wilde directs his own *Panic in the Year Zero*. Instead of a bomb it's pollution and a virus causing famine and the collapse of civilization. An English family tries to reach a safe fortress and encounters destructive motorcycle gangs with horned helmets and rifles. Wilde's wife, Jean Wallace, stars with Nigel Davenport (with an eyepatch). Also with Lynn Frederick and George Coulouris. **(R)**

NO GREATER SIN: See *18 AND ANXIOUS.*

NO HOLDS BARRED
1952 Monogram (B&W)
PRODUCER: Jerry Thomas
DIRECTOR: William Beaudine
SCREENWRITERS: Tim Ryan, Jack Crutcher,
Bert Lawrence

Magic turns the Bowery Boys into professional wrestlers. With Marjorie Reynolds, Henry Kulky, and Hombre Montana. Leo Gorcey and Huntz Hall star.

NO MAN'S LAND
1964 Cinema-Video International (B&W)
PRODUCER/DIRECTOR/SCREENWRITER:
Russ Harvey

Russ Harvey of *Dungeons of Harrow* plays Corporal Jerry Little in this Korean War picture. He meets an Oriental girl walking her dog and marries her after killing a sniper. Made in San Antonio, Texas, and released the same month as Harvey's other feature. Associate producer—Pat Boyette. Co-starring Kim Lee as Anna Wong, with Lee Morgan, Val Martinez, Henry Garcia and Captain, Tom Lytle. Musical director Jaime Mendoza-Nava is involved in a lot of third-rate stuff, from *Shell Shock* to *Fever Heat*. —CB

NO PLACE LIKE HOMICIDE: See *WHAT A CARVE UP!*

NO SURVIVORS, PLEASE
1963 Shorcht (Germany)
PRODUCER: Hans Albin
DIRECTORS: Hans Albin, Peter Berneis
SCREENWRITER: Peter Berneis

Lots of interesting German cheapies turn up late at night. It's hard to track down information on the many that were imported strictly for TV packages. Here, a reporter and a beautiful secretary investigate alien forces that are using the bodies and minds of murdered scientists. About every 15 seconds there's a new scene with new characters.

Robert Cunningham and Maria Perschy star. Watch for similar treats like *The White Spider* and *The Invisible Terror*. Albin and Berneis also made one called *Games of Desire*. —CB

NO TEARS FOR THE DAMNED

1968 Gold Star (B&W)
PRODUCER: Oliver Drake
DIRECTOR: William Collins
SCREENWRITERS: June and Oliver Drake

Robert Dix (*Blood of Dracula's Castle*) is a Las Vegas playboy who marries a prostitute and is driven berserk by her two-timing. He kills two girls, beats a homosexual for making a pass, then turns on his domineering mother. Made in Las Vegas. With Gillian Simpson, Liz Marshall, Gay Conway, and John Cardos. —CB

NO TIME TO BE YOUNG

1957 Columbia (B&W)
PRODUCER: Wallace McDonald
DIRECTOR: David Lowell Rich
SCREENWRITERS: John McPortland, Raphael Hayes

Robert Vaughn, Roger Smith of *77 Sunset Strip*, and Tom Pittman of *High School Big Shot* play three youths who hold up a supermarket. Roger and Tom don't get far, but Vaughn, who kills a cashier, almost makes it to the Mexican border before he is killed when his stolen getaway truck crashes. A Columbia "new faces" presentation featuring Dorothy Green, Merry Anders, and Kathy Nolan (Kate McCoy on *The Real McCoys*). —CB

NOCTURNA, GRANDDAUGHTER OF DRACULA

1979 Compass International
PRODUCER: Vernon Becker
DIRECTOR/SCREENWRITER: Harry Tampa

Ex-belly dancer Nai Bonet stars as the rebellious granddaughter of Dracula (John Carradine). She runs off to New York with an English musician and the 73-year-old vampire follows. More a disco-comedy than a horror movie. Filmed in Manhattan. Yvonne De Carlo co-stars as "Jugulia." Pretty pathetic in every way. It played with Nai's other cardboard hit, *Hoodlums*. With Brother Theodore. This feature was made possible by the financial backing of ex-actor/embezzler William Callahan, who was slain gangland-style in 1981.

THE NORLISS TAPES

1973 TV
PRODUCER/DIRECTOR: Dan Curtis
SCREENWRITER: William F. Nolan

Before *Kolchak, The Night Stalker* became a series, Curtis made a third pilot in which Roy Thinnes plays a serious investigator after a demon-statue. ABC went ahead with the original concept and this NBC one was forgotten. With Angie Dickinson, Claude Akins, and Hurd Hatfield.

NOSFERATU, THE VAMPYRE

1979 20th Century-Fox
PRODUCER/DIRECTOR/SCREENWRITER:
  Werner Herzog
ALSO RELEASED AS: *Nosferatu, Phantom der Nacht*

Since neither director Werner Herzog nor the cast of *Nosferatu* spoke English, it was only logical for financier 20th Century-Fox to request that this remake of the old story be filmed in English. Actually, Herzog filmed in both English and German, and the English version, which was never released, is said to be a laff-riot. Instead, we get the German version with subtitles, which is slow-moving even by Herzog standards, perhaps because the story is so familiar by now. Klaus Kinski stars as Dracula. With Isabelle Adjani as

Klaus Kinski is Nosferatu, the Vampyre.

Lucy Harker and Bruno Ganz as Jonathan Harker. Music by Popol Vuh. –BM

NOT OF THIS EARTH

1956 Allied Artists (B&W)
PRODUCER/DIRECTOR: Roger Corman
SCREENWRITERS: Charles Griffith, Mark Hanna

Corman's most enjoyable science-fiction film stars Paul Birch as a blank-eyed anemic alien vampire wearing wraparound black shades and a business suit. He hires an unsuspecting nurse (Beverly Garland) to give him blood injections and sends specimens of "lower-class" Earth life to his home planet in a matter-transformation machine. Victims include drunks he picks up in the park and a Chinaman. Jonathan Haze as his suspicious chauffeur and Dick Miller as a vacuum cleaner salesman provide humorous touches. Morgan Jones is the hero cop. Great fast-paced nonsense with a flying, head-crushing bat creature and a mistaken transfusion of dog's blood. The alien didn't know the doctor was a veterinarian! Special effects by Paul Blaisdell. Originally co-billed with *Attack of the Crab Monsters.*

NOTHING BUT THE NIGHT

1972 Cinema Systems (England)
PRODUCER: Anthony Nelson-Keys
DIRECTOR: Peter Sasdy
SCREENWRITER: Brian Hoyles
ALSO RELEASED AS: *The Resurrection Syndicate*

The first and last product of Christopher Lee's own production company was this mystery/horror film about killer children who have dead people's memories. Lee is a Scotland Yard inspector. Peter Cushing and Diana Dors co-star. It was never released to theaters in America.

THE NUDE BOMB

1980 Universal
PRODUCER: Jennings Lang
DIRECTOR: Clive Donner
SCREENWRITERS: Arne Sutton, Bill Dana, Leonard B. Stern
ALSO RELEASED AS: *The Return of Maxwell Smart*

Get Smart was a welcome half-hour on TV each week from 1965 to 1970. Ten years later, Don Adams was back as Maxwell Smart in a film without Agent 99 or the Chief (Ed Platt had died). It was greeted with indifference. Andrea Howard plays Smart's new partner. Vittorio Gassman is a stump-handed killer. With Sylvia Kristel (*Emmanuelle*), Rhonda Fleming, Pamela Hensley, Bill Dana (one of the writers), Maxwell Smart clones, and a tour of Universal Studios.

NURSE SHERRI

1978 Independent International
PRODUCER: Mark Sherwood
DIRECTOR: Al Adamson
ALSO RELEASED AS: *Beyond the Living*

A friendly 21-year-old nurse (Jill Jacobsen) becomes possessed by the spirit of a religious fanatic who died on the operating table. Everyone who participated in his surgery must die. Sherri, armed with meat cleavers and a pitchfork, goes to work. With Geoffrey Land and Marilyn Joi (*Ilsa, Harem Keeper of the Oil Sheiks*). By the director of *Horror of the Blood Monsters*.(R)

THE NUTTY PROFESSOR

1963 Paramount
PRODUCER: Ernest D. Glucksman
DIRECTOR: Jerry Lewis
SCREENWRITERS: Jerry Lewis, Bill Richmond

Jerry Lewis directs a hit! Awkward Professor Kelp develops a Jekyll-Hyde formula and transforms himself into the slicked-down stud Buddy Love (who bears an uncanny resemblance to Dean Martin). Stella Stevens is the sexy bright-eyed student who decides she prefers the shy professor. Jerry's son Gary (who can't get a recording contract) now lives in Lakewood, Ohio, where he revealed in an exclusive interview with the *Lakewood Post* that Jerry and he haven't talked for five years. C'mon Gary, call your dad and tell him you still care.

NYOKA AND THE LOST CITY OF HIPPOCRATES: See THE PERILS OF NYOKA.

Vampire-like alien Paul Birch threatens starlet Beverly Garland in Not of This Earth.

O.K. CONNERY: See OPERATION KID BROTHER.

OSS 117 — DOUBLE AGENT
1968 UPA (France/Italy)
DIRECTOR: André Hunebelle
ORIGINALLY RELEASED AS:
 Niente Rose per OSS 117

Psycho co-star John Gavin, currently our Ambassador to Mexico, pretends he's James Bond, battling an assassination bureau in the Mideast. This role may have been decisive in proving his qualifications for a diplomatic appointment. With Margaret Lee, Curt Jurgens, and Luciana Paluzzi.

OSS 117 — MISSION FOR A KILLER
1965 Embassy (France/Italy)
PRODUCER: Paul Cadeac
DIRECTOR: André Hunebelle
SCREENWRITERS: Jean Halin, Pierre Foucaud, André Hunebelle
ORIGINALLY RELEASED AS:
 Furia A Bahia Pour Oss 117

The French James Bond, played by the Austrian Frederic Stafford (*Topaz*), goes to Rio and discovers a world-domination plot involving hypnotic drugs derived from a rare plant. With Mylene Demongeot. One of a half-dozen or more OSS 117 films, most of which star different 117's.

THE OBLONG BOX
1969 AIP (U.S./England)
PRODUCER/DIRECTOR: Gordon Hessler
SCREENWRITERS: Lawrence Huntington, Christopher Wicking

Planned as a project by the late Michael Reeves, this lame Poe adaptation was the first of three Vincent Price films directed by American Gordon Hessler in England. Price as Julian Markham has a deranged, deformed brother (Alastair Williamson) whom he decides to bury alive. The masked brother is dug up and begins killing people. With Hillary Dwyer, Rupert Davies, Judy Geeson, and Christopher Lee in a small role as a doctor. Also with a witch doctor called N'galo and the Oh! Ogunde dancers. The buried-alive promo art was very close to *The House of Usher* ads. (M)

OBSESSION
1976 Columbia
PRODUCERS: George Litto, Harry N. Blum
DIRECTOR: Brian DePalma
SCREENWRITER: Paul Schrader

Between his psychic-power hits *Carrie* and *The Fury*, DePalma directed this mostly ignored Hitchcock copy. Alfred himself was reportedly not too happy with the way DePalma and scriptwriter Paul Schrader lifted his *Vertigo* plot. Cliff Robertson's wife and daughter are kidnaped by his ex-partner (John Lithgow). Years later, Cliff meets and falls in love with Geneviève Bujold in Italy. He thinks she's his wife but she's really his (guess). Originally to be called *Déjà Vu*. With a very loud Bernard Herrmann score. Filmed on location in Florence and New Orleans.

OCTAMAN
1971 Filmers Guild
PRODUCERS: Joel Freeman, Harry Essex
DIRECTOR: Harry Essex
SCREENWRITER: Leigh Chapman

Direct-to-TV disaster directed by *The Creature from the Black Lagoon*'s scriptwriter. Kerwin Matthews, Pier Angeli, and Jeff Morrow all come out of semi-retirement to discover a monster and go through the low-budget love-triangle moves. The unique upright octopus man was an early creation of Rick Baker (who later did *American Werewolf* and the star creature in *Star Wars*). Angeli, making a Hollywood comeback, died of a barbiturate overdose during filming.

She once had a well publicized affair with James Dean.

OF LOVE AND DESIRE
1963 20th Century-Fox
PRODUCER: Victor Stolloff
DIRECTOR: Richard Rush
SCREENWRITERS: Laslo Gorog, Richard Rush

This comeback attempt for Merle Oberon is literally a home movie filmed in her 16th-century Mexico City villa. Steve Cochran, John Agar, and Steve Brodie are invited to be the playmates of a nymphomaniac Mexico City socialite (Merle). Her life is a horror story even before brother Curt Jurgens confesses his forbidden desires. "If you are an adult in every sense of the word . . . ," you are qualified to see this movie, according to the ads. Sammy Davis, Jr., massacres "Katherine's Theme." Rush went on to *Hell's Angels on Wheels* and *The Stunt Man.* —CB

OKEFENOKEE
1960 Filmservice (B&W)
PRODUCER: Aaron Danches
DIRECTOR: Roul Haig
SCREENWRITER: Jess Abbott

Henry Brandon and swamp-dive owner Peggy Maley run aliens and dope into the country with Seminole guides and air boats. Peter Coe's girl is shamed by one of Brandon's henchmen and she stares into the sun until blind. This, along with the gangsters' habit of eliminating their helpers, leads to an attack by 50 Indian braves. With Serena Sande. Filmed on location in Florida, co-released with *The Monster of Piedras Blancas.* See *The Wacky World of Dr. Morgus.* —CB

OKLAHOMA WOMAN
1955 AIP (B&W)
PRODUCER/DIRECTOR: Roger Corman
SCREENWRITER: Lou Rusoff

Horror Heap from the Nuclear Trash!

OCTAMAN

starring
KERWIN MATHEWS
PIER ANGELI

co-starring
JEFF MORROW   JERRY GUARDINO   NORMAN FIELDS   ROBERT WARNER   DAVID ESSEX

produced by MICHAEL KRAIKE   directed by HARRY ESSEX   written by LAWRENCE MORSE   a FILMERS GUILD PRODUCTION   IN COLOR

Corman's first. He directed four quickie Westerns in a row. This one stars Peggie Castle as the woman the ads identified as the "queen of the outlaws . . . queen of sin!" She runs the gambling house/saloon and the local elections. "No man could tame her," including Richard Denning, Michael "Touch" Connors, Jonathan Haze, and Dick Miller. She and Cathy Downs fight "with all the fury of savage wildcats!"

THE OLD DARK HOUSE
1932 Universal (B&W)
PRODUCER: Carl Laemmle, Jr.
DIRECTOR: James Whale
SCREENWRITER: Ben Levy

Boris Karloff as the drunken butler comforts Lillian Bond, a visitor to The Old Dark House.

1932 James Whale movie. Charles Addams did the main title pictures. A confused Tom Poston (*Zotz*) is a salesman stranded in a mansion where murder is a way of life. Robert Morley is Roderick Femm. Peter Bull (*Dr. Strangelove*) has a dual role as Caspar and Jaspar. Janette Scott is the nice daughter. Fenella Fielding is the seductive kooky one. One relative waiting for the floods has built an ark in the backyard. The mother sleeps with knitting needles through her neck. With Mervyn Johns (star of *Dead of Night*). For some reason it was shown in theaters in black-and-white but it's in color on TV.

OLD DRAC: See OLD DRACULA.

OLD DRACULA

1973 AIP (England)
PRODUCER: Jack H. Wiener
DIRECTOR: Clive Donner
SCREENWRITER: Jeremy Lloyd
ALSO RELEASED AS: *Vampira, Old Drac*

David Niven stars in a vampire comedy unfairly called a copy of *Young Frankenstein*. It was made before that film and released afterward with a new title. Niven's castle is now a tourist trap where *Playboy* bunnies pose. He revives his love, Vampira, with a blood transfusion, but it turns her black. Ex-*Laugh-In* comedienne Teresa Graves plays the surprised vampire's mate. In the end Niven turns black! From the director of *What's New Pussycat?* With Hammer stars Linda Hayden, Veronica Carlson, and Freddie Jones.

Originally advertised as "another Whale of a picture . . . with KARLOFF—the Frankenstein monster himself." Boris looks great as Morgan, the bearded and scarred mute butler, but he's just one of many stars. Melvyn Douglas, Charles Laughton, Gloria Stuart, Raymond Massey, and Lillian Bond are stranded during a storm at the home of a family Charles Addams must have loved. Effeminate Ernest Thesiger has a 102-year-old father, a pyromaniac brother, and a religious fanatic sister. Whale makes fun of haunted-house mysteries here the way he was to make fun of monster movies a few years later in *The Bride of Frankenstein*. It's only 71 minutes long.

THE OLD DARK HOUSE

1963 Hammer/Universal (England)
PRODUCERS: William Castle, Anthony Hinds
DIRECTOR: William Castle
SCREENWRITER: Robert Dillon

William Castle went to England to film this remake of J.B. Priestley's novel about the crazed Femm Family. A fun macabre comedy with *Addams Family*–style touches, it's nothing like the

OLD MOTHER RILEY MEETS THE VAMPIRE: See MY SON, THE VAMPIRE.

THE OMEGA MAN

1971 Warner Brothers
PRODUCER: Walter Seltzer
DIRECTOR: Boris Sagal
SCREENWRITERS: John William,
Joyce H. Corrington

Second version of Richard Matheson's *I Am Legend* (*The Last Man on Earth* was the first). This end-of-the-world saga stars Charlton Heston in between his other end-of-the-world films (*Planet of the Apes* and *Soylent Green*). Thinking he's the last healthy human left in the Los Angeles of 1975, he discovers a cure for the plague that's killing off the population and protects himself with a rifle that has an infra-red scope. The film is very early '70s: the mutants led by Anthony Zerbe are mostly black albinos and are members of a Manson-like cult called the Family; the bored Heston re-watches *Woodstock* endlessly in a vacant theater—a fate worse than death. With Rosalind Cash.

THE OMEGANS

1968 Paramount-TV (U.S./Philippines)
PRODUCER/DIRECTOR: W. Lee Wilder
SCREENWRITERS: Waldon Wheeland,
W. Lee Wilder

An extremely obscure horror/science-fiction film. A strange tribe is immune to radioactive water that causes disfigurement and life after death. An artist makes his wife and her lover pose in the water. It stars horror queen Ingrid Pitt and Keith Larsen.

THE OMEN

1976 20th Century-Fox (England)
PRODUCER: Harvey Bernhard
DIRECTOR: Richard Donner
SCREENWRITER: David Seltzer

I never thought Gregory Peck would end up in big-budget sensationalist horror movies, but here he is as the stepfather of the Antichrist who was "born unto a jackal." David Warner is decapitated in a scene more explicit than any 42nd Street gore feature. The part where Damien's nanny hangs herself in full view of a group of small children at a birthday party is also unsettling. And don't forget the priest skewered on a lightning rod, Lee Remick falling off a balcony, a monkey attack, a dog attack . . . Aiming for the religion-traumatized masses, the film was successfully sneak-previewed on Sundays. With Billie Whitelaw, Leo McKern, and little Harvey Stevens. By the director of *Superman*. *Damien: Omen II* was the first sequel. **(R)**

ON HER BED OF ROSES

1966 Famous Players (B&W)
PRODUCER: Robert Caramico
DIRECTOR/SCREENWRITER: Albert Zugsmith

A teenage girl (Sandra Lynn) goes to Dr. Krafft-Ebing (Ric Marlowe) after her fiancé (Stephen Long) murders his mother, passing motorists, and himself. Flashbacks show the mother-dominated man with a rose fetish discovering he's impotent during a garden seduction scene and "becoming filled with a desire to commit evil acts." Zugsmith's terrible movies were a lot more fun when they featured Mickey Rooney and Mamie Van Doren.

ON HER MAJESTY'S SECRET SERVICE

1969 United Artists (England)
PRODUCERS: Harry Saltzman,
Albert R. Broccoli
DIRECTOR: Peter Hunt
SCREENWRITER: Richard Maibaum

A commercial disappointment due to the absence of Sean Connery, this 007 film is less gimmicky than its predecessors and features ex-*Avengers* star Diana Rigg as the best of the "Bond girls." She plays the gambling suicidal daughter of Draco, an international gangster.

007 saves her life, marries her, and cries when she's shot by the seemingly indestructible Blofeld (Telly Savalas). The story concerns skis, bobsleds, and a plan to destroy the world by making the population sterile. With Bessie Love, Julie Ege, Catherina Von Schell and, uh . . . George Lazenby as James Bond. Louis Armstrong sings "We Have All the Time in the World." Music by John Barry. The TV version was severely re-edited. After this, the series should have ended it all. (M)

ON THE BEACH

1959 United Artists (B&W)
PRODUCER/DIRECTOR: Stanley Kramer
SCREENWRITER: John Paxton
Nuclear war breaks out in 1964! The only people alive are either in Australia or on Gregory Peck's submarine. He and Ava Gardner remain civil till the end, when we learn "there is still time." With nervous Anthony Perkins and Fred Astaire. Filmed in Australia. It made "Waltzing Matilda" a big U.S. hit. The year's other serious look at the future was *The World, The Flesh and the Devil*. Many of us preferred to watch *The Tingler* and *The Wasp Woman*.

ONCE UPON A SPY

1980 TV
PRODUCER: Jay Daniel
DIRECTOR: Ivan Nagy
SCREENWRITER: Jimmy Sangster
TV-movie in the "James Bond tradition," featuring *Man with the Golden Gun* star Christopher Lee as Marcus Valorium, a mad scientist with a shrinking machine. Don't expect too much. With Ted Danson, Mary Louise Weller, and Eleanor Parker.

ONE BODY TOO MANY

1944 Paramount (B&W)
PRODUCERS: William Pine, William Thomas
DIRECTOR: Frank McDonald
SCREENWRITERS: Winston Miller, Maxwell Shayne
Bela Lugosi plays another sinister butler in a murder comedy starring Jack Haley as an insurance salesman hired to guard the body of an eccentric millionaire the night his will is to be read. With Jean Parker, Lyle Talbot, Blanche Yurka, Dorothy Granger, and Fay Helm.

ONE GIRL'S CONFESSION

1953 Columbia (B&W)
PRODUCER/DIRECTOR/SCREENWRITER: Hugo Haas
Waitress Cleo Moore goes to prison for robbing her boss who had robbed her father. After serving time she goes to work for Hugo Haas and nearly kills the unfortunate director-star. With Glenn Langan, Ross Conway, and a touching ending.

ONE HOUR TO DOOMSDAY: See CITY BENEATH THE SEA.

ONE MILLION B.C.

1940 United Artists (B&W)
PRODUCER: Hal Roach
DIRECTORS: Hal Roach, Hal Roach, Jr.
SCREENWRITERS: Mickell Novak,
George Baker, Joseph Frickert
ALSO RELEASED AS: Cave Man

The ads bellowed: "The most exciting adventure in a million years!" Victor Mature (in his first starring role) and Carole Landis grunt, fall in love, and fight dinosaurs in this exciting prehistoric epic. Lon Chaney, Jr., plays the scared leader of the warlike rock people and gets attacked by a big ox. Effective scenes of lizards doubling as dinosaurs have been reused countless times in low-budget films. The most startling scene shows people being covered with lava. D. W. Griffith had something to do with it but had his name removed from the final credits.

ONE MILLION YEARS B.C.

1966 Hammer/20th Century-Fox
(England/U.S.)
PRODUCER/SCREENWRITER: Michael Carreras
DIRECTOR: Don Chaffey

The rock people are fighting the shell people again. The dinosaurs are animated this time (by Ray Harryhausen) and blond Raquel Welch got a lot of publicity for wearing a brief fur bikini, getting picked up by a pterodactyl, and grunting. With John Richardson, Martine Beswick, and a giant turtle. To cut costs a real spider and iguana were used. With false eyelashes and no spoken dialogue.

ONE MORE TIME

1970 United Artists (England)
PRODUCER: Milton Ebbins
DIRECTOR: Jerry Lewis
SCREENWRITER: Michael Pertwee

Sammy Davis, Jr., and Peter Lawford (the executive producers) star as nightclub owners in this comedy sequel to *Salt and Pepper.* Unbilled Christopher Lee and Peter Cushing appear as Dracula and Dr. Frankenstein. Lawford plays two roles: with a *2001* take-off.

ONE OF OUR SPIES IS MISSING

1966 MGM
PRODUCER: Boris Ingster
DIRECTOR: Darrell Hallenbeck
SCREENWRITER: Howard Rodman

Vera Miles, owner of a fashionable dress salon, wants to revitalize her elder-statesman lover (Maurice Evans) with a rejuvenation serum. T.H.R.U.S.H. agents intervene. Napoleon (Robert Vaughn) and Ilya (David McCallum) come to the rescue. A *Man from U.N.C.L.E.* feature put together from TV episodes. With Leo G. Carroll, Yvonne Craig, and James Doohan (Scotty on *Star Trek*).

ONE SPY TOO MANY

1966 MGM
PRODUCER: David Victor
DIRECTOR: Joseph Sargent
SCREENWRITER: Dean Hargrove

Rip Torn is Alexander the Greater in the *Man from U.N.C.L.E.* feature made from two TV episodes. See Robert Vaughn tied to a stone slab in a "Pit and the Pendulum" parody. See Torn attempt to conquer the world with gas. Dorothy Provine is the villain's wife. With David McCallum, Leo G. Carroll, and Yvonne Craig.

1,000 YEARS FROM NOW: See CAPTIVE WOMEN.

ONE WAY TICKET TO HELL

1956 Eden (B&W)
PRODUCER/DIRECTOR/SCREENWRITER:
Bamlet L. Price, Jr.

The ads promised: "The shocking truth about narcotics and teenage vice!" Girl from broken home joins pothead motorcycle gang. She tries to make a clean break by marrying her childhood sweetheart but is soon back with the gang, landing in the hospital after a barbiturate-influenced car crash. On her escape, she is forced to sell dope for Mr. Big, but when the police start closing in she heads for the border with two Mexican boys. Cold turkey in desert forces surrender. The cast includes Barbara Marks, Robert A. Sherry, Robert Norman, and Joe Popovich, plus Bamlet L. Price, Sr. and Jr.   –CB

THE ONLY WAY OUT IS DEAD: See THE MAN WHO WANTED TO LIVE FOREVER.

OPERATION BIKINI
1964 AIP (B&W with color sequences)
PRODUCERS: James N. Nicholson, Lou Rusoff
DIRECTOR: Anthony Carras
SCREENWRITER: John Tomerlin
Despite the cast, this is not to be confused with AIP's beach movies. It's a serious World War II story about a navy demolition team led by Tab Hunter, who falls for *Beach Party* star Eva Six as Reiko. Also on the low-budget sub are Frankie Avalon, who sings, and Scott Brady, Jim Backus, Gary Crosby, and Jody McCrea, who don't.

OPERATION DAMES
1959 AIP
PRODUCER: Stanley Kallis
DIRECTOR: Louis Clyde Stouman
SCREENWRITER: Ed Lasko
Russ Meyer's wife Eve heads a USO troupe caught behind enemy lines in Korea. A UN patrol led by Chuck Henderson locates the missing entertainers; romance, nude bathing, and freedom follow. With Don Devlin, Ed Craig, and Cindy Girard. Screenwriter Ed

Lasko wrote the songs. Originally a double feature with *Tank Commandos*. –CB

OPERATION KID BROTHER
1967 United Artists (Italy)
PRODUCER: Dario Sabatello
DIRECTOR: Alberto De Martino
SCREENWRITERS: Paul Levi, Frank Walker, Canzio
ALSO RELEASED AS: *O.K. Connery*
A 007 spinoff starring Sean Connery's untalented brother Neil (as himself) and leftovers from Bond films. Connery, a plastic surgeon/hypnotist/archer who works for the secret service, fights villain Adolfo Celi (*Thunderball*), loves Daniela Bianchi (*From Russia with Love*), and takes orders from Bernard Lee (all Bond films) whose secretary is Lois Maxwell (ditto). With Guido Lollobrigida.

OPERATION M: See HELL'S BLOODY DEVILS.

ORCA THE KILLER WHALE
1977 Paramount
PRODUCER: Luciano Vincenzoni
DIRECTOR: Michael Anderson
SCREENWRITERS: Luciano Vincenzoni, Sergio Donati
More laughable nonsense presented by Dino De Laurentiis. This tasteless mixture of *Jaws* and *Moby Dick* features a giant whale after the killers of his pregnant mate. Richard Harris and Charlotte Rampling star. The multi-talented Bo Derek has her leg eaten by Orca. Keenan Wynn is dragged underwater by Orca, and Robert Carradine is saved by Orca, who eats the shark that was attacking him. With Will Sampson (*The White Buffalo*). *Orca* was released between Dino's giant gorilla and giant buffalo epics. All were financial disappointments. Music by Ennio Morricone.

ORGY OF THE DEAD

1965 F.O.G. Distributors
PRODUCER/DIRECTOR: Stephen C. Apostoloff
SCREENWRITER: Ed Wood, Jr.

Wonderful dated nudie horror film with a screenplay by Ed Wood, Jr.! It features Criswell and strippers like Texas Starr and Bunny Glaser. It takes place on a cemetery set where a couple show up to find material for a novel. The Master of the Dead (Criswell) and the Princess of Darkness (Fawn Silver) have them tied to posts and make them watch sinners being judged. Two "native" men in striped skirts get to beat their former slave owner, a topless blonde. A topless murderess has to marry a skeleton. One woman is turned into a gold statue and another is turned into a cat (she wears a leopard suit with holes for her breasts to stick out). With a werewolf, a mummy, and even better dialogue than *Plan 9 from Outer Space*.

ORGY OF THE GOLDEN NUDES: See *HONEYMOON OF HORROR*.

ORLAK, EL INFIERNO DE FRANKENSTEIN

1960 Columbia (Mexico) (B&W)
PRODUCER/DIRECTOR: Rafael Baledon
SCREENWRITERS: Alfredo Ruanova,
Carlos E. Taboada

It's Frankenstein—Mexican style! After the mad doctor (with the help of his faithful servant Pedro) creates the ultimate man he discovers that the 100,000-volt operation has melted its face! So the monster, whose face looks like the plastic puke you can buy in novelty stores, spends most of the time with a steel box on its head. One of the more entertaining south-of-the-border horrors. Not dubbed into English, but who cares, you'll figure it out.

ARE YOU HETEROSEXUAL...?

ORGY OF THE DEAD

THE FILM THAT WILL SATISFY EVERY OVER-SEXAGESIMAL ADULT!

IN GORGEOUS AND SHOCKING ASTRAVISION and SEXICOLOR

with CRISWELL and A BEVY of GORGEOUS GIRLS..!

THE OTHER

1972 20th Century-Fox
PRODUCER/DIRECTOR: Robert Mulligan
SCREENWRITER: Tom Tryon

This chilling supernatural tale set in the '30s looks like *The Waltons* as a horror movie. A young boy and his evil, dead (?) brother disrupt the hick relatives and neighbors. Executive producer Tom Tryon, a former actor who played alien in *I Married a Monster from Outer Space*, wrote the screenplay based on his similarly titled novel. With Uta Hagen, Diana Muldaur, and Chris and Martin Udvarnoky as the twins.

THE OTHER SIDE OF BONNIE AND CLYDE

1968 Dal-Art (B&W)
PRODUCER/DIRECTOR: Larry Buchanan
Documentary-style. See actual footage of the bloody ambush scene, listen

in on the questioning of gang member Floyd Hamilton, visit with Texas Ranger Frank Hamer and his family. When the director of *Naughty Dallas* and *Creature of Destruction* runs out of newsreel, he drops in a couple of scenes with Jo Enterentree and Lucky Mosley as Parker and Barrow. Burl Ives narrates. —CB

THE OTHER WOMAN
1955 20th Century-Fox (B&W)
PRODUCER/DIRECTOR/SCREENWRITER: Hugo Haas

In his seventh one-man production Haas plays a second-string director who gets himself in big trouble by letting Cleo Moore audition for a bit part. He passes her over, so she becomes crazed and lures him into a compromising situation complete with spiked drink. Unless he comes up with 50 grand she will inform his wife of their torrid love, which resulted in unwed motherhood. A peddler charged with the subsequent strangling is freed when Hugo's guilty conscience intervenes, and the actor-director apologizes for the unhappy ending from his new prison home. See *Bait* and *Strange Fascination*. Lance Fuller, Lucille Barkley, and John Qualen co-star. —CB

OUR MAN FLINT
1966 20th Century-Fox
PRODUCER: Saul David
DIRECTOR: Daniel Mann
SCREENWRITERS: Hal Fimberg, Benn Starr

Star James Coburn makes this one of the best of the James Bond spoofs. He's the ultimate spy/stud (he works for Z.O.W.I.E.), carries a multipurpose cigarette lighter, and saves the world from three mad scientists who have control of the weather. The theme music is great and the part about zombie girls being trained for pleasure on an island is unforgettably absurd. With Lee J. Cobb, Edward Mulhare, and Gila Golan. Coburn also starred in *In Like Flint* ('67).

OUR MOTHER'S HOUSE
1967 MGM (England)
PRODUCER/DIRECTOR: Jack Clayton
SCREENWRITERS: Jeremy Brooks, Haya Marareet

More chilling children from the director of *The Innocents*. The seven Hook children live in a Victorian house where they listen to their bedridden mother read from the Bible every night during "mothertime." When she dies they secretly bury her and commune with her spirit. Life goes on as usual until their rotten father (Dirk Bogarde) shows up, squanders their money, and makes the mistake of telling them the truth about their mother. The kids include Pamela Franklin and Mark Lester, both of whom ended up playing many similar roles.

OUT OF SIGHT
1966 Universal
PRODUCER: Bart Patton
DIRECTOR: Lennie Weinrib
SCREENWRITER: Larry Hovis

A teenage/secret agent/musical comedy with a fair about to be sabotaged by Big Daddy (John Lawrence) who's been "driven mad by rock 'n' roll." The fair features six hit acts but no hit songs. With the Turtles, the Astronauts, the Knickerbockers, Dobie Gray, Gary Lewis and the Playboys, and bottom-of-the-barrel Brit rock by Freddie and the Dreamers. Featuring the girl from F.L.U.S.H., beautiful spies named Scuba, Wipeout, and Tuff Bod, midget Billy Curtis, Bob Eubanks from *The Newlywed Game*, and Jamie Farr. Jonathan Daly and Karen Jensen star.

OUT OF THE DARKNESS:
See *NIGHT CREATURE*.

THE OUTER SPACE CONNECTION

1975 Sunn Classics
DIRECTOR/SCREENWRITER: Fred Warshofsky

Aliens will return on December 24, 2011. How old will you be? Sunn Classic Films return with another highly questionable "documentary" based on the idea that aliens are responsible for every unexplained event in history. Somehow they got Rod Serling to lend credibility as narrator. An American sequel to *Chariot of the Gods?*.

OUTLAND

1981 Ladd Company/Warner Brothers
PRODUCER: Richard A. Roth
DIRECTOR/SCREENWRITER: Peter Hyams

Hyams, whose *Capricorn One* was the first SF movie without any SF, further documents his contempt for the genre (and insults Western fans, too) by setting his remake of *High Noon* in outer space. Sean Connery is the Federal District Marshall of the mining colony on Io, third moon of Saturn. Connery learns that an epidemic of crazed violence has been caused by a superamphetamine drug ring; to silence him, company goons are headed for the colony via the noon shuttle. Hyams' primitive idea of futurized suspense is typified by repeated shots of a digital clock readout superimposed on the Ionian landscape. The effects are excellent, however, and seem to draw inspiration from the designs of *Alien* (a major Alan Ladd, Jr., project from his 20th Century-Fox days, just prior to the formation of the Ladd Company). In published interviews, Hyams went to great lengths to deny this, but off-the-record statements by effects crewmembers indicate that the resemblance was not at all coincidental. With Frances Sternhagen and Peter Boyle. **(R)** –BM

OUTLAW MOTORCYCLES

1967 Gillman
PRODUCER/DIRECTOR: Titus Moody

Weddings, funerals, and vacations, mondo-cycle-style. Producer-director Moody also appears as Titus Moede in *Rat Pfink and Boo Boo* and *The Skydivers*, among others. Other Gillman films: *Airborne* and *Passion Street U.S.A.* –CB

OUTLAW TREASURE

1955 ARC (AIP) (B&W)
PRODUCER/SCREENWRITER: John Carpenter
DIRECTOR: Oliver Drake

John Forbes stars as an army troubleshooter who crosses paths with lawless Adele Jergens while investigating a series of gold-shipment heists. "He could tame the West but had difficulty with a blonde bombshell!" When her ringleader boyfriend (Glenn Langan) retaliates by going after the hero's elderly father (also played by Forbes), she defects to the side of justice. With Frank "Red" Carpenter, Michael Whalen, and Harry Lauter. –CB

THE OUTLAWS IS COMING

1965 Columbia (B&W)
PRODUCER/DIRECTOR: Norman Maurer
SCREENWRITER: Elwood Ullman

The Three Stooges in their last film join future *Batman* Adam West out west where they defeat famous gunfighters and outlaws with the help of Annie Oakley (Nancy Kovac). With Stooge regular Emil Sitka in three roles and Henry Gibson. Moe appeared in two more films—*Don't Worry We'll Think of a Title* and *Doctor Death, Seeker of Souls*. The producer-director (Moe's son-in-law) also wrote the story on which this was based.

PACTO DIABOLICO
1968
PRODUCER: Luis Enrique Vergara
DIRECTOR: Jaime Salvador
SCREENWRITERS: Ramon Obon, Jr.,
Adolpho Torres Portillo

A Mexican version of *Dr. Jekyll and Mr. Hyde*. John Carradine plays an old scientist who drinks a potion made with extracts from living women and becomes a young and Mexican killer (Miguel Angel Alvarez). With Regina Thorne. Probably never dubbed into English. Made at the same time as *La Señora Muerte*.

PAJAMA PARTY
1964 AIP
PRODUCERS: James M. Nicholson,
Samuel Z. Arkoff
DIRECTOR: Don Weis
SCREENWRITER: Louis M. Heyward

A follow-up to *Beach Party*. As the Martian Go-Go, Tommy Kirk arrives on Earth and falls in love with Annette Funicello. It must have been the inspiration for *Mork and Mindy*. With Elsa Lanchester as an eccentric aunt with a hidden fortune, Jesse White as a crook, Buster Keaton as Chief Rotten Eagle, Dorothy Lamour (in her last theatrical feature), Harvey Lembeck, Donna Loren, Susan Hart, and bits by Don Rickles and Frankie. Music by the Nooney Ricket Four and Annette, who sings "Where Did I Go Wrong."

PANIC AT LAKEWOOD MANOR: See *IT HAPPENED AT LAKEWOOD MANOR*.

PANIC BUTTON
1964 Gorton Associates (Italy) (B&W)
PRODUCER: Ron Gorton
DIRECTOR: George Sherman
SCREENWRITER: Hal Biller

Seventy-six-year-old Maurice Chevalier plays a forgotten old actor cast as Romeo in a TV pilot film made in Italy. A starlet with a voluptuous body but no talent (Jayne Mansfield) is cast as Juliet. The idea is to make a certified flop—as in *The Producers*. Akim Tamiroff is hired as director. The film's investor (Michael Connors) and his ex-wife (Eleanor Parker) disguise themselves as nuns and take a print of this *Romeo and Juliet* to the Venice Film Festival where it takes all the honors as best comedy.

Akim Tamiroff tries to direct Jayne Mansfield in Panic Button.

PANIC IN THE CITY

1968 Commonwealth United
PRODUCER: Earl Lyon
DIRECTOR: Eddie Davis
SCREENWRITERS: Eddie Davis,
  Charles E. Savage

Communist conspirators Nehemiah Persoff and Anne Jeffries plan to detonate an atom bomb in L.A. Government agent Howard Duff sacrifices himself to save the city. Nuclear horrors with Linda Cristal, Steven McNally, Dennis Hopper, John Hoyt, and Stanley Clements.

PANIC IN THE YEAR ZERO!

1962 AIP
PRODUCERS: Arnold Houghland, Lou Rusoff
DIRECTOR: Ray Milland
SCREENWRITERS: Jay Simms, John Morton
ALSO RELEASED AS: *The End of the World*

Ray Milland directed five of his own films but this is the one to look for, even if you're not an end-of-the-world movie completist. The Baldwin family is going on a fishing trip. Ray is the dad. Jean Hagen is the mom. Mary Mitchell is the 17-year-old daughter and Frankie Avalon is the son. They hear an explosion and realized that L.A. has been leveled by a nuclear attack! Looters and killers are everywhere. Not one to give up, Dad holds up a store for supplies and hides the family in a cave. A group of young toughs rape the daughter. All this would be very depressing except for the raucous music by Les Baxter and the bad acting by Frankie. Listen to the kids have friendly arguments about whether the canned food is radioactive or not. Don't worry, Ray was soon back in two more AIP hits directed by Roger Corman.

PANIC OFFSHORE: See *THE INTRUDER WITHIN*.

PANTHER GIRL OF THE CONGO

1955 Republic (B&W)
PRODUCER/DIRECTOR: Franklin Adreon
SCREENWRITER: Ronald Davidson
ALSO RELEASED AS: *The Claw Monsters*

Only Columbia and Republic continued making serials into the '50s. The last were the worst, and this was one of the last. Phyllis Coates (the original Lois Lane) isn't much of a heroine. She usually faints and lets Myron Healey do the fighting. A scientist (Arthur Space) turns lobsters into giant back-projected "claw monsters" to scare the local natives away from a diamond mine. The natives scare easily; one gunshot sends them running through the jungle. The tree-swinging footage was taken from the 1941 serial *Jungle Girl* to save time and money.

PARADISE ALLEY

1962 Pathe-America (B&W)
PRODUCER/DIRECTOR/SCREENWRITER:
  Hugo Haas
ALSO RELEASED AS: *Stars in Your Backyard*

Czech-born Hugo Haas, the director-star of a series of wonderfully trashy

movies in the '50s, fittingly ended his career by playing an elderly, once-great film director, in this eccentric morality play. He moves to a seedy L.A. boarding house filled with various unhappy unfortunates and announces he's making a film starring them called *The Chosen and the Condemned*. He neglects to tell them he doesn't have any film in the camera. Eventually a studio discovers his plans and finances a real film. In real life nobody ever backed Hugo again. With Marie Windsor, William Schallert, the elderly Corinne Griffith, Margaret Hamilton, Almira Sessions, and comedians Billy Gilbert and Chester Conklin. Don Sullivan (*Teenage Zombies*) and Carol Morris are the teen stars. Sylvester Stallone had a lot of nerve stealing the title for his directorial debut.

PARADISE — HAWAIIAN STYLE

1966 Paramount
PRODUCER: Hal B. Wallis
DIRECTOR: Michael Moore
SCREENWRITERS: Allan Weiss,
    Anthony Lawrence

Elvis, in Hawaii again, is Rick, a helicopter-charter-service pilot surrounded by beautiful girls. He gets grounded because of canine interference. With Suzanna Leigh, Marianna Hill, Philip Ahn, Grady Sutton, and Linda Wong. Hear Elvis sing "It's a Dog's Life" and "Queenie Washine's Papaya."

PARADISIO

1962 Fanfare (England) (B&W, 3-D)
PRODUCER: Jacques Henrici
SCREENWRITERS: Lawrence Zeitlin,
    Henri Haile, Jacques Henrici

An Oxbridge University professor in Austria comes into possession of a special pair of sunglasses. They make every-body appear naked! And sometimes in 3-D! Nobody seems to know who directed this oddity and it may have been made as early as 1956. Leslie Howard's brother Arthur stars with Eva Waegner. For more 3-D nudie confusion, see *The Playbirls and the Bellboy*.

PARANOIA

1968 Fanfare (France/Italy)
PRODUCER: Salvatore Alabiso
DIRECTOR: Umberto Lenzi
SCREENWRITERS: Ugo Moretti,
    Umberto Lenzi, Marie Clair Solleville
ORIGINALLY RELEASED AS: *Orgasmo*

As a socialite widow in Italy, Carroll Baker is the victim of a scheme to gain control of her inheritance. She's seduced by a young man who drugs her and makes her participate in orgies which are photographed for blackmailing. Soft-core sex and psychological horror with one of the stars of *The Greatest Story Ever Told*. (X)

PARANOIAC

1963 Hammer/Universal (England)
PRODUCER: Anthony Hinds
DIRECTOR: Freddie Francis
SCREENWRITER: Jimmy Sangster

Oliver Reed makes a great psycho who plays an organ in the chapel for the mummy of the baby brother he has killed. His sister (Janette Scott) thinks she's going crazy because the dead brother shows up alive. Full of deceptions and plotting, it's one of the better early *Psycho*-inspired films.

PARASITE

1982 Embassy (3-D)
PRODUCER/DIRECTOR: Charles Band
SCREENWRITERS: Alan Adler, Michael Shoob, Frank Levering

Advertised as "the first futuristic monster movie in 3-D," this slow-moving dud concerns a scientist (Robert Gladini) hiding out in what looks like a set for an old Western, trying to study and destroy a parasitic monster copied from *Alien*. The slimy creature burrows through the body of '50s musical star Vivian Blaine and ex-Runaways singer Cherie Currie, and occasionally leaps out at the audience. The effects and acting are mediocre at best. Producer-director Band is more successful selling other people's films on videocassette. He created Media Video and Wizard Video. Both are great sources for home exploitation and horror. **(R)**

THE PARASITE MURDERS: See THEY CAME FROM WITHIN.

PARATROOP COMMAND

1959 AIP
PRODUCER/SCREENWRITER: Stan Shpetner
DIRECTOR: William Witney

The ads promised: "The deadly thrill of jump and kill!" from this story of World War II African invasion crises.

Richard Bakalyan accidentally kills a soldier who called him a coward. He clears his name by tripping a series of land mines to open a path for a much-needed radio generator, giving his life in the process. Ken Lynch, Jack Hogan, and Jimmy Murphy complete the mission. Witney came to AIP after 21 years at Republic. A double bill with *Submarine Seahawk*.   –CB

PARIS PLAYBOYS

1954 Allied Artists (B&W)
PRODUCER: Ben Schwalb
DIRECTOR: William Beaudine
SCREENWRITER: Elwood Ullman

Huntz Hall is mistaken for a French scientist who discovers atomic sourcream fuel. With Leo Gorcey and the other Bowery Boys. Director Beaudine did *More for Peace* for the Protestant Film Commission the same year.

PARTS: THE CLONUS HORROR

1979 Group I
PRODUCERS: Myrl A. Schreibman, Robert S. Fiveson
DIRECTOR: Robert S. Fiveson
SCREENWRITER: Myrl A. Schreibman
ALSO RELEASED AS: *The Clonus Horror*

An extremely low-budget but effective feature with Tom Donnelly as a rebellious clone trying to expose a massive conspiracy. Duplicates of politicians and industrial magnates are kept hanging in plastic bags in a giant refrigerator for spare parts. More fun than the major release *Coma*. With Peter Graves, Keenan Wynn, and Dick Sargent. **(R)**

THE PARTY CRASHERS

1958 Paramount (B&W)
PRODUCER: William Alland
DIRECTOR/SCREENWRITER: Bernard Girard

They're "Kids running wild because their parents run wilder!" according to the ads. Mark Damon and his goons crash a square teen gathering, where he talks Connie Stevens away from her date. They make their way to a swank motel party and run into Damon's alcoholic mother, who falls down a flight of stairs while being escorted out. Featuring '30s bad girl Frances Farmer, with Denver Pyle, Onslow Stevens, and child Oscar winner Bobby Driscoll. –CB

PASSAGE TO MARSEILLE
1944 Warner Brothers (B&W)
PRODUCER: Hal B. Wallis
DIRECTOR: Michael Curtiz
SCREENWRITERS: Casey Robinson, Jack Moffitt

After *The Maltese Falcon*, Warner Brothers made *Across the Pacific* (with Bogart, Greenstreet, and Mary Astor), *All Through the Night* (with Bogart, Lorre, and Conrad Veidt), *Casablanca* (with Bogart, Greenstreet, Lorre, Claude Rains, and Conrad Veidt), *Background to Danger* (with Lorre and Greenstreet), and *then* this flashback-filled film about five fugitive Frenchmen. They escape from Devil's Island to join the Free French and fight Nazis. The not-too-surprising cast includes Bogart, Lorre, Greenstreet, and Rains as well as French leading lady Michèle Morgan, Austrian Helmut Dantine, Dutch Philip Dorn, British John Loder, Italian Eduardo Ciannelli, and Yank George Tobias. By the Hungarian director of *Casablanca*. Cinematography by James Wong Howe.

PATRICK
1979 Filmways (Australia)
PRODUCERS: Anthony I. Ginnane,
Richard Franklin
DIRECTOR: Richard Franklin
SCREENWRITER: Everett De Roche

The electrical accident that killed his mother has left Patrick in a coma for four years. When a cute nurse starts to work on his floor, Patrick transmits psychic mash notes to her typewriter.

Patrick, it turns out, is Carrie in a coma. The coma deepens in the badly dubbed U.S. version. Starring Susan Penhaligon and Robert Helpman. Music by Brian May (*Road Warrior*). Franklin later directed *Psycho II*. (**R**)   –BM

THE PATSY
1964 Paramount
PRODUCER: Ernest D. Gluckman
DIRECTOR: Jerry Lewis
SCREENWRITERS: Jerry Lewis, Bill Richmond

Inept bellboy Stanley Belt (Jerry Lewis) is made into a star celebrity by the management team of a singer who has just died. The starmakers include Everett Sloan, Phil Harris, Keenan Wynn, Peter Lorre (as a director), John Carradine (as a valet), and Ina Balin. Stanley becomes a hit by appearing on the Ed Sullivan Show and lip-syncing "I Lost My Heart in a Drive-in Movie." Besides Ed, George Raft, Hedda Hopper, Mel Tormé, Rhonda Fleming, and Ed Wynn play themselves. Also with Hans Conreid, Richard Deacon, Nancy Kulp, Neil Hamilton, Phil Foster, Scatman Crothers, and Lloyd Thaxton. Lorre died four days after filming his scenes.

PEARL OF DEATH
1944 Universal (B&W)
PRODUCER/DIRECTOR: Roy William Neill
SCREENWRITER: Bertram Millhauser

Rondo Hatton debuts in his famous role as the Oxton creeper, a back-breaking brute who leaves a trail of smashed bric-a-brac in his wake. Hatton suffered from acromegaly, a progressive disease that causes enlargement and distortion of the bones, so he was able to play the gruesome creeper without makeup. This Sherlock Holmes movie is based on *The Adventure of the Six Napoleons*. One of the Napoleon busts contains the Borgia pearl. Evelyn Ankers stole it. Miles Mander wants it. Basil Rathbone and

—Karlheinz—Boehm), a cameraman who moonlights taking nudie shots, is fascinated by physical imperfections and kills models with a spiked tripod while filming them. He also documents the police investigations that follow the murders, and finally his own suicide. Mark's childhood was similarly documented by his sadistic psychologist father (played by Powell), who used him as a guinea pig for fear experiments. Formerly known only to some lucky late-night TV viewers and completist horror fans, this film received belated critical acclaim when Martin Scorsese arranged for a limited rerelease in 1980. Don't miss it. Naive Anna Massey and her blind but perceptive mother (Maxine Audley) are the boarders in Mark's house. Moira Shearer is a dancer victim. With Shirley Ann Field and famous '50s nudie model Pamela Green.

UPI 8/10/75: Evelyn Ankers, an English citizen born in Chile, was a popular movie actress in the 1940s. Here Evelyn is seen in 1944 (the year she starred in Pearl of Death) wearing sarape and sombrero to celebrate being named the No. 1 pinup girl of her native country. Today, she is pursuing a second career—wife (of actor Richard Denning), mother, and grandmother—on the Hawaiian island of Maui.

PENETRATION
1976 Mishkin (Italy/U.S.)
PRODUCER: William Mishkin
DIRECTOR: Roberto Montero

Nigel Bruce are faced with 20 unsolved murders. With Dennis Hoey as the slow-witted Lestrade and Mary Gordon as Mrs. Hudson. Universal next put the incredible Rondo in *Jungle Captive*.

PEEPING TOM
1960 Anglo Amalgamated/Astor
(England)
PRODUCERS: Michael Powell, Albert Fennell
DIRECTOR: Michael Powell
SCREENWRITER: Leo Marks
ALSO RELEASED AS: *Face of Fear*
Like Tod Browning's *Freaks*, this fascinating and unflinching horror classic pretty much ruined the career of popular director Michael Powell. Mark (Karl

MORE HORRIBLE THAN HORROR! MORE TERRIBLE THAN TERROR!

marked for death by PEEPING TOM—TO LOOK MEANT DANGER TO SMILE MEANT DEATH!

ASTOR PICTURES presents **peeping tom**

CARL BOEHM · MOIRA SHEARER · ANNA MASSEY · MAXINE AUDLEY
An original story and screenplay by Leo Marks · Produced and Directed by MICHAEL POWELL
EASTMAN **COLOR**

WARNING! Don't see "PEEPING TOM" unless you are prepared to see the screaming shock and raw terror in the faces of those marked for death! SEE IT FROM THE BEGINNING!

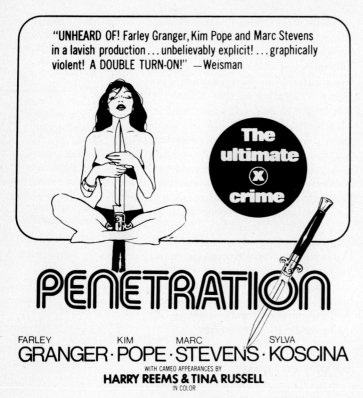

"UNHEARD OF! Farley Granger, Kim Pope and Marc Stevens in a lavish production...unbelievably explicit!...graphically violent! A DOUBLE TURN-ON!" —Weisman

The ultimate **X** crime

PENETRATION

FARLEY **GRANGER** · KIM **POPE** · MARC **STEVENS** · SYLVA **KOSCINA**

WITH CAMEO APPEARANCES BY

HARRY REEMS & TINA RUSSELL

IN COLOR

Farley Granger in a hard-core sex movie? Well, sort of. He played a cop trailing after a killer in an Italian feature, which was shown here under the charming title of *The Slasher is the Sex Maniac*. That film was given a second life when it was re-edited and retitled. Now Farley looks for women having affairs (because they're always the killer's victims) and in his search encounters porno footage shot in America with Tina Russell, Harry Reems, Kim Pope, and others. An example of the irritating "insert" method of film-making. With Sylvia Koscina. (X)

THE PEOPLE

1972 TV

PRODUCER: Gerlad I. Isenberg
DIRECTOR: John Korty
SCREENWRITER: James M. Miller

A teacher in a small California town (Kim Darby) discovers the locals are peaceful aliens with powers of ESP and levitation. With William Shatner, Diane Varsi, and Dan O'Herlihy. An American Zoetrope production on which Francis Ford Coppola had executive producer credit.

THE PEOPLE THAT TIME FORGOT

1977 Amicus/AIP (England)
PRODUCER: John Dark
DIRECTOR: Kevin Conner
SCREENWRITER: Patrick Tilley

Okay sequel to *The Land That Time Forgot*. During World War I, Patrick Wayne (yes, John's son and star of *Sinbad and the Eye of the Tiger*, released the same year) flies to the lost continent of Caprona to rescue a bearded Doug McClure, still lost from the '75 movie. Wayne finds a tribe of Na-Gas warriors, a city of skulls, some fairly silly dinosaurs, and (since David Bowie failed to make her a rock star) Dana Gillespie in some pretty revealing fur outfits. With Thorley Walters, Sarah Douglas, and strongman Milton Rird.

PEOPLE WHO OWN THE DARK

1975 Newcal (Spain)
EXECUTIVE PRODUCER: Salvadore Romero
DIRECTOR/SCREENWRITER: Armando de Ossorio
ORIGINALLY RELEASED AS: *Planeta Ciego*

A science-fiction/horror film about the end of the world. You wouldn't know it from the deceptive 1980 American ads, but the stars are Paul Naschy, Maria Perschy, and Tony Kendall. (R)

PERCY

1971 MGM (England)
PRODUCER: Betty E. Box
DIRECTOR: Ralph Thomas
SCREENWRITER: Hugh Leonard

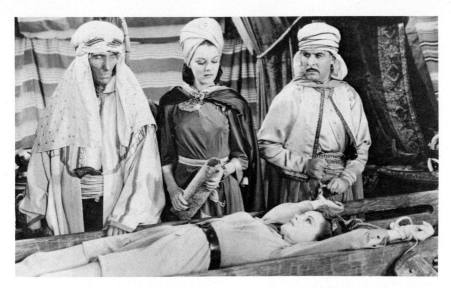

Charles Middleton and Lorna Gray (as Vultura) provide one of The Perils of Nyoka *(played by Kay Aldridge).*

Percy ties with the American-made *Amazing Transplant* as the first penis-transplant feature. Hywel Bennett tries to find the donor of his new tool. Elke Sommer and Britt Ekland are interested, too. With Denholm Elliott and Tracy Reed. Ray Davies and the Kinks provided a better sound track than this nonsense deserved. The sequel was shown as *It's Not the Size That Counts.*

PERCY'S PROGRESS:
See *IT'S NOT THE SIZE THAT COUNTS.*

PERFORMANCE
1969 Warner Brothers (England)
PRODUCER: Sanford Lieberson
DIRECTORS: Donald Cammell, Nicholas Roeg
SCREENWRITER: Donald Cammell
The ads read: "This film is about madness. And sanity. Fantasy. And reality. Death. And life. Vice. And versa." Pretty pretentious, but Warners must have had a really hard time trying to market this magical, disturbing movie. It's hard to find an uncut version, but the opening scenes with gangster James Fox include some extremely sadistic violence. Fox, badly disguised as a juggler, rents a room at the townhouse of Turner (Mick Jagger), a reclusive rock star. He's offered Anita Pallenberg, Michele Breton, and some pretty strong mushrooms leading to a literal personality switch and death. Jagger sings "Memo From Turner," one of the best songs he's ever done, during a particularly drug crazed scene. Other great music is by Randy Newman, Jack Nitzsche, and the Last Poets. Cammell later directed *Demon Seed.* Roeg's next feature was *Walkabout.* (**X**)

PERILS FROM THE PLANET MONGO: See *FLASH GORDON CONQUERS THE UNIVERSE.*

THE PERILS OF NYOKA
1942 Republic (B&W)
ASSOCIATE PRODUCER: W.J. O'Sullivan
DIRECTOR: William Witney
SCREENWRITERS: Ronald Davidson, Norman S. Hall, William Lively, Joseph O'Donnell, Joseph Poland
ALSO RELEASED AS: *Nyoka and the Lost City of Hippocrates*

Nyoka (Kay Aldridge), considered a white goddess by African natives, helps Clayton Moore (*The Lone Ranger*) and his expedition find sacred tablets containing the secret of life. As the evil Vultura, Lorna Gray sends her Arab followers and Satan the gorilla to stop them. With Tristam Coffin and Charles Middleton as Cassib. A feature version of this 15-chapter serial was released in '66. It was a sequel to *Jungle Girl* ('40)

PERILS OF PAULINE
1967 Universal
PRODUCER: Herbert B. Leonard
DIRECTORS: H.B. Leonard, Joshua Shelley
SCREENWRITER: Albert Beich
Silly made-for-TV movie based on the 1914 serial. It stars Pam Austin, TV's "Dodge Rebellion" girl. A gorilla falls in love with her and Russians try to embalm her with Lenin. Pat Boone is the hero. Terry-Thomas is a villain. With Edward Everett Horton, Hamilton Camp, and Kurt Kasznar. Somehow it managed to get released theatrically in the U.S.

PERSECUTION
1973 Paragon (England)
PRODUCER: Kevin Francis
DIRECTOR: Donald Chaffey
SCREENWRITERS: Robert B. Hutton,
Rosemary Wootten
ALSO RELEASED AS: *Terror of Sheba*
Lana Turner plays a crippled, possessive mom in a pantsuit in this sadistic tale of murder and cat funerals. With Ralph Bates, Trevor Howard, Olga Georges-Picot, and a lot of cats, all named Sheba. Lana later refered to this, her first feature after *The Big Cube*, as "a bomb."

PETE KELLY'S BLUES
1955 Warners
PRODUCER: Mark VII Ltd.
DIRECTOR: Jack Webb
SCREENWRITER: Robert L. Breen

Webb's second feature and probably his best. He stars as a trumpeter in a '20s Kansas City area jazz band under contract pressure from gangster Edmond O'Brien. Peggy Lee was nominated for an Oscar for her portrayal of O'Brien's alcoholic girlfriend—who eventually falls down a stairway and ends up in a mental hospital. Also with Janet Leigh, Andy Devine, Lee Marvin, Jayne Mansfield, Martin Milner, and Ella Fitzgerald. —CB

PHANTASM
1979 Avco Embassy
PRODUCERS: D.A. Coscarelli,
Paul Pepperman
DIRECTOR/SCREENWRITER: Don Coscarelli
A unique and fascinating horror hit with more satisfying surprises than you could find in a dozen other recent offerings. It's a fantasy-horror movie with a science-fiction twist. Though aimed at kids (the hero, Michael Baldwin, is 15), it had to be cut to avoid an X rating. There's a cemetery sex scene, a ghostly undertaker, a mortuary with a link to another dimension, and an unforgettable flying metal sphere. The sphere imbeds itself into a victim's face with jagged spikes, drills a hole through the head, and causes all his blood to gush out a hole on the other side! A sound track album is available. Director Coscarelli made his first feature, *Jim—the World's Greatest*, at the age of 18! His second, *Kenny and Co.*, was about a Halloween party. In 1982 he did *The Beastmaster*. **(R)**

PHANTOM FIEND: See THE LODGER.

PHANTOM FIEND: See THE RETURN OF DR. MABUSE.

PHANTOM FROM SPACE

1953 United Artists (B&W)
PRODUCER/DIRECTOR: W. Lee Wilder
SCREENWRITERS: Bill Raynor, Myles Wilder

Pretty forgettable science fiction about an invisible alien trapped in the Griffith Observatory. When the big muscle-bound alien dies and becomes visible we see a "naked man" (he has tight shorts on) with a bulbous head. With Ted Cooper, Noreen Nash, and Michael Mark.

THE PHANTOM FROM 10,000 LEAGUES

1955 ARC (B&W)
PRODUCERS: Jack and Dan Milner
DIRECTOR: Dan Milner
SCREENWRITER: Lou Rusoff

Spies, an underwater death ray, and a laughable puppet monster are dispersed by hero Kent Taylor. It was co-billed with Corman's *The Day the World Ended*, making that movie look great by comparison. With Cathy Downs and Michael Whalen.

THE PHANTOM KILLER

1943 Monogram (B&W)

A remake of Monogram's *The Sphinx*, a Lionel Atwill mystery. John Hamilton (TV's Perry White) is the killer. With Dick Purcell, Joan Woodbury, and dumb Warren Hymer. Advertised as a horror film.

THE PHANTOM OF CHINATOWN

1940 Monogram (B&W)
PRODUCER: Paul Malvern
DIRECTOR: Phil Rosen
SCREENWRITER: Joseph West

Key Luke, usually seen in Charlie Chan movies, took over the Mr. Wong role for the last in that series after Boris Karloff quit. Karloff looked as Chinese as—well, Boris Karloff. Luke was the only Chinese person to star in one of the countless cheap Oriental detective movies popular in the '30s and '40s. With Grant Withers and Lotus Long.

THE PHANTOM OF HOLLYWOOD

1974 TV
PRODUCER/DIRECTOR: Gene Levitt
SCREENWRITERS: Robert Thom, George Shenk

Jack Cassidy plays Otto Vonner, who turns out to be the killer phantom living on the MGM back lot. Wearing an executioner's costume with studded wristbands, he goes crazy when he finds out his home is going to be destroyed. I think he lost it when he saw the list of co-stars in this misfired nostalgia: Broderick Crawford, Jackie Coogan, Peter Lawford, Kent Taylor, Regis Toomey, Billy Halop, and John Ireland. Skye Aubrey, daughter of the one-time MGM president, is the lady in distress.

PHANTOM OF PARIS: See *THE MYSTERY OF MARIE ROGET.*

THE PHANTOM OF SOHO

1964 Producers Releasing Organization (W. Germany) (B&W)
PRODUCER: Arthur Brauner
DIRECTOR: Franz Josef Gottlieb
SCREENWRITER: Ladislas Foder
ORIGINALLY RELEASED AS: *Das Phantom von Soho*

Scotland Yard investigates murders committed by a hooded killer in a skull mask. With a strip-club setting, lots of suspects, and a rather unpleasant revelation about the victims. From a novel by Bryan (not Edgar) Wallace.

PHANTOM OF TERROR: See *THE BIRD WITH THE CRYSTAL PLUMAGE.*

THE PHANTOM OF THE OPERA

1943 Universal
PRODUCER: George Waggner
DIRECTOR: Arthur Lubin
SCREENWRITERS: Eric Taylor,
Samuel Hoffenstein

Respectable technicolor remake of the Lon Chaney classic ('25) with Claude Rains as the acid-scarred composer Erique, living below the Paris Opera House. Rains is good and there's a great crystal-chandelier scene but too much opera for some. Susanna Foster is the singer helped by the phantom. With Nelson Eddy, Hume Cronyn, and Leo Carrillo. Miss Foster and the Phantom stage returned the next year in *The Climax*, a somewhat similar Karloff feature.

THE PHANTOM OF THE OPERA

1962 Hammer/Universal (England)
PRODUCER/SCREENWRITER: Anthony Hinds
(John Elder)
DIRECTOR: Terence Fisher

After successfully revitalizing Dracula, the Frankenstein monster, and the Mummy, Hammer Studios turned to the Phantom. Herbert Lom stars as the acid-scarred composer living beneath the opera house. New attractions are a dwarf assistant, a comical rat catcher, and a black museum, but all that didn't improve things much. Michael Gough claims he wrote "Saint Joan" but we know it was Lom. With Heather Sears, Thorley Walters, and Edward De Souza.

THE PHANTOM OF THE PARADISE

1974 20th Century-Fox
PRODUCER: Edward R. Pressman
DIRECTOR/SCREENWRITER: Brian De Palma

A hit-and-miss musical comedy/horror film with a lot of good ideas. Paul Williams, a songwriter and TV non-star, is hard to take as an eternally young evil rock music magnate, and Jessica Harper doesn't make it as a "rock superstar." But some of the visuals are exciting and the record-industry gags are prety funny. As the phantom, William Finley (also in *Sisters*) is mangled in a record-pressing plant. A Kiss-like group dismembers a fan in the audience and Gerrit Graham plays a sissy Frankenstein monster singing star. With De Palma's usual Hitchcock references. All references to Swan Song Records had to be optically removed because Led Zeppelin's company sued. That's why wavy lines appear around the logos.

PHANTOM OF THE RUE MORGUE

1954 Warner Brothers (3-D)
PRODUCER: Henry Blanke
DIRECTOR: Roy Del Ruth
SCREENWRITERS: Harold Medford,
James R. Webb

House of Wax had just been a big hit for Warner Brothers, so they decided to follow it with this 3-D remake of Poe's "Murders in the Rue Morgue." The results are pretty pathetic. In 19th-century Paris Karl Malden overacts as never before as a mad zoologist who hypnotizes an ape (Charles Gremora, who was also in the '32 version, *Murders in the Rue Morgue*) to kill when it hears church bells. Steve Forrest (brother of Dana Andrews and star of *S.W.A.T.*) is blamed for the monkeyshines so that Karl can take away his girlfriend (Patricia Medina). Co-starring everybody's favorite talk-show host Merv Griffin in one of his rare film roles. With Claude Dauphin, Henry Kulky, and the Flying Zacchinis.

THE PHANTOM PLANET

1961 AIP (B&W)
PRODUCER: Fred Gebhardt
DIRECTOR: William Marshall
SCREENWRITERS: William Telaak,
Fred de Gortner, Fred Gebhardt

In the future (1980) an astronaut (Dean Fredricks) crash-lands on an asteroid named Rheton where the inhabitants are six inches tall. He shrinks to their size, falls for a mute girl (who later regains her speech in the excitement), and helps fight the solarites. The ridiculous dog-faced monster/solarites are led by giant Richard Kiel. Francis X. Bushman (then 79 years old) is Seaom, the Rheton leader. Anthony Dexter (star of the '51 *Valentino*) is another leader. Both were in *Twelve to the Moon* two years earlier. With Coleen Gray (*The Leech Woman*) and Dolores Faith.

PHANTOM SHIP: See THE MYSTERY OF THE MARIE CELESTE.

THE PHARAOH'S CURSE

1957 United Artists (B&W)
PRODUCER: Howard W. Koch
DIRECTOR: Lee Sholem
SCREENWRITER: Richard Landau
An Egyptian kills off members of an archaeological expedition as he ages thousands of years. A boring *Mummy*-like movie with Mark Dana, Ziva Rodann, and Kurt Katch.

PHASE IV

1974 Paramount
PRODUCER: Paul B. Radin
DIRECTOR: Saul Bass
SCREENWRITER: Mayo Simon
Great science-fiction thriller starring countless real ants. Because of chemical pollution and ecological imbalance, ants in Arizona band together and attack. They can strip the flesh of animals (or humans) in seconds, hypnotize people and destroy computers and machines by chewing wires. Two scientists and a farm girl fight a losing battle in the desert. Directed by title designer

Saul Bass. The *2001*-style ending was drastically cut by the studio. With Nigel Davenport, Michael Murphy, and Lynn Frederick. Music by Stomu Yamashta. Filmed in England.

PHILOSOPHY IN THE BOUDOIR: See EUGÉNIE... THE STORY OF HER JOURNEY INTO PERVERSION.

PHOBIA

1980 Magder/Paramount (Canada)
PRODUCER: Zale Magder
DIRECTOR: John Huston
SCREENWRITERS: Lew Lehman, James Sangster, Peter Bellwood
Put together the director of *The Maltese Falcon* and the star of *Starsky and Hutch* and this is what you get. Paul Michael Glaser is a doctor treating the psychotic fears of a group of convicted murderers. The doctor's therapy is interrupted, however, when someone starts killing off his patients one by one, using their greatest fears as the instrument of murder. Deemed unfit for wide theatrical release after a few test engagements, *Phobia* later showed up on some cable services. **(R)**　　　–BM

THE PHOENIX

1980 21st Century (Hong Kong)
PRODUCER: Frank Wong
DIRECTORS: Richard Caan, Sadamasa Arikawa
SCREENWRITER: F. Kenneth Lin
Richard ("Jaws") Kiel plays Steel Hands, a giant who helps a fisherman battle the evil queen Flower Fox for possession of a magic vessel and a book of spells. With a stone warrior, a tidal wave, and the big bird of the title.

THE PHYNX

1970 Warner Brothers
PRODUCERS: Bob Booker,
George Foster
DIRECTOR: Lee M. Katzin
SCREENWRITER: Stan Cornyn

An athlete, a campus militant, a negro model, and an American Indian are picked by a computer (shaped like a woman) to form a rock group called the Phynx and go on tour in Albania where American show business people have been kidnaped by Communists. So bad that the studio decided not to release it at the last minute. *Some* of the stars that the phony band rescues: Johnny Weissmuller and Maureen O'Sullivan, Leo Gorcey and Huntz Hall, Ed Sullivan, Colonel Harlan Sanders, Xavier Cugat, Trini Lopez, Dick Clark, Richard Pryor, Harold "Oddjob" Sakata, George Jessel, and Rona Barrett! Want more? Why not? Patty of the Andrew Sisters, Edgar Bergen, Busby Berkeley, Andy Devine, Guy Lombardo, Butterfly McQueen, Jay Silverheels, Rudy Vallee, Marilyn Maxwell, Pat O'Brien, Dorothy Lamour, Patsy Kelley, Ruby Keeler, Louis Hayward, Cass Daley, Fritz Feld, and James Brown! Also with the following, who don't get kidnaped: Michael Ansara, Joan Blondell, Martha Raye, and Ultra Violet! Sound good? Wanna see it? Write your local TV station or revival theater.

PICKUP

1951 Columbia (B&W)
PRODUCER/DIRECTOR/SCREENWRITER:
Hugo Haas

At age 50, Czechoslovakian character actor Hugo Haas decided to become a producer-director-screenwriter, and over the next ten years he turned out over a dozen low-budget features, usually starring himself. In most of his trashy soap operas he plays a lonely middle-aged man fatally attracted to a cheating young dame. In this, his first effort, Haas is a hardworking widower living in the desert who marries young Beverly Michaels and soon becomes deaf. His unfaithful wife tries to have him killed, but he regains his hearing when a car knocks him down. With Allan Nixon (*Mesa of Lost Women*). Beverly and Hugo were soon back in *Girl on the Bridge*.

PICTURE MOMMY DEAD

1966 Embassy Pictures
PRODUCER/DIRECTOR: Bert I. Gordon
SCREENWRITER: Robert Sherman

Bert I. Gordon, who had given bit parts to his daughter Susan, decided to put her in a starring role. Thanks, Dad! Susan leaves an asylum where she's been in shock over the fiery death of her mother (Zsa Zsa Gabor). Dad Don Ameche has a new wife (Martha Hyer), who only married him for the money left by Zsa Zsa. Susan is still haunted by her mother's memory, and her stepmother is conspiring with her lover, the caretaker, to get the troubled girl to lead them to Zsa Zsa's jewels. If you're familiar with Bert's work, you know what to expect. With Wendell Corey and Signe Hasso.

PICTURE OF DORIAN GRAY

1945 MGM (B&W with color sequence)
PRODUCER: Pedro S. Berman
DIRECTOR/SCREENWRITER: Albert Lewin

The classic version of Oscar Wilde's novel stars Hurd Hatfield as the handsome, wealthy 19th-century Londoner who stays young while his portrait ages and shows the effects of his decadent life-style. George Sanders is great as Dorian's cynical friend, Lord Henry, who puts all those evil thoughts in the impressionable young man's head and introduces him to the artist who does the incredible likeness. The actual painting was by Ivan Albright, whose "Maggot Realism" pieces can be viewed at the Whitney and the Museum of Modern Art. Unlike the 1970 remake, this one leaves a lot to your imagination, but you can tell what Dorian does with his spare time. Hatfield later repeated his most famous role in a typically silly segment of *The Wild Wild West* in the late '60s. He looked just as he did in '45, though. Also with Angela Lansbury, Donna Reed, Peter Lawford, and Bernard Gorcey. Cedric Hardwicke narrates.

PICTURE OF DORIAN GRAY

1973 TV
PRODUCER: Dan Curtis
DIRECTOR: Glenn Jordan
SCREENWRITER: John Tomerlin
A surprisingly good version starring Shane Briant who was briefly a star of British Hammer films. Originally shown in two 90-minute segments, it'll be trimmed a lot if repeated. With Nigel Davenport and Vanessa Howard.

THE PIED PIPER

1972 Paramount (England/
    W. Germany)
PRODUCERS: David Puttnam,
    Sandford Lieberson
DIRECTOR: Jacques Demy
SCREENWRITERS: Andrew Berkin,
    Jacques Demy, Mark Peploe
It's too bad this grim fantasy got such limited distribution because it's a classic not aimed at kids. Forget *Willard*; the rats shown here bringing the plague to a 14th-century English town are scary. Pop singer Donovan (who unfortunately hasn't been taken seriously for years) stars as the piper and provides the music. Donald Pleasence is the inept baron. As his despicable son, John Hurt is about to marry an 11-year-old girl. Her crippled friend (Jack Wild) is the apprentice to the alchemist who is

burned at the stake. Also with Diana Dors.

PIER 5, HAVANA

1959 United Artists (B&W)
PRODUCER: Robert E. Kent
DIRECTOR: Edward Cahn
SCREENWRITER: James B. Gordon
Cameron Mitchell and Allison Hayes help save Castro's headquarters in Havana from bombing by Batista sympathizers. A pre-Bay of Pigs feature filmed on location. Cahn directed *The Four Skulls of Jonathan Drake*, *Riot in Juvenile Prison*, *Invisible Invaders*, *Vice Raid*, and *Inside the Mafia* the same year. How many have you seen?

THE PILL: See TEST TUBE BABIES.

PILLOW OF DEATH

1945 Universal (B&W)
PRODUCER: Ben Pivar
DIRECTOR: Wallace Fox
SCREENWRITER: George Bricker
Is Lon Chaney, Jr., smothering people to death? Does his dead wife tell him to? Is this another *Inner Sanctum* mystery? Yeah, and it features Brenda Joyce and Rosalind Ivan.

PIRANHA

1978 New world
PRODUCER: Jon Davidson
DIRECTOR: Joe Dante
SCREENWRITER: John Sayles
A great modern horror movie with thrills, blood, laughs, and a cast picked to please the fans. The government has created mutant, man-eating fish to use against the North Vietnamese, but they escape into a resort lake and tear apart vacationing teens and kids. Bradford Dillman (*Bug*, *Swarm*) is the hero. Kevin McCarthy is the scientist who developed the toothy killers. Barbara Steele is Dr. Mengers, a military officer.

Lost River Lake was a thriving resort - until they discovered...

PIRANHA

A NEW WORLD PICTURE

With Heather Menzies (*Sssss*), Kennan Wynn, Dick Miller, Bruce Gordon, Richard Deacon, and Paul Bartel, director of *Eating Raoul*. Roger Corman was the executive producer. Producer Jon Davidson did *Hollywood Boulevard* with Dante. A sound track album by Pino Donaggia (*Dressed to Kill*) is available. (**R**)

THE PIRATES OF BLOOD RIVER
1962 Hammer/Columbia (England)
PRODUCER: Anthony Nelson-Keys
DIRECTOR/SCREENWRITER: John Gilling

Christopher Lee is great as the pirate Laroche. He wears all black, including an eyepatch, and even with a useless left arm is completely in control of a ship of cutthroats. He forces Kerwin Matthews to take him to a Huguenot settlement in the Caribbean to steal a solid gold statue. With Glen Corbett, Oliver Reed, and Andrew Keir. Matthews, best known for starring in *The Seventh Voyage of Sinbad*, also was in *Maniac* for Hammer.

THE PIT AND THE PENDULUM
1961 AIP
PRODUCER/DIRECTOR: Roger Corman
SCREENWRITER: Richard Matheson

In the follow-up to the successful *House of Usher*, Vincent Price returns as Nicholas Medina, a 16th-century Spanish nobleman who goes crazy when he thinks his wife has been buried alive. He actually "becomes" his own father, an inquisitor. Barbara Steele is great in her first American role; she plays Elizabeth, Price's scheming "dead" wife who eventually gets hers in an iron maiden. The massive torture chamber including the fabled razor-sharp pendulum which almost cuts John Kerr (as Elizabeth's brother) in half provides a visual highlight. Luana Anders (as Price's sister) and Anthony Carbone (as Steele's lover) are there to remind you that despite Poe and a new-found respectability, this is still an AIP picture.

PIT STOP
1969 Goldstone (B&W)
PRODUCER/DIRECTOR/SCREENWRITER: Jack Hill

From the director of *Blood Bath* and *Spider Baby*, the story of an ambitious young stock-car driver who forces his competitors into major crack-ups so he can steal their women. Richard Davalos of *East of Eden* stars, with Brian Donlevy as his wealthy sponsor and Ellen McRae (later Burstyn) as the track wife he makes a widow. Filmed in 1967 in and around L.A., with scenes from the Phoenix International. Also with Sid Haig. Roger Corman was executive producer. (R)   –CB

PLAGUE
1978 Group I (Canada)
PRODUCERS/SCREENWRITERS: Ed Hunt, Barry Pearson
DIRECTOR: Ed Hunt
ORIGINALLY RELEASED AS: *Plague–M3: The Gemini Strain*

A weak imitation of David Cronenberg's *Rabid* starring Daniel Pilon and Kate Reid. A scientist experiments with DNA and discovers a contagious bacteria that causes fatal convulsions.

PLAGUE–M3: THE GEMINI STRAIN: See PLAGUE.

PLAGUE OF THE ZOMBIES
1966 Hammer/20th Century-Fox (England)
PRODUCER: Anthony Nelson-Keys
DIRECTOR: John Gilling
SCREENWRITER: Peter Bryan

A pretty good horror film with an incredible dream sequence showing a blank-eyed zombie rising from a grave. The rest of the less scary-looking corpses are revived by a Cornish squire to work his tin mine. With André Morell, Diane Clare, and Brook Williams. When it was first shown in theaters with *Dracula, Prince of Darkness* girls received free zombie eyes (glasses) and boys got vampire fangs.

PLAN 9 FROM OUTER SPACE
1959 DCA (B&W)
PRODUCER/DIRECTOR/SCREENWRITER: Edward D. Wood, Jr.

The merits of this incredible film have not been exaggerated. It's not actually the worst film ever made, but it's the most entertaining bad one you'll find. The story was built around a few minutes of Bela Lugosi footage shot just days before he died (in '56). The scene of old Bela visiting the grave of an imaginary dead wife is really pretty sad to

Tor Johnson in Ed Wood, Jr.'s Plan 9 from Outer Space.

watch. But as soon as aliens arrive and revive the wife (Vampira), a policeman (Big Tor Johnson), and "Bela" (played by a chiropractor friend of the director hiding his face with a cape), it's all laughs. Audiences stare in disbelief at the studio floor under the moving grass in the cemetery, flying saucers made of paper plates, night constantly changing to day and back again, and a jet-cockpit set that elementary school kids could have designed for a play. TV psychic Criswell narrates ("Can you prove it didn't happen?"). In fact, he says it all: "There comes a time in every man's life when he just can't believe his eyes." Gregory Walcott and Mona McKinnon play the modern couple living near the graveyard. Dudley Manlove (!) plays the effeminate Eros the Alien, aided by Joanna Lee, now a rich TV writer. Lyle Talbot (in his third Wood film) plays a general with a little Washington office. Wood was also in charge of the special effects and the editing. Worth watching nine times.

PLANET EARTH
1974 TV
PRODUCER: Robert H. Justman
DIRECTOR: Marc Daniels
SCREENWRITERS: Gene Roddenberry, Juanita Bartlett

A pilot film starring John Saxon as Dylan Hunt, a 20th-century man in the year 2133. It was a sequel/remake of *Genesis II*. The plot, about Saxon as a prisoner of an all-female future society, is hilarious. With Saxon's manly help, the male slaves (Dinks) convince the women to let them go in time to help fight off some Nazilike mutants. Saxon saves the future of mankind in the bedroom, of course. Wearing long blond hair and a headband, Ted "Lurch" Cassidy is Saxon's sidekick. With Diana Muldaur and Janet Margolin. Saxon was

at it again the next year in *Strange New World*, a third pilot. Gene Roddenberry of *Star Trek* was executive producer.

PLANET OF BLOOD: See QUEEN OF BLOOD.

PLANET OF DINOSAURS
1978 Filmpartners
PRODUCER/DIRECTOR: James K. Shea
SCREENWRITER: Ralph Lucas

Stop-motion animation fans should look for this independent feature with several well-done dinosaurs and other creatures. Starring James Whitworth of *The Hills Have Eyes*.

PLANET OF HORRORS: See GALAXY OF TERROR.

PLANET OF THE APES
1968 20th Century-Fox
PRODUCER: Arthur P. Jacobs
DIRECTOR: Franklin J. Schaffner
SCREENWRITERS: Rod Serling, Michael Wilson

Rod Serling's screenplay was based on Pierre Boulle's novel. The makeup by Ben Nye and Dan Striepere (designed by John Chambers) was quite a feat, even though I got pretty tired of hearing about it when the initial media blitz was on. Charlton Heston and Linda Harrison as a mute slave girl are the star humans. Kim Hunter, Roddy McDowall, Maurice Evans, James Whitmore, and James Daly are the lead apes. In the end, which was really a surprise when this was new, Heston finds the ruins of the Statue of Liberty. Someday in Cleveland, they'll dig under the Beef Corral Parking Lot at 117th and Detroit and find the remains of the theater I saw this in back in '68.

PLANET OF THE VAMPIRES

1965 AIP (Italy/Spain)
PRODUCER: Fulvio Lucianso
DIRECTOR: Mario Bava
SCREENWRITERS: Catillo Cosulich,
Antonio Roman, Alberto Bevilacqua,
Mario Bava, Rafael J. Salvia
ORIGINALLY RELEASED AS: *Terrore Nello Spazio*
ALSO RELEASED AS: *Demon Planet*

Most Italian science-fiction movies are as exciting to watch as a blank screen. Here's an exception. Earth astronauts led by Barry Sullivan land on a misty volcanic planet. Crew members go crazy and fight each other. They find ruins of an alien ship and giant skeletons. The astronauts wear shiny black leather suits. When they die they're "buried" upright in transparent bags. Disembodied aliens take over the corpses, turning them into space vampires intent on conquering Earth. Ib Melchior wrote the American script.

PLANET ON THE PROWL: See *WAR BETWEEN THE PLANETS.*

PLATINUM HIGH SCHOOL

1960 MGM (B&W)
PRODUCER: Albert Zugsmith
DIRECTOR: Charles Haas
SCREENWRITER: Robert Smith
ALSO RELEASED AS: *Rich, Young and Deadly, Trouble at 16*

Mickey Rooney arrives on a private-military-school island to claim his son's body and find out how the boy died. Nobody will cooperate. Everybody tells him lies or won't talk at all. If you can stay awake during this boring film you'll discover the awful truth! When the school's commander (Dan Duryea) shows Rooney a photo of his "son," it's really a picture of young Mickey himself. With Terry Moore, Yvette Mimieux (who had just debuted in *The Time Machine*), and Conway Twitty

(who sings the theme song), Jimmy Boyd, Richard Jaeckel, and Warren Berlinger as students. Elisha Cook, Jr., flips burgers.

A dead astronaut returns in Mario Bava's Planet of the Vampires.

PLANETS AGAINST US

1961 Teleworld (Italy/France)
PRODUCERS: Alberto Chimenz, Vico Pavoni
DIRECTOR: Romano Ferrara
SCREENWRITERS: Romano Ferrara,
Piero Pierotti
ORIGINALLY RELEASED AS: *I Pianeti Contro di Noi*
ALSO RELEASED AS: *The Man with the Yellow Eyes*

Earthbound science fiction with some surprising special effects. Michel Lemoine plays identical alien humanoid robots with hypnotic eyes and the touch of death.

THE PLANTS ARE WATCHING: See *THE KIRLIAN WITNESS.*

PLAY IT COOL

1962 Allied Artists (England) (B&W)
PRODUCER: David Deutsch
DIRECTOR: Michael Winner
SCREENWRITER: Jack Henry

Sir Charles (Dennis Price) sends his daughter away to keep her apart from a singer, but she ends up with another, Billy Fury as Billy Universe. They visit London nightclubs and watch Bobby Vee, Shane Fenton and the Fentones, Jimmy Crawford, Helen Shapiro, and other names foreign to American ears and charts.

PLAY MISTY FOR ME
1971 Universal
PRODUCER: Robert Daly
DIRECTOR/SCREENWRITER: Clint Eastwood
Clint Eastwood directs himself as a Monterey late-night disc jockey who makes the mistake of dating a possessive female psycho (Jessica Walter). Effective shocks with Donna Mills, Jack Ging, and Don Siegel as a bartender. Music by Errol Garner. **(R)**

PLAYGIRL AFTER DARK: See TOO HOT TO HANDLE.

PLAYGIRL KILLER
1965 (Canada)
PRODUCER: Max A. Sendel
DIRECTOR: Enrick Santamaran
ALSO RELEASED AS: Decoy for Terror

Although not released theatrically in America, this astonishingly bad Canadian mad-artist feature has long been a graveyard-shift favorite on local television. Star William Kirwin has trouble making his models stand still. The obvious solution is to kill them and freeze the bodies in a meat locker. A worthy contribution to the inept hilarity is early '60s pop star Neil Sedaka singing, "If You Don't Wanna, You Don't Hafta" and "Waterbug." Get out your tape recorders (or videotape recorders for the full effect) so you can enlighten your friends who keep normal hours.

THE PLAYGIRLS AND THE BELLBOY
1958/62 United Producers Releasing Organization (W. Germany/U.S.) (B&W/color, 3-D)
PRODUCERS: Wolfgang Hartwig, Harry Ross
DIRECTORS: Fritz Umgelter, Francis Ford Coppola
SCREENWRITERS: Dieter Hildebrandt, Margh Malina
ORIGINALLY RELEASED AS: Mit Eva Fing die Sunde
ALSO RELEASED AS: The Bellboy and the Playgirls

This is basically a black-and-white German voyeur sex comedy for which Coppola wrote and shot new 3-D color sequences featuring starlets like June Wilkinson. *Paradisio* was 1962's other 3-D nudie. This one features a bellboy using various disguises to spy on lingerie models staying at a hotel. June was described in ads as "Staggering—magnificent—mighty—sensational (43-22-36)."

THE PLAYGIRLS AND THE VAMPIRE
1960 Fanfare (Italy) (B&W)
PRODUCER: Tiziano Longo
DIRECTOR/SCREENWRITER: Piero Regnoli
ORIGINALLY RELEASED AS: L'Ultima Preda del Vampiro
ALSO RELEASED AS: Curse of the Vampire

A fun pseudo-nudie film with showgirls (usually in sheer nighties) being terrorized by vampires. The action takes place at the castle of Count Kernassy (Walter Brandi), whose identical ancestor is a vampire living (?) in the underground tomb. Soon lots of lovely future female vampires are chained up in the crypt. The sexy vampires have *very* long teeth. Presented by Richard Gordon. Brandi was at it again a year later in *The Vampire and the Ballerina*.

THE PLAYGROUND

1965 Jerand (B&W)
PRODUCER/DIRECTOR: Richard Hilliard
SCREENWRITER: George Garrett

An atheist actor tries to scare his religious prostitute date by lying in a grave and swearing. He dies of a heart attack. His wife is killed in a motorcycle accident that paralyzes his director, who later dies when the actor's other girlfriend pulls a plug and goes off to swing in a park. The prostitute's psychiatrist schedules a lobotomy. For adults only! Rees Vaughn, Inger Stratton, and Edmon Ryan star. —CB

PLEASE DON'T EAT MY MOTHER

1972 Box Office International
PRODUCER/DIRECTOR: Carl Monson
SCREENWRITER: Jack Beckett
ALSO RELEASED AS: *Hungry Pets, Glump*

A soft-core remake of Corman's *Little Shop of Horrors.* Buck Kartalian plays a middle-aged guy living with his hypochondriac mother. The original flower shop is gone so he grows his man-eating plant at home. The plant is actually better than the original. Since it is a sex comedy, when the hero isn't feeding people to his plant he's an active voyeur. With René Bond. From the director of *I Dismember Mama.* (X)

POCOMANIA

1939 Lenwal (B&W)
PRODUCER/DIRECTOR: Arthur Leonard
SCREENWRITER: George Terwilliger
ALSO RELEASED AS: *Devil's Daughter*

This obscure voodoo feature filmed in Jamaica is one of the rarest items now available on videocassette. It's an all-black remake of an equally rare film called *Ouanga.* Nina Mae McKinney stars as a voodoo priestess who puts a curse on a rival. McKinney had starred in King Vidor's all-black musical *Hallelujah* (1929) and later toured European

nightclubs as "the black Garbo." With Jack Carter, Ida James, and Hamtree Harrington. *Son of Ingagi,* a black horror film, was produced the same year.

POINT OF TERROR

1971 Crown International
PRODUCERS: Chris Marconi,
Peter Carpenter
DIRECTOR: Alex Nicol
SCREENWRITERS: Tony Crechales,
Ernest A. Charles

Shoddy horror from the makers of *Blood Mania,* starring Peter Carpenter (the co-producer) and Dyanne Thorne, better known for the incredible *Ilsa* films. Carpenter wakes up from dreaming about 80 minutes of sickness to find it's really happening! (R)

POLTERGEIST

1982 MGM/UA
PRODUCERS: Steven Spielberg,
Frank Marshall
DIRECTOR: Tobe Hooper
SCREENWRITERS: Steven Spielberg,
Mark Grais, Michael Victor

Some excellent special effects highlight this ghost story set (like *E.T.*) in a modern, upper-middle-class California suburb. Except for one shocking scene

Buck Kartalian in Please Don't Eat My Mother, *the adults-only remake of* Little Shop of Horrors.

of a face falling apart, it's almost a throwback to the silly but fun thrills of William Castle's *13 Ghosts*. Jobeth Williams and Craig T. Nelson are the typical young dope-smoking American parents of the '80s. The real stars are the kids, especially little Heather O'Rourke, who stays up nights watching a possessed television. Tiny clairvoyant Zelda Rubenstein saves the day and rescues the child from another dimension. With scenes from *A Guy Named Joe*, a World War II fantasy which Spielberg plans to remake. James Karen of *Frankenstein Meets the Space Monster* fame plays the realtor. The ending wasn't happy in real life for the teenage daughter (Dominique Dunne) who was murdered by her live-in boyfriend shortly after the film's release.

POLYESTER
1981 New Line
PRODUCER/DIRECTOR/SCREENWRITER:
John Waters

The first feature in "Odorama"! Unlike the earlier *Scent of Mystery*, *Polyester* features number-coded scratch-and-sniff cards of scents you could do without, and you can enjoy them months later in the privacy of your own home! Divine stars as Francine Fishpaw, a housewife whose life is a shambles because of her cheating porno-theater-owner husband, her glue-sniffing, angel-dusted son, and her wild, pregnant daughter. Her only friend is her retarded ex-maid Edith Massey. She drinks herself into a constant stupor. Her dog commits suicide. But her life perks up when handsome playboy Todd Tomorrow (Tab Hunter) shows up. This hilarious comedy is filled with references to exploitation, porno, and art films. It should have been Waters' biggest hit, but the humor in this bid for mass (pre-midnight) acceptance is a little too close to home. Characters in his earlier mov-

ies (like *Pink Flamingos*) seemed totally unreal to most, but the suburban family shown here is all too familiar. Made in Baltimore. With Mink Stole and Stiv Bators. Tab, who was 50 when this was filmed, also sings the theme song.

POOR ALBERT AND LITTLE ANNIE: See I DISMEMBER MAMA.

POOR DEVIL
1973 TV
PRODUCER: Robert Stambler
DIRECTOR: Robert Scheerer
SCREENWRITERS: Arne Sultan,
   Earl Barrat, Rich Baker

Christopher Lee as the Devil sends disciple Sammy Davis, Jr., up to Earth to bring down gambler Jack Klugman. A comedy pilot with Sammy talking to manhole covers and trying to earn his horns. With Adam West and Madlyn Rhue. Lee was also with Sammy in *One More Time*.

POOR WHITE TRASH
1957 United Artists (B&W)
PRODUCER: M.A. Ripps
DIRECTOR: Harold Daniels
SCREENWRITER: Edward L. Femler
ORIGINALLY RELEASED AS: *Bayou*

After this tale of Northern architect Peter Graves fighting sadistic illiterate Timothy Carey for the hand of 15-year-old bayou girl Lita Milan failed at the box office, M.A. Ripps, its executive producer, bought it from United Artists. He re-released it in 1961 under the new title *Poor White Trash* and, because of an ingenious ad campaign including uniformed police keeping unescorted children out of theaters, it became a giant exploitation hit that continued playing into the early '70s. Also featuring Douglas Fowley and Jonathan Haze. Ripps also bought Corman's *The Intruder*, retitled it *Shame*, and co-billed

it with this earlier hit. In '76 Ripps was back with *Poor White Trash II*, an unrelated feature also known as *Scum of the Earth*. It's about a deranged Vietnam vet coming home and killing his backwoods neighbors.

POP GEAR: See
GO GO MANIA.

PORT SINISTER
1952 RKO (B&W)
PRODUCERS/SCREENWRITERS:
Jack Pollexfen, Aubrey Wisberg
DIRECTOR: Harold Daniels
ALSO RELEASED AS: *Beast of Paradise Island*
An earthquake causes a sunken pirate ship to rise to the surface. Giant crabs attack the cast. James Warren stars with Lynne Roberts, William Schallert, and House Peters, Jr. Albert Zugsmith was the associate producer.

PORTNOY'S COMPLAINT
1972 Warner Brothers
PRODUCER/DIRECTOR/SCREENWRITER:
Ernest Lehman

Richard Benjamin jacks off. John Carradine is the voice of God. Portnoy's penis talks, too. Lee Grant is Portnoy's dominating mother. A major flop with Karen Black, Jill Clayburgh, and Kevin Conway. From Philip Roth's scandalous bestseller of the same name. Lehman wrote the script for *The Sound of Music*.

PORTRAIT IN TERROR
1965 AIP
DIRECTOR: Jack Hill
Patrick Magee plays a brooding, sadistic hit man who checks into a seedy hotel in Venice, California. At one point he's eating at an outdoor café and a dancing girl flirts with him. He flicks out a stiletto and cuts off her brief costume. There's an impressive chase scene, a few murders, and some sex. William Campbell is a deranged artist trying to steal a Titian painting. All very moody and strange. Scenes from this forgotten little movie show up in *Blood Bath*, a paste-up horror film which shows Magee (uncredited) covered with wax. With Anna Pavane. Look for it.

THE POSEIDON ADVENTURE
1972 20th Century-Fox
PRODUCER: Irwin Allen
DIRECTOR: Ronald Neame
SCREENWRITERS: Sterling Silliphant, Wendell Mayes
"Combining the talents of 15 Academy Award winners." Well—the special effects are good as various stars forget which way is up in a capsized ocean liner. Shelley Winters is an ex-swimming champ married to Jack Albertson. It's one of her heaviest roles in both senses of the word. Ernest Borgnine is a detective with an ex-prostitute wife (Stella Stevens). Gene Hackman gets top billing as a minister. With Carol Lynley as a "pop singer," Red Buttons, Roddy McDowall, Angela

Cartwright, Arthur O'Connell, Pamela Sue Martin, and Leslie Nielsen as the captain. Remember—"There's got to be a morning after." Music by John Williams.

THE POSSESSED
1977 TV
PRODUCER: Philip Mandelker
DIRECTOR: Jerry Thorpe
SCREENWRITER: John Sacret Young
Another bad made-for-television *Exorcist* ripoff. James Farentino stars as a defrocked priest at an isolated girls' school. With Joan Hackett, Harrison Ford, and P. J. Soles.

THE POSSESSION OF JOEL DELANEY
1972 Paramount
PRODUCER: Martin Poll
DIRECTOR: Waris Hussein
SCREENWRITERS: Matt Robinson, Grimes Grice
Rich New York socialite Shirley Mac-Laine is surprised to find out that brother Perry King (who's living on East 1st Street) has been taken over by the spirit of his dead friend, a Puerto Rican murderer who liked to decapitate people. Caribbean voodoo in Manhattan wasn't a film topic that viewers flocked to, but you should watch for it on television. (R)

THE POSTAL INSPECTOR
1936 Universal (B&W)
PRODUCER: Robert Presnell
DIRECTOR: Otto Brower
SCREENWRITERS: Robert Presnell, Horace McCoy
Ricardo Cortez investigates a mail robbery committed by nightclub owner Bela Lugosi. Including an exposé of fraudulent products, such as electric hair growers, sold through the mail.

THE POWER
1968 MGM
PRODUCER: George Pal
DIRECTOR: Byron Haskin
SCREENWRITER: John Gay
Underrated science fiction with similarities to the recent *Scanners*. George Hamilton is the chief suspect of inspector Gary Merrill after Arthur O'Connell is murdered in a space-endurance device. One of the scientists involved in a research project is an evil superhuman with telekinetic powers. Hamilton, his only clue the name Adam Hart, goes about finding the murderer. It could be Suzanne Pleshette, Earl Holliman, Nehemiah Persoff, Michael Rennie, or Richard Carlson. Also with Yvonne De Carlo, Aldo Ray, Ken Murray, and Barbara Nichols. Music by Miklos Rosza.

PREHISTORIC WOMEN
1950 Eagle-Lion
PRODUCER: Albert J. Cohen
DIRECTOR: Greg Tallas
SCREENWRITERS: Sam X. Abarbanel, Greg Tallas
The ads promised: "Savage struggle! Primitive passion! In gorgeous Cinecolor." An adults-only feature with beauties in animal-skin dresses and lipstick, who capture men, destroy a dragon, and get carried around by a hairy giant. A narrator tells us about the advancing civilization and informs us that "these girls invented the swan dive before the swan." With Allan Nixon (*Mesa of Lost Women*), Laurette Luez, and Mara Lynn. Watch for it on late-night TV.

PREHISTORIC WOMEN
1967 Hammer/20th Century-Fox (England)
PRODUCER/DIRECTOR/SCREENWRITER: Michael Carreras
ALSO RELEASED AS: *Slave Girls*

A blond slave serves Martine Beswick in Hammer's Prehistoric Women ('67).

Laurette Luez carrying her meal of raw meat up a ladder to her tree in Prehistoric Women ('50).

The Brits prove they can make 'em as funny as we did 17 years earlier (see previous entry). This quickie was made with sets from *One Million Years B.C.* and stars one of its cave girls, Martine Beswick, as the cruel Queen Kari. Her tribe of dark-haired women in animal-skin bikinis use blond rhino-worshipping women as their slaves. A hunter (Michael Latimer) stumbles into the all-female gold mine and falls for Edina Ronay, a slave. Martine and Edina fight over the dreaming(?) male.

PREHISTORIC WORLD: See TEENAGE CAVEMAN.

PREMATURE BURIAL
1962 AIP
PRODUCER/DIRECTOR: Roger Corman
SCREENWRITERS: Charles Beaumont, Ray Russell

UPI 6/8/77: French director Louis Malle talks to Brooke Shields and Keith Carradine during the filming of the scene in Paramount's Pretty Baby *where the prostitutes are ousted by the police from their district of New Orleans, circa 1917.*

Corman's third Poe picture and the only one not starring Vincent Price. Ray Milland plays Guy Carrell, a 19th-century man obsessed with the idea that he will be buried alive while in a state of catalepsy, as his father was. He marries Hazel Court (in her first American role) but only thinks of his new custom-built coffin with special escape devices. His fears become reality and an insidious plot is discovered. A moody, serious movie, with Richard Ney, Heather Angel, Alan Napier, and Richard Miller (as Mole, a grave robber).

THE PREMONITION

1976 Avco Embassy
PRODUCER/DIRECTOR: Robert Allen Schnitzer
SCREENWRITER: Anthony Mahon
An interesting, Mississippi-shot feature about a couple using parapsychology to locate their missing adopted daughter. An active dead mother, a mime, and a graveside organ recital all figure in the plot. Sharon Farrell stars as the haunted foster mother and Jeff Corey as the investigating cop. With Richard Lynch.

THE PRESIDENT'S ANALYST

1967 Paramount
PRODUCER: Stanley Rubin
DIRECTOR/SCREENWRITER: Theodore J. Flicker
Spies chase the President's shrink for info in this political satire featuring an all-powerful phone company run by robots and an FBI run by midgets. Starring James Coburn, with Godfrey Cambridge, Pat Harrington, Will Geer, Arte Johnson, and Barry McGuire (*The Eve of Destruction*). The hippie band Clear Light is featured as a hippie band and performs two songs. Clear Light's publicity claims that "forty other groups were rejected." The TV version has new scenes to replace the nudity and violence in the original prints. Some say part of it was left over from the unfinished third Derek Flint movie. Kurt Neuman (*The Fly*) was the assistant director.

PRETTY BABY

1978 Paramount
PRODUCER/DIRECTOR: Louis Malle
SCREENWRITER: Polly Platt
A beautifully photographed, slow, matter-of-fact look at a pre–World War I New Orleans brothel. Starring Keith Carradine as a photographer who marries 12-year-old prostitute Brooke Shields. With Susan Sarandon (*Atlantic City*), Barbara Steele, Gerrit Graham, and Frances Faye. **(R)**

PRETTY POISON

1968 20th Century-Fox
PRODUCER: Lawrence Turman
DIRECTOR: Noel Black
SCREENWRITER: Lorenzo Semple, Jr.
Tuesday Weld plays a small-town New England high school drum majorette. She meets an unhinged arsonist who works at a chemical factory (Anthony Perkins). She helps him try to destroy the polluting factory and drowns a night watchman. The perfect couple are about

to leave town when Tuesday's mom (Beverly Garland) shows up. Weld is great and makes Perkins seem almost harmless. The unusual Tuesday-Anthony team were together again in the dark *Play It As It Lays*. Screenwriter Semple later sold out to Dino De Laurentiis, writing *King Kong*, *Flash Gordon*, and *Hurricane*.

THE PRIME TIME
1960 Essanjay (B&W)
PRODUCER/DIRECTOR: Hershell Gordon Lewis
SCREENWRITER: Robert Abel

Lewis' first, pre-gore film made in Chicago under the name Gordon Weisenborn. Thrill-seeker JoAnn LeCompte borrows her boyfriend's car to drive to a date with a detective at the apartment of a beatnik artist. She's surprised by the artist (Ray Gronwold) who ties her up and forces her to pose nude. LeCompte blackmails the crooked detective (Frank Roche) into marriage following Gronwold's death at the hands of teenage vigilantes. Featuring seminude midnight swim parties and wild music. With James Brooks, Maria Pavelle, Betty Senter, and Karen Black (in her film debut).   —CB

PRIMITIVE LOVE
1964 American Film Distributors
PRODUCERS: Dick Randall, Joel Holt, Fulvio Luciano, Pietro Paulo Giordani
SCREENWRITERS: Luigi Scattini, Armedeo Sollazzo
ORIGINALLY RELEASED AS: *L'Amore Primitivo*

THIS IS THE TIME OF THE VIOLENT PLUNGE INTO ADULTHOOD...

THIS IS THE PRIME TIME

...OF YOUTH, LIFE AND LOVE!

Here is all the passion, the pain the poignance of emotional awakening ...Here are all the wild excitements of youth discovering their purpose on earth!

starring JO ANN LeCOMPTE FRANK ROCHE

Jayne Mansfield in another of her obscure European comedies. She plays Jayne, an anthropologist who had made a film showing that love is universally primitive. It illustrates sexual practices and marriage customs. When a handsome professor views the film and isn't convinced, Jayne decides to use a more direct teaching tool and strips for him (and two leering porters)! With Jayne's musclebound husband, Mickey Hargitay. It includes scenes of Jayne judging a beauty contest, going to a nightclub, and visiting a massage parlor later used in *The Wild Wild World of Jayne Mansfield.*

PRISONER OF WAR
1954 MGM (B&W)
PRODUCER: Henry Berman
DIRECTOR: Andrew Marton
SCREENWRITER: Allen Rivkin

UPI 2/5/54: Pretty Nancy Davis displays wifely concern for her husband's appearance as she buttons his shirt. He happens to be Ronald Reagan (in case you didn't recognize him) and his face is all dirtied-up for his part in Prisoner of War.

A tale of POWs in the Korean War with Ronald Reagan, who is mistaken for a Communist. Oscar Homolka is in charge of brainwashing Americans. With Steve Forrest, Harry Morgan, and Darryl Hickman. By the director of *Birds Do It* (with Soupy Sales), *Crack in the World,* and *Clarence the Cross-eyed Lion.*

PRIVATE EYES
1953 Allied Artists (B&W)
PRODUCER: Ben Schwalb
DIRECTOR: Edward Bernds
SCREENWRITERS: Edward Bernds, Elwood Ullman

After he gets hit on the head Huntz Hall can read minds. With Lee Van Cleef and Emil Sitka as spies. Also with Myron Healy, Leo Gorcey, and the other Bowery Boys.

THE PRIVATE FILES OF J. EDGAR HOOVER
1978 AIP
PRODUCER/DIRECTOR/SCREENWRITER: Larry Cohen

A very entertaining low-budget epic covering the career of Hoover. It spans five decades and shows his relationships with various presidents, the media, and women. Broderick Crawford stars as the older Hoover. Rip Torn holds the story together as an FBI agent. With José Ferrer, Michael Parks (as Robert Kennedy), Ronee Blakely, Celeste Holm, Raymond St. Jacques (as Martin Luther King), Howard Da Silva, Jack Cassidy, Dan Dailey, Lloyd Nolan, Jennifer Lee, and Michael Sacks. Music by Miklos Rosza.

THE PRIVATE LIFE OF SHERLOCK HOLMES
1970 United Artists (England/U.S.)
PRODUCER/DIRECTOR: Billy Wilder
SCREENWRITERS: Billy Wilder, I.A.L. Diamond

The most intimate look at the famous detective features a plot involving the Loch Ness monster, missing midgets, Queen Victoria, cocaine, and doubts about Holmes' manliness. Robert Stephens is Holmes. Colin Blakely is Watson. Christopher Lee is a bald Mycroft Holmes. Geneviève Page is the doomed love interest. With Stanley Holloway. Music by Miklos Rosza. A great, long (over two hours) Holmes film that totally flopped at the box office.

THE PRIVATE LIVES OF ADAM AND EVE

1959 Universal (B&W with color sequence)
PRODUCER: Red Doff
DIRECTORS: Albert Zugsmith, Mickey Rooney
SCREENWRITER: Robert Hill

Tacky soap opera with bizarre tinted fantasy sequences in the Garden of Eden. With a typical Zugsmith cast. Mickey Rooney (as the Devil!) sends Fay Spain (as Lilith) to the Garden. Adam and Eve are played by Marty Milner and Mamie Van Doren! Also with Tuesday Weld, Paul Anka, Mel Tormé, Ziva Rodann, June Wilkinson, and Cecil Kellaway. Amazing. In "Spectacolor." It was condemned by the Catholic Legion of Decency, but it's real harmless stuff.

THE PRIVATE LIVES OF ELIZABETH AND ESSEX

1939 Warner Brothers
ASSOCIATE PRODUCER: Robert Lord
DIRECTOR: Michael Curtiz
SCREENWRITERS: Norman Reilly Raine, Aeneas Mackenzie

A swashbuckling reworking of history with Bette Davis as Queen Elizabeth, who tires of the antics of the Earl of Essex (Errol Flynn) and has his head cut off. The scene of Errol's execution was cut before the release. With Olivia de Havilland, Vincent Price (as Sir Walter Raleigh), Henry Daniell, Leo G. Carroll, and Alan Hale. Music by Erich Wolfgang Korngold. In color.

PRIVATE PARTS

1972 MGM
PRODUCER: Gene Corman
DIRECTOR: Paul Bartel
SCREENWRITERS: Philip Kearney, Les Rendelstein

A funny, neglected mixture of *Peeping Tom* and *Homicidal* set in a seedy L.A. hotel. A young runaway girl (Ann Ruymen) goes on a date with a nice guy (Stanley Livingston—Chip from *My Three Sons*) but is more drawn to an older photographer (John Ventantonio) who lives in her aunt's hotel. Her aunt (Lucille Benson) is a professional funeral patron who photographs corpses. A guy named Reverend Moon down the hall entertains muscular young men at night. The photographer puts a head shot of the girl on his water-filled sex doll and injects it with his own blood after a little foreplay. Lots of fast-paced, kinky surprises. Bartel later directed *Eating Raoul.*

PRIVATE PROPERTY

1960 Citation (B&W)
PRODUCER/DIRECTOR/SCREENWRITER: Leslie Stevens

The creator and executive producer of *The Outer Limits* made this in his home on a budget of $60,000. His beautiful real-life wife Kate Manx stars as a woman troubled by two beatnik drifters (Corey Allen and Warren Oates) who keep her under surveillance from the house next door. Allen poses as a gardener to set her up for Oates, whose sexuality is in question. When Oates fails the test Allen takes him outside to the pool and drowns him. High-art cinematography by Oscar winner Ted McCord.   —CB

PRIVILEGE

1967 Universal (England)
PRODUCER: John Hyman
DIRECTOR: Peter Watkins
SCREENWRITER: Norman Bogner

Set in the near future of 1970, this is a documentary-style film about a popular singer used by a church-and-state coalition government to control England's youth. As Stephan Shorter, ex–Manfred Mann singer Paul Jones begins with a mock-violent stage act that was pretty exciting at the time. He sings "Free Me" as uniformed cops handcuff, beat, and jail him. Later he sings evangelical rock songs next to a cross in a stadium full of marching boy scouts and giant pictures of himself. Model Jean Shrimpton is an artist who urges him to stop being a phony symbol for the government. A powerful, well-made film by the director of *The War Game* (which was made for and banned by the BBC). Great music by Mike Leander.

PROBE

1972 TV
PRODUCER/SCREENWRITER: Leslie Stevens
DIRECTOR: Russ Mayberry

The pilot film for a short-lived series starring Hugh O'Brian. He's a space-age detective monitored by mission control with miniature TV cameras while investigating a gem robbery. Burgess Meredith and Angel Tompkins costar and were also in the series. With guests Elke Sommer, John Gielgud, Kent Smith, and Jaclyn Smith (in a bit part).

THE PROFILE OF TERROR: See THE SADIST.

PROJECT M–7

1953 Universal (England) (B&W)
PRODUCER: Anthony Darnsborough
DIRECTOR: Anthony Asquith
SCREENWRITER: William Fairchild
ALSO RELEASED AS: *The Net*

A spaceman discovers he's in orbit with an enemy agent who's trying to kill him. Static British science fiction with Phyllis Calvert, James Donald, and Herbert Lom.

PROJECT MOONBASE

1953 Lippert (B&W)
PRODUCER: Jack Seamon
DIRECTOR: Richard Talmadge
SCREENWRITER: Robert Heinlein

Episodes of an unsold television series edited into a feature. In the future (1970) a spaceship leaves an orbiting station for the Moon. A Communist saboteur destroys its chances of returning, but a surviving couple are married and congratulated by the female President on a TV screen. The commanding officer is a woman, too. The best part is the spacesuits: shorts, T-shirts, boots, and skull caps! With Donna Martell, Ross Ford, and Hayden Rourke.

PROJECT X

1968 Paramount
PRODUCER/DIRECTOR: William Castle
SCREENWRITER: Edmund Morris

In the year 2118 *Rat Patrol* star Christopher George is a secret agent who knows how to stop the immediate destruction of the West by "Sino-Asia," but he has amnesia. To probe his memory, scientists convince him that he's a bank robber in the 1960s. His subconscious unleashes a deadly mass animated by the Hanna-Barbera Studios. With Monte Markham, Greta Baldwin, Henry Jones, and Key Luke. Unlike any other Castle film.

THE PROJECTED MAN

1966 Universal (England)
PRODUCERS: Maurice Foster,
John Croydon
DIRECTOR: Ian Curteis
SCREENWRITERS: John C. Cooper,
Peter Bryan

Professor Steiner (Bryant Halliday) uses laser power for matter-transportation experiments. As in the *Fly* movies, things go wrong. A guinea pig sent from one room to another emerges charged with electricity. In the midst of a blackmail-and-sabotage plot, Steiner projects himself and emerges with a deadly electric touch, a warped mind, and one of the most disgusting disfigured half-faces ever filmed. With Mary Peach and Tracy Crisp. Richard Gordon was executive producer.

THE PROJECTIONISTS

1968 Maglon
PRODUCER/DIRECTOR/SCREENWRITER:
Harry Hurwitz

A New York City movie projectionist (Chuck McCann) imagines himself as superhero Captain Flash. With lots of rare film clips and Rodney Dangerfield as the mean theater owner. The film's comic theme is disrupted by some war-atrocity footage.

PROM NIGHT

1980 Avco Embassy (Canada)
PRODUCER: Peter Simpson
DIRECTOR: Paul Lynch
SCREENWRITER: William Gray

Another *Halloween* copy with Jamie Lee Curtis. A hooded killer is bumping off all the kids who were involved in the death of Jamie's little sister years before. I wouldn't ruin the end of a good movie—it was her brother! He's the deejay at the prom! He kills people during 12-inch versions of disco songs! Jamie dances like John Travolta! A head gets cut off and rolls on the dance floor!

Robert Silverman as the janitor in Prom Night.

Part of the plot is stolen from *Carrie!* Leslie Nielsen is wasted. David Cronenberg fans should watch for Robert Silverman (*Scanners, The Brood*) as a weird janitor. NBC managed to get this seven months after its theatrical release. They even beat out the cable stations. (**R**)

PROMISES! PROMISES!

1963 NDT (B&W)
PRODUCERS: Tommy Noonan,
Donald F. Taylor
DIRECTOR: King Donovan
SCREENWRITERS: William Welch,
Tommy Noonan

Jayne Mansfield bares all (almost) in her first nudie comedy. Jayne can't get pregnant because her husband (co-producer Tommy Noonan) is impotent. They decide a restful ocean cruise will make a difference, but in the next cabin are a muscleman (Jayne's real-life hus-

"THIS IS THE FIRST TIME I'VE EVER APPEARED **COMPLETELY NUDE!**" JAYNE MANSFIELD in **PLAYBOY MAGAZINE**

Promises! Promises!

UNCUT! UNCENSORED! EUROPEAN VERSION!

starring
JAYNE MANSFIELD · MARIE McDONALD · TOMMY NOONAN

mote the film. Because of a few seconds of Jayne naked in bed having a bad dream, it was shown only in "art" theaters. It was banned outright in Cleveland.

THE PROPER TIME
1960 Lopert (B&W)
PRODUCER/DIRECTOR/SCREENWRITER:
   Tom Laughlin
Laughlin plays a college freshman with a speech problem who is hit with a moral crisis when his girl's promiscuous roommate tries to seduce him. The cast includes Nira Monsour, Rich Shannon, and Norma Quine. Shelley Manne did the music. Tom made one more, *The Young Sinner*, before *Billy Jack*. –CB

PROPHECY
1979 Paramount
PRODUCER: Robert L. Rosen
DIRECTOR: John Frankenheimer
SCREENWRITER: David Seltzer
Blame screenwriter David Seltzer (*The Omen*) for not quitting while he was ahead. Pregnant concert violinist Talia Shire (*Rocky*) and her doctor husband (Robert Foxworth) hightail to the authorities with an incredibly ugly baby bear cub, proof that chemical pollution is mutating the wildlife in the timberlands of Maine. Meanwhile, an equally misshapen giant Mama Bear is on their trail. Great ugliness engineered by the Tom Burman Studios is lost in the boredom of it all. With George Clutesi and Armand Assante. –BM

THE PROWLER
1981 Sandhurst
PRODUCERS: Joseph Zito,
   David Streit
DIRECTOR: Joseph Zito
SCREENWRITER: Glenn Leopold
ALSO RELEASED AS: *Rosemary's Killer*
Another crazed-killer-returning-to-the-scene-of-his-original-crime movie fea-

band, Mickey Hargitay) and his beautiful wife (Marie "The Body" McDonald). The two couples have drinking parties and exchange mates. Or maybe not— they can't remember. But both women become pregnant. With Fritz Feld, female impersonator T.C. Jones, and Imogene Coca as herself. Jayne sings "Promise Her Anything" (originally the title) and "Lu-Lu-Lu-I'm in Love." Partially filmed on the *S.S. Independence*. Jayne posed for *Playboy* to pro-

turing graphic gore effects by Tom Savini. A World War II soldier who killed his unfaithful girlfriend and her new lover with a pitchfork during a graduation dance returns 35 years later (wearing his helmet) to mutilate modern teens. Shocking scenes of a head blowing up and a bayonet going through a head are cut from some prints. Farley Granger is the sheriff. With Vicky Dawson and Laurence Tierney. Pretty bad. (**R**)

THE PSYCHIC

1977 Group I (Italy)
PRODUCER: Franco Cuccu
DIRECTOR: Lucio Fulci
SCREENWRITERS: Lucio Fulci,
    Roberto Gianuiti
ORIGINALLY RELEASED AS: *Seite Note in Mero*
Jennifer O'Neill has a vision of a murder in a typical dull Italian mystery disguised as a horror film. With Gabriele Ferzetti (*L'Avventura*). Only O'Neill reads her lines in English. By the director of *Zombie*. (**R**)

PSYCHIC KILLER

1976 Avco Embassy
PRODUCER: Mardi Rustam
DIRECTOR: Ray Danton
SCREENWRITERS: Greydon Clark,
    Mike Angel, Ray Danton
Jim Hutton, well known for his portayal of likable innocents, is wrongly placed in a mental institution where a fellow inmate who happens to practice voodoo teaches him the fine art of astral projection. After being released with the help of a friendly psychiatrist (Julie Adams), he brings destruction to all who had victimized him—without even leaving his apartment. As a butcher, Neville Brand puts his arm in a meat grinder. Cop Paul Burke investigates. This sometimes funny thriller is the best feature directed by actor Danton and includes Whit Bissell, Rod Came-

ron, Aldo Ray, Della Reese, and Nehemiah Persoff.

PSYCHO

1960 Paramount (B&W)
PRODUCER/DIRECTOR: Alfred Hitchcock
SCREENWRITER: Joseph Stefano
Time to check into the Bates Motel again. *Psycho* is the best-known movie of the best-known director in the world. It's one of the most influential movies ever made—and Alfred said he made it as a joke! Every situation in the plot has been copied and parodied to death. Bernard Herrmann's effectively irritating music has been swiped countless times. The film remains unsettling after more than 20 years. People still argue about who was responsible for which plot twists and why it was shot in black-and-white. Norman's first victim Janet Leigh wouldn't let her daughter Jamie (Lee Curtis) watch it on TV. Now her daughter is typecast in horror films that wouldn't exist if it weren't for this one. Anthony Perkins, appearing at a screen-

Anthony Perkins as Norman Bates in Hitchcock's Psycho.

ing in Cleveland, said, "You know I *have* been in other films." Most of the audience couldn't recall any of them. With John Gavin, our Ambassador to Mexico, as the hardware store owner/ boyfriend, Vera Miles as the sister, Martin Balsam as Arbogast, John McIntire as the sheriff, and Simon Oakland as the psychiatrist who explains what a transvestite is. At first-run showings in 1960 no one was allowed to enter the theater after the picture had begun. Scriptwriter Joseph Stefano went on to produce *The Outer Limits*. The story was based on Robert Bloch's novel. In 1982, *Psycho II* was finally being shot with Perkins and Miles repeating their roles.

PSYCHO-CIRCUS

1967 AIP (England)
PRODUCER/SCREENWRITER: Harry Alan Towers
DIRECTOR: John Moxey
ALSO RELEASED AS: *Circus of Fear*

Based on an Edgar Wallace story, this is a circus murder mystery made to compete with *Berserk*, released the same year. A Scotland Yard inspector (Leo Genn) has lots of suspects in a murder case. Christoper Lee is Gregor, the lion tamer who wears a black mask to cover his scarred face. Heinz Drache is the ringmaster. Anthony Newlands owns the circus. With Klaus Kinski, Margaret Lee, Suzy Kendall, Victor Maddern, and a dwarf named Mr. Big (Skip Martin). A German-language version was also shot at the same time with a different director. Although it was filmed in color, the U.S. prints are in black-and-white.

PSYCHO KILLER: See THE PSYCHO LOVER.

PSYCHO–KILLERS: See MANIA.

THE PSYCHO LOVER

1970 Medford
PRODUCER/DIRECTOR/SCREENWRITER: Robert Vincent O'Neil
ALSO RELEASED AS: *The Loving Touch, Psycho Killer*

Mad psychiatrist uses patient to kill his alcoholic wife after his mistress tells him what she learned about brainwashing from viewing *The Manchurian Candidate*. The wife puts the mistress in her place, and the mistress and the patient are electrocuted by a TV set. With Lawrence Montaigne, Joanne Meredith, Elizabeth Plumb, and Frank Cuva. Presented by the Isley Brothers of "Twist and Shout" fame. O'Neil also directed *Blood Mania*. (X)   —CB

PSYCHOMANIA

1963 Victoria Films (B&W)
PRODUCER: Del Tenney, Margot Hartman
DIRECTOR: Richard Hilliard
SCREENWRITER: Robin Miller, Margot Hartman
ALSO RELEASED AS: *Violent Midnight*

The screenwriter of the unforgettable *Horror of Party Beach* steps out to direct his own horror movie. Like the other Del Tenney projects, it was filmed in Stamford, Connecticut, but this one was for adults only! The lead psycho (Lee Philips) is an artist. Shepperd Strudwick is his lawyer. The real reason to watch is to see James Farentino and, best of all, *Eight Is Enough* star Dick Van Patten as a cop. If you've ever witnessed him gushing on talk shows about his wonderful family, who live in adjoining California mansions, you'll really enjoy seeing his roots. Also with Sylvia Miles.

PSYCHOMANIA

1972 Scotia International (England)
PRODUCER: Andrew Donally
DIRECTOR: Don Sharp
SCREENWRITER: Julian Halevy
ALSO RELEASED AS: *The Death Wheelers*

Incredible, to say the least. The leader of a motorcycle gang (Nicky Henson) learns the secret of immortality. He kills himself, and his gang (the Living Dead!) places him in a grave on his bike. He comes back to life, drives out, and heads for his incredulous girlfriend. Soon he convinces the rest of the gang, and bikers are committing suicide all over the place only to return to murder and terrorize—forever! Weird horror comedy(?) by the director of other interesting horrors, including *Kiss of the Vampire* and *The Curse of the Fly*. The "adult" stars are Beryl Reid and George Sanders as devil worshipers. Sanders killed himself shortly after making this movie, but did not return on a motorcycle.

THE PSYCHOPATH

1966 Amicus/Paramount (England)
PRODUCERS: Max J. Rosenberg,
Milton Subotsky
DIRECTOR: Freddie Francis
SCREENWRITER: Robert Bloch

A good shocker. An inspector (Patrick Wymark) is investigating a series of brutal murders (weapons include a blowtorch) in which a doll of each victim is found at the scene. The dolls, it turns out, were purchased by the crippled Mrs. Von Sturm (Margaret Johnson), whose home is overcrowded with a doll collection. Her pale, wide-eyed, neurotic son (John Standing) is the prime suspect. As the daughter of one of the victims, Judy Huxtable discovers the shocking truth.

THE PSYCHOPATH

1973 Brentwood
PRODUCER/DIRECTOR/SCREENWRITER:
Larry Brown
ALSO RELEASED AS: *An Eye for an Eye*

This cheap little California film has a unique theme: a children's TV show host protects kids by killing the parents who beat and mistreat them. Tom Basham, the young man who plays Mr. Rabbey, acts like an infantile Anthony Perkins. His incredible performance makes this less-than-great movie a must. When re-released in 1980 all the bizarre murders (with a baseball bat, a lawnmower, etc.) were cut out, leaving only Basham riding his bike, putting on puppet shows, pouting, rolling his eyes, playing with kids at a park, throwing tantrums, being cuddled by his female producer, and making this amateurish sleaze bearable.

THE PSYCHOTRONIC MAN

1980 International Harmony
PRODUCER: Peter Spelson
DIRECTOR: Jack M. Sell
SCREENWRITERS: Peter Spelson, Jack M. Sell

An extremely low-budget independent from Chicago. The producer, whose main occupation is running an insurance business, stars as Rocky Foscoe, the psychic barber. Unknown forces cause him to blink at people, who die instantly or jump out of windows. Reports suggest it's good for laughs. Great title though.

PSYCH-OUT

1968 AIP
PRODUCER: Dick Clark
DIRECTOR: Richard Rush
SCREENWRITERS: E. Hunter Willit,
Betty Ulius, Betty Tusher

The *best* Haight-Ashbury drug film. Susan Strasberg as a deaf 17-year-old runaway looking for her missing brother is "helped" by the hippie team of Dean Stockwell, Jack Nicholson (as Stoney), Adam Roarke, and Max Julien. They get her beads and a mini to replace her square clothes and give her some STP, which sends her wandering in the traffic. The lost brother turns out to be a totally crazed, long-haired Bruce Dern

Max Julien, Susan Stras-berg, and Jack Nicholson in Psych-Out.

walking around like a mysterious Christ figure. With lots of bad rock music by phony bands plus one terrible real band —the Strawberry Alarm Clock. One influential flower/punk band, the Seeds, (featuring Sky Saxon), does a good song at a be-in. Cinematography by Laszlo Kovacs. By the director of *The Stunt Man.* With Robert Kelljan, director of the Count Yorga films.

PURPLE DEATH FROM OUTER SPACE: See FLASH GORDON CONQUERS THE UNIVERSE.

THE PURPLE MONSTER STRIKES

1945 Republic (B&W)
ASSOCIATE PRODUCER: Ronald Davidson
DIRECTORS: Spencer Bennet, Fred Brannon
SCREENWRITERS: Royal Cole, Albert di Mondi, Basil Dickey, Lynn Perkins, Joseph Poland, Barney Sarecky
ALSO RELEASED AS: *D-Day on Mars*
Mota the Martian (Roy Barcroft) arrives on Earth wearing a silly outfit with a hood and threatens humans with an "electroannihilator." He also has a "distance eliminator" (closed-circuit TV) and can take over other bodies. Dennis Moore and Linda Sterling are the Earth protectors in this condensed serial. Mary Moore is a female Martian. James Craven is Dr. Bryant. Mota returned in *Flying Disc Man from Mars* ('51).

PURSUIT

1972 TV
PRODUCER: Robert L. Jacks
DIRECTOR: Michael Crichton
SCREENWRITER: Robert Dozier
A madman threatens to use nerve gas to kill everybody at the Republican presidential convention in San Diego. Ben Gazzara stars with E.G. Marshall, William Windom, Joseph Wiseman (*Dr. No*), and Martin Sheen. It was the first film directed by Crichton.

PURSUIT OF THE GRAF SPEE

1957 (England)
PRODUCERS/DIRECTORS/SCREENWRITERS: Michael Powell, Emeric Pressburger
ALSO RELEASED AS: *The Battle of the River Plate*
Another high-quality film directed by the team responsible for *Stairway to Heaven, The Red Shoes,* and *Black Narcissus.* British forces follow a German battleship to South America where the locals offer no help at all. The British cast includes John Gregson, Anthony Quayle, Peter Finch, Ian Hunter, Bernard Lee (M in Bond movies), Patrick Macnee, and Christopher Lee.

PURSUIT TO ALGIERS

1945 Universal (B&W)
PRODUCER/DIRECTOR: Roy William Neill
SCREENWRITER: Leonard Lee
Holmes and Watson (Basil Rathbone and Nigel Bruce) escort a Far Eastern prince aboard an ocean liner. As Mirko,

Martin Kosleck leads a group of political assassins. With John Abbott and Marjorie Riordan. Based on *The Return of Sherlock Holmes*.

THE PUSHER

1960 United Artists (B&W)
PRODUCERS: Gene Milford, Sidney Katz
DIRECTOR: Gene Milford
SCREENWRITER: Harold Robbins

A police lieutenant's addict daughter is implicated in the death of a Puerto Rican teenager whose body is found near a broken hypo in the basement club room of a tenement gang. Cold turkey for Kathy Carlyle as Lt. Douglas F. Rodgers investigates with the help of her fiancé, Robert Lansing of *Twelve O'Clock High*. Filmed in New York City from a screenplay by *the* Harold Robbins, based on a novel by Evan Hunter, author of *The Blackboard Jungle*. With Felice Orlandi and Sloan Simpson.–CB

PUSSYCAT: See FASTER PUSSYCAT! KILL! KILL!

PYGMY ISLAND

1950 Columbia (B&W)
PRODUCER: Sam Katzman
DIRECTOR: William Berve
SCREENWRITER: Carroll Young

Jungle Jim (Johnny Weissmuller) teams up with pygmies (really white dwarfs) to defeat enemy agents seeking war supplies. He also fights a crocodile and a man in a gorilla suit and finds a lost WAC (Ann Savage). With David Bruce, Billy Curtis, and Billy Barty.

PYRO

1964 AIP (U.S./Spain)
PRODUCERS: Sidney W. Pink,
  Richard C. Meyer
DIRECTOR: Julio Coll
SCREENWRITER: Sidney Pink
ORIGINALLY RELEASED AS: *Fuego*
ALSO RELEASED AS: *Pyro—the Thing Without a Face*

Barry Sullivan stars as a British engineer who snaps after his wife and daughter die in a fire set by his mistress. Disfigured while trying to save his family, he puts together a disguise and goes after the mistress and her little girl. Martha Hyer and Sherry Moreland co-star. With Soledad Miranda.

PYRO — THE THING WITHOUT A FACE: See PYRO.

THE PYX

1973 Cinerama (Canada)
PRODUCERS: Maxine Samuels,
  Julian Roffman
DIRECTOR: Harvey Hart
SCREENWRITER: Robert Vezier

Christopher Plummer investigates the death of prostitute Karen Black, who wears an upside-down cross. Flashbacks involving a black mass provide a solution. Karen also sings. (R)

Q

1982 United Film Distribution
PRODUCER/DIRECTOR/SCREENWRITER:
Larry Cohen
ALSO RELEASED AS: *The Winged Serpent*

Q is Quetzalcoatl (featured in PRC's old *The Flying Serpent*), a giant flying serpent-bird god worshiped by the Aztecs (and now animated by David Allen). Q makes a nest in the top of New York's famous Art Deco Chrysler Building, occasionally flying around to decapitate construction workers. Meanwhile priests are sacrificing victims by removing their skins. The highlight of this low-budget tale is Michael Moriarty (*Bang the Drum Slowly*) giving a great oddball performance as Jimmy Quinn, a smalltime crook, ex-junkie, and would-be musician who stumbles on the creature's hiding place. Candy Clark is his girlfriend. David Carradine and Richard Roundtree are detectives. Presented by Samuel Z. Arkoff. A sound track album is available. **(R)**

QUATERMASS AND THE PIT: See *FIVE MILLION MILES TO EARTH.*

THE QUATERMASS CONCLUSION

1980 TV (England)
PRODUCER: Ted Childs
DIRECTOR: Piers Haggard
SCREENWRITER: Nigel Kneale

A four-hour TV special later edited into a feature. As Professor Quatermass, John Mills comes out of retirement when the young people of England riot and decide to worship a destructive alien beam. They gather at Stonehenge, where the beam fries them. By the director of *The Fiendish Plot of Fu Manchu* (Peter Sellers' last film) and *Venom.*

QUATERMASS II: See *ENEMY FROM SPACE.*

THE QUATERMASS XPERIMENT: See *THE CREEPING UNKNOWN.*

QUEEN OF BLOOD

1966 AIP
PRODUCER: George Edwards
DIRECTOR/SCREENWRITER: Curtis Harrington
ALSO RELEASED AS: *Planet of Blood*

Here's the story from Curtis Harrington himself (quoted from Corman's biography): "Roger Corman had acquired some spectacular Russian footage of spaceships. I saw the footage and wrote a screenplay around it. We shot the film in seven and a half days at a cost of $65,000." Dr. Farraday (Basil Rathbone) leads an expedition to Mars to rescue a crashed spaceship. The only survivor is a green-skinned alien woman with glowing eyes (Florence Marly). On the trip back she completely drains the blood from assorted crew members. John Saxon and Dennis Hopper are aboard as well as Forrest J Ackerman in a bit part. Pretty good, considering, and Marly is a memorable bloodsucker. Rathbone hung around long enough to film similar scenes for *Voyage to the Prehistoric Planet.* Stephanie Rothman was associate producer.

QUEEN OF OUTER SPACE

1958 Allied Artists
PRODUCER: Ben Schwalb
DIRECTOR: Edward Bernds
SCREENWRITER: Charles Beaumont

Famous laff riot that's right up there with *Attack of the 50 Ft. Woman* in illustrating the battle of the sexes. Everyone's favorite Miss Hungary, Zsa Zsa Gabor, plays a rebel Venusian in a slit skirt who actually likes the four Earth men her queen wants destroyed. The queen (Laurie Mitchell) hates all males because her face, which she hides behind a glittering mask, was scarred in war with them. Three of the captive Earth astronauts, handsome *Rawhide* star Eric Fleming, young Patrick Waltz, and comic Dave Wilcox, go nuts over the sexy dames. Choice dialogue: "How'd you like to drag that one to the high school prom?" Older, dumpy Paul Birch mostly blushes. Fans will recognize leftover spacesuits from *Forbidden Planet*, sets and a spider from *World Without End*, and a rocket from *Flight to Mars*. From a story by Ben Hecht. In color and Deluxe CinemaScope! By the director of Three Stooges movies.

QUEEN OF THE GORILLAS: See *BRIDE AND THE BEAST.*

QUEEN OF THE NILE
1962 Colorama Features (Italy)
PRODUCER: Ottavio Poggi
DIRECTOR: Fernando Cerchio
SCREENWRITERS: John Byrne, Ottavio Poggi
ORIGINALLY RELEASED AS: *Nefertite, Regina del Nilo*

Italy imports Americans to play Egyptians. Vincent Price as Benakon, the high priest, forces his daughter Nefertiti (Jeanne Crain) to marry the heir to the throne, who happens to be insane. She wants to marry a sculptor, played by Edmund Purdom (star of *The Egyptian*), whom Price tries to keep in jail. Vincent also made *Rage of the Buccaneers* in Italy the same year.

THE QUESTOR TAPES
1973 TV
PRODUCER: Howie Horowitz
DIRECTOR: Richard A. Colla
SCREENWRITERS: Gene Roddenberry, Gene L. Coon

Questar (Robert Foxworth) is an android created to prevent the destruction of Earth. Mike Farrell is his human scientist friend. A good pilot that led nowhere and is surprisingly cynical for a television movie. With Lew Ayres

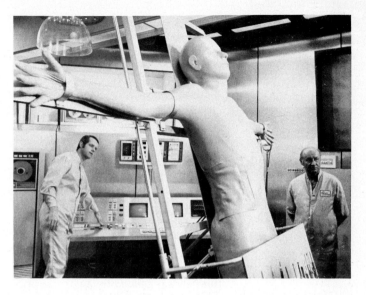

and John Vernon. Gene Roddenberry (*Star Trek*) was executive producer.

QUICKSAND
1950 United Artists (B&W)
PRODUCER: Mort Briskin
DIRECTOR: Irving Pichel
SCREENWRITER: Robert Smith

Mickey Rooney as a tragic small-time criminal in love with James Cagney's sister Jeanne. Peter Lorre as a blackmailing penny arcade owner, Barbara Bates, and Minerva Urecal also appear.

QUINTET
1979 20th Century-Fox
PRODUCER/DIRECTOR: Robert Altman
SCREENWRITERS: Frank Barhydt, Robert Altman, Patricia Resnick

An end of the world/ice age movie. Paul Newman, Vittorio Gassman, Bibi Andersson, and others play a game in which they try to kill each other. Fernando Rey is the referee. Brigitte Fossey is Newman's wife. If you've seen other recent Altman films you know why this one disappeared so fast. Music by John Williams. (**R**)

Mike Farrell and Robert Douglas prepare for the activation of Questor, an ambulatory computer capable of all human functions, in The Questor Tapes.

RABID

1977 New World (Canada)
PRODUCER: John Dunning
DIRECTOR/SCREENWRITER: David Cronenberg
ALSO RELEASED AS: *Rage*

Porn actress Marilyn Chambers goes "legit," sort of, playing a woman severely injured in a motorcycle accident who receives an experimental graft of "morphologically neutral" skin. Because she's lost a good deal of intestine as well, the neutral skin develops into a digestive organ—an ugly, phallus-shaped projection that sucks nourishment from the blood of her sleeping lovers. She only takes a little at a time, so she figures she can live with it (which is why Cronenberg's first treatment for this film was called *Mosquito*). But the diseased vampiric organ soon touches off an epidemic, and the city of Montreal goes rabid! With Joe Silver (**R**)   –BM

A cooled-off victim of Marilyn Chambers in Rabid.

RACE WITH THE DEVIL

1975 20th Century-Fox
PRODUCER: Wes Bishop
DIRECTOR: Jack Starrett
SCREENWRITERS: Lee Frost, Wes Bishop

An action-packed car-chase movie billed as horror about four vacationers in a trailer pursued by devil worshipers in cars and trucks. With Peter Fonda, Warren Oates, and Loretta Swit. Starrett also directed biker films like *Run Angel Run* and is a busy character actor.

RACING FEVER

1964 Allied Artists
PRODUCER/DIRECTOR/SCREENWRITER:
  William Grefe

Hot hydroplanes and the wildmen who ride them. Joe Morrison stars as Lee Gunner, whose father is run down in his last race by alcoholic playboy Gregg Stevenson. Joe falls in love with Connie Stevenson when she and her mother come around to offer their condolences. And Joe's pregnant sister shoots Gregg when she realizes his promises were nothing but lies. From the ads: "The action! The thrills! The spills!" Charles G. Martin, Barbara Biggart, and Maxine Carroll co-star; Gerry Granahan performs the twist-hit title song. With endless blazing boat action from Miami Marine Stadium in Pelican Harbor. Watch for Grefe's other Florida cheapsters including *The Checkered Flag*, *Death Curse of Tartu*, and *Sting of Death*. Required.   –CB

RADAR MEN FROM THE MOON

1951 Republic (B&W)
ASSOCIATE PRODUCER: Franklin Adreon
DIRECTOR: Fred C. Brannon
SCREENWRITER: Ronald Davidson
ALSO RELEASED AS: *Retik, the Moon Menace*

Commando Cody, Sky Marshall of the Universe (George Wallace), goes to the Moon to stop Retik (Roy Barcroft) from conquering Earth with an atomic gun. Made right after *Destination Moon* ushered in the science-fiction-film era, it was the first serial since the *Flash Gordon* series to take place in outer space. Cody's bullet-shaped metal helmet and rocket-powered backpack were originally used in *King of the Rocketmen* ('49). Action scenes from that serial were also reused here. Aline Towne is Cody's assistant. Clayton Moore (*The Lone Ranger*) helps Retik. The condensed feature was released in '66. Cody returned in *Zombies of the Stratosphere*.

RAGE: See *RABID*.

RAGE OF THE BUCCANEERS
1962 Colorama Features (Italy)
PRODUCER: Ottavio Poggi
DIRECTOR: Mario Costa
SCREENWRITERS: John Byrne, Ottavio Poggi
ORIGINALLY RELEASED AS: *Gordon il Pirata Nero*
ALSO RELEASED AS: *The Black Buccaneer*
In San Salvador, Gordon the Black Buccaneer (Ricardo Montalban, the white actor) is imprisoned by the evil governor's secretary (Vincent Price). Price is secretly leader of the slave trade and Montalban is a former slave. Price made *Queen of the Nile* in Italy at about the same time.

RAIDERS OF THE LOST ARK
1981 Paramount
PRODUCER: Frank Marshall
DIRECTOR: Steven Spielberg
SCREENWRITER: Lawrence Kasdan
The world's most expensive and best-looking "serial" and another top-grossing feature for Spielberg and executive producer George Lucas. From a story by Lucas and Philip Kaufman, who was once expected to direct. As archaeologist Indiana Jones, *Star Wars* hero Harrison Ford travels around the world searching for the ark of the covenant.

Karen Allen (*Animal House, The Wanderers, Cruising*) is his tough but reluctant partner in Nazi, Arab, and snake fighting. Expect several sequels and many imitations.

RAISE THE TITANIC
1980 AFD (England)
PRODUCER: William Frye
DIRECTOR: Jerry Jameson
SCREENWRITER: Adam Kennedy
Laughable special effects highlight this dull $36 million adventure starring Jason Robards as a crooked admiral salvaging the famous liner. With Richard Jordan, David Selby (*Dark Shadows*), and Alec Guinness. A Sir Lew Grade Production and money loser of catastrophic proportions. Music by John Barry.

RANSOM: See *MANIAC!*

RASPUTIN AND THE EMPRESS
1932 MGM (B&W)
PRODUCER: Irving Thalberg
DIRECTOR: Richard Boleslavsky
SCREENWRITER: Charles MacArthur
All three Barrymores star in this big-budget drama about the "mad monk" and his effect on Russia's monarchy before the Revolution. Lionel as Rasputin is finally killed by John as Prince Chegodieff (it takes poison cakes, a poker, and drowning). Sister Ethel is the czarina, and Ralph Morgan is the czar. The real czar's niece (and cousin) Princess Irina Yousoupoff sued MGM for slander. She settled out of court. Diana Wynward played her in the film.

RASPUTIN, THE MAD MONK
1966 Hammer/20th Century-Fox (England)
PRODUCER: Anthony Nelson-Keys
DIRECTOR: Don Sharp
SCREENWRITER: Anthony Hinds

No other Rasputin film was ever like this! Christopher Lee as the almost supernatural debauched monk chops off an opponent's hand in a fight, throws acid in another guy's face, and hypnotizes and seduces his way into the family of Nicholas II. When plotters try to kill him they find the task nearly impossible. Lee was good as the bearded Russian, but the movie wasn't very popular. When it showed in America, some lucky viewers were given free Rasputin beards at the box office! Boys got blue beards, girls received red ones. I can imagine a matinee audience of bearded kids throwing candy at the screen. With Barbara Shelley, Richard Pasco, Francis Mathews, and Suzan Farmer. Filmed with the same sets, crew, and stars as *Dracula, Prince of Darkness*.

RAT FINK
1965 Cinema Distributors (B&W)
PRODUCER: Lewis Andrews
DIRECTOR/SCREENWRITER: James Landis
ALSO RELEASED AS: *My Soul Runs Naked*
Landis' follow-up to *The Nasty Rabbit* is the story of a nameless rock 'n' roll singer who tries to sleep his way to the top. He steals money from an older woman's purse to get to Hollywood, where he takes on a teenager and his agent's wife. When little Judy Hughes

WIN A LIVE RAT
FOR YOUR MOTHER-IN-LAW!

gets pregnant he takes her to an animal hospital. Starring Schuyler Hayden, with Hal Bokar, Warrene Ott, and the Futuras. Don Snyder sings "One on Every Corner" and the original title song, "My Soul Runs Naked." Cinematography by William (originally, and later, Vilmos) Zsigmond.   –CB

RAT PFINK BOO BOO
1966 Craddock (B&W)
PRODUCER/DIRECTOR: Ray Dennis Steckler
SCREENWRITER: Ronald Haydock

Rock singer and gardener transform themselves into superheroes to rescue the singer's girl (Carolyn Brandt) from evil. Vin Saxon and Titus Moede star, with George Caldwell, Mike Kannon, James Bowie, and Kogar the swinging ape. See also *The Lemon Grove Kids Meet the Monsters*.   –CB

THE RATS ARE COMING! THE WEREWOLVES ARE HERE!
1972 William Mishkin Motion Pictures
PRODUCER: William Mishkin
DIRECTOR/SCREENWRITER: Andy Milligan
Awful cheapie about a family of werewolves in 19th-century England. The daughter raises man-eating rats. Filmed on Staten Island and in England. Do-it-all Mishkin was also his own cinematographer. The rat sequences were added after *Willard* achieved popularity.

THE RAVAGERS
1965 Hemisphere (U.S./Philippines) (B&W)
EXECUTIVE PRODUCER: Kane W. Lynn
DIRECTOR: Eddie Romero
SCREENWRITERS: Cesar Amigo, Eddie Romero
One of the many war films Romero made before he turned to more lucrative horror movies. As American Captain Kermit Dowling, John Saxon leads a group of native guerrillas against the Japanese. His ex-convict partner (Fer-

*Boris Karloff and Vincent
Price in* The Raven *('63).*

nando Poe, Jr.) infiltrates a convent
and falls in love with a woman being
hidden there by the nuns. Romero did
one more war drama, *Flight to Fury*.

THE RAVAGERS

1979 Avco Embassy
PRODUCER: John W. Hyde
DIRECTOR: Richard Compton
SCREENWRITER: Donald S. Sandford
Richard Harris wanders through a postholocaust 1991 searching for a place
called "Genesis." He finds Ernest Borgnine living in an oil tanker. Executive
producer Saul David also made *Logan's
Run* possible. Nothing good has been
said about this end-of-the-world movie,
which also features Ann Turkel, Art
Carney, and Woody Strode.

THE RAVEN

1935 Universal (B&W)
ASSOCIATE PRODUCER: David Diamond
DIRECTOR: Louis Friedlander
SCREENWRITERS: David Boehm, Jim Tully
Bela Lugosi in one of his greatest roles
as Dr. Vollin, a brilliant, eccentric plastic surgeon obsessed by the works of
Poe. He saves the life of actress Irene
Ware (she appears in a musical Poe
number). Her judge father (Samuel
Hinds) laughs at Bela's request to marry
her. The spurned madman invites his
"Lenore," her father, and her approved
fiancé to his electrically operated home
to try out his collection of torture devices. Besides his own pit-and-pendu-
lum there's a bedroom/elevator and a
room with crushing walls. Best of all is
the doctor's new assistant, an escaped
criminal (Boris Karloff) who showed
up for a new face and was turned into a
mutilated, partially paralyzed instrument of revenge. Lugosi tortures Karloff
further by debuting his new "face" in a
room lined with full-length mirrors.
The plot is quite similar in some ways
to that of the same year's *Mad Love*,
from MGM.

THE RAVEN

1963 AIP
PRODUCER/DIRECTOR: Roger Corman
SCREENWRITER: Richard Matheson

Corman's enjoyable comedy-fantasy about three 15th-century magicians brought together Karloff, Price, and Lorre, and, unlike most multi-horror-star hits, it worked. Dr. Erasmus Craven (Vincent Price), a retired sorcerer, is visited by a talking raven that turns out to be an inept, drunken magician, Dr. Adolphus Bedlo (Peter Lorre). He had been transformed by the evil magician Dr. Scarabus (Boris Karloff), whose mistress Lenore (Hazel Court) is Craven's wife, thought to be dead. Jack Nicholson is sufficiently silly as Bedlo's son, Rexford. Olive Sturgess is Craven's daughter. It all ends in a dynamic duel between the evil and the good magicians. Boris turns Vincent into a jar of jam. Some of the funniest moments are provided by Lorre, who ad-libbed much of his dialogue.

RAW MEAT

1972 AIP (England)
PRODUCER: Paul Maslansky
DIRECTOR: Gary Sherman
SCREENWRITER: Ceri Jones
ALSO RELEASED AS: *Deathline*

Descendants of an 1892 tunnel disaster are now living underground and eat-

Jack Nicholson (with striped pants and vertical exhaust) in Rebel Rousers.

ing London subway riders for dinner. Donald Pleasence stars as a police official in this semi-serious, fairly mild horror tale. Co-star Christopher Lee only has a brief cameo. With David Ladd, Sharon Gurney, and Norman Rossington. It would have been scarier if set in New York City, where thousands of homeless people live in subway tunnels. (R)

REBEL ANGEL

1962 Hoffman
PRODUCER: James J. Gannon
DIRECTOR: Lamont Douglas
SCREENWRITERS: Denny Ross, Elliott Tyne

Patricia Manning is a high school student torn between Richard Flynn and Tom Falk—until one of them murders a child she is baby-sitting. Music by the Stardusters. Manning had a bit part in *A House is Not a Home*; producer Gannon financed *Every Sparrow Must Fall*.   –CB

REBEL ROUSERS

1967 Four Star Excelsior
PRODUCER/DIRECTOR: Martin B. Cohen
SCREENWRITERS: Abe Polsky, Michael Kars, Martin B. Cohen

Shortly before *Easy Rider* and international fame, Jack Nicholson played his last outlaw-biker role. Along for the ride is Bruce Dern. The next year they were both in the classic LSD epic *Psych-Out*. The incredible Cameron Mitchell is Mr. Collier, an architect. The gang of lawless rebels captures his pregnant girlfriend (Dern's real-life wife for a while—Diane Ladd) and have a drag race to see who will win her. Cameron gets frantic and Bruce warns Jack to stop wearing striped pants. The couple is rescued by a family of irate Mexicans with pitchforks. Filmed in Arizona and L.A. by Laslo Kovacs. With Harry Dean Stanton. Not released until 1970.

THE REBEL SET

1959 Allied Artists (B&W)
PRODUCER: Earl Lyons
DIRECTOR: Gene Fowler, Jr.
SCREENWRITERS: Lou Vittes, Bernard Girard
ALSO RELEASED AS: *Beatsville*

Beatnik coffeehouse proprietor Edward Platt recruits Gregg Palmer, John Lupton, and Don Sullivan to help with a million-dollar armored-car heist. The caper goes off as planned during a four-hour train layover, but Platt springs a double cross. Kathleen Crowley, Ned Glass, and I. Stanford Jolley co-star. Platt was the chief on *Get Smart*, and Fowler directed *I Married a Monster from Outer Space.*   —CB

REBEL WITHOUT A CAUSE

1955 Warner Brothers
PRODUCER: David Weisbart
DIRECTOR: Nicholas Ray
SCREENWRITER: Stewart Stern

From the ads: "Teenage terror torn from today's headlines!" This classic pre-rock 'n' roll teen drama stars James Dean, Natalie Wood, and Sal Mineo as mixed-up young misfits. See how much fun the '50s really were. Middle-class kids with everything cope with maladjusted parents and a terrifying vision of Earth exploding. Other students are played by Dennis Hopper, Nick Adams, and Corey Allen (as Buzz, loser of a chicken run). Jim Backus, Ann Doran, Rochelle Hudson, and William Hopper are parents. With Paul Birch and Edward Platt as cops. Key scenes filmed at the Griffith Park Planetarium. All three of the stars died unnatural deaths. *Blackboard Jungle* was released the same year.

REBELLION IN CUBA

1961 International Film Distributors (B&W)
PRODUCER/DIRECTOR: Albert C. Gannaway
SCREENWRITER: Frank Graves
ALSO RELEASED AS: *Chiuato, Betrayer*

Raging Bull left out Jake LaMotta's acting career. He was in some real fringe stuff. As Julio in this obscure anti-Castro item, he teams up with Lon Chaney, Jr., and Bill Fletcher to aid a revolt against the Communists on the Isle of Pines. Filmed in Miami and Cuba. It would make a great double bill with the equally rare Errol Flynn movie, *Cuban Rebel Girls.*

THE RED BARON

1970 United Artists
PRODUCER: Gene Corman
DIRECTOR: Roger Corman
SCREENWRITERS: John and Joyce Corrington
ALSO RELEASED AS: *Von Richthoven and Brown*

As a Canadian garage-mechanic-turned-pilot, Don Stroud defeats the honorable old-fashioned German ace Von Richthoven (John Phillip Law). With Hurd Hatfield, Barry Primus, Karen Huston, Stephen McHattie, and a lot of flying sequences. A nude love scene was deleted after audiences laughed at it. All the German voices were dubbed in after the film was finished. It was the last movie directed by Corman, who had just formed his New World Pictures company.

THE RED HANGMAN: See *THE BLOODY PIT OF HORROR.*

RED HELL: See *TWO BEFORE ZERO.*

RED PLANET MARS

1952 United Artists (B&W)
PRODUCER: Anthony Veiller
DIRECTOR: Harry Horner
SCREENWRITERS: John L. Balderston, Anthony Veiller

Christian science-fiction from the Mc-Carthy era. Mars, a utopian planet, is ruled by God! Married scientists Peter Graves and Andrea King find out the shocking facts by communicating with the planet via a supertransmitter left behind by a crazed Nazi (Herbert Berghof). When the news get out, religious revolutionaries overthrow the Communist government in Russia! I'm sure the folks who made it were sincere, but the ludicrous plot twists make it impossible to take seriously. An anti-Communist classic with Marvin Miller, Morris Ankrum, and Walter Sande.

THE REDEEMER

1978 Dimension
PRODUCER: Sheldon Tromberg
DIRECTOR: Constantine S. Gochis
From the ads: "First THE OMEN . . . now THE REDEEMER." Six sinner graduates from the class of '67 are graphically mutilated and killed by a skull-faced angel from hell (T.G. Finkbinder). Twisted moralizing, exploitation style. **(R)**

REFLECTION OF FEAR

1971 Columbia (Canada)
PRODUCER: Howard B. Jaffe
DIRECTOR: William A. Fraker
SCREENWRITERS: Edward Hume,
Lewis John Carlino
ALSO RELEASED AS: *Labyrinth*
A young girl (Sondra Locke) lives in a fantasy world with Aaron, a doll she believes can kill people. Her father (Robert Shaw) returns after 10 years. Sally Kellerman is her new stepmother. Mary Ure is her mother. Many of the cast members die. This *Psycho*-ish tale sat on the shelf for two years before being released in a cut version. A very effective, well-photographed surprise thriller.

REFLECTIONS OF MURDER

1974 TV
PRODUCER: Aaron Rosenberg
DIRECTOR: John Badham
SCREENWRITER: Carol Sobieski
Joan Hackett, Tuesday Weld, and Sam Waterston prove themselves in this remake of *Diabolique*. Nerve-case Joan and louse husband Sam run a boys' school on an island in Puget Sound. Best friend Tuesday offers to help somebody murder somebody else. Beautifully shot on location in Washington State. Genuinely suspenseful. —CB

REFORM SCHOOL GIRL

1957 AIP (B&W)
PRODUCER: Robert J. Gurney, Jr.
DIRECTOR/SCREENWRITER: Edward Bernds
From the ads: "Caged boy-hungry wildcats gone mad!" Edd "Kookie" Byrnes ditches Luana Anders to take Gloria Castillo on a wild joyride in a stolen car. Castillo is framed in the death of a pedestrian. Byrnes then gets Anders out of the way by having a third girl turn her in for car stripping. Luana thinks that Castillo is responsible and tensions between the two rack the cellblock. Teenage tramps include Diana Darrin, Yvette Vickers, Donna Jo Gribble, and Sally Kellerman. Originally distributed with *Rock Around the World* and rereleased in 1959 to cash in on Byrnes' TV success. —CB

THE REINCARNATE

1971 Meridian (Canada)
PRODUCER/SCREENWRITER: Seelig Lester
DIRECTOR: Don Haldane
The ads promise: "No one ever dies." A struggling young sculptor agrees to let a dying lawyer transfer his spirit to the sculptor's body in an occult ritual involving the sacrifice of a young virgin and black cats. The dead girl is reincarnated as the baby of the now successful sculptor.

THE REINCARNATION OF PETER PROUD

1975 Cinerama
PRODUCER: Frank P. Rosenberg
DIRECTOR: J. Lee Thompson
SCREENWRITER: Max Ehrlich

Michael Sarrazin begins to realize he's the reincarnation of a man who was drowned years ago. The dead man's daughter (Jennifer O'Neill) falls in love with him. The dead man's wife (Margot Kidder in old-age makeup) wants him out of the way. Sound interesting? Not very. With some really embarrassing dialogue. A Bing Crosby production. With Cornelia Sharpe. Based on a novel by Max Ehrlich. (**R**)

THE RELUCTANT ASTRONAUT

1966 Universal
PRODUCER/DIRECTOR: Edward J. Montagne
SCREENWRITERS: Jim Fritzell,
Everett Greenbaum

Don Knotts as a nervous NASA janitor afraid of heights is sent into space to prove how efficient U.S. space capsules are. A made-for-TV feature released instead to theaters. With Leslie Nielsen, Joan Freeman, Jesse White, Jeanette Nolan, and Arthur O'Connell.

THE REPTILE

1966 Hammer/20th Century-Fox (England)
PRODUCER: Anthony Nelson-Keys
DIRECTOR: John Gilling
SCREENWRITER: John Elder

In 19th-century Cornwall, Jacqueline Pierce turns into a snake creature because of a Malayan curse. The '50s-style monster has fangs, big pop eyes, and a scaly face, but she's got a human's body and hair. With Noel Willman, Jennifer Daniel, and Ray Barrett. Made at the same time as *Plague of the Zombies*.

REPTILICUS

1962 AIP (Denmark)
PRODUCER/DIRECTOR: Sidney Pink
SCREENWRITERS: Ib Melchior, Sidney Pink

Oil drillers find a hunk of dinosaur flesh that grows into a giant flying reptile that attacks Copenhagen! The laughable sub-Japanese monster is actually a jerky puppet. Starring people named Carl, Asjorn, and Bent. Filmed in "Cinemagic," from a story by producer-director Pink.

REPULSION

1965 Royal (England) (B&W)
PRODUCER: Gene Gutowski
DIRECTOR: Roman Polanski
SCREENWRITERS: Roman Polanski,
Gerard Brach

Catherine Deneuve as a young Belgian woman working as a manicurist in London is repelled by sex. When her roommate-sister (Yvonne Furneaux) leaves for a vacation with her married boyfriend (Ian Hendry), she quits her job and shuts herself in the apartment. Her mental state deteriorates as she sees arms reaching out of the wall to grab her, and she kills her would-be boyfriend (John Fraser) and a lecherous landlord (Patrick Wymark). Polanski's first English-language feature is an essential classic. Music by Chico Hamilton. Watch for Polanski playing spoons.

REQUIEM FOR A SECRET AGENT

1965 CPT (Italy)
DIRECTOR: Sergio Sollima

After co-starring in a great James Bond movie (*From Russia with Love*), Daniela Bianchi went to Italy and co-starred in two of the worst Bond imitations, *Operation Kid Brother*, and this one featuring Stewart Granger. Granger spends most of the movie slapping and punching female cast members. With Peter Van Eyck and Giorgia Moll.

THE RESTLESS ONES

1965 World Wide
PRODUCER/DIRECTOR: Dick Ross
SCREENWRITER: James F. Collier

Johnny Crawford's parents find faith while doing research for a television script on wayward youth. He escapes to Palm Springs with a pregnant friend. Kim Darby, who has come along to meet her trucker fiancé, slashes her wrists when he doesn't show. This is enough for Johnny; at Billy Graham's next Los Angeles revival he stands proud in the light. With Jean Engstrom, Lurene Tuttle, I. Standford Jolley, Bob Random, and Robert Clarke. Robert Sampson of *For Pete's Sake* and Georgia Lee of *Wiretapper* are the parents, Mr. and Mrs. Winton. —CB

RESURRECTION

1981 Universal
PRODUCERS: Renee Missel,
  Howard Rosenman
DIRECTOR: Daniel Petrie
SCREENWRITER: Lewis John Carlino

Ellen Burstyn briefly "dies" after a car collision and catches a glimpse of life-after-death—which is sort of like a big family reunion held in a disco that plays soft electronic music. Thereafter, she discovers that she has the ability to feel the sickness of others, and heal by touch. Putting aside the stern morality of her father (played by Robert Blossom, the mass murderer of Allan Ormsby's *Deranged*), she lets Sam Shepard, the rebellious son of a hell-and-brimstone preacher, muscle his way into her bedroom. Later, Shep can't get it up because he's convinced that Burstyn is Christ returned; he shoots her in an effort to prove it. The tear-prone should bring lots of Kleenex. —BM

THE RESURRECTION OF ZACHARY WHEELER

1971 Gold Key Entertainment
PRODUCER: Bob Stabler
DIRECTOR: Robert Wynn
SCREENWRITERS: Jay Sims, Tom Rolf

Reporter Leslie Nielsen discovers a clone factory in New Mexico where scientists blackmail their revived patients to gain power. A senator (Bradford Dillman) gets new vital organs after a car accident. Shot on videotape and sold directly to television. With Angie Dickenson, Jack Carter, and James Daly.

THE RESURRECTION SYNDICATE: See NOTHING BUT THE NIGHT.

RETIK, THE MOON MENACE: See RADAR MEN FROM THE MOON.

THE RETURN

1980 Greydon Clark Productions
PRODUCER/DIRECTOR: Greydon Clark
SCREENWRITERS: Jim Wheat, Ken Wheat,
  Curtis Burch

Twenty years ago, two children and a prospector were zapped by a saucer. Now, the kids have grown up to be Cybill Shepherd, the scientific-genius daughter of high-tech industrialist Raymond Burr, and Jan-Michael Vincent, deputy to Martin Landau, the marshal of the desert town of Little Creek. The prospector (Vinnie Schiavelli, the whining inmate from *One Flew Over the Cuckoo's Nest*) hasn't aged at all; he's living in a cave near Little Creek and has taken to mutilating people and Neville Brand's cattle with a glowing rod that burns flesh, and throwing spare parts through a weird glowing tunnel that is his direct line to the saucer people. Shepherd and Vincent eventually learn that the saucer folks are okay after all—Schiavelli just misunderstood their instructions. Director Clark apparently didn't know whether he wanted to make a horror film or another *Close Encounters*; the result is a lot of contradictory nonsense with a few flashy effects scenes. Never released to theaters, though it's been seen on TV. *Without Warning* (by the same director) was, believe it or not, better. —BM

RETURN FROM THE PAST: See *DR. TERROR'S GALLERY OF TERRORS.*

RETURN FROM WITCH MOUNTAIN

1978 Buena Vista
PRODUCERS: Ron Miller, Jerry Courtland
DIRECTOR: John Hough
SCREENWRITER: Malcolm Marmorstein

The two alien kids with psychic powers from *Escape to Witch Mountain* return to Earth and are used by mad scientist Christopher Lee and partner Bette Davis to rob a museum and destroy a nuclear reactor. Excellent special effects highlight this science-fiction adventure. With Denver Pyle, Jack Soo, and Dick Bakalyan.

THE RETURN OF CAPTAIN MARVEL: See THE ADVENTURES OF CAPTAIN MARVEL.

THE RETURN OF CAPTAIN NEMO: See THE AMAZING CAPTAIN NEMO.

THE RETURN OF CHANDU

1934 Principal (B&W)
PRODUCER: Sol Lesser
DIRECTOR: Ray Taylor
SCREENWRITER: Barry Barringer

As the hero magician with occult powers, Bela Lugosi goes to the magic island of Lemuria to rescue Princess Nadji from a cat-worshiping cult. The first four chapters of this independent serial were condensed into this feature, and the last eight into another (*Chandu on Magic Island*). All 12 are now available on one videocassette. See Lugosi actually save the leading lady (Maria Alba), gaze into his crystal ball, and use his yoga powers to become invisible! With sets (and the great wall) left over from *King Kong*. Iron Eyes Cody is Bela's native assistant. Bela played the villain in the earlier *Chandu the Magician.*

THE RETURN OF CHARLIE CHAN: See HAPPINESS IS A WARM CLUE.

THE RETURN OF COUNT YORGA

1971 AIP
PRODUCER: Miachael Macready
DIRECTOR: Bob Kelljan
SCREENWRITERS: Bob Kelljan,
  Yvonne Wilder

Count Yorga made so much money that this quick sequel was rushed out. Robert Quarry again stars, this time stalking around an orphanage in San Francisco. Roger Perry is again the hero. Mariette Hartley (of Polaroid camera TV ads) is the Count's main interest. Edward Walsh is Brudah again and the producer's dad, George Macready, appears as a professor in his last role. Quarry went on to *Dr. Phibes Rises Again, Madhouse,* and unemployment. Director Kelljan made *Scream, Blacula, Scream.*

THE RETURN OF DR. MABUSE

1961 A Jay Films
(W. Germany/France/Italy) (B&W)
PRODUCTION SUPERVISOR: Wolf Brauner
DIRECTOR: Harald Reinl
SCREENWRITERS: Ladislas Foder, Marc Behm
ORIGINALLY RELEASED AS:
Im Stahlnetz des Dr. Mabuse
ALSO RELEASED AS: *Phantom Fiend*

Dr. Mabuse (Wolfgang Preiss), working with the Chicago Mafia, uses hypnotism and drugs to make mindless slaves of the inmates and staff of a prison. Gert Frobe as Inspector Lohmann, Lex Barker as a CIA man, and Daliah Lavi as the daughter of the professor who invented the drug rush to prevent an attack on a nuclear reactor. By the director of *Blood Fiend*.

RETURN OF DR. X

1939 Warner Brothers (B&W)
PRODUCER: Bryan Foy
DIRECTOR: Vincent Sherman
SCREENWRITER: Lee Katz

Humphrey Bogart as a vampire! Actually he's the notorious Dr. Xavier, electrocuted for a few murders but returned to life by John Litel. The living-dead Bogey has a shock of white hair, wears striped pants, and carries a scalpel because he needs blood. Potential victims include Rosemary Lane, Dennis Morgan, Wayne Morris, Huntz Hall, William Hopper, Creighton Hale, and Glenn Langan. Bogart did not receive top billing and hated the role. You might not, though.

THE RETURN OF DRACULA

1958 United Artists (B&W with color sequence)
PRODUCERS: Jules V. Levy, Arthur Gardner
DIRECTOR: Paul Landres
SCREENWRITER: Pat Fielder
ALSO RELEASED AS: *Curse of Dracula*

As Dracula, Francis Lederer arrives in contemporary Southern California impersonating a visiting artist and proceeds to vampirize the locals. Probably because of *Horror of Dracula* (released the same year), we get to see a little blood when this creature of the night is staked. He also turns into a bat and a wolf. With Norma Eberhardt and Ray Stricklyn.

THE RETURN OF MAJIN

1966 Daiei/AIP-TV (Japan)
PRODUCER: Masaichi Nagata
DIRECTORS: Kenji Misumi, Yoshiyuki Kuruda
SCREENWRITER: Tetsou Yoshida

The giant warrior statue Majin returns in a sequel, almost identical to the original—*Majin, Monster of Terror*. Kenji Misumi later directed *Shogun Assassin*.

THE RETURN OF MAXWELL SMART: See THE NUDE BOMB.

THE RETURN OF MR. MOTO

1965 20th Century-Fox
PRODUCERS: Robert Lippert, Jack Parsons
DIRECTOR: Ernest Morris
SCREENWRITER: Fred Eggers

A failed attempt to put a 1930s character into the modern James Bond world. Henry Silva, a Puerto Rican, plays the Japanese sleuth (now an Interpol agent) without makeup. He exposes a world-domination plot involving oil sheiks and ex-Nazis. With Martin Wyldeck and Suzanne Lloyd.

RETURN OF THE APE MAN

1944 Monogram (B&W)
PRODUCERS: Jack Dietz, Sam Katzman
DIRECTOR: Phil Rosen
SCREENWRITER: Robert Charles

Sixty minutes of vintage Monogram nonsense. Bela Lugosi as Professor Dexter brings a prehistoric man (former boxer Frank Moran) to life and gives it the brain of his co-worker (John Carradine). The creature (first seen frozen in plastic-wrap "ice") plays piano and shows his underwear under his animal skins! Wonderful. Third-billed George Zucco isn't even in it (he was going to play the ape man). It has nothing to do with the previous year's *The Apeman*, but it's just as funny.

RETURN OF THE BLIND DEAD

1973 (Spain)
DIRECTORS: Armando De Ossorio
ORIGINALLY RELEASED AS:
El Ataque de los Muertos sin Ojos
You loved the ancient rotting zombies in *The Blind Dead*. Here they are again, back to attack Tony Kendall and all his beautiful European girlfriends. Since you still couldn't get enough of the lovable flesh-eating ghouls, they returned yet again in *Horror of the Zombies*.

RETURN OF THE FLY

1959 20th Century-Fox (B&W)
PRODUCER: Bernard Glasser
PRODUCER/SCREENWRITER: Edward L. Bernds
The sequel to the color hit *The Fly* is a more standard black-and-white retelling of the same story. Andre's grown son, Phillip (Brett Halsey), dusts off the matter transmitter and, thanks to a spy, becomes a human fly like dad did. This time the monster has a huge head, spends a lot more time onscreen, and goes after the hysterical wife (Danielle Demetz). Vincent Price is back as the concerned uncle and there's one good silly/sick scene worthy of the original: a man is put in the machine with a guinea pig, resulting in a dead guy with white paws. Director Bernds is best known for his work with the Three Stooges.

THE RETURN OF THE GIANT MONSTERS

1967 Daiei/AIP-TV (Japan)
PRODUCER: Hidemasa Nagata
DIRECTOR: Noriaki Yuasa
SCREENWRITER: Fumi Takahashi
ORIGINALLY RELEASED AS: *Gamera tai Gyaos*
In the third Gamera the Flying Turtle movie, the giant world protector fights Gyaos, a winged reptile with laser-beam breath.

RETURN OF THE LIVING DEAD: See *DEAD PEOPLE*.

RETURN OF THE TERROR

1934 Warner Brothers (B&W)
PRODUCTION/SUPERVISOR: Sam Bischoff
DIRECTOR: Howard Bretherton
SCREENWRITERS: Eugene Solow, Peter Milne
A remake of *The Terror* (1928), which was the first sound horror film. The inventor of the super X-ray machine escapes from the asylum and the murders start. Mary Astor and Lyle Talbot are the romantic stars. Frank McHugh is comic relief. With J. Carrol Naish, Irving Pichel, and Frank Reicher. It was based on an Edgar Wallace story.

THE RETURN OF THE VAMPIRE

1943 Columbia (B&W)
PRODUCER: Sam White
DIRECTOR: Lew Landers
SCREENWRITER: Griffith Jay
Despite his fame as a bloodsucker, Bela Lugosi only played a real vampire three times and once it was in a comedy (*Abbott and Costello Meet Frankenstein*). Greedy Universal wouldn't let Columbia call him Dracula, so he's called Armand Tesla here. He's a Rumanian vampire in London who gets revived when World War II German bombs hit a cemetery. His assistant (Matt Willis) is a werewolf! Frieda Inescort runs an

asylum and tries to destroy the vampire. With Nina Foch and Miles Mander. The director, originally known as Louis Friedlander, had also done *The Raven* with Lugosi.

RETURN TO BOGGY CREEK

1977 777 Distributors
PRODUCER: Bob Gates
DIRECTOR: Tom Moore
SCREENWRITER: Dave Woody
The hairy man-in-a-suit creature from *The Legend of Boggy Creek* helps some kids lost in a storm. With Dawn Wells (Mary Ann on *Gilligan's Island*).

REVENGE

1971 TV
PRODUCER: Mark Carliner
DIRECTOR: Jud Taylor
SCREENWRITER: Joseph Stephano
Shelley Winters stars as a deranged mother in her first TV movie! She thinks Bradford Dillman caused her daughter's death, so Brad goes in the jail cell in the basement. His wife (Carol Rossen) uses ESP to find him. With Stuart Whitman and Roger Perry.

THE REVENGE OF FRANKENSTEIN

1958 Hammer/Columbia (England)
PRODUCER: Anthony Hinds
DIRECTOR: Terence Fisher
SCREENWRITER: Jimmy Sangster
Peter Cushing returns as Dr. Frankenstein. He now calls himself Dr. Stein and runs a charity hospital for the poor. It's an ideal situation for the "good" doctor, who takes body parts from his peasant patients whenever he feels like it. With the help of his assistant (Francis Mathews), he puts the brain of Karl, a crippled man who rescued him from the guillotine in the opening sequence, into a new body. The creature (Michael Gwynn) looks like a normal human with stitches. With Eunice Grayson and Lionel Jeffries as a body snatcher. An American ad warned: "If you go alone . . .you'll find yourself running all the way home!"

REVENGE OF THE CREATURE

1955 Universal (3-D, B&W)
PRODUCER: William Alland
DIRECTOR: Jack Arnold
SCREENWRITER: Martin Berkeley
The popular gill man returns, only to be captured by John Agar, taken to Florida, and thrown in a Marineland fish tank. Agar, with co-workers Lori Nelson and John Bromfield, uses electric cattle prods to help in his study of the chained creature. The angry amphibian (Ricou Browning) is once again after the leading lady. He follows her to a swingin' dance, which quickly ends when the party-goers spot the scaly square from South America. Although filmed in 3-D, it was usually projected flat. With Nestor Paiva and, in his first screen role, Clint Eastwood as a lab technician with a mouse in his pocket. In 1982 a New Orleans showing made

John Agar and Lori Nelson watch John Bromfield inject clams in Revenge of the Creature.

it the first feature broadcast in 3-D on commercial television.

REVENGE OF THE DEAD: See *NIGHT OF THE GHOULS*.

REVENGE OF THE LIVING DEAD: See *THE MURDER CLINIC*.

REVENGE OF THE SCREAMING DEAD: See *DEAD PEOPLE*.

REVENGE OF THE STEPFORD WIVES
1980 TV
PRODUCER: Scott Rudin
DIRECTOR: Robert Fuest
SCREENWRITER: David Wiltse

A totally useless "sequel" to a pretty useless feature. A reporter (Sharon Gless) discovers the truth about the seemingly perfect wives in a New England bedroom community. With Julie Kavner (*Rhoda*) and Arthur Hill.

REVENGE OF THE ZOMBIES
1943 Monogram (B&W)
PRODUCER: Lindsley Parsons
DIRECTOR: Steve Sekely
SCREENWRITERS: Edmund Kelso, Van Norcross

More wartime horrors. Down in the bayou scientist John Carradine creates a zombie army for the Nazis. His wife (Veda Ann Borg), also a zombie, puts a stop to his friendly plans. *My Little Margie* star Gale Storm and future Batman Robert Lowery snoop around and Mantan Moreland is funny. With Bob Steele. *I Walked with a Zombie* had just been a hit for RKO. The director, whose real name was Istvan Szekely, did features in Hungary and Germany before moving to America in 1940.

The 'WALKING DEAD' are the most DEADLY!

THE SHAW BROTHERS PRESENT

REVENGE of the ZOMBIES

One of the most shocking and bizarre films of the year!

A W RLD NORTHAL FILM   **R**

REVENGE OF THE ZOMBIES
1981 World Northal (Hong Kong)
PRODUCER: Run Run Shaw
DIRECTOR: Horace Menga
ALSO RELEASED AS: *Black Magic II*
Called "the ultimate exploitation film" by Manhattan fans who are hard to please, this modern-day black-magic movie features more madness, sickness, gore, and fun than a dozen recent American films. A 125-year-old evil sorcerer stays young by drinking human milk. There's a good white magician, zombies with spikes through their heads, alligators, cannibals, kung fu, and sex. Look for it at your local martial-arts theater. With Ti Lung and Lily Tu. **(R)**

REVOLT OF THE ZOMBIES
1936 Academy (B&W)
PRODUCER: Edward Halperin
DIRECTOR: Victor Halperin
SCREENWRITERS: Howard Higgins, Rollo Lloyd, Victor Halperin
The makers of *White Zombie* try unsuccessfully for a repeat hit. They even reused shots of Bela Lugosi's eyes. During World War I young Dean Jagger creates zombie soldiers in Cambodia for the French. With Dorothy Stone. A rare independent feature that looks like it was made in the '20s. Dean Jagger still helps create monsters (see *Alligator*).

REVOLUTION
1969 United Artists
PRODUCER/DIRECTOR/SCREENWRITER: Jack O'Connell
The director of *The Greenwich Village Story* moves west to document Haight Ashbury. A young middle-class girl drops out and changes her name to Today. The ads tell you all you need to know about her newfound way of life. "Today panhandles and sells underground newspapers with an equal sense of absurdity." "Today believes that napalm is more harmful than LSD." Hippies and opposing establishment types are interviewed. If you're a San Francisco music fan, you'll love the sound track with music by Country Joe and the Fish, Mother Earth, the Steve Miller Band, and the Quicksilver Messenger Service featuring the guitar of John Cippolina.

RICH, YOUNG AND DEADLY: See *PLATINUM HIGH SCHOOL*.

RICHARD

1972 Aura City
PRODUCER: Lorees Yerby
DIRECTORS: Lorees Yerby, Harry Hurwitz
SCREENWRITERS: Bertrand Castelli,
   Lorees Yerby, Harry Hurwitz

A real-life horror comedy that mixes newsreel footage with scenes of Nixon imitator Richard M. Dixon. John Carradine is a surgeon. With Mickey Rooney as an angel, Kevin McCarthy, and Paul Ford.

RIDE THE WILD SURF

1964 Columbia
PRODUCER/SCREENWRITER: Jo Napoleon
DIRECTOR: Don Taylor

Columbia makes a beach movie. With heartthrobs Fabian and Tab Hunter, the multitalented Shelley Fabares, Barbara Eden, and Susan Hart; plus James Mitchum as Eskimo! Great theme song by Jan and Dean. Filmed in Hawaii. *Beach Party* over at AIP proved more popular.

RIDERS TO THE STARS

1954 United Artists
PRODUCER: Ivan Tors
DIRECTOR: Richard Carlson
SCREENWRITER: Curt Siodmak

Documentary-style unsensational science fiction based on probable future space problems. Astronauts go on a meteor hunt. With William Lundigan, Herbert Marshall, Richard Carlson (who also directed), Martha Hyer, Dawn Addams, and King Donovan. Kitty White sings the theme song.

THE RIGHT HAND OF THE DEVIL

1963 Cinema-Video International (B&W)
PRODUCER/DIRECTOR/SCREENWRITER:
   Aram Katcher

Katcher did everything on this film, including star. He plays a crook who engineers the successful robbery of the Hollywood Sports Arena, then dumps his accomplices into a bathtub filled with acid and escapes to Rio. He faces death when he returns to L.A. with another heist in mind. Lisa McDonald co-stars, with Brad Trumbull, Chris Randall, and James V. Christy.   –CB

RING-A-DING RHYTHM

1962 Amicus/Columbia (England) (B&W)
PRODUCER/DIRECTOR: Richard Lester
SCREENWRITER: Milton Subotsky
ALSO RELEASED AS: *It's Trad, Dad*

Richard Lester displays a few of the skills he brought to the Beatles movies in this musical with a trivial plot about a mayor who bans rock 'n' roll and jazz music. Helen Shapiro and Craig Douglas put on a show and change his mind. The big attractions here are Gene Vincent, Del Shannon, Gary "U.S." Bonds, and Gene McDaniels. Also with Chubby Checker, the Paris Sisters, Kenny Ball, Acker Bilk, and lots of lame British

Today visits an 80-year-old Haight Ashbury resident who claims to love hippies in Revolution.

Dixieland and jazz groups. Vincent does "Space Ship to Mars" and Bonds sings "Seven Day Weekend."

RING OF TERROR
1962 Ashcroft (B&W)
PRODUCER: Alfeo Bocchicchio
DIRECTOR: Clark Paylow
SCREENWRITER: Lewis Simeon,
  G.J. Zinnamon

An allegedly true story about the evils of fraternity hazing. Premed student George Mather is known around campus for his courage, having lived through class dissections as well as a run-in with an angry rattler in lovers' lane. To get into the right frat, he must steal a ring from the finger of a corpse. He dies of shock. Mather, star of *Pattern for Murder*, is supported by Esther Furst, Austin Green, Joseph Conway, and June Smavey.   —CB

RIO 70
1970 (Spain/Germany/U.S.)
PRODUCER/SCREENWRITER:
  Harry Allan Towers
DIRECTOR: Jesus Franco

Shirley Eaton is back in this spectacular sequel to the wonderful *Million Eyes of Sumaru*. She has an all-female village in the Amazon jungle and is trying to take over the world again. George Sanders co-stars. With Maria Rohm and Richard Wyler.

RIOT
1968 Paramount
PRODUCER: William Castle
DIRECTOR: Buzz Kulik
SCREENWRITER: James Poe

After *Rosemary's Baby*, William Castle produced this violent prison adventure filmed at the Arizona State Penitentiary. Ex–Cleveland Browns star Jim Brown reluctantly helps fellow prisoner Gene Hackman start a riot to cover their escape. Ben Carruthers is a psy-

chopathic Indian. Featuring the prison's real warden, personnel, and inmates. By the director of *The Explosive Generation*. Written by the late James Poe, who had been married to Barbara Steele. **(R)**

RIOT AT LAUDERDALE: See HELL'S PLAYGROUND.

RIOT IN JUVENILE PRISON
1959 United Artists (B&W)
PRODUCER: Robert E. Kent
DIRECTOR: Edward L. Cahn
SCREENWRITER: Orville H. Hampton

A public outcry arises from the shooting of two youngsters during a breakout. Psychologist Jerome Thor, appointed by the governor to keep an eye on warden John Hoyt and his sadistic guards, turns the institution coed and tries very hard, but Scott Marlowe starts fights and screws everything up. With Marcia Henderson, Ann Doran, and Dorothy Provine.   —CB

RIOT ON SUNSET STRIP
1967 AIP
PRODUCER: Sam Katzman
DIRECTOR: Arthur Dreifuss
SCREENWRITER: Orville H. Hampton

The ads claim it's "The most shocking film of our generation!" Aldo Ray stars as police lieutenant Lorimer, sympathetic to the kids on the Strip but pressured by businessmen to clear them out. Tim Rooney and his friends convince Mimsy Farmer to hang out. At Pandora's Box they watch the Standells (who do the theme song) and the Chocolate Watchband. The Watchband was a great drug/punk band with a Mick Jaggeresque lead singer. The dire tale continues as the kids go to a party in an abandoned house and a movie star's son puts acid in the naive Mimsy's drink. After her choreographed freakout, she is gang-raped (off-screen).

Aldo, who is the father she hasn't seen in years, reacts with punches, and cries of "police brutality" start the riot of the title. Great theme song lyrics: "Just doesn't seem fair/To bug ya 'cause ya got long hair. . ."

RITUAL OF EVIL
1970 TV
PRODUCER: David Levinson
DIRECTOR: Robert Day
SCREENWRITER: Robert Presnell, Jr.
The second pilot for a projected series called *Bedeviled* starring Louis Jourdan and Wilfrid Hyde-White as psychic investigators. They look into the apparent suicide of a young heiress involved with witchcraft. With Diana Hyland, Belinda Montgomery, and Carla Borelli.

THE ROAD BUILDER: See THE NIGHT DIGGER.

ROAD GAMES
1981 Avco Embassy (Australia)
PRODUCERS: Richard Franklin, Barbi Taylor
DIRECTOR: Richard Franklin
SCREENWRITER: Everett Deroche
An Australian trucker, traveling through the outback en route to Sidney, has found that it breaks the monotony if you murder an attractive female hitchhiker every few hundred miles. Stacy Keach, another trucker whose brain seems to have been addled by too much speed and/or solitude, is mistaken for the murderer. Jamie Lee Curtis is an attractive female hitchhiker. The Hitchcockian concept is underlined by a few unsubtle references to the late director, but that unfortunately only emphasizes how far Franklin (who also directed

Psycho II) is from being Hitchcock. He's a lot closer than DePalma, though. **(R)**   –BM

ROAD TO NASHVILLE
1966 Crown International
PRODUCER: Robert Patrick
DIRECTOR/SCREENWRITER: Will Zens
Country music exploitation movie from the director of *Spy Squad*. Doodles Weaver is a Hollywood agent who makes many new friends among the Nashville personalities but forgets that he's been sent to sign them for an upcoming feature. What a jam when film crews arrive to find a deserted theater. Connie Smith, Marty Robbins, Webb Pierce, Waylon Jennings, Johnny Cash, Kitty Wells, Porter Wagoner, Dottie West, Hank Snow, and others rise to the rescue. Songs include "El Paso," "Skid Row Joe," "A Woman Half My Age," and "Just a Faded Petal From a Beautiful Bouquet." Cinematography by Vilmos Zsigmund.   –CB

THE ROAD WARRIOR
1982 Warner Brothers (Australia)
PRODUCER: Byron Kennedy
DIRECTOR: George Miller
SCREENWRITERS: Terry Hayes, George Miller, Brian Hannant
ORIGINALLY RELEASED AS: *Mad Max II*
The riveting nonstop sequel to *Mad Max* also stars Mel Gibson (*Gallipoli*) as the sullen, leather-clad loner Max, roaming the futuristic wastelands of Australia in his souped-up Mustang, searching for gas. He finds himself reluctantly helping a peaceful community escape from a tribe of muscle-bound punked-out killers on wheels. With lots of interesting characters, stirring music by Brian May, and the greatest motorized chase scenes ever. The best action film in years. Don't miss it. Director

Miller's next project was a segment of the *Twilight Zone* movie. (R)

THE ROADRACERS
1959 AIP (B&W)
PRODUCER/SCREENWRITER: Stanley Kallis
DIRECTOR: Arthur Swerdloff
Young Joel Lawrence is suspended from U.S. car-racing competition following an accident that claims the life of another driver. Returning after two very successful years in Europe, he sets out to get Sumner Williams for stealing his girl. With Marian Collier, Sally Fraser, and Skip Ward of *The Mad Room*. Action footage from the U.S. Grand Prix.   –CB

ROBINSON CRUSOE ON MARS
1964 Paramount
PRODUCER: Aubrey Schenck
DIRECTOR: Byron Haskin
SCREENWRITERS: Ib Melchior,
 John C. Higgins
Astronaut Paul Mantee saves an alien humanoid slave (Vic Lundin) who in turn helps him survive the harsh planet. Adam "Batman" West is the astronaut who never makes it to Mars. Filmed in Death Valley. The spaceships were left over from *The War of the Worlds*. Mona the Woolly Monkey plays herself.

ROBOT MONSTER
1953 Astor (3-D, B&W)
PRODUCER/DIRECTOR: Phil Tucker
SCREENWRITER: Wyott Ordung
ALSO RELEASED AS: *Monsters from the Moon*
Belly laughs meet stark terror as the last six "hu-mans" in existence are caught in a death struggle with the dreaded Ro-man, a bogus gorilla in a plastic diving helmet. The hairy invader is under pressure to figure out why his calcinator death ray is ineffective against professor Gregory Moffett and his crew, which consists of George Nader, Claudia Barrett, two horrible children, and Selena Royle—the high-class moll who taught Joan Crawford manners in *The Damned Don't Cry*. Ro-man strangles the professor's little girl, pummels Nader, and is about to do something really subhuman to Claudia when he gets an important call from his superior. The Great One punishes Ro-man for his incompetence by unleashing a devastating U-ray; cities and dinosaurs fall in the subsequent orgy of stock-footage destruction. Already something of a legend, *Robot Monster* was shot in four days in Hollywood's Bronson Canyon for under $20,000. Ro-man's interplanetary receiver is a standard war-surplus job on a kitchen table which fills the air with bubbles when in use. Music by Elmer Bernstein (*To Kill a Mockingbird*). Stock scenes from *One Million B.C.* and *Flight to Mars*. Movies don't come any better.   –CB

THE ROBOT VS. THE AZTEC MUMMY
1959 K. Gordon Murray Productions (Mexico) (B&W)
PRODUCER: William C. Stell
DIRECTOR: Raphael Portillo
SCREENWRITER: Alfred Salazar
ORIGINALLY RELEASED AS: *La Momia Contra el Robot Humano*
This bizarre sequel to *The Aztec Mummy* features Dr. Krupp, a mad scientist after the treasure buried in the mummy's tomb. He creates a tin-can robot with a human head looking through a face window (and light bulbs for ears) that battles the zombie-like mummy attired in shredded cloth. Lots of American kids sat through this at '60s Saturday matinees. The Mexican *momia* was soon back in *Curse of the Aztec Mummy*.

ROCK ALL NIGHT

1957 AIP (B&W)
PRODUCER/DIRECTOR: Roger Corman
SCREENWRITER: Charles B. Griffith

From the ads: "Some gotta dance, some gotta kill!" The Cloud Nine, a rock 'n' roll bar, is invaded by two desperate killers (Russell Johnson and Jonathan Haze) who hold guns on the patrons and make them act like nothing is wrong. Abby Dalton is forced to sing rock hits (accompanied by the jukebox). Dick Miller, as Shorty, an oddball with a striped jacket, is the hero. The all-star Corman players in this 62 minute, one-set, five-day wonder include Bruno Ve Sota, Mel Welles, Ed Nelson, and Beach Dickerson. The Platters and the Blockbusters sing in an unrelated open-ing segment. It was originally co-billed with *Dragstrip Girl*.

ROCK AROUND THE CLOCK

1956 Columbia (B&W)
PRODUCER: Sam Katzman
DIRECTOR: Fred Sears
SCREENWRITERS: Robert E. Kent,
James B. Gordon

The year after *Blackboard Jungle's* open-ing credits introduced rock music to filmgoers, Sam Katzman (first with every trend) made the first movie *about* rock 'n' roll. Some cities banned it. Projectionists were told to turn down the sound track. In England some audiences "rioted." The story shows the mostly fictional rise of Bill Haley and the Comets, discovered rockin' with a new beat in a mountain village. They're brought to the attention of New York deejay Alan Freed and, despite inter-ference from booker Alix Talton who loves their new manager, Johnny Johns-ton, they make it big. Haley sure couldn't act but his band really cooks doing nine songs. With the Platters doing the wonderful "Great Pretenders" and some incredible dancing. Also with Freddie Bell and the Bellboys. See you later, Alligator.

ROCK AROUND THE WORLD

1957 AIP (England) (B&W)
PRODUCERS: Peter Rogers,
Herbert Smith
DIRECTOR: Gerard Bryant
SCREENWRITER: Norman Hudis
ALSO RELEASED AS: *The Tommy Steele Story*

England's first Elvis copy, Tommy Steele, stars in this cinematic artifact, which shows how heavily American rock 'n' roll hit over there. American teens watching pre-Beatle British rock films must have wondered who the hell these guys were. Steele's biggest hit (in Eng-land) was a cover of "Singin' the Blues." L.A. disc jockey Hunter Hancock provides the introduction. With lots of skiffle and calypso music, still popular in England at the time.

ROCK BABY, ROCK IT

1957 Freebar (B&W)
PRODUCER: J. G. Tiger
DIRECTOR: Murray Douglas Sporup
SCREENWRITERS: Herbert Margolis,
William Raynor

Dallas-made obscurity with cult following. Syndicate bookies want space that teens are using as club headquarters. Kids put on benefit, save club, and expose gangsters. Johnny Carroll, Don Coats, and Kay Wheeler star; music segments feature the Bon Aires, Cell Block Seven, and Preacher Smith's Deacons.   –CB

ROCK 'N' ROLL HIGH SCHOOL

1979 New World
PRODUCER: Michael Finnell
DIRECTORS: Alan Arkush, Joe Dante
SCREENWRITERS: Richard Whitley,
Russ Dvonch, Joseph McBride

The best teen drive-in movie in years! P. J. Soles lives for the Ramones. They're about to give a concert but in the meantime high school has to be endured. Clint Howard (from the *Gentle Ben* series) is the school's supplier of

Riff Randall (P. J. Soles) and the Ramones in the halls of Vince Lombardi High, a.k.a. Rock 'n' Roll High School.

everything, including make-out lessons for jock Vincent Van Patten. Mary Woronov (*Chelsea Girls*) is Miss Togar, the tough new principal. Dey Young discovers rock 'n' roll. So does a giant lab mouse. The Ramones play in a theater, in the halls of the school, and in a shower. The school blows up. Audiences cheer. With Dick Miller and Paul Bartel. Roger Corman was executive producer.

ROCK, PRETTY BABY

1957 Universal (B&W)
PRODUCER: Edmond Chevie
DIRECTOR: Richard H. Bartlett
SCREENWRITERS: Herbert Margolis,
William Raynor

John Saxon needs an electric guitar for a new combo with drummer Sal Mineo and bassman Rod McKuen. Mineo takes time out from trying to separate Caryl Volkman from her twin sister Susan to set up a benefit rock fest. The new guitar goes into hock to pay off property damages resulting from riot scene but is reclaimed after the Fraternal Order of Bisons offers a two-week summer-camp engagement. With Luana Patten, Edward Platt, Fay "King Kong" Wray (as Saxon's mom), and Shelley Fabares as Twinkey. Music by Jimmy Daley and his Ding-a-lings and Henry Mancini. *Summer Love* was a sequel.   –CB

ROCK ROCK ROCK

1956 DCA (B&W)
PRODUCERS: Milton Subotsky,
Max J. Rosenberg
DIRECTOR: Will Price
SCREENWRITER: Milton Subotsky

Thirteen-year-old Tuesday Weld stars as a schoolgirl who devises a money-lending scheme to earn cash for a prom dress after dad takes her charge account away. The story is below TV situation-comedy level but most of the bands are great. Little Frankie Lymon and the

Teenagers take top honors. The legendary Johnny Burnette Trio make their only film appearance. With the king of rock 'n' roll Alan Freed, Laverne Baker, Chuck Berry, the Moonglows, the Flamingos, and others. Connie Francis provides the singing voice for little Tuesday. It took nine days to film—in the Bronx. An extremely rare sound-track album was issued by Chess records.

ROCKABILLY BABY

1957 20th Century-Fox (B&W)
PRODUCER/DIRECTOR: William F. Claxton
SCREENWRITERS: Will George,
 William Driskill

A rockabilly movie with music by Les Brown? Two teens are forced out of town by local bigots when their mother (Virginia Field) is exposed as an ex-fan dancer. With Irene Ryan (*The Beverly Hillbillies*), Ellen Corby, Douglas Kennedy, Susan and Caryl Volkman, and Gene Roth.

ROCKET ATTACK U.S.A.

1960 Exploit Films (B&W)
PRODUCER/DIRECTOR: Barry Mahon

An amazing low-budget feature with tacky sets, great stock footage, and a romantic subplot. United States Intelligence sends spy John Mackay to obtain Sputnik secrets: the Soviets retaliate by launching a missile against New York. Manhattan is leveled. "Don't let this be—the end" is the finale title card. With Monica Davis, Dan Kern, and Edward Czerniuk. Davis and Mackay also appear in Mahon's *The Dead One*.

–CB

THE ROCKET MAN

1954 20th Century-Fox (B&W)
PRODUCER: Leonard Goldstein
DIRECTOR: Oscar Rudolph
SCREENWRITERS: Lenny Bruce, Jack Henley

Lenny Bruce co-wrote the screenplay for this comedy starring George "Foghorn" Winslow as a little boy whose space gun forces people to tell the truth. The honest cast includes Charles Coburn, Spring Byington, John Agar, Anne Francis, Beverly Garland, and Stanley Clements.

ROCKET SHIP: See *FLASH GORDON*.

595

George "Foghorn" Winslow with frog and space gun salutes in The Rocket Man.

ROCKET TO THE MOON: See CAT WOMEN OF THE MOON.

ROCKETSHIP X-M

1950 Lippert (B&W with color sequence)
PRODUCER/DIRECTOR/SCREENWRITER:
Kurt Neumann.

When United Artists and George Pal announced that *Destination Moon* was about to be shot, Robert Lippert's company quickly made *Rocketship X-M* (*Expedition Moon*) and got it out first, making it the first serious postwar science-fiction movie. The plot is simple—four men and one woman take off to the Moon, run into a meteor shower, and are knocked off course. They land on Mars (which is tinted pink), a planet devastated by atomic warfare and populated by deadly radiation-scarred mutants. All the astronauts die. The special effects team of Jack Rabin and Irving Block went on to other '50s hits like *Captive Women* and *Flight to Mars*. Cinematographer Karl Struss worked on *Island of Lost Souls* and many Neumann films. The music by Ferde Grofe (who wrote the "Grand Canyon Suite") was orchestrated by Albert Glasser and features a theremin, which was soon to be overused in other features. A sound-track album is available through *Starlog* magazine. The astronauts are Lloyd (*Sea Hunt*) Bridges, Osa Massen, Hugh (*Wyatt Earp*) O'Brian, John Emery, and Noah Beery, Jr. Morris Ankrum stays home. In 1978 Wade Williams shot new special effects scenes (in color) and added them to the restored original print. The long shots include actors dressed to look like the original cast. The "special edition" is available on videocassette; the original still plays on local television stations.

THE ROCKY HORROR PICTURE SHOW

1975 20th Century-Fox (England)
PRODUCER: Michael White
DIRECTOR: Jim Sharman
SCREENWRITERS: Jim Sharman,
Richard O'Brien

If this is the first film you're looking up, you probably know more about it than I do. You might also enjoy *Basket Case*, *Shriek of the Mutilated*, and *Strange Behavior*. (**R**)

RODAN

1957 Toho/DCA (Japan)
PRODUCER: Tomoyuki Tanaka
DIRECTOR: Inoshiro Honda
SCREENWRITERS: Takeshi Kimura,
Takeo Murata

Japanese miners are upset when they run into giant bugs in a cave. Then a *really* big pterodactyl hatches from an egg, eats the bugs, and flies around, causing untold destruction just by flapping its wings. Soon another big bird joins the fun. Cities crumble. People run (and scream).

ROGUE'S REGIMENT

1948 Universal (B&W)
PRODUCER/SCREENWRITER: Robert Buckner
DIRECTOR: Robert Florey

As an army intelligence officer in the French Foreign Legion, Dick Powell tries to track down an ex-Nazi officer (Stephen McNally) in the Orient. Vincent Price, ridiculous with a German accent, is a double-dealing antiques dealer. With Marta Toren, Carol Thurston, Richard Loo, and Philip Ahn.

ROLLERBALL

1975 United Artists
PRODUCER/DIRECTOR: Norman Jewison
SCREENWRITER: William Harrison

In the year 2018, James Caan is a star player of a violent elimination sport called Rollerball who becomes too popular for the totalitarian government. This mostly dull science-fiction dud, based on an *Esquire* short story, features ponderous classical music, Maud Adams, Ralph Richardson, John Houseman, and John Beck. *Death Race 2000*, made by New World for a fraction of *Rollerball's* budget, was far more successful in relation to its cost. **(R)**

ROLLERCOASTER

1977 Universal
PRODUCER: Jennings Lang
DIRECTOR: James Goldstone
SCREENWRITERS: Richard Levinson,
    William Link

George Segal and Richard Widmark try to catch madman Timothy Bottoms as he sabotages rollercoasters across the country. Though it's in Sensurround, it's not your usual disaster movie. The clever cult band *Sparks* is featured doing "Big Boy." With Henry Fonda, Susan Strasberg, Harry Guardino, and Tom Baker. Filmed on location at various amusement parks.

ROPE OF SAND

1949 Paramount (B&W)
PRODUCER: Hal B. Wallis
DIRECTOR: William Dieterle
SCREENWRITER: Walter Doninger

Another *Casablanca* imitation, with three of its stars. Burt Lancaster stars as a game hunter in Diamondstad, South Africa. Paul Henreid is his old enemy, a sadistic police commandant. Claude Rains runs the local diamond mine. Peter Lorre is Toady. With Corinne Calvet (making her U.S. film debut), Sam Jaffe, John Bromfield, and Mike Mazurki.

ROSEMARY'S BABY

1968 Paramount
PRODUCER: William Castle
DIRECTOR/SCREENWRITER: Roman Polanski

Polanski's classic witchcraft thriller based on Ira Levin's novel still looks great, even on TV. When Mia Farrow and her actor husband John Cassavetes move into the Dakota Apartments at 72nd and Central Park West, his career soars—but the price is high. The next-door neighbors (Ruth Gordon and Sidney Blackmer) seem like noisy eccentrics but they (and all the other older people except for Maurice Evans) are much more. Mia and John should have known something was wrong when they find out Elisha Cook, Jr., is the super. When Rosemary meets a woman in the laundry room she tells her she resembles actress Victoria Vetri. It's an inside joke because she really *is* Vetri, a former *Playboy* playmate (Miss September 1967) and star of *When Dinosaurs Ruled the Earth*, now using the name Angela Dorian. With Ralph Bellamy, Patsy Kelly, Hope Sommers, Charles Grodin, Almira Sessions, and the voice of Tony Curtis. Ruth Gordon won an Oscar. Producer Castle is seen in a phone booth. After his first big success, Polanski, whose wife had just been killed, went into a noncommercial period that resulted in *Macbeth* and *What?*

ROSEMARY'S BABY II: See LOOK WHAT HAPPENED TO ROSEMARY'S BABY.

ROSEMARY'S KILLER: See THE PROWLER.

ROUSTABOUT
1964 Paramount
PRODUCER: Hal B. Wallis
DIRECTOR: John Rich
SCREENWRITERS: Anthony Lawrence, Allan Weiss

Presley and Stanwyck! Elvis is Charlie Rogers, a handyman for Barbara Stanwyck's carnival. He likes to fight (he knows karate!), ride his motorcycle, and sing. His singing saves the ailing carnival and he wins the love of Joan Freeman. With Leif Erickson, Sue Ann Langdon, Pat Buttram, and Joan Staley (*Playboy's* Miss November 1958). Costumes by Edith Head. He sings 11 songs including "Poison Ivy League," "Wheels on my Heels," and "Big Love, Big Heartache." Watch for Raquel Welch in her film debut. Barbara Stanwyck's next was William Castle's *Night Walker.*

A ROYAL SCANDAL
1945 20th Century-Fox (B&W)
PRODUCER: Ernest Lubitsch
DIRECTOR: Otto Preminger
SCREENWRITER: Edwin Justis Mayer

Tallulah Bankhead as Catherine the Great, Czarina of Russia. Her lovers include William Eythe and Vincent Price as the French ambassador. Her court includes Charles Coburn, Sig Ruman, Anne Baxter, and Mischa Auer (a real Russian!). With Eva Gabor, Grady Sutton, Henry Victor, and various palace stooges and lackeys. Ernst

Lubitsch started directing it before calling in Preminger.

RUBY
1977 Dimension
PRODUCER: George Edwards
DIRECTORS: Curtis Harrington, Stephanie Rothman
SCREENWRITERS: George Edwards, Barry Schneider

Piper Laurie's career was revitalized when she played the fanatical mother in *Carrie.* She returned the next year to star in *Ruby,* as the owner of a drive-in theater who was once a gangster's moll. As her daughter, Janet Baldwin is possessed by a dead hood. Bullet holes appear on her face. People die. The drive-in screen shows *Attack of the 50 Ft. Woman.* The projectionist is found hanging from the film. A corpse is stuffed into a Coke machine. With Stuart Whitman and Roger Davis. Harrington was fired before the feature was done. (R)

RUMBLE ON THE DOCKS
1956 Columbia (B&W)
PRODUCER: Sam Katzman
DIRECTOR: Fred Sears
SCREENWRITERS: Lou Morheim, Jack Dewitt

A Katzman-Sears delinquency exposé, made to support their second Bill Haley party, *Don't Knock the Rock.* Teenage gang leader James Darren tries to get in with waterfront mobsters but wakes up when they terrorize his crippled father. With Laurie Carroll, Michael Granger, Jerry Janger, Dan Terranova, Tim Carey, and Bobby Blake (*Baretta*). Music by Freddie Bell and his Bellboys.
–CB

RUN ANGEL RUN
1969 Fanfare
PRODUCER: Joe Soloman
DIRECTOR: Jack Starrett
SCREENWRITERS: Jerome Wish, Valerie Starrett

Angel (big William Smith) quits the Devil's Advocates motorcycle gang after selling a biker-exposé story to a national magazine (*Like*). He settles on a California sheep ranch with his girlfriend (Valerie Starrett), but four of his sadistic ex-riding buddies show up seeking vengeance. Tammy Wynette sings the title song. The Soloman/Starrett/Smith team made *The Losers* next. (R)

RUN FOR THE HILLS
1953 Realart (B&W)
DIRECTOR: Lew Landers

Obscure H-bomb feature with Sonny Tufts (*Cat Women of the Moon*) as an insurance clerk who buys a cave and moves in with his family in order to survive an imagined nuclear attack. He worries when his funds run out, but a mild earthquake loosens a rock, revealing gold. A happy ending for Sonny and wife Barbara Payton. From the director of *Jungle Jim in the Forbidden Land*.

RUN, STRANGER, RUN: See HAPPY MOTHER'S DAY, LOVE GEORGE.

RUNAWAY DAUGHTERS
1956 AIP (B&W)
PRODUCER: Alex Gordon
DIRECTOR: Edward L. Cahn
SCREENWRITER: Lou Rusoff

From the ads: "The revolt of the teenagers!" Three itchy high schoolers lift a car and head for Hollywood, fleeing parents who are too strict, too lenient, and too drunk. Tragedy follows. One roars off a cliff in the heat of a highspeed chase; another must marry a serviceman to give her baby a name. The third returns to a reformed household with hope for a better tomorrow. Marla English, Anne O'Neal, and Gloria Castillo star, with Lance Fuller, Anna Sten, Adele Jergens, John Litel, and

Frank Gorshin. Originally a double feature with *Shake, Rattle and Rock*. —CB

RUNNING WILD
1955 Universal (B&W)
PRODUCER: Howard Pine
DIRECTOR: Abner Biberman
SCREENWRITER: Leo Townsend

Racketeer Keenan Wynn heads a gang of juvenile car thieves from his servicestation front. Rookie highway patrolman William Campbell infiltrates and gets to romance bad girl Mamie Van Doren while gathering evidence. Hotcar hoods include John Saxon, Jan Merlin, and Kathleen Case. —CB

RUSSIAN ROULETTE: See TWO BEFORE ZERO.

SST — DEATH FLIGHT
1977 TV
PRODUCER: Ron Roth
DIRECTOR: David Lowell Rich
SCREENWRITERS: Robert L. Joseph,
Meyer Dolinsky, William Roberts
ALSO RELEASED AS: SST—*Disaster in the Sky; Death Flight*

Peter Graves, Susan Strasberg, Regis Philbin, Bert Convy, Lorne Greene, Burgess Meredith, Doug McClure, Tina Louise, Martin Milner, Season Hubley, George Maharis, Billy Crystal, Barbara Anderson, Brock Peters, and Robert Reed are on America's first supersonic transport and they're headed for death! Would you miss any of them?

SST — DISASTER IN THE SKY: See SST — DEATH FLIGHT.

SABAKA: See THE HINDU.

SABU AND THE MAGIC RING
1957 Allied Artists
PRODUCER: Maurice Duke
DIRECTOR: George Blair
SCREENWRITERS: Sam Roeca,
Benedict Freedman, John Fenton Murray

Thirty-three-year-old Sabu Dastagir, the former "elephant boy," gets his name in the title (an honor previously reserved for Lugosi and Karloff) in this re-edited unsold television series by the director of *The Hypnotic Eye*. In a nod to *The Thief of Baghdad*, Sabu has a genie (William Marshall, of *Blacula*) to help fight the bad guys. With Vladimir Sokoloff and Daria Massey.

THE SAD SACK
1957 Paramount (B&W)
PRODUCER: Hal B. Wallis
DIRECTOR: George Marshall
SCREENWRITERS: Edmund Beldin,
Nate Monaster

Jerry Lewis comedy based on the *Sad Sack* comic strip with Phyllis Kirk, David Wayne, Gene Evans, Yvette Vickers, and Peter Lorre as Abdul, an Arab. It was Jerry's second film without Dino. Also with Shepperd Strudwick and Abraham Sofaer.

THE SADIST
1963 Fairway International (B&W)
PRODUCER: L. Steven Snyder
DIRECTOR/SCREENWRITER: James Landis
ALSO RELEASED AS: *The Profile of Terror*

NEVER BEFORE A MOTION PICTURE RAMPACKED WITH...

SUSPENSE... TERROR... SUDDEN SHOCK, AS THE **SADIST**

STARRING **ARCH HALL, JR.**

CO-STARRING
HELEN HOVEY • RICHARD ALDEN
MARILYN MANNING • DON RUSSELL
Written and Directed by JAMES LANDIS
Produced by L. STEVEN SNYDER

A FAIRWAY-INTERNATIONAL
IMPACT PICTURE!

WHAT FIENDISH PASSION TWISTED HIS MIND—MADE HIM TORMENT, TORTURE, KILL?

Teenage psychos terrorize three small-town high school teachers whose car has broken down near a deserted garage. Helen Hovey, Richard Alden, and Don Russell—en route to Dodger Stadium—are under the hood when Arch Hall, Jr., and Marilyn Manning appear. Arch shoots two motorcycle patrolmen, two teachers, and his companion before falling into a rattlesnake pit. Cinematography by Vilmos Zsigmond.   —CB

SAFARI DRUMS
1953 Allied Artists (B&W)
PRODUCER/DIRECTOR/SCREENWRITER:
Ford Beebe
Bomba (Johnny Sheffield) catches a killer with help from his animal friends. With Douglas Kennedy and Barbara Bestar.

SAGA OF THE VIKING WOMEN AND THEIR VOYAGE TO THE WATERS OF THE GREAT SEA SERPENT
1957 AIP (B&W)
PRODUCER/DIRECTOR: Roger Corman
SCREENWRITER: Louis Goldman
ALSO RELEASED AS: Viking Women and the Sea Serpent
Wins the awards for longest title and lowest budget for a historical spectacle with a sea monster. The cast (mostly in blonde wigs) includes Abby Dalton, Susan Cabot, Betsy-Jones Moreland, Jonathan Haze, Richard Devon, Gary Conway, June Kenney, and Michael Forrest. The statuesque Viking women rescue their men, who are prisoners on an island. Seventy minutes of "Huh?!"

THE ST. VALENTINE'S DAY MASSACRE
1967 20th Century-Fox
PRODUCER/DIRECTOR: Roger Corman
SCREENWRITER: Howard Browne

Not only is this Al Capone vs. Bugs Moran story reportedly pretty accurate, it also happens to be very entertaining in an odd way. Jason Robards stars as Capone. Ralph Meeker is Bugs. A narrator gives us precise time and location information leading up to the famous massacre. Some of the many other actors are George Segal, Jean Hale, Harold J. Stone, John Agar, Celia Lovsky, Alex D'Arcy, Bruce Dern, Jack Nicholson (as a chauffeur), Dick Miller, Jonathan Haze, and Barboura Morris. At the end, the narrator informs us: "Though no one is ever brought to trial for the slaughter, the killers all die violent deaths within 22 months."

THE SAINT'S DOUBLE TROUBLE
1940 RKO (B&W)
PRODUCER: Cliff Reid
DIRECTOR: Jack Hively
SCREENWRITER: Ben Holmes
George Sanders plays Simon Templar and his double, a smuggler. As a fellow crook, Bela Lugosi spends most of his time in a basement hideout. It was the fourth in a series of nine features. Pretty shoddy.

SALEM'S LOT
1979 TV
PRODUCER: Richard Kobritz
DIRECTOR: Tobe Hooper
SCREENWRITER: Paul Monash
A good but overlong TV horror movie from a novel by the incredibly popular Stephen King. Barlow (Reggie Nalder), a vampire patterned after Nosferatu, lives in a spooky New England mansion in the hometown of a successful writer (David Soul). James Mason is the bloodsucker's human aide. Mason's real-life wife, Clarissa Kaye, is a female

vampire. With Lew Ayres, Elisha Cook, Jr., Fred Willard (*Fernwood Tonight*), Marie Windsor, and Kenneth McMillan. Soul's young partner in vampire-hunting (Lance Kerwin) is a horror movie fan who fills his bedroom with monster models and posters. Originally a four-hour miniseries, it was released in Europe as a feature with stronger scenes added. *Frankenstein: The True Story*, James Mason's other TV movie, was given the same treatment. The bloodier theatrical version of *Salem's Lot* is shown on cable.

SAMSON

1961 Telewide (Italy)
DIRECTOR: Giafranco Parloni
ORIGINALLY RELEASED AS: *Sansone*

Brad Harris is Samson. Alan Steel is Samson's son. Brigitte Corey is Jamine. Alan Steel also played Hercules (and Maciste). Figure it out if you dare (or care). With Walter Reeves (not George or Steve) and Serge Gainsbourg (without Jane Birkin).

SAMSON AND THE SEVEN MIRACLES OF THE WORLD

1961 AIP (Italy)
PRODUCERS: Ermanno Donati, Luigi Carpentieri
DIRECTOR: Riccardo Freda
SCREENWRITERS: Oreste Biancoli, Duccio Tessari
ORIGINALLY RELEASED AS: *Maciste alla Corte del Ghan Khan*

Former Tarzan Gordon Scott plays Maciste, but he ends up being called Samson in the American prints. He goes to China, saves a princess (Yoko Tani), and fights Tartar rebels. It all ends when he causes an earthquake by moving a mountain in which he was buried alive.

SAMSON AND THE SLAVE QUEEN

1964 AIP (Italy)
PRODUCER: Fortunato Misiano
DIRECTOR: Umberto Lenzi
SCREENWRITERS: Guido Malatesa, Umberto Lenzi
ORIGINALLY RELEASED AS: *Zorro Contra Maciste*

Maciste (Alan Steel), called Samson in the dubbed version, fights Zorro (Pierre Brice) in the 15th century. They decide to join forces and defeat an evil queen. A major rewrite of historical legends, mixing times and continents.

SAMSON IN THE WAX MUSEUM

1963 AIP-TV (Mexico) (B&W)
PRODUCER: Alberto López
DIRECTOR: Alfonso Corona Blake
SCREENWRITERS: Fernando Galiana, Julio Porter

A mad scientist turns people into monsters and disguises them as exhibits in his wax museum. Santo the silver-masked wrestling hero (called Samson in the dubbed prints) defeats them all in five rounds. A K. Gordon Murray production.

SAMSON VS. THE GIANT KING

1964 Alexander Films (Italy) (B&W)
PRODUCER: Luigi Rovere
DIRECTOR: Amerigo Anton
SCREENWRITERS: Mario Moroni, Alberto de Rossi, Tanio Boccia
ORIGINALLY RELEASED AS: *Maciste alla Corte della Zar*

Kirk Morris as Samson (actually Maciste) has been frozen for centuries under the Russian tundra. Anthropologists thaw him out. He goes to St. Petersburg and leads the people in a revolt against the cruel czar. Maciste really gets around. It was shot in color but the American company was too cheap to make color prints.

SAMSON VS. THE VAMPIRE WOMEN

1961 AIP-TV (Mexico) (B&W)
PRODUCER: Luis Garcia DeLeon
DIRECTOR/SCREENWRITER:
Alfonso Corona Blake
ORIGINALLY RELEASED AS: *Santo Contra las Mujeres*

Sexy vampire women keep muscular male slaves on slabs in their atmospheric crypt. Santo the masked wrestling hero (called Samson in the dubbed version) defeats them all. A K. Gordon Murray production.

SAMURAI PIRATE: See THE LOST WORLD OF SINBAD.

SANDOKAN THE GREAT

1964 MGM (France/Italy/Spain)
PRODUCER: Solly V. Bianco
DIRECTOR: Umberto Lenzi
SCREENWRITERS: Fulvio Gicca,
Umberto Lenzi

As Sandokan, Steve Reeves takes his muscles to 19th-century North Africa, where he leads revolutionaries against the British, who have slaughtered his family. Featuring headhunters and a kidnaped British woman who decides she loves the Arab hero. It was the last of over a dozen juvenile historical adventures made in Italy starring the American-born ex-Mr. Universe. He made one more, *A Long Ride from Hell*, an R-rated Western.

SANTA CLAUS

1959 Azteca (Mexico)
PRODUCER: William Calderon
DIRECTOR: René Cardona
SCREENWRITERS: René Cardona,
Adolpho Portillo

Ho! Ho! Ho! Every winter for years K. Gordon Murray has dusted off his dubbed prints of this creaky south-of-the-border cheapie and made a bundle. From the ads: "See . . . the all-time-great Christmas classic! Seen by millions—bring the whole family." Santa teams up with Merlin the magician to fight the dreaded red devil. The devil, in tights and horns and the worst Spock ears ever seen, would fit right into a silent-era comedy. If Santa plays at your local shopping mall this year, by all means go and experience holiday exploitation at its finest.

SANTA CLAUS CONQUERS THE MARTIANS

1964 Embassy
PRODUCER: Paul Jacobson
DIRECTOR: Nicholas Webster
SCREENWRITER: Glenville Mareth

As bad as the Mexican *Santa Claus* is, residents of our own Long Island proved they could make a more inept, embarrassing movie and reap an even bigger profit! The spirit of Christmas shines through in one of the worst movies of any kind ever made. Santa and two Earth kids are kidnaped by green Martians and a robot. On Mars Santa is forced to make toys (by pushing buttons), is impersonated, plots a mini-rebellion, and returns to his happy dwarf elves "just in time for Christmas." The sets, props, and acting are all bottom-of-the-budget-barrel. Some cast members were from Broadway shows. Some of you might recognize little green Pia Zadora as Girmar. "Hooray for Santa Claus," the theme song, was released as a single and the exciting story was retold in a Dell comic book.

THE SATAN BUG

1965 United Artists
PRODUCER/DIRECTOR: John Sturges
SCREENWRITERS: James Clavell,
Edward Anhalt

Richard Basehart plays a modern mad scientist planning to wipe out the population of L.A. with a deadly virus serum. He practices on a Florida town first. Edward Asner and Frank Sutton help. George Maharis as a government agent and Anne Francis as General Dana Andrews' daughter try to stop the deadly organism. With John Anderson, Russ Bender, and Simon Oakland.

THE SATANIC RITES OF DRACULA
1973 Hammer/Dynamite
PRODUCER: Roy Skeggs
DIRECTOR: Alan Gibson
SCREENWRITER: Don Houghton
ALSO RELEASED AS: *Count Dracula and His Vampire Bride; Dracula Is Dead and Well and Living in London*

Christopher Lee, playing Dracula for the last time, has a brief speaking role in this modern day follow-up to *Dracula A.D. 1972.* Not content with his female vampire followers, he wants to control the entire world with the help of a scientist and black-death bacteria. As a descendant of Van Helsing, Peter Cushing stops Dracula, who ends up in a thornbush. Warner Brothers decided not to bother releasing the violent film, which sat around for five years before being released here by Dynamite. **(R)**

SATANIK
1968 (Spain/Italy)
PRODUCER: Romano Mussolini
DIRECTOR: Piero Vivarelli
SCREENWRITER: Eduardo M. Brochero

Ugly Magda Konopka uses a potion to become beautiful, but it backfires as usual, turning her into a horrible monster.

SATAN'S CHEERLEADERS
1977 World Amusements
PRODUCER: Alvin L. Fast
DIRECTOR: Greydon Clark
SCREENWRITERS: Greydon Clark, Alvin L. Fast

Four high school cheerleaders and a lady teacher are captured by hooded backwoods satanists led by sheriff John Ireland. His wife (Yvonne De Carlo) prays to a big eye fixed to a wooden star until dogs kill her. Yvonne's best dialogue: "Kill! Mutilate! Destroy!" One of the girls turns out to be a real witch and admonishes Ireland for ruining the maiden sacrifice by raping the only virgin—the teacher. With John Carradine as a crazy bum and Sydney Chaplin (*Land of the Pharoahs*) as a comic devil worshiper. The nonsense ends with the girls using satanic powers to help their football team. **(R)**

SATAN'S MISTRESS
1978 Manson International
PRODUCER/DIRECTOR: James Polakof
ALSO RELEASED AS: *Fury of the Succubus; Demon Rage; Dark Eyes*

Lana Wood stars as a bored rich California housewife who spends most of this movie naked while writhing around with an invisible spirit. Britt Ekland (who received star billing) has a small role as a psychic and John Carradine has an even smaller role as a priest (see *The Sentinel*). There's a guillotine in the basement and a few laughs to relieve the boredom. With Kabir Bedi. **(R)**

SATAN'S SADISTS
1969 Independent-International Films
PRODUCER/DIRECTOR: Al Adamson
SCREENWRITER: Dennis Wayne

The ads touted this one as a portrait of: "Human garbage—in the sickest love parties!" Russ Tamblyn stars in his second psychotic-biker role of 1969 (see *Free Grass*). He and his gang pass the time killing and raping college girls after putting LSD in their coffee. They're finally taught a lesson by a hitchhiking Vietnam vet. With misused oldtimers Scott Brady and Kent Taylor. The incredible Regina Carrol is "the freak-

out girl." Also with John Cardos, Robert Dix, Gary Kent, Bambi Allen, and future director Greydon Clark as Acid. Music by "The Nightriders." The sound track was on the Smash label. Probably the grossest biker movie of them all. (R)

SATAN'S SATELLITES: See ZOMBIES OF THE STRATOSPHERE.

SATAN'S SCHOOL FOR GIRLS
1973 TV
PRODUCERS: Aaron Spelling,
Leonard Goldberg
DIRECTOR: David Lowell Rich
SCREENWRITER: Arthur A. Ross
Pamela Franklin enrolls as a student at a private school in order to investigate the suicide of her sister. She discovers a satanic cult! Led by professor Roy Thinnes in a hooded cloak! With future *Charlie's Angels* Kate Jackson and Cheryl Ladd, Lloyd Bochner, and Jo Van Fleet.

SATAN'S SKIN: See THE BLOOD ON SATAN'S CLAW.

SATAN'S SLAVE
1976 Crown International (England)
PRODUCERS: Les Young, Richard Crafter
DIRECTOR: Norman J. Warren
SCREENWRITER: David McGillivay
Michael Gough leads a coven of witches in a gory shocker featuring Martin Potter (*Fellini Satyricon*). Warren later directed *Inseminoid*. (R)

SATAN'S TRIANGLE
1975 TV
PRODUCER: James Roykos
DIRECTOR: Sutton Roley
SCREENWRITER: William Read Woodfield
Helicopter pilots Doug McClure and Alejandro Rey visit the popular Bermuda triangle to rescue shipwrecked Kim Novak. A Danny Thomas production, not a Sunn Classic. With Jim Davis.

SATELLITE IN THE SKY
1956 Warner Brothers (England)
PRODUCERS: Edward J. and
Harry Lee Danziger
DIRECTOR: Paul Dickson
The world's first satellite is about to explode. Scientists rush to disarm a bomb and save the crew. With Kieron

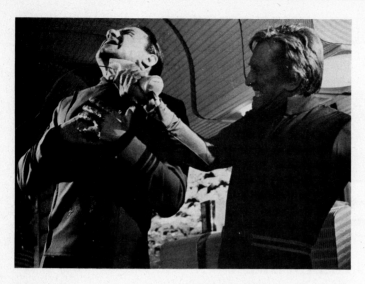

Kirk Douglas stabs Harvey Keitel with a plastic bottle in Saturn 3.

Moore, Lois Maxwell, and Donald Wolfit. Talky science fiction.

SATURDAY THE 14TH

1981 New World
PRODUCER: Julie Corman
DIRECTOR/SCREENWRITER: Howard R. Cohen
Despite the title, this is more a parody of old monster movies than of newer slasher films. Real-life husband and wife Richard Benjamin and Paula Prentiss play a couple who move into a haunted house. Their little boy (Kevin Brando) accidentally conjures up some creatures (left over from *Galaxina*), and some vampires pay a visit. With Severn Darden as Van Helsing, and Rosemary DeCamp (the 1949–50 edition of the *Life of Riley* series). Not to be confused with *Thursday the 12th*, a spoof directed by Alfred Sole, which is also known as *Pandemonium*.

SATURN 3

1980 Associated Film Distribution (England)
PRODUCER/DIRECTOR: Stanley Donen
SCREENWRITER: Martin Amis
Kirk Douglas and Farrah Fawcett run a hydroponic food factory on the third moon of Saturn. They get an unexpected visit from Harvey Keitel (whose Brooklyn accent, through the miracle of dubbing, has been replaced by a British one) and a robot named Hector. Harvey proves to be a psychopath on the run from Earth—and Hector shares his personality. John Barry, the production designer on *Star Wars* and the first *Superman* film, conceived the story and was director for the first two weeks of shooting, but "creative differences" with producer Donen sent him packing. He then joined the crew of the *Star Wars* sequel, and died of spinal meningitis before its completion. At least he escaped any blame for the boredom *Saturn 3* eventually generated. Though *Saturn 3* includes the only known film footage of Farrah Fawcett's bare right breast, two scenes were clipped prior to release in the interest of good taste— one where a drug-crazed Kirk Douglas imagines that he has killed Harvey Keitel, and one in which the psychotic robot tears Keitel into little pieces. **(R)** –BM

THE SAVAGE BEES

1976 TV
PRODUCER/DIRECTOR: Bruce Geller
SCREENWRITER: Guerdon Trueblood
Killer African bees go to Mardi Gras! They sting sheriff Ben Johnson, hero Michael Parks, bee expert Horst Buchholz, and Gretchen Corbett. This low-key TV movie is better than the B-epics that followed—*The Swarm* and *The Bees*—but that's not saying much. Don Kirshner was the co-producer. A theatrical release in Europe.

SAVAGE DRUMS

1951 Lippert (B&W)
DIRECTOR: William Berke
Sabu vs. commies who have taken over his mythical island country. Spies kill a visiting prince while Sabu is studying

in America. He rushes home with Sid Melton and a monkey to save the island paradise from the Reds. With H.B. Warner and Lita Baron. Former child star Sabu got top billing in a series of comical '50s adventures, then faded into supporting roles in the early '60s.

SAVAGE MUTINY

1953 Columbia (B&W)
PRODUCER: Sam Katzman
DIRECTOR: Spencer Gordon Bennett
SCREENWRITER: Sol Shor
Jungle Jim (Johnny Weissmuller) rounds up natives to flee their island, a site for A-bomb testing. Enemy agents tell the natives to stay. With Angela Greene and Lester Mathews.

THE SAVAGE SEVEN

1968 AIP
PRODUCER: Dick Clark
DIRECTOR: Richard Rush
SCREENWRITER: Michael Fisher
One of the best biker films features hero cyclists. Biker Chisum (Adam Roarke) loves Indian waitress Marie Little Hawk (Joanna Frank). Her brother (Robert Walker, Jr.) disapproves. The two groups join forces but crooked businessmen scheme to have them at each other's throats again. With Duane Eddy, Larry Bishop, John Cardos, and Beach Dickerson. The theme song, "Anyone for Tennis," is by Cream. Iron Butterfly are heard playing their classic "Iron Butterfly Theme." Clark and Rush made *Psych-Out* earlier in the year.

SAVAGES

1972 Angelika
PRODUCER: Ismael Merchant
DIRECTOR: James Ivory
SCREENWRITER: George W. S. Trow
In this satirical look at civilization, the savage mud people follow a croquet ball to an empty mansion. They gradually adopt modern dress and the appearance and manners of 20th-century idle rich people, then revert to their original state. The cast includes Thayer David, Ultra Violet, Sam Waterston, Susan Blakely (in her first screen role), and Lewis J. Stadlen. Filmed in Tarrytown, New York. By the director of *The Wild Party* and *Roseland*. **(R)**

SAVAGES FROM HELL

1968 Trans-International
PRODUCER: K. Gordon Murray
DIRECTOR: Joseph Prieto
SCREENWRITER: Reuben Guberman
ALSO RELEASED AS: *Big Enough and Old Enough*
High Test, leader of the Black Angels cycle gang, kidnaps a migrant farmworker's daughter after beating her brother for attracting his steady girl. Starring William P. Kelley as High Test, with Viola Lloyd, Bobbie Byers, Cyril Poitier, and Diwaldo Myers. Test is killed when he tries to rape his beautiful hostage. Filmed in Florida. **(R)** —CB

SCALPEL: See FALSE FACE.

SCANNERS

1981 Filmplan/Avco Embassy (Canada)
PRODUCER: Claude Heroux
DIRECTOR/SCREENWRITER: David Cronenberg

Robert Silverman as the crazed sculptor in David Cronenberg's Scanners.

A new strain of telepathic humankind is capable of such antisocial acts as taking control of other people's bodies and blowing up folks' heads in colorful liquid explosions. Dr. Ruth (*Secret Agent* man Patrick McGoohan) is a scientist with the ConSec Corporation, and has a vested interest in finding and controlling the mutant "scanners." Ruth sends a docile scanner to infiltrate the scanners' "terrorist underground," and to face his greatest enemy, Darryl Revok (Michael Ironside, the psychopath of *Visiting Hours*). The concluding scenes of telepathic battle benefit greatly from excruciating effects engineered by Dick (*The Exorcist*) Smith. Cronenberg did *Videodrome* next. **(R)**   –BM

SCARED STIFF

1953 Paramount (B&W)
PRODUCER: Hal B. Wallis
DIRECTOR: George Marshall
SCREENWRITERS: Herbert Baker, Walter de Leon

Dean Martin and Jerry Lewis in a remake of *The Ghost Breakers*, a 1940 Bob Hope mystery-comedy also directed by Marshall. The plot involves gangsters, ghosts, and a zombie on a Caribbean island. Lizabeth Scott is the love interest for Dino. Jerry imitates and sings with Carmen Miranda. Hope and Crosby put in guest appearances. Songs include "The Bongo Bingo" and "The Enchilada Man."

SCARED TO DEATH

1947 Screen Guild
PRODUCER: William B. David
DIRECTOR: Christy Cabanne
SCREENWRITER: W.J. Abbott

This almost surreal little film is remarkable for three reasons: it's in color, it's narrated by a woman's corpse, and it's the closest thing to a horror movie released in the lean year of 1947. Bela Lugosi (in a crooked, wide-brimmed hat and a Colonel Sanders tie) acts like he's in a trance. He lurks around peering in windows with dwarf pal Angelo Rossitto. Angelo, who was in two other Lugosi movies, also appeared in *Freaks* and played an alien in *Galaxina*. With villain George Zucco, idiot Nat Pendleton, one-time star Joyce Compton, and Douglas Fowley (who later directed *Macumba Love*). It's only 65 minutes long. Watch it closely and decide: Had the actors ever seen the script? Were some of them under the influence of a very disorienting drug? Fascinating in a different way from Bela's Ed Wood films.

SCARED TO DEATH

1980 Lone Star Films
PRODUCERS: Rand Marlis, Gil Shelton
DIRECTOR/SCREENWRITER: Bill Malone
ALSO RELEASED AS: *The Terror Factor*

Look out! It's a SynGenOr! It's in the sewers of your city! And it's out to get you! A modernized Frankenstein tale in which a DNA experiment run wild results in a SYNthetic GENetic ORganism (that's SynGenOr for short—it closely resembles the creature in *Alien*). The monster escapes the lab in Los Angeles and sticks its long sucking tongue down victim's throats. Lots of low-budget fun as the authorities, unable to cope with the unseen monster's strange M.O., put a hard-boiled private eye on the case. Director Malone and his filmmaking partner Bob Short were last seen attempting to launch a feature film based on TV's *The Man from U.N.C.L.E.* **(R)**   –BM

SCARFACE, SHAME OF A NATION

1931 United Artists (B&W)
PRODUCER/DIRECTOR: Howard Hawks
SCREENWRITERS: Ben Hecht, Seton I. Miller, John Lee Mahin, W.R. Burnett, Fred Pasley

Paul Muni is a thinly disguised Al Capone in this gangster classic featuring Boris Karloff as a rival hood who gets machine-gunned to death in a bowling alley. With Ann Dvorak, George Raft, and Karen Morley. Brian DePalma directed a 1983 remake starring Al Pacino.

THE SCARLET BLADE: See THE CRIMSON BLADE.

THE SCARLET CLAW

1944 Universal (B&W)
PRODUCER/DIRECTOR: Roy William Neill
SCREENWRITER: Edmund L. Hartman

Touted as "Holmes vs. Monster!" Well, not exactly, but it's one of the best Holmes movies. In La Morte Rouge, Canada, the detective exposes a phantom killer. With Gerald Hamer and Paul Cavanagh.

THE SCARS OF DRACULA

1970 Hammer/American Continental
Films (England)
PRODUCER: Aida Young
DIRECTOR: Roy Ward Baker
SCREENWRITER: Anthony Hinds

Christopher Lee is given more screen time than in other Dracula films. He also looks real pasty and dead. There's more sex and sadism than before and the special effects are awful. Somehow it's hard to take seriously a scene of a rubber bat on a string drooling into a coffin in order to revive his master. There are lots of phony big bats and death by lightning for Dracula. Dennis Waterman is the hero. Jenny Hanley is the main potential pinup victim. (R)

THE SCAVENGERS

1959 Valiant (B&W)
PRODUCER/SCREENWRITER: Eddie Romero
DIRECTOR: John Cromwell

Far East intrigue produced by Philippine blood-movie mogul Eddie Romero. Vince Edwards of *Ben Casey* stars as a former smuggler who spots missing wife Carol Ohmart in Hong Kong. New friends have gotten her involved with hard drugs as well as foreign bonds stolen from the Chinese Nationalist Government. Paramount tried to make Ohmart into Marilyn Monroe for a while. She played another drug addict in *Wild Youth*. Director Cromwell was a Hollywood veteran fallen on hard times. His films include the 1934 *Of Human Bondage*, with Bette Davis, and *The Goddess*, a 1958 dissection of a Monroe-like star, with Kim Stanley.

–CB

SCENT OF MYSTERY

1960 Scent of Mystery Productions
(England)
PRODUCER: Michael Todd, Jr.
DIRECTOR: Jack Cardiff
SCREENWRITER: William Roos
ALSO RELEASED AS: *Holiday in Spain*

Mike Todd, Jr., presented this technical marvel in "Glorious Smell-O-Vision!" It was originally planned by his late father. Only audiences in New

UPI 12/14/59: With a microphone poised overhead to pick up the sound, movie producer Michael Todd, Jr., gets an expensive shoe shine on the set in Hollywood. Requiring a shoe shine sound effect for his forthcoming Smell-O-Vision movie, Scent of Mystery, *Todd auditioned bootblacks from all over Southern California. Leroy Daniel (left) and Henry Carrier (center) proved to be the best cloth snappers and brush wielders around, so they got the job. The lucky bootblacks received $100 for less than an hour's work.*

York, Chicago, and L.A. had a chance to experience over 30 aromas, sent from the "Smell-O-Vision brain" through plastic tubes attached to each theater seat. Scents included wine, seafood, garlic, peppermint, bananas, pipe tobacco, perfume, and gunsmoke. The mystery feature filmed in Spain stars Peter Lorre as Smiley, a taxi driver, Diana Dors, Denholm Elliott, Paul Lukas, and Leo McKern. It was rereleased scentless in '62 and hasn't been shown much anywhere or any way since. A special cartoon co-feature called *The Tale of Old Whiff* was narrated by Bert Lahr. Until *Polyester* in '81 it was the only feature film that smelled.

SCHIZO

1977 Niles International (England)
PRODUCER/DIRECTOR: Pete Walker
SCREENWRITER: David McGillivray
ALSO RELEASED AS: *Amok; Blood of the Undead*

Lynne Frederick (Peter Sellers' last wife) stars as a woman hunted by a maniac. When she was a child she saw him murder her mother. With knife murders, a shower scene, a psychic brotherhood, and a surprise ending. With John Leyton, Stephanie Beacham, and John Fraser. At some showings, free smelling salts were handed out. (R)

SCHIZOID

1971 AIP (Italy/France/Spain)
PRODUCER: Edmondo Amati
DIRECTOR: Lucio Fulci
SCREENWRITERS: Lucio Fulci,
   Roberto Gianviti,
   José Luis Martinez Molla, Andre Tranche
ORIGINALLY RELEASED AS: *Una Lucertola con la Pelle di Donna*

A female killer and drug-induced hallucinations enhance this Euro-psycho movie filmed in London. Starring Stanley Baker and Florinda Bolkan. With Leo Genn and Jean Sorel. (R)

SCHIZOID

1980 Cannon
PRODUCERS: Menahem Golan,
   Yoram Globus
DIRECTOR/SCREENWRITER: David Paulsen
ALSO RELEASED AS: *Murder by Mail*

Some people thought hardworking Klaus Kinski would break away from cheap horror items after he achieved international fame in Werner Herzog films. Forget it. He just graduated to better-distributed cheap horror films. In this one he's a psychiatrist in sunny California who seems to be murdering his group-therapy patients with scissors. It appears that before each killing he mails threatening paste-up notes to Marianna Hill, a patient who writes a newspaper advice column. A ludicrous hit with hot tubs and a surprise (!) ending. (R)

SCHLOCK

1972 Jack Harris
PRODUCER: James C. O'Rourke
DIRECTOR/SCREENWRITER: John Landis
ALSO RELEASED AS: *The Banana Monster*

This first effort by the guy who hit the big time with *Animal House* mostly played midnight shows. Landis (then 22) also stars as a prehistoric ape man in this low-budget spoof. The convincing ape suit was designed by Rick Baker. Forrest J Ackerman, makeup expert John Chambers, and producer Jack Harris have bit parts. Including a *2001* spoof.

THE SCORPIO LETTERS

1967 TV
PRODUCER/DIRECTOR: Richard Thorpe
SCREENWRITERS: Adrian Spies, Jo Eisinger

Shirley (*Goldfinger*) Eaton and Alex Cord are spies after Scorpio, head of an international blackmail ring. Oscar Beregi is the bad guy in this TV Bond copy.

SCREAM AND DIE: See THE HOUSE THAT VANISHED.

SCREAM AND SCREAM AGAIN

1970 Amicus/AIP. (England)
PRODUCERS: Max J. Rosenberg, Milton Subotsky
DIRECTOR: Gordon Hessler
SCREENWRITER: Christopher Wicking

Wild and confusing horror with a great title and a mostly wasted cast. Vincent Price keeps busy creating perfect beings using limb and organ transplants. In a small role as a Nazilike foreign agent, Peter Cushing backs the project. Christopher Lee is also in a small role as a British agent. The best part is when Michael (*The Devils*) Gothard as a young creation drains the blood from

Klaus Kinski and axe in Schizoid.

some girls, is handcuffed by police, tears off his hand to escape, and jumps into a vat of acid. Later much of the cast ends up in the same vat. With Judy Huxtable and the Amen Corner.

SCREAM BABY SCREAM

1969 Westbury
PRODUCER/DIRECTOR: Joseph Adler
SCREENWRITER: Lawrence Robert Cohen

A demented artist kidnaps people and surgically disfigures them to provide models for his creepy paintings. Various students go to his mansion searching for missing friends and become "hideous creatures." Filmed in Miami. With Ross Harris. Music by the Odyssey. **(R)**

SCREAM BLACULA SCREAM

1973 AIP
PRODUCER: Joseph T. Naar
DIRECTOR: Bob Kelljan
SCREENWRITERS: Joan Torres, Raymond Koenig, Maurice Jules

This inevitable sequel, directed by the guy who did the Count Yorga films, pits Blacula (William Marshall) against a voodoo priestess (Pam Grier). The results are pretty laughable. Set in modern-day L.A., with parties, mod clothes, and a lot of new vampires. With Don Mitchell (from the *Ironside* series) and Richard Lawson.

SCREAM BLOODY MURDER

1972 Indepix
PRODUCER/DIRECTOR/SCREENWRITER:
  Robert J. Emery

A laughable tale of a killer with a hook hand. He lost his real hand while killing his father with a tractor. He kidnaps a prostitute after killing his mother and stepfather. From the ads: "Filmed in violent vision and gory color!" "So horrifying you need a blindfold to see it!" Theater patrons were given free blindfolds. (R)

SCREAM FREE: See FREE GRASS.

SCREAM OF FEAR

1960 Hammer/Columbia (England) (B&W)
PRODUCER/SCREENWRITER: Jimmy Sangster
DIRECTOR: Seth Holt
ALSO RELEASED AS: *Taste of Fear*

Hammer Films did a lot of less than thrilling psychological thrillers inspired by *Psycho*, but this was their first and it's great. You'll never figure out the ending or anticipate some of the plot twists. Susan Strasberg has her best role as Penny Appleton, a frightened woman in a wheelchair visiting her father's French villa. Stepmother Ann Todd tells her that Dad is away, but his dead body keeps showing up in odd places. Only Penny sees it. A doctor (Christopher Lee) tries to calm her down. An especially good scene concerns Dad's discovery at the bottom of the swimming pool. In nice, dark black-and-white.

SCREAM OF THE BUTTERFLY

1965 Emerson (B&W)
DIRECTOR: Ebar Lobato

Ray Dennis Steckler shot this story of a nymphomaniac who is murdered by her lover after explaining that she plans to stay on with her millionaire husband. The district attorney must decide whether to send Nick Novarro to prison or to a mental institution. Nelida Lobato is the victim, William Turner is her husband. Steckler directed *The Thrill Killers* the same year.   –CB

SCREAM OF THE DEMON LOVER

1971 New World (Italy/Spain)
PRODUCER/DIRECTOR: José Louis Merino
SCREENWRITERS: José Louis Merino,
  Enrico Columbo

A 19th-century baron has killer dogs and a monstrous brother scarred by fire. With Agostina Belli and a lot of anglicized names. It was co-billed with *Velvet Vampire*. (R)

SCREAM OF THE WOLF

1974 TV
PRODUCER/DIRECTOR: Dan Curtis
SCREENWRITER: Richard Matheson

A phony werewolf movie with Clint Walker as a macho sportsman trying to get his former best "pal" Peter Graves to leave his girlfriend (Jo Ann Pflug) and writing career so the two of them can go live in the woods together. Unexpected ideas from screenwriter Matheson.

SCREAM PRETTY PEGGY

1973 TV
PRODUCER: Lou Morheim
DIRECTOR: Gordon Hessler
SCREENWRITERS: Jimmy Sangster,
  Arthur Hoffe

Ted Bessell, co-star of the *That Girl* series, gets to prove how good he can act as a famous sculptor with a crazy sister. But since this is a substandard *Psycho* copy, he's the sister too! And Bette Davis is his overprotective mom! Sian-Barbara Allen is Peggy, who screams. By the director of *Scream and Scream Again*.

SCREAMERS
1979 New World (Italy)
PRODUCER: Lawrence Martin
DIRECTORS: Sergio Martino, Dan T. Miller
SCREENWRITERS: Sergio Donati,
Cesare Frugoni, Sergio Martino
ALSO RELEASED AS: *Isle of the Fishmen*,
Something Waits in the Dark

"Warning: In this film you will actually see a man turned inside out!" This tag line from the ads is totally untrue, made up to get people to see a childish Italian fantasy which New World brought over here and added new footage to. Some gory killings by a fish monster are featured in the new scenes. Some things never change. The stellar exploitation cast includes Barbara Bach, Richard Johnson, Beryl Cunningham, Joseph Cotten, Cameron Mitchell, and Mel Ferrer. Cameron and Mel are in the new American scenes. (R)

SCREAMING MIMI
1958 Columbia (B&W)
PRODUCERS: Harry Joe Brown,
Robert Fellows
DIRECTOR: Gerd Oswald
SCREENWRITER: Robert Blees

A great neglected sleazy psychological horror film starring Anita Ekberg. She sees a man get shot moments after he tried to knife her in a shower (two years before *Psycho*), so she goes to a psychiatrist (Harry Townes) for therapy. He falls in love with her and takes over her life, although she insists on continuing her career at the El Madhouse nightclub. Great filler is provided by Anita doing a very erotic strip/dance

to steamy music by the Red Norvo Trio. The club's tough owner (Gypsy Rose Lee) sings an incredibly bad song when Anita is late one night. The traumatized Anita is suspected of a series of murders. Each victim had purchased a contorted sculpture of a woman called the Screaming Mimi, which was created by her step-brother. He's the one who had shot her attacker. Handsome columnist Philip Carey figures it all out. Includes interesting photography and a killer dog named Devil. Based on the novel of the same title by Frederic Brown. The director later worked on *The Outer Limits* show.

THE SCREAMING SKULL
1958 AIP (B&W)
PRODUCER/SCREENWRITER: John Kneubuhl
DIRECTOR: Alex Nicol

A man tries to drive his new wife insane by placing skulls all over his Southern mansion, but the plan backfires. Some good moments with skulls popping up in a murky pool and screeching birds everywhere. The director plays the servant. The music is by Alex Gold, who did the score for *Exodus*. With John Hudson, a.k.a. William Hudson (Harry in *Attack of the 50 Ft. Woman*), and Peggy Weber.

THE SCREAMING WOMAN
1972 TV
PRODUCER: William Frye
DIRECTOR: Jack Smight
SCREENWRITER: Merwin Gerard

Olivia de Havilland, just out of the asylum, hears a voice from the ground. Of course nobody believes her when she tries to get help to dig up the unfortunate speaker. A real downbeat version of a Ray Bradbury story set in a very unfriendly Middle America.

With Ed Nelson, Joseph Cotten, and Walter Pidgeon.

SCREAMS OF THE WINTER NIGHT
1979 Dimension
PRODUCERS: Richard Wadsack, James L. Wilson
DIRECTOR: James K. Wilson
SCREENWRITER: Richard Wadsack

A 16mm feature shot in Natchitoches, Louisiana, consisting of several stories told by teenagers around a campfire. They feature a haunted house, a psychic killer, and the ever-popular Big Foot. Most people who have seen this probably own the videocassette.

THE SEARCH FOR BRIDEY MURPHY
1956 Paramount (B&W)
PRODUCER: Pat Duggan
DIRECTOR/SCREENWRITER: Noel Langley

An unsensational version of the best-selling book, supposedly based on a true incident. Louis Hayward hypnotizes Teresa Wright, who regresses and re-members her previous life as a 19th-century Irish woman. Every day, record-ings are made to document her past. With Kenneth Tobey, Nancy Gates, and Richard Anderson. The public couldn't get enough reincarnation and hypnotism during the next few years. See: *I've Lived Before, The Undead, Hold That Hypnotist, Spell of the Hypnotist.*

SEARCH FOR THE GODS
1975 TV
PRODUCER: Wilford Lloyd Baumes
DIRECTOR: Jud Taylor
SCREENWRITER: Ken Pettus

Kurt Russell goes to Taos, New Mex-ico, fights bad guys, and takes mesca-line. A pilot film for a series inspired by Erik von Däniken's books. With Ralph Bellamy, Stephen McHattie, and Raymond St. Jacques.

SEASON OF THE WITCH: See HUNGRY WIVES.

THE SECOND BEST SECRET AGENT IN THE WHOLE WIDE WORLD
1965 Embassy (England)
PRODUCER: Joseph E. Levine
DIRECTOR: Lindsay Shonteff
SCREENWRITERS: Howard Griffiths, Lindsay Shonteff
ALSO RELEASED AS: *Licensed to Kill*

An 007 copy with Tom Adams as agent Tom Vine. He and assistant Veronica Hurst protect Swedish scientist Karel Stepanek and his antigravity machine from the Russians. With Peter Bull and Judy Huxtable. Sammy Davis, Jr., sings the theme song, heard only in the American version. Adams was back in *Where the Bullets Fly.*

SECOND FIDDLE TO A STEEL GUITAR
1965 Marathon
ASSOCIATE PRODUCER: Edward R. Neely
DIRECTOR: Victor Duncan
SCREENWRITER: Seymour D. Rothman

Arnold Stang puts together a country music show after the cancellation of an Italian opera company his socialite wife (Pamela Hayes) has lined up for a benefit. The crowd is won over by Kitty Wells, Homer and Jethro, Webb Pierce, Faron Young, Minnie Pearl, Dottie West, Lefty Frizzell, Sonny James, George Hamilton IV, Del Reeves and friends, but stagehands Leo Gorcey and Huntz Hall get into mischief by fool-ing with the opera wardrobe. Stang thinks the dread Italians have arrived and goes after a musketeer with a mallet. Filmed in Nashville. Songs include "Hello Walls," "Honky Tonk Angels," and "Born to Lose."   –CB

SECOND HOUSE FROM THE LEFT: See *THE NEW HOUSE ON THE LEFT.*

SECONDS

1966 Paramount (B&W)
PRODUCER: Edward Lewis
DIRECTOR: John Frankenheimer
SCREENWRITER: Lewis John Carlino

A chilling tale of a bored middle-aged Scarsdale banker who undergoes plastic surgery and various transplants, emerging as Rock Hudson. The new, younger-looking man leaves his family (they think he died), moves to California to be an artist, and falls in love with Salome Jens. To his horror, he discovers that the corporation he paid to change him has other demands. With John Randolph as the pre-operation man, Will Geer, Jeff Corey, Richard Anderson, and Murray Hamilton. Great cinematography by James Wong Howe.

SECRET AGENT

1936 Gaumont (England) (B&W)
PRODUCERS: Michael Balcon, Ivor Montagu
DIRECTOR: Alfred Hitchcock
SCREENWRITER: Charles Bennett

A comic spy thriller with John Gielgud as a British agent come to Switzerland to kill an enemy agent. Madeleine Carroll pretends to be his wife. Peter Lorre (in his second Hitchcock movie) is a sexually twisted Eastern European disguised as a curly-headed Mexican with an earring. Robert Young, as the innocent American in love with Miss Carroll, turns out not to be what he seems and the wrong man is killed. With Lilli Palmer and Sebastian Cabot. Based on stories by Somerset Maugham.

SECRET AGENT SUPER DRAGON

1966 United Screen Arts (France/Italy/ W. Germany)
PRODUCER: Roberto Ambroso
DIRECTOR: Calvin Jackson Padget
SCREENWRITERS: Bill Coleman, Mike Mitchell, Remigio del Grosso, Roberto Ambroso
ORIGINALLY RELEASED AS: *New York Appelle Super Dragon*

A Venezuelan criminal starts conquering America by giving drugged candy and gum to college students in Michigan. Agent Super Dragon (Ray Danton) tracks the villain to Amsterdam. With Marisa Mell and Margaret Lee.

THE SECRET INVASION

1964 United Artists
PRODUCER: Gene Corman
DIRECTOR: Roger Corman
SCREENWRITER: R. Wright Campbell

UA gave Corman his biggest budget to date ($590,000!) to direct this World War II drama with a plot similar to *The Dirty Dozen* (which didn't come out until '67). Stewart Granger leads five criminals (Henry Silva, a killer, Raf Vallone, a gangster, Mickey Rooney, a demolitions expert, Edd Byrnes, a forger, and William Campbell, an art thief) in a mission to rescue an Italian general from a Nazi prison. Filmed on location in Yugoslavia. Who would have expected *this* in between Poe pictures? It was probably the best film role Edd "Kookie" Byrnes ever had.

THE SECRET LIFE OF WALTER MITTY

1947 RKO
PRODUCER: Sam Goldwyn
DIRECTOR: Norman Z. McLeod
SCREENWRITERS: Ken Englund, Everett Freeman

In his best movie, Danny Kaye plays a timid proofreader of pulp novels who imagines himself in heroic situations. Boris Karloff is great as a villain/ psychiatrist. Virginia Mayo is the girlfriend. With Milton Parsons, Frank Reicher, and Ann Rutherford. From James Thurber source material.

THE SECRET OF DR. ALUCARD: See A TASTE OF BLOOD.

THE SECRET OF DR. MABUSE

1964 (W. Germany/Italy/France) (B&W)
PRODUCER: Filmkunst
DIRECTOR: Hugo Fregonese
SCREENWRITERS: Ladislas Fodor, Brian Edgar Wallace
ORIGINALLY RELEASED AS: *Die Totesstrahlen der Dr. Mabuse*

The evil Dr. Mabuse (Wolfgang Preiss) gets his hands on a death ray in the last of six German-made Mabuse thrillers from the early '60s. Peter Van Eyck stars (it was his third appearance in the series) with Yvonne Furneaux (*The Mummy*—1959) and Toko Yani.

THE SECRET OF DORIAN GRAY: See DORIAN GRAY.

THE SECRET OF THE BLUE ROOM

1933 Universal (B&W)
DIRECTOR: Kurt Neumann

Advertised as: "The 10-star mystery drama!" Three men after the same woman are asked to spend the night in the room of a castle where a murder took place. The main stars are Lionel Atwill, Paul Lukas, Gloria Stuart (*The Old Dark House*), Edward Arnold, and Onslow Stevens. If it looks overly familiar, maybe you've seen one of the remakes: *The Missing Guest* ('38) or *Murders in the Blue Room* ('42). By the director of *The Fly*.

THE SECRET OF THE TELEGON

1960 Toho/Herts-Lion (Japan)
PRODUCER: Tomoyuki Tanaka
DIRECTOR: Jun Fukuda
SCREENWRITER: Shinichi Sekizawa
ORIGINALLY RELEASED AS: *Denso Ningen*

An electric man can teleport himself anywhere, kill people, and return unnoticed.

SECRETS OF A SOUL: See CONFESSIONS OF AN OPIUM EATER.

SEE NO EVIL

1971 Columbia (England)
PRODUCERS: Martin Ransohoff, Leslie Linder
DIRECTOR: Richard Fleischer
SCREENWRITER: Brian Clemens

A blind girl (Mia Farrow) goes to stay at her uncle's mansion. On the way, the uncle's car splashes mud on a young man's cowboy boots. Later, while Mia is out, the man with muddy boots slaughters the entire family. When she returns, he's ready and waiting. Written by Brian Clemens (*The Avengers* series).

SEED OF TERROR: See GRAVE OF THE VAMPIRE.

SEEDS OF DESTRUCTION

1952 Astor (B&W)
DIRECTOR: Frank Strayer

Kent Taylor stars as a Communist spy who assumes the identity of an imprisoned missionary and travels to the United States to spread destructive ideas. However, his brain is infected with Americanism and he renounces his former beliefs on an international radio broadcast. The missionary listens in his lonely cell. Featuring Gene Lockhart, Gloria Holden, and David Bruce. —CB

SEEDS OF EVIL
1974 KKI Films
ASSOCIATE PRODUCER:
Chalmer Kirkbride, Jr.
DIRECTOR/SCREENWRITER: Jim Kay
ALSO RELEASED AS: *The Gardener*

A talky fantasy filmed in Puerto Rico with ex-Warhol superstar Joe Dallesandro. As Carl, he grows odd plants for a rich Yankee woman living in South America while exercising a mental hold over her. All his previous employers died mysteriously. Some of his plants emit deadly fumes. In the end the pony-tailed Dallesandro turns into a tree. With Rita Gam and Katharine Houghton (*Guess Who's Coming to Dinner*). Terrible.

SEIZURE
1974 Cinerama (Canada)
PRODUCERS: Garrard Glenn,
Jeffrey Kapelman
DIRECTOR: Oliver Stone
SCREENWRITERS: Edward Mann, Oliver Stone

A badly distributed horror film made in Quebec starring ex-*Dark Shadows* vampire Jonathan Frid as a writer whose dreamed-up creations come to life. The incredible subconscious trio consists of Martine Beswick as the Queen of Evil, Henry Baker as a giant black executioner, and little Herve Villechaize as an evil bearded dwarf. Victims include Troy Donahue, Mary Woronov, Christina Pickles, and a dog. It was the first feature by the director of *The Hand*.

THE SENDER
1982 Paramount (England)
PRODUCER: Edward S. Feldman
DIRECTOR: Roger Christian
SCREENWRITER: Thomas Baum

A superior shocker that got lost amid the glut of early '80s slasher films and big-buck fantasies. Yugoslavian-born Zeljiko Ivanek plays a young mental-

GARDEN OF LOVE.... GARDEN OF DEATH, HE PLANTS THE

SEEDS OF EVIL

hospital patient known only as John Doe. He has a mysterious link with his ghostly mother (Shirley Knight) and the uncontrollable ability to make others experience his nightmares. Visions of rats, roaches, flames, and more unusual horrors are experienced without lasting physical harm. Kathryn Harrold (*Yes, Giorgio*) is a sympathetic doctor trying to remain rational while helping the troubled patient. A British production, partially filmed in Atlanta, Georgia. Director Christian did art di-

Jonathan Frid is manhandled by a product of his subconscious in Seizure.

rection for *Alien* and set decoration for *Star Wars*. **(R)**

LA SEÑORA MUERTE
1968 Columbia
PRODUCER: Luis Enrique Verarga
DIRECTOR: Jaime Salvador
SCREENWRITER: Ramon Obon, Jr.
A Mexican horror movie with John Carradine as a mad scientist who blackmails a horribly scarred woman (Regina Torne) into killing people. As a reward she becomes temporarily beautiful again. Probably never dubbed into English. With Elsa Cardenas and a Frankenstein monster. Made at the same time as *Pacto Diabolico*.

SENSUOUS VAMPIRES: See THE VAMPIRE HOOKERS.

THE SENTINEL
1977 Universal
PRODUCERS: Michael Winner, Jeffrey Konvitz
DIRECTOR/SCREENWRITER: Michael Winner
Another loser directed by Winner. This shocker filmed in Brooklyn Heights hits new lows in bad taste, which would be okay if it were any good, but . . . John Carradine as a mute priest guards the gate of Hell (in the basement of a nice brownstone). For all the acting he does they could have used a picture of John Carradine. When oddball tenant Burgess Meredith releases the small population of Hell, they turn out to be a mixture of actors with effective gory makeup by Dick Smith (*The Exorcist*) and real freaks, which is pretty unsettling. Another highlight is when nude lesbian cannibals Sylvia Miles and Beverly D'Angelo enjoy their dinner. Most of the movie is spent with Cristina Rains and Chris Sarandon as a modern couple with marital problems. Some of the many cast members with small, useless parts include Martin Balsam, Jose Ferrer, Ava Gardner, Arthur Kennedy, Eli Wallach, Christopher Walken (*The Deerhunter*), and Deborah Raffin. **(R)**

SERENADE
1956 Warner Brothers
PRODUCER: Henry Blanke
DIRECTOR: Anthony Mann
SCREENWRITERS: Ivan Goff, Ben Roberts, John Twist
Mario Lanza stars in a CinemaScope musical soap opera based on James M. Cain's novel. Mario sings a lot and is torn between Joan Fontaine and Sarita Montiel. Vincent Price is a cruel worldly impresario. With Vince Edwards and Edward Platt.

SERGEANT DEADHEAD THE ASTRONAUT!
1965 AIP
PRODUCERS: James H. Nicholson, Samuel Z. Arkoff
DIRECTOR: Norman Taurog
SCREENWRITER: Louis M. Heyward
An Air Force comedy with a *Beach Party* cast. Frankie Avalon gets to stumble through two roles again. As Sergeant Deadhead, he accidentally goes into orbit with a chimp and returns with an

aggressive new personality. His double (Sergeant Donovan), substituted to keep the embarrassing mistake quiet, is about to marry Deadhead's fiancée (Deborah Walley). With Harvey Lembeck, John Ashley, Buster Keaton, Eve Arden (who sings), Cesar Romero, Gale Gordon, Fred Clark, and two *Playboy* Playmates.

SERPENT ISLAND
1954 (B&W)
PRODUCER/DIRECTOR/SCREENWRITER:
Bert I. Gordon
Before the amazing *King Dinosaur*, Mr. B.I.G. made this voodoo thriller. Sonny Tufts (*Cat Women of the Moon*, *Run for the Hills*) stars with Mary Munday. Pretty memorable.

THE SERVANT
1963 Landau (England) (B&W)
PRODUCER/DIRECTOR: Joseph Losey
SCREENWRITER: Harold Pinter
A harrowing look at a master-servant relationship gone awry. As an efficient scheming Cockney valet, Dirk Bogarde manages to dominate the home of rich James Fox. He brings in "sister" Sarah Miles to be the maid and seduce Fox away from highborn fiancée Wendy Craig. The master ends up a wifeless mindless drunk, unable to control his servant's orgies. With Catherine Lacy, Patrick Magee, and screenwriter Pinter. Fox, who later went through another personality switch in *Performance*, must have taken these roles pretty seriously. He retired from acting in the early '70s and was "born again," only to announce a return to acting in the early '80s.

SERVICE DE LUXE
1938 Universal (B&W)
ASSOCIATE PRODUCER: Edmund Grainger
DIRECTOR: Rowland V. Lee
SCREENWRITERS: Gertrude Purcell,
Leonard Spigelgass
Twenty-seven-year-old Vincent Price makes his film debut opposite Constance Bennett in a "screwball" comedy about a New York City service bureau for the ultra rich. Charles Ruggles hires Bennett to keep his hayseed nephew (Price) from visiting him. Vinnie and Constance fall in love and marry. The next year Price was in *Tower of London*, by the same director.

THE SEVEN BROTHERS MEET DRACULA: See *THE LEGEND OF THE SEVEN GOLDEN VAMPIRES.*

SEVEN DAYS IN MAY
1964 Paramount (B&W)
PRODUCER: Edward Lewis
DIRECTOR: John Frankenheimer
SCREENWRITER: Rod Serling
A modern political horror story. As Chairman of the Joint Chiefs of Staff, Burt Lancaster plans a military coup when the President (Fredric March) signs a nuclear treaty with the Soviet Union. As a patriotic general, Kirk Douglas discovers the plot involving a secret missile base in Texas. With Ava Gardner, Edmond O'Brien, Martin Balsam, and, to remind you of its science-fiction overtones, Whit Bissell, Hugh Marlowe, George Macready, and Richard Anderson.

SEVEN DAYS TO NOON
1950 Mayer-Kingsley (England) (B&W)
PRODUCERS/DIRECTORS: John and
Roy Boulting
SCREENWRITERS: Frank Harvey, Roy Boulting
In this early antinuclear thriller, London is evacuated when a scientist (Barry Jones) threatens to destroy the city if the government doesn't ban the weapon he helped create. With Andre Morell and Olive Stone.

THE SEVEN FACES OF DR. LAO
1964 MGM
PRODUCER/DIRECTOR: George Pal
SCREENWRITER: Charles Beaumont

Excellent fantasy with Tony Randall as an old Chinese showman setting up his magic circus in a small Western town and changing the lives of its inhabitants. Randall also appears as Merlin the Magician, the blind Apollonius, the snake-haired Medea, Pan, and the Abominable Snowman. The seventh face is an animated serpent. As a librarian, Barbara Eden (*I Dream of Jeannie*) sees Pan as her secret love, newspaper editor John Ericson. Bad guy Arthur O'Connell sees himself as the snake. With an incredible scene showing a tiny fish growing into the Loch Ness Monster. Jim Danforth was one of the animators. For his contribution to this film, William Tuttle won the first of two Special Oscars for makeup (the second went to *Planet of the Apes* in '68) before makeup was established as a regular category in 1981. Also with Minerva Urecal, Lee Patrick, and Noah Beery. Tony Randall didn't like it. Includes scenes from Pal's *Atlantis, the Lost Continent*.

Professor Willingdon (Barry Jones) on the run in Seven Days to Noon.

THE SEVEN MINUTES
1971 20th Century-Fox
PRODUCER/DIRECTOR: Russ Meyer
SCREENWRITER: Richard Warren Lewis

After the success of *Beyond the Valley of the Dolls*, Meyer attempted a serious film about censorship and pornography based on Irving Wallace's similarly titled novel. The result is a mixture of boredom and laughs. Yvonne De Carlo stars as a senator from California. With Philip Carey (*Screaming Mimi*), Harold J. Stone, Edy Williams, Barry Kroeger (*Nightmare in Wax*), Alex D'Arcy, Wayne Maunder (the *Custer* TV series), Marianne McAndrew, Tom Selleck, and John Carradine as a drunken poet.

THE SEVEN PER-CENT SOLUTION
1976 Universal (England)
PRODUCER/DIRECTOR: Herbert Ross
SCREENWRITER: Nicholas Meyer

1976 was a big year for Sherlock Holmes. There was a TV-movie with Roger Moore (*Sherlock Holmes in New York*), Gene Wilder's spoof (*The Adventures of Sherlock Holmes' Smarter Brother*), and a touring revival of the play (*Sherlock Holmes*) with Leonard Nimoy. This one's the best of the Holmes offerings. Nicholas Meyer wrote the screenplay based on his bestselling novel (he later turned director with *Time After Time* and *Star Trek II: The Wrath of Khan*). Nicol Williamson is the famous detective. Watson (Robert Duvall) and Moriarty (Laurence Olivier) team up to trick Holmes into going to Vienna to meet Sigmund Freud (Alan Arkin). It seems Freud alone can cure Holmes' coke habit and Moriarty is a master villain only in Sherlock's mind. Vanessa Redgrave is kidnaped. Charles Gray is Mycroft. With Joel Grey and Samantha Eggar.

Tony Randall and Barbara Eden in George Pal's Seven Faces of Dr. Lao.

THE SEVENTH VICTIM

1943 RKO (B&W)
PRODUCER: Val Lewton
DIRECTOR: Mark Robson
SCREENWRITERS: Dewitt Bodeen,
    Charles O'Neal

Many consider this the best of Val Lewton's finely detailed low-budget thrillers. A devil cult in Greenwich Village is intent on eliminating former member Jean Brooks. Her sister (Kim Hunter) arrives to locate the missing woman and finds an apartment furnished with a chair and a noose. Darkness, loneliness, a restaurant called Dante's, and a surprising shower scene are all part of an amazingly grim story. With Tom Conway, Isabel Jewell, and Hugh Beaumont.

THE SEVENTH VOYAGE OF SINBAD

1958 Columbia
PRODUCER: Charles H. Schneer
DIRECTOR: Nathan Juran
SCREENWRITER: Kenneth Kolb

The best animated film since *King Kong* is set in an ancient fantasy world where anything can and does happen. Ray Harryhausen created the incredible giant cyclops that roasts men on a spit, a giant roc with a two-headed chick, a fire-breathing guardian dragon, and the famous skeleton warrior. As the evil magician Sokurah, Torin Thatcher shrinks Princess Parisa (Kathryn Grant) to six inches as part of a plan to obtain the magic lamp held by her fiancé, Sinbad (Kerwin Matthews). Sokurah creates a horrified snake woman and an invisible shield. The little princess meets the genie (Richard Eyer) in his colorful lamp prison and learns the magic words to free him. Nonstop wonders with a Bernard Herrmann score, still available on Varèse Saraband Records.

SEX KITTENS GO TO COLLEGE

1960 Allied Artists
PRODUCER/DIRECTOR: Albert Zugsmith
SCREENWRITER: Robert Hill
ALSO RELEASED AS: *Beauty and the Robot,*
    Beauty and the Brain

After producing *High School Confidential* and producing and directing *College Confidential*, the notorious Albert

Zugsmith was responsible for this all-star mess. As in his other school pictures, the star is Mamie Van Doren. She's a stripper with a high I.Q. who gets picked by Thinko the robot to head a university science department. As if Mamie weren't enough to handle, the cast is crowded with Tuesday Weld, Mijanou Bardot (Brigitte's sister), Mickey Shaughnessy, Louis Nye, Pamela Mason, Marty Milner, Jackie Coogan (Uncle Fester!), John Carradine, Vampira, Conway Twitty (he sings!), and two talented sons—Charles Chaplin, Jr., and Harold Lloyd, Jr. Woo Woo Grabowski plays himself.

SEX ON THE GROOVE TUBE: See CASE OF THE FULL MOON MURDERS.

THE SEXORCISTS: See THE TORMENTED.

SHADOW IN THE SKY
1952 MGM (B&W)
PRODUCER: William H. Wright
DIRECTOR: Fred Wilcox
SCREENWRITER: Ben Maddow
World War II vet Ralph Meeker returns home a shellshocked psychopathic wreck. His selfless sister (future First Lady Nancy Davis) lets him move in with her suburban family, but Meeker goes nuts every time it rains. James Whitmore, who had already starred with Nancy in The Next Voice You Hear, is the husband. With Eduard Franz and Jean Hagen (Night of the Blood Beast).

SHADOW OF CHINATOWN
1936 Victory (B&W)
PRODUCER: Sam Katzman
DIRECTOR: Robert F. Hill
SCREENWRITERS: Isador Bernstein, Basil Dickey
ALSO RELEASED AS: Yellow Phantom

Bela Lugosi is Victor Poten, a scientist criminal who hates Chinese and Caucasians. He is hired by San Francisco dragon lady Luana Walters to help keep tourists out of Chinatown. Bela, sometimes disguised as an Oriental, uses a hypnotism machine, bombs, and poisoned darts. Hero Herman Brix (Bruce Bennett) fights him. A feature version of this ridiculous 15-chapter serial was also released.

SHADOW OF EVIL
1964 Seven Arts (France/Italy)
PRODUCER: Paul Cadéac
DIRECTOR: André Hunebelle
SCREENWRITERS: Pierre Foucard, Raymond Borel, André Hunebelle, Michel Lebrun, Richard Caron, Patrice Rondard
ORIGINALLY RELEASED AS: Banco à Bangkok Pour O.S.S. 117
Kerwin Matthews as superagent OSS 117 goes to Bangkok and discovers a plot devised by Dr. Sinn (Robert Hossein) to exterminate "inferior races" with a deadly virus. Pier Angeli is rescued and loved by the famous Bond imitator. The world is saved and Dr. Sinn is thrown into a pit of contaminated rats. One of a series starring different actors. Matthews and Angeli were reunited six years later in Octaman.

SHADOW OF TERROR
1945 PRC (B&W)
ASSOCIATE PRODUCER: Jack Grant
DIRECTOR: Lew Landers
SCREENWRITER: Arthur St. Clair
Scientist Richard Fraser develops the A-bomb and dodges spies for 60 minutes. In true exploitation manner, this film was released right after the bombing of Hiroshima, beating out the competition. The mushroom cloud footage was added at the last minute. See Beginning or the End.

SHADOW OF THE CAT
1961 Universal (England) (B&W)
PRODUCER: Jon Pennington
DIRECTOR: John Gilling
SCREENWRITER: George Baxt

When André Morell and his servant murder his wife for her money, her pet cat successfully seeks revenge. The deaths of the terrified killers are shown through the eyes of the avenging kitty. With Barbara Shelley, Freda Jackson, and William Lucas.

SHADOW OF THE HAWK
1976 Columbia (Canada)
PRODUCER: John Kemeny
DIRECTOR: George McGowan
SCREENWRITER: Norman Thaddeus Vane

Canadian Indian legend fantasy filmed in Vancouver. Jan-Michael Vincent leaves the city with his reporter girl-friend (Marilyn Hassett) to discover his Indian roots. He finds old Chief Dan George and a lot of active evil spirits to fight.

SHADOW ON THE LAND
1968 TV
PRODUCER: Matthew Rapf
DIRECTOR: Richard C. Sarafin
SCREENWRITER: Nedrick Young

In the near future America is run by a fascist government! Two people plot a revolution. Various military types are played by Jackie Cooper, John Forsythe, and Myron Healey. With Gene Hackman and Carol Lynley. By the director of *Vanishing Point*.

SHADOW ON THE WALL
1950 MGM (B&W)
PRODUCER: Robert Sisk
DIRECTOR: Patrick Jackson
SCREENWRITER: William Ludwig

Nancy Davis (Reagan) has one of her best roles as Dr. Caroline Canford, a psychiatrist. Eight-year-old Gigi Perreau develops amnesia after witnessing

Nancy Davis (Reagan) as a psychiatrist in Shadow on the Wall.

her stepmother's murder. Her father (Zachary Scott) is blamed, convicted, and about to be executed! Can Nancy probe the child's mind in time to reveal the identity of the real killer? With Ann Sothern, John McIntire, Jimmy Hunt (*Invaders from Mars*) and Barbara Billingsley as Olga.

SHADOWMAN
1973 New Line (France)
PRODUCER: Raymond Froment
DIRECTOR: Georges Franju
SCREENWRITER: Jacques Champreux
ORIGINALLY RELEASED AS: *Nuits Rouges*

A red-masked supercriminal (Jacques Champreux) and his accomplice (Gayle Hunnicutt) are after the missing half of a treasure map. It was condensed to 88 minutes for a limited U.S. release. With Josephine Chaplin, Gert Frobe, and an army of revived corpses. From the director of *The Horror Chamber of Dr. Faustus* and *Judex*. Watch for it. An eight-chapter television serial (*L'Homme sans Visage*) with the same cast and characters was aired in 1974.

Fred MacMurray with his son, The Shaggy Dog.

THE SHAGGY DOG
1959 Buena Vista
PRODUCER: Walt Disney
DIRECTOR: Charles Barton
SCREENWRITERS: Bill Walsh, Lillie Hayward
The first Walt Disney live-action fantasy. It looks pretty good after over 20 years of increasingly unfunny variations of the same formula. As the son of mailman Fred MacMurray, Tommy Kirk finds a ring that turns him into a sheep dog. As such, he captures some spies. With Jean Hagen (*Panic in the Year Zero*), Annette Funicello, Cecil Kellaway, Tim Considine, and Strother Martin. Tommy and Fred returned in *The Absent-Minded Professor*.

SHAKE RATTLE AND ROCK
1956 AIP (B&W)
PRODUCER: James H. Nicholson
DIRECTOR: Edward Cahn
SCREENWRITER: Lou Rusoff
From the ads: "Rock 'n' roll vs. the squares." Deejay Michael "Touch" Connors tries to help teens open a rock club. The father (Sterling Holloway) of his girlfriend (Lisa Gaye) objects and takes the matter to court. An old newsreel showing snobbish Margaret Dumont as a Charleston dance contestant decides the case. (The same idea was used in

Don't Knock the Rock.) The kids win. Fats Domino sings "Ain't That a Shame" and "I'm in Love Again." With Joe Turner, Annita Ray, and others. It played with *Runaway Daughters*.

SHAME: See
THE INTRUDERS.

SHANKS
1974 Paramount
PRODUCER: Steven North
DIRECTOR: William Castle
SCREENWRITER: Ranald Graham
The last film directed by William Castle is an odd, uneven story starring Marcel Marceau as a mute puppeteer working for an old wrinkled scientist (also Marceau) who brings dead animals back to life with electricity. When the old man dies, his corpse (and a few others) are revived by the puppeteer and used against his enemies. Co-stars Tsilla Chelton and Philippe Clay are also mimes. Castle, who died in '77, has a cameo role.

THE SHAPE OF THINGS TO COME
1979 Film Ventures
PRODUCER: William Davidson
DIRECTOR: George McGowan
SCREENWRITER: Martin Lager
Another mindless *Star Wars* clone that has nothing to do with H. G. Wells except the use of the name Cabal. Jack Palance is the ridiculous Emperor/villain Omus. Carol Lynley is from the Moon. Barry Morse and John Ireland are older good guys. With cute robots. Harry Alan Towers was executive producer.

SHARK KILL
1976 TV
PRODUCER: Barry Weitz
DIRECTOR: William A. Graham
SCREENWRITER: Sandor Stern

Man vs. great white shark in a *Jaws* clone TV-movie with Richard Yniguez, Jennifer Warren, and Phillip Clark. By the director of *Change of Habit*.

SHAROD OF ATLANTIS: See UNDERSEA KINGDOM.

SHATTER: See CALL HIM MR. SHATTER.

SHE

1935 RKO (B&W)
PRODUCER: Merian C. Cooper
DIRECTORS: Irving Pichel,
  Lansing C. Holden
SCREENWRITER: Ruth Rose

The ads describe *She* as: "Young and beautiful for 500 years . . . and wicked every one of them!" In her only film role, future Congresswoman Helen Gahagan stars as "She who must be obeyed" in this incredible art-deco fantasy set in the lost kingdom of Kor. The cast of 5,000 dances and writhes around in *Flash Gordon*-style costumes on massive sets that would suit a Busby Berkeley film. Randolph Scott is the lucky explorer chosen for eternal life. Helen Mack, in a getup you won't believe, is prepared for sacrificing by high priest Gustav Von Seyffertitz. With Nigel Bruce and Noble Johnson. From H. Rider Haggard's novel. Music by Max Steiner.

SHE

1964 Hammer/MGM (England)
PRODUCER: Michael Carreras
DIRECTOR: Robert Day
SCREENWRITER: David T. Chantler

Ursula Andress is the beautiful Ayesha —"She who must be obeyed"— in Hammer's cut-rate version of H. Rider Haggard's novel. Two-thousand-year-old Ayesha rules the lost city of Kuma and wants adventurer John Richardson (whom she believes to be the reincarnation of her lover) to enter the flame of eternal youth. Major Holly (Peter Cushing) tries to calm things down, while Billali, the priest (Christopher Lee), has fun offering sacrifices. But Haumeid (Andre Morell) has a hard time controling the black slaves. *The Vengeance of She* was a sequel, without Andress.

THE SHE BEAST

1965 Europix (Italy/Yugoslavia)
PRODUCER: Paul M. Maslansky
DIRECTOR: Michael Reeves
SCREENWRITER: Michael Byron
ORIGINALLY RELEASED AS: *La Sorella di Satana*

The first feature by England's Michael Reeves (then 21) stars Barbara Steele as a tourist in Transylvania possessed by a vengeful ugly witch. Ian Ogilvy is her husband. Lots of odd gags about Communists in modern Eastern Europe make this a unique thriller. With John Karlson and Mel Welles (as the innkeeper). Unfortunately you only get to see Steele for about 15 minutes.

THE SHE CREATURE

1956 AIP (B&W)
PRODUCER: Alex Gordon
DIRECTOR: Edward L. Cahn
SCREENWRITER: Lou Rusoff

The ads tell you she was "Reincarnated as a monster from Hell!" When the great Lombardi (Chester Morris) hypnotizes sexy Marla English, her prehistoric sea-monster former self emerges from the sea to kill. Lombardi becomes famous by predicting the murders and splits the showbiz profits with rich partner Tom Conway. The highlight is the monster created by Paul Blaisdell. It has skin like the bottom of a dried lake, stringy blond hair, a tail, claws in its stomach, wings, and very large breasts! The popular creature was back without the breasts in *Voodoo Woman*,

also with Miss English. This reincarnation-craze horror movie also features Frieda Inescort and Lance Fuller. A double feature with *It Conquered the World*, it was remade as *Creature of Destruction*.

SHE DEMONS

1958 Astor (B&W)
PRODUCER: Arthur A. Jacobs
DIRECTOR: Richard E. Cunha
SCREENWRITERS: Richard E. Cunha,
 H.E. Barrie

A ridiculous Nazi war criminal turns beautiful women into ugly-faced monsters on his private island. The women, kept in bamboo cages, do a great ritual dance, and even the transformed ones retain their perfect bodies and wear brief animal-skin bikinis. Former *Sheena, Queen of the Jungle* Irish McCalla (39-24-37) shows up with Tod Griffin (the hero) and Victor Sen Young (ethnic comedy relief) to do battle with the bad guys (who have horrible German accents) in front of the very phony-looking sets. A true wonder. By the director of *Missile to the Moon*.

SHE DEVIL

1957 20th Century-Fox (B&W)
PRODUCER/DIRECTOR: Kurt Neumann
SCREENWRITERS: Kurt Neumann,
 Carroll Young

Mari Blanchard has TB. She's cured by a serum. Unfortunately it turns her into an indestructible chameleon-like killer! With Jack Kelly, who faced similar problems in *Cult of the Cobra* the same year, Albert Dekker, Blossom Rock (Grandma on *The Addams Family*), and X Brands.

SHE-DEVILS ON WHEELS

1968 Mayflower
PRODUCER/DIRECTOR: Herschell Gordon Lewis
SCREENWRITER: Louise Downe

Members of the "Man-Eaters," a violent female motorcycle gang, choose men from a "stud line" and battle hot rodders with chains. A character named Joe-Boy is decapitated; Honey-Pot is initiated during an orgy. A very popular gory movie by the director of *Blood Feast*. With Ruby Tuesday.

SHE FREAK

1966 Sonney-Friedman
PRODUCER/SCREENWRITER: David F. Friedman
DIRECTOR: Byron Mabe

A waitress (Claire Brennen) marries the owner of a seedy freak show and has an affair with a sadistic Ferris-wheel operator. Husband kills rival—goes to jail—waitress takes over show—fires "Shorty"—the freaks turn her into "one of them." A sleazy partial remake of *Freaks* from the producer of *Two Thousand Maniacs* and *Blood Feast*.

SHE GODS OF SHARK REEF

1956 AIP
PRODUCER: Ludwig H. Gerber
DIRECTOR: Roger Corman
SCREENWRITERS: Robert Hill, Victor Stoloff

Two brothers finds a tropical island inhabited entirely by pearl-diving women. The bad brother (Don Durant) tries to steal pearls and ends up as shark food. The good brother (Bill Cord) falls for a local maiden (Lisa Monteil) and saves her from a tribal sacrifice. This color adventure movie was filmed back to back with *Naked Paradise* on the island of Kauai and features some nice print bathing suits. Decca released the theme song, "Nearer My Love to You."

The She Demons *escape.*

THE SHE MAN

1967 Southeastern (B&W)
PRODUCER: Charles W. Brown, Jr.
DIRECTOR: Bob Clark
SCREENWRITERS: Bob Clark, Jeff Gillen

Army deserter hides under women's clothing and forces hormone pills on his former lieutenant, who must help "Dominita" run an extortion racket when not busy with French-maid duties. Starring Dorian Wayne, with Leslie Marlow and Wendy Roberts. Southeastern also distributed *The Wild Wild World of Jayne Mansfield*. Clark later hit the big time with *Porky's* in 1982.   —CB

SHE WAITS

1972 TV
PRODUCER/DIRECTOR: Delbert Mann
SCREENWRITER: Art Wallace

The dead Dorothy McGuire possesses the body of Patty Duke, the new wife of widower David McCallum. Lew Ayres is a doctor. From the director of *Marty*.

SHE WAS A HIPPY VAMPIRE: See *THE WILD WORLD OF BATWOMAN.*

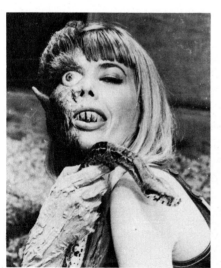

UPI 12/12/66: Hollywood makeup men are still transforming pretty girls into monsters for horror films. Starlet Claire Brennan is the latest to make the big switch for her role in She Freak.

Beautiful maidens in a LUSH TROPICAL PARADISE ruled by a HIDEOUS STONE GOD!

SHE GODS OF SHARK REEF

WIDE VISION COLOR

SHE'S WORKING HER WAY THROUGH COLLEGE

1952 Warner Brothers
PRODUCER: William Jacobs
DIRECTOR: Bruce Humberstone
SCREENWRITER: Peter Milne

Virginia Mayo is an ex-burlesque queen attending college. See Ronald Reagan as her meek professor get roaring drunk, fight Don Defore (Mr. Baxter on *Hazel*), defend showbiz people in a defiant speech, and put on a musical about inflation! Songs include "Give 'Em What They Want," "Love is Still for Free," and the title tune, lifted from *Golddiggers of 1937*. With Phyllis Thaxter, Gene Nelson, and Roland Winters. It was a remake of *The Male Animal* ('42). By the director of *Charlie Chan at the Opera* and *Tarzan's Fight for Life*. Nelson later directed *The Hand of Death*.

SHE-WOLF OF LONDON

1946 Universal (B&W)
PRODUCER: Ben Pivar
DIRECTOR: Jean Yarbrough
SCREENWRITER: George Bricker

Is June Lockhart, mother of Will and Penny (not to mention Timmy and Lassie), a murdering werewolf? Nope. Neither is Don Porter, Martin Kosleck, Dennis Hoey, or Lloyd Corrigan.

THE SHERIFF OF FRACTURED JAW

1959 20th Century-Fox (England)
PRODUCER: Daniel M. Angel
DIRECTOR: Raoul Walsh
SCREENWRITER: Arthur Dales

Jayne Mansfield out West. As saloon owner Kate, she rides, shoots, and sings —sort of. Connie Francis supplied the voice, Jayne moved her mouth. It's a British-produced sagebrush comedy shot in Spain starring Kenneth More as the English gent who becomes a sheriff. With Robert Morley, William Campbell, Henry Hull, and Bruce Cabot (*King Kong*).

SHERLOCK HOLMES AND THE DEADLY NECKLACE

1962 Screen Gems (W. Germany)
DIRECTORS: Terence Fisher,
  Frank Witherstein
SCREENWRITER: Curt Siodmak
ORIGINALLY RELEASED AS:
  Sherlock Holmes und das Halsband des Todas
ALSO RELEASED AS: *Valley of Fear*

Hammer stars and a Hammer director went to Germany to make this seldom seen Holmes adventure. Christopher Lee is Sherlock Holmes but somebody else dubbed his voice. Thorley Walters is Dr. Watson. Dr. Moriarty escapes at the end. It's considered an interesting failure. With Senta Berger. Lee went on to play Sherlock's brother in *The Private Life of Sherlock Holmes*.

SHERLOCK HOLMES AND THE SECRET WEAPON

1942 Universal (B&W)
ASSOCIATE PRODUCER: Howard Benedict
DIRECTOR: Roy William Neill
SCREENWRITERS: Edward T. Lowe,
  W. Scott Darling, Edmund L. Hartmann

Patriotic World War II propaganda with the evil Professor Moriarty (Lionel Atwill) joining the Nazis only to be foiled again by Sherlock Holmes (Basil Rathbone) most of whose blood has been drained. It was the second of three Universal war-themed Holmes films. The bad guys are after a new bomb, divided into four units and held secretly by four scientists. Based (loosely) on *The Adventure of the Dancing Men* by Arthur Conan Doyle. With regulars Dennis Hoey (as Lestrade) and Mary Gordon (as Mrs. Hudson). Also with Paul Fix and Philip Van Zandt as Nazis and William Post, Jr., as the inventor of the bomb. Director Neill did 11 Holmes films in four years.

SHERLOCK HOLMES AND THE SPIDER WOMAN
1944 Universal (B&W)
PRODUCER/DIRECTOR: Roy William Neill
SCREENWRITER: Bertram Millhauser

One of the most popular and bizarre Basil Rathbone Holmes movies. As the Spider Woman, the wonderful Gale Sondergaard keeps a black dwarf (Angelo Rossitto) in her suitcase and causes a series of "pajama suicides." She returned in '46 (with the Creeper Rondo Hatton) in *The Spider Woman Strikes Back*. This one is based on Arthur Conan Doyle's *The Sign of the Four*. Watch for great World War II propaganda in the finale at the carnival with Holmes tied behind a shooting gallery cut-out of Hitler. Watson is given a loaded rifle. With series regulars Gordon and Hoey.

SHERLOCK HOLMES AND THE VOICE OF TERROR
1942 Universal (B&W)
ASSOCIATE PRODUCER: Howard Benedict
DIRECTOR: Jack Rawlins
SCREENWRITERS: Lynn Riggs, Robert D. Andrews

Angelo Rossitto and Gale Sondergaard in Sherlock Holmes and the Spider Woman.

In the first of the Universal series, Sherlock Holmes and Watson find themselves inexplicably transported to World War II England where they're summoned by the British inner council to stop dangerous Nazi radio broadcasts. Holmes rounds up the saboteurs and delivers a stirring propaganda speech. Rathbone and Bruce soon returned in 11 more "modern" adaptations of Conan Doyle's stories. With Evelyn Ankers as Kitty, a dance-hall girl, Reginald Denny, Montagu Love, Henry Daniell, Thomas Gomez, and Mary Gordon as Mrs. Hudson. Based on *His Last Bow*.

SHERLOCK HOLMES FACES DEATH
1943 Universal (B&W)
ASSOCIATE PRODUCER/DIRECTOR: Roy William Neill
SCREENWRITER: Bertram Millhauser

After leaving Nazi villains behind and combing his hair, Sherlock Holmes (Basil Rathbone) and Watson (Nigel Bruce) began a series of more traditional adventures. This one, based on *The Musgrave Ritual*, concerns murders committed when the clock strikes 13 and a chessboard with human chess pieces. The underground crypt is the same set used in the 1931 *Dracula*. To remind viewers that a war was on, Milburn Stone shows up as a soldier. With Hillary Brooke, Peter Lawford, and series regulars Mary Gordon and Dennis Hoey. Director Neill did *Frankenstein Meets the Wolfman* the same year.

SHERLOCK HOLMES IN NEW YORK

1976 TV
PRODUCER: John Cutts
DIRECTOR: Boris Sagal
SCREENWRITER: Alvin Sapinsley

Roger Moore as Sherlock Holmes? In love with Charlotte Rampling? Not as bad as it sounds. Holmes and Watson (Patrick Macnee) save the world's gold supply, hidden under Union Square. John Huston is Moriarty. With Gig Young and Jackie Coogan. It was television's answer to *The Seven Per-Cent Solution*.

SHERLOCK HOLMES IN WASHINGTON

1943 Universal (B&W)
ASSOCIATE PRODUCER: Howard Benedict
DIRECTOR: Roy Neill
SCREENWRITERS: Bertram Millhauser, Lynn Riggs

In the third and last of the Holmes World War II–theme films, the detective is more out of place than ever. In 20th-century Washington, D.C., the sleuth tracks down vital microfilm documents hidden in a matchbook cover. George Zucco and Henry Daniell (who both played Moriarty) are the Axis villians. With Marjorie Lord. For some reason Rathbone had a very weird haircut in the three anti-Nazi movies.

THE SHINING

1980 Warner Brothers
PRODUCER/DIRECTOR: Stanley Kubrick
SCREENWRITERS: Stanley Kubrick, Diane Johnson

Jack Nicholson is great in this unconventional and chilling horror film destined to be regarded as a classic once the initial criticism is forgotten. Scenes and dialogue will linger in your mind years later. The massive Overlook Motel (actually sets) stars, along with Shelley Duvall, Scatman Crothers, little Danny Lloyd, and Barry Nelson. Based on Stephen King's novel. The Bela Bartok music is played by Wendy Carlos. See it again. **(R)**

SHOCK

1946 20th Century-Fox (B&W)
PRODUCER: Aubrey Schenck
DIRECTOR: Alfred Werker
SCREENWRITER: Eugene Ling

Vincent Price in his first starring role, and wouldn't you know that he plays a wife-killer psychiatrist. As Dr. Cross, he and his nurse (Lynn Bari) kill his wife, but a neighbor (Anabel Shaw) witnesses the crime. When the neighbor's husband (Frank Latimore) arrives home from a Japanese prison camp, Price easily convinces him that his wife is crazy and has her locked away. In the end justice prevails. This unsavory portrayal of a psychiatrist outraged serious critics at the time.

SHOCK: See BEYOND THE DOOR 2.

SHOCK CORRIDOR

1963 Allied Artists (B&W)
PRODUCER/DIRECTOR/SCREENWRITER: Samuel Fuller

Newspaper writer Peter Breck will do anything to win the Pulitzer Prize. He convinces stripper girlfriend Constance Towers to pose as his sister and have him committed to a mental institution in order to investigate the murder of a patient. He meets a devastating collection of traumatized Americans, is given shock therapy, exposes the killer orderly, wins the coveted prize, and becomes irreversibly insane. This amazing movie includes some of the most effective hallucination footage ever seen. Part of it was filmed by Fuller as early as 1955 and saved. With Gene Evans as a former nuclear scientist who now has the mind of a six-year-old, Philip Ahn, James Best (The Killer Shrews), and Hari Rhodes. Fuller's next was *The Naked Kiss*.

SHOCK TREATMENT
1964 20th Century-Fox (B&W)
PRODUCER: Aaron Rosenberg
DIRECTOR: Denis Sanders
SCREENWRITER: Sydney Boehm

Asylum fun with Lauren Bacall as a psychiatrist trying to trick patient Roddy McDowall into revealing where a fortune is hidden. Roddy, a gardener, had decapitated his rich employer with garden shears. An actor (Stuart Whitman) pretends he's crazy and is committed so he can find out Roddy's secret. Then he goes and falls in love with manic-depressive Carol Lynley. The scheming Bacall ends up a patient in her own hospital. You would, too. Director Sanders later did *Invasion of the Bee Girls*.

SHOCK WAVES
1977 Cinema Shares
PRODUCER: Reuben Trane
DIRECTOR: Ken Wiederhorn
SCREENWRITERS: John Harrison, Ken Wiederhorn
ALSO RELEASED AS: *Death Corps*

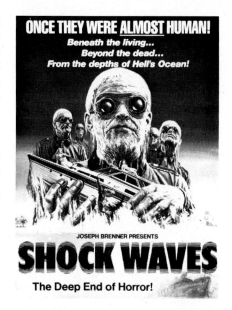

ONCE THEY WERE ALMOST HUMAN!
Beneath the living...
Beyond the dead...
From the depths of Hell's Ocean!

JOSEPH BRENNER PRESENTS

SHOCK WAVES
The Deep End of Horror!

A surprisingly good independent feature from Florida. An old sea captain (John Carradine) goes down with his ship during a storm but the survivors (including Brooke Adams and Luke Halperin of *Flipper*) find themselves stranded on a tropical island. Peter Cushing, a former S.S. officer, lives there with an army of blond super-Nazi zombies who live underwater. The scary creatures rise from their liquid graves and attack the cast. An effective old-fashioned non-gore movie. Alan Ormsby did the makeup.

SHOGUN ASSASSIN
1974/80 Toho/New World (Japan/U.S.)
PRODUCERS: Shintaro Katsu, Hisaharu Matsubara, David Weisman (U.S. version)
DIRECTORS: Kensi Misumi, Robert Houston
SCREENWRITERS: Robert Houston, David Weisman, Kazuo Koike

A Japanese film called *Baby Cart at River Styx* was shortened, dubbed, and re-edited for an American release. It's a gory surprise hit, with fight scenes

Lone Wolf and son in Shogun Assassin.

bloodier and more graphic than anything in a George Romero film. In Japan it was second in a series about Lone Wolf, a vengeance-seeking executioner who totes his little baby around in a specially rigged wooden cart. This 14th-century Oriental sword-and-sorcery adventure is better than most kung-fu films and pretty humorous (the baby narrates). An electronic sound track was added by Mark Lindsay, once singer with Paul Revere and the Raiders. Also with footage from *Sword of Vengeance*, the first Lone Wolf film. Based on a Japanese comic book. (R)

SHORT WALK TO DAYLIGHT
1972 TV
PRODUCER: Edward J. Montagne
DIRECTOR: Barry Shear
SCREENWRITERS: Philip H. Reisman, Jr., Gerald DiPego
New York City is destroyed by an earthquake! Eight people are trapped in a subway tunnel. With James Brolin, Don Mitchell, and about six others. From the director of *Wild in the Streets*.

THE SHOTGUN WEDDING
1963 Arkota
PRODUCER/DIRECTOR: Boris L. Petroff
SCREENWRITER: Edward D. Wood, Jr.
Wood's screenplay is about love trouble for a shanty-boat family stuck in the same mud for 30 years. One member wants to marry a fugitive carnival girl who loves a phony preacher. His son is locked into a Romeo-and-Juliet situation with a cantankerous moonshiner's daughter. Featuring Jenny Maxwell, Valerie Allen, Nan Peterson, J. Pat O'Malley, and Peter Colt. —CB

SHRIEK OF THE MUTILATED
1974 AM Films
PRODUCER: Ed Adlum
DIRECTOR: Michael Findlay
SCREENWRITERS: Ed Adlum, Ed Kelleher
The mutilated of the title are college students searching for Bigfoot. Serves 'em right. The white yeti creatures are actually men in fluffy costumes and one is the kids' professor (Tawn Ellis of *Cat Women of the Moon*). They're both cannibals! This inept New York State gore film is the perfect cure for viewers bored by endless "In search of the abominable big-footed yeti" docudramas. Including death by toaster, an Indian named Laughing Crow, and the hit song "Hot Butter." By the writer of *Invasion of the Blood Farmers* and the director of *Snuff*. With Jennifer Stock.

THE SHUTTERED ROOM
1967 Warner Brothers (England)
PRODUCER: Phillip Hazelton
DIRECTOR: David Greene
SCREENWRITERS: Nathaniel Tanchuck, Alex Jacobs

Filmed versions of H.P. Lovecraft stories usually don't quite make it. This one is no exception. Gig Young and Carol Lynley inherit an old mill house on an island off the coast of New England. As Aunt Agatha, Flora Robson knows the "horrible" secret of the locked room. Oliver Reed is a local troublemaker who helps make life miserable for the couple from New York City.

THE SIDEHACKERS: See FIVE THE HARD WAY.

THE SILENCERS

1966 Columbia
PRODUCER: Irving Allen
DIRECTOR: Phil Karlson
SCREENWRITER: Oscar Saul

No James Bond films came out in '66, so instead you could go to *Our Man Flint* or, if you were really desperate, one of two Matt Helm films starring Dean Martin and his exploding buttons and lame sex jokes. This, the first of the series, pits Dino against Tung-tze (Vic-

tor Buono), a supervillain from the Big O organization that wants to sabotage American atomic missiles. He also gets involved with Stella Stevens, Daliah Lavi, Nancy Kovack, Cyd Charisse (who sings the title song), and Beverly Adams as his secretary. With Arthur O'Connell, Robert Webber, and Richard Devon.

THE SILENT FLUTE: See CIRCLE OF IRON.

SILENT NIGHT, BLOODY NIGHT

1972 Cannon
PRODUCERS: Ami Artzi, Jeffrey Konvitz
DIRECTOR: Theodore Gershuny
SCREENWRITERS: Theodore Gershuny, Jeffrey Konvitz, Ira Teller, Ami Artzi
ALSO RELEASED AS: *Night of the Dark Full Moon, Death House*

Muddled but interesting shocker filmed in Oyster Bay, Long Island. Guest star Patrick O'Neal plays an ill-fated lawyer spending the night in an old mansion he's been hired to sell. James Patterson is the hulking owner. The horrible history of the ex-asylum is told in dark flashbacks in which a group of New York underground movie veterans (Ondine, Jack Smith, Tally Brown, and Candy Darling) play mental patients who take over the place. The modern scenes feature Mary Woronov, John Carradine as a mute newspaper editor, and a bloody axe. Producer Konvitz later wrote *The Sentinel*.

SILENT NIGHT, EVIL NIGHT

1974 Warner Brothers (Canada)
PRODUCERS: Bob Clark, Gerry Arbeid
DIRECTOR: Bob Clark
SCREENWRITER: Roy Moore
ALSO RELEASED AS: *Black Christmas; Stranger in the House*

Christmas Eve murders in a sorority house from the director of *Deathdream*

A cannibal snowman from Shriek of the Mutilated.

and *Porky's*. Olivia Hussey of *Romeo and Juliet* is the star screamer. With Keir Dullea, Margot Kidder, John Saxon (as a cop), and Andrea Martin (*SCTV*). The end is a real surprise. (**R**)

SILENT RUNNING

1971 Universal
PRODUCER: Michael Gruskoff
DIRECTOR: Douglas Trumbull
SCREENWRITERS: Deric Washburn, Mike Cimino, Steve Bochco

Bruce Dern, an expert at playing various demented characters, is a botanist-astronaut who resorts to murder in order to save the only Earth greenery left in the 21st century. A domed forest in a massive spaceship orbiting Saturn is to be destroyed by order of the government. To save it, Dern kills the other three crew members and lives with only three robots as companions. The friendly "drone" machines, actually containing legless human amputees, are incredibly lifelike. The director of this thoughtful, underrated look at a possible bleak future worked on the special effects for *2001: A Space Odyssey*. With Cliff Potts, Ron Rifkin, and Jesse Vint. TV viewing hint: turn off your volume every time Joan Baez warbles on the sound track, which is still in print.

SILENT SCREAM

1980 American Cinema Releasing
EXECUTIVE PRODUCERS:
Joan and Denny Harris
DIRECTOR: Denny Harris
SCREENWRITERS: Ken and Jim Wheat

A family with a horrible secret takes in college roomers. People die gory deaths. Cameron Mitchell and Avery Schreiber are an unlikely cop team who try to solve the crimes. The mad family includes Yvonne DeCarlo as the mother and Barbara Steele in a silent but very active role. A flashback showing a pregnant girl hanging herself reaches new heights of tastelessness. With Rebecca Balding. (**R**)

SILK STOCKINGS

1957 MGM
PRODUCER: Arthur Freed
DIRECTOR: Rouben Mamoulian
SCREENWRITERS: Leonard Gershe, Leonard Spigelgass

Musical remake of *Ninotchka* starring Fred Astaire and Cyd Charisse in the Melvyn Douglas and Greta Garbo roles. Peter Lorre, Joseph Buloff, and Jules Munshin (*On the Town*) are dancing comrades of the Russian woman. At one point they sing "We've got the red blues." It was the last completed film by the director of *Dr. Jekyll and Mr. Hyde* ('32).

SIMON, KING OF THE WITCHES

1971 Fanfare
PRODUCER: David Hammond
DIRECTOR: Bruce Kessler
SCREENWRITER: Robert Phippeny

Bearded Andrew Prine plays a modern warlock with a magic mirror. His home is a Los Angeles storm sewer. The ads claim that "He curses the Establishment." The psychedelic-trip plot confuses the audience. With Ultra Violet as the leader of a Satanic cult. Joe Solomon was executive producer. Prine went on to hits like *Grizzly* and *Centerfold Girls*. (**R**)

SINBAD AND THE EYE OF THE TIGER

1977 Columbia
PRODUCERS: Charles Schneer, Ray Harryhausen
DIRECTOR: Sam Wanamaker
SCREENWRITER: Beverly Cross

The third Sinbad adventure features some of Ray Harryhausen's best animated creations. There's a chess-playing baboon, a giant walrus, a friendly one-horned troglodyte, a mechanical gold minotaur, a sabre-tooth tiger, and three scary bug-eyed ghouls. Patrick Wayne is Sinbad this time. Also starring Taryn Power (daughter of Tyrone), Jane Seymour (as Princess Farah), and Margaret Whiting (as the evil Zenobia). It was the eleventh feature for the Schneer-Harryhausen team.

SING AND SWING

1963 Universal (England) (B&W)
PRODUCER/DIRECTOR: Lance Comfort
SCREENWRITER: Lyn Fairbanks
ALSO RELEASED AS: *Live It Up*
A pre-*Blowup* David Hemmings as a post-office messenger boy promises his father to disband his group, the Smart Alecs, if their tape doesn't make them successful. He loses the tape but later finds it, plays it for an American producer, and signs a contract. Inspirational. Gene Vincent is a guest star. Steve Marriott (of the Small Faces) and European rock star Heinz also sing and act.

SING, BOY, SING!

1958 20th Century-Fox (B&W)
PRODUCER/DIRECTOR: Henry Ephron
SCREENWRITER: Claude Binyon
Tommy Sands, as a Presley-style rock 'n' roll star, nearly cracks under the pressure of a crooked manager. With Edmond O'Brien (*The Girl Can't Help It*), John McIntire, and Lili Gentle. Based on a Kraft Playhouse TV show. Sands later married Nancy Sinatra. She had more hits.

SINGLE ROOM FURNISHED

1968 Crown International
PRODUCER/DIRECTOR: Matteo Ottaviano
SCREENWRITER: Michael Musto
Jayne Mansfield met Matteo Ottaviano (alias Matt Cimber) while co-starring with Mickey Hargitay in a Yonkers Playhouse production of *Bus Stop*. Smitten with raging love, Matt replaced Mickey

THE EVIL SPIRIT MUST CHOOSE EVIL!
THE BLACK MASS...THE SPELLS...THE INCANTATIONS...
THE CURSES...THE CEREMONIAL SEX...

JOE SOLOMON Presents
SIMON-KING of the WITCHES
Starring
ANDREW PRINE · BRENDA SCOTT
and GEORGE PAULSIN · NORMAN BURTON · GERALD YORK with ULTRA VIOLET
Executive Producer JOE SOLOMON · Produced by DAVID HAMMOND · Associate Producer THOMAS J. SCHMIDT
Directed by BRUCE KESSLER · Screenplay by ROBERT PHIPPENY · Music Composed and Conducted by STU PHILLIPS
METROCOLOR   PRODUCED AND RELEASED BY THE FANFARE CORPORATION

in the Pink Palace and soon found himself directing a movie. (Brianne Murphy, a woman cinematographer, claims that she and not Cimber directed this film, but I've never seen her name in the credits.) Jayne plays a young bride who dyes her hair and changes her name to wait tables after her husband leaves her pregnant. She changes her name again and becomes a prostitute. The downbeat feature ends when a sailor proposes, then shoots himself as Jayne humiliates him with taunts of "Monkee, mon-kee!" Jayne and Cimber had a tiff during the shooting and the production closed down while she took off for Florida to cool off. Her fatal car crash outside New Orleans occurred as she was on her way back to L.A. to resume her role. To compensate for her loss, footage is padded out with a side plot involving neighbors Flo (Dorothy Keller) and Charley (Fabian Dean). The photography is by Laszlo Kovacs. With Bruno Ve Sota as Mr. Donald Duck from Duluth and a lengthy introduction by Walter Winchell. Cimber followed with 49 positions of sexual intercourse in *Man and Wife* and Pia Zadora's *Butterfly*.   –CB

THE SINISTER URGE

1959 Headliner (B&W)
PRODUCER/DIRECTOR/SCREENWRITER:
Edward D. Wood, Jr.
ALSO RELEASED AS: *The Young and the Immoral; Hellborn*

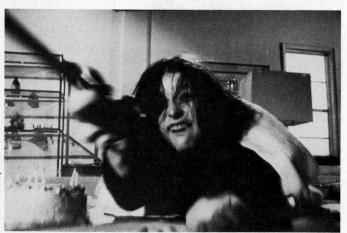

Margot Kidder in Brian DePalma's Sisters.

From the headline school of advertising: "Another sex maniac murder! Smut picture racket blamed! Police seek Dirk Williams!" Dino Fantini goes berserk watching a sex film and corners the leading lady in a city park. Police lieutenant Kenne Duncan and Sergeant James Moore seek to eliminate the killer and the film that caused the crime. With Jean Fontaine, Carl Anthony, Jeanne Willardson, Toni Costello, and April Lynn. The last film directed by the creator of *Plan 9 from Outer Space* is a fascinating adults-only time piece exploiting the field of pornography. Wood himself appears in a fight scene and posters for his movies decorate the wall of Johnny Ryde, the porn director, who claims he used to make good films. With an undercover cop in drag, one very brief nude scene, and a judge who warns us all about the price pornographers must pay.   –CB

SIREN OF ATLANTIS

1948 United Artists (B&W)
PRODUCER: Seymour Negenzul
DIRECTORS: Arthur Ripley, Douglas Sirk, John Brahm
SCREENWRITERS: Roland Leigh, Robert Lay
Maria Montez, in one of her last films, is the queen of the lost city of Atlantis. Jean-Pierre Aumont arrives with his legionnaires and love blossoms. With Henry Daniell, Dennis O'Keefe, and Allan Nixon. The editor got credit for directing. The real directors were too embarrassed.

SISTERS

1973 AIP
PRODUCER: Edward R. Pressman
DIRECTOR: Brian De Palma
SCREENWRITERS: Brian De Palma, Louisa Rose
Great first horror shocker by De Palma. Reporter Jennifer Salt is convinced that Danielle (Margot Kidder) is a killer. Danielle is/was a Siamese twin sepa-

rated from her sister by a creepy doctor lover (Bill Finley). Split-screen double images and some wonderful flashbacks and dream sequences tell the perverse story, which ranges from a bloody birthday celebration to the top of a telephone pole. Music by Bernard Herrmann. With Charles Durning and Lisle Wilson. Filmed on Staten Island. From a story by De Palma. (R)

THE SIX-MILLION DOLLAR MAN
1973 TV
PRODUCER/DIRECTOR: Richard Irving
SCREENWRITER: Henri Simoun
The pilot film for the popular series (1974–78) starring Lee Majors as the remade bionic test pilot. With Martin Balsam, Darren McGavin, and Barbara Anderson.

16 FATHOMS DEEP
1948 Monogram
PRODUCERS: James S. Burnett, Irving Allen
DIRECTOR: Irving Allen
SCREENWRITER: Max Trell
The ads promise "Spine-chilling thrills in the monster-ridden world beneath the sea!" With an odd cast including Arthur ("Dagwood") Lake, Lon Chaney, Jr., Lloyd Bridges (the future star of *Sea Hunt*), and Tanis Chandler. It's in "startling Ansco color!" It was a remake of an early-'30s Monogram feature, also with Chaney.

SKI FEVER
1967 Allied Artists (U.S./Austria/Czechoslovakia)
PRODUCERS: Wolfgang Schmidt, Mark Cooper
DIRECTOR: Curt Siodmak
SCREENWRITERS: Curt Siodmak, Robert L. Joseph
From the post-beach teen ski craze that never was, the misadventures of an American working his way through college as a ski instructor at a swinging Austrian resort. The employees, under contract to entertain female guests during off hours, wire one bed into a pinball machine and gamble their wages on fast scores. *Adam 12's* Martin Milner avoids the monkey business but has trouble proving it when Dean Martin's daughter Claudia becomes his raging desire. Vivi Bach, Dorith Dom, Dietmar Schonherr, and downhill champ Toni Sailor are featured. Watch for the choice Milner-inspired musical dream sequence. —CB

SKI PARTY
1965 AIP
PRODUCER: Gene Corman
DIRECTOR: Alan Rafkin
SCREENWRITER: Robert Kaufman
If you can get past Frankie Avalon and Dwayne Hickman in drag, you may enjoy wild musical action featuring the Hondells, James Brown and the Flames doing "I Got You (I Feel Good)," and

Lesley Gore. Frankie and Dwayne are Los Angeles college students on vacation in Sun Valley. They cross-dress to find out why all the best girls are interested in Aron Kincaid. Their cover is blown and a chase through Sawtooth National Forest follows. Co-starring Deborah Walley and Yvonne Craig, with Robert Q. Lewis and Annette Funicello.   —CB

SKI TROOP ATTACK

1960 Filmgroup (B&W)
PRODUCER/DIRECTOR: Roger Corman
SCREENWRITER: Charles Griffith

Frank Wolff and his men penetrate Germany's Huertgen forest and are trapped by enemy fire near their railroad-bridge objective. The mission is accomplished following a hair-raising encounter with Fräulein Sheila Carol, who shelters and then tries to poison them. Shot on location in Deadwood, South Dakota, where Michael Forrest, Wally Campo, Richard Sinatro, and the others defeated *The Beast from Haunted Cave*. Special guests—Roger Corman and team skiers from Deadwood and Lead high schools. As the ads put it, "They turned a white hell red with enemy blood!"   —CB

SKIDOO

1968 Paramount
PRODUCER/DIRECTOR: Otto Preminger
SCREENWRITER: Doran William Cannon

Most of the bad directors featured in this book work for small independent companies with impossibly low budgets and are unknown to the general public. Not so Otto Preminger, a famous, respected hack who was turning out incredibly bad films until very recently. This misguided counterculture comedy is his worst. A gangland boss recruits retired gangster Jackie Gleason to kill an imprisoned mobster (Mickey Rooney) who is about to testify to the Senate. Planted in the prison, Gleason takes acid, has some ridiculous hallucinations, and decides that violence is evil. To escape, Jackie spikes the prison soup with LSD and, while everybody goes nuts, he floats away in a garbage can held aloft by plastic-bag balloons. Carol Channing sings the title song and strips. John Phillip Law is Stash. Nilsson wrote the music and plays a drugged guard. With Frankie Avalon, Frank Gorshin, Peter Lawford, Burgess Meredith, George Raft, Cesar Romero, Arnold Stang, Slim Pickens, and Richard Kiel. Groucho Marx (totally wasted and unfunny in his last role) plays "God." Costumes designed by Rudi Gernreich. Assistant director—Erich von Stroheim, Jr.

THE SKULL

1965 Amicus/Paramount (England)
PRODUCERS: Milton Subotsky,
    Max J. Rosenberg
DIRECTOR: Freddie Francis
SCREENWRITER: Milton Subotsky

Robert Bloch's "The Skull of the Marquis De Sade" was the basis for this Peter Cushing horror film. Cushing plays a professor who buys a stolen skull from dealer Patrick Wymark. He soon wishes he hadn't. The evil skull floats around and wills him to murder people. With an impressive supporting cast and interesting photography. The long end sequence contains no dialogue. With Christopher Lee, Nigel Green, Michael Gough, George Coulouris, Patrick Magee, and Jill Bennett.

SKULLDUGGERY

1969 Universal
PRODUCER: Saul David
DIRECTOR: Gordon Douglas
SCREENWRITER: Nelson Gidding

Burt Reynolds tries to save a tribe of cute missing links found in New Guinea from being sold as slaves. He takes the case and the ape people to court. to prove they're human. The mix of comedy and social commentary just doesn't work. Vercors, the author of the novel this film is based on, had his name removed. If you wonder why Universal made this, remember that *Planet of the Apes* was a hit the previous year. The cast includes Susan Clark, Wilfrid Hyde-White, William Marshall, Pat Suzuki, and 24 University of Djakarta students as the "Tropis."

THE SKYDIVERS

1963 Crown International (B&W)
PRODUCER: Anthony Cardoza
DIRECTOR/SCREENWRITER: Coleman Francis
From the creator of *The Beast of Yucca Flats*. Newlywed jump-school owners are terrorized by a rich girl who's been jilted by her husband. She tries to destroy their business and their lives by monkeying with plane wiring and sabotaging chutes with corrosives. No happy ending for Tony Cardoza and his wife Beth (Kevin Casey). Marcia Knight, Eric Tomlin, and Titus Moede co-star; Jimmy Bryant and his Night Jumpers perform "Ha-So," "Tobacco Worm," and "Stratosphere Boogie."   –CB

SLAUGHTER HOTEL

1971 Hallmark (Italy)
PRODUCERS: Armando Novelli, Tizio Longo
DIRECTOR: Fernando Di Leo
SCREENWRITERS: Fernando Di Leo, Nino Latino
ORIGINALLY RELEASED AS: *La Bestia Uccide a Sangue Freddo*
ALSO RELEASED AS: *Asylum Erotica*
Klaus Kinski at his craziest, running a private asylum where inmates are tortured, decapitated, etc. With Margaret Lee and Rosalba Neri. Ads promised "The Slasher Massacre of eight innocent nurses!" **(R)**

SLAUGHTER OF THE VAMPIRES

1962 Pacemaker (Italy) (B&W)
PRODUCER: Dino Sant'Ambrogio
DIRECTOR/SCREENWRITER: Roberto Mauri
ORIGINALLY RELEASED AS: *La Stage dei Vampiri*
ALSO RELEASED AS: *Curse of the Blood Ghouls*
Yet another carbon-copy Italian vampire film. The bloodsuckers live in a castle and are defeated by a doctor with iron stakes. With Dieter Eppler and Walter Brandi (*The Vampire and the Ballerina*). Graziella Granata is a great-looking female vampire.

SLAUGHTER ON TENTH AVENUE

1957 Universal (B&W)
PRODUCER: Albert Zugsmith
DIRECTOR: Arnold Laven
SCREENWRITER: Lawrence Roman
Violence results when gangsters use brute force to subvert New York dockworkers' union. Richard Egan is the D.A. Great music, courtroom drama, and a waterfront battle. With Walter Matthau, Dan Duryea, Jan Sterling, Mickey Shaughnessy, Julie Adams, and Mickey Hargitay as "Big John."

SLAUGHTERHOUSE FIVE

1972 Universal
PRODUCER: Paul Monash
DIRECTOR: George Roy Hill
SCREENWRITER: Stephen Geller
As Billy Pilgrim, Michael Sachs is unstuck in time. His most memorable moments are spent in World War II Dresden, where his only real friend is shot by the Germans for not handing over a porcelain statue found in the ruins. Back in postwar America, he suffers through a prosperous but boring life with an irritating wife and a long-haired son (Perry King) who knocks over tombstones for fun. Then he finds happiness living with an actress (Valerie

Perrine) he once saw in a drive-in movie. They're both specimens living under a glass dome on an alien planet. The constant time changes are accompanied by Bach. Based on *Slaughterhouse Five or the Children's Crusade* by Kurt Vonnegut, Jr. With Robert Blossom (the star of *Deranged*). **(R)**

THE SLAVE
1962 MGM (Italy)
DIRECTOR: Sergio Corbucci
SCREENWRITERS: Adriano Bolzoni, Bruno Corbucci, Giovanni Grimaldi
ORIGINALLY RELEASED AS: *Il Figlio di Spartacus*
ALSO RELEASED AS: *Son of Spartacus*
Steve Reeves as Randus, son of Spartacus, leads a slave revolt in 48 B.C. The evil Grassus dies when molten gold is poured on his face. With Gianna Maria Canale.

SLAVE GIRLS: See PREHISTORIC WOMEN ('67).

SLAVE OF THE CANNIBAL GOD
1977 New Line (Italy)
PRODUCER: Luciano Martino
DIRECTOR: Sergio Martino
ORIGINALLY RELEASED AS: *Il Montagna di Dio Cannibale*
Stacy Keach helps the always sexy Ursula Andress search for her lost husband in the New Guinea jungle. After surviving many perils (including a giant python), they discover the lost man, dead and now worshiped as a deity by a cannibal tribe. In a scene later recreated in Ursula's one-time husband John Derek's *Tarzan* movie, she's stripped and painted by the natives in preparation for a ceremony that never happens. John and Bo must have studied this mediocre adventure for inspiration. With Helmut Berger. **(R)**

SLEEPER
1973 United Artists
PRODUCER: Jack Grossberg
DIRECTOR: Woody Allen
SCREENWRITERS: Woody Allen, Marshall Brickman
Greenwich Village health-food store owner Woody Allen goes to the hospital with ulcers and wakes up in 2173, disguises himself as a robot, and is sold to Diane Keaton. Lots of great gags and props are used in this inventive science-fiction comedy. Too bad Allen didn't anticipate how it would look on television. An often visible boom mike at the top of the screen is very distracting.

THE SLIME PEOPLE
1964 Hansen Enterprises (B&W)
PRODUCER: Joseph F. Robertson
DIRECTOR: Robert Hutton
SCREENWRITER: Vance Skarstedt
One solid hour of laughs as prehistoric creatures resembling rotten vegetables emerge from a sewer and take over Los Angeles. The monsters "from the bowels of the Earth" terrorize the tiny cast led by hero/director Robert Hutton. With Susan Hart, Les Tremayne, and Tom Laughlin.

SLITHIS
1978 Fabtrak
PRODUCERS: Stephen Traxler, Paul Fabian
DIRECTOR/SCREENWRITER: Stephen Traxler
ALSO RELEASED AS: *Spawn of the Slithis*
A '50s-style scaly monster, a product of nuclear pollution, attacks people in Venice, California. A good independent project with a fun publicity campaign. Free *Slithis* survival kits were given out at theaters and you could sign up for the *Slithis* fan club and receive a free photo.

SLUMBER PARTY MASSACRE

1982 New World Pictures
PRODUCERS: Amy Jones,
  Aaron Lipstadt
DIRECTOR: Amy Jones
SCREENWRITER: Rita Mae Brown

A short (77-minute), humorous, and gory no-frills slasher movie. A group of high school girl basketball players (and a few awkward male crashers) are attacked at a slumber party by a demented-looking, wide-eyed killer with a portable power drill. The guy just shows up; there's no time wasted on past events, revenge plots, or police. The script by feminist novelist Rita Mae Brown (*Rubyfruit Jungle*) makes the characters a bit more human than the usual stupid, drugged-out losers featured in most of these films, and parodies the clichés without sacrificing the pace or excitement. A classic of its kind. With Michele Michaels and Robin Stille. **(R)**

THE SNAKE PEOPLE

1968 Columbia (Mexico/U.S.)
PRODUCERS: Luis Enrique Vergara,
  Juan Ibañez
DIRECTORS/SCREENWRITERS: Jack Hill,
  J. Ibañez
ORIGINALLY RELEASED AS: *La Muerte Viviente*
ALSO RELEASED AS: *Isle of the Snake People*

Boris Karloff is Damballah, a voodoo cultist on an island, in one of the four quickie movies he shot scenes for in L.A. shortly before his death. With zombies, an evil dwarf, and Kalaea, the reptile woman.

THE SNAKE WOMAN

1961 United Artists (England)
PRODUCER: George Fowler
DIRECTOR: Sidney J. Furie
SCREENWRITER: Orville H. Hampton

On the moors during the 19th century Susan Travers kills by turning herself into a deadly cobra. It's all because her father injected her mother with snake venom. Scotland Yard man John Mc-Carthy investigates. Furie went on to direct *The Ipcress File* and *Lady Sings the Blues*.

SNAPSHOT: See THE DAY AFTER HALLOWEEN.

THE SNIPER

1952 Columbia (B&W)
PRODUCER: Stanley Kramer
DIRECTOR: Edward Dmytryk
SCREENWRITER: Harry Brown

Arthur Franz plays a homicidal maniac who murders women. He realizes his problem and seeks help. With Adolphe Menjou, Gerald Mohr, and Marie Windsor. See *Targets* and *The Deadly Tower* for more of the same. It was Dmytryk's first film since 1947 when he was branded one of the Hollywood Ten.

THE SNORKEL

1958 Hammer (England) (B&W)
PRODUCER: Michael Carreras
DIRECTOR: Guy Green
SCREENWRITERS: Peter Myers, Jimmy Sangster

Peter Van Eyck stars as a wife killer in a murder mystery made by Hammer just

UPI 5/5/78: It is final exam time on college campuses across the country. Students are occupied with passing grades and have little time for anything else. In this case, anything else is just the average monster out for a walk. It drew little more than a second glance from these two University of Nebraska students. The monster, a Slithis, *was in town to promote a movie.*

before the company began to concentrate on horror. With Betta St. John.

SNOW CREATURE
1954 United Artists (B&W)
PRODUCER/DIRECTOR: W. Lee Wilder
SCREENWRITER: Myles Wilder

Another inept feature by Billy Wilder's brother. An abominable snowman (a tall man wearing sewn-together furs covering everything but his face) is brought to Los Angeles and escapes! With Paul Langton and Leslie Denison. It was the first and possibly the worst abominable snowman film.

SNOW DEMONS: See SNOW DEVILS.

SNOW DEVILS
1965 MGM (Italy)
PRODUCERS: Joseph Fryd,
    Antonio Margheriti
DIRECTOR: Antonio Margheriti
    (Anthony Dawson)
SCREENWRITERS: Charles Sinclair,
    William Finger, I. Reiner, Moretti
ORIGINALLY RELEASED AS: I Diavoli dello Spazio
ALSO RELEASED AS: Snow Demons

Explorers Giacomo Rossi-Stuart (Jack Stuart) and Ombretta Colli (Amber Collins) discover humanoid survivors of the planet Aytia (abominable snowmen). Very boring.

SNOW WHITE AND THE THREE STOOGES
1961 20th Century-Fox
PRODUCER: Charles Wick
DIRECTOR: Walter Lang
SCREENWRITERS: Noel Langley,
    Elwood Ullman

Larry, Moe, and Curly Joe are traveling puppeteers who've adopted Prince Charming in this sappy version of the Grimm fairy tale. Patricia Medina is the witch/queen. Gul Rolfe is her advisor. Skating star Carol Heiss is Snow White. With Buddy Baer and Blossom Rock, but not enough insults and eye-gougings. It was a box-office failure.

SNOWBEAST
1977 TV
PRODUCER: Wilfred Lloyd Baumes
DIRECTOR: Herb Wallerstein
SCREENWRITER: Joseph Stephano

A Jaws inspired abominable-snowman TV-movie. The beast terrorizes a ski resort. Bo Svenson plays husband to Yvette Mimieux, who encountered scarier creatures in The Time Machine. With Sylvia Sydney and Clint Walker. You never even get to see the monster.

SNOWMAN: See LAND OF NO RETURN.

SNUFF
1976 Selected Pictures (Argentina/U.S.)
DIRECTOR: Allan Shackerton

Morbid curiosity tricks millions into paying to see dull unconvincing film! Irate film reviewers provide maximum publicity by condemning phony movie! Tacked on to a 1971 Argentinian picture called Slaughter was a new, badly done sequence in which a woman, hired to act in a movie, is shown being cut apart. The badly done special effects fooled no one except reviewers who hadn't even watched the film. Patrons were taught not to believe what they read in the papers. Snuff ended up second-billed to The Slasher with Farley Granger, but is now a favorite of sick videocassette collectors. (X)

SO SAD ABOUT GLORIA
1973 Centronics
PRODUCER/DIRECTOR: Harry Thomason
SCREENWRITER: Marshal Riggan

A disturbed woman (Lori Saunders) is being driven insane (again) by a phony apparition and Dean Jagger. Pretty useless axe-murder cheapness by the makers of *Encounters with the Unknown.*

SOLARIS

1972 Magna (U.S.S.R.)
DIRECTOR: Andrei Tarkovsky
SCREENWRITERS: Andrei Tarkovsky,
Friedrich Gorenstein

Excellent 2 hour and 45 minute long Soviet science-fiction epic based on a novel by Stanislaw Lem. Astronauts on an alien planet are confronted by illusions from their subconscious memories. Better than *2001.*

SOLE SURVIVOR

1970 TV
PRODUCER: Walter Burr
DIRECTOR: Paul Stanley
SCREENWRITER: Guerdon Trueblood

A general (Richard Basehart) returns to the Libyan site of a World War II air crash he survived. The ghosts of the crew members appear and accuse him of desertion. With Vince Edwards, William Shatner, and Patrick Wayne.

SOME CALL IT LOVING

1973 Cine Globe
PRODUCER/DIRECTOR/SCREENWRITER:
James B. Harris

Jazz musician Zalman King buys a sleeping beauty (Tisa Farrow) from a seedy carnival. A strange fantasy with a drugged-out Richard Pryor and a bald nun. By the director of *The Bedford Incident.* (R)

SOME GIRLS DO

1969 United Artists (England)
PRODUCER: Betty E. Box
DIRECTOR: Ralph Thomas
SCREENWRITERS: David Osborn,
Liz Charles-Williams

Richard Johnson returns as the space-age Bulldog Drummond. James Villiers

and his army of beautiful female robots try to conquer the world. With Daliah Lavi, Sydne Rome. Vanessa Howard, and guest star Robert Morley.

SOME MAY LIVE: See IN SAIGON, SOME MAY LIVE.

SOMEONE BEHIND THE DOOR

1971 Avco Embassy (France/England)
PRODUCER: Raymond Danon
DIRECTOR: Nicolas Gessner
SCREENWRITERS: Jacques Robert, Marc Behm,
Nicholas Gessner, Lorenzo Ventavoli

Mad brain surgeon Anthony Perkins takes home amnesia victim Charles Bronson and reprograms his memory so he'll kill Perkins' wife Jill Ireland. Perkins is his usual nervous, flighty self but seeing Bronson act like a disoriented zombie is pretty strange.

SOMEONE IS WATCHING ME

1978 TV
PRODUCER: Anna Cottle
DIRECTOR/SCREENWRITER: John Carpenter

A Peeping Tom with a telescope has bugged Lauren Hutton's high-rise apartment and terrorizes her with phone calls. Nobody believes her but friend Adrienne Barbeau, who tries to help. A superior made-for-TV thriller with some obvious similarities to *Rear Window.* With David Birney.

SOMETHING EVIL

1972 TV
PRODUCER: Alan Jay Factor
DIRECTOR: Steven Spielberg
SCREENWRITER: Robert Clouse

Sandy Dennis, Darren McGavin, and their kids move into a possessed Pennsylvania farmhouse. Their son is Johnny Whittaker (Jody on *Family Affair*). This early Spielberg effort shares some similarities with his later production, *Poltergeist.* With Jeff Corey, Ralph Bellamy, and, in bit parts, AIP regular Bruno Ve Sota and the director himself.

SOMETHING IS OUT THERE: See DAY OF THE ANIMALS.

SOMETHING WAITS IN THE DARK: See SCREAMERS.

SOMETHING WEIRD

1966 Mayflower
PRODUCER/SCREENWRITER: James F. Hurley
DIRECTOR: Herschell Gordon Lewis
A love story about an ugly witch restoring the handsome face of a man scarred in a high-tension-wire accident. The accident gave him extrasensory perception and the power of telekinesis. He becomes a famous fortune-teller and goes to Chicago to help police solve a crime. One of Lewis' obscure non-hit horror movies.

SOMEWHERE IN TIME

1980 Universal
PRODUCER: Stephen Deutsch
DIRECTOR: Jeannot Szwarc
SCREENWRITER: Richard Matheson

Playwright Christopher Reeve is transported into the past to be with his true love, stage actress Jane Seymour. A romantic fantasy that, despite the presence of Superman and some critical acclaim, was ignored by the paying moviegoers of America. It went on to become a smash hit in Japan, however. With Christopher Plummer. Music by John Barry. —BM

SON OF BLOB

1972 Jack Harris Enterprises
PRODUCER: Anthony Harris
DIRECTOR: Larry Hagman
SCREENWRITERS: Jack Woods, Anthony Harris
ALSO RELEASED AS: *Beware! The Blob*

Some smartass recently re-released this comedy sequel as "the movie J.R. shot!" That's right, Larry Hagman actually directed and has a bit part as a hobo consumed by the blob. As in the original, a teen couple (Robert Walker, Jr., and Gwynne Gilford) are the ones who warn the town, but it's not the '50s anymore and even the presence of guest stars as victims doesn't help much. Godfrey Cambridge starts the story by accidentally drinking part of the blob. He's eaten from the inside out. The pulsating, featureless creature next invades a party and a bowling alley. Carol Lynley, Shelly Berman, and Burgess Meredith (as Hagman's companion) also show up as blob food. With Cindy Williams.

SON OF DR. JEKYLL

1951 Columbia
DIRECTOR: Seymour Friedman
SCREENWRITER: Edward Heubsch
As the son, Louis Hayward sets out to prove Dad was no killer, but then he becomes one himself. Horror films were

not fashionable in 1951. This one's pretty restrained. It turns out that Hayward only *imagines* that he becomes Mr. Hyde. With Alexander Knox and Jody Lawrence.

SON OF DRACULA
1943 Universal (B&W)
PRODUCER: Ford Beebe
DIRECTOR: Robert Siodmak
SCREENWRITER: Eric Taylor

A neglected highlight of Universal's horror years stars Lon Chaney, Jr., as Count Alucard (the backward-spelled name was copied many times in inferior movies). He goes to Louisiana and recruits the willing Louise Allbritton as his vampire bride. Robert Paige is her confused ex-boyfriend, Evelyn Ankers her sister. Chaney can turn into mist or a bat in this atmospheric one-shot, which makes no attempt to tie in with the other Universal Dracula films. No son of Dracula is involved.

SON OF DRACULA
1974 Cinemation (England)
PRODUCER: Ringo Starr
DIRECTOR: Freddie Francis
SCREENWRITER: Jay Fairbanks

Ringo's horror-comedy flop stars Harry Nilsson as Count Down, son of Dracula. Pretty funny so far. Ringo is Merlin the Magician. Also with Dennis Price as Van Helsing, dead rock drummers Keith Moon and John Bonham, and the still living Peter Frampton. It premiered in Atlanta.

THE SON OF FLUBBER
1962 Buena Vista (B&W)
PRODUCER: Walt Disney
DIRECTOR: Robert Stevenson
SCREENWRITERS: Bill Walsh, Don Da Gradi

Fred MacMurray returns in his *Absent-Minded Professor* role, helps the Medfield football team win with "flubbergas," breaks all the glass in town with a weather gun, loses his wife (Nancy Olson), and is taken to court by Keenan Wynn. Protégé Tommy Kirk went on to star in *The Misadventures of Merlin Jones*. With Ed Wynn, Charlie Ruggles, William Demarest, Paul Lynde, and Stuart Erwin.

SON OF FRANKENSTEIN
1939 Universal (B&W)
PRODUCER/DIRECTOR: Rowland V. Lee
SCREENWRITER: Willis Cooper

Basil Rathbone stars as Wolf in the last of the Karloff/Frankenstein trilogy. He revives his father's creation, mute again and with a new furry vest. Bela Lugosi steals the show as Igor, the vengeful shepherd who uses the monster to kill members of the jury who sentenced him to hang. As inspector Krogh, Lionel Atwill loses his arm to the monster. The "friendly giant" kidnaps Wolf's little boy to insure cooperation. All the sets are twisted and photographed with strong shadows, making it a unique film to look at, as well as the last in Universal's Frankenstein series to make much sense. Lugosi returned as Igor in *The Ghost of Frankenstein*, but without Karloff, the monster became a stumbling cliché.

SON OF GODZILLA
1968 Toho/AIP-TV (Japan)
PRODUCER: Tomoyuki Tanaka
DIRECTOR: Jon Fukuda
SCREENWRITERS: Shinichi Sekizawa, Kazue Shiba
ORIGINALLY RELEASED AS: *Godzilla no Musuko*

An egg hatches and out comes a cute little dinosaur, Minya. Godzilla is a she!? Mom(?) protects the new kid from a giant spider and giant praying mantises. They both go into hibernation in the snow. The most juvenile, comical Godzilla movie to that time.

From Son of Ingagi, *an early all-black horror film.*

This instant, light-hearted sequel to *King Kong* was made in a rush, on half the original's budget. Carl Denham (Robert Armstrong) flees the ruins of midtown Manhattan and heads back to Skull Island. The crew mutinies and sets Denham, the captain, the Chinese cook, and a stowaway circus girl from Java (Helen Mack) adrift in a rowboat. They find a smaller, friendly white gorilla stuck in quicksand. It was nowhere near the hit the original *Kong* was, sealing the fate of animated fantasies for years. With Frank Reicher, Noble Johnson, and Victor Wong from the earlier film. The special effects were again by Willis O'Brien and the music by Max Steiner. Merian C. Cooper was executive producer.

SON OF SAMSON

1960 Medallion (France/Italy/Yugoslavia)
PRODUCERS: Ermando Donati,
Luigi Carpentieri
DIRECTOR: Carlo Campogalliani
SCREENWRITER: Oreste Bioncoli
ORIGINALLY RELEASED AS: *Maciste Nella Valle dei Re*

Mark Forest as Maciste (son of Samson) fights an evil queen and leads a slave revolt. The American muscleman Forest played Maciste in a half-dozen Italian quickies. By the time the films got to America, Maciste always had a new name (Hercules, Samson, Goliath, Fred, etc.).

SON OF INGAGI

1940 Sack Amusement (B&W)
PRODUCER/DIRECTOR: Richard C. Kahn
SCREENWRITER: Spencer Williams, Jr.

Ingagi, a 1930 roadshow hit, was a phony "African documentary" featuring an ape carrying around topless native women. Its success led to many imitations. This totally unrelated film features an all-black cast and is about love-starved apeman Ingeena (Zack Williams) who kidnaps a bride and takes her to his basement laboratory. It's described as a mystery-comedy. Laura Bowman, Alfred Grant, and Spencer Williams star with the Four Toppers. Williams (who wrote the story) later played Andy on *The Amos 'n' Andy Show.*

SON OF KONG

1933 RKO (B&W)
ASSOCIATE PRODUCER: Archie Marshek
DIRECTOR: Ernest B. Schoedsack
SCREENWRITER: Ruth Rose

SON OF SINBAD

1953 RKO (3-D)
PRODUCER: Robert Sparks
DIRECTOR: Ted Tetzlaff
SCREENWRITER: Aubrey Wisberg,
Jack Pollexfen
ALSO RELEASED AS: *Nights in a Harem*

Howard Hughes presents Sinbad (Dale Robertson) and his comical sidekick Omar Khayyam (Vincent Price) battling the forty thieves. In typical Hughes fashion the thieves are all beautiful women and they're in "Superscope"! The veiled lovelies include Sally Forrest, former stripteaser Lili St. Cyr, and Mari Blanchard. Kim Novak is also in there somewhere. Hughes held up the release for two years, letting it get a reputation as a "hot" film. A group of sexy "Sinbadettes" toured the country by train promoting it. The movie was just a pathetic way for Hughes to keep his promises to an endless line of young starlets.

SON OF SPARTICUS: See THE SLAVE.

THE SONG OF BERNADETTE
1943 20th Century-Fox (B&W)
PRODUCER: William Perlberg
DIRECTOR: Henry King
SCREENWRITER: George Seaton
As a French peasant girl in 1858, Jennifer Jones sees a vision of the Virgin Mary (Linda Darnell). As the prosecutor who tries to have her put in an asylum, Vincent Price gets cancer. The cast includes Lee J. Cobb, Gladys Cooper, Sig Ruman, Jerome Cowan, Alan Napier, Edward Van Sloan, Fritz Leiber, Dickie Moore, and many, many others.

THE SORCERERS
1967 Tigon/Allied Artists (England)
PRODUCERS: Patrick Curtis,
Tony Tenser
DIRECTOR: Michael Reeves
SCREENWRITERS: Michael Reeves, Tom Baker
Twenty-three-year-old Michael Reeves directs 70-year-old Boris Karloff as Professor Monserrat in an interesting tale of mind control. Boris and his wife (Catherine Lacy) offer a new psychedelic experience to a bored swinging young Londoner (Ian Ogilvy). Using a mesmerizing light machine, they gain total control of him and can experience

everything he does. The elderly woman gets carried away with the vicarious thrills and wills the mod zombie to steal and murder. Filmed in London. With Susan George (*Straw Dogs*).

SORORITY GIRL
1957 AIP (B&W)
PRODUCER/DIRECTOR: Roger Corman
SCREENWRITERS: Ed Waters,
Lou Lieberman
They're "Rich, smart, pretty—and all bad!" promise the ads. Sabra, Tina, and Rita are your guides to the dark side of sisterhood—where hair-pulling, paddling, and blackmail are the favored pastimes. Witness their "shock by shock confessions!" Rejected pledge Susan Cabot gets revenge by ruining other girls with rumors and innuendo. Barboura Morris, June Kenney, and Dick Miller also star. Originally released on a double bill with *Motorcycle Gang*.   –CB

SOULS FOR SALE: See CONFESSIONS OF AN OPIUM EATER.

SOUND OF HORROR
1964 Europix (Spain)
PRODUCER: Gregory Siechristian
DIRECTOR: José Antonio Nieves Conde
SCREENWRITERS: San-X-Abar Banel,
Gregory Siechristian
A prehistoric dinosaur makes a lot of noise and kills people but the damned thing's invisible. Soledad Miranda and Ingrid Pitt run for their lives. It played here with *Kill Baby Kill*.

SOYLENT GREEN
1973 MGM
PRODUCERS: Walter Seltzer, Russel Thatcher
DIRECTOR: Richard Fleischer
SCREENWRITER: Stanley R. Greenberg
In 2022 New York City is in *really* bad shape and a nosy cop (Charlton Heston in his fourth end-of-the-world

movie in five years) discovers that the overcrowded populace has been fed little squares of dead people for years. Edward G. Robinson (in his last role) is a police researcher friend whose death leads Charlton to the awful truth. With Leigh Taylor-Young as a piece of furniture, Joseph Cotton, Chuck Connors, Brock Peters, Whit Bissell, and Mike Henry.

THE SPACE CHILDREN
1958 Paramount (B&W)
PRODUCER: William Alland
DIRECTOR: Jack Arnold
SCREENWRITER: Bernard C. Schoenfeld

An alien brain in a cave uses mental telepathy to help the children of rocket-base personnel stop the launching of a nuclear warhead. The kids include little Johnny Crawford (*The Rifleman*) and Sandy Descher. The adults heading for destruction include Jackie Coogan and Russell Johnson.

SPACE MASTER X-7
1957 20th Century-Fox (B&W)
PRODUCER: Bernard Glasser
DIRECTOR: Edward Bernds
SCREENWRITERS: George Worthing Yates,
   Daniel Mainwaring

An alien fungus brought back by a space probe is mixed with blood and becomes deadly "blood rust." If that doesn't tempt you, how about Moe Howard playing a cabdriver in a serious film? The Stooges' contract for making shorts had just expired, so Moe did this rare solo appearance before returning with Larry and a new Curly in *Have Rocket, Will Travel*. Bill Williams, Paul Frees, Thomas B. Henry, and others managed to get better billing than the aging comedian.

SPACE MEN: See ASSIGNMENT OUTER SPACE.

SPACE MISSION OF THE LOST PLANET: See HORROR OF THE BLOOD MONSTERS.

SPACE MONSTER
1965 AIP-TV (B&W)
PRODUCER: Burt Topper
DIRECTOR/SCREENWRITER: Leonard Katzman

Francine York (*Curse of the Swamp Creature*) and Russ Bender find their rocketship in a fish tank containing crabs. They meet a spaceman with an exposed brain left over from *The Wizard of Mars*. Amazing.

SPACE SOLDIERS: See FLASH GORDON.

SPACE SOLDIERS CONQUER THE UNIVERSE: See FLASH GORDON CONQUERS THE UNIVERSE.

SPACESHIP: See THE CREATURE WASN'T NICE.

SPACESHIP TO THE UNKNOWN: See FLASH GORDON.

SPACEWAYS
1953 Hammer-Lippert
   (England) (B&W)
PRODUCER: Michael Carreras
DIRECTOR: Terence Fisher
SCREENWRITERS: Paul Tabori,
   Richard Landau

A science fiction/murder mystery based on a radio show. A scientist (American actor Howard Duff) is accused of murdering his wife and her lover and sending their bodies up in an orbiting satellite. To prove his innocence he has to go up in a rocketship to bring back the satellite. It's strange to hear characters worrying that Englishmen might not be the first to conquer space. With

Eva Bartok and footage from *Rocketship X-M*.

SPAWN OF THE SLITHIS: See SLITHIS.

SPECTRE
1977 TV
PRODUCER: Gordon L. T. Scott
DIRECTOR: Clive Donner
SCREENWRITERS: Gene Roddenberry, Samuel B. Peebles

Robert Culp as a criminologist and Gig Young as his alcoholic doctor partner go to an English mansion owned by John Hurt. The inhabitants, one of whom is actually a green lizard man, follow Druid priests. Lots of kinky sex is implied by having models dressed as little girls, a dominatrix, etc. Another unsold pilot film from story provider and executive producer Gene Roddenberry. It was Young's last English language feature.

THE SPECTRE OF EDGAR ALLAN POE
1974 Cinerama
PRODUCER/DIRECTOR/SCREENWRITER: Mohy Quandor

Cesar Romero stars as the owner of an asylum with a snake pit and torture devices in the basement. Edgar Allan Poe (Robert Walker, Jr.) brings his beloved Lenore to stay there and ends up going mad himself. Carol Ohmart is an axe murderess. With Tom Drake. Pretty bad independent feature by the multi-talented Mr. Q.

SPEED CRAZY
1959 Allied Artists (B&W)
PRODUCER: Richard Bernstein
DIRECTOR: William Hole, Jr.
SCREENWRITERS: Richard Bernstein, George Waters

The ads promised: "Jet-hot thrills!" As the killer of a gas station attendant, Brett Halsey competes in events on the American sportscar circuit. Meanwhile police pore over tire tracks left at the scene of the crime. The authorities come around just as Brett is about to run new employer Charles Wilcox off the track for stealing his girl. With Yvonne Lime, Regina Gleason, and Slick Slavin—who sings the title song.
                                    –CB

SPEED LOVERS
1968 Jemco
PRODUCER/DIRECTOR/SCREENWRITER: William McGaha

A track mechanic's young son decides to become a stock-car driver after watching real-life champ Fred Lorenzen tear up tracks in Atlanta, Riverside, Charlotte, Darlington, and Daytona Beach. The cast includes David Marcus, Peggy O'Hara, Glenda Brunson, and the director; Billy Lee Riley sings the title song.   –CB

SPEEDWAY
1968 MGM
PRODUCER: Douglas Lawrence
DIRECTOR: Norman Taurog
SCREENWRITER: Philip Skuken

Steve Grayson (Elvis), a stock-car racing champ, is in trouble with the IRS, which sends agent Susan Jacks (Nancy Sinatra) to collect. They fall in love. Bill Bixby is Elvis' manager. With Gale Gordon and Carl Ballantine. Elvis and/or Nancy sing "He's Your Uncle, Not Your Dad," "Your Groovy Self," "There Ain't Nothing Like a Song," and three others.

THE SPELL
1977 TV
PRODUCER: David Manson
DIRECTOR: Lee Philips
SCREENWRITER: Brian Taggert

As the ads tell you, this movie is about "A taunted overweight teenager with a mysterious power to destroy her enemies!" A *Carrie* for television with Susan Myers turning on her tormentors and eventually on mother Lee Grant (*The Omen*). The same TV season provided more cheap psychic horror in *The Possessed* and *Good Against Evil*.

SPELL OF THE HYPNOTIST

1956 Exploitation Productions (B&W)
PRODUCER/DIRECTOR: W. Lee Wilder
SCREENWRITER: Myles Wilder
ALSO RELEASED AS: *Fright*

From the ads: "One murder committed twice—a century apart!" Nancy Malone misses her flight for London, having gotten stuck in a traffic jam caused by criminal psychopath Frank Marth's attempt to jump off the Queensboro bridge. Psychiatrist Eric Fleming restores the doomed killer to police custody, but Malone is strangely affected. In a subsequent hypnosis session she insists she is Austrian Crown Prince Rudolph's illicit lover, who died with him in a Mayerling suicide pact in 1889. Fleming falls in love but the troubled girl disappears in a trance. Marth gets her back by impersonating the prince. With Humphrey Davis and Dean Almquist. Fleming was also Gil Favor on *Rawhide*. —CB

SPERMULA

1975 PPFC (France)
PRODUCER: Bernard Lenteric
DIRECTOR/SCREENWRITER: Charles Matton

In the tradition of *Emmanuelle* and *The Story of O*, an atmospheric, well-made erotic horror film about a society of beautiful females from outer space living in a giant plush castle. They're vampires who live on sperm instead of blood. Dayle Haddon stars with Udo Kier. (R)

THE SPIDER

1958 AIP (B&W)
PRODUCER/DIRECTOR: Bert I. Gordon
SCREENWRITERS: Laszlo Gorog,
George Worthing Yates
ALSO RELEASED AS: *Earth vs. the Spider*

The ads warned: "It must eat you to live!" A high school biology teacher finds a "dead" giant spider and puts it in the gym. The music of the band practicing for the prom wakes up the monster. It hates rock 'n' roll and decides to stomp the town and turn the citizens into dried-up corpses! Two teens get stuck in a spiderweb in a cave. Will they be rescued? Wow! With June Kenney, Edward Kremer, Gene Roth, and Mickey Finn. Originally co-billed with *The Brain Eaters*.

SPIDER BABY

1964 American General Pictures (B&W)
PRODUCERS: Paul Monka, Gil Laskey
DIRECTOR/SCREENWRITER: Jack Hill
ALSO RELEASED AS: *The Liver Eaters, Cannibal Orgy or the Maddest Story Ever Told*

Lon Chaney, Jr., is a member of a demented family of adults who have become cannibals because of inbreeding. This seldom-seen horror cheapie also stars Carol Ohmart, Mantan Moreland, and Sig Haig. What a cast! And get the alternate titles! Lon also sings the theme song.

THE SPIDER WOMAN STRIKES BACK

1946 Universal (B&W)
PRODUCER: Howard Welsch
DIRECTOR: Arthur Lubin
SCREENWRITER: Eric Taylor

Gale Sondergaard, star of *Sherlock Holmes and the Spider Woman*, and Rondo Hatton from the Holmes film *Pearl of Death* team up to drain the blood of young women in order to keep some plants alive. Sherlock isn't around to stop them, but Milburn Stone and

Kirby Grant are. Brenda Joyce is an almost-victim.

SPIDERMAN

1977 TV

PRODUCER: Edward J. Montagne
DIRECTOR: E. W. Swackhamer
SCREENWRITER: Alvin Boretz

Nicholas Hammond is Peter Parker, who doubles as a web-spinning superhero. With Michael Pataki, Bob Hastings, and Thayer David. It's about a mind-control plot. *The Incredible Hulk*, which aired two months later, proved more popular. *Spiderman* led to a succession of specials but not a series. It was a theatrical feature in Europe.

SPIES-A-GO-GO: See THE NASTY RABBIT.

SPINOUT

1967 MGM

PRODUCER: Joe Pasternak
DIRECTOR: Norman Taurog
SCREENWRITER: Theodore J. Flicker
ALSO RELEASED AS: *California Holiday*

Elvis is Mike McCoy, a race-car driver who leads a hot combo featuring Jimmy Hawkins, Jack Mullaney, and Deborah Walley (on drums). Shelley Fabares is the rich Cynthia Foxhugh. She wants Elvis. Diane McBain is Diane St. Claire, author of *The Perfect American Male*. Elvis is he. Dodie Marshall and Walley want him, too. Solution: He "marries" all four. With Cecil Kellaway, Will Hutchins, Warren Berlinger, Carl Betz, and Una Merkel. It was the sixth Elvis movie directed by Norman Taurog. Elvis only has time to sing five songs, including "All that I Am" and "Am I Ready."

THE SPIRAL STAIRCASE

1946 RKO (B&W)

PRODUCER: Dore Schary
DIRECTOR: Robert Siodmak
SCREENWRITER: Mel Dinelli

A psycho who kills women with physical defects pursues mute servant girl Dorothy McGuire in an old New England mansion during a thunderstorm. With Ethel Barrymore as a bedridden old lady, Kent Smith as a friendly doctor, Elsa Lanchester as a frightened servant, Rhonda Fleming, and Gordon Oliver.

THE SPIRAL STAIRCASE

1974 (England)

DIRECTOR: Peter Collinson

Remake of the classic 1946 thriller. Jacqueline Bisset is the mute servant caring for an invalid lady in a house that also harbors a killer. With Christopher Plummer, John Phillip Law, Sam Wanamaker, Gayle Hunnicutt, and Elaine Stritch (*Who Killed Teddy Bear?*) as the old lady.

THE SPIRIT IS WILLING

1967 Paramount

PRODUCER/DIRECTOR: William Castle
SCREENWRITER: Ben Star

Sid Caesar and Vera Miles rent a haunted New England house. Son Barry Gordon gets blamed for the destruction caused by three ghosts. With Harvey Lembeck, John McGiver, Doodles Weaver, Nestor Paiva, Jesse White, Jill Townsend, and John Astin as a psychiatrist. It's a comedy.

SPIRITS OF THE DEAD

1968 AIP (France/Italy)

DIRECTORS: Roger Vadim,
Louis Malle, Federico Fellini
SCREENWRITERS: Roger Vadim, Pascal Cousin,
Louis Malle, Federico Fellini,
Bernardino Zapponi
ORIGINALLY RELEASED AS:
Histoires Extraordinaires

The idea of having three interesting European directors each adapt a Poe short

Jane Fonda in Roger Vadim's segment of Spirits of the Dead.

ment is great. Terence Stamp is a disheveled drugged/drunk English movie star who nods acceptance as the Italian press and his producers fawn over him. All of Fellini's usual grotesque characters (and his humor) are present in this unforgettable horror story, which was also released separately. Mario Bava was the cinematographer and second unit director. With music by Nino Rota and Ray Charles singing "Ruby." The other two segments pale by comparison. "Metzengerstein" was going to be Roger Vadim's feature follow-up to *Barbarella*, again starring his then-wife Jane Fonda. As countess Frederica, Jane wears provocative costumes and spends most of her time organizing orgies. When her cousin/neighbor Baron Wilhelm (brother Peter) resists her advances, she sets fire to his stable. He dies but lives on spiritually in a wild black stallion with which the countess becomes obsessed. Fairly shoddy-looking and with obvious hints of incest and bestiality. "William Wilson" is a haunting story of a sadistic Austrian student (Alain Delon) with an exact double whom he later kills. A scene of kids lowering a screaming boy into a tub of rats is unsettling. Brigitte Bardot is flogged after losing a card game. Vincent Price narrates the English version. **(R)**

THE SPIRITUALIST
1948 Eagle Lion (B&W)
PRODUCER: Ben Stoloff
DIRECTOR: Bernard Vorhaus
SCREENWRITERS: Muriel Ross Bolton, Ian McLellan Hunter
ALSO RELEASED AS: *The Amazing Mr. X*
Fake spiritualist Turhan Bey creates some very convincing ghosts to fool rich clients. The writers must have seen the previous year's *Nightmare Alley*. With Lynn Bari, Richard Carlson, and Cathy O'Donnell.

story to the screen is great, but the results are mixed. "Toby Dammit," also known as "Never Bet the Devil Your Head," by Fellini is brilliant. Even if you're not a Fellini fan and think his films are overlong nonsense, his seg-

WELL KNOWN STAR PHOTOGRAPH DELETED BY ORDER OF THE SUPERIOR COURT OF THE STATE OF CALIFORNIA

The deleted star is Juliet Prowse in Spree.

THE SPLIT: See *THE MANSTER.*

SPOOK BUSTERS
1946 Monogram (B&W)
PRODUCER: Jan Grippo
DIRECTOR: William Beaudine
SCREENWRITERS: Edmond Seward, Tim Ryan
A mad scientist (Douglass Dumbrille) wants to put Huntz Hall's brain into a gorilla. With Charles Middleton, Bernard Gorcey as Louie, and the Bowery Boys (Leo Gorcey, Bobby Jordan, Gabriel Dell, et. al.).

SPOOK CHASERS
1957 Allied Artists (B&W)
PRODUCER: Ben Schwalb
DIRECTOR: George Blair
SCREENWRITER: Elwood Ullman
Huntz Hall, Stanley Clements, and the Bowery Boys are involved with phony ghosts again. Not to be confused with other East Side Kids/Bowery Boys classics: *Spooks Run Wild, Hold That Ghost, The Ghost Creeps, Spook Busters,* and *Ghost Chasers.*

SPOOKS RUN WILD
1941 Monogram (B&W)
PRODUCER: Sam Katzman
DIRECTOR: Phil Rosen
SCREENWRITERS: Carl Foreman,
　Charles R. Marion
This is one of two movies Bela Lugosi made with the East Side Kids (early Bowery Boys). Nardo the magician (Lugosi dressed as Dracula) and his dwarf assistant (Angelo Rossitto) terrorize Muggs (Leo Gorcey), Gimpy (Huntz Hall), and their pals in a haunted house. This wonderfully cheap Monogram Studios B-movie also features Sammy Morrison and Bobbi Jordan. They were all back in *Ghosts on the Loose* ('43).

UPI 2/4/77: As "Jaws," massive Richard Kiel is "equipped with a set of deadly steel teeth that can rip apart furniture" in the film The Spy Who Loved Me. "Jaws" is indeed a formidable opponent for 007 Secret Agent James Bond, played by Roger Moore.

A documentary about Las Vegas featuring Jayne Mansfield singing and stripping, Juliet Prowse doing a Cleopatra takeoff, Vic Damone singing, plus cockfighting and bare-fisted boxing with Jayne's husband, Mickey Hargitay. Jayne sings "Promise Her Anything."

THE SPY IN THE GREEN HAT

1966 MGM
PRODUCER: Boris Ingster
DIRECTOR: Joseph Sargent
SCREENWRITER: Peter Allan Fields
Episodes of *The Man from U.N.C.L.E.* are edited into another feature. Jack Palance plans to divert the Gulf Stream with a sonic destruction mechanism! Robert Vaughn and David McCallum are sent by Leo G. Carroll to stop him. The all-star cast includes Janet Leigh, Elisha Cook, Jr., Maxie Rosenbloom, Allen Jenkins (*Chained for Life*), Letitia Roman (*Fanny Hill*), Joan Blondell, Jack La Rue, and Eduardo Ciannelli.

SPY IN YOUR EYE

1966 AIP (Italy)
PRODUCERS: Fulvio Fucisano, Lucio Marcuzzo
DIRECTOR: Vittorio Sala
ORIGINALLY RELEASED AS: *Berlino, Appuntamento per le Spie*
Dana Andrews has a tiny camera implanted in his eye and battles Russians over a death ray and a kidnaped daughter. Espionage shenanigans with Brett Halsey and Pier Angeli.   —CB

THE SPOOKY MOVIE SHOW: See *THE MASK.*

SPREE

1962 United Producers Releasing Corporation
PRODUCERS: Carroll Case, Hal Roach, Jr.
DIRECTORS: Mitchell Leisen, Walon Green
SCREENWRITER: Sydney Field
ALSO RELEASED AS: *Las Vegas by Night*

SPY SQUAD

1961 States Rights (B&W)
PRODUCER/DIRECTOR/SCREENWRITER: Will Zens
ALSO RELEASED AS: *Capture That Capsule!*
Bumbling Communist spies play into the hands of American intelligence agents by retrieving a phony nosecone from waters off the coast of California.

The capsule's secret transmitter leads our boys to a '59 Buick convertible parked outside Marineland. A thrilling land-and-sea chase follows. Dick Miller of *Bucket of Blood* fame stars. The cast includes Dick O'Neill, Richard Jordahl, Pat Bradley, Carl Rogers, and Dorothy Schiller. The assistant director was David Bradly (*They Saved Hitler's Brain*).   —CB

THE SPY WHO LOVED ME

1977 United Artists (England)
PRODUCER: Albert R. Broccoli
DIRECTOR: Lewis Gilbert
SCREENWRITERS: Christopher Wood,
  Richard Maibaum

It was the biggest if not the best. Playing 007 for the third time, Roger Moore stops Stromberg (Curt Jurgens) from destroying the world with his stolen atomic subs. As Russian agent Anya Amasoua, Barbara Bach helps. It features the largest set ever built (to that time) for a movie. It also features the biggest villains, seven-foot two-inch Richard Kiel as the steel-toothed Jaws and Hammer vet Milton Reid as Sandor. Caroline Munro also stars. Carly Simon sings the hit "Nobody Does It Better." Music by Marvin Hamlish. William Grefe (*Stanley*) was the second unit director.

THE SPY WITH MY FACE

1966 MGM
PRODUCER: Sam Rolfe
DIRECTOR: John Newland
SCREENWRITERS: Clyde Ware,
  Joseph Cavelli

See Robert Vaughn as Napoleon Solo fight Robert Vaughn as a THRUSH clone in this *Man from U.N.C.L.E.* feature expanded from "The Double Affair" episode. Most of the action takes place in Switzerland, where Senta Berger and her cronies have a super-nuclear weapon. With Leo G. Carroll

and Nancy Hsueh. Directed by the creator of *One Step Beyond*.

SQUIRM

1976 AIP
PRODUCER: George Manasse
DIRECTOR/SCREENWRITER: Jeff Lieberman
Pretty bad film about electrified earthworms in Georgia that have teeth and make noises like horses. It does have an amazing scene with long worms burrowing through a man's face. Whole rooms are filled with what looks like thick spaghetti. Don Scardino is the studious young hero. The ads claimed there were "250,000 real worms" in the film. From the director of *Blue Sunshine*. (R)

SSSSSSS

1973 Universal
PRODUCER: Dan Striepeke
DIRECTOR: Bernard Kowalski
SCREENWRITER: Hal Dresner
(Don't say it, hiss it.) Mad scientist Strother Martin turns his daughter's lover (Dirk Benedict) into a killer cobra man who ends up in a freak show. A

Sheriff Jack Ging (center) helps mad scientist Strother Martin and daughter Heather Menzie with a sick boa constrictor in SSSSSSS.

giant python swallows a man and hundreds of various snakes slither around. It's all to benefit mankind. With Heather Menzies and a mongoose.

STAIRWAY TO HEAVEN

1945 Universal (England) (B&W with color sequence)

PRODUCERS/DIRECTORS/SCREENWRITERS: Michael Powell, Emeric Pressburger

ORIGINALLY RELEASED AS: *A Matter of Life and Death*

Excellent romantic fantasy. David Niven as a downed RAF pilot finds himself ascending to heaven in an operating room on an escalator! Once there, he has to stand trial and prove his death was a mistake. The tears of Kim Hunter are valuable evidence. With Raymond Massey, Robert Coote, Richard Attenborough, and Abraham Sofaer. With some amazing special effects that range from awesomely surreal to just plain silly.

STAKEOUT!

1962 Crown International (B&W)

PRODUCERS: Robert Hughes, William Hughes, Joe R. Gentile

DIRECTOR/SCREENWRITER: James Landis

On release from prison, Bing Russell retrieves his 10-year-old son and tries to set up a decent life, but his record keeps him bouncing from job to job. In desperation he talks a jailbird buddy into helping kidnap the son of oilman Bill Hale. Made in Texas with financing from Robert Hughes, who plays Sautu, and William Hughes, whose son Billy plays Joey. With Jack Harris and William Foster.   –CB

STAKEOUT ON DOPE STREET

1958 Warners (B&W)

PRODUCER: Andrew J. Fenady

DIRECTOR: Irvin Kershner

SCREENWRITERS: Irvin Kirshner, Irwin Schwartz, Andrew J. Fenady

Yale Wexler, Jonathan Haze, and Morris Miller find two pounds of uncut heroin and try to sell it, thinking their futures are assured. Abby Dalton, Herschel Bernardi, and John Savage (*The Deer Hunter*) appear. The music is by the Hollywood Chamber Jazz Group. Kershner also directed *The Young Captives* and *The Empire Strikes Back*. Photographed by Haskell Wexler. Roger Corman was executive producer. –CB

STANLEY

1972 Crown International

PRODUCER/DIRECTOR: William Grefe

SCREENWRITER: Gary Crutcher

Ben—with snakes. Chris Robinson (of *General Hospital* and *Diary of a High School Bride*) is a young Seminole veteran with many enemies. Steve Alaimo of *Where the Action Is* and Alex Rocco (*The Godfather*) poach snakes for a snake-products tycoon, who was involved in the killing of Robinson's father while Robinson was away in Vietnam. Then there's the father's former lover, whose "Cleopatra" nightclub act climaxes with her biting off the head of an asp. Chris forces his reptile friends to do his dirty work and one day they draw the line. See *Mako*.   –CB

STAR PILOT

1966 Monarch (Italy)

PRODUCERS: Aldo Calamara, Ermanno Curti

DIRECTOR: Pietro Francisci

SCREENWRITERS: Pietro Francisci, Ermanno Curti, Girolami

ORIGINALLY RELEASED AS: *2 + 5 Missione Hydra*

In 1977 this terrible, then 11-year-old space opera was retitled and released in America to cash in on the *Star Wars* mania. Kirk Morris and Gordon Mitchell, both known for flexing muscles in sub-Hercules spectacles, appear with lesser-known Italians and a laughable tin-foil spaceship that lands in Rome.

STAR TREK: THE MOTION PICTURE

1979 Paramount
PRODUCER: Gene Roddenberry
DIRECTOR: Robert Wise
SCREENWRITER: Harold Livingston

Wise directed the classic *The Day the Earth Stood Still* and *The Andromeda Strain*, so he seemed like the perfect choice to do this film. But, unfortunately, Paramount wasted much of the alleged $42 million budget in overtime salaries for the effects crew, who were involved in a race against the clock to deliver the completed film to theaters on the guaranteed date. The story is a combination of a few episodes of the television show: "The Immunity Syndrome," "The Doomsday Machine," and especially "The Changeling." A massive, all-powerful machine sucks up everything in its path as it seeks out its creator. The *Enterprise* is overhauled and its crew reassembled to search out and stop this force from reaching Earth. Admiral Kirk relieves the *Enterprise*'s current Captain Decker to regain what he has lost and Spock fails his Vulcan final exam and returns to the position he left. The crew gains a new alien, a beautiful bald woman named Ilia (Persis Khambatta). One of the high points of this film is the fantastic score by Jerry Goldsmith, but overall it's a major disappointment. With series regulars William Shatner, Leonard Nimoy, DeForest Kelley, James Doohan, George Takei, Majel Barrett (Mrs. Roddenberry), Walter Koenig, Michelle Nichols, Grace Lee Whitney, and Mark Leonard. *Star Trek II: The Wrath of Khan* was the first sequel. Special effects by Douglas Trumball and John Dykstra (*Star Wars*). Fifteen extra minutes of footage were added to the network TV showing, adding to the boredom.   –AF

UPI 12/6/79: *William Shatner, Persis Khambatta, and Stephen Collins are shown in a scene from Paramount's* Star Trek: The Motion Picture. *The movie comes to 850 theaters in the U.S. and Canada on December 7th and promoters say it will sell.*

STAR TREK II: THE WRATH OF KHAN

1982 Paramount
PRODUCER: Robert Sallin
DIRECTOR: Nicholas Meyer
SCREENWRITER: Jack B. Sowards

A long-haired Ricardo Montalban recreates his role as a genetically engineered supervillain from the 1967 "Space Seed" episode in the second *Star Trek* movie. Probably because it cost only $11 million ($40 million was reportedly spent on the first feature), it retains more of the feel of the series. The aging crew combines humor with heroics while experiencing the horrors of space. The entire main cast of regulars returns, with the addition of Paul Winfield, Bibi Besch as Captain Kirk's old flame, and Kirstie Alley as a pointy-eared Vulcan. Spock dies and receives a space funeral, but scriptwriters should have no trouble reviving him for future sequels.

UPI 7/28/78: Darth Vader, villain in the film Star Wars, gets a hero's welcome from youngsters at Tallahassee's airport recently. Youngsters yelled, "May the Force be with you!" as he left the airport. Darth was in town for a personal appearance at a theater that has run the movie for a full year.

From a vast and distant galaxy. . . A Space Adventure for all Time!

STAR CRASH

STAR WARS

1977 20th Century-Fox
PRODUCER: Gary Kurtz
DIRECTOR/SCREENWRITER: George Lucas

Mark Hammill (*Corvette Summer, The Big Red One*), Harrison Ford (*Zabriskie Point, American Graffiti*), and Carrie Fisher (daughter of Eddie Fisher and Debbie Reynolds) star with two robots and an upright dog in the film that changed the look of science-fiction features and created a multi-million-dollar industry. British horror star Peter Cushing makes a great villain as usual, and David Prowse (Cushing's monster in *Frankenstein and the Monster from Hell*) is Darth Vader (with the help of James Earl Jones's voice). Alec Guinness is Ben Kenobi. Music by John Williams. A total of nine sequels and prequels are planned.

STARCRASH

1979 New World Pictures (Italy)
PRODUCERS: Nat and Patrick Wachsberger
DIRECTOR: Luigi Cozzi (Lewis Coates)
SCREENWRITERS: Luigi Cozzi (Lewis Coates), Wa Ohberger
ALSO RELEASED AS: *Stella Star*
Star Emperor Christopher Plummer finds his kingdom under attack by evil Space Count Joe (*Maniac!*) Spinell, so he sends his best rocket jockey, Caroline (*Maniac!*) Munro to check out the situation in the Empire's farthest reaches. Caroline's accompanied by robot Judd Hamilton (her real-life husband) and superpowered alien Marjoe (ex-evangelist) Gortner. Despite a criminally low budget, Cozzi and his associates manage to squeeze in every kind of effect imaginable; stop motion, matte paintings, and so on. They range in quality from adequate to almost good, but the psychedelic Christmas-tree look of the spacecraft makes these sequences garishly attractive, especially to young children and people under the influence of controlled substances. John Barry, usually busy scoring James Bond films, supplied the music. With Nadia Cassini and Robert Spinell. **(R)** –BM

STARK FEAR

1963 B.H.S./Ellis Films (B&W)
PRODUCERS: Joe E. Burke,
Ned Hockman, Dwight V. Swain
DIRECTOR: Ned Hockman
SCREENWRITER: Dwight V. Swain

A one-shot homemade production filmed in Oklahoma and Arkansas. Fifties horror star Beverly Garland is married to sadistic, unemployed Skip Homeier. After he lets his best friend beat her, she leaves to be with her kind boss (Kenneth Tobey). Low-budget Southwest feminism, with music performed by the Oklahoma City Symphony Orchestra.

STARLIGHT SLAUGHTER: See EATEN ALIVE.

STARS IN YOUR BACKYARD: See PARADISE ALLEY.

STARSHIP INVASIONS

1977 Warner Brothers (Canada)
PRODUCERS: Norman Glick,
Ed Hunt, Ken Gord
DIRECTOR/SCREENWRITER: Ed Hunt

Funny, childish science fiction that actually looks like an old serial in color. Christopher Lee has a nonspeaking role as evil alien Captain Ramses. He wears black tights, a square-topped hood, and a dragon on his chest. Good aliens with large bald heads kidnap UFO expert Robert Vaughn. Ramses aims a suicide ray at Earth. Scenes of people suddenly strangling themselves or running in front of cars are pretty strange. With Helen Shaver.

STAY AWAY, JOE

1968 MGM
PRODUCER: Douglas Laurence
DIRECTOR: Peter Tewksbury
SCREENWRITER: Michael A. Hoey

In his first nonformula film since *Wild in the Country*, Elvis Presley is Joe Lightcloud, a half-Navajo, girl-chasing rodeo rider. This embarrassing, totally out-of-it comedy also stars Burgess Meredith as Elvis' Indian father, Joan Blondell as a tavern owner, Thomas Gomez as an old Indian, and L.Q. Jones. Elvis the Indian barbecues a prize bull, thinking it's a cow, and sings two songs. Jerry Reed sings "U.S. Male."

STELLA STAR: See STARCRASH.

THE STEPFORD WIVES

1975 Columbia
PRODUCER: Edgar J. Scherick
DIRECTOR: Bryan Forbes
SCREENWRITER: William Goldman

Former actor Forbes (he was in the original Quatermass films) directs an Ira Levin story about suburban wives turned into obedient robots by their husbands. Katharine Ross stars as a newcomer to town who wonders why the local women are always happy and talk like they're in TV commercials. Paula Prentiss is her only normal friend. Nanette Newman and Tina Louise are perfect neighbors. Patrick O'Neal runs the husbands' secret organization. Ross ends up with new, larger breasts courtesy of makeup man Dick Smith. Sort of a feminist *Invasion of the Body Snatchers*. Filmed in Westport, Connecticut.

STING OF DEATH

1966 Thunderbird International
PRODUCER: Hank Rifkin
DIRECTOR: William Grefe
SCREENWRITER: Richard S. Flink

Grefe's first horror film, about a marine biologist's assistant who conducts Portugese man-of-war experiments in an underwater cave. He thinks he'll discover something to help his melted face, but instead he turns into a monster and terrorizes vacationers with his hydrozoan brothers. Doug Hobart of *Death Curse of Tartu* takes over from John Vella for the creature scenes; Joe Morrison of *Racing Fever*, Valerie Hawkins, and Jack Nagle co-star. Special musical guest— Neil Sedaka. —CB

STOLEN FACE
1952 Hammer/Lippert (England) (B&W)
PRODUCER: Anthony Hinds
DIRECTOR: Terence Fisher
SCREENWRITERS: Martin Berkeley,
Richard H. Landau

Terence Fisher (1904–1980) was best known for directing Hammer horror films, but he had also been an editor and actor in England since the '30s. This prehorror oddity stars Paul Henreid as a plastic surgeon who falls in love with Lizabeth Scott. He can't have her, so he somehow transforms a Cockney prison inmate into an exact replica. The always wonderful and sexy Scott gets to play two roles in this unlikely story.

STONE COLD DEAD
1980 Dimension (Canada)
PRODUCERS: George Mendeluk, John Ryan
DIRECTOR/SCREENWRITER: George Mendeluk

Terrible, ineptly produced thriller about a psycho killing prostitutes with a high-powered rifle. Cop Richard Crenna tracks him down. Featuring Paul Williams (that's right, the tiny terror of trashy television and maudlin music), Linda Sorenson, and Belinda J. Montgomery.

STOP, LOOK AND LAUGH
1960 Columbia (B&W)
PRODUCER: Harry Romm
DIRECTORS: Jules White, Charley Chase, Edward Bernds, Del Lord, Don Apel
SCREENWRITERS: Felix Adler, Edward Bernds, Elwood Ullman

After the success of *Have Rocket, Will Travel* Columbia threw together scenes of Larry, Curly, and Moe from seven old shorts and added scenes of ventriloquist Paul Winchell (with Jerry Mahoney) and the Marquis chimps (remember *The Hathaways?*) acting out "Cinderella." The result was 78 minutes of unrelated muck and a lawsuit by the Three Stooges. A settlement was reached, but Moe and Larry never got a cent for any of the old shorts that are always being aired on television (Curly died before the TV showings).

STORM WARNING
1951 Warner Brothers (B&W)
PRODUCER: Jerry Wald
DIRECTOR: Stuart Heisler
SCREENWRITERS: Daniel Fuchs, Richard Brooks

A good film about the Ku Klux Klan with Ronald Reagan as a district attorney. Ginger Rogers, a New York model, travels south to visit her sister (Doris Day), who is married to a Klan member (Steve Cochran, star of *The Beat Generation*). Ginger witnesses his involvement in a murder and is about to be horse-whipped beneath a burning cross for talking when hero Reagan shows up and embarrasses local businessmen by recognizing them under the sheets. Despite the topic, there are no black characters.

THE STORY OF MANKIND
1957 Warner Brothers
PRODUCER/DIRECTOR/SCREENWRITER:
Irwin Allen

Back before he was the king of empty-headed disaster films and moronic TV series, Irwin Allen tried to be the new Cecil B. DeMille, whose *Ten Commandments* had come out in '56. Here Allen tells, as the ads put it, "The whole story of men and their women from creation until now!" Just look at that cast. Who else would sign the three Marx Brothers and not put them in any scenes together? Who else would have the foresight to cast Vincent Price as the Devil? The insight to cast Dennis Hopper as Napoleon? Peter Lorre as Nero? Hedy Lamarr (in her last role) as Joan of Arc? Because man has discovered the H-Bomb too early, the spirit of man (Ronald Colman in his last role) and the devil debate our future, citing past events. More of the "50 big names" are John Carradine as a pharoah, Agnes Moorehead, Anthony Dexter, Cedric Hardwicke, Cesar Romero, Marie Windsor, Ziva Rodann, Henry Daniell, Angelo Rossitto, William Schallert, Francis X. Bushman, Edward Everett Horton, and Robert Watson, who played Hitler in at least six films. With stock footage from *Land of the Pharoahs*. Unbelievable! Don't miss it!

STOWAWAY TO THE MOON

1975 TV
PRODUCER: John Cutts
DIRECTOR: Andrew V. McLaglen
SCREENWRITERS: John Boothe,
   William R. Shelton
An 11-year-old boy (Michael Link) hides on a spaceship headed for the Moon. Good for kids. With Lloyd Bridges as an astronaut, John Carradine, and Keene Curtis.

STRAIGHT ON TILL MORNING

1972 Hammer (England)
PRODUCER: Roy Skeggs
DIRECTOR: Peter Collinson
SCREENWRITER: Michael Peacock
One of the many '70s Hammer Studios movies that never got much distribu-

JUST KEEP SAYING TO YOURSELF: "IT'S ONLY A MOVIE...IT'S ONLY A MOVIE...IT'S ONLY A MOVIE...IT'S ONLY A... IT'S ONLY...IT'S

STRAIT-JACKET
FROM THE AUTHOR OF 'PSYCHO', THE DIRECTOR OF 'HOMICIDAL' AND THE CO-STAR OF 'WHAT EVER HAPPENED TO BABY JANE?'
STARRING
JOAN CRAWFORD
SETS A NEW HIGH IN HARROWING SHOCK-SUSPENSE!

WARNING! 'STRAIT-JACKET' VIVIDLY DEPICTS AX MURDERS!

WHEN THE AX SWINGS THE EXCITEMENT BEGINS! WE URGE YOU TO SEE 'STRAIT JACKET' FROM THE BEGINNING IN ORDER TO BRACE YOURSELF FOR THE SURPRISE ENDING!

CO-STARRING
DIANE BAKER · LEIF ERICKSON · HOWARD ST. JOHN
With JOHN ANTHONY HAYES ROCHELLE HUDSON Written by ROBERT BLOCH Produced and Directed by WILLIAM CASTLE · A WILLIAM CASTLE PRODUCTION
A COLUMBIA PICTURES RELEASE

tion in America (if any). This one was released directly to American TV. Shane Briant is a young guy living in a London apartment with a mirrored bedroom and drawers full of money. His new girl is Rita Tushingham, a "shy ugly duckling" who isn't prepared for his bizarre ways of showing "how much he cares."

STRAIT-JACKET
1964 Columbia (B&W)
PRODUCER/DIRECTOR: William Castle
SCREENWRITER: Robert Bloch

This slasher film was promoted by the precautionary school of advertising: "Warning! STRAIT-JACKET vividly depicts axe murders!" It also depicts Joan Crawford in a black wig just released from an asylum and convinced she's returning to her old habit of decapitating people. She has a nightmare of having the heads of her late husband and his lover in bed with her. Sculptress daughter Diane Baker just wants to get married and help Joan lead a normal life. Doesn't she? With Leif Erickson, George Kennedy, and Rochelle Hudson. Joan made *I Saw What You Did* for Castle next. The great gimmick ad line ("Just keep saying to yourself—it's only a movie—it's only a movie . . .") was later appropriated by the producers of *Last House on the Left*. Lucky theater patrons were given little cardboard bloody axes.

A STRANGE ADVENTURE
1956 Republic (B&W)
ASSOCIATE PRODUCER: William O'Sullivan
DIRECTOR: William Witney
SCREENWRITER: Houston Branch

From the ads: "Captive of killers in a white nightmare!" Young hotrod enthusiast Ben Cooper falls in love with an out-of-town girl and is forced at gunpoint to drive her and her two accomplices into the Sierras after an armored car holdup/homicide. Marla English, Joan Evans, Jan Merlin, and Nick Adams co-star.　　　　　　–CB

THE STRANGE AND DEADLY OCCURENCE
1974 TV
PRODUCER: Sandor Stern
DIRECTOR: John Llewellyn Moxie
SCREENWRITERS: Lane Sloan, Sandor Stern

Occult "accidents" plague Robert Stack and Vera Miles in their remote new home. With L.Q. Jones and Herb Edelman.

STRANGE BEHAVIOR
1980 World Northal
PRODUCERS: Anthony I. Ginnane, John Barnett
DIRECTOR: Michael Laughlin
SCREENWRITERS: Michael Condon, Michael Laughlin
ORIGINALLY RELEASED AS: *Dead Kids*

An interesting, original horror film about students in a small Midwestern town who subject themselves to psychological experiments for money and are turned into programmed killers. Dan Shor stars as the main human guinea pig. Michael Murphy (*Manhattan*) is his police-chief father. With Fiona Lewis (who blew up in *The Fury*), Louise Fletcher, Arthur Dignam, Dey Young, Scott Brady as a Chicago cop, and a slasher in a Tor Johnson mask. The music is a mixture of New Wave, Tangerine Dream, and Lou Christie. Filmed in New Zealand. Based on *School Days*, by Robert Hughes. **(R)**

STRANGE CARGO
1940 MGM (B&W)
PRODUCER: Joseph L. Mankiewicz
DIRECTOR: Frank Borzage
SCREENWRITER: Lawrence Hazard

Atmospheric-allegorical adventure of whores and Christ-figures involved in a Devil's Island penal-colony escape.

With Joan Crawford, Clark Gable, Ian Hunter, Peter Lorre (as M'sieur, Pig), and Albert Dekker. Different and recommended. It was condemned by the Catholic Legion of Decency.

THE STRANGE CASE OF DR. JEKYLL AND MR. HYDE

1968 TV (U.S./Canada)
PRODUCER: Dan Curtis
DIRECTOR: Charles Jarrott
SCREENWRITER: Ian McClellan Hunter
Originally a two-part special, this videotaped feature made in London stars Jack Palance. Since Palance already looks like Mr. Hyde, a special satyrlike makeup was designed by Dick Smith to make Hyde weirder-looking than Jekyll. Billie Whitelaw is good as the dance-girl. With Delholm Elliott, Torin Thatcher, Oscar Homolka, and Leo Genn.

THE STRANGE CASE OF DR. RX

1942 Universal (B&W)
ASSOCIATE PRODUCER: Jack Bernhard
DIRECTOR: William Nigh
SCREENWRITER: Clarence Upson Young
A murder mystery advertised as a horror movie. Lionel Atwill with thick glasses is Dr. Fish. Patric Knowles is a detective who almost has his brain put in the body of a gorilla! With Anne Gwynne, Mantan Mooreland, Shemp Howard, and Samuel S. Hinds.

STRANGE CONFESSION

1945 Universal (B&W)
PRODUCER: Ben Pivar
DIRECTOR: John Hoffman
SCREENWRITER: M. Coates Webster
Remake of *The Man Who Reclaimed His Head* ('34). J. Carrol Naish is a drug manufacturer who steals scientist Lon Chaney, Jr.'s formula and his wife. Lon retaliates by cutting Naish's head off. With Brenda Joyce, Milburn Stone, and

Lloyd Bridges. An "Inner Sanctum" mystery.

THE STRANGE DOOR

1951 Universal (B&W)
PRODUCER: Ted Richmond
DIRECTOR: Joseph Pevney
SCREENWRITER: Jerry Sackheim
Shoddy historical horror based on a Robert Louis Stevenson story. Charles Laughton is a sadistic 17th-century nobleman who imprisons his brother for marrying a woman they both loved. As Voltan, his servant, Boris Karloff rebels when Sally Forrest, thrown in the dungeon with her father, is about to be crushed to death. With Michael Pate and Alan Napier. It was a real low point for Laughton, who soon faced Abbott and Costello when they met Captain Kidd.

STRANGE FASCINATION

1952 Columbia (B&W)
PRODUCER/DIRECTOR/SCREENWRITER:
Hugo Haas
Middle-aged pianist Hugo Haas moves to America and marries a flirtatious young dancer (blond Cleo Moore). He maims his hand for insurance money. The plan backfires and he ends up on the Bowery, a broken, lonely man—all because of a woman! With Mona Barrie and Rick Vallin. Cleo Moore returned to use and humiliate Hugo in six more sleazy features. *One Girl's Confession* was next.

THE STRANGE MR. GREGORY

1946 Monogram (B&W)
PRODUCER: Louis Berkoff
DIRECTOR: Phil Rosen
From the ads: "Love thief by day . . . fiend by night." Edmund Lowe stars as a villainous hypnotist who pretends to be dead to win Jean Rogers. With Frank Reicher and Jonathan Hale.

UPI 7/9/75: Neil, a 400-pound, 11-year-old male lion, relaxes while actor John Saxon studies his script for the new ABC-TV movie Strange New World. Neil, who eats more than 15 pounds of meat a day, has been a film actor since he was four years old. He has been in more than ten films, as well as numerous commercials and television shows. The animal's trainer warns that although Neil is generally amiable, he is prone to moodiness and should always be handled with respect.

STRANGE NEW WORLD
1975 TV
PRODUCER: Robert E. Larson
DIRECTOR: Robert Butler
SCREENWRITERS: Walon Green,
Ronald F. Graham, Al Ramos

A third unsuccessful pilot film for Gene Roddenberry's *Genesis II* series. John Saxon (who also played in attempt number two—*Planet Earth*) is a man who wakes up 180 years in the future. This time, Kathleen Miller and Keene Curtis are with him. This "movie" is just two episodes of the never-produced series strung together. The heroes go to "Eterna," where eternal clones are being made, and to another land where zoo keepers battle hunters. With Martine Beswick.

THE STRANGE POSSESSION OF MRS. OLIVER
1977 TV
PRODUCER: Stan Shpetner
DIRECTOR: Gordon Hessler
SCREENWRITER: Richard Matheson

Bored housewife Karen Black takes on the personality of a woman believed to be dead. The new Karen is a swinging blonde. For fans of Karen Black and George Hamilton only. Director Hessler doesn't have any fans.

THE STRANGER
1973 TV
PRODUCERS: Alan A. Armer, Gerald Sanford
DIRECTOR: Lee H. Katzin
SCREENWRITER: Gerald Sanford

A science-fiction pilot film about an astronaut landing on Earth's twin planet. With Cameron Mitchell, Glenn Corbett (*Homicidal*), Lew Ayres, Dean Jagger, and George Coulouris. A Bing Crosby production. Similar to the much better *Journey to the Far Side of the Sun*.

A STRANGER CAME HOME: See THE UNHOLY FOUR.

STRANGER FROM VENUS
1954 Rich & Rich (England) (B&W)
PRODUCERS: Burt Balaban, Gene Martel
DIRECTOR: Burt Balaban
SCREENWRITER: Hans Jacoby
ALSO RELEASED AS: *Immediate Disaster*

A few years after *The Day the Earth Stood Still* appeared, Patricia Neal went to England to star in what's basically a cheap uncredited remake. Helmut Dantine is a man from Venus who comes to warn Earth of nuclear danger. A flying saucer arrives for negotiations, but Earthlings try to ambush it.

STRANGER IN OUR HOUSE
1978 TV
PRODUCERS: Pat and Bill Finnegan
DIRECTOR: Wes Craven
SCREENWRITERS: Max A. Keller,
Glenn M. Benest
ALSO RELEASED AS: *Summer of Fear*

In her fifth TV-movie, Linda Blair is a schoolgirl whose boyfriend and family are taken over by a back woods cousin who is a witch. Only Linda's horse and occult expert Macdonald Carey can sense the truth. A surprise TV-movie by Craven, who had just done *The Hills Have Eyes*. With Lee Purcell, Jeremy Slate, and Carol Lawrence. It was a theatrical release in Europe.

STRANGER IN THE HOUSE:
See *SILENT NIGHT, BLOODY NIGHT.*

A STRANGER IS WATCHING
1982 MGM
PRODUCER: Sidney Beckerman
DIRECTOR: Sean Cunningham
SCREENWRITERS: Earl MacRauch,
  Victor Miller

The producer/cowriter of *Last House on the Left* and producer/director/writer of *Friday the 13th* makes his bid for respectability with the film adapation of a novel by Mary Higgins Clark. This story of a mother-daughter kidnaping under New York's Grand Central Station engineered by extremely weird psychotic Rip Torn belies Cunningham's reputation for relentless violent. It includes only one senseless rape-murder, two knife killings, and a vicious screwdriver wound, played against a pervasive atmosphere of sadism. Plot considerations are ignored right and left, but Cunningham does achieve an appropriate level of nerve-racking suspense. (R)   –BM

STRANGER ON THE THIRD FLOOR
1940 RKO (B&W)
PRODUCER: Lee Marcus
DIRECTOR: Boris Ingster
SCREENWRITER: Frank Partos

Credited as being "the first true *film noir* film." The testimony of New York reporter John McGuire convicts taxi driver Elisha Cook, Jr. of a brutal murder. Soon McGuire begins to suspect that an elusive stranger with a scarf (Peter Lorre) is really the killer and has horrible dreams of himself being sent to the chair. This sleeper, which was influenced by German Expressionism, had Van Nest Polglase for art director. The next year he worked on *Citizen Kane*, also for RKO. Lorre and Cook worked together the next year in *The Maltese*

Falcon. With Margaret Tallicet. It's 64 minutes long.

THE STRANGER WITHIN
1974 TV
PRODUCER: Neil T. Maffed
DIRECTOR: Lee Philips
SCREENWRITER: Richard Matheson

In between being a genie and a resident of Harper Valley, Barbara Eden had an experience of the fourth kind, became extremely pregnant, and ended up with an alien baby. The story includes elements from *The Exorcist* and *Rosemary's Baby*. With Joyce Van Patten, Nehemiah Persoff, and David Doyle (ugh).

THE STRANGLER
1964 Allied Artists (B&W)
PRODUCERS: Samuel Bischoff,
  David Diamond
DIRECTOR: Burt Topper
SCREENWRITER: Bill S. Ballinger

Victor Buono stars as an overweight hospital lab technician who murders nurses. His possessive mother (Ellen Corby) is constantly attended by nurses.

Psychopathic killer Rip Torn holds Kate Mulgrew (left) and Shawn von Schreiber hostage in the tunnels beneath Grand Central Station in MGM's A Stranger Is Watching.

With David McLean as a lieutenant, Diane Sayer, and Davey Davidson.

STRANGLER OF THE SWAMP
1945 PRC (B&W)
ASSOCIATE PRODUCER: Raoul Pagel
DIRECTOR/SCREENWRITER: Frank Wisbar

Charles Middleton, formerly Ming the Merciless, is a vengeful white-faced ghost haunting a swamp. A remake of a German movie by the same director, it's said to be the best production from PRC. The cast includes future producer-director Blake Edwards and Rosemary La Planche.

STRANGLER OF VIENNA: See THE MAD BUTCHER.

STRANGLERS OF BOMBAY
1960 Hammer/Columbia (England) (B&W)
PRODUCER: Anthony Hinds
DIRECTOR: Terence Fisher
SCREENWRITER: David Z. Goodman

A religious cult that workships Kali in 1820 India tortures and kills British soldiers. A notoriously sadistic film with tongues and limbs cut off and implied castrations. With Marie Devereux in charge of the mutilations, Guy Rolfe, and Andrew Cruikshank. Filmed in "Stranglescope"!

STUDENT BODIES
1981 Paramount
PRODUCER: Allen Smithee
DIRECTOR/SCREENWRITER: Mickey Rose

A terrible spoof of *Halloween*-type teen-slasher movies. The only really funny part is the "producer" appearing on the screen and saying that since there's no onscreen sex or violence in this movie, the only way to get an R rating is to swear. He does. Jokes about a retarded double-jointed janitor who doesn't understand the purpose of toilets are more offensive than anything in the films this makes fun of. The writer-director used to collaborate on Woody Allen scripts. **(R)**

THE STUDENT NURSES
1970 New World
PRODUCERS: Charles S. Swartz, Stephanie Rothman
DIRECTOR: Stephanie Rothman
SCREENWRITER: Don Spencer

As the ads said, "They're learning fast." This was the second production after *Angels Die Hard* from executive producer Roger Corman's New World Company, now the largest independent in the business. Four beautiful young nurses are involved with a dying patient, a Chicano revolutionary, an accidental drug overdose, and a secret abortion. Elaine Giftos stars with Brioni Farrell, Barbara Leigh, Richard Rust, and Karen Carlson as Phred. From the director of *Velvet Vampire*. The success of this sex-tease drive-in time-waster led to *Private Duty Nurses*, *Night Call Nurses*, *The Young Nurses*, *Candy Stripe Nurses*, *Tender Loving Care*, and, for a change of pace, *The Student Teachers*, *Summer School Teachers*, *Fly Me*, *Cover Girl Models*, and other variations from assorted quick-buck companies. **(R)**

A STUDY IN TERROR
1965 Columbia (England/U.S.)
PRODUCER: Henry G. Lester
DIRECTOR: James Hill
SCREENWRITERS: Donald and Derek Ford

From the ads: "Holy terror! Sherlock Holmes vs. Jack the Ripper!" John Neville, who later played Holmes on Broadway, discovers who the Ripper really is. Donald Huston is Dr. Watson. With Anthony Quayle, John Fraser, Adrienne Cori, Robert Morley as Mycroft Holmes, and Frank Finlay as Lestrade. The same idea was later explored in *Murder by Decree* (also with

Quayle and Finlay). Herman Cohen was executive producer.

SUBMARINE SEAHAWK
1959 AIP (B&W)
PRODUCER: Alex Gordon
DIRECTOR: Spencer G. Bennett
SCREENWRITERS: Lou Rusoff, Owen Harris

Nobody much likes crew commander John Bentley until he heads a successful attack on a Japanese aircraft carrier. Brett Halsey, Wayne Heffley, and Steven Mitchell co-star. Originally released with *Paratroop Command* to comprise one of AIP's war-festival duals. See also *Tank Commandos* and *Hell Squad*. Bennett was an old-timer from B-studio Westerns. —CB

THE SUBTERRANEANS
1960 MGM
PRODUCER: Arthur Freed
DIRECTOR: Ranald McDougall
SCREENWRITER: Robert Thom

A free-loving French girl (Leslie Caron) falls in love with the poet-saint of the beatniks in San Francisco (George Peppard), hears a lot of jazz, and gets pregnant. See and hear Gerry Mulligan, Shelly Manne, Art Farmer, Art Pepper, Red Mitchell, and Carmen MacRae. With Janice Rule, Roddy McDowall, Jim Hutton, Scott Marlowe, and Arte Johnson. Based on what the ads called "the Jack Kerouac book that shocked conventional America!" Tunes include "Coffee Time," "Look Ma, No Clothes," and "Analyst."

SUCCUBUS
1968 Trans-American (W. Germany)
PRODUCER: Adrian Hoven
DIRECTOR: Jesse Franco
SCREENWRITER: Pier A. Caminneci
ORIGINALLY RELEASED AS:
Necronomicon—Geträumte Sunden

Called "perversely funny and incredibly pretentious" in *Castle of Frankenstein*

THESE ARE
The Subterraneans
TODAY'S YOUNG REBELS—
WHO LIVE AND LOVE IN A WORLD OF THEIR OWN
THIS IS THEIR STORY TOLD TO THE
HOT RHYTHMS OF
FABULOUS JAZZ!

I'm LEO:
"Why can't I love two people, and three people and four? I want everyone to love everyone!"

I'm MARDOU:
"They drove my mother out of town...yelling and tearing at her!"

I'm YURI:
"Life is a party and everyone alive is a party-crasher!"

I'm ADAM:
"I painted all the beautiful things I knew...and the police said they were wicked..."

I'm ROXANNE:
"If what I've done tonight is wrong...don't let me find out until tomorrow!"

METRO-GOLDWYN-MAYER presents
AN ARTHUR FREED PRODUCTION
starring
LESLIE CARON
GEORGE PEPPARD
JANICE RULE · RODDY McDOWALL with GERRY MULLIGAN · CARMEN McRAE · ANDRÉ PREVIN
Screen Play by ROBERT THOM Based On the Novel by JACK KEROUAC · In CinemaScope and METROCOLOR · Directed by RANALD MacDOUGALL

FROM THE JACK KEROUAC BOOK THAT SHOCKED CONVENTIONAL AMERICA!

magazine, this early X-rated sexy horror film was sometimes advertised without its name. You could call the theater for the shocking title. Janine Reynaud stars as a kinky nightclub performer. Every night she tortures and fondles a manacled victim on stage, then pretends to kill him. Having a hard time distinguishing fantasy from reality, she visits a psychiatrist. She believes a demon controls her actions. After an

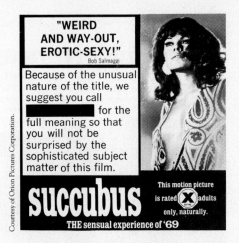

From the ads: "To hell with orders—we attack!" A list of guerrillas who have joined the Allies is hidden in the underground vault of a captured U.S. outpost in the Philippines. If Axis soldiers get their hands on the list, the men named on it will be killed. Major Mike "Touch" Connors leads John Ashley, Russ Bender, Scott Peters, Walter Maslow, Bing Russell, and Jewell Lain into enemy territory to retrieve the document. With Jan Englund, Sammee Tong of *Bachelor Father*, and Hawaiian entertainer Hilo Hattie. Originally paired with *Jet Attack*. —CB

orgy she kills her female lover. At the next show she stops faking the sex and killing. Includes dream sequences, animated mannequins, and a jazz score. With Howard Vernon, Jack Taylor, Michele Lemoine, and Adrian Hoven, who later made the *Mark of the Devil* films. (X)

SUGAR HILL

1974 AIP
PRODUCER: Elliott Schick
DIRECTOR: Paul Maslansky
SCREENWRITER: Tim Kelly
ALSO RELEASED AS: *Voodoo Girl*
Sugar Hill (Marki Bey) makes a deal with Baron Samedi (Don Pedro Colley), a character lifted from *Live and Let Die*. She finds him a bride and he provides an army of black Haitian zombies to wipe out the white Mafiosi who killed her boyfriend. The cobweb-covered zombies with blank eyes and machetes are pretty scary in one of the better movies from the blaxploitation craze. With Robert Quarry. Music by the Originals.

SUICIDE BATTALION

1958 AIP (B&W)
PRODUCER/SCREENWRITER: Lou Rusoff
DIRECTOR: Edward L. Cahn

SUMMER LOVE

1957 Universal (B&W)
PRODUCER: William Grady, Jr.
DIRECTOR: Charles Haas
SCREENWRITERS: William Raynor, Herbert Margolin
John Saxon is back as combo leader Jimmy Daley in a sequel to *Rock, Pretty Baby*. Daley's Ding-a-Lings (including bassist Rod McKuen) are hired to play at a summer camp. Rock music and romance with Molly Bee, Jill St. John, and Shelley Fabares. Fay Wray repeats her role from the first film.

SUMMER OF FEAR: See STRANGER IN OUR HOUSE.

SUNSET COVE

1978 Cal-Am
PRODUCER: Harry Hope
DIRECTOR: Al Adamson
SCREENWRITERS: Cash Maintenant, Dudd Donnelly
Crooked condo developers plan to ruin a popular teen beach spot. The kids use sex and blackmail to embarrass the sheriff and businessmen. A drive-in comedy with guest star John Carradine. (R)

SUPERARGO AND THE FACELESS GIANTS

1967 Fanfare (Italy/Spain)
DIRECTOR: Paolo Bianchini
SCREENWRITER: Julio Buchs
ORIGINALLY RELEASED AS: *Superargo e I Giganti Senza Volto*

A mad scientist turns athletes into mummified robots. Superargo, the wrestling spy in tights, joins with an ex-lama who teaches him to levitate—and the world is saved. With Ken Wood, Liz Barrett, and Guy Madison. It was a sequel to *Superargo vs. Diabolicus*.

SUPERARGO VS. DIABOLICUS

1966 Columbia (Italy/Spain)
PRODUCERS: Ottavio Poggi, J.J. Balcazar
DIRECTOR: Nick Nostro
SCREENWRITERS: Giarda and J.J. Balcazar
ORIGINALLY RELEASED AS: *Superargo Contra Diabolicus*

A European imitation of Mexican wrestling-hero films. Giovanni Cianfriglia (Ken Wood in the American credits) saves the world while wearing a mask and tights. Gerhard Tichey is the villain who manufactures gold. Good for laughs. Ads stressed—"Not a cartoon!"

SUPERBEAST

1972 United Artists (Philippines)
PRODUCER: Aubrey Schenck
DIRECTOR/SCREENWRITER: George Schenck

A no-star *Most Dangerous Game*-inspired dud about a doctor who experiments on criminals, then turns into a hairy-ape-like monster. It was co-billed with *Daughters of Satan*. With Antoinette Bower. **(R)**

SUPERCHICK

1973 Crown International
DIRECTOR: Ed Forsythe

Joyce Jillson is Tara B. True, a blond stewardess who doubles as a karate-expert crime-fighter on the ground. It's a comedy. John Carradine plays a surgeon. **(R)**

SUPERMAN

1978 Warner Brothers
PRODUCER: Pierre Spengler
DIRECTOR: Richard Donner
SCREENWRITERS: Mario Puzo, David Newman, Leslie Newman, Robert Benton

The man of steel reaches the screen for the first time since '57 (when the TV series ended). Christopher Reeve and Margot Kidder star with Marlon Brando, top-billed as Jor-El. Watch the train sequence with little Lois Lane. Her mother (Noel Neill) played Lois in the serials and on TV. Her father (Kirk Alyn) was Superman in two serials. Alyn was cut out of the theatrical version but you can see him in the reconstructed TV version, which includes 40 minutes of previously discarded footage. Donner's previous credits include directing the action segments of the *Banana Splits* show. Music by John Williams. *Superman* cost an astounding $55 million.

UPI 7/7/77: Passersby stare at the name "Daily Planet" over the doorway of the New York Daily News *building as the fictitious paper from the comic strip* Superman *comes to life for a day for the cinema world. Movie crews used the front of the News and lobby for a movie set.*

SUPERMAN II

1981 Warner Brothers
PRODUCER: Pierre Spengler
DIRECTOR: Richard Lester
SCREENWRITERS: Mario Puzo, David Newman, Leslie Newman

Most of the original cast except for profit-eating Marlon Brando return in this sequel. Terence Stamp and the krypton criminals get more screen time, which is good, but for all those millions (54) couldn't they make the effects more convincing? Insiders say *Superman* director Richard Donner actually directed about 75 percent of this feature before he was fired. Watch for *Superman III*.

SUPERMAN AND THE MOLE MEN

1951 Lippert (B&W)
PRODUCER: Barney A. Sarecky
DIRECTOR: Lee Sholem
SCREENWRITER: Richard Fielding

George Reeves plays Superman for the first time. He helps a small group of "mole men" disturbed by an oil well. The subterraneans are dwarves with furry pajamas, enlarged heads, and a radioactive ray gun that looks like a vacuum cleaner. George started the popular TV series the next year and this 67-minute feature later turned up as a two-parter called "Unknown People." With Phyllis Coates as Lois, Billy Curtis as a mole man, Jeff Corey, and Walter Reed.

SUPERNATURAL

1933 Paramount (B&W)
PRODUCERS: Victor and Edward Halperin
DIRECTOR: Victor Halperin
SCREENWRITERS: Harvey Thew, Brian Marlow

Carole Lombard is possessed by the spirit of an executed criminal! Vivienne Osborne is a ghost, H.B. Warner a doctor, and Randolph Scott a hero in this old horror movie from the Halperin brothers, producers of *White Zombie*.

SUPERSONIC MAN

1979 Topar (Spain)
DIRECTOR: Juan Piquer
SCREENWRITERS: Juan Piquer, Sebastian Moi

Cameron Mitchell stars as the mad Dr. Gulk in this terrible superhero film. He battle Kronos, the Supersonic Man,

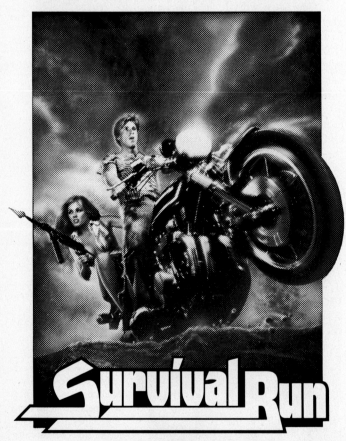

**No place to hide-No place to run…
Six kids become killers to live!!!**

Survival Run

SPIEGEL · BERGMAN PRODUCTIONS AND MEXICO FILM INTERNATIONAL Present
PETER GRAVES · RAY MILLAND · VINCENT VAN PATTEN in "SURVIVAL RUN" Starring PEDRO ARMENDARIZ, JR.

sent to Earth to cash in on the success of the previous year's *Superman*. With Michael Coby.

SURF PARTY
1964 20th Century-Fox (B&W)
PRODUCER/DIRECTOR: Maury Dexter
SCREENWRITER: Harry Spaulding
Bobby Vinton stars as the operator of a surf shop. Jackie DeShannon is a vacationer in Malibu Beach. Songs include "Firewater" and "If I Were an Artist." With the Astronauts and the Routers as themselves.

SURF TERROR: See THE BEACH GIRLS AND THE MONSTER.

SURVIVAL RUN
1980 Film Ventures
PRODUCER: Lance Hool
DIRECTOR: Larry Spiegel
SCREENWRITERS: Larry Spiegel, G.M. Cahill
Teenagers, violence, drugs, nudity, and mobsters with young Vincent Van Patten on a motorcycle. Also with exploitation experts Ray Milland and Peter Graves as bad guys. (R)

SURVIVE!
1977 Paramount (Mexico)
PRODUCER/DIRECTOR/SCREENWRITER:
René Cardona, Jr.
When a jet liner crashes in the Andes, the survivors stay alive by eating the frozen bodies of people they were busy relating to during the flight. The best known of Cardona's inept spectacles. With Pablo Ferrez and Hugo Stiglitz (also in Cardona's *Tintorera* and *Guyana, Cult of the Damned*).

SURVIVOR
1980 (Australia)
PRODUCER: Anthony I. Ginnane
DIRECTOR: David Hemmings
SCREENWRITER: David Ambrose

A jumbo jet crashes, but the only survivor, pilot Robert Powell, can't remember a thing. A *Twilight Zone*-type story released directly to cable television in America. Jenny Agutter co-stars as a psychic and Joseph Cotten has a bit part. Music by Brian May. Director Hemmings and Powell were in *Harlequin* the same year.

SUSPIRIA
1976 International Classics
(20th Century-Fox) (Italy)
PRODUCER: Claudio Argento
DIRECTOR/SCREENWRITER: Dario Argento
Nonstop shocks confront Jessica Harper when she arrives at Tanz Akadamie in Freiburg run by Joan Bennett (*Dark Shadows*) and Alida Valli. A colorful, stylish horror movie with a witch, bats, and totally unexpected elements, like a fall into a room full of barbed wire and maggots dropping from the ceiling onto sleeping girls. The sound track by the rock group Goblin is the loudest

The Only Thing More Terrifying Than The Last 12 Minutes Of This Film Are The First 80.

SUSPIRIA

Once You've Seen It You Will Never Again Feel Safe In The Dark

R RESTRICTED   RELEASED BY INTERNATIONAL CLASSICS

you'll ever hear. With Udo Kier and Stefania Casini. (R)

SVENGALI

1931 Warner Brothers (B&W)
PRODUCER: Warner Brothers
DIRECTOR: Archie Mayo
SCREENWRITER: J. Grubb Alexander

John Barrymore is great as the wild-eyed bearded hypnotist in turn-of-the-century Paris. He controls the life and singing career of blond Marian Marsh as Trilby. With Bramwell Fletcher. Barrymore followed this role with a similar one in *The Mad Genius*, the same year.

SVENGALI

1955 MGM (England)
PRODUCER: George Minter
DIRECTOR/SCREENWRITER: Noel Langley

Donald Wolfit, star of *Blood of the Vampire*, gets to wear lots of eyeliner again as the famous love-starved French hypnotist. Hildegarde Neff is Trilby.

SWAMP DIAMONDS: See SWAMP WOMEN.

SWAMP FIRE

1946 Paramount
PRODUCERS: William Pine, William Thomas
DIRECTOR: William Pine
SCREENWRITER: Geoffrey Holmes

Once again the ads tell the story: "Twin water wizards clash in deadly bayou love feud!" The world's two most famous Olympic swimming champs-turned-matinee-idol-heroes appear together for the first time! Navy man Johnny Weissmuller fights bayou king Buster Crabbe on land and (of course) in alligator-infested waters for "a tiger girl's love." Except for cameo appearances as himself in other films, it was Weissmuller's only role outside of the *Tarzan* and *Jungle Jim* series. With Virginia Grey, Carol Thurston, and young David Janssen.

THE SWAMP THING

1982 Embassy
PRODUCERS: Benjamin Melniker, Michael E. Uslan
DIRECTOR/SCREENWRITER: Wes Craven

Despite some unintentional laughs, this comic-book adaptation is enjoyable and deserved to do better than it did. A scientist (Ray Wise) working on a secret project in the Louisiana bayou is doused with his new animal/vegetable formula and becomes the strong but tragic Swamp Thing. Bad guy Arcane (Louis Jourdan) eventually steals the formula and becomes the Arcane monster for an anticlimactic battle of silly-looking men in monster suits. The best parts involve government agent Adrienne Barbeau hiding from Arcane's henchmen with the help of a young swamp-wise black kid. Sick cinema fans will recognize David Hess (Craven's *Last House on the Left*) and Nicholas Worth (*Don't Answer the Phone*) as the inept bad guys. Barbeau fans will enjoy her first onscreen topless bathing scene. "Swampmania" items, including books, records, shirts, bubble-gum cards, toys, games, and underwear, mostly sat on shelves collecting dust.

SWAMP WOMEN

1956 Woolner
PRODUCER: Bernard Woolner
DIRECTOR: Roger Corman
SCREENWRITER: David Stern
ALSO RELEASED AS: *Swamp Diamonds, Cruel Swamp*

Policewoman Carole Matthews poses as a gun moll to get in with prisoners Beverly Garland, Marie Windsor, and Jill Jarmyn—"the Nardo Gang"—who have a fortune in stolen diamonds tucked away in the Louisiana bayou country. There's a rigged breakout and the four end up in the swamp, where they meet geologist/oil explorer Mike "Touch" Connors and his fiancée. Con-

nors has a strong effect on the lonely women, who fight tooth and nail for his favor. The fiancée and Garland are both killed before the police arrive to clear the way for Carole and our hero. With Lou Place, Jonathan Haze, and alligators. Filmed in a Louisiana swamp. —CB

SWARM
1978 Warner Brothers
PRODUCER/DIRECTOR: Irwin Allen
SCREENWRITER: Sterling Silliphant
A wonderful cast of well-known stars try to outdo each other while reading terrible dialogue and being stung. Michael Caine, a B-movie hero if there ever was one, is top-billed as a scientist who saves Houston by duplicating the sound of bees mating. Katharine Ross

loves him. Olivia de Havilland, a school teacher, is involved in a love triangle with Ben Johnson and Fred MacMurray before being stung to death. Henry Fonda, Richard Chamberlain, and José Ferrer are doctors. Richard Widmark, Bradford Dillman, and Cameron Mitchell represent the military. Other stars carefully selected for this multi-million-dollar flop include Slim Pickens, Lee Grant, and Patty Duke Astin. It's long, it's funny, and it features posters for *The Towering Inferno*.

SWEET KILL
1972 New World
PRODUCER: Tamara Asseyeu
DIRECTOR/SCREENWRITER: Curtis Hanson
ALSO RELEASED AS: *The Arousers*

The *Los Angeles Times* called it "a milestone in Tab Hunter's career." He stars as an impotent California gym teacher who masturbates while a prostitute plays his dead mother. *Psycho*-type thrills are promised. (R)

THE SWEET RIDE
1968 20th Century-Fox
PRODUCER: Joe Pasternak
DIRECTOR: Harvey Hart
SCREENWRITER: Tom Mankiewicz
Surfers, tennis bums, and bikers in Malibu all figure in this mess, which would be better off without Tony Franciosa as a tennis bum and Michael Sarrazin as his roommate. Jacqueline Bisset and Bob Denver (in one of his Maynard-type roles) can stay. With Michael Wilding, Percy Rodriguez, Warren Stevens, Pat Buttram, and a sadistic bald biker called Mr. Clean. Music by Dusty Springfield and Moby Grape.

SWEET SAVAGE
1979 Evolution Films
DIRECTOR: Ann Perry
Aldo Ray stars as a bad guy in his first hard-core Western. He had previously distinguished himself in hits like *Nigger Lover*. Indians and cowboys have sex. When poor Aldo starts taking his clothes off, a man rushes in the room and pushes him out the window. Carol Conners (*Deep Throat*, *The Gong Show*) sings and dances. Beth Anna is the real star. Laughable porno featuring real Indians dancing and various Caucasian and black women playing Indians for the sex scenes. (X)

SWEET SWEET RACHEL
1971 TV
PRODUCER: Stan Shpetner
DIRECTOR: Sutton Roley
SCREENWRITER: Anthony Lawrence
Alex Dreier, a former newscaster, stars as an ESP expert searching for a psy-chic killer in this pilot for *The Sixth Sense* series (1972). With Stefanie Powers and Pat Hingle. Gary Collins starred in the series.

A SWINGIN' AFFAIR
1963 Emerson (B&W)
PRODUCER/SCREENWRITER: Gunther Collins
DIRECTOR: Jay O. Lawrence
William Wellman, Jr., tries to finance a college education while his waitress love waits on the sidelines. Sandra Gale Bettin and Arline Judge co-star along with Dick Dale and the Del Tones. Emerson Film Enterprises eventually found sex movies less of a headache than the likes of this, *Monstrosity*, and *Manos—Hands of Fate*. —CB

SWINGIN' ALONG
1962 20th Century-Fox
PRODUCER: Jack Leewood
DIRECTOR: Charles Barton
SCREENWRITER: Jameson Brewer

Tommy Noonan and Peter Marshall were a comedy team in a series of forgotten films. In this, their last together, Noonan ends up winning first prize in a songwriting contest. With Barbara Eden, Ted Knight (as a priest), Mike Mazurki, and Ray Charles, Roger Williams, and Bobby Vee as themselves. Noonan later made nudies with Mansfield and Van Doren. Peter Marshall has been the host of *Hollywood Squares* since 1966.

THE SWINGIN' SET: See GET YOURSELF A COLLEGE GIRL.

A SWINGIN' SUMMER
1965 United Screen Arts
PRODUCER: Reno Carell
DIRECTOR: Robert Sparr
SCREENWRITER: Leigh Chapman

William Wellman, Jr., plans to make millions with partner James Stacy by booking dynamite acts into a Lake Arrowhead dance pavillion. But the owner says no to the likes of the Rip Chords, the Righteous Brothers, Gary Lewis and the Playboys, Mr. Personality Donnie Brooks, and Jody Miller—until his girlfriend (Quinn O'Hara) arranges for her father to put up security. Wellman acts typically stupid when the secret leaks out, but he gets over it in time for opening night, which is such a success that three friends of a jealous lifeguard (Martin West) try to make off with the cashbox. The performers ignore their hits in favor of "Justine," "Penny the Poo," "Red Hot Roadster," "Out to Lunch," and "Nitro"; bookish Raquel Welch finally takes off her glasses in all the excitement. Miller sings the title song. With Michael Blodgett (*Beyond the Valley of the Dolls*).

–CB

SWORD AND THE DRAGON

1956 Valiant (U.S.S.R.)
PRODUCER/DIRECTOR: Alexander Ptushko
SCREENWRITER: V. Kotochnev
ORIGINALLY RELEASED AS: *Ilya Mourometz*

Charming fantasy epic with 11th-century Russian hero Ilya Mourometz using his magic sword to slay a three-headed dragon. With a wind demon and other legendary creatures. Starring Boris Andreyev. By the director of *The Magic World of Sinbad*.

THE SWORD AND THE SORCERER

1982 Bedford
PRODUCERS: Brandon Chase, Marianne Chase
DIRECTOR: Albert Pyun
SCREENWRITER: Tom Karnowsky

This bloody, low-budget moneymaker is in many ways better than *Conan* and *Excalibur* (as ad quotes claimed). It includes some great shocking special effects and lots of action, but have fun trying to follow the plot. Hero Lee Horsley (the *Matt Houston* series) helps Kathleen Beller (who likes to kick men in the groin) rescue her brother from the evil Cromwell's torture chamber. George Maharis co-stars. With Richard Lynch as Cromwell, a scary demon from Hell, and a triple-bladed, jet-propelled supersword. It was the first feature for the 26-year-old director. (R)

THE SWORD OF ALI BABA

1965 Universal
PRODUCER: Howard Christie
DIRECTORS: Arthur Lubin, Virgil W. Vogel
SCREENWRITERS: Oscar Brodney, Edmund Hartmann

Supposedly up to 70 percent of this feature was taken from the 1944 *Ali Baba and the Forty Thieves*. Frank Puglia as Prince Cassim remains from the 21-year-old footage. The new "star" is Peter Mann. With Jocelyn Lane, Gavin MacLeod (later captain of *The Love Boat*), and Frank De Kova.

SWORD OF SHERWOOD FOREST

1960 Hammer/Columbia (England)
PRODUCER: Sidney Cole
DIRECTOR: Terence Fisher
SCREENWRITER: Alan Hackney

TV's Robin Hood, Richard Greene, vs. Peter Cushing as the Sheriff of Nottingham (a role once played by Basil Rathbone). With Oliver Reed and Nigel Green. Filmed in Ireland.

THE T.A.M.I. SHOW
1964 AIP (B&W)
PRODUCER: Lee Savin
DIRECTOR/SCREENWRITER: Steve Binder

That's "Teenage Awards Music International," the ultimate rock 'n' roll movie. An Electronovision (videotape) production with no subplots or acting—it's just one wonderful all-star live show. Starting with the least impressive and moving up: the Barbarians are the only bad group. They only do one (nonhit) song but you can see drummer Moulty's famous hook hand. Billy J. Kramer and the Dakotas and Gerry and the Pacemakers are good, but pale compared to the other acts. Chuck Berry's great as usual, but he's in lots of movies. Jan and Dean, the comical hosts, wear striped T-shirts and ride skateboards, but they don't do their best songs. Lesley Gore does "It's My Party" and "You Don't Own Me," both still popular anthems. The best of Motown is represented by Marvin Gaye ("Hitchhike"), Smokey Robinson and the Miracles ("Shop Around"), and the Supremes, featuring Diana Ross' eyes ("Baby Love"). The Rolling Stones do a great "Time Is on My Side" but they really can't follow James Brown and the Fabulous Flames. James dances like nobody else in the business and sings "Please, Please, Please," throwing off his cape and repeatedly returning for more until you think he'll drop. It's the best "teen" film ever made. The seldom-shown 117-minute version also features the Beach Boys. Jack Nitzsche was the musical director.

THX-1138
1971 Warner Brothers
PRODUCER: Lawrence Sturhahn
DIRECTOR: George Lucas
SCREENWRITERS: George Lucas, Walter Murch

See how the director of *Star Wars* really feels about things. As a film student at USC, Lucas made a short called *THX 1138 4EB*. Francis Coppola saw it, liked it, and helped him raise money to make this feature version, which became the first American Zoetrope production. (Coppola takes executive producer credit). It's a classic, chilling look at a dehumanized future. Robert Duvall, as THX, is arrested for not taking his tranquilizing drugs. He and an unwanted companion (Donald Pleasence) go to prison, an all-white void where robot guards poke bald prisoners with cattle prods. THX finds the embryo of his unborn child, discovers his illegal lover (Maggie McOmie) is dead, and escapes in a jet car. With Don Pedro Colley, Sid Haig, Marshall Efron, Johnny Weissmuller, Jr. (a robot), mutant hairy dwarfs, holograms, and a *Wizard of Oz*–style religious leader. Partialy shot in San Francisco's BART tunnels.

TABOOS OF THE WORLD
1965 AIP (Italy)
PRODUCER: Guido Giambartolomei
DIRECTOR/SCREENWRITER: Romolo Marcellini
ORIGINALLY RELEASED AS: *I Tabu*

Vincent Price narrates another *Mondo Cane* imitation with lepers, atom-bomb victims, drug addicts selling their babies, blood drinking, and childbirth!

A TALE OF TWO CITIES
1958 Rank (England) (B&W)
PRODUCER: Betty E. Box
DIRECTOR: Ralph Thomas
SCREENWRITER: T.E.B. Clarke

Dirk Bogarde stars in this version of Dickens' story. Christopher Lee, who soon found international fame in *Horror of Dracula*, plays the decadent marquis.

On Christmas Eve, Jo-
anne (Joan Collins) is visited by an unwanted Santa
(Oliver MacGreevy) in
Tales From the Crypt.

TALES FROM THE CRYPT

1972 Amicus/Cinerama (England)
PRODUCERS: Milton Subotsky,
Max J. Rosenberg
DIRECTOR: Freddie Francis
SCREENWRITER: Milton Subotsky

An attempt to bring five E.C. horror
comics to the screen with Ralph Richardson holding things together as the
cryptkeeper. "Poetic Justice" features
Peter Cushing as Grimsdyke, an old
man who returns from the grave to seek
revenge. "Blind Alleys" features Patrick Magee as a victimized blind man
who arranges for Nigel Patrick to run
down a narrow dark hallway lined with
razor blades. "All Through the House,"
with Joan Collins and Chloe Frank, is
about a psycho Santa. In "Reflection
of Death" Ian Hendry plays a man who
doesn't realize he's dead. "Wish You
Were Here" finds Richard Greene
brought back to life in a variation of
"The Monkey's Paw." Its success led
to *Vault of Horror* the next year.

TALES FROM THE CRYPT II:
See *THE VAULT OF HORROR.*

TALES OF TERROR

1962 AIP
PRODUCER/DIRECTOR: Roger Corman
SCREENWRITER: Richard Matheson

After three Poe hits, Roger Corman did
this three-in-one Poe movie. Vincent
Price stars in all three, but the big news
was Peter Lorre and Basil Rathbone returning to horror films and making their
first AIP appearances. In "Morella," a
story similar to "Tomb of Ligea," Price
is killed by his daughter, Lenora, who
is possessed by his dead wife, Morella.
"The Black Cat" (which includes the
story "The Cask of Amontillado")
begins with a comical wine-tasting
contest between Lorre and Price. When
the drunken Lorre discovers wife Debra
Paget has been fooling around with
Price, he bricks them up in the cellar
along with an unnoticed cat. With
Wally Campo. In "Facts in the Case of
M. Valdemar" mesmerist Rathbone
keeps Price alive in a trance. When he
forces Price's wife (Debra Paget) to
marry him, Price rises, begins melting
into an oozing faceless mess, and scares
his nemesis to death.

If you ever wondered where the director of *They Saved Hitler's Brain* got his start, look no further. His feature debut was this film starring Nancy Davis (Reagan) and future politician George Murphy as husband and wife. The happy citrus-growing couple are upset when their son (Billy Gray of *Father Knows Best*) finds his dog dead. A new (foreign) man in town (Kurt Kasznar) is blamed for the canine caper. Gossip leads to the poor man being accused of a murder. With Lewis Stone. Critical reactions range from "unbelievably poor" (*Variety*) to "disturbing, expressionistic" (*Film Noir*, Overlook Press).

TAM LIN: See THE DEVIL'S WIDOW.

TANK BATTALION

1958 AIP (B&W)
PRODUCER: Richard Bernstein
DIRECTOR: Sherman A. Rose
SCREENWRITERS: Richard Bernstein, George W. Waters

Advertised as: "A raging inferno of war!" Don Kelly, Marjorie Hellen, Frank Gorshin, and Edward G. Robinson, Jr., are somewhere in Korea. A tank with a broken gearbox is pinned against a sheer cliff by enemy fire. Robinson risks death by setting out for spare parts. Operation Spider is saved. A double with *Hell Squad*. Rose also directed *Target Earth*. —CB

TALES THAT WITNESS MADNESS

1973 Amicus/Paramount (England)
PRODUCER: Norman Priggen
DIRECTOR: Freddie Francis
SCREENWRITER: Jennifer Jayne

Four horror stories related by patients in a clinic. The stars include Kim Novak in her first role since '69, Jack Hawkins in his last role (he died in '73), Donald Pleasence, Joan Collins, Suzy Kendall, and Donald Houston. The stories involve cannibalism, a living plant, an imaginary tiger, and a time-machine bicycle. (R)

TALK ABOUT A STRANGER

1952 MGM (B&W)
PRODUCER: Richard Goldstein
DIRECTOR: David Bradley
SCREENWRITER: Margaret Fitts

TANK COMMANDOS

1959 AIP (B&W)
PRODUCER/DIRECTOR/SCREENWRITER: Burt Topper

From the ads: "The guts and dynamite demolition squad!" In World War II Italy Robert Barron and his crew search for a bridge used by the Germans for heavy-artillery transport. Barron spends off hours with Red Cross nurse Maggie Lawrence while his GIs chase Italian girls. With Wally Campo and Donato Faretta. A dual release with *Operation Dames.*   —CB

TANYA'S ISLAND

1980 Fred Baker Films (Canada)
PRODUCER/SCREENWRITER: Pierre Brousseau
DIRECTOR: Alfred Sole

This unique fantasy did terribly at the box office but, like Sole's *Alice, Sweet Alice*, it's surprisingly well made for its small budget and deserves another look. The sometimes pretentious screenplay presents gorgeous dark-skinned model D.D. Winters as Tanya, a film technician with an abusive unemployed live-in artist-lover. His primitive paintings help inspire her dream about living on a beautiful tropical island where he acts surly and paints as usual and she mostly rides naked along the shoreline. She finds and befriends a gentle ape with blue eyes. Her jealous boyfriend can't accept the platonic relationship, locks the ape in a bamboo cage, and, when he escapes, locks up Tanya. The sometimes humorous battle continues as man and ape man imitate each other and fight for the woman who eventually wakes up screaming. The extremely realistic ape costume was designed by Rick Baker and Rob Bottin. Filmed in Puerto Rico. With clips from *Mighty Joe Young.* (**R**)

TAP ROOTS

1948 Universal
PRODUCER: Walter Wanger
DIRECTOR: George Marshall
SCREENWRITER: Alan Lemay

Van Heflin and Southern belle Susan Hayward are would-be lovers in Mississippi during the Civil War. Boris Karloff is Tishomingo, a friendly Indian with braids. With Ward Bond, Julie London, Richard Long, and Arthur Shields.

Mara Corday and John Agar in Jack Arnold's Tarantula.

TARANTULA

1955 Universal (B&W)
PRODUCER: William Alland
DIRECTOR: Jack Arnold
SCREENWRITERS: Robert M. Fresco, Martin Berkeley

Professor Leo G. Carroll experiments with artificial food in his desert lab. It causes lab animals to grow large but gives people acromegaly. Crazed deformed assistant Eddie Parker destroys the lab, unleashing the 100-foot-tall tarantula, which kills cattle, then people. John Agar and Mara Corday (as "Steve") try to help the ugly, dying professor and destroy the tarantula before it attacks the town. Air Force pilot Clint Eastwood (in a very small role) drops an effective bomb on the monster. One of the better giant-creature movies, it was based on an episode of the *Science Fiction Theatre* TV show. With Nestor Paiva.

TARANTULAS, THE DEADLY CARGO
1977 TV
PRODUCER: Paul Freeman
DIRECTOR: Stuart Hagmann
SCREENWRITERS: Guerdon Trueblood, John Groves

A Southwestern town is attacked by tarantulas that escape from a crashed cargo plane. With Claude Akins and Pat Hingle. It was a theatrical release in Europe. *Kingdom of the Spiders* was released the same year. It's better.

TARGET EARTH
1954 Allied Artists (B&W)
PRODUCER: Herman Cohen
DIRECTOR: Sherman A. Rose
SCREENWRITER: William Raynor

Only six people are left in Chicago after robots from Venus attack—and some of them are selfish gangsters! Richard Denning and Kathleen Crowley are the ones to cheer for. A tall robot with corrugated legs, really broad square shoulders, ice tongs for hands, and a death-ray eye is one of filmdom's best. In addition, this movie has Whit Bissell, Virginia Grey, Arthur Space, and House Peters, Jr. The science-fiction gangster theme later showed up in *The Day the World Ended* and *The Astounding She-Monster*. First-time producer Cohen was 23 when this was made.

TARGET: HARRY
1969 ABC Pictures International
PRODUCER: Gene Corman
DIRECTOR: Henry Neill (Roger Corman)
SCREENWRITER: Bob Barbash
ALSO RELEASED AS: *What's in It for Harry?*; *How to Make It*

A TV-movie deemed too violent to air. It played in Europe with some nude scenes added and showed up in some American theaters in 1980. It's a James Bondish spy film with a *Maltese Falcon* plot, filmed partially in Monte Carlo and Istanbul. Vic Morrow stars as Harry. Victor Buono is after plates stolen from the British Mint. So is double-crossing Suzanne Pleshette. Also with Cesar Romero, Stanley Holloway, Charlotte Rampling, Michael Ansara, and Milton Reid. Music by Les Baxter.

TARGETS
1968 Paramount
PRODUCER/DIRECTOR/SCREENWRITER: Peter Bogdanovich

Excellent first feature by Bogdanovich, a former assistant to Roger Corman, who was executive producer. Tim O'Kelly, a handsome California WASP, buys a rifle with a telescopic lens, then goes home and slaughters his family. After picking off motorists from atop a gasoline tank he hides out behind the screen at a drive-in and starts shooting people in their cars. Meanwhile aging horror star Brian Orlock (Boris Karloff) arrives to promote his new film and confronts the sniper, who gets so confused at seeing the real and the reel Orlock that the police are able to close in and arrest him. Boris is great in what should have been his last role (he made five more films, all pathetic). Bogdanovich, who also plays the writer-director of Boris' film-within-the-film, pulls off a contemporary horror classic. In comparison the tame supernatural shocks of old movies, represented here by clips from *The Terror* and a 1931 Karloff film, *The Criminal Code*, seem incredibly dated. With Nancy Hsueh, Sandy Baron, Mike Farrell, Jack Nicholson, and Dick Miller. Cinematography by Laszlo Kovacs.

TARZAN AND HIS MATE
1934 MGM (B&W)
PRODUCER: Bernard H. Hyman
DIRECTORS: Cedric Gibbons, Jack Conway
SCREENWRITER: James Kevin McGuinness

In the great sequel to *Tarzan the Ape Man*, more white men invade the jungle paradise, greedy for ivory. Tarzan fights a rhino and a giant crocodile, and is helped by a herd of elephants and a group of men in unconvincing gorilla suits. Johnny Weissmuller and Maureen O'Sullivan got to wear their brief loincloths for the last time. Too much thigh, ruled the Hays office. An "offensive" scene in which Jane's breast was revealed got cut to please the censors. With Neil Hamilton repeating his role as Jane's dejected admirer and Paul Cavanagh.

TARZAN AND THE AMAZONS
1945 RKO (B&W)
PRODUCER: Sol Lesser
DIRECTOR: Kurt Neumann
SCREENWRITER: Hans Jacoby,
Marjorie L. Pfaelzer

A new Jane (Brenda Joyce) joins Tarzan (Johnny Weissmuller) and Boy (Johnny Sheffield) in a story about a lost tribe of white women led by old Maria Ouspenskaya, better know as an expert on lycanthropy. Barton Maclane is a villain. Advertised as: "Lovely pagans vs. white man's evil!" For some reason, black natives virtually disappeared from the jungle in the six RKO/Weissmuller Tarzan movies.

TARZAN AND THE GREAT RIVER
1967 Paramount
PRODUCER: Sy Weintraub
DIRECTOR: Robert Day
SCREENWRITER: Bob Barbash

Tarzan (Mike Henry) joins a grizzled Jan Murray, Michael Padilla, Jr., as Pepe, a pet lion, and Dinky the chimp to defeat the Leopard Men. Filmed on location in Brazil. The most juvenile Tarzan in years.

TARZAN AND THE GREEN GODDESS
1938 Principal (B&W)
PRODUCERS: George W. Stout,
Ben S. Cohen, Ashton Dearholt,
Edward Rice Burroughs
DIRECTOR: Edward Kull
SCREENWRITER: Charles F. Royal

A re-edited version of *The New Adventures of Tarzan*, with some previously unused footage added. Herman Brix stars.

TARZAN AND THE HUNTRESS
1947 RKO (B&W)
PRODUCER/DIRECTOR: Kurt Neumann
SCREENWRITERS: Jerry Gruskin,
Rowland Leigh

This was the last time around for Johnny Sheffield as Boy. He went on to play Bomba in eleven awful adventures. It was also the second-to-the-last for Johnny Weissmuller. Tanya, the huntress of the title is Patricia Morison. Brenda Joyce is Jane. Tarzan issues a call to all the animals of the jungle to stop the bad guy hunters led by Barton Maclane.

TARZAN AND THE JUNGLE BOY
1968 Paramount (U.S./Switzerland)
PRODUCER: Robert Day
DIRECTOR: Robert Gordon
SCREENWRITER: Stephen Lord

Mike Henry, the modern Tarzan, does one last filmed-in-Brazil entry. He helps Alizia Gur find a lost white jungle boy. Henry was supposed to star in the TV series, but resigned from the role before the first of his three Tarzan films was even released. His next film was *The Green Berets*.

TARZAN AND THE LEOPARD WOMAN

1946 RKO (B&W)
PRODUCER/DIRECTOR: Kurt Neumann
SCREENWRITER: Carroll Young

By the mid-40s the Tarzan series needed help: Maureen O'Sullivan was long gone, Johnny Sheffield was getting too big to be called Boy, and things were becoming pretty dull in the RKO jungle. Unlike other entries at the time, this one is great because of a plot worthy of Edgar Rice Burroughs and Aquanetta as the high priestess of the leopard cult. She was probably the most exotic-looking actress in the '40s. You might remember her as Paula the Ape Woman in *Jungle Captive* and *Jungle Woman*. Johnny Weissmuller stars with Brenda Joyce as a blond Jane, Edgar Barrier, Dennis Hoey, and the "beast-claw men."

TARZAN AND THE LOST SAFARI

1957 MGM
PRODUCER: John Croydon
DIRECTOR: Bruce Humberstone
SCREENWRITERS: Montgomery Pittman, Lillie Hayward

Gordon Scott in the second of his six Tarzan movies. It was the first in color and involves a millionaire playboy and his friends crashing in the jungle. Nobody plays Jane. The British cast includes George Coulouris, Wilfrid Hyde-White, Yolande Donlan, and Robert Beatty. It was filmed entirely on location in Africa and features "14 different tribes," according to the studio publicity.

TARZAN AND THE MERMAIDS

1948 RKO (B&W)
PRODUCER: Sol Lesser
DIRECTOR: Robert Florey
SCREENWRITER: Carroll Young

Sad, but true—after making the jungle safe for 16 years, Johnny Weissmuller was forced to retire. For this, his last appearance, RKO hired a good director, Robert Florey (*Murders in the Rue Morgue, Beast with Five Fingers*), and shot on location in Mexico. Tarzan leaves Jane (Brenda Joyce) behind and helps Linda Christian and her native islander people revolt against their evil, living god, who resides in a pyramid. With the great villain George Zucco and an octopus fight! Music by Dimitri Tiomkin. Later the same year, Weissmuller became "Jungle Jim," who he went on to play in 16 horrendous features and a TV series. Lex Barker took over as Tarzan.

TARZAN AND THE SHE DEVIL

1953 RKO (B&W)
PRODUCER: Sol Lesser
DIRECTOR: Kurt Neumann
SCREENWRITERS: Karl Kamb, Carroll Young

Monique Van Vooren stars as Lyra, the seductive "she devil" who has Tarzan whipped. Raymond Burr as Vargo and Tom Conway as Fidel are her evil, ivory-stealing partners. Joyce Mackenzie is Jane. It was the last and funniest Lex Barker/Tarzan movie. That year Barker married Lana Turner, becoming the fourth of her seven husbands. Gordon Scott took over the apeman role next. From the director of *The She Devil*, an unrelated '57 feature.

TARZAN AND THE SLAVE GIRL

1950 RKO (B&W)
PRODUCER: Sol Lesser
DIRECTOR: Lee Sholem
SCREENWRITERS: Hans Jacoby, Arnold Belgaro

Tarzan (Lex Barker) is made a slave of the lost tribe of Lionians. Jane is Vanessa Brown. The cast includes Robert Alda, Arthur Shields, Eva Gabor,

TARZAN AND THE TRAPPERS

1958 TV
PRODUCER: Sol Lesser
DIRECTOR: Bruce Humberstone
SCREENWRITER: Thomas Hal Phillips

For anybody who cares, this one is missing from most complete Tarzan lists. It's a combination of three TV pilots. The same cast and director Humberstone did *Tarzan's Fight for Life* the same

TARZAN AND THE VALLEY OF GOLD

1966 AIP
PRODUCER: Sy Weintraub
DIRECTOR: Robert Day
SCREENWRITER: Clair Huffakep

Cheeta, Johnny Weissmuller, and Maureen O'Sullivan in Tarzan Escapes.

683

Ex-pro football star Mike Henry was the 14th screen Tarzan. After doing three features, he sued the producer for physical and mental injury (Dinky the chimp bit him). This, the first of Henry's series, features Nancy Kovack, a bald Don Megowan (*Creation of the Humanoids*), and Michael Padilla, Jr., as Ramel, the kidnaped boy rescued by the updated Tarzan. Filmed in Mexico. With Carlos Rilas (*They Saved Hitler's Brain*).

TARZAN ESCAPES
1936 MGM (B&W)
PRODUCER: Sam Zimbalist
DIRECTORS/SCREENWRITERS: James McKay, John Farrow, Richard Thorpe

One of the best Tarzan films, it would have been really great if left in its original form. Called "The Capture of Tarzan," it featured giant vampire bats, pygmies, and lizards. The studio decided it was too scary. Scenes were altered, reshot, or totally deleted. Three directors worked on the feature, including John Farrow, who married star Maureen O'Sullivan after being fired. Most of one awesome scene remains: the Ganelonis natives tie bent trees to the limbs of spread-eagled victims, causing their bodies to sail through the air in several directions at once. The plot concerns evil hunters tricking Jane into leaving the jungle and a heartbroken Tarzan (Johnny Weissmuller) giving up and locking himself in an iron cage. The elaborate treehouse appears for the first time and Jane wears a new one-piece dress to replace her old, revealing two-piece. With an elephant stampede, the crocodile fight from *Tarzan and His Mate*, and a one-fanged native called Bomba, played by Darby Jones of *I Walked with a Zombie*. John Buckler is Captain Frye.

TARZAN FINDS A SON!
1939 MGM (B&W)
PRODUCER: Sam Zimbalist
DIRECTOR: Richard Thorpe
SCREENWRITER: Cyril Hume
In the original print of MGM's fourth Tarzan adventure, Jane dies. Before it was released Edgar Rice Burroughs said they had no right to kill off his character. The ending was refilmed and Maureen O'Sullivan was talked into doing two more entries (i.e. paid more). Five-year-old Johnny Sheffield is Boy, who falls out of the sky to keep Tarzan and Jane company. The plot concerns a safari to find the lost Boy, hostile natives, and yet another elephant stampede. Incredibly, the scene of Johnny Weissmuller fighting a crocodile was used for the third film in a row. Screenwriter Hume also did *Forbidden Planet*. With Ian Hunter, Frieda Inescort, and Henry Wilcoxon.

TARZAN GOES TO INDIA
1962 MGM (U.S./England/Switzerland)
PRODUCER: Sy Weintraub
DIRECTOR: John Guillermin
SCREENWRITERS: Robert Hardy Andrews, John Guillerman
Jock Mahoney, the villain in *Tarzan, the Magnificent*, becomes the hero in this adventure shot on location. Ravi Shankar wrote the Indian music. Tarzan saves a herd of elephants from drowning because of a dam project. Leo Gordon and Mark Dana are the thoughtless contractor villains. With Jai the Elephant Boy and Peter Cooke. Director Guillermin later made *The Towering Inferno* and *King Kong*.

TARZAN THE APE MAN
1932 MGM (B&W)
PRODUCER: Irving Thalberg
DIRECTOR: W.S. Van Dyke
SCREENWRITERS: Cyril Hume, Ivor Novello

Above left: *Denny Miller stars in Al Zimbalist's Tarzan, the Ape Man re-make ('59).*

Below left: *Maureen O'Sullivan as Jane in Tarzan and His Mate ('34).*

Below right: *Bo Derek and friend in the latest* Tarzan, the Ape Man *fiasco ('81).*

Twenty-eight-year-old Olympic swimming champ Johnny Weissmuller makes screen history in the first all-talking Tarzan picture. Made partially with leftover footage from the 1931 hit *Trader Horn*, by the same director, it led to five more MGM Tarzans. Maureen O'Sullivan, 20 years old when she started, played Jane in all of them. The story, bearing little relation to Burroughs' novel, features a safari led by Jane's father (C. Aubrey Smith) after ivory in the legendary Elephant's Graveyard. A tribe of pygmies lower Tarzan into a pit containing Zumangani, a huge gorilla. Elephants stampede the native village and the Englishwoman Jane Parker stays in the jungle with her apeman lover. Despite the studio sets, it's a classic adventure. With Neil Hamilton. *Tarzan and his Mate* was an immediate sequel.

TARZAN, THE APE MAN
1959 MGM
PRODUCER: Al Zimbalist
DIRECTOR: Joseph Newman
SCREENWRITER: Robert Hill

The worst Tarzan movie ever! Produced by the man responsible for *Robot Monster*, it stars ex-UCLA basketball star Denny Miller. The blond first-time actor made $175 a week. He made more on *Wagon Train* a few years later. This remake features endless chunks of the 1932 version, *Tarzan and His Mate* and *King Solomon's Mines*. The old black-and-white Weissmuller shots are tinted. The horrible new portions featuring Joanna Barnes and Cesare Danova are in color. The pygmies are played by Los Angeles high school kids! A laugh riot.

TARZAN, THE APE MAN
1981 MGM/UA
PRODUCER: Bo Derek
DIRECTOR: John Derek
SCREENWRITERS: Tom Rowe,
Gary Goddard

Lots of us were suckered into seeing this silly, dull remake because of the totally manufactured Bo Derek mania. As Jane's father, Richard Harris rants. As Jane, Bo has her body painted white. John Phillip Law takes pictures, and Tarzan fights a snake in slow motion. The best acting is by Steven Strong as the native king. Somebody plays Tarzan. The estate of Edgar Rice Burroughs sued, creating more publicity. **(R)**

TARZAN THE FEARLESS
1933 Principal (B&W)
PRODUCER: Sol Lesser
DIRECTOR: Robert Hill
SCREENWRITERS: Basil Dickey,
George Plympton, Walter Anthony

Buster Crabbe was the first spinoff Tarzan to cash in on the success of Weissmuller's *Tarzan, the Ape Man* ('32). Like Weissmuller, "perfect man" Crabbe was an Olympic swimming star and had already played a pseudo-Tarzan in *King of the Jungle*. This delightful, ancient-looking artifact was released as a 12-chapter serial and then as a feature edited from the first four chapters. Let Buster tell the story: "We shot most of ours on the back lot in six weeks and we only had a few animals: a chimp, an old elephant, and a lion, which fortunately didn't have a tooth in his head." Includes men-in-suit gorillas, white natives that dress like Egyptians, and Mischa Auer as the high priest of Zar. Jacqueline Wells, later known as Julie Bishop, plays the Jane role. Guaranteed fun. Producer Lesser turned up five years later with another Weissmuller rival in *Tarzan's Revenge*. With Darby Jones.

TARZAN THE MAGNIFICENT
1960 Paramount (England)
PRODUCER: Sy Weintraub
DIRECTOR: Robert Day
SCREENWRITERS: Berne Giler, Robert Day

In his fifth and final Tarzan appearance, Gordon Scott escorts a criminal (Jock Mahoney—the next Tarzan) to jungle police. With Lionel Jeffries, Betta St. John, and everybody's fave star—John Carradine. A hit follow-up to *Tarzan's Greatest Adventure*, filmed in Africa and London. Scott went on to Italy to play Hercules types.

TARZAN TRIUMPHS

1943 RKO (B&W)
PRODUCER: Sol Lesser
DIRECTOR: William Thiele
SCREENWRITERS: Ray Chanslor, Carroll Young

Johnny Weissmuller as Tarzan and Johnny Sheffield as Boy leave MGM and Jane for RKO and a battle with Nazis! Frances Gifford, who was Burroughs "Jungle Girl" in a 1941 serial, is Princess Zandra and she needs help from the patriotic ape man. With Stanley Ridges, Sig Ruman, Pedro De Cordoba, and Cheetah—as herself. Great dialogue as usual: "Now Tarzan make war!"

TARZAN'S DEADLY SILENCE

1970 National General
PRODUCER: Leon Benson
DIRECTOR: Robert L. Friend
SCREENWRITERS: Lee Edwin,
Jack A. Robinson,
John and Tom Considine

Were you tricked into paying to see these strung-together TV episodes? Ex-Tarzan Jock Mahoney plays the general, a villain with a whip. With Woody Strode and Nichelle Nichols (Lt. Uhura from *Star Trek*). See *Tarzan's Jungle Rebellion* for the regulars.

TARZAN'S DESERT MYSTERY

1943 RKO (B&W)
PRODUCER: Sol Lesser
DIRECTOR: William Thiele
SCREENWRITER: Edward T. Lowe

Tarzan (Johnny Weissmuller) fights Nazis again in a quickie follow-up to *Tarzan Triumphs*. After rescuing an American magician (Nancy Kelly) from hanging in an Arab city, he encounters dinosaur footage from *One Million B. C.* and throws a few of der Führer's men to a giant spider! Generally considered the most ridiculous of the series, it features Otto Kruger, Joe Sawyer, Robert Lowery, Johnny Sheffield as Boy for the fifth time, and a man-eating plant.

TARZAN'S FIGHT FOR LIFE

1958 MGM
PRODUCER: Sol Lesser
DIRECTOR: Bruce Humberstone
SCREENWRITER: Thomas Hal Phillips

Gordon Scott is the jungle hero. Eve Brent is Jane. Tarzan helps white doctors battle black magic. Partially filmed in Africa. With Woody Strode as Ramo. The same cast made some TV pilots, later released as *Tarzan and the Trappers*.

TARZAN'S GREATEST ADVENTURE

1959 Paramount (England)
PRODUCER: Sy Weintraub
DIRECTOR: John Guillermin
SCREENWRITERS: Berne Giler,
John Guillermin

One of the best Tarzan adventures, it was filmed in Africa and London and features Sean Connery and Anthony Quayle as villains. At the time it was considered quite "adult" for a Tarzan movie. Gordon Scott stars with Sara Shane and Scilla Gabel. No Jane or Cheetah. In Cinemascope.

TARZAN'S HIDDEN JUNGLE

1955 RKO (B&W)
PRODUCER: Sol Lesser
DIRECTOR: Harold Schuster
SCREENWRITER: William Lively

Tarzan's New York Adventure.

Gordon Scott, a former lifeguard whose real name is Gordon Werschkull, is Tarzan for the first of six times. Vera Miles co-stars as Jill Hardy. Scott married her after this cheap, substandard adventure movie was finished. Peter Van Eyck is a doctor and Jack Elam is Burger (a bad guy). Rex Ingram is Sukulu Makumwa. Besides starring in *Green Pastures* and *The Thief of Baghdad*, Ingram was in the very first Tarzan movie in 1918. This was the last of the dozen RKO Tarzans.

TARZAN'S JUNGLE REBELLION

1970 National General
PRODUCER: Steve Shagan
DIRECTOR: William Witney
SCREENWRITER: Jackson Gillis

People paid to go see this feature made from episodes of the TV series (1966–69) starring Ron Ely. Suckers! With Sam Jaffe, William (*Blacula*) Marshall, Jason Evers, Manuel Padilla, Jr. (left over from the Mike Henry features),

as Jai, Packy the elephant, and Cheetah. The six-foot four-inch Ely now hosts TV game shows. His Tarzan yell was actually provided by a Johnny Weissmuller sound track from over 30 years earlier.

TARZAN'S MAGIC FOUNTAIN

1949 RKO (B&W)
PRODUCER: Sol Lesser
DIRECTOR: Lee Sholem
SCREENWRITERS: Curt Siodmak,
  Harry Chandler

For the first time, Lex Barker puts on the loincloth vacated by Johnny Weissmuller. Brenda Joyce returns as Jane for the fifth and last time. The plot is right out of *Lost Horizon*. Evelyn Ankers never grows old after she crash-lands in a magic jungle. "Dr. Cyclops" himself (Albert Dekker) is on hand as the villain. Edgar Rice Burroughs was on the set during filming. He died a few months later. The film was not a hit. With Alan Napier, Henry Kulky, and Elmo Lincoln in a bit part.

TARZAN'S NEW YORK ADVENTURE

1942 MGM (B&W)
PRODUCER: Frederick Stephani
DIRECTOR: Richard Thorpe
SCREENWRITERS: William R. Lipman,
Myles Connolly

Even if you hate Tarzan movies you might like this nonjungle adventure. It was a commercial flop when released and Maureen O'Sullivan quit the series after acting in it. When Boy is kidnaped by some low-life promoters and taken to Brooklyn, his family (with scene-stealing Cheetah) flies to New York to find him. Tarzan (Johnny Weissmuller in a business suit) has to put up with hotels, skyscrapers, nightclubs, and the clean 1942 subway. After swinging from tall buildings, jumping off the Brooklyn Bridge, and causing random trouble, Tarzan is hauled into court, where is is accused of not properly adopting Boy and not being married. Having had enough of the crazy white man's laws, he picks up the prosecuting attorney and throws him at the jury! At the same time as it moralizes about civilization vs. the simple life, it features blacks (including Mantan Moreland) in typically demeaning roles as porters and maids. Tarzan can't relate to the "Stone jungle" blacks. With Virginia Grey, Chill Wills, and a bit by Elmo Lincoln, the original Tarzan. The crocodile fight scene from *Tarzan and his Mate* was used for the fourth time! The series moved to RKO and got even cheaper.

TARZAN'S PERIL

1951 RKO (B&W)
PRODUCER: Sol Lesser
DIRECTOR: Byron Haskin
SCREENWRITERS: Samuel Newman,
Francis Swann

The third of five films with Lex Barker as Tarzan. Two escaped convicts try to kill Tarzan. Virginia Huston is Jane. As Queen Melmendi, Dorothy Dandridge (*Porgy and Bess*) is kidnaped, tied to the stake, and rescued by the jungle hero. With George Macready, Douglas Fowley, and Alan Napier. It was the first Tarzan filmed on location in Africa.

TARZAN'S REVENGE

1938 20th Century-Fox (B&W)
PRODUCER: Sol Lesser
DIRECTOR: Ross Lederman
SCREENWRITERS: Robert Lee Johnson,
Jay Vann

After *Tarzan Escapes* it was three years before MGM finished the next Johnny Weissmuller feature. To fill the void, 20th Century-Fox made this one-shot disaster with Olympic decathlon champ Glenn Morris. Morris retired from acting. Producer Lesser eventually got to make Weissmuller films at RKO. Eleanor Parker is the love interest. Also with Joe Sawyer and Hedda Hopper. It's generally thought to be one of the worst Tarzan movies ever. Nobody but Weissmuller played the jungle hero again until 1949.

Dorothy Dandridge as the Queen in Tarzan's Peril. Note the bald makeup jobs on her subjects.

TARZAN'S SAVAGE FURY

1952 RKO (B&W)
PRODUCER: Sol Lesser
DIRECTOR: Cy Enfield
SCREENWRITERS: Cyril Hume,
Hans Jacoby, Shirley White

Patric Knowles impersonates Tarzan's cousin in a plot to find diamonds. Lex Barker stars with Dorothy Hart as Jane and a "Boy" substitute called Joey. The first Tarzan film with a Communist villain (Charles Korvin).

TARZAN'S SECRET TREASURE

1941 MGM (B&W)
PRODUCER: B.P. Fineman
DIRECTOR: Richard Thorpe
SCREENWRITERS: Myles Connolly,
Paul Gangelin

More evil white men show up in the jungle and kidnap Jane and Boy to force Tarzan to lead them to some gold. Johnny Weissmuller, Maureen O'Sullivan, and Johnny Sheffield star in a follow-up to *Tarzan Finds a Son*. With Tom Conway, Reginald Owen, and Barry Fitzgerald.

TARZAN'S THREE CHALLENGES

1963 MGM
PRODUCER: Sy Weintraub
DIRECTOR: Robert Day
SCREENWRITERS: Berne Gilor, Robert Day

Jock Mahoney plays Tarzan for the second and final time. He travels to Thailand to help an heir to the throne claim his rightful place. Woody Strode stars in two roles as brothers. The highlight is the bad Woody fighting Tarzan on a net over a pit of coals. Filmed in Thailand. Mahoney, the 13th Tarzan, is Sally Field's stepfather.

A TASTE OF BLOOD

1967 Ajay Films
PRODUCER/DIRECTOR: Herschell Gordon Lewis
SCREENWRITER: Donald Stanford
ALSO RELEASED AS: *The Secret of Dr. Alucard*

A two-hour-long low-budget vampire epic, which some feel is as bad as they come. An American businessman (Bill Rogers) drinks some British brandy and is transformed into a vampire. He goes to England to claim a land inheritance and avenge his ancestor's (Count Dracula) death. Back home in Florida, he hypnotizes his wife (Elizabeth Wilkinson) and kills a stripper named Vivacious Vivian. A Dr. Howard Helsing (Otto Schlesinger) arrives to drive the stake in. It sometimes shared a bill with *Teen-age Strangler*. Filmed in Miami.

A TASTE OF EVIL

1971 TV
PRODUCER: Aaron Spelling
DIRECTOR: John Llewellyn Moxie
SCREENWRITER: Jimmy Sangster

A drive-her-crazy, psychological thriller written by Hammer Films vet Jimmy Sangster. Barbara Parkins returns from an asylum and faces Barbara Stanwyck and William Windom. Roddy McDowall is her doctor. With Arthur O'Connell.

TASTE OF FEAR: See SCREAM OF FEAR.

TASTE THE BLOOD OF DRACULA

1970 Hammer/Warner Brothers (England)
PRODUCER: Aida Young
DIRECTOR: Peter Sasdy
SCREENWRITER: Anthony Hinds

Satanist Ralph Bates convinces three respectable citizens he met at a bordello to go to a desecrated chapel for a blood-drinking ceremony. The men beat him to death but he "becomes" Dracula (Christopher Lee) and takes over their sons and daughters, who then kill their depraved dads. More than ever before, Dracula is the hero. Linda Hayden and Ilsa Blair are vampirized daughters. Lee's brief appearance as the count was his fourth for Hammer; this was the last worthwhile entry in the series. *Scars of Dracula* came next.

THE TATTERED DRESS
1957 Universal
PRODUCER: Albert Zugsmith
DIRECTOR: Jack Arnold
SCREENWRITER: George Zuckerman
Crooked lawyer Jeff Chandler goes to a California desert town to defend a rich but unpopular society figure accused of killing the man who had assaulted his wife. Chandler wins the case but finds himself on trial for bribing a juror. Jack Carson is the local sheriff. With Jeanne Crain, Gail Russell, Edward Platt, Paul Birch, William Schallert, and Elaine Stewart as the tease whose frock gets shredded. Arnold directed *The Incredible Shrinking Man* for Zugsmith the same year.

TATTOO
1981 20th Century-Fox
PRODUCER: Richard P. Levine
DIRECTOR: Bob Brooks
SCREENWRITER: Joyce Bunuel
Bruce Dern returns to the type of demented psycho role that made him such a great character actor in the 60s. As a tattooed ex-soldier living in Hoboken, New Jersey, he kidnaps beautiful Manhattan model Maud Adams. He tattoos her body, they fuck, she stabs him with the tattoo machine. They tried to push this dud with a publicity campaign emphasizing the nudity. Most people yawned and ignored it. **(R)**

JOHN BRINKLEY · ED NELSON · PAT GEORGE
Produced by STAN BICKMAN · Directed by RICHARD HORBERGER
Screenplay by JOHN BRINKLEY and TONY MILLER

T-BIRD GANG
1959 Filmgroup (B&W)
PRODUCER: Roger Corman
DIRECTOR: Richard Harbinger
SCREENWRITERS: John Brinkley, Tony Miller
A youth syndicate run by sadistic Ed Nelson is infiltrated by John Brinkley, a recent high school graduate cooperating with authorities to avenge his father's murder. Gang operations break down when Nelson's right-hand man turns to save Brinkley's neck. The ads promised "Fast cars, fast girls, and no place to go!" With Pat George, Tony Miller (who co-wrote the screenplay with Brinkley), and Beach Dickerson of *Shell Shock*. Score by Shelley Manne. This and co-feature *High School Big Shot* were Filmgroup's first releases. —CB

TEACHER'S PET
1958 Paramount (B&W)
DIRECTOR: George Seaton
SCREENWRITERS: Michael and Fay Kanin

Newspaper editor Clark Gable romances journalism teacher Doris Day. Watch it for Mamie Van Doren and Nick Adams. With Gig Young and Charles Lane.

TEENAGE BAD GIRL

1957 DCA (England) (B&W)
PRODUCER/DIRECTOR: Herbert Wilcox
SCREENWRITER: Felicity Douglas
ALSO RELEASED AS: *Bad Girl*

Sylvia Syms stars as the teen of the title. One of the better juvenile-delinquency films. With Wilfrid Hyde-White, Anna Neagle, and Norman Wooland. Originally co-billed with *Teenage Wolfpack* from Germany.

TEENAGE CAVEMAN

1958 AIP (B&W)
PRODUCER/DIRECTOR: Roger Corman
SCREENWRITER: R. Wright Campbell
ALSO RELEASED AS: *Prehistoric World*

Robert Vaughn plays the rebellious "boy" who breaks his tribal rules, finds "the monster that kills with a touch," and discovers that his prehistoric society is really a postholocaust society. In an

interview Vaughn called it "one of the worst films of all time." He probably said that before starring in *Starship Invasions*. With Jonathan Haze, Robert Shayne, Frank De Korva, and Darrah Marshall, a former Miss Teenage America. Dinosaur footage, courtesy *One Million B.C.* Beach Dickerson actually plays four roles (including a bear) and gets killed three times!

TEEN-AGE CRIME WAVE

1955 Columbia (B&W)
PRODUCER: Sam Katzman
DIRECTOR: Fred F. Sears
SCREENWRITER: Ray Buffum

Advertised as: "The screen-scorching story of today's immoral youth!" An innocent joyride turns into a trip to reform school. Mollie McCart introduces Sue Englund to Tommy Cook and James Ogg on the way to an armed robbery. The four share adventures, including a farmhouse siege and a climactic shootout with the law, in the shadow of a familiar observatory. As the ads claimed, "Teenage terror straight from the sidewalk jungle!"   –CB

TEENAGE DOLL

1957 Allied Artists (B&W)
PRODUCER/DIRECTOR: Roger Corman
SCREENWRITER: Charles B. Griffith
ALSO RELEASED AS: *The Young Rebels*

Advertised as: "The scorching truth about today's thrill-mad hellcats!" (See *Teen-age Crime Wave* for striking contrast.) June Kenney stabs a gang-girl rival in a struggle for the affections of Vandals leader John Brinkley. Kenney escapes to the Vandals' city-dump hideout where she finds the guys engaged in debauchery with their counterpart Vandalettes. All concerned prepare for a major confrontation with the Black Widows and their Tarantula boyfriends. More advertising creativity: "This is not a pretty story, but it's true!" With

Contributing to the Teenage Crime Wave.

Collette Jackson, Ed Nelson, Ziva Rodann, Bruno Ve Sota, Barboura Morris, Richard Devon, and an unbelievable geeklike mother. Original cofeature: *Undersea Girl*. A Woolner Brothers production.　　　　–CB

TEENAGE MILLIONAIRE

1961 United Artists
(B&W with color sequence)
PRODUCER: Howard B. Kreitsek
DIRECTOR: Lawrence F. Doheny
SCREENWRITER: H. B. Cross

Millionaire Jimmy Clanton is cared for by his aunt (Zasu Pitts) and his bodyguard Rocky (Rocky Graziano). He sneaks his own record on the family radio station and it's a hit. At the happy ending he's drafted. Watch it for performances by Dion, Jackie Wilson, Marv Johnson, Chubby Checker, and Bill Black's Combo. Includes 20 songs. With Jack Larson (TV's Jimmy Olsen).

693

TEENAGE MONSTER

1957 Howco (B&W)
PRODUCER/DIRECTOR: Jacques Marquette
SCREENWRITER: Ray Buffum
ALSO RELEASED AS: *Meteor Monster*

Terrible slow science-fiction horror set in the 19th-century West. A boy turns into a hairy murdering moron after being exposed to a meteor. Loving mother Anne Gwynne hides the ugly killer from the sheriff. With Gloria Costello. Gilbert Perkins is the monster.

TEENAGE PSYCHO MEETS BLOODY MARY: See THE INCREDIBLY STRANGE CREATURES WHO STOPPED LIVING AND BECAME CRAZY MIXED-UP ZOMBIES.

TEENAGE REBELLION

1967 (B&W)
PRODUCER/DIRECTOR/SCREENWRITER:
Norman Herman
ALSO RELEASED AS: *Mondo Teeno*

World youth in revolt! Burt Topper narrates as the young go mad on drugs, sex, rock music, and wild fashions. Brit-ish scenes directed by Richard Lester; additional footage from the U.S., Sweden, Italy, France, and Japan.   –CB

TEEN-AGE STRANGLER

1964 Ajay
PRODUCER/SCREENWRITER: Clark Davis
DIRECTOR: Bill Posner

Made in West Virginia in 1964, starring Bill A. Bloom, Jo Canterbury, John Ensign, Jim Asp, Bill Mills, and Johnny Haymer. It has something to do with a high school Bluebeard. In 1967 this obscurity showed up as a co-feature with Herschell Gordon Lewis' A *Taste of Blood.*   –CB

TEENAGE THUNDER

1958 Howco (B&W)
PRODUCER: Jacques Marquette
DIRECTOR: Paul Helmick
SCREENWRITER: Rudy Makoul

From the ads: "How can you tell them to be good—they've too many reasons to be bad!" Filling-station employee Charles Courtney's father doesn't share his son's enthusiasm for drag racing until he wins the big race in the station owner's machine. David Houston sings "Teenage Kisses." Cast includes Melinda Byron, Robert Fuller, Tyler McVey, and Paul Bryar of *Squad Car.* Helmick also directed *Thunder in Carolina.* Stunts by Frank Huszar and his Throttle Merchants.   –CB

REVVED-UP YOUTH ON A THRILL-RAMPAGE!

TEEN AGE THUNDER

"CHICKEN is not just a word ...it's MURDER!

Starring
CHARLES COURTNEY · MELINDA BYRON · ROBERT FULLER

TEENAGE ZOMBIES

1957 Governor (B&W)
PRODUCER/DIRECTOR: Jerry Warren
SCREENWRITER: Jacques Le Cotier

Katherine Victor, a mad doctor on an isolated island uses nerve gas to turn water-skiing teenagers into mindless slaves. Older mindless zombie Chuck

Niles and a mindless gorilla help. Don Sullivan, star of *The Giant Gila Monster*, is the hero. Shot in 1957, it wasn't released until 1960, a bit late for the teen/horror craze.

TEENAGERS FROM OUTER SPACE

1959 Warner Brothers (B&W)
PRODUCER/DIRECTOR/SCREENWRITER:
  Tom Graeff

"They blast the flesh off humans!" claimed the ads. A young alien (David Love) falls for a teenage earth girl (Dawn Anderson) and ruins the plans of his invading cohorts by blowing them up. The invaders, who arrived in a flying saucer, carry deadly ray guns and breed giant lobster monsters for food. Only the shadow of one of the creatures is shown in this extremely low-budget feature picked up by Warners. Some of the music later was heard in *Night of the Living Dead*.

THE TEMPTER

1974 Avco Embassy (Italy)
PRODUCER: Edmondo Amati
DIRECTOR: Alberto DiMartino
SCREENWRITERS: Alberto De Martino,
  Vincenzo Mannino
ORIGINALLY RELEASED AS: *Anticristo*

It took it a while to get here, but this was the first blatant *Exorcist* copy produced. Carla Gravina is a 20-year-old cripple possessed by a witch ancestor. The leering woman with blackened eyes and short, punk blond hair kills her father (Mel Ferrer) and seduces her brother. Arthur Kennedy and George Coulouris are priests. With Alida Valli and the usual green bile, floating bodies, and an orgy in hell. Music by Ennio Morricone. **(R)**

THE TEN COMMANDMENTS

1956 Paramount
PRODUCER/DIRECTOR: Cecil B. DeMille
SCREENWRITERS: Aeneas Mackenzie,
  Jesse L. Lasky, Jr., Jack Guriss,
  Fred M. Frank

Captivating 219-minute all-star epic with Charlton Heston as Moses parting the Red Sea with the help of special effects master John P. Fulton. The last movie directed by the legendary, then 75-year-old DeMille, it was a remake of his 1923 hit. The story is about the Jewish slaves being freed, but other matters take up most of the time. Will evil overlord Edward G. Robinson spoil slave girl Debra Paget for true love John Derek? Will architect Vincent Price flog Derek to death? Will Yul Brynner become Pharaoh Cedric Hardwicke's number-one son? With Anne Baxter, Yvonne DeCarlo, H. B. Warner, Robert Vaughn, Michael Ansara, Clint Walker, Judith Anderson, Woody Strode, Nina Foch—and John Carradine turning staffs into snakes. The next year Irwin Allen tried to top old C.B. with his ridiculous *The Story of Mankind* (also with Price, Carradine, and Hardwicke). In VistaVision, Technicolor, and stereophonic sound. Music by Elmer Bernstein (*Robot Monster*).

TEN LITTLE INDIANS

1965 7 Arts (England)
PRODUCER: Harry Alan Towers
DIRECTOR: George Pollock
SCREENWRITERS: Harry Alan Towers,
  Peter Yeldham

Agatha Christie's *Ten Little Niggers*, previously filmed as *And Then There Were None*, is given a more acceptable title for this British version set in an Austrian castle. As the judge, Wilfrid Hyde-White turns out to be the guilty host. Hugh O'Brian and Shirley Eaton star with Dennis Price, Daliah Lavi, Stanley Holloway, and the unlikely Fabian.

Includes a "who dunit break" in which audiences were supposed to guess who the killer was.

TEN LITTLE INDIANS

1976 Avco-Embassy (Italy, Spain, France, W. Germany)
PRODUCER: Corona/Comeci
DIRECTOR: Peter Collinson
SCREENWRITERS: Enrique Llouet, Erich Krohnke

Murder on the Orient Express was a big hit in '74. It had a big international cast and was based on an Agatha Christie novel. So is this quickie, the third version of Agatha Christie's *Ten Little Niggers*. For some reason the setting is changed from England to Iran! It features Elke Sommer, Oliver Reed, Charles Aznavour, Gert Frobe, Herbert Lom, Richard Attenborough, and the voice of Orson Welles. Executive producer Harry Alan Towers also backed the 1965 version.

THE TENANT

1976 Paramount (France)
PRODUCER: Andrew Braunsberg
DIRECTOR: Roman Polanski
SCREENWRITERS: Roman Polanski, Gerard Brach

Excellent psychological horror film starring director Polanski as Trelkovsky, an out-of-place Polish file clerk in Paris with a new apartment. The previous tenant (a woman) died slowly in a hospital after jumping out her window. Trelkovsky seems doomed to repeat her final act. He jumps twice (in drag) while his neighbors watch. A disturbing and visually fascinating film with some subtle touches impossible to catch in one viewing. With Isabelle Adjani, Melvyn Douglas, Jo Van Fleet, Shelley Winters, Claude Dauphin, a tooth in a hole in the wall, a bouncing Polanski head, and (in a film clip) Bruce Lee. (R)

TENDER FLESH

1973 Brut Productions
PRODUCERS: Jack Cushingham, Steven North
DIRECTOR: Laurence Harvey
SCREENWRITER: Wallace C. Bennett
ALSO RELEASED AS: *Welcome to Arrow Beach*

From the ads: "He killed more than he could eat." The year he died Lithuanian-born Laurence Harvey directed himself as a Santa Barbara man living with his sister (Joanna Pettet). They're both cannibals. Hippie Meg Foster finds out and goes to the cops Stuart Whitman and John Ireland but they don't believe her. You won't either. Warner Brothers decided not to release it at the last minute, so a cut version ended up on the exploitation circuit in '76. With Jesse Vint. Harvey also functioned as executive producer. (R)

TENNESSEE'S PARTNER

1955 RKO
PRODUCER: Benedict Borgeaus
DIRECTOR: Allan Dwan
SCREENWRITERS: Milton Krims,
  D.D. Beauchamp, Graham Baker,
  Teddi Sherman

As unusual, popular Western with Ronald Reagan as a lonesome cowboy helped by gambler John Payne. Rhonda Fleming runs the elaborate whorehouse where much of the action takes place. With Coleen Gray, Morris Ankrum, Leo Gordon, Myron Healy, and Angie Dickinson as "a girl." After this, Reagan made only one more theatrical feature —*Hellcats of the Navy*.

TENTACLES

1977 AIP (Italy)
PRODUCER: E.F. Doria
DIRECTOR: Oliver Hellman
  (Olvidio Assonitis)
SCREENWRITERS: Jerome Max, Tito Carpi,
  Steve Carabatsos

The director of *Beyond the Door*, an Italian *Exorcist* copy filmed in California, returns with an Italian *Jaws* copy. It's hard to convey just how boring and useless this octopus-attack film is. John Huston and Shelley Winters star as Mr. & Mrs. Turner. Henry Fonda has a mercifully brief role. With Bo Hopkins, Cesare Danova, and Claude Akins.

THE TENTH VICTIM

1965 Embassy (Italy/France)
PRODUCER: Carlo Ponti
DIRECTOR: Elio Petri
SCREENWRITERS: Elio Petri, Ennio Flaiano,
  Tonino Guerra, Giorgio Salvione
ORIGINALLY RELEASED AS: *La Decima Vittima*

A very '60s look at the 21st century when "the big hunt" has replaced war and Ursula Andress is assigned to kill Marcello Mastroianni. The murder is to be filmed for a tea commercial. The opening sequence features Ursula killing a man with her shooting bra in a New York art gallery. In short blond hair and shades, Marcello eventually falls for his would-be assassin but the legalized killing must go on. With Elsa Martinelli.

TERMINAL ISLAND

1973 Dimension
PRODUCER: Charles Swartz
DIRECTOR: Stephanie Rothman
SCREENWRITERS: Stephanie Rothman,
  Charles Swartz, Jim Barnett

An action feature about four women prisoners being banished to an island housing two camps of male death row convicts. It's a variation on the usual sadistic prison movie with sex and a little feminism added. Ena Hartmen leads a band of rebels. The cast includes Barbara Leigh, Don Marshall, Phyllis Davis (later on *Love, American Style*) and Tom Selleck as a mercy killer doctor. (R)

THE TERMINAL MAN

1974 Warner Brothers
PRODUCER/DIRECTOR/SCREENWRITER:
  Mike Hodges

George Segal, as a man with a psychotic fear of machines, has a small computer planted in his brain to control his violent urges. The operation backfires and the lobotomized Segal goes on a killing spree. Clothing in all black or white adds an arty look to this adaptation of a Michael Crichton novel. With Joan Hackett as a doctor and Jill Clayburgh as a stripper. Hodges later directed *Flash Gordon* for Dino De Laurentiis.

TERRIFIED

1963 Crown International (B&W)
PRODUCER/SCREENWRITER: Richard Bernstein
DIRECTOR: Lew Landers

A hooded phantom fiend who is also a ventriloquist kills people in a ghost town. With Rod Lauren and Tracy Olsen as young fools visiting the town, plus Denver Pyle and Angelo Rossitto. It was the last film by Lew Landers, whose career reached back to the silents.

THE TERROR

1963 AIP-Filmgroup
PRODUCER/DIRECTOR: Roger Corman
SCREENWRITERS: Leo Gordon, Jack Hill

Roger Corman is famous for turnin' 'em out fast. This one was supposedly done in three days! *The Raven* was finished early. The sets were still there and Boris Karloff was still under contract. So why not? Quickly written scenes were handed out to five other directors even though only Corman got screen credit. The others were Francis Ford Coppola, Monte Hellman, Jack Hill, Dennis Jacob, and even star Jack Nicholson. As Lieutenant André Duvalier, Nicholson is totally unconvincing. Lost on the Baltic coast, he follows beautiful woman (ghost?) Sandra Knight to the castle of Baron von Leppe (Karloff). Nicholson and Knight were married at the time. With Corman regulars Dick Miller, as the baron's servant Stephan, and Jonathan Haze as the halfwit Gustan, who lives with a witch. Of course it's disjointed, but think of it as an exercise in economy and speed. A legendary mess.

TERROR

1978 Crown International (England)
PRODUCERS: Les Young, Richard Crafter
DIRECTOR: Norman J. Warren
SCREENWRITER: David McGillvray

In London a man makes a movie showing how his family had burned a witch a hundred years ago. After a private screening relatives and technicians begin to die in various ways. With a floating car and a woman skewered to a tree. Starring John Nolan and Carolyn Courage. It was double-billed with the famous *Dracula's Dog*. (R)

TERROR AT RED WOLF INN: See THE FOLKS AT RED WOLF INN.

TERROR BENEATH THE SEA

1966 Toei/Teleworld (Japan)
EXECUTIVE PRODUCER: Masafumi Soga
DIRECTOR: Hajimo Sato
ORIGINALLY RELEASED AS: *Kaitei Daisenso*

An odd Japanese science-fiction movie about a mad scientist in an underwater city who turns humans into water-breathing robot monsters. The reporter hero is Sinichi "Sonny" Chiba, now known as the streetfighter in martial-arts films. Fun to watch and the transformation scenes are incredible! With Mike Daneen.

TERROR BY NIGHT

1946 Universal (B&W)
PRODUCER/DIRECTOR: Roy William Neill
SCREENWRITER: Frank Gruber

Basil Rathbone and Nigel Bruce as Holmes and Watson attempt to protect the Star of Rhodesia diamond on a train traveling from London to Edinburgh. Alan Mowbray is a friend of Dr. Watson. Skelton Knaggs hides in a coffin. As Lestrade, Dennis Hoey is puzzled.

TERROR CASTLE: See HORROR CASTLE.

TERROR CIRCUS: See BARN OF THE NAKED DEAD.

TERROR CREATURES FROM THE GRAVE

1965 Pacemaker (Italy/U.S.)
PRODUCER: Frank Merle
DIRECTOR: Ralph Zucker (Massimo Pupillo)
SCREENWRITERS: Roberto Natale,
Romano Migliorini
ORIGINALLY RELEASED AS: Cinque Tombe per un Medium

Barbara Steele is the widow of a murdered occultist living in a turn-of-the-century European villa. The husband whom she had helped to kill returns as a ghost and summons dead medieval plague victims to avenge him. Walter Brandi and Marilyn Mitchell (as Steele's daughter) are the romantic survivors.

TERROR EYES: See NIGHT SCHOOL.

THE TERROR FACTOR: See SCARED TO DEATH.

TERROR FROM THE YEAR 5,000

1958 AIP (B&W)
PRODUCER/DIRECTOR/SCREENWRITER: Robert Gurney, Jr.

A favorite '50s cheapie about scientists on an island playing around with a time machine. They receive a futuristic cat with four eyes and later a gorgeous woman who rivals *The Astounding She Monster* for Frederick's of Hollywood–style sexiness. She disguises herself as a nurse and hypnotizes people with her glittery fingernails. Starring Ward Costello, Joyce Holden, and Beatrice Furdeaux. When a couple goes to the mainland to see a movie, it's AIP's *I Was a Teenage Frankenstein*. Part of the sound track was later used for *Night of the Living Dead*.

TERROR FROM UNDER THE HOUSE

1971 Hemisphere (England)
PRODUCER: George Brown
DIRECTOR: Sidney Hayers
SCREENWRITER: John Kruse
ORIGINALLY RELEASED AS: Revenge
ALSO RELEASED AS: After Jenny died,
Inn of Frightened People

The American release company had to devise a deceptive ad campaign and a new scary title to get patrons for this one. Two men whose daughters had been molested and killed discover that the police have released the prime suspect. They kidnap him, beat him, and leave him, thinking he's dead, in the cellar of a pub one of them owns. Most of the time is spent trying to keep the constables and the drinking patrons from discovering their captive, while James Booth, Joan Collins, and their family yell at one another.

TERROR HOUSE: See THE FOLKS AT RED WOLF INN.

TERROR IN THE CRYPT

1963 AIP (Italy/Spain) (B&W)
PRODUCER: William Mulligan
DIRECTOR: Thomas Miller
(Camillo Mastrocinque)
SCREENWRITERS: Maria Del Carment
Martinez Roman, Jose L. Monter
ALSO RELEASED AS: Crypt of Horror
ORIGINALLY RELEASED AS: La Maldicion de los Karnstein

An interesting version of *Carmilla* by J. Sheridan Le Fanu. Christopher Lee (who filmed his scenes in English) stars as Count Karnstein. He consults an exorcist because he thinks his daughter is possessed by a dead witch. The story had previously been filmed as *Blood and Roses*.

TERROR IN THE HAUNTED HOUSE

1958 Howco International (B&W)
PRODUCER/DIRECTOR: William S. Edwards
SCREENWRITER: Robert C. Dennis
ALSO RELEASED AS: *My World Dies Screaming*

The story about a man taking his new wife to the house of her nightmares is no big deal, but when originally released this film used the "Psychorama" process. Words and pictures of skulls and snakes were flashed on the screen for 1/50 of a second to cause subliminal shudders. The process, proven to work by advertisers who "suggested" that audiences buy their products at the concession stand, was banned later in the year. Gerald Mohr and Cathy O'Donnell star.

TERROR IN THE SKY

1971 TV
PRODUCER: Matthew Rapf
DIRECTOR: Bernard Kowalski
SCREENWRITERS: Richard Nelson, Stephen and Elinor Karpf

Television's answer to *Airport* was a remake of *Zero Hour*, the same film that *Airplane* was based on. Troubled ex-helicopter pilot Doug McClure lands a plane when the crew gets food poisoning. With Roddy McDowall, Leif Erickson, Kenneth Tobey (also in *Airport*), Lois Neddleton, and Jack Ging.

TERROR IN THE WAX MUSEUM

1973 Cinerama
PRODUCER: Andrew J. Fenady
DIRECTOR: George Fenady
SCREENWRITER: Jameson Brewer

A badly made rehash of old movies, starring Ray Milland as the sculptor and manager of a mysterious wax museum. It's a Bing Crosby production. Crosby must have wanted to help out-of-work friends—Patric Knowles (*The Wolfman*), Louis Hayward (*Son of Dracula*), Elsa Lanchester (*Bride of Frankenstein*), Broderick Crawford (*10-4*), and Maurice Evans. John Carradine, however, is never out of work: this was his "415th movie"! It's better than the pathetic *Nightmare in Wax* with Cameron Mitchell, but as in that disaster you can see the wax figures breathing.

TERROR IS A MAN

1959 Valiant (U.S./Philippines) (B&W)
EXECUTIVE PRODUCERS: Kane Lynn, Eddie Romero
DIRECTOR: Gerry De Leon
SCREENWRITER: Harry Paul Harber
ALSO RELEASED AS: *Blood Creature*

The original and best Filipino horror film. A mad doctor (Francis Lederer) on Blood Island surgically turns a leopard into a horrible leopard/man. It's basically *The Island of Dr. Moreau* with only one creature. Executive producer Eddie Romero later reworked the theme into a series of John Ashley films. A buzzer warned audiences when a bloody incision was about to be made (a shocking scene at the time). With Greta Thyssen and Richard Derr.

Broderick Crawford (left) offers to buy the wax museum from John Carradine as assistant Steven Marlo stirs the wax cauldron in Terror in the Wax Museum.

THE TERROR OF
DR. MABUSE

1962 Thunder Pictures (W. Germany)
PRODUCER: Artur Brauner
DIRECTOR: Werner Klinger
SCREENWRITERS: Ladislaus Fodor,
Robert A. Stemmle
ALSO RELEASED AS: *Terror of the Mad Doctor*
ORIGINALLY RELEASED AS: *Das Testament des
Dr. Mabuse*

A remake of Fritz Lang's 1933 Dr. Mabuse film. As the head of an asylum, Walter Rilla is being controlled by the dead Dr. Mabuse (Wolfgang Preiss), who had hypnotized him. As Inspector Lohmann, Gert Frobe tries to learn the truth about the apparent return of the late master criminal. With Senta Berger, Helmut Schmid, and Walter Rilla.

TERROR OF FRANKENSTEIN:
See VICTOR FRANKENSTEIN.

THE TERROR OF GODZILLA

1975 Toho/Bob Conn Entertainment
(Japan)
DIRECTOR: Inoshiro Honda
SCREENWRITER: Yukiko Takayama
ORIGINALLY RELEASED AS: *Meka-Gojira no
Gyakusyu*

The most recent Godzilla film at this writing (it's the 15th). It features Mecha-Godzilla and a new birdlike creature called Chitanoceras. Aliens put the controls to the bad metal monster inside an innocent woman, who commits suicide to save Earth.

TERROR OF ROME AGAINST
THE SON OF HERCULES

1964 Avco Embassy-TV (Italy/France)
DIRECTOR: Mario Ciano
SCREENWRITERS:
Amendola and Alfonso Brescia
ORIGINALLY RELEASED AS: *Maciste, Gladia-
tore di Sparta*

The son of Hercules is Maciste (Mark Forest), but he's called Poseidon here.

THE MIGHTY TITAN OF TERROR in his MOST INCREDIBLE ADVENTURE!

ALL NEW! NEVER BEFORE SEEN!

KING of the MONSTERS

The Terror of GODZILLA

a TOHO PRODUCTION in association with TOHO-EIZO COMPANY, LTD.
Distributed by BOB CONN ENTERPRISES   In COLOR and WIDESCREEN   G

The terror of Rome is a skinny ape man. They fight in the gladiatorial arena. Marilu Tolo watches.

TERROR OF SHEBA: See
PERSECUTION.

TERROR OF THE
BLOODHUNTERS

1962 ADP Productions
PRODUCER/DIRECTOR/SCREENWRITER:
Jerry Warren
Jerry Warren, who usually Americanized foreign horror films, occasionally made dismal original features like this one. Robert Clarke (*The Hideous Sun*

Demon) stars as Steven Duval, a French writer sent to the Devil's Island penal colony. He escapes through Jivaro Indian country with the commandant's daughter (Dorothy Haney).

TERROR OF THE MAD DOCTOR: See THE TERROR OF DR. MABUSE.

TERROR OF THE TONGS

1961 Hammer/Columbia (England)
PRODUCER: Kenneth Hyman
DIRECTOR: Anthony Bushell
SCREENWRITER: Jimmy Sangster
Christopher Lee is Chung King, a tong leader in 1910 Hong Kong. His "drug-crazed hatchetmen" brutally kill anybody who stands in the way of his slave and opium sales. A merchant seaman (Geoffrey Toone) whose daughter and servant had been murdered by Chung's men teams up with a former slave (Yvonne Monlaur) to get revenge. Milton Reid (Hammer's resident fat, scary strongman) plays a bald prison guard who shoves long needles into inmates. A good violent adventure. Better than Christopher Lee's Fu Manchu films. With some early Chinese kung fu fighting scenes featuring Burt Kwouk of the Pink Panther series.

TERROR ON THE BEACH

1973 TV
PRODUCER: Allan Jay Factor
DIRECTOR: Paul Wendkos
SCREENWRITER: Bill Suande
The Hills Have Eyes, TV-style. Dennis Weaver, Estelle Parsons, and family take their trailer to the beach for a nice vacation. A Manson-style gang shows up to terrorize them (especially daughter Susan Dey).

TERROR ON THE 40TH FLOOR

1974 TV
PRODUCER: Ed Montagne
DIRECTOR: Jerry Jameson
SCREENWRITER: Jack Turley
TV's *Towering Inferno* copy, with people trapped in the penthouse of a burning skyscraper. The hot cast includes John Forsythe, Joseph Campanella, and Anjanette Comer.

TERROR OUT OF THE SKY

1978 TV
PRODUCER: Peter Nelson
DIRECTOR: Lee H. Katzin
SCREENWRITERS: Guerdon Trueblood, Peter Nelson, Doris Silverton
Remember *The Savage Bees* from '76? (If you can tell one TV bee movie from another, you probably watch too much television.) This is supposed to be a sequel. As bee specialists, Efrem Zimbalist, Jr., and Dan Haggerty fight an attack of the little stingers.

TERROR TRAIN

1981 20th Century-Fox (Canada)
PRODUCER: Harold Greenberg
DIRECTOR: Roger Spottiswoode
SCREENWRITER: Y. T. Drake
Jamie Lee Curtis screams again, as a crew of college kids holding a party aboard a train are terrorized and murdered one by one by a former classmate out for revenge. A few things make this worth enduring the familiar slaughter-movie elements: Stanley Kubrick's favorite cinematographer, John Alcott, is aboard, doing a fine job, despite the problems of shooting within the confines of an actual train; the plot has a couple of bizarre twists that keep the whodunit aspect going till the final reel; and Ben Johnson plays the fatherly conductor. With magician David Copperfield and the required disco scene. **(R)**   –BM

THE TERRORNAUTS

1967 Amicus/Embassy (England)
PRODUCERS: Milton Subotsky,
Max J. Rosenberg
DIRECTOR: Montgomery Tully
SCREENWRITER: John Brunner

Undistinguished British science-fiction adventure. An entire building containing research scientists is transported to another planet. There, a robot who gives intelligence tests takes the Earthlings to yet another planet, populated with green humanoids, to show them the fate of Earth. With Simon Oates and Zena Marshall (*Dr. No*).

TEST TUBE BABIES

1953 Screen Classics (B&W)
PRODUCER: George Weiss
DIRECTOR: Merle Connell
SCREENWRITER: Richard McMahan
ALSO RELEASED AS: *The Pill*

A famous, often banned adults-only sex-instruction shocker from the director of *The Flesh Merchants* and the producer of *Glen or Glenda*. John Maitland stars with Monica Davis of *The Dead One*. Reworked and re-released in 1967 as *The Pill*.   —CB

THE TEXAS CHAINSAW MASSACRE

1974 Bryanston
PRODUCER/DIRECTOR: Tobe Hooper
SCREENWRITERS: Kim Henkel, Tobe Hooper

This crowd-pleasing, low-budget phenomenon is loosely based on the real-life exploits of Ed Gein (see *Deranged*). Three ex-slaughterhouse employees and an ancient grandfather live in a remote farm house full of bones, occult items, and spare body parts (including a human-arm lamp). When two young couples and a crippled friend in a van stupidly stop there looking for gas, the action never stops. Leatherface (Gunnar Hansen, wearing a human skin mask) provides the best moments

with his chainsaw, chasing Marilyn Burns. Filmed in Texas. Director Hooper had previously made an anti-Vietnam war movie and a documentary about Peter, Paul, and Mary! In 1982 a Texas Chainsaw video game was marketed. (**R**)

A moment of terror in The Texas Chainsaw Massacre.

THANK YOU MR. MOTO

1937 20th Century-Fox (B&W)
EXECUTIVE PRODUCER: Sol M. Wurtzel
DIRECTOR: Norman Foster
SCREENWRITERS: Willis Cooper, Norman Foster

As Mr. Moto, Peter Lorre tracks down a scroll that when joined with six others reveals "the golden secret of Kubla Khan"! With Sidney Blackmer, Sig Ruman, John Carradine (as a helpful butler), Philip Ahn (as Prince Chung), Thomas Beck, and Pauline Frederick.

Jack Hawkins and theater critic Robert Morley clutching his beloved twin poodles in Theatre of Blood.

THEATRE OF BLOOD

1973 United Artists (England)
PRODUCERS: John Kohn, Stanley Mann
DIRECTOR: Douglas Hickok
SCREENWRITER: Anthony Greville-Bell

Vincent Price's whole career is a preparation for this wonderful gory revenge comedy. Although inspired by the *Dr. Phibes* films, it's a better production in every way. Price plays Edward Lionheart, a Shakespearean actor who murders theatrical critics using famous death scenes from *Macbeth*, *Richard III*, etc., as models. He's aided by his faithful daughter (Diana Rigg) and a group of tramps. Each killing involves elaborate planning and disguises, with Rigg sometimes playing men. Jack Hawkins is driven to murder his wife (Diana Dors), as in *Othello*. As an outrageously gay critic, Robert Morley is fed his own twin poodles (*Titus Andronicus*). Other victims are Dennis Price, Arthur Lowe, Robert Coote, Madeline Smith, and Harry Andrews. With Ian Hendry and Coral Brown (Mrs. Vincent Price). **(R)**

THEATRE OF DEATH

1967 Hemisphere (England)
PRODUCER: Michael Smedley-Astin
DIRECTOR: Samuel Gallu
SCREENWRITERS: Ellison Kadisous,
Roger Marshall
ALSO RELEASED AS: *Blood Fiend*

Christopher Lee is Phillippe Daruas, director of Grand Guignol horror plays in Paris. The mean, domineering man is a prime suspect in a series of vampirelike killings. Lelia Goldoni and Jenny Till are roommate actresses. A good mystery with a perfect background of faked gore and murders. A slightly risqué voodoo dance segment is often cut. Cinematography by Gilbert Taylor (*Star Wars*).

THEM!

1954 Warner Brothers (B&W)
PRODUCER: David Weisbart
DIRECTOR: Gordon Douglas
SCREENWRITER: Ted Sherdemann

This classic science-fiction film was the first of the oversized-bug movies.

Twelve-foot-high (mechanical) ants caused by radiation are discovered in New Mexico and head for the sewers of L.A. James Whitmore is top-billed as the self-sacrificing police sergeant. FBI agent James Arness and scientist Joan Weldon provide the romantic interest. Edmund Gwenn is Weldon's entomologist father. The movie's great, but the fun of spotting the supporting players makes it even better. The humorous drunk in the alcoholic ward (Olin Howard) was the first victim in *The Blob*. The little girl (Sandy Descher) who can only say "Them!—Them!" was one of Jack Arnold's *Space Children*. The airline pilot who saw the ants is Fess Parker (*Daniel Boone*). Also look for William Schallert (Mr. Lane on *The Patty Duke Show* as well as the voice of "Milton the Toaster"), Onslow Stevens (*The House of Dracula*), Dub Taylor, and Leonard Nimoy. After *Them's* success we were quickly offered *Tarantula*, *The Black Scorpion*, *The Deadly Mantis*, etc.

THESE ARE THE DAMNED

1961 Hammer/Columbia (England)
PRODUCER: Anthony Hinds
DIRECTOR: Joseph Losey
SCREENWRITER: Evan Jones
ALSO RELEASED AS: *The Damned*

A multi-faceted Orwellian classic that received critical acclaim despite cuts by the producer and a total lack of promotion. Macdonald Carey, an American businessman in a British coastal town, is beaten by a gang of Teddy Boys led by Oliver Reed and discovers a secret military installation where radioactive children are taught by closed-circuit television how to survive the inevitable atomic war. Alexander Knox is the cold-blooded man in charge of the project. His former lover, Viveca Lindfors, spends her time sculpting mutant creatures. Shirley Ann Field tries to escape her overprotective, violent brother (Reed). The theme song goes: "Black leather, black leather rock-rock-rock. . ." The end offers no hope at all.

THESE DANGEROUS YEARS: See *DANGEROUS YOUTH.*

THEY CAME FROM BEYOND SPACE

1967 Amicus/Embassy (England)
PRODUCERS: Max J. Rosenberg, Milton Subotsky
DIRECTOR: Freddie Francis
SCREENWRITER: Milton Subotsky

Silly science fiction with forgotten American star Robert Hutton (*The Slime People*) as an astrophysicist. He's got a metal plate in his head, which makes him immune to alien takeover. Everybody else is taken over by astral beings who want slaves to help repair a ship that crashed on the Moon. Hutton and his girl (Jennifer Jayne) go to the

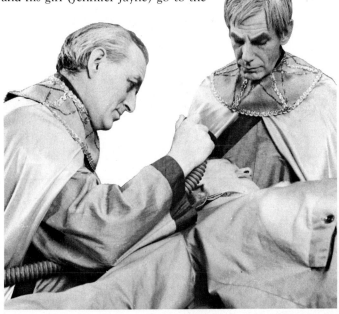

Michael Gough as the alien leader in They Came From Beyond Space.

Moon, meet Michael Gough, and work everything out.

THEY CAME FROM WITHIN

1975 Trans American (Canada)
PRODUCER: Ivan Reitman
DIRECTOR/SCREENWRITER: David Cronenberg
ALSO RELEASED AS: *The Parasite Murders*
ORIGINALLY RELEASED AS: *Frissons*
The first of Cronenberg's unique commercial features has horrible, scientifically created aphrodisiac parasites that live in the stomachs of tenants at a sterile apartment complex on an island near Montreal. Paul Hampton, Joe Silver, and Lynn Lowry star. Barbara Steele receives a parasite while taking a bath. A bloody, queasy, and very personal horror film. Cronenberg's next was *Rabid*. **(R)**

THEY LOVE AS THEY PLEASE: See GREENWICH VILLAGE STORY.

THEY MET IN BOMBAY

1941 MGM (B&W)
PRODUCER: Hunt Stromberg
DIRECTOR: Clarence Brown
SCREENWRITERS: Edwin Justis Mayer, Anita Loos, Leon Gordon
Clark Gable and Rosalind Russell are jewel thieves in a romantic-comedy adventure. Peter Lorre co-stars as Captain Chang, a double-crossing Chinese cargo ship skipper.

THEY RAN FOR THEIR LIVES

1968 Color Vision International
PRODUCER: Samuel Ray Calabrese
DIRECTOR: John Payne
SCREENWRITER: Monroe Manning
Ludicrous desert-chase yarn featuring Luana Patten as a dead oil geologist's daughter who is plagued by thugs lusting after secret documents of some sort. Scott Brady, Jim Davis, and Anthony Eisley run into complications when Luana teams up with strategist John Payne, who also directed. "This oughta slow them down," Payne says as he plants a can of peaches on the trail. Sure enough. The geologist's former partner John Carradine arrives and almost gets the upper hand before Payne's dog Bravo edges him off a cliff. Filmed in the Valley of Fire near Las Vegas. Great title song by the Knickerbockers, who stole much of it from their smash "Lies." —CB

THEY SAVED HITLER'S BRAIN

1963 Crown International (B&W)
PRODUCER: Carl Edwards
DIRECTOR: David Bradley
SCREENWRITERS: Richard Miles, Steve Bennett
ALSO RELEASED AS: *Madmen of Mandoras*
This classic bad movie has been amazing late-night TV viewers for years. Some of it seems to have been shot in the Philippines, some of it in America at a different time, and a car crash was "borrowed" from *Thunder Road*. The incoherent story is about an American neurobiologist who disappears with one of his daughters. Another daughter and her husband fly to a Caribbean island to look for him and find Nazis taking orders from Hitler's head, which has been kept alive on top of a mechanical box. They plan to take over the world with nerve gas and find a new body for der Führer. Hero Walter Stocker was in *Lassie's Greatest Adventure*. Police chief Nestor Paiva is in dozens of science-fiction movies. Hero's wife Audrey Caire went on to greater heights as the wife of the executive in *Joe*. The director was a contributor to *Famous Monsters of Filmland* and directed Charlton Heston in his first role, in a 1941

amateur production of *Peer Gynt.* This production, on the other hand, is *professional.*

THEY'RE COMING TO GET YOU: See DRACULA VS. FRANKENSTEIN.

THE THIEF
1952 United Artists (B&W)
PRODUCER: Clarence Greene
DIRECTOR: Russell Rouse
SCREENWRITERS: Clarence Greene, Russell Rouse
If you don't like too much talking in your movies, here's one without any. Made as an experiment, it features a silent Ray Milland as an atomic scientist forced by a commie spy to microfilm top-secret formulas. Rita Gam, Martin Gabel, and Harry Bronson also keep their mouths closed.

THE THIEF OF BAGHDAD
1940 United Artist (England)
PRODUCER: Alexander Korda
DIRECTORS: Michael Powell, Ludwig Berger, Tim Whelan
SCREENWRITERS: Miles Malleson, Lajos Biro
This classic Arabian Nights spectacle in early Technicolor is still the best fantasy film ever produced. It features a white, winged horse, a giant spider, a flying carpet, and massive sets by William Cameron Menzies (*Things To Come, Invaders from Mars*). Rex Ingram (De Lawd in *Green Pastures*) is the giant flying djinni from the bottle and the great Conrad Veidt is the evil magician Jaffar. Sabu stars in his second film with June Duprez and John Justin. Production in England was stopped by World War II and had to be resumed in Hollywood. It was a remake of a Douglas Fairbanks silent movie and has since been filmed two more times. Music by Miklos Rosza.

THE THIEF OF BAGHDAD
1959 MGM (Italy/France)
PRODUCER: Bruno Vailati
DIRECTOR: Arthur Lubin
SCREENWRITERS: Augusto Frassinetti, Filippo San Just, Bruno Vailati
ORIGINALLY RELEASED AS: *Il Ladro di Bagdad*
The third version of the Arabian Nights fantasy stars Steve (*Hercules*) Reeves. It's not bad at all; it has a winged horse, faceless warriors, and at one point an army of Steve Reeves doubles. With Giorgia Moll and Arturo Dominici.

THE THIEF OF BAGHDAD
1978 TV (England)
PRODUCER: Aida Young
DIRECTOR: Clive Donner
SCREENWRITER: A.J. Carothers
A good cast couldn't save this dull fourth version of the popular Arabian Nights fantasy. Kabir Bedi is the prince. Roddy McDowall is the thief. Terence Stamp is the evil Wazir. With Peter Ustinov, his daughter Paula, Frank Finlay, Ian Holm, and Daniel Emilfork.

THE THIEF OF DAMASCUS
1951 Columbia
PRODUCER: Sam Katzman
DIRECTOR: Will Jason
SCREENWRITER: Robert E. Kent
Paul Henreid says "open sesame." Aladin, Sinbad, and Ali Baba join forces. With Lon Chaney, Jr., Elena Verdugo, and John Sutton.

THIN AIR: See THE BODY STEALERS.

THE THING
1982 Universal
PRODUCERS: David Foster, Lawrence Turman
DIRECTOR: John Carpenter
SCREENWRITER: Bill Lancaster
The ultimate special-effects horror movie. Highly publicized transformation scenes in other recent shockers pale

James Arness as The Thing.

in comparison to the many astounding and often gross and disturbing changes in this one, as an alien presence takes over the bodies of dogs and men stranded at an Antarctic military research post. The 1951 version of John Campbell's *Who Goes There?* was impossible to top in the dialogue department. This version doesn't even try, with star Kurt Russell playing a man of few words. But visually this is real nightmare material. Special effects by Rob Bottin (*The Howling*) and Roy Arbogast (*Jaws*). Partially filmed in Alaska and British Columbia. Music by Ennio Morricone. Script by Burt Lancaster's son. (R)

THE THING (FROM ANOTHER WORLD)
1951 RKO (B&W)
PRODUCER: Howard Hawks
DIRECTOR: Christian Nyby
SCREENWRITER: Charles Lederer
A science-fiction classic that still hasn't been topped. It has all the elements of a barely passable SF movie (small, nonstar cast, a monster, a pretty low budget), but it surpasses them in every way. A flying saucer is discovered (under the ice) by an Arctic research team. They take its frozen alien inhabitant (James Arness) indoors where it thaws out. The plant creature uses human blood to nurture its seeds, and some of the scientists at the base help them to grow. The more sensible military leader (Kenneth Tobey of *The Whirleybirds* television show) puts a stop to that nonsense. Great dialogue and acting, with a strong female lead (Margaret Sheridan). With George Fenneman from *The Groucho Show*. "Watch the skies!"

THE THING THAT COULDN'T DIE
1958 Universal (B&W)
PRODUCER/DIRECTOR: Will Cowan
SCREENWRITER: David Duncan
The living head of a devil worshiper buried by Sir Francis Drake takes over the minds of people on a ranch. The girl that found it discovers the body in a casket and puts the pieces together. Pretty bad. With William Reynolds and Andra Martin.

THE THING WITH TWO HEADS

1972 AIP

PRODUCER: Wes Bishop
DIRECTOR: Lee Frost
SCREENWRITERS: Lee Frost, Wes Bishop, James Gordon White

The ultimate blaxploitation horror movie, not to be confused with the previous year's all-white *Incredible Two-Headed Transplant.* Both are from AIP. This, believe it or not, features Ray Milland as a racist brain surgeon with terminal cancer. Milland first creates a two-headed gorilla (designed by Rick Baker). Then he arranges to have his head transplanted onto the healthy body of a volunteer convict from death row. When he awakens from his operation he finds his head on Rosey Grier's body. You've got to see him (them) running around, riding a motorcycle, yelling at each other, and punching each other in the face. Poor Ray Milland is occasionally spared acting on Grier's shoulder when a dummy head is substituted for action shots. Chelsea Brown is the convict's surprised girlfriend. With Roger Perry, who is also in both *Count Yorga* movies, and William Smith. Music by Jerry Butler. Director Frost worked on lots of '60s "adults only" films.

THINGS TO COME

1936 United Artists (B&W)

PRODUCER: Alexander Korda
DIRECTOR: William Cameron Menzies
SCREENWRITER: H.G. Wells

Science-fiction epic with a screenplay by H.G. Wells—and another classic British Korda production. The story, which spans nearly 100 years, begins during what we now call World War II (predicted by Wells). The war drags on, leaving all the known world in ruins and local tribal dictators in control. In the '70s huge black airships (Wings Over The World) arrive, stop the war, and begin a new age of technology. By 2036 everyone lives in enormous Art Deco underground cities, but problems arise when the first space shot is about to take place. This antique vision of the future features awesome sets and future marvels like TV and jets. The only other movie this can be compared to is *Metropolis.* Raymond Massey stars as Oswald Cabal and as his grandfather, John. With Ralph Richardson as the warlord, Sir Cedric Hardwicke as Theotocopolous, who tries to stop progress, and Margaretta Scott, also in two roles.

THINK FAST, MR. MOTO

1937 20th Century-Fox (B&W)

EXECUTIVE PRODUCER: Sol M. Wurtzel
DIRECTOR: Norman Foster
SCREENWRITERS: Howard Ellis Smith, Norman Foster

Things to Come.

Peter Lorre starred in eight Mr. Moto films in just two years. They're actually better than most of the similar "Charlie Chan" films that were being made by the same studio. In the first entry, the Japanese master of disguises trails diamond smugglers from San Francisco to Shanghai. With Virginia Field, Sig Ruman, J. Carrol Naish, and Thomas Beck. Based on John P. Marquand's novel of the same name. When this was filmed, only one Moto feature was planned.

THIRST

1979 New Line Cinema (Australia)
PRODUCER: Anthony I. Ginnane
DIRECTOR: Rod Hardy
SCREENWRITER: John Pinkney
Beautiful career woman Chantal Contouri is kidnaped and brought to the secret headquarters of a worldwide organization. The group's seductive ringleader (David Hemmings) explains that members of the Hyma Brotherhood believe that their superiority over the rest of humanity stems from the ritualistic consumption of human blood, harvested from a human herd and distributed in milk cartons. A crisp and classy production, despite script holes wide enough to invite freeway construction. With Henry Silva. **(R)**   –BM

THE THIRSTY DEAD

1974 International Amusement (Philippines)
PRODUCER: Wesley E. Depue
DIRECTOR: Terry Becker
SCREENWRITER: Charles Dennis
Laughable horror with captive women fighting each other to become the bride of eternally young jungle cultist John Considine. His slaves kidnap the sexy females for blood sacrifices. The cave sets are pretty unbelievable. With Jennifer Billingsley (*White Lightning*) and

a canoe ride through the sewers of Manila.

13: See EYE OF THE DEVIL.

13 FRIGHTENED GIRLS

1963 Columbia
PRODUCER/DIRECTOR: William Castle
SCREENWRITER: Robert Dillon
A spy adventure aimed at preteens. As the daughter of diplomat Hugh Marlowe, Kathy Dunn has a crush on CIA agent Murray Hamilton. She becomes involved with Chinese Communists and discovers a body in a freezer. With Khigh Dhiegh and a bunch of bratty girls.

THIRTEEN GHOSTS

1960 Columbia (B&W with two color sequences)
PRODUCER/DIRECTOR: William Castle
SCREENWRITER: Robb White
Fun scares about a haunted house filmed in "Illusion-O." Viewers were given a card with two transparent colored plastic squares. The "ghost viewer" square was red. The "ghost remover" square was blue. (So were the ghosts.) Margaret Hamilton is the housekeeper. With Donald Woods, Martin Milner, Rosemary DeCamp, and Jo Morrow. With a flaming skeleton, a headless lion tamer, a lion, and the popular Dr. Zorba.

THE THIRTEENTH CHAIR

1929 MGM (B&W)
PRODUCER/DIRECTOR: Tod Browning
SCREENWRITER: Elliot Clawson
Two years before *Dracula* Bela Lugosi made his first all-sound film for *Dracula*'s director. Browning was known at the time for his Lon Chaney hits. This version of a popular stage play stars Margaret Wycherly as a medium. As Inspector Delzante, Bela helps catch a murderer. With Leila Hyams and Joel McCrea.

It had been filmed before in 1919 and was remade in 1937.

THE 13TH CHAIR
1937 MGM (B&W)
PRODUCER: J.J. Cohn
DIRECTOR: George B. Seitz
SCREENWRITER: Marion Parsonnet
A third version of a mystery play about fake seances. Bela Lugosi was in a 1929 version. This one features Dame May Whitty, Lewis Stone, Henry Daniell, and Elissa Landi.

THE THIRTEENTH GUEST
1932 Monogram (B&W)
PRODUCER: M.H. Hoffman
DIRECTOR: Albert Ray
SCREENWRITERS: Francis Hyland, Arthur Hoerl
A black-hooded killer in a creepy old house electrocutes people by telephone. A mystery that was revived several times because of star Ginger Rogers (in her second film). Lyle Talbot is a detective. Remade as *The Mystery of the 13th Guest*.

-30-
1959 Warner Brothers
PRODUCER/DIRECTOR: Jack Webb
SCREENWRITER: William Bowers
Another Thursday night shift at the *Los Angeles Banner*. Jack Webb arrives late from his weekly visit to the graves of his wife and son to settle in with city editor William Conrad for eight hours of cigarettes and stale coffee. David Nelson and friends relax with "Copy Boy" for voice and bongos, while assorted newsroom types await progress reports on a 5-year-old girl lost in the city's storm-drain system. Cannon and Friday's backups include Richard Bakalyan, Joe Flynn of *McHale's Navy*, and *Hazel's* Whitney Blake. —CB

THE THIRTY FOOT BRIDE OF CANDY ROCK
1959 Columbia (B&W)
EXEC. PRODUCER: Edward Sherman
DIRECTOR: Sidney Miller
SCREENWRITERS: Rowland Barber, Arthur Ross
After he split from Abbott, Costello made this one film alone before he died. A very light counterpart to *The Attack of the 50-Foot Woman*, it features Lou as a meek inventor who turns his girlfriend (Dorothy Provine) into a 30-foot woman. He also has an unusual time machine he uses to turn soldiers into cavemen. With Gale Gordon and Doodles Weaver.

THE 39 STEPS
1959 20th Century-Fox (England)
PRODUCER: Betty E. Box
DIRECTOR: Ralph Thomas
SCREENWRITER: Frank Harvey
Kenneth More and Taina Elg take the star roles in this faithful color remake of Hitchcock's classic. With Barbara Steele. From the director of *It's Not the Size That Counts*. Another version was made in 1978.

THIS HOUSE POSSESSED
1981 TV
PRODUCER/SCREENWRITER: David Levinson
DIRECTOR: William Wiard
A mysterious force controls the surveillance system of a country home owned by a rich rock star! Ex-"Hardy Boy" Parker Stevenson stars with Joan Bennett (as the rag lady) and Slim Pickens.

THIS IS NOT A TEST
1962 Modern (B&W)
PRODUCERS: Frederic Gadette, Murray De'Atlevi
DIRECTOR: F. Gadette
SCREENWRITERS: Peter Abenheim, Betty Lasky, Frederic Gadette

An end-of-the-world atomic-attack movie that has to be seen to be believed. A state trooper stops a small group of travelers; the radio announces an atomic attack. The travelers hide in the back of their van and live. The trooper stays outside and dies. With Seamon Glass and Mary Morlas.

THIS ISLAND EARTH
1955 Universal
PRODUCER: William Alland
DIRECTOR: Joseph Newman
SCREENWRITERS: Franklin Coen,
   Edward G. O'Callaghan

The first serious interplanetary science-fiction epic. Earth scientist Dr. Cal Meacham (Rex Reason) assembles an interociter (a futuristic two-way television) sent to him from the Planet Metaluna. The inquisitive doctor soon finds himself prisoner at a remote research mansion run by Exeter (Jeff Morrow), a superintelligent agent from the dying alien planet. When Dr. Cal and Ruth Adams (Faith Domergue) try to escape, they find themselves in a state of suspended animation aboard Exeter's flying saucer, headed for the horrors of war-torn Metaluna. There, the couple is threatened with space lobotomies (by the good guys), attacked by an incredible mutant insect-man (Eddie Parker), and dodging meteors guided by the destructive Zahgons. They survive with the help of the noble, compassionate Exeter (he likes to listen to Mozart). Although directed by Newman, most of the excitement can probably be credited to unbilled co-director Jack Arnold and producer Alland. Makeup ace Bud Westmore created the famous mutant with the pulsating exposed cranium at a cost of $24,000. Herman Stein wrote the music. Most of the technicians continued to work with the Arnold-Alland team on other superior science-fiction hits. Faith Domergue (a personal discovery of Howard Hughes) made *It Came from Beneath the Sea* and *Cult of the Cobra.* Originally co-billed with *Abbott and Costello Meet the Mummy.* With Russell Johnson and Lance Fuller.

THIS REBEL AGE: See BEAT GENERATION.

THIS REBEL BREED
1960 Warner Brothers (B&W)
PRODUCER: William Rowland
DIRECTOR: Richard L. Bare
SCREENWRITER: Morris Lee Green
ALSO RELEASED AS: *Lola's Mistake*

Blacks vs. whites vs. Mexicans as high school gangs slice each other, push dope, terrorize innocent citizens, and turn young girls into tramps. Two police-academy graduates are assigned an undercover investigation. The cast includes Mark Damon, Rita Moreno, Gerald Mohr, Dyan Cannon, Jay Novello, and Richard Rust. Richard Bare was staff director of *Green Acres* from 1965–69. This film was re-released as an exploitation item in 1965.   –CB

A THOUSAND AND ONE NIGHTS
1945 Columbia
PRODUCER: Samuel Bischoff
DIRECTOR: Alfred E. Green
SCREENWRITERS: Richard English,
   Jack Henley, Wilfred H. Pettit

Aladdin (Cornel Wilde) finds a lamp with a female genie (Evelyn Keyes) in this Technicolor Arabian Nights comedy. Rex Ingram repeats his genie role from *The Thief of Baghdad.* Shelley Winters is a harem girl. With Phil Silvers, Nestor Paiva, and Adele Jergens.

THE 1,000 EYES OF DR. MABUSE

1960 Ajay Films (W. Germany/Italy/France) (B&W)
PRODUCER: Arthur Brauner
DIRECTOR: Fritz Lang
SCREENWRITERS: Fritz Lang, Heinz Oskar Wuttig
ORIGINALLY RELEASED AS: *Die Tausend Augen Des Dr. Mabuse*
ALSO RELEASED AS: *Eyes of Evil*

Fritz Lang returned in his last film to the master-criminal character he had brought to the screen in Germany in 1922 and 1933. His postwar success led to a whole series of Dr. Mabuse thrillers by other directors. They're all fun to watch but this one is a low-budget classic. The Hotel Luxor is completely bugged with hidden TV cameras and see-through mirrors. Commissioner Kraugs (pre-*Goldfinger* Gert Frobe) is investigating 15 murders connected with the hotel, which is run by Jordon (Wolfgang Preiss), a master criminal who thinks he's the reincarnation of the long-dead Mabuse. The bugged-hotel idea was derived from Nazi plans to observe foreign dignitaries visiting Germany after they had won the war. With Peter Van Eyck, Dawn Addams, and Howard Vernon as "Number 12."

THREE BAD SISTERS

1956 United Artists (B&W)
PRODUCER: Howard Koch
DIRECTOR: Gilbert L. Kay
SCREENWRITER: Gerald Drayson Adams

From the ads: "What they did to men was nothing compared to what they did to each other!" Evil Kathleen Hughes wants all of her father's estate for herself. She beats and disfigures her sister, Marla English. Marla commits suicide when she sees her new face. Then Hughes encourages her late father's pilot, John Bromfield, to help unravel sister number two, Sara Shane, promising him a cut. He agrees but instead falls in love with Sara and marries her. The enraged Hughes tells Sara that she and the husband are having a torrid affair. Sara prepares to dive from a cliff as sister and husband fight for the wheel of a speeding car. With Brett Halsey   —CB

THE THREE MUSKETEERS

1948 MGM
PRODUCER: Pandro S. Berman
DIRECTOR: George Sidney
SCREENWRITER: Robert Ardrey

Gene Kelly is D'Artagnan. The musketeers are Van Heflin, Gig Young, and Robert Coote. Lana Turner is Milady, in Technicolor for the first time. Vincent Price is Richelieu. With June Allyson, Angela Lansbury, Keenan Wynn, and Frank (*The Wizard of Oz*) Morgan as King Louis. Lana is decapitated in the end.

THE THREE MUSKETEERS

1973 20th Century-Fox (England)
PRODUCER: Alexander Salkind
DIRECTOR: Richard Lester
SCREENWRITER: George McDonald Fraser

An excellent all-star comedy adventure with Oliver Reed, Richard Chamberlain, and Frank Findlay as the musketeers and Michael York as D'Artagnan. Raquel Welch has her best role as a clumsy servant of spy Faye Dunaway. Christopher Lee has a very good one as the evil Rochefort. Producer Alexander Salkind tricked the cast by filming two movies at once and paying them for one. When *The Four Musketeers* was released the next year, they sued and were awarded substantially more than their original salaries, though not twice as much. Salkind later tried to pull off the same scam for *Superman* and *Superman II*. Also with Geraldine Chaplin, Charlton Heston, Michael Gothard, Spike Milligan, Sybil Danning, and Roy Kinnear (*Help*).

Enjoying a nutritious breakfast in the adults-only Three Nuts in Search of a Bolt

Carolyn Thompson looks at the blood-stained body of her girlfriend in Three on a Meathook.

THREE NUTS IN SEARCH OF A BOLT

1964 Harlequin International (B&W with color sequence)

PRODUCERS/SCREENWRITERS: Tommy Noonan, Ian McGlashan

DIRECTOR: Tommy Noonan

Tommy Noonan, who had once starred with Monroe (in *Gentlemen Prefer Blondes*), went on to Jayne Mansfield (in *Promises, Promises*), and finally Mamie in this "adults only" comedy.

Three "nuts"—Mamie Van Doren (as Saxie Symbol), Paul Gilbert, and John Cronin—can't afford to go to an expensive psychiatrist, so they pay an actor (Tommy Noonan) to go and act out each of their personalities so that all will have their problems solved for the price of one. His session is filmed because Dr. Myra Von (Ziva Rodann) thinks he has a rare triple personality. The film is accidentally aired on TV, making him a celebrity. He becomes rich and is happy ever after with Saxie. With Alvy Moore and T. C. Jones.

THREE ON A MEATHOOK

1973 Studio One

PRODUCERS: John Asman, Lee Jones

DIRECTOR/SCREENWRITER: William Girdler

Like *Deranged* and *The Texas Chainsaw Massacre*, this horror movie is partially based on the deeds of real-life killer Ed Gein. Charles Kissinger (*Asylum of Satan*) is a cannibalistic madman who ends up like Tony Perkins in *Psycho*. His innocent son (James Pickett) is blamed for the murders of several young girls. A very gory movie with a lot of comic dialogue. Shot in Louisville, Kentucky. (R)

THE THREE STOOGES GO AROUND THE WORLD IN A DAZE

1963 Columbia (B&W)
PRODUCER/DIRECTOR: Norman Maurer
SCREENWRITER: Elwood Ullman

Larry, Moe, and Curly Joe are servants of Phileas Fogg III and join him when he makes the same bet his great-grandfather did. The group experiences endless wacky adventures around the world and wins the bet. With Joan Freeman and Emit Sitka. It premiered in Cleveland. Producer-director Maurer is Moe's son-in-law.

THE THREE STOOGES IN ORBIT

1962 Columbia (B&W)
PRODUCER: Norman Maurer
DIRECTOR: Edward Bernds
SCREENWRITER: Elwood Ullman

The Three Stooges play themselves hosting a TV show. The sponsor is "N Yuk N Yuks—breakfast of Stooges." They visit a nutty scientist (Emit Sitka) who lives in an old castle and has a flying submarine/tank. Martians that look like Frankenstein monsters with extra-big heads arrive to steal the invention, but the Stooges intervene. With Carol Christensen and Nestor Paiva as the Martian leader.

THE THREE STOOGES MEET HERCULES

1962 Columbia (B&W)
PRODUCER: Norman Maurer
DIRECTOR: Edward Bernds
SCREENWRITER: Elwood Ullman

A time machine transports the Three Stooges from Ithaca, New York to Ithaca, Greece, in 961 B.C. They pass off their nervous inventor friend as Hercules until the real strongman shows up. The Stooges become galley slaves and look great in togas and headbands with 20th-century shoes and white

Copyright © 1962 Normandy Productions, Inc. Courtesy of Columbia Pictures.

Curly Joe, Larry, and Moe entertain Carol Christensen as Emil Sitka watches in The Three Stooges in Orbit.

socks. With a ridiculous Siamese cyclops, Emil Sitka, Gene Roth, and Samson Burke as Hercules.

THREE STRANGERS

1946 Warner Brothers (B&W)
PRODUCER: Wolfgang Reinhardt
DIRECTOR: Jean Negulesco
SCREENWRITERS: John Huston, Howard Koch

After *The Maltese Falcon*, Warner Brothers continued to team Peter Lorre and Sidney Greenstreet. The ads repeatedly refer to them as "the little monster" and "the fat man"—very subtle. In this one, three partners holding a winning sweepstakes ticket pray to the goddess Kwan Yin on the Chinese new year. Greed and deception result. Geraldine Fitzgerald is a deserted wife, Lorre a small-time criminal, and Greenstreet a crooked lawyer.

THE THREE WORLDS OF GULLIVER

1960 Columbia
PRODUCER: Charles H. Schneer
DIRECTOR: Jack Sher
SCREENWRITER: Arthur Ross, Jack Sher

Kerwin Matthews follows his *Seventh Voyage of Sinbad* role, starring in another fantasy with Ray Harryhausen animated effects and Bernard Herrmann music. The effects are great, but they mostly involve tiny or huge people and props. With Jo Morrow, Peter Bull, a giant alligator, and a giant squirrel.

THE THRILL KILLERS
1965 Hollywood Star (B&W)
PRODUCER: George J. Morgan
DIRECTOR: Ray Steckler
SCREENWRITERS: Ray Steckler, Gene Pollock
ALSO RELEASED AS: *The Maniacs Are Loose, The Monsters Are Loose*

Cash Flagg a.k.a. Ray Dennis Steckler stars in his less-known follow-up to *The Incredibly Strange Creatures.* As Mad Dog Glick, he runs around killing people and kidnaps ex-stripper Liz Renay. Meanwhile three escapees from a mental hospital are on a decapitation spree. Some lucky theater patrons saw it in "Hallucinogenic Hypno-vision"! A special prologue with a "real" hypnotist explains that when you see a spiraling wheel on the screen you will be convinced that the maniacs are leaping out of the screen into the audience. Ushers with hoods, cardboard axes, and Cash Flagg masks ran up the aisles terrorizing the audience. Even without the gimmicks it's a weird, well-photographed bit of culture that you should see. With Carolyn Brandt, Atlas King, Ron Haydock, and Brick Bardo. When Liz Renay reached her 40s, she headed the only mother/daughter strip-tease act.

THUNDER ALLEY
1967 AIP
PRODUCER: Burt Topper
DIRECTOR: Richard Rush
SCREENWRITER: Sy Salkowitz

Fabian stars as a stock-car driver who is forced to join Jan Murray's thrill circus after his blackouts cause a fatal accident that gets him thrown off the circuit. He shows Pete's daughter (Annette Funicello) and her boyfriend (Warren Berlinger of *The Life of Riley*) everything he knows. Berlinger takes up with Fabian's girl (Diane McBain) after winning his first time out. They are fierce rivals by the next race, during which Fabian remembers driving over his brother with a go-kart and Berlinger hits the wall. "Days of screaming wheels, nights of reckless pleasure!" were promised in the ads. —CB

THUNDER IN CAROLINA
1960 Howco
PRODUCER: J. Francis White
DIRECTOR: Paul Helmick
SCREENWRITER: Alexander Richards

From the ads: "He had a way with fast cars and women!" Moonshine-runner-turned-stock-car-ace Rory Calhoun looks up an old garage-owner buddy after ruining his car and his leg in a smash-up. John Gentry and wife Connie Hines have taken over the business. Race-weary Calhoun teaches Gentry the tricks of the track, then finds he's created a monster. With Alan Hale, Ed McGrath, Troyanne Ross, and Trippie Wisecup. Action sequences filmed at the Southern 500. A Darlington Production. —CB

THUNDER IN DIXIE
1965 MPI (B&W)
PRODUCER/DIRECTOR: William T. Naud
SCREENWRITER: George Baxt

Vengeance stalks the high bank oval of the Dixie 400 as Ticker Welsh (Mike Bradford) grinds metal with the man he blames for the death of his beloved fiancée. Ticker's new girlfriend Nancy Berg (Karen Mallet) knows what he has in mind, as does the intended victim's wife, but they don't do anything about it. Just as well, because by the time

Ticker gets out of the hospital he has an old friend and a new fiancée. Starring Harry Millard. Bob Wills is the track announcer, stocks champ Richard Petty and stripper Sheri Benet play themselves, and Barry Darval sings "Maybe Tomorrow." See *Hot Rod Hullabaloo*. —CB

THUNDER OVER HAWAII: See *NAKED PARADISE*.

THUNDER ROAD

1958 United Artists (B&W)
PRODUCER: Robert Mitchum
DIRECTOR: Arthur Ripley
SCREENWRITER: James Atlee Phillips

The hot-car-and-moonshine archetype, engineered by Robert Mitchum—who wrote the original story, produced, composed the title song, sings it, and plays the lead. Mitchum is Lucas Doolin, a Korean War vet caught between T-men and mobsters as he hot-freights loads of corn liquor through the Tennessee hills to tax-beating buyers in Memphis. Mitchum's real-life son Jim plays the little brother who itches for action of his own. Keely Smith is the girl who waits behind. With Gene Barry, Sandra Knight, Randy Sparks, and Peter Breck. And the hopped-up Fords sound the way they're supposed to. For a closer look, see Richard Thompson's essay in *Kings of the Bs*. The footage of Mitchum's crash into a power transformer was used in *They Saved Hitler's Brain*. —CB

THUNDERBALL

1965 United Artists (England)
PRODUCER: Kevin McClory
DIRECTOR: Terence Young
SCREENWRITERS: Richard Maibaum, John Hopkins

The fourth Bond movie really ushered in the '60s spy mania. Soon we had films with Matt Helm, Derek Flint, Harry Palmer, and endless European

UPI 4/7/65: Sean Connery, who plays Secret Agent 007 in the James Bond films, clowns with actress Claudine Auger on the set of the latest Bond thriller Thunderball, which is currently being filmed in the Bahamas. Miss Auger is Connery's leading lady in the movie.

imitations and spoofs. *Get Smart*, *I Spy*, and *The Girl from U.N.C.L.E.* joined *The Man from U.N.C.L.E.* on television. Plastic suitcases with hidden daggers and revolvers were must-have items for the hip elementary school student. *Playboy* showed us the Bond girls in scenes that were never in the movies. This time, Claudine Auger is Domino, the ward of SPECTRE villain Largo (Adolfo Celi with an eye patch). SPECTRE hijacks a NATO plane with hydrogen bombs and threatens to destroy Miami and Cape Kennedy unless a ransom in diamonds is paid. 007 (Sean Connery) loves Domino, who joins his side, and Fiona (Luciana Paluzzi), who doesn't. Lots of underwater scenes with hydroplanes and sharks. Music by John Barry. Tom Jones sings the theme song. Desmond Llewelyn joins the regulars at headquarters as Q. With Rik Von Nutter as CIA agent Felix Leiter and Martine Beswick.

THUNDERBIRDS ARE GO

1966 United Artists (England)
PRODUCER: Sylvia Anderson
DIRECTOR: David Lane
SCREENWRITERS: Gerry and Sylvia Anderson

A feature based on Gerry and Sylvia Anderson's super marionation space series. The Tracy family and Lady Penelope fly to Mars in *Zero X* and fight the Hood, an interplanetary criminal, and Martian rock serpents. The special-effects miniatures are better than in most movies with real people. The puppet heroes returned in *Thunderbird Six.* Cliff Richard and the Shadows (seen as puppets) provide the music. Other shows by the same crew were *Supercar* and *Stingray.*

THUNDERBIRD SIX

1968 United Artists (England)
PRODUCER: Sylvia Anderson
DIRECTOR: David Lane
SCREENWRITERS: Gerry and Sylvia Anderson

The puppet family Tracy and Lady Penelope test a new spaceship in the 21st century and battle the Black Phantom. More great super marionation thrills from Gerry and Sylvia Anderson. Sylvia, the producer, provides Penelope's voice.

THY NEIGHBOR'S WIFE

1953 20th Century-Fox (B&W)
PRODUCER/DIRECTOR/SCREENWRITER:
Hugo Haas

The popular Hugo Haas–Cleo Moore team take their soap-opera stories to the 19th century. Hugo is a ruthless judge who hangs for killing the lover of his young wife (Cleo). With Ken Carlton and Katherine Hughes.

TICKLE ME

1965 United Artists
PRODUCER: Ben Schwalb
DIRECTOR: Norman Taurog
SCREENWRITERS: Elwood Ulmann, Edward Bernds

Julie Adams hires singer rodeo rider Elvis (as "Lonnie") to work at her all-girl health spa/dude ranch. He ends up discovering gold in a ghost town filled with villains disguised as monsters and marrying phys-ed teacher Jocelyn Lane. Elvis sings "Dirty, Dirty Feeling" and "Slowly But Surely," and leads the young beauties in aerobic dances. With Merry Anders and Allison Hayes. The screenwriters are better known for their work on Three Stooges features.

TICKLED PINK: See *THE MAGIC SPECTACLES.*

TIDAL WAVE

1973/5 Toho/New World (Japan/U.S.)
PRODUCER: Max E. Youngstein
DIRECTORS: Shiro Moritani, Andrew Meyer
SCREENWRITER: Andrew Meyer

The Submersion of Japan, a two-and-a-half hour epic, was the most popular film in Japan up to the time of its

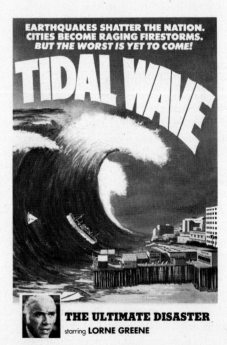

EARTHQUAKES SHATTER THE NATION. CITIES BECOME RAGING FIRESTORMS. BUT THE WORST IS YET TO COME!

TIDAL WAVE

THE ULTIMATE DISASTER
starring LORNE GREENE

release. It features the evacuation of the country, which took two years to sink into the ocean, and subplots involving the prime minister, a prince, scientists, and young lovers. The scenes of destruction (by the people who've been wrecking cities with Godzilla for years) are excellent. For the American release New World cut out more than an hour of plot and added cheap scenes with Lorne Greene, who had been in *Earthquake* (which was produced after this was released in its original form). What's left is nonsense. Roger Corman was executive producer.

TIGER MAN: See THE LADY AND THE MONSTER.

TIME AFTER TIME
1979 Warner Brothers (England)
PRODUCER: Herb Jaffe
DIRECTOR/SCREENWRITER: Nicholas Meyer
Malcolm McDowall stars in a good romantic adventure-fantasy that mixes elements of *The Time Machine* and *Jack the Ripper*. As H.G. Wells, McDowall accidentally allows the Ripper (David Warner) to escape the police in his time-travel machine. The guilt-ridden Victorian inventor follows Jack to modern-day San Francisco and falls in love with a bank clerk (his soon-enough offscreen wife Mary Steenburgen), whose life is suddenly threatened by the famous killer. The music by Miklos Rosza, is available on a sound track album.

THE TIME BANDITS
1981 Embassy (England)
PRODUCER/DIRECTOR: Terry Gillam
SCREENWRITERS: Terry Gillam, Michael Palin
An excellent comic adventure-fantasy from the Monty Python people that's fun for adults or kids. Little Craig Warnock escapes the dull British suburban home of his telly-addicted parents by traveling through time and space with a gang of dwarf thieves, including David Rappaport and Kenny Baker (R2D2 in *Star Wars* films). David Warner is great as the theatrical evil genius, Ralph Richardson is the business-suited supreme being, and Sean Connery is the heroic Agamemnon. With Python members John Cleese and Michael Palin, Shelley Duvall, Ian Holm, and Kathryn Helmond *(Soap)*. The great special effects include a massive giant, an ogre, and time portals. Ex-Beatle George Harrison was one of the executive producers and provides songs.

THE TIME KILLER: See THE NIGHT STRANGLER.

THE TIME MACHINE
1960 MGM
PRODUCER/DIRECTOR: George Pal
SCREENWRITER: David Duncan
A wonderful version of H.G. Wells' amazing story with Rod Taylor leaving his comfortable turn-of-the-century life to explore the horrors of the future. He passes through two world wars, atomic destruction (in 1966), and stops in the year 802,701. The beautiful passive Eloi spend their brief lives eating fruit and lounging around waiting for the ugly nocturnal Morlock's siren. The horrible cannibals with whips live in caves below a giant monument. Rod decides to teach the human cattle how to fight back and to stay in the future with Weena (Yvette Mimieux). The 1900 sequences feature Alan Young, Sebastian Cabot, and Whit Bissell as doubting friends. A special effects Oscar winner.

THE TIME MACHINE
1978 TV
PRODUCER: James Simmons
DIRECTOR: Henning Schallerup
SCREENWRITER: Wallace Bennett

Yvette Mimieux with monster in The Time Machine.

A Sunn Classics TV version of H.G. Wells' novel. John Beck travels back from the '70s and encounters lots of stock footage involving cowboys and witches. In the future he meets Weena (Priscilla Barnes). George Pal, who did the 1960 theatrical feature, considered suing. Whit Bissell is in both versions. With Rosemary DeCamp and Jack Kruschen. Originally an NBC "Big Event."

THE TIME OF THEIR LIVES
1946 Universal (B&W)
PRODUCER: Val Burton
DIRECTOR: Charles Barton
SCREENWRITERS: Val Burton, Walter De Leon, Bradford Ropes
An Abbott and Costello comedy that's different in a number of ways and actually worth watching. It's a ghost comedy with Costello and Marjorie Reynolds as spooks killed for spying during the Revolutionary War. They haunt a modern-day home, trying to clear their names and rest in peace. Gale Sondergaard is a medium. Abbott, not cast as the straight man of a team for a change, doesn't have much to do.

A TIME TO RUN: See THE FEMALE BUNCH.

THE TIME TRAVELERS
1964 AIP
PRODUCER: William Redlin
DIRECTOR/SCREENWRITER: Ib Melchior
Good, imaginative science-fiction adventure with Dr. Erik Von Steiner (Preston Foster) and his assistants (Philip Carey and Merry Anders) traveling through a time portal 107 years in the future. They find a barren underground postnuclear-war society run by John Hoyt. The remaining humans fight off mutants while using androids to build a spaceship to take them to a new planet. The impressive androids are bald and noseless with round ear and mouth holes. The scientists attempt to flee back through the portal and find themselves trapped in time. With Forrest J. Ackerman as a technician. Cinematography by Vilmos Zsigmond and

Laszlo Kovacs. A minimalist remake, *Journey to the Center of Time*, came out in '67. Irwin Allen's *Time Tunnel* was also obviously inspired by this little time-travel epic.

THE TIME TRAVELERS

1975 TV
PRODUCER: Irwin Allen
DIRECTOR: Alex Singer
SCREENWRITER: Jackson Gillis

A forgettable rehash of old ideas thrown together as a pilot film. Sam Groom and Tom Hallick travel back to the great Chicago fire of 1871 and dodge old tinted footage from *In Old Chicago* (1938). With Richard Basehart and Trish Stewart. From a story by Irwin (*Time Tunnel*) Allen and Rod Serling.

TIMESLIP: See THE ATOMIC MAN.

THE TINGLER

1959 Columbia (B&W and red)
PRODUCER/DIRECTOR: William Castle
SCREENWRITER: Robb White

William Castle discovers the primal scream and makes a brilliant legendary gimmick film. Doctor Vincent Price discovers a large insectlike creature that grows on spinal cords of terrified people. If the people scream the tingler is destroyed. If they don't it kills them by pinching their nerves. He isolates one of the creatures and it gets loose in a movie theater. This is where "Percepto" comes in. Selected seats were wired to give mild shocks. If that didn't make people scream the film stopped, the house lights came on, and ushers carried a planted employee out of the theater in a dead faint! On screen, Price yells that you'll die if you don't scream. Of course the people you're watching in the theater on the screen are all screaming too. There's also a plot to scare a deaf-mute woman to death (she

Vincent Price in William Castle's The Tingler.

runs a theater that only shows silent films). She sees a ghoul and a bathtub filling up with blood from which an arm reaches out for her! That scene was tinted red. With Darryl Hickman, Philip Coolidge, and a scene with Price freaking out after injecting hallucinogenic drugs.

TINTORERA...BLOODY WATERS

1977 United Film Distribution (Mexico/England)
PRODUCER: Gerald Green
DIRECTOR: René Cardona, Jr.
SCREENWRITER: Ramon Bravo

A bloody *Jaws* copy from the director of *Guyana, Cult of the Damned.* Two shark hunters want Susan George. They both get her and a chance to hunt the great white shark. With Jennifer Ashley and Fiona Lewis. (**R**)

TO LOVE A VAMPIRE: See LUST FOR A VAMPIRE.

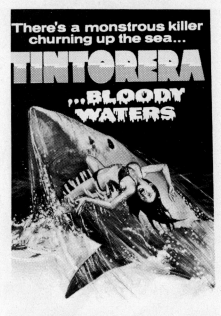

There's a monstrous killer churning up the sea...

TINTORERA ...BLOODY WATERS

TO THE DEVIL— A DAUGHTER

1976 Hammer/Cine Artists (England)
PRODUCER: Roy Skeggs
DIRECTOR: Peter Sykes
SCREENWRITER: Chris Wicking

If this satanic movie gets any attention in the future it'll be because of 16-year-old Nastassia Kinski in an early role. The story, based on a Dennis Wheatley novel, presents Christopher Lee as an ex-priest arranging for Nastassia (as a nun) to have the Devil's baby. When she does it's a bloody little hand puppet. Richard Widmark, as the famous author of "The Devil Walks Among Us," tries to put a stop to the devilish nonsense. With Honor Blackman and Delholm Elliott. (R)

TO THE SHORES OF HELL

1966 Crown International
PRODUCER/DIRECTOR: Will Zens
SCREENWRITERS: Will Zens, Robert McFadden

Marine Major Donohue (Marshall Thompson) flies into Da Nang and is granted permission to search for his cap-tured brother Dr. Gary Donohue (Robert Dornan) with help from a sol-dier, a native, and a priest. Gary will be killed by the Vietcong for refusing to treat their casualties unless his res-cuers can make their way through am-bushes and booby traps in time. The Donohue brothers are reunited to see their courageous friends receive proper burial. With Kiva Lawrence, Richard Arlen, Jeff Pearl, Richard Jordahl, and Dick O'Neill of *Spy Squad.*   –CB

TO TRAP A SPY

1966 MGM
PRODUCER/SCREENWRITER: Sam Rolfe
DIRECTOR: Don Medford

Originally called *The Vulcan Affair,* this pilot episode for *The Man from U.N.-C.L.E.* series was first shown in Septem-ber '64, and then expanded into a the-atrical feature. Napoleon Solo (Robert Vaughn) and Illya Kuryakin (David McCallum) use their best James Bond moves to save the president of a new African state (William Marshall) from evil Fritz Weaver and his Vulcan Chem-ical Company. Vaughn and Patricia Crowly are hung by the wrists for interfering. With Luciana Paluzzi and Ivan Dixon. The popular TV series lasted four years. In 1968 it was replaced by *Laugh-In.* Boo!

TOBOR THE GREAT

1954 Republic (B&W)
PRODUCER: Richard Goldstone
DIRECTOR: Lee Sholem
SCREENWRITERS: Phillip MacDonald,
  Richard Goldstone

A tall robot with emotions saves its in-ventor and his grandson (Billy Chapin) from spies. Creaky science-fiction thrills aimed at kids. Featuring Lyle Talbot, William Schallert, Henry Kulky, Rob-ert Shayne, Charles Drake, and Karin Booth.

tom thumb
1958 MGM (England)
PRODUCER: George Pal
DIRECTOR/SCREENWRITER: Ladislas Foder

Good children's fantasy with Russ Tamblyn as the five-and-a-half inch-tall hero of the Grimms' fairy tale. Terry-Thomas and Peter Sellers are the villains. Featuring Alan Young and Jessie Mathews. With Puppetoon sequences of dancing toys and songs by Peggy Lee.

THE TOMB OF LIGEA
1964 AIP (England)
PRODUCER/DIRECTOR: Roger Corman
SCREENWRITER: Robert Towne

Corman's last Poe picture, also his last horror film. Vincent Price looks great as the 19th-century nobleman in a black suit and dark, antique wraparound glasses. Unlike the other Poe films, much of it was shot outdoors, as an experiment by the director. The plot involving a dead wife's spirit taking over a new wife and something about a cat is confusing, and some of Price's dialogue is laughable (note the cabbage scene). Basically, Corman should have stopped with *Masque of the Red Death*. Choice scenes later turned up in Scorsese's *Mean Streets*. Screenwriter Towne got better later with *Chinatown*. With Elizabeth Sheperd.

TOMB OF THE LIVING DEAD: See *MAD DOCTOR OF BLOOD ISLAND*.

TOMB OF TORTURE
1963 Trans-Lux (Italy) (B&W)
PRODUCER: Frank Campitelli
DIRECTOR: Antonio Boccaci
SCREENWRITERS: Antonio Boccaci, Georgio Simonelli
ORIGINALLY RELEASED AS: *Metempsycose*

Another Italian horror film with phony anglicized credits to hide the fact that it's dubbed. It's about a girl troubled by nightmares who might be a dead countess. The countess's butler, still running the family torture chamber in the basement, is the film's highlight. Half his face is moldy and sinking. One eye is down near his mouth! With Annie Albert and Adriano Micantoni. Richard Gordon was executive producer of the English version.

UPI 12/25/58: If these 11 men and women look like midgets, the giant paint brush and key ring they're holding are only part of the reason—the other part is the fact that they actually are midgets. To combat the loss of advertising due to New York's newspaper strike, MGM dispatched the pint-sized people into the Times Square area to ballyhoo the film tom thumb, *currently playing in over 100 New York theaters.*

TOMBS OF THE BLIND DEAD: See THE BLIND DEAD.

THE TOMMY STEELE STORY: See ROCK AROUND THE WORLD.

TOO HOT TO HANDLE

1960 Topaz Films (England)
PRODUCER: Phil C. Samuel
DIRECTOR: Terence Young
SCREENWRITER: Herbert Kretzmer
ALSO RELEASED AS: *Playgirl After Dark*

One of Jayne Mansfield's British films (*It Takes a Thief* was made the same year). Jayne is Midnight Franklin, a stripper in a seamy Soho club. The club's owner (Leo Genn) is plagued with blackmailers, his manager (Christopher Lee) is in league with local hoodlums, a French journalist (Karl Boehm) is hanging around trying to pick up a mysterious German dancer, and a 15-year-old girl named Pony Tail is used as bait for a gangster. Jayne wears a see-through sequined net dress. Need we say more? With Ian Fleming.

THE TOOL BOX MURDERS

1978 Selected
PRODUCER: Tony Didio
DIRECTOR: Dennis Donnelly
SCREENWRITERS: Robert Easter,
Ann N. Kindberg

Cameron Mitchell in his ultimate exploitation sickie. This one's pretty strong stuff. As the crazed super of a California apartment building, Cameron puts on a ski mask and takes his tool box along to kill "sinful" women. A screwdriver is driven through a head, skulls are mashed, and in the most shocking scene he repeatedly shoots a naked woman (porno star Kelly Nichols) with a powerful nail gun. Later he kidnaps a young neighbor girl (Pamelyn Ferdin), ties her to a bed, and sings "Sometimes I Feel Like a Motherless Child" as he sucks on a lollipop. Mitchell's performance is indescribable. Aneta Corseau (Helen Crump on *The Andy Griffith Show*) plays Pamelyn's barmaid mom. Saturday morning television watchers will recognize Wesley Ure from *Land of the Lost* and Pamelyn Ferdin from *Space Academy*. **(R)**

TOPPER

1937 MGM (B&W)
PRODUCER: Hal Roach
DIRECTOR: Norman Z. McLeod
SCREENWRITERS: Jack Jevne,
Eric Hatch, Eddie Moran

When Cary Grant, Constance Bennett, and their dog are killed in a car crash, they return as ghosts who have to perform a good deed in order to rest in peace. They decide to help Cosmo Topper (Roland Young) who's henpecked by wife Billie Burke. Excellent comedy produced by Hal Roach (*Our Gang* and Laurel and Hardy shorts). With Hedda Hopper, Alan Mowbray, Arthur ("Dagwood") Lake, and Doodles Weaver. Music by Hoagy Carmichael. Roach also produced two sequels.

TOPPER

1979 TV
PRODUCER: Robert A. Papazian
DIRECTOR: Charles S. Dubin
SCREENWRITERS: George Kirgo,
Maryanne Kasica, Michael Scheff

A late, lame attempt by the husband-and-wife team of Kate Jackson and Andrew Stevens (*The Fury*) to create a new series with Jack Warden as Topper. It had already been a series (1953–56) with Anne Jeffreys, Robert Sterling, and Leo G. Carroll, and there was also a 1974 pilot.

TOPPER RETURNS

1941 United Artists (B&W)
PRODUCER: Hal Roach
DIRECTOR: Roy Del Ruth
SCREENWRITERS: Jonathan Latime,
Gordon Douglas

Topper (Roland Young) and a new ghost (Joan Blondell) solve a murder mystery in an old house. Billie Burke is Mrs. Topper again. Eddie "Rochester" Anderson, George Zucco, Carole Landis, Patsy Kelly, Dennis O'Keefe, and H. B. Warner are also featured.

TOPPER TAKES A TRIP

1939 United Artists (B&W)
PRODUCER: Hal Roach
DIRECTOR: Norman Z. McLeod
SCREENWRITERS: Eddie Moran,
Jack Jevne, Corey Ford

Constance Bennett returns as the ghost of Marion Kirby and tries to help Cosmo Topper (Roland Young) with his marital problems. Billie Burke is his wife. With Franklin Pangborn, Irving Pichel, Alex D'Arcy, and Alan Mowbray.

IT'S VERY LATE...
YOU'RE ALL ALONE...
YOU HEAR STRANGE SOUNDS...
who's there?
The Tormented
A 21ST CENTURY DIST. CORP. RELEASE
R
IN COLOR

TORMENTED

1960 Allied Artists (B&W)
PRODUCERS: Bert I. Gordon,
Joe Steinberg
DIRECTOR: Bert I. Gordon
SCREENWRITER: George Worthing Yates

In Bert Gordon's most "adult" horror film, Richard Carlson pushes his mistress (Juli Reding) to her death from his lighthouse. He's haunted by parts of her ghost (a crawling hand, a floating head) and a seaweed-covered body turns up at his wedding. Tacky fun with Gene Roth and Bert's daughter Susan. Bert also wrote the story and helped with the special effects.

THE TORMENTED

1977 Tiberia Film International (Italy)
PRODUCER: Justin Reid
DIRECTOR: Mario Gariazzo
ALSO RELEASED AS: *The Sexorcists, Eeerie Midnight Horror Show*

Sex-horror nonsense about a young female art student in Italy who steals a life-size statue of one of the crucified thieves from a church. The possessed statue comes to life and seeks relief from centuries of chastity. With Stella Carnachia, Chris Auram, and Lucretia Love. (**R**)

THE TORNADO OF DOOM: See FIGHTING DEVIL DOGS.

TORSO

1975 Joseph Brenner Associates (Italy)
PRODUCER: Antonio Cervi
DIRECTOR: Sergio Martino
SCREENWRITERS: Ernesto Gastaldi,
Sergio Martino

A hooded psycho-rapist killer with a hacksaw turns out to be John Richardson in this boring shocker. With Suzy Kendall and Tina Aumont. No one was admitted during the last 10 minutes, when the killer is unmasked. (**R**)

Staten Island residents play dress-up in Torture Dungeon.

THE TORTURE CHAMBER OF DR. SADISM: See BLOOD DEMON.

TORTURE DUNGEON

1970 Mishkin
PRODUCER: William Mishkin
DIRECTOR: Andy Milligan
SCREENWRITERS: Andy Milligan,
John Borske

Cheap gore film from Staten Island. The evil Duke of Norwich murders and tortures the successors to the throne in front of sets representing medieval England. Filmed "in dripping blood color." It opened on a double bill with Milligan's *Bloodthirsty Butchers*.

TORTURE GARDEN

1967 Amicus/Columbia (England)
PRODUCERS: Max J. Rosenberg,
Milton Subotsky
DIRECTOR: Freddie Francis
SCREENWRITER: Robert Bloch

A clever horror anthology featuring Burgess Meredith as Dr. Diablo, a sideshow owner who narrates the fates of four people. A man is willed by his cat to kill people so it can eat their heads! A starlet (Beverly Adams) discovers that movie star Robert Hutton is a robot! A doctor makes her into one, too. Barbara Ewing falls in love with a famous pianist, but his jealous piano kills her! As a collector of Edgar Allan Poe relics, Jack Palance kills another collector (Peter Cushing) for an unpublished manuscript and is faced with Poe himself who had been resurrected by Cushing. Theater patrons were given a packet of "fright seeds" to grow their own "torture garden."

TOUCH OF EVIL

1958 Universal (B&W)
PRODUCER: Albert Zugsmith
DIRECTORS: Orson Welles, Harry Keller
SCREENWRITER: Orson Welles

A brilliant look at corruption and despair in a Mexican border town. After a millionaire is blown up in his car, honeymooning Mexican narcotics officer Charlton Heston neglects his American bride (Janet Leigh) to investigate. Hank Quinlan (Orson Welles), a gross, cigar-chomping American detective, frames a man for the crime. When the honest Heston interferes, his wife is kidnaped and shot up with junk by punks led by Mercedes McCambridge. The cast includes Akim Tamiroff, Marlene Dietrich, Ray Collins, Dennis Weaver, Zsa Zsa Gabor, Keenan Wynn, and Joseph Cotten. Filmed in Venice, California. Some additional scenes were added by the studio after Welles was finished. The complete version runs 107 minutes. Albert Zugsmith was the last person to produce a Welles film in America.

THE TOUCH OF MELISSA: See THE TOUCH OF SATAN.

THE TOUCH OF SATAN

1971 Futurama International
PRODUCER: George E. Carey
DIRECTOR: Don Henderson
SCREENWRITER: James E. McLarty
ALSO RELEASED AS: *The Touch of Melissa,*
Night of the Demon

A young man gets lost and is allowed to stay at a farm. He falls in love with a pretty young girl (Emby Mellay) who says she's a witch. Not only is she a 127-year-old witch, but her "parents" are actually her sister's children. Her sister, also an old witch, looks her age and occasionally escapes from the attic to hack up the locals. An interesting, extremely low-budgeted movie, still playing theaters under different titles.

TOURIST TRAP

1978 Compass
PRODUCER: J. Larry Carroll
DIRECTOR: David Schmoeller
SCREENWRITERS: David Schmoeller,
J. Larry Carroll

A bizarre movie that makes no sense at all. Chuck Connors (*The Rifleman*) stars as a psycho with telekinetic powers. At his out-of-the-way vacation spot he traps four young people in his wacky world of mannequins. Store-window dummy parts are everywhere. Some mannequins come alive. Some people become mannequins. Sharp objects fly through the air. Future *Charlie's Angel* Tanya Roberts is stabbed in the head. An interesting misfire. The music by Pino Donaggio is available on a sound track album.

TOWER OF EVIL: See
HORROR ON SNAPE ISLAND.

TOWER OF LONDON

1939 Universal (B&W)
PRODUCER/DIRECTOR: Rowland V. Lee
SCREENWRITER: Robert N. Lee

Great historical-horror film teaming Basil Rathbone (as the evil Richard III) with Boris Karloff (as his executioner). Karloff is awesome as the bald, club-footed Mord, torturing prisoners in the well-equipped dungeon, chopping off heads with an enormous axe, and drowning Vincent Price in a vat of wine. (Price graduated to the Richard III role in the Roger Corman remake of 1962.) All this was considered shockingly violent 40 years ago and some torture sequences were cut before the release. (The music was the score written for *Son of Frankenstein,* which director Lee did the same year, also with Rathbone and Karloff.) Lee retired from filmmaking in 1945, explaining in an interview: "The fun had gone out of the picture business entirely. People were coming into the business who had been making safety pins."

TOWER OF LONDON

1962 United Artists (B&W)
PRODUCER: Gene Corman
DIRECTOR: Roger Corman
SCREENWRITERS: Leo V. Gordon,
F. Amos Powell, James B. Gordon

Corman strayed from AIP to make this minor Poe-like historical drama. Vincent Price (who had played a duke drowned in wine in the much superior 1939 version) stars as Richard the Ruthless, hunchbacked brother of King Edward IV. With the help of Michael Pate and a torture chamber he destroys everyone standing between him and the throne. Richard becomes more deranged, hallucinates a lot, and during a battle (provided by stock footage) sees the ghosts of all his victims. With Joan Freeman and Sandra Knight. Francis Ford Coppola was the dialogue director.

TOWER OF TERROR: See IN
THE DEVIL'S GARDEN.

THE TOWERING INFERNO

1974 Warner Brothers/20th Century-Fox
PRODUCER: Irwin Allen
DIRECTOR: John Guillermin
SCREENWRITER: Sterling Silliphant

It took two studios and two novels to make Irwin Allen's biggest hit. It has the biggest stars of any disaster movie and proves that, if paid enough, few actors can refuse taking second place to special effects and being fried to a crisp in a burning 138-story hotel. Paul Newman is the building architect and Steve McQueen is the fire chief. With Faye Dunaway (magazine editor), William Holden (building developer), Fred Astaire (con man), Richard Chamberlain (it's all his fault), Susan Blakely (his wife), Jennifer Jones (art dealer), Robert Vaughn (senator), Robert Wagner (P.R. man), and O. J. Simpson (token). Music by John Williams. Maureen McGovern sings the theme song (she also sang the theme for *The Poseidon Adventure*). It won three academy awards. The director next did another disaster, *King Kong*.

THE TOWN THAT DREADED SUNDOWN

1977 AIP
PRODUCER/DIRECTOR: Charles B. Pierce
SCREENWRITER: Earl E. Smith

Americana horror from the producer of *The Legend of Boggy Creek*. A man who killed five people in '46 returns with a hood over his face to terrorize the population of Texarkana. With Ben Johnson, Andrew Prine, (*Simon, King of the Witches*), Dawn Wells (*Gilligan's Island*), and the director as a cop. Based on a true story. **(R)**

TRACK OF THE MOONBEAST

1976 Cinema Shares
DIRECTOR: Richard Ashe

A young minerologist becomes an interesting-looking lizard monster because of a meteor fragment. A nonstar, "we can't act" hit that shows up on television once in a while. The soon-to-be-famous Rick Baker designed the beast.

TRACK OF THE VAMPIRE: See BLOOD BATH.

TRACK OF THUNDER

1967 United Artists
PRODUCER: E. Stanley Williamson
DIRECTOR: Joe Kane
SCREENWRITER: Maurice J. Hill

A feud between two top stock-car drivers, fabricated by syndicate track owners to increase attendance and gambling income, turns real as boyhood chums Tommy Kirk and Ray Stricklyn compete for the same girl. As Tommy's mother, Faith Domergue marries his rival's dad. Young Brenda Benet must decide whether she would rather be a track wife or live on a farm. Apparently Kane's last release, made, as was his previous film *Country Boy*, by Ambassador Films of Nashville. With H.M. Wynant, Chet Stratton, James Dobson, and Majel Barrett—Nurse Chapel on the Starship *Enterprise*.   –CB

TRAINED TO KILL: See WHITE DOG.

TRANSATLANTIC TUNNEL

1935 Gaumont (England) (B&W)
PRODUCER: Michael Balcon
DIRECTOR: Maurice Elvery
SCREENWRITERS: Clemence Dane,
  L. DuGarde Peach

In the future (1940s) a huge tunnel connecting England and America is dug under the Atlantic. Hard-working designer Richard Dix spends years under the Earth, only seeing his wife on the television/phone. Leslie Banks stays in England and comforts her. Disasters kill workers but the work goes on. With

Walter Huston, George Arliss, and C. Aubrey Smith.

THE TRANSVESTITE: See GLEN OR GLENDA.

TRAUMA
1962 Parade (B&W)
PRODUCER: Joseph Cranston
DIRECTOR/SCREENWRITER:
Robert Malcolm Young

A forgotten psychological horror film with a 21-year-old girl (Lorie Richards) suffering from amnesia after witnessing the murder of her aunt ('40s star Lynn Bari). She returns to the mansion where it happened with her new husband (John Conte) and discovers the truth, which involves a caretaker and a retarded relative.

THE TREASURE OF SAN TERESA: See LONG DISTANCE.

THE TRIAL
1962 Astor (France/Italy/W. Germany) (B&W)
PRODUCERS: Yves Laplanche, Miguel Salkind
DIRECTOR/SCREENWRITER: Orson Welles
ORIGINALLY RELEASED AS: Le Procès

A neglected masterpiece by Orson Welles. Anthony Perkins stars as Kafka's Joseph K. a doomed bank clerk trying to save himself after being arrested for unspecified crimes. Welles appears as a defense attorney who never gets around to the case. With Romy Schneider, Jeanne Moreau, Elsa Martinelli, and Akim Tamiroff (also in Welles' previous great nonhit Touch of Evil).

THE TRIAL OF LEE HARVEY OSWALD
1964 Falcon (B&W)
PRODUCER/DIRECTOR/SCREENWRITER:
Larry Buchanan

As it might have been. Defense pleads not guilty, then not guilty by reason of insanity. Twenty-three witnesses take the stand. As in Buchanan's Free, White and 21 and Under Age, the verdict is up to you. Arthur Nations, George Russell, George Edgley, and Charles W. Tessmer are featured; Charles Mazyrack is Lee. In 1977 a television movie of the same name covered the same ground. —CB

THE TRIBE
1974 TV
PRODUCER: George Eckstein
DIRECTOR: Richard A. Colla
SCREENWRITER: Lane Slate

One Million B.C. without dinosaurs. Victor French, Henry Wilcoxon, and others represent Neanderthals and Cromagnons. A new low or high for television movies, depending on your taste.

TRILOGY OF TERROR
1975 TV
PRODUCER/DIRECTOR: Dan Curtis
SCREENWRITERS: William F. Nolan, Richard Matheson

Karen Black plays four (actually three) different women in three tales serving as a pilot film for a series to have been called Dead of Night. The stories are all by Richard Matheson, who also wrote the script for "Prey," the third and best. In it Karen buys a sharp-toothed Zuni doll that comes to life and attacks. She tries to drown it and burn it in the oven but the horrible noisy doll keeps returning. The stories all have surprise endings.

THE TRIP
1967 AIP
PRODUCER/DIRECTOR: Roger Corman
SCREENWRITER: Jack Nicholson

From the ads: "LSD—a lovely sort of death." Confused TV-commercial director Peter Fonda asks bearded friend

with it, man." Would you trust Bruce Dern? The best scene is Fonda grooving on the washing machines in a laundromat. Music by the Electric Flag. With Susan Strasberg, Dick Miller, Barboura Morris, Luana Anders, Peter Bogdanovich, and Angelo Rossitto. Various combinations of *The Trip*'s stars were in *Psych-Out* and *Easy Rider*.

TROG

1970 Warner Brothers (England)
PRODUCER: Herman Cohen
DIRECTOR: Freddie Francis
SCREENWRITER: Aben Kandel
Anthropologist Joan Crawford shows up in the city with a troglodyte (affectionately called Trog). The economical monster is a man with hair around his waist and on his chest, and a monkey head. Michael Gough, an irate land developer, lets the missing link loose so it can impale a butcher on a meat hook, throw some pedestrians around, and kidnap a little girl. Joan still loves and understands Trog, who enjoys classical music but goes berserk when he hears rock 'n' roll. When Trog's brain is tapped, he "remembers" old footage from Irwin Allen's *Animal World*. When Trog is found in a cave a crowd gathers to watch and drink Pepsis! It was Joan's last feature.

THE TROJAN HORSE

1961 Colorama (France/Italy)
PRODUCER: Gianpaolo Bigazzi
DIRECTOR: Giorgio Ferroni
SCREENWRITER: Giorgio Stegani
ORIGINALLY RELEASED AS: *La Guerre de Troie*
A favorite matinee feature starring Steve Reeves as the hero Aeneas. John Drew Barrymore is Ulysses. With lots of fighting, the giant wooden horse, and characters named Ajax, Paris, Achilles, etc. With Juliette Mayniel and Arturo Dominici.

Bruce Dern to be the guide on his first trip. They cop from Dennis Hopper at a party and return to Dern's split-level pad with an indoor pool. Fonda experiences visions of sex, death, strobe lights, flowers, dancing girls, witches, hooded riders, a torture chamber, and a dwarf. He panics but Dern tells him to "go

THE TROLLENBERG TERROR: See *THE CRAWLING EYE.*

TROPIC ZONE

1953 Paramount
PRODUCERS: William H. Pine,
William C. Thomas
DIRECTOR/SCREENWRITER: Lewis R. Foster

The last of three low-budget adventures starring Ronald Reagan and Rhonda Fleming (all directed by Foster). This time Ron is a reformed bum who helps save a South American banana plantation from outlaws. With Noah Beery and Estelita.

TROUBLE AT 16: See *PLATINUM HIGH SCHOOL.*

THE TROUBLE WITH GIRLS (AND HOW TO GET INTO IT)

1969 MGM
PRODUCER: Lester Welch
DIRECTOR: Peter Tewksbury
SCREENWRITERS: Arnold and Lois Peyser

Elvis, in his second-to-last acting role, only sings two songs. The year is 1927. Elvis is the manager of a traveling cultural show and involved in a murder. The pint-sized star of the show is Anissa Jones (Buffy on *Family Affair*). Vincent Price is Mr. Morality. John Carradine is Mr. Drewcolt, a member of the troupe. With Marlyn Mason, Sheree North, Nicole Jaffe, and Edward Andrews. This is a rock 'n' roll idol?

THE TURN OF THE SCREW

1974 TV
PRODUCER/DIRECTOR: Dan Curtis
SCREENWRITER: William F. Nolan

Lynn Redgrave stars as the new governess in this videotaped TV version of the chilling Henry James story, previously filmed as *The Innocents*. Megs Jenkins repeats her servant role from the '61 film. This 3-hour Curtis remake was originally shown in two parts.

12 TO THE MOON

1960 Columbia (B&W)
PRODUCER: Fred Gebhardt
DIRECTOR: David Bradley
SCREENWRITER: Dewitt Bodeen

An international expedition to the Moon finds Moon men who threaten to freeze Earth with a ray. Most of the movie is devoted to examining the astronauts and their petty, boring personal problems. With Anthony Dexter, Francis X. Bushman, Tom Conway, Ken Clark, and Robert Montgomery, Jr. From the director of *They Saved Hitler's Brain*. Anthony and Francis X. both returned in *Phantom Planet*.

20TH CENTURY OZ

1977 BEF (Australia)
PRODUCER/DIRECTOR/SCREENWRITER: Chris Lofven

A rock musical version of *The Wizard of Oz*? 'Fraid so. From the ads: "The Scarecrow is a surfer—the Tin Man is a greaser—the Lion is a biker—the Good Fairy is gay." Sounds great, right? **(R)**

20 MILLION MILES TO EARTH

1957 Columbia (B&W)
PRODUCER: Charles H. Schneer
DIRECTOR: Nathan Juran
SCREENWRITERS: Bob Williams,
Christopher Knopf

When astronaut William Hopper crash-lands off the coast of Italy, a gelatinous egg he brought from Venus is found by a young boy. He takes it to an old zoologist and his daughter (Joan Taylor). The little creature in the egg is the Ymir, one of Ray Harryhausen's greatest animated creations. Earth's atmosphere causes the hellish snake-tailed monster to grow at a rapid rate. The soon giant creature is captured by scientists, escapes, battles an animated elephant, kills a lot of horrified Italians, and faces the military from the top of the Colosseum in Rome. A Harryhausen favorite!

THE 27TH DAY
1957 Columbia (B&W)
PRODUCER: Helen Ainsworth
DIRECTOR: William Asher
SCREENWRITER: John Mantley

Cold-war science fiction with an incredible ending. Five Earthlings from different countries (including Gene Barry and Valerie French) are given capsules by an alien (Arnold Moss). If opened within 27 days each capsule is capable of killing the population of Earth. The Russian is tortured by the KGB and when the Communists open his capsule, the entire population of the Soviet Union is wiped out! The free world lives on. An early effort by the director of AIP's beach movies. Includes film clips from *Earth vs. the Flying Saucers*. Originally co-billed with *20 Million Miles to Earth*.

20,000 LEAGUES UNDER THE SEA
1954 Buena Vista
PRODUCER: Walt Disney
DIRECTOR: Richard Fleischer
SCREENWRITER: Earl Fenton

As Captain Nemo, James Mason uses his luxurious 19th-century atomic submarine the *Nautilus* to destroy the world's war ships. An excellent version of Verne's story and the best live-action film from the Disney Studios. Harpoonist Kirk Douglas, professor Paul Lukas, and assistant Peter Lorre are taken hostage aboard the sub, where they dine on "unborn octopus." With a convincing giant squid, a native attack, and an explosive ending. Douglas sings "Mermaid Millie."

TWICE TOLD TALES
1963 United Artists
PRODUCER/SCREENWRITER: Robert E. Kent
DIRECTOR: Sidney Salkow

AIP had just scored with Vincent Price in a Poe trilogy (*Tales of Horror*) so UA decided to use him in three Nathaniel Hawthorne stories. "Dr. Heidegger's Experiment" is about an elixir of youth that keeps Sebastian Cabot and Price young and brings Mari Blanchard (*The She Devil*) back to life—for a while. In "Rappaccini's Daughter" Price makes his daughter's touch deadly poison. With Brett Halsey and Abraham Sofaer. In "The House of the Seven Gables" Price is Gerald Pyncheon, who searches for his family fortune and discovers deadly ghosts. Beverly Garland is his new wife. With Richard Denning and Gene Roth. Back in 1940 Price was the young hero in the same story. George Sanders was the troubled nobleman.

TWILIGHT PEOPLE
1972 New World (Philippines)
PRODUCERS: Eddie Romero, John Ashley
DIRECTOR: Eddie Romero
SCREENWRITERS: Eddie Romero, Jerome Small

In 1959 Eddie Romero tried to remake the classic *Island of Lost Souls* as *Terror Is a Man*. He was the executive producer then. For *this* version of that tale of a mad scientist creating animal/people on a remote island, he's both producer and director. (Roger Corman handled executive producer chores.) Like most Romero duds, it stars former American teen actor John Ashley (who co-produced). The panther woman is played by Pam Grier! This boring quasi-remake includes an ape man, antelope man, flying bat man, wolf woman, and a tree woman(?), a Nazi, bad makeup, and some pretty gory scenes.

TWINS OF EVIL

1971 Hammer/Universal (England)
PRODUCERS: Harry Fine, Michael Style
DIRECTOR: John Hough
SCREENWRITER: Tudor Gates

More 19th-century vampire sex based on *Carmilla*. This one features Mary and Madeleine Collinson, *Playboy*'s first twin playmates (October '70), who were in *The Love Machine* the same year. There are witch burnings, vampires, and black magic ceremonies. Peter Cushing, repeating his *Vampire Lovers* role, shows up to decapitate the vampire twin who bites female victims on the breast.

TWIST ALL NIGHT

1961 AIP (B&W)
PRODUCER: Maurice Duke
DIRECTOR: William Hole, Jr.
SCREENWRITER: Berni Gold
ALSO RELEASED AS: *The Continental Twist, The Young and the Cool*

This patch job beat Katzman's Chubby Checker feature to the theaters by 15 days. Enjoy the nine minute TWIST CRAZE prologue in color, then the best of Sam Butera and the Witnesses and Louis Prima—who breaks an art-theft ring while turning his club into a goldmine. June Wilkinson is Louis' girl. Hear all the big dance hits: "The Continental Twist," "Twistin' the Blues," "Tag That Twistin' Dollie," "When the Saints Go Twistin' In," "Better Twist Now Baby," and "Oh Mama, Twist."
—CB

TWIST AROUND THE CLOCK

1961 Columbia (B&W)
PRODUCER: Sam Katzman
DIRECTOR: Oscar Rudolph
SCREENWRITER: James B. Gordon

Five years after "Rock Around the Clock" real rock music was already gone. There were still great artists and records, but many of the originators were dead, "tamed," or ruined by scandals. This remake of the early Katzman hit exploits the dance craze, which was fun but hardly as exciting as the new sounds in '56. Countless twist songs by Chubby Checker include "Merrytwist-mas." With Alvy Moore, the Marcels, and, best of all, Dion. He sings "Runaround Sue" and "The Wanderer," both classics. It was followed by the feared but inevitable *Don't Knock the Twist*.

TWISTED BRAIN: See HORROR HIGH.

TWISTED NERVE

1969 National General (England)
PRODUCER: John Boulting
DIRECTOR: Roy Boulting
SCREENWRITERS: Roy Boulting, Leo Marks

A good psychological chiller, with Hywel Bennett as 21-year-old Martin, who sometimes "becomes" six-year-old Georgie. Martin/Georgie has a mongoloid brother, kills his stepfather (Frank Findlay), and moves into the

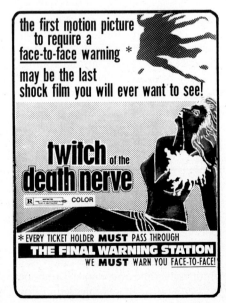

the first motion picture to require a face-to-face warning * may be the last shock film you will ever want to see!

twitch of the death nerve

R COLOR

* EVERY TICKET HOLDER MUST PASS THROUGH
THE FINAL WARNING STATION
WE MUST WARN YOU FACE-TO-FACE!

Courtesy of Orion Pictures Corporation.

home of Hayley Mills and her mother (Billie Whitelaw). The older woman tries to seduce him with disastrous results and Hayley returns home to find Georgie, a teddy bear, and an axe. His problems are blamed on a chromosome imbalance. Music by Bernard Herrmann. The Boulting brothers, who produced and directed, are twins. After finishing this feature, Roy Boulting married Hayley Mills, who is 23 years younger than he is.

TWITCH OF THE DEATH NERVE
1972 Hallmark (Italy)
PRODUCER: Giuseppe Zacciarello
DIRECTOR: Mario Bava
SCREENWRITERS: Mario Bava, Carlo Reali
ALSO RELEASED AS: *Last House on the Left Part II*
ORIGINALLY RELEASED AS: *Antefatto*
A strong body-count movie that greatly influenced the inferior *Friday the 13th*. It includes "13 periods of intense shock" (a.k.a. gore murders) and when originally released theater patrons were warned "face to face" about the content. Despite the new title it was re-released under in a cut version, it has nothing to do with *Last House on the Left*. With Claudine Auger and a surprise ending. Director Bava served as his own cinematographer. (R)

TWO BEFORE ZERO
1962 Ellis Films
PRODUCER: Fred A. Niles
DIRECTOR: William Faralla
ALSO RELEASED AS: *Red Hell, Russian Roulette*
An anti-communist allegory/fantasy/documentary with a black-robed Basil Rathbone narrating the history of Marxism (with film clips). Mary Murphy (star of *The Wild One*) is Everywoman in a white robe. She interrupts Rathbone with questions. It was released during the month (October) of the Cuban missile crisis.

THE TWO FACES OF DR. JEKYLL: See HOUSE OF FRIGHT.

TWO LOST WORLDS
1950 United Artists (B&W)
PRODUCER: Boris Petroff
DIRECTOR: Norman Dawn
SCREENWRITER: Tom Hubbard
Nineteenth-century Australian pirates kidnap a girl (Laura Elliot). The hero (James Arness) arrives and they're all shipwrecked on a desert island enlivened by stock footage from *One Million B.C.* With Bill Kennedy, now a Midwest TV movie-show host. Only 63 minutes long.

TWO ON A GUILLOTINE
1965 Warner Brothers (B&W)
PRODUCER/DIRECTOR: William Conrad
SCREENWRITERS: Henry Slesar, John Kneubuhl
Connie Stevens has to spend a week in a creepy haunted mansion before she can collect her inheritance. Cesar Romero is her demented magician father and Dean Jones is a nosy reporter. With John Hoyt and Virginia Gregg. —CB

2001: A SPACE ODYSSEY
1968 MGM (U.S./England)
PRODUCER/DIRECTOR: Stanley Kubrick
SCREENWRITERS: Stanley Kubrick, Arthur C. Clarke
"The ultimate trip"—and for once the ads were correct. It revolutionized the look of cinematic space travel (and ape suits). It also was responsible for making "Thus Spake Zarathustra" the most overused tune known to man. With Keir Dullea, Gary Lockwood, and William Sylvester. Douglas Rain is the voice of HAL.

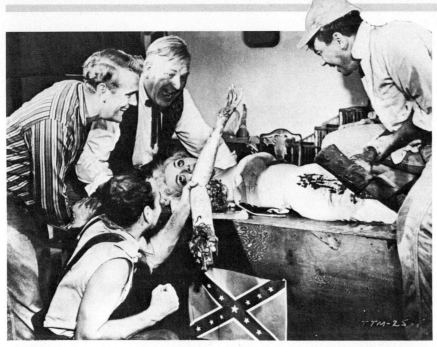

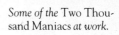
Some of the Two Thousand Maniacs *at work.*

TWO THOUSAND MANIACS

1964 Box Office Spactaculars

PRODUCER: David Friedman

DIRECTOR/SCREENWRITER: Herschell Gordon Lewis

After the incredible *Blood Feast*, gore master H.G. Lewis made this unique look at Southern hospitality. The small town of Pleasant Valley, wiped out by the Union during the Civil War, magically returns every hundred years for a celebration and revenge. Six vacationing Northerners are greeted by the jovial mayor and made guests of honor. One woman is dismembered, another crushed by a boulder. One man is barbecued, another rolled down a hill in a barrel lined with nails. As in the first Lewis gore film, *Playboy* playmate Connie Mason escapes. The unsettlingly graphic effects still make it hard for many people to take. The corny banjo music is provided by the Pleasant Valley Boys, who play themselves. EEE-HAH! Historical horror with Thomas Wood and Jeffrey Allen. Filmed in St. Cloud, Florida. Lewis also photographed and wrote the musical score.

THE TWONKY

1953 United Artists (B&W)

PRODUCER/DIRECTOR/SCREENWRITER: Arch Oboler

A wonderful anti-television comedy nightmare. Hans Conreid's square TV set with rabbit-ear antennae comes to life, walks (very awkwardly), does household chores with electronic beams, hypnotizes anyone who tries to stop it, and tries helpfully to take over Hans' life. Director Oboler was more effective on the radio (*Lights Out*). He was also responsible for the first post-nuclear war film (*Five*). Although this is a comedy, it makes a more startling statement than the recent *Network*. With Gloria Blondell and Billy Lynn.

UFO

1956 United Artists (B&W with color sequences)
PRODUCER: Clarence Greene
SCREENWRITER: Francis Martin
ALSO RELEASED AS: *Unidentified Flying Objects*

Tom Powers narrates this very dated and slow documentary with many obviously staged sequences. Includes what the ads called "actual color films of UFOs kept top secret until now!"

THE UFO INCIDENT

1975 TV
PRODUCER/DIRECTOR: Richard A. Colla
SCREENWRITERS: S. Lee Pogostin,
  Hesper Anderson

This well-done TV-movie tells the story of Betty and Barney Hill, who said they were taken aboard a UFO and examined by little green men. It includes facts that many UFO fanatics claim to be undisputable evidence. Director Colla later went on to *Battlestar Galactica*. With James Earl Jones and Estelle Parsons as the traumatized couple. –AF

UFO:TARGET EARTH

1974 Centrum International
PRODUCER/DIRECTOR:
  Michael A. De Graetono

A pretty funny feature made for $70,000. Most of the budget went for the computer graphics used to show the pure-energy form-shifting aliens discovered in a spaceship submerged in a lake.

THE ULTIMATE WARRIOR

1974 Warner Brothers
PRODUCERS: Fred Weintraub, Paul Heller
DIRECTOR/SCREENWRITER: Robert Clouse

After the plague in the 21st century, New York City consists of several armed communes and crazed, wandering street people. Yul Brynner (in between *Westworld* films) is a knife fighter looking for a better life. Max Von Sydow (in between *Exorcist* films) is the baron, leader of the biggest tribe, who hoards luxuries like books, cigars, and alcohol. Yul escapes with pregnant Joanna Miles through deserted subway tunnels, kills a lot of people, and loses his hand before surfacing at 14th Street. Similar to *Escape from New York*. With William Smith (*Grave of the Vampire*) and Stephan Mchattie. From the producer and director of Bruce Lee's *Enter the Dragon*. **(R)**

ULYSSES

1955 Paramount (Italy)
PRODUCERS: Dino De Laurentiis,
  Carlo Ponti
DIRECTOR: Mario Camerini
SCREENWRITERS: Franco Brusati,
  Mario Camerini, Ennio De Concini,
  Hugh Gray, Ben Hecht, Ivo Perilli,
  Irwin Shaw
ORIGINALLY RELEASED AS: *Ulisse*

A bearded Kirk Douglas takes forever to return to his wife, Silvana Mangano. He fights a giant cyclops and Anthony Quinn and sees his men turned into pigs by Circe (also Mangano). With Rossana Podesta.

THE UNCANNY

1977 (England/Canada)
PRODUCERS: Claude Heroux, Rene Dupont
DIRECTOR: Denis Heroux
SCREENWRITER: Michael Parry

Another horror anthology, with three stories linked by appearances of Ray Milland, Peter Cushing, and some killer cats. With Samantha Eggar, Chloe Franks, Susan Penhaligon, and Donald Pleasence as De'Ath. Not released to American theaters.

UNCLE WAS A VAMPIRE

1959 Embassy (Italy)
PRODUCER: Mario Cecchi Gori
DIRECTOR: Stefano Steno
SCREENWRITERS: Eduardo Anton, Dino Verde, Sandro Continenza
ORIGINALLY RELEASED AS: *Tempi Duri per i Vampiri*

Christopher Lee, fresh from *Horror of Dracula*, plays a vampire who bites his impoverished Italian nobleman cousin (comedian Renato Rascel), who is busy working as a porter in his castle/hotel. A comedy with Sylvia Koscina as a lady gardener. It was the first of many European Christopher Lee movies.

THE UNCONQUERED

1947 Paramount
PRODUCER/DIRECTOR: Cecil B. DeMille
SCREENWRITERS: Charles Bennett, Frederic M. Frank, Jack Lasky, Jr.

A ludicrous historical epic about American Indians (led by Boris Karloff as Chief Guyasuta) vs. the colonists. Technicolor fun starring Gary Cooper and Paulette Goddard, previously teamed in DeMille's *Northwest Mounted Police*. With Howard Da Silva, Cecil Kellaway, Ward Bond, Mike Mazurki, Alan Napier, Lloyd Bridges, Lex Barker, and Charles Middleton.

THE UNDEAD

1956 AIP (B&W)
PRODUCER/DIRECTOR: Roger Corman
SCREENWRITERS: Charles Griffith, Mark Hanna

Corman's quickie reincarnation movie starring Pamela Duncan as a 1950s prostitute who goes to a shrink and finds herself in medieval times, condemned as a witch. Allison Hayes is a real witch who can turn into a cat. Bruno Ve Sota is killed with an axe. With dancing witches, a dwarf (Billy Barty), and the Devil (Richard Devon)! Also with Richard Garland, Mel Welles, and Dick

Miller. Orginally billed with *Voodoo Woman*.

UNDER AGE

1964 AIP (B&W)
PRODUCER: Harold Hoffman
DIRECTOR: Larry Buchanan
SCREENWRITERS: Larry Buchanan, Harold Hoffman

Divorcée Anne MacAdams is accused of encouraging her 14-year-old daughter to transgress with a Mexican boy and finds herself on trial for rape under Texas law. "The Turtledove Song" and "Boil Them Cabbage Down" are heard in the background as daughter Judy Adler, aunt Tommie Russell, and young Roland Royter paint Mom into a corner on the stand. But, as in *The Trial of Lee Harvey Oswald*, the final decision is yours. –CB

UNDERSEA GIRL

1957 Allied Artists (B&W)
PRODUCER: Norman T. Herman
DIRECTOR: John Peyser
SCREENWRITER: Arthur V. Jones

Advertised as: "Skin-diving mermaid vs. ruthless frogmen in a whirlpool of crime!" Mara Corday finds money on the body of a murdered tuna fisherman, then helps the police and the Navy tie up a case involving $2 million lost in the sinking of a World War II destroyer. Originally co-billed with *Teenage Doll*. Featuring Pat Conway of *Tombstone Territory*, Myron Healey of *Wyatt Earp*, Dan Seymour, and Brick Sullivan. –CB

UNDERSEA KINGDOM

1936 Republic (B&W)
PRODUCER: Nat Levine
DIRECTORS: B. Reeves Easton, Joseph Kane
SCREENWRITERS: John Rathmell, Maurice Geraghty, Oliver Drake
ALSO RELEASED AS: *Sharod of Atlantis*

Great *Flash Gordon*-style serial about war in the lost city of Atlantis. As the

A MACABRE STORY OF TWO MOTORCYCLE-RIDING, KNIFE-WIELDING, SHIV-SHAVING, EYE-GOUGING, ARM-TWISTING, CHAIN-LASHING, SCALPEL-FLASHING, ACID-THROWING, GUN-SHOOTING, BONE-BREAKING, PATHOLOGICAL NUTS AND THEIR PAL THE UNDERTAKER...

In the tradition of Herschell Gordon Lewis gore films but with more attempts at humor. Two maniacs with motorcycles and chains butcher women to create business for an undertaker (Ray Dannis) who provides cut-rate funerals with trading stamps. Parts of the victims are served in a diner, which offers specialties like leg of lamb (from a Miss Lamb). A stupid detective who loses several secretaries with food names investigates. Terrible acting and totally tasteless black comedy. A classic of its kind. With Robert Lowery (a serial *Batman*). When triple-billed with *The Corpse Grinders* and *The Embalmer*, a nurse was on duty in the theater to give blood-pressure checks and patrons received a "certificate of assurance" to sign. The theater was not responsible for death, insanity, or coronaries suffered during or following a viewing of the demented triple bill.

evil Khan, Monte Blue fights the forces of Sharad (William Farnum). Ray "Crash" Corrigan (as himself) is the muscular hero from the surface of Earth. With spiked tanks, warriors on horseback, a disintegration machine, ray guns, and the popular Republic robots. With Lon Chaney, Jr., as Hakur, Lois Wilde, and C. Montague Shaw. A feature version was released in 1961.

THE UNDERTAKER AND HIS PALS

1967 Howco
PRODUCER/DIRECTOR: David C. Graham
SCREENWRITER: T.L.P. Swicegood

THE UNDERWATER CITY

1962 Columbia
PRODUCER: Alex Gordon
DIRECTOR: Frank McDonald
SCREENWRITER: Owen Harris
Dull account of the world's first underwater city and the personal lives of its inhabitants. With William Lundigan, Julie Adams (*Creature from the Black Lagoon*), and Paul Dubov.

THE UNDYING MONSTER

1942 20th Century-Fox (B&W)
PRODUCER: Bryan Foy
DIRECTOR: John Brahm
SCREENWRITERS: Lillie Hayward, Michael Jacoby
A wealthy British family living near the moors is cursed. The male heir (John Howard) becomes a werewolf. The wolfman is seen only briefly in this at-

mospheric mystery. With Heather Angel, Bramwell Fletcher, James Ellison, and Holmes Herbert. It was made because of the success of Universal's *The Wolf Man* the previous year.

THE UNEARTHLY

1957 Republic (B&W)
PRODUCER/DIRECTOR: Brooke L. Peters
SCREENWRITERS: Geoffrey Dennis, Jane Mann
Advertised as: "Guaranteed to frighten!" In one of Republic's last productions, mad scientist John Carradine lures mentally disturbed patients to his house in Georgia for treatment. He uses them for experiments with eternal life which always backfire and cause his basement to fill up with mutants. His servant Lobo (Tor Johnson) turns on him and rescues sexy Allison Hayes and her new love, escaped convict Myron Healy. Originally co-billed with *Beginning of the End*. It's similar to but more fun than the previous year's period horror film, *The Black Sleep*.

THE UNGUARDED MOMENT

1956 Universal
PRODUCER: Gordon Kay
DIRECTOR: Harry Keller
SCREENWRITERS: Herb Meadow, Larry Marcus
High school psycho under influence of misogynist father intimidates buxom teacher with series of mash notes. She tries to help him. The boy is finally freed from his mania when the crazed parent dies of heart seizure after being discovered rummaging through the teacher's apartment. John Saxon and swimming great Esther Williams star as student and teacher, with George Nader, Edward Andrews, and Les Tremayne. One of the screenwriters was actually Rosalind Russell under a pseudonym.   –CB

Tor Johnson grabs hero Myron Healy in The Unearthly.

THE UNHOLY FOUR

1954 Lippert (England)
PRODUCER/SCREENWRITER: Michael Carreras
DIRECTOR: Terence Fisher
ALSO RELEASED AS: *A Stranger Came Home*
Early effort by Hammer Films director Fisher. William Sylvester (*Devil Doll*) is an amnesiac accused of murder. With Paulette Goddard who didn't act again for 12 years after this.

UNIDENTIFIED FLYING OBJECTS: See UFO.

THE UNINVITED

1944 Paramount (B&W)
PRODUCER: Charles Brackett
DIRECTOR: Lewis Allen
SCREENWRITERS: Frank Partos, Dodie Smith
A supernatural shocker about a brother and sister (Ray Milland and Ruth Hussey) who rent a haunted house on the Cornish coast of England. A young medium (Gail Russell) tries to exorcise

a spirit, which appears as ectoplasm. A serious American ghost movie was a unique idea in the '40s. No others were made until *The Haunting* (1963). The cast includes Alan Napier, Donald Crisp, and Cornelia Otis Skinner. Original ads compared it to *Rebecca*.

THE UNKISSED BRIDE: See MOTHER GOOSE-A-GO-GO.

THE UNKNOWN

1946 Columbia (B&W)
PRODUCER: Wallace MacDonald
DIRECTOR: Henry Levin
SCREENWRITERS: Malcolm Stuart Boylan, Julian Harmon

An "I Love a Mystery" feature based on the CBS radio show. Private detectives capture a cloaked grave robber at a haunted Southern mansion. Jim Bannon and Barton Yarborough star. With Karen Morley.

THE ULTIMATE HIDDEN TERROR!

A WORLD NORTHAL FILM

THE UNSEEN starring BARBARA BACH

R

UNKNOWN ISLAND

1948 Film Classics
PRODUCER: Albert Jay Cohen
DIRECTOR: Jack Bernhard
SCREENWRITERS: Robert T. Shannon, Jack Harvey

A lost-world movie with hilarious man-in-a-suit dinosaurs walking around a desert. With Richard Denning, Virginia Grey, Barton Maclane, and a man in a gorilla suit playing a prehistoric sloth. All this and Cinecolor too!

THE UNKNOWN TERROR

1957 20th Century-Fox (B&W)
PRODUCER: Charles Stabler
DIRECTOR: Charles Marquis Warren
SCREENWRITER: Kenneth Higgins

A mad scientist in the Caribbean turns locals into silly foam-covered monsters. Mala Powers enters the "cave of death" and explores "the secrets of hell." Legendary non-scares with John Howard, Paul Richards, and Sir Lancelot—King of the Calypsos (from *I Walked with a Zombie*).

UNKNOWN WORLD

1950 Lippert (B&W)
PRODUCERS: Jack Rabin, Irwin Block
DIRECTOR: Terrell O. Morse
SCREENWRITER: Millard Kaufman

A newsreel about a "Society to Save Civilization" shows members claiming there is no hope of surviving an inevitable nuclear war. After obtaining some last minute funds, the Morley expedition boards the cyclotron, a giant traveling drill vehicle, and heads for the center of the Earth (actually Carlsbad Caverns) to find a safe place for humans. After a strong beginning this film really slows down. With Bruce Kellogg, Marilyn Nash, and Victor Kilian.

UNNATURAL
1952 DCA (W. Germany)
DIRECTOR: Arthur Maria Rabenalt
SCREENWRITER: Fritz Rotter
ORIGINALLY RELEASED AS: *Alraune*

Scientist Erich von Stroheim uses artifical insemination to create a soulless woman (Hildegarde Neff). With Karl Boehm. A popular German story, it had previously been filmed three times.

THE UNSEEN
1945 Paramount (B&W)
DIRECTOR: Lewis Allen
SCREENWRITERS: Hagar Wilde,
  Raymond Chandler

A forgotten follow-up to *The Uninvited*. As a young governess, lovely Gail Russell suspects her employer of being a killer. With Joel McCrea, Herbert Marshall, and Phyllis Brooks. No ghosts this time, though.

THE UNSEEN
1981 World Northal
PRODUCER: Anthony Unger
DIRECTOR: Peter Foleg
SCREENWRITER: Michael L. Grace

Barbara Bach stars as an L.A. TV newswoman spending the night at the mansion of a weird museum manager (Sidney Lassick of *One Flew Over the Cuckoo's Nest*). Hidden in the basement is a murderous retarded overweight full-grown baby (Steven Furst of *Animal House*). Barbara's two friends are killed and she's next. An underrated and perverse horror non-hit. **(R)**

UNTAMED MISTRESS
1960 Brenner
PRODUCER/DIRECTOR/SCREENWRITER:
  Ron Ormand

Allan Nixon, the charismatic star of *Prehistoric Women* and *Mesa of Lost Women*, returns in another incredible independent. The ads claim it's "a picture that would shock Dr. Kinsey!" and show an ape fondling starlet Jacqueline Fontaine (who was later in *Guess Who's Coming to Dinner*). She's a female Tarzan type. The big question is: "Which will be her mate . . . man or beast?" It was originally co-billed with *One Way Ticket to Hell*, a teenage-narcotics exposé.

UNTAMED WOMEN
1952 United Artists (B&W)
PRODUCER: Richard Kay
DIRECTOR: W. Merle Connell
SCREENWRITER: George W. Sayre

From the ads: "Savage beauties who feared no animal . . . yet fell before the

touch of men!" Four healthy 20th-century American males find themselves on an uncharted island ruled by priestess Sandra and her tribe of beautiful Druids! The only males there are hairy, mentally deficient warriors. The Americans are captured by the women for breeding, but carnivorous plants, the hairy opposition, and stock footage of dinosaurs keep them too busy to have any fun. A classic. With Mikel Conrad,

Lyle Talbot, and Doris Merrick. Choice dialogue: "Shoot anything with hair that moves!"

UNTAMED YOUTH
1957 Warners (B&W)
PRODUCER: Aubrey Schenck
DIRECTOR: Howard W. Koch
SCREENWRITER: John C. Higgins
The ads promised a look "Inside a juvenile prison farm!" Two entertainer sisters are picked up hitchhiking and get 30 days' labor at a reform school/cotton farm run by senile lady judge Lurene Tuttle and lascivious tyrant John Russell. Russell's labor scam blows up after Yvonne Lime miscarries and dies from overwork. "Starring the girl built like a platinum powerhouse" (Mamie Van Doren), with Lorie Nelson as her sister. Musical sequences feature Eddie Cochran and the Hollywood Rock 'n' Rollers, with incidental themes by Les Baxter.   –CB

UNWED MOTHER
1958 Allied Artists (B&W)
PRODUCER: Joseph Justman
DIRECTOR: Walter Doniger
SCREENWRITERS: Anson Bond, Alden Nash
Norma Moore, a small-town girl new to Los Angeles, sees a bright future when Robert Vaughn, a nice boy from a wealthy family, promises to make her dreams come true. Then he asks her to help him rob a movie theater. "Snagged by unguided emotions!" as the ads put it. From the director of over 200 episodes of *Peyton Place*. With Diana Darrin, Billie Bird, and Ron Hargrave —who sings the title song.   –CB

UP FROM THE DEPTHS
1979 New World (Philippines)
PRODUCER: Cirio H. Santiago
DIRECTOR: Charles B. Griffith
SCREENWRITER: Alfred Sweeny

Your vacation is about  to end!!!

UP FROM THE DEPTHS

starring
SAM BOTTOMS
SUSANNE REED
VIRGIL FRYE • KEDRIC WOLFE
CHARLES HOWERTON
Directed by CHARLES GRIFFITH
Produced by CIRIO SANTIAGO
Written by ANNE DYER ● NEW WORLD PICTURES

R | RESTRICTED
UNDER 17 REQUIRES ACCOMPANYING PARENT OR ADULT GUARDIAN

Another *Jaws*-inspired movie about a big prehistoric fish. With Sam Bottoms, Virgil Frye, and Suzanne Reed. Director Griffith wrote many of Roger Corman's best movies. "Your vacation is about to end!" cried the ads. (**R**)

UP IN CENTRAL PARK
1948 Universal (B&W)
PRODUCER/SCREENWRITER: Karl Tunberg
DIRECTOR: William A. Seiter
A musical with singing Deanna Durbin and reporter Dick Haymes exposing the corrupt 19th-century "Boss Tweed" (Vincent Price). Just try and sit through it. Durbin retired from acting after one more picture.

UP IN SMOKE
1958 Allied Artists (B&W)
PRODUCER: Richard Heermance
DIRECTOR: William Beaudine
SCREENWRITER: Jack Townley
Huntz Hall sells his soul to Satan (Byron Foulger). He does it to win at the races. With Stanley Clements. The Bowery Boys did only one more movie. Hall had been playing basically the same roll since the 1937 movie (and play) *Dead End*. He was a 38-year-old boy when the series ended.

THE VAGABOND KING

1956 Paramount
PRODUCER: Pat Duggan
DIRECTOR: Michael Curtiz
SCREENWRITERS: Ken Englund, Noel Langley

Kathryn Grayson and Oreste (an opera tenor) in a musical remake of *If I Were King* (1938). Vincent Price narrates. With Rita Moreno and Sir Cedric Hardwicke. In VistaVision.

VALLEY OF FEAR: See SHERLOCK HOLMES AND THE DEADLY NECKLACE.

THE VALLEY OF GWANGI

1969 Warner Brothers
PRODUCER: Charles H. Schneer
DIRECTOR: James O'Connolly
SCREENWRITERS: William E. Bast,
Julian More

This Ray Harryhausen project is one of *the best* animated movies ever made. It's a prehistoric dinosaur vs. cowboys story set in Mexico that *King Kong* animator Willis O'Brien wrote and wanted to make himself. When a traveling circus captures the title creature they display him in a stadium (a sequence originally planned for *Kong*). The action takes a while to start, but hang in there and you'll see a tiny prehistoric horse, a pterodactyl, Gwangi fighting another dinosaur and an elephant, and Gwangi terrorizing a church. Never before or since have animated creatures looked so convincing. Less convincing are James Franciscus, Gila Golan, and '50s science-fiction star Richard Carlson. Scriptwriter Bast was a roommate and biographer of James Dean.

VALLEY OF THE DRAGONS

1961 Columbia (B&W)
PRODUCER: Bryon Roberts
DIRECTOR/SCREENWRITER: Edward Bernds

Cesare Danova and Sean McClory are having a 19th-century duel when a windstorm sweeps them onto a passing comet. On that tiny prehistoric globe they find the river people fighting the cave-people mutants, dinosaur footage from *One Million B.C.*, the spider from *World Without End*, and some friendly cavewomen, Joan Stanley (*Playboy*'s Miss November 1958), and Danielle DeMetz. The men become pals and unite the warring tribe. Based on a Jules Verne novel.

VALLEY OF THE HEADHUNTERS

1953 Columbia (B&W)
PRODUCER: Sam Katzman
DIRECTOR: William Berke
SCREENWRITER: Edward Bernds

Jungle Jim (Johnny Weissmuller) helps a government representative make a deal with natives for mineral deposits. With Christine Larson.

VALLEY OF THE ZOMBIES

1946 Republic (B&W)
ASSOCIATE PRODUCERS/SCREENWRITERS:
Dorrell and Stuart McGowan
DIRECTOR: Philip Ford

Ian Keith plays an insane doctor who returns from the dead and steals blood to stay alive. Non-thrills with Robert Livingston, Adrian Booth, and a total lack of zombies.

VAMPIRA: See OLD DRACULA.

LAS VAMPIRAS

1969 Columbia (Mexico)
PRODUCER: Luis Enrique Vergara
DIRECTOR: Frederico Curiel
SCREENWRITERS: Adolfo Torres Portillo,
Frederico Curiel

The last of four horror movies John Carradine made in Mexico. This one features wrestling superhero Mils Mascaras fighting a group of female vampires in body stockings with wings.

Señor Carradine, the vampire leader, is overthrown by Maria Duval (*Santa vs. the Vampire Woman*) and locked in a cage.

THE VAMPIRE (*'32*): See VAMPYR.

THE VAMPIRE

1957 United Artists (B&W)
PRODUCERS: Arthur Gardner, Jules Levy
DIRECTOR: Paul Landres
SCREENWRITER: Pat Fielder
ALSO RELEASED AS: *Mark of the Vampire*

A doctor (John Beal) becomes a crusty monster when he takes some pills. Billed as "a new kind of horror." Right. With Coleen Gray and Kenneth Tobey.

THE VAMPIRE

1957 K. Gordon Murray (Mexico) (B&W)
PRODUCER: Abel Salazar
DIRECTOR: Fernando Mendez
SCREENWRITERS: Henrique Rodriguez, Ramón Obón
ORIGINALLY RELEASED AS: *El Vampiro*

While Americans were concerned with atomic bombs and space invaders, Mexico got busy copying our '30s and '40s horror movies. German Robles is Count Lavud, an impressive-looking vampire with very long fangs and a nice crypt. Producer Abel Salazar was the top-billed hero. *The Vampire's Coffin* was a sequel.

VAMPIRE

1979 TV
PRODUCER: Gregory Hoblit
DIRECTOR: E.W. Swackhammer
SCREENWRITERS: Steve Bocho, Michael Kozell

In response to the Frank Langella *Dracula*, ABC gave us this TV-movie with Richard Lynch terrorizing modern-day San Francisco, where of course he visits a disco. Jason Miller (*The Exorcist*) is the hero. E.G. Marshall is the Van Helsing type. Jessica Walter (*Play Misty for Me*) has an attractive neck. Like the vampire in *Brides of Dracula*, this one is blond.

THE VAMPIRE AND THE BALLERINA

1960 United Artists (Italy) (B&W)
PRODUCER: Bruna Bolognesi
DIRECTOR: Renato Polselli
SCREENWRITERS: Renato Polselli, Ernesto Castaldi, Giuseppe Pellegrini
ORIGINALLY RELEASED AS: *L'Amante del Vampiro*

Lost in the woods in a storm, two members of a ballet troupe find a castle in which to spend the night. The castle is owned by a contessa who is really a vampire. She and her vampire servant (with a rotted, leathery face) terrorize the dancers, who are built more like strippers than ballerinas. Great cheap thrills. With Helene Remy, Walter Brandi, and Maria Luisa Rolando.

VAMPIRE BAT

1933 Majestic (B&W)
PRODUCER: Phil Goldstone
DIRECTOR: Frank Strayer
SCREENWRITER: Edward T. Lowe

Lionel Atwill is the mad Dr. Otto von Niemann in this poverty-row horror that tries hard to make you think it's from Universal. That studio's sets were borrowed, Lionel Belmore repeats his *bürgermeister* role from *Frankenstein*, and, best of all, idiot batkeeper Dwight Frye looks and acts like Renfield in *Dracula*. Atwill sends Robert Fraser out for victims to nourish a blob of living tissue he keeps in a tank. Fay Wray (in her third film with Atwill) is the star almost-victim. Melvyn Douglas is the hero. A very strange and extremely outdated exploitation film.

THE VAMPIRE BEAST CRAVES BLOOD

1968 Tigon/Pacemaker (England)
PRODUCER: Arnold L. Miller
DIRECTOR: Vernon Sewell
SCREENWRITER: Peter Byran
ALSO RELEASED AS: *The Blood Beast Terror*

Robert Fleming is a 19th-century entomologist whose daughter (Wanda Ventham) is actually a giant moth (!) that needs human blood to survive. They go to a fishing village so Fleming can work quietly on creating a mate for his "daughter." Because of the mounting deaths, an inspector (Peter Cushing) arrives with his daughter (Vanessa Howard) who is soon captured by the moth woman. Basil Rathbone was signed to play the father but died before filming started.

VAMPIRE CIRCUS

1972 Hammer/20th Century-Fox (England)
PRODUCER: Wilbur Stark
DIRECTOR: Robert Young
SCREENWRITER: Judson Kinberg

A supernatural circus run by a vampire plays in the 19th century European town where his cousin had been killed. The population is entertained, then horrified, by a man who turns into a panther, acrobatic twins who become bats, and a tiger woman. With Adrienne Cori, Thorley Walters, John Moulder-Brown, and David Prowse. An interesting variation on themes from Hammer. It originally played with *Countess Dracula*.

THE VAMPIRE HAPPENING

1971 Acquila Films (W. Germany)
PRODUCER: Pier A. Caminneci
DIRECTOR: Freddie Francis
SCREENWRITER: August Rieger
ORIGINALLY RELEASED AS: *Gebissen Wird Nur Nachts*

Ferdy Mayne, the vampire in *The Fearless Vampire Killers*, plays another comic bloodsucker. This time he's surrounded by beautiful women and rides in a "bat copter."

THE VAMPIRE HOOKERS

1979 Capricorn Three (Philippines)
PRODUCER: Robert E. Waters
DIRECTOR: Cirio H. Santiago
SCREENWRITER: Howard Cohen
ALSO RELEASED AS: *Sensuous Vampires*

John Carradine is a 73-year-old vampire with a harem of female vampires who bring victims to his tacky hidden crypt. I think it's supposed to be funny. Carradine was another aged bloodsucker the same year in *Nocturna*. (R)

THE VAMPIRE LOVERS

1970 Hammer/AIP (England)
PRODUCERS: Harry Fine, Michael Style
DIRECTOR: Roy Ward Baker
SCREENWRITER: Tudor Gates

It might look tame now, but this was Hammer's first horror film with nudity, and its lesbian-vampire theme was soon used in quite a few European imitations. Based on Sheridan Le Fanu's *Carmilla*, it stars Polish-born Ingrid Pitt as Mircalla Karnstein, an ageless vampire who seduces her mostly female victims before draining their blood. She returns to plague the village of Styria, using the names Mircalla and Marcilla. Pippa Steel, Madeline Smith, and Kate O'Mara are three of the victims who have nightmares about a giant bloodsucking cat. Peter Cushing (as General Spielsdorf) and Douglas Wilmer (as Baron Hartog) know how to stop the vampires— decapitate them. With Jon Finch, Dawn Addams, and Ferdy Mayne. The sequel was *Lust for a Vampire*. (R)

VAMPIRE MEN OF THE LOST PLANET: See HORROR OF THE BLOOD MONSTERS.

VAMPIRE OVER LONDON: See *MY SON, THE VAMPIRE.*

THE VAMPIRE PEOPLE: See *THE BLOOD DRINKERS.*

VAMPIRE PLAYGIRLS: See *THE DEVIL'S NIGHTMARE.*

VAMPIRE PLAYGIRLS: See *DRACULA'S GREAT LOVE.*

THE VAMPIRES: See *GOLIATH AND THE VAMPIRES.*

THE VAMPIRE'S COFFIN

1958 K. Gordon Murray (Mexico) (B&W)
PRODUCER: Abel Salazar
DIRECTOR: Fernando Mendez
SCREENWRITERS: Ramón Obón, Javier Mateos
ORIGINALLY RELEASED AS: *El Ataud del Coffin*

Sequel to *The Vampire*, with German Robles returning as Count Lavud, a vampire who dies as a bat pinned to the wall by a spear. Abel Salazar is the hero again. It played some American theaters as part of a "giant scream show" with *The Robot vs. the Aztec Mummy* and people dressed like monsters running through the aisles.

THE VAMPIRE'S GHOST

1945 Republic (B&W)
ASSOCIATE PRODUCER: Rudy Abel
DIRECTOR: Lesley Selander
SCREENWRITERS: Leigh Brackett,
John K. Butler

John Abbott, an underworld leader on the west coast of Africa, turns out to be sort of a vampire. He can't be killed by bullets and he carries Peggy Stuart around. Slow horror with Grant Withers and Charles Gordon. The most notable fact about this quickie is that a woman co-wrote the screenplay.

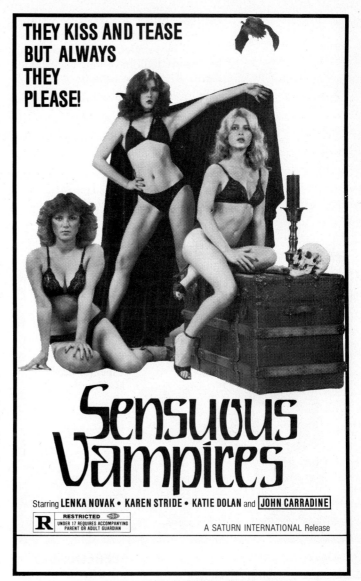

THEY KISS AND TEASE BUT ALWAYS THEY PLEASE!

Sensuous Vampires

Starring **LENKA NOVAK** • **KAREN STRIDE** • **KATIE DOLAN** and **JOHN CARRADINE**

R — RESTRICTED — UNDER 17 REQUIRES ACCOMPANYING PARENT OR ADULT GUARDIAN

A SATURN INTERNATIONAL Release

THE VAMPIRE'S NIGHT ORGY

1973 International Amusement (Spain)
PRODUCER: Jose Frade
DIRECTOR: Leon Klimovsky
SCREENWRITERS: Gabriel Burgos,
Antonio Fos
ORIGINALLY RELEASED AS: *La Orgia Nocturna de los Vampiros*

Also released as: Vampire Hookers.

Not-bad thriller about people visiting an unusual European town totally inhabited by vampires. Jack Taylor and his friends don't have long to live. Director Klimovsky usually does Paul Naschy vehicles. (R)

VAMPYR

1932 Klang Film (France/Germany) (B&W)
PRODUCERS: Carl Dreyer, Nicholas De Gunzburg
DIRECTOR: Carl Dreyer
SCREENWRITERS: Carl Dreyer, Christian Jul
ALSO RELEASED AS: *Castle of Doom, The Vampire*

A nightmarish art house classic based loosely on *Carmilla* by Sheridan Le Fanu. The Danish Dreyer filmed it silently in Paris and added a German sound track in Berlin. The cast is made up of his artist and writer friends. Baron Nicolas de Gunzberg financed the project and plays David Gray, who watches himself being buried alive in a coffin with a glass window. Polish cinematographer Rudolph Mate later directed *When Worlds Collide*.

VAMPYRES, DAUGHTERS OF DRACULA

1975 Cambist (England)
PRODUCER: Brian Smedley-Aston
DIRECTOR: Joseph Larraz
SCREENWRITER: D. Daubeney

Anulka and Marianne Morris are fangless but beautiful bisexual vampires who lure men to their castle for sex-and-blood orgies. One man happily stays for the nightly romps until he finally dies from lack of blood. The only female victim is an artist living in a trailer on the grounds of the castle with her husband. Anulka was the May '73 *Playboy* foldout. With lots of nudity and gore. The ultimate erotic vampire movie. (R)

THE VANISHING BODY: See THE BLACK CAT.

VANISHING POINT

1971 20th Century-Fox
PRODUCER: Norman Spencer
DIRECTOR: Richard Sarafian
SCREENWRITER: Guillero Cain

Petrocelli star Barry Newman is Kowalski, an ex-cop Vietnam hero who bets he can drive his Dodge Challenger from Denver to San Francisco in 15 hours. Roadblocks are set up to stop him. Loaded with amphetamines, he races

"More Sex Appeal Per Puncture Than Any Dracula Outing On Record!"
—Playboy Magazine

"Suspense! Sex! Mayhem! Unusually Erotic!"
—Variety

"Scary as Hell"
—Flick

LEE HESSEL presents

VAMPYRES

REFRESHINGLY ORIGINAL!
—SIR!

Daughters of Dracula

on, encountering an old prospector (Dean Jagger) and a naked girl on a motorcycle on the way. An almost successful metaphysical statement that's worth catching. With Cleavon Little as "Supersoul," the blind deejay, and John Amos. Charlotte Rampling was in the original uncut version, not shown in America. Music by Delaney and Bonnie and others.

VARAN THE UNBELIEVABLE

1958 Toho/Crown International (Japan/U.S.) (B&W)

PRODUCER: Tomoyuki Tanaka
DIRECTOR: Inoshiro Honda
SCREENWRITERS: Shinichi Sekizawa, Sid Harris
ORIGINALLY RELEASED AS: *Daikaiju Baran*

A Godzilla-esque monster with a spiked back emerges from a lake to destroy everything in its path. In new American scenes Myron Healy stars as a commander responsible for reviving the prehistoric terror.

THE VAULT OF HORROR

1973 Amicus/Cinerama (England)

PRODUCERS: Milton Subotsky, Max J. Rosenberg
DIRECTOR: Roy Ward Baker
SCREENWRITER: Milton Subotsky
ALSO RELEASED AS: *Tales from the Crypt II*

Five horror stories adapted from William Gaines *E.C.* comics of the '50s. Five doomed men tell their nightmares. "Midnight Mess" is a comic vampire tale with Daniel and Anna Massey playing what they are—brother and sister. "The Neat Job" stars Terry-Thomas as an insufferably neat man whose new wife (Glynis Johns) can't stand it anymore. Edward Judd double-crosses Michael Craig in "Bargain in Death." In "This Trick'll Kill You" Curt Jurgens steals a rope trick in India and regrets it. "Drawn and Quartered" stars

Tom Baker as an artist who uses voodoo to eliminate his enemies.

THE VEIL

1958

PRODUCER: Hal Roach

Two years before the *Thriller* series, Boris Karloff hosted and sometimes starred in a syndicated show that is forgotten even in Karloff biographies. At least three features were culled from it. The others were *Destination Nightmare* and *Jack the Ripper*. each containing four of the episodes. Confusion arose because at least one story turned up in two different features. With Patrick Macnee.

THE VEIL: See *HAUNTS*.

SHE'S WAITING TO LOVE YOU...TO DEATH

Climax after climax of terror and desire...

where the living change places with the dead.

IN METROCOLOR

THE VELVET VAMPIRE

STARRING Michael Blodgett · Sherry Miles and Celeste Yarnall A NEW WORLD PICTURES RELEASE

VELVET HOUSE: See CRUCIBLE OF HORROR.

THE VELVET VAMPIRE

1971 New World
PRODUCER: Charles S. Swartz
DIRECTOR: Stephanie Rothman
SCREENWRITERS: Maurice Jules,
Charles S. Swartz, Stephanie Rothman

The ads promised "Climax after climax of terror and desire . . ." Sherry Miles and Michael Blodgett (*Beyond the Valley of the Dolls*) go through endless psychedelic sexual changes when they stay with vampire Diana Le Fanu, (Celeste Yarnall) at her Mojave desert home. Hippies with crosses save the day. Pretty laughable. With dune buggies, dreams, and snakebites. (**R**)

THE VENETIAN AFFAIR

1967 MGM
PRODUCERS: Jerry Thorpe, E. Jack Newman
DIRECTOR: Jerry Thorpe
SCREENWRITER: E. Jack Newman

Robert Vaughn stars as a former CIA man/reporter in Venice to investigate the deaths of some diplomats. Reasons to watch this *Man from U.N.C.L.E.* copy: Boris Karloff (in a wheelchair

UPI 3/22/66: Actor Robert Vaughn, alias Napoleon Solo of the Man From U.N.C.L.E. *TV series, manfully shoulders a couple of gonks which he received from his fans at his press conference this morning. Vaughn is due to commence work in Venice next month on a new movie,* The Venetian Affair.

again) plays Dr. Vaugiroud, and Karl Boehm (star of *Peeping Tom*) plays an enemy agent who shoots people up with a serum that turns them into brainwashed robots. With Elke Sommer (sometimes disguised as a nun), Edward Asner, Felicia Farr, Roger C. Carmel, and Luciana Paluzzi.

VENGEANCE: See THE BRAIN.

THE VENGEANCE OF FU MANCHU

1967 Anglo Amalgamated/Warner
Brothers-7 Arts (England)
PRODUCER/SCREENWRITER: Harry Alan Towers
DIRECTOR: Jeremy Summers

The third Christopher Lee/Fu Manchu film with the usual cast of Douglas Wilmer as Sir Nayland Smith, Howard Marion Crawford as Dr. Petrie, and Tsai Chin as Lin Tang. From his palace in China, Fu arranges the kidnaping of a famous surgeon and his daughter and forces the doctor to transform a prisoner into an exact double of Nayland Smith. He also allies himself with the Mafia to form a new crime syndicate. With Horst Frank, Maria Rohm, and Tony Ferrer. A color film for some reason shown here in black-and-white. "The world will hear from me again," says Fu at the end. (We heard from him two more times, actually.)

VENGEANCE OF SHE

1967 Hammer/20th Century-Fox
(England)
PRODUCER: Aida Young
DIRECTOR: Cliff Owen
SCREENWRITER: Peter O'Donnell

Olinka Berova is tricked into thinking she is the immortal Ayshea of Kuma in the mediocre sequel to *She*. John Richardson (who also starred in *She, One*

Million B.C., and *Black Sunday*) is the king searching for her. With Edward Judd. *She* returned again in 1983, this time starring Sandahl Bergman from *Conan the Barbarian*.

VENOM: See THE LEGEND OF SPIDER FOREST.

VENOM
1982 Paramount (England)
PRODUCER: Martin Bregman
DIRECTOR: Piers Haggard
SCREENWRITER: Robert Carrington

An all-star suspense film with a deadly black mamba snake thrown in . As a German criminal, Klaus Kinski kidnaps a rich American boy in London. Servants Oliver Reed and Susan George help. Sarah Miles is a toxicologist. Michael Gough is a snake expert at the zoo. With Cornelia Sharpe, Sterling Hayden, and Nicol Williamson. Tobe Hooper started the project but was replaced. From the director of *Blood on Satan's Claw*. Reed was back with more snakes in *Spasms*. **(R)**

VENUS IN FURS
1970 AIP (Italy/Germany/England)
PRODUCER: Harry Alan Towers
DIRECTOR: Jesse Franco
SCREENWRITERS: Jesus Franco, Malvin Wald
ORIGINALLY RELEASED AS: *Paroxismus*

Incredible fusion of sex and sadism with horror overtones and a totally unexpected cast. Jazz musician James Darren (possibly still in the *Time Tunnel*) sees the horrible murder of Wanda (Maria Rohm) by three people in Istanbul. He goes to Rio and has an affair with nightclub singer Barbara McNair. Venus (who looks just like Wanda!) arrives and seduces one of Wanda's killers (Dennis Price), who is a homosexual. He dies of a heart attack. Then she makes it with Olga (Margaret Lee), who kills herself. Back in Istanbul, Ahmed (Klaus Kinski) dies while enacting a slave-mistress story at a party. Manfred Mann plays at the party. Poor James, obsessed with deadly Venus, trails her to a cemetery and finds her fur on Wanda's grave! Back on the beach he finds his own body! Wow! Not to be confused with the '67 American or the other '70 Italian film of the same name. **(R)**

THE VERDICT
1946 Warner Brothers (B&W)
PRODUCER: William Jacobs
DIRECTOR: Don Siegel
SCREENWRITER: Peter Milne

Don Siegel's first feature as a director was the last teaming of Sidney Greenstreet and Peter Lorre. In 19th-century London Greenstreet is an ex-Scotland Yard superintendent plotting the perfect murder. Best friend Lorre is suspicious. With Joan Lorring, George Coulouris, and Arthur Shields. Based on *The Big Ben Mystery* by Israel Zangwill, also filmed as *The Perfect Crime* (1928) and *The Crime Doctor* (1934).

DER VERLONE
1951 (W. Germany)
PRODUCER: Arnold Pressburger
DIRECTOR: Peter Lorre
SCREENWRITERS: Peter Lorre,
  Axel Eggebrecht, Benno Vigny

After 18 years Peter Lorre returned to the country where he first rose to fame and directed a strongly anti-Nazi film. He stars as a scientist in bombed-out Hamburg who becomes a killer. It was unsuccessful in Germany and wasn't released here. Lorre returned to Hollywood to continue playing mostly cliché parts in light films and started putting on weight. He gained over 100 pounds in the early '50s and didn't work for three years. *Der Verlone* later became appreciated in Europe but was never

Martin Stephens stars in Village of the Damned.

dubbed into English. It can be seen at U.C.L.A.

VICE RAID

1960 United Artists (B&W)
PRODUCER: Robert E. Kent
DIRECTOR: Edward Cahn
SCREENWRITER: Charles Ellis

Mamie Van Doren stars in this sordid caper with Rich Coogan, Brad Dexter, and Barry Atwater. Mamie also acted in *Girls, Guns and Gangsters*, and *Pier 5, Havana* for Cahn.

VICTOR FRANKENSTEIN

1975 FAW (Sweden/Ireland)
PRODUCER/DIRECTOR: Calvin Floyd
SCREENWRITERS: Yvonne and Calvin Floyd
ALSO RELEASED AS: *Terror of Frankenstein*

A pretty dull but faithful version of Mary Shelley's novel by the director of *In Search of Dracula*. With Per Oscarsson and Leon Vitali. In English.

THE VIKING QUEEN

1967 Hammer/20th Century-Fox (England)
PRODUCER: John Temple-Smith
DIRECTOR: Don Chaffey
SCREENWRITER: Clarke Reynolds

Don Murray loves statuesque Viking Queen Carita but he's a Roman military man and has to stop her from fighting the Druids. A sensational-sex-tease costume drama with Andrew Kier, Adrienne Corri, and Donald Huston. If you look hard, you can see one character wearing a wristwatch.

VIKING WOMEN AND THE SEA SERPENT: See THE SAGA OF THE VIKING WOMEN AND THEIR VOYAGE TO THE WATERS OF THE GREAT SEA SERPENT.

VILLAGE OF THE DAMNED

1960 MGM (England) (B&W)
PRODUCER: Ronald Kinnoch
DIRECTOR: Wolf Rilla
SCREENWRITERS: Sterling Silliphant, Wolf Rilla, George Barclay

Excellent British science fiction based on *The Midwich Cuckoos* by John Wyndham. Twelve superintelligent, emotionless, blond, fair-skinned children with telepathic powers are born at the same time in a small village. The mothers raise the mysterious, alien-sired kids as their own. Their puzzled, angry "dads" are totally demoralized except for George Sanders, who becomes their teacher, then tries to stop their plan of domination. His unwanted "son" Martin Stevens (*The Innocents*) is the leader. Some think the sequel, *Children of the Damned*, is even better.

VILLAGE OF THE GIANTS

1965 Embassy Pictures
PRODUCER/DIRECTOR: Bert I. Gordon
SCREENWRITER: Alan Caillou

From the ads: "See them burst out of their clothes and bust up a town!" Bert Gordon actually claims this absurd giant-teenager comedy was based on *Food of the Gods* by H.G. Wells. (Gordon is responsible for the film's "story" and "visual effects" as well as producing and directing it.) At least it's more fun than his 1976 version with Marjoe. This one's got real stars like Tommy

Kirk (just given his walking papers by Walt Disney), Johnny Crawford (no more *Rifleman* shows and his rock 'n' roll career didn't do so hot), Beau Bridges, Tisha Sterling, Tim Rooney, Toni Basil, Joseph Turkel, and little Ronnie Howard as Genius, the kid who causes all the sudden growth. Some of the female cast members grow 30 feet tall so guys can climb on their breasts. Good music by the Beau Brummels, Freddie Cannon, and Jack Nitzsche. Filmed in "Perceptovision" (Gordon's usual below-par special effects).

VIOLATED
1954 Palace (B&W)
PRODUCER: Wim Holland
DIRECTOR: Walter Strate
SCREENWRITER: William Paul Mishkin
Detective hires psychopathologist to help in case of hair-fetish killer. Mitchell Kowal interrogates a sleaze photographer who has shots of some of the victims; Wim Holland, the movie's producer, is given truth serum and explains how he became a maniac. With Lili Dawn, Vicki Carlson, William Martel, and Jason Niles. Harmonica score by Tony Mottola.　　　　　　–CB

VIOLENT JOURNEY: See THE FOOL KILLER.

VIOLENT MIDNIGHT: See PSYCHOMANIA.

THE VIOLENT ONES
1967 Feature Films
PRODUCER: Robert W. Stabler
DIRECTOR: Fernando Lamas
SCREENWRITERS: Doug Wilson, Charles Davis
The gringo implicated in the sex death of a small-town New Mexico girl could be any one of three available strangers, so the victim's father thinks it best to lynch them all. Deputy Lamas must suppress his anti-white sentiments to save Aldo Ray, David Carradine, and Tommy Sands from vigilante justice. With Lisa Gaye and Melinda Marx. Filmed in Lone Pine, California, and the Mojave Desert.　　　　　–CB

TEEN-AGERS ZOOM TO SUPERSIZE AND TERRORIZE A TOWN!
See...The Wildest, Weirdest "Party-Rumble" Of 'Em All!

VILLAGE OF THE GIANTS

Based on "The Food Of The Gods" By H.G. WELLS

STARRING
TOMMY　JOHNNY　RONNY
KIRK · CRAWFORD · HOWARD
GUEST STARS—THE　FREDDY　MIKE
BEAU BRUMMELS · CANNON · CLIFFORD
PRODUCED & DIRECTED BY　　SCREENPLAY BY
BERT I. GORDON · ALAN CAILLOU
A **BERT I. GORDON** PRODUCTION
An Embassy Pictures Release IN **COLOR**

Hear! "WOMAN"
"WHEN IT COMES TO YOUR LOVE"
"LITTLE BITTY CORRINE"
"MARIANNE"

THE VIOLENT YEARS

1956 Headliner Productions (B&W)
PRODUCERS: O'Camp and A.O. Bayer
DIRECTOR: Franz Eichorn
SCREENWRITER: Ed Wood, Jr.
ALSO RELEASED AS: *Female*

From the ads: "Untamed thrill-girls of the highway!" The innocent-looking daughter of a prominent newspaperman organizes a girl gang. She and her young hellions hold up filling stations, molest men in the park, and vandalize their high school. Then they hold a torrid mixed pajama party with heavy petting, capped off by a commando raid resulting in the murder of a cop. Jean Moorehead dies in prison giving birth to an illegitimate child. The key phrase is: "So what." Co-starring Barbara Weeks, Glen Corbett, Gloria Parr, Lee Constant, Art Millan, and I. Stanford Jolley. A recently re-discovered classic, written by the director of *Plan 9 from Outer Space*. Don't miss.   —CB

THE VIRGIN WITCH

1970 Tigon/Joseph Brenner Associates (England)
PRODUCER: Ralph Solomons
DIRECTOR: Ray Austin
SCREENWRITER: Klaus Vogel
ALSO RELEASED AS: *Lesbian Twins*

Two girls (Ann Michelle and Patricia Haines) go to London to become models. They meet a lesbian who initiates them into the world of soft-core sex and witchcraft, complete with white robes and voodoo ceremonies. It played with the re-released *The Devil's Rain*. (R)

VIRGINS AND VAMPIRES

1972 Box Office International (France)
PRODUCER: Sam Selsky
DIRECTOR: Jean Rollin
ORIGINALLY RELEASED AS: *Vièrges et Vampires*
ALSO RELEASED AS: *Caged Virgins, Crazed Vampire, Dungeons of Terror*

A lot of vampire movies with sex scenes were released in the '70s. This, however, is a sex film with vampire scenes, the fourth in a series that included *The Vampire's Rape*, *The Naked Vampire*, and *The Vampire's Thrill*. It's the only one that got much exposure here and features two girls with braids and miniskirts trapped by the vampire king in his castle. Includes a bat biting the girls between their legs. (X)

VIRUS

1980 Toho (Japan)
PRODUCER: Haruki Kadokawa
DIRECTOR: Kinji Fukasaku
SCREENWRITERS: Tosi Takada, Gregory Knapp, Kinji Fukasaku

From the ads: "The entire world is a graveyard!" An epic $17 million end-of-the-world movie with music by Janis Ian. Many of America's finest actors went to Japan because they wanted to make a film for the company that made *Godzilla*. The dying human race living on Antarctica is represented by Chuck Connors, Glenn Ford, Henry Silva, Bo Svenson, Robert Vaughn, Oliva Hussey, and George Kennedy. Also with Sonny Chiba. Sold directly to cable TV in America.

VISIT TO A SMALL PLANET

1960 Paramount (B&W)
PRODUCER: Hal B. Wallis
DIRECTOR: Norman Taurog
SCREENWRITERS: Edmund Beloin, Henry Garson

Jerry Lewis as Kreton, an alien with superhuman powers, lands on Earth, where he encounters beatniks, falls in love with Joan Blackman, the daughter of right-wing news commentator Fred Clark, and generally wreaks havoc. With Earl Holliman, Barbara Lawson as a dancing beatnik, and John Williams as the alien chief. Special effects by John P. Fulton. Based (loosely) on a play by Gore Vidal.

THE VISITOR
1980 International Picture Show (Italy/U.S.)
DIRECTOR: Giulio Paradisi (Michael J. Paradise)
SCREENWRITERS: Lou Comici, Robert Mundi
ORIGINALLY RELEASED AS: *Il Visitatore*
A terrible thriller about a young Antichrist from the makers of *Tentacles*. They've assembled a typical "just pay us and we'll do it" cast: Mel Ferrer (as an alien), Glenn Ford, Shelley Winters, and in cameo roles: Sam Peckinpah and John Huston. Filmed partially in Atlanta. Presented by Ovido Assonitis.

VIVA LAS VEGAS
1964 MGM
PRODUCERS: Jack Cummings, George Sidney
DIRECTOR: George Sidney
SCREENWRITER: Sally Benson
Elvis is race-car driver Lucky Jackson. He needs a new engine, so he takes a waiter job and falls for swim instructress Ann-Margret. So does rival Count Mancini (Cesare Danova). William Demarest is Ann-Margret's understanding dad. Typical nonsense saved by some hot musical scenes featuring A-M go-going like nobody's business in black tights and spike heels. With Regina Carrol. From the director of *Bye Bye Birdie*.

VON RICHTHOVEN AND BROWN: See THE RED BARON.

VOODOO GIRL: See SUGAR HILL.

SERUM OF SATAN
One drop...and a raging monster is unleashed to kill ...and kill again in an unending lust for blood!

VOODOO HEARTBEAT

RAY MOLINA · PHILIP AHN · ERN DUGO
FORREST DUKE · EBBY RHODES · MIKE ZAPATA
RAY MOLINA, JR. · STAN MASON · MARY MARTINEZ · MIKE MEYERS

WARNING! BE SURE YOU ARE MATURE ENOUGH TO WITNESS THE SHOCKING DETAILS OF THIS MOTION PICTURE!

VOODOO HEARTBEAT
1972 TWI
PRODUCER: Ray Molina
DIRECTOR/SCREENWRITER: Charles Nizet
Producer Molina stars as a man turned into a blood-drinking monster with fangs. With his greasy hair and long sideburns, Molina resembles an aged Southern rockabilly singer. Philip Ahn is the only name star, but this cheapie features the funniest dialogue you'll ever

encounter plus voodoo ceremonies with black women doing the frug in tiger-skin bikinis. Also with Ray Molina, Jr. Filmed in Las Vegas. (R)

VOODOO ISLAND
1957 United Artists (B&W)
PRODUCER: Howard W. Koch
DIRECTOR: Reginald Leborg
SCREENWRITER: Richard Landau

In one of Karloff's worst movies he investigates the island of the title, sees some of his men turned into zombies, and discovers "woman-eating cobra plants." With Rhodes Reason, Elisha Cook, Jr., Beverly Tyler, and Murvyn Nye. It was filmed in Hawaii.

VOODOO MAN
1944 Monogram (B&W)
PRODUCER: Sam Katzman
DIRECTOR: William Beaudine
SCREENWRITER: Robert Charles

In this great example of Monogram horror Bela Lugosi is Dr. Marlowe, who wears a goatee and a robe covered with mysterious symbols. He kidnaps girls in order to find one "on the same mental plane" as his wife, who is in a permanent trance. After undergoing the doctor's mind-transfer process, the girls always become zombies and are taken to the basement by idiot John Carradine. Gas-station owner George Zucco tricks victims into driving over to Bela's house. Wanda Mckay is an almost zombie rescued by her boyfriend, who decides the whole ordeal will make a great script for a Lugosi film. As Lugosi says, "Ramboona never fails!" Sixty-two minutes long.

VOODOO TIGER
1952 Columbia (B&W)
PRODUCER: Sam Katzman
DIRECTOR: Spencer Gordon Bennet
SCREENWRITER: Samuel Newman

Jungle Jim (Johnny Weissmuller) fights Nazis, headhunters, and gangsters. With Jean Byron and Tamba the Chimp.

VOODOO WOMAN
1957 AIP (B&W)
PRODUCER: Alex Gordon
DIRECTOR: Edward L. Cahn
SCREENWRITERS: Russel Bender, V.I. Voss

A horror quickie made with leftovers from *The She Creature*. When mad scientist Tom Conway turns Marla English into a monster, the She Creature suit gets a new head, a sack dress, and a blond wig. Jungle terror with Michael "Touch" Connors, Lance Fuller, Paul Dubov, and Paul Blaisdell as the creature (again).

VORTEX: See THE DAY TIME ENDED.

VOYAGE TO THE BOTTOM OF THE SEA
1961 20th Century-Fox
PRODUCER/DIRECTOR: Irwin Allen
SCREENWRITERS: Irwin Allen, Charles Bennett

Irwin Allen's best film and the one that led to his popular, ridiculous TV series of the same name. Admiral Nelson (Walter Pidgeon) saves the world from the Van Allen radiation belt with the Seaview, his giant supersub. Joan Fontaine is a psychiatrist/saboteur. Barbara Eden is the admiral's secretary, Robert Sterling (from the *Topper* series) is Captain Crane. Peter Lorre is a shark-loving marine biologist. With Frankie Avalon (who sings the theme song), Michael Ansara as a religious fanatic, Henry Daniell, and Regis Toomey. The impressive sets were economically reused on the TV version. Underwater photography by John Lamb (*Mermaids of Tiburon*).

VOYAGE TO THE END OF THE UNIVERSE

1963 AIP (Czechoslovakia)
PRODUCER: Rudolph Wohl
DIRECTOR: Jindřich Polak
SCREENWRITERS: Pavel Juráček, Jindřich Polak
ORIGINALLY RELEASED AS: *Ikarie X.B.I.*

A small group of space travelers spend months in a vast spaceship searching for a planet less corrupt than their own. They discover a ghost ship with a group of finely dressed corpses seated around a table, are engulfed by a space nebula, and finally discover a friendly planet to settle on. Guess which planet. A superior Czechoslovakian science-fiction film with excellent special effects. Twenty-six minutes were cut for its U.S. release. Starring Zdenek Stepanek and Francis Smolen.

VOYAGE TO THE PLANET OF PREHISTORIC WOMEN

1968 AIP-TV
PRODUCER: Norman D. Wells
DIRECTOR: Derek Thomas
   (Peter Bogdanovich)
SCREENWRITER: Henry Ney

This one takes a while to explain. First read the entry on *Voyage to the Prehistoric Planet*. Done? Okay. This is the same Soviet footage in its third feature. The new scenes shot by Bogdanovich (using pseudonym) are astounding. He also narrates. The new star is Mamie Van Doren! She's the leader of a tribe of alien women who wear clamshell bikinis, worship the pterodactyl (it's dead and a bit limp in the new scenes), and lie around the beach communicating by means of telepathic voice-overs. They never meet the poor comrades who've been wandering around for six years. A very disorienting experience for everyone involved.

VOYAGE TO THE PREHISTORIC PLANET

1965 AIP-TV
PRODUCER: George Edwards
DIRECTOR/SCREENWRITER: John Sebastian
   (Curtis Harrington)

In 1962, the Leningrad Studio of Popular Science Films (really) made a serious science-fiction film called *Planeta Bura* (Planet of Storms). It featured Soviet cosmonauts with a giant robot exploring Venus. The special effects were excellent, including a pterodactyl and a land rover similar to the one later used on *Lost in Space*. AIP and executive producer Roger Corman (being your typical greedy capitalists) bought the Russian movie, hired Curtis Harrington to shoot new scenes with Basil Rathbone and Faith Domergue, and released it to television as a new movie. Rathbone plays basically the same earthbound role he had in *Queen of Blood*, which was also built around Russian footage.

THE VULTURE

1966 Paramount (England/U.S./Canada)
PRODUCER/DIRECTOR/SCREENWRITER:
   Lawrence Huntington

Unbelievable embarrassment in which Akim Tamiroff uses atomic energy to combine himself with a dead bird buried with an 18th-century witch. The result is a big killer vulture with Tamiroff's head! And Broderick Crawford plays an English squire! And Robert Hutton (*The Slime People*) is the hero! A color film released here in black-and-white. With Diane Claire.

W

1974 Cinerama (England)
PRODUCER: Mel Ferrer
DIRECTOR: Richard Quine
SCREENWRITERS: Gerald Di Pego, James Kelly
ALSO RELEASED AS: *I Want Her Dead*

Twiggy in her first dramatic role! She plays an ex-model who's terrorized by her insane ex-husband (Dirk Benedict). He's supposed to be in jail for killing her, but she's alive and remarried. Her new husband is played by her real-life husband, Michael Witney.

THE WACKY WORLD OF DR. MORGUS

1962 (B&W)
DIRECTOR: Raoul Haig
SCREENWRITERS: Noel and Raoul Haig

Dr. Morgus (Sid Noel), a popular television horror movie host in New Orleans, stars in a movie about an "instant-people" machine that turns humans into sand, then revives them. The evil ruler of Microvania uses it to fill the United States with 300 spies. Reporter Pencils McCane talks a top lady agent into a double cross. Filmed in Kiln, Mississippi, Kenner, Louisiana, and New Orleans. With Dana Barton, Jeanne Teslof, and David Kleinberger. See *Okefenokee.* —CB

WALK THE DARK STREET

1956 Dominant
PRODUCER/DIRECTOR/SCREENWRITER:
Wyott Ordung

Rifleman star Chuck Connors is a big-game hunter who holds Army officer Don Ross responsible for his GI brother's fatal heart attack. He hatches a scheme whereby he and Ross will track each other through the streets of downtown L.A. with novel camera guns, the winner taking a reward. As Connors is cornered he realizes the weapons have been switched and Ross has the camera with the bullet. He dies of heart failure. Producer-director-writer Ordung appeared in *Fixed Bayonets* and wrote the screenplay for *Robot Monster.* —CB

THE WALKING DEAD

1936 Warner Brothers (B&W)
PRODUCER: Lou Edelman
DIRECTOR: Michael Curtiz
SCREENWRITERS: Ewart Adamson,
Peter Milne, Robert Andrews,
Lillie Hayward

Ex-con Boris Karloff is framed for a murder, goes to the chair, and is electronically brought back to life as a piano-playing zombie by doctor Edmund Gwenn. Karloff, with a white streak in his hair, leads his enemies to violent deaths. Ricardo Cortez, Marguerite Churchill, Barton Maclane, and Warren Hull also star. Karloff later made a series of similar films at Columbia, but this one is the best.

THE WALLS OF HELL

1964 Hemisphere (U.S./Philippines)
PRODUCER: Eddie Romero
DIRECTORS: Gerardo De Leon, Eddie Romero
SCREENWRITERS: Ferde Grofe, Jr.,
Cesar Amigo, Eddie Romero

American lieutenant Jock Mahoney leads an attack against Japanese soldiers holding thousands of Filipinos captive in an ancient walled city. With Fernando Poe, Jr. From the makers of *Moro Witch Doctor.*

WAR BETWEEN THE PLANETS

1965 Fanfare (Italy)
PRODUCERS: Joseph Fryd,
Antonio Margheriti, Walter Manley
DIRECTOR: Anthony Dawson
(Antonio Margheriti)
SCREENWRITERS: Ivan Reiner, Moretti
ORIGINALLY RELEASED AS:
Missione Planète Errante
ALSO RELEASED AS: *Planet on the Prowl*

Astronauts try to stop the orbit of a planet that's causing earthquakes and disasters on Earth. Boring science fiction with Giacomo Rossi-Stuart and others using anglicized names.

WAR IS HELL
1964 Allied Artists (B&W)
PRODUCER/DIRECTOR/SCREENWRITER:
Burt Topper

A demented sergeant lies and murders his way to honor during the final days of the Korean War. Director Topper, who started at AIP with *Hell Squad* and *Tank Commandos*, co-stars with Baynes Barron, Wally Campo, and Judy Dan. Tony Russell is Sergeant Keefer. —CB

WAR OF THE COLOSSAL BEAST
1958 AIP (B&W with color sequence)
PRODUCER/DIRECTOR: Bert I. Gordon
SCREENWRITER: George Worthing Yates

The Amazing Colossal Man didn't die after all! In this Bert Gordon follow-up he's alive in Mexico but half his face is ruined. His right eye socket is empty. Giant Colonel Manning (this time played by Dean Parkins) goes on the rampage again, ugly and crazier than ever. The army catches him and chains him to a giant straw bed in an airplane hangar but soon the "beast" is loose, throwing buses and trucks. When his sister makes him feel guilty he commits suicide by grabbing high-tension wires. Funnier than the original! With special effects by producer-director Gordon, as usual.

WAR OF THE FOOLS
1964 Czechoslovakia (B&W)
DIRECTOR: Karel Zeman
SCREENWRITERS: Karel Zeman, Pavel Juráčcek
ORIGINALLY RELEASED AS: *Blaznova Kronika*

A historical antiwar fantasy from the creator of *The Fabulous World of Jules Verne*. In 1625 three people search for

Action from The Walls of Hell.

a land without war. Live action is combined with animation and sets based on engravings made during the Thirty Years' War.

WAR OF THE GARGANTUAS
1967 Toho/UPA (Japan)
EXECUTIVE PRODUCERS: Tomoyuki Tanaka, Henry G. Saperstein, Reubon Bercovitch
DIRECTOR: Inoshiro Honda
SCREENWRITERS: Inoshiro Honda, Kaori Mabuchi
ORIGINALLY RELEASED AS: *Sanda tai Gailah*

In one of the funniest Japanese monster bashes, American scientist Russ Tamblyn tries to act very serious and concerned about two giant, ugly ape-like gargantuas. He feels responsible for the destruction they're causing because he once studied a baby gargantua (a kid in a silly monkey suit) that escaped. Then an atomic blast made the cells of the friendly brown creature grow into a twin green one. During a nightclub scene a girl sings a wonderful song called "The Words Get Stuck in My Throat" until a gargantua smashes the building. The band Devo used to do the song at live performances. The movie was intended as a sequel to *Frankenstein Conquers the World* but American re-editing obscures the connection.

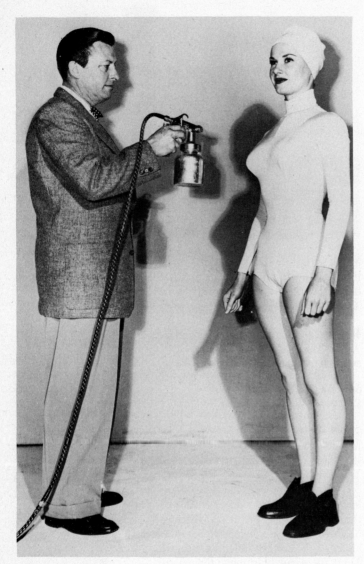

UPI 9/14/52: Earth-bound beauty Ann Robinson prepares to be transformed into a dweller of Mars by means of the spray applied by makeup man Wally Westmore on the Paramount lot, for her appearance in the new film, War of the Worlds.

WAR OF THE PLANETS

1965 MGM (Italy)
PRODUCERS: Joseph Fryd,
Antonio Margheriti, Walter Manley
DIRECTOR: Anthony Dawson
(Antonio Margheriti)
SCREENWRITERS: Ivan Reiner, Moretti
ORIGINALLY RELEASED AS: *I Diafanoidi Portano la Mort*

Martians made of light inhabit Earthlings during the 21st century. Forgettable thrills with Tony Russell and Lisa Gastoni.

WAR OF THE SATELLITES

1957 Allied Artists (B&W)
PRODUCER/DIRECTOR: Roger Corman
SCREENWRITER: Lawrence Louis Goldman

Two months after the first Russian sputnik went up, this eight-day exploitation item was in the theaters. *Life* magazine actually gave it a good review! Aliens take over the body of astronaut Richard Devon and he sabotages a space flight. Dick Miller is the hero. With Susan Cabot, Beach Dickerson, and Bruno Ve Sota. It is one of Corman's dullest.

WAR OF THE WORLDS

1953 Paramount
PRODUCER: George Pal
DIRECTOR: Byron Haskin
SCREENWRITER: Barré Lydon

Great updating of H.G. Wells' novel to contemporary Southern California with Gene Barry as a research scientist on the run with Ann Robinson when flying Martian warships attack. Humans and tanks disintegrate, major cities around the world are destroyed, even atomic bombs fail to stop the invaders. The incredible, briefly seen, one-eyed Martians eventually die from Earth germs outside a church. One of the most religious science-fiction films. With Carolyn Jones, Les Tremayne, Alvy Moore, and Paul Birch. Cedric Hardwicke narrates. When it was re-released

WAR OF THE MONSTERS

1966 Daiei/AIP-TV (Japan)
PRODUCER: Masaichi Nagata
DIRECTOR: Shigeo Tanaka
SCREENWRITER: Nizo Takahashi
ORIGINALLY RELEASED AS: *Gamera tai Barugon*

In the second Gamera-the-flying-prehistoric-turtle movie, the hero reptile fights Baragon, a dinosaur who can project a freezing rainbow.

with *When Worlds Collide*, audiences were surprised to see the exact same scene of people in a store listening to a radio in both movies.

WAR OF THE ZOMBIES

1963 AIP (Italy)
PRODUCERS: Ferruccio De Martino, Massimo De Rita
DIRECTOR: Giuseppe Vari
SCREENWRITERS: Piero Pierotti, Marcello Sartarelli
ORIGINALLY RELEASED AS: *Roma Contra Roma*
ALSO RELEASED AS: *Night Star*, *Goddess of Electra*

John Drew Barrymore in a robe and beard is Aderbal, the evil magician using revived corpses of Roman soldiers to conquer the world! The hero Gaius puts out the eye of his giant idol and destroys his power.

WARD 13 : See HOSPITAL MASSACRE.

Copyright © 1965 American International Pictures. Courtesy of Orion Pictures Corporation.

WAR-GODS OF THE DEEP

1965 AIP (England)
PRODUCER: Daniel Haller
DIRECTOR: Jacques Tourneur
SCREENWRITERS: Charles Bennett, Louis M. Heyward
ALSO RELEASED AS: *City Under the Sea*

Another AIP Poe adaptation. Corman didn't want to do any more, so it became the last feature for Jacques Tourneur. Tab Hunter, David Tomlinson, and a pet rooster discover an underwater city while searching for Susan Hart. She had been kidnaped by one of the gillmen and taken to the city because the ruling captain (who else but Vincent Price?) thinks she's the reincarnation of his dead wife. A dull and unconvincing adventure film with underwater photography by the director of *Mermaids of Tiburon*.

THE WARLORD

1937 Warner Brothers (B&W)
PRODUCTION SUPERVISOR: Bryan Foy
DIRECTOR: John Farrow
SCREENWRITER: Crane Wilbur
ALSO RELEASED AS: *West of Shanghai*

Boris Karloff stars as a renegade Chinese General named Wu Yen Fang. He captures a town and takes the Americans there prisoner. Ricardo Cortez is the real villain. With Gordon Oliver, Richard Loo, and Beverly Roberts. The story had been filmed (as *The Bad Man*) twice before. Previous versions were set in Mexico.

WARLORDS OF ATLANTIS

1978 Amicus/Columbia (England)
PRODUCER: John Dark
DIRECTOR: Kevin Connor
SCREENWRITER: Brian Hayles

Doug McClure stars in this lost-world kiddie adventure film, his fourth in a row. This one has turn-of-the-century

John Drew Barrymore in War of the Zombies.

explorers finding the lost cities of Atlantis, 55-year-old Cyd Charisse as high priestess Atsil, a giant octopus, and other unconvincing creatures. With Daniel Massey and Michael Gothard.

WARNING FROM SPACE

1956 Daiei/AIP-TV (Japan)
PRODUCER: Masaichi Nagata
DIRECTOR: Koji Shima
SCREENWRITER: Hideo Oguni
ORIGINALLY RELEASED AS: *Uchujin Tokyo Arawaru*
ALSO RELEASED AS: *Mysterious Satellite*

Friendly aliens who look like giant one-eyed starfish travel to Earth disguised as humans to warn us of the dangers of the H-bomb. If you think Japanese science-fiction movies are all the same, this should be a big surprise.

THE WASP WOMAN

1959 Allied Artists (B&W)
PRODUCER/DIRECTOR: Roger Corman
SCREENWRITER: Leo Gordon

She's advertised as: "A beautiful woman by day—a lusting queen wasp by night!" As the head of a cosmetics firm, Susan Cabot uses wasp enzymes for her rejuvenation formula. She becomes a ludicrous bug-eyed monster probably inspired by the previous year's *The Fly*. A fun Corman feature with Anthony Eisley, Barboura Morris, Michael Mark, and Bruno Ve Sota. Music by Fred Katz. A Filmgroup presentation.

WATCHER IN THE WOODS

1981 Buena Vista
PRODUCER: Ron Miller
DIRECTOR: John Hough
SCREENWRITERS: Brian Clemens, Harry Spaulding, Rosemary Anne Sisson

Cute teen Lynn-Holly Johnson (*For Your Eyes Only*) is convinced that something is watching her from the woods surrounding the ancient mansion that has become her home during her family's stay in England. That something turns out to be another cute teen who got caught in a time knot some 30 years before and is trying to get back to her mom, Bette Davis. In a final bid to shake its "kiddie film" image, the Disney folks decided to make this in the style of a gothic horror film, but somehow the horror got left out. Also left out was a sequence involving a bizarre, bat-winged alien creature and a trip to his native planet. The studio spent almost $200,000 developing the "other world" sequence, but decided that *Watcher* wasn't worth the expense of completing it. Instead, they rewrote the ending (badly). With Carroll Baker. Di-

Publisher Bennett Cerf (left) shows sons Jonathan and Christopher the joys of filmmaking on the set of Watusi. *Star George Montgomery introduces the family to a pair of "Watusis."*

rector Hough left Disney and did *Incubus* next.   –BM

THE WATTS MONSTER: See DR. BLACK AND MR. HYDE.

WATUSI
1959 MGM
PRODUCER: Al Zimbalist
DIRECTOR: Kurt Neumann
SCREENWRITER: James Clavell
In 1950, Stewart Granger starred in a popular version of H. Rider Haggard's *King Solomon's Mines*. Nine years later, leftover footage from that feature was frugally added to new scenes featuring George Montgomery as the son of the original great white hunter. This cheap, phony sequel includes UCLA basketball players as Watusi tribesmen, and a trip to the land of fire by Dinah Shore's then husband George in a pith helmet. With Rex Ingram, Finnish actress Taina Elg, and David Farrar. Originally co-billed with *The Mysterians*. Director Neumann died before it was released. Some good resulted from it, though: the Orlons had a hit single, "The Wah-Watusi," and a new dance craze swept the nation for a few weeks.

WAY WAY OUT
1966 20th Century-Fox
PRODUCER: Malcolm Stuart
DIRECTOR: Gordon Douglas
SCREENWRITERS: William Bowers, Laslo Vadnay
Science-fiction sex comedy set on the Moon in 1984. As a platonic married couple, Jerry Lewis and Connie Stevens replace American weathernauts who went crazy over sexy Russian Anita Ekberg. Anita's troublesome Soviet partner is Dick Shawn. The four of them drink instant vodka, the Russians marry, and at the end of the film the two couples happily decide to race to have the first baby born on the Moon.

With some really futuristic clothes and a giant TV screen showing the 1931 *Frankenstein*.

THE WAYWARD BUS
1957 20th Century-Fox (B&W)
PRODUCER: Charles Brackett
DIRECTOR: Victor Vicas
SCREENWRITER: Ivan Moffait
An adaptation of a John Steinbeck novel with a busload of California types, including Jayne Mansfield playing it straight as a former stripper and Dan Dailey as a drunken salesman. With Joan Collins and Rick Jason.

THE WAYWARD GIRL
1957 Republic (B&W)
PRODUCER: William J. O'Sullivan
DIRECTOR: Lesley Selander
SCREENWRITERS: Houston Branch, Frederic Louis Fox
Marcia Henderson cools her evil stepmother's lascivious boyfriend with an iron. Stepmom Katherine Barrett, having heard the whole thing, finishes him off and railroads the youngster into prison, where Marcia finds the hair-tugging inmates victims of a prostitution scam. With Peter Walker, Whit Bissell, Barbara Eden, Rita Lynn, and Francis De Sales. At this point in his career Selander had been cranking out around six movies a year for 21 years.   –CB

WE SHALL RETURN
1963 Cinema-Video International (B&W)
PRODUCER: Robert M. Carson
DIRECTOR: Philip S. Goodman
SCREENWRITER: Pat Frank
Cesar Romero stars as a prominent Cuban landowner who flees to Miami with his anti-Castro activist younger son, then learns that his elder son is working to sabotage the Bay of Pigs invasion. Tony Ray, Linda Libera, and Ramon Rodrigues co-star. Shot on location in St. Augus-

tine and Daytona Beach, Florida, in 1961.   –CB

THE WEB
1947 Universal (B&W)
PRODUCER: Jerry Bresler
DIRECTOR: Michael Gordon
SCREENWRITERS: William Bowers, Bertram Millhauser

Crooked industrialist Vincent Price arranges for bodyguard Edmond O'Brien to be blamed for a homicide. New York police lieutenant William Bendix has doubts. Ella Raines is Price's secretary.

WEB OF THE SPIDER
1972 Cinema Shares (Italy)
PRODUCER: Giovanni Adessi
DIRECTOR: Anthony Dawson (Antonio Margheriti)
SCREENWRITERS: Antonio Margheriti, Giovanni Adessi
ORIGINALLY RELEASED AS: *Nella Stretta Morsa del Ragno*
ALSO RELEASED AS: *In the Grip of the Spider*

Margheriti remakes his own *Castle of Blood* ('62) without Barbara Steele but with the talents of Klaus Kinski as Edgar Allan Poe, Tony Franciosa, and Michele Mercier.

WEEKEND OF FEAR
1966 J.D. Productions (B&W)
PRODUCER/DIRECTOR/SCREENWRITER: Joe Danford

Widow Ruth Trent hires deaf mute to terrorize and eliminate girlfriend of attractive local boy. Kenneth Washman co-stars, with Tory Alburn, Micki Malone, and Dianne Danford. Filmed on location in the Los Angeles area. –CB

WEEKEND REBELLION
1970 CineWorld
PRODUCER: Barry Mahon
DIRECTOR: Frank Willard

Producer Barry Mahon took the 1968 feature *Mondo Daytona* and added footage of that new sensation, Grand Funk Railroad, to make this "new" movie, which includes the long-haired Michigan trio plowing through "Paranoia" and "On Time" and the original *Mondo* stars mixed with "documentary" footage of students on a spring break.

THE WEIRD ONES
1962 Colonial International (B&W)
PRODUCER/DIRECTOR/SCREENWRITER: Pat Boyette

Two press agents hire a "cosmos-cutie" to help capture an alien "astronik." Mike Braden, Rudy Duran, Phyliss Warren, and Lee Morgan star; the director credit for this very obscure San Antonio feature is not definite. See *Dungeons of Harrow* and *No Man's Land*.   –CB

WEIRD WOMAN
1944 Universal (B&W)
PRODUCER: Oliver Drake
DIRECTOR: Reginald Le Borg
SCREENWRITER: Brenda Weisberg

From the ads: "She strikes with the curse of voo doo!" This first version of Fritz Leiber's *Conjure Wife* was part of the "Inner Sanctum" series. Later it was filmed as *Burn Witch Burn*. It's interesting to compare the different approaches to the story of a woman using witchcraft to help the career of her professor husband. Lon Chaney, Jr., and Anne Gwynne are Mr. and Mrs. With Evelyn Ankers, Ralph Morgan, and Elizabeth Russell.

WELCOME TO ARROW BEACH: See *TENDER FLESH.*

WELCOME TO BLOOD CITY
1977 EMI (England/Canada)
PRODUCER: Marilyn Stonehouse
DIRECTOR: Peter Sasdy
SCREENWRITER: Stephen Sohneck

A *Westworld*-inspired science-fiction tale about a computer-programmed Western-town. Residents are either citizens or slaves. Jack Palance is the

WHAT WAS THE TERRIFYING SECRET OF THE KILLER MONSTER?

BEAUTIES! The prey of a Monster's Desires!

WHAT IS IT?

WEREWOLF IN A GIRLS' DORMITORY
(THE GHOUL IN SCHOOL)

with BARBARA LASS · CARL SCHELL · Directed by RICHARD BENSON

A NEW HIGH IN HORROR!

marshall. Samantha Eggar creates a double of herself to spend time with Keir Dullea. Barry Morse is in charge of a project to find able warriors. The film never made it to America.

THE WEREWOLF
1956 Columbia (B&W)
PRODUCER: Sam Katzman
DIRECTOR: Fred F. Sears
SCREENWRITERS: Robert E. Kent, James B. Gordon

Scientists' serum "accidentally" turns tormented family man Steven Richie into a werewolf. He looks like the werewolf in *Return of the Vampire* from the same studio. Don Megowan is the sheriff. With Joyce Holden. Originally co-billed with *Earth vs. the Flying Saucers.*

THE WEREWOLF AND THE YETI: See *NIGHT OF THE HOWLING BEAST.*

WEREWOLF IN A GIRL'S DORMITORY
1961 MGM (Italy/Austria) (B&W)
EXECUTIVE PRODUCER: Guido Giambartolomei
DIRECTOR: Richard Benson (Paolo Heusch)
SCREENWRITER: Ernesto Gastaldi
ALSO RELEASED AS: *Lycanthropus*

Curt Lowens as Mr. Swift, the superintendent of a school for wayward girls, turns out to be a ferocious werewolf. The monster has fangs and lots of eye makeup, but not much facial hair. The scriptwriter must have seen the 1957 American *Blood of Dracula.* The theme song is "The Ghoul in School." A subplot involves blackmail. Carl Schell (brother of Maximilian) is the hero.

WEREWOLF OF LONDON
1935 Universal (B&W)
PRODUCER: Stanley Bergerman
DIRECTOR: Stuart Walker
SCREENWRITER: James Colton

Henry Hull as The Werewolf of London.

The original wolfman. Henry Hull, a botanist in Tibet, is bitten by a werewolf (Warner Oland). Back in London, the two cursed doctors fight over the moon flower that is the only known cure. Hull visits a real wolf in the zoo while on a nightly rampage and fears that he'll kill his wife (Valerie Hobson), "the one he loves most." Some of the best scenes feature two drunken cockney women. Universal rewrote the werewolf rules for their better-known '41 film.

WEREWOLF OF WASHINGTON

1973 Diplomat
PRODUCER: Nina Schulman
DIRECTOR/SCREENWRITER:
Milton Moses Ginsberg
A sometimes effective satire, partially inspired by Watergate, with the President's press secretary (Dean Stockwell) becoming a werewolf. As a Chinese diplomat watches in disbelief, Stockwell is transformed into a hairy creature and bites the President (Biff McGuire). Michael Dunn plays Dr. Kiss, a scientist who uses a secret door in a White House men's room to enter a hidden lab and create monsters. Director-writer Ginsberg also edited the film.

THE WEREWOLF VS. THE VAMPIRE WOMAN

1970 Ellman Enterprises (Spain/W. Germany)
PRODUCER: Plata Films
DIRECTOR: Leon Klimovsky
SCREENWRITERS: Jacinto Molina, Hans Munkell
ORIGINALLY RELEASED AS: *La Noche de Walpurgis*
Waldemar Daninsky, El Hombre Lobo (Paul Naschy), returns to life after a silver bullet is removed during an autopsy. As the wolfman, he's a snarling vicious killer. As Waldemar, he joins two female students searching for the tomb of a witch. The revived vampire/witch turns one of the girls into a vampire, and the monsters of the title fight. Ads warned: "Those easily nauseated approach with caution." With Gaby Fuchs and Patty Shepard. A big hit in Europe, it led to an onslaught of Spanish horror movies. **(R)**

WEREWOLVES ON WHEELS

1971 Fanfare
PRODUCER: Paul Lewis
DIRECTOR: Michel Levesque
SCREENWRITERS: Michel Levesque, David M. Kaufman
Satanists turn two bikers into werewolves. They're shown for about two minutes. Lots of violence, rock music, and stupidity with Barry (*Eve of Destruction*) McGuire, Billy (*Father Knows Best*) Gray, and biker-movie regulars. It was billed with *Simon, King of the Witches*. Joe Soloman was executive producer. **(R)**

WEST OF SHANGHAI: See THE WARLORD.

WESTWORLD

1973 MGM
PRODUCER: Paul Lazarus, Jr.
DIRECTOR/SCREENWRITER: Michael Crichton

The ultimate adult amusement park turns into a nightmare when the android population malfunctions. Yul Brynner is great in a silent role as the gunslinger that paying customers can "kill" over and over without fear of being harmed themselves—until things go wrong. Richard Benjamin and James Brolin aren't so great in speaking roles as patrons of the fantasy park. With Dick Van Patten (*Eight is Enough*) having his way with a robot hooker and Stephen Franken (Chatsworth on *Dobie Gillis*) as a mechanic. *Futureworld*, a sequel, came out in '76 and there was a mercifully short TV series.

WETBACKS

1956 Banner
DIRECTOR: Hank McCune

Two government secret agents working with U.S. Immigration employ a former Coast Guardsman having trouble making payments on his charter fishing boat. Smugglers John Hoyt and Harold Peary are trying to hire him, too. Starring Lloyd Bridges—whose similar *Sea Hunt* character debuted one year later. With Nancy Gates and Barton MacLane.   —CB

WHAT!

1963 Futurama Releasing
(Italy/England/France)
EXECUTIVE PRODUCER: John Oscar
(Elio Scardamaglia)
DIRECTOR: Mario Bava (John M. Old)
SCREENWRITERS: Ernesto Gastaldi,
Ugo Guerra, Luciano Martino
ORIGINALLY RELEASED AS: *La Frusta e il Corpo*
ALSO RELEASED AS: *Night is the Phantom*

A seldom shown Bava film that was banned in Italy for its sado-sexual theme. It was heavily censored before release elsewhere. During the 19th-century the sadistic Kurt Menliff (Christopher Lee) returns to his father's castle. When his brother's new wife (Daliah Lavi) spurns his advances, he follows her to the beach and whips her into unconsciousness. Soon afterward Kurt is discovered dead. More people are killed and the family believes that the bad son has returned from the crypt. The uncut version was reportedly excellent, but what remains is a bit incoherent. With Tony Kendall.

WHAT A CARVE UP!

1961 Embassy (England)
PRODUCERS: Robert S. Baker, Monty Berman
DIRECTOR: Pat Jackson
SCREENWRITERS: Ray Cooney, Tony Hilton
ALSO RELEASED AS: *No Place Like Homicide*

A comedy version of *The Ghoul*, a 1933 Karloff film. It's time to read the will of Uncle Gabriel, a proofreader of horror and sex novels. Donald Pleasence is the sinister solicitor. Michael Gough is the clubfooted butler. Starring Kenneth Conner, Sidney James, Shirley Eaton, Dennis Price, and pop star Adam Faith.

WHAT BECAME OF JACK AND JILL?

1971 Amicus (England)
PRODUCERS: Max J. Rosenberg,
Milton Subotsky
DIRECTOR: Bill Bain
SCREENWRITER: Roger Marshall

Vanessa Howard and Paul Nicholas star as lovers who terrorize a meddling grandmother played by Mona Washbourne (the old lady in the 1964 version of *Night Must Fall*). This psycho story was originally billed here with *The Strange Vengeance of Rosalie*.

WHAT EVER HAPPENED TO AUNT ALICE?

1969 Cinerama
PRODUCER: Robert Aldrich
DIRECTOR: Lee H. Katzin
SCREENWRITER: Theodore Aspin

As Aunt Alice, Ruth Gordon applies for the job of housekeeper in the Tucson, Arizona home of widow Geraldine Page in order to find out what happened to a missing friend. The crazed Page, left only a stamp album by her husband, takes money from her housekeepers, kills them, and buries the bodies in her garden. Alice is a widow too. So is neighbor Rosemary Forsyth. Lots of widows in this *Baby Jane* spinoff. (M)

WHAT EVER HAPPENED TO BABY JANE?

1962 Warners Brothers (B&W)
PRODUCER/DIRECTOR: Robert Aldrich
SCREENWRITER: Lukas Heller

A Hollywood horror story starring Bette Davis as the guilt-ridden ex-child star Baby Jane Hudson. Joan Crawford is her older sister Blanche, a former movie star confined to a wheelchair after an accident Jane believes she caused. The reclusive middle-aged women have been tormenting each other for years. Jane sings "I've Written a Letter to Daddy" in grotesque little-girl makeup, accompanied by 24-year-old Victor Buono (in his first film), and serves her sister a dead parakeet for dinner. In perfect black-and-white. Includes 1930s film clips from the real past of both stars. Based on Henry Farrell's novel. This innovative, often-imitated hit revived the careers of Davis and Crawford and set the precedent for aging female stars playing unhinged human monsters. Bette followed with *Dead Ringer*, Joan with *Straightjacket*. Aldrich made his own follow-up (with Davis), *Hush Hush . . . Sweet Charlotte*.

WHAT THE PEEPER SAW

1971 Avco Embassy (England)
PRODUCER: Graham Harris
DIRECTOR: James Kelly
SCREENWRITER: Trevor Preston
ORIGINALLY RELEASED AS: *Night Hair Child*

Young problem child Mark Lester (*Who Slew Auntie Roo?*) plays Britt Ekland's stepson. His mother had been electrocuted in a bathtub. A psycho mystery from executive producer Harry Alan Towers, filmed in Spain. With Hardy Kruger, Lilli Palmer, and Harry Andrews. (R)

WHAT'S A NICE GIRL LIKE YOU . . . ?

1971 TV
PRODUCER: Norman Lloyd
DIRECTOR: Jerry Paris
SCREENWRITER: Howard Fast

Vincent Price appears on TV all the time, but this is his only TV-movie. Brenda Vaccaro stars as a kidnaped Bronx girl forced to impersonate a socialite. It's a comedy. With Roddy McDowall, Jack Warden, Edmond O'Brien, and Jo Anne Worley. Directed by the dentist neighbor on *The Dick Van Dyke Show*.

WHAT'S IN IT FOR HARRY?: See *TARGET: HARRY.*

WHAT'S THE MATTER WITH HELEN?

1971 United Artists
PRODUCER: George Edwards
DIRECTOR: Curtis Harrington
SCREENWRITER: Henry Farrell

The Midwestern mothers of two teenage Leopold and Loeb—like murderers move to Hollywood in the 1930s and open a dancing school for would-be Shirley Temples. Debbie Reynolds falls in love with a Texas millionaire (Dennis Weaver), but Helen (Shelley Winters) turns to an evangelist (Agnes Moorehead) and goes off the deep end. With Pamelyn Ferdin and Fatty Arbuckle's look-alike son. Shelley was back the same year in *Who Slew Auntie Roo?*

WHAT'S UP FRONT

1964 Fairway-International
PRODUCER: Anthony M. Lanza
DIRECTOR: Bob Wehling
SCREENWRITERS: Bob Wehling,
　Arch Hall, Sr.
ALSO RELEASED AS: *The Fall Guy*
Frederick's of Hollywood supplied the merchandise for this story of an Indiana boy who becomes the world's greatest door-to-door bra salesman. The Johnson Bra Company's sales manager tries to snare the boss's daughter by taking credit for Homer L. Pettigrew's success and even gets him arrested by the FBI, but it all works out in the end. Tommy Holden stars, with Carolyn Walker as Pamela, Marilyn Manning as secretary Candy Cotton, and William Watters as the old man. Watters, who also was the executive producer (using a pseudonym), is actually Arch Hall, Sr., of *Eegah!* fame. Vilmos Zsigmond was cinematographer. —CB

WHAT'S UP, TIGER LILY?

1964/6 AIP (U.S./Japan)
EXECUTIVE PRODUCERS: Henry G. Saperstein,
　Tomoyuki Tanaka
DIRECTOR: Senkichi Taniguchi
SCREENWRITERS: Woody Allen,
　Frank Buxton, Len Maxwell,
　Louise Lasser, Mickey Rose,
　Bryna Wilson, Julie Bennett
Woody Allen took a Toho spy film (*Kagi no Kagi*), had it reedited, and overdubbed hilarious new dialogue. The Japanese hero becomes Phil Moskowitz. He's taken to a mythical country and asked to help retrieve the world's best egg-salad recipe. With Mie Hama as

Terri Yaki. The Lovin' Spoonful are good but their musical intrusions really slow down an otherwise great comedy. The scriptwriters also supply the voices. Allen appears at the beginning and the end with China Lee (*Playboy*'s Miss August '64 and wife of Mort Sahl). Don't miss.

WHEN A STRANGER CALLS

1979 Columbia
PRODUCERS: Doug Chapin, Steve Feke
DIRECTOR: Fred Walton
SCREENWRITERS: Steve Feke, Fred Walton
The ultimate in baby-sitter terror. Carol Kane takes a job looking after someone's kid and is victimized by a murderous phone caller who always seems to be one step ahead of everyone else. Not satisfied with this one night of nail-biting horror, the psycho makes a return engagement years later when Kane is happily married with children and baby-sitters of her own. Although fairly predictable, it's still suspenseful and is helped by a strong cast that includes such troupers as Charles Durning, Rachel Roberts, Colleen Dewhurst, and Ron O'Neal (*Superfly*). Based on the director's '77 short, *The Sitter*. (R) –BM

WHEN DINOSAURS RULED THE EARTH

1970 Hammer/Warner Brothers
　(England)
PRODUCER: Aida Young
DIRECTOR/SCREENWRITER: Val Guest
In the follow-up to *One Million Years B.C.*, blond *Playboy* playmate Victoria Vetri takes over from Raquel Welch as the star cavewoman. Jim Danforth did the excellent stop-motion animation, including a baby dinosaur hatching from an egg, a pterodactyl, a triceratops, and giant crabs. The dialogue consists of 27 words. "N'dye krasta m'kan neecro tedak" means "Come fast kill evil flying

monster." The Moon is torn from the Earth, causing tidal waves, human sacrifices, and pagan rites. Sex scenes seem to have been cut before the release.

WHEN MICHAEL CALLS

1972 TV (Canada)
EXECUTIVE PRODUCER: Victor J. Sherrick
DIRECTOR: Philip Leacock
SCREENWRITER: James Bridges

A psycho hypnotizes a kid and makes him call his sister (Elizabeth Ashley) and impersonate their dead brother. With a bee attack and a Halloween murder. Starring Ben Gazzara and Michael Douglas. A favorite of Stephen King. Based on a novel by John Ferris (*The Fury*).

WHEN THE BOYS MEET THE GIRLS

1965 MGM
PRODUCER: Sam Katzman
DIRECTOR: Alvin Ganzler
SCREENWRITER: Robert E. Kent

A remake of *Girl Crazy*, filmed in '32 and '43 (with Judy Garland and Mickey

Rooney). Rich playboy Harve Presnell helps poor Nevada ranch girl Connie Francis open a dude ranch for divorcees. In between Gershwin songs sung by the leads, popular bands and singers perform. With Sam the Sham and the Pharaohs, Herman's Hermits, Louis Armstrong, and Liberace. It was the only film appearance of the underrated Sam the Sham ("Woolly Bully").

WHEN THE GIRLS TAKE OVER

1962 Parade Releasing
PRODUCER/DIRECTOR: Russell Hayden
SCREENWRITER: Samuci Roeca

Revolutionaries try to break Hondo-Rica on the Caribbean by holding the First Minister's daughter hostage for a ransom of arms. Rescue attempts fail until island beauties show up in 26 pink Jeeps filled with food and wine. Robert Lowery stars as Maximo Toro, with Marvin Miller, Jackie Coogan, Jimmy Ellison, Ingeborg Kjeldsen, and Tommy Cook of *Teen-age Crime Wave*.   –CB

WHEN THE SCREAMING STOPS

1973 Independent Artists (Spain)
PRODUCERS: Ricardo Sanz,
 Ricardo Munoz Suay
DIRECTOR/SCREENWRITER: Armando De Ossorio
ORIGINALLY RELEASED AS: *La Garras de Loreley*

A beautiful woman turns into a toothy reptile monster and rips the hearts out of naked girls. A gory Spanish film from the director of *The Blind Dead* series. With Tony Kendall and Helga Line. A red flasher warns viewers of the bloody segments. **(R)**

WHEN TIME RAN OUT

1980 Warner Brothers
PRODUCER: Irwin Allen
DIRECTOR: James Goldstone
SCREENWRITERS: Carl Foreman,
 Sterling Silliphant

Only Irwin Allen could make a $20 million disaster movie with Paul Newman heading an all-star cast—and have it go totally ignored! Not willing to admit the public had gotten sick of these things, he tried to get away with just one more. With Jacqueline Bisset, William Holden, Red Buttons, Ernest Borgnine, James Franciscus, Burgess Meredith, Barbara Carrera, John Considine, ex-football star Alex Karras, and a volcano and tidal wave destroying an island in Hawaii. It was announced in *Variety* ads as "the most important film of the decade."

WHEN WOMEN HAD TAILS

1970 European International (Italy)
PRODUCER: Silvio Clementelli
DIRECTOR: Pasquale Festa Campanile
SCREENWRITERS: Lina Wertmüller,
Ottavio Jemma, Marcello Costa,
Pasquale Festa Campanile
ORIGINALLY RELEASED AS: *Quando le Donne Avevano la Coda*

When Dinosaurs Ruled the Earth made money, so why not throw out the dinosaurs and add more sex? That's what the Italians did. Senta Berger stars as a sexy cavewoman with a tail who's dis-

covered on an island by seven horny cavemen. It's a comic version of *Snow White*. It even had a sequel—*When Women Lost Their Tails*. Music by Ennio Morricone. With Frank Wolff. (R)

WHEN WORLDS COLLIDE

1951 Paramount
PRODUCER: George Pal
DIRECTOR: Rudolph Mate
SCREENWRITER: Sydney Boehm

1951 was a banner year for good, major-studio science fiction, including *The Thing*, *The Day the Earth Stood Still*, and this end-of-the-world epic based on a novel by Philip Wylie and Edwin Balmer. It's Armageddon time as the passing of the planet Zyra causes volcanoes to erupt on Earth and tidal waves to submerge Manhattan. (Academy Award–winning special effects show Herald Square with a giant wave coming up Broadway.) Before the star Bellus collides with Earth, a modern ark/spaceship must take off for the good life on the pastoral planet Zyra. Meanwhile Richard Derr and Peter Hanson fight over Barbara Rush, and ruthless crippled millionaire John Hoyt plots to gain passage on the streamlined space ark and eliminate excess human cargo. Director Mate (from Poland) was the cameraman for *Vampyr* (1932). With Stuart Whitman.

WHERE HAVE ALL THE PEOPLE GONE

1974 TV
PRODUCER: Gerald Isenberg
DIRECTOR: John L. Moxey
SCREENWRITERS: Lewis John Carlino,
Sandor Stern

Peter Graves and his cliché family unit emerge from a cave while on a camping trip to discover they're in an end-of-the-world movie. A solar flare-up (not a bomb for a change) caused the destruction and turned most of the popu-

UPI 8/6/70: Actress Senta Berger has a "hang-up" in a scene from the film, When Women Had Tails. *The man she is stringing up is Italian actor Giuliano Gemma.*

lation into sand. With Verna Bloom and Kathleen Quinlan. It was the unlucky 13th made-for-TV feature by Moxey.

WHERE THE BULLETS FLY
1966 Embassy (England)
PRODUCER: S.J.H. Ward
DIRECTOR: John Gilling
SCREENWRITER: Michael Pittock
Tom Adams is back as agent Tom Vine in a sequel to *The Second Best Secret Agent*. He and Dawn Addams, his Air Force officer girlfriend, stop the Russians from stealing spurium, a lightweight metal used for nuclear aircraft. With Sidney James (the *Carry On* series), Wilfrid Brambell (*A Hard Day's Night*), and Michael Ripper (*Revenge of Frankenstein*).

WHERE TIME BEGAN
1977 Almena (Spain)
PRODUCER/DIRECTOR: Juan Piquer
SCREENWRITERS: Carlos Puerto, John Melson, Juan Piquer
ORIGINALLY RELEASED AS: *Viaje al Centro de la Tierra*
ALSO RELEASED AS: *Journey to the Center of the Earth*

Rhonda Fleming confronts John Drew Barrymore as the lipstick killer in Fritz Lang's While the City Sleeps.

Badly made juvenile Jules Verne adventure with giant turtles, a big ape, and rubber dinosaurs projected behind Kenneth More and the rest of the cast. From the director of *The Supersonic Man*.

WHILE THE CITY SLEEPS
1956 RKO (B&W)
PRODUCER: Bert Friedlob
DIRECTOR: Fritz Lang
SCREENWRITER: Casey Robinson
Vincent Price as Walter Kyne, Jr., inherits his late father's newspaper and announces to his editors a competition to find "the lipstick killer." They all turn to women to gain influence and information. Reporter Dana Andrews helps city editor Thomas Mitchell investigate by using girlfriend Sally Forrest as bait. Wire service editor George Sanders sends mistress Ida Lupino to charm information from Andrews. Photo editor James Craig is having an affair with Kyne's wife (Rhonda Fleming). The killer turns out to be John Barrymore, Jr., a confused delivery boy who reads comic books. Top-notch Lang, despite what you might read.

WHIPHAND
1951 RKO (B&W)
PRODUCER: Lewis J. Rachmil
DIRECTOR: William C. Menzies
SCREENWRITERS: George Bricker, Frank L. Moss
Nazis-turned-Communists plan to wipe out the entire U.S. population via germ warfare! A secret lab is set up in a New England village and the insidious work begins. This astounding anti-commie shock feature was originally filmed as *The Man He Found*, a story about Hitler relocating to America after the war. Under orders of studio head Howard Hughes, much of the footage was cut, new footage was shot, and the title and plot were changed. The results are inter-

esting, to say the least. Carla Balenda, Elliott Reid, Edgar Barrier, and Raymond Burr star. As in all his unique features (*The Maze, Invaders from Mars*), director Menzies was also production designer.

WHISPERING GHOSTS

1942 20th Century-Fox (B&W)
EXECUTIVE PRODUCER/DIRECTOR:
Alfred Werker
SCREENWRITER: Lou Breslow
Milton Berle is a radio detective investigating the murder of a sea captain with the help of Willie Best. John Carradine is one of the nonsupernatural scares. With Brenda Joyce, Grady Sutton, and Milton Parsons. It was "inspired" by Red Skelton's *Whistling in the Dark.*

THE WHITE BUFFALO

1977 United Artists
PRODUCER: Pancho Kohner
DIRECTOR: J. Lee Thompson
SCREENWRITER: Richard Sale

Advertised as being "From the creators of KING KONG," this was an even bigger flop presented by Dino De Laurentiis! Charles Bronson is the Polish Wild Bill Hickok after a giant albino buffalo. With Jack Warden, Kim Novak (in her first role since *Tales That Witness Madness*), Stuart Whitman, John Carradine, Slim Pickens, and Will Sampson (Chief Bromden in *One Flew Over the Cuckoo's Nest*). Dino also gave us *Orca* the same year. Music by John Barry.

WHITE DOG

1982 Paramount
PRODUCER: John Davidson
DIRECTOR: Sam Fuller
SCREENWRITERS: Sam Fuller, Curtis Hanson
ALSO RELEASED AS: *Trained to Kill*
Kristy McNichol adopts a dog. Suspecting that it's been killing on the sly, she takes it to animal training specialists. Paul Winfield and Burl Ives discover that the dog has been trained since birth

to attack and kill—but only black people. They try to deprogram the racist but otherwise friendly dog. After finally finding somebody to direct this controversial project, Paramount chickened out and decided not to release it. *White Dog* has played to good reviews in Europe and will eventually play here in a cut version on cable TV. Based on a *Life* magazine story by Romain Gary, the ex-husband of ill-fated Jean Seberg. With Dick Miller.

THE WHITE GORILLA
1947 Special Attractions (B&W)
PRODUCER: Adrian Weiss
DIRECTOR: Harry L. Fraser
One of the cheapest and funniest features ever made. Using advanced techniques later perfected by Roger Corman and Al Adamson, the producers managed to create a "new" film by shooting around a 1927 silent. The original footage is from *Perils of the Jungle* starring Frank Merril and featuring black natives worshiping one-eyed statues with beards. The new footage features Ray "Crash" Corrigan as a big ape thrown out of his tribe for being the wrong color. Narration was supplied in an attempt to hold things together. See men in different-colored gorilla suits fight, carry a girl around, and react to actors filmed two decades earlier. Incredible.

WHITE PONGO
1945 PRC (B&W)
PRODUCER: Sigmund Neufeld
DIRECTOR: Sam Newfield
SCREENWRITER: Raymond L. Schrock
A poverty-row quickie starring a man in a big fluffy white gorilla suit as the missing link. From the director of *Nabonga, Terror of Tiny Town,* and *Harlem on the Prairie.* With Robert Fraser and the wonderful Maris Wrixon.

WHITE VOICES
1964 Rizzoli (France/Italy)
PRODUCERS: Luciano Peruglia, Nello Meniconi
DIRECTOR: Pasquale Festa Campanile
SCREENWRITERS: Pasquale Festa Campanile, Massimo Franciosa, Luigi Magni
ORIGINALLY RELEASED AS: *Le Voci Bianche*
A comedy about a man (Paolo Ferrari) in 18th-century Rome who sells his brother to the Vatican Choir. The brother escapes and the man takes his place, pretending he's been castrated in order to sing soprano. He's caught fooling around with the wives of old noblemen and is faced with decapitation or castration. With Sandra Milo, Anouk Aimee, Barbara Steele, and Rosalba Neri.

THE WHITE WARRIOR
1959 Warner Brothers (Italy)
PRODUCER: Majestic-Lovcen
DIRECTOR: Riccardo Freda
SCREENWRITERS: Gino De Santis, Akos Tolnay
ORIGINALLY RELEASED AS: *Agi Murad, Il Diavolo Bianco*
Tolstoy's "Khadzhi-Murat" is given the Hercules treatment. A bearded Steve Reeves stars as a 19th-century tribal chieftain who defies Czar Nicholas of Russia. He also fights a villainous rival for possession of Sutanet. Director Freda did *Caltiki* next.

WHITE WOMAN
1933 Paramount (B&W)
PRODUCER: E. Lloyd Sheldon
DIRECTOR: Stuart Walker
SCREENWRITERS: Samuel Hoffenstein, Gladys Lehman
After *Island of Lost Souls,* Paramount put Charles Laughton in a similar role in this seldom-seen adventure. The incredible sets from the first film were reused. Decapitated heads are kicked around. Laughton is an evil jungle ruler

with a bushy mustache. With Carole Lombard, Kent Taylor, Charles "Ming" Middleton, Noble Johnson, and Charles Bickford. When it was showing as an "adults only" feature, the newspaper ads promised "Woman Hunger. Crazed Men Who Lived Without Love—Sly Whispers!" It was remade as *Island of Lost Men* in '39.

WHITE ZOMBIE

1932 United Artists (B&W)
PRODUCER: Edward Halperin
DIRECTOR: Victor Halperin
SCREENWRITER: Garnett Weston

The original zombie movie! In 1929 a book called *The Magic Island* introduced the word zombie to America. A play called *Zombie* hit New York in 1932. Everyone was talking about zombies. For this film the Halperin Brothers, independent producers, borrowed sets (from *Frankenstein*, *Dracula*, *The Hunchback of Notre Dame*, and *King of Kings*) and Universal's master makeup man Jack Pierce. Best of all, they signed Bela Lugosi, who had just hit in *Dracula*, to play Murder Legendre, creator and ruler of zombies in Haiti. The result is a unique, ancient-looking but fascinating low-budget horror movie which made millions. Lugosi, who must have had awful agents, walked away with $800. His eyes and hands are prominently featured. In addition to great sets and lots of the living dead, there's weird music, some of it by Xavier Cugat. With silent star Madge Bellamy.

WHO?

1974 Allied Artists (England)
PRODUCER: Barry Levinson
DIRECTOR: Jack Gold
SCREENWRITER: John Gould

FBI man Elliott Gould has to find out if a cybernetic man (Joseph Bova) created by East Germans is really the top

American physicist who had been in a car crash near the Berlin wall. Trevor Howard is a Communist agent. An unusual science-fiction espionage film.

WHO FEARS THE DEVIL: See THE LEGEND OF HILLBILLY JOHN.

WHO KILLED "DOC" ROBBIN

1948 United Artists
PRODUCER: Robert F. McGowan
DIRECTOR: Bernard Carr
SCREENWRITERS: Maurice Geraghty, Dorothy Reid
ALSO RELEASED AS: *Curley and His Gang in the Haunted Mansion*

A haunted-house comedy featuring George Zucco as a mad scientist using "an atomic firing chamber." It's a Hal Roach production in "gay new Cinecolor." With Virginia Grey, Don Castle, and a man in a gorilla suit. It was a sequel to *The Adventures of Curley and His Gang*. The features were an attempt by Roach to create a new *Little Rascals*-type series.

WHO KILLED TEDDY BEAR?

1965 Magna (B&W)
PRODUCER: Everett Rosenthal
DIRECTOR: Joseph Cates
SCREENWRITERS: Leon Tokatyan,
   Arnold Drake

Really grimy obscene-phone call chiller with a New York discotheque background. Busboy Sal Mineo, guardian to a brain-damaged sister, writhes in bed while club hostess/deejay Juliet Prowse worries on the other end of the line. Jan Murray of the vice squad tries to investigate and acts so creepy that Juliet thinks he's the maniac. With Frank Campanella, Margot Bennett, and Elaine Stritch as Juliet's lesbian boss, who tries to help in her own way. Title song and discotheque hits written by Al Kasha and Bob Gaudio (of the Four Seasons).   –CB

WHO SLEW AUNTIE ROO?

1971 AIP (U.S./England)
PRODUCERS: Samuel Z. Arkoff, James H.
   Nicholson
DIRECTOR: Curtis Harrington
SCREENWRITERS: Jimmy Sangster,
   Robert Blees, Gavin Lambert
ALSO RELEASED AS: *Whoever Slew Auntie
   Roo?*

Shelley Winters plays a kind but crazed American widow living in England in the 1920s. She misses her late daughter so much that she keeps her mummified corpse around and kidnaps a little girl (Chloe Franks) who resembles her. The girl's brother (Mark Lester) thinks Shelley is the witch in "Hansel and Gretel" and decides to duplicate the ending of the fairy tale. With Ralph Richardson, Lionel Jeffries, Hugh Griffith, and Michael Gothard (*The Devils*).

WHOEVER SLEW AUNTIE ROO?: See *WHO SLEW AUNTIE ROO?*.

WHY MUST I DIE?

1960 AIP (B&W)
PRODUCER: Richard Bernstein
DIRECTOR: Roy Del Ruth
SCREENWRITERS: George Waters,
   Richard Bernstein

An *I Want to Live* retread starring Terry Moore of *Mighty Joe Young*. She's a nightclub singer whose comeback is cut short when an associate of her petty-crook father comes around with a safecracking girlfriend and a plan. Debra Paget shoots the club owner

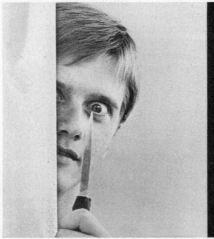

Split-screen action in Wicked, Wicked *featuring star psycho Randy Roberts and singer Tiffany Bolling.*

during the big job but owns up only after Moore goes to the chair. Juli Reding of *Pattern for Murder* and Bert Freed co-star. —CB

WICKED, WICKED

1973 MGM
PRODUCER/DIRECTOR/SCREENWRITER:
Richard L. Bare

A comic psycho movie in "Duo-vision." The entire feature employs the split-screen technique used in parts of *Sisters* and *Woodstock*. As a handyman at a seacoast hotel Randolph Roberts wears a monster mask while he kills and dismembers women with blond hair. From the ads: "See the hunter, see the hunted both at the same time." Cast members include Tiffany Bolling as a singer, Scott Brady as a detective, Diane McBain, Arthur O'Connell, and Edd "Kookie" Byrnes as a lifeguard. The music is the organ score for the silent *Phantom of the Opera*. It was not a hit.

THE WICKER MAN

1972 Warner Brothers (England)
PRODUCER: Peter Snell
DIRECTOR: Robin Hardy
SCREENWRITER: Anthony Shaffer

Led by Christopher Lee, the inhabitants of a Scottish island practice pagan rites. The title refers to a giant, hollow sacrificial wicker statue that burns with a meddlesome police sergeant in it. This movie has a reputation as a neglected classic—see it and decide for yourself. With Hammer horror actress Ingrid Pitt and Britt Ekland, whose nude dance was the reason for the R rating. Screenwriter Anthony Shaffer also did *Sleuth* and *Frenzy*. It was released several times by different companies. (R)

THE WILD ANGELS

1966 AIP
PRODUCER/DIRECTOR: Roger Corman
SCREENWRITER: Charles Griffith

UPI 7/24/79: *Peter Fonda stands in front of a huge poster blowup of himself in a scene from* The Wild Angels *during an affair at the Museum of Modern Art honoring American International Pictures' 25th anniversary.*

Peter Fonda stars as Heavenly Blues, a sulking, leather-clad Hell's Angel leader. The sometimes shocking events in this incredible movie were based on stories told by the real California Angels, who appear as themselves. Afterward they sued for defamation of character! After an attack on a Mexican biker club, Heavenly's best friend Loser (Bruce Dern) is wounded and ends up in a hospital. Gang members kidnap him from the hospital. He dies, and during his funeral service they tie up the preacher and have a stoned-out orgy in the church (with fast bongo music). Dern attends, propped up on a bench with a joint in his mouth. At the end Fonda stays behind, explaining: "There's nowhere to go." True, but after *The Trip* Fonda made *Easy Rider* and became a cult hero (for a while). Literally dozens of biker films followed, some more violent and meaningless but few better. With Nancy Sinatra as Mike, Michael J. Pollard as Pygmy, Gayle Hunnicutt, Diane Ladd, Dick Miller, and Peter Bogdanovich (the assistant director). "Blues Theme" by the Arrows was a hit single and two albums of the Fuzztone instrumental music were released.

new French stepmother (Noëlle Adam) was once a stripper at a burlesque club. She goes there and becomes involved with the club's sleazy owner (Christopher Lee). With David Farrar, Nigel Green, and Oliver Reed as a dissatisfied youth. Great music by the John Barry Seven.

WILD GUITAR

1962 Fairway-International (B&W)
PRODUCER: Nicholas Merriwether
DIRECTOR: Ray Dennis Steckler
SCREENWRITERS: Nicholas Merriwether, Bob Wehling

Arch Hall, Jr., motorcycles to Hollywood where a young dancer tips him to a TV talent show. Unscrupulous agent William Watters (a.k.a. Arch Hall, Sr. of *Eegah!*) catches the act and sets out to line his own pockets with gold. Arch, Jr., and Alan O'Day wrote the songs. The co-stars are Nancy Czar, Cash Flagg (a.k.a. Steckler), and Marie Denn.   —CB

Oliver Reed (left) dances in Wild For Kicks.

WILD FOR KICKS

1960 Victoria Films (England) (B&W)
PRODUCER: George Willoughby
DIRECTOR: Edmond T. Greville
SCREENWRITER: Dail Amber
ALSO RELEASED AS: *Beat Girl*

A hot British teen movie with beatniks, strippers, murder, and music. Rock star Adam Faith was the big attraction, but the story centers on Gillian Hills (later one of the girls in *Blow-Up*) as a young girl who likes to hang out at a beatnik dive with Faith and Shirley Ann Field, who both sing. She finds out that her

WILD HARVEST

1961 Sutton (B&W)
PRODUCER: Aubrey Schenck
DIRECTOR: Jerry Baerwitz
SCREENWRITER: Sid Harris

Female migrant workers eat dirt at the hands of a sadistic ranch foreman (Dean Fredericks of *The Phantom Planet*) during grape harvesting season in the San Joaquin Valley. His mistress changes sides after Susan Kelly (*Playboy*'s Miss May 1961) is killed delivering a petition to the ranch owner. She supplies a key to Fredericks' hideout, where he is attacked and mutilated with pruning shears. Dolores Faith, Robert Harrow, Arlynn Greer, Kathleen Freeman, and Ivy Thayer co-star, with narration by Walter Winchell. Filmed on location in Homestead, Florida.   —CB

WILD IN THE COUNTRY

1961 20th Century-Fox
PRODUCER: Jerry Wald
DIRECTOR: Philip Dunne
SCREENWRITER: Clifford Odets

In this serious drama, Elvis Presley is Glen Tyler, a rebellious country boy who is sent to live with a crooked uncle. He is gossiped about, fought over, accused of a murder, and ends up going to college. As his widow psychiatrist, Hope Lange tries to kill herself when she hears Elvis has "murdered" the son (Gary Lockwood) of her ex-fiancée (John Ireland). Tuesday Weld is great as Elvis' seductive cousin, complete with an illegitimate kid. Millie Perkins is his long-suffering childhood sweetheart. With Alan Napier, Jason Robards, and Christina Crawford as Monica. Elvis sings four songs.

WILD IN THE STREETS

1968 AIP
PRODUCERS: James H. Nicholson, Samuel Z. Arkoff
DIRECTOR: Barry Shear
SCREENWRITER: Robert Thom

Richard Pryor applauds for Christopher Jones in Wild in the Streets.

Max Frost (Christopher Jones), a millionaire rock star, becomes the President of the United States after managing to have the voting age lowered to 14. He decrees that citizens over 30 be sent to concentration camps where they're forced to take LSD. This wacky political youth satire is a hit-and-miss affair that mixes wit with embarrassment. Shelley Winters gives an unrestrained performance as Max's thoughtless mother. Hal Holbrook is a liberal Congressman whose appeal to youth backfires. Walter Winchell, Melvin Belli, and Dick Clark play themselves. The familiar voice of Paul Frees narrates. With Ed Begley, Diane Varsi, Richard Pryor (as Stanley X), Kevin Coughlin, and Millie Perkins. Based on a story in *Esquire*. "The Shape of Things to Come" by Max Frost and the Troopers was a hit single. It was AIP's biggest-budgeted film to that time.

WILD IS MY LOVE

1963 Mishkin (B&W)
PRODUCER/DIRECTOR: Richard Hilliard
SCREENWRITER: Otto Lemming

A *pre-*Deer Hunter *Russian roulette sequence in* Wild Is My Love.

Hilliard's follow-up to *Psychomania.* Relations among three college chums studying for makeup exams are strained when one invites a stripper to spend a weekend on the deserted campus. Miss Queenie leaves after tensions lead to Russian roulette; Ben, Aga, and Zero resume their friendship. Paul Hampton, Ray Fulmer, and Bob Alexander star.

—CB

WILD JUNGLE CAPTIVE: See JUNGLE CAPTIVE.

WILD ON THE BEACH
1965 20th Century-Fox (B&W)
PRODUCER/DIRECTOR: Maury Dexter
SCREENWRITER: Harry Spalding
Frankie Randall and Sherry Jackson both lay claim to a beach house for student boarders. Problems arise when both boys and girls show up to live there. They're soothed by the music of Sonny and Cher, Jackie and Gayle, Sandy Nelson, and the Astronauts. With Russ Bender. Songs include "Pyramid Stomp" and "Gods of Love."

THE WILD ONE
1953 Columbia (B&W)
PRODUCER: Stanley Kramer
DIRECTOR: Laslo Benedek
SCREENWRITER: John Paxton
Mary Murphy: "What are you rebelling against?" Marlon Brando: "What ya got?" Thirty bikers take over a small town and terrorize the locals while fighting each other. With Lee Marvin, Robert Keith, Jay C. Flippen, Jerry Paris, and Bruno Ve Sota. Banned in England, it was only a sample of the discontent to come.

WILD ONES ON WHEELS
1962 Emerson (B&W)
PRODUCER: Fred Charles
DIRECTOR: Rudolph Cusumano
ORIGINALLY RELEASED AS: *Drivers to Hell*
Sportscar gang murders ex-con and forces his wife to help them locate $240,000 buried in the Mojave Desert. With Francine York, Edmund Tontini, and Robert Blair. Emerson also released *Creation of the Humanoids,* and *Manos, the Hand of Fate.*

—CB

THE WILD PARTY

1956 United Artists
PRODUCER: Sidney Harmon
DIRECTOR: Harry Horner
SCREENWRITER: John McPartland

Demented ex-football hero Anthony Quinn and his jazzed-out drug-addict friends hold a young socialite and her fiancé hostage in a sleazy beatnik hangout in downtown L.A. Carol Ohmart and Arthur Franz are terrorized and humiliated by Jay Robinson, Nehemiah Persoff, and Kathryn Grant. Music by the Buddy De Franco Quartet. Originally a package with *Four Boys and a Gun*. Horner directed *Red Planet Mars*. —CB

THE WILD RACERS

1968 AIP
PRODUCER: Joel Rapp
DIRECTOR: Daniel Haller
SCREENWRITER: Max House

If you liked Corman's *The Young Racers* back in '62, here's a reworking of the same themes, again with race scenes filmed in Europe. Fabian stars as Jo-Jo, a driver who changes women like tires. Mimsy Farmer (*Riot on Sunset Strip*) lasts for about 45 minutes. With Dick Miller, Alan Haufrect, and Talia Coppola. Her brother Francis, who did the sound on *The Young Racers*, advanced to second-unit director on this one. He had already directed *You're a Big Boy Now* and *Dementia 13*. Roger Corman was executive producer.

THE WILD REBELS

1967 Crown International
ASSOCIATE PRODUCER: Joseph Fink
DIRECTOR/SCREENWRITER: William Grefe

From the ads: "They live, love, and even kill for kicks!" Lieutenant Dorn (Walter Philben) talks a stock-car racer (Steve Alaimo) into accepting an offer from Satan's Angels Fats (Jeff Gillen), Banjo (Willie Pastvano), and Jeeter (John Vella) to drive the getaway car in a bank job. He tips the authorities as planned, but the gang slips away to an abandoned lighthouse and prepares for battle. Grefe (who directed episodes of *Sea Hunt*, *Flipper*, and *Gentle Ben*) turned this out between *Death Curse of Tartu* and *The Hooked Generation*. With southern Florida's Birdwatchers. Steve Alaimo sings "You Don't Know Like I Know." —CB

Brando's gang in The Wild One.

THE WILD RIDE
1960 Filmgroup (B&W)
PRODUCER/DIRECTOR: Harry Berman
SCREENWRITERS: Ann Porter,
   Marion Rothman

Jack Nicholson runs down two motor-cycle cops, then tries to ruin the life of a reformed friend by kidnaping his girl. At the drags, Georgianna Carter watches Jack win by killing the competition. Robert Bean attempts a rescue during the wild victory celebration. The subsequent high-speed chase ends in tragedy. *The Girl in Lovers' Lane* was the original co-feature. Roger Corman was the executive producer.   –CB

WILD WHEELS
1969 Fanfare
PRODUCER: Budd Dell
DIRECTOR: Kent Osborne
SCREENWRITERS: Kent Osborne, Ralph Luce

WILD BIKE RIDERS-VS DUNE BUGGY BOYS!
The Original California Gang!
WILD WHEELS
HEAR 5 NEW TUNES!
COLOR
Starring
DON EPPERSON • ROBERT DIX Co-starring CASEY KASEM • DOVIE BEAMS
TERRY STAFFORD • JOHENNE LEMONT • Introducing BRUCE KIMBLE as "BOOMER"
Produced by BUDD DELL • Written by KENT OSBORNE and RALPH LUCE • Directed by KENT OSBORNE
Released by FANFARE FILM PRODUCTIONS, INC. – R

Big 16mm biker vs. dune buggy war at Pismo Beach. Robert Dix of *Seven Bloody Graves* and his Roadrunners are accused of raping a local girl during a pot-and-stolen-liquor orgy. Dix joins the more peaceful four-wheelers after his biker buddies are apprehended by police. Don Epperson and Casey Kasem co-star, with Dovie Beams, Terry Stafford, Evelyn Guerrero, Byrd Holland, Three of August, Billie & Blue, Saturday Revue, and Thirteenth Committee. **(R)**   –CB

WILD WILD PLANET
1965 MGM (Italy)
PRODUCERS: Joseph Fryd,
   Antonio Margheriti
DIRECTOR: Anthony Dawson
   (Antonio Margheriti)
SCREENWRITERS: Ivan Reiner, Renato Moretti
ORIGINALLY RELEASED AS: *I Criminali della Galassia*

Fun, cheap science-fiction adventure with an alien mad scientist sending female agents in tight leather pants to shrink humans. The tiny people are taken in suitcases to a futuristic city with mutants, dwarves, and four-armed androids. With Tony Russel and Franco Nero.

THE WILD, WILD WEST REVISITED
1979 TV
PRODUCER: Robert L. Jacks
DIRECTOR: Burt Kennedy
SCREENWRITER: William Bowers

Ten years after the original show's demise, Robert Conrad and Ross Martin returned in this feature as agents James West and Artemus Gordon. Good idea. Michael Dunn, who played Dr. Loveless, had died, so they got singer Paul Williams to play his son.

Terrible idea. With Harry Morgan, René Auberjonois, and Skip Homier. *More Wild, Wild West* was offered the next year.

WILD, WILD WINTER

1966 Universal
PRODUCER: Bart Patton
DIRECTOR: Lennie Weinrib
SCREENWRITER: David Macolm

Another song fest, this time featuring the Beau Brummels, the Astronauts, Jay and the Americans, Dick and Dee Dee, and Jackie and Gayle. Fraternity boys chase sorority beauties at a small college in the hills. With Gary Clarke, Don Edmonds, Les Brown, Jr., Chris Noel, Vicky Albright, and Dick Miller. Songs include "Heartbeats," "Two of a Kind," "Snowball," "A Change of Heart," and "Just Wait and See." Weinrib also made *Beach Ball* and *Out of Sight*.

THE WILD, WILD WORLD OF JAYNE MANSFIELD

1968 Blue Ribbon
PRODUCER: Dick Randall
DIRECTOR: Arthur Knight
SCREENWRITER: Charles Ross

Knight and his mondo eye revisit some favorite locations from *Around the World with Nothing On* in the company of the faded star. From nude island resorts to the standard big-city drag bars, strip joints, cruise areas, and drug markets, Jayne knows where to look for action no matter where she goes. Special features include a wild outdoor twist party with Rocky Roberts and his Airdales, a visit with the topless Ladybirds combo, and Mickey Hargitay's guided tour of the legendary Pink Palace—where a pair of Jayne's heels wait by the foot of the bed. Insulting footage of the fatal car crash is included, of course. Worth seeing.   –CB

WILD WOMEN OF WONGO

1958 Wolcott
PRODUCER: George R. Black
DIRECTOR: James Wolcott
SCREENWRITER: Cedric Rutherford

This unbelievable Pathecolor production is the most obscure (and the funniest) entry in the wonderful subgenre of scantily-clad-prehistoric-women movies. The isle of Wongo is populated by beautiful cavewomen and ugly bearded-neanderthals. On the nearby island of Goona, handsome, muscular, clean-shaven men live with ugly females. After a lot of spear chucking and a few sacrifices to an alligator, the tribes exchange mates and live happily ever after. A must for anthropology students. With future Italian Hercules Ed Fury and Adrienne Bourbeau as Wang. We strongly suspect that this is former nudie model and *Maude* star Adrienne Barbeau, who doesn't like to give her age.

THE WILD WORLD OF BATWOMAN

1966 ADP Productions
PRODUCER/DIRECTOR/SCREENWRITER:
Jerry Warren
ALSO RELEASED AS: *She Was a Hippy Vampire*

This is said to be Jerry Warren's worst film, which would make it really unbelievable. He was sued for using the name Batwoman, so he changed the title to *She Was a Hippy Vampire*. Smart move, Jerry. He lost so much cash fighting the lawsuit that he never again blessed us with his cinematic charms. Very few people have seen this picture. A few more would like to. Slightly overage Katherine Victor stars in a tight black costume with a cheap mask, teased hair, and a rubber bat glued to her chest. She and her batgirls battle Dr. Neon and Ratfink who are after a hearing aid/atomic bomb and use laughter pills. With Steve Brody and Lloyd Nelson.

WILD YOUTH

1961 Cinema Associates (B&W)
PRODUCER: John Bushelman
DIRECTOR: John Schreyer
SCREENWRITERS: Robert J. Black, Jr., Lester William Berke, Dean Romano
ALSO RELEASED AS: *Naked Youth*

The New Mexican desert explodes as two escapees from an honor farm and a fugitive murderer fight over a doll filled with heroin. Robert Arthur is Frankie, Steve Rowland is blade-happy Switch. Co-starring John Goddard, Robert Hutton, Jan Brooks, and Carol Ohmart as Goddard's addict moll. Produced by John Bushelman of *Day of the Nightmare*.   —CB

WILL SUCCESS SPOIL ROCK HUNTER?

1957 20th Century-Fox
PRODUCER/DIRECTOR/SCREENWRITER: Frank Tashlin

Tashlin's follow-up to *The Girl Can't Help It* is based on a play about Hollywood. They changed it to a movie about television advertising and retained its star, Jayne Mansfield. Ad man Tony Randall signs Rita Marlowe (Jayne) to endorse Stay Put lipstick, but the publicity nearly ruins his life. Jayne's real life is satirized in this semi-fictional account. Known for her terrible films, Rita Marlowe will do anything for more publicity. Mickey Hargitay plays her jealous TV-jungle-man lover. With Joan Blondell as her companion-servant, John Williams as Randall's boss, anti-TV gags, big-breast jokes, and Groucho Marx.

WILLARD

1971 Cinerama
PRODUCER: Mort Briskin
DIRECTOR: Daniel Mann
SCREENWRITER: Gilbert A. Ralston

Bruce Davison's Willard is a typical lonely, pushed-around office boy until he trains two superintelligent rats to lead their pals and attack his enemies. Everybody loved the scene of the cruel boss Ernest Borgnine being attacked by rats, even though it looks as if offscreen crew members were throwing them at him. Willard makes the mistake of falling in love (with Sandra Locke) and neglects rat leaders Socrates and Ben. Willard dies, but the movie made millions, so *Ben* was back the next year. With Elsa Lanchester (*The Bride of Frankenstein*) as Willard's mother and 50 real rats.

WILSON

1944 20th Century-Fox
PRODUCER: Darryl F. Zanuck
DIRECTOR: Henry King
SCREENWRITER: Lamar Trotti

President Woodrow Wilson (Alexander Knox) tries to get America into the League of Nations. The long, expensive historical drama with 143 speaking parts was a big financial flop. A few of those 143 were Vincent Price as the President's son-in-law and Secretary of the Treasury, Cedric Hardwicke, Geraldine Fitzgerald, Sidney Blackmer, George Macready, Francis X. Bushman, and Thomas Mitchell. The action focuses on the years from 1909 to 1920.

THE WINGED SERPENT: See Q.

WINK OF AN EYE
1958 United Artists (B&W)
PRODUCER: Fernando Carrere
DIRECTOR: Winston Jones
SCREENWRITERS: Robert Radnitz,
Robert Presnell, Jr., James Edmiston
A chemist in a perfume factory (Jonathan Kidd) seems to have killed his wife, cut her up, and stuck her remains in the freezer. A comic horror film with an interesting ending. With Doris Dowling and Barbara Turner.

THE WINNING TEAM
1952 Warner Brothers (B&W)
PRODUCER: Bryan Foy
DIRECTOR: Lewis Seiler
SCREENWRITERS: Ted Sherdeman,
Seeleg Lester, Mervin Gerrard
Ronald Reagan stars as Grover Cleveland Alexander, a baseball great with double vision and epilepsy. Everybody thinks he's an alcoholic, including his wife (Doris Day), who leaves him (temporarily). With young Russ Tamblyn and Frank Lovejoy. Its numerous songs include "Take Me Out to the Ball Game" and "Ain't We Got Fun." Ron and Doris had been in *Storm Warning* the year before. It was the last of Reagan's 40 films for Warners. By the director of *Tugboat Annie Sails Again* and *Charlie Chan in Paris*.

WINTER A-GO-GO
1965 Columbia
PRODUCER/SCREENWRITER: Reno Carell
DIRECTOR: Richard Benedict
William Wellman, Jr., turns an inherited ski lodge into something groovy

with Joni Lyman, the Astronauts, the Hondells, the Reflections, and the Nooney Rickett Four. Sedaka collaborator Howie Greenfield wrote "King of the Mountain," "Ski City," and the title song; "Do the Ski," "I'm Sweet on You," and "Hip Square Dance" were written by Tommy Boyce/Bobby Hart and friends. With James Stacy, Beverly Adams, Jill Donohue, and Tom Nardini.   –CB

THE WITCH
1966 G.G. Productions (Italy) (B&W)
PRODUCER: Alfredo Bini
DIRECTOR: Damiano Damiani
SCREENWRITERS: Damiano Damiani,
Ugo Liberatore
Historian Richard Johnson takes a job at a castle and falls in love with a young woman who turns out to be a witch. With Rosanna Schiaffino and Gian Maria Volonte.

A WITCH WITHOUT A BROOM
1966 Producers Releasing Organization (Spain/U.S.)
PRODUCER: Sid Pink
DIRECTOR: Jose E. Lorietta (Joe Lacy)
SCREENWRITERS: José Luis Navarro Basso,
Howard Berk
ORIGINALLY RELEASED AS: *Una Bruja sin Escoba*
Jeffrey Hunter went to Spain to play a professor involved with a blond witch (Maria Perschy). She accidentally transports him to the stone age, the 16th century, and Mars. *Bewitched* must have hit Spain that year. Produced by Sidney Pink of *Journey to the 7th Planet* fame. With lots of sex jokes. Not bad.

WITCHCRAFT
1964 20th Century-Fox (England) (B&W)
PRODUCER: Robert L. Lippert
DIRECTOR: Don Sharp
SCREENWRITER: Harry Spalding

When a cemetery containing the bodies of witches burned during the 17th century is bulldozed, the Whitlock family, led by Lon Chaney, Jr. (in his only really decent '60s role) seeks revenge. Yvette Rees is a memorable revived witch in the Barbara Steele tradition. Theater patrons were given a round "witch deflector" to save them "from the eerie web of the unknown." After this successful film it was back to routine Westerns and unspeakably bad horror films for old Lon.

Beautiful witch Warene Ott initiates Thordis Brandt into the coven of Luther the Berserk in The Witchmaker.

THE WITCHES: See *THE DEVIL'S OWN.*

THE WITCHES' MIRROR

1960 K. Gordon Murray (Mexico) (B&W)
PRODUCER: Abel Salazar
DIRECTOR: Chano Urveta
SCREENWRITER: Alfredo Ruanova
ORIGINALLY RELEASED AS: *El Espejo de la Bruja*

A man is haunted by the ghost of his first wife who makes him disfigure his new wife. He uses skin from corpses to restore her face. The ghost can change into an owl or a cat. With a dwarf and a witch. Pretty strange.

WITCHES' MOUNTAIN

1970 Avco Embassy-TV (Spain)
DIRECTOR: Raul Artigot
ORIGINALLY RELEASED AS: *En Monte de la Brujas*

A news photographer is sent to the site of a witch burning. Obscure and low-budget. With Patty Shepard, John Caffari, and Monica Randall.

THE WITCHFINDER GENERAL: See *THE CONQUEROR WORM.*

THE WITCHMAKER

1969 Excelsior
PRODUCER/DIRECTOR/SCREENWRITER: William O. Brown
ALSO RELEASED AS: *Legend of Witch Hollow*

Interesting low-budget thriller with Alvy Moore taking a small research team to the swamps to investigate the murders of eight women. *Green Acres* regular Moore (also the associate producer) is charmingly enthusiastic in his Van Helsing–type role. John Lodge plays "Luther the Berserk," a warlock supplying blood to a 200-year-old witch. Anthony Eisley is the hero. Thordis Brandt is the witch. Filmed in Louisiana. With three former *Playboy* playmates and television horror host Seymour. (M)

THE WITCH'S CURSE

1960 Medallion (Italy)
PRODUCERS: Ermano Donati,
Luigi Carpentieri
DIRECTOR: Riccardo Freda
SCREENWRITERS: Eddy H. Given,
Oreste Biancoli, Piero Pierotti
ORIGINALLY RELEASED AS: *Maciste al Inferno*

American muscleman Kirk Morris plays Italian hero Maciste. Somehow he ends up in 17th-century Scotland, where he rips up a tree and climbs down a hell hole. He goes to blazes to find the witch who had put a curse on Loch Lake. By the director of *The Horrible Dr. Hichcock.*

WITHOUT WARNING: See THE INVISIBLE MENACE.

WITHOUT WARNING

1980 Filmways
PRODUCER/DIRECTOR: Greydon Clark
SCREENWRITERS: Lyn Freeman,
Daniel Grodnik, Ben Nett,
Steve Mathis

An all-star terrible movie from the director of *Satan's Cheerleaders*. An alien that looks like a leftover from *The Outer Limits* lands in a remote rural area and battles gas-station owner Jack Palance. The invader uses frisbeelike flesh-eating parasites for weapons. Guest victims include Martin Landau as a Vietnam vet, Cameron Mitchell, Neville Brand, Larry Storch as a cub scout leader, Ralph Meeker, and Sue Ann Langdon. Director Clark started out playing bit parts in Al Adamson hits. (R)

THE WIZARD OF GORE

1970 Mayflower
PRODUCER/DIRECTOR: Herschell Gordon Lewis
SCREENWRITER: Allan Kahn

The director of *Blood Feast* makes a gory hit reminiscent of *The Hypnotic Eye.*

Ray Sager stars as Montag the Magician. His show includes sawing a woman in half and driving a spike through the head of another. The volunteer victims leave the theater in one piece but experience horrible delayed deaths when they go home. Appearing on a TV show, Montag hypnotizes the entire audience but is killed by the hero (Wayne Ratay) before any damage is done. With Sherry Carson and lots of laughable acting and effects. The inspired Zen ending is not to to believed. (R)

WIZARD OF MARS

1964 American General Pictures
PRODUCER/DIRECTOR/SCREENWRITER:
David L. Hewitt

Cheap and pretty boring science fiction about four astronauts who crash on Mars and wander around until they find the Wizard of Mars, played by John Carradine. Pretty short on ideas, considering it's vaguely a takeoff of *The Wizard of Oz*. With Roger Gentry and Vic McGee.

THE WIZARD OF OZ

1939 MGM (Color and B&W)
PRODUCER: Mervyn Le Roy
DIRECTOR: Victor Fleming
SCREENWRITERS: Noel Langley,
Florence Ryerson, Edgar Allan Woolf

Since it used to be on TV every year, *Oz* has probably been seen more times by more people than any movie ever made. A high point of my junior high years was playing bits of Munchkin dialogue (taped the night before) at select times during math class. Guaranteed to totally disrupt the learning process. Director Fleming followed it with *Gone with the Wind* and *Dr. Jekyll and Mr. Hyde*. Wicked witch Margaret Hamilton was only 20 years old at the time.

WOLFEN

1981 Orion/Warner Brothers
PRODUCER: Rupert Hitzig
DIRECTOR: Michael Wadleigh
SCREENWRITERS: David Frye,
Michael Wadleigh

A series of incredibly brutal killings keeps rebellious Manhattan cop Dewey Martin (Albert Finney) guessing. Terrorists? Wild dogs? Amerindian werewolves? The audience knows that it's the Wolfen—a hitherto undiscovered species of wolf that holds a grudge against the white settlers who took their land, and is now prepared to settle an old score. Whitley Streiber's so-so novel has been transformed into a classy, thoughtful, but not very frightening horror film.

Albert Finney hadn't made a feature in years, and neither had *Woodstock* director Wadleigh, when both were signed by Orion for *Wolfen*. After Wadleigh delivered his cut of the picture, Orion decided they didn't trust him, and set a battery of editors to work to "save" a picture that they thought was in trouble. Ultimately, the picture that was released was pretty much Wadleigh's work, with some special-effects footage (the Steadicam work) reshot. (R)   –BM

THE WOLF MAN

1941 Universal (B&W)
PRODUCER/DIRECTOR: George Waggner
SCREENWRITER: Curt Siodmak

A horror classic starring Lon Chaney, Jr. As Larry Talbot, he returns home to his father's Welsh estate and becomes a tormented killer. It made Chaney a star and created a folklore concerning wolfbane, pentagrams, silver, and the Moon. The excellent cast includes Claude Rains as Sir John Talbot, the Russian Maria Ouspenskaya as Maleva the Gypsy, Bela Lugosi as her son Bela, Ralph Bellamy, Evelyn Ankers, Warren Williams, Patric Knowles, and Fay Helm. Lon was back in *Frankenstein Meets the Wolfman* in '43.

THE WOLFMAN

1979 E.D. Corp.
PRODUCER: Earl Owensby
DIRECTOR/SCREENWRITER: Worth Keeter

North Carolina drive-in movie mogul Earl Owensby has been the topic of reports on *60 Minutes* and in *Esquire*, but nobody outside of the Confederacy seems to have seen any of his movies. This one's set in 1910 Georgia, where Earl's usual star (Earl) plays a cursed rich man who becomes a werewolf. The budget was very low. It made money without even playing or being reviewed in New York. See *Living Legend*. In '82 Owensby joined the new 3-D race with *Rottweiler*.

THE WOMAN EATER

1959 Columbia (England) (B&W)
PRODUCER: Guido Coen
DIRECTOR: Charles Saunders
SCREENWRITER: Brandon Fleming

Interesting title for a pretty horrible movie about a mad doctor (George Coulouris) feeding women to his tall flesh-eating plant and trying to revive the dead. With Vera Day.

THE WOMAN IN GREEN
1945 Universal (B&W)
PRODUCER/DIRECTOR: Roy William Neill
SCREENWRITER: Bertram Millhauser
Women are found murdered with their right forefingers missing. As the nefarious Lydia, Hillary Brooke teams with Dr. Moriarty (Henry Daniell) to defeat Sherlock Holmes (Basil Rathbone) with hypnotism. Adapted from *The Adventure of the Empty House*. With Nigel Bruce and Mary Gordon.

THE WOMAN IN WHITE
1948 Warner Brothers (B&W)
PRODUCER: Henry Blanke
DIRECTOR: Peter Godfrey
SCREENWRITER: Stephen Morehouse Avery
Sidney Greenstreet plays a villanous count in this gothic mystery about twin sisters. Agnes Moorehead is his wife. Starring Alexis Smith, Eleanor Parker, and Gig Young. Based on a popular novel by Wilkie Collins, which had been filmed four times during the Silent era.

WOMEN AND BLOODY TERROR
1970 Howco
PRODUCER: Albert J. Salzer
DIRECTOR: Joy N. Houck, Jr.
SCREENWRITERS: Joy N. Houck, Jr., Robert A. Weaver, Albert J. Salzer
ALSO RELEASED AS: *His Wife's Habit*
Howco drifts off-color as Georgine Darcy enjoys Mardi Gras by having relations with a bellboy, a hustler, the son of the tenant whose apartment she and the bellboy used, and Gerald McRaney, the boyfriend of her daughter, Christa Hart. Later mother and daughter are terrorized by parking-lot attendant Marcus J. Grapes and his sidekick Michael Anthony (as "Zool"). Shot in New Orleans. With music by Gary Le Mel, the Armadillo, and Cleveland's Sonny Geraci (of the Outsiders and Climax), who sings "Come on In" and "Mr. Funky." **(M)** —CB

WOMEN IN CHAINS
1972 TV
PRODUCER: Edward K. Milkis
DIRECTOR: Bernard Kowalski
SCREENWRITER: Rita Larkin
The first women's prison TV-movie stars Ida Lupino as a sadistic warden (see *Women's Prison* of '55). Lois Nettleton is a parole officer posing as an inmate to expose brutal conditions, but she can't prove her identity when she wants to be released. With Jessica Walter and Belinda Montgomery.

WOMEN OF ALL NATIONS
1931 Fox (B&W)
PRODUCER: Fox Film Corp.
DIRECTOR: Raoul Walsh
SCREENWRITER: Barry Connors
One of a series of comic adventures starring Edmond Lowe and Victor McLaglen as Sergeants Flagg and Quirt. In his first film released after *Dracula*, Bela Lugosi plays a bearded Turkish prince. He orders the invaders of his harem castrated. With Humphrey Bogart.

THE WOMEN OF THE PREHISTORIC PLANET
1965 Realart
PRODUCER: George Gilbert
DIRECTOR/SCREENWRITER: Arthur C. Pierce
Ultracheap science fiction with shoddy sets, man-eating plants, giant lizards,

and a huge spider. It also has Wendell Corey and John Agar, ridiculous as astronauts who bring together Linda and Tang (the oriental Adam and Eve) and name the planet they explored Earth! Linda and Tang presumably begat all mankind in this tacky studio-set Eden. Produced by Jack Broder. (*Bela Lugosi Meets a Brooklyn Gorilla*). With Leith Larsen, Merry Anders, Adam Roarke, Lyle Waggoner, and Stuart Margolin (*The Rockford Files*).

WOMEN'S PRISON
1955 Columbia (B&W)
PRODUCER: Bryan Foy
DIRECTOR: Lewis R. Seiler
SCREENWRITERS: Crane Wilbur, Jack Dewitt
Inside a coed hell, Warren Stevens' secret off-limits visit is discovered by sadistic and power-mad warden Ida Lupino. Audrey Totter is punished until she miscarries and almost dies. Cleo Moore and Jan Sterling, habitual offenders, organize a prisonwide riot and in the storm of teargas and bullets that follows Stevens tracks down the butchering warden. The ads promised: "Gals on rampage! Shock after shock!" When the smoke clears she is found—a hopeless raving lunatic. With Phyllis Thaxter and Howard Duff.   –CB

THE WONDERS OF ALADDIN
1961 MGM (France/Italy)
PRODUCER: Joseph E. Levine
DIRECTOR: Henry Levin
SCREENWRITER: Luther Davis
Aladdin (Donald O'Connor) rubs a magic lamp and Vittorio De Sica pops out and grants him three wishes. Not too thrilling. With Michele Mercier, Noelle Adam, Milton Reid, and Mario Girotti, later famous as Terence Hill. Mario Bava was the second-unit director.

WONDER WOMAN
1974 TV
PRODUCER: John Stephens
DIRECTOR: Vincent McEveety
SCREENWRITER: John D.F. Black
A disastrous first attempt at a Wonder Woman pilot starring Cathy Lee Crosby in a starred zip-up-the-front minidress battling evil Ricardo Montalban. The setting was changed to modern times. ABC tried again next year with an entirely new concept and cast. With Andrew Prine.

WONDER WOMEN
1973 General Film Corporation (Philippines)
PRODUCER: Ross Hagen
DIRECTOR: Robert O'Neill
SCREENWRITER: Lou Whitehill
Flower Drum Song star Nancy Kwan is the evil Dr. Su, whose all-female army kidnaps the world's top athletes to dismember and use for spare parts. Their organs are sold to aging millionaires. An insurance investigator arrives at the doctor's island fortress to stop the lady cutups. Producer Ross Hagen gave himself the hero role. With some pitiful monsters and Sid Haig.

THE WONDERFUL WORLD OF THE BROTHERS GRIMM
1962 MGM
PRODUCER: George Pal
DIRECTOR: Henry Levin
SCREENWRITERS: David P. Harmon, Charles Beaumont, William Roberts
Laurence Harvey and *Peeping Tom* star Karl Boehm are the Grimm brothers in this fantasy cinerama release featuring Pal's puppetoons and an animated dragon. A biographical story is combined with three fairy tales. "The Dancing Princess" stars Yvette Mimieux, with Russ Tamblyn and Jim Backus. "The

Cobbler and the Elves" stars Harvey. "The Singing Bone" features Terry-Thomas, Buddy Hackett, and Otto Kruger. With Claire Bloom, Walter Slezak, Barbara Eden, Oskar Homolka, and Arnold Stang.

THE WORLD OF ABBOTT AND COSTELLO

1965 Universal (B&W)
PRODUCERS: Max J. Rosenberg, Milton Subotsky

If you can't take whole Bud and Lou features, you might go for this compilation with scenes from 18 of their films (all made by Universal from 1940 to 1956). It even includes the "Who's on first" routine. Narrated by Jack E. Leonard.

THE WORLD OF VAMPIRES

1960 AIP-TV (Mexico) (B&W)
PRODUCER: Abel Salazar
DIRECTOR: Alfonso Corona Blake
SCREENWRITER: Ramon Obon
ORIGINALLY RELEASED AS: El Mundo de los Vampiros

A caped vampire controls his converts by playing eerie music on his Vocallion organ, built mostly with human bones and skulls. Also with a great-looking vampire woman with just the right eyeliner. Mauricio Garces and Silvia Fournier star.

THE WORLD, THE FLESH AND THE DEVIL

1958 MGM (B&W)
PRODUCER: George Englund
DIRECTOR/SCREENWRITER: Ranald McDougall

Harry Belafonte emerges from a mine accident to discover it's panic-in-the-year-zero time. He heads for a deserted New York City and finds Inger Stevens and Mel Ferrer—of course, a racist. They argue, fight, and finally decide to live in harmony. Corman's Last

Woman on Earth had a more likely conclusion. Music by Miklos Rosza. The world premiere was held in Cleveland!

WORLD WAR III

1982 TV
PRODUCER/SCREENWRITER: Robert L. Hudson
DIRECTOR: David Green

From the ads: "The world is on the brink. Any one of them can push it over the edge." In 1987, when Russia, led by Brian Keith (Meteor), invades Alaska, President Rock Hudson (Avalanche) tries to avoid a nuclear war. Two hours of human drama and small-scale battles in a feature kicked off by Boris Sagal (he died in a helicopter accident). The American forces are led by David Soul. Cathy Lee Crosby is an intelligence officer.

WORLD WAR THREE BREAKS OUT: See THE FINAL WAR.

WORLD WITHOUT END

1955 Allied Artists
PRODUCER: Richard Heermance
DIRECTOR/SCREENWRITER: Edward Bernds

American astronauts head for Mars, enter a time warp, and end up on 21st-century Earth (which of course has undergone a nuclear war). They fight a big phony spider and mutant cavemen and discover an underground civilization with angular tunnels and people in tights and tunics. The sets, props, and plot were all recycled from other movies, but this one is in CinemaScope and Technicolor! With Hugh Marlowe, Rod Taylor, and Nancy Gates. Popular pin-up-girl artist Alberto Vargas designed the costumes for the alien women.

THE WORLD'S GREATEST SINNER

1962 Frenzy Productions (B&W)
PRODUCER/DIRECTOR/SCREENWRITER:·
Timothy Carey

Frank Zappa did the music for this oddity about an insurance salesman who decides he's God and becomes a rock 'n' roll evangelist to spread the word. Timothy Carey, the man who assassinated the race horse in *The Killing*, stars as well as producing, directing, and writing the screenplay. With Gil Baretto, Betty Rowland, Doris and George F. Carey, James Farley as the Devil, and Titus Moede. Made in Vancouver. Ray Dennis Steckler was one of the cameramen.   –CB

THE WORM EATERS

1977 New American
PRODUCER: T.V. Mikels
DIRECTOR/SCREENWRITER: Herb Robins

Advertised as: "An immortal film of our time." Director Robins stars as Ungar, a clubfooted worm breeder, in this weird horror comedy with terrible acting by people who actually eat worms on screen. At the Las Vegas premiere there was a worm-eating contest. Some cast members become "worm people" and as such wiggle around on the floor.

THE WRECKING CREW

1968 Columbia
PRODUCER: Irving Allen
DIRECTOR: Phil Karlson
SCREENWRITER: William McGivern

The last Matt Helm film—finally! Sharon Tate plays a beautiful but bumbling secret agent helping Dino recover gold stolen by villain Nigel Green. With Elke Sommer and Nancy Kwan as female villains and Tina Louise, who gets killed by an exploding bottle of Scotch. It's hard to believe Dean Martin got away with playing himself in four of these sub-Bond spoofs.

THE WRESTLING WOMEN VS. THE AZTEC MUMMY

1965 AIP-TV (Mexico) (B&W)
PRODUCER: Guillermo Calderon Stell
DIRECTOR: René Cardona
SCREENWRITER: Abel Salazar
ORIGINALLY RELEASED AS: *Las Luch Adoras Contra la Momia*

Sometimes Mexican filmmakers come up with great original ideas. Imagine a series about wrestling women! They wrestle monsters. Maybe you caught them in *Doctor of Doom*. Xochitl, the mummy, can turn into a snake or a bat, which are hard to get half-Nelsons on. Lorena Vasquez is Loreita, the Golden Ruby, who joins her sister to battle the evil Prince Fugiyata and her Oriental female wrestlers. The mummy is also female and on the good side of the struggle.

THE X FROM OUTER SPACE
1967 AIP (Japan)
DIRECTOR: Nazui Nihomatsu
SCREENWRITERS: Eibi Motomuchi,
Moriyoshi Ishida, Kazui Nihonmatsu
ORIGINALLY RELEASED AS: *Uchu Daikaiju
Guilala*

An explorer spaceship brings back an organism that grows into a giant lizard/chicken and levels Tokyo.

X — THE MAN WITH THE X-RAY EYES
1963 AIP
PRODUCER/DIRECTOR: Roger Corman
SCREENWRITERS: Robert Dillon, Ray Russell
In one of his best-remembered roles Ray Milland is Dr. Xavier. He experiments on himself with X-ray vision eyedrops. He can see through skin, diagnose a patient's internal physical damage, easily win when gambling, and (in a party scene) see through clothes. All the naked people are discreetly covered by plants or furniture. After accidentally killing a colleague, he hides out as a mind reader at a carnival. Don Rickles is his boss. The pair of wise guys in the audience are Corman regulars Jonathan Haze and Dick Miller. Ray's sight gets increasingly stronger until he can see through everything—to eternity! And it hurts! At a revival meeting the preacher yells out—"If thy eye offend thee . . ." With Diana Van Der Vlis, Harold J. Stone, and John Hoyt.

X THE UNKNOWN
1956 Hammer/Warner Brothers
(England) (B&W)
PRODUCER: Anthony Hinds
DIRECTOR: Leslie Norman
SCREENWRITER: Jimmy Sangster
This early Hammer science fiction is one of the first pulsating-blob movies. Living radioactive mud from the center of the earth surfaces in Scotland, where it dissolves people while absorbing radioactive material. With Dean Jagger (token American for box-office draw), Leo McKern, and Anthony Newley. Not to be confused with the Quatermass films. Originally co-billed with *The Curse of Frankenstein.*

YAMBAO: See CRY OF THE BEWITCHED.

YEAR 2889: See IN THE YEAR 2889.

YELLOW PHANTOM: See SHADOW OF CHINATOWN.

YETI
1977 (Italy)
PRODUCERS: Mario Di Nardo,
Gianfranco Parolini
DIRECTOR: Frank Kramer
SCREENWRITER: Mario Di Nardo
An unconvincing man in a Bigfoot suit turns out to be friendly and helps a lost mute boy and his little dog. Filmed in Canada. Not released theatrically in America

YOG — MONSTER FROM SPACE
1970 Toho/AIP (Japan)
PRODUCER: Tomoyuki and Fumio Tanaka
DIRECTOR: Inoshiro Honda
SCREENWRITER: Ei Ogawa
Advertised as having "Twice the monsters! Twice the terror!!!!" Well, maybe twice the monsters. An alien force takes over Earth creatures, making them grow and destroy. An octopus, crabs, and bats attack a Pacific island.

YONGARY, MONSTER FROM THE DEEP
1967 AIP-TV (S. Korea/Japan)
DIRECTOR: Kiduck Kim
SCREENWRITER: Yungsung Suh
ORIGINALLY RELEASED AS: *Dai Koesu Yongkari*

Here's your chance to be able to say you've seen a Korean film. Yongary is a rather eccentric city crusher. A giant monster, it is unleashed by an earthquake in China. It drinks gasoline and stops stomping to dance to rock 'n' roll music. Ever heard Korean rock music?

YOU ONLY LIVE TWICE
1967 United Artists (England)
PRODUCERS: Albert R. Broccoli,
Harry Saltzman
DIRECTOR: Lewis Gilbert
SCREENWRITER: Roald Dahl

A few months after *Casino Royale*, the fifth real James Bond movie was released. 007 (Sean Connery) goes to Japan, fakes his own death, gets married, and stops SPECTRE villain Blofeld (Donald Pleasence) from starting World War III. Blofeld, a bald, scarred man who loves cats, had been intercepting U.S. and Russian space capsules. The female leads include Mie Hama (as Kissy Sukuki) and Akiko Wakabayashi. Both had been in *What's Up, Tiger Lily?* and *King Kong vs. Godzilla*. With Charles Gray, Robert Hutton, Karin Dor, and *Fu Manchu* series regular Tsai Chin. Nancy Sinatra sang the theme song, which should have been a big hit. Music by John Barry. Connery quit the series, only to return four years later in *Diamonds Are Forever*.

YOU'LL FIND OUT
1940 RKO (B&W)
PRODUCER/DIRECTOR: David Butler
SCREENWRITER: James V. Kern

Advertised as: "A seance in swing with the ha-ha-horror boys." The boys are Peter Lorre, Boris Karloff, and Bela Lugosi (in a turban as Prince Saliano). They're trying to kill young heiress Helen Parrish. A slice of pop history with Dennis O'Keefe and Ish Kabibble. The real star is band leader Kay Kyser with his Kollege of Musical Knowledge.

Kyser's band does five numbers. The wasted trio is blown up at the end. Music by Johnny Mercer.

YOU'LL LIKE MY MOTHER
1972 Universal
PRODUCER: Mort Briskin
DIRECTOR: Lamont Johnson
SCREENWRITER: Jo Heims

Richard Thomas of *The Waltons* stars as a psycho/rapist. Patty Duke is a pregnant widow visiting her mother-in-law (Rosemary Murphy) in Minnesota.

UPI 8/9/77: What's afoot? Visitors at a Rome film studio get an advance look at Yeti recently. Following in the footsteps of King Kong, you might say, the monster—some 30 feet tall and 4,960 pounds—is to be the star of an upcoming movie.

While trapped by a blizzard she discovers horrible secrets. With Sian Barbara Allen. A Bing Crosby Production.

YOUNG AND DANGEROUS
1957 20th Century-Fox (B&W)
PRODUCER/DIRECTOR: William F. Claxton
SCREENWRITER: James Landis

From the ads: "Why can't our parents understand us?" Mark Damon goes square to get in with a nice girl. Lili Gentle, Edward Binns, Paul Bryar, Frances Mercer, Ann Doran, and Connie Stevens appear. Very tame. Claxton ended up directing for *Bonanza* and *Little House on the Pairie*. Screenwriter Landis later worked for Fairway-International. See *Deadwood '76.* –CB

YOUNG AND EVIL: See CRY OF THE BEWITCHED.

THE YOUNG AND THE COOL: See TWIST ALL NIGHT.

THE YOUNG AND THE IMMORAL: See THE SINISTER URGE.

YOUNG AND WILD
1958 Republic (B&W)
PRODUCER: Sidney Picker
DIRECTOR: William Witney
SCREENWRITER: Arthur Horman

Summer in suburban L.A. stinks of beatings, rape, and hit-and-run homicide as Robert Arthur and Carolyn Kearney are terrorized by Scott Marlowe and his thrill-seeking goons. With Gene Evans, Morris Ankrum, and John Zaremba. In Naturama. Originally co-billed with Witney's *Juvenile Jungle.*–CB

THE YOUNG ANIMALS
1968 AIP
PRODUCER/DIRECTOR: Maury Dexter
SCREENWRITER: James Gordon White
ALSO RELEASED AS: *Born Wild*

A Mexican-American student organization, pushing for the dismissal of bigot coach Russ Bender finds itself at war with David Macklin and his goons after his girlfriend Patty McCormack takes up with a Chicano (Tom Nardini). Arson, rape, torture, and death follow. Eventually Patty and Tom get cornered in an airplane junkyard by Macklin, who's at the controls of a giant steel claw. Songs include "Love Has Got Me Down" by the American Revolution and "In Big Letters" by the Orphan Egg. With Zoey Hall (*I Dismember Mama*). –CB

THE YOUNG CAPTIVES
1959 Paramount (B&W)
PRODUCER/SCREENWRITER: Andrew J. Fenady
DIRECTOR: Irvin Kershner

The ads tell the story: "Two kids who couldn't stop loving, held by a kid who couldn't stop killing!" Tom Selden and Luana Patten pick up a hitchhiker on their way to Mexico. More ad copy: "Teenage elopers' love turns to terror as they battle crazed killer!" Steven Marlo, sought in the murder of his oilfield foreman, announces his intent to kill Tom and claim Luana. In case you haven't got the picture yet, the ads continue: "Violent death threatened their young romance!" Marlo drives into the side of a warehouse trying to escape the law. With Herb Armstrong and Ed Nelson. By the director of *The Empire Strikes Back.* –CB

YOUNG DILLINGER
1965 Allied Artists (B&W)
PRODUCER: Al Zimbalist
DIRECTOR: Terry O. Morse
SCREENWRITERS: Donald Zimbalist, Arthur Hoerl

Young Dillinger (Nick Adams) meets Pretty Boy Floyd (Robert Conrad), Baby Face Nelson (John Ashley), and Homer Van Meter (Dan Terranova)

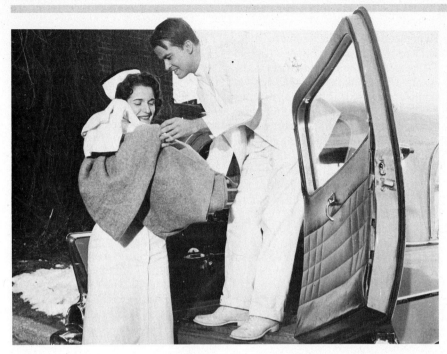

while in prison for robbing his girlfriend's father's safe. With help from Victor Buono, these guys and their girlfriends become legendary desperados. John Hoyt, Reed Hadley, Anthony Caruso, Ted Knight, Patty Joy Harmon, and Beverly Hills wear 1965 street clothes (the film is set in the '30s, of course); the music is by Shorty Rogers. Also "introducing brilliant new star Mary Ann Mobley."   –CB

THE YOUNG DOCTORS

1961 United Artists (B&W)
PRODUCERS: Stuart Miller, Lawrence Turman
DIRECTOR: Phil Karlson
SCREENWRITER: Joseph Hayes
Ronald Reagan narrates this hospital drama filmed in New York. The American Medical Association assisted. Ben Gazzara, a new doctor on the pathology staff, opposes the methods of stubborn old doctor Fredric March, who makes some serious mistakes. Other doctors are

Dick Clark, Eddie Albert, and George Segal. With Ina Balin and Phyllis Love.

THE YOUNG DON'T CRY

1957 Columbia (B&W)
PRODUCER: Phil A. Waxman
DIRECTOR: Alfred L. Werker
SCREENWRITER: Richard Jessup
From the ads: "Too tough for tears!" Sal Mineo, "the screen's most dynamic teen-age star," is a loner who helps an escaped murderer (James Whitmore). With J. Carrol Naish and Paul Carr.

YOUNG DRACULA: See ANDY WARHOL'S DRACULA.

YOUNG FRANKENSTEIN

1974 20th Century-Fox (B&W)
PRODUCER: Michael Gruskoff
DIRECTOR: Mel Brooks
SCREENWRITERS: Gene Wilder, Mel Brooks
Some good laughs in this spoof of Universal's Frankenstein movies. In black-and-white and with electronic

equipment designed by Kenneth Strick-fadden, it looks right, but then so did *Flesh Gordon*. Gene Wilder stars as the young Dr. Frankenstein. He has on hand a copy of the original doctor's book, *How I Did It*. As the monster, Peter Boyle sings and dances. Madeline Kahn becomes his willing bride. With Gene Hackman as the blind hermit, Kenneth Mars as the one-armed inspector, Marty Feldman as the hunchback Igor, Cloris Leachman, and Teri Garr.

THE YOUNG HELLIONS: See HIGH SCHOOL CONFIDENTIAL.

THE YOUNG RACERS

1963 AIP
PRODUCER/DIRECTOR: Roger Corman
SCREENWRITER: R. Wright Campbell
Roger Corman made this Grand Prix adventure while in Europe on a vacation/work trip. William Campbell is Joe Machin, a race driver who uses any means to win and spends his spare time having extramarital affairs. When another driver (Mark Damon) discovers Machin with his girlfriend, he vows to write a book and expose him. Campbell's real-life brother Robert plays his film brother. Patrick Magee is Sir William Dragonet. With Luana Anders. Sound man Francis Ford Coppola retained the main cast members and directed *Dementia 13* after this was finished. Filmed in France, England, Belgium, and Monaco. With the "International Playgirls." Future producer-director Menachem Golan was the property master.

THE YOUNG REBELS: See TEENAGE DOLL.

THE YOUNG SINNER

1965 United Screen Arts (B&W)
PRODUCER/DIRECTOR/SCREENWRITER:
Tom Laughlin
ORIGINALLY RELEASED AS: *Among the Thorns*
Seen in preview as early as 1961, this was apparently Laughlin's second self-made feature, after *The Proper Time*. He stars as Chris Wotan, a once-promising high school athlete whose fall from grace is shown via confessional flashbacks. Highlights include getting caught in the sack with a girl by her wealthy parents and a degrading experience in a church loft with a 14-year-old. Stefanie Powers, William Wellman, Jr., Linda March, James Stacy, and Chris Robinson are friends, Charles Heard and Dorothy Downey are parents, Jack Starrett is Coach Jennings. Part one of an aborted trilogy to be called *We Are All Christ*. –CB

THE YOUNG SWINGERS

1963 20th Century-Fox (B&W)
PRODUCER/DIRECTOR: Maury Dexter
SCREENWRITER: Harry Spalding
Molly Bee tries to save the Vanguard nightclub from being torn down by her mean real-estate-agent aunt. She falls in love with star attraction Rod Lauren. They sing "Mad, Mad, Mad" and "Watusi Surfer." The club burns down and Molly turns 21. With Jack Larson (television's Jimmy Olsen). Director Dexter followed with *Surf Party* and *Wild on the Beach*.

YOUNG TORLESS

1966 Kanawha (France/W. Germany) (B&W)
PRODUCER: Frank Seitz
DIRECTOR/SCREENWRITER: Volker Schlöndorff
ORIGINALLY RELEASED AS: *Der Junge Torless*

Torless, a boarding-school student in the prewar Austro-Hungarian Empire, is a fascinated observer as his friends visit the local prostitute (Barbara Steele) and turn one student into a humiliated and tortured slave. A critically acclaimed look at the seeds of Nazism. "Artistic supervisor" Louis Malle used Steele as a prostitute again in *Pretty Baby*. The director later did *The Tin Drum*. Based on the novel of the same title by Robert Musil.

YOUR MONEY OR YOUR WIFE

1960 Ellis Films (England) (B&W)
PRODUCER: Norman Williams
DIRECTOR: Anthony Simmons
SCREENWRITER: Ronald Jeans

A domestic comedy about a couple who take in boarders to pay the rent on their large house. Barbara Steele is a prospective lodger. Peggy Cummins (*Gun Crazy*) and Donald Sinden star. Released in America in '65.

YOU'VE GOT TO BE SMART

1967 Producers Releasing Organization
ARRANGED BY: Stan Worth
DIRECTOR/SCREENWRITER: Ellis Kadison

Thirty-four-year-old Mamie Van Doren in her last movie. Fourth billing as a secretary who fools around with the star (Tom Stern) of this unheard-of little opus was a step down even from *Navy vs. the Night Monsters*, so she retired from the screen. *Smart* is about a nine-year-old singing Ozark preacher being exploited on television by Stern, a sleazy publicist. The kid (called Methuselah Jones) and his brother musicians are played by "The Bantams," a real brother act. With Roger Perry of the *Count Yorga* movies, Gloria Castillo, and "rockabilly music." In 1982, Mamie was one of the quartet of nostalgia stars in the touring show *4-Girls-4*. The same year, she and her latest husband opened a private club bearing her name in Cannery Village, Newport Beach, California. The club, said a press release, "will cater to those wanting a better life-style, with a swarm of Ph.D.s backing Mamie with their services." *You've Got to be Smart* turned out to be a prophetic title.

Z.P.G.

1971 Paramount (England)
PRODUCER: Thomas F. Madigan
DIRECTOR: Michael Campus
SCREENWRITERS: Max Erlich, Frank DeFelitta
ALSO RELEASED AS: *Zero Population Growth*

In the 21st century everyone wears gas masks. The state provides robot dolls for couples who want children. Oliver Reed and Geraldine Chaplin defy the government by having a real baby. A dim view of the future that got zero distribution.

ZAAT: See THE BLOOD WATERS OF DR. Z.

ZARDOZ

1974 20th Century-Fox
PRODUCER/DIRECTOR/SCREENWRITER:
John Boorman

Box-office flop that is now a cult favorite. In the year 2293, a huge stone head flies out of the sky and brings guns to the Exterminators in the outlands. Zed (Sean Connery in a role originally planned for Burt Reynolds), an Exterminator, stows aboard the head to infiltrate the Vortex, a place where the eternally young, sexless intellectuals live. He is captured by them and found to be genetically superior and therefore a threat to their existence. Saved by Friend (John Alderton), he falls in love with Charlotte Rampling and they set about bringing an end to the intellectuals' rule. Boorman uses Beethoven's Seventh Symphony and Geoffrey Unsworth's brilliant cinematography to create a stunning, thought-provoking film, but don't take it too seriously: "Zardoz" is a contraction of "Wizard of Oz," and, as Friend says, "It was all just a joke." —AF

ZERO HOUR!

1957 Paramount (B&W)
PRODUCER: John Champion
DIRECTOR: Hall Bartlett
SCREENWRITER: Arthur Hailey

The crew of a trans-Canadian passenger plane is overcome by food poisoning. Neurotic World War II pilot Dana Andrews lands it safely in the fog and is reunited with old flame Linda Darnell, a stewardess. Sterling Hayden advises him from Vancouver. A classic air near-disaster movie, based on a 1956 *Alcoa Hour* TV show. It was later the basis for *Airplane*. With John Ashley as a TV singer, Jerry Paris, Maxine Cooper, and Elroy "Crazy Legs" Hirsch. By the director of *Jonathan Livingston Seagull*.

ZERO POPULATION GROWTH: See Z.P.G.

ZOMBIE

1980 Jerry Gross Organization (Italy)
PRODUCERS: Ugo Tucci, Fabrizio De Angelis
DIRECTOR: Lucio Fulci
SCREENWRITER: Elisa Briganti
ORIGINALLY RELEASED AS: *Zombie 2*
ALSO RELEASED AS: *Zombie Flesh Eaters*

In Italy *Dawn of the Dead* was called *Zombie*. This unrelated phony sequel is *Zombie 2*. American ads implied that flesh-eating zombies invade New York City. Forget it. The cliché action mostly takes place on a tropical island. One funny scene has an underwater zombie fighting a shark. There's the expected gut-munching and one incredible shot of a piece of splintered wood going through an eyeball. With Richard Johnson, Mia Farrow's sister Tisa, and Ian McCulloch (*Dr. Butcher M.D.*). West Coast audiences were given *Zombie* barf bags. The even gorier European version is available on videocassette. *Gates of Hell* was Fulci's next gory American release. (self-imposed **X**)

ZOMBIE FLESH EATERS: See ZOMBIE.

ZOMBIES ON BROADWAY
1945 RKO (B&W)
PRODUCER: Ben Stoloff
DIRECTOR: Gordon Douglas
SCREENWRITER: Lawrence Kimble

I Walked with a Zombie was an RKO hit, so the studio execs figured a zombie comedy would be even bigger. A New York nightclub run by gangsters advertises that it has real zombies. The comedy team of Brown and Carney is sent to the West Indies to get them. Bela Lugosi, as Dr. Renault, creates the living dead with injections. Darby Jones, the tall zombie in the earlier film, repeats his role. So does Sir Lancelot, the calypso singer. Bela turns pudgy Alan Carney into a bug-eyed zombie and almost does the same to Anne Jeffries. A very strange film. With Sheldon Leonard.

ZOMBIES OF MORA TAU
1957 Columbia (B&W)
PRODUCER: Sam Katzman
DIRECTOR: Edward Cahn
SCREENWRITERS: Raymond T. Marcus

Zombies guard an underwater treasure. The underwater effect is produced by a wavy image and bubbles. Autumn Russel is the doomed heroine. Allison Hayes joins the zombies. With Morris Ankrum, Gene Roth, and Gregg Palmer.

ZOMBIES OF THE STRATOSPHERE
1952 Republic (B&W)
ASSOCIATE PRODUCER: Franklin Adreon
DIRECTOR: Fred C. Brannon
SCREENWRITER: Ronald Davidson
ALSO RELEASED AS: *Satan's Satellites*

Commando Cody (Judd Holdren) returns in another serial wearing his rocket suit and saving Earth from aliens. One of the aliens in hooded, medieval-looking suits is named Narab and played by Leonard Nimoy. Aline Towne is Cody's assistant. Nearly everything in this serial was left over from earlier Republic productions. The great clunky cylinder robot was from *The Mysterious Dr. Satan* ('40). The flying-man footage was from *King of the Rocket Men* ('49). The feature version was thrown together in '58. Holdren continued as Cody on television in even cheaper adventures. All 12 chapters are now available on one videocassette.

WE ARE GOING TO EAT YOU!

ZOMBIE

...THE DEAD ARE AMONG US!

Bela Lugosi in Zombies on Broadway.

ZONTAR, THE THING FROM VENUS

1966 AIP-TV

PRODUCER/DIRECTOR: Larry Buchanan
SCREENWRITERS: Larry Buchanan, H. Taylor

An incredible remake of *It Conquered the World*. It was one of seven science-fiction films AIP made in a row and sold to television in a bargain package. John Agar stars. He tries to stop Anthony Huston, who gives an historic performance as a scientist dominated by an alien bat. When he fires his laser gun the film turns negative! Most of the cast members end up with brain-control devices on the back of their necks. This inept hit is so popular that SCTV did a takeoff and there's a Boston-based magazine named after it.

ZOTZ!

1962

PRODUCER/DIRECTOR: William Castle
SCREENWRITER: Ray Russell

Great title! But this William Castle comedy doesn't really make it. Tom Poston is a professor who finds an ancient coin that gives him magic powers. If he points at somebody, it causes pain. If he says the movie's title, everything slows down. If he points at someone *and* says "Zotz!" they die! The Pentagon thinks he's crazy, but the commies know he's got a great weapon so they send spies to get it. With Jim Backus, Fred Clark, Cecil Kellaway, Margaret Dumont, Julia Meade, Louis Nye, and a Khruschev lookalike. Scriptwriter Russell did X—*The Man with the X-Ray Eyes*. Plastic *Zotz* coins were given to the first theater patrons.

RECOMMENDED READING

BOOKS

The American Film Institute Catalog (1961–1970). New York: R. R. Bowker, 1976.

Bojarski, Richard. The Films of Bela Lugosi. Secaucus, N. J.: Citadel, 1980.

Bojarski, Richard, and Kenneth Beals. The Films of Boris Karloff. Secaucus, N.J.: Citadel, 1974.

Brooks, Tim, and Earl Marsh. The Complete Directory to Prime Time Network TV Shows. New York: Ballantine, 1981.

De Coulteray, George. Sadism in the Movies. U.S. translation. Secaucus, N.J.: Castle, 1965.

Di Franco, Phillip. The Movie World of Roger Corman. New York and London: Chelsea, 1979.

Dowdy, Andrew. Films of the Fifties. New York: Morrow, 1975.

Esso, Gabe. Tarzan of the Movies. New York: Citadel, 1968.

Everson, William K. Classics of the Horror Film. Secaucus, N.J.: Citadel, 1974.

Gerani, Gary, and Paul Schulman. Fantastic Television. New York: Harmony, 1977.

Halliwell, Leslie. Filmgoers Companion. New York: Hill and Wang, 1977.

Hirschhern, Clive. The Warner Brothers Story. New York: Crown, 1979.

Hogan, David. Who's Who of the Horrors. San Diego: Barnes, 1980.

Howard, Moe. Moe Howard and the Three Stooges. Secaucus, N.J.: Citadel, 1977.

Jenkinson, Philip, and Alan Warner. Celluloid Rock. London: Lorrimer, 1974.

Lee, Walt. Reference Guide to Fantastic Films. Los Angeles: Chelsea, 1972.

Marrill, Alvin H. Movies Made for Television. New York: De Capo, 1980.

Martin, Leonard. Movie Comedy Teams. New York: Signet, 1970.

McCartny, Todd, and Charles Flynn. Kings of the B's. New York: Dutton, 1977.

Miller, Don. B Movies. New York: Curtis, 1973.

Parish, James. The Great Movie Series. Cranbury, N.J.: Barnes, 1971.

Parish, James, and Steven Whitney. Vincent Price Unmasked. New York: Drake, 1974.

Pirie, David. A Heritage of Horror, The English Gothic Cinema. London: Equinox, 1973.

Pitts, Michael. Horror Film Stars. Jefferson, N.C.: McFarland, 1981.

Saxon, Martha. Jayne Mansfield and the Fabulous Fifties. Boston: Houghton Mifflin, 1975.

Shipman, David. The Great Movie Stars, The International Years. New York: St. Martin's, 1973.

Silver, Alan, and Elizabeth Ward. Film Noir. Woodstock: Overlook, 1979.

Thomas, Tony. Ronald Reagan—The Hollywood Years. Secaucus, N.J.: Citadel, 1980.

Turner, George E., and Marshall H. Price. Forgotten Horrors. Cranbury, N.J.: Barnes, 1979.

Variety International Showbusiness Reference. New York and London: Garland, 1981.

Youngkin, Steve D., James Bigwood, and Raymond Cabana, Jr. *The Films of Peter Lorre.* Secaucus: Citadel, 1982.

Zmijewsky, Steven and Boris Zmijewsky. *Elvis—The Films and Career of Elvis Presley.* Secaucus: Citadel, 1976.

MAGAZINES

Castle of Frankenstein. New York: 1958–1970.

Cinefantastiques. Oak Park, Ill.: 1971–

Confessions of a Trash Fiend. Old Bridge, N.J.: 1982–1984, bi-weekly.

Famous Monsters of Filmland. Philadelphia: 1958–1983, bi-monthly.

Fangoria. New York: 1979– , 8 times a year.

Fear of Darkness. Columbus, Ohio: 1982–1983, irregular.

Film Journal. New York: 1934– , bi-weekly.

Gore Gazette. Montclair, N.J.: 1980– , bi-weekly.

Motion Picture Exhibitor. Philadelphia: 1919–1968, weekly.

Motion Picture Herald. New York: 1907–1972, weekly.

Sleazoid Express. New York: 1980– , irregular.

Trashola. San Francisco: 1981–1984, bi-weekly.

TV Guide. Radnor, PA: 1952– , weekly.

Weekly Variety. New York: 1906– , weekly.

PICTURE CREDITS

The following companies and individuals kindly granted permission to use the photographs and illustrations in this book. Columbia Pictures Corporation, Embassy Pictures Corporation, and Orion Pictures Corporation also permitted the use of pictures owned by them; the appropriate copyright and courtesy lines appear next to these pictures, at their request. To these film companies and to those listed below, the author and the publisher gratefully acknowledge their debt.

MGM release "FREAKS" Copyright © 1932 Metro-Goldwyn-Mayer Distributing Corporation. Renewed 1959 by Loew's Incorporated. Photograph from "GALAXINA" Courtesy of Crown International Pictures. Photograph from "THE GEORGE RAFT STORY" Courtesy of Lorimar Productions. Photograph from "THE GIRL ON THE BRIDGE" Copyright © 1951 Twentieth Century-Fox Film Corporation. All Rights Reserved. Courtesy of Twentieth Century-Fox. Photograph from "GIRLS ON THE LOOSE" Copyright © by Universal Pictures, a Division of Universal City Studios, Inc. Courtesy of MCA Publishing, a Division of MCA Communications, Inc. Advertisement for "GOD TOLD ME TO" Copyright © 1977 The Georgia Company. Photograph from "THE GODSEND" A Golan-Globus Production for The Cannon Group, Inc. Advertisement for "GODZILLA ON MONSTER ISLAND" Courtesy of Cinema Shares International Television Ltd. Advertisement for "GOLIATHON" Courtesy of World Northal Corporation. Advertisement for "GRIZZLY" Copyright © Film Ventures International. Photograph from "GUYANA, CULT OF THE DAMNED" Copyright © by Universal Pictures, a Division of Universal City Studios, Inc. Courtesy of MCA Publishing, a Division of MCA Communications, Inc. Photograph from "HALLOWEEN" Copyright © 1978 Falcon International Pictures. Courtesy of Compass International Pictures. Photographs from "HALLOWEEN II" and "HALLOWEEN III" Copyright © by Universal Pictures, a Division of Universal City Studios, Inc. Courtesy of MCA Publishing, a Division of MCA Communications, Inc. Photograph from "HAND OF DEATH" Copyright © 1961 Twentieth Century-Fox Film Corporation. All Rights Reserved. Courtesy of Twentieth Century-Fox. Photograph from "HAWK THE SLAYER" Courtesy of Roger Corman. Photograph from "HELL NIGHT" Copyright © 1981 BLT Productions, Ltd. Courtesy of Compass International Pictures. Photograph from "THE HILLS HAVE EYES" Copyright © 1977 The Blood Relations Co. Photograph from "HOLD BACK TOMORROW" Copyright © by Universal Pictures, a Division of Universal City Studios, Inc. Courtesy of MCA Publishing, a Division of MCA Communications, Inc. Advertisement for "HOLLYWOOD BOULEVARD" Copyright © 1976 New World Productions. Photograph from "HORROR OF THE BLOOD MONSTERS" Copyright © Independent-International Pictures Corporation. Photograph from "HOSPITAL MASSACRE" A Golan-Globus Production for The Cannon Group, Inc. Advertisement for the MGM release "HOT RODS TO HELL" Copyright © 1966 Metro-Goldwyn-Mayer, Inc. and Four Leaf Productions, Inc. Photograph from "HOW TO MAKE A MONSTER" Copyright © Sunset Productions. Photograph from "THE HYPNOTIC EYE" Courtesy of Lorimar Productions. Advertisement for "I DRINK YOUR BLOOD" and "I EAT YOUR SKIN" Property of Monarch Releasing Corporation. Advertisement for "I WAS A TEENAGE FRANKENSTEIN" Copyright © Santa Rosa Productions. Advertisement for "I WAS A TEENAGE WEREWOLF" Copyright © Sunset Productions. Photograph from "IMMORAL TALES" Courtesy of New Line Cinema. Photograph from "THE INCREDIBLE MELTING MAN" Copyright © 1977 Quartet Productions. Courtesy of Max J. Rosenberg, Producer. Photograph from "THE INCREDIBLE SHRINKING MAN" Copyright © by Universal Pictures, a Division of Universal City Studios, Inc. Courtesy of MCA Publishing, a Division of MCA Communications, Inc. Photograph from "THE INDESTRUCTIBLE MAN" Courtesy of Lorimar Productions. Advertisement for "INVASION OF THE BEE GIRLS" Courtesy of Motion Picture Marketing, Inc. Advertisement for "INVASION OF THE BLOOD FARMERS" Courtesy of NMD Film Distributing Co., Inc. "INVASION OF THE SAUCERMEN" Copyright © Malibu Productions. Photograph from "THE INVISIBLE INVADERS" Copyright © 1959 Premium Pictures, Inc. All Rights Reserved. Released through United Artists Corporation. Publicity photograph from "IT CAME FROM OUTER SPACE" Copyright © by Universal Pictures, a Division of Universal City Studios, Inc. Courtesy of MCA Publishing, a Division of MCA Communications, Inc. Photograph from "JUNGLE WOMAN" Copyright © by Universal Pictures, a Division of Universal City Studios, Inc. Courtesy of MCA Publishing, a Division of MCA Communications, Inc. Advertisement for "KILL BABY KILL" Courtesy of NMD Film Distributing Co., Inc. Photograph from "KING KONG ('33)" Courtesy of RKO General Pictures. Advertisement for

"KING KONG VS. GODZILLA" Copyright © by Universal Pictures, a Division of Universal City Studios, Inc. Courtesy of MCA Publishing, a Division of MCA Communications, Inc. Photograph from the MGM release "KISSIN' COUSINS" Copyright © 1964 Metro-Goldwyn-Mayer, Inc. and Four Leaf Productions, Inc. Advertisement for "LADY FRANKENSTEIN" Copyright © 1972 Mel Welles and Condor International Films. Advertisement for "LAST RITES" A Cannon Film Release. Photograph from "LIVE FAST, DIE YOUNG" Copyright © by Universal Pictures, a Division of Universal City Studios, Inc. Courtesy of MCA Publishing, a Division of MCA Communications, Inc. Photograph from "MACHINE GUN KELLY" Copyright © El Monte Productions. Advertisement for "MAD DOG MORGAN" Courtesy of Cinema Shares International Television Ltd. Photograph from "THE MAGNETIC MONSTER" Copyright © 1953 A-Men Productions, Inc. Renewed 1981. All Rights Reserved. Released through United Artists Corporation. Photograph from "MAN MADE MONSTER" Copyright © by Universal Pictures, a Division of Universal City Studios, Inc. Courtesy of MCA Publishing, a Division of MCA Communications, Inc. Photograph from the MGM release "MARK OF THE VAMPIRE" Copyright © 1935 Metro-Goldwyn-Mayer Corporation. Renewed 1962 by Metro-Goldwyn-Mayer, Inc. Photograph from "MARTIN" Copyright © 1977 Braddock Associates. Photograph from "THE MINOTAUR" Copyright © 1961 Agliani-Mordini-Illira Film. All Rights Reserved. Released through United Artists Corporation. Photograph from "THE MOLE PEOPLE" Copyright © by Universal Pictures, a Division of Universal City Studios, Inc. Courtesy of MCA Publishing, a Division of MCA Communications, Inc. Photograph from "MOTHER'S DAY" Copyright © 1980 Mother's Day Co. Courtesy of United Film Distribution Co. Photograph from "THE MUNSTERS' REVENGE" Copyright © by Universal Pictures, a Division of Universal City Studios, Inc. Courtesy of MCA Publishing, a Division of MCA Communications, Inc. Photograph from "THE NESTING" Copyright © 1980 The Nesting Company. Armand Weston Producer/Director. Photograph from "NEW YEAR'S EVIL" A Golan-Globus Production for The Cannon Group, Inc. Photograph from the MGM release "THE NEXT VOICE YOU HEAR" Copyright © 1950 Loew's Incorporated. Renewed 1977 by Metro-Goldwyn-Mayer, Inc. Advertisement for "NIGHT OF THE COBRA WOMAN" Copyright © 1972 New World Pictures, Inc. Photograph from "NIGHT OF THE LIVING DEAD" Copyright © 1978 Image Ten, Inc. Advertisement for "NIGHT OF THE ZOMBIES" Courtesy of NMD Film Distributing Co., Inc. Photograph from "NIGHTMARE IN WAX" Courtesy of Crown International Pictures. Photograph from "NOSFERATU, THE VAMPYRE" Copyright © 1979 Twentieth Century-Fox Film Corporation. All Rights Reserved. Courtesy of Twentieth Century-Fox. Photograph from "NOT OF THIS EARTH" Copyright © 1956 Los Altos Productions, Inc.; All Rights Reserved. Photograph from "THE OLD DARK HOUSE" Copyright © by Universal Pictures, a Division of Universal City Studios, Inc. Courtesy of MCA Publishing, a Division of MCA Communications, Inc. Advertisement for "ON THE BEACH" Copyright © 1959 Lomitas Productions, Inc. All Rights Reserved. Released through United Artists Corporation. Advertisement for "PENETRATION" Copyright © William Mishkin Motion Pictures, Inc. Advertisement for "PIRANHA" Copyright © 1978 The Pacific Trust d.b.a. Piranha Productions. Photograph from "RABID" Copyright © 1976 The Dibar Syndicate. Advertisement for "THE RATS ARE COMING! THE WEREWOLVES ARE HERE!" Copyright © William Mishkin Motion Pictures, Inc. Photograph from "REVENGE OF THE CREATURE" Copyright © by Universal Pictures, a Division of Universal City Studios, Inc. Courtesy of MCA Publishing, a Division of MCA Communications, Inc. Advertisement for "REVENGE OF THE ZOMBIES" Courtesy of World Northal Corporation. Advertisement for "ROCK ALL NIGHT" Copyright © Sunset Productions. Photograph from "ROCK 'N' ROLL HIGH SCHOOL" Copyright © 1979 New World Pictures, Inc. Photograph from "THE ROCKET MAN" Copyright © 1954 Twentieth Century-Fox Film Corporation. All Rights Reserved. Courtesy of Twentieth Century-Fox. Advertisement for "SATAN'S SADISTS" Copyright © Independent-International Pictures Corporation. Photograph from "SCHIZOID" A Golan-Globus Production for The Cannon

INDEX

*t*his index lists over 400 names that show up frequently in *The Psychotronic Encyclopedia of Film*. Included are notable producers and directors, big stars, famous character actors, cult favorites, and a few select special-effects experts, screenwriters, authors, and composers. The author extends his thanks and best wishes to everyone listed here and hopes that their contributions to the world of *Psychotronic* movies will be remembered and preserved.   —MW

Towers, Harry Alan (Peter Welbeck), 90, 107, 132, 203, 221, 229, 241, 340, 341, 406, 470, 511, 521, 522, 568, 590, 624, 695, 696, 750, 751, 768

U

Ulmer, Edgar G., 11, 32, 53-54, 60, 78, 159, 374, 389, 450

V

Valli (Alida), 328, 339, 364, 671, 695
Vampira (Maila Nurmi), 45, 446, 512, 552
Van Cleef, Lee, 42, 130, 219, 282, 379, 562
Van Doren, Mamie, 45, 56, 82, 100, 101, 124, 255, 280, 282, 320, 413, 503, 504, 529, 563, 599, 622, 692, 714, 742, 752, 757, 799
Van Sloan, Edward, 49, 62, 142, 170, 171, 173, 203, 207, 256, 282, 464, 489, 647
Van Voren, Monique, 15, 234, 682
Vaughn, Robert, 38, 104, 175, 750, 754
Veidt, Conrad, 8, 106, 475
Vernon, Howard, 4, 9, 31, 74, 186, 195
Ve Sota, Bruno, 18, 27, 34, 85, 118, 123, 138, 149, 174, 232, 236, 282, 299, 306, 313, 334, 370, 449, 517, 593, 636, 644, 693, 737, 760, 762, 780
Victor, Katherine, 101, 138, 149, 342, 694, 783
Von Stronheim, Erich, 11, 141-42, 179, 295, 356, 410, 464, 741
Von Sydow, Max, 126, 224, 225, 244, 517, 736

W

Walker, Pete, 127, 188, 189, 262, 343, 610
Walley, Deborah, 40, 92, 192, 381, 638, 651
Warner, David, 262, 375, 485, 529, 719
Warren, Jerry, 27, 137, 149, 229, 361, 367, 449, 701, 783
Webb, Jack, 154, 207, 208, 417, 544, 711
Weissmuller, Johnny, 100, 103, 180, 266, 393-94, 395, 399, 460, 548, 571, 607, 612, 676, 681, 682, 684, 686, 687, 688, 689, 690, 744, 756
Welch, Raquel, 47, 79, 231-32, 304, 446, 496, 531, 598, 713
Weld, Tuesday, 430, 431, 560, 563, 580, 594, 595, 622, 779
Welles, Mel, 3, 26, 123, 320, 323, 410, 425, 625, 737
Welles, Orson, 107, 162, 390, 418, 454, 504, 696, 736, 729
Whale, James, 88, 255, 256, 451, 527, 528
Whitman, Stuart, 99, 109, 120, 135, 163, 176, 214, 280, 299, 305, 337, 430, 455, 458, 480, 513, 586, 598, 631, 697, 751, 773
Wilder, W. Lee, 401, 456, 529, 545, 642, 650
Wilkinson, June, 100, 554, 563, 733
Williams, John (Johnny), 122, 212, 213, 217, 231, 266, 298, 310, 338, 381, 388, 416, 558, 658, 669, 728
Windsor, Marie, 3, 110, 114, 161, 280, 393, 538, 602, 641, 661, 672
Winner, Michael, 518, 553, 618
Winters, Shelley, 76, 120, 182, 216, 352, 390, 444, 513, 557, 586, 696, 712, 755, 769, 776, 779
Wise, Robert, 13, 29, 79, 147, 269, 307, 657
Wood, Ed, Jr., 50, 88, 89, 284, 385, 512, 533, 551, 552, 632, 636, 754
Wood, Lana, 102, 187, 252, 260, 261, 282, 520, 604
Woronov, Mary, 324, 594, 617, 633
Wray, Fay, 120, 198, 209, 269, 311, 402, 485, 499, 594, 668, 745

Y

Yarbrough, Jean, 92, 139, 320-21, 340, 384, 405, 465, 628
York, Michael, 428, 432, 713

Z

Zsigmond, Vilmos (William), 122, 169, 241, 332, 363, 478, 479, 502, 503, 576, 591, 601, 720
Zucco, George, 5, 62, 108, 127, 165, 196, 250, 251, 340, 349, 437, 442, 444, 452, 480, 485, 489, 490, 495, 585, 608, 630, 682, 725, 756, 775
Zugsmith, Albert, 45, 56, 104, 124, 127, 198, 231, 235, 281, 282, 319, 361, 370, 488, 514, 529, 553, 557, 563, 621-22, 639, 691, 726, 769

ABOUT THE AUTHOR

MOVIES HAVE ALWAYS BEEN A MAJOR PART OF MY LIFE. MY EARLIEST MEMORIES ARE OF SITTING IN FRONT OF A TELEVISION WATCHING OBSCURE 1930S MYSTERIES AND COMEDIES. I FELT THAT TELEVISION EXISTED TO SHOW ME AS MANY MOVIES AS POSSIBLE. THOSE SHORT NEW PROGRAMS WERE JUST FILLER.

THEATERS WERE EVEN BETTER. MY PARENTS OR GRAND-PARENTS TOOK ME TO MAJOR RELEASES ONE NIGHT A WEEK AND I JOINED SCHOOL FRIENDS EVERY WEEKEND AT DOUBLE FEATURE MATINEES. AT THE TIME WE HAD A HALF DOZEN THEATERS WITHIN WALKING DISTANCE TO CHOOSE FROM.

MY FIRST FAVORITES WERE MONSTER MOVIES. I'M TOLD I HID BEHIND A STUFFED CHAIR WHEN THE MUMMY FIRST THREATENED FROM THE T.V. SCREEN. WHEN MY FATHER TOOK ME TO SEE THE SEVENTH VOYAGE OF SINBAD (WHILE MY MOTHER WAS IN THE HOSPITAL ABOUT TO HAVE MY FIRST BROTHER) I ENDED UP HAVING NIGHTMARES FOR WEEKS. I COULDN'T WAIT TO SEE SOMETHING ELSE THAT SCARY.

LATER I WENT TO MIDNIGHT UNDERGROUND SHOWS, REVIVAL HOUSES, FOREIGN LANGUAGE THEATERS, AND BEST OF ALL, CLEVELANDS DOWNTOWN GRINDHOUSES WHERE THE MOST SHOCKING CINEMATIC BLOOD, GUTS AND SEX (IN AN ERA OF EXTREME CENSORSHIP) COULD BE ENJOYED. MUSIC (TOP FORTY), MOVIES, AND THE MYSTERIES OF SEX WERE MY PRIME CONCERNS. SINCE THESE TOPICS WEREN'T DISCUSSED OR TOLERATED BY TEACHERS, I CONSIDERED MOST OF MY DAYS BEHIND SMALL DESKS A WASTE.

IF I SEE A GREAT MOVIE, I WANT TO TELL PEOPLE ABOUT IT. IF I'M IN A BAD MOOD, THE RIGHT FEATURE SNAPS ME OUT OF IT. I LOVE INEPT, BADLY MADE MOVIES AS WELL AS EFFECTIVE WELL-CRAFTED ONES. SELECTIVE MOVIE WATCHING CAN IMPROVE YOUR LIFE. TAKE SOMEONE TO A THEATER TONIGHT.

— MICHAEL J. WELDON